MW01010485

THE RUSSIAN CONQUEST OF CENTRAL ASIA

The Russian conquest of Central Asia was perhaps the nineteenth century's most dramatic and successful example of European imperial expansion, adding 1.5 million square miles and at least 6 million people – most of them Muslims – to the Tsar's domains. Alexander Morrison provides the first comprehensive military and diplomatic history of the conquest to be published for over a hundred years. From the earliest conflicts on the steppe frontier in the 1830s to the annexation of the Pamirs in the early 1900s, he gives a detailed account of the logistics and operational history of Russian wars against Khoqand, Bukhara and Khiva, the capture of Tashkent and Samarkand, and the bloody subjection of the Turkmen, as well as Russian diplomatic relations with China, Persia and the British Empire. Based on archival research in Russia, Kazakhstan, Uzbekistan, Georgia and India, memoirs and Islamic chronicles, this book explains how Russia conquered a colonial empire in Central Asia, with consequences that still resonate today.

ALEXANDER MORRISON is Fellow and Tutor in History at New College, Oxford. His publications include *Russian Rule in Samarkand 1868–1910: A Comparison with British India* (2008).

THE RUSSIAN CONQUEST
OF CENTRAL ASIA

A Study in Imperial Expansion, 1814–1914

ALEXANDER MORRISON
New College, Oxford

CAMBRIDGE
UNIVERSITY PRESS

CAMBRIDGE
UNIVERSITY PRESS

University Printing House, Cambridge CB2 8BS, United Kingdom

One Liberty Plaza, 20th Floor, New York, NY 10006, USA

477 Williamstown Road, Port Melbourne, VIC 3207, Australia

314–321, 3rd Floor, Plot 3, Splendor Forum, Jasola District Centre, New Delhi – 110025, India

79 Anson Road, #06–04/06, Singapore 079906

Cambridge University Press is part of the University of Cambridge.

It furthers the University's mission by disseminating knowledge in the pursuit of education, learning, and research at the highest international levels of excellence.

www.cambridge.org
Information on this title: www.cambridge.org/9781107030305
DOI: 10.1017/9781139343381

© Alexander Morrison 2021

This publication is in copyright. Subject to statutory exception and to the provisions of relevant collective licensing agreements, no reproduction of any part may take place without the written permission of Cambridge University Press.

First published 2021

Printed in the United Kingdom by TJ Books Limited, Padstow Cornwall

A catalogue record for this publication is available from the British Library.

ISBN 978-1-107-03030-5 Hardback

Cambridge University Press has no responsibility for the persistence or accuracy of URLs for external or third-party internet websites referred to in this publication and does not guarantee that any content on such websites is, or will remain, accurate or appropriate.

In memory of John Malcolm Morrison (1949–2017)

CONTENTS

     Afterwards': The Conquest of Transcaspia, 1869–85   409

10   Aryanism on the Final Frontier of the Russian Empire: The
     Exploration and Annexation of the Pamirs, 1881–1905   476

     Epilogue: After the Conquest   531

     Sources and Bibliography   540
     Index   593

ILLUSTRATIONS

MAPS

TABLES

ACKNOWLEDGEMENTS

This book has been ten years in the making, during which I have had three different jobs and worked in archives and libraries in six different countries. I have made many friends and accumulated many scholarly debts along the way, and will try to remember them all as best I can.

In what was then still the *School* of History at the University of Liverpool I would like to thank Paul Booth, Harald Braun, Marios Costambeys, Alex Drace-Francis, Charles Esdaile, Michael Hopkins, Michael Hughes, Richard Huzzey, Stephen Kenny, Eve Rosenhaft, Benedetta Rossi, Nigel Swain and Dmitri van den Bersselaar for many years of advice, support and guidance in what was my first academic job. I could not have asked for better colleagues or a more supportive environment as I adjusted to full-time teaching and the dreary requirements of the 'Research Excellence Framework'. During my time at Liverpool I also held a fifty-pound Fellowship at All Souls College, Oxford, which was of great assistance to my research: my thanks to the Warden and Fellows.

The School of Humanities and Social Sciences at Nazarbayev University in what I will continue to call Astana was a remarkable place to work and a unique intellectual community – well on the way to becoming the most important centre for Central Asian studies in the world after barely a decade of existence. Thanks to my friends and colleagues Erika Alpert, Zhuldyz Amankulova, the late Sofiya An, Aiganym Ayazbayeva, Alima Bissenova, Daniel and Zohra Beben, Elliott Bowen, Aziz Burkhanov, Mwita Chacha, Zachary Cofran, Neil Collins, Eric Espinoza, Andrei Filchenko, David Hammerbeck, Michael Hancock-Parmer, Meruert Ibrayeva, Saniya Karpykova, Meiramgul Kusseinova, Yoshiharu Kobayashi, Kevin Lam, Jack Lee, Don Leggett, Laura Makhulbayeva, Gwen McEvoy, Gabriel McGuire, James Nikopoulos, Loretta O'Donnell, Brendan Pietsch, Duncan Priestley, Daniel and Christina Pugh, Nurlan Qabdilhaq, Danielle Ross, Rosario and Aida Ronga, Edwin Sayes, Caress Schenk, Daniel Scarborough, Uli Schamiloglu, John Schoeberlein, Francesco Sica, Charles Sullivan, Victoria Thorstensson, Alexei Trochev, Nikolai Tsyrempilov, Siegfried van Duffel, Stephen Wheatcroft, Chris Whitsel, the late Matthew Wilhite, Spencer Willardson, Zbigniew Wojnowski, Mahire Yakup and Almira Zholamanova – and to my students

Alibek Akhmetov, Alen Askar, Laura Berdikhojaeva, Madina Bizhanova, Yerkebulan Dosmakhambet, Yuan Gao, Inzhuna Karazhanova, Galiya Khassenkhanova, Dmitri Melnikov, Nursultan Nurmukhanov, Xeniya Prilutskaya, Makhabbat Sadykova, Aliya Tazhibayeva, Adina Tulegenova, Di Wang, Kamshat Yermaganbetova and Ademi Zhakyp. There is nothing like teaching *History of Kazakhstan* semester after semester to help you refine and focus your ideas about Central Asia's past.

I have also benefited hugely from being part of the wider community of Kazakhstani historians during my time in Astana and since: thanks to Miras Abdrakhim, Meruert Abusseitova, Mikhail Akulov, the late Timur Beisembiev, Assylkhan Bikenov, Karlygash Bizhigitova, Gianluca Bonora, Tenlik Dalayeva, Irina Erofeeva, Gulbanu Izbassarova, Nikolai Kropivnitskii, Zhanar Jampeissova, Ablet Kamalov, Svetlana Kovalskaya, Galina Ksenzhik, Yerlan Medeubaev, Ashirbek Muminov, Gulnara Musabalina, Arailym Musagalieva, Gulmira Orynbaeva, Pavel Shabley, Dina Sharipova, Anar Smagulova, Gulmira Sultangalieva, Zhuldyz Tulibaeva, Saule Uderbaeva and Marziya Zhylysbaeva.

In Oxford David Parrott made me feel at home at New College from the moment I arrived, and has been unfailingly kind and patient with the many idiotic queries I have put to him since. I would also like to thank Roy Allison, Katya Andreyev, Robert Beddard, James Belich, Nigel Biggar, the late Jeremy Catto, Erica Charters, Nicholas Cole, Sarah Crook, the late John Davis, Michael Feener, John-Paul Ghobrial, Adrian Gregory, Dan Healey, Edmund Herzig, Rob Johnson, Catriona Kelly, Colin Kidd, Robin Lane-Fox, Noel Malcolm, Julia Mannherz, Katie McKeogh, Andy Meadows, Asli Niyazioğlu, Sofya Omarova, Ali Parchami, Christian Sahner, Beatrice Teissier, Hannah Theaker, Christopher Tyerman, David Washbrook, the late Mark Whittow, Peter Wilson, George Woudhuysen, John Vickers and Andrei Zorin.

I began the research for this book in 2009 thanks to a small research grant from the British Academy, which also funded a conference on the Russian conquest of Central Asia at the University of Liverpool in 2012. This did much to form my ideas and resulted in a special issue of *Central Asian Survey* on the topic. In 2011, together with Dr Berny Sèbe of the University of Birmingham, I was awarded an AHRC early career research grant, 'Outposts of Conquest', for a comparative study of colonial fortresses in the steppe and the Sahara which funded an important field trip to the Syr-Darya region. In 2012 I was awarded a Philip Leverhulme Prize by the Leverhulme foundation, which funded trips to Moscow, St Petersburg and Amsterdam, as well as a semester of leave at Liverpool. Most recently I have benefited from funding from the History Faculty at Oxford for a monograph workshop in the summer of 2018, which did much to finally get me over the finishing line, and a subvention from the Ludwig Humanities Research Fund at New College to pay for the drawing of maps and the inclusion of additional illustrations. My thanks to all these funding bodies.

Thanks to Michael Watson, Emily Sharp and Lisa Carter of Cambridge University Press, for their understanding and patience during this book's very long gestation, and to Steven Holt for his eagle-eyed copy-editing. Portions of the Introduction and of Chapters 2, 3 and 5 first appeared as articles in *Ab Imperio, Central Asian Survey, The Journal of the Economic & Social History of the Orient* and *Modern Asian Studies*. My thanks to the editors of those journals for permission to re-publish. I would also like to thank Teona Iashvili, Arnur Karymsakov and Tat'yana Burmistrova, the directors respectively of the National Archives of Georgia, the Central State Archive of the Republic of Kazakhstan and the Russian State Military-Historical Archive, for permission to reproduce images of documents from these archives. Especial thanks to Natasha Bregel for permission to base Map 1 on her father Yuri Bregel's teaching map of Central Asia at the beginning of the nineteenth century.

I began writing this book in 2010 on a Visiting Fellowship at the Slavic Research Centre of Hokkaido University, where I was hosted by Uyama Tomohiko, an inexhaustible fount of knowledge on everything to do with the history of the Qazaqs. It was he who told me I needed to explain not just why the conquest of Central Asia happened, but why it happened *when* it did. Dominic Lieven's work has long been an inspiration, and for the last twenty years he has encouraged me to persist with the diplomatic and military history of the Russian empire in the teeth of academic fashion. Scott Levi has always been ready to enlighten me on abstruse points of Central Asian military terminology over a beer or two. David Schimmelpenninck van der Oye has been generous with his insights on Turkestan generals and explorers, and in sharing sources. When I was in Astana David McDonald offered unstinting moral and practical support in the face of the more surreal aspects of NU's bureaucracy, as well as much sound academic advice there and as a very generous host in Madison. Over the last four years it has been a great privilege to be able to discuss the nomadic economy, the vacuousness of the 'Silk Road' and the dietary benefits of horsemeat with Anatoly Khazanov.

Neither this book nor any of my other research would have been possible without the endless kindness and hospitality of Misha Labovsky and Olga Vinogradova, who for two decades now have been offering me a home from home on Malaya Bronnaya whenever I have needed to work in Moscow: I am deeply grateful to them. Also in Moscow I would like to thank Vladimir Bobrovnikov, Tatiana Kotiukova, Evgenii Kozhokin, Andrey Larin and Dmitrii Vasil'ev. In St Petersburg Sergei Abashin, Alfrid Bustanov, Boris Kolonitskii, Roman Pochekaev and Alexander Semyonov have provided academic support and unfailingly stimulating ideas, and Olga and Emmanuel Berard much-needed relaxation at their picture-perfect dacha. In Orenburg

Sergei Liubichankovskii was an exemplary host and allowed me to present my work on the Orenburg customs to an expert audience.

In Tashkent and Samarkand I am grateful to Bakhtiyar Babajanov for his generous hospitality and incisive conversation, as well as Evgenii Abdullaev, Raushan Abdullaev, Hushnud Abdurasulov, Akmal Bazarbaev, Said Gaziev, Muhayo Isakova, Alisher Khaliyarov, Oybek Mahmudov, Sherzodhon Mahmudov, Jalol Nasirov, Hilola Nazirova, Sirojiddin Nurmatov, Azim Malikov, Ludmila Pak, Oksana Pugovkina, Elena Pustovaya, Sanobar Shadmanova, Uktambek Sultonov, Gulchehra Sultonova, Nuryoghdi Toshev, Abduvahob Vahidov and Qahramon Yaqubov. In Khujand Inomjon Mamadaliev and Nabijon Rahimov were kind and generous hosts. In Bishkek and Karakol I would like to thank Gulzada Abdalieva, Gulnara Aitpaeva, Christopher Baker, Janyl Bokontoeva, Svetlana Jacquesson, Adyl Kanimetov, Aziza Suiumbaevna, Medet Tiulegenov and Cholpon Turdalieva. In Tbilisi Timothy Blauvelt took me to the sulphur baths, while Anton Vacharadze showed that post-Soviet archives *can* be accessible and user-friendly when they have the right person running them.

In Delhi, Bhola and Promodini Varma, Manik Varma and Sachi Srivastava have been encouraging my scholarship for nearly two decades. I am deeply grateful to them, and to Madhavan Palat.

For invitations to speak, assistance in archives, conversations at conferences, discourses at dinners, comments and challenges I would also like to thank Sergei Andreyev, Ingeborg Baldauf, Matthias Battis, Evrim Binbash, Assel Bitabarova, Vladimir Boyko, Ian Campbell, Chida Tetsuro, Aminat Chokobaeva, Sally Cummings, William Dalrymple, David Darrow, Devin DeWeese, Simon Dixon, Nicola Di Cosmo, Rossen Djagalov, Askar Djumashev, Cloé Drieu, Jipar Duishembieva, Stéphane Dudoignon, Jeff Eden, Tim Epkenhans, Olivier Ferrando, Svetlana Gorshenina, Jörn Happel, John Heathershaw, Philippa Hetherington, Rosemary Hill, Geoff Humble, Ali Iğmen, Hamid Ismailov, Clare Jackson, Catherine Poujol, Artemy Kalinovsky, Jennifer Keating, Michael Kemper, David Kenrick, Adeeb Khalid, Kimura Satoru, Masha Kirasirova, Komatsu Hisao, Jo Laycock, Zeev Levin, Lhamsuren Munkh-Erdene, Rachel Lin, Morgan Liu, Thomas Loy, Olga Maiorova, Azim Malikov, Virginia Martin, Nick Megoran, David Moon, Robert Middleton, Naganawa Norihiro, Timothy Nunan, Isabelle Ohayon, Elena Paskaleva, Jürgen Paul, Joe Perkins, Niccolò Pianciola, Madeleine Reeves, Philipp Reichmuth, Flora Roberts, Montu Saxena, Yue Shi, Shioya Akifumi, Eric Schluessel, Ron Sela, Nariman Skakov, Elena Smolarz, Heather Sonntag, John Steinberg, Rory Stewart, Ronald Suny, Tommaso Trevisani, Gabrielle van den Berg Denis Volkov, Nick Walmsley, Kim Wagner, Franz Wennberg and Paul Werth.

Especial thanks to those who read and commented on individual chapters to help me avoid the worst howlers: Ulfatbek Abdurasulov, Bakhtiyar Babajanov,

Daniel Beben, Victoria Clement, Markus Hauser, Anton Ikhsanov, Ablet Kamalov, Oybek Mahmudov, Robert Middleton, James Pickett, Daniel Prior and Paul Richardson. Paolo Sartori and Marianne Kamp read the entire manuscript at the monograph workshop in Oxford in 2018 and provided detailed comments. I am deeply grateful to them for taking the trouble. I would also particularly like to thank Daniel Beben, Tom Welsford and Paolo Sartori for assistance with documents in Chaghatai and for correcting my execrable Persian. Tom also read the entire manuscript, providing line by line commentary, proof-reading and copy-editing. If this book is readable at all it is thanks to him. The remaining errors are of course my own responsibility.

Berny Sèbe also deserves special thanks for his acute observational skills, brilliant photography and unflagging cheerfulness during our journey from the Aral Sea along the valley of the Syr-Darya in search of fortresses in the summer of 2012. My memories of that trip are all the more precious since the third member of our party was my dear friend Alim Sabitov, whose death in 2019 has left a void that can never be filled. Every one of the many trips I have made to Almaty since 2005 has been a *prazdnik* thanks to him and Gulnara Abikeyeva.

My mother, Penny, and brother Nicholas have reminded me that there is more to life than academia – for cricket, theatre, birds and bumblebees my thanks and love.

My wife, Beatrice Penati, was healthily sceptical about this book from the beginning – too many men with moustaches and not enough numbers or Excel spreadsheets. She has been striving heroically for the last ten years to turn me into a *poryadochnyi chelovek*, and along the way we have shared many things which are much more important than this book. The fact that I have finished it is a testimony to her patience, support and love.

My father, John Morrison, encouraged me to become a historian rather than follow in his footsteps as a journalist because I never use one word where six will do. He did not live to see the completion of this book, but I know that he would have thought it far too long. I dedicate it to his memory.

NOTE ON TRANSLATION, TRANSLITERATION
AND DATES

For the transliteration of Russian terms and proper names I have used the simplified library of Congress system without diacritics, apart from ' to indicate the soft sign (ь), and using *ya* rather than the misleading *ia* for я. Terms and names in Central Asian languages are generally transliterated from historic spellings in the Arabic script, again using a simplified system without diacritics except for ' to indicate *'ain* (ع) and ' for *hamza* (ء). Where familiar versions of a name already exist in English I have stuck with the established spelling (e.g. Samarkand not Samarqand). Where a direct English equivalent exists, technical terms have been translated, notably *oblast'* (province) and *uezd* (district). Unless otherwise indicated, all translations from Russian, French and Persian are my own, while all translations from Chaghatai are by a friend who prefers to remain anonymous, but whose assistance I gratefully acknowledge.

Before 14 February 1918 the Russian empire operated according to the Julian calendar, which was thirteen days behind the Gregorian calendar used in the rest of Europe, and now worldwide. Almost all dates in this book are Old Style (O.S.), but when the Russians were dealing directly with the British I have also given Gregorian dates. All dates in the footnotes are those given in the original document, which in most cases means they are O.S.

ABBREVIATIONS

Archives

F. – *Fond* (Fund); **Op.** – *Opis'* (Catalogue); **D.** – *Delo* (File); **l.** – *list'* (folio); ***ob*** – *oborot'* (verso).

AV   *Arkhiv Vostokovedov Sankt-Peterburgskogo Filiala Instituta Vostokovedenii RAN* (St Petersburg Filial of the Oriental Institute of the Russian Academy of Sciences, Archive of Orientalists)

AVPRI   *Arkhiv Vneshnei Politiki Rossiiskoi Imperii* (Archive of the Russian Empire's Foreign Policy, Moscow).

BL   British Library, London.

GAOO   *Gosudarstvennyi Arkhiv Orenburgskoi Oblasti* (State Archive of Orenburg Province, Orenburg)

GARF   *Gosudarstvennyi Arkhiv Rossiiskoi Federatsii* (State Archive of the Russian Federation, Moscow).

IAOO   *Istoricheskii Arkhiv Omskoi Oblasti* (Historical Archive of Omsk Province, Omsk)

IOR   India Office Records (British Library, London)

IISH   International Institute for Social History, Amsterdam

NAG   National Archives of Georgia (Tbilisi)

NAI   National Archives of India (New Delhi)

RGIA   *Rossiiskii Gosudarstvennyi Istoricheskii Arkhiv* (Russian State Historical Archive, St Petersburg)

RGIMOPI   *Rossiiskii Gosudarstvennyi Istoricheskii Muzei, Otdel Pis'mennykh Istochnikov* (Russian State Historical Museum, Division of Written Sources, Moscow)

RGVIA   *Rossiiskii Gosudarstvennyi Voenno-Istoricheskii Arkhiv* (Russian State Military-Historical Archive, Moscow).

TsGARKaz   *Tsentral'nyi Gosudarstvennyi Arkhiv Respubliki Kazakhstan* (Central State Archive of the Republic of Kazakhstan, Almaty).

TsGARUz   *Tsentral'nyi Gosudarstvennyi Arkhiv Respubliki Uzbekistan* (Central State Archive of the Republic of Uzbekistan, Tashkent).

Document Collections

AKAK   *Akty, sobrannye Kavkazskoi Arkheograficheskoi Kommissii* (Tiflis: Tip. Glavnogo Upravleniya Namestnika Kavkazskogo, 1881)

KRO   F. N. Kireev (ed.): *Kazakhsko-russkie otnosheniya v XVIII–XIX vekakh (1771–1867 gody): sbornik dokumentov i materialov* (Alma-Ata: Nauka, 1964)

MPITT	V. V. Struve, A. K. Vorovkov & A. A. Romaskevich (ed.) *Materialy po Istorii Turkmen i Turkmenii* Vol. II (Moscow–Leningrad: Izd. AN SSSR, 1938).
PP	*Parliamentary Papers*
PSZ	*Polnoe Sobranie Zakonov Rossiiskoi Imperii*
PT	A Il'yasov (ed.) *Prisoedinenie Turkmenii k Rossii. Sbornik Arkhivnykh Dokumentov* (Ashkhabad: Izd. AN Turkmenskoi SSR, 1960)
RTO	S. G. Agadzhanov & A. Il'yasov (ed.) *Russko-Turkmenskie otnosheniya v XVIII–XIX vv. (do prisoedineniya Turkmenii k Rossii). Sbornik arkhivnykh dokumentov* (Ashkhabad: Izd. AN Turkmenskoi SSR, 1963)
Serebrennikov *Sbornik*	A. G. Serebrennikov (ed.) *Sbornik Materialov dlya istorii zavoevaniya Turkestanskogo Kraya* 1839 g–1845 g (Tashkent: Tip. Sht. Turkestanskogo V.O., 1908–1912) 4 Vols & *Turkestanskii Krai. Sbornik Materialov dlya istorii ego zavoevaniya* 1846 g–52 g, 1864 g–66 g (Tashkent: Tip. Shtaba Turkestanskogo Voennogo Okruga, 1914–15) 13 Vols
SIRIO	*Sbornik Imperatorskogo Russkogo Istoricheskogo Obshchestva*
VPR	*Vneshnyaya Politika Rossii XIX i nachala XX veka: Dokumenty Rossiiskogo Ministerstva inostrannykh del* Series I & II (Moscow: Gos. izd-vo polit. lit-ry, 1960–1995)
Zagorodnikova *Bol'shaya Igra*	T. N. Zagorodnikova, (ed.): *'Bol'shaya igra' v Tsentral'noi Azii: 'Indiiskii pokhod' russkoi armii. Sbornik arkhivnykh dokumentov* (Moscow: Institut Vostokovedeniya, 2005)

Chronicles

Donish *Risala*	Ahmad Makhdum-i Donish: *Risala ya Mukhtasari az Ta'rikh-i Saltanat-i Khanadan-i Manghitiyya* (*c.* 1898) ed. Abulghani Mirzoev (Stalinabad: Nashriyat-i Daulati-yi Tajikistan, 1960)
TA	Mullah Muhammad Yunus Jan Shighavul Tashkandi: *Ta'rikh-i 'Aliquli Amir-i Lashkar* (*c.* 1903) ed. & trans. T. K. Beisembiev as *The Life of 'Alimqul. A Native Chronicle of Nineteenth-Century Central Asia* (London: RoutledgeCurzon, 2003)
TJT	Muhammad Salih Khwaja Tashkandi: *Ta'rikh-i Jadidah-yi Tashkand* (*c.* 1886) Al-Biruni Institute of Oriental Studies, Uzbekistan Academy of Sciences Manuscript No. 11073/II, portions transcribed by Bakhtiyar Babajanov at http://zerrspiegel.orientphil.uni-halle.de/t386.html
TSh	*Mullah Niyaz Muhammad b. 'Ashur Muhammad Khoqandi: Ta'rikh-i Shahrukhi* (1871) ed. Nikolai Pantusov as *Taarikh Shakhrokhi. Istoriya Vladetelei Fergany* (Kazan': Tip. Imp. Universiteta, 1885).

TSM   Mirza 'Abd al-'Azim Sami: *Ta'rikh-i Salatin-i Manghitiyya*. (c. 1907) ed. &
             trans. L. M. Epifanova as *Istoriya Mangitskikh Gosudarei Pravivshikh
             v Stolitse, Blagorodnoi Bukhare* (Moscow: Izd. Vostochnoi Literatury,
             1962).

Journals and Publications

AHR   *American Historical Review*
AI   *Ab Imperio*
AS   *Asiatische Studien*
CAC   *Cahiers d'Asie Centrale*
CAS   *Central Asian Survey*
CSSH   *Comparative Studies in Society & History*
EcHR   *Economic History Review*
EHR   *English Historical Review*
GJ   *The Geographical Journal*
HJ   *The Historical Journal*
IIRGO   *Izvestiya Imperatorskogo Russkogo Geograficheskogo Obshchestva*
IJMES   *International Journal of Middle-East Studies*
IS   *Iranian Studies*
IV   *Istoricheskii Vestnik*
IZ   *Istoricheskie Zapiski*
JAH   *Journal of Asian History*
JBFGO   *Jahrbücher für Geschichte Osteuropas*
JESHO   *Journal of the Economic and Social History of the Orient*
JGH   *Journal of Global History*
JIS   *Journal of Islamic Studies*
JMH   *Journal of Military History*
JPS   *Journal of Persianate Studies*
JRGS   *Journal of the Royal Geographical Society*
JWH   *Journal of World History*
Kritika   *Kritika: Explorations in Russian and Eurasian History*
MAS   *Modern Asian Studies*
MES   *Middle-Eastern Studies*
PPV   *Pis'mennye Pamyatniki Vostoka*
PRGS   *Proceedings of the Royal Geographical Society*
RA   *Russkii Arkhiv*
RS   *Russkaya Starina*
RV   *Russkii Vestnik*
SEER   *Slavonic & East European Review*
SR   *Slavic Review*
St Pb.   St Petersburg

TKLA	*Protokol zasedaniya i soobshcheniya chlenov Turkestanskogo Kruzhka Liubitelei Arkheologii*
TOUAK	*Trudy Orenburgskoi Uchenoi Arkhivnoi Komissii*
TRHS	*Transactions of the Royal Historical Society*
TVOIRAO	*Trudy Vostochnogo Otdeleniya Imperatorskogo Russkogo Arkheologicheskogo Obshchestva*
TS	*Turkestanskii Sbornik*
TV	*Turkestanskie Vedomosti*
VE	*Vestnik Evropy*
VIRGO	*Vestnik Imperatorskogo Russkogo Geograficheskogo Obshchestva*
VS	*Voennyi Sbornik*
ZIRGO	*Zapiski/Zhurnal Imperatorskogo Russkogo Geographicheskogo Obschestva*
ZVOIRAO	*Zapiski Vostochnogo Otdeleniya Imperatorskogo Russkogo Arkheologicheskogo Obshchestva*

GLOSSARY

'Adat – customary law, applied in the Russian Empire to the law used by nomads.

Aul – a nomadic encampment or winter settlement.

Aqsaqal – 'white-beard'. An elder, a village headman.

Arba – a high, two-wheeled cart.

Ariq – an irrigation canal.

Batyr – a warrior or hero, cognate of *Bahadur* (Persian) and *Bogatyr* (Russian).

Bek/Beg – a title of respect, (sometimes) governor of a province.

Berdanka – affectionate term for the Berdan rifle, introduced in the Russian army after 1870.

Bii – a Kyrgyz or Qazaq judge or figure of authority.

Dadkhwah – a Khoqandi court rank, literally meaning a 'petitioner for justice'.

Dasht-i Qipchaq– 'the field of the Qipchaqs'. Name used for the steppe between the twelfth and nineteenth centuries.

Desyatina– Russian measurement of area, equivalent to 2¾ acres or 1.09 hectares.

Diwan – Qazaq term for the administrative divisions created by the Russians in the steppe in the 1820s, but with the broader meaning of a court or political centre.

Diwan-begi – chief minister (Khiva).

Dungan – Han Chinese Muslims, many of whom migrated to Russian Turkestan in the 1880s.

Fazany – 'pheasants' – a contemptuous term for aristocratic officers who secured a transfer to Central Asia when there was a campaign and a chance of medals or promotion.

Jigit – Turkic term meaning a mounted warrior, used by the Russians for mounted messengers, bodyguards etc.

Jungharia – what is now northern Xinjiang in western China.

Khan – a royal title indicating (in principle) both Chingissid descent and widespread recognition of a right to rule. By the nineteenth century only Qazaq Khans were genuinely Chingissids.

Khoja or *Khwaja* – a religious honorific indicating descent from the prophet's kin, and (sometimes) membership of a Sufi lineage.

Kibitka – term used by the Russians for nomadic households and *yurts*.

Kirgiz – The generic term used by the Russians for both Qazaqs and Kyrgyz in Central Asia. I have preserved it in quotations from primary sources, while referring to Qazaqs and Kyrgyz in the main body of the text.

Inorodtsy – literally 'those of a different birth'. A term used to describe some of the non-Russian peoples of the empire. As a legal category it denoted those excluded from Russian citizenship.

Ishan – a religious leader, whose authority could derive from personal charisma, or from blood descent from or being taught by a famous saint. Associated with Sufism, although not all *ishans* belonged to a Sufi order.

Lazutchik – scout or spy.

Manap – a figure of authority among the Kyrgyz.

Mawara' al-nahr – 'the land beyond the river'. The river in question is the Oxus or Amu-Darya. This was the classic Arabic term for the settled lands of Central Asia, lying roughly between the Amu-Darya and the Syr-Darya.

Oblast' – a province, with a population of a million or more. Known as a *guberniya* in European Russia.

Okrug – a military district.

Otdel – an administrative division.

Pood – Russian measurement of weight, equivalent to 36 lbs.

Pristav – in this period the officer in charge of a region whose administration has not yet been regularised.

Qazi-Kalan – the chief Islamic judge of a city.

Qush-begi – Chief Minister (Bukhara).

Sarbaz – infantry drilled according to modern methods in the armies of Bukhara and Khoqand.

Sart – a generic term used both by Russians and by nomads for the settled population of Central Asia.

Sayyid – one claiming descent from the tribe of the Prophet.

Shaika – raiding band.

Sotnya – a company of Cossack cavalry, usually 100–120 men.

Stanitsa – a Cossack settlement.

Sultan – a title which among Qazaqs indicates Chingissid descent, i.e. membership of the 'white bone' aristocracy.

Taranchi – 'farmer' – the name by which the modern Uyghurs were known in the nineteenth and early twentieth century.

Töre/Tura – a title of respect, indicating membership of the 'white bone' Chingissid aristocracy among Qazaqs.

Trakt – highway or post-road.

Tuzemtsy – 'natives'. The general term used by Russians to describe the local population.

Uezd – a district, which in Turkestan could have a population of 250,000 or more.

'ulama – the collective term for Muslim clergy and theological scholars, plural of *alim*.

Verst – Russian measurement of distance, equivalent to about two-thirds of a mile.

Volost' – an administrative division, in Central Asia usually with about 2,000 households.

Zakat – the Islamic tax on goods, 1/40th of their value – widely applied to livestock in Central Asia.

Zhuz – 'hundred', usually translated as 'horde'. Name for the three political divisions of the Qazaqs.

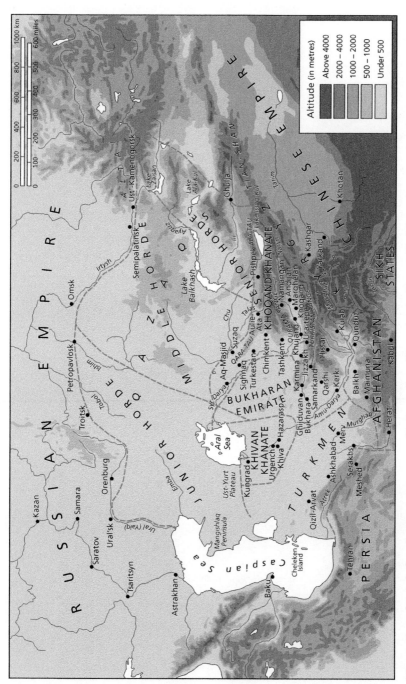

Map 1 Central Asia before the Russian conquest. (Redrawn from 'Central Asia: First Half of the 19th Century'. © Yuri Bregel, with the kind permission of Natasha Bregel.)

~

Introduction

Russia's movement to the East had already begun at the time of the Tatar Yoke.

Mikhail Afrikanovich Terent'ev, *History of the Conquest of Central Asia* (1906)

This book tells the story of how Central Asia became Russian. With the fall of Kazan in 1552 Medieval Muscovy had extended its frontier to the Volga. It reached the Caspian in 1556, with the capture of Astrakhan, and by the end of the sixteenth century had expanded beyond the Urals, with the destruction of the khanate of Sibir'. Over the following 200 years Russian rule in Siberia and the Urals was gradually consolidated, but until the 1820s the Russian Empire's southern frontier in Asia remained more or less unchanged, a string of fortified outposts along the Ural and Irtysh rivers. By the early twentieth century it lay almost 1,800 miles further south; 1.5 million square miles and perhaps 6 million new subjects had been added to the Tsar's domains. Russian Central Asia stretched from the Altai and Ala-Tau mountains in the east of what is now Kazakhstan to the deserts of Transcaspia (Turkmenistan) in the west, with a southern frontier which ran through the lofty plateaus of the Pamirs and along the Amu-Darya, the Oxus of antiquity. The basins of Central Asia's other great rivers – the Syr-Darya, the Zarafshan, the Ili, the Murghab – all lay wholly or partially in Russian territory, as did the whole of the Aral Sea and almost the whole of the Caspian shore. The states which had existed in southern Central Asia – the khanate of Khoqand in Ferghana, the khanate of Khiva in Khwarazm and the emirate of Bukhara in the Zarafshan valley – had in the first case been destroyed, and in the latter two transformed into Russian protectorates.[1]

For some contemporaries this subjugation of the lands and peoples between Siberia and the Oxus was a form of revenge for the 'Tatar Yoke' of the

[1] See Yuri Bregel, 'The New Uzbek States: Bukhara, Khiva and Khoqand *c.* 1750–1886', in *The Cambridge History of Inner Asia: The Chingissid Age* ed. Nicola Di Cosmo, Allen J. Frank & Peter B. Golden (Cambridge: Cambridge University Press, 2009), 392–411 for a more detailed description of the political geography of Central Asia before the Russian conquest.

thirteenth and fourteenth centuries, when Muscovy had been subject to the Turco-Mongol Golden Horde.[2] It was also seen as part of a wider civilising mission, which saw Russia take her place among the other European colonial empires that dominated the nineteenth-century world;[3] as a means of championing the spread of Orthodox Christianity in a region most of whose population were Muslims;[4] and as a reconquest by 'Aryans' of a region long dominated by Turkic peoples.[5] Above all, it was perhaps the pre-eminent assertion of Russia's status as a Great Power in the nineteenth century. The pace and scale of Russian territorial expansion attracted the admiration and apprehension of Russia's rivals, and formed an important part of the 'myth of conquest' which underpinned the authority of the Russian monarchy.[6] Central Asia's conquest was the most spectacular example of such expansion: it was by far the most substantial territory added to the Russian empire between the Congress of Vienna and the First World War. While the individual campaigns of conquest were usually fairly brief, taken together they spanned almost a century – from the end of the Napoleonic Wars, when Russian attention began to shift away from Europe towards the empire's Asian frontier, to the early 1900s when the last formal territorial annexation took place in the Pamirs.

Russia's new Central Asian possessions comprised a bewildering variety of landscapes, climatic zones and peoples. The steppe grasslands of the Sary-Arqa – Qazaq for 'yellow back' – which stretched across the provinces of Ural'sk, Turgai,

[2] M. A. Terent'ev, *Istoriya zavoevaniya Srednei Azii s kartami i planami* (St Pb.: A. V. Komarov, 1906), I, 1. See also V. V. Grigor'ev, 'Russkaya politika v otnoshenii k Srednei Azii', in *Sbornik Gosudarstvennykh Znanii* I ed. V. P. Bezobrazov (St Pb.: Tip. V. P. Bezobrazov, 1874), 233–61; S. M. Seredonin, 'Istoricheskii ocherk zavoevaniya aziatskoi Rossii', in *Aziatskaya Rossiya* (St Pb.: Izd. Pereselencheskago Upravleniya, 1914), I, 1–2.

[3] P. P. Semenov, 'Znachenie Rossii v kolonizatsionnom dvizhenii evropeiskikh narodov', *IIRGO* 38 (1892), 349–69; Adeeb Khalid, 'Culture and Power in Colonial Turkestan', in *CAC.* Vols. 17–18. *Le Turkestan russe: Une colonie comme les autres?* ed. Svetlana Gorshenina & Sergej Abašin (Tashkent & Aix-en-Provence: IFEAC, Éditions De Boccard,2009), 413–47; Ulrich Hofmeister, *Die Bürde des Weißen Zaren: Russische Vorstellungen einer imperialen Zivilisierungsmission in Zentralasien* (Stuttgart: Franz Steiner, 2019).

[4] N. P. Ostroumov, *Kitaiskie emigranty v Semirechenskoi Oblasti Turkestanskogo Kraya i rasprostranenie sredi nikh Pravoslavnogo Khristianstva* (Kazan: Tip. Imperatorskogo Universiteta, 1879); Bakhtiyar Babajanov, 'How Will We Appear in the Eyes of *inovertsy* and *inorodtsy*? Nikolai Ostroumov on the Image and Function of Russian Power', *CAS* 33/ 2 (2014), 270–88.

[5] M. I. Veniukov, 'Postupatel'noe dvizhenie Rossii v Srednei Azii', in *Sbornik Gosudarstvennykh Znanii* III ed. V. P. Bezobrazov (St Pb.: Tip V. Bezobrazova, 1877), 60; Marlène Laruelle, *Mythe aryen et rêve impérial dans la Russie du XIXe siècle* (Paris: CNRS Éditions, 2005), 138–9.

[6] Richard Wortman, *Scenarios of Power: Myth and Ceremony in the Russian Monarchy.* Vol. I. *From Peter the Great to the Death of Nicholas I* (Princeton, NJ: Princeton University Press, 1995), 26–30, 42–51; Vol. II. *From Alexander II to the Abdication of Nicholas II* (Princeton, NJ: Princeton University Press, 2000), 6–15.

Akmolinsk and Semipalatinsk – shaded into the lakes and pine forests of Siberia on their northern fringe. To their south lay the Turkestan governor-generalship, whose two northernmost provinces, Semirechie and Syr-Darya, also included much steppe country: in Semirechie this was bounded by the Ili river and the shallow waters of Lake Balkhash in the north, and by the snow-capped Tian-Shan range in the south, while in Syr-Darya the grassland and saxaul-studded scrub faded into the Qizil-Qum (Red Sands) south-east of the Aral Sea. All of this territory was inhabited primarily by nomadic or semi-nomadic Qazaqs, apart from scattered fortresses and small urban settlements with mixed Russian and Tatar populations. At the southern tip of Syr-Darya province lay Tashkent, the largest city of Central Asia and the administrative centre of the Turkestan governor-generalship. It sat on the threshold between the nomadic regions to the north – historically known as the *Dasht-i Qipchaq*, or 'Plain of the Qipchaqs' – and the irrigated basin between the Syr-Darya and Amu-Darya, known by the Arabic name of *Ma wara' al-nahr*, or 'the land beyond the river' – Transoxiana in English – where most of Central Asia's historic cities were located. By the nineteenth century the most agriculturally rich region of the sedentary zone was the Ferghana valley, core of the brash new khanate of Khoqand, whose population had probably overtaken that of the Zarafshan valley – with its ancient urban centres of Bukhara and Samarkand – in the late eighteenth century, as it grew rich on trade with Qing China.[7] The third of the great agricultural oases of Central Asia was Khwarazm, a relatively isolated region in the delta of the Amu-Darya, south of the Aral Sea, alternating desert and marshland and centred on the city of Khiva. The settled oases of Central Asia were gentle landscapes of poplars and irrigation canals, intensively cultivated and managed as peasant smallholdings interspersed with compact villages and walled towns. Their inhabitants were known generically by the Russians as 'Sarts' – a term of disputed origin which by the late nineteenth century was used as a blanket label for the Turkic-speaking sedentary population of Central Asia.[8] The ruling dynasties and elites of Bukhara, Khoqand and Khiva were Uzbeks, descended from a group of Qipchaq Turkic tribes which had migrated from the steppe to Transoxiana in the sixteenth century. In Khwarazm there were also Qaraqalpaqs (a settled people speaking a language similar to Qazaq) and Turkmen. These groups were all Turkic-speaking Sunni Muslims of the Hanafi school, but in Bukhara and Samarkand there were also significant numbers of Tajiks (i.e. Persian-speakers), Jews and *Iranis* (Shi'i

---

[7] Scott Levi, *The Rise and Fall of Khoqand 1709–1876: Central Asia in the Global Age* (Pittsburgh, PA: Pittsburgh University Press, 2017), 23; Laura Newby, *The Empire and the Khanate: A Political History of Qing Relations with Khoqand c. 1760–1860* (Leiden: Brill, 2005), 184–209.

[8] On the 'Sart' question see Adeeb Khalid, *The Politics of Muslim Cultural Reform: Jadidism in Central Asia* (Berkeley, CA: University of California Press, 1998), 187–90; Sergei Abashin, *Natsionalizmy v Srednei Azii: V poiskakh identichnosti* (St Pb.: Aleteia, 2007), 99–176.

Muslims, the descendants of Persian slaves). To the east of the Zarafshan and Ferghana valleys lay the great mountain massif of the Tian-Shan and Turkestan ranges, and ultimately the Pamir plateau and the Himalayas. These mountains were largely inhabited by Kyrgyz pastoralists, although some valleys along the upper Zarafshan and at the edges of the Pamir plateau had populations of sedentary agriculturalists, most of whom spoke dialects of Persian and followed the Isma'ili branch of Shi'i Islam. To the west, beyond the Amu-Darya and towards the Caspian, the Zarafshan and Khwarazm oases gave way to the harshness of the Qara-Qum (Black Sands), with cultivable areas along the Atrek and Murghab rivers and in the Akhal-Teke oasis at the foot of the Köpet Dagh mountains, mostly populated by Turkmen.

The conquest of Central Asia presented the Russian empire with a vast, almost exclusively Muslim territory which, unlike earlier Asian conquests in Siberia, remained stubbornly 'alien' (chuzhoi) and turned out to be permanently unassimilable to the Russian 'core'. The military elite that conquered Central Asia also governed it for the fifty-odd years of Tsarist rule that preceded the revolutions of 1917, and fundamentally shaped its administration. This helped to ensure that until the fall of the Tsarist regime Central Asia would remain outside the main civic structures of the empire, and its very difference encouraged Russian statesmen to think of it as a colony analogous to French North Africa or British India – a colony which by the early twentieth century was subject to elaborate plans for economic exploitation and increased Russian settlement.[9] In the Soviet period Russian colonialism would be replaced by an extraordinary experiment in nation-building, in which Central Asia once again represented the greatest challenge because of its perceived 'backwardness' and distance from European civilisational norms.[10]

---

[9]   Daniel Brower, *Turkestan and the Fate of the Russian Empire* (London: Routledge, 2003), 140–5; Jeff Sahadeo, *Russian Colonial Society in Tashkent, 1865–1923* (Bloomington, IN: Indiana University Press, 2007); A. S. Morrison, *Russian Rule in Samarkand 1868–1910: A Comparison with British India* (Oxford: Oxford University Press, 2008); Willard Sunderland, 'The Ministry of Asiatic Russia: The Colonial Office That Never Was but Might Have Been', *SR* 69/1 (2010), 120–50; Alexander Morrison, 'Metropole, Colony and Imperial Citizenship in the Russian Empire', *Kritika* 13/2 (2012), 327–64; Paolo Sartori, *Visions of Justice: Sharī'a and Cultural Change in Russian Central Asia* (Leiden: Brill, 2016).

[10]   Terry Martin, *The Affirmative Action Empire: Nations and Nationalism in the Soviet Union, 1923–1939* (Ithaca, NY: Cornell University Press, 2001), 125–81; Shoshana Keller, *To Moscow, not Mecca: The Soviet Campaign against Islam in Central Asia, 1917–1941* (New York: Praeger, 2001); Arne Haugen, *The Establishment of National Republics in Soviet Central Asia* (Basingstoke: Palgrave Macmillan, 2003); Adrienne Edgar, *Tribal Nation: The Making of Soviet Turkmenistan* (Princeton, NJ: Princeton University Press, 2004); Francine Hirsch, *Empire of Nations: Ethnographic Knowledge and the Making of the Soviet Union* (Ithaca, NY: Cornell University Press, 2005), 160–86; Marianne Kamp, *The New Woman in Uzbekistan: Islam, Modernity and Unveiling under Communism* (Seattle, WA: University of Washington Press, 2006); Paul Bergne, *The Birth of Tajikistan: National Identity and the Origins of the Republic* (London: I.B. Tauris, 2007); Jeremy

Both Tsarist Russia and the Soviet Union would have been very different states without their Central Asian territories.

However, while its importance for the course of Russian history is beyond dispute, the conquest of Central Asia deserves also to be studied in its own right, not as an incidental outcome of the great power politics of the nineteenth century, or a minor appendage to the history of the Russian Empire. Its real significance is to be found in Central Asia itself, where its legacy was 130 years of Russian and Soviet rule, and an unequal political and cultural relationship with Russia which continues to this day. Understanding the course and consequences of the Russian conquest in and for Central Asia is at the heart of this book. The sources that can allow us to gain this understanding – both in Russian and in Central Asian languages – are almost embarrassingly abundant, though heavily skewed towards the Russian perspective. A brief glance at the bibliography will show that, even before former Soviet archives and manuscript collections were opened to foreign researchers after 1991, there was a huge amount of published material available – military memoirs, collections of documents, official histories, editions and translations of chronicles in Persian and Chaghatai.[11] Despite this, while there are excellent recent studies in English of the conquest of the Caucasus and Russian expansion in the Far East, the Russian conquest of Central Asia remains neglected and misunderstood.[12] There are no modern works which seek to explain its motives, processes and outcomes of the kind that we have for British and French conquests in Asia and Africa in the same period.[13] There is nothing

Smith, *Red Nations: The Nationalities Experience in and after the USSR* (Cambridge: Cambridge University Press, 2013), 76–84; Adeeb Khalid, *Making Uzbekistan: Nation, Empire and Revolution in the Early USSR* (Ithaca, NY: Cornell University Press, 2015).

[11] Two very useful Soviet-era guides to this material are L. M. Epifanova, *Rukopisnye istochniki po istorii Srednei Azii perioda prisoedineniya ee k Rossii* (Tashkent: Nauka, 1965) and L. G. Levteeva, *Prisoedinenie Srednei Azii k Rossii v memuarnykh istochnikakh* (Tashkent: FAN, 1986).

[12] Moshe Gammer, *Muslim Resistance to the Tsar: Shamil and the Russian Conquest of Chechnia and Daghestan* (London: Frank Cass, 1994); V. O. Bobrovnikov, *Musul'mane Severnogo Kavkaza: Obychai, pravo, nasilie* (Moscow: Vostochnaya Literatura, 2002); Michael Khodarkovsky, *Bitter Choices: Loyalty and Betrayal in the Russian Conquest of the North Caucasus* (Ithaca, NY: Cornell University Press, 2011); Mark Bassin, *Imperial Visions: Nationalist Imagination and Geographical Expansion in the Russian Far East, 1840–1865* (Cambridge: Cambridge University Press, 1999); David Schimmelpenninck van der Oye, *Toward the Rising Sun: Russian Ideologies of Empire and the Path to War with Japan* (DeKalb, IL: Northern Illinois University Press, 2001).

[13] Notably R. Robinson and J. Gallagher's classic study of the 'Scramble for Africa': *Africa and the Victorians: The Official Mind of Imperialism* (London: Collins 1965). See also Benjamin Brower, *A Desert Named Peace: The Violence of France's Empire in the Algerian Sahara 1844–1902* (New York: Columbia University Press, 2009); Randolf G. S. Cooper, *The Anglo-Maratha Campaigns and the Contest for India: The Struggle for Control of the South Asian Military Economy* (Cambridge: Cambridge University Press, 2003); John

comparable to Peter Perdue's magnificent account of the Qing dynasty's Inner Asian campaigns against the Junghars 100 years earlier.[14] This is partly because, as Dominic Lieven has observed, the military and diplomatic history of the Russian empire have been thoroughly out of fashion for the past thirty years.[15] It is also because, as discussed below, there have long been certain ready-made, facile explanations of why the conquest happened which historians have been happy to invoke unquestioningly without bothering to delve further. While there are some recent studies of specific episodes and campaigns, which will be referred to in the relevant chapters, the only works in English that attempt to understand the conquest of Central Asia as a whole were published in the 1960s and 1970s and are brief and outdated.[16] David Mackenzie's biographical study of General Mikhail Grigor'evich Chernyaev (1828–1898) is perhaps the best of the existing scholarship, but is understandably focused on his principal protagonist, and is wedded to an explanation of the conquest as the outcome of disobedience which is in the end inadequate.[17] With the exception of Robert Baumann and Alex Marshall, who concentrate on tactics, the conquest of Central Asia has been equally neglected by military historians.[18] We have some books that offer a grand geopolitical perspective on Russian expansion, but they suffer from a lack of detailed local studies on which to base these generalisations, which leads to frequent errors and the casting of a retrospective smoothness and rationality over Russian actions

Darwin, 'Imperialism and the Victorians: The Dynamics of Territorial Expansion', *EHR* 112 (1997), 614–42; Michael H. Fisher, *The Politics of the British Annexation of India 1757–1857* (Delhi: Oxford University Press, 1997); Douglas Porch, *The Conquest of the Sahara* (London: Jonathan Cape, 1984); A. S. Kanya-Forstner, *The Conquest of the Western Sudan: A Study in French Military Imperialism* (Cambridge: Cambridge University Press, 1969).

[14] Peter C. Perdue, *China Marches West: The Qing Conquest of Central Eurasia* (Cambridge, MA: Belknap Press, 2005).

[15] Dominic Lieven, 'Introduction', in *The Cambridge History of Russia* ed. Dominic Lieven (Cambridge: Cambridge University Press, 2006), II, 3.

[16] In particular the articles in Alexander Morrison (ed.), *The Russian Conquest of Central Asia*. Special Issue of *CAS* 33/2 (2014); Hélène Carrère d'Encausse, 'Systematic Conquest, 1865 to 1884', in *Central Asia: A Century of Russian Rule* ed. Edward Allworth (New York: Columbia University Press, 1967), 131–50; Seymour Becker, *Russia's Protectorates in Central Asia: Bukhara and Khiva 1865–1924* (Cambridge MA: Harvard University Press, 1968), 1–45.

[17] David MacKenzie, 'Expansion in Central Asia: St Petersburg vs. the Turkestan Generals (1863–1866)', *Canadian Slavic Studies* 3/2 (1969), 286–311 and *The Lion of Tashkent: The Career of General M. G. Cherniaev* (Athens, GA: University of Georgia Press, 1974).

[18] Robert F. Baumann, 'The Conquest of Central Asia', in *Russian-Soviet Unconventional Wars in the Caucasus, Central Asia, and Afghanistan*. Leavenworth papers No. 20 (Fort Leavenworth, KS: Combat Studies Institute, 1993), 49–115; Alex Marshall, *The Russian General Staff and Asia, 1800–1917* (Abingdon: Routledge, 2006), 46–66; Bruce Menning, *Bayonets before Bullets: The Imperial Russian Army 1861–1914* (Bloomington, IN: Indiana University Press, 1992), 12.

which is often deeply misleading.[19] The closest equivalent to a holistic explanation for Russian imperialism as comprehensive as Cain and Hopkins's 'Gentlemanly Capitalism' thesis for the expansion of the British Empire is Dietrich Geyer's pioneering analysis of the interaction of Russian domestic and foreign policy from the 1860s, but unlike the former work, which has sparked more than three decades of intense debate and revision, Geyer's arguments have produced little in the way of engagement or response – and his book does not cover the period of Russian expansion in Central Asia before 1860 in any case.[20]

Virtually all of the scanty Anglophone historiography tends to concentrate on the fall of Tashkent in 1865 and the campaigns which followed it, not least because this coincided (and it was no more than a coincidence) with the global cotton famine during the American Civil War which supposedly provided the main spur for the Russian conquest.[21] Tashkent is almost 1,000 miles to the south of Orenburg and Omsk, the centres of Russian power in the northern steppe at the end of the Napoleonic Wars. How did the Russians come to be in the city's vicinity by the 1860s? How did the vast expanse of the Qazaq steppe come to be conquered?[22] In fact the Russian empire had been pursuing an aggressive and expansionist policy in Central Asia since the late 1830s, and the most crucial stages of the Russian advance – from Orenburg to the Syr-Darya in the west, and from Omsk and Semipalatinsk across the Ili River into Semirechie in the east – took place in the 1840s and 1850s. Tashkent's capture was only the culmination of an advance which began twenty-five years earlier, and which would probably have been completed much sooner had the Crimean War not intervened. Whilst understanding the long-term thinking behind the annexation of Tashkent, the first major city taken by the Russians in the settled regions of Central Asia, is obviously important, as is understanding the reasons why the advance continued so relentlessly thereafter, the original motives which launched Russia on the path of conquest have to be sought in an

---

[19] William C. Fuller, *Strategy and Power in Russia 1600–1914* (Toronto: the Free Press, 1992), 289–92; J. P. LeDonne, *The Russian Empire and the World, 1700–1917: The Geopolitics of Expansion and Containment* (Oxford: Oxford University Press, 1997); John P. LeDonne, *The Grand Strategy of the Russian Empire, 1650–1831* (Oxford: Oxford University Press, 2004); Alfred J. Rieber, *The Struggle for the Eurasian Borderlands: From the Rise of Early Modern Empires to the End of the First World War* (Cambridge: Cambridge University Press, 2014), 395–415.

[20] P. J. Cain & A. G. Hopkins, *British Imperialism: Innovation and Expansion 1688–1914* (London: Longmans, 1990); Dietrich Geyer, *Russian Imperialism: The Interaction of Domestic and Foreign Policy 1860–1914* trans. Bruce Little (Leamington Spa: Berg, 1987).

[21] LeDonne, indeed, claims that the conquest of Central Asia *began* in 1864: *Grand Strategy*, 235.

[22] The only study of this in English is Janet Kilian, 'Allies and Adversaries: The Russian Conquest of the Kazakh Steppe' (Ph.D. Dissertation, The George Washington University, 2013).

earlier period. The men who took the crucial decisions that began the Russian conquest of Central Asia were not the 'disobedient' generals of the 1860s, but the generation of statesmen and soldiers that came of age during the war against Napoleon, something explored in Chapter 1.

The literature in Russian on the conquest is much more extensive, but – as we will see – most of it is distorted by the Soviet insistence that imperialism was primarily driven by economic motives, and some recent publications are marked by unapologetic jingoism.[23] Writing from the Tsarist period is often of much higher quality, but inevitably compromised by its proximity to events, and by the need to construct an appropriately heroic narrative: much of it, indeed, was produced under the direct sponsorship of the War Ministry. This is the case for the only previous history of the Russian conquest of Central Asia worthy of the name, that of General Mikhail Afrikanovich Terent'ev (1837–1909), whose opening line provides the epigraph for this introduction.[24] Terent'ev's book is in many ways an astonishing achievement. He spent over thirty years research-ing and writing it, beginning it as a young man serving under the first Turkestan Governor-General, Konstantin Petrovich von Kaufman (1818–1882), who com-missioned it from him in 1871. Its eventual publication in three volumes in 1906 came thanks to the support of War Minister General Alexei Nikolaevich Kuropatkin (1848–1925), another *Turkestanets* (old Turkestan hand).[25] Terent'ev's is the only truly comprehensive history of the conquest, beginning with the winter invasion of Khiva in 1839–40, and culminating with the Anglo-Russian agreement to divide the Pamirs in 1895. It deals exhaustively with the decision-making behind Russian campaigns, their planning and organisation, and the many foibles and flaws of the personalities involved. It provides vivid descriptions of battles, marches through steppe and desert, triumphs and tra-gedies of Russian arms in Central Asia. Terent'ev knew most of the principal actors on the Russian side personally, and many of his insights are based on conversations, mess gossip and what we would now call oral history, though he was also an assiduous archival researcher. As I worked through piles of corres-pondence, campaign diaries and memoranda in the reading room of the Military-Historical Archive in Moscow (formerly that of the Tsarist Ministry of War), I frequently had the distinct sense that Terent'ev had been there before me – never more vividly than when, after congratulating myself on finding the Chaghatai original of a remarkable letter of defiance from a Kyrgyz leader called 'Abdullah Bek to General Mikhail Dmitr'evich Skobelev (1843–1882), I opened

[23] For example Evgenii Glushchenko, *Rossiya v Srednei Azii: Zavoevaniya i preobrazovaniya* (Moscow: Tsentropoligraf, 2010).
[24] M. A. Terent'ev, *Istoriya zavoevaniya Srednei Azii s kartami i planami* (St Pb.: Tip. A. V. Komarova, 1906) 3 vols.
[25] On this and other aspects of the Tsarist military historiography of the conquest, see Alexander Morrison, 'The 'Turkestan Generals' and Russian Military History', *War in History* 26/2 (2019), 153–84.

INTRODUCTION 9

the relevant chapter of Terent'ev to find that he had clearly read exactly the same file and had included the Russian translation of the letter in his history (see Chapter 8).[26] I will refer to Terent'ev throughout this book, and there will be times when I rely on him for details that might once have been part of the common lore of the *Turkestantsy*, but which are now only available in Terent'ev's *History*. Nevertheless, it is high time his work was superseded. Terent'ev was a participant in the campaigns of conquest himself, and did not even pretend to emotional detachment from the events he described. To the usual prejudices and beliefs of a Russian officer of his day he added violent prejudices against the British – often blamed for their aggression and Machiavellian manoeuvring in a manner highly reminiscent of later Soviet historiography; against officers of German descent (including his erstwhile patron, von Kaufman); and against officers of the Caucasian corps. This led him, for instance, to excoriate von Kaufman's massacre of the Yomud Turkmen after the conquest of Khiva in 1873 (Chapter 7), but to turn a blind eye to the equally brutal and unnecessary violence committed by Skobelev against unarmed civilians during the Ferghana campaign of 1875–6 – indeed Skobelev was one of the all-Russian heroes of Terent'ev's narrative: the verdict on him in this book is very different.[27] Terent'ev had little interest in Russia's Central Asian opponents, apart from occasional unflattering character sketches of rulers such as Khudoyar Khan of Khoqand or Amir Sayyid Muzaffar of Bukhara. The 'natives' are described in his work using the usual tropes of his day – as savage, untrustworthy and often cowardly. He was almost entirely blind to the reliance of the Russians on Qazaq auxiliaries as guides, and as suppliers of the camels without which the Russian conquest would never even have begun. Above all Terent'ev was not really able to explain *why* the Russians conquered Central Asia – he made occasional references to the intransigence of Central Asian rulers and the aggression of the British, but was really too wholeheartedly wrapped up in the details of his story and settling scores with his enemies to spend much time analysing motives, or the unspoken assumptions that under-pinned Russian policy. The chief of these assumptions was perhaps the most significant – that conquering and subduing your weaker neighbours was simply what was expected of a Great Power – especially when those neighbours were as turbulent and insolent as those in Central Asia. This is a theme I will return to.

To outside observers at the time the motivation for the conquest seemed quite clear. The British saw it as the pre-eminent example of Russian

[26] Terent'ev, *Istoriya zavoevaniya*, II, 418.
[27] Terent'ev, *Istoriya zavoevaniya* II, 267–279, 405–10. For an unadulterated hagiography (designed to stimulate patriotic feelings during the First World War) see E. Tolbukhov, 'Skobelev v Turkestane (1869–1877 g.)', *IV* (1916) No. 10, pp. 107–32; No. 11, pp. 369–403; No. 12, pp. 638–67. More broadly on the posthumous cult of Skobelev see Hans Rogger, 'The Skobelev Phenomenon: The Hero and his Worship', *Oxford Slavonic Papers* 9 (1976), 46–7.

aggression and territorial acquisitiveness, directed primarily at their own empire in India.[28] Later Soviet historians believed (or were forced to argue) that it was economically motivated, fuelled by a desire for captive markets and secure sources of raw materials. Both of these are misconceptions. Russian motives were rarely constant, and did not rest on any kind of 'grand strategy', whether political or economic. One great merit of Terent'ev's history was that he focused mainly on Russian relations with Central Asian rulers and peoples. He was not in thrall to any of the grand narratives that have consistently blighted most attempts to write about the subject, of which the most infuriatingly persistent is the 'Great Game'.

I.1   The 'Great Game'

We all began to explain the Central Asian question off-hand, flinging army corps from the Helmund to Kashmir with more than Russian recklessness.

Rudyard Kipling 'A Conference of the Powers' (1890)

Russia was too big and was pointing in the direction of India

W. C. Sellar & R. J. Yeatman *1066 & All That* (1933)

Kipling's Anglo-Indian short story and Sellar and Yeatman's brilliant satire on the teaching of British history were written for very different purposes more than forty years apart, but between them they illustrate the enduring hold which the 'Great Game' between Britain and Russia has had on the way English-speakers view Central Asia and its history.[29] The most potent of historical clichés, this imagined nineteenth-century Cold War has spawned an entire school of historical writing based on the same narrow group of (mostly published) English-language sources, and consisting largely of a series of anecdotes of adventure and derring-do by heavily moustachioed officers and explorers against a picturesque but badly drawn Central Asian backdrop.[30] There is a more scholarly tradition which explores the foreign policy of British

---

[28]   Rob Johnson, '"Russians at the Gates of India": Planning the Strategic Defence of India, 1884–1899', *JMH* 67 (2003), 697–743; M. E. Yapp, 'British Perceptions of the Russian Threat to India', *MAS* 21/4 (1987), 647–65.

[29]   Portions of this and the following section were first published in Alexander Morrison, 'Introduction: Killing the Cotton Canard and Getting Rid of the Great Game: Rewriting the Russian Conquest of Central Asia, 1814–1895',*CAS* 33/2 (2014), 131–42 and reappear here by kind permission of the publisher.

[30]   The best-known of these is Peter Hopkirk, *The Great Game: On Secret Service in High Asia* (London: John Murray, 1990), but see also Karl Meyer & Shareen Brysac, *Tournament of Shadows: The Great Game and the Race for Empire in Asia* (Washington D.C.: Counterpoint, 1999); Rob Johnson, *Spying for Empire: The Great Game in Central and South Asia 1757–1947* (London: Greenhill, 2006); John Ure, *Shooting Leave: Spying out Central Asia in the Great Game* (London: Constable, 2010).

India and relations with Russia, most notably the work of Garry Alder, Edward Ingram and Malcolm Yapp, but even this is hampered by a lack of access to Russian sources, and a focus not on Central Asia itself but on how the British imagined it.[31] Evgenii Sergeev's *The Great Game*, published in both English and Russian, is the only book on the topic to make extensive use of both British and Russian archives, but it falls into many of the same traps.[32] In Sergeev's account every advance made by the Russians in Central Asia is a response to something the British had done, and he largely ignores Russian relations with Central Asian rulers and peoples. His insistence on the centrality of Anglo-Russian rivalry frequently leads him into errors of chronology, usually because of a failure to appreciate that any Russian military expedition in Central Asia required months of planning and a lengthy decision-making process before it was actually launched. Sergeev's book also opens only in the aftermath of the Crimean War, when many of the most decisive Russian moves in Central Asia had already been undertaken.

The broader problem with the 'Great Game' narrative is that it marginalises or ignores completely Central Asian rulers, states and peoples, which become little more than an incidental detail in a story of 'Great Power' rivalry.[33] Consciously or unconsciously this reproduces the nineteenth-century European assumption that Central Asians were savage, backward, barbarous and unamenable to any form of diplomacy or negotiation.[34] In fact British and Russian 'players' of the 'Great Game' had shared assumptions about the inferiority and exoticism of 'Asiatics', and the benefits of Europe's civilising mission. Where the 'Game' was played at all, it was in a spirit as much of cooperation as of competition, as travellers, envoys and spies on both sides recognised the same imperial ethos in their opposite numbers – something that was particularly clear during the last phase of Russian expansion into the Pamirs (Chapter 10).[35] This would culminate in the 1907 Anglo-Russian

---

[31] G. J. Alder, *British India's Northern frontier 1865–95; a Study in Imperial Policy* (London: Longmans, 1963); Edward Ingram, *The Beginning of the Great Game in Asia, 1828–1834* (Oxford: Clarendon Press, 1979) and *In Defence of British India: Great Britain in the Middle East, 1774–1842* (London: Cass, 1984); M. E. Yapp, *Strategies of British India: Britain, Iran and Afghanistan, 1798–1850* (Oxford: Clarendon Press, 1980).

[32] Evgeny Sergeev, *The Great Game 1856–1907* (Washington, D.C.: Woodrow Wilson Centre & Johns Hopkins University Press, 2013); E. Sergeev, *Bol'shaya Igra: Mify i realii rossiisko-britanskikh otnoshenii v Tsentral'noi i Vostochnoi Azii* (Moscow: KMK, 2012)

[33] Benjamin Hopkins, *The Making of Modern Afghanistan* (Basingstoke: Palgrave Macmillan, 2008), 34–47.

[34] The only attempt to apply international relations theory to Central Asia in this period combines these prejudices with a truly jaw-dropping lack of primary research: Joseph Mackay, 'International Politics in Eighteenth- and Nineteenth-Century Central Asia: Beyond Anarchy in International Relations Theory', *CAS* 32/2 (2013), 210–24.

[35] Alexander Morrison, 'Russian Rule in Turkestan and the Example of British India', *SEER* 84/4 (2006), 689–91; Ian W. Campbell, '"Our Friendly Rivals": Rethinking the Great Game in Ya'qub Beg's Kashgaria, 1867–77', *CAS* 33/2 (2014), 199–214.

agreement which in principle demarcated the two empires' relative spheres of influence and divided Central Asia's territory between them.[36] The relative ease with which these long-standing disagreements were apparently resolved took the Germans by surprise, and put the coping-stone on the alliance system that would have such fateful consequences in the summer of 1914.[37] As Jennifer Siegel has shown, the Russian empire continued to encroach into Northern Persia before and during the First World War, producing continued tensions with Britain – but the most likely consequence of this would have been a further mutually agreed territorial partition, this time of Persia, not an open conflict. The priority for both empires by this date lay in Europe with their common fear of Germany.[38]

The 'Great Game' will doubtless continue to fascinate monoglot British historians, but its glamour always exceeded its practical importance, and its long-term consequences even for the security of British India turned out to be fairly negligible.[39] For Russia herself the rivalry with Britain was important primarily in ideological terms: Britain was the leading 'Great Power' against which she measured her own imperial and diplomatic achievements, and whose global reach and clout she sought to emulate. It was this resentment of and desire to 'get even' with Britain, rather than any rational calculation of strategic advantage, which led to the one authorised attempt by the Russians to invade India, Paul I's despatch of 20,000 Cossacks in 1801.[40] Significantly enough, this was launched by a Tsar of doubtful sanity, and it was fortunate for the Cossacks sent on this hare-brained enterprise that they were halted near Saratov, before they had penetrated the steppes of Emba and the Ust-Yurt plateau, which would prove the doom of V. A. Perovskii's expedition to Khiva forty years later. In practical, strategic terms though, attempts to play on British fears of Russian expansion towards India, and Russia's own fear of British expansion in Central Asia, only really came to prominence at the time of the First and Second Anglo-Afghan Wars (1839–42 and 1878–80).[41] Otherwise, as we will see, it is remarkable how seldom British India featured in the calculations of the Russian soldiers

[36] F. Kazemzadeh, 'Anglo-Russian Convention of 1907', in *Encyclopædia Iranica*, II/1, 68–70.
[37] Rudolf A. Mark, *Im Schatten des „Great Game": Deutsche „Weltpolitik" und russischer Imperialismus in Zentralasien 1871–1914* (Paderborn: Ferdinand Schoeningh, 2012), 329–39.
[38] Jennifer Siegel, *Endgame: Britain, Russia and the Final Struggle for Central Asia* (London: I.B. Tauris, 2002).
[39] M. E. Yapp, 'The Legend of the Great Game', *Proceedings of the British Academy* 111 (2001), 179–98.
[40] David Schimmelpenninck van der Oye, 'Paul's Great Game: Russia's Plan to Invade British India', *CAS* 33/2 (2014), 143–52.
[41] See Alexander Morrison, 'Twin Imperial Disasters: The Invasions of Khiva and Afghanistan in the Russian and British Official Mind, 1838–1842', *MAS* 48/1 (2014), 253–300 and 'Beyond the "Great Game": The Russian Origins of the Second Anglo-Afghan War', *MAS* 51/3 (2017), 686–735.

and statesmen who planned and undertook the conquest of Central Asia: when the British were considered, it was usually as a restraining factor, as the Ministry of Foreign Affairs wanted to avoid provoking tensions in Europe through adventurism in Central Asia. Any study of this period requires a more profound understanding of Russian intentions, motivations and actions than is possible when viewing them through the British lens of 'The Defence of India'. After all, the fundamental fact about the 'Great Game', if this is understood as some sort of contest for the control of Central Asia, is that British influence in the region was negligible. Accordingly, in this book the energetic explorers and paranoid proconsuls of British India have been pushed back to the margins of the story, where they belong.

I.2 Economic Theories of Expansion and the 'Cotton Canard'

The British capitalists are exerting every effort to develop cotton growing in *their* colony, Egypt [. . .] the Russians are doing the same in *their* colony, Turkestan.

V. I. Lenin, *Imperialism, The Highest Stage of Capitalism* (1916)

The *main determining factor* in assessing the progressive significance of the inclusion of the peoples of Central Asia in the Russian Empire is that, in spite of the will and desire of tsarism, they 'entered into relations with the Russian people, with the Russian working class – a powerful revolutionary force'.

N. A. Khalfin, *The Policy of Russia in Central Asia* (1960)

Soviet historians also employed a variant of the 'Great Game' argument, claiming that the conquest of Central Asia by Tsarist Russia was a 'lesser evil', as otherwise the region would have fallen into the rapacious hands of the British.[42] From the late 1940s onwards they did not even call it a conquest (*zavoevanie*), being obliged to refer instead to a 'uniting' (*prisoedinenie*) of Central Asia to Russia, generally claiming that this had had a 'progressive significance' (*progressivnoe znachenie*).[43] Unsurprisingly though, the standard Soviet explanation for the conquest was economic. Owing to a partial misreading of Lenin's ideas (which were actually meant to be applied to a much later period of imperial expansion),[44] the annexation of Turkestan was held to have been carried out at the behest of the capitalist 'big bourgeoisie'. These were the

---

[42] For example A. L. Popov, 'Bor'ba za sredneaziatskii platsdarm', *IZ* (1940) No. 7, 182–235.
[43] N. A. Khalfin, *Politika Rossii v Srednei Azii (1857–1868)* (Moscow: Izd. Vostochnoi Literatury, 1960), 234. On the enforcement of this orthodoxy, which still finds many adherents in Russia today, see Lowell Tillett, *The Great Friendship: Soviet Historians on the Non-Russian nationalities* (Chapel Hill, NC: University of North Carolina Press, 1969), 32–4, 174–190.
[44] Eric Stokes, 'Late Nineteenth-Century Colonial Expansion and the Attack on the Theory of Economic Imperialism: A Case of Mistaken Identity?', *HJ* 12/2 (1969), 285–301.

textile manufacturers of Moscow, supposedly panicked by the cotton famine of the 1860s caused by the American Civil War, and desirous of obtaining both a secure domestic supply of raw materials and a captive market for shoddy Russian industrial goods.[45] The Moscow textile 'barons' were thus meant to have played the same Machiavellian role in provoking the conquest of Central Asia as J. A. Hobson's Jewish financiers in South Africa did in engineering the Boer War, an argument which fitted snugly into official Marxism-Leninism, unsurprisingly given Lenin's considerable debt to Hobson.[46] The influence of these ideas has proved long-lasting, such that otherwise excellent recent works still give primacy to economic motives for the conquest of Turkestan in the 1860s, with the chief role being played by cotton hunger.[47] Central Asia figures prominently in Sven Beckert's ambitious account of the growth of cotton cultivation and textile production worldwide, as it appears to provide a case in point for his wider thesis about cotton remaking the global economy and driving imperial expansion.[48] However, cotton *cannot* have been the spur for a conquest which began in the 1830s, well before Russia even had a significant cotton textile industry, and which would probably have come to an end much sooner had it not been for the Crimean War. The notion that in the 1860s Russia's fledgling industrial capitalists were somehow pulling the strings of the autocracy's foreign policy behind the scenes is so inherently implausible that the onus is on those who believe in it to produce solid evidence – and none has ever been found. The Soviet historian N. A. Khalfin, the chief proponent of an economic, cotton-driven explanation for the Russian conquest of Central Asia, was able to point to a grand total of two articles in the metropolitan press from the middle of the nineteenth century which showed an interest in the economic resources of Central Asia. One of these was written by an official from the Ministry of Finance, and neither of them directly advocated either conquering the oasis regions of Central Asia or establishing Russian-controlled cotton plantations there.[49] Had the Russians felt that they needed to encourage or force the local population to grow more cotton in the 1860s, they would

---

[45] Khalfin, *Politika Rossii v Srednei Azii*, 154–64 and *Prisoedinenie Srednei Azii k Rossii* (Moscow: Nauka, 1965), 31–43; Z. D. Kastel'skaya, *Iz istorii Turkestanskogo kraya* (Moscow: Nauka, 1980), 10–12; G. A. Mikhaleva, *Torgovye i posol'skie svyazi Rossii so sredneaziatskimi khanstvami cherez Orenburg* (Tashkent: FAN, 1982), 48–53.

[46] A. M. Eckstein, 'Is There a "Hobson–Lenin Thesis" on Late Nineteenth-Century Colonial Expansion?', *EcHR* 44/2 (1991), 306–7.

[47] Marko Buttino, *Revoliutsiya naoborot* (Moscow: Zven'ya, 2007), 18; Bregel, 'The New Uzbek States', 405–11; Richard Pomfret, *The Central Asian Economies in the Twenty-First Century: Paving a New Silk Road* (Princeton, NJ: Princeton University Press, 2019), 55.

[48] Sven Beckert, 'Emancipation and Empire: Reconstructing the Worldwide Web of Cotton Production in the Age of the American Civil War', *AHR* 109/5 (2004), 1405–38 and *Empire of Cotton: A New History of Global Capitalism* (London: Allen Lane, 2014), 345–7.

[49] Khalfin, *Politika Rossii*, 151–3; Gavriil Kamenskii, 'Angliya strashnyi sopernik Rossii v torgovle i promyshlennosti', *Vestnik Promyshlennosti* (1859) No. 2, 141–61; G[agemeister,

have invaded Ferghana, the centre of the later cotton economy, but at this stage they tried hard to maintain it as a protectorate, annexing it only after a revolt in 1875. They could, in any case, have created cotton plantations in Transcaucasia, most of which had been under Russian rule since 1813, and where the land and climate are equally well-suited to cotton growing, without the need for further conquests at all.[50] There is no suggestion in any official Russian correspondence on the cotton shortage of the 1860s that expensive conquest and annexation might be needed to maximise the Asian supply. Instead, as we will see in Chapters 3, 5 and 6, Russian officials were well aware that the shortage was temporary, and demand for Central Asian cotton plummeted as soon as the American Civil War ended in 1865. Cotton would not be widely cultivated in Turkestan until the 1890s, and even then the 'Cotton Boom' of the early 1900s was largely an accidental by-product of tariff and taxation policies introduced for other reasons.[51] Julia Obertreis suggests that 'the importance of cotton as a stimulus for conquest should be signifi-cantly downgraded',[52] and I would go further and say that it should be rejected altogether, as it was already long ago in some English-language publications.[53] Even for M. K. Rozhkova, the leading Soviet historian of Russian–Central Asian trade, the conspiratorial Hobson–Lenin thesis was too much to stomach, although she continued to uphold the primacy of economic motives in the Russian conquest.[54] This renders the persistence of this Soviet-era canard all the more baffling: it is high time it too was laid to rest.

If the desire for a captive cotton plantation can be safely dismissed as a motive for the Russian conquest, the question of trade, and the importance of the Central Asian market for Russia, deserve more scrutiny. Russian officials frequently referred to the need to protect trade caravans, and sometimes

Iu. A.], 'O torgovom znachenii Srednei Azii v otnoshenii k Rossii', *RV* Vol. 41 (1862) No. 10, 706–36.

[50] Some half-hearted attempts were made to grow cotton in the Caucasus in the 1840s, but imported cotton was better and cheaper. See M. K. Rozhkova, *Ekonomicheskiya politika tsarskogo pravitel'stva na srednem vostoke vo vtoroi chetverti XIX veka i Russkaya burz-huaziya* (Moscow & Leningrad: Izd. AN SSSR, 1949), 113.

[51] Beatrice Penati, 'The Cotton Boom and the Land Tax in Russian Turkestan (1880s–1915)', *Kritika* 14/3 (2013), 741–74.

[52] Julia Obertreis, *Imperial Desert Dreams: Cotton Growing and Irrigation in Central Asia* (Göttingen: V & R Unipress, 2017), 52.

[53] John Whitman, 'Turkestan Cotton in Imperial Russia', *American Slavic and East European Review* 15/2 (1956), 190–205; Seymour Becker, 'Russia's Central Asian Empire, 1885–1917', in *Russian Colonial Expansion to 1917* ed. Michael Rywkin (London: Mansell Publishing, 1988), 235–56. Sven Beckert cites both Whitman and a draft version of Obertreis's work, but appears to deliberately ignore their conclusions because they do not fit his thesis: *Empire of Cotton*, 345–7.

[54] M. K. Rozhkova, *Ekonomicheskie svyazi Rossii so Srednei Azii 40–60e gody XIX veka* (Moscow: Izd. AN SSSR, 1963), 199–201.

outlined more ambitious aims for control of major routes as a means of
national enrichment.[55] As Scott Levi has shown, the eighteenth century saw
a significant growth in the north–south caravan trade across the Qazaq steppe,
which linked Russian markets to India and supplanted the older route across
the Caspian and up the Volga. The most important entrepôt on the steppe
frontier was the *Menovoi Dvor*, a caravanserai specifically for Central Asian
merchants outside Orenburg.[56] By far the best account of how this exchange
developed in the nineteenth century is by Rozhkova, who provides detailed
statistical analysis of Russian trade with Asia – not just with the Qazaq steppe
and the Central Asian khanates, but also with China, Persia and the Ottoman
Empire. These figures and her often shrewd analysis of them (within the limits
prescribed by Soviet historical orthodoxy) remain useful today, and have
inspired at least one innovative interpretation of the changing terms of trade
between Russia and Central Asia, namely Madhavan Palat's claim that the
1860s saw the khanates slip into an unequal, exploitative and colonial economic relationship, as they moved from being exporters of manufactures to
importers, and became producers of raw materials.[57] However, while the
economic relationship with Russia was clearly of growing importance for
Central Asia in this period, it is less clear whether the reverse was true.

    As even Khalfin was forced to admit, Central Asia accounted for only 2.5%
of Russia's external trade in the early 1850s, when the Russians first seized
territory from Khoqand with the capture of Aq Masjid ('White Mosque' –
modern Kyzylorda, on the Syr-Darya).[58] It is true that between 1820 and 1850
the Asian market absorbed between 88% and 99% of all Russia's textile exports,
but Central Asia was not the main destination for these: in 1825 56% were
destined for Persia and Turkey, and in 1850 52% were destined for China.[59]
Asian trade received a boost when European markets were cut off during the
Crimean War, when Russian exports to Asia rose to a peak of 27% of the total
in 1855, falling back to 6% once the war ended, although they remained at a
permanently higher level than before. Between 1856 and 1867 the proportion
of Russian exports across the Asian frontier rose from 6.7% to 10.6% of the
total, and more than doubled in absolute value from 10,594,000 roubles to
26,640,000 roubles. The value of this trade was increased still further as it
consisted primarily of manufactured goods, a much higher proportion than for
any other external market.[60] Between 1820 and 1860, the largest portion of

[55] Gagemeister, 'O torgovom znachenii', 722–4.
[56] Scott Levi, 'India, Russia, and the Transformation of the Central Asian Caravan Trade',
    JESHO 42/4 (1999), 519–48.
[57] Rozhkova, *Ekonomicheskie svyazi*, 66–9; Madhavan K. Palat, 'Tsarist Russian
    Imperialism', *Studies in History* 4/1–2 (1988), 157297.
[58] Khalfin, *Politika Rossii*, 39.
[59] Rozhkova, *Ekonomicheskaya politika*, 66; Palat, 'Tsarist Russian Imperialism', 229.
[60] Rozhkova, *Ekonomicheskie svyazi*, 58–9.

Table I.1 *Value of exports through the Orenburg customs, 1859–64 (roubles)*[a]

Year	Total	Of which textiles
1859	2,160,047	895,001
1860	2,014,606	819,711
1861	2,916,394	979,693
1862	4,530,142	1,207,390
1863	7,190,214	2,145,712
1864	6,358,537	2,004,300

[a] Calculated from figures in RGIA F.19 Op.1 D.961-4, 999, 1074.

Russia's Asian exports (40%–65%) was destined for China, mostly through Kiakhta in Siberia, although a growing proportion was passing through Semipalatinsk to Ili and Chinese Turkestan.[61] Exports to the steppe and the Central Asian khanates rose substantially in the 1860s, to a peak of 67% of Asian trade in 1867, though much of this was probably ultimately destined for China. As Rozhkova says, this increase may have been partly a result of the improved security and conditions for Russian traders brought about by the military advance along the line of the Syr-Darya between 1853 and 1864, but this is not to say that this was the *reason* such annexations were undertaken, as she argues.[62] The data for imports through the Orenburg customs tell a similar story – of a steady increase in the value of trade throughout the 1860s, although the proportion made up by textiles actually fell slightly in the same period (see Table I.1 and Figure I.1). However, as we will see in Chapters 3, 4 & 5, there is no evidence that trade played any significant role in Russian official decision-making in the 1850s and 1860s.

Looking at imports from Central Asia to Russia, the records of the Orenburg and Siberian customs show that throughout the first half of the nineteenth century these were dominated by animal products – principally livestock for meat, but also wool, leather, *pukh* (fluffy goat hair for a particular type of shawl made in Orenburg), tallow and even the horns of the Saiga antelope, which were used in Chinese medicine. From 1858 to 1861 the value of livestock imports through the Orenburg customs posts was almost three times that of

---

[61] Di Wang, 'The Unofficial Russo-Qing Trade on the Eastern Kazakh Steppe and in Northern Xinjiang in the First Half of the 19th Century' (M.A. Thesis, Nazarbayev University, 2018) (https://nur.nu.edu.kz/handle/123456789/3316).

[62] Rozhkova, *Ekonomicheskaya politika*, 49, 60, 64–5.

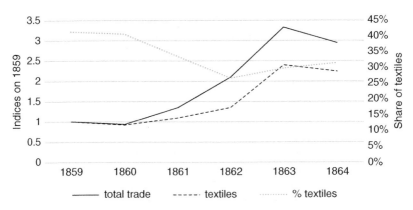

Figure I.1 Value of exports through the Orenburg customs, 1859–64.

raw cotton imports from Bukhara and Khiva, but strangely enough nobody has ever suggested that Central Asia was conquered for its sheep.[63] It was not until 1863 that the value of Central Asian cotton imported through Orenburg exceeded that of livestock from the Qazaq steppe. Market stimuli were quite sufficient to encourage Central Asian merchants to vastly increase the amount of cotton they brought to the Russian market, without any coercion required: in 1862 the value of cotton imports from Central Asia quadrupled, and overall between 1858 and 1864 they trebled in volume and increased in value by a factor of ten (see Table I.2 and Figure I.2).[64] This confirms that, in the best traditions of informal empire, the Russians were already getting pretty much what they wanted from Central Asia without formal annexation, as imports of raw cotton and exports of cotton textiles rose, whilst imports of the latter dwindled.[65] There was no need to conquer Central Asia to bring about this change.

The Central Asian market was also limited in size because of the region's small population, something many Russian commentators realized. Julius Hagemeister, an advocate of free trade and head of the Chancery of the Ministry of Finance from 1847 to 1858, was one of the few metropolitan

---

[63] 'Vedomost' Orenburgskoi Pogranichnoi Tamozhni za 1858 g.', RGIA F.19 Op.1 D.933 ll. 1220–7.

[64] Head of the Orenburg Customs Region to the Department of External Trade of the Ministry of Finance, 09/01/1863 RGIA F.19 Op.3 D.963 ll. 296–7; Head of the Orenburg Customs Region to the Department of External Trade of the Ministry of Finance, 14/01/1863 RGIA F.19 Op.3 D.964 ll. 29*ob.*–30*ob.*

[65] Palat, 'Tsarist Russian Imperialism', 234–41, using figures from Rozhkova *Ekonomicheskie svyazi*, 66–7; R. Robinson & J. Gallagher, 'The Imperialism of Free Trade', *EcHR* 4/1 (1953), 1–15.

Table I.2 *Value of imports through the Orenburg customs, 1858–64 (roubles)[a]*

Year	Total	Raw Cotton	Livestock
1858	3,402,543	647,488	1,011,311
1859	3,445,982	445,891	1,310,098
1860	4,910,485	661,327	2,069,680
1861	4,013,655	475,383	2,051,400
1862	5,364,302	1,829,208	2,087,132
1863	5,785,272	2,360,868	1,722,277
1864	9,049,903	6,473,006	802,911

[a] Calculated from figures in RGIA F.19 Op.1 D.961–4, 999, 1074.

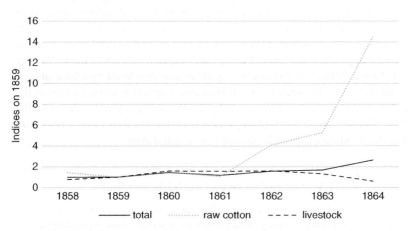

Figure I.2 Value of imports through the Orenburg customs, 1858–64.

commentators to take an interest in Central Asia's economic potential. He believed the region's population to be over eight million (almost certainly a substantial overestimate), and considered that Russia's Central Asian trade was more important than that with China or Persia, but even he acknowledged that overall it was of small value and that the empire could easily manage without it.[66] When a special committee headed by Baron Reutern, the finance minister, met in 1865 to discuss the possibility of moving the Asian customs boundary from Orenburg to the Syr-Darya line, it noted that the vast distances in Central

[66] Gagemeister, 'O torgovom znachenii', 715–17.

Asia rendered European imports uneconomic, and that the khanates were too primitive and backward to allow such trade to flourish.[67] There was greater interest in using Central Asia as a springboard to penetrate the larger Chinese, Indian and Persian markets, but even this remained a vague ambition rather than a developed plan. Geyer's study of the links between Russian domestic and foreign policy does not cover the period before 1860, but he concluded that even for the later period, when Russia had industrialised more fully, there is no evidence to suggest that economic interests played a role in the renewal of the advance into Central Asia after 1863: instead what mattered was the wider competition with Britain and a desire to restore prestige after defeat in the Crimean War.[68] Thus, while Russian officials often referred piously to the importance of trade, they saw it primarily as an instrument of policy, a means of projecting power by non-military means, and usually had only the vaguest idea of what the real prospects for trade in Central Asia actually were. Equally, despite Russian paranoia on this point, there is absolutely no evidence to suggest that British financial or trading elites had any significant interest in the region.[69] Much work remains to be done on the role that Central Asia played within the economy of the Russian empire and Soviet Union, but it is clear that in purely fiscal terms the region brought a net loss to the exchequer until at least 1909, with revenue falling short of expenditure by a total of over 85 million roubles between 1868 and 1881 alone, largely because the cost of the garrison of occupation had to be met by the War Ministry and paid for by the centre.[70] Economic theories of imperial expansion are thus of little relevance for understanding the Russian conquest of Central Asia.

I.3   Disobedience and the 'Official Mind'

Tashkent has been taken by General Chernyaev. No one knows why and for what [. . .] there is something erotic (*nechto eroticheskoe*) about everything we do on the far-flung periphery of the empire.

P. A. Valuev, Minister of Internal Affairs, 1865

The only remaining explanation offered in the existing historiography is that of disobedience – the conquest as accident, brought about by ambitious men on the spot, powerful 'local atamans' hungry for glory, medals and promotion,

---

[67] 'Kommisiya dlya razsmotreniya voprosov do aziyatskoi torgovli otnosyashchiksya Zasedaniya 08/04/1865', GAOO F.339 Op.1 D.50 'O perenesenii Orenburgskoi Tamozhennoi cherty na Syr-Dar'inskuiu liniu', ll.109*ob.*–10.

[68] Geyer, *Russian Imperialism*, 86–100.

[69] Kamenskii, 'Angliya strashnyi sopernik'; Morrison, 'Twin Imperial Disasters', 259–61.

[70] Morrison, *Russian Rule in Samarkand*, 293–4; Ekaterina Pravilova, *Finansy Imperii* (Moscow: Novoe Izd., 2006), 271–301.

whose actions were then weakly accepted as a *fait accompli* in St Petersburg.[71] This was an argument which some Tsarist military historians were happy to endorse retrospectively.[72] It is associated above all with the capture of Tashkent by Mikhail Grigor'evich Chernyaev, and in particular the well-known *bon mot* from Valuev's diary quoted above.[73] This idea of imperial expansion as something atavistic, an irrationally aggressive and anachronistic impulse by a militarised aristocratic ruling class in a modern capitalist society, is reminiscent of the theories of Joseph Schumpeter, which have long been a useful corrective to economic determinism in understanding why and when the European empires expanded.[74] It also has a long pedigree in understanding other episodes of European imperial expansion by 'prancing proconsuls', ambitious military officers or string-pulling civil servants, the *locus classicus* being the British occupation of Egypt in 1882 which triggered the 'Scramble for Africa'.[75] In Central Asia there were indeed some episodes – particularly in the late 1860s, which was the focus of Mackenzie's research – when local commanders did seek battle and annex territory without authorisation from above – these are covered in Chapter 6. Nevertheless, as an explanation for the whole course of Russian expansion from the 1830s to the early 1900s it does not hold water.

As Svetlana Gorshenina has suggested, the idea of the 'man on the spot' out of control absolved Russian statesmen of responsibility, allowing them to claim that Russia had been helplessly sucked into conquest after conquest. This is a narrative of which we should instinctively be suspicious, not least because it resembles so closely contemporary British claims that the conquest of India in the eighteenth and early nineteenth centuries had been unwilling or accidental, which was clearly not the case.[76] This explanation is also heavily dependent on seeing the fall of Tashkent as the beginning of the conquest – which, as we have

---

[71] Mackenzie, 'Expansion in Central Asia'; David Alan Rich, *The Tsar's Colonels: Professionalism, Strategy, and Subversion in Late Imperial Russia* (Cambridge, MA: Harvard University Press, 1998), 91; Bakhtiyar Babadzhanov, *Kokandskoe Khanstvo: Vlast', politika, religiya* (Tashkent & Tokyo: TIAS, 2010), 280–1.

[72] A. E. Snesarev, *Indiya kak glavnyi faktor v sredneaziatskom voprose* (St. Pb.: A. Suvorin, 1906), 51; Terent'ev, *Istoriya zavoevaniya*, I, 297–8.

[73] Diary entry 20/07/1865, in P. A. Zaionchkovskii (ed.), *Dnevnik P. A. Valueva* (Moscow: Izd. AN SSSR, 1961), II, 60–1.

[74] Joseph Schumpeter, 'Imperialism and Capitalism', in *Imperialism and Social Classes* ed. Paul Sweezy & trans. Heinz Norden (Oxford: Basil Blackwell, 1951), 83–5.

[75] Afaf Lutfi al-Sayyid Marsot, *Egypt and Cromer: A Study in Anglo-Egyptian Relations* (London: John Murray, 1968); John S. Galbraith and Afaf Lutfi al-Sayyid Marsot, 'The British Occupation of Egypt: Another View', *IJMES* 9/4 (1978), 471–88; Alexander Schölch, 'The "Men on the Spot" and the English Occupation of Egypt in 1882', *HJ* 19/3 (1976), 773–85; A. G. Hopkins, 'The Victorians and Africa: A Reconsideration of the Occupation of Egypt, 1882', *Journal of African History* 27/2 (1986), 363–91.

[76] Svetlana Gorshenina, *Asie Centrale: L'invention des frontiers et l'heritage russo-soviétique* (Paris: CNRS Editions 2012), 51–63; Fisher, *British Annexation of India*, 5–7, 15–20.

seen, leaves unexplained the means and motives for the Russian advance 1,000 miles south to the Syr-Darya and the Ili over the previous two decades. As I argue in Chapter 5, even the fall of Tashkent was not, in fact, as unexpected or unauthorised as Valuev believed.[77] While the Russian conquest was indeed often as chaotic and dominated by short-term thinking as the disobedience thesis would suggest, and it was usually the men on the frontier who first suggested a further advance, in almost all cases it had to be authorised in St Petersburg before anything would happen on the ground. One very simple reason for this was that any expedition required a budget – as we shall see below, this was particularly true if it was in steppe or desert conditions where large numbers of baggage animals were required. The bulk of any original archival file dealing with a military expedition into Central Asia is made up of estimated expenditure, requests for the assignment of funds (generally in silver roubles, which had to be physically transported to the relevant spot), accounts of purchases and wages and final accounts indicating whether any funds remained unspent. Before even this stage could be reached, there would have been a regular flow of letters back and forth between, say, Orenburg and St Petersburg, to secure permission. This would start with the original request from the local governor or military commander to despatch a punitive exped- ition, build a fortress, or capture a town. Sometimes this was rejected outright and the project would be revived only some months or years later. Sometimes numerous explanations of why this was necessary or desirable would be requested, and always an estimate of the cost. This would typically be sent to the Ministries of War, Foreign Affairs and Finance. At a certain point a *soveshchanie* or gathering would be convened, usually by the Minister of War, under whose jurisdiction the whole of the Central Asian frontier fell, attended by the other two ministers or their representatives, and sometimes by the frontier governors or commanders if they were present in St Petersburg. Detailed minutes of the subsequent discussion almost invariably revealed the same pattern: the Minister of Finance would say that it was too expensive, the Minister of Foreign Affairs would say that it might upset the British, and the Minister of War would argue that there was an immediate, urgent military necessity and overrule these objections.[78] The committee's conclusions would be presented to the Tsar, and only once he had annotated the file – usually with the phrase '*byt' po semu*' (so be it) – would the proposed expedition, construc- tion or annexation go ahead. The chain of command in Tsarist Russia was

[77] Matthew Jamison, 'Weakness, Expansion and "Disobedience": The Beginnings of Russian Expansion into the Heart of Central Asia, 1864–1865' (D.Phil. Thesis, University of Oxford, 2007).
[78] This dynamic was identified long ago by P. A. Zaionchkovskii in a paper that was published posthumously: 'K voprosu zavoevaniya Srednei Azii', in *Petr Andreevich Zaionchkovskii: Sbornik statei i vospominanii k stoletiiu istorika* ed. L. G. Zakharova *et al.* (Moscow: ROSSPEN, 2008), 36–95.

centralised, hierarchical – and overwhelmingly skewed towards the needs (or imagined needs) of the military. This ensured that they usually got their own way. It did not mean that expansion was uncontrolled.

What this does suggest is that the key to understanding Russian motives for conquering Central Asia is careful attention to the process of decision-making, insofar as this is revealed in the documentary record – whether decisions were consciously made at all, and if so how, when, why and by whom.[79] In this book I have sought to adapt the concept of the 'official mind' developed by Ronald Robinson and Jack Gallagher in their pioneering study of the 'Scramble for Africa', and subsequently refined by other historians, to understand the parallel case of Russian expansion into Central Asia.[80] Strategic considerations, economic motives, personal ambition, local initiative, peripheral instability and plain blundering could all have a role to play in determining imperial policy, but a crucial part of any analysis of the dynamics of expansion has to be an examination of the correspondence and memoranda of those who took the decisions, and an assessment of the individual personalities involved.[81] The limitations of this approach have long been clear to diplomatic historians: it does not always distinguish clearly between motive and desired outcome, it cannot penetrate the subconscious wishes and fears of historical figures, and it must always take account of delusions and deceptions.[82] As James Joll argued long ago with reference to the outbreak of the First World War, we need to assess the 'unspoken assumptions' of diplomats, soldiers, officials and other decision-makers, and this requires an understanding of the cultural and educational milieu which formed them.[83] The 'official mind' is not a single, coherent, omniscient, rational actor which carefully weighs up the available information and then makes a decision on the basis of its assessment of state interest (and it is doubtful whether Robinson and Gallagher would have recognised this description of their argument either).[84] Still less is it Cain and Hopkins's 'gentlemanly capitalist', making decisions on the basis of a narrower, but equally 'rational' calculation of the economic advantage that

---

[79] Joseph Frankel, 'Towards a Decision-Making Model in Foreign Policy', *Political Studies* 7/1 (1959), 2.

[80] Robinson & Gallagher, *Africa and the Victorians*, 19–26.

[81] T. G. Otte, 'Introduction: Personalities and Impersonal Forces in History', in *Personalities, War and Diplomacy: Essays in International History* ed. T. G. Otte and Constantine A. Pagedas (London: Frank Cass, 1997), 8–9 and *The Foreign Office Mind: The Making of British Foreign Policy, 1865–1914* (Cambridge: Cambridge University Press, 2011).

[82] Zara S. Steiner, *The Foreign Office and Foreign Policy, 1898–1914* (Cambridge: Cambridge University Press, 1969), x.

[83] James Joll, *1914: The Unspoken Assumptions: An Inaugural Lecture Delivered 25 April 1968* (London: Weidenfeld & Nicholson, 1968).

[84] Eric Stokes 'Bureaucracy and Ideology: Britain and India in the Nineteenth Century', *TRHS* 30 (1980), 133–4.

24INTRODUCTION

will accrue to an individual or his class.[85] Rather, the 'official mind' should be
seen as a bundle of prejudices, assumptions, ambition and ignorance, generally
with very imperfect access to information, deeply affected by rumour, often
reacting wildly and erratically to the pressure of 'events', and with multiple
different identities and perspectives, of which that at the centre – whether
London or St Petersburg – was not necessarily the most important.[86] The
Russian 'official mind' – the assumptions, prejudices, and mental universe of
its ruling military elite – was in many ways remarkably similar to its British
counterpart. Like their mid-Victorian counterparts, Russian officers sported
luxuriant moustaches and extravagant whiskers worthy of Merv Hughes, as a
visible expression of martial masculinity. Like the British, the Russians saw
Central Asia's states not as rational, sovereign polities open to the usual
niceties of diplomacy and negotiation, but as savage, backward, unreliable
and amenable only to force. And like the British they aimed above all to
maintain Russia's status and prestige as a great power, both in the eyes of
these 'Asiatics' and in those of its European rivals.

I.4   Great Power Prestige and 'Asiatic' Insolence

What an unreliable thing prestige is: it suffers decisively from every trifle!

M. A. Terent'ev, *Istoriya zavoevaniya Srednei Azii* (1906), Vol. III, 250–1

Terent'ev was referring here to the fragility of the British sense of prestige, but
he could equally well have been talking about Russia. British and Russian
officials, whether in the metropole or 'on the spot', shared a common military–
bureaucratic institutional culture, common patterns of prejudice and ignorance, and a sense of sheer entitlement that came from their self-identification
as agents of European 'Great Powers'. The latter concept, which in its original
form as '*Die grossen Mächte*' is usually attributed to Leopold von Ranke, had
come into increasingly widespread use after the Congress of Vienna in 1814–
15, initially as a means of categorising European states.[87] The political

---

[85]   Cain & Hopkins *British Imperialism: Innovation and Expansion*, 42–52; Raymond Dumett
'Introduction', in *Gentlemanly Capitalism and British Imperialism: The New Debate on
Empire* ed. Raymond Dumett (London: Longmans, 1999), 10–11 has a similar query.
[86]   David Reynolds *Britannia Overruled: British Policy and World Power in the Twentieth Century*
(London: Longmans, 1991), 57; Darwin 'Imperialism and the Victorians', 622, 640–2.
[87]   Leopold Ranke, 'Die grossen Mächte', *Historisch-Politische Zeitschrift* II (1833), 1–51; the
term seems to have been used by statesmen and diplomats well before it was adopted by
historians. See Paul Kennedy, *The Rise and Fall of the Great Powers* (London: Unwin
Hyman, 1988), xxiv–xxv. By the 1830s, together with its concomitant 'lesser powers', it
was already current in Anglophone historiography: see Sir Archibald Alison, *History of
Europe from the Commencement of the French Revolution [...] to the Restoration of the
Bourbons* (Edinburgh: Wm Blackwood, 1835–42) I, 157; II, 254–6, 288–95, 599–600; V,
305–7; X, 57, 196, 201, 382, 521, 769, 979.

settlement of 1815 had left just two powers with the ability to act on a global, and not merely European, stage, namely Britain and Russia: as we will see in Chapter 1, their future rivalry was already anticipated by many in the Russian ruling elite even before Napoleon's 'hundred days'. Certain patterns of behaviour were expected of these mutually identified 'Great Powers' in order to uphold that elusive quality, imperial prestige.[88] This led to a cycle of competitive emulation, in which a perceived gain by one power was seen as a loss of prestige for the other, which had to be redeemed by some fresh aggressive action. Paul Kennedy has argued that there is a certain remorseless logic to 'Great Power' status, the maintenance of which becomes an end in itself, requiring ever-greater military resources as competition increases, which in many cases eventually leads to growing economic weakness.[89] It could also prompt states into annexations of territory that had little economic or strategic value. This was partly because territorial size was seen as a measure of power, but also because the very consciousness of Great Power status created a neurotic obsession among ruling elites with the maintenance of prestige in the face of challenges not only from great power rivals, but also from weaker or more 'backward' states. This desire to maintain prestige, rather than any rational calculation of advantage, is visible in most Russian decision-making relating to Central Asia. As a 'Great Power', the default option (with one intriguing and revealing exception in Ghulja in the upper Ili Valley, discussed in Chapter 4) was always to advance and expand, and once a claim to sovereignty had been made, it had to be permanent or there would be a further loss of prestige.

This form of Great Power neurosis became all the more acute when the potential challengers were non-Europeans. In the course of the nineteenth century what were previously more symbiotic relationships between European and 'Asiatic' or 'native' states, as well as those with local elites in existing colonies, were increasingly couched in terms of overwhelming European cultural and eventually racial superiority. As many scholars have argued in relation to Britain and France, this growing arrogance and intolerance played an important (if sometimes exaggerated) role in stimulating and justifying imperial expansion and dominion.[90] What is less often acknowledged is that these attitudes could also provoke intelligence failures and 'information panics' that led to an underestimation of non-European foes and undermined imperial control: we will see examples of both in this book.[91]

---

[88] Alison, *History of Europe*, X, 1016–17; Kennedy, *Rise and Fall*, 138–9; C. A. Bayly, *The Birth of the Modern World 1780–1914* (Oxford: Blackwell, 2004), 99, 112–13, 125–9.

[89] Kennedy, *Rise and Fall*, xxiii–xxiv, 539–40.

[90] Edward Said, *Orientalism: Western Conceptions of the Orient* (London: Routledge & Kegan Paul, 1978).

[91] C. A. Bayly, *Empire and Information: Intelligence Gathering and Social Communication in India, 1780–1870* (Cambridge: Cambridge University Press, 1996), 143–9, 171–9, 315–17, 365–76.

Russian imperialism is still sometimes held to have been qualitatively different
from that of the West, owing to a sense of cultural and ethnic 'kinship' with Asians
and a hybrid identity that lay mid-way between Europe and Asia.[92] In this
interpretation Russia is held to be largely free of the original sin of European
'Orientalism' or of a profound sense of difference from the Asian 'other'.[93] The
corollary of this, at least for some contemporaries, was that Russia's expansion was
merely an organic absorption of neighbouring territories with which she already
had strong cultural ties. In the words of Prince Esper Ukhtomskii – tutor to
Nicholas II, promoter of the Transsiberian Railway, newspaper proprietor and
enthusiast for Buddhism – 'Russia, in reality, conquers nothing in the East, since all
the alien races visibly absorbed by her are related to us in blood, in traditions, in
thought; and we are only knitting together closer the bonds between us and that
which in reality was always ours.'[94] This idea has proved attractive in modern
Russia, where there is still strong hostility to the idea that Russia was ever a colonial
empire.[95] However, Ukhtomskii was not characteristic even of Russian scholarly
and intellectual attitudes towards Central Asia, let alone those of the bureaucracy
and military. They saw Central Asia's territories and peoples as alien to Russia –
Muslim where Russia was Christian, savage where Russia was civilised – and were
generally startlingly ignorant and contemptuous of Central Asian cultural, social
and political structures. The following passage from Terent'ev's introduction can
stand for many, in its invocation of Russia's long suffering at the hands of 'savage
nomads', and its unambiguous reference to racial difference:

> Most of this territory has now been conquered by us, and our current frontiers
> are reasonably satisfactory, but we came to them only after three hundred
> years of stubborn struggle. Russia endured many terrible attacks by savage
> nomads, coming from that same Central Asia. That evil figure with slanted
> eyes and high cheekbones was long familiar to our ancestors. But as soon as
> Russia gathered and consolidated her lands they left off their raiding.[96]

It is interesting to set this alongside the similar language – used to very
different purpose – in Alexander Blok's famous 1918 poem *Skify*: 'Yes, we are

[92] See, for instance, Orlando Figes, *Natasha's Dance: A Cultural History of Russia* (London: Allen Lane, 2002), 358–429; Mark Bassin, 'Geographies of Imperial Identity', in *Cambridge History of Russia*, ed. Lieven, II, 60–3.
[93] Nathaniel Knight, 'Grigor'ev in Orenburg, 1851–1862: Russian Orientalism in the Service of Empire?', *SR* 59/1 (2000): 74–100; S. N. Abashin, 'Osobennosti rossiiskogo orienta-lizma', in *Tsentral'naya Aziya v sostave Rossiiskoi Imperii* ed.S. N. Abashin, D. A. Arapov & N. A. Bekmakhanova (Moscow: Novoe Literaturnoe Obozrenie, 2008), 332–3.
[94] Prince E. E. Ookhtomsky, *Travels in the East of Nicholas II, Emperor of Russia when Cesarewitch 1890–1* trans. Robert Goodlet (Westminster: Constable, 1896), II, 54–5. See further Morrison, 'Russian Rule in Turkestan and the example of British India', 677–82.
[95] Alexander Morrison, 'Russia's Colonial Allergy', *eurasianet.org* 19/12/2016 (https://eurasianet.org/russias-colonial-allergy).
[96] Terent'ev, *Istoriya zavoevaniya*, I, xv–xvi.

Scythians! Yes, we are Asiatics, with slanted, greedy eyes!' Sometimes interpreted as an expression of Russia's ambivalent identity between Europe and
Asia, Blok's real target was the Orientalisation of Russia (and of Bolshevism) by
western Europeans; he and his 'Scythianist' compatriots embraced the kind of
pejorative language the Russians themselves often used about Asians in general
and nomads in particular.[97] As Blok's poem suggests, Russian literature, music
and art by no means consistently denigrated the 'Orient' or sought to separate
themselves from it.[98] The conquest of the Caucasus in the first half of the
nineteenth century produced highly ambivalent literary responses to the
extension of Russian power in the work of Pushkin, Lermontov, Bestuzhev-
Marlinskii and Tolstoy, all of whom found ways of celebrating the freedom of
the Caucasian peoples and lamenting the crushing of their resistance by the
autocracy.[99] The music of Alexander Borodin celebrated Central Asian
themes, while the brilliant Orientalist canvases of Vasilii Vereshchagin
(1842-1904) - which illustrate some points in this book - both represented
the 'east' as savage and exotic, and contained a melancholy message on the
futility of war and conquest.[100] None of this is to suggest that Russia was
somehow not 'Orientalist', in the western European sense, as the crude binary
opposition proposed by Edward Said was not always true of the British or
French empires either.[101] In response to General M. D. Skobelev's bloody
victory over the Akhal-Teke Turkmen at Gök-Tepe, Feyodor Dostoevskii
famously announced that Russia's destiny lay in conquering and subduing
Asia, as a means of emancipating herself from a sense of inferiority vis-à-vis
Europe (see Chapter 9).[102] Whatever the case in literature or art, in Russian
official attitudes and state ideology a strong sense of 'Europeanness' and superiority to Asia predominated throughout most of the nineteenth century.[103]
Crucially, Russia's elites also espoused fully European or Westphalian ideas of

[97] Figes, *Natasha's Dance*, 416-20; David Schimmelpenninck van der Oye, *Russian Orientalism: Asia in the Russian Mind from Peter the Great to the Emigration* (Newhaven, CN: Yale University Press, 2010), 222.
[98] Schimmelpenninck van der Oye, *Russian Orientalism*, 194.
[99] Susan Layton, *Russian Literature and Empire: Conquest of the Caucasus from Pushkin to Tolstoy* (Cambridge: Cambridge University Press, 1994).
[100] David Schimmelpenninck van der Oye, 'Vasilij V. Vereshchagin's Canvases of Central Asian Conquest', *CAC* 17/18 (2009), 179-209; Schimmelpenninck van der Oye, *Russian Orientalism*, 76-91, 199-211; Vahan D. Barooshian, *V. V. Vereshchagin, Artist at War* (Gainesville, FA: University Press of Florida, 1993), 20-50.
[101] Alexander Morrison, '"Applied Orientalism" in British India and Tsarist Turkestan', *CSSH* 51/3 (2009), 619-47.
[102] See Milan Hauner, *What Is Asia to Us? Russia's Asian Heartland Yesterday and Today* (London: Routledge, 1990), 1-26.
[103] Adeeb Khalid, Nathaniel Knight and Maria Todorova, 'Ex Tempore - Orientalism', *Kritika* 1/4 (2000), 691-727; Vladimir Bobrovnikov, 'Pochemu my marginaly? Zametki na poliakh russkogo perevoda "Orientalizma" Edwarda Saida', *AI* (2008) No. 2, 325-44.

sovereignty, as something clearly defined and territorially bounded. As we will
see in the account of Russian–Qazaq relations in Chapter 1, the absence of such
clear boundaries in Central Asia was deeply frustrating for Russia's rulers, and
acted as a recurrent source of mutual misunderstanding in their diplomatic
relations in Central Asia from at least the beginning of the eighteenth century.

A variation on the theme of Russia's absorption of neighbours with whom
she already had close cultural ties is to see the conquest of Central Asia as an
extension of the Russian empire's earlier relationships with other Muslim
peoples in the Volga–Ural region.[104] The Empire had had substantial groups
of Muslim subjects since the sixteenth century, and the Kazan Tatars in
particular did play a crucial role as intermediaries with Central Asian peoples
with whom they shared language and faith. Muscovy's diplomatic relations
with the Central Asian nomads and khanates had begun in the same period,
and until the eighteenth century these had been on a relatively equal footing,
with a degree of mutual understanding.[105] Nevertheless, the amount of real
cultural exchange remained limited, as did Central Asia's significance for
Russia in these centuries.[106] By the early 1800s what little ethnographic
knowledge had been accumulated through these early diplomatic exchanges
was lost or buried in the archives, and even when records were rediscovered by
historians in the later nineteenth century it was only for the purpose of
constructing narratives of the unremitting hostility of Central Asian rulers to
trade and diplomatic relations with Russia.[107] Central Asia was not familiar
territory to Russia's rulers, and their knowledge and understanding became
ever vaguer the further their forces penetrated. While everyday interaction and
exchange certainly continued on the steppe frontier itself, at the elite level in
Russian relations with Central Asian states and peoples a term which recurs
over and over again is *derzost'* – 'insolence'. They were not prepared to view
them as diplomatic equals, and saw any attempt to assert or argue for their own
legitimate interests as an affront to Russia's great power status.

---

[104] Robert D. Crews, *For Prophet & Tsar: Islam and Empire in Russia and Central Asia*
(Cambridge, MA: Harvard University Press, 2006), 241–92.

[105] Edward Keenan, 'Muscovy and Kazan: Some Introductory Remarks on the Patterns of
Steppe Diplomacy', *SR* 26/4 (1967), 548–58.

[106] Ron Sela, 'Prescribing the Boundaries of Knowledge: Seventeenth-Century Russian
Diplomatic Missions to Central Asia', in *Writing Travel in Central Asian History* ed.
Nile Green (Bloomington, IN: Indiana University Press, 2014), 69–88.

[107] Paolo Sartori, 'Archival Silences: On 18th-Century Russian Diplomacy and the
Historical Episteme of Central Asian Hostility', *Itinerario* (forthcoming). See e.g. Peter
Lerch, *Khiva oder Kharezm: Seine historischen und geographischen Verhältnisse* (St Pb.,
Verlag der Kaiserlichen Hofbuchandlung, 1873); Johann Garber, *Journal von der Reise
aus Astrachan nach Chiwa und Bucharen, 1732* (St Pb.: Buchdruckerei der kaiserlichen
Akademie der Wissenschaften, 1902). My thanks to Paolo Sartori for these observations
and references.

I.5 Weapons, Organisation and Tactics in Russian and Central Asian Armies

In the Russian campaigns in Central Asia it has generally been the same. Energy and resolution have been the watchword. The procedure has been rather to overawe the enemy by a vigorous offensive than to bring against him a mighty force, and the result speaks for itself. Prestige is everything in such warfare. It is the commander who recognizes this, and who acts upon it, who conquers inferior races absolutely and for good.

C. A. Callwell, *Small Wars: Their Principles and Practice* (1899)

The Russian campaigns in Central Asia figured prominently in Charles Callwell's *Small Wars*, the ur-text for modern counter-insurgency studies, and Callwell greatly admired what he called 'the extraordinary successes which the Russians have achieved' as a model for the British to follow in their own colonial wars.[108] Soviet military leaders also looked to these earlier campaigns for guidance when Central Asia was reconquered by the Bolsheviks between 1919 and 1922, and even during the war in Afghanistan in the 1980s.[109] I do not believe that there is much to be gained from this approach: when historical research is driven by contemporary policy or 'security' agendas it generally produces both bad policy and bad history.[110] Understanding how the Russians were able to conquer Central Asia is considerably simpler than understanding why they did so, but circumstances have changed so fundamentally that it is unlikely any useful lessons could be learned even if this were considered desirable.

As James Belich and Dierk Walter have shown, we should not assume that European colonial armies always enjoyed technological and tactical superiority over their opponents – indeed, it was often their very weakness and inability to bring their enemies to what they considered a decisive battle which led to their use of indiscriminate violence against civilians.[111] As we shall see, for logistical

---

[108] C. E. Callwell, *Small Wars: Their Principles and Practice* 2nd ed. (London: HMSO, 1899), 58, 80. See Alexander Morrison, '"The Extraordinary Successes Which the Russians Have achieved" – the Conquest of Central Asia in Callwell's *Small Wars*', *Small Wars and Insurgencies* 30/4–5 (2019), 913–36.

[109] Alex Marshall, 'Turkfront: Frunze and the Development of Soviet Counter-insurgency in Central Asia', in *Central Asia: Aspects of Transition* ed. Tom Everett-Heath (London: Routledge, 2003), 5–29.

[110] Kim Wagner, 'Seeing Like a Soldier: The Amritsar Massacre and the Politics of Military History', in *Decolonization and Conflict: Colonial Comparisons and Conflicts* ed. Martin Thomas and Gareth Curless (London: Bloomsbury Academic, 2017), 24–37. See further Huw Bennett, Michael Finch, Andrei Mamolea & David Owen-Morgan, 'Studying Mars and Clio: Or How Not to Write about the Ethics of Military Conduct and Military History', *History Workshop Journal* 88 (2019), 274–80.

[111] Dierk Walter, *Colonial Violence: European Empires and the Use of Force* trans. Peter Lewis (London: Hurst & Co., 2017), 56–7, 116–19; James Belich, *The New Zealand Wars*

reasons there were indeed severe limits to the forces the Russians could deploy in Central Asia, but these still proved more than equal to the task. As Callwell noted, this was partly because Russia's opponents tended obligingly to meet the Russians head on in pitched battles or sieges, and rarely resorted to guerrilla warfare.[112] The latter was much more difficult for the Russians to deal with, as the ten-year resistance of the Qazaq leader Kenesary Qasim-oghli [Qasimov] (1802–1847) to their control of the northern steppe demonstrates (see Chapters 1 and 3), but in Central Asia (unlike in the Caucasus) this was exceptional. Russian forces enjoyed a significant superiority over their Central Asian opponents in infantry training, firearms and artillery, which only grew more marked with time. The most obvious indication of this is the very low casualties they generally suffered, despite the apparently enormous disparity in numbers between their (usually tiny) forces and those of their Central Asian opponents. Writing in 1897, A. Grebner provided a collation of figures for attackers, defenders and casualties in Russian military engagements in Central Asia, most of which were sieges, though some were battles fought in the open (see Table I.3).

The numbers of defenders which Grebner gave were often implausible and clearly intended to exaggerate the scale of Russian victories – but there is little doubt that the figures he gives for Russian forces and the casualties they suffered are accurate. They amount to 677 killed and 2,282 wounded over thirty years. Even by the standards of colonial conquests elsewhere, this is remarkably low, and is dwarfed even by minor campaigns in the other wars the Russian empire fought in the nineteenth century: as a comparison, 2,278 men were killed and another 4,948 wounded during a single unsuccessful attempt to storm the Turkish fortress of Kars during the Crimean War, where a certain K. P. von Kaufman first saw military action.[113] As Grebner's table suggests, only a minority of engagements during the Russian conquest were fought in the open – though these included the most decisive Bukharan defeats, at Irjar, Chupan-Ata and Zirabulak. Most Russian victories in Central Asia were assaults on fortified positions, and Grebner identified three distinctive types of these over the previous forty years – those on 'steppe fortresses' with small garrisons such as Aq Masjid, Pishpek or Chimkent, taken by classic siege tactics through digging parallel trenches up to their walls, sapping and mining; those on fortified towns, such as Tashkent, Jizzakh and Khujand, where artillery was used to create a breach, followed by a frontal assault; and those on towns with no substantial fortifications, such as Andijan, where instead the attackers had to negotiate a series of walled gardens in the outskirts of the city. The attack on the Turkmen

---

  and the Victorian Interpretation of Racial Conflict (Auckland: Auckland University Press, 1986).
[112] Callwell, *Small Wars*, 6, 10, 79–80.
[113] A. Korsakov, 'Vospominaniya o Karse', *RV* 34 (1861), 338.

Table I.3 *Sieges and battles in the Russian conquest of Central Asia, 1853–81[a]*

Year	Name	Russian forces		Russian casualties				Enemy forces		Enemy casualties		Duration (days)
		Men	Guns	Killed	Wounded/contused	Total	%	Men	Guns	Total	% killed	
1853	Aq Masjid	2,350	17	30	74	104	4.4	400	3	242		26
1860	Uzun-Agach[b]	1,050	6	1	32	33	3	20,000	10[d]	1,500	7.5	N/A
1860	Pishpek	1,800	13	1	6	7	0.4	442	16	20	4.5	5
1861	Yangi-Qurghan	969	11	1	3	4	0.5	120	0	4	3.3	2
1862	Pishpek	1,500	8	13	4	17	1.1	554	9			13
1864	Turkestan	1,150	12	5	33	38	3.3	1,500				3
1864	Chimkent	1,950	17	8	50	58	3	10,000	31			3
1864	Tashkent (first assault)	1,550	20	6	8	14	0.37					1
1865	Tashkent (second assault)	1,950	12	25	117	142	7.2	30,000	63			2
1866	Irjar[b]	2,850	20	1	11	12	0.4	30,000	12	1,000	3.3	N/A
1866	Khujand	2,700	18	11	122	133	5		73	2,500		6
1866	Ura-Tepe	3,825	28	17	217	227	5.9		38	2,000		5
1866	Jizzakh	3,225	20	6	92	98	3	10,000	53	6,000	60	6
1868	Chupan-Ata[b]	3,500	16	2	38	40	1		21			N/A
1868	Defence of Samarkand[c]	658	4	49	172	221	26	55,000	0			3

Table I.3 (cont.)

		Russian forces		Russian casualties				Enemy forces		Enemy casualties		Duration
Year	Name	Men	Guns	Killed	Wounded/contused	Total	%	Men	Guns	Total	% killed	(days)
1868	Zirabulak[b]	3,600	14	0	37	37	1	21,000	14			
1870	Kitab	1,725	12	19	109	128	7.4	8,000	29	600	7.5	3
1875	Makhram	3,750	20	6	8	13	0.37	50,000	39	1,000		
1875	Andijan	1,350	8	8	56	64	4.7	25,000	0			1
1879	Denghil-Tepe (first assault)	3,000	12	185	268	453	8.9					1
1881	Denghil-Tepe (second assault)	7,000	79	283	825	1,108	15.8	30,000	3	6,500	21.7	20

a From A. Grebner, 'Osady i shturmy sredne-aziatskikh krepostei i naselennykh punktov', Inzhenernyi Zhurnal (1897), 33. Grebner's table is not complete – it omits some smaller sieges, such as that of Toqmaq, and omits the campaign against Khiva.
b Indicates a battle fought in the open.
c Indicates a siege where the Russians were the defenders.
d The Khoqandis at Uzun-Agach in fact had no guns as they had been forced to leave all their artillery behind.

fortress of Denghil-Tepe (Gök-Tepe), he added, belonged in a fourth category of its own, owing both to its size and to the huge material resources that were needed.[114] This typology is riddled with inconsistencies. Some steppe fortresses, such as Toqmaq, had surrendered after a few hours' bombardment without the need for siege works. Chimkent was not simply a steppe fortress, as Grebner described it, but a substantial town and market centre. Grebner's generally triumphalist account also paid scant attention to those sieges – Aq Masjid in 1852, Tashkent in 1864, Gök-Tepe in 1879 – where a premature frontal assault had been beaten off, in the latter case with quite heavy casualties. Such setbacks were rare, however, and the overall picture which emerges is that the Russians conquered Central Asia with mere handfuls of men, and were usually heavily outnumbered. Their success was largely owing to the weaknesses of their opponents, rather than any particular tactical or technological brilliance on their part.

The natural advantages enjoyed by Central Asian mounted warriors over their sedentary neighbours were always highly contingent on political and technological factors and the availability of pasture, and relative to the technology and organisational skills of neighbouring settled societies. From the early eighteenth century the growing reliability of firearms meant that the technological advantage shifted decisively towards sedentary polities with the capacity to produce them.[115] Despite this, until the early nineteenth century the armies even of Central Asia's sedentary states were still made up largely of irregular cavalry, which helps to explain why they were so powerless to resist Nadir Shah's invasion of 1742.[116] Wolfgang Holzwarth has argued that the admiration of the first Manghit ruler of Bukhara, Muhammad Rahim Khan, for the ruthless military order represented by Nadirid Persia led to a drive towards military centralisation in Bukhara which would later be copied by Khoqand.[117] This sort of military modernisation and synthesis was widespread in South Asia in this period, with the leading Indian example the creation of the formidable Sikh *Khalsa* by Ranjit Singh in Punjab.[118] The same thing seems to have happened on a smaller scale in Central Asia. In Bukhara Amir Nasrullah (r. 1827–1860) succeeded in reducing the power of

[114] Grebner, *Osady i shturmy*, 2.
[115] Dennis Sinor, 'The Inner Asian Warriors', *Journal of the American Oriental Society* 101/2 (1981), 133–44; Nicola di Cosmo, 'Introduction: Inner Asian Ways of Warfare in Historical Perspective', in *Warfare in Inner Asian History* ed. Nicola Di Cosmo (Leiden: Brill, 2002), 1–12.
[116] Ron Sela, *The Legendary Biographies of Tamerlane: Islam and Heroic Apocrypha in Central Asia* (Cambridge: Cambridge University Press, 2011), 117–35.
[117] Wolfgang Holzwarth, 'Relations between Uzbek Central Asia, the Great Steppe and Iran, 1700–1750', in *Shifts and Drifts in Nomad–Sedentary Relations* ed. Stefan Leder & Bernard Streck (Wiesbaden: Ludwig Reichert, 2005), 201–4.
[118] Kaushik Roy, 'Military Synthesis in South Asia: Armies, Warfare and Indian Society, c. 1740–1849', *JMH* 69/3 (2005), 651–90.

34

INTRODUCTION

Uzbek tribal elites and creating a standing army in which irregular cavalry was gradually superseded by the foot-soldier or *sarbaz*, trained by military adventurers from India, Persia and Russia.[119] Flintlocks were introduced from the 1840s onwards, though these were limited to the small number of regular *sarbaz* soldiery, perhaps 1,000 men out of a total force of 4,000 infantry and 20,000 cavalry, with the remainder of the infantry equipped only with matchlocks. The quantity of artillery remained small: in the 1820s the Bukharans had just ten cannon, under the command of a Russian deserter.[120] Reliance on foreign experts remained heavy throughout the 1830s–1860s. Alexander Burnes refers to a deserter from the 24th Bengal Native Infantry (who had formerly served the *Bek* of Qunduz) serving in the Bukharan army as a gunner in 1833.[121] According to a British intelligence report, Bukhara's crushing defeat of neighbouring Khoqand in 1852 was largely thanks to 'the presence of a single Regiment of Infantry raised & commanded by an adventurer from Hindoostan called Abdool Summud Khan, who had formerly served under some of the French Officers in the Punjab'.[122] The Russian orientalist Nikolai Khanykov (1822–1878) also mentioned 'Abd al-Samad, whom he described as a Persian military adventurer from Tabriz who entered Bukharan service after fleeing Afghanistan: 'he persuaded the Amir to introduce regular troops into the country, and by that means gained such an ascendancy over Nasr-Ullah, that at present he is one of the most influential men in the Khanat'.[123]

The Ming dynasty in Khoqand was not far behind. As Scott Levi has shown, in the early nineteenth century 'Alim Khan (r. 1799–1811) and 'Umar Khan (r. 1811–1822) successfully created a new 20,000-strong standing army, the *Sipah-i jadid*, made up largely of *Ghalchas* – Tajik mountain-dwellers from the Pamir and Alai ranges. Mocked as 'donkey jockeys' by the Uzbek elites of Khoqand, they proved their worth in battle by conquering first Tashkent and

---

[119] O. D. Chekhovich, 'O nekotorykh voprosakh istorii Srednei Azii XVIII–XIX vekov', *Voprosy Istorii* (1956) No. 3, 84–95; Wolfgang Holzwarth, 'The Uzbek State as Reflected in Eighteenth-Century Bukharan Sources', *AS* LX/2 (2006), 325–6; Andreas Wilde, *What Is Beyond the River? Power, Authority and Social Order in Transoxiana in the 18th–19th Centuries* (Vienna: Verlag der Österreichischen Akademie der Wissenschaften, 2016), II, 758–61.

[120] Wolfgang Holzwarth, 'Bukharan Armies and Uzbek Military Power, 1670–1870: Coping with the Legacy of a Nomadic Conquest', in *Nomad Military Power in Iran and Adjacent Areas in the Islamic Period* ed. Kurt Franz & Wolfgang Holzwarth (Wiesbaden:Ludwig Reichert Verlag, 2015), 291–2, 317, 328–35.

[121] NAI/Foreign/S.C./6 June 1833/Nos. 1–10, *Burnes (Captain) on the Political and Military Status of Bokhara*, 2517–18; Alexander Burnes, *Travels into Bokhara* (London: John Murray, 1834), I, 286–7.

[122] NAI/Foreign/S.C./24 November 1854/Nos. 1–22, *Account of the Khanate of Kokand*, 183–4.

[123] N. A. Khanikoff, *Bokhara, Its Amir and People* trans. A Clement de Bode (London: James Madden, 1845), 306–7. For a biography of this remarkable figure see Wilde, *What Is Beyond the River*, II, 768–71.

then most of the Syr-Darya Valley between 1807 and 1834.[124] In 1839 Muhammad 'Ali Khan despatched an envoy called Zahid Khwaja to the Ottoman Sultan, requesting military assistance in the form of artillery, infantry and cavalry officers, and failing that books of military science, to help Khoqand resist encirclement by Russia, China and Bukhara.[125] While this seems to have been unsuccessful, in 1854 an ambassador sent from Khoqand to the East India Company to request military assistance against the Russians reported that the then Khan, Khudoyar (r. 1852–1858, 1866–1875) had two battalions of troops with European training:

> Those men who belonged to – Campbell's[126] battalion and who after-wards came to Kokund. The uniform of these men is similar to that of the British troops. Broadcloth (blue) coat Pantaloons of red broadcloth. The cap was also English, but it being inconvenient at the time of reading prayers, it was replaced by the Kura Koolee or the long Persian Cap. Each of these battalions consists of 1,000 men who are armed with muskets of various workmanship.[127]

Among these men may have been Jemadar Na'ib, a former sepoy of Ranjit Singh's army who left Punjab after its annexation by the British in 1849. From 1860 to 1865 he commanded Khoqand's artillery, and then served the Khoqandi adventurer Yaqub Beg in the same capacity during the latter's reign in Kashgar (1865–1877), before retiring to his native Peshawar in the late 1870s.[128] Many Russian soldiers also deserted from frontier garrisons to serve Central Asian rulers, where their skills were in high demand. In 1860 a Russian intelligence report noted that Malla Khan, the then ruler of Khoqand, was preparing an infantry unit, which currently numbered 800 men wearing identical uniforms with red caps, pikes and firearms, and drilled by 'some Tatar deserter'.[129] When the Russians captured Pishpek the same year, they found five Russian deserters among its garrison (Chapter 4), and in the 1860s the Bukharan infantry and artillery were also commanded by two Russian desert-ers who had converted to Islam, Osman and Bogdanov (Chapter 6). In 1869 Khudoyar Khan had a Cossack called Vlasov serving him as a cavalry drill-master, and it seems to have been his continued attempts to expand his

---

[124] Levi, *The Rise and Fall of Khoqand*, 82–92.
[125] Written record of the verbal petition of Zahid Khwaja, 15/03/1839 in *The History of Central Asia in Ottoman Documents*. Vol. I. *Political and Diplomatic Relations* ed. Shahin Mustafayev & Mustafa Serin (Samarkand: IICAS, 2001), 157–8.
[126] A marginal note in the file explains that 'Campbell was formerly an officer in the Bengal Native Infantry and for many years under the name of Shere Mahomed has been in the service of the Ameer [of Afghanistan]. S^d/J[ohn]. L[awrence].'
[127] NAI/Foreign/S.C./24 November 1854/Nos. 1–22, p. 235.
[128] T. K. Beisembiev (ed.), *The Life of 'Alimqul: A Native Chronicle of Nineteenth-Century Central Asia* (London: RoutledgeCurzon, 2003), 64.
[129] 'Zapiska o slukakh i sobytiyakh v Srednei Azii', 29/01/1860 RGVIA F.1433 Op.1 D.7 ll. 6–7.

military establishment on European lines, even after Khoqand had become a
Russian protectorate, which led to his overthrow in 1875 (Chapter 8).[130]

These core forces of *sarbaz* infantry (Figure I.3) and artillery were still
accompanied on the battlefield by great crowds of irregular cavalry, and in
some cases (such as Chupan-Ata in 1868) civilian levies as well, which partly
explains the huge numbers of the enemy always listed in Russian battle
accounts. As Belich reminds us, we should treat one-sided accounts of
European victories in colonial wars with a degree of caution, particularly
their tendency to exaggerate enemy numbers and casualties. As he shows, in
New Zealand the Maori managed to hold their own against numerically

Figure I.3 Khudoyar Khan's *sarbaz* infantry on parade before the palace gate, Khoqand
(Turkestan Album, 1871).[131]

---

[130] A. P. Khoroshkhin, *Sbornik statei kasaiushchikhsya do Turkestanskogo kraya* (St Pb.: Tip.
A Transhelya, 1876), 57.
[131] 'Kokanskoe khanstvo: Vorota khanskago dvortsa v g. Kokane', in *Turkestanskii al'bom: Po
rasporiazheniiu Turkestanskago General-Gubernatora General-ad'iutanta K. P. fon
Kaufmana 1-go.* ed. A. L. Kun. Pt. 2. *Chast' etnograficheskaya* ed. A. L. Kun (Tashkent:
Litografiya Voenno-Topograficheskogo Otdela Turkestanskogo Voennogo Okruga, 1871–
2), Vol. 2, plate 158, No. 486 (Library of Congress, Prints & Photographs Division, LC-DIG-
ppmsca-09953-00225).

superior European forces through bold forms of tactical innovation.[132] There is no evidence of anything comparable in Central Asia.

Even the reformed armies of Bukhara and Khoqand (Khiva still relied entirely on Turkmen and Qazaq irregular cavalry) would prove no match for Russian forces. This was partly because the quality of their firearms was poor – a motley collection of unrifled matchlock and flintlock muskets and smoothbore artillery, most of it originating on the subcontinent. It is also because both states were weakened by the wars they fought against each other, while Khoqand suffered from chronic internal rivalry between sedentary 'Sarts' and nomadic and semi-nomadic Qipchaqs and Kyrgyz following Amir Nasrullah's brief conquest of the Khanate in 1842. This rivalry and bloodshed continued even as the Russian threat grew; one of the most important Khoqandi chronicles, a biography of the Qipchaq military leader 'Alimqul, records how he spent at least as much time fighting Khudoyar Khan and his Bukharan sponsors as the Russians.[133] Finally, Russia's Central Asian opponents never developed innovative tactics that could cope with superior Russian firepower. The closest was perhaps the construction by the Akhal-Teke Turkmen of their great fortress at Gök-Tepe, which did allow them to repel the Russians once in 1879, and to inflict heavy casualties on them when they finally took it in 1881. Otherwise, as we shall see, most battles and sieges were extremely one-sided.

The decisive phases of the conquest of Central Asia, between the 1840s and the 1860s, took place before the introduction of those technologies that Daniel Headrick identified as crucial to late-nineteenth-century European colonial expansion, namely the breech-loading rifle and the sealed brass cartridge.[134] While Russian weapons technology lagged behind that of western Europe in the first half of the nineteenth century, it was much superior to anything the armies of Bukhara or Khoqand could muster. The first tests with rifled weapons in the Russian army took place in the 1830s in the Finnish Guards regiment, but it took much longer for these advanced weapons to filter through to the Central Asian frontier, and even longer for the army to settle on a single pattern of rifle.[135] In 1839, at the time of the first Khiva expedition, the infantry in Orenburg were still equipped with the 1828 model smooth-bore, flintlock musket and smooth-bore field artillery. General Perovskii's force did, however, march with several batteries of a Russian variant of the Congreve Rocket developed by General Karl Andreevich Shil'der.[136] Percussion-cap muskets

---

[132] Belich, *The New Zealand Wars*, 311–35.
[133] *TA* trans. 35–7, 19–29, 44, 50–9.
[134] Daniel R. Headrick, *The Tools of Empire: Technology and European Imperialism in the Nineteenth Century* (Oxford: Oxford University Press, 1981), 83–104.
[135] V. V. Mavrodin, *Iz istorii otechestvennogo oruzhiya: Russkaya Vintovka* (Leningrad: Izd. Leningradskogo Universiteta, 1981), 15–16.
[136] Anon., 'Khivinskaya ekspeditsiya 1839 goda', *RS* 7/2 (1873), 245.

were introduced across the Russian army between 1845 and 1849, a period
which also saw the introduction of a primitive muzzle-loading rifle called the
'Littich Stutzer', a design borrowed from the army of Braunschweig, which was
adopted by sharpshooter (*strelkovye*) battalions after 1843. Both this and the
'Gartung Stutzer' relied on little wings on the bullet that fitted the rifling
grooves, making them difficult to load. In 1849 only 20,756 of these had
been produced – a drop in the ocean of the Russian army and its million
men.[137] With the exception of sharpshooter battalions, the Russian army
remained primarily equipped with smooth-bore muzzle-loading muskets
until after the Crimean War.[138] However, as the Stutzers were superseded in
European Russia by more advanced designs, such as the 1854 and 1856 model
rifled percussion muskets, they seem to have been used to re-equip rifle
battalions on Russia's Asian frontiers in the Urals and Siberia, and hence
were used during the Central Asian campaigns of the 1860s. At the siege of
Pishpek in 1860 Colonel Zimmerman referred to the withering Stutzer fire
(*shtutsernyi ogon'*) unleashed on the garrison, and they were still in use at the
battle of Zirabulak against Bukhara in 1868.[139] Whatever the limitations of this
weapon, it was still much better than those of the Russians' Bukharan,
Khoqandi and Khivan opponents, who were still limited to smooth-bore
flintlock – or more commonly matchlock – muskets. Numerous accounts
attest to Russian infantry being able to wreak terrible execution on their
Central Asian opponents through volley fire while remaining beyond effective
range of their enemies' weapons. In 1864 Aulie-Ata fell to Chernyaev almost
without casualties because, as he casually remarked in a letter to his father, it
was raining and the Khoqandi garrison's matchlocks were unusable.[140]

The introduction of the famous Berdan rifle (affectionately known as the
Berdanka) after 1870 underlined this superiority still further. The .45 calibre
Berdan, based on an American design by inventor Hiram Berdan, with a simple
and robust sliding bolt mechanism, was the first successful purpose-built breech-
loading weapon introduced into the Russian army, and immediately became a
firm favourite with officers and men because of its ruggedness and simplicity. It
was also the first Russian rifle to be machine-produced, using American

---

[137] The former was a muzzle-loader of 17.78 mm calibre, weighed 4.34 kg with a length of
124.2 cm, fired a round ball weighing 33 g, and had a 1,200-pace effective range:
Mavrodin *Russkaya Vintovka*, 21–5.

[138] Joseph Bradley, *Guns for the Tsar: American Technology and the Small Arms Industry in
Nineteenth-Century Russia* (DeKalb, IL: Northern Illinois University Press, 1990), 18–19.

[139] *Opisanie voennykh deistvii v Zailiiskom krae v 1860 godu i zhurnal osady Khokandskoi
kreposti Pishpek* (St Pb.: Tip. V. Spiridionova, 1861), 25–6; N. N. Karazin 'Zarabulakskie
Vysoty' [1874], reprinted in N. N. Karazin *Pogonya za nazhivoi* (St Pb.: Lenizdat, 1993),
478.

[140] M. G. Chernyaev to Grigorii Nikitich Chernyaev 27/06/1864, Aulie-Ata. IISH Archief M.
G. Cernjaev, Folder 17.

techniques, under contract with the Colt company. It is not clear exactly when all Russian garrisons in Central Asia were re-equipped with them – by 1872, of the 870,000 rifles in use in the Russian army only 30,000 were *Berdankas*. Full re-equipment was not completed until 1874, and unsurprisingly forces stationed in Europe, where the technological competition was much fiercer, had priority – even so, during the Russo-Turkish War of 1877–8 some Russian infantry regiments were still equipped solely with inferior converted Krnka breech-loaders, which were far out-ranged by Turkish Peabody-Martinis. However, *Berdankas* were certainly used during the conquest of Khiva in 1873, and praised for their performance in that campaign.[141] With an effective range of up to 1,500 paces and a firing rate of six to eight rounds per minute, the *Berdanka* was vastly superior to anything Russia's opponents in Central Asia could call upon. The importance of this advantage was underlined by the loss of 600 Berdan rifles and ammunition to the Akhal-Teke Turkmen during the failed assault on Gök-Tepe in 1879, which probably led to the Russians suffering much heavier casualties when they attacked again in 1881.[142] Even though it was superseded by the Mosin rifle (which used smokeless ammunition) in the mid 1890s, many regiments in Central Asia seem to have retained the *Berdanka*, and they were still in use during the suppression of the 1916 Central Asian Revolt.

While aristocratic officers from Guards regiments would descend on Turkestan during campaigns (they were known disparagingly as *fazany* – pheasants – by local officers), the conquest was undertaken by ordinary infantry line and sharpshooter battalions (initially from Orenburg and Western Siberia, later renamed Turkestan line battalions; Figure I.4), Ural, Orenburg and West Siberian (later Semirechie) Cossacks and their associated batteries of horse artillery.[143] The regular long-service infantry line battalions of the Russian army were a formidable opponent for largely irregular Central Asian forces, partly because of their discipline and training, but also because they were bound by extremely strong ties of internal solidarity, such that Belich's 'military tribes, warrior guilds' seems as appropriate a way to describe them as it would be for a British regular regiment.[144] In his discussion of the Khiva campaign of 1873, Terent'ev repeated what he claimed was the common 'native' view of the relative strength and importance of the infantry and cavalry arms in Central Asia: 'The local asiatics do not rate Cossacks at all, if they are not accompanied by rockets or cannon; they regard the infantry with great respect. A platoon of Russian sharpshooters is far more alarming to them than

[141] Bradley, *Guns for the Tsar*, 107–10, 127; Mavrodin, *Russkaya Vintovka*, 70–80.
[142] Terent'ev, *Istoriya zavoevaniya*, III, 21, 24.
[143] Regimental histories for these humble units are few and far between, but see V. N. Zaitsev, *Istoriya 4-ogo Turkestanskogo Lineinogo Batal'ona za period s 1771 do 1882 god kak material k dvizheniiu russkikh v Sredniuiu Aziiu* (Tashkent: n.p., 1882); Anon., *Kratkaya istoriya 6-ogo Turkestanskogo Strelkovago Batal'ona* (Samarkand: Tip. Trud, 1904).
[144] Belich, *The New Zealand Wars*, 23.

Figure I.4 Soldiers Uchaev, Butarev, and Kochergin, and NCOs Arkhipov of the 1st Turkestan Sharpshooter Battalion, Private Tiutrin and NCOs Naidin and Tolstyakov of the 4th Turkestan Line Battalion, awarded the St George's cross for bravery at the Battle of Irjar, 8 May 1866 (Turkestan Album, 1871).[145]

three *sotnya*s of Cossacks [. . .] the native says "The Cossack is a rich man, everything he has is his own; because of this he values his life. The *aq-gemlek* – white shirt (as they call the infantryman) – is a *baigush*, i.e. a pauper, he has nothing but his weapon, and even this is not his, but the treasury's; because of this he has nothing to lose and does not value his life.'[146]

There were no regular Russian cavalry forces in Central Asia: the Ural Cossacks, who participated in almost all the Central Asian campaigns, were the most 'wild' of all the Cossack regiments and the closest to their original hybrid, Slavic/Turkic character. Until the 1870s many of them were Muslim Tatars and Bashkirs, and a large proportion were Old Believers with an ambivalent relationship to the Tsarist state: a rebellion in 1871 saw many of them exiled to the Aral Sea region.[147] Comparing them with the Orenburg Cossacks during the march to Khiva in 1873,

[145] 'Georgievskie kavalery imieiushchie znaki otlichiya voennago ordena: Za delo pod Irdzharom 8-go maia 1866 g.', in *Turkestanskii al'bom: Po rasporiazheniiu Turkestanskago General-Gubernatora General-ad'iutanta K. P. fon Kaufmana 1-go* ed. A. L. Kun. Pt. 4 *Chast' istoricheskaya* ed. M. A. Terent'ev (Tashkent: Litografiya Voenno-Topograficheskogo Otdela Turkestanskogo Voennogo Okruga, 1871–2), plate 33 No. 62 (Library of Congress, Prints & Photographs Division, LC-DIG-ppmsca-09957-00062).

[146] Terent'ev, *Istoriya zavoevaniya*, II, 177.

[147] E. Kalbanova, 'Les Cosaques de l'Oural au Karakalpakistan', *CAC* 10 (2002), 239–47.

Count Petr Shuvalov observed that the latter looked more or less like regular troops, 'while the Ural Cossack – is a *jigit* ', using the Turkic word for a freebooting horseman.[148] Their close resemblance to the irregular cavalry that made up the bulk of their opponents' forces in Central Asia was not coincidental, and meant that they held few terrors for them. While the figure of the Cossack was important to the romantic imaginary of the Russian conquest, in battle their role was largely limited to scouting, skirmishing and pursuing the defeated enemy.

Thus both Russian and Central Asian sources attest that infantry volley fire and artillery (especially *kartechnyi* – canister shot) was what conferred a decisive advantage on Russian forces. In the early nineteenth century Russian artillery had a much better reputation among its opponents than either cavalry or infantry. The forces sent into Central Asia in the 1840s and 1850s were generally equipped with light batteries of horse artillery, consisting of 6 lb cannon with a 3.76 inch smooth bore and a range of 1,200 yards, 9 lb (quarter-*pood*) howitzers with a range of 900 yards, firing explosive shells, and lighter weapons such as *edinorogy* (unicorns) firing a 3 or 4 lb ball.[149] These were sometimes supplemented with heavier artillery – 12 lb cannon and 4½ *pood* howitzers – for attacking fortresses, but heavy siege trains were both impossible to move and unnecessary in Central Asian campaigns. From the 1860s Central Asian expeditionary forces began to be equipped with rifled artillery, but this simply reinforced an existing superiority, although it did make the destruction of fortifications easier.[150]

Russian tactics in Central Asia reflected both this technological superiority and the small size of the forces involved. General Dragomirov, in his standard 1867 work on tactics for infantry officers, recommended that the advance guard of a large force should be a mixed formation, made up of three infantry battalions, four cavalry squadrons, six foot and two horse artillery guns, which would march in a column a mile long.[151] This corresponds more or less to the total size and composition of the expeditionary forces with which the Russians conducted their Central Asian campaigns, which rarely exceeded 5,000 men and were usually considerably fewer. As Alex Marshall has shown, these forces would move in expeditionary columns with a small advance guard that remained in sight of the main column, and flanked by pickets of infantry or cavalry. This was designed to protect both the column and its enormous baggage train from surprise attack. At night they created temporary defensive positions (*Wagenburg*) using their wagons

---

[148] Shuvalov to Grand Duke Alexei Alexandrovich, Letter 4 24/05/1873 BL Add. MS. 47841 f. 81*ob.*

[149] John Shelton Curtiss, *The Russian Army under Nicholas I 1825–1855* (Durham, NC: Duke University Press, 1965), 148.

[150] Baumann, 'The Conquest of Central Asia', 61.

[151] M. I. Dragomirov, *Kurs Taktiki, dlya gg. ofitserov uchebnogo pekhotnogo bataliona* (St Pb., 1867), quoted in *The Military–Naval Encyclopaedia of Russia and the Soviet Union* ed. David R. Jones (Gulf Breeze, FL: Academic International Press, 1978), Vol. 4, 107–8.

if they had any, or else simply the bodies of their camels.[152] It was sometimes necessary to break up the column into several echelons owing to shortages of water and forage – this occurred during the 1873 Khiva expedition. In principle it made Russian forces vulnerable to attack while on the move, but it usually occurred in terrain that was so hostile and remote that it was also all but inaccessible to their opponents.[153] In battle in open country Russian infantry remained in close formations, supported by artillery, that proved almost impossible for Central Asian cavalry to overrun. Cossacks also frequently dismounted and fought as infantry in close formation on foot, as in the celebrated battle at Iqan in 1864, where they held off a much larger force of Khoqandis for almost two days (Chapter 5). As Gök-Tepe showed, when military leadership and decision-making were poor the Russians could still be beaten, but they were more or less guaranteed victory if their commander kept his head – and above all if they could actually reach their enemy in the first place.

I.6   Camels and Commissariat

Camels were probably the principal sufferers from the forward policy in Central Asia.

M. A. Yapp, *Strategies of British India* (1980)

Given this crushing technological superiority in weaponry, the main challenges the Russians faced in Central Asia were always logistical. Finding enough supplies and enough animals to carry them was of crucial importance in Central Asian campaigns. Peter Perdue has noted that it was the key factor which determined the initial failure and ultimate success of the Qing campaigns against the Junghars between the 1730s and 1750s. Their ability first to control the grain market in regions neighbouring the Junghar confederation, and then to find nomadic allies who would supply the necessary transport (60,000 horses and 34,000 camels in the initial plans of the 1730s, a number which subsequently rose), finally allowed the Qing to prevail. They had to adapt to what Perdue calls 'the political ecology of frontier conquest' in an arid and sparsely populated region, which involved vast expenditure and careful and elaborate planning before any technological or tactical advantages could be brought to bear on the enemy.[154] One hundred years later little had changed, but this aspect of Russia's Central Asian campaigns has been almost entirely overlooked in both Tsarist and modern historiography.[155] Terent'ev paid little attention to it, simply taking

---

[152] Marshall, *Russian General Staff*, 53–5; Baumann, 'The Conquest of Central Asia', 60–1.

[153] Baumann, 'The Conquest of Central Asia', 65; Marshall, *Russian General Staff*, 53.

[154] Perdue *China Marches West*, 331–2, 520–4.

[155] This section summarises arguments in Alexander Morrison, 'Camels and Colonial Armies: The Logistics of Warfare in Inner Asia in the Early 19th century', *JESHO* 57 (2014), 443–85 and reappears here by kind permission of the publisher. The only other

for granted the fact that steppe expeditions required baggage animals and that the lack of them often caused problems, but never considering just how fundamentally the whole enterprise of conquest depended on them and those who bred and managed them. Colonel A. G. Serebrennikov (1863–?), in his celebrated collection of documents relating to the conquest, rarely included the mundane details relating to the carriage of ammunition, rations and forage, or the lengthy, complex and expensive business of rounding up the necessary animals. In almost all cases these would be camels, usually of the double-humped Bactrian variety, although single-humped dromedaries are also found in southern Central Asia. My introduction to the topic came when I ordered an 800-folio file in the Kazakhstan state archives in Almaty, promisingly entitled 'On the despatch of a military expedition to Khiva' – and discovered that virtually all of it consisted of correspondence between Qazaq Sultans of the Junior Horde (*Kishi zhuz*) and the Orenburg Frontier Commission on the collection of the 10,000 camels for the 1839–40 winter invasion of Khiva, a process which took eighteen months.[156] There will be an awful lot of camels in this book, and I make no apology for this.

Thus Russia's invading armies might be equipped with the latest in available military technology, but they were nevertheless dependent on local knowledge and resources when it came to actually moving around. The camel caravan was an apparently startlingly archaic means of projecting European power into Asia, but, as William McNeill has shown, it would be a mistake even in the nineteenth century to think of camel transport as an anachronistic, ineffective survival from an earlier era, although it is true that by the 1830s its days were numbered.[157] In the early nineteenth century camels were still the principal form of long-distance land transport in the Maghreb, the Ottoman Empire, Persia, Central Asia and North-Western India (further east, where the damper climate did not suit them, they yielded to bullocks), and there were very good reasons for this. A single camel could carry a load of between 150 and 350 kg (this varied greatly with size and breed of camel and the nature of the terrain), more than twice as much as a horse or donkey.[158] Camels have an unusually low energy cost from locomotion

---

historian to have devoted any attention to this is vital question is Marshall, *The Russian General Staff*, 53–6.

[156] TsGARKaz F.4 Op.1 D.2167, 'Materialy ob otpravke v Khivu voennogo otryada dlya osvobozhdeniya russkikh plennykh'.

[157] Despite its title Niels Steensgaard, *The Asian Trade Revolution of the Seventeenth Century: The East India Companies and the Decline of the Caravan Trade* (Chicago: Chicago University Press, 1973) reveals the resilience of much caravan transport in the face of maritime competition; see further Levi, 'India, Russia, and the Transformation of the Central Asian Caravan Trade', 524–6.

[158] Michel Tuchscherer, 'Some Reflections on the Place of the Camel in Ottoman Egypt', in *Animals and People in the Ottoman Empire* ed. Suraiya Faroqhi (Istanbul: Eren, 2010), 177–81; Hilde Gauthier-Pilters & Anne Innis Dagg *The Camel: Its Evolution, Ecology, Behaviour and Relationship to Man* (Chicago: University of Chicago Press, 1981), 109–10.

compared with other mammals, and this is not proportionally increased by the addition of a load.[159] The camel caravan was fantastically efficient, required hardly any infrastructure, and was capable of carrying goods very long distances very cheaply at a steady 4 km an hour in flat country.[160] This was in part because camels could graze as they travelled and carried a substantial supply of fat, making the transport of large quantities of fodder unnecessary. Most caravans consisted of no more than a few strings of six camels, meaning that they were unlikely to totally denude any route they passed across, and even the largest caravans in the Middle East had no more than 1,000.[161] However, a Russian expeditionary column of 5,000 men – such as that for the winter invasion of Khiva – needed 10,000 camels or more. Under these circumstances, many of the economies associated with caravan travel simply broke down, because even the richest landscape could not sustain that number of animals passing through it. Whilst they could travel for up to a week without eating, in order to remain in good condition each camel would need 10–20 kg of plant matter a day,[162] meaning a total daily requirement of 100–200 tonnes for the Khiva expedition's camels. To transport even the lower amount would itself require another 330 camels, adding another 3.3 tonnes of fodder to the army's daily requirements – accordingly, even assuming the minimum consumption of fodder and a 300 kg load per camel (close to the upper limit possible), if every one of the 10,000 camels on the march had carried nothing but fodder, it would have sufficed for only thirty days. This makes it clear enough why it was essential that the camels lived off the land during the march and were well fed before it, but such grazing was not always available, even assuming the camels would be given time to feed properly. To this were added problems with climate, loading and management, which together added up to very high mortality rates for British as well as Russian expeditions into Central Asia.[163] The death from cold of almost all the camels during the 1839 winter invasion of Khiva guaranteed the campaign's failure (Chapter 2).

[159] In one experiment camels carrying loads weighing 21%–34% of their body mass increased their metabolic rate by just 18%: M. K. Yousef, M. E. D. Webster & O. M. Yousef, 'Energy Costs of Walking in Camels, *Camelus dromedarius*', *Physiological Zoology* 62/5 (1989), 1080–8.
[160] Indeed, so regular is the camel's pace that James Rennell, the first surveyor of Bengal, thought that it could be used to calculate distances in regions where obtaining fixed points by celestial observations was difficult: James Rennell, 'On the Rate of Travelling, as Performed by Camels: And Its Application, as a Scale, to the Purposes of Geography', *Philosophical Transactions of the Royal Society of London* 81 (1791), 129–45.
[161] William H. McNeill, 'The Eccentricity of Wheels, or Eurasian Transportation in Historical Perspective', *AHR* 92/5 (1987), 1111–26. The classic exploration of the revolutionary effect of the development of camel transport is Richard W. Bulliet, *The Camel and the Wheel* (Cambridge, MA: Harvard University Press, 1975).
[162] Gauthier-Pilters & Dagg, *The Camel*, 36.
[163] Yapp, *Strategies of British India*, 391.

Writing in 1876 General Nikolai Lomakin (1830–1902), then commander of the Transcaspian Division, summed up the structural limitations which reliance on camel transport placed on Russian forces, and some of the reasons why, once they had been accumulated with so much difficulty, they then proceeded to die in vast numbers:

> The sole means of transport here for troops is the camel. But each year we have more and more reasons to be certain that, just as this useful beast is suitable and essential for trade caravans, it is unsuitable and impractical for troops. I will give just a few main facts to support these thoughts: in the main actions against Khiva in 1873, out of 10,000 camels with the Turkestan column, only 1,500 reached Khiva, the remainder fell. In General Verevkin's column out of 8,000 camels 6,000 died, and out of my 2,000 camels [with the Mangishlaq column] only 900 remained, and Colonel Markozov lost more than 4,000 dead and injured, in total more than 20,000 in the last four years. One can imagine what a heavy burden this sad circumstance is on the economic situation of our Central Asian possessions, and especially on the nomadic way of life of our Kirgiz and Turkmen. We vainly seek to explain this terrible mortality among the camels through climatic conditions: heat, lack of water and lack of food are not so terrible to a camel on the march as the breach of the usual conditions under which trade caravans travel, when camels always have the time to rest and feed themselves – these conditions are impossible when troops are moving. Normally trade caravans set off around midnight, and march until around 8 am, covering 25 *versts* (i.e. one *manzil*), they then wait and rest until one in the afternoon; – thus having managed in these five hours to feed their camels well, they then make another *manzil* from 2 until 7; after which they usually unload the camels and they sleep until midnight. This order of march is impossible for troops.[164]

Lomakin was almost certainly correct in his diagnosis that forced marches in the heat of the day and lack of time for the beasts to feed were a major cause of camel fatalities: Richmond Shakespear, a British envoy to Khiva forty years earlier, observing the practices of his Turkmen guides, had written that 'the native plan of dividing the distance to be crossed in the twenty-four hours into two stages, is a good one; and should another army of the Indus leave India, I think they would find this plan answer. Your camels and your cattle have the cool of the morning and evening for work, and the middle of the day to feed, and they have a good night's rest, instead of being loaded or harnessed in the middle of the night.'[165] However, neither the British nor the Russians were prepared to adapt their order of march to the practices used by trade caravans,

---

[164] Lomakin to Franchini 20/11/1876 NAG F.545 Op.1 D.1255 l. 34*ob*.

[165] Richmond Shakespear, 'A Personal Narrative of a Journey from Heraut to Ourenbourg, on the Caspian [*sic*] in 1840', *Blackwood's Edinburgh Magazine* 51 (June 1842), 704; Morrison, 'Camels and Colonial Armies', 472.

and their camels continued to die in their thousands, whether on Lomakin's march to the Akhal-Teke oasis in 1879 or on Lord Roberts's march to Qandahar and Kabul in the same year.[166]

The Russians chafed at the restrictions on their freedom of movement imposed by dependence on camel transport, and through this on 'native' camel-breeders and drivers. To complicate matters further, in Transcaspia it was the Turkmen themselves who were simultaneously the main breeders of camels and the main objects of Russian aggression, and they were understandably reluctant to supply them.[167] During the 1873 Khiva campaign this constraint had compelled the Russians to divide their forces into four different columns, one of which, from Krasnovodsk, was forced to turn back after antagonising the Turkmen along the Atrek, who refused to supply the necessary beasts.[168] Lomakin urged the construction of a railway to overcome this constraint, and it was begun in 1880, reaching Samarkand in 1888: it played a key role in General Skobelev's final victorious campaign against the Turkmen in 1881. However, the railway came too late for most nineteenth-century Central Asian campaigns, whether British or Russian.

When Captain Alexei Nikolaevich Kuropatkin – later Skobelev's chief of staff, then Governor of Transcaspia and Minister of War – produced a report on his official mission to the French Army in Algeria in 1874, he commented admiringly on the French system of maintaining a permanent force of 800 camels for desert expeditions, and compared it unfavourably with the system of temporary requisitions in place in Turkestan.[169] His mission there followed swiftly after the second Russian expedition against Khiva in 1873, which this time was successful, but which endured great logistical difficulties and, as we have seen, huge mortality in camels. The preparations for the expedition prompted General M. I. Ivanin, who had been commissariat-master during Perovskii's winter invasion of Khiva, to send a memorandum to the War Ministry urging a new system for the recruitment of camels which revealed that the frustrations of 1839–40 were still keenly felt, but that the real lesson of

---

[166] James Hevia, *Animal Labor and Colonial Warfare* (Chicago: University of Chicago Press, 2018), 27–49.

[167] Lomakin to the head of the Kavkazskoe Gorskoe Upravlenie 20/11/1876 NAG F.545 Op.1 D.1255 l. 34*ob*.

[168] Astrabad Consul to Russian Legation, Tehran 25/09/1872 F.5 Op.1 D.2241 ll. 275–9*ob*.

[169] A. N. Kuropatkin, *Alzhiriya* (St Pb.: Tip. V. A. Poletiki, 1877), 285–309. The Russians were also interested in the experiments made by the U. S. army in Texas in the 1850s: A. A. Katenin, 'O pokhodnykh dvizhenii pekhota po stepi' 06/12/1858 RGVIA F.483 Op.1 D.49 ll. 23–*ob*, referring to Jefferson Davis, *Report of the Secretary of War, Communicating, in Compliance with a Resolution of the Senate of February 2, 1857, Information Respecting the Purchase of Camels for the Purposes of Military Transportation* (Washington, D.C.: A. O. P. Nicholson, 1857), which described experiments undertaken with camels imported from Asia Minor and North Africa to Texas.

the campaign – the need to listen to the expertise of the Qazaq pastoralists who bred and managed the army's pack animals – had not been learned:

> At the moment when there is a steppe expedition, we hire camels and camel drivers, a great deal of time is lost in this; the secret of the expedition gets out; the enemy has time to take measures to impede or slow down the collection of camels, and to establish the proposed plan of the expedition. With this system of collecting camels, there is no way of knowing their strength, carrying capacity or familiarity with packs, with that certainty which is essential for military enterprises, and thus calculate with accuracy what quantity of supplies it is possible to carry on camels gathered by this means; what length of stages it is possible to make with them, and what distance they can travel without feeding. Beyond this we also have to hope that during the vicissitudes of war the Kirgiz drivers will not leave with the camels, or go over to the enemy, and abandon the force in the steppe in a hopeless situation.[170]

His solution to this problem was to find a means of transporting infantry using camels, thus both speeding up the progress of steppe expeditions (meaning fewer provisions and thus fewer baggage camels were needed) and obviating the need for unreliable Qazaq drivers. This was a revival of an idea first put forward in 1858 by General Katenin, the Governor of Orenburg, who proposed hanging a cumbersome wooden armchair on each side of the camel, allowing it to carry two infantrymen at a time: it had been approved as an experiment by the Tsar; however, while the published report suggested that this system should be used for all expeditions where speed was essential, it never seems to have been put into practice.[171] Ivanin also thought greater use could be made of steppe horses, and proposed establishing stud farms for them along the Ural and Terek rivers to improve the breed and make them more fit for military use.[172] Above all, however, he advocated rearing and maintaining a permanent reserve of 40,000 camels for military purposes, along the lines (so he believed) of what he still referred to as the East India Company and the Chinese Empire. Ivanin's proposals were rejected by the cavalry remount division, and by the Regional Staff in Orenburg, who wrote that improving the breed of the steppe horses was a slow process, and above all that as soldiers and Cossacks alike

---

[170] M. I. Ivanin, 'Ob ustroistve otryadov na verbliudakh dlya voennykh tselei v Srednei Azii', 22/03/1873 RGVIA F.400 Op.1 D.340 ll. 1–*ob*.

[171] A. A. Katenin, 'O pokhodnykh dvizhenii pekhota po stepi', 06/12/1858; Lieven to Bezak 09/04/1861 RGVIA F.483 Op.1 D.49 ll. 3–17; 114–18; 'Pokhody v stepi: Upotreblenie verbliudov dlya voennykh nadobnostei', *VS* (1862) No. 2, 357–88.

[172] 'Ob uluchshenii pochve i porody loshadei v Prikaspiiskikh stepyakh ot r. Tereka do r. Urala', 27/01/1873 RGVIA F.400 Op.1 D.340 ll. 3–5*ob*; on the use of Central Asian horses by the Russian military see Carole Ferret, 'Des chevaux pour l'empire', in *CAC*. Vols. 17–18. *Le Turkestan russe: Une colonie comme les autres?* ed. Svetlana Gorshenina and Sergej Abašin (Tashkent & Aix-en-Provence: IFEAC, Éditions De Boccard, 2009), 211–53.

were unable to manage, let alone rear, camels, it was necessary to remain with the current system of hiring them from the Qazaqs; now that Khiva had fallen there was no longer any reason to fear treachery.[173] Ivanin died a year later, and some of his conclusions on the logistics of Central Asian warfare, which were based on a study of the campaigns of Chingis Khan, Tamerlane and Nadir Shah, were published posthumously by the General Staff, but they do not seem to have been interested in putting them into practice.[174]

This basic structural constraint on military campaigning in Central Asia thus persisted throughout the entire period of the conquest: once away from the line of rail, troops could be kept supplied only by camel, and these in turn could be provided and effectively managed only by the pastoralists who reared them – who in some cases (such as the Turkmen in the 1880s) were precisely the group against whom the campaign was directed. The role of this factor in determining the dynamics of Central Asian warfare and conquest in the nineteenth century has been severely underestimated: railways came to this region only after most of it had already been conquered by Britain or Russia. This meant that, even as the products of industrialised warfare – rockets, rifled firearms and artillery, explosive shells – were employed against Central Asian peoples in increasingly unequal campaigns, the means of transportation remained the same: the camel. Before every campaign in the barren lands of the North-West Frontier and the steppes and deserts of Central Asia pastoralist groups would have to supply thousands of these, whether for money or under coercion. This had important political consequences. After the failure of the winter invasion of Khiva in 1839–40 the Russians were forced to change their tactics for steppe campaigns; they never again attempted to send so large an expedition over so long a distance, and instead concentrated on building permanent fortresses and supply bases much deeper in nomadic territory, along the Syr-Darya and the frontier with China:[175] these represented a more concrete assertion of sovereignty in the region, and helped to create a new and inexorable logic of conquest (see Chapter 3).[176]

Even with this new infrastructure the numbers of troops involved in Central Asian expeditions remained small – in the Russian case usually around 3,000 men. This was sufficient to overcome the limited opposition the Russians met

[173] Head of Cavalry Remounts to the Head of the General Staff 14/05/1873; Head of the Orenburg Regional Staff to the Head of the General Staff 15/06/1873 RGVIA F.400 Op.1 D.340 ll. 11–2.
[174] M. I. Ivanin, *O voennom iskusstve i zavoevaniyakh mongol-tatar i sredne-aziyatskikh narodov pri Chingis-Khane i Tamerlane* ed. N. S. Golitsyn (St Pb., Tip. Obshchestvennaya Pol'za, 1875), 237–43; Marshall, *The Russian General Staff*, 47–8, 53.
[175] This also echoes the tactics used by the Qing 100 years earlier: Perdue, *China Marches West*, 522–3.
[176] Alexander Morrison, '"Nechto eroticheskoe?" "Courir après l'ombre?" Logistical Imperatives and the Fall of Tashkent, 1859–1865', *CAS* 33/2 (2014), 153–69.

from Central Asian states and nomadic groups, but not to defeat another European power. Logistics ensured that the Russian and British armies would never confront each other directly in Central Asia. The idea of a Russian conquest of India, so beloved of 'Great Game' theorists then and now, was a chimera precisely because of these constraints – something Russian Generals often stated in public (to the incredulity of British journalists),[177] and which in fact reflected their conclusions in internal documents whenever the topic of making a 'demonstration' against the British in India was discussed at the highest political level. A serious invasion force would have needed at least 150,000 men – and at least 300,000 camels to transport supplies.[178] This was a physical impossibility, something that by the 1890s British Military Intelligence in London seems to have understood, but which continued to be stubbornly ignored by the General Staff in India.[179] This also means that one of the most popular theories regarding Russian expansion in Central Asia – that it was undertaken by 'men on the spot' without sanction from the centre – was only rarely true.[180] The transport arrangements for steppe and desert expeditions required months of preparation, together with a substantial budget that had to be approved in St Petersburg, and this did not lend itself to spontaneous acts of aggression along the frontier. As Peter Perdue has noted of the Qing conquest of Inner Asia 100 years previously, local environmental, animal and human factors – grain, fodder, camels and the pastoralists who bred and drove them – were more decisive than the desires of statesmen or the tactics of generals in determining the success or failure of military conquest in these arid regions.[181]

I.7   From Grand Narrative to Microhistory

I do not wish to replace the failed grand narratives of the 'Great Game' and 'Cotton Canard' with a new overarching explanation of Russian expansion in Central Asia. One thing which became abundantly clear while researching this book is that every decision to advance was taken with a unique combination of factors involved: the personalities would vary on the Russian side and so would the opponents they faced in Central Asia. The level of violence employed

---

[177] Charles Marvin, *The Russian Advance towards India: Conversations with Skobeleff, Ignatieff, and Other Distinguished Russian Generals and Statesmen, on the Central Asian Question* (London: W. H. Allen & Co, 1882), 103–4.

[178] D. A. Miliutin, 'Ministerstvo Voennoe doklad po glavnomu shtabu chast' Aziatskaya', 08/04/1878 NAG F.545 Op.1 D.1154 ll. 174–9*ob* & AVPRI F.161 I-5 Op.4 1878 No. 1 ll. 1–9.

[179] James Hevia, *The Imperial Security State: British Colonial Knowledge and Empire-Building in Asia* (Cambridge: Cambridge University Press, 2012), 164–72.

[180] MacKenzie, 'Expansion in Central Asia'.

[181] Perdue, *China Marches West*, 37–8.

fluctuated hugely, from the massacres perpetrated against the Yomud and
Akhal-Teke Turkmen and the Sarts and Qipchaqs of Ferghana, to the almost
entirely peaceful annexation of the Pamirs. The wider international situation
also varied – until the 1870s the British usually found out about Russian
campaigns only after they had happened, but in the 1880s and 1890s they
sometimes became directly involved. Sometimes the Russians were also dealing
with the Chinese, Afghan and Persian states, and sometimes they were wholly
occupied with just one Central Asian ruler. Perhaps the most important variations were environmental: would this campaign be fought across steppe, desert,
mountain, or the easier cultivated terrain of the riverine oases of southern
Central Asia? Could the troops live off the land, or would they have to bring
all their supplies with them? Would they experience extremes of heat, or of cold?
Would there be forage for their baggage animals? And could they get hold of
those animals in the first place? The only ever-present factor was the Russian
official mind, with its prejudices, paranoia and anxieties about prestige. This
helped ensure that the default option was always to advance and annex more
territory, but, considered in isolation, it does not carry much explanatory power.
As Artemy Kalinovsky has shown for the Soviet war in Afghanistan 100 years
later, one should not expect to find a single coherent or rational motive, let alone
some sort of 'grand strategy', behind Russian or Soviet decision-making regarding Central Asia – these things only ever existed in the minds of their 'Great
Power' opponents, whether Anglo-Indian Staff officers or American Cold
Warriors. Instead, in both cases we find confused and hurried reactions to
events, constant anxiety about prestige, and a considerable degree of Central
Asian agency.[182] Rather than seeking yet another easily disprovable grand theory
to explain the Russian conquest, this book consists of a series of microhistories of
the different campaigns, structured partly chronologically and partly geograph-
ically. There are also a number of themes that recur throughout: conflicting ideas
of sovereignty between Russian and Central Asian elites; the importance of
imperial prestige to the Russians; the role of local agency and circumstances in
precipitating events; the surprisingly inconsistent use of violence; the role of
personality and relations between individuals; the importance of environmental
factors; and, of course, camels.

I refer throughout this book to 'Central Asians' and 'Russians' as if these
were uniform and undifferentiated categories, when of course they were not. I
tried at the beginning of this introduction to give some sense of the many
different peoples and languages of Central Asia, and I hope some more details
will become clear as the book progresses. On the other side, the word 'Russian'
in English translates two distinct terms: *Russkii* and *Rossiiskii*. The first refers
to Russians as an ethnicity, the second to the Russian state, its institutions and

[182] Artemy Kalinovsky, *A Long Goodbye: The Soviet Withdrawal from Afghanistan*
(Cambridge, MA: Harvard University Press, 2011), 11–12.

its agents.[183] Almost without exception, when I use the term 'Russian' or refer to 'the Russians' in this book it is in the second sense. The conquest of Central Asia was a Russian *imperial* enterprise, whose agents were sometimes Russian by ethnicity, but almost equally often German, Polish, Tatar, Ukrainian, Bashkir, Georgian, Armenian or Finnish. They were predominantly Orthodox Christians, but also Lutherans, Catholics, Monophysites and, in some cases, Muslims. This did not mean they identified any the less with Russian state interests – nor does it vitiate the generally European character of the Russian conquest. Viewing this or any other aspect of pre-twentieth-century Central Asian history through the prism of modern nationality is unhelpful.[184]

Beyond these necessary simplifications, I am only too aware of this book's many other deficiencies, the chief of which is that it gives an overwhelmingly Russian perspective on events. I have tried to use Central Asian accounts of what it was like to be on the receiving end of the Russian conquest wherever possible, but a substantial imbalance remains – especially when assessing individual biographies and personalities, where the sources allow one to give a much fuller account of the character of Russian than of Central Asian protagonists. A truly comprehensive history of the conquest written from the Central Asian perspective would require a historian with much greater linguistic skills. There is a lot of material detail in this book, there are a lot of empirical claims, and there is a lot of narrative. I should be the first to admit that none of these things makes for particularly sophisticated or innovative history. There are many other histories of the Russian conquest of Central Asia that could and I hope will one day be written – through the prisms of literature, gender or medicine, for example – but, given the current state of research, I do not think that is what this topic demands at the moment. This is an enormously complicated story, about a part of the world that is not particularly well-known to an English-speaking audience, which has never before been fully told in English. In this book I will tell it as completely as I can.

---

[183] Geoffrey Hosking, *Russia, People and Empire 1552–1917* (London: HarperCollins, 1997), xix.
[184] On this see Abashin, *Natsionalizmy v Srednei Azii*, 13–35.

1

Russia's Steppe Frontier and the Napoleonic Generation

> Millions of men, renouncing their human feelings and reason, had to go from west to east to slay their fellows, just as some centuries previously hordes of men had come from the east to the west slaying their fellows.
>
> Leo Tolstoy, *War and Peace*, Book IX, Chapter 1, trans.
> Louise & Aylmer Maude

Citing Tolstoy at the beginning of a book like this is perhaps a bit foolhardy. Apart from this glancing reference to the Mongol conquests, he does not mention Central Asia anywhere in *War and Peace*. Tolstoy also famously decried the pretensions of historians, soldiers and memoirists to determine the causes of the events which formed the backdrop to his great novel. It was a delusion, he wrote, to suppose that the actions or decisions of one man or group of men could explain the outcome of the battle of Borodino or any other historical moment. You would need to trace the lives of every person who participated, all of the factors that went into their upbringing and formation, all the impersonal elements which also came to bear, and then trace the actions of every single one of these over the course of that day to begin to arrive at a truly historical explanation, and this was plainly impossible. As Isaiah Berlin put it: 'After disposing of the heroic theory of history, Tolstoy turns with even greater savagery on scientific sociology, which claims to have discovered laws of history, but cannot possibly have found any, because the number of causes upon which events turn is too great for human knowledge or calculation.'[1]

> To us their descendants, who are not historians and are not carried away by the process of research, and can therefore regard the event with unclouded common sense, an incalculable number of causes present themselves. The deeper we delve in search of these causes the more of them we find; and each separate cause or whole series of causes appears to us equally valid in itself and equally false by its insignificance compared to the magnitude of the events, and by its impotence – apart from the co-operation of all the other coincident causes – to occasion the event. [...]

---

[1] Isaiah Berlin, 'The Hedgehog and the Fox: An Essay on Tolstoy's View of History', in *Russian Thinkers* ed. Henry Hardy (London: Penguin, 2013), 45–6.

Without each of these causes nothing could have happened. So all these causes – myriads of causes – coincided to bring it about.[2]

Logically this would lead to the conclusion that nothing about the past could be truly known or understood – a conclusion not dissimilar to that which some historians later drew from the 'linguistic turn', though proceeding from very different roots: 'due not to some inherent inaccessibility of first causes, only to their multiplicity, the smallness of the ultimate units, and our own inability to see and hear and remember and record and co-ordinate enough of the available material'. Tolstoy's tragedy, as Berlin brilliantly showed, was that – like Archilochus's fox – he could see the extraordinary complexity of history with almost painful clarity, yet, hedgehog-like, he believed that there should be a single, overarching explanation or theory that would bind them together, which he was never able to identify.[3]

This book consists mainly of attempts to establish chains of causation, focusing above all on the decision-making and actions of small groups of elite men, and as such is precisely the kind of exercise Tolstoy would have despised. Why invoke him at all? Partly it is as a reminder of the need for humility in all historical enquiry: the problems that Tolstoy illustrated in trying to identify historical causes are real and have never gone away. I will not be able to overcome all of them in this book, and any immediate causes for the Russian conquest of Central Asia which I put forward will of course be subject to Tolstoy's 'multiplication effect' if pursued back in time. It is also because nothing illustrates the hold which the Napoleonic campaigns exercised over the nineteenth-century Russian imagination like *War and Peace*. Understanding the impact which the Napoleonic Wars had not just on the Russian empire's standing as a 'Great Power', but on the self-perception of its ruling elites, is central to understanding why Russia conquered Central Asia when it did.

For over 100 years the effective boundaries of Russian sovereignty in Central Asia were the fortified lines along the Ural and Irtysh rivers, and the Presnogorskaya line between them, all constructed between 1710 and 1735 and at this date consisting mostly of wooden fortresses. In 1716 Peter I ordered an invasion of Khiva by a force under Prince Bekovich-Cherkasskii to support a simultaneous advance along the western shore of the Caspian into the Caucasus and Persia. Both proved abortive, as Bekovich-Cherkasskii's entire force was massacred, and the Russian empire also returned the territories it

---

[2] Leo Tolstoy, *War and Peace*. Vol. II trans. Louise Maude & Aylmer Maude (Oxford: Humphrey Milford for Oxford University Press, 1942), 256–7.
[3] Berlin, 'The Hedgehog and the Fox', 50, 57–8, 92; see further the essays in Rick McPeak & Donna Tussing Orwin, *Tolstoy on War: Narrative Art and Historical Fiction in 'War and Peace'* (Ithaca, NY: Cornell University Press, 2012).

had annexed in the Caucasus under the treaty of Ganja in 1735.[4] The Russians did not attempt to conquer Khiva again until Perovskii's winter expedition of 1839–40 – they were unsuccessful once more, but this time failure ushered in a series of advances and annexations that would end only in 1895, with the delineation of the Pamir boundary. What explains this relative eighteenth-century stability? And how do we explain the renewed advance, when it came?

As we shall see, there were specific local circumstances in the first half of the nineteenth century – notably Khiva's enslavement of Russian subjects, the expansion of the Khoqand khanate into the steppe, and Sultan Kenesary Qasimov's resistance to Russian attempts to consolidate their rule among the Qazaqs – that helped to trigger an advance far beyond the limits of settled cultivation, to which the Russians had hitherto largely confined themselves, and into the almost purely nomadic territory of the Asian steppe. However, these circumstances were not unprecedented in their nature: as Michael Khodarkovsky has shown, since the sixteenth century Russia's steppe frontier had been a place of violence and contested sovereignty, only partly mitigated by cultural exchange.[5] Since at least the late eighteenth century, and arguably for some time before, Russia had had a clear sense of a *mission civilisatrice* in the region, something seen very clearly, for instance, in D. V. Volkov's letters to Catherine the Great when he was Governor of Orenburg in 1763, where he wrote of the need to demonstrate the superiority of Russian civilisation to the Qazaqs and convert them to settled agriculture.[6] Instability, blurred sovereignty, raids on trade caravans, nomadic rebellions and slave-raiding were endemic on Russia's steppe frontier throughout the eighteenth century. The Pugachev rebellion of 1773–5, which almost destroyed the Russian state, was a far greater threat to security and stability than anything that happened on the steppe in the nineteenth century.[7] The question, then, is why the response of the Russian state to these persistent factors became more aggressive and

[4] René Létolle, 'Les expéditions de Bekovitch-Tcherkassky en Turkestan (1714–1717) et le début de l'infiltration russe en Asie centrale', in *CAC*. Vols. 5–6. *Boukhara la noble* (Tashkent &Aix-en-Provence: IFEAC, Éditions De Boccard, 1998), 259–85.

[5] Michael Khodarkovsky, *Russia's Steppe Frontier: The Making of a Colonial Empire 1500–1800* (Bloomington, IN: Indiana University Press, 2002).

[6] 'Zapiska ob Orenburgskom krae' (D. V. Volkov to Catherine the Great, Moscow, 26/04/1763), in 'Dmitrii Vasil'evich Volkov: Materialy k ego biografii 1718–1785', *RS* (1874) No. 9, 491–3; Khodarkovsky, *Russia's Steppe Frontier*, 225–6; Harsha Ram suggests that Lomonosov's Khotin ode of 1739 marks the first literary recognition of the Russian sense of superiority over Asia: Harsha Ram, *The Imperial Sublime: A Russian Poetics of Empire* (Madison, WN: University of Wisconsin Press, 2003), 23–4, 77–8.

[7] The standard account remains John T. Alexander, *Autocratic Politics in a National Crisis: The Imperial Russian Government and Pugachev's revolt, 1773–1775* (Bloomington, IN: Indiana University Press, 1969). See also Alan Bodger, *The Kazakhs and the Pugachev Uprising in Russia, 1773–1775* (Bloomington, IN: Research Unit for Inner Asian Studies, Indiana University, 1988).

ambitious in the early 1800s, leading to the outright annexation of vast but for the most part extremely unremunerative territories.

Part of the explanation lies in broader historical trends common to much of Europe: the balance of power and military technology on the steppe shifted decisively in Russia's favour in the late eighteenth century, as the last serious nomadic threat to Russian security, the Crimean Khanate, was conquered in 1774 and annexed in 1783.[8] Nevertheless, as the fate of Perovskii's expedition shows, immense logistical difficulties continued to hamper the application of these military advantages in the Asian steppe until the railway finally superseded the camel in the last decade of the nineteenth century: the Russians certainly did not conquer Central Asia because it had suddenly become easy to do so.

Another factor was a changed geopolitical balance, which saw the significant expansion of British power in the Indian subcontinent during the Revolutionary and Napoleonic Wars (a period Christopher Bayly called Britain's 'Imperial Meridian').[9] If the Central Asian frontier had remained in more or less the same place for most of the eighteenth century, this was at least in part because Russian expansionist ambitions had been directed towards other, more obviously valuable territories, most notably the Baltic coastline, the Pontic Steppe and latterly the Caucasus. These were also the areas where she came into conflict with her most important international rivals, which in the eighteenth century were Poland, Sweden, Prussia and the Ottoman Empire. In contrast, for most of the nineteenth century Russia's main rival would be Britain – and, just as for the British, so for the Russians the Napoleonic victory added to a serene assurance of superiority the arrogance and sense of entitlement born of pure power, and led to a significant shift in attitudes, mentality and self-perception within the official mind. It reinforced a sense that Russia was engaged in a global contest with other European imperial powers, and that her policies would need to measure up to a common standard with those of Britain and France, whether it came to the maintenance of her prestige or the development of her civilising mission. The implications of this for Russia's position in Europe are well known, and have been extensively studied, but its impact on the Central Asian frontier remains under-explored.[10] My contention is that the ruling elite of the Russian empire became much less willing to tolerate what it saw as the insolence and insubordination of steppe nomads and the khanates that lay beyond them. For the

---

[8] Alan W. Fisher, *The Annexation of Crimea by the Russian Empire* (Cambridge: Cambridge University Press, 1970); Kelly O'Neill, *Claiming Crimea: A History of Catherine the Great's Southern Empire* (Newhaven, CN: Yale University Press, 2017).

[9] C. A. Bayly, *Imperial Meridian: The British Empire and the World, 1780–1830* (London: Longmans, 1989).

[10] D. C. B. Lieven, 'Russia and the Defeat of Napoleon (1812–14)', *Kritika* 7/2 (2006), 283–308; LeDonne, *Grand Strategy*, 216–17.

Napoleonic generation the steppe world of multiple allegiances, shifting sovereignty and indeterminate borders had to be forced to acknowledge both the superiority of Russian civilisation and the reality of Russian power.

1.1   The Napoleonic Generation

> ... this interesting epoch, which should decide the fate of Germany, the happiness of Europe and in consequence that of Russia, gives birth to a host of ideas which seem in keeping with the circumstances, with the fine role played by Your Majesty, and above all with the grandeur and magnanimity which have characterised all your actions, since you undertook to become the Liberator of Europe.
>
> A. I. Chernyshev to Alexander I, 1813[11]

The experience of fighting Napoleon and his armies across Europe had a profound effect on a whole generation of Russia's ruling elite. A war which had begun in part because Alexander I could no longer endure the repeated humiliations which Napoleon's foreign policy heaped upon Russia in the unequal alliance forged at Tilsit[12] ended in a triumph that, in the short term, could hardly have been better stage-managed.[13] It inspired patriotic sentiments, certainly, but also admiration for the technological, agricultural and political advances which many officers and men had witnessed in western Europe, and frustration at Russia's failure to emulate these. Many of the Decembrists had fought in these campaigns, and their patriotism would take the form of rebellion to secure what they saw as a better political future for their country, but not all reacted as they did.[14] For much of Russia's ruling class the victory of 1814 was instead an affirmation of conservative, monarchical politics, which underwent a significant revival in the 1820s and 1830s and helped to underpin the 'Holy Alliance' between Russia and the conservative

---

[11] '... cette intéressante époque, qui doit décider du sort de l'Allemagne, du bonheur de l'Europe et par conséquent de celui de la Russie, fait naître une foule d'idées qui paraissent être analogues aux circonstances, au beau rôle que joue Votre Majesté et surtout à la grandeur et magnanimité qui ont caractérisé toutes vos démarches, Sire, depuis que Vous avez entrepris d'être le libérateur de l'Europe'. 'Copie d'un mémoire présenté à Sa Majesté l'Empereur par l'aide-de-camp général Tchernichef, à l'arrivée du grand quartier général à Francfort sur le Main vers la fin du mois de décembre 1813', in 'Bumagi A. I. Chernysheva za Tsarstvovanie Imperatora Aleksandra I', *SIRIO* Vol. 121 (St Pb., 1906), 232.

[12] Charles Esdaile, *Napoleon's Wars: An International History 1803–1815* (London: Allen Lane, 2007), 432–3; LeDonne, *Grand Strategy*, 157–8.

[13] Dominic Lieven, *Russia against Napoleon: The Battle for Europe, 1807–1814* (London: Allen Lane, 2009), 516–17.

[14] Janet M. Hartley, *Russia 1762–1825: Military Power, the State and the People* (Westport, CN & London: Praeger, 2008), 65–7; Bitis, *Russia and the Eastern Question*, 63–72.

monarchies of Austria and Prussia.[15] Above all, Napoleonic victory was understood as a clear indication that Russia was now the world's greatest land power, even as Britain controlled the seas, and this helped to paper over many underlying weaknesses that would not be fully revealed until forty years later, during the Crimean War.[16]

The decisions to advance ever deeper into Central Asia were taken in the 1830s, 1840s and 1850s by a very small group of men, all of whom could be said to belong to Russia's 'Napoleonic Generation' – that is, they had risen to distinction, and in most cases come of age, during the Napoleonic Wars. Having gained the favour of Alexander I, they proved adept at maintaining their positions when his brother assumed the throne, and between them succeeded in dominating not just Russian policy in Asia, but most of the highest echelons of the Russian state, until the 1850s, by which time they were old men.[17] They were proud of their role in Napoleon's defeat and jealous of Russia's consequent status as the liberator of Europe and guarantor of order and legitimacy there: in Asia the mission could be extended still further, with Russia the bringer of civilisation *tout court*. Whether of ethnic Russian or foreign origin, they wrote almost exclusively in French: for Russia's ruling class in this period, that was, quite literally, the language of self-description.[18]

On the Central Asian frontier the central figure was General (later Count) Vasilii Alexeevich Perovskii (1794–1857). Perovskii was the illegitimate (but acknowledged) son of one of Russia's greatest magnates, Count A. K. Razumovskii (1752–1838), a former Minister of Education, and Anna Mikhailovna, the estranged (but not divorced) wife of Count V. P. Sheremetev. He was brought up on his mother's estate at Pochep in Chernigov province, and then educated at Moscow University, leaving at the age of seventeen to fight the French. He lost part of a finger at Borodino, and was then captured with the Russian rearguard at the fall of Moscow, forced as a captive to walk to France, and held prisoner until the fall of Paris in 1814, whereupon he escaped.[19] After the war he was ennobled in his own right by Alexander I, and in 1818 he became *aide-de-camp* to the Tsar's brother, the then Grand Duke Nikolai Pavlovich.[20] He would accompany the future Nicholas

---

[15] Alexander Martin, *Romantics, Reformers, Reactionaries: Russian Conservative Thought and Politics in the Reign of Alexander I* (DeKalb, IL: Northern Illinois University Press, 1997), 143–68.

[16] Fuller, *Strategy and Power*, 218–19.

[17] W. Bruce Lincoln, *Nicholas I: Emperor and Autocrat of All the Russias* (DeKalb, IL: Northern Illinois University Press, 1989), 161–5.

[18] On the need to understand the empire on its own terms (and the simultaneous dangers of simply accepting the latter at face value) see Ilya Gerasimov, Jan Kusber & Alexander Semyonov (eds.), *Empire Speaks Out: Languages of Rationalization and Self-Description in the Russian Empire* (Leiden & Boston: Brill, 2009), 23–5.

[19] 'Iz zapisok Gr. Vasiliya Alekseevicha Perovskago o prebyvanii ego v plenu u frantsuzov 1812–1814', *RA* (1865) No. 3, 258–86.

[20] Terent'ev, *Istoriya zavoevaniya*, I, 94; V. F. Novitskii (ed.), *Voennaya entsiklopediya* (St Pb.: Tip. Tovarishchestva I. D. Sytina, 1915), XVIII, 372–3.

I on his educational tours of Europe and Russia, and personally protected him on St Isaac's Square during the Decembrist Revolt, where he was lightly wounded.[21] He subsequently served with distinction in the Russo-Turkish War of 1828, where he was chief of staff for the force which took Varna, and was severely wounded in the chest, Foreign Minister Count K. V. Nesselrode (1780–1862) writing that Perovskii had exposed himself to Turkish fire with foolhardy bravery, and that for many days they had despaired of his life.[22] The Perovskii legend included not only his reckless disregard for danger, but also supposedly a talent for rubbing people up the wrong way – he was reputed to be so moody and 'lacking in ambition' that he did not give thanks for the orders or promotions he received, while he was willing to tell the Tsar things that nobody else would risk. One such story, related to his biographer, Zakhar'in, by an old comrade-in-arms called N. N. Velyaminov in February 1891, concerned a very highly placed personage who had won more than half a million roubles at cards from a well-known tycoon. The St Petersburg gossip had it that there was something less than honourable about this story, and the emperor needed to be told: only Perovskii dared to do so, making himself a number of enemies as a result.[23]

Zakhar'in suggests that these enemies came from the 'German party' within the Russian elite, which stood for the rigid upholding of autocracy, Prussian military doctrine and drill, and the maintenance of alliances with conservative absolutist states in Europe.[24] His romantic image of Perovskii has him associated with the 'Russian party', a patriotic liberal who scorned foreign influences, rather like A. P. Yermolov (see below). Perovskii was first appointed Governor of Orenburg in 1833 at the age of just thirty-nine, and Zakhar'in describes this as a ploy by his enemies in the 'German party' to have him removed to what was still then a place of exile.[25] It seems more likely, however, that it was meant as a promotion. Perovskii's loyalty to Nicholas I is not in doubt, and more importantly it is clear that the latter trusted him implicitly. As we will see over the next two chapters, the Tsar would lend a ready ear both to Perovskii's proposal for an invasion of Khiva in 1839 (Chapter 2) and, fourteen years later (during his second tenure as Governor of Orenburg), to the project to seize the Khoqandi fortress of Aq Masjid and create a line of fortresses along the Syr-Darya (Chapter 3). For this he was made a Count in 1855, whilst Aq Masjid became the first (but not the last)

---

[21] 'Graf Vasilii Alekseevich Perovskii', *RA* (1878) No. 3, 373–4; I. N. Zakhar'in (Yakunin), *Graf V. A. Perovskii i ego zimnii pokhod v Khivu* (St Pb.: Tip. P. P. Soikina, 1901), 1–4; Lincoln, *Nicholas I*, 42.

[22] K. V. Nesselrode to Marie Nesselrode 04/09/1828, in *Lettres et papiers du Chancelier Comte de Nesselrode 1760–1850: Extraits de ses archives*. Vol. VII. *1828–1839* ed. A. de Nesselrode (Paris: A Lahure, 1908), 87.

[23] Zakhar'in, *Graf V. A. Perovskii*, 8–9.

[24] Bitis, *Russia and the Eastern Question*, 90–7.

[25] Zakhar'in, *Graf V. A. Perovskii*, 9.

Central Asian settlement to be renamed after its conqueror. Perovskii would be seen by subsequent generations of Turkestan Generals as the man who laid the foundations of Russian rule in Central Asia, and a dramatic portrait of his handsome but haggard features was the opening photograph of the 'Historical Section' of K. P. von Kaufman's *Turkestan Album* (Figure 1.1).[26]

Many of the stories related to Zakhar'in by old soldiers in Orenburg were probably apocryphal (and out of all proportion to Perovskii's actual military achievements in the region),[27] but they are in themselves a testament to the legend he left behind him. Perovskii seems to have had remarkable charisma: one old resident of Orenburg remembered how, when the city's centenary was celebrated in 1843, a year after Perovskii's recall to St Petersburg, the volume and enthusiasm of the toast in his honour far outshone that accorded to his more

Figure 1.1 General Count V. A. Perovskii in the 1850s. Note the gold fillet replacing the left forefinger lost at Borodino (Turkestan Album, 1871).

[26] A. L. Kun (ed.), 'Orenburgskii general gubernator i komanduiushchii voiskami Orenbur. Korpusa: General-ad'iutant Graf V. A. Perovskii', in *Turkestanskii al'bom: Po rasporiazheniiu turkestanskago General-Gubernatora General-ad'iutanta K. P. fon Kaufmana 1-go.* Pt. 4. *Chast' istoricheskaya 1871–1872 g.* ed. M. A. Terent'ev (Tashkent: Litografiya Voenno-Topograficheskogo Otdela Turkestanskogo Voennogo Okruga, 1871–2), plate 1, No. 1 (Library of Congress, Prints & Photographs Division LC-DIG-ppmsca-09957-00001). On the *Turkestan Album* see further Morrison, 'The Turkestan Generals', 162–3.
[27] Apart from the Khiva debacle, at least one later, iconoclastic military historian chided him for extreme caution in the conduct of the siege of Aq Masjid: M. L. Iudin, *Vzyatie Ak-Mecheti v 1853 godu kak nachalo zavoevaniya Kokandskogo khanstva* (Moscow: Izd. Vladimira Bolasheva, 1917).

modest successor, General V. A. Obruchev (1795–1866).[28] Tolstoy, who had intended to include him in a putative novel about the Decembrists, saw him as almost emblematic of his age: 'that great figure, who became Nikolai Pavlovich's shadow, the most significant and *à grands traits* figure, – brings to mind in full *that time*.'[29] Zakhar'in's description of Perovskii as 'this illegitimate boy, without a name and, one might say, without birth or family'[30] is clearly a romantic exaggeration: as we learn clearly enough in *War and Peace*, illegitimacy had legal implications but otherwise carried relatively little stigma in early-nineteenth-century Russia. Perovskii and his brother, Lev, Minister of the Interior from 1841 to 1852, 'occupied the very top of the imperial pyramid', and were unusually close to the imperial family.[31] For both brothers the fact that they could not inherit anything and therefore had to make a career based entirely on service to the state may account for the favour they were shown by Nicholas I – their loyalty could be assured. In Vasilii Perovskii's case it also seems to have produced a high degree of sensitivity for the dignity both of his office and of Russia herself. This, as we shall see in the next chapter, proved important in determining his reaction to the political situation in Central Asia which he found on his arrival in Orenburg.

Although Perovskii's name would subsequently come to be seen as synonymous with Russian policy in Central Asia in this period, he was far from being the only 'man on the spot' whose views mattered. Perovskii was more of a soldier than a legislator, and by far the most important development in Russian attempts to administer the Qazaqs in this period was the introduction after 1822 of the *Regulations for the Siberian Kirgiz*, which were a legacy of Mikhail Mikhailovich Speranskii's (1772–1839) tenure as Governor of Western Siberia.[32] Speranskii, the son of a priest, was possibly the most important Russian statesman of the early nineteenth century, another who passed the formative period of his career during the conflict with Napoleon, whom he met at Erfurt in 1809. He was accused of attacking noble privileges, and became a bugbear to Russian conservatives, receiving a deeply unflattering portrait in *War and Peace*.[33] While his despatch to the harsh climate and surroundings of Omsk was a consequence of the loss of imperial favour, it is striking to find this apostle of the Russian liberal bureaucracy, Perovskii's

[28] S. N. Sevast'yanov, 'Grigorii Fedorovich Gens', *TOUAK*. Vyp. XIX (1907), 163–4.
[29] L. N. Tolstoy to Countess A. A. Tolstoya, 1878, printed in Zakhar'in, *Graf V. A. Perovskii*, 113–14.
[30] Zakhar'in, *Graf V. A. Perovskii*, 8.
[31] Alexander Etkind, *Internal Colonization: Russia's Imperial Experience* (Cambridge: Polity Press, 2001), 152.
[32] 'Ustav o sibirskikh Kirgizakh' 22/07/1822, in *PSZ*. 2nd Series, Vol. 38, No. 29127, 417–41; Virginia Martin, *Law and Custom in the Steppe: The Kazakhs of the Middle Horde and Russian Colonialism in the Nineteenth Century* (Richmond: Curzon Press, 2001), 146; Marc Raeff, *Siberia and the Reforms of 1822* (Seattle: University of Washington Press, 1956), 112–28.
[33] Martin, *Romantics, Reformers, Reactionaries*, 54–6.

antithesis, at the heart of the first serious attempt to impose administrative control over the Qazaqs. It suggests that the ideological cleavages between liberals and conservatives mattered much less when it came to making policy on the steppe frontier, where reformers and reactionaries alike shared assumptions about the superiority of Russian (or more broadly European) civilisation.

Russian policy in Central Asia in this period was closely tied to that in the Caucasus and Persia, and often cannot be understood independently of it. Here a prominent role was played by another proconsul who had first made his name fighting Napoleon, General Alexei Petrovich Yermolov (1777–1861), who had been one of the principal opponents of Barclay de Tolly's (ultimately highly successful) strategy of retreat in 1812.[34] Yermolov was one of the best-known and most popular figures in the Russian army in the immediate post-Napoleonic period, being seen by many as the embodiment of the patriotic 'Russian party' which opposed Count Arakcheev's domestic policy and Nesselrode's foreign policy. It was apparently for this reason that Alexander I sent him to command the Georgian corps in 1816, where he subsequently made a great name for himself in the Russo-Persian Wars and in the brutal suppression of Muslim resistance to Russian rule in the North Caucasus.[35] As with Perovskii, in Yermolov's case a military reputation forged in battle against Napoleon translated into an aggressive policy of expansion and extension of colonial rule on Russia's Asian frontier.

Continuing the roll-call of 'men on the spot' on Russia's Asian frontier, Count I. O. Simonich (1792–1855), the Russian envoy to Tehran from 1833 until 1838, was originally from Dalmatia and had been captured whilst fighting with Napoleon's armies, entering Russian service on his release. He distinguished himself fighting under Paskevich in the Russo-Persian war of 1827–8, where many credited him with the attack that led to a Russian victory at the battle of Elizavetpol, where he was wounded.[36] Despite having switched his allegiance, he had retained a good Bonapartist's loathing for British power, and would play an important role in provoking the First Anglo-Afghan War.[37] General V. A. Obruchev, Governor of Orenburg in the interregnum between

[34] Lieven, *Russia against Napoleon*, 141–3 – this episode of course features prominently in *War and Peace*.
[35] Bitis, *Russia and the Eastern Question*, 75–8, 219–35; Alexander Mikaberidze, 'Ermolov, Alexei Petrovich', in *The Russian Officer Corps in the Revolutionary and Napoleonic Wars, 1795–1815* (Staplehurst: Spellmount, 2005), 95–7. See Ermolov's memoirs: A. P. Ermolov, *Materialy dlya istorii voiny 1812 goda: Zapiski Alekseya Petrovicha Ermolova* (Moscow: Tip V. Got'e, 1863); N. P. Ermolov (ed.), *Zapiski Alekseya Petrovicha Ermolova*. Part I. *1801–1812 g.* & Part II. *1816–1827 g.* (Moscow: Universitetskaya Tipografiya, 1865–8).
[36] Bitis, *Russia and the Eastern Question*, 215.
[37] 'Avtobiografiya A. O. Diugamelya', *RA* (1885) No. 5, 90–1; A. O. Diugamel, Simonich's successor in Tehran, described him as an 'ardent Bonapartist' with a powerful hostility towards the British, and whilst his memoir is not entirely reliable, there is plenty of corroborative evidence for this. See Morrison, 'Twin Imperial Disasters', 262–7.

Perovskii's terms in office, and the initiator of the Russian 'fortress strategy' on the steppe, also received his formative military experiences fighting Napoleon (when he was adjutant to General Diebitsch, future head of the Main Staff), and came of age with Russia's victory.[38] Finally, General Petr Dmitr'evich Gorchakov (1785–1868), Governor of Western Siberia from 1836 until 1854, fought throughout the Napoleonic campaigns of 1813–15, as well as in the Russo-Turkish Wars of 1806–12 and 1828–9, and in Abkhazia, where he served under Yermolov. As Perovskii and Obruchev's counterpart and rival in Omsk, he would play an important role in the campaigns in the eastern part of the Qazaq steppe in the 1840s and early 1850s.[39]

Although Perovskii often reported directly to the Tsar, his immediate superiors in the chain of command were the War Minister, Count (later Prince) A. I. Chernyshev (1786–1857) and Foreign Minister Nesselrode, who together with whoever happened to be the Governor of Western Siberia at the time sat on the Asiatic committee which deliberated all proposed advances in Central Asia. Chernyshev was another golden boy of the Napoleonic generation. As his biographer put it, 'In the course of the memorable fifteen years in which Napoleon tried to force his way to the mastery of Europe, and Alexander strove for the preservation of rights, sanctified by centuries, there appeared in each state men of war and counsel, the movers of the age. One might excel in war, another in relations with foreign powers, a third in the field of civil affairs. But to very few did it fall to gain renown in all three.'[40] Chernyshev hailed from a less exalted (but legitimate) noble background than Perovskii: he had lost his parents young, and had supposedly first come to Alexander I's attention at the age of fifteen whilst dancing the Écossaise at a ball at Prince Kurakin's palace in Moscow, greatly impressing the then twenty-four-year-old Tsar in conversation. Thereafter Chernyshev seems to have enjoyed the Tsar's unbroken personal favour. He attended the Corps de Pages, and was commissioned as a cornet in the Chevalier Guards shortly afterwards in 1802. Having distinguished himself at Austerlitz in 1805, he first met Napoleon at the Tuileries in 1808, after the treaty of Tilsit.[41] He subsequently conducted a series of celebrated diplomatic missions to Napoleon in 1810–12 (during which he built up a strong personal relationship with the French Emperor) and would go on to be one of the war's most dashing cavalry commanders, leading a flying column of Cossacks which managed to wreak havoc on Napoleon's lines of communication, making him

---

[38] Novitskii (ed.), *Voennaya entsiklopediya*, XVII, 81.

[39] A. V. Remnev, '"Omskii pasha" – general-gubernator knyaz' P. D. Gorchakov', *Izvestiya Omskogo Gosudarstvennogo Istoriko-kraevedcheskogo Muzeya* (2008) No. 14, 179–96.

[40] A. I. Chernyshev, 'Zhizneopisanie Grafa Aleksandra Ivanovicha Chernysheva', *SIRIO* Vol. 122 (St Pb., 1905), 1.

[41] *Ibid.*, 2–9.

perhaps the war's most successful 'partisan' leader.[42] After the war he was entrusted with various diplomatic missions, most importantly in the Netherlands, where he worked hard to counter British influence. As War Minister from 1832 (when he more or less created the post)[43] until his death in 1857, Chernyshev oversaw and authorised most of the Central Asian advances in this period, motivated, at least in part, by his powerful dislike of the British.[44]

The cautious and emollient Nesselrode advocated a less aggressive Russian policy in Asia and a rapprochement with Britain. Partly as a result of this, and also because of his long-standing conviction that Russia's foreign interests were best secured through alignment with the conservative monarchical regimes of Prussia and Austria, his patriotism was doubted by some. His cosmopolitan German background (he was born in Lisbon, the product of a mixed Protestant and Catholic marriage, and baptised an Anglican)[45] made him an easy target for the scorn of a later generation of ethnic Russian nationalists,[46] but as early as 1814 his wife was warning him not to become too close to Metternich, as it was provoking malicious gossip that he was betraying Russia's interests.[47] Nesselrode was at least sufficiently carried away by the drama of 1812 to write to his wife Marie that 'when one mentions to a Frenchman the name of Russia, he immediately becomes as pale as the snow which has caused him so much chagrin'. As the *de facto* foreign minister, he was at the heart of what he himself described as the 'immense things' which the small coterie around Alexander I were engaged in after the occupation of Paris in 1814, something he clearly looked back on as the greatest experience of his life.[48] In the late 1830s and early 1840s, when the confrontation with Britain in Asia was reaching a crisis, Nesselrode did his best to restrain the aggression of Perovskii and Simonich and bring about

---

[42] Bruce Menning, 'A. I. Chernyshev: A Russian Lycurgus', *Canadian Slavonic Papers* 30/2 (1988), 191–6; Mikaberidze, 'Chernyshev, Alexander Ivanovich', in *The Russian Officer Corps*, 58–9; Dominic Lieven, 'Tolstoy on War, Russia, and Empire', in *Tolstoy on War* ed. McPeak & Orwin, 20; Lieven *Russia against Napoleon*, 172, 299; [A. I. Chernyshev], *Voennye deistviya otryada General Ad'iutanta Chernysheva v 1812, 1813 i 1814 godakh* (St Pb.: Voennaya Tip., 1839).

[43] Chernyshev, 'Zhizneopisanie Grafa Aleksandra Ivanovicha Chernysheva', 133–6, 189–90.

[44] Annotating an article from a French newspaper deploring the spread of revolutionary tendencies in Europe ('C'est aux perfidies de l'Angleterre et à la faiblesse des gouvernements continentaux que les maux que l'Europe souffre maintenant doivent être attribués!') Chernyshev apparently wrote: 'Cet article a l'air d'avoir été écrit sous ma dictée', see 'Perepechatka iz "La Gazette de France" ot 5 mars 1834', *SIRIO* Vol. 122, 377–82.

[45] K. V. Nessel'rode, 'Zapiski Grafa Karla Vasil'evicha Nessel'rode', *RV* Vol. 59 (1865), 519.

[46] See E. Shumigorskii, 'Odin iz revnosteishikh nasaditelei nemetskago zasil'ya v Rossii: Graf Karl Vasil'evich Nessel'rode', *RS* Vol. 161 (1915) No. 1, 160–5, reflecting anti-German hysteria during the First World War.

[47] Marie Nesselrode to K. V. Nesselrode 09/04/1814, in A. de Nesselrode (ed.) *Lettres et papiers*. Vol. V. *1813–1818* (Paris: A. Lahure, 1907), 188–90.

[48] K. V. Nesselrode to Marie Nesselrode 03/01/1814; K. V. Nesselrode to Marie Nesselrode 04/04/1814, in A. de Nesselrode *Lettres et papiers*, V, 2, 184; Nessel'rode 'Zapiski', 566–7.

a rapprochement, but never advocated doing so at the expense of what he too saw as Russia's legitimate trade and political interests in the region.[49] His cosmopolitan reputation and legacy are perhaps best embodied in the elaborate iced pudding named after him which became a firm favourite on middle- and upper-class tables across Europe.

Finally, there was the Tsar himself. Nicholas I, contrary to many myths about exuberant officers on the frontier exceeding their authority, exercised full control over the actions of his governors and officials in the region, and personally authorised each and every stage of the Russian advance into Central Asia during his reign, even if he did not initiate them. His consistent prioritisation of military interests on Russia's Asian frontiers is another manifestation of the way in which the ethos and culture of the military – 'paradomania' – permeated and controlled the very highest echelons of government in Nikolaevan Russia.[50]

1.2   Russia, Persia and Afghanistan, 1814–41

As the Napoleonic Wars finally drew to a close, many Russian statesmen realised immediately that, for all that it had been Russian, Prussian and Austrian troops who had marched into Paris, the main outcome of the war would be an enormous increase in British power.[51] Alexander I initially hoped that the conjunction of interests and forces that had allowed Russia and Britain to 'deliver the continent of Europe' from Bonapartist oppression would endure into the peace.[52] Chernyshev was considerably more sceptical, as he wrote to the Tsar in 1814:

> ... if following the fall of Napoleon Europe has an oppression to fear, it is solely on the part of England. The immense advantages which this power has gained from all the past wars, the augmenting of her land forces, constantly combined with her maritime means, her establishment since the last peace in Holland, in the Low Countries, in Hanover, do they not presage that she is seeking to become a Continental power? [...] everything she has acquired since [1640] on the Mediterranean, on the ocean, in Africa, in America, in India, on the road to China, has been taken by her during the wars which she has engendered or prolonged in Europe.[53]

---

[49] Harold N. Ingle, *Nesselrode and the Russian Rapprochement with Britain, 1836–1844* (Berkeley, CA: University of California Press, 1976), 72–95.

[50] Lincoln, *Nicholas I*, 169–71; LeDonne, *Grand Strategy*, 215–19, 227.

[51] Lieven, *Russia against Napoleon*, 524.

[52] Alexander I to Prince Kh. A. Lieven, ambassador to London, 15/12/1814, *VPR* I/VIII, 139–44.

[53] ' ... si depuis la chute de Napoléon l'Europe a une oppression à craindre, c'est unique-ment de la part de l'Angleterre. Les avantages immenses qu'a retiré cette puissance de toutes les guerres passées, l'accroissement de ses forces de terre, constamment combinées avec ses moyens maritimes, son établissement depuis la dernière paix en Hollande, dans

Chernyshev's fears for the establishment of a powerful British influence on the continent proved exaggerated – after the creation of Belgium in 1830 the British rarely intervened directly in European affairs – but his remarks about her global reach proved more prescient. The question was how, given her hopeless naval inferiority, Russia could challenge and emulate Britain, and the Asian frontier appeared to provide possibilities. The settlement at Vienna had removed any imminent threat to Russia's frontiers in Europe and left her free to concentrate on settling various outstanding questions in Asia. The most urgent of these related to the Ottoman Empire, with which Russia had been at war for most of the last three decades of the eighteenth century, and to the Caucasian frontier, where the Russians had recently fought against both the Ottoman Empire and Persia in 1810–13.[54] For the first three decades of the nineteenth century Central Asia came a poor third to Ottoman Turkey and Qajar Persia in Russian diplomatic and military priorities: the Orenburg and Siberian lines had just twenty-four infantry battalions allocated to them in the 1820s, while the much shorter Caucasian frontier had a nominal strength of forty-five battalions.[55] Subduing Persia was important because of the need to secure Russian control of Georgia, which had been annexed in 1801, while ensuring that the Ottoman Empire remained pliant and was not replaced by a more formidable military and naval power was vital to Russian interests in the control of the Straits leading from the Black Sea to the Mediterranean – the origins of the much-studied 'Eastern Question'.[56] As Chernyshev put it:

> It would be superfluous to repeat that which has been said so often about the importance of the geographical position of Constantinople, of the Bosphorus and of its outlets to the two seas. These precious possessions, which one can justly consider to be the vital key to the heart of Russia, can only rest in the hands of the Turks, or be at our disposition. No one would wish to contest that we will never be able to tolerate the establishment there, even potentially, of any other foreign power.[57]

les Pays-Bas, le Hanovre, ne présagent-ils pas qu'elle cherche à devenir puissance continentale [. . .] tout ce qu'elle a acquis depuis [1640] sur la Méditerranée, sur l'Océan, en Afrique, en Amérique, dans l'Inde, sur le chemin de la Chine, a été enlevé par elle pendant des guerres qu'elle avait suscitées ou prolongées en Europe.' 'Dokladnaya zapiska A. I. Chernysheva Imperatoru Aleksandru I' in 'Bumagi A. I. Chernysheva za Tsarstvovanie Imperatora Aleksandra I' n.d. (1814), SIRIO Vol. 121 (St Pb., 1906), 280–1.

[54] Brian L. Davies, The Russo-Turkish War, 1769–1774 (London: Bloomsbury, 2016); Bitis, Russia and the Eastern Question, 26–33, 190–6; LeDonne, Grand Strategy, 168–9.

[55] LeDonne, Grand Strategy, 197; Bitis, Russia and the Eastern Question, 212.

[56] The standard account of this from the British perspective remains M. S. Anderson, The Eastern Question 1784–1923: A Study in International Relations (London: Macmillan, 1966).

[57] 'Il serait superflu de répéter ce qui a été dit si souvent sur l'importance de la position géographique de Constantinople, du Bosphore et de ses débouches dans les deux mers. Ces précieuses possessions, que l'on peut considérer a juste titre, comme la clef vitale du midi de la Russie, ne peuvent rester qu'entre les mains des Turcs, ou être à notre

While both wars began badly, the decisive defeat of Persia in 1828 and of the Ottoman Empire in 1829 allowed Russia to consolidate her position in Georgia and on the Black Sea by annexing substantial territories in the south Caucasus.[58] The Ottoman Empire was thrust into still greater dependence on Russia under the Treaty of Unkiar-Skelessi in 1833, after Nicholas I had rescued the Sultan from the rebellious ruler of Egypt, Muhammad 'Ali, and would remain largely quiescent until the 1850s.[59] Meanwhile Qajar Persia became something close to a Russian client state after the 1828 Treaty of Turkmanchai.[60] The destruction of the Russian mission in Tehran and the murder of Alexander Griboedov in 1829 were only a temporary setback to the growth of Russian power in Persia, since it was based on the presence of overwhelming military forces in Transcaucasia.[61] Muriel Atkin has argued that Russia's two successful wars with Persia were the product of accident rather than design, and were certainly not originally intended to form part of a drive towards British India.[62] Nevertheless, the Russian legation in Tehran rapidly became a listening-post for (not always very accurate) intelligence from across Central Asia, and a centre of anti-British intrigue. This was largely owing to the appointment as envoy in 1832 of Count I. O. Simonich, while shortly afterwards V. A. Perovskii took up his appointment as Governor of Orenburg. Although there is no evidence that the two men ever met, they shared remarkably similar views on the need for a more aggressive Russian policy in Asia.

In June 1832 Nesselrode wrote to Simonich in Tehran stating that he believed the British had acquiesced to the terms of the Treaty of Turkmanchai, and that he did not foresee any serious political differences emerging between Britain and Russia in Persia.[63] This judgement turned out to be overly sanguine. Instead Russia's dominance at the Qajar court was viewed with growing alarm in London and Calcutta as a threat to Indian security, which had come to be seen as vital to sustaining Britain's status as the world's

---

disposition. Personne ne voudra contester, que nous ne saurions jamais y tolérer l'établissement, même éventuel, d'aucune autre puissance étrangère.' 'Vsepoddanneishii doklad grafa Chernysheva Imperatoru Nikolaiu I' 03/12/1829 *SIRIO* Vol.122 (St Pb., 1905), 304–307.

[58] Bitis, *Russia and the Eastern Question*, 155–61, 372–7.

[59] *Ibid.*, 467–79.

[60] Muriel Atkin, *Russia and Iran, 1780–1828* (Minneapolis, MN: University of Minnesota Press, 1980), 162–6; Bitis, *Russia and the Eastern Question*, 200, 253–61.

[61] Laurence Kelly, *Diplomacy and Murder in Tehran: Alexander Griboyedov and Imperial Russia's Mission to the Shah of Persia* (London: I.B. Tauris, 2002); LeDonne, Grand Strategy, 208–9.

[62] Atkin, *Russia and Iran, 1780–1828*, 162–6.

[63] Nesselrode to Simonich, 7 June 1832, *AKAK* Vol. 8, No. 795, p. 906; Volodarsky, 'The Russians in Afghanistan', 65.

greatest power since the end of the Napoleonic wars.[64] The British were particularly alarmed by the second Persian siege of Herat, which began in 1837. They believed that this was undertaken on Russian initiative, and whilst Simonich's despatches from Tehran indicate that this was untrue, they also make it quite clear that, once Muhammad Shah Qajar had decided to attack Herat, the Russian envoy did everything possible to encourage it, writing to Nesselrode that 'If I take it so much to heart to see these projects succeed, it is precisely because the English are opposing them with all their means.'[65] At this stage he claimed to be unaware of why the proposed invasion seemed to worry the British so much: six weeks later, in a letter to the head of the Asiatic Department, Rodofinikin, he wrote (perhaps disingenuously) that it was only over the previous few days that he had realised that English jumpiness and paranoia had arisen owing to their fears over their precarious position in India, where the natives would be prepared to rise up at the approach of a power that could liberate them from the English yoke. He offered this both as an example of how the English misjudged Russia and also as a diplomatic opportunity to be exploited.[66]

In 1835 Nesselrode had advocated a cautious response to the emissaries which Russia had begun to receive from India and Afghanistan requesting assistance in fighting off English aggression, writing that, whilst there were obvious trade advantages to be had in the region, Russia was not in a position to assist them directly, and there was little sense in arousing English suspicions needlessly.[67] In 1836 this policy was put to the test with the arrival in Orenburg of an ambassador from Dost Muhammad Khan of Kabul, Hussain 'Ali, in the company of Perovskii's young protégé, the exiled Polish nobleman Jan Vitkevich (Witkiewicz).[68] Hussain 'Ali carried letters requesting Russian assistance in the face of increasing pressure from the Government of India.[69]

[64] Bitis, *Russia and the Eastern Question*, 270–3; Ingram, *In Defence of British India*, 130–217; Robinson and Gallagher, *Africa and the Victorians*, 10–14.
[65] Simonich to Nesselrode 03/04/1836, AVPRI F.133 Op.469 (1836) D.204 'Dépêches reçues de Téhéran en 1836 (Cte. Simonich)', l. 79ob.
[66] Simonich to Rodofinikin 20/04/1836, AVPRI F.133 Op.469 (1836) D.204 ll. 153–4.
[67] 'O poslannikakh iz Afganistana i Indii' 27/05/1835, AVPRI F.161 I-1 Op.781 D.75 ll. 32–3ob.
[68] Witkiewicz, whose name is usually russified to Vitkevich, was exiled to Orenburg from Vil'na at the age of fourteen for participating in a nationalist secret society. He learnt to speak Turki and Persian fluently, and was promoted to officer rank by Perovskii's predecessor, Sukhtelen (Morrison 'Twin Imperial Disasters', 273–9). He had met Hussain 'Ali in Bukhara, where he had been sent on a diplomatic mission by Perovskii, the account of which is published as 'Zapiska, sostavlennaya po rasskazam Orenburgskogo Lineinoga Batal'ona No. 10 Praporshchika Vitkevicha otnositel'no puti ego v Bukharu i obratno', in *Zapiski o Bukharskom khanstve* ed. N. A. Khalfin (Moscow: Nauka, 1983), 12–129.
[69] Amir Dost Muhammad Khan Ghazi to Emperor Nicholas I and to Count V. A. Perovskii, translated from the Persian (late October 1835), AVPRI, F.161 I-5 Op.5 D.2 'O priezde v S-Peterburge Kabulskogo Poslannika Gussein Ali, tut zhe ob otpravlenii Poruchika

Perovskii immediately proposed that Vitkevich should be despatched to Dost Muhammad with offers of Russian support, and put forward the following arguments to counter objections raised by Nesselrode:

> This state of affairs, without doubt, is undesirable for Russia, because the rule of the English in the East is threatening to spread. [...] The English maintain their devotees, or those whom they have bought, not only in Kabul, but even in Bukhara itself. They act against us; use every circumstance in order to harm us and our trade.[70]

Vitkevich was duly despatched with a letter from the Tsar, and, as is well known, his arrival in Kabul in 1837, almost simultaneously with a British envoy, Alexander Burnes, was one of the chief factors which persuaded Lord Auckland, the Governor-General of India, to mount the ultimately disastrous British invasion of Afghanistan in 1839.[71] When rumours began to circulate that the British were planning an invasion, Simonich swung rapidly from confidence to despair, and rather melodramatically foresaw the complete eclipse of Russian power in Central Asia. He argued strongly for the creation of a powerful Afghan buffer state under Persian suzerainty and Russian protection, something he attempted to bring about himself by guaranteeing (on his own authority and initiative) a treaty between the Qajar Shah and Dost Muhammad's brothers, the rulers of Qandahar.[72] In August 1837 Simonich was removed from his post and replaced by A. O. Diugamel (1801–1880), the former Russian envoy to Egypt, who had been a staff officer during the Russo-Turkish War, and would later become governor of Western Siberia.[73] It is not clear whether Simonich's dismissal was because of insubordination, not least because Simonich himself seems to have been anxious to leave Tehran and rejoin his wife and ten children in Tiflis.[74] Diugamel had not yet been explicitly instructed to repudiate Simonich's guarantee of the treaty with the rulers of Qandahar: to begin with, he sent

Vitkevicha v Kabul dlya vstupleniya v blizhaishiya snosheniya s Avganistanom', ll. 10*ob*, 12–13.

[70] Perovskii to Nesselrode 05/05/1836, AVPRI F.161 I-5 Op.5 D.2 ll. 7–8.
[71] 'Instruktsiya Poruchik Vitkevichu, ot 14-ogo maya 1837 goda No. 1218', *AKAK* Vol. 8 No. 874, 944–5 (original in NAG F.11 Op.1 D.731 'O poruchike Vitkeviche i Avgantse Gussein Ali, proekhavshikh v Persii', ll. 44–7*ob*). On Vitkevich's mission and the conflict it provoked see Yapp, *Strategies*, 240–52, 270–303; Morrison, 'Twin Imperial Disasters', 267–82; Andrei Larin, 'Yan Vitkevich: Raporty iz Afganistana', in *Istoriya i istoriografiya zarubezhnogo mira v litsakh*. Vyp. IX ed. V. V. Kutyavin (Samara: Izd. 'Samarskii Universitet', 2009), 171–95.
[72] Simonich to Nesselrode 13/10/1836, AVPRI F.133 Op.469 (1836) D.204 l. 258*ob*.
[73] Curtiss, *The Russian Army under Nicholas I*, 206.
[74] Diugamel claimed that this was indeed why Nesselrode had appointed him in his place, but it is notable that even Diugamel, who disliked Simonich and did his best to discredit him in his memoirs, wrote that Nicholas I approved of Russian support for the Herat expedition. 'Avtobiografiya A. O. Diugamelya', *RA* (1885) No. 5, 84, 91.

repeated requests to Nesselrode asking whether he should recognise it, and more broadly whether Russia should offer further support to Dost Muhammad against British aggression. In December 1838 he wrote that

> Some sort of decision is no less urgent, indispensable, if we do not wish to lose the credit in which we currently rejoice in Asia [...] if after all this we today abandon the Barakzai brothers to the vengeance of their enemies, believe me, M. le Comte, that the Russian name will suffer a taint, which centuries will not suffice to efface, in the opinion of the peoples of Central Asia: a retrograde step will be considered as a sign of weakness.[75]

Here we see clearly the fear of being perceived as weak, of the diminution of the 'prestige' which was thought to be so crucial in Asia, and which governed so many Russian actions in these years. In 1839 it became clear that the British were going to invade Afghanistan, and at this stage the hollowness of Russia's pretensions to be able to give direct assistance to Dost Muhammad Khan was clearly revealed. Simonich would be condemned for having provoked the British invasion, which until the final disaster of 1842 the Russians believed to have been a success, permanently establishing British power in Central Asia to their detriment. This would prompt Simonich to defend himself in a personal memoir penned in 1841, before the scale of the Afghan catastrophe became apparent:

> I have been reproached with having wished to bring about a war with England. As the accused I am not a competent judge of my own cause, but I will permit myself some observations [...] the position of Russia in Persia was so imposing, at the beginning of 1838, that in order to set India on fire, she had but to wish it [...] *the fate of India was in our hands.*[76]

---

[75] Diugamel to Nesselrode 23/12/1838 (Draft) AVPRI F.194 'Missiya v Persii' Op. 528/1 D.182 'za 1838g.' ll.58*ob*, 59*ob*; exactly the same sentiments are found in Diugamel to Golovin 23/12/1838 NAG F.11 Op.1 D.760 l.23: 'J'ignore complètement jusqu'à présent si notre Gouvernement a l'intention de maintenir la garantie donnée par le Comte Simonitch ou non [...] nous ne pouvons pas les abandonner a la vengeance de leurs ennemies, sans que le nom Russe en Asie n'en souffre une sévère atteinte'. Characteristically, Diugamel disguised this in his memoirs, claiming that on his arrival he had immediately taken steps to repudiate Simonich's actions and establish better relations with Britain: 'Avtobiografiya A. O. Diugamelya' *RA* (1885) No.5, 104–5.

[76] 'On m'a reproché d'avoir voulu entrainer mon pays dans une guerre avec l'Angleterre. Inculpé je ne suis pas juge competent dans ma cause, cependant je me permettrai quelques observations. [...] La position de la Russie en Perse, était tellement imposant, au commencement de 1838, que pour mettre la combustion dans les Indes, elle n'avait qu'a le vouloir [...] *le sort des Indes était en nos mains.*' I. O. Simonich, 'Précis historique de l'Avènement de Mahomed-Schah au Trône de Perse par le Comte Simonich, ex-Ministre plénipotentiaire de Russie à la cour de Téhéran. Varsovie, l'année 1841', 359–61. AV 1-i razryad Op.6 D.1 ll. 193–4.

Simonich's sense that a great opportunity had been missed was shared by his successor in Tehran. Throughout 1841 Diugamel sent ever more gloomy despatches, warning that the British were now on the point of extending their commercial and political influence towards the Caspian, and that 'to permit the English to establish themselves at any point on the littoral of the Caspian Sea would be to paralyse for all time both our commerce and the legitimate preponderance which we ought to exercise over that sea'.[77] These gloomy prognostications later interested Count N. P. Ignat'ev (1832–1908), who would lead an important Russian mission to Khiva and Bukhara in 1858, and remained suspicious of British influence in Central Asia throughout his distinguished diplomatic career – notes from Diugamel's despatches can be found in his private papers.[78] However, at the time Nesselrode sought a rapprochement with Britain: the return to Tehran of the abrasive Sir John McNeill, the British envoy whose alarmist despatches had done much to trigger the invasion of Afghanistan, prompted him to warn Diugamel to make special efforts to conciliate him.[79] Nesselrode would repeatedly insist that Russia's interests in Persia were purely commercial, and that her policies were intended to bring about the peace and security needed for commerce to flourish.[80] He clearly found both British paranoia and what he perceived as the chaotic nature of Persian politics distinctly trying. When advising the Russian minister in London, Baron Brunnow, on the wisdom of backing Muhammad Shah against machinations at the Qajar Court, he wrote that the most important thing was 'not to compromise the dignity of Russia through too pronounced an intervention in a cause which at bottom is not our own, where Russia in the midst of a maze of Asiatic perfidy will bring only a measure of good faith'. He added, rather plaintively, that

> It would be more in conformity with the dignity of Russia to see the English Government, after all the tergiversations in its policy, seek our influence in Asia rather than that we should forcibly interpose our intervention from today, when all seems to indicate that our most disinterested intentions will be suspected and falsely interpreted.[81]

---

[77] Diugamel to Nesselrode 05/02/1841, AVPRI F.133 Op.469 (1841) D.213 'Téhéran (Affaires de l'Asie)', l. 56.

[78] GARF F.730 Op.1 D.517 l. 1.

[79] Nesselrode to Diugamel 02/06/1841, AVPRI F.133 Op.469 (1841) D.184 'Tegeran', l. 79ob.

[80] Nesselrode to Diugamel (draft) 11/10/1841, AVPRI F.133 Op.469 (1841) D.184 l. 92.

[81] 'Il sera plus conformé à la dignité de la Russie, de voir le Gouvt. Anglais après toutes les tergiversations de sa politique, rechercher notre appui en Asie que de nous efforcer à interposer notre intervention dès aujourd'hui même, où tout semble indiquer que nos intentions les plus désintéressées seraient méconnues et faussement interprétées' Nesselrode to Brunnow 13/06/1841 (draft), AVPRI F.133 Op.469 (1841) D.184 l. 153ob.

As Nesselrode indicated here, it was Russia's dignity and good faith which were at stake, rather than any vital strategic or economic interests. For the time being Russia was a satisfied power on her Caucasian frontier – she might have failed in Afghanistan (though, as it turned out, not nearly as disastrously as the British), but Russia remained dominant in Persia, which was in no position to challenge for the territories she had lost in what would become Russian Armenia and Azerbaijan, while the Ottoman Empire also remained subdued until the 1850s. The significance of these early passages of rivalry with Britain has generally been misunderstood in existing scholarship. On the British side they may have ushered in almost seventy years of paranoia regarding a Russian threat to India, but for the Russians the contest was understood largely in terms of relative prestige, not as an initial attempt to threaten the British empire in Asia. Equally, what the Russians feared from Britain was not so much a threat to their own Asian territories as diplomatic humiliation. The fear expressed here by Simonich and Diugamel would re-echo in Russian despatches until the early 1900s: that of appearing weak, or foolish, or diminished in the eyes of their 'Asiatic' neighbours and their British rivals, a form of universal 'Great Power' neurosis.

This was also at play on the steppe frontier, to which the focus shifted as relations with the Ottoman Empire and Persia became more peaceful in the 1830s, and which had a long and complex history of its own. In December 1841 Nesselrode composed a despatch to the Russian ambassador in London, Baron Brunnow, to be passed on to the British:

> We repeat: strangers to all projects of conquest and aggrandisement, without thinking of making the slightest attempt against the independence of the states of Central Asia, without wishing to impose Russian garrisons on them, we must and we wish to maintain a respect for our power, and this with the aim of putting our frontier in a state of tranquillity, and to contain in obedience the Kirgiz and other nomadic tribes who are habituated to living from rapine and brigandage, to open at last outlets for our industry, in assuring the free passage of caravans which sustain our commercial communications with Central Asia.[82]

However, it was precisely this tranquillity, obedience and respect which were so hard to come by on the steppe frontier, at least in any form which the Russians recognised as sufficient. For Perovskii in Orenburg and Gorchakov in Omsk, the need to make Russian authority felt beyond the early-eighteenth-century Orenburg and Siberian lines had never been greater.

---

[82] '... et cela dans le but de mettre à convert la tranquillité de notre frontière, de contenir dans l'obéissance les kirghises et autres tribus nomades habitués à vivre de rapine et de brigandage ...', Nesselrode to Brunnow 03/12/1841 (draft), AVPRI F.133 Op.469 (1841) D.184 l. 172ob.

1.3   The Russian Empire and the Steppe Frontier, 1731–1837

While the Russian encounter with the steppe had begun in the sixteenth century in conflicts with the Crimean Tatars, Nogais, Bashkirs and Qalmyqs, most of the Black Sea and Caspian Steppe frontier was closed and pacified in the late eighteenth century.[83] This left the long frontier on the Asian steppe, along the Ural and Irtysh rivers, where the key Russian interlocutors were the Qazaqs, a nomadic confederation which had emerged from the collapse of the Golden Horde in the middle of the fifteenth century, and in the eighteenth century was still ruled by Chinggissids – descendants of Genghis Khan. In Soviet historiography the Qazaqs were said to have voluntarily 'united' with Russia in 1731, after which they all became Russian subjects more or less overnight. This interpretation placed enormous weight on the supposed 'submission' of Abu'l-Khayr Khan (1693–1748) of the Junior Horde to the Empress Anna Ioannovna that year, supposedly because he needed protection from the Junghars – an Oirat (western Mongol) nomadic confederation which had repeatedly raided the Qazaqs in the late seventeenth and early eighteenth centuries.[84] It is possibly a too literal reading of this account which has led so many historians to assume that the conquest of the settled regions of southern Central Asia in the nineteenth century could be undertaken by the Russian empire *without* first conquering the Qazaq steppe.[85] In fact, the conquest and absorption of the Qazaqs and their pastures into the Russian empire is better understood as a process than as a single event – a process which may have begun in 1731, but would not be completed until the 1860s, and had many twists and turns along the way.

Abu'l-Khayr Khan certainly initiated a new phase in Qazaq relations with Russia when he first wrote to the Empress Anna in 1730. In the seventeenth century there had been diplomatic relations between Muscovy and the Qazaq khans (the earliest mention of the division of the Qazaqs into three hordes (*zhuzes*) comes from a Russian source in 1616), but contact was intermittent until the early eighteenth century, and there was no suggestion of a subordinate relationship.[86] Now Abu'l-Khayr wrote asking for the empress's mediation in his conflicts with the Bashkirs (who were nominally at least already Russian subjects), requesting her protection and saying that his people were ready to 'bow their heads and fulfil your requests' (*yarliq*). A key phrase in

---

[83] Khodarkovsky, *Russia's Steppe Frontier*, 126–83; Michael Khodarkovsky, *Where Two Worlds Met: The Russian State and the Kalmyk Nomads 1600–1771* (Ithaca, NY: Cornell University Press, 1992), 207–41.

[84] Alan Bodger, 'Abulkhair, Khan of the Kazakh Little Horde, and His Oath of Allegiance to Russia of October 1731', *SEER* 58/1 (1980), 40–57 contains a useful summary and critique of Soviet historiography.

[85] See for instance Carrère d'Encausse, 'Systematic Conquest 1865–1884'.

[86] Allen J. Frank, 'The Qazaqs and Russia', in *The Cambridge History of Inner Asia* ed. di Cosmo, Frank & Golden, 365.

this letter was translated into Russian at the time as 'wishing to be with all my domains subject to your imperial majesty' (*zhelaiu byt' so vsem moim vladeniem v V. I. V. poddanstve*), and in Soviet times as 'wishing to be entirely under your Majesty's power' (*zhelaya byt' sovershenno podvlastnym Vashemu Velichestvu*).[87] In fact, the Chaghatai original is better translated as 'wishing to be under the shadow of your Majesty', a subtle but important difference, while Abu'l-Khayr's letter does not refer anywhere to 'subjects' or 'subjecthood' (*poddanstvo*), instead using the Turkic term *qaracha* or 'black [ordinary] people' to describe the non-Chinggissid Qazaqs of the Junior Horde.[88] While this initial mistranslation was far from the only determining factor, mutual misunderstanding – both over the nature of sovereignty and over what each side was actually proposing – would create many problems for the Russian–Qazaq relationship in the future.[89]

In response to this letter, the College of Foreign Affairs despatched Kutlu-Muhammad Tevkelev, from an old Tatar noble family, to negotiate with Abu'l-Khayr – something which as a Turki-speaker he was able to do directly. Tevkelev's report and diary of his mission provides a vivid, if uncorroborated, account of what passed between them which is key to understanding the real relationship between the Russian empire and the Qazaq khans until the early nineteenth century. Tevkelev noted that the situation at Abu'l-Khayr's *stavka* (royal camp) was chaotic – he had to meet the Khan secretly, by night, as most of the elite of the Junior Horde were deeply hostile to the presence of a Russian envoy. Abu'l-Khayr had sent his letter and requested Russian protection alone, without consulting the sultans and *batyrs* (warriors) who hemmed in his freedom of action as khan. It transpired that this was his reason for approaching the Russians in the first place:

> Abu'l-Khayr Khan among other khans had been held in high regard among them, but now they are all filled with malice, because he alone requested to enter into all-Russian subjecthood (*v poddanstve vserossiiskom*). And I learnt the long-term intentions of Abu'l-Khayr through long conversation, and he informed me, why he on his own without the agreement of others asked to be an all-Russian subject: firstly, because amongst them khans are not autocratic (*nesamovlastnye*) – and secondly, because they are not hereditary, and he, Abu'l-Khayr, wishes that the protection of Her Imperial Majesty should render him autocratic, and that

---

[87] Abu'l-Khayr Khan to the Empress Anna Ioannovna recd. 20/07/1731, AVPRI F.122 Op.1, 1730–1731 gg. ll. 45ob–47 trans. R. M. Peigumbari, in *Kazakhsko-russkie otnosheniya v XVI–XVIII vekakh (1594–1770)* ed. F. N. Kireev et al. (Alma-Ata: Nauka, 1961), 36.

[88] Abu'l-Khayr Khan to the Empress Anna Ioannovna recd. 20/07/1731 trans. T. K. Beisembiev, in *Epistolyarnoe nasledie kazakhskoi pravyashchei elity 1675–1821 godov* ed. I. V. Erofeeva (Almaty: abdi, 2014) I, 106–7.

[89] Gregory Afinogenov, 'Languages of Hegemony on the Eighteenth-Century Kazakh Steppe', *The International History Review* 41/5 (2018), 1022.

his children might succeed after him, just as Ayuka-Khan exercises his will over his Qalmyqs.[90]

The Junghars – who loomed large in the Soviet interpretation of Abu'l-Khayr's motives, largely because they could be characterised as a 'foreign' threat, outside the Soviet family of nations – were marginal in Tevkelev's account. The Junghar threat had receded over the previous decade, partly thanks to Abu'l-Khayr's own victories over them at Bulanty and Angkhrai, and would disappear entirely in the 1750s with their destruction by the Qing.[91] Abu'l-Khayr did request protection, but from the Bashkirs and Qalmyqs, both of whom were – at least nominally – Russian subjects. Instead it is clear from Tevkelev's account that Abu'l-Khayr sought to use a relationship with Russia to strengthen his internal authority over the unruly sultans of the Junior Horde. There is further evidence of this in the account by the Anglo-Prussian adventurer John Castle, who visited Abu'l-Khayr on a demi-official mission in 1736, and noted the khan's pleasure at his arrival, since this renewed evidence of Russian favour and interest 'would give him cause for forbidding his subjects from joining the conjunction that they were planning with the Kilmeck [Qalmyq] rebels'.[92] The existence of a powerful and unruly Chinggissid aristocracy among the Qazaqs – the *Töre* or *Aq Suyek* (white bone), who distinguished themselves from the *Qara Suyek* (black bone) or common people, has long been clear to historians and anthropologists.[93] The creation of centralised authority in a nomadic society was far more difficult than in a sedentary one, because the main assets – animals – were mobile and could not be controlled and taxed in the same way as immovable crops and land; this in turn explains why longer-lasting nomadic states are almost

[90] Muhammad Tevkelev, 'Donoshenie perevodchika Kollegii inostrannykh del A. I. Tevkeleva v Kollegiiu inostrannykh del o priniatii rossiiskogo poddanstva kazakhami Mladshego i Srednego zhuzov ot 5 ianvaria 1732 g.', in *Istoriya Kazakhstana v russkikh istochnikakh XVI–XX vekov*. Vol. III. *Zhurnaly i sluzhebnye zapiski diplomata A. I. Tevkeleva po istorii i etnografii Kazakhstana* ed. I. V. Erofeeva (Almaty: Daik-Press, 2005), 58–9.
[91] Bodger, 'Abulkhair, Khan of the Kazakh Little Horde', 42–56; Kilian, 'Allies and Adversaries', 90–1; Perdue, *China Marches West*, 270–89.
[92] John Castle, 'Journal von der AO 1736 aus Orenburg zu dem Abul Geier Chan der Kirgis-Kaysak tartarischen Horda', in *Materialen zu der russischen Geschichte* (Riga: n.p., 1784) trans. Sarah Tolley & ed. Beatrice Teissier as *Into the Kazakh Steppe: John Castle's Mission to Khan Abu'lkhayir (1736)* (Oxford: Signal Books, 2014), 41–3.
[93] Virginia Martin, 'Using Turki-Language Qazaq Letters to Reconstruct Local Political History of the 1820s–30s', in *Explorations in the Social History of Modern Central Asia* ed. Paolo Sartori (Leiden: Brill, 2013), 210–14. The suggestion by David Sneath in *The Headless State: Aristocratic Orders, Kinship Society, and Misrepresentations of Nomadic Inner Asia* (New York, NY: Columbia University Press, 2007), 71–84 that the existence of a Qazaq aristocracy has somehow been overlooked or suppressed in the existing literature is a straw man. See the review by Anatoly Khazanov in *Social Evolution & History* 9/2 (2010), 135–8.

invariably based on the conquest of neighbouring sedentary societies.[94] Even in the sixteenth century it seems probable that there could be more than one khan ruling at a time ruling the Qazaqs, and that their rule was constrained by the need to secure agreement from a powerful and numerous aristocracy of Chinggissid sultans.[95] The weakness of their authority became still more marked as the nomadic military advantage on the steppe was eroded by the spread of fortifications and gunpowder weaponry, but the encroachment of sedentary powers – Russia and China – also offered the possibility of exploiting diplomatic relations to bolster khanal authority, through the provision of gifts, trading relationships or titles that would increase their prestige and allow them to exercise patronage. This was the touchstone of all relations between Qazaq khans and neighbouring sedentary powers in the eighteenth and early nineteenth centuries. It was what Abu'l-Khayr sought in 1731, and what his successors as khans of the Junior Horde would seek thereafter. While Tevkelev used the language of 'subjecthood' throughout his description of the negotiations, it is clear that Abu'l-Khayr understood the agreement he had signed with Russia not as a permanent cession of sovereignty, but rather as a temporary alliance whose main aim was to strengthen his authority as khan.[96] While initially Abu'l-Khayr cooperated with the Orenburg expedition of 1735, which sought to establish Russian control over the Bashkirs, by 1743, angered by the holding of his son as an *amanat* or hostage in the newly founded fortress town of Orenburg, he was in full rebellion against Russia.[97]

Thus, while 1731 marks the point at which Russian rulers began *claiming* the Qazaqs as Russian subjects, it did not signal any real control over either the people or the territory where they grazed their animals, nor did it mean that their independent relations with other powers and peoples ceased.[98] Even in the Junior Horde the Russian authorities did not collect taxes or impose Russian laws, and in the Middle Horde (*Orta zhuz*), whose submission was also claimed by Tevkelev in 1731, Russian rule was even less of a reality. The same motives which prompted Abu'l-Khayr to approach Russia in 1731

---

[94] Anatoly Khazanov, *Nomads and the Outside World* (Madison, WI: University of Wisconsin Press, 1994), 228–62.

[95] Thomas Welsford, 'The Disappearing Khanate', in *Turko-Persian Cultural Contacts in the Eurasian Steppe: Festschrift in Honour of Professor István Vásáry* ed. B. Péri and F. Csirkes (Leiden: Brill, forthcoming).

[96] I. V. Erofeeva, *Khan Abulkhair: Polkovodets, pravitel', politik* (Almaty: Daik-Press, 2007), 217–39; Khodarkovsky, *Russia's Steppe Frontier*, 152–6.

[97] Erofeeva, *Khan Abulkhair*, 361–83; Frank, 'The Qazaqs and Russia', 368–9.

[98] I am more sceptical of Gregory Afinogenov's argument that Russian officials themselves continued to see their relationship with the Kazakhs as purely diplomatic, rather than one of putative vassalage – but he is certainly correct that in practice until the early nineteenth century it continued to be a diplomatic relationship based on negotiation and compromise with no real attempt to assert Russian sovereignty. See Afinogenov, 'Languages of Hegemony'.

prompted Ablai (1711–1781), the khan of the Middle Horde, to write to the Qing Emperor in 1757, after the fall of the Junghar confederation had brought Chinese military power to the fringes of the Qazaq steppe. Ablai offered his submission as the emperor's *albatu* (servant), a sentiment he repeated in 1779 in a letter to the Chinese military governor of Ili, when he wrote that he and his people would 'never leave the hem of the golden coat'.[99] He accepted the title of khan from the Qing, but refused a similar offer from Russia, which would have entailed taking up residence under Russian supervision in the frontier fortress of Petropavlovsk. Ablai was able to maintain stable and independent diplomatic relations with both Qing China and the Russian empire until his death, and it was only shortly before this, in 1778, that he accepted a *gramota* conferring a khanal title on him from Catherine the Great – even then he refused to come to Petropavlovsk to receive it, forcing the Russian envoy to come to him, much to official annoyance.[100] Correspondence between Qazaq sultans of the Middle Horde and the Qing continued into the 1820s, demonstrating clearly that they did not consider their relationship with Russia to be exclusive.[101] Russian relations with the Qazaqs were conducted entirely through their own Chinggissid elites who, as Virginia Martin has shown, became very accustomed to communicating with and making use of Russian power.[102] Not until after 1786, when the then governor of Orenburg Baron Osip Igel'strom created the Orenburg Frontier commission, did the Qazaqs of the Junior Horde come under anything resembling Russian administration – and even then this was still an organ of the Ministry of Foreign Affairs. Under Catherine the Great the Russian authorities espoused a policy of using settled, literate Muslims, mainly Tatars, as 'civilising' agents amongst the Qazaqs, apparently judging that the moment for their Russification had not yet come.[103] It would not be until 1822, with the introduction of Mikhail Speranskii's *Regulations for the Siberian Kirgiz*, that the Russians began to

---

[99] *Albatu* is a Mongol term meaning something like liege-man – see the documents and analysis in *A Collection of Documents from the Kazakh Sultans to the Qing Dynasty* ed. Noda Jin & Onuma Takahiro (Tokyo: TIAS, 2010), 12, 40, 114–17.

[100] 'Predstavleniya Sultana Ablaya Imp. Ekaterine II s pros'boi ob utverzhdenii ego khanskom zvanii' 28/02/1778, AVPRI F.122 Op.1 D.1 ll. 42–6, in *KRO*, 87–8; I. G. Andreev, *Opisanie srednei ordy Kirgiz-kaisakov* [1790] (Almaty: Gylym, 1998), 36; Ian Campbell, *Knowledge and the Ends of Empire: Kazak Intermediaries and Russian Rule on the Steppe, 1731–1917* (Ithaca, NY: Cornell University Press, 2017), 18–20.

[101] Noda & Onuma, *A Collection of Documents*, 81–4.

[102] Virginia Martin, 'Engagement with Empire as Norm and in Practice in Kazakh Nomadic Political Culture (1820s–1830s)', *CAS* 36/2 (2017), 175–94. Martin, 'Using Turki-Language Qazaq Letters', 216–18.

[103] A. Dobromyslov, 'Zaboty Imperatritsy Ekateriny II o prosveshchenii Kirgizov', *TOUAK* Vyp. IX (1902), 51–63; see further Dov Yaroshevski, 'Imperial Strategy in the Kirghiz Steppe in the Eighteenth Century', *JBFGO* 39/2 (1991), 221–4.

build fortresses and attempted to levy taxation and administer justice in the territories of the Middle Horde in the northern part of the steppe.[104]

Speranskii's new regulations formalised the status of Qazaqs as Russian subjects with the legal status of *inorodtsy* (those of a different birth), created an administrative structure of 'inner' and 'outer' districts (based on their distance from the old frontier line) and a hierarchy of rule under Chinggissid elites. The basic unit of administration was the *aul* or nomadic settlement. These were grouped into *volosts* under a sultan, and in turn into larger districts under a senior or *agha* sultan who held Russian military rank and could attain Russian noble status. The new regulations thus retained a key role for Chinggissids as elite intermediaries between the Russian authorities and the Qazaqs. However, they also entailed the abolition of the khanship of the Middle Horde, and in the longer term would see a progressive erosion of Chinggissid authority in Qazaq society.[105] More than anything else, Speranskii's statute aimed to regulate the mobility of the Qazaqs, both across the Russian frontier line and between the new *okruzhnye prikazy* or *diwans* (administrative divisions) which were now created in the territory of the Middle Horde, each centred on a newly constructed Russian fortress: Kokshetau, Karkaralinsk, Ayaguz, Akmolinsk, Bayan-aul, Uch-Bulak, Aman-Karagai and Kokpekti.[106] In 1824 a similar set of regulations – the *Mnenie ob Orenburgskikh Kirgizakh* – abolished the khanship of the Junior Horde and extended the authority of the Orenburg Frontier Commission over what were now called the 'Orenburg Kirgiz', with a similar role played by Chinggissid elites – in this case known as *sultan-praviteli* – and a similar attempt at territorialisation of control and the limiting of mobility.[107] Qazaq leaders had long maintained independent relations with the Central Asian khanates, while the annual pastoral transhumance of many groups within the Junior and Middle Hordes over whom the Russians claimed sovereignty took them far to the south of Russian fortified lines in winter, as they pastured their flocks along the Syr-Darya, in regions claimed by Khiva and Khoqand. This movement was now seen by the Russians as illegitimate and a source of chronic instability – accusations that the Central Asian rulers were interfering with and claiming control over 'our' Qazaqs would become a staple complaint. For the first time, the sovereignty which the Russians had claimed for so long over the Qazaqs was beginning to bite, and while many Qazaq Chinggissids chose to cooperate

---

[104] Martin, *Law and Custom*, 2, 34–47; Raeff, *Siberia and the Reforms of 1822*, 112–28; D. V. Vasil'ev, *Rossiya i kazakhskaya step': Administrativnaya politika i status okrainy XVIII–pervaya polovina XIX veka* (Moscow: Rosspen, 2014), 208–44.

[105] Khazanov, *Nomads*, 217; Virginia Martin, 'Kazakh Chinggisids, Land and Political Power in the Nineteenth Century: A Case Study of Syrymbet' *CAS* 29/1 (2010), 79–102.

[106] 'Ustav o Sibirskikh Kirgizakh' 22/07/1822 *PSZ* 2nd Series, Vol. 38, No. 29127, 417; Martin 'Engagement with Empire', 181–7.

[107] Frank, 'The Qazaqs and Russia', 372–3.

with the Russian state – such as Aighanym, the widow of Vali, last Khan of the
Middle Horde – others chose to resist.[108] The most notable of these was Sultan
Kenesary Qasimov (1802–1847), a grandson of Ablai Khan.

No Qazaq leader of the nineteenth century has been more mythologised than
Kenesary. For the Russians at the time he was the *myatezhnyi* (rebellious) sultan. In
Soviet times he was condemned as a 'feudal' reactionary, while in modern
Kazakhstan he has been canonised as both the last Qazaq khan and the leader of
a modern 'national-liberation' movement.[109] None of these is really helpful for
understanding the nature of the authority which he exercised on the Qazaq steppe
from 1837 until his death ten years later, or his relations with Russia. That Kenesary
was resisting growing Russian encroachments on the territory of the Middle Horde
is clear, and in some ways his movement can be seen as a last attempt to create
a nomadic confederation on the steppe, along the lines of the Junghars 100 years
earlier, or the sixteenth- and seventeenth-century Qazaq khans. He benefited from
the failure of the 1839–40 winter expedition to Khiva, which seemed to reveal the
limits of Russian power in the steppe, and from a period of political chaos in
Khoqand from 1842 until 1844, when the Qipchaqs seized power.[110] At different
times most of the Middle Horde and some tribes of the Junior Horde acknowledged
his authority, and he built up strong relationships with the Khoqandi governors of
Tashkent, who often gave him shelter. His attempts to win over the Kyrgyz in
Semirechie were less successful, though it gave us one of the few examples of his
political message not to be filtered through Russian archives:

> The Russians are a numerous people who crush enemies that oppose them.
> They have become like a rising flood, crossing the Idil [Volga] and the Yayiq
> [Ural] rivers and the Ural mountains, taking over the innumerably teeming
> Qazaqs of the Sary-arqa. Their divisions are the toughest and their soldiers
> are exceedingly numerous. From the beginning, in foreign and military
> affairs, we Kirgiz and Qazaqs have for the most part shared equally in our
> blessings, good and bad, and in our prosperity; we are a mingled people, in
> a material as well as in a spiritual sense. Let us prepare to make war together.
> If we Qazaq and Kirgiz unite, then Tashkent, Qoqand, and Samarqand will
> not be able to avoid our power for long. [. . .] If you do not unite with us,
> a large force will come.[111]

---

[108] Martin, 'Engagement with Empire', 175–81 and 'Kazakh Chinggisids', 84–6.

[109] The classic (and still the best-researched) account of Kenesary's movement is
E. Bekmakhanov, *Kazakhstan v 20–40 gody XIX veka* (Alma-Ata: Kazakhskoe
Ob"edinennoe Gosudarstvennoe Izd., 1947), which was suppressed soon after publication
for characterising the revolt as 'progressive'. It plays an enormously important role in modern
Kazakh historiography: see Stephen Sabol, 'Kazak Resistance to Russian Colonization:
Interpreting the Kenesary Kasymov Revolt 1837–1847', *CAS* 22/2–3 (2003), 231–52.

[110] Levi, *The Rise and Fall of Khoqand*, 159–66.

[111] 'Qaligul G. on Kenesari's Incursion of 1846' trans. Daniel Prior, in Daniel Prior (ed. &
trans.), *The Shabdan Baatyr Codex: Epic and the Writing of Northern Kirghiz History*
(Leiden: Brill, 2013), 335.

Instead it was the Kyrgyz who would kill him in 1847, and he would be remembered among them as a brutal aggressor.[112] At the same time Kenesary's correspondence with the Russian authorities makes it clear that what he wanted above all was their recognition and confirmation of his title as Khan and a return to the status quo which had existed under his grandfather, Ablai (whom he frequently invoked).[113] A characteristic example of this comes in a letter to P. D. Gorchakov, then governor of Western Siberia, from 1845:

> We inform you that in the time of our grandfathers and fathers we did not turn away from the grace of the Emperor, and did not produce disorders, but having seen that it was proposed to place fortresses on the lands where we had our summer pastures, we encountered annoyances and were unable to enter them, and for this reason we were compelled to turn with requests to the local commander. But if you now graciously concede to us Ulu-Tau, Sary-Su and Chekengur as far as the Elanchi Torghai, then we are prepared to take the pledged oath and maintain it, in whatever form presented, to never arm ourselves against the people who are under the power of the Emperor.[114]

In a letter to V. A. Obruchev, the governor of Orenburg, the same year, he made similar complaints about the construction of fortresses (*diwans*), and promised to maintain order and cease his raids if these were removed.[115] It is true that these letters come from when Kenesary's power was waning, but the reference to the good relations between Chinggissid elites and the Russian empire in the past, before the construction of fortresses in the steppe, is also found in a well-known letter which his father, Qasim, had addressed to the Russian authorities in 1824 after the construction of the first *diwan* at Kokshetau.[116] Neither he nor Kenesary objected to the Russian presence *per se*, but they wanted to be able to use their connection with the Russians to support their own claims to leadership, as previous Qazaq khans had done. This was no longer enough for the Russian imperial authorities. What had previously been an arm's length relationship with Qazaq Chinggissid elites, which entailed a grudging acceptance of blurred and overlapping sovereignty, was to be replaced with one of hard borders and direct territorial control. As we will see in Chapter 3, Kenesary's 'rebellion' against these new arrangements, his frequent raids on Qazaqs whom the Russians claimed as subjects, and his independent relations with Khiva and Khoqand would come to be frequently cited as a factor necessitating Russian expansion southwards into the steppe.

---

[112] 'The Story of Kenesari', in Prior (ed. & trans.), *The Shabdan Baatyr Codex*, 147–57.
[113] See further Kilian, 'Allies and Adversaries', 200–10.
[114] Kenesary to P. D. Gorchakov (n.d. – 1845) RGVIA F.483 Op.1 D.14 ll. 234–5.
[115] Kenesary to V. A. Obruchev 03/06/1845, TsGARKaz F.4 Op.1 D.2232 'Materialy o vosstanii K. Kasymova i o stroitel'stve ukreplenii Irgiz i Turgai', ll. 480–*ob*.
[116] Martin, 'Engagement with Empire', 175–6.

1.4 Beyond the Qazaq Steppe

As this last point suggests, the sedentary states and rulers of the oasis regions to the south of the steppe also loomed increasingly large in the Russian official mind in the 1820s and 1830s. Here again questions of prestige and sovereignty were paramount, rather than direct economic or strategic interest. As we have seen, Russian trade with the region remained very limited until the 1850s, but most of what existed was with Bukhara – 4,800,000 roubles' worth of imports through Orenburg between 1787 and 1796, more than ten times the value of trade with Khiva in the same period.[117] It was the Minister of Commerce, N. P. Rumyantsev, rather than the foreign ministry, who despatched the first Russian mission to Bukhara of Alexander I's reign in 1802, and his instructions to the envoy, Lt Gaverdovskii, were mild – to assure the Bukharan Amir Haidar of Russian friendship, to request him to give up Russian fugitives from justice, and above all to smooth the path for Russian merchants, ideally by establishing an equivalent of Orenburg's *Menovoi Dvor* for them in Bukhara.[118] Bukharan envoys regularly travelled to Orenburg, where once again the talk was mainly of facilitating trade. Governor Volkonskii, writing of the arrival of an envoy called Muminjan with a proposal for a trade agreement in February 1815, emphasised the need to secure trading rights for Russian Christian merchants. They were heavily dependent on Tatar agents whom he suggested could not be relied on to uphold Russian trading rights because they had too many interests in common and often intermarried with their co-religionists in Bukhara.[119] Further Russian missions were despatched in 1809, 1819, 1824, 1834 (under P. I. Desmaisons), 1836 (Witkiewicz) and 1839, and, while they did not succeed in opening up Bukhara to Christian Russian merchants, Tatars who were Russian subjects continued to trade freely.[120] Russian relations with Bukhara remained on a fairly even keel throughout the thirty-year reign of Amir Nasrullah (1827–1860), who became notorious as a cruel fanatic in the English-speaking world for his execution of the Indian Army officers Charles Stoddart and Arthur Conolly in 1842, but who is better understood as the most powerful and successful Bukharan ruler of the nineteenth century. While Bukhara was an expansionist power under Nasrullah, his aggression was directed against city-states such as Shahrisabz and Hissar which defied his authority, and towards territory contested with his

---

[117] Mikhaleva, *Torgovye i posol'skie svyazi*, 42.

[118] 'Instruktsiya otpravlyaiushchemusya v Bukhariiu Porutchika Gaverdovskogo ot minis-tra kommertsii' 07/11/1802, *VPR* I/2, 332–7.

[119] 'Zamechaniya Orenburgskogo General-Gubernatora G. S. Volkonskago na zapisku bukharskogo poslannia A. Muminzhanova' 08/02/1815, *VPR* I/8, 203–4.

[120] S. V. Zhukovskii, *Snosheniya Rossii s Bukharoi i Khivoi za poslednee trekhsotletie* (Petrograd: Obshchestvo Russkikh Orientalistov, 1915), 96–112. On Desmaisons (1807–1873), a Sardinian in Russian service, see Khalfin (ed.), *Zapiski o Bukharskom khanstve*, 7–11.

sedentary neighbours in Khiva (Merv, Charjui) and Khoqand (Khujand, Ura-Tepe), rather than towards the steppe; he did not make the direct claims to sovereignty over the Qazaqs which would increasingly bring Khiva and Khoqand into conflict with Russia.[121]

Between 1807, when Tashkent fell to Khoqandi forces under the future 'Umar Khan,[122] and 1834, when a Chitrali mercenary called Lashkar Qushbegi established the fortress of Aq Masjid on the lower Syr-Darya, Khoqand expanded to become a major steppe power. This advance was marked by the construction of a series of fortresses in what the khanate's own historians always called the *Dasht-i Qipchaq*: Suzaq, Chulaq-Qurghan, Yangi-Qurghan, Julek and Aq Masjid, which the Khoqandis used as trading posts and for the collection of *zakat*[123] on the livestock of Qazaq nomads over whom Russia also claimed sovereignty.[124] In 1827 the Asiatic committee received a report from General Essen, the then Governor of Orenburg, that the Khoqandis had constructed two new fortresses on the Syr-Darya – probably Yangi-Qurghan and Julek. Each supposedly had over 100 houses and was home to a garrison of 700 men, although Essen thought these numbers were exaggerated. While the committee was concerned that this might lead to disruption of caravan traffic and disturbances amongst the Qazaqs, they vetoed sending a punitive expedition to destroy the fortresses, arguing that the Khoqandis would just rebuild them. 'Such a measure', they wrote, 'can only be put into action with the desired effect when we have succeeded in bringing the Khivan Khanate into peaceful and close relations with us, and when the dominion (*vladychestvo*) of the Russian Empire is unquestionably established on the Syr-Darya and further into the East as far as the Altai mountains.'[125] As this indicates, there was a long-term goal to advance the empire's frontier to the south, and the chief focus of Russian suspicion and hostility was Khiva.

In 1826 Major-General F. M. Verigin, the head of the Orenburg customs, wrote a lengthy memorandum in which he argued that Russia was in danger of losing the hard-won gains and glory of the Napoleonic Wars, as her trade and manufactures were outstripped by other countries, notably Britain. One way to

[121] Wilde, *What Is beyond the River?*, II, 745–80.
[122] O. D. Chekhovich, 'Skazaniya o Tashkente', *PPV* (1970), 173–6.
[123] The Islamic tax on goods, one-fortieth of their value, which was widely applied to livestock in Central Asia.
[124] Levi, *The Rise and Fall of Khoqand*, 82–90, 119–24; Scott Levi, 'The Ferghana Valley at the Crossroads of World History: The rise of Khoqand 1709–1822', *JGH* 2/2 (2007), 213–32; T. K. Beisembiev, 'Vysshaya administratsiya Tashkenta i iuga Kazakhstana v period Kokandskogo khanstva: 1809–1865', in *Istoriko-kul'turnye vzaimosvyazi Irana i Dasht-i Kipchaka v XIII–XVIII vv.* (Almaty: Daik-Press 2004), 291–313; Timur Beisembiev, *Ta'rikh-i Shakhrukhi kak istoricheskii istochnik* (Alma-Ata: Nauka, 1987), 17; Babadzhanov, *Kokandskoe khanstvo*, 117–83.
[125] 'Zhurnal aziatskago komiteta 10 avgusta 1827 o postroenii kokantsami pri Syr-Dar'e dvukh krepostei na kirgizskikh zemlyakh', AVPRI F.161 I-1 Op.781 D.491 ll. 68–9ob.

counter this would be to open up new markets and trade routes in Central Asia, whose commerce with Russia was currently fairly insignificant, but which he thought could be transformed into a secure market for Russian goods if only its troublesome states and inhabitants could be properly pacified.[126] Verigin made an explicit link between the newfound status Russia had gained from her Napoleonic victories and the need to pacify the steppe frontier and curb the insolence of Central Asian peoples and states:

> After the wonderful victory achieved by Russia in 1812 and the following years, over the enemies of the whole of Europe, it seemed that all peoples should have a proper sense of the terrible strength of her mightiness and fear to arouse her righteous wrath; but, notwithstanding all these hopes, on the contrary we see that, close to the boundaries of our realm, the insignificant, but perfidious Khivan people [. . .] have dared once again to raise an armed force to attack one of our commercial caravans, despatched to Bukhara in 1824.[127]

He went on to ask how it could be that in the course of the past 100 years the Russians had never managed to subdue Khiva, when the British, with a population of just 12 million people, had in the same time managed to rule 80 million Indians. He attributed this to the British having clear plans of conquest which they had pursued with determination and firmness throughout. Half measures would not do – nothing less than an outright conquest of Khiva and the deposition of its ruler was worthy of the dignity of Russia and her Emperor. The rapid approach of the British was also a source of worry in itself, as they might begin to foment further trouble for the Russians in Central Asia. In imposing her commercial supremacy by force, and at the same time attempting to use trade as a tool to expand her political influence, Russia would be doing no more than what Britain had been doing in the Mediterranean over the previous twenty years.[128] While commercial considerations played a part in Verigin's reasoning, once again the spirit of prestige and competitive emulation was paramount. At the time official attention was still primarily directed towards the Caucasian Frontier, and Verigin's memorandum produced little in the way of reaction, but it would be revived ten years later as Russia began preparations to snuff out Khivan insolence once and for all.

---

[126] 'Kratkoe izlozhenie myslei General-maiora Verigina o neobkhodimosti zanyat' Khivu, kak edinstvennoe sredstvo dlya rasprostraneniya i privedeniya v bezopasnost' nashei torgovli v srednei chasti Azii, predstavlennoe Ego Imperatorskomu Velichestvu 5 fevralya 1826 goda', in Serebrennikov, *Sbornik*. Vol. 2, *1840 g.*, Doc.5, 4–6.

[127] 'Kratkoe izlozhenie myslei General-maiora Veriginа', 8.

[128] 'Kratkoe izlozhenie myslei General-maiora Veriginа', 9.

2

'Pray for the Camels': The Winter Invasion of Khiva, 1839–41

Ici il faut agir à l'anglaise, et cela d'autant plus que c'est contre les Anglais qu'on agit.

V. A. Perovskii, 1840[1]

General V. A. Perovskii's attempt to invade Khiva in the winter of 1839–40 was seen by most Tsarist historians as the first decisive step in the Russian conquest of Central Asia. A state secret at the time, from the 1860s numerous publications and memoirs by participants appeared describing the expedition and its tragic failure.[2] The tone was set by the earliest comprehensive account, drawn up by General M. I. Ivanin on Perovskii's instructions, which is largely a description of Khivan perfidy and a celebration of Russian heroism and endurance, together with a certain amount of score-settling with Ivanin's fellow officers.[3] For subsequent military historians, the 1839 disaster assumed

---

The bulk of this chapter was first published, with additional material, in 'Twin Imperial Disasters: The Invasions of Khiva and Afghanistan in the Russian and British Official Mind, 1839–1842', *MAS* 48/1 (2014), 253–300 and in 'Camels and Colonial Armies: The Logistics of Warfare in Inner Asia in the Early 19th Century', *JESHO* 57 (2014), 443–85. It reappears here by kind permission of both journals. I would like to thank the Slavic Research Centre of Hokkaido University, where I wrote the initial version while on a Visiting Fellowship in 2010, and in particular Professor Uyama Tomohiko for his comments.

[1] 'Here we must act in the English way, all the more so because it is against the English that we are acting': Perovskii to Bulgakov, 4 February 1840, 'Pis'ma Grafa V. A. Perovskago k A. Ya. Bulgakovu', *RA* (1878) No. 7, Letter 9, 309.

[2] Apart from the accounts by Dal', Ivanin and Peslyak described below, see Anon., 'Voennoe predpriyatie protiv Khivu', *Chteniya v Imperatorskom obshchestve istorii i drevnostei rossiiskikh pri Moskovskom Universitete* (January–March 1860), Kn. 1, 147–66; S. Zykov, 'Khivinskiya dela s 1839–1842', *Russkoe Slovo* (March 1862), 1–58; E. M. Kosyrev, 'Pokhod v Khivu v 1839 godu (iz zapisok uchastnika)', *IV* (1898), No. 8, 538–45.

[3] This was first published by Captain D. Golosov, who found the manuscript in the Orenburg archive and, not realising that the author was still alive, sent it to the specialist military journal *Voennyi Sbornik* as his own work, although he had only added notes and a historical introduction: see M. Ivanin/D. Golosov, 'Pokhod v Khivu v 1839 godu otryada russkikh voisk, pod nachal'stvom General-Ad'yutanta Perovskago', *VS* (1863), No. 1, 3–72; No. 2, 309–58 and No. 3, 3–71. On the article's publication, Ivanin alerted the editors of the journal, who published an explanation: 'Neobkhodimoe ob"yasnenie', *VS* (1863), No. 3, 73–5. This account was then translated into English: *A Narrative of the*

a symbolic significance as a tragic, heroic sacrifice, which showcased Russian hardiness and endurance and enabled the army to learn important lessons that would render the later conquest of Central Asia possible.[4] It was no coincidence that the first two volumes of Serebrennikov's enormous early-twentieth-century collection of documents on the Russian conquest of Central Asia were largely devoted to the 'winter expedition to Khiva'.[5] In the Soviet period, as a clear example of Russian aggression which long pre-dated the expansion of Moscow's textile industry, it fitted poorly both into the sanctioned narrative of 'prisoedinenie' and into that of the cotton canard. When mentioned, it was usually considered a legitimate response to British machinations and aggression in Central Asia, especially the visits of Captain James Abbott and Lieutenant Richmond Shakespear to Khiva in 1839–40.[6]

The immediate cause of the expedition's failure – the severe winter conditions on the Orenburg steppe and the Ust-Yurt plateau – has long been clear. As it was indeed the first Russian attempt to conquer the sedentary regions of Central Asia since Bekovich-Cherkasskii's failed effort in 1717, in many ways it also deserves the important place given to it in Tsarist-era historiography as the starting-point for Russian expansion in Central Asia. This still leaves many questions unanswered, not least why the expedition was launched at that particular moment, when Russian grievances against Khiva were of such long standing. How far were the Russians acting to counter the British, who launched their invasion of Afghanistan in the same year? The opening quotation from Perovskii suggests that there was a connection, though his reference to 'acting in the English way' suggests that emulating Russia's rival was as important as presenting a challenge to her. We might also ask why Khiva was singled out as the first object of Russian aggression, rather than Khoqand, which had expanded rapidly into the steppe in the 1820s and 1830s. What were

Russian Military Expedition to Khiva under General Perofski, in 1839. Translated from the Russian for the Foreign Department of the Government of India (Calcutta: Office of the Superintendent of Government Printing, 1867). Ivanin published his own, revised version of the text a few years later: M. Ivanin, *Opisanie zimnego pokhoda v Khivu v 1839–40 g.* (St Pb.: Tip. Obshchestvennaya Pol'za, 1874).

[4] The canonical versions are I. N. Zakhar'in, *Khiva: Zimnii pokhod v Khivu Perovskago v 1839 godu, – i 'Pervoe posol'stvo v Khivu' v 1842 godu* (St Pb.: Tip P. P. Soikina 1898); I. N. Zakhar'in, *Graf V. A. Perovskii i ego zimnii pokhod v Khivu* (St Pb.: Tip. P. P. Soikina, 1901), which are based not on archival sources, but on oral accounts collected by the author from veterans in Orenburg in the 1890s, and Terent'ev, *Istoriya zavoevaniya*, I, 92–172.

[5] Serebrennikov, *Sbornik*. Vol. 1. *1839 g.* & Vol. 2. *1840 g.* (1908–12).

[6] Khalfin, *Rossiya i khanstva Srednei Azii*, 280–7. See James Abbott, *Narrative of a Journey from Heraut to Khiva, Moscow and St Petersburgh during the Late Russian Invasion of Khiva, with Some Account of the Court of Khiva and the Kingdom of Khaurism* (London: W. H. Allen & Co., 1843) 2 volumes; Shakespear, 'A Personal Narrative of a Journey from Heraut to Ourenbourg'.

Russia's plans in the event of a successful outcome? How did the Russians cope with the logistical challenges presented by long-distance warfare across the steppe? And how did Perovskii's failure alter Russian strategy in Central Asia and tactical approaches to steppe warfare? This chapter will attempt to answer these questions, while also illustrating just how important new-found Russian arrogance towards Central Asian peoples was both to the launching of the expedition and to its failure.

2.1 The Genesis of the Khiva Expedition

At the time the Russian invasion of Khiva was seen as justified by substantial grievances even by the British. The Russians could point to Khivan raids on caravan traffic and repeated attempts to extract revenue from Qazaqs over whom the Russians claimed sovereignty. The more historically minded could also invoke the massacre of Prince Bekovich-Cherkasskii's expedition in 1717, or the supposed 'political testament' of Peter the Great, which called for the subjugation of Khiva.[7] Madhavan Palat has argued that the presence of what were variously estimated as hundreds or thousands of Russian slaves in the Khanate, who had been captured by Qazaq or Turkmen raiders along the Orenburg line and the Caspian coast, played a crucial role in legitimising and motivating the Russian advance. He notes that this was despite the fact that the number of Russian slaves was grossly exaggerated, that Russia itself was engaged in slave trafficking in the Caucasus in the same period, and that there was no systematic Khivan policy of enslaving Russians, who were described in contemporary documents not as slaves – *raby* – but as *plenniki* – captives – taken during border raids.[8] Elena Smolarz has pointed out that this semantic distinction indicated the opposite of what Palat believed – namely that the taking of Russian captives by nomads was illegal, and should not be recognised or accepted as part of the established system of slavery which existed in Khiva, Bukhara and Afghanistan.[9] What is clear is that the number of Russian captives/slaves seems to have been consistently exaggerated. The overwhelming majority of the khanate's slaves were Shi'i Persians who provided much of the agricultural labour in Khwarazm, something which prompted the Qajars to send a number of unsuccessful missions to Khiva aimed at freeing them. As Jeff Eden has shown, captive-taking was a normal outcome of warfare and raiding on the steppe in this period, indulged in by all participants – including the Russians themselves – so the singling out of Khiva

---

[7] Létolle, 'Les Éxpeditions de Bekovitch-Tcherkassky'; Schimmelpenninck van der Oye, 'Paul's Great Game', 143–4.

[8] Palat, 'Tsarist Russian Imperialism', 163–6.

[9] Elena Smolarz, 'Speaking about Freedom and Dependency: Representations and Experiences of Russian Enslaved Captives in Central Asia in the First Half of the 19th Century', *Journal of Global Slavery* 2 (2017), 47–60.

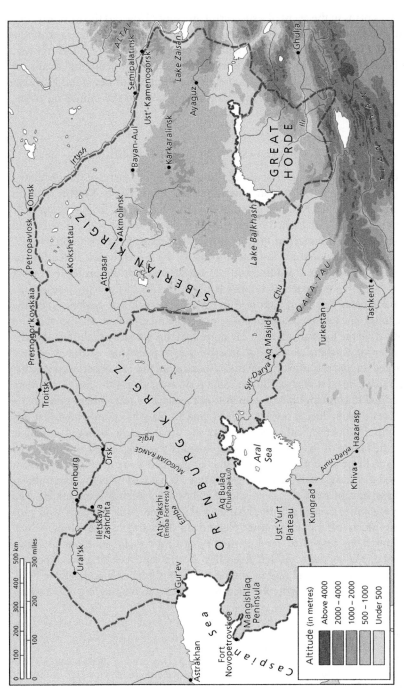

Map 2 The northern steppe

as a slave state involved a degree of double standards.[10] However the effectiveness of these complaints in a diplomatic sphere dominated by the rhetoric of anti-slavery can be seen in the Government of India's acknowledgment that it was a legitimate justification for a punitive expedition, even though it feared that a permanent Russian presence in Khiva might be damaging to Indian security.[11] The presence of Russian slaves in Khiva was nothing new, but, as we saw in the previous chapter, what gave these reasons for attacking Khiva force and urgency within Russia was the new, self-conscious sense among the administrative and military elite that they were the servants of a European 'Great Power' with prestige and standards to maintain, a tendency Michael Khodarkovsky identified on the steppe frontier as early as the 1750s, and which reached its apotheosis in 1814, when Alexander I marched into Paris.[12]

The attack on Khiva had a lengthy genesis: in 1804 Prince G. S. Volkonskii, the then governor of Orenburg, proposed a punitive expedition to Alexander I, although at that time there were other pressing foreign policy priorities.[13] In 1819 Captain N. N. Murav'ev was despatched on a mission to Khiva across the Caspian from Tiflis, and succeeded not only in traversing the Turkmen country to reach the Khivan oasis, but also, more remarkably, in returning alive, but without procuring any lasting agreement or securing the release of any Russian prisoners, of which there were then supposed to be 3,000.[14] In 1831 the head of the Orenburg Frontier Commission, General G. F. Gens, wrote a strongly worded memorandum on the plight of the Russian prisoners in Khiva, which in 1833 prompted Nesselrode to acknowledge that an expedition ought to be sent to free them, although he was concerned about the cost and the difficulties of the route.[15] Thus there was agreement in principle to some sort of punitive expedition well before Perovskii's arrival in Orenburg, although its feasibility had yet to be established. As Zakhar'in recounted it, on taking up his post in 1833 on the death of Governor Sukhtelen, Perovskii was shocked to discover that Qazaqs around the Ural River, while nominally acknowledging Russian sovereignty, were still in the habit of capturing

---

[10] Jeff Eden, *Slavery and Empire in Central Asia* (Cambridge: Cambridge University Press, 2018), 17–19, 38–47, 55; Arash Khazeni, 'Across the Black Sands and the Red: Travel Writing, Nature and the Reclamation of the Eurasian Steppe *circa* 1850', *IJMES* 42/4 (2010), 591–614.

[11] Torrens to Macnaghten, 25/05/1840, IOR/L/P&S/G10/3 No. 6, p. 8; see Richard Huzzey, *Freedom Burning: Anti-Slavery and Empire in Victorian Britain* (Ithaca, NY: Cornell University Press, 2012), 51–65, 206–10.

[12] Khodarkovsky, *Russia's Steppe Frontier*, 225–6; Lieven, 'Russia and the Defeat of Napoleon'.

[13] S. N. Sevast'yanov, 'Sobytiya v Orenburgskom krae podgotovivshiya ekspeditsiiu v Khivu 1839–1840 gg.', *TOUAK* Vyp. XVI (1906), 108–14.

[14] N. N. Murav'ev, *Puteshestvie v Turkmeniiu i Khivu v 1819 i 1820 godakh* (Moscow: Tip. Avgusta Semena, 1822), 143–4; Eden, *Slavery and Empire*, 50.

[15] Sevast'yanov, 'Sobytiya v Orenburgskom krae', 125–6, 131–2, 140–2.

Russian subjects and selling them into slavery in Khiva. One particularly affecting tale concerned a Cossack officer's widow who was kidnapped from Orenburg itself in 1825, on the eve of the first visit to the town by Alexander I. Thanks to the latter's intervention she was eventually found and brought back, but even the autocrat of all the Russias had been forced to offer a large sum to her captors.[16] Whether this story was true or not, Perovskii clearly felt a strong, almost personal, sense of affront and moral outrage at Khiva's enslavement of Russians. In 1834 he asked the Orenburg Frontier Commission to prepare a list of known Russian prisoners held in Khiva, which eventually amounted to 599 names, of which 20 were women and 57 clearly Muslim.[17] Early the following year he sent a melodramatic memorandum to St Petersburg, advocating a punitive expedition and invoking the common civilising mission of the European powers in the Muslim world:

> The guilt of the Dey of Algiers against the King of the French pales into insignificance in comparison with the crimes carried out by whole generations of Khivan Khans against the Emperors of Russia [...] there a single, momentary, and in reality bloodless insult to the Consul; here in the course of a whole century constantly accumulating perfidy which increases day by day, deliberate malice, robbery, banditry and disrespectful abuse of Majesty; here the blood of Russians is spilled, has been flowing for a whole century [...] thousands have suffered and suffer now under the yoke of slavery [...] France demanded millions for the conquest of Algeria, and has retained for all time her conquests beyond the restitution of what she has spent. For Russia the conquest of Khiva would not cost one tenth of this; but all of Central Asia would be revived, would rise up from its torpor with the introduction of an educated, beneficial government.[18]

The sense of competitive imperial emulation emerges clearly: Russia could not be left behind by Britain and France, nor could one of Europe's Great Powers continue to tolerate the insults of a petty Asiatic state like Khiva. Curiously enough, in 1830 Chernyshev had despatched a memorandum 'on the usages and customs adopted in our Eastern Wars' to the Quai d'Orsay to assist the French in their preparations for the attack on Algiers.[19] Now his

---

[16] Zakhar'in, *Khiva*, 20–2.

[17] Perovskii to the Orenburg Frontier Commission (OPK) 30/04/1834; OPK to Perovskii, 02/06/1834, TsGARKaz F.4 Op.1 D.1567 'Spisok Russikh plennykh nakhoodyashchikhsya v sredneaziatskikh khanstvakh', ll. 1, 3–25ob.

[18] 'Zapiska o snosheniyakh Rossii s Khivinskim khanstvom i o protivnykh narodnym pravam postupkakh khanov Khivinskikh protiv Rossii', Perovskii to Chernyshev, ?/01/1835, in Serebrennikov, *Sbornik*. Vol. 1. *1839 g.* Doc.6, 28.

[19] This drew on Russia's experiences in the recently concluded war with Persia: Sébastien Haule, "'... us et coutumes adoptées dans nos guerres d'orient": L'expérience coloniale russe et l'expédition d'Alger', *CMR* 45/1–2 (2004), 293–320.

response to Perovskii's reference was enthusiastic: he wrote that the tsar was entirely in agreement with the memorandum's sentiments and wished to see a detailed plan for an expedition: once again, Perovskii's close personal connection with Nicholas I had borne fruit.[20] The first practical consequence of this was an imperial decree of 1836 ordering the detention of over 350 Khivan merchants in the *Menovoi Dvor* (Asian caravanserai) outside Orenburg and a total suspension of Russian trade with the Khanate.[21] The Khivan Khan, Allah Quli (1794–1842), responded with a letter asking why the Russians had broken off friendly relations, not just by detaining his merchants but also by constructing a new fortress at Novo-Alexandrovsk on the Caspian, in what he considered to be Khivan territory; for the Russians this matter was not even negotiable.[22]

Military preparations were temporarily postponed owing to a rebellion among the Qazaqs, and to what Allah Quli Khan would later describe to James Abbott as genuine efforts to reach a diplomatic settlement by freeing some of the Russian slaves.[23] Ivanin wrote that the Russians simply saw these as delaying tactics, possibly inspired by British interference.[24] The Khivan historian Agahi, in the *Riyaz ud-Daulat*, his chronicle of Allah Quli Khan's reign, while referring in triumphant tones to Khivan success in capturing slaves on the Russian frontier, also made it clear that the Khivans viewed the detention of their merchants as an attempt by the Russians to bargain, by swapping them for Russian slaves in Khiva.[25] Perovskii, while paying lip-service to the idea that the trade embargo might be used to bring Khiva to the negotiating table, made it clear that nothing less than the immediate and unconditional release of what he still claimed were 3,000 Russian prisoners in the Khanate would do: 'the Khivans meet their guests with knives, poison or the shackles of a prisoner'.[26] In practice he was not really prepared to negotiate: when two Khivan envoys arrived with five freed Russian prisoners in August 1838, Perovskii refused to receive them, had them detained with the

---

[20] Chernyshev to Perovskii, 14/01/1835, in Serebrennikov, *Sbornik*. Vol. 1 *1839 g.* Doc.6, 28–9.

[21] Perovskii to the Orenburg Frontier Customs, 14/08/1836, GAOrO F.153 Op.1 D.153 'Perepiska s Orenburgskim Voennym Gubernatorom i Orenburgskim tamozhnym okrugom o zaderzhanii khivintsev', ll. 1, 5–12ob.

[22] Khwarazmshah to Perovskii (Russian translation), ?/11/1836 GAOrO F.167 Op.1 D.35 'Pis'mo Khorezmskogo Shakha o narushenii russkimi druzhestvennykh otnoshenii s Khorezmom', ll. 1–2ob.

[23] Abbott, *Narrative*, I, 108–10.

[24] Ivanin/Golosov, 'Pokhod v Khivu', *VS* (1863), No. 1, 70–1; Anon., *Russian Military Expedition to Khiva*, 52–69.

[25] *MPITT* Vol. II, 473; the Chaghatai original is in the *Riyaz ud-Daulat* MS IVANP No.D123 ff. 226b–7b.

[26] Perovskii Memorandum, 18/09/1836, GAOrO F.167 Op.1 D.27 'O vzaimotnosheniyakh Khivy i Bukhary s Rossiei', ll. 1–4.

merchants, and interrogated the ex-slaves for useful information.[27] This and other opportunities to resolve the dispute peacefully were deliberately ignored – the preparations for the expedition were already under way.

In March 1839 a special committee, consisting of Perovskii himself, Nesselrode and Chernyshev, met to consider Perovskii's proposal for a military expedition. They added a further consideration:

> ... beyond its stated principal aim, it must have another, still more important: to establish and consolidate the influence of Russia in Central Asia, weaken the long-standing impunity of the Khivans, and especially that constancy with which the English government, to the detriment of our industry and trade, strives to spread its supremacy in those parts. [...] however, bringing into consideration the current state of affairs in Central Asia, we consider it more convenient to postpone the mission to Khiva until the end of the expedition undertaken by the Governor-General of the British possessions in India against the ruler of Kabul, Dost Muhammad.[28]

In other words, while they hoped that the Khiva expedition would combat British influence by reviving both Russia's trade and her prestige in Central Asia, they were anxious to avoid an open clash.[29] The committee added that alluding to the concurrent British invasion of Afghanistan would be a sufficient response to any British complaints, but it would be better to wait until the outcome there had been decided. In April 1840, Nesselrode wrote to Perovskii to let him know the substance of what had passed between the Russian Foreign Ministry and the British government, which evidently regarded the Khivan expedition with suspicion, seeing it as a response to their invasion of Afghanistan and an attempt to meddle with their affairs. Nesselrode claimed to have dispelled these fears by explaining Russia's grievances against Khiva and categorically denying that the expedition had anything to do with the invasion of Afghanistan.[30] As we have seen, to a large extent this was true – the invasion of Khiva had been proposed and agreed in principle long before the British decided to invade Afghanistan or the Russians became aware of it.

However, the committee also cited Afghanistan when it came to the expedition's aims, one of which would be to depose Allah Quli Khan, and replace him with a Russian client: 'this measure, which is not against the customs of the

---

[27] Gub. Sek. Aitov to the OPK, 10/08/1838; *Zhurnal* OPK, 15/08/1838, TsGARKaz F.4 Op.1 D.333 'O pribyvshikh iz Khivy dvukh poslantsev', ll. 14, 35–46, 52–*ob*.

[28] 'Zhurnal Komiteta, razsmotrivavshago predpolozheniya Orenburgskogo voennogo gubernatora o poiske na Khivu', 11/03/1839, in Serebrennikov, *Sbornik*. Vol. 1. *1839 g*. Doc.12, 33.

[29] For more on the intertwined nature of these two expeditions see Morrison, 'Twin Imperial Disasters'.

[30] Nesselrode to Perovskii, 05/04/1840, in Serebrennikov, *Sbornik*. Vol. 2. *1840 g*. Doc.64, 104–6.

Asiatics, would be entirely consistent with the actions of the British in their current expedition against Dost Muhammad Khan, the declared purpose of which [. . .] lies in the deposition of its ruler and the restoration of its former Shah, Shuja ul-Mulk'.[31] However, the proposed candidate, Sultan Bai Muhammad Aichuvakov, head of the western section of the Orenburg Qazaqs, wisely turned down the opportunity to become the Russian Shah Shuja (although he would later accompany the expedition). Instead Perovskii proposed replacing Allah Quli with his younger brother, Rahman Quli Inaq, who was rumoured to be 'a very reasonable man, and, so far as is known, secretly wishes the friendship and patronage of Russia'.[32] There was no indication of where this information had come from, or indeed of whether the Khan's brother had been made aware of the honour in store for him. The Russians did not even know his name, referring to him simply as 'Inaq', which was not a name but a title conventionally bestowed on the younger brother of the khan.[33] Richmond Shakespear, who met Rahman Quli at Hazarasp in 1840, certainly had no inkling that he was under consideration as a potential Russian ally.[34] Despite this, Nesselrode endorsed the proposal, reiterating that preserving the same dynasty in power would render the replacement of their ruler agreeable to the understanding of 'Asiatics', and again pointed to parallels with British policy in Kabul.[35] As with Perovskii's original invocation of the French invasion of Algeria when proposing the expedition, it is clear that the emulation of imperial competitors was at least as important as any notional challenge to them – 'agir à l'anglaise', as Perovskii would later put it. Any further details seem to have become swamped in the sheer logistical complexity of sending a military force into the barren steppe in winter, and the plans for Khiva's future government in the event of the expedition's success remained vague until its departure. One of the few indications that any thought had been given to this was a small (and, as it turned out, very premature) pamphlet published in 1840 which contained wildly inaccurate claims about the wealth and resources of Khiva which would accrue to Russia after its conquest.[36]

[31] 'Zhurnal komiteta, razsmotrivavshago predpolozheniya Orenburgskogo voennogo gubernatora o poiske na Khivu', 11/03/1839, in Serebrennikov, *Sbornik*. Vol. 1. *1839 g.* Doc.12, 35.

[32] Perovskii to Nesselrode, 30/09/1839, in Serebrennikov, *Sbornik*. Vol. 1. *1839 g.* Doc.93, 148–50.

[33] T. K. Beisembiev, *Annotated Indices to the Kokand Chronicles* (Tokyo: ILCAAS, 2008), 727. The Uzbek Qungrat dynasty of Khiva had been established by Muhammad Amin Inaq in 1770–1 when he recaptured the khanate from the Yomut Turkmen, although the fiction of Chinggissid rule would be preserved until 1804: see Yuri Bregel (ed. and trans), *Firdaws al-Iqbal: History of Khorezm* (Leiden: Brill, 1999), 95–122.

[34] Shakespear, 'Narrative', 702.

[35] 'Zhurnal komiteta, razsmatrivavshavo predpolozhenie Orenburgskogo voen. Gubernatora o poiske v Khivu', 10/10/1839, in Serebrennikov, *Sbornik*. Vol. 1. *1839 g.* Doc.101, 158–63.

[36] Ivan Koritskii, *Khiva, ili geograficheskoe i statisticheskoe opisanie Khivinskago khanstva, sostoyashchago teper' v voine s Rossiei* (Moscow: Universitetskaya Tip., 1840).

Because the Khiva expedition was halted by the weather, Perovskii was later able to claim that it remained militarily undefeated, while Zakhar'in attributed its failure partly to the disloyalty of the Qazaq guides, but also to the brutality and machinations of General Tsiolkovskii, one of the column commanders and an exiled Pole, who undermined morale.[37] Because of this and other conspiracy theories, the political and military planning and intelligence behind the expedition received far less scrutiny than that of the British in Afghanistan, where European troops had been very publicly worsted by supposedly 'savage' tribesmen. Instead the Russians emphasised the few skirmishes they had with the Khivans, in which they had managed to drive them off: in his address to the troops on announcing the decision to retreat, Perovskii made great play of the 'contemptible' and 'cowardly' nature of the enemy with which the Russians had failed to come to grips.[38] Although the Russian force was indeed almost certainly superior to anything Allah Quli could have put in the field, it was still small, and it seems likely that, even if the weather had been more favourable, it would have been exhausted and in severe need of supplies by the time it reached the cultivated lands of the Khanate. The outcome would by no means have been certain, and the Khivans were well prepared.

If James Abbott's account is to be believed, Allah Quli Khan was well aware of the size of the advancing force (4,000 to 5,000 men) and of the fact that by January 1840 they were stuck fast in the snow.[39] Even if other rumours had not reached him before, the khan would have been alerted to the preparation of the expeditionary force when the lengthy and complicated process of assembling the 10,000 camels required for transport began in August 1838 (see below). At this stage the cover for the preparations remained a 'scientific expedition', but, given the prodigious numbers involved, this soon wore rather thin: Ivanin described how already in March 1839 the female traders of the Orenburg bazaar knew that an expedition against Khiva was being prepared, while 'false' rumours about Russian movements were circulating in the steppe.[40] By May 1839 the Qazaqs clearly knew that a military expedition was being prepared, as the *Biis* (judges) of the Nazarov division wrote to General Gens expressing their relief on learning that it was not intended to chastise them: 'it is not unknown to your Excellency that our people were afraid of the force which you are sending out, not knowing the reason' – Gens, however, refused

---

[37] Zakhar'in, *Graf V. A. Perovskii*, 53–67, 104–6, 134–5.

[38] 'Prikaz po otryadu voisk Khivinskoi ekspeditsii', 01/02/1840, in Serebrennikov, *Sbornik.* Vol. 2. *1840 g.* Doc.22, 42; an English translation of this document can be found in Anon., *Narrative*, 165–6.

[39] Abbott, *Narrative*, 110.

[40] M. Ivanin, 'Zametki po povodu napechatannoi vo 2 i 3 numerakh "Voennago Sbornika" nyneshnago goda stat'i "pokhod v Khivu 1839 g."', *VS* (1863), No. 4, 490; Ivanin/Golosov, 'Pokhod v Khivu', *VS* (1863), No. 2, 352; Anon., *Russian Military Expedition to Khiva*, 119.

the request to be told the route the expedition would take.[41] Rumours of these preparations spread far ahead, as Alexander Burnes had already heard of them in garbled form from his agent in Bukhara in October 1839.[42] Allah Quli thus had ample warning of the Russian advance and had made preparations to resist it.[43] The *Riyaz ud-Daulat* records that a Khivan force of 7,000 men, consisting mainly of cavalry recruited from among the Qazaqs, Turkmen and Qaraqalpaqs and led by Ata Murad Qushbegi Avaz Khwaja, had set off from Khiva across the Ust-Yurt on the 10 November 1839 – it would return after ninety-six days, after mounting an unsuccessful attack on the Russian forces at Aq Bulaq.[44] After the Khiva expedition's failure, the commander of the Novo-Alexandrovsk fortress in Mangishlaq reported that one of his spies, Tolmach Turpaev, had given him a proclamation in 'Tatar' (Figure 2.1) which bore the Khan of Khiva's seal, and which urged Qazaq and Turkmen *Biis* and *Batyrs* to join him in fighting against the Russians:[45]

> We, the father of victory and aided by God in war, Shah of Khwarazm [*Khwarazmshah*],[46] enjoin our loyal subjects and truly devoted Qaraqul Bai-Bii, Hakim-Bii, Mai-Bii, Bute-Qare-Bii, Tuman-Bahadur, Nila-Bii, Qalbe Mullah, Chapuka, Dusqana, 'Umar-Bai, Aisare, Churah, Qaldman Kaja Ali-Bii, Nazar Bii, [Biktadu, Tasqul-Bai, va Tura va Bai] Ishat-Bii, commander [*ataliq-i lashkar*] of the Adami Bikbuli-Bii and all those who see this letter to our famous *batyrs* [*bahadurlar*] and *Biis*. We have sent Musulman Bai [to take charge of] the first part [*birinchi fauj*] of the assembled army [*lashkar-i bahadur-i nusrat-athar jumlah-si-din*] for battle with the Russians [*urus urushi uchun*]. In the case of necessity, according to the wishes of Almighty God, we ourselves will advance with our innumerable hosts, with heroic swords [*qilij-i bahadur*] in their hands. But before we ourselves advance, {all you who are my famous subjects}, you should gather up your tribal leaders and *batyrs* [*naukarlar va bahadurlar*] {with weapons in hands} and give them [the army] the help and service which is due to them. Be certain, that

[41] *Biis* of the Nazarov division to Gens, 25/05/1839; Gens to the *Biis* of the Nazarov division, 26/05/1839 TsGARKaz F.4 Op.1 D.2167 ll. 33*ob*–36.
[42] 'Translation [by Alexander Burnes] of a letter from Nazir Khan Oollah, at Bokhara to the address of the British Envoy and Minister at Cabool dated 15th Rajab 24th Sept. 1839', NAI/Foreign/S.C./18 December 1839/No. 6 'Russian Agent Reported to Have Arrived at Bokhara', 3. Yapp was puzzled as to how rumours of Russian troop movements could have reached the British at Kabul months before the Khivan expedition actually set out in November 1839 (see *Strategies*, 391–2), but, given how far ahead the preparations were initiated, the explanation is quite simple.
[43] Abbott, *Narrative*, I, 97.
[44] *MPITT*, II, 473; *Riyaz ud-Daulat* ff. 226b–7b. My thanks to Shioya Akifumi for alerting me to this reference.
[45] Likhamerstov to Perovskii 24/05/1840 TsGARKaz F.4 Op.1 D.2182 l. 15.
[46] Bregel notes that the Khans of Khiva continued to use this ancient title frequently in official documents and on their seals right down to the nineteenth century. Bregel, *Firdaws al-Iqbal*, viii.

Figure 2.1 Allah Quli Khan of Khiva's proclamation of resistance to the Russians. TsGARKaz F.4 Op.1 D.2182 l. 16*ob* © Central State Archive of the Republic of Kazakhstan.

for the service and labour of each you will receive worthy royal favours, and will remain in honour with exalted heads.[47]

Perovskii's scheme to depose a khan who seems to have been a fairly popular ruler was based, as in the parallel case of Lord Auckland's removal of Dost Muhammad, on a mixture of prejudice and poor (or non-existent) intelligence. If at first sight the Russians appeared to have a stronger case for invading Khiva than the British had had in Afghanistan, their specific grievances against Allah Quli Khan were only part of the story. Like the British, they came to see their

---

[47] Enclosure in Likhamerstov to Perovskii, 24/05/1840 TsGARKaz F.4 Op.1 D.2182 ll. 16*ob* (original Turki document), 19–*ob* (Russian translation). Note: I have translated this from the Russian, and then compared this with such parts of the Turki that I have been able to decipher with the assistance of a friend who prefers to remain anonymous. Those parts in square brackets, [ ], are taken from the Turki text; those parts in wavy brackets, { }, occur only in the Russian translation.

invasion as a means of countering a threat from another Great Power in Asia and, like the British, they had devised an ill-thought-out scheme to impose a ruler of their choice on a neighbouring state, in the expectation that, as 'Asiatics', the population would simply submit. Both powers also indulged in dubious legal justifications for their acts of aggression – the British by claiming that Dost Muhammad was a usurper, while Ivanin later asserted that in the eighteenth century the Khivans had chosen five Khans in succession who were 'Russian subjects' by virtue of being 'Kirgiz' (Qazaq – these were the Chinggissid puppets in whose name the Qunghrats had ruled until 1804), and that therefore Russia had an 'indisputable claim' to sovereignty over Khiva.[48] However, the political failings of the Russian plans for Khiva were never revealed as starkly as those of the British occupation of Afghanistan, because the Russian forces never reached their destination. The most significant aspect of the Khiva expedition was that it first introduced the Russians to the sheer logistical difficulties of campaigning in the steppe – and their overwhelming reliance on the humble camel.

2.2   Pray for the Camels

By comparison with the 21,000 men who in 1839 marched from Hindustan into Afghanistan with the army of the Indus (which faced its own massive logistical challenges),[49] General V. A. Perovskii's expedition to Khiva was relatively small, with only 5,000 men, but it had to cross some of the most hostile territory on the planet, carrying all of its supplies, as there was no possibility of living off the land. The main challenges to the expedition were thus always logistical rather than military, as Perovskii had predicted at the outset: 'the success of the military enterprise against Khiva will be founded almost exclusively on the correct assessment and consideration of the means and methods for the supplying of men and horses'.[50] Everything – not just supplies for the men, but forage for the pack animals – had to be carried with the force, which would really be a gigantic caravan.[51] Perovskii's plan for the invasion involved sending out a substantial advance party of troops with Bashkir sappers under the command of Colonel Geke to construct two temporary fortifications which would act as supply depots for the main column at Aty-Yakshi on the Emba and at Chushqa-Kul on the river Aq Bulaq, at the edge of the Ust-Yurt plateau. Some indication of what lay in store for the expedition could be seen in the fate of this force. Although out of 7,878 men

[48] Ivanin/Golosov, 'Pokhod v Khivu', VS (1863), No. 3, 34; Anon., Narrative, 39.
[49] On this see Morrison, 'Camels and Colonial Armies', 462–76.
[50] 'Vsepoddaneishii doklad General-ad'iutanta Perovskago' 7/02/1839, in Serebrennikov, Sbornik. Vol. 1. 1839 g. Doc.6, 12.
[51] Ivanin/Golosov, 'Pokhod v Khivu', VS (1863), No. 2, 322–3; Anon., Russian Military Expedition to Khiva, 95.

only 193 died (most of them Bashkir auxiliaries), out of the 23,290 horses used for transport no fewer than 8,869 died or were lost.[52] This underlined the fact that the only feasible means of transport for this colossal quantity of material through the steppe was the camel.

Initially it was proposed to purchase the camels from the Qazaqs for 150 roubles each, and to hire the drivers separately, but Perovskii soon wrote to say that it would make much more sense to hire the camels together with drivers, as buying them was prohibitively expensive, whilst 'without the careful attentions of their actual owners the greater part will not survive the campaign'.[53] In principle this was sensible: fifty years later the British army's chief expert on camels would write that 'There can be no question about this. To look after camels you require men who have owned, bred, and driven camels all their lives – who know their ways, habits and characteristics most thoroughly, and who understand all their peculiarities and peccadilloes', though this was a precept the British themselves had rarely followed.[54]

Initially Perovskii hugely underestimated the numbers of camels that would be needed, stating that one camel for every 8–10 men would be sufficient. He anticipated a force of just over 6,000 men, with 2,207 horses, 400 Qazaqs to look after the livestock, and just 1,712 camels.[55] The Russians had never before attempted to send such a large expedition so deep into Central Asia, and at this stage they had no idea of the real numbers of camels that would be required. Eventually 10,400 camels would set off from Orenburg, although by then the estimated requirement for the expedition had risen to 12,000; the process of collecting them began in August 1838 and would last for almost eighteen months. The head of the Orenburg Frontier Commission, General Gens, sent out a series of orders to the Qazaq Sultans of the Junior Horde instructing them to collect fixed numbers of camels from the different sections under their authority, and bring them to Orenburg on a particular date.[56] The Russians were prepared to pay only ten silver roubles for the hire of each camel, five roubles less than the going rate for a caravan journey to Khiva or Bukhara, and this, combined with what Perovskii described as intransigence on the part of certain Qazaq tribes, meant that gathering the 8,000 camels he then estimated would be needed was taking

---

[52] Perovskii to Chernyshev 14/11/1839, in Serebrennikov, *Sbornik.* Vol. 1. *1839 g.* Doc.112, 174–5.

[53] Anon., 'Khivinskaya ekspeditsiya 1839 goda', *RS* (1873), Vol. 7, No. 2, 248; Perovskii to Chernyshev 09/05/1839, in Serebrennikov, *Sbornik.* Vol. 1. *1839 g.* Doc.24, 49.

[54] Arthur Glyn Leonard, *The Camel: Its Uses and Management* (London: Longmans, Green & Co., 1894), 254.

[55] 'Vsepoddaneishii doklad General-ad'iutanta Perovskago' 7/02/1839, in Serebrennikov, *Sbornik.* Vol. 1. *1839 g.* Doc.6, 15, 19–20.

[56] Gens to Sultan Bai Muhammad Aichuvakov 27/08/1838; Sultan Bai Muhammad Aichuvakov to Gens 12/09/1838 TsGARKaz F.4 Op.1 D.2167 'Materialy ob otpravke v Khivu voennogo otryada dlya osvobozhdeniya russkikh plennykh', ll. 1, 3ob–4ob.

longer than expected.[57] General Ivanin, Perovskii's commissariat chief, later claimed that only the Qazaqs of the Baiuli tribe refused to provide their quota and were duly chastised, but other groups also failed to produce theirs by the time of departure, suggesting that resistance and reluctance were rather more widespread than he was willing to admit in his published account.[58] Another indication of dissent comes from a letter sent by the *Biis* of the Nazarov division of the Junior Horde, who drew attention to the contribution they had made, but clearly disagreed with Perovskii's aggressive intentions towards Khiva and resented the disruption of trade caused by the interning of Khivan merchants which Perovskii had ordered in 1836:

> For the forces of his Majesty the Emperor which have set out we gave 2,500 sheep, 200 camels, 200 horses and 4 camp guides to accompany the force to Khiva. If there is some other assignment for us, then we are always ready to carry it out. In the letter to us sent with Davletkildi Bishbaev your Excellency was pleased to say that we should detain Khivan merchants with us, but this is entirely unjust, which is known to Sultan Yusuf.[59]

Eventually 18 influential Qazaqs would be decorated with gold and silver medals for the crucial role they had played in assembling the necessary camels, while 131 were listed as having made important contributions.[60] This highlights the total dependence of the Russian forces on the livestock and local knowledge supplied by the steppe's permanent inhabitants. Without huge efforts on the part of Qazaq sultans who owed allegiance to Russia, the Khiva expedition would never have left Orenburg at all. As we shall see in Chapter 7, this would be true for the successful 1873 expedition to Khiva as well. Nevertheless, while Ivanin acknowledged how indispensable the Qazaq drivers were (Figure 2.2), he would later write that 'on account of their knowledge of the characteristics of the camels, being accustomed to loading them and ministering to them, and also of their acquaintance with the steppe, their trustworthiness and loyalty to us were doubtful, and, in the case of a hostile attack, it would be necessary to take measures of precaution to prevent them not only from running away, but also from having any intercourse with the hostile Kirgiz and Khivans'.[61] This deep-rooted distrust of the Qazaqs as 'savages' and 'Muslim fanatics' would have disastrous consequences when the expedition faced its crisis in January 1840.

[57] Perovskii to Chernyshev 24/06/1839, in Serebrennikov, *Sbornik*. Vol. 1. *1839 g*. Doc.51, 80.

[58] Ivanin/Golosov, 'Pokhod v Khivu', *VS* (1863), No. 2, 354–5; Anon., *Russian Military Expedition to Khiva*, 121–2.

[59] The *Biis* of the Nazarov division to the head of the OPK, 30/01/1840 TsGARKaz F.4 Op.1 D.2167 l. 343.

[60] 'Spisok ordyntsev, okazavshykh userdie pri sbore verbliudov dlya uchenoi ekspeditsii' n. d. TsGARKaz F.4 Op.1 D.2167 ll. 213–19*ob*.

[61] Ivanin/Golosov, 'Pokhod v Khivu', *VS* (1863), No. 2, 323; Anon., *Narrative*, 96.

Figure 2.2 Camels carrying packs with rusks and oats. Note the Qazaq driver (Ivanin, *Opisanie zimnego pokhoda*, 1874).

In June 1839 Perovskii reported that other preparations were proceeding well; despite the poor harvest in the Orenburg region large quantities of *sukhari* (rusks) and pickled cabbage were being prepared, together with heavy woollen clothing for the soldiers.[62] However the 780 *pood*s of compressed gelatine made according to the 'Darset' (Dorset?) process which Perovskii asked for, and which had to be sent from central Russia, could not be prepared in time, and he had to be content with just 200.[63] Eventually the expedition would set off with the supplies listed in Table 2.1.

Alongside these staples the column carried salted cabbage and cucumbers, *salo* (in the steppe this was always sheep's tail fat, known as *dumba* or *kurdak*) and hog's lard, and onions, pepper, vinegar, honey, horseradish and other anti-scorbutics. Each camel must have been carrying at least 18 *pood*s (300 kg), which was towards the upper limit of what they could manage – by the 1860s the standard load for a camel on a military expedition in Orenburg was just 15 *pood*s, and in Siberia just 10.[64] It also suggests that over 7,000 camels were carrying fodder alone.

[62] Perovskii to Chernyshev 24/06/1839, in Serebrennikov, *Sbornik*. Vol. 1. *1839 g.* Doc.51, 78–81.
[63] Perovskii to Chernyshev 29/06/1839; Chernyshev to Perovskii 25/07/1839, in Serebrennikov, *Sbornik*. Vol. 1. *1839 g.* Docs.54 & 65, 83, 103.
[64] Miliutin to Diugamel 09/02/1864, in Serebrennikov, *Sbornik*. *1864 g.* Pt. *I* Doc.20, 45. While Leonard wrote that Bactrian camels could carry heavier loads than dromedaries, he

Table 2.1 *Supplies for the Khiva expedition*[a]

Item	Quantity
Sukhari (rusks)	11,653 *chetvert*'s (2,447,000 litres)
Krupy (buckwheat)	3,223 *chetvert*'s (677,000 litres)
Wine/vodka	8,286 *vedros* (101,000 litres)
Meat	13,954 *poods* (228 tonnes)
Salt	3,406 *poods* (56 tonnes)
Animal fodder (barley, oats, hay)	130,000 *poods* (2,100 tonnes)

[a] Ivanin/Golosov, 'Pokhod v Khivu', *VS* (1863), No. 2, 335, 337; Anon., *Narrative*, 108, 125; Ivanin, *Opisanie zimnego pokhoda*, 63–4; 1 *pood* = 16.4 kg; 1 *chetvert*' = 210 l; 1 *vedro* (bucket) = 12.3 l.

Colonel E. M. Kosyrev recalled the troops grumbling at the lack of vodka, although it was clearly listed (in abundant quantities) amongst the expedition's provisions. The great Russian lexicographer Vladimir Dal' (1801–1872), who accompanied the expedition in his capacity as Perovskii's secretary, certainly had access to some vodka, as he used it to play a trick on one of the scientists accompanying the expedition by making it appear that the snow had caught fire.[65] The men were also provided with immense quantities of warm clothing, much of it in imitation of the winter wear of the Qazaqs. Kosyrev later reminisced that, once wrapped up in their many layers of swaddling, great-coats, Qazaq woollen underpants, black broadcloth caps with visors and enormous felt boots, 'the soldiers were awkward and fat to the point of ugliness, and with a mask and a weapon in the left hand a soldier had already entirely lost his human form' (Figure 2.3).[66]

Despite the vast number of camels and the other preparations for the expedition, there was one commodity which could not be carried in anything like sufficient quantities, and that was water. It was largely for this reason that Perovskii made the fateful decision to launch the exped-ition in winter, when there would be snow to compensate for this defi-ciency. In this he was taking a calculated risk. The Russians were well aware of the probable effects of intense cold and wet, not only on the

did not believe the 'Brobdingnagian' figure of 480–880 lbs (200–400 kg) which Russian accounts of steppe expeditions claimed (*The Camel*, 205), but this suggests it was not so far from the truth.

[65] 11/01/1840 Dal', 'Pis'ma k druzyam', *RA* (1867), Vyp. 4, 618; Kosyrev, 'Pokhod v Khivu', 539–40.

[66] Kosyrev, 'Pokhod v Khivu', 539.

Figure 2.3 Orenburg Cossacks and line infantry in winter uniform (Ivanin, *Opisanie zimnego pokhoda*, 1874).

soldiers, but also on their transport. As Ivanin later wrote, one of the difficulties the Russians encountered was that

> As camels cannot endure cold, dampness and wet, they are mostly kept in the southern part of the steppe. This would naturally retard and render more difficult the collection of camels and their transmission to Orenburg, all the more so, as the southern Kirgiz tribes were less under Russian subjection than those in the north, being more amenable to the influence of Khiva.[67]

Had the Russians been in any doubt about the effects of cold and wet weather on the camels, their Qazaq guides and drivers would have told them. Already in September there were signs that the winter ahead would be an exceptionally harsh one. As Sultan Yusuf Nuraliev,[68] head of the middle section of the Orenburg Qazaqs, wrote:

[67] Ivanin/Golosov, 'Pokhod v Khivu', *VS* (1863), No. 2, 349; Anon., *Narrative*, 118.

[68] Nuraliev's *Formulyarnyi spisok* (record of service) reveals that he held the honorary rank of *Voiskovoi Starshina* and was fifty-three years old in 1839, having been in Russian service since 1830. TsGARKaz F.4 Op.1 D.1635, in *Istoriya Kazakhstana v russkikh istochnikakh XVI–XX vekov*. Vol. VIII. Pt. 2. *O pochetneishikh i vliyatel'neishikh ordynt-sakh* ed. B. T. Zhanaev (Almaty: Daik-Press, 2006), Doc.217, 17–20.

Figure 2.4   Cossack light horse (*sic*) artillery (Ivanin, *Opisanie zimnego pokhoda*, 1874).

With the onset of cold and foul weather for the camels under my jurisdiction, collected from the *Nazarovtsy*, hide blankets are essential for their
protection against frost and rain, which is what the Kirgiz usually use to save
their camels from falling victim, when they meet severe or cold weather. And
as here there are no hides, it would be desirable for the frontier commission
to order the delivery of these camels to the line or directly to the
Commission, as otherwise there could be severe losses amongst them.[69]

The illustrations accompanying Ivanin's account show that the expedition's
camels would indeed be provided with heavy leather jackets (Figure 2.4),
giving them the appearance of oddly shaped pantomime horses.
Nevertheless, the whole expedition was a gamble on the weather. As somebody
(possibly Dal') put it in a hastily written note on the expedition's departure:

With our arrival on the Ust-Yurt, pray that there will be snow, but not too
much; that the ground will not be frozen; that the storms will not last too
long; do not worry about frost in calm weather, but in general, for all that
they are animals and not Christians, pray for the camels as you would for
us sinners; without them there is no salvation for us.[70]

---

[69] Sultan Yusuf Nuraliev to Gens 9/09/1839, TsGARKaz F.4 Op.1 D.2167 l. 126.
[70] A letter without addressee or signature, probably from Vladimir Dal', Orenburg 18/11/
1839, in Serebrennikov, *Sbornik*. Vol. 1. *1839 g.* Doc.119, 191.

2.3   The Road to Aq Bulaq

Dal''s letters are probably the most vivid testimony we have of the hardships of the march as it progressed. In them we can trace the deteriorating condition of the camels, and with it the expedition's chances of success. Dal' was well aware both of the dependence of the expedition on its camels and of its consequent dependence on Qazaq drivers to manage them, not least because the drivers had to clear away the snow before the camels could eat. He expressed some misgivings about this, but concluded that there had been surprisingly few desertions.[71] He described how, even in the early stages, fuel was so scarce that they were burning 'the fresh dung from underneath the camels'.[72] They rose at 2 am, travelled for 15–23 *versts*, and then unloaded the camels and horses and turned them loose for 1½ to 2 hours to allow them to forage, having cleared away as much snow as they could from the ground.[73] On the 8 December the column ran into a terrible storm which halted the march altogether:

> The heavens are dull, the sun swims in a sort of semi-transparent dusk, pale and colourless. The horses stand in their frozen leather blankets as if in armour, hanging their heads and waiting for oats, their manes hanging down in icicles, drifts of snow cover their backs, the camels lie like dead things on their bedding, one alongside the other, like bales, like giant bundles or trunks, they chew what they ate yesterday, and today God willing![74]

Two weeks later Dal' wrote that almost a fifth of the camels were already sick and unfit to work, and a couple of days after that he estimated that, even including the sick ones, the expedition had only 8,000 of the 10,400 camels it started with. The force halted for almost a month at the fortification on the Emba, where an attempt was made to recover the strength of men and beasts whilst waiting for a break in the weather, but none came. The column was dependent on Qazaqs not only for transport, but also for its communications with Orenburg, which were carried by Qazaq messengers. By late December these too were coming under severe strain:

> In carrying out the request of the authorities I sent out at different times several Kirgiz [Qazaqs] in the wake of the force which has set out into the steppe with the Orenburg Military Governor and his companions, in order to take to them items and despatches sent from Orenburg; but up until now not one of these envoys has returned. [. . .] because of the great distance and because of the powerful storms and still more because of the

---

[71] 21/12/1839; 23/12/1839 Dal', 'Pis'ma k druzyam', *RA* (1867), Vyp. 3, 417, 424–5.
[72] 05/12/1839 Dal', 'Pis'ma k druzyam', *RA* (1867), Vyp. 3, 407–8.
[73] 05/12/1839 Dal', 'Pis'ma k druzyam', *RA* (1867), Vyp. 3, 408–9.
[74] 08/12/1839 Dal', 'Pis'ma k druzyam', *RA* (1867), Vyp. 3, 411.

emptiness in this expanse between my camp and the Aty-Yakshi *auls* near the fortress, constructed on the branch of the river Emba, these Kirgiz who were sent ahead may have lost their lives and thus also have lost state property. [. . .] All those whom I had prepared to carry designated packages have already been sent after the force which set out into the steppe. Now the Kirgiz ask me to represent to the authorities that they should give us an exemption from undertaking such hardships, owing to the distance and *aul*-lessness [i.e. lack of nomadic encampments] of these places.[75]

Throughout his later memoir of the expedition, Ivanin referred to the Qazaqs on whom the force relied for the management of its camels in the most disparaging terms, as 'Asiatics unworthy of entire confidence', and bemoaned the lack of reliable information about routes to Khiva because 'the testimony on these points of the Asiatics who have been there, because of their inclination to deceit [*obman*] and exaggeration, can in no degree be relied upon'.[76] He often noted the possibility that they might mutiny or go over to the Khivans. It was at this point that the only brush with Khivan forces occurred. On the 13 December the force of cavalry which had been despatched from Khiva a month earlier by Allah Quli Khan attacked the small garrison of 130 men which had been left to await the arrival of the main column in the fortress on the river Aq Bulaq. This was under the command of Captain Egor Petrovich Kovalevskii (1809–1868), who would go on to have a distinguished career as a traveller and diplomat – from 1856 until 1861 he would be director of the Asiatic Department of the Ministry of Foreign Affairs, and participated in many of the most crucial decisions relating to the Central Asian advance.

In a pattern that would be repeated in later steppe campaigns, the Khivan cavalry made several fruitless frontal attacks, but were beaten off by musket and artillery fire without loss to the garrison. The Khivan force then attacked an advance column of 140 men of the 1st Orenburg Line Battalion, 70 Ural Cossacks and 230 camels which had been sent forward from Aty-Yakshi to Aq Bulaq under Lt Erofeev, but squandered the advantage of surprise by attempting to carry off its camels and horses rather than attacking directly. Erofeev's force was without artillery and did not have the protection of fortifications, but was still able to drive them off with musketry, losing five killed in the process.[77] The enormous advantage which Russian infantry enjoyed over the irregular cavalry which at this date made up the bulk of the armed forces of the Central Asian khanates had been very clearly demonstrated, though in this case it would avail the Russians very little. During the attack, Ivanin claimed, some horsemen approached close enough to try to persuade the Qazaqs and Tatars

---

[75] Sultan Yusuf Nuraliev to General Gens 22/12/1839 TsGARKaz F.4 Op.1 D.2167 ll. 265–6.
[76] Ivanin/Golosov, 'Pokhod v Khivu', *VS* No. 2 (1863), 324–5; Anon., *Russian Military Expedition to Khiva*, 97.
[77] Ivanin, *Opisanie zimnego pokhoda*, 122–5; a terse description of the attack is also to be found in the *Riyaz ud-Daulat*, f. 227b: *MPITT*. Vol. II, 473.

with the force to abandon the Russians and join their fellow-believers, but without success.[78] This instance of loyalty does not seem to have moderated his suspicion of them, which was shared by Perovskii and would soon have disastrous consequences.

Matters came to a crisis when the main columns prepared to move off from the fortification at Aty-Yakshi on the river Emba, which they had reached only with the greatest difficulty, through still deeper snow to the advanced post at Aq Bulaq:

> Rumours had spread amongst the *Kaisaki* [Qazaqs] about the closeness of the Khivan forces in overwhelming numbers, about the uniting of the Khoqand troops with them & c. The enemy's spies made use of this, it would seem, and sought to shake their nerve with terrible threats from the Khivan Khan and with the undoubted preponderant numbers of his forces. In consequence of this the camel drivers of the whole column, more than 300 people, at the very moment of departure positively and unanimously stated that they would go no further, but would return with the camels to their *auls*. Every exhortation was in vain; I exhausted every spoken persuasion, but succeeded in nothing. The suggestions of Sultan Aichuvakov also had no effect. The crowd grew larger, noisy groups summoned their comrades; the disorder grew from minute to minute. [. . .] As Kirgiz [Qazaqs] from other columns began to join the crowd I had it surrounded, and told them that they would all be shot if they persisted in this disobedience. To this some of the most vehement, coming forward, stated that they were all prepared to die, but that to go on was against their faith, and that caravans never travelled when there was such a frost.[79]

Two of the ringleaders were shot, and the crowd dispersed. Revealingly, when Perovskii reminisced about this incident during a recuperative sojourn in Rome, he transformed it into a grotesque anecdote about a 'mullah' accompanying the expedition, who refused to obey orders and yielded only once Perovskii had shot two of his sons and was about to send the third to the firing-squad.[80] He had chosen to remember it as an instance of Islamic 'fanaticism', an interpretation echoed in other Russian accounts of the 'mutiny' and subsequent executions: Terent'ev and Zakhar'in refer to this as a moment of crisis, where Perovskii's decisive action saved the column from being stranded in the steppe by their unreliable Qazaq allies.[81] In his account Ivanin attributed the rebellion to Qazaq 'fanaticism' stimulated by Khivan propaganda. His description of this incident is clearly based on Perovskii's official despatch, and in places echoes it almost word for word. However, he placed a greater emphasis

---

[78] Ivanin, *Opisanie zimnego pokhoda*, 124.
[79] Perovskii to Chernyshev, 06/01/1840, in Serebrennikov, *Sbornik*. Vol. 2. *1840 g.* Doc.4, 3.
[80] 'Pis'ma Grafa V. A. Perovskago k A. Ya. Bulgakovu', *RA* No. 7 (1878), 314.
[81] Terent'ev, *Istoriya zavoevaniya*, I, 150–1; Zakhar'in, *Graf V. A. Perovskii*, 85–8.

on Khivan machinations and the 'wild shouts' of the Qazaqs, and said nothing about the more practical objections of the drivers to proceeding any further.[82] The Polish exile Peslyak testified that it was the freezing conditions that caused the Qazaq drivers to try to halt the expedition, although he also wrote that after two had been shot 'as an example' the rest then carried on with 'Asiatic fanaticism' and fatalistic indifference to life.[83] Dal', however, says that the Qazaqs claimed the camels were simply not up to the journey.[84] There is also a contradiction between what Perovskii originally reported the Qazaqs to have said and the reasons he and Ivanin then adduced for the mutiny. It seems clear that it was the sheer insanity of trying to travel in the steppe under such conditions that had aroused the drivers to such a dangerous step, not fears of a possible Khivan attack. In effect, they were telling Perovskii what he would belatedly discover for himself a month later. By that time, not only would over half his camels be dead, but also almost half his men would be either dead or incapacitated by frostbite and scurvy.

Despite these growing difficulties, at the beginning of January, as the force advanced to Aq Bulaq, Dal' was still full of bombast, writing that 'the camels cannot perish suddenly; we may lose a third on the way, or a half – and we will carry on until the last',[85] but just three days later he was forced to admit that the camels were now so tired, and progress so slow, that 'if we are going to move *like this*, then we will never reach it. Only yesterday, with a grieving heart, was I forced to accept this sad truth.'[86]

It was not until three weeks later, however, that Perovskii finally admitted that they could advance no further, and announced to the force that they would retreat to the Emba.[87] Two days later Dal' wrote that a further 2,000 camels had perished since advancing to Aq Bulaq – he quoted the Qazaqs as saying that many of the beasts supplied to the Russians had been sickly in the first place.[88] Perovskii himself wrote to his friend Bulgakov from Aq Bulaq the following day that 'The expedition has failed completely – our camels, which were not sustained by the moral force which had made us advance up to the *ne plus ultra* [!], have become enfeebled with frightening speed; we have lost more than a half, and the

[82] Ivanin/Golosov, 'Pokhod v Khivu', *VS* (1863), No. 3, 32–3; Anon., *Russian Military Expedition to Khiva*, 149; Ivanin, *Opisanie zimnego pokhoda*, 125–6.

[83] Peslyak, 'Zapiski', 586.

[84] 27/12/1839 Dal', 'Pis'ma k druzyam', *RA* (1867), Vyp. 3, 430–1.

[85] 08/01/1840 Dal', 'Pis'ma k druzyam', *RA* (1867), Vyp. 4, 612.

[86] 11/01/1840 Dal', 'Pis'ma k druzyam', *RA* (1867), Vyp. 4, 615–16.

[87] 'Prikaz po otryadu voisk Khivinskoi ekspeditsii' 01/02/1840, in Serebrennikov, *Sbornik.* Vol. 2. *1840 g.* Doc.22, 42; Ivanin/Golosov, 'Pokhod v Khivu', *VS* (1863), No. 3, 49. An English translation of the latter document can be found in Anon., *Military Expedition to Khiva*, 165–6.

[88] 03/02/1840 Dal', 'Pis'ma k druzyam', *RA* (1867), Vyp. 4, 624.

Гєн.Адъютъ Перовскій.   Ген.М. Ціолковскій.   Полковн.Кузьминскій. Офицеръ Оренбург Казачьяго Войска.   Н.В.Ханыковъ.В.И.Даль.

Figure 2.5 L–R, Perovskii, Tsiolkovskii, Col. Kuz'minskii, Orenburg Cossack Officer, N. V. Khanykov, V. I. Dal' (Ivanin, *Opisanie Zimnego Pokhoda*, 1874).

remainder have definitively refused to march with their loads.'[89] This would hugely hamper their retreat, which began the following day.

On the return march from Aq Bulaq to the Emba thousands more camels died, and Dal' wrote that, of those which were left, only 700 were fit, and he did not expect them to last long. The remainder were all invalids, many suffering from frostbitten legs and feet despite having been shod with warm boots. Mortality among the men was also high – among the 2,930 infantry 400, or one-seventh, were already dead.[90] Sultan Bai Muhammad Aichuvakov was sent out to round up as many camels as he could from the neighbouring Qazaq groups, and Perovskii wrote to Orenburg to urgently request that at least another 3,500 be rounded up and sent to the expedition's aid, but this proved extremely difficult.[91] As he wrote a month later, revealing both the desperate straits his force was in and the degree of coercion which had been required to secure the necessary camels in the first place:

> When the means and strength of this region were still fresh, and not used up, it was only with great difficulty that over eight months, in place of the 12,000 camels we had demanded, we gathered 10,400. These camels, hired for fairly negligible rates, or, to be more accurate, demanded, have perished; out of them only about a tenth have survived; the loss has been so significant that it extends to a million and a half [roubles], and the nomads

[89] '... les chameaux, qui n'étaient pas soutenus par la force morale qui nous a fait avancer jusqu'au *ne plus ultra* ...', Perovskii to Bulgakov 04/02/1840, 'Pis'ma Grafa V. A. Perovskogo k A. Ya. Bulgakovu', *RA* (1878), No. 7, 307.

[90] 21/02/1840 Dal', 'Pis'ma k druzyam', *RA* (1867), Vyp. 4, 636–7.

[91] Perovskii to Chernyshev 20/02/1840, in Serebrennikov, *Sbornik*. Vol. 2. *1840 g.* Doc.33, 57; Ivanin/Golosov, 'Pokhod v Khivu', *VS* (1863), No. 3, 52–3; Anon., *Russian Military Expedition to Khiva*, 168–70; 08/03/1840 Dal', 'Pis'ma k druzyam', *RA* (1867), Vyp. 4, 638.

[*ordyntsy*], of course, are unwilling to submit to a similar transaction and now it will be essential to send light military forces into the steppe for the purpose.[92]

In the same letter, however, he stubbornly continued to insist that late autumn and winter were still the only time when campaigning in the steppe was possible. The Khivans did not despatch another force of cavalry to Aq-Bulaq until March, when the thaw had begun. The *Riyaz ud-Daulat* records that the party of Chaudar Turkmen under 'Abdullah Yasawulbashi arrived on the 2 April to find the fortress deserted and the Russians gone.[93]

The remnants of the Khiva expedition would eventually limp home at the beginning of July 1840: 1,054 soldiers (and an unknown number of Qazaq drivers) had been 'buried on the steppe', and of those who were left over 600 were suffering from scurvy and the after-effects of frostbite: Kosyrev describes horrendous scenes in the military hospital at Orenburg, where the smell of rotting flesh rose from the bandaged stumps of their limbs.[94] He also attests to the devastating human impact the heavy mortality had in the small, highly militarised community of this frontier town. It is not clear what the effects of the camel holocaust were on the overall camel population of the steppe: in 1900 there were approximately 470,000 camels in the four northern steppe provinces, but it is very difficult to project this back fifty years.[95] In the early 1860s, when there was a boom in trade between Russia and Central Asia owing to increased demand for raw cotton during the American Civil War, between 15,000 and 25,000 camels arrived annually in Orenburg bearing goods from the south.[96] The volume of Russian trade with Central Asia was substantially higher in those years than it had been twenty-five years previously,[97] so the 10,000 camels lost in 1839–40 were probably the equivalent of or slightly more than the total number engaged in the caravan trade with Orenburg over an entire year. As we shall see, in 1845, when Governor-General Obruchev instructed the Orenburg Frontier Commission to secure 1,000 camels with Qazaq drivers to carry supplies to the new fortresses the Russians had constructed on the Irgiz and Turgai rivers, they faced immense difficulties in finding enough of them, as the shortage was still acute.[98]

---

[92] Perovskii to Chernyshev 21/03/1840, in Serebrennikov, *Sbornik*. Vol. 2. *1840 g.* Doc.60, 98.
[93] *MPITT*. Vol. II, 474; *Riyaz ud-Daulat*, f. 230b.
[94] Kosyrev, 'Pokhod v Khivu', 543–4.
[95] V. P. Semenov (ed.), *Rossiya: Pol'noe geograficheskoe opisanie nashego otechestva*. Vol. XVIII. *Kirgizskii krai* (St Pb.: Izd. A. F. Devriena, 1903), 241.
[96] 'Otchety Nachal'nikov Orenburgskogo Tamozhennogo Okruga', 1860, 1861, 1862, 1863 RGIA F.19 Op.3 D.961 l. 299; D.962 l. 287; D.963 l. 295; D.964 l. 28.
[97] Rozhkova, *Ekonomicheskie svyazi Rossii so Srednei Azii*, 58–69.
[98] Obruchev to the OPK 25/07/1845; OPK to Obruchev 09/08/1845 TsGARKaz F.4 Op.1 D.2344 ll. 1–*ob*, 36–47.

2.4   Ignoring the 'Native Voice'

To justify the Russian decision to retreat from Aq Bulaq, Ivanin referred to the British retreat from Kabul in the winter of 1842 as an example of what can happen to an exhausted and demoralised army set upon even by a militarily inferior enemy.[99] What this did not acknowledge, however, was that while the failure of the expedition was perhaps inevitable, given the climatic conditions, Perovskii's refusal to listen to his Qazaq drivers when they urged him to turn back at the Emba hugely increased both the human and the animal cost of this failure. By the time he himself decided to retreat a month later, half his camels were dead and the rest dying, while a third of his men were also either dead or incapacitated by frostbite and scurvy. In ignoring the views of those who actually lived on the steppe and failing to turn back earlier, when most of his camels were still alive, Perovskii was guilty of a folly almost as great as that of Macnaghten and Elphinstone at Kabul the following year. Well before this, Perovskii entirely ignored the repeated attempts of Allah Quli Khan to reach a negotiated settlement of the outstanding grievances between Russia and Khiva. As we have seen, the Russians responded to these overtures (which Ivanin would later describe as a typical instance of Oriental untrustworthiness) by detaining all Khivan ambassadors and merchants and refusing further dialogue.[100] The Russians shared this arrogance with their British competitors. In his parallel correspondence with the British, Allah Quli Khan had sent a straightforward response to a letter from Eldred Pottinger, the Political Officer in Herat, that had asked him to satisfy Russia's grievances by releasing the slaves at Khiva. After first pointing out that Yar Muhammad Khan, who ruled Herat under British auspices, was also a keen slave trader, Allah Quli Khan wrote that he was preparing for conflict with Russia and asked the British to send him some experienced artillerymen as a mark of their good faith.[101] The Government of India consistently refused to offer anything other than empty assurances of friendship. As the prime minister (*mehtar*) of Khiva bluntly told Abbott: 'What then have you come hither for? If you will grant none of our demands, of what use is it to call yourselves our allies?'[102]

As Kim Wagner has shown, although 'native informants' remained important to the British in the early nineteenth century and were often invoked to add authority to intelligence reports, the raw information they provided was increasingly ignored or woven into new and fantastical forms if it did not

---

[99] Ivanin/Golosov, 'Pokhod v Khivu', *VS* (1863), No. 3, 47–8; Anon., *Russian Military Expedition to Khiva*, 164.

[100] Ivanin/Golosov, 'Pokhod v Khivu', *VS* No. 1 (1863), 70–1; Anon., *Russian Military Expedition to Khiva*, 52–69.

[101] 'Firman addressed by the Khan Huzrut of Khiva to the British Envoy at Herat', recd. 10 December 1839, IOR/L/P&S/20/G10/3 No. 14, 9–10.

[102] Abbott, *Narrative*, I, 100.

coincide with official preconceptions.[103] Beyond the frontiers of the East India Company's territory, increasingly the crucial figure was not the independent local 'newswriter', but the British agent who reinterpreted his missives to suit his own purposes and repackaged them for Calcutta, of which Alexander Burnes was the pre-eminent example.[104] As Bayly and Hopkins have concluded, the growing British tendency to disregard information from 'native sources' was a crucial factor in the colossal intelligence failures that surrounded the First Anglo-Afghan War.[105] That Russian attitudes were very similar is confirmed by the failure of the Khiva expedition, which only got as far as it did thanks to the expertise of its Qazaq auxiliaries, and ended in disaster thanks to a refusal to listen to them. Whether we view Britain and Russia's aims in Central Asia as being primarily those of territorial annexation or dominance, or take at face value the claims made by their leaders that all they sought were stable frontiers, the protection of trade and the release of slaves, it is clear that both powers systematically undermined these aims through their failure to regard either Central Asian rulers or Central Asian informants as worthy of serious consideration as equal partners, and instead to assume their 'fanaticism', ignorance and bad faith from the very outset. This was to be a recurring pattern in Russian relations with Central Asian states and peoples over the next four decades.

Khiva would not fall to a Russian army until 1873, while, after the punitive expedition they sent to avenge the army of the Indus in the autumn of 1842, it would be almost forty years before the British were once again drawn into meddling in Afghanistan's internal affairs. Yapp has argued that both the British and the Russians suffered severe rebuffs in 1839–41 and realised that the costs of a 'forward strategy' in Central Asia outweighed the likely benefits.[106] While this might be true in the British case, the lessons Russia learned from the Khivan disaster were more complicated than those the British learnt in Afghanistan. First, it was not until 1842 that it became clear that the British adventure in Afghanistan had been a catastrophe. Until then, the Russians felt that they had been comprehensively outmanoeuvred (or at any rate out-spent) by the British in Central Asia. In January 1840 Major-General Verigin urged that the occupation of Khiva be made permanent once the expedition reached its destination, claiming that otherwise – 'instigated by the English and with the aid of their skilled officers' – the khanate would improve its defences and prove resistant to

[103] Kim Wagner, *Thuggee: Banditry and the British in Early Nineteenth-Century India* (Basingstoke: Palgrave Macmillan, 2007), 217–26.
[104] Hopkins, *Afghanistan*, 13–18, 41–5.
[105] Bayly, *Empire and Information*, 128–40; Hopkins, *Afghanistan*, 78–81.
[106] Yapp, *Strategies*, 413–18, 460.

future attacks.[107] The expedition's failure rendered such a scheme impossible
and deepened Russian worries still further. Perovskii wrote vehemently to
Nesselrode that, once Afghanistan had fallen, Bukhara could be next.[108]
Diugamel also wrote from Tehran that British influence would soon spread
from Afghanistan to the Caspian littoral, snuffing out Russian trade and
other interests and compromising its security.[109] In the same despatch
Diugamel also complained about Richmond Shakespear's activities in
Khiva. Russian paranoia was reinforced by the presence of British agents
beyond the Oxus. However inept James Abbott's mission to Khiva appears
with hindsight, he certainly succeeded in annoying Perovskii, who fulmin-
ated over his presumption and the flimsiness of his credentials.[110] Perovskii
and Nesselrode agreed that as Abbott's reception in Khiva did not appear to
have been particularly friendly or to have achieved a great deal, it would be
unwise to worsen relations with Britain by punishing him for what they
regarded as an illegitimate intrusion into Russia's foreign affairs.[111] In
September 1840, however, came the unwelcome news that Richmond
Shakespear had turned up at the Novo-Alexandrovsk fortress with 416
liberated Russian slaves: this was a more substantial blow, as he appeared
to have achieved single-handedly what the winter expedition of 1839–40 had
failed to.[112] Although Ishniyaz Mashetniyazov, an envoy from Allah-Quli
Khan who arrived in Orenburg in May 1841, assured Perovskii that the
decision to release Russian slaves had nothing to do with English pressure
or bribes, the humiliation remained.[113]

As this suggests, the failure of military force led to renewed Russian attempts
at diplomatic negotiation with Khiva, though in the long term these too would
be undermined by arrogance. In the spring of 1841 Captain Nikiforov of the
Main Staff was sent on a new mission to the Khan of Khiva, with instructions to
also proceed on to the Amir of Bukhara if possible, and to offer his services in
mediation between the two rulers if necessary in order to ward off future
conflict between them. The latter injunction by Nesselrode seems puzzling in
view of later Russian fears that the Central Asian khanates might combine
against Russia – by the 1850s conflict between Khiva and Bukhara was seen as

[107] 'Dopolnenie k zapiske Gen-m Verigina, predstavlennoi im v 1826 godu', 13/01/1840,
Serebrennikov, *Sbornik*. Vol. 2. *1840 g.* Doc.5, 15.
[108] Perovskii to Nesselrode 06/05/1841, AVPRI F.161 I-9 D.5 ll. 483–7 in *KRO*, 293–4.
[109] Diugamel to Nesselrode 5 February 1841, AVPRI, F.133 Op.469 1841 g. D.213 'Téhéran
(affaires de l'Asie)', ll. 54ob–56.
[110] Perovskii to Nesselrode 28/05/1840, in Serebrennikov, *Sbornik*. Vol. 2. *1840 g.* Doc.92,
146–47.
[111] Nesselrode to Perovskii 05/04/1840; Perovskii to Nesselrode, 08/07/1840, in
Serebrennikov, *Sbornik*. Vol. 2. *1840 g.* Docs.106 & 108, 180–5.
[112] Perovskii to Chernyshev 26/11/1840, in Serebrennikov, *Sbornik*. Vol. 2. *1840 g.* Doc.133,
217.
[113] Perovskii to Nesselrode 19/05/1841, in Serebrennikov, *Sbornik*. Vol. 3. *1841 g.*, 57–8.

in Russian interests – but is explained by his concern to prevent Khiva attacking Bukharan caravans, which were important for trade through Orenburg.[114] Nikiforov had participated in the attempted winter invasion of Khiva, where despite his junior rank he had effectively been Perovskii's chief of staff and right-hand man – Ivanin, who clearly disliked him, accused him of having intrigued to exclude a more experienced officer, Colonel Zhemchuzhnikov, from the post.[115] Both his closeness to Perovskii and his choice to lead the mission to Khiva are explained by a background in the Guards, from which Nikiforov had been expelled to an Orenburg line battalion for refusing to fight a duel, reputedly to protect a lady's name.[116] Accompanied by two surveyors and an escort of twelve Cossacks and ten Qazaq irregulars, bearing gifts that included a silver samovar and tea-service, he set out in mid May, and reached Khiva two months later. The aims of Nikiforov's mission were almost identical to those the Russians had hoped to achieve by military force – the release of any remaining Russian captives and an end to what the Russians saw as Khivan meddling among the Qazaqs over whom they claimed sovereignty, and to attacks on caravans.[117] An additional, though less urgent goal, was to secure the release of Persian slaves held in Khiva.[118] The incomplete transcription of Nikiforov's conversation with Allah Quli Khan suggested a bland but cordial exchange (which curiously enough was mostly devoted to discussion of the First Opium War between Britain and China).[119] Zakhar'in, who had access to oral testimony from one of the surveyors who witnessed Nikiforov's audience, wrote that in fact his mission was a complete failure because of the proud and arrogant way in which he had conducted himself towards the Khan, apparently with the idea of impressing him with the extent of Russian power: 'you must stick as closely to Russia as a shirt does to a body, because Russia is a great power, which, if it falls on you, will crush you utterly just as my shoe does a small beetle on the road' – something which was unlikely to seem convincing so soon after the failure of the winter invasion.[120] His own report concentrated mainly on describing the city of Khiva and the region around the Syr-Darya, but he did record one interesting remark from Allah Quli Khan:

> Khan Allah-Quli in his justification told me one day when I said to him
> that Khiva alone acts with such hostility to Russia, buying Russian

---

[114] Nesselrode to Nikiforov 19/02/1841, in Serebrennikov, *Sbornik*. Vol. 3. *1841 g.*, 27–9.

[115] Ivanin, *Opisanie*, 78.

[116] I. N. Zakhar'in, 'Posol'stvo v Khivu v 1842 godu (po rasskazam i zapiskam ochevidtsa)', *IV* (1894), No. 11, 428–9.

[117] Perovskii to Nikiforov 12/05/1841; Nikiforov to Perovskii 17/07/1841, in Serebrennikov, *Sbornik*. Vol. 3. *1841 g.*, 47–50, 80; I. Zalesov, 'Posol'stvo v Khivu Kapitana Nikiforova v 1841 g.', *VS* (1861), No. 11, 41–92.

[118] Eden, *Slavery and Empire*, 43–4.

[119] 'Kratkii otchet o peregovorakh Kap. Nikiforova s khanom Alla-Kulom', 15/08/1841, in Serebrennikov, *Sbornik*. Vol. 3. *1841 g.*, 94–5.

[120] Zakhar'in, 'Posol'stvo v Khivu', 430.

prisoners from the Turkmen, and that the Amir of Bukhara does not do
this: – 'You think that only Khiva does this to Russia? All Muslims by right
can trade, buy and keep Russians in captivity. I do not want to be an
informer, but you will find out that there are many Russian prisoners in
Bukhara.'[121]

Nikiforov's low rank and lack of plenipotentiary powers also indicated that the
Russians were not interested in negotiating on equal terms, and instead still
sought to intimidate.

Another Russian mission to Khiva, led by Lt-Col. Danilevskii, set out from
Orenburg in August 1842, arriving in mid October. The embassy was complicated
by the fact that Allah Quli Khan died not long after it arrived, and his successor
Rahim Quli Khan showed considerable hostility to his Russian guests and repeatedly delayed his meeting with them. After being warned by a runaway Russian
soldier (of whom there seem to have been many in Khiva) that the new Khan was
planning a Bekovich-Cherkasskii-style massacre of the Russian mission,
Danilevskii threatened Russian reprisals. In the end he was not only able to depart
unmolested, but secured a commercial agreement whereby Khiva undertook to
limit Turkmen raiding and protect caravan traffic, and was accompanied by
a Khivan ambassador who was then permitted to proceed to St Petersburg.[122]
The other concrete achievement of the embassy was a surreptitious survey of the
routes to Khiva and the geography of the city undertaken by Zelenin, the
topographer who accompanied the embassy. Zakhar'in's jaundiced conclusion
was that any attempt to treat with the Khivans on equal terms was simply taken as
a sign of weakness, and that the Khivans never had any intention of upholding
even the limited agreement they had reached with Danilevskii.[123] It is true that
Muhammad 'Ali Khan, a Qajar ambassador who was in Khiva at the same time as
Danilevskii, attempting to secure the release of Persian slaves, seems to have found
the Khivans just as intransigent and difficult to negotiate with as the Russians did,
so this was not purely a matter of European cultural prejudice.[124] Raids and
slaving continued unabated, and the Khivans did not respect the agreement signed
with Danilevskii – but then again, neither did the Russians, who had undertaken
to recognise the Syr-Darya as Khiva's north-eastern boundary, but who nevertheless conquered this region from 1847 onwards. They would not send another
embassy to Khiva until 1858, when the Ignat'ev mission arrived backed by
gunboats of the Aral Sea Flotilla, designed to awe and intimidate.[125] Under
those circumstances it is hardly surprising that the then Khan, Sayyid

---

[121] Nikiforov to Perovskii 02/10/1841, in Serebrennikov, *Sbornik*. Vol. 3. *1841 g.*, 117–19.
[122] N. Zalesov, 'Posol'stvo v Khivu Podpolkovnika Danilevskogo v 1842 g.', *VS* (1866), No. 5,
41–75; Zakhar'in, 'Posol'stvo v Khivu', 431–47.
[123] Zakhar'in, 'Posol'stvo v Khivu', 446–7.
[124] Eden, *Slavery and Empire*, 41–7.
[125] Ignat'ev to Kovalevskii 25/10/1857 GARF F.730 Op.1 D.287 ll. 18, 24–5; Ignat'ev to
Kovalevskii 24/05/1858 GARF F.730 Op.1 D.289 l. 151.

Muhammad, informed Ignat'ev that he had no record of any agreement signed with Danilevskii, prompting Ignat'ev to dismiss this and all agreements signed with Central Asian rulers as 'political fluff' (*politicheskii puf*).[126]

As this suggests, the Russian response to the failure of the winter invasion of Khiva was not confined to, or even primarily reliant on, diplomacy. Even before the remains of the Khivan expedition had returned to Orenburg, officials were raising the question of how to maintain Russia's prestige in Central Asia and counter perceptions of weakness. Prince Menshikov proposed a fort on the Syr-Darya as a means of responding to the debacle: 'The taking of Kabul by the English and the approach of their forces to Bukhara must now, without doubt, be considered the main factor opposed to our influence', and that the best means of combating it was to project Russian influence deep into the steppe through fortifications.[127] As we shall see in the following chapter, this would indeed become the cornerstone of future Russian policy in Central Asia. While the British were so scarred by their experience in Afghanistan that they left it alone for forty years, the Russians drew practical lessons from the failure of the Khivan expedition and did not abandon their determination to subdue both the nomadic peoples who populated the empire's southern frontier and the sedentary states beyond them, which they assumed were responsible for most of the military problems they encountered in the steppe. As Ivanin put it in a dyspeptic response to the unauthorised publication of his reminiscences, the expedition had at least taught some tactical lessons about steppe warfare.[128] The ease with which Kovalevskii's tiny force had repelled a much larger number of Khivan attackers from behind the hastily erected fortifications at Chushqa-Kul told its own story. Perovskii's failure had shown that the difficulties of movement and maintaining supply lines needed for steppe campaigning meant that long-distance expeditions were not feasible. Instead the Russians would push their frontier south by building a new line of fortresses, beginning in 1845 with the construction of small forts on the rivers Irgiz and Turgai by Perovskii's successor as governor of Orenburg, General V. A. Obruchev.

[126] Zakhar'in, 'Posol'stvo v Khivu', 447; N. P. Ignat'ev, *Missiya v Khivu i Bukharu v 1858 g.* (St Pb.: Gosudarstvennaya Tip., 1897), 188; John W. Strong, 'The Ignat'ev Mission to Khiva and Bukhara in 1858', *Canadian Slavonic Papers* 17/2–3 (1975), 251–5. Ignat'ev was similarly dismissive of the 1841 mission to the 'cunning' Amir of Bukhara, Nasrullah: GARF F.730 Op.1 D.289 l. 15.
[127] 'Zapiska knyazya Menshikova o predpolozhenii osnovat' na r. Syr-Dar'e sil'noe ukreplenie s poseleniem', 04/03/1840, in Serebrennikov, *Sbornik*. Vol. 2. Doc.43, 72–3.
[128] Ivanin, 'Zametki', 484.

3

'This Particularly Painful Place': The Failure of the Syr-Darya Line as a Frontier, 1841–63

> This Fortress is a Talisman which is the first gateway into the land of the People of Islam of *Ma wara' al-nahr*
>
> Mullah Niyaz Khoqandi, *Ta'rikh-i Shahrukhi* (1871)

The capture of Aq Masjid in 1853 deserves to stand alongside the fall of Tashkent as a central event of the Russian conquest of Central Asia. This small fortress, constructed by the Chitrali mercenary Lashkar Qushbegi during the latter part of the reign of the Khoqandi ruler Muhammad 'Ali Khan (r. 1823–1842), represented the northernmost limit of the khanate's authority in the *Dasht-i Qipchaq*.[1] Unlike Turkestan or Aulie-Ata to the south, Aq Masjid was not a fortified town and contained no religious monuments, and its importance was almost entirely strategic and fiscal, as it served as a centre for the levying of *zakat* on the livestock of Qazaqs over whom the khanate claimed sovereignty, and as a base for a Khoqandi garrison. Whilst earlier Russian forts at Irgiz, Turgai and Raim were all built on virgin sites, this represented the first which had been seized by force of arms from the enemy. For both Tsarist and Central Asian historians, the taking of Aq Masjid was a triumph of Russian arms which would leave Turkestan wide open to further Russian conquests. As we saw in Chapter 1, the historical volume of General Konstantin Petrovich von Kaufman's 1871 *Turkestan Album* opened with a dramatic portrait of Perovskii, presented as having redeemed his failure against Khiva in 1839–40 with this successful siege. The album also contained reproductions of the maps and sketches of the old Khoqandi fortress, together with images of the new fortifications the Russians had constructed. Aq Masjid was the first Central Asian settlement to have its very name replaced and Russianised, and until 1918 it would be known as Perovsk, after its conqueror (not until 1912 and 1915 would Generals Skobelev and Chernyaev be similarly honoured with the short-lived renamings of, respectively, New Marghelan and Chimkent).[2] Writing forty years later, the iconoclastic military historian

---

[1] Beisembiev, *Ta'rikh-i Shakhrukhi*, 17; Levi, *The Rise of Khoqand*, 132.
[2] Although the original name continued in use in the vernacular, at least until the 1880s: *TJT*, f. 113b.

114

M. L. Iudin was highly critical of Perovskii's handling of the siege, but even he saw the fall of Aq Masjid as a crucial turning-point, as Russian attention turned away from Khiva and towards Khoqand and Bukhara.[3] For Mullah Niyaz Muhammad Khoqandi, writing with the benefit of hindsight in 1871, after the reduction of Khoqand to a rump in the Ferghana valley, but before the khanate's final annexation, the fall of Aq Masjid signalled nothing less than the conquest of the whole of the sedentary regions of Central Asia:

> The unbelievers [kuffar], having taken the fortress, began to talk among themselves. 'Is this how to rule the world? This fortress is a talisman which is the first gateway into the land of the people of Islam of Ma wara' al-nahr [ke inchonin qala talesmat ra, ke avval darvaza-i mulk-i ahl-i islam-i ma wara' al-nahr ast]. This fortress, with an abundance of all the products of nature, they allowed it to slip from their hands. They ignored this province, and those brave men, who together with their wives did not want to be taken prisoner and attained martyrdom. This province – is the gateway to all Muslim domains; it is the navel of the Qipchaq lands [naf-i zamin-i dasht-i qipchaq ast]; one can say that to him who rules this fortress will belong the whole of the Dasht-i Qipchaq. They should have resisted us at this place: if the Bukharans, Urganjis [Khivans] and Khoqandis had entered into discussions with each other, and put their enmity to one side, had united and from all three directions come here [Agar misahat midashtand yakdigar khusumat-i khudha-ra bar taraf namuda va yakdala kardid, bukharayi va urganji va khoqandi dar inja az se taraf rasid dakhl mikardand], it would have been very easy for them to resist us, as among those things essential for an army we had neither clothing nor food. Now we can receive both from this very province; now it will be difficult for these kingdoms to repel us.' Thus they spoke among each other.[4]

Apart from the divisions between Bukhara, Khiva and Khoqand which Khoqandi bemoaned here, Khoqand also suffered from internal political rivalry between its sedentary ('Sart') and nomadic ('Qipchaq) elements, each of which had their partisans in the Khanate's historiography.[5] Coming just

---

[3] M. L. Iudin, *Vzyatie Ak-Mecheti v 1853 godu kak nachalo zavoevaniya Kokandskogo khanstva* (Moscow: Izd. Vladimira Bolasheva, 1917), 45. Soviet historians paid little attention to it, however, as it was a clear instance of unprovoked Russian aggression in Central Asia, and did not fit their preposterous economic explanation for the conquest. See Khalfin, *Politika Rossii*, 26.

[4] *TSh*, 199–200; V. V. Bartol'd, 'Tuzemets o russkom zavoevanii', in *Sochineniya* II (2) (Moscow: Izd. Vostochnoi Literatury, 1964), 335–7; T. K. Beisembiev, *Kokandskaya istoriografiya: Issledovanie po istochnikovedeniiu Srednei Azii XVIII–XIX vekov* (Almaty: TOO Print-S, 2009), 272.

[5] In 1842 the Qipchaqs under Musulmanqul had deposed and exiled the young Khudoyar Khan, who was then restored after a rebellion and massacre of the Qipchaqs in 1852. The *TSh* is strongly pro-Khudoyar Khan, whereas the *TA* is a pro-Qipchaq narrative: Beisembiev, *Annotated Indices*, 21–2.

one year after the fall of the Qipchaq ascendancy in the Khoqand Khanate and the restoration of Khudoyar Khan, Khoqandi considered the loss of the fortress so shameful that in his history he deliberately misdated it to 1856, so that he could blame it on the negligence of Khudoyar's brother, Malla Khan, who became governor of Tashkent in that year, and would eventually overthrow him in 1858.[6] The fall of the fortress to the Russians prompted the Khoqandis to send an embassy to the East India Company at Peshawar, in an (ultimately fruitless) plea for military assistance,[7] and contributed significantly to the chronic political instability from which Khoqand suffered during the last twenty years of its existence.

3.1   V. A. Obruchev and the Initiation of a Fortress Strategy

In 1860 the famous steppe strategist and military geographer Mikhail Veniukov (1832–1901) published an article in *Voennyi Sbornik* in which he described the difficulties of steppe warfare, and the solutions which, he argued, had been found for some of them during the 1840s.[8] He quoted with approval an unidentified manuscript on the subject of 'steppe expeditions' by a brother officer which concluded that decisive victories were well-nigh impossible to achieve, as, even if you found the enemy, he would flee as soon as the artillery opened up. Instead, the path to the control of the steppe was the punitive destruction of nomadic *auls* (although this should be done with moderation, as it could generate bitterness) and, above all, the construction of fortresses. To this Veniukov himself added that these fortifications should not be considered mere passive defensive positions, but be employed as supply bases for constant punitive expeditions into the steppe. In cases where the garrison was besieged, fortifications gave Russian troops an overwhelming advantage, and he cited in evidence the assault by 13,000 Khoqandis on a Russian garrison of just 700 in Fort Perovskii in 1854, which led to the enemy suffering enormous casualties and losing most of their artillery. He wrote that he would not enlarge on the political significance of these fortresses, but like most of his contemporaries he dated the shift in Russian strategy towards the building of fortifications in the

---

[6] 'After the fourteenth year since the accession of Khudoyar Khan [1856–7] Malla Khan [his brother] was appointed governor of the province [*vilayat*] of Tashkent. [. . .] Malla Khan did not concern himself with the defence of the *Dasht-i Qipchaq*, and did not receive any news on the condition in which the commanders of the local fortresses found themselves.' *TSh*, 199; Bartol'd, 'Tuzemets o russkom zavoevanii', 335; Beisembiev, *Ta'rikh-i Shakhrukhi*, 131.

[7] NAI/Foreign/S.C./24 November 1854/Nos. 1–22, *Account of the Khanate of Kokand*, 32–3.

[8] On Veniukov see A. V. Remnev, 'U istokov Rossiiskoi Imperskoi geopolitiki: Aziyatskie pogranichnye prostranstva v issledovaniyakh M. I. Veniukova', *IZ* 4/122 (2001), 344–69; A. Kuznetsova, 'M. I. Veniukov i Imperskie proekty Rossii v Srednei Azii', *Vestnik Evrazii* 4/19 (2002), 72–84.

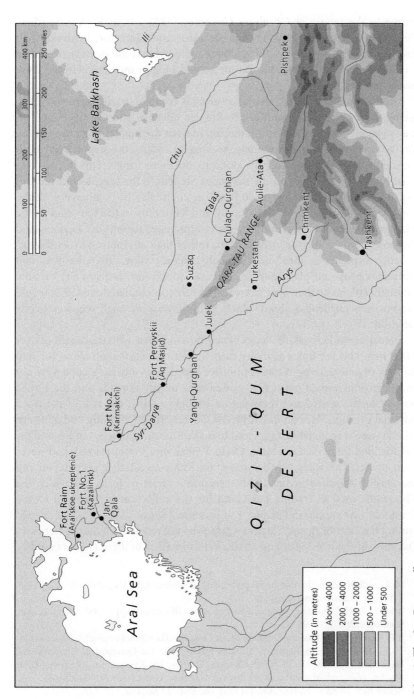

Map 3 The Syr-Darya valley

steppe to the tenure as Orenburg Governor (1842–51) of V. A. Obruchev. Veniukov noted that Obruchev's predecessor and successor, Perovskii, had strongly disagreed with the change, but concluded that the strategy of mobile forces based in fixed fortifications represented a happy medium between these two schools of thought.[9]

Although to some extent Veniukov and his contemporaries were correct in seeing this as a turning-point in the Russian advance into Central Asia,[10] in many ways it was only a logical extension of what the Russians had been doing for the previous 100 years: namely, seeking to control the steppe from what were effectively fortified *kasbahs* along its northern fringe. This in turn was what Muscovy had done on the Black Sea Steppes in the seventeenth century with the creation of the Belgorod line.[11] It could also be compared with the 'siege strategy' of Generals Veliaminov and Yermolov in the Caucasus in the 1820s, which involved surrounding the mountainous regions of Chechnya and Daghestan with a ring of fortifications, rather than attempting to send long-distance expeditions into such difficult terrain.[12] The difference was that Obruchev proposed placing these fortresses much further from any existing Russian settlement than had previously been contemplated, and this would present new challenges about which Veniukov, as we shall see, was overly sanguine.

The failure of Perovskii's winter expedition to Khiva, with the deaths of over 1,000 men and ten times as many camels, carried a clear message to Russian military planners. Long-distance punitive expeditions into the steppe were not an effective means of projecting power over unruly nomads and the settled powers to the south, and their failure brought with it the risk of damaged imperial prestige. At the same time the Governors of Orenburg and Western Siberia were convinced that the need to make Russian authority felt beyond the old fortified lines via Orenburg, Orsk, Troitsk and Petropavlovsk had never been greater. This was partly because of the Khoqand Khanate's expansion into the *Dasht-i Qipchaq* in the 1830s, creating a series of fortresses which the Khoqandis used as trading posts and for the collection of *zakat* on Qazaq livestock.[13] As we saw in Chapter 1, it was also because of the disorder created among the Orenburg and Siberian Qazaqs by the rebellion of Sultan Kenesary Qasimov in the late 1830s and 1840s. Whilst neither of these factors could be

---

[9] M. Veniukov, 'Zametki o stepnykh pokhodakh v Srednei Azii', *VS* (1860), No. 12, 294–6.
[10] Terent'ev, *Istoriya zavoevaniya*, I, 203.
[11] Brian L. Davies, *Warfare, State and Society on the Black Sea Steppe 1500–1700* (London: Routledge, 2007), 78–95.
[12] J. F. Baddeley, *The Russian Conquest of the Caucasus* (London: Longmans, Green & Co., 1908), 106–64; Moshe Gammer, 'Russian Strategies in the Conquest of Chechnia and Daghestan 1825–1859', *The North Caucasus Barrier: The Russian Advance towards the Muslim World* ed. Marie Bennigsen Broxup (London: Hurst & Co., 1992), 45–61.
[13] Beisembiev *Ta'rikh-i Shakhrukhi*, 17; Levi *The Rise of Khoqand*, 119–122.

said to constitute a really serious military threat to Russia's existing frontier, both disrupted caravan traffic across the steppe and, perhaps more importantly, challenged Russia's claim to sovereignty over the Qazaqs of the Junior and Middle Hordes. To this was added, as a distant background note, the vague threat of expanding British influence in Central Asia, although Russian fears on this score were calmed, at least temporarily, by the disastrous retreat from Kabul in the winter of 1841–2. Relations with Kenesary and with Khoqand were a much more pressing concern.

Kenesary first came to Russian attention in 1837, when he attacked and destroyed their fortress at Aqtau, causing over 38,000 roubles worth of damage.[14] In 1838, he attacked a caravan heading from Bukhara to Troitsk, and burnt down part of the Russian post at Akmolinsk. The customs authorities clamoured for military measures to be taken against him, but this proved easier said than done.[15] Over the next seven years he became a ubiquitous figure in Russian reports, invoked whenever a frontier raid had taken place even if there was no direct evidence of his involvement. At the same time, his raids – which were mainly aimed at carrying off livestock and hostages – were used as a pretext by the Russians to engage in exactly the same behaviour as that which they condemned. In November 1839 Colonel Ladyzhenskii, the head of the Siberian frontier administration, reported to P. D. Gorchakov with evident satisfaction the success of a Cossack raiding party led by Captain Mochul'skii against the 'rebellious Kirgiz' in carrying off almost 3,000 horses, 150 cows, 220 camels and 400 sheep and goats, as well as capturing the 'traitor' Sultan Baigary, his two wives, son, grandson and three daughters.[16] The following summer saw a systematic series of raids by Cossacks all along the Siberian frontier, ostensibly to punish 'rebellious Kirgiz' who followed Kenesary, but clearly aimed primarily at collecting horses for use as cavalry remounts, and other livestock as food or baggage animals for frontier garrisons (Table 3.1).

These figures are probably an underestimate – by August 1840 there were apparently 9,000 captured sheep at Karkaralinsk alone awaiting redistribution. As this indicates, these were not simply being seized as punishment, but for use – forty-three of the horses seized from the descendants of Kenesary's brother, Sarzhan, in the Karkaralinsk raid were considered suitable for use as military remounts, while the sheep were destined to be eaten by the troops of

---

[14] Compensation Commission to Gorchakov 30/10/1839 IAOO F.6 Op.1 D.108 'O voznagrazhdenii za ubytki, ponesennye ot myatezhnykh kirgizov' l.21ob.

[15] 'Donesenie nachal'nika Sibirskogo tamozhennogo okruga ministru finansov o napadenii sultana Kenesary Kasymova na torgovye karavany i o neobkhodimosti prinyat' reshitel'nye mery protiv nego' 20/03/1838 TsGARKaz F.806 Op.1 D.74 ll.184–192 in KRO, 288–291.

[16] Ladyzhenskii to Gorchakov 03/11/1839 IAOO F.6 Op.1 D.107, 'O skote, otbitom u myatezhnykh kirgizov', ll. 6–10.

Table 3.1 *Livestock seized on the Siberian Frontier, June–July 1840*[a]

Region/tribe	Horses	Cattle	Camels	Sheep and goats
Akmolinsk	–	88	213	4,722
Atbasar	112	–	56	405
Karkaralinsk	190	41	219	478
Kokshetau	–	14	31	3,720
Qipchaq	229	52	527	3,955
Baidaly-Suyunduk	–	32	32	6,505
Totals	531	227	1,078	19,785

[a] Compiled from figures in IAOO F.6 Op.1 D.115 ll. 3, 12–13, 84–85*ob*; D.121 l. 5, D.123 ll. 8–*ob*, 31; D.131 l. 6.

the 7th Cossack Regiment and the 7th and 8th Siberian Line Battalions.[17] In Kokshetau 600 of the captured sheep were given to selected loyal Qazaqs as a reward, 155 were eaten during the expedition, 130 died *en route*, and 400 were assigned to feed the garrison at Atbasar, while those seized in Akmolinsk were used to feed garrisons at Akmolinsk itself, Zhargalinsk and Petropavlovsk.[18] One imagines that the Qazaqs of the Middle Horde, if they had not been inclined to support Kenesary before, certainly would be after suffering these losses to their ostensible protectors.

As Virginia Martin has noted, *baramta* – the seizing of livestock in order to force the settlement of a dispute – was sanctioned under Qazaq customary law, or *'adat*, but had been criminalised under Speranskii's *Regulations for the Siberian Kirgiz* of 1822.[19] Its continuation among the Qazaqs, and in particular its use by Kenesary, was one of the principal grievances the Russian authorities complained of on their steppe frontier, a mark of the lack of civilisation of nomadic peoples. In 1840–1 the Siberian Frontier Commission recorded multiple cases of *baramta* every month, although few of them netted the

[17] 'Vedomost' o chisle skota otbitago otryadom sotnika Rebrova u detei Sarzhana 3 chisla iiulya'; Danilevskii to Gorchakov 17/08/1840 IAOO F.6 Op.1 D.115, 'O skote otbitom u kirgizov otryadom Sotnika Rebrova v 1840 g.', ll. 3, 12–13, 84–85*ob*, 92.

[18] 'Vedomost' o chisle otbitago skota iz volostei Sultana Kenesary Kasimova' 07/07/1840 IAOO F.6 Op.1 D.121, 'O skote otbitom u kirgizov otryadom Sotnika Volkova', ll. 5, 21–2*ob*; 'Vedomost' 06/06/1840; Maj.-Gen. Gaius, 'Raport', 17/06/1840 IAOO F.6 Op.1 D.123, 'O skote otbitom u myatezhnykh kirgizov Atbasarskim voennym otryadom', ll. 8–*ob*, 31; 'Vedomost' skotu', 20/06/1840; Faletskii to Gorchakov 02/10/1840 IAOO F.6 Op.1 D.131, 'O skote sobrannom na stepi otryadom Sotnika Lebedeva', ll. 6, 26–8.

[19] Virginia Martin, 'Barimta: Nomadic Custom, Imperial Crime', in *Russia's Orient. Imperial Borderlands and Peoples* ed. Daniel Brower & Edward Lazzerini (Bloomington, IN: Indiana University Press, 1997), 249–70; Martin, *Law and Custom in the Steppe*, 140–55.

quantities of livestock seized in Russian raids.[20] The latter were presented as a punitive measure enjoined by military necessity, but in fact, as we see here, raiding for livestock and captives was a normal part of the steppe economy in which the Russians themselves wholeheartedly engaged.[21] The difference was that the Russians conceived of their sovereignty over people, animals and territory as absolute, not contingent on their ability to protect them, and thus Kenesary's use of the same tactics was seen as unbearable insolence and a violation of that sovereignty – a pattern very similar to that which had prompted the winter expedition to Khiva a few years before.

While Russian punitive expeditions netted plenty of sheep, they did not succeed in capturing Kenesary himself. Veniukov noted that Kenesary's ability to evade the punitive expeditions which the Russians sent out into the steppe against him soon became legendary.[22] In 1841, in a rather catty letter to Gorchakov, with whom he had a bitter personal rivalry,[23] Perovskii had concluded that

> Many years' experience has demonstrated the uselessness of the efforts of the troops of the Siberian corps in the Kirgiz steppe against the rebel Kenesary. On the one hand, the difficulty of searching the steppe, and on the other the ease with which the Kirgiz can escape the military forces, sufficiently prove the uselessness of such enterprises; no less than this, the band of the rebel sultan grows each year, sometimes very considerably over the previous number, and in the future there are few hopes of limiting these disorders. Expeditions against Kenesary, whilst they carry no threat to him, have given cause for the punishment of entire Kirgiz tribes and have thus only increased the hatred of this people for Russia.[24]

He did not, however, propose any alternative military strategy, instead advocating that an offer from Kenesary to cease his raids in return for protection against the Khoqandis be taken seriously. Much as Perovskii might have wished otherwise, the Sultan's depredations were not limited to the Siberian jurisdiction, and the Orenburg forces were no more effective at chastising him. Perovskii was transferred from his post early in 1842, and left the problem of Kenesary to be solved by his successor in Orenburg, V. A. Obruchev.

In 1843 the Orenburg Frontier Commission received a series of petitions from the Qazaqs under its jurisdiction complaining of raids by Kenesary on their livestock, and that 'the Russian forces sent out into the steppe have done

---

[20] See IAOO F.3 Op.2 D.1879, 'Vedomosti o proisshestviyakh po Kirgizskoi stepi', 11/02/1840–08/03/1841.

[21] Eden, *Slavery and Empire*, 19.

[22] Veniukov 'Zametki o stepnykh pokhodakh', 278.

[23] Bekmakhanov, *Kazakhstan v 20–40 gody XIX veka*, 358–9.

[24] Perovskii to P. D. Gorchakov 21/11/1841, in Serebrennikov, *Sbornik*. Vol. 3. *1841 g.* Doc.69, 136.

nothing.'[25] In August–November 1844 a new expedition was prepared under the leadership of Colonels Dunikovskii and Kovalevskii, including a force of 200 Qazaqs under the leadership of Sultan Ahmad Jan Tura, ruler of the eastern section of the horde, who was one of the original petitioners.[26] One column from Orenburg, under the command of *Voiskovaya Starshina* (Lt-Col.) Lebedev, attempted to match Kasimov's speed and mobility by dispensing with the cumbersome baggage train of camels which normally accompanied Russian forces, instead having his Cossacks carry light rations on their horses, but he proved unable to find Kenesary, attacked an innocent *aul* and was discharged, meaning this experiment was not repeated.[27] In February 1844 a force of Siberian Cossacks under Esaul Rybin succeeded in finding Kenesary's *aul* in the Aqchita depression. Kenesary himself was absent, and they managed to take the 500 or so men who had been left to guard the camp unawares by pretending to be his force returning, holding up a 'Kirgiz standard' which they had captured. Dispersing resistance with a salvo of case-shot, they succeeded in capturing Kenesary's senior wife, Qunymjan, together with twenty-three other women and several children. Kenesary responded with an emollient letter, asking Esaul Rybin, as a brave man, to return the women and children: 'for quieting the tears of these unfortunates you will receive reward in the hereafter.'[28] Once again demonstrating their understanding of steppe norms regarding captive-taking, the Russians held them hostage until Kenesary agreed to give up his own prisoners, which he did in January 1845.[29] The Russians then sent an embassy to his *aul* to return his wife, giving Kenesary the opportunity to remind the Russian envoy, Dolgov, that he was a grandson of Ablai Khan and rightful ruler of all the Qazaqs – which as we have seen was a recurring theme in all Kenesary's correspondence. Obruchev concluded that, while Kenesary had behaved 'honourably' in giving up his prisoners, the policy of engagement with him hadn't worked, as he had soon resumed raiding.[30] General Zhemchuzhnikov, chief of staff of the Western Siberian Corps, outlined the principal reasons for Russian failure in

[25] Petitions from the *Biis* of the Chumkeevskii lineage, from Sultan Sapali Murzaaliev and Sultan Ahmad Janturin to the OPK, 29/10/1843, 21/10/1843, 04/01/1844 TsGARKaz F.4 Op.1 D.2232 ll. 287–*ob*, 296–*ob*, 349–52.

[26] 'Formulyarnyi spisok o sluzhbe i dostoinstve pravitelya Vostochnoi chasti orenburgskikh kazakhov Sultana Akhmeda Dzhantiurina', in *Istoriya Kazakhstana v russkikh istochnikakh XVI–XX vekov*. Vol. 8, Pt. 2. *O pochetneishikh i vliyatel'neishikh ordyntsakh* ed. B. T. Zhanaev & I. V. Erofeeva (Almaty: Daik-Press, 2006), No. 221, 43–5.

[27] Bekmakhanov, *Kazakhstan v 20–40 gody XIX veka*, 260–1.

[28] Vishnevskii to Gorchakov 25/04/1844; Kenesary to Rybin n.d. IAOO F.6 Op.1 D.164, 'Ob imushchestve, loshadyakh i verbliudakh, otbitykh otryadom pod komandoiu Esaula Rybina, u myatezhnago Sultana Kenesary Kasimova', ll. 3, 6.

[29] Obruchev to Chernyshev 02/01/1845, in Serebrennikov, *Sbornik*. Vol. 4. *1845 g.*, 50–3.

[30] Dolgov to the OPK recd. 09/05/1845 RGVIA F.483 Op.1 D.14 l. 203; Obruchev to Chernyshev 29/05/1845, in Serebrennikov, *Sbornik*. Vol. 4. *1845 g.*, 126–9.

a series of notes on the campaigns against Kenesary in the summer of 1844: 'Kenesary's advantage over our forces in terms of speed of movement constitutes the most important factor against us [. . .] our forces, moving on the same horses across vast distances, are usually completely exhausted already before any clash with Kenesary.' The latter, he claimed, had over 20,000 horses and could always be sure of fresh mounts. Only in early Spring, when his horses would be tired from the winter and some normally dry river-beds were rendered impassable by melting snow, could there be any chance of coming up with him.[31]

The conclusion reached by Obruchev was that punitive expeditions were pointless – at least if understood as a means of suppressing Kenesary's rebellion rather than of feeding and mounting steppe garrisons on the cheap. Instead he argued that during the summer months the Russians should establish fortified posts much deeper in the steppe than hitherto, and he suggested three sites: one at the junction of the rivers Irgiz and Turgai, one on the river Irgiz opposite the desert of Air-Qizil-Kum, and a third near Airiuk, in the western part of the Mugojar mountains. These were only to be occupied temporarily, and would be abandoned during the winter months each year when movement on the steppe almost ground to a halt.[32] After Chernyshev pronounced himself in favour,[33] Obruchev's initial proposal was accepted in revised form by the Asiatic committee, whose other members were Gorchakov and Nesselrode. They considered that attempting to establish three far-flung temporary posts of this kind in the Qazaq steppe carried significant political risks and, perhaps more importantly, at an estimated annual cost of 60,000 silver roubles, would be much too expensive. Instead they authorised the establishment of two *permanent* fortresses, whose sites were eventually fixed, with one on the river Turgai between the sands of Tusun and the heights of Talpaq, and the other on the Irgiz near Air-Qizil, as originally proposed, the third site being rejected by Nesselrode.[34] Welcoming this decision, Obruchev drew attention to the particular challenges posed by constructing fortresses so far from the nearest Russian settlements, or indeed from areas with arable crops:

[31] General Zhemchuzhnikov, 'Zapiska o deistviyakh sibirskikh otryadov v stepi, v techenii leta 1844 goda', 16/11/1844 RGVIA F.483 Op.1 D.14 ll. 2–4; also published in Serebrennikov, *Sbornik*. Vol. 4. *1844 g.* Doc.12, 24–6.

[32] General V. A. Obruchev, 'O merakh k prekrashcheniiu grabitel'stvo proizvodimykh myatezhnym Sultanom Kenisary Kasimovym v kirgizskoi orde Orenburgskago vedomstva i k unichtozheniiu po vosmozhnosti vliyaniya ego', 14/11/1844 RGVIA F.483 Op.1 D.14 l. 13ob; also published in Serebrennikov, *Sbornik*. Vol. 4. *1844 g.* Doc.14, 28–44.

[33] Chernyshev to Nesselrode 28/11/1844, in Serebrennikov, *Sbornik*. Vol. 4. *1844 g.* Doc.17, 47.

[34] Asiatic Committee to Obruchev 23/03/1845; Chernyshev to Obruchev 02/04/1845; Obruchev to Chernyshev 27/04/1845; Nesselrode to P. D. Gorchakov 28/04/1845 RGVIA F.483 Op.1 D.14 ll. 55–ob, 65–73ob, 75–7ob, 94; this correspondence was published in Serebrennikov, *Sbornik*. Vol. 4. *1845 g.*, 69–95.

> The Orenburg Kirgiz steppe represents an entirely flat plain, the greater
> part of which is made up of saline and waterless areas [...] many of the
> rivers contain bitter water, and only in some places along the course of
> rivers is there abundant pasture. In consequence, there is a dearth of local
> means for the erection of permanent forts. Not only building materials,
> but also living supplies and even fuel are not plentiful.[35]

Accordingly everything for the initial construction and future supply of the
fortresses would have to be brought from the Orenburg and Siberian lines,
over 400 *versts* away. Obruchev instructed the Orenburg Frontier Commission
to hire 1,000 camels at a rate of three roubles each from the Orenburg Qazaqs
for the carriage of supplies. Owing to a harsh winter, and also perhaps to the
continued after-effects of the terrible mortality amongst the camels of the
Khiva expedition five years earlier, only 543 could eventually be found, even
though Sultan Muhammad 'Ali Tauke, the assistant to the Sultan of the
western section of the Orenburg Cossacks, claimed to have offered as much
as ten roubles per camel.[36] These numbers were merely a foretaste of the
growing transport needs generated by the two new fortresses in the future:
by 1847 the annual caravan despatched from the Orenburg line to supply them
consisted of 1,500 camels.[37]

The fortress on the Turgai river was built by men of the 6th Orenburg Line
Battalion, and was hence often confusingly known as the 'Orenburgskoe
ukreplenie'; that on the Irgiz was built by Ural Cossacks, under the command
of Lt-Col. Nazarov, a veteran of the Khiva expedition, and was known as the
'Ural'skoe ukreplenie'. The total cost of construction for the two was estimated
at 65,059 roubles, and Obruchev wrote that he believed part of this would be
compensated for by increased receipts for the *kibitochnyi sbor* (the tax on
kibitkas, or nomadic households) on the local Qazaqs. Nesselrode dismissed
this, saying that costs had already risen to 18,000 roubles more than
Obruchev's original estimate, and that, as the average total receipts for the
kibitochnyi sbor over the previous few years had rarely amounted to more than
60,000 roubles, there would clearly be a shortfall. These objections were
brushed aside, although some semblance of fiscal responsibility was maintained when the Ministry of Finance asked for customs agents to be posted in
the new fortifications to develop and regulate trade with the Qazaqs. In June
the Tsar gave his approval to the plans, and by the end of July both

---

[35] Obruchev to Chernyshev 19/05/1845 RGVIA F.483 Op.1 D.14 ll. 114*ob* –5, also published
in Serebrennikov, *Sbornik*. Vol. 4. *1845 g.* Doc.20, 95–105.

[36] Obruchev to the OPK 25/07/1845; Muhammad 'Ali Tauke to the OPK. 31/07/1845; Col.
Isaev to the OPK 06/10/1845 TsGARKaz F.4 Op.1 D.2344, 'O naime 1000 verbliudov dlya
svoza prodovolstvennykh pripasov v vnov' zavodim na r.r. Turgai i Irgiz ukrepleniya', ll.
1–*ob*, 19, 133–40.

[37] I. F. Blaramberg, *Vospominaniya* ed. N. A. Khalfin (Moscow: Izd. Vostochnoi Literatury,
1978), 285.

fortifications were complete, and had been occupied by their garrisons 'with beat of drum (*s barabannym boem*)' even before the interior buildings had been erected.[38] These were small fortifications: the Ural'sk fortress on the Irgiz had a rectangular earthen breastwork 80 sazhens by 60 (150 × 200 yards) and a garrison of 280 men. The interior buildings were of clay, although at least they had wooden roofs, a luxury lacking further south in the steppe, and there was a small brick church whose roof was thatched with reeds.[39] By 1863 this had been replaced by a small stone church with an iron roof, although the other buildings were still constructed with unbaked bricks.[40]

Even as the first two forts were being completed, Obruchev was arguing for the construction of a new fortress much deeper in the steppe, which would allow the Russians to control the mouth of the Syr-Darya and explore the possibilities of steam navigation on that river and the Aral Sea in preparation for a renewed attack on Khiva. In 1846 a small reconnoitring expedition under Captain Lemm, who had a training in astronomy and had undertaken topographical work in Persia, and Captain Schulz of the Main Staff, was despatched to find a suitable spot. They reported enthusiastically that the Raim peninsula, near the point where the Syr-Darya debouched into the Aral, was both strategically desirable and sufficiently fertile to be able to provide up to a million *poods* of wheat.[41] There was initial reluctance from St Petersburg, where Nesselrode argued that constructing a new fortress so far from the Orenburg line was premature, as the Khivans and Bukharans had still not fully digested the effects of the Orenburg and Ural'sk fortresses, and that it would be enormously expensive.[42] However, Nicholas I expressed personal enthusiasm for the project, suggesting that funds and materials set aside for a fortress on the river Temir could be better employed at Raim, and Obruchev further urged the political benefits which would flow from controlling the mouth of the Syr-Darya, both in terms of influence over Khoqand and Khiva, and also by invoking the spectre of British influence.[43] Fort Raim was more massively constructed than either Irgiz or Turgai, as it was considerably more remote: 1,300 camels were required to carry supplies when the fortress was built in 1847, and several Qazaq leaders were rewarded with medals and titles for their

---

[38] Obruchev to Chernyshev 19/05/1845; Nesselrode to P. D. Gorchakov n.d.; Chernyshev to Obruchev 06/06/1845; Department of International Trade, Ministry of Finance to the War Ministry 08/06/1845; Obruchev to Chernyshev 13/08/1845 & 17/08/1845 RGVIA F.483 Op.1 D.14 ll. 121, 139, 164*ob*–5, 196–*ob*, 197–*ob*, 238*ob*, 242*ob*.

[39] A. N. Gren, 'Pis'ma iz Forta Perovskii (Ak-Mechet') 31/08/1859', *VS* (1859), No. 12, 455, 458.

[40] Fedor Lobysevich, 'Syr-Dar'inskaya liniya', *VS* (1864), No. 6, 401.

[41] Obruchev to Chernyshev 24/12/1846, in Serebrennikov, *Sbornik*. Vol. 4. *1846 g.*, 306–13.

[42] Nesselrode to Chernyshev 16/01/1847, in Serebrennikov, *Sbornik*. Vol. 5. *1847 g.*, 12–14.

[43] Chernyshev to Obruchev 20/01/1847; Obruchev to Chernyshev 31/01/1847, in Serebrennikov, *Sbornik*. Vol. 5. *1847 g.*, 14–17, 21–8; Blaramberg, *Vospominaniya*, 278–9; Iudin, *Vzyatie Ak-Mecheti*, 41; Kilian, 'Allies and Adversaries', 215–19.

assistance in the enterprise.[44] I. F. Blaramberg described vividly the 'colossal caravan' of camels and *telegas* which set off from Orenburg in May 1847 under Obruchev's personal command carrying supplies to last a garrison of 700 men for a year, together with all the building materials for constructing the new fortress. These included disassembled schooners and barques, three windmills, barrels of tar, canvas, oars, masts and yards, bricks for building stoves and lime, of which there was a shortage in the southern steppe: 'it was a mobile colony, carrying with it everything for distant settlement'. The spot which had been chosen was a Qazaq burial ground, and it took its name of 'Raim' (or, more correctly, Rahim) after the tomb of Raim *Batyr* which stood there. Obruchev found that the water supply was sufficient, but the ground surrounding was barren clay or marsh. It was, however, good for brick-making, and 1,500 workmen, soldiers, Bashkirs and Qazaqs were soon employed in erecting fortifications and barracks.[45] The wood for the buildings had to be brought from Bashkiria, over 1,000 *versts* distant, as the marshy surroundings of the Syr-Darya estuary yielded little in the way of either building materials or supplies: 'the surroundings of Raim abound with rushes: there are no meadows and the horses are fed on young reeds and barley, bought from the Qazaqs nomadising nearby. It may be that, with time, meadows of the kind existing in Khiva, Bukhara and Persia can be created by irrigation. Reeds are also used in place of fuel.'[46] By the end of 1847 the fortifications were complete, and the schooners had been launched on the Aral. These wooden vessels were joined in 1853 by a pair of iron steamships (named *Obruchev* and *Perovskii*), made in England and assembled in a temporary slipway on the Syr-Darya below the walls of Fort Raim by Captain Alexei Butakov. These ships would enable Butakov to carry out the first complete survey of the shores of the Aral Sea in 1848–9.[47] The artist who accompanied this expedition was none other than the exiled Ukrainian poet Taras Shevchenko, whose sketches form the main visual record of Raim and its surroundings at that time (Figure 3.1[48]). The Aral Sea flotilla would also

---

[44] Zhanaev & Erofeeva (ed.), *O pochetneishikh i vliyatel'neishikh ordyntsakh*, 117, 198, 254, 261, 564.

[45] Blaramberg, *Vospominaniya*, 286–7; the remains of the fortifications are still visible above the small fishing village of Raim. See E. Iu. Demidova, A. S. Morrison & A. R. Sabitov, 'Rossiiskie ukreplennye poseleniya Raim i Vernyi: Graficheskaya rekonstruktsiya', *Vestnik TiumGASU* (2015), No. 3, 73–9.

[46] *Voenno-statisticheskoe obozrenie Rossiiskoi Imperii*. Vol. 14, Pt. 3. *Zemli Kirgiz-kaisakov vnutrennei (Bukeevskoi) i zaural'skoi (Maloi) Ordy, Orenburgskogo vedomstva* ed. I. F. Blaramberg (St Pb.: n.p., 1848), 115–16.

[47] Alexey Butakoff, 'Survey of the Sea of Aral', *JRGS* 23 (1853), 93–101; N. L. Korzhenevskii (ed.), *Dnevnye zapiski plavaniya A. I. Butakova po Aral'skomu Moriu v 1848–1849 gg.* (Tashkent: Izd. AN UzSSR, 1957).

[48] Taras Shevchenko, *Polnoe sobranie sochinenii v 10-i tomakh*. Vol. 8 (Kiev: Izd. AN USSR, 1962), No. 11, p. 10.

Figure 3.1 Taras Shevchenko, Interior of Fort Raim, with the Ruined Mausoleum of Raim Batyr in the Foreground (1848). © National Museum of Taras Shevchenko, Kyiv, inv. No. Г-449.

be used for reconnoitring the upper reaches of the Syr-Darya and (eventually) transporting N. P. Ignat'ev's embassy to Khiva and Bukhara in 1858.

By 1847, then, the Russians had established a permanent presence at the mouth of the Syr-Darya and were exploring the possibilities that steam navigation offered of liberating them from their perennial need for slow and expensive camel transport. There were already signs, however, that Fort Raim might cause as many problems as it solved. As early as August 1847, Batyr Jan Khoja Nurmuhammadov wrote to the commander of the Fort, Lt-Col. Erofeev, to tell him that since its construction his relations with Khiva and Khoqand had worsened, and that his people had been forced to migrate to the left bank of the Syr-Darya to avoid their depredations. The punitive expedition sent out by Erofeev along the valley of the Syr-Darya managed to drive off a group of Khivan forces near the fortress of Jan-Qala, but without inflicting a decisive defeat.[49] In 1849 Obruchev reported rumours of an impending Khivan attack on the fortress itself, which seemed to be as much a provocation as a deterrent.[50] Whilst Raim provided an excellent base for exploring the Aral Sea and the great rivers which flowed into it, its usefulness in

[49] Jan Khoja Nurmuhammad to Erofeev 20/08/1847; Obruchev to Nesselrode AVPRI F.161 I-9 D.5 ll. 671–79, 681–3, published in *KRO*, 339–40, 343–4. In 1856 Jan Khoja Nurmuhammad would rebel against the Russians, suggesting that his request for support was more opportunistic than anything else.

[50] Obruchev to Chernyshev 14/03/[1849] RGVIA F.483 Op.1 D.22 ll. 13–14, published in *Prisoedinenie Kazakhstana i Srednei Azii k Rossii (XVIII–XIX veka): Dokumenty* ed. N. E. Bekmakhanova (Moscow: Institut Rossiiskoi Istorii RAN, 2008), Doc.42, 141–2. Bekmakhanova misdates this letter to 1839, something quite impossible as this would be three years before Obruchev became Governor and eight years before Fort Raim was even constructed.

securing the frontier against either Khiva or Khoqand was limited. Obruchev soon began to advocate further conquests.

In March 1851 Obruchev sent a lengthy report to the War Ministry in which he referred to an article in the *Allgemeine Augsburger Zeitung* stating that the British were planning to advance in Afghanistan again, and might soon be launching vessels on the Amu-Darya. To counter this 'threat' (which it is hard to imagine he really believed in), he advocated a twin-pronged advance, with the main thrust along the Amu-Darya towards Khiva, but with another force to seize Aq Masjid 'through which we will defend our Kirgiz [. . .] and beyond this acquire strong influence over Tashkent and Khoqand' without, so he argued, facing any significant military difficulties. He received a blunt refusal from St Petersburg, as Chernyshev informed him that the Emperor was firmly opposed to the idea.[51] As we shall see, when the same proposal was put forward by his favourite, Perovskii, a year later, the Tsar would prove more accommodating. On his return to Orenburg as Governor-General in May 1851, Perovskii was initially contemptuous of Obruchev's 'fortress strategy' in the steppe (as he was of almost all his predecessor's undertakings), writing in November that year that 'unfortunately the experience of several years has shown all too clearly how little steppe fortresses bring about a reduction in *baramta* and raiding amongst the Qazaq tribes'.[52] In January 1852, however, in response to a suggestion from Gustav Khristianovich Gasfort (1794–1874), the Governor of Western Siberia, the Tsar authorised the creation of a new frontier line along a string of lakes which was thought to link the most advanced Siberian outposts with the Syr-Darya (Russian understanding of the geography of the region was still extremely vague). When Gasfort enquired about the feasibility of extending the Orenburg frontier to meet the proposed new limits of Siberian jurisdiction on the River Chu, Perovskii responded coolly:

> The experience of several years has shown that in their current location the permanent occupation of points is insufficient for the suppression of internecine strife in the horde, and that in order to maintain peace there mobile forces are more useful than fortresses, which rarely unite in themselves the first necessities of self-sufficiency: good water for the garrison and sufficient fodder for the horses.[53]

Whilst he continued to maintain that the steppe fortresses of the Orenburg line were not particularly useful in their current state, Perovskii came to use this as an argument for the further consolidation and expansion of Russian influence in the region, rather than a retreat. However, where Obruchev had seen the best line of advance as lying along the Amu-Darya towards Khiva, by 1852 St Petersburg had decided that suppressing Khoqand's influence in the

[51] Obruchev to Chernyshev 27/03/1851, in Serebrennikov, *Sbornik*. Vol. 8. *1851 g.*, 49–52.
[52] Perovskii to Chernyshev 06/11/1851, in Serebrennikov, *Sbornik*. Vol. 8. *1851 g.*, 155.
[53] Perovskii to Gasfort 20/01/1852, in Serebrennikov, *Sbornik*. Vol. 8. *1852 g.*, 7.

steppe was the priority, and that the line of the Syr-Darya could become a firm new frontier with good communications (aided by the recent launch of the two steamers on the Aral) which would serve to contain that khanate.[54] Even before the assault on Aq Masjid had been authorised, plans were already well advanced to move part of the Russian garrison from the bleak and exposed surroundings of Fort Raim to a more sheltered location at Kazaly, slightly upstream along the Syr-Darya, something to which the Tsar gave his assent without demur, provided Perovskii himself inspected the site to ensure its suitability.[55] At the same time a series of raids by parties of horsemen, whom Perovskii believed had been despatched from the Khivan fortress of Khoja-Niyaz and the Khoqandi fortresses of Aq Masjid and Julek, started to direct his attention towards the necessity of eliminating these challenges to Russian sovereignty.[56] In June there came further apparent provocation when a small surveying party of eighty men under Lt Golov was warned by the commander of Aq Masjid that any attempt to proceed further up the Syr-Darya would be countered with force. In response Perovskii ordered an experienced military topographer of Prussian origin, Colonel I. F. Blaramberg, to proceed upriver with a stronger reconnaissance column of 125 infantry and 200 Cossacks. Although ostensibly once again their purpose was to carry out a survey of the Syr-Darya, Perovskii gave him discretion to attack and destroy Aq Masjid if it proved to be on the right bank of the river (the Russians still did not know), as if so it would be an obstacle to the proposed new frontier line between the Syr-Darya and the Chu. Blaramberg duly made an initial assault on Aq Masjid in July 1852, but it was unsuccessful (according to Blaramberg's own account) because his column did not have proper siege equipment:

> Some soldiers rushed towards the gates of the citadel. However, the Khoqandis during the previous night had erected a thick wall (traverse) using large quantities of moist clay blocks, which closed off the gates of the citadel, leaving only a narrow passage for them along both walls. I gave orders to roll two guns into the outer fortress, set them at a distance of about 15 *sazhen*s in front of the traverse and tried to destroy it; but the shells embedded themselves in the clay wall, as if it were soft soap, and remained sticking out of it; even 10-pound grenades, when they exploded, caused little damage to the traverse.[57]

[54] Iudin, *Vzyatie Ak-Mecheti*, 43–4.
[55] 'Obshchaya vedomost' o materialakh, potrebnykh dlya vozvedeniya postroek v Kazalinskom forte', 30/12/1851; Dolgorukov to Perovskii 13/02/1852 RGVIA F.1441 Op.1 D.47, 'O vozvedenii na reke Syr Dar'e forta Kazaly (No. 1go)', ll. 6–9, 18; Perovskii to Dolgorukov 29/01/1852, in Serebrennikov, *Sbornik.* Vol. 8. *1852 g.*, 9–10.
[56] Perovskii to Dolgorukov 23/12/1851; Perovskii to Dolgorukov 06/04/1852, in Serebrennikov, *Sbornik.* Vol. 8. *1852 g.*, 187–8, 75–6.
[57] Blaramberg, *Vospominaniya*, 306.

The premature frontal assault failed with the loss of ten dead and forty wounded. Blaramberg may have exaggerated the size and extent of Aq Masjid's defences in order to exonerate himself, but the garrison's successful resistance under Muhammad Riza Bahadur-bashi, the deputy of the then governor Yaqub Beg (1820–1877) (who hastened with a large force from Tashkent to lift the siege), was remembered as a particularly heroic episode by the Khoqandi historian Mullah Yunus Tashkandi in his *Ta'rikh-i 'Aliquli* fifty years later.[58] To the Russians it was clear that prestige demanded both that this setback be quickly overcome, and that no further chances could be taken the second time around – the Tsar himself wrote on Perovskii's report that 'I am apprehensive that this latest mishap will make the Asiatics still more insolent; we must wait for the end of the expedition to decide what to do; in any case it follows that we should not begin a new expedition without means that will unquestionably give us victory.'[59]

3.2 The Siege of Aq Masjid and the Creation of the Syr-Darya Line

In January 1853 Perovksii presented a new proposal to Prince V. A. Dolgorukov (1804–1868), who had succeeded Chernyshev as War Minister in 1852, for the construction of four new fortresses along the right bank of the Syr-Darya. It included the well-nigh obligatory assertion that, despite the considerable initial expense (which he estimated at 173,000 roubles, with an annual maintenance and supply cost of 330,000 roubles), this would soon pay for itself, as it would open up 'a new and rich source of revenue', both from increased receipts from the *kibitochnaya podat'* (the household tax on the Qazaqs) and from greater security for caravans:

> Furthermore, knowing the terrain well, I can put forward a positive assurance that all means employed in establishing us solidly on the Syr-Darya should be considered as money placed very advantageously: not three years will have passed before the Kirgiz will have paid all the capital and interest of the advances that we will make. The profit which will be yielded to commerce by the complete security of caravans will also be immediate and much more considerable.[60]

---

[58] *TA* trans. 35, text ff. 23a–b; Mullah Yunus no doubt also placed particular emphasis on the defence of Aq Masjid as it was one of the last achievements which could be credited to the Qipchaq regime in Khoqand.

[59] Perovskii to Dolgorukov 16/08/1852 (postscript), in Serebrennikov, *Sbornik.* Vol. 8. *1852 g.* Doc.40, 136–42.

[60] 'De plus, connaissant bien le terrain [*sic*] je puis émettre l'assurance positive que toute soins employée à nous établir d'une manière solide sur le S[yr]. D[arya]. doit être considérée comme de l'argent placé très avantageusement: il ne passera pas trois ans et les Quirguiz auront payée [tout le] capital et intérêts des avances que nous allons faire. Le profit qu'en retira le commerce par la sécurité complète des caravanes, sera aussi

This would turn out to be hopelessly optimistic; it was clear that Perovskii saw the main importance of Aq Masjid as strategic rather than fiscal, and was offering this spurious financial argument to sweeten the pill of military necessity. Fort Raim, he argued, was unable to protect Russian Qazaqs from Khivan and Khoqandi raids, and a more advanced frontier would make it much easier to wield influence over those two khanates.[61] The key was Aq Masjid, which he considered 'especially important from the strategic point of view'.[62] The War Ministry agreed, adding that punishing the Khoqandis for Blaramberg's defeat the year before was essential to maintain Russian prestige.[63] Perovskii's close personal relationship with Nicholas I meant that, in stark contrast to Obruchev's experience, obtaining the Tsar's approval presented few difficulties, as Dolgorukov reported:

> The Emperor has received with considerable interest, my dear General, your project concerning the occupation of the Syr-Darya, and has deigned to trace with his own hand the decisions which have been suggested to him by the attentive examination of this important question. [...] I believe I must reiterate to you that our August Master, in giving you full latitude for your operations on the Syr, relies on your experience only to attempt enterprises of which the success can be guaranteed by the means of action of which you dispose. All those things which you have demanded of the Emperor are accorded to you, and his Majesty has but to await the notice of your definite intentions. [...] Your constant solicitude for the soldier offers to the Emperor the assurance that you have already thought to furnish the garrisons destined to winter in the new forts with anti-scorbutic rations, such as horseradish, garlic, pepper, vinegar, lemon juice, in sufficient quantities, and it would also be desirable that they will not want for fresh meat.[64]

---

immédiat et bien plus considérable.' Perovskii to Dolgorukov, 29/01/1853 RGVIA F.483 Op.1 D.31 ll. 51ob-2.

[61] Iudin, *Vzyatie Ak-Mecheti*, 77.

[62] 'Predpolozhenie o zanyatii reki Syr-Dar'i', RGVIA F.483 Op.1 D.31 ll. 4, 7.

[63] Memorandum from the War Ministry 18/02/1853 RGVIA F.483 Op.1 D.31 ll. 65-ob.

[64] 'L'Empereur à accueilli avec beaucoup d'intérêt, mon cher General, votre projet concernant l'occupation du Syr-Daria, et a daigné tracer de sa propre main les décisions que lui a suggéré l'examen attentif de cette question importante. [...] je crois devoir vous réitérer ici que notre Auguste Maitre, en vous donnant pleine latitude pour vos opérations sur le Syr, s'en remet à votre expérience pour ne tenter que les entreprises dont le succès sera garanti par le moyens d'action, dont vous disposes. Tous ceux que Vous avez demandés à l'Empereur Vous sont accordés et sa Majesté n'a plus qu'à attendre l'avis de vos déterminations définitives. [...] Votre constante sollicitude pour le soldat offre à l'Empereur l'assurance que vous avez déjà pensé à fournir les garnisons destinées a hivernée dans les nouveaux forts de comestibles anti-scorbutiques, tels que: raifort, ail, poivre, vinaigre, jus de citron, en quantités suffisantes, il serait encore à desirée que la viande fraiche ne leur manquât pas.', Dolgorukov to Perovskii [n.d., Feb. 1853] RGVIA F.483 Op.1 D.31 ll. 77-ob.

The latter part of the letter vividly suggests both the personal interest the Tsar took in the enterprise and the degree to which it was already well understood that a lengthy stint in a steppe fortress was akin to embarking on a long ocean voyage, with an accompanying risk of scurvy. Perovskii was confident enough of success to include plans of the fortifications he proposed to build superimposed over the existing Khoqandi fortress, but he was anxious not to repeat Blaramberg's errors of the year before. A frontal assault with scaling-ladders might be successful, but without a breach in the defences it would certainly entail considerable loss of life. Artillery was useless against earthen walls, which simply absorbed the shot, so he proposed sapping, mining and blowing them up instead. Supplies would be carried along the Syr-Darya on the newly assembled steamships of Captain Butakov's flotilla, and Perovskii particularly praised Butakov's energy and efficiency.[65] Despite his own failing health (as the spring advanced Perovskii wrote that he was prostrated by asthma, so much so that he could hardly breathe), he remained confident of success, writing that every precaution humanly possible had been taken.[66] The campaign's keynote was indeed caution, as Perovskii was clearly anxious to avoid the errors both of the Khivan expedition of 1839–40 and of Blaramberg's assault the previous year. In explanation of why the force had halted for so long at Fort Raim to prepare for the assault, he wrote that 'I cannot help but remember the remarkable observation of the late Duke of Wellington on the unhappy Khivan expedition of 1839: that however great the difficulties of a winter expedition in the steppe, the difficulties of a similar expedition in summer [...] are incomparably greater.'[67] His preparations may have been slow, but they were effective. Despite the heat, which rose to over 42 degrees in the shade by June, Perovskii's force of 750 infantry, 550 Cossacks, 300 Bashkir auxiliaries and ten guns, together with the 1,400 camels transporting those supplies which could not be carried on Butakov's ships (as always, with Qazaq guides and drivers), had reached Aq Masjid by the 2 July without any signifi-cant losses owing to sickness.[68] Perovskii reported that he had sent a small party to parley with the Khoqandis, who had allowed them to approach close to the fortress walls and then opened fire without warning, wounding two horses but missing the men. The following account was given by Mullah Yunus Tashkandi, whose critical attitude towards 'Abd al-Vali, the new Khoqandi

---

[65] 'Predpolozhenie o zanyatii reki Syr-Dar'i'; Perovskii to Dolgorukov 29/01/1853 RGVIA F.483 Op.1 D.31 ll. 28ob–32, 38ob.

[66] Perovskii to Dolgorukov 20/04/1853 & 28/05/1853 RGVIA F.483 Op.1 D.31 ll. 198–9, 236–7.

[67] Perovskii to Dolgorukov 17/06/1853 RGVIA F.483 Op.1 D.31 l. 261. For Wellington's observations on the Khivan expedition see 'Copie d'une dépêche du Baron de Brunnow, en date de Londres, le 23 avril/5 mai 1840', in Serebrennikov, Sbornik. Vol. 2. 1840 g. Doc.71, 113–15.

[68] Kilian, 'Allies and Adversaries', 234.

commander appointed by Khudoyar Khan, is explained by the pro-Qipchaq nature of his narrative:

> At that time one great commander of the Russian army with some quantity of soldiers and artillery came to besiege 'Abd al-Vali at Aq Masjid. Though the afore-mentioned military chief sent a messenger to 'Abd al Vali [with the suggestion that]: 'To fight is not good. Whatever has happened let us make peace,' 'Abd al-Vali behaved with enmity and therefore sent a man to the Russian chief [with the following message]: 'You come up to the fortress and we, the two of us, will negotiate, come to an agreement and make peace.' The Russian military chief believed his words and without bringing his guns and sabres, unarmed and calm approached the fortress with his officers. 'Abd al-Vali, conducting himself in a treacherous way, sent all the marksmen to the fortress wall. They all took aim and after the command to 'Fire in volleys!' fired at the Russians. But the Most High protected them and not one bullet hit either the Russians or their horses. They all moved to a place of safety. The Russian military chief said to 'Abd al-Vali: 'By committing treachery and meanness [shedding] your blood has become lawful for me.' [He] reinforced the siege, made sapping operations towards the gates, put in gunpowder and breached the wall. The army rushed into the city through the gap. 'Abd al-Vali fell with some of his subordinates while others were wounded. When the Russian soldiers had overpowered the enemy they flooded the city.[69]

The bombardment and siege works in fact began six days after the first ultimatum had been rejected, and progress was slow but steady. On the 13 July the Khoqandis rejected another ultimatum to surrender, saying that the Russians had sent their expedition to the fortress without a declaration of war or any attempt to settle differences through negotiation, and the work of digging zig-zag trenches to approach the walls continued (Figure 3.2).[70]

On the 15 July Perovskii wrote to say that the men were getting rather impatient, having expected the fortress to fall at once, but they would not have too long to wait.[71] The mine was finally sprung on the 28 July, and Aq Masjid was stormed within four hours. Resistance had been fierce – Perovskii wrote of the desperate, stubborn fight which the garrison put up even after the breach had been made and the Russians had entered the fortress.[72] Khoqandi portrayed it as nothing less than a holy war:

---

[69] *TA* trans. 39 text ff. 27b–8b.

[70] 'Plan osady i shturma kreposti Ak-Mecheti s 5-go po 28-e iiulia 1853 g.', in Kun (ed.), *Turkestanskii al'bom*. Part 4 plate 15 no. 14 (Library of Congress, Prints & Photographs Division LC-DIG-ppmsca–09957–00014).

[71] Perovskii to Dolgorukov 09/07/1853 & 15/07/1853 RGVIA F.483 Op.1 D.31 ll. 273–6, 282–3*ob*.

[72] Perovskii to A. Ya. Bulgakov 28/07/1853 in I. Zakhar'in, 'Nachalo zavoevaniya Kokanda (k 25-letiiu prisoedineniya Ferganskoi oblasti', *IV* No. 6 (1901), 1072.

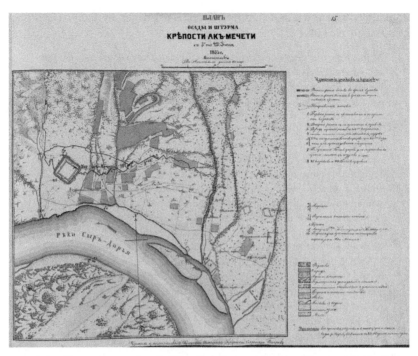

Figure 3.2 Plan of siege and assault on the fortress of Aq Masjid, 5–28 July 1853 (*Turkestan Album*, 1871).

A mass of Russian unbelievers [*bi din*], full of hate, laid siege to Aq Masjid, the greatest fortress of that region. The commander of Aq Masjid was Muhammad 'Ali, a relative of the murdered Mingbashi Shadi. He fought hard for three days; finally, he ran out of supplies of powder and lead, essential materials of war and for the defence of fortresses. The unbelievers found out about this, dug a mine beneath the walls, filled it with gunpowder, lit it, destroyed and entered the fortress [*atesh sardada qala-ra bar dashtand va be darun-i qala bar amadand*]. The besieged, men and women, throwing aside guns and bullets, took up knives and swords [*zan va mard hama yakbara tir tufang ra par tafta dasteha-ra bar qabza tegh buda*]. There followed a terrible battle such as no eyes have witnessed from the time of Adam. Finally the souls of all the men and women in the fortress through the blood of their martyrdom [*az khun-i shahidan*] attained the fortress of paradise.[73]

Russian losses were 34 killed and 130 wounded, but out of the garrison of approximately 300 men 226 were killed (together with four women and two children) and 35 wounded, indicating that Khoqandi had not exaggerated the

---

[73] *TSh*, 199; Bartol'd, 'Tuzemets o russkom zavoevanii', 335–6.

Figure 3.3 View of Aq Masjid after its capture on the 28 July 1853 (*Turkestan Album*, 1871).

fierceness of the resistance. Most of the survivors were women and children, and the Russians captured eighty-three of the former and sixty-five of the latter.[74] Khoqandi's claim that the Russians had martyred the defenders of Aq Masjid apparently circulated widely in Turkestan and was used to stir up anti-Russian feeling.[75] No doubt as part of his wider anti-Khudoyar and pro-Qipchaq agenda, Mullah Yunus Tashkandi went out of his way to exonerate Perovskii of this, writing that he saw that all the women were repatriated to Khoqand and that the wounded were properly cared for.[76] Figure 3.3 shows the fort after its capture, with one of Obruchev's steamers in the background.[77]

[74] Terent'ev, *Istoriya zavoevaniya*, I, 227.
[75] *TSh*, 199; Beisembiev, *The Life of Alimqul*, 12.
[76] *TA* trans. 39–40, text ff. 28b–9a.
[77] 'Syr-dar'inskaya oblast': Vid kokanskoi kreposti Ak-Mecheti posle shturma 28 iiulya 1853', in Kun (ed.), *Turkestanskii al'bom*. Part 4, plate 13 No. 12 (Library of Congress, Prints & Photographs Division LC-DIG-ppmsca–09957–00012).

Khudoyar Khan responded by sending two expeditions to recapture the fort, both of which failed ignominiously, and by sending an embassy to the East India Company at Peshawar to request military and technical assistance. The ambassador, an Afghan princeling called Shahzada Sultan Muhammad Khan, who had taken refuge in Khoqand when the Anglo-Sadozai regime in Kabul collapsed in 1842, had this to say about the siege:

> Ak-musjid is a fort belonging to Kokan occupied by 500 men. It stands on the river Sir which flows also near Kokan. The Kuzzauks [Qazaqs], subjects of Russia, come there every winter from the country of Kizzilpir and Shummeh. They are wandering tribes whose wealth consists in horses and goats. After a siege of 40 days the Russians took the fort of Ak-musjid. The defence was obstinate, the garrison threw boiling water and oil down on the assailants, & often times drove them back. But the Feringees returned to the charge again and again, and at last after many hundred had fallen on both sides – the place was taken by an unheard of stratagem. A fire-cart was driven up against the gate, which set fire to it, and let the besiegers in. Ak-musjid since then has been occupied by about 1,500 Russians & they control about 15 miles of the surrounding country. There was no dispute which led to this attack. It was an aggression with the intention of clearing the way to take Kokan itself. The boundary between Kokan and Russia was previously Kizzilpir – now it is Ak-musjid. [. . .] The Padshah of Kokan now wishes to ally himself with the British and not with the Russians.[78]

Some of the commanders responsible were forced to dress up in women's clothing as a humiliation, and a few paid for the defeat with their lives.[79] Russian intelligence reports the following June suggested that Khudoyar also blamed Yaqub Beg, the previous commander of Aq Masjid, for provoking the Russian attack through excessive raids on the Qazaqs under Russian jurisdiction.[80] The fall of Aq Masjid was a considerable blow to the shaky legitimacy of the newly restored Khudoyar Khan, the first of a series of defeats which would lead to his overthrow by his brother, Malla Khan, in 1858, and to the murder of the latter and another Qipchaq takeover in 1862.

Aq Masjid, renamed Fort Perovskii by imperial decree and eventually reconstructed, would become the central point of a new fortified line along the Syr-Darya, with three other fortresses hurriedly constructed between it and the Aral fortress at Raim during September 1853. These were known, imaginatively, as Forts Nos. 1, 2 and 3 (names chosen by Nicholas I himself),[81]

---

[78] NAI/Foreign/S.C./24 November 1854/Nos. 1–22, 10–11.

[79] *TA* trans. 40–1, text ff. 30b–1a; Beisembiev, *Ta'rikh-i Shakhrukhi*, 241.

[80] 'Zapiska o slukhakh i sobytiyakh v sredneaziyatskikh vladeniyakh', 01/06/1854 TsGARKaz F.382 Op.1 D.1 l. 54*ob*.

[81] 'Vedomost' o rabotakh, proizvedennykh s 21go sentyabrya do 1go chisla oktyabruya mesyatsa v kreposti Ak Mecheti'; War Minister to Perovskii 02/11/1853 RGVIA F.1441 Op.1 D.60, 'O vozvedenii ukreplenii na levom flange Syr-Dar'inskoi linii', ll. 109–11, 170.

although the first two were equally often referred to by their Qazaq names as Kazalinsk (Kazaly) and Karmakchi, whilst the last was soon abandoned as unnecessary, as was Fort Raim in 1855. If the forts on the Irgiz, on the Turgai and at Raim had been isolated outposts of the Orenburg line, these new fortresses represented a permanent advance of the Russian frontier to a point over 600 miles into the steppe, and accordingly new administrative arrangements would also be needed. Even before the assault, Perovskii had written to Dolgorukov envisaging the new line as a semi-autonomous command:

> I think also that the Syr-Darya line is much too far from Orenburg not to have its own commander. The commandants of Aralsk, of Ak-Mechet, of the forts in between to that of the flotilla, in order to act with ease, especially in unforeseen cases, cannot ask for orders [...] they would be awaiting them for two months or more sometimes. It seems to be, thus, entirely indispensable to appoint to this effect a superior officer, colonel or general, who will receive instructions from the chief of the corps.[82]

The Syr-Darya Line was thus established as a separate command, held successively by Major-General A. I. Fitingof (1854–7), Col. A. L. Danzas (1857–9), Col. V. D. Dandevil' (1859), Col. A. O. Debu (1859–62) and Col N. A. Verevkin (1862–4) – interestingly all but the last of these were of non-Russian descent.[83] The garrisons of the new line were small: in February 1854 Fort Perovskii was the headquarters for a total of 1,345 men, divided between Perovskii itself, Fort No. 2 (Karmakchi) and the soon-to-be abolished Fort No. 3 (Table 3.2).

These forces were supplemented by the sailors of Butakov's flotilla, one 12-pounder gun, two six-pounders, two light 'unicorn' guns, two ten-pounder and two three-pounder 'gornye' and three mortars. Fort Perovskii had a garrison of 1,055 men (635 infantry, 237 Cossacks, 95 artillerymen and 42

---

[82] 'Je pense aussi, que la ligne de Syr-Darya est beaucoup trop éloignée d'Orenbourg pour ne pas avoir son chef spécial. Les commandants d'Aralsk, d'Ak-Metchet, des forts intervenées à celui de la flotille, pour agir avec aise, surtout dans les cas imprévues, ne peuvent demander des ordres [...] ils les attendraient près de deux mois d'avantage quelquefois. Il me parait, donc, tout à fait indispensable de nommer à cet effet un off. supérieure, colonel ou général, qui recevrait ses instructions du chef du corps.' Perovskii to Dolgorukov, 29/01/1853 RGVIA F.483 Op.1 D.31 ll. 37ob-8.

[83] Fitingof (von Viettinghoff) was of an old Livonian noble family, Alexander Loginovich Danzas (1810–1880) came from a noble Kurland family, and was known as a 'reforming' officer close to Miliutin. Viktor Dezidierevich Dandevil' (1826–1907) was the son of a French prisoner of war, Desiré d'Andeville, who had become a Russian subject and joined the Orenburg Cossacks. He would later distinguish himself in the Russo-Turkish War of 1878. Alexander Osipovich Debu (1802–1862), a veteran of the war in the Caucasus, was descended from a French naval doctor called De Desbout who had entered Russian service in the 1780s. All biographical details are taken from Novitskii, *Voennaya entsiklopediya*.

Table 3.2 *Garrisons of the Syr-Darya line, February 1854*[a]

Unit	Staff officers	Higher-ranking officers	NCOs	Musicians	Other ranks	Non-combatants	Totals
1st Company, 4th Orenburg Line Battalion	2	3	24	6	222	5	262
2nd Company, 4th Orenburg Line Battalion	–	5	21	4	227	5	262
3rd Company, 4th Orenburg Line Battalion	–	7	21	4	223	1	256
Ural Cossacks	2	9	14	–	290	1	316
Orenburg Cossacks	–	1	3	–	96	–	100
Bashkir auxiliaries	–	1	2	–	49	–	52
Orenburg horse artillery	–	1	10	–	84	2	97
Totals	4	27	95	14	1,191	14	1,345

[a] 'Raport o sostoyanii garnizona forta "Perovskii" s nakhodyashchimsya v fortakh No. 2 i 3', 01/02/1854 RGVIA F.1433, 'Upravlenie komanduiushchego Syr-Dar'inskoi liniei', Op.1 D.1, 'Stroevye raporta sostoyanii garnizona forta Perovskogo i nakhodyashchikhsya v fortakh No. 1go i No. 2go na 1854 g.', ll. 29–30.

sailors),[84] whilst Fort No. 2 was home to two officers, seven NCOs and 100 men of the Ural Cossacks and the Orenburg line battalions.[85]

The Russians adapted and continued to use the existing fortifications at Aq Masjid until 1858–9, when they were replaced. Until this time a small mosque

[84] Terent'ev, *Istoriya zavoevaniya*, I, 230.
[85] 'Stroevyi raport o sostoyanii garnizona forta No. 2', 28/02/1854 RGVIA F.1433 Op.1 D.1 ll. 73–4, 197–8.

and the house of the former Khoqandi *Bek* were also preserved, but thereafter the only reminder of the Khoqandi fortress was a single bastion, left within the new fortifications and used as a flagstaff and clock-tower.[86] The new fortifications were low, and constructed largely of earth, whilst the buildings were still of sun-baked mud-brick mixed with straw (*pakhsa*). Finding sufficient wood for building was a perennial problem, as along most of the Syr-Darya all that grew were reeds, which could only be used for thatch, and saxaul, which was an excellent fuel but useless for construction.[87] A. Gren, one of the engineers who oversaw the rebuilding of the edifices within the fortifications along the Syr-Darya line in 1859, wrote that all the wood had to be brought from the Nuruzumskaya forests north of Orenburg, at a cost of 12 roubles 27 kopeks per log.[88] Gren considered that almost all the structures he and his men had replaced were jerry-built and liable to collapse at a moment's notice, whether through natural wear and tear caused by the huge variations of temperature and the weight of snow in winter, or because of the activities of the garrison: he referred to a group of sailors of the Syr-Darya flotilla who had eroded the walls of their barracks by watering the pea plants they had sown alongside them.[89] Although he claimed that the structures he and his men had erected in their place were more solid, it is not clear whether they fared any better: in 1863 the traveller Lobysevich still found that most structures in the fortresses were mud-brick buildings which crumbled easily and never survived more than two or three years, and although he described certain amenities for the officers, these were not extended to the majority of the fortresses' inhabitants.[90]

In 1866 a group of Cossack settlers petitioned the Commander of Fort No. 1 to say that their houses had been built on insufficient foundation, whilst the wood used in their construction had rotted, and that this year they had collapsed completely, and they could not afford to rebuild them themselves.[91] As this suggests, the new fortresses of the line were intended to be more than just military strongpoints. They were supposed to become flourishing settlements of hardy Russian colonists, beacons of a superior sedentary civilisation which would persuade the surrounding Qazaq population to abandon their misguided nomadic ways, important transit points for

[86] A. Gren, 'Zametki ob ukrepleniyakh v Orenburgskom krae voobshche i na Syr-Dar'inskoi linii v osobennosti', *Inzhenernyi Zhurnal* (1861), No. 5, 433–4; a photograph of this bastion can be found in the *Turkestan Album*: 'Syr-dar'inskaya oblast': Ostatki byvshei kokanskoi kreposti vnutri forta perovskago', in Kun (ed.), *Turkestanskii al'bom* (1871) Part 4 plate 14 No. 13(Library of Congress, Prints & Photographs Division LC-DIG-ppmsca-09957–00013).

[87] Yonnei to Perovskii 09/10/1853 RGVIA F.1441 Op.1 D.60 ll. 164–5.

[88] Gren, 'Zametki', 451.

[89] *Ibid.*, 455.

[90] Lobysevich, 'Syr-Dar'inskaya liniya', *VS* (1864), No. 6, 404.

[91] 'Semeinykh nizhnikh chinov prozhivaiushchikh pri forte No. 1', 23/05/1866 TsGARKaz F.385 Op.1 D.30 l. 45.

trade and centres for the collection of intelligence and information about events in the steppe and in the Central Asian khanates beyond. If the immediate military and intelligence objectives of the line were to a large extent realised, albeit not always in the form the Russians desired, these broader aims were not.

3.3   The Failure of a Frontier

In 1857 the new commander of the Syr-Darya Line, Colonel A. L. Danzas (1810–1880), wrote a series of private letters to the Governor-General of Orenburg in which he complained at length of the hopeless state of the fortresses under his charge:

> Proceeding from Fort No. 1 to Fort Perovskii and going carefully into all parts of the administration of the Syr-Darya line, I was overcome with vexation and bitterness at the thought that so much human capital, strength and hardship has been spent uselessly. The forts cannot in any way be described as strongpoints charged with defending our territory. [...] One can sink into a powerful sleep on the laurels of former victories, the awakening from which is sometimes painful [...].[92]

He complained that the fortifications were poorly designed, and that in any case Fort Perovskii was so surrounded by temporary structures, which even encroached on the glacis, that there was no clear field of fire. The interior of the fort was cluttered with half-derelict temporary structures, and the whole thing needed to be pulled down and started afresh. The garrison was no better prepared than the fortifications:

> The greater part of the garrison lives outside the fort. The fort cannot be locked up at night, and in consequence the soldiers wander around where they like; the reason the fort cannot be locked up is that throughout the entire fort there isn't a single privy [here Danzas used the vulgar term *otkhozhoe mesto*, which is probably best translated as 'bog']; for their natural needs the garrison go a *verst* out into the fields or make filth wherever it so happens. The commanders of the forts are economists, caterers, planters, artillerymen, salesmen, whatever you want, only not commanders. It would appear that it has never occurred to a single one of them to think about their primary duty, for the fulfilment of which they are paid. They know nothing about construction or about the defence of the forts entrusted to them.[93]

The infantry did not know how to look after their weapons and performed very poorly in rifle drill, whilst the Cossacks were still worse: 'the Kirgiz fear

---

[92] Danzas to Katenin 11/10/1857 RGVIA F.67 Op.1 D.242 l. 1*ob.*
[93] Danzas to Katenin 11/10/1857 RGVIA F.67 Op.1 D.242 ll. 2–*ob.*

them not as soldiers, but as thieves'. They had a reputation as cowards, although Danzas remarked that he was not prepared to believe this, as Russian men were 'brave by their very nature'. Their officers he considered to be very poor, as well as the quality of their mounts and weapons.[94] By the time he wrote his third letter two months later, his anger seems to have given way to despair: 'I would rather organise five new lines than have to sort out the stagnant mess which has established itself on the Syr-Darya over the years.'[95]

Danzas's complaints (which came just four years after the fall of Aq Masjid) would be echoed by his successors even after Fort Perovskii had been rebuilt and put into better order. The earliest photographs of the fortresses of the Syr-Darya line come from the *Turkestan Album* of 1871, by which time their military significance had declined and was about to disappear altogether with the conquest of Khiva. Nevertheless, they give some idea of what their appearance must have been like ten years before, when the military importance of the line was at its height. Alongside the pictures of fortifications, barrack blocks, churches and white-jacketed soldiers, often with the masts and spars of the Aral flotilla in the background, some of the images also reveal the clusters of bazaar stalls and housing which sprang up outside their walls, which by the 1860s had turned Fort Perovskii and Fort No. 1 into the small towns of Perovsk and Kazalinsk. In 1863 Lobysevich gave an enthusiastic description of the bustling surroundings of Fort No. 1, where he remarked on the number of mills in the settler *sloboda* and the extent of boat traffic on the Syr-Darya.[96] Despite Danzas's objections to these encroachments, it was in fact the presence of traders (Figure 3.4)[97] which made the Russian fortifications on the steppe possible.

Danzas's notes on the trade around Fort Perovskii in 1858 reveal the numerical dominance of Bukharan traders, who were the main suppliers of the imported grain on which the garrisons depended – by 1858 there were forty-eight of them, as opposed to just three Russian merchants.[98] The trade they engaged in was fairly small-scale, as the creation of the line does not appear to have had a major effect on the caravan routes across the steppe, not least because the Russians did not attempt to move the customs boundary there. When this was proposed in 1862, the conclusion was that it made little sense as the area between the fortresses was almost completely unpopulated and virtually impossible to monitor and police, whilst caravans would be reluctant to halt their journey in the middle of the steppe, far short of their

---

[94] Danzas to Katenin 11/10/1857 RGVIA F.67 Op.1 D.242 l. 6ob.

[95] Danzas to Katenin 01/12/1857 RGVIA F.67 Op.1 D.242 l. 12ob.

[96] Lobysevich, 'Syr-Dar'inskaya liniya', 402.

[97] 'Syr-dar'inskaya oblast' g. Kazalinsk: Torgovye ryady (bazar)', in Kun (ed.) *Turkestanskii al'bom* (1871), Part 2, Vol. 1 plate 47, No. 123 (Library of Congress, Prints & Photographs Division LC-DIG-ppmsca-09951-00123).

[98] RGVIA F.67 Op.1 D.63, 'Zapiski Danzasa "O torgovli Forta Perovskii"', l. 1.

Figure 3.4 Syr-Darya Province. Kazalinsk Town. Trading lines (bazaar) (*Turkestan Album*, 1871).

actual trading destination.[99] The presence of a significant Qazaq, Tatar, Bukharan and even Khoqandi population around the fortresses of the line suggests that it had the potential, at least, to develop some of the characteristics of the Terek frontier examined by Thomas Barrett, a 'middle ground' which was not always or only a site of military conflict, but a site of cultural and economic exchange.[100] Although in the North Caucasus much of this disappeared as warfare mounted in bitterness and intensity in the 1840s and 1850s,[101] the picture painted by Barrett of shifting allegiances and identities has certain parallels on the Syr-Darya in this period, something seen particularly in the complex Russian relationship with the local Qazaq population.

[99] Bezak to the head of the Orenburg Customs Region 16/08/1862; Chernyaev to the same 31/10/1862 GAOrO F.339, 'Kantselyariya Nachal'nika Orenburgskogo Tamozhennogo Okruga', Op.1 D.50, 'O perenesenii Orenburgskoi tamozhennoi cherty na Syr Dar'inskuiu liniiu', ll. 1, 5–6ob.

[100] Thomas M. Barrett, 'Lines of Uncertainty: The Frontiers of the North Caucasus', in *Imperial Russia: New Histories for the Empire* ed. David Ransel & Jane Burbank (Bloomington, IN: Indiana University Press, 1999), 158–73.

[101] See Khodarkovsky, *Bitter Choices*.

While the military commander was in overall charge of the Syr-Darya line, in principle a civilian official from the Orenburg frontier commission was appointed to administer the local Qazaq population. From 1853 until his death this was the Polish Court Counsellor Iosif (Efim) Yakovlevich Osmolovskii (1820–1862), a graduate of the Oriental Faculty of Kazan University, who began his career in the Asiatic Department of the Ministry of Foreign Affairs in 1844 before being sent to Orenburg as a translator in 1848. On his death he was succeeded by another Pole, Court Counsellor Gruzdz', who had no university education but had served the Orenburg Frontier Commission on the steppe since 1840, spending a number of years as clerk to Sultan Arslan Jan Tura.[102] Each rejoiced in the title of 'Administrator of the Syr-Darya Kirgiz'. In practice, as the Russians made little attempt either to collect taxes or to administer justice in the region, their duties were largely concerned with building an intelligence network which sought to gather information both on immediate military threats to the Syr-Darya line and its Qazaq population, and on more distant developments in Khoqand, Bukhara, Khiva and Afghanistan.

In 1849 an article in the *Journal of the Imperial Russian Geographical Society* had complained of the paucity of accurate information which the Russians had on the lower reaches of the Amu-Darya and Syr-Darya, remarking that, whilst Tatar merchants constituted one of the major sources of information on the steppe and the khanates that lay beyond it, the accounts they gave were 'indistinct and in places contradictory', and that separating the accurate and false information and comparing it with other sources was a thankless task. Instead most of the information on the Amu-Darya in particular was drawn from British sources.[103] The building of the new fortresses provided new opportunities for gathering information about the great rivers of Central Asia, and the territory and peoples of Bukhara, Khiva and Khoqand, which could meet both immediate military needs and ostensibly more objective, scholarly concerns. From 1854 until 1865, the most detailed and accurate information which St Petersburg received on events in Central Asia came from the monthly reports 'on rumours and events' which the administrator of the Syr-Darya Kirgiz made to the Governor-General in Orenburg. He produced these compilations partly through receiving and interpreting rumours and reports of raids, partly by interrogating passing merchants and

---

[102] Zhanaev & Erofeeva (ed.), *Istoriya Kazakhstana v russkikh istochnikakh*. Vol. 8, Pt. 2, 566–7, 570–1. On his death Osmolovskii's effects included three kaftans, a Muslim skull-cap and two silver koumiss-cups, suggesting that he saw himself very much as an intermediary between Russian and Qazaq culture: Debu to Karlov 2/05/1862 TsGARKaz F.383 Op.1 D.231, 'O smerti kollezhskogo sovetnika Osmolovskogo i o peredache ego del nadvornomu sovetniku Gruzdz'', ll. 1, 3–4.

[103] P. Chikhachev, 'O issledovanii vershin Syr i Amu-dar'i i nagornoi ploshchadi Pamir', *ZIRGO* Kn. III (1849), 28–9.

groups of nomads, but also through the active recruitment of Qazaqs as spies, or *lazutchiki*, who if literate produced written reports (usually short documents in Tatar) and if not were debriefed orally. Their duties ranged from the gathering of camels to the relaying of rumours from the steppe, out-and-out spying in Khoqandi fortresses and long-distance expeditions into the heartlands of the Khanates, often at considerable personal risk. In 1851 the standard rate of pay for a spy was 8–12 silver roubles per month, later reduced to 5–8 roubles, together with one *funt* of meat and two of grain, with special awards for outstanding service.[104] Long-distance journeys carried special payments, and were often undertaken under the cover of trade. A Qazaq who in January 1860 brought intelligence of Khivan movements in the vicinity of Fort No. 1 had twice been paid 50 silver roubles for undertaking special missions to Bukhara, and was now about to set off there again 'for his own trading purposes' and being paid a further 60 roubles for collecting information for the Russians whilst he was there.[105] This emphasises the fact that crossing the notional frontier between Russian, Khoqandi and Khivan territory did not in itself incite suspicion, nor indeed did the identification of a trader or traveller as a Khivan, Bukharan or Russian subject: Khoqandi traders lived and worked in the bazaar at Fort Perovskii even as their leaders were engaged in fighting against the Russians. In any case the line between merchant and spy was blurred: the Russians obtained much of their intelligence from questioning recently arrived caravans, and it is probable the Khoqandis did the same. Osmolovskii also attempted to collect reports of the rumours which were being relayed by Khoqandi spies.[106]

This porousness and constant movement across the steppe meant that Russian intelligence regarding Khoqand's military preparations was often both timely and accurate, not least because it was impossible to gather the thousands of horses needed by the Khoqandi cavalry without revealing that something was in the wind. In April 1854 Perovskii could report to Dolgorukov that the Khoqandis had prepared a force of 8,000 horsemen for an attack on the newly built fortresses of the line later that spring, possibly in cooperation with Khivan forces from Khoja Niyaz, and he had been able to send reinforcements accordingly.[107] In June 1860 the Russians received intelligence that the Khoqandis were planning a renewed attack on the

---

[104] Perovskii to the OPK 23/07/1851 TsGARKaz F.4 Op.1 D.2614 l. 7ob.
[105] Debu to Osmolovskii 30/01/1860 RGVIA F.1433 Op.1 D.7, 'O slukakh i sobytiyakh v sredne-aziatskikh vladeniyakh', l.4.
[106] 'Zapiska o polozhenii del v sredneaziatskikh khanstvakh', 11/10/1854 TsGARKaz F.382 Op.1 D.1 l. 120ob.
[107] Perovskii to Dolgorukov 06/04/1854 RGVIA F.483 Op.1 No. 32, 'Perepiska po otnosheniyam komandire otdel'nykh korpusov: Orenburgskogo i Sibirskogo o namereniyakh i prigotovleniyakh kokantsev vtorgnut' nashe predely i o prinyatykh po etomu merakh', ll. 1–ob.

Russian positions of the Siberian line from Sultan Taichik, a relative of Kenesary, who had been summoned to Tashkent by Malla Khan with all the other *sipahi* commanders for a council of war. This was confirmed in late July by a spy who had just returned from Turkestan, who reported that Malla Khan was preparing his forces and buying up the best horses to be found in the Tashkent bazaar for the campaign. An attack on the fortress of Merke by 6,000 Khoqandis followed soon after, but was easily beaten off by its Russian garrison.[108]

Intelligence on the internal politics of the khanates was patchier: Bekmakhanov notes that Qazaq scouts often made up facts or repeated rumours without any verification, as they were reluctant to run the risk of travelling too far into enemy territory.[109] As might be expected, the information the Russians received became progressively less reliable according to the distance from their frontier of the power concerned. The length of Khoqand's frontier on the steppe meant that events in that khanate usually reached the Russians sooner and in more complete form than for Khiva, whilst Bukharan news tended to be tardier and fuzzier than either. The modern history of Khoqand was reasonably well known in Russia, and in particular the poor relations which existed between that Khanate and Bukhara, Amir Nasrullah's invasion of the Ferghana valley in 1842, the Qipchaq ascendancy in Khoqand which followed thereafter and the overthrow of Musulmanqul in 1852 after another Bukharan invasion.[110] However, even the news from Khoqand often contained significant inaccuracies and exaggerations. In 1858, for instance, the Russians received a report that Khudoyar Khan had been overthrown by his brother, Malla Bek, with the assistance of the Ferghana Kyrgyz (which was true), but also that Khudoyar had been killed (which was not).[111] Much of the intelligence was falsified, magnified or reflected Russian fears rather than Central Asian realities, and the rumours concerning the activities of the British were usually particularly fantastical.[112] Towards the end of 1854, for instance, scouts reported a bizarre rumour that the British 'have become so cunning' that they were extracting gold from the waters of the Amu-Darya and

---

[108] 'Zapiska o slukhakh i sobytiyakh v Srednei Azii', 14/06/1860, 28/07/1860, 18/08/1860 RGVIA F.1433 Op.1 D.7 ll. 76, 91, 97.

[109] Bekmakhanov, *Kazakhstan v 20–40 gody*, 34.

[110] V. V. Velyaminov-Zernov, 'Istoricheskiya izvestiya o Kokanskom khanstve ot Mukhammed-Ali do Khudoyar Khana', *TVOIRAO* Part 2 (St Pb., 1856), 333–9, 353. Velyaminov-Zernov's sources included an account of events in the khanate in 1852 by a Russian merchant based in Tashkent.

[111] 'Zapiska o slukhakh i sobytiyakh v Srednei Azii', 14/12/1858 TsGARKaz F.383 Op.1 D.82, 'Zapiska o polozhenii del v sredneaziyatskikh khanstvakh za 1858–1859 gg.', l. 10.

[112] Although characteristically Khalfin repeats these, and even more unlikely, stories of Ottoman agents in the steppe, as if they were an established threat which justified the Russian conquest. Khalfin, *Politika Rossii*, 50–3.

coining money from it to pay their forces.[113] The Russians were also particularly concerned at suggestions that the three khanates might forge an alliance and present a united front against them. In 1854 there were rumours of an embassy from Khoqand to Bukhara in response to a plea by the Ottoman Sultan for the Central Asian khanates to unite against the Russian threat, although Amir Nasrullah was said to have rejected these overtures on the grounds that the Khoqandis could not be trusted, and that in any case war against the Russians was a futile enterprise.[114]

For all their limitations in describing events within the khanates, the intelligence networks run by Osmolovskii and Gruzdz' proved more than adequate as an early-warning system against potential attacks on the fortresses of the line, and when these came they were easily beaten off. The Russians not only maintained their military security with relative ease, but also, between 1853 and 1862, successfully attacked and destroyed the Khivan fortresses of Jan-Qala and Khoja Niyaz and the Khoqandi fortresses of Yangi-Qurghan and Julek, refortifying and occupying the latter in 1861.[115] Communications along the line were also rendered easier by the presence of the river, although it was not really navigable in the summer months, and in 1863 it still took six days to travel by steamer from Fort Perovskii to Julek.[116]

Preventing raids on livestock proved a more intractable problem. As we have seen, in the 1840s at least, the Russians were not above engaging in the practice themselves, but along the Syr-Darya frontier, *baramta* was seen by the Russians not merely as an 'imperial crime', but as a violation of sovereignty which could not be tolerated, for reasons of prestige, if nothing else.[117] This was compounded by the difficulty of establishing precisely who was responsible for a particular raid. Although the Russian military authorities always claimed that their principal aim in Central Asia was to defend Qazaqs under Russian sovereignty from Khoqandi depredations (a version of events which would become canonical in the Soviet period), the reality was inevitably more complex. The shifting allegiances of the steppe meant that conflicts did not divide along notional state or ethnic lines. Many of the raids on the line of forts were indeed directed by Khoqandi forces against the Qazaqs: in 1855, for instance, a party of 1,500 horsemen, led by the Khoqandi *Bek* of

---

[113] 'Zapiska o polozhenii del v sredneaziatskikh khanstvakh', 31/12/1854 TsGARKaz F.382 Op.1 D.1 l. 168.

[114] 'Zapiska o polozhenii del v sredneaziatskikh khanstvakh', 11/06/1854 TsGARKaz F.382 Op.1 D.1 ll. 61–2ob.

[115] Katenin to Miliutin 08/11/1859 RGVIA F.1441 Op.1 D.109, 'O vozvedenii ukreplenii Dzhuleka i Dzhan Kaly', ll. 9–21. For Mullah Yunus Tashkandi's description of the siege and destruction of Yangi Qurghan see *TA* trans. 42–3 text ff. 34a–5a, for Bezak's report on the same A. P. Bezak, 'Yany-Kurgan', *VS* (1861), No. 12, 511–25.

[116] Lobysevich, 'Syr-Dar'inskaya liniya', 408.

[117] Martin, 'Barimta', 258.

Yangi-Qurghan, attacked a Qazaq *aul*, killing six, wounding thirty, seven severely, and carrying off six into captivity.[118] In January 1863 the Russians were once again reminded of their inability to guarantee the security of the line, but this time the raiders were a group of 50 Qazaqs who carried off a total of 103 camels and 64 horses from *auls* near Fort Perovskii. In November of that year 300 Qazaq raiders carried off 9,100 sheep, 300 camels and 100 horses, as well as two *kibitkas* with all their inhabitants and property: in both cases Gruzdz' claimed that they were acting on orders from Khoqand and that the raids were at 'Alimqul's instigation, but they could equally have been cases of *baramta*.[119] Nomadic raids on caravans were also a perennial problem, and also generally blamed by the Russians on the instigation of either Khiva or Khoqand, although there was rarely any proof of this. In 1860 a Qazaq of the Niyazov lineage working for a Russian merchant, Matvei Putilov, trading at Fort No. 1, reported that a caravan of fifty-two people and eighty camels carrying Russian goods to Bukhara, which he was escorting, had been attacked by a group of Turkmen near Yangi Qurghan, who announced that they were from the Chaudar tribe but made no mention of Khiva.[120]

At the same time many of the punitive expeditions the Russians sent out into the steppe after such raids contained substantial numbers of Qazaq horsemen: Veniukov remarked that their presence alongside Russian forces in the steppe was always desirable, provided that they were drawn from amongst those whose sultans were loyal to Russia. He considered that they were often superior to Cossacks as scouts and often displayed great loyalty and bravery, but characteristically claimed that they fought well only when supported by Russian troops.[121] Veniukov's condescension is only to be expected, but there is little doubt that many Qazaqs did fight loyally in Russian service: in 1864, for instance, a party of 40 Cossacks and Qazaqs under the joint command of Cornet Rannev and Sultan Taichik Kenesarin successfully beat off a party of 300 Khoqandi horsemen between Julek and Fort Perovskii , an engagement in which the Sultan was wounded.[122] Some Qazaq leaders switched sides – Jan Khoja Nurmuhammadov, who had been appealing for Russian protection at Fort Raim in 1847, was in open rebellion against the Russians ten years later.[123] All this suggests that, while there was rarely any

[118] Fitingof to Perovskii 07/08/1855 TsGARKaz F.383 Op.1 D.17 ll. 8–9.
[119] Verevkin to Gruzdz' 16/11/1862; Gruzdz' to Verevkin 12/01/1863; Gruzdz' to Verevkin 29/11/1863 TsGARKaz F.383 Op.1 D.206 ll. 25; 37–8ob; 56.
[120] 'Zapiska o slukhakh v sosednikh khanstvakh', 08/01/1860 RGVIA F.1433 Op.1 D.7 ll. 22–3.
[121] Veniukov, 'Zametki o stepnykh pokhodakh', 287–8.
[122] 'Izvestiya s Syr-Dar'inskoi linii', *VS* (1864), No. 4, 191.
[123] Perovskii to the War Ministry 04/02/1857 & 11/02/1857 RGVIA F.483 Op.1 D.40, 'Delo po doneseniyam Komandira Otdel'nogo Orenburgskogo Korpusa o voennykh prois-shestviyakh vo vverennom emu krae i o polozhenii del' na Syr-Dar'inskoi linii', ll. 6, 10.

serious military threat to the Russian line, the stability, peace and freedom from raiding which the Syr-Darya fortresses were supposed to bring to the Qazaq population proved harder to achieve, whilst there was always a certain ambiguity over who was friend and who was foe.

Neither military nor intelligence considerations represented the greatest challenge to sustaining the Syr-Darya line. The principal problem was keeping its fortresses supplied, and the bulk of the records from the twenty-odd years of its existence are concerned with securing sufficient quantities of food, fuel and construction materials to maintain the Russian military presence in near-desert conditions. The 1,000 camels General Obruchev had needed for the supply of the first small fortifications the Russians had built on the Irgiz and Turgai rivers were multiplied several times over once this was extended to Fort Raim, and then Fort No. 1 (Kazalinsk), Fort No. 2 (Karmakchi), Fort Perovskii and eventually Julek, all of which were larger and lay still further from the Orenburg line. This had not been the original intention: one of the reasons why the valley of the Syr-Darya had been chosen as a frontier was because it was believed that the presence of the river would render it more fruitful than localities further north in the steppe. As early as 1841 Captain Nikiforov, then returning from his failed embassy to Khiva, had written to his friend the orientalist Nikolai Khanykov that, despite the barren appearance of the lower reaches of the Syr-Darya, the *solonchak* (saline soil) there was similar to that on the banks of the Amu in Khiva, and could be made fruitful through irrigation and the settlement of Qazaq agriculturalists and, eventually, Russians.[124] General A. A. Katenin (1803–1860), the governor of Orenburg from 1856 until 1860, and his successor A. P. Bezak (1800–1868) both believed that with the right policies of encouragement the Syr-Darya could be made into a fruitful colony, populated by settled Qazaqs and incoming Russians.[125] This was a fantasy – in the event, the valley of the lower Syr-Darya consistently failed to produce sufficient grain even to feed the permanent garrison of 300–1,000 men, and whilst in principle meat supplies presented fewer prob-lems, these too became acutely difficult at times. Katenin estimated that in the course of the summer of 1856 alone over 450,000 *pood*s of supplies of various kinds had been sent out into the steppe from Orenburg, and the costs had been inflated still further because of Russian reliance on two or three rich merchants who controlled the caravans.[126] The desire to encourage trade (and in particu-lar Russian merchants) often came into conflict with the demands of food security for the garrisons. Visiting Fort Perovskii in 1863, ten years after its establishment, Lobysevich gave a glowing description of cabbages and potatoes growing in irrigated fields surrounding it, but the prices he quoted told their

[124] Nikiforov to Khanykov 18/10/1841, in Serebrennikov, *Sbornik.* Vol. 3. *1841 g.,* 131.
[125] Campbell, *Knowledge and the Ends of Empire,* 41–2.
[126] Katenin to Danzas 04/01/1858 RGVIA F.67 Op.1 D.74 l. 25*ob.*

own tale – whilst the high prices of luxuries such as sturgeon and caviar were only to be expected and of concern just to a few, flour 'of the third sort' cost 1 silver rouble 50 kopeks per *pood*, and, even more disturbingly, almost all of it was imported from Bukhara rather than Russia, and controlled by Bukharan merchants. In general the cost of goods was two and a half times that in Orenburg.[127]

Successive Governors of Orenburg and commanders of the Syr-Darya line realised that the only way to ensure its food security and reduce the dangerous reliance on long lines of communication with the Urals region to the north, and on trade with the khanates to the south, was to encourage local agriculture. There were essentially two ways of doing this – one was to persuade the local Qazaqs to turn to cultivating crops, and the other was to encourage the growth of Russian (or more usually Cossack) settlement. Both required the extension of irrigation from the Syr-Darya, as rain fell but rarely, and this would require far more labour and expenditure than the Russians realised. The first priority was to increase the local supply of grain. In principle there was already plenty of it available: the 1,300–1,500 men of the Syr-Darya garrisons would have had an annual consumption of, at most, 30,000–35,000 *pood*s of grain. The most optimistic estimates by Russian officials suggested that in the early 1860s about 8,000 households of Qazaqs of the Syr-Darya region cultivated 100,000 *desyatina*s of land, most of it in areas periodically flooded by the Syr-Darya or at the end of small inundation canals, producing up to 4.8 million *pood*s of grain annually.[128] In all likelihood these figures were a substantial overestimate, fuelled by a fantasy of sedentarising the steppe.[129] Whatever the true size of the annual harvest of grain produced by the Qazaqs of the Syr-Darya region, most of it seems to have been intended either for their own consumption, or else for sale to nomadic groups of Qazaqs. Something which emerged clearly was the Qazaq preference for millet, as it was hardier than the other grains, and required only a fifth as much seed as wheat to produce a comparable harvest. However, the Russian military authorities wanted wheat, barley and rye. Of these only barley (which was mainly used for fodder) seems ever to have been obtainable in sufficient quantities, and even then it was rare for the entire annual supply to be obtained locally.[130] Thus neither the quantity nor the type

[127] Lobysevich, 'Syr-Dar'inskaya liniya', 404–6.
[128] L. Meier (sostavitel'), *Kirgizskaya step' Orenburgskago vedomstva: Materialy dlya geografii i statistiki Rossii sobrannye ofitserami General'nago Shtaba* (St Pb.: Tip. E. Veimar & F. Person, 1865), 111. The estimates for 1860 were made by one Staff-Captain Starkov, and Meier himself states that they were probably very inaccurate, though there was a bad harvest that year. Those for 1861 are taken from reports by Osmolovskii and his assistant Karamyshev, those for 1862 from a report by Debu.
[129] Campbell, *Knowledge and the Ends of Empire*, 42–3.
[130] 'O khlebopashchestve Kirgiz', n.d. TsGARKaz F.383 Op.1 D.203 ll. 6–7ob; Meier, *Kirgizskaya step'*, 115–16.

of these crops was sufficient to satisfy the needs of the new Russian garrisons. For meat supplies the Russians relied on the surrounding Qazaqs, paying roughly 1 rouble 70 kopeks per sheep in the late 1850s and early 1860s, whilst a fat bullock cost 16 silver roubles and a cow between 8 and 12 roubles. In 1857 Danzas complained that the process of negotiating and purchasing a sufficient supply of beasts was cumbersome and time-consuming, requiring as it did sending an armed convoy out into the steppe to *auls* that were often at a considerable distance from the fortress, and then the gathering of vast quantities of fodder to feed the beasts which were brought back. During the winter months each cow required 30 *funts* of hay per day, and each sheep 10 *funts*, a total of 211,087 *poods* for each of the five winter months – 528 men had had to be sent out to gather this amount in the late summer. Danzas concluded that it would be better to farm the meat supply out to a private contractor, if some means of ensuring real competition could be found.[131] At least one attempt was made to do this and at the same time promote the husbandry of the local Cossack settlers, but this also proved an ignominious failure.[132]

In response to these difficulties a series of schemes was proposed to extend irrigation, boost yields of wheat and barley, introduce improved tools, persuade more nomads to take to a settled existence and encourage Russian (principally Cossack) settlement. These uniformly failed: responding to a proposal to give the Syr-Darya Qazaqs firmer land rights as a means of encouraging them to settle, Osmolovskii warned (correctly) that only the poorest Qazaqs ever turned to agriculture out of necessity, and that the irrigated areas along the Syr-Darya which were the only possible sites of cultivation were currently held not as private property but in common by particular lineages.[133] In 1863 the distribution of a circular in Russian and Tatar extolling the benefits of settled agriculture to Qazaqs currently pasturing their animals along the Syr-Darya line threw them into panic, as rumours spread that they would be forcibly sedentarised and they fled deep into the steppe.[134] Russian colonisation was no more successful: even in 1866 Fort No. 2 had only six families, whilst the Commander of Fort No. 1, the site of the most substantial existing settlement, reported that the European population

[131] 'Zapiska o zatrudneniyakh, vstrechaemykh Nachal'nikami chastei pri zagotovlenii portsionnogo skota dlya voisk Syr-Dar'inskoi Linii' 14/11/1857; Osmolovskii to Danzas 17/11/1857 RGVIA F.67 Op.1 D.74 ll.7–18.

[132] 'Konditsii na postavku myasnykh portsii, dlya garnizonov stepnykh ukreplenii i fortov v 1861 i 1862 godakh' TsGARKaz F.384 Op.1 D.17 'O postavke myasnykh portsii dlya garnizoni Forta No.1 postoyannami onogo-zhe forta v prodolzhenii 1861 i 1862 godakh' ll.5–6, 18*ob*, 169.

[133] Bezak to Debu 29/10/1861; Osmolovskii to Debu 08/01/1862 TsGARKaz F.382 Op.1 D.42 'Perepiska ob osedlosti kazakhskogo naseleniya' ll.1–2*ob*, 5–7.

[134] OPK to Verevkin 05/06/1863; Gruzdz' to Verevkin 10/07/1863 TsGARKaz F.382 Op.1 D.42 ll.19, 21; Commander of Fort No.1 to Verevkin 21/06/1863 TsGARKaz F.382 Op.1 D.60 l.5.

was just 245 men and 233 women.[135] A visitor in 1866 confirmed the disappointing results of Russian colonisation around Fort Perovskii, remarking also that it had led to disputes with the Qazaq population as the Cossack settlers often encroached on their fields or stole their water.[136] Attempts at Russian colonisation thus remained limited in scope, partly because of continued security fears, but also because those Cossacks who did settle around what would become the towns of Kazalinsk and Perovsk stubbornly refused to become sturdy agriculturalists and instead engaged in more lucrative activities such as petty trade or the carriage of goods.

Overall, as Danzas's letters suggest, the Syr-Darya line was an absolutely miserable place to be stationed, and this affected the morale of officers and men alike. Rates of sickness were high: in February 1854 out of the 107 men of the garrison of Fort No. 2, 12 were sick, and this was by no means unusual. Mortality rates were noticeably higher amongst the Bashkirs than amongst the Russian troops: in October 1854 six died at Fort Perovskii, followed by another seven in November.[137] Five years later visiting engineer A. Gren attributed this to the exceptionally hard labour they were forced to undertake: most of the construction work along the line was done by Bashkirs without any additional pay, and he suggested that both this and their working conditions ought to be improved.[138] Lobysevich described the climate at Fort Perovskii as 'murderous'. The temperature climbed to 40 degrees, whilst a powerful wind blew fine dust into every crevice and horseflies bit people, horses and cattle alike during the day, to be replaced by millions of mosquitoes at night, whilst the steppe surrounding it abounded in camel spiders, scorpions and tarantulas.[139]

> The quarters are poor, the food relatively worse, the climate dangerous and decidedly without any entertainments suitable for the soldier. There is nowhere even to drink a cup of vodka. The soldiers receive six cups of spirits a month, and there is no free sale of wine. The majority, suffering from the lack of women, have recourse to the Kirgiz women nomadising near the fort, who, forced into prostitution through poverty, even for a piece of bread, spread syphilis amongst the military.[140]

[135] D. I. Romanovskii (Military Governor of the Turkestan *Oblast'*) to the temporary commander of the town of Turkestan 14/06/1866; Commander of Fort No. 2 to Romanovskii 22/03/1867; Commander of Fort No. 1 to Romanovskii 07/06/1867; TsGARKaz F.385 Op.1 D.30, 'Perepiska o vodvorenii russkikh pereselentsev v Turkestanskoi oblasti', ll. 8–*ob*, 20, 26, 45.

[136] Bolotov, 'S Syr-Dar'i', 177–8.

[137] 'Stroevyi raport o sostoyanii garnizona Forta No. 2', 28/02/1854 RGVIA F.1433 Op.1 D.1 ll. 261, 268.

[138] Gren, 'Zametki ob ukrepleniyakh', 447.

[139] Lobysevich, 'Syr-Dar'inskaya liniya', 406; current temperatures are comparable, though exacerbated by the loss of the Aral Sea.

[140] Lobysevich, 'Syr-Dar'inskaya liniya', 404.

This problem with syphilis proved predictably difficult to control. In 1863 the commander of Fort Perovskii wrote to Colonel Verevkin, the then commander of the Syr-Darya line, saying that Private Fyodor Rogochin had caught a venereal disease after frequenting the Bukharan bazaar in the Qazaq *aul* near the fort, and asked that in future all *auls* be kept at a distance of 10 *versts*. Verevkin peremptorily refused, writing that it might provoke severe discontent amongst the Qazaqs.[141] In 1863 the War Minister wrote at length to the Governor of Orenburg, A. P. Bezak, about the problems of the line, in particular crime and indiscipline amongst the troops, sentiments which Bezak passed on:

> Service in the forts is so difficult that soldiers deliberately commit crimes in order to be delivered from the steppe, and it is necessary to find means to eliminate this evil – now Colonel Chernyaev has confirmed to me that there have been two such cases amongst the other ranks.[142]

His conclusion was that enforced inactivity was the main problem, and he recommended that they be sent out on expeditions into the steppe more regularly. Officers were not immune to the misery of service on the Syr-Darya either, and bad temper and ferocious disputes were common. The Colonel Chernyaev mentioned in Bezak's letter above was of course Mikhail Grigor'evich Chernyaev (1828–1898), who would find fame as the conqueror of Tashkent in 1865. Chernyaev was the son of Lt-Col. Grigorii Nikitich Chernyaev, a veteran of 1812, and his French wife, Aimée Esther Charlotte Lecuyer. His family were minor nobles with a small estate called Tubyshki in what is now Belarus, where Chernyaev grew up. Despite (or perhaps because of) these modest origins, he affected a highly aristocratic ethos. Arrogant, irascible, highly strung and thin-skinned, Chernyaev notoriously got on very badly with his superior, Danzas, something chronicled in their private correspondence, carefully preserved by Chernyaev in his private archive, in which Danzas accused Chernyaev of impugning his personal honour.[143] In 1861 Lt General Debu issued a stinging rebuke to the Commander of Fort No. 1 after the latter had written directly to the Orenburg supply commission over difficulties with the meat contractors rather than going through him (he made his feelings known by scribbling '*Durak*' (Idiot) in the margin of the letter).[144] Sheer boredom was a considerable problem: although military

---

[141] Commander of Fort Perovskii to Verevkin 15/10/1863; Verevkin to the Garrison Commander of Fort Perovskii 20/10/1863 TsGARKaz F.382 Op.1 D.59 'Perepiska po voprosu o tainykh snosheniyakh kazakhskogo naseleniya s sredneaziyatskimi khanstvami, zabolevanii venericheskoi bolezniiu i dr.', ll. 16–17.

[142] Bezak to Verevkin ?/09/1863 TsGARKaz F.382 Op.1 D.47, 'O budushchikh deistviyakh nashikh v Srednei Azii', l. 29*ob.*

[143] Danzas to Chernyaev 30/12/1858 RGIM OPI F.208 Op.1 D.5 ll. 42–3*ob.*

[144] Debu to the Commander of Fort No.1 29/12/1860 TsGARKaz F.384 Op.1 D.17 l. 58*ob.*

memoirs of life in the steppe understandably concentrated on moments of battle and excitement, these were fleeting moments in an existence remarkable largely for its discomfort and tedium. Lobysevich concluded that

> Society here in Fort Perovskii is fairly large; but social life is very stagnant, although, by comparison with the other forts, it would appear to be more varied. A sort of apathy is imprinted on all faces, and noticeable in all activities.[145]

There was also the looming but generally unspoken fear of desertion by the ordinary soldiers of the garrison. Some of these were Tatar or Bashkir Muslims, but even Orthodox Christians might seek to escape the horrible tedium and brutal discipline of garrison duty in the steppe by escaping to the other side. As early as 1855 eight Qazaqs were given rewards of between 12 and 50 silver roubles for having captured Russian soldiers who had attempted to desert from Fort Perovskii.[146] In January 1860 a Qazaq spy reported that an NCO called Bakaushin was now in Turkestan, where

> he has adopted the Muslim faith and studies the Arab language, they call him Mullah-Musulmanin, he goes about in a *khalat* and turban, and ceaselessly prays and repeats 'Ya Allah' (O God). [...] Bakaushin has recounted at Turkestan that he is not an ordinary Cossack, but an officer, and that he had a significant post in Fort Perovskii, and that because of this the Russians will demand him. Having left Fort Perovskii, he went on foot along the bank of the Syr-Darya and around Julek met with three Kirgiz, who wanted to present him to me, but he said that he was an officer, and that there was a Russian force following in his rear, and that because of this they should not delay him.[147]

Instead he had been able to proceed, and convinced the *Bek* of Turkestan that he was a genuine deserter, and not a spy. A survey by Veniukov of Khoqandi garrisons revealed they relied at least in part on Russian deserters to man their artillery.[148] This was almost certainly true in some cases: one of the Khoqandi artillerymen, known as 'Christian Osman', was a deserter from the Siberian Cossacks who had taken service with 'Alimqul in 1863. After being captured by the Bukharans in 1865 he became one of the commanders of Amir Muzaffar's forces against the Russians (see Chapter 6).[149] Such suspicions

---

[145] Lobysevich, 'Syr-Dar'inskaya liniya', 404.
[146] Report 07/08/1855 TsGARKaz F.383 Op.1 D.17 l. 13.
[147] 'Zapiska o slukakh i sobytiyakh v Srednei Azii', 29/01/1860 RGVIA F.1433 Op.1 D.7 ll. 7–8.
[148] 'Kokanskaya voennaya liniya', 15/07/1860 RGVIA F.1449 Op.1 D.7, 'O dostyzhenii General-Kvartirmeisteru Glavnogo Shtaba Ego Imperatorskogo Velichestva, opisanie kokandskoi voennoi linii na r. Chu, sostavlennago General'nogo Shtaba Kapitanom Veniukovym', ll. 2–3.
[149] *TSM* trans. 74–5, text ff. 77a–8b.

could also extend to Tatar or Bashkir Muslim officers: in 1863 two Cornets of the Orenburg Cossacks, Niyaz Muhammad and Shah Murad Kucherbaev (who was a translator) were accused of having treacherously misdirected a force from Fort Perovskii under the command of Colonel M. G. Chernyaev so that it became vulnerable to attack by the Khoqandis.[150] On the Syr-Darya line, as on all frontiers, 'borders were crossed and allegiances shifted continually'.[151] Qazaqs served both Russia and Khoqand and fought both sides on their own account for good measure, whilst some Russians and Tatars preferred service with a Muslim power to the dreariness and boredom of garrison service on the line.

Thus, while in purely military and intelligence terms the Syr-Darya line functioned reasonably well as a frontier, when it came to questions of morale, food, agriculture and Russian colonisation the problems were much more intractable. The climatic and soil conditions were so harsh, the local population so unreasonably (as the Russians saw it) wedded to a pastoral rather than an agricultural way of life, and the few settlers so feckless and lacking in skill and initiative, that it was clear that it could not be made self-sustaining. The Russians would have to continue to rely either on food, military and building supplies transported from Orenburg at immense cost, or on long-distance trade with the very khanates which constituted their principal foes. By the late 1850s and early 1860s a whole host of factors were pushing the Russians to reconsider the position of their fortified line along the Syr-Darya, acquired with such fanfare and high hopes just a few years before. It was too difficult to supply, too expensive and above all too unpleasant a place to become a permanent military frontier. The question was, should the Russians advance to find a new frontier, or retreat to their old one? Various considerations, strategic and economic, would be brought to bear on this decision, but one of the most important was simply to fix the frontier in a well-forested area with a settled agrarian population, in order to ensure a steady supply of food and building materials to the Russian garrisons along the line.

3.4   The Lure of Tashkent

Russia's defeat in the Crimean War in 1856 had made it clear that further expansion in the Balkans would have to be suspended for the foreseeable future, whilst the capture of Shamil in 1859 rendered the Caucasian frontier more tractable than hitherto. Both these factors contributed to a renewed interest in resolving the difficulties the Tsarist state was encountering on its

---

[150] Verevkin to Gruzdz' ?/07/1863 & 14/05/1864 TsGARKaz F.383 Op.1 D.244, 'Po obvineniiu Khorunzhego Niyaza Mukhamedova i perevodchika Kucherbaeva v izmenicheskikh snosheniyakh s Turkestanskim Bekom', ll. 1–*ob*, 87*ob*–90*ob*.

[151] Barrett, 'Lines of Uncertainty', 149.

southern frontier in the steppe, whilst in the process, perhaps, regaining some lost military prestige.[152] The first manifestation of this was the decision to send N. P. Ignat'ev on an embassy to Bukhara and Khiva in 1858–9 which, whilst it achieved little in diplomatic terms (there was never much likelihood of either khanate allying itself with Khoqand, as the Russians feared), greatly improved Russian intelligence of the upper Amu-Darya, and confirmed the opinion that neither state had significant military resources.[153] A more permanent solution to the perennial problem of frontier security was put forward by General Katenin in September 1858: namely the uniting of the Syr-Darya line (whose woes had been so eloquently recounted to him by Danzas) with that of Western Siberia by means of an advance south through Julek, Yangi-Qurghan and Aulie-Ata to Tashkent.[154] He received support from Gustav Gasfort, the Governor of Western Siberia, who in January 1859 advised St Petersburg that a further advance was necessary on the Siberian line in order to seize the Khoqandi fortresses of Toqmaq, Pishpek, Aulie-Ata, Suzaq and the upper reaches of the river Chu 'in order to unite the southern forward line of Western Siberia with that of Orenburg on the Syr-Darya [. . .] and in this way obtain a firm state boundary [*poluchit' tverduiu gosudarstvennuiu granitsu*]'.[155] This would bring a halt to Khoqandi raiding and firmly establish Russian sovereignty over the Qazaqs of the Great Horde. The state advisory council's verdict on this note, confirmed by the Tsar, was that further reconnaissance of the territory and more detailed estimates of the forces required were needed before an assault on Pishpek could be sanctioned.[156] By late July Mikhail Veniukov had carried out his survey of the upper valley of the Chu, and after several months of preparations and the gathering of supplies and transport in December the attack was finally authorised by the Tsar's own hand (see Chapter 4).[157] The question was whether this advance should become permanent, and thus be met by one from the Syr-Darya line. Accordingly Katenin formed a committee of members of the staff of the Orenburg Corps, who were asked to give their views 'on Russian influence in Asia and the means of

---

[152] Geyer, *Russian Imperialism*, 94–5.

[153] Ignat'ev to Alexander II, 01/1859 GARF F.730 Op.1 D.300 ll. 1–26; Ignat'ev *Missiya v Khivu i Bukharu*, 274–5; Strong 'The Ignat'ev Mission', 258.

[154] 'Vsepoddanneishee donesenie A. A. Katenina', 22/09/1858 cited in Khalfin, *Politika Rossii*, 120.

[155] 'Zapiska Komandira Otdel'nogo Sibirskogo Korpusa i General Gubernatora Zapadnoi Sibiri o neobkhodimosti zanyatiya verkhov'ev r. Chu i predvaritel'nykh k tomu rasporyazheniyam', 21/01/1859 RGVIA F.483 Op.1 D.51 ll. 4–5ob.

[156] This consisted of Prince A. M. Gorchakov (Foreign Ministry), N. O. Sukhozanet (War Ministry), A. F. Knyazhevich (Finance Ministry), Baron V. K. Lieven, E. P. Kovalevskii (former Director of the Asiatic Department), N. P. Ignat'ev (current Director of the same), Katenin and Gasfort himself. 28/01/1859 RGVIA F.483 Op.1 D.51 ll. 12–14ob.

[157] 'Sobstvenno EGO VELICHESTVA rukoyu pisana karandashym: Soglasen', 20/12/1859 RGVIA F.483 Op.1 D.51 l. 241.

increasing it', a file on which the Tsar had written (rather unhelpfully, given the wide range of views therein) 'There is much which is judicious.'

State Counsellor Artsimovich presented the most pessimistic viewpoint: 'The many years in which the Qazaq steppe of the Orenburg agency has been subject to Russia have demonstrated that the steppe brings not only no benefit to the state, but obvious harm. Its revenues do not suffice to cover the expenses of its administration, and maintaining it in a state of calm each year requires the expenditure of vast sums, to the detriment of other aspects of administration in the empire.' He poured scorn on the argument that the establishment of this or that fortified point in the steppe would suddenly bring the long-awaited trade benefits, and also the prospect of any serious competition with Britain in the region. All that was left was the question of a secure frontier, and he considered that 'any conquest along the vast frontiers of Russia is an evil [. . .] and I cannot depart from my conviction that the sole and eternal security for our frontier must be where the limits of Russian population end'. In other words, he advocated a retreat to the original Orenburg and Siberian fortified lines, and he claimed that his views were shared by almost everyone who had spent any time on the administration of the Orenburg region.[158]

Rear-Admiral A. I. Butakov, the creator of the Aral Sea flotilla and a man whose career had been made by the advance along the Syr-Darya and the use of his steamers in the assault on Aq Masjid, was almost equally pessimistic, but came to a rather different conclusion:

> I will not seek to judge whether there was really any necessity to take Fort Perovskii and create the Syr-Darya line. Our expansion to the East along the Syr-Darya into this particularly painful place in the Orenburg *krai* has given us the while nothing but unproductive expenditure. Be that as it may, the Syr-Darya line exists. We cannot abandon it without injury to the honour of Russia; we are obliged to protect the new nomadic subjects of Russia, acquired at a very high price, and it would be shameful of us to abandon them once again to the arbitrariness and exactions of the Khoqandis.' (emphasis in original)[159]

He considered the possibility of carrying on south-eastwards as far as Tashkent, but concluded that it would be too difficult to administer. Instead, predictably enough, he advocated a further advance, but along the Amu-Darya towards Khiva rather than along the Syr towards Khoqand, something that would guarantee a starring role for his flotilla. Butakov wrote that Russia should annex Khiva and establish control over what he fondly imagined

---

[158] Statskii Sovetnik Artsimovich, 'O vliyanie Rossii v Srednei Azii i merakh k uvelichenii', 1859 RGVIA F.483 Op.1 D.53 ll. 1–5ob.

[159] Rear Admiral A. I. Butakov, 'O budushchikh deistviyakh Rossii v Srednei Azii', 1859 RGVIA F.483 Op.1 D.53 ll. 9–ob.

would be an all-water route to the Afghan frontier because it would worry Britain more than any other action Russia could take, and he cited the opinions of Arthur Conolly and James Abbott in the 1830s on this point.[160] Russia should take advantage of the shock which the Indian 'Mutiny' had dealt to British confidence: 'If the English had these misgivings at a time when they were unshakeably certain of the firmness of their rule in India, and when our affairs in the Caucasus were going worse than ever, then what will they do now, when recent events in India have shown them how little they have established themselves there?'[161] He also cited a comparison of the relative merits of the Amu and the Syr, and a description of the water routes to Kungrad by Colonel M. G. Chernyaev. At this stage the future conqueror of Tashkent was also a firm advocate of the Amu-Darya route, writing that the lower reaches of the Syr were unknown territory, and that the lines of supply from Orenburg would be so long that the Russians would in any case be confronted with a choice between advancing further to annex more fertile regions to the south, or annexing the lower reaches of the Amu, which were already known to be productive, in order to use their resources to supply the Syr-Darya line.[162] The orientalist V. V. Grigor'ev, at that time the head of the Orenburg Frontier Commission, was against any advance whatsoever, writing that it would serve only to stir up the fanaticism of the inhabitants of Khoqand and Bukhara, especially if the Russians were to seize Turkestan, site of the mausoleum of Khwaja Ahmad Yasavi.[163] However, Colonel Dandevil', the then commander of the Syr-Darya line, was quite certain that the Russians should advance along the Syr-Darya and take Tashkent, extending their frontier as far as the River Chirchik. This would counter British influence and trade in the neighbouring regions of China and Persia, would allow the Russians to dominate all three khanates, and should provide a firmer, and above all cheaper, frontier than the one they had at present.[164]

---

[160] Arthur Conolly, *Journey to the North of India Overland from England through Russia, Persia and Affghaunistan* (London: Richard Bentley, 1834) 2 volumes; Abbott, *Narrative of a Journey from Heraut to Khiva.*

[161] Butakov, 'O budushchikh deistviyakh Rossii v Srednei Azii', 1859 RGVIA F.483 Op.1 D.53 ll. 10*ob*–11.

[162] Chernyaev, 'Sravnitel'nyi ocherk Amu i Syra', RGVIA F.483 Op.1 D.53 ll. 40–1. In Chernyaev's private papers the same text appears as 'Dokladnaya zapiska General'nogo Shtaba Podpolkovnika Chernyaeva G-nu Komandiru Otdel'nogo Orenburgskogo Korpusa 1858 g.', RGIM OPI F.208 Op.1 D.4, 'Materialy kasaiushchii 1858 g. po Syr-D. linii', ll. 48–9. Chernyaev's description of the routes to Kungrad is on ll. 10–35 of this file, and as cited by Butakov in RGVIA F.483 Op.1 D.53 ll. 19–28. It was published in *Russkii Arkhiv* in 1905.

[163] V. V. Grigor'ev, 'Chto predstavlyaetsya vygodneishim dlya nas: Zanyatie del'ty Amy, ili dvizhenie vverkh po Syru do Tashkenta vkliuchitel'no?', RGVIA F.483 Op.1 D.53 ll. 42–57. See Knight, 'Grigor'ev in Orenburg, 1851–1862', 86–9.

[164] Dandevil', 'O deistviyakh nashikh v Srednei Azii', RGVIA F.483 Op.1 D.53 ll. 58–83.

Thus already in 1859, well before the outbreak of the American Civil War and consequent cotton famine, some voices were calling for the annexation of Tashkent, but there was still considerable disagreement as to whether this was necessary or desirable. Discussion was dominated, above all, by the practicalities of reducing expenditure, guaranteeing easy supplies and ensuring security. As discussed in the Introduction, big capitalist lobbying for the securing of captive markets and supplies of raw material for Russian industry in Central Asia, so beloved of Soviet historians and those who thoughtlessly reproduce their Leninist (or Hobsonian) arguments, was never mentioned.[165] Trade considerations did play a role in Russian decision-making, although in military correspondence in particular it is likely that officers often merely paid lip-service to its importance, and in most cases saw it as a means of furthering political interests rather than an end in itself. In 1859 Osmolovskii produced a lengthy memorandum on Russia's position in Central Asia in which he discussed the competition between British and Russian goods in the Bukharan market, and British ambitions to create a 'great Afghanistan' under their influence which would include parts of the territory of Khiva, Khoqand and Bukhara. He nevertheless concluded that, however useful some Central Asian products such as cotton might be, 'regardless of all success in this regard, the low population of the Central Asian khanates will always be a reason why our trade with them cannot develop on a large scale'. Instead he thought trade with Chinese Turkestan a much more promising prospect; however, in order to penetrate this market a further advance would be necessary:

> For the consolidation of our trade with Chinese Turkestan it is essential to establish our sovereignty, not on the steppe amongst wandering nomads, but in the settled regions – neighbouring Tashkent, which we would then be able to quickly develop as an entrepôt and focus for our Central Asian trade; then the improvement of routes of communication would no longer be utopian, but an essential requirement, and, despite the unenterprising nature of our merchants, seeing their interests in a clear and tangible way, they would no longer fear to invest their capital.[166]

In other words, it was the long-distance trade with neighbouring regions which mattered more than that with the Central Asian khanates itself, and the state was to be the facilitator of sluggish private enterprise, not the servant of powerful commercial interests. Such considerations could be invoked to convince sceptical officials at the Ministry of Finance of the need for further annexations, but they were not the crucial factor behind the decision to renew the Russian advance in 1860–1. Neither was it anything to do with

---

[165] Khalfin, *Politika Rossii*, 154–64; Beckert, *Empire of Cotton*, 345–7.
[166] 'Zapiska o slukhakh i sobytitakh v Srednei Azii', 31/12/1859 RGVIA F.1433 Op.1 D.7 ll. 12–15.

a supposed threat from the British in India, who were still recovering from the effects of the 1857 rebellion, and under the cautious Viceroyalty of Sir John Lawrence from 1864–9 were not about to launch an aggressive policy in Central Asia, as the Russians were well aware. In 1864, after rumours that British agents had appeared in Bukhara with the intention of launching steamers on the Amu-Darya, Governor Bezak, who was certainly no dove in Central Asian affairs, and as we shall see had not long since enthusiastically endorsed the uniting of the Syr-Darya and Siberian lines and the capture of Tashkent, made the following revealing arguments about the folly of extending Russian rule any further south:

> The very carriage of heavy and burdensome parts of iron steamers, such as the hull, across the Hindu Kush, is probably not possible, and even if it were, what benefit would [the English] gain if they managed with enormous effort to float a few steamers on the Amu Darya? In my view none at all. Through the agency of Afghan merchants English goods even without this are already able to spread [...] from India to the Central Asian khanates; but this trade can never become significant or particularly profitable because of the poverty of the inhabitants of these countries, who have little demand for textile products; even for us trade with the Bukharans is not profitable, thanks to their carriage of large amounts of coin from Russia; if at the moment they are essential for our factories in supplying them with cotton, this will only last as long as the war in America.
>
> Turning to the political side, I am very doubtful whether the English really have any desire to extend their power over the Central Asian khanates; they are of course sure that in such a case they will come into conflict in Asia prematurely with Russia, at a time when they do not have the means to throw them back on the other side of the mountains, and apart from this it would oblige [the Russians] to advance their frontier closer to India, something which the English without doubt wish to avoid as far as they possibly can. Finally, the loss in the 1840s in Afghanistan of an army of 20,000 men, and their decision not to attempt again the invasion of that country, allows us to posit that the English will not enter the desert khanates of Central Asia, and that the rumours of their measures to construct a flotilla on the Amu-Darya, so long as they remain unconfirmed, are no more than rumours.[167]

This memorandum neatly dismisses both the 'Great Game' theory and the 'Cotton Canard' argument for the Russian advance in two paragraphs, although it is easy to see how, quoted out of context, it might be manipulated to confirm both of them. It is in fact one of the rare references to cotton in debates among the military, and, as we can see, a negative one: even before the end of the American Civil War, nobody thought the cotton famine would last

---

[167] Bezak to Miliutin 27/02/1864, in Serebrennikov, *Sbornik. 1864 g. Pt. 1*, Doc.37, 73.

forever. The campaign to unite the Syr-Darya and Siberian lines of fortresses in
Central Asia did not proceed from rational economic calculation, rivalry with
Britain, local aggression, or 'men on the spot', but was instead the outcome of
a sustained debate between Orenburg, Omsk and the highest levels of government in St Petersburg, a debate which focused primarily on military security,
logistics and what the Russians saw as the immediate threat from the Central
Asian khanates, in which the major players were the new Governors of
Orenburg and Western Siberia – A. P. Bezak and A. O. Diugamel – and the
new War Minister, Dmitrii Alexeevich Miliutin (1816–1912). The latter was
one of the greatest statesmen of the post-1861 reform era, whose diaries and
voluminous memoirs, composed during a long retirement, are also one of the
key sources for understanding decision-making at the highest levels of Russian
government in this period.

3.5   Uniting the Lines

Although he was fairly guarded on the subject both in his private and public
correspondence, it seems clear that Miliutin strongly favoured a further
advance, primarily for strategic reasons, and was not in favour of trying to
maintain a frontier on the Syr-Darya. A letter from him which was circulated
by Bezak to the officers of the Line contained the following telling sentiments:
'The construction of such fortresses is expensive, brings little benefit (as the
fortress remains in a passive state) and will restrict us still further in future.'[168]
As he later recalled, 'in the Central Asian borderlands our situation appeared
to be somewhat undefined; we did not even have a definite state border'.[169]
Thus the receipt late in 1861 of a lengthy memorandum from Bezak, arguing
for the unsustainability of the Syr-Darya line as a frontier, is likely to have been
welcome to him.

   Bezak began his review of the situation along the line with an account of how
at one time Obruchev's 'system of separate fortresses in the steppe, taking the
place of the frequent and expensive despatch of forces, was the best means of
defending our frontiers at the time from predatory Kirgiz'. Neither these, nor
the Syr-Darya fortresses, were adequate any longer, however:

> The construction of these fortresses, on account of a lack of local means,
> and through errors in the initial design, has turned out to be extraordin-
> arily expensive. At the moment expenditure on the forts in the steppe, and
> on the garrisons which occupy them, amounts to up to 700,000 silver
> roubles a year, whilst the levy on *kibitkas* brings in no more than 200,000.

[168] 'Vypiska iz pis'ma Voennogo Ministra', n.d. (after Dec. 1862), TsGARKaz F.382 Op.1
D.47, 'O budushchikh deistviyakh nashikh v Srednei Azii', l. 2ob.
[169] D. A. Miliutin, *Vospominaniya 1860–1862* ed. L. G. Zakharova (Moscow: Rossiiskii
Arkhiv, 1999), 208.

In consequence the government has doomed itself to an annual subsidy of almost half a million, not counting expenditure on the administration of the region, which comes to another 100,000 silver roubles.

The government, wanting to escape from this undesirable state of affairs, gave instructions for the establishment of Russian colonies near the forts; but the experience of the settlements at Fort No. 1, and also at the Ural'sk and Orenburg fortresses [Irgiz and Turgai] and Kara-Butak, proved not to be durable. Settled Cossacks, unaccustomed to carrying out the heavy labour associated with cultivation in the steppe, came to occupy themselves largely with carriage and trade, thus the Government's aim has not been realised, and hopes for the creation of Russian settlements on the Syr, and for the development of agriculture remain unrealised. If we can expect more grain to be sown in the steppe at all, then it is more likely to be by the Kirgiz themselves; but this will take a great deal of time, because even the poorest *ichins* (ploughmen) grow grain only as a last resort, and so long as the Kirgiz are satisfied with nomadic life in our or neighbouring jurisdictions they do not turn to agriculture.[170]

The annual expenses were now approaching 1,300,000 silver roubles, and there was still no firm frontier, either to the west, across the Aral Sea, or to the east, from Julek, the southernmost fortress of the Syr-Darya, to the Siberian Line.

We can only escape from this situation on the Eastern frontier by driving on up the Syr-Darya in order to take more fertile areas with a settled native population, where there is abundant grain productivity, and where there are standing forests which are essential to the support of our fortresses on the Syr-Darya. [. . .] Between Turkestan and Tashkent, according to those of our merchants who have been there, grain cultivation is in a flourishing state.[171]

He was not proposing that any advance take place immediately, not least because extensive reconnaissance would be necessary, but he felt sure that this would chime with the views of the Tsar. Bezak referred to how ten years before, in the time of Count Perovskii, Nicholas I had expressed the desirability of uniting the Siberian and Orenburg lines, saying it was of the greatest importance, and urging the benefits it could bring to Russian trade with China. This could now be done either by taking Turkestan or by pushing on to Tashkent, but he favoured the latter. If they took Tashkent,

Then Russia would obtain on this side an excellent state boundary [. . .] it gives us the possibility to cheaply supply our forts on the Syr-Darya with provisions and wooden materials, with the aid of our flotilla. [. . .] As Tashkent is the most important manufacturing town in those parts, through which pass all the trade routes between Bukhara, China and

---

[170] Bezak to Miliutin 29/11/1861 RGVIA F.483 Op.1 D.62 ll. 6*ob*–7.
[171] Bezak to Miliutin 29/11/1861 RGVIA F.483 Op.1 D.62 ll. 8–*ob*.

Russia, and as Khoqand is only 150 *versts* distant from it, if we ruled
Tashkent, we would not only have a decisive influence over the Khanate of
Khoqand, but would strengthen our influence over Bukhara, which would
significantly develop our trade.[172]

He also believed that Tashkent itself might bring in revenues of up to
1,350,000 silver roubles, basing his assertion on a description of the
Khoqand Khanate published in the *Journal of the Imperial Geographical
Society* in 1849.[173] He did not think this was likely to cause any particular
problems with the British, as 'I do not think, incidentally, that the English
seriously fear an expedition of ours to India, in my view this is a chimera
which they will not yield to, being a highly practical people', and he
considered they would probably accept Russian arguments about the need
to protect their Qazaq subjects: in any case, Russia could not afford to
allow her policy in Central Asia to be dictated by Britain's likes and
dislikes.[174] Miliutin referred approvingly to Bezak's plan in his memoirs,
but simply as the prelude to the capture and destruction of the Khoqandi
fortress of Yangi Qurghan later that year: he mentioned neither Bezak's
proposal to seize Tashkent, nor the reasons he had advanced for doing
so.[175]

Bezak's letter provoked a cautious reaction from Ignat'ev, the current head
of the Asiatic Department of the Ministry of Foreign Affairs and a more
enthusiastic one from his predecessor Kovalevskii, but Diugamel, the new
Governor of Western Siberia, was bitterly opposed. Tashkent could perhaps
be taken, he wrote, but it would require the construction of two more fortresses
at a cost of over 700,000 roubles, and he was sceptical about the quantity of
revenue the city would yield. There would be no material benefits, and any
political ones would take a long time to manifest themselves. He expressed
himself still more forthrightly in a letter in French to Prince A. M. Gorchakov
(1798–1883) , the Minister of Foreign Affairs, on which Alexander II had
written 'C'est fort sage et juste':

> It is impossible for me to share the opinion put forth by Adj.-General
> Bezak and Lt-Gen. Kovalevskii on the urgency and utility of conquering
> the province of Tashkent. I'm afraid that we are embarking on a bad
> business, of which the final consequences cannot even be predicted at this

[172] Bezak to Miliutin 29/11/1861 RGVIA F.483 Op.1 D.62 ll. 13–*ob*; Khalfin cites the copy of
this memorandum made by Serebrennikov from his *Fond* in the Tashkent archives, and
(I can only assume) invents a line about 'valuable mineral deposits for national industry'
which is not in the original. Khalfin, *Politika Rossii*, 142.

[173] 'Obozreniya Kokanskogo khanstva v nyneshnem ego sostoyanii', *ZIRGO*. Kn. III (1849),
96–116.

[174] Bezak to Miliutin 29/11/1861 RGVIA F.483 Op.1 D.62 l. 15.

[175] Miliutin, *Vospominaniya 1860–1862*, 208.

moment. To organise distant conquests instead of developing the resources of the Transsiberian country which, with colonists other than Cossacks, could become very flourishing, is to abandon reality to chase after shadows.[176]

Gorchakov forwarded this letter to Miliutin, drawing his attention to the Tsar's annotation, whilst observing that 'Je souffre d'un violent accès de goutte qui me rends pour le moment inhabile pour tout travail sérieux.'[177] The inclusion of such personal details, together with the use of French throughout this correspondence, emphasises that this matter was being debated within the very highest circles of Russian government. Miliutin (who in his memoirs referred to Diugamel as 'the embodiment of inertia')[178] then attempted to convince the Governor of Siberia of the need for a forward policy, dropping all reference to Tashkent but pointing out that even the region around Aulie-Ata was said to be sufficiently fertile to sustain a settled population. Diugamel was still sceptical: 'The further and deeper we go into the interior of Asia, the greater are the expenses.' However, he now put forward an alternative proposal: the separation of Tashkent from Khoqandi rule, and its re-establishment as an independent khanate, with a Russian client as its ruler.[179] The Central Asian Committee, consisting of Gorchakov, Bezak, Miliutin, Reutern, Vershinin, Kovalevskii and Ignat'ev, met on the 28 February 1863 to consider these proposals, and its written conclusions appeared on the 2 March. Whilst acknowledging that the decision to establish the Syr-Darya line of fortresses might have been a mistake, 'we must acknowledge that it is a historical fact, and now limit ourselves to considering what measures we can take to improve and consolidate our position in that distant region,' the cost of whose maintenance they estimated at 600,000 roubles a year. 'Remaining in the north, we control the poorest, most infertile places, when neighbouring them is a rich region, plentiful in good things.' This meant the unification of the two lines – the question was what form it should take: the conquest of Turkestan and Tashkent, or the creation of a client khanate in the latter city? The latter option

---

[176] 'Il m'est impossible de partager l'opinion émise par l'Aide de camp Général Bézak et le Lt. General Kovalevsky sur l'urgence et l'utilité de conquérir la province de Tachkent. Je crains que nous nous embarquons là dans une mauvaise affaire, dont les dernières conséquences ne sont même pas à prévenir dans ce moment. Convoquer des conquêtes lointaines, au lieu de développer les resources de la contrée transsibérienne qui avec d'autres colons que des Cosaques, pourrant devenir très florissante, c'est abandonner la réalité pour courrir après l'ombre.' Diugamel to A. M. Gorchakov 26/ 05/1862 RGVIA F.483 Op.1 D.62 ll. 70–ob.

[177] 'I am suffering from a violent attack of gout which renders me for the moment incapable of all serious work'. A. M. Gorchakov to Miliutin 15/06/1862 RGVIA F.483 Op.1 D.62 l. 72.

[178] Miliutin Vospominaniya 1860–1862, 36.

[179] Miliutin to Diugamel 28/06/1862; Diugamel to Miliutin 04/09/1862; Diugamel Memorandum 23/01/1863 RGVIA F.483 Op.1 D.62 ll. 77–85ob, 89, 128–30.

would be cheaper and attract less attention from other European powers, and could be endorsed by reference to the imperial rival Russia most sought to emulate: 'the English direct a similar system which has brought beneficial results in India'. The Minister of Finance, Baron Reutern, agreed with Miliutin that Russia's previous actions in establishing the Syr-Darya line and conquering the Qazaq steppe now belonged to history, 'and it is now too late to debate whether or not this region was really necessary for us. Fully recognising that Russia must not concede or abandon those places which she already rules, the Minister of Finance finds that we must therefore be still more careful and prudent in future with each new forward step in Central Asia.' He opposed any further advance, saying that, whilst the areas proposed for annexation might be fertile, Russia at present did not have the resources and capital to develop them properly.[180] Gorchakov concluded by saying that it was also important to preserve good relations with Russia's neighbours, and the committee's overall conclusion, much to Bezak and Miliutin's disgust, was that, however desirable the uniting of the lines might be, it would have to be postponed, at least until the following year. In the interim, however, Colonel Chernyaev was authorised to conduct a reconnaissance from Julek towards Turkestan along the line of the proposed frontier, and to send a 'flying column' to probe the defences of the Khoqandi fortress of Suzaq.[181] Zaionchkovskii notes that after Diugamel had left St Petersburg Miliutin made some changes to the committee's recommendations, altering Chernyaev's orders from 'not to undertake any military actions whatsoever' to 'avoid all conflicts with the Khoqandis as far as possible'.[182] As we will see in Chapter 5, the ambitious Chernyaev knew only too well how to take advantage of such ambiguities.

Whilst the Russian advance was being planned in St Petersburg, relative peace prevailed with Khoqand. Although tsarist historians generally claimed that Russian attacks were always provoked by Khoqandi aggression, the view from the other side was different. According to the *Ta'rikh-i 'Aliquli*, even as the Russians made their plans for the uniting of the fortresses and the annexation of more Khoqandi territory, the leadership of the khanate was contemplating a rapprochement. Mullah Yunus remembered advising 'Alimqul in March 1864 that, as there had been a period of peace with Russia (which was how he interpreted the lull after the capture of Julek in 1860), now was the time to send an embassy of four respected *'ulama* (scholars) with connections amongst the Tatar merchants in Russia in order to negotiate peace. 'Alimqul said that he would consider this, but in the interim a diplomatic crisis emerged

---

[180] Thus rather scuppering Khalfin's theory that Reutern saw the conquest of Central Asia as a means of restoring the Imperial finances after the Crimean War: Khalfin, *Politika Rossii*, 60–2. Zaionchkovskii correctly noted Reutern's opposition to Miliutin's plan: Zaionchkovskii, 'K voprosu zavoevaniya Srednei Azii', 39.

[181] 02/03/1863 RGVIA F.483 Op.1 D.62 ll. 160–78.

[182] Zaionchkovskii, 'K voprosu zavoevaniya Srednei Azii', 41.

in Kashgar, where the Khoqandi ambassador had been detained by Yaqub Beg. Mullah Yunus was sent to resolve this, but when he had returned 'Alimqul said to him: 'We are very glad and satisfied with your actions. But you were too long of a journey. [Therefore] the opportunity [to send an ambassador] has passed. Turkistan has been lost [to the Russians].'[183]

As this suggests, the Russian decision to call a halt did not last long: in June Bezak wrote to Miliutin to say that Chernyaev had taken Suzaq with surprisingly little effort and cost, and that now 'it seems to me that the most rational form of action' would be to carry on reconnaissance of the routes towards Aulie-Ata, to determine whether the land was as fertile as Chernyaev's forces had reported the area around Suzaq to be, and therefore whether it would be suitable for the future frontier.[184] This in turn prompted Miliutin to write a belligerent letter to Gorchakov, urging once again the importance of uniting the line, the possibilities it gave of reducing the garrisons in its most difficult sections and moving them to more fertile areas and thus reducing costs, and also its usefulness in diplomatic terms: 'In the case of a European war we must especially value the occupation of a region which brings us closer to the northern borders of India, and renders easier our access to that country. Ruling in Khoqand, we will be able to permanently threaten the East Indian possessions of England. It is still more important as it is *only here* that we can be dangerous to this enemy of ours.' This 'Great Game' argument (which, we should note, Miliutin invoked only *after* the emphasis on the immediate military needs of the frontier had failed to move the Foreign Ministry) finally convinced Gorchakov, as the latter wrote that it did indeed seem to be a good idea to take advantage of the momentum created by Chernyaev's easy victory at Suzaq, and unite the two lines along the summit of the Qara-Tau range, through Aulie-Ata.[185] On the 1 August Miliutin and Gorchakov presented Alexander II with their joint conclusion that the lines should be united forthwith, although omitting Miliutin's arguments about threatening Britain, and the Tsar approved the plan. Miliutin sent the substance of their reasoning to Bezak a week later:

> In uniting the line, and with the establishment of our frontier on the summit of the Qara-Tau, we are not broadening our frontiers, but on the contrary restricting their extent, and coming closer to the fertile regions of Central Asia; as a consequence we will be able to use the resources of these lands, guaranteeing the sustenance of the garrisons of our steppe fortresses, and only then will the Syr-Darya line obtain the significance which is its due, when it can be satisfied by local resources, rather than supplies brought from the interior of Russia. The fulfilment of this union

[183] *TA*, trans. 61–3. text. ff. 64a–7a.
[184] Bezak to Miliutin 11/06/1863 & 25/06/1863 RGVIA F.483 Op.1 D.62 ll. 189–97.
[185] Miliutin to A. M. Gorchakov 01/?/1863 RGVIA F.483 Op.1 D.62 ll. 198ob–9ob.

represents the furthest development of the idea, stated in the Journal of
the Special Committee of the 2 March this year (confirmed by his Imperial
Majesty) and considered by your Excellency and the Commander of the
Siberian Corps. At that time the Committee could not accept the aforesaid
proposal, partly because of the lack of precision of the proposed measures
and anticipated expenses, and also because of the impossibility of recon-
ciling your opinion on the necessity of taking Tashkent with the conclusion of General Diugamel, proposing that it would be more beneficial for
us to turn Tashkent into an independent khanate. Because of this the
Committee concluded with the thought that 'the actual uniting of
the Orenburg and Siberia Lines, *however desirable it might be*, must for
the time being be set aside, limiting ourselves for the immediate future
exclusively to putting a barrier around those Kirgiz who are already under
our jurisdiction, and studying the area which divides the two advanced
lines'. Now, the situation of the question has fundamentally changed. The
successful action of Colonel Chernyaev, without any special expenditure
or casualties, has brought us significantly closer to the fulfilment of our
principal aim.[186]

Thus, in the final resort, a small successful action by an officer on the frontier
was enough to tip the scale and push the more cautious members of the
Committee towards Miliutin's point of view (much to his evident satisfaction
and Diugamel's disgust).[187] Chernyaev had powerful supporters both in
Orenburg and in St Petersburg, whom he knew would endorse his actions.
The final outcome of the campaign to 'unite the line' is well known, though not
without its own controversies, which will be dealt with in Chapter 5. However,
the consistent factor informing all Russian decisions in 1859–63 was the need
to solve the Syr-Darya line's urgent problems of security, morale and, above all,
supply.

The classic justification for the Russian conquest of Central Asia, repeatedly
invoked by historians, remains that given by Foreign Minister Prince
A. M. Gorchakov in his famous circular to European Governments of 1864,
which emphasised the instability of the existing frontier, and Russia's responsibility, shared with other 'civilised' powers, of disciplining and controlling the
savage tribes on her frontiers. Whilst these considerations did play an important part in Russian deliberations over advancing the line of their frontier, they
were neither the sole, nor the decisive ones. These were in fact mentioned by
Gorchakov, but have never received the same degree of attention from
historians:

> It was essential that the line of our advanced forts thus completed should
> be situated in a country fertile enough, not only to insure their supplies,

---

[186] Miliutin to Bezak 12/08/1863 TsGARKaz F.382 Op.1 D.47, 'O budushchikh deistviyakh
nashikh v Srednei Azii', ll. 33*ob*–4*ob*.

[187] 'Avtobiografiya A. O. Diugamelya', *RA* (1885), No. 10, 161, 163.

but also to facilitate the regular colonization, which alone can prepare a future of stability and prosperity for the occupied country, by gaining over the neighbouring populations to civilized life. [...] By the adoption of this line we obtain a double result. In the first place, the country it takes in is fertile, well wooded, and watered by numerous water-courses; it is partly inhabited by various Kirghize tribes, which have already accepted our rule; it consequently offers favourable conditions for colonization, and the supply of provisions to our garrisons. In the second place, it puts us in the immediate neighbourhood of the agricultural and commercial populations of Khoqand.[188]

The decision of the Russians to move their frontier far to the south so that it would run through the settled regions of Central Asia was motivated by a number of factors. Prestige – the refusal to countenance frontier raids, or to be seen to retreat or abandon territory – was one. The desire for a firmly demarcated, secure frontier was another. The expansion of trade was a third, although arguably rather less important, and mainly aimed at tapping the larger markets of India, China and Persia that lay beyond Central Asia itself. But one crucial factor, and one which is rarely, if ever, referred to, is that in the 1840s and 1850s they had chosen the worst possible place to try to build a frontier – a particularly painful place, in Butakov's words – which was too expensive and difficult to maintain precisely because it lay mid-way between the limits of Russian settlement to the north and the riverine oases to the south. Within a few years of the fall of Aq Masjid the Russians had realised this, and instead wanted a frontier that ran through a region with a sedentary, rather than a nomadic, population, with an ample supply of grain and wood, and with a climate and surroundings that did not sap and destroy the morale of their officers and men. They could obtain this only by either retreating to their original fortified line at Orenburg, or advancing to the oases around Aulie-Ata, Chimkent and, above all, Tashkent itself. The former option was proposed by some, but ruled out for reasons of prestige, so they chose the latter. Whilst the final decision to take Tashkent had not yet been made in 1863–4, the logic which led to it is clearly illustrated in the official debates on the subject. At the very least, further conquests meant that the Russians would no longer have to base a frontier on a line of flyblown, crumbling and expensive fortresses strung out along the edge of the Qizil-Qum.

---

[188] 'Circular Dispatch Addressed by Prince Gortchakow to Russian Representatives Abroad', 21 November 1864, *PP* Central Asia No. 2 (1873), *Correspondence Respecting Central Asia* C.704, 70–5. Miliutin later echoed these sentiments, which, as we have seen, originated with the War Ministry: D. A. Miliutin, *Vospominaniya 1863–1864* (Moscow: ROSSPEN, 2003), 520–1.

4

From Ayaguz to Almaty: The Conquest and Settlement of Semirechie, 1843–82

> *Zhaghana duan tusken song*
> *Suingdy orys ishken song*
> *Ayaghöz suy kaghyndy*
>
> When the Tsar took her banks,
> When Russians drank her water,
> The very water of the Ayagoz shivered
>
> Dulat Babataiuli, *Sayir zherden airylyp*, translation
> © Gabriel McGuire

The annexation of the region known historically as Jeti-su, or in Russian Semirechie – the Land of the Seven Rivers – is often overlooked in histories of the conquest of Central Asia. Its name refers to the relatively well-watered nature of the region, lying in what is now south-eastern Kazakhstan and northern Kyrgyzstan, where the steppe grasslands merge into the fertile and forested foothills of the snowy Ala-Tau mountains, the original homeland of the humble and ubiquitous apple, where today some of the finest apricots in Central Asia are also cultivated. The most important of the eponymous seven rivers is the Ili, which flows into Lake Balkhash. Beyond the Ala-Tau, encircled by mountains, lies one of the world's largest alpine lakes, Issyq-Kul, whose warm and slightly saline waters never freeze even in the depths of winter.[1] The complexity of the history of Semirechie in this period – inhabited largely by Qazaqs and Kyrgyz, but contested between Russia, Qing China and the Khanate of Khoqand – has made the creation of straightforward narratives of imperial heroism or national resistance more difficult. In most accounts of the Russian advance in the 1840s and 1850s the principal focus is instead on the campaigns launched from Orenburg, Russia's key garrison town on the north-western fringes of the steppe.[2] As we saw in the previous chapter, in the Orenburg region the Russian advance took on an almost wholly military character: repeated attempts to colonise the Syr-Darya with

---

My thanks to Ablet Kamalov and Daniel Prior for their detailed comments on this chapter.

[1] The best summary of Semirechie's history from the first century to the middle of the eighteenth century remains that of Vasilii Bartol'd, 'Ocherk istorii Semirech'ya', in *Sochineniya*. Vol. II, Part 1 (Moscow: Izd. Vostochnoi Literatury, 1963), 23–106.

[2] Terent'ev, *Istoriya zavoevaniya*, I, 212–59.

Cossacks and Russian peasants from the Urals or Siberia failed. This made it impossible for the Syr-Darya fortresses to become self-sufficient, and these logistical difficulties would become the driving force behind the Russian decision to renew the advance towards Tashkent in 1863, leading to the fall of that city in 1865. This final steppe campaign was intended to unite two fortified lines to create a new and supposedly 'natural' frontier.[3] However, General M. G. Chernyaev, who in capturing Aulie-Ata, Chimkent and Tashkent in quick succession laid the groundwork for the new frontier, was under the Western Siberian command when he began this final campaign in 1864. He and his troops set out not from Fort Perovskii, but from Fort Vernoe, which had been founded one year after its counterpart on the Syr-Darya, in 1854, as the centre of what the Russians then called the Trans-Ili region (*Zailiiskii krai*) or the Alatau district (*Alatauskii okrug*), which would become Semirechie Province (*Semirechenskaya oblast'*) after 1867. Well before the fall of Tashkent, and in stark contrast to the Syr-Darya region, Semirechie already had the makings of the Russian settler colony which it was to become in the second half of the nineteenth century. The present chapter will explore this second, lesser-known prong of the Russian advance into Central Asia from Western Siberia, which was directed from Omsk. This saw Russian settlements extended south-east from Semipalatinsk on the Irtysh, first to the steppe fortress of Ayaguz in 1831, then Lepsinsk in 1843, Kapal in 1847, and the establishment of Fort Vernoe in the valley of the Almaty rivers in 1854. I argue that environmental factors were decisive in determining the nature of this stage of the advance, which, whilst it also had a military and violent character (most obviously seen in the key battle of Uzun-Agach in 1860, the one episode in Semirechie referred to by Terent'ev),[4] was, to a much greater extent than on the line of advance from Orenburg, an extension of earlier patterns of colonisation in Western Siberia.[5] Another prominent factor in Semirechie was the existence of multiple, fluid frontiers and sovereignty contested between many different parties – the Russians, Khoqand, the Northern Kyrgyz, the Qazaqs of the Great Horde (*Uli zhuz*) and another great, if declining power – Qing China. The effect of the Russian advance would be to create a new frontier with China, which, with very minor alterations, remains in place to this day.[6] The existence of these frontiers created

---

[3] See the following chapter and Alexander Morrison, 'Russia, Khoqand, and the Search for a Natural Frontier, 1863–1865', *AI* (2014), No. 2, 165–92.

[4] Terent'ev, *Istoriya zavoevaniya*, II, 252–8.

[5] Probably the best published account of this advance is that by Irina Erofeeva in M. K. Kozybaev (ed.), *Istoriya Kazakhstana s drevneishikh vremen do nashikh dnei*. Vol. III. *Kazakhstan v Novoe Vremya* (Almaty: Atamura, 2010), 362–90. See also B. Z. Galiev, 'Prodvizhenie rossiiskikh voisk po territorii iuzhnogo Kazakhstana', in *Istoriya kolonizatsii Kazakhstana v 20–60x godakh XIX veka* ed. B. Z. Galiev & S. F. Mazhitov (Almaty: Mektep, 2009), 111–30.

[6] The classic description is Owen Lattimore, *Inner Asian Frontiers of China* (New York, NY: American Geographical Society, 1940), 151–205. See also Joseph Fletcher, 'Ch'ing Inner Asia c. 1800', in *The Cambridge History of China*. Vol. 10 (Cambridge: Cambridge University Press, 1978), 58–90.

political conflict and difficult choices for the Qazaqs and Kyrgyz caught between them, but at the same time presented them with opportunities. A recurring pattern in Semirechie is that of Qazaqs migrating between different jurisdictions to avoid taxation, and Qazaq and Kyrgyz leaders affirming their loyalty to Khoqand, Russia or China in turn, depending on what seemed most beneficial at the time.

It was also on this frontier that we see the only instance during the Russian conquest of the voluntary cession of territory already annexed: the occupation of the Ili valley in 1871, and its return to China ten years later. This episode, which created new patterns of migration that had profound consequences for Semirechie's demography, has been the subject of several previous studies.[7] It deserves reconsideration here because the decision to hand this territory back tells us something important about the broader motivations and logic of the Russian advance in Central Asia.

4.1   Early Explorations and Chinggissid Contacts

Russian geographical knowledge of Semirechie prior to and during their advance into the region was considerably superior to their knowledge of the Aral Sea and the Syr-Darya, which would be described and mapped only after occupation: as we have seen, early enthusiastic descriptions of the fertility and capacity for supporting colonists of the latter region turned out to be ill-founded. In contrast, Semirechie was first explored by Grigorii Karelin and Alexander Shrenk in 1839–45, then most famously by Petr Petrovich Semenov (1827–1914), who would acquire the sobriquet 'Tian-Shanskii' thanks to his explorations in the mountains of that name.[8] From our perspective the most interesting and best-informed accounts of the region and its population are those by the famous Qazaq officer and ethnographer Choqan Valikhanov

---

[7] Charles and Barbara Jelavich (eds.), *Russia in the East 1876–1880* (Leiden: E. J. Brill, 1959); Immanuel C. Y. Hsü *The Ili Crisis: A Study of Sino-Russian Diplomacy 1871–1881* (Oxford: Clarendon Press, 1965); S. C. M. Paine, *Imperial Rivals: China, Russia, and Their Disputed Frontier* (Armonk, NY: M. E. Sharpe, 1996), 107–74; Alexei D. Voskressenski, *The Sino-Russian St Petersburg Treaty of 1881: Diplomatic History* (Commack, NY: Nova Science Publishers, 1996); S. V. Moiseev, *Rossiya i Kitai v Tsentral'noi Azii (vtoraya polovina XIX v.–1917 g.)* (Barnaul: AzBuka, 2003); S. V. Moiseev, *Vzaimootnosheniya Rossii i uigurskogo gosudarstva Iettishar, 1864–1877 gg.* (Barnaul: AzBuka, 2006); Gorshenina, *Asie Centrale*, 95–132.

[8] P. P. Semenov, 'Pervaya poezdka na Tian'-shan ili nebesnyi khrebet do verkhov'ev r. Yaksarta ili Syr-Dar'i v 1857 g.', *VIRGO* Chast' 23, Otd. 2 (1858), 1–25; P. P. Semenov Tian-Shanskii, *Puteshestvie v Tian'-Shan' v 1856–7 godakh* ed. L. S. Berg (Moscow: OGIZ, 1946), translated as *Travels in the Tian-Shan 1856–1857* ed. Colin Thomas (London: The Hakluyt Society, 1998). I will refer to the English edition throughout. Gerasim Alexeevich Kolpakovskii, the first governor of Semirechie, had a manuscript copy of this account among his private papers: 'Puteshestvie P. Semenova vo vnutreniuiu Aziiu v 1857', TsGARKaz F.825 Op.1 D.2.

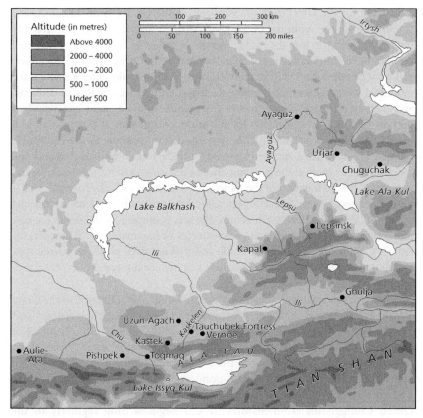

Map 4 Semirechie

(1835–1865),[9] though at the time these were less influential than those by the military geographer Mikhail Veniukov, whom we encountered in the previous chapter as a theorist of steppe warfare.[10] Alongside lyrical descriptions of the snow-capped Ala-Tau and Tian-Shan mountain ranges and the lush pastures in their foothills, their writings gave ethnographic descriptions of the region's mainly Qazaq and Kyrgyz inhabitants, and mapped the main routes that could be used by Russian forces.

Russian interest in and contacts with Semirechie predated even these explorations. As early as 1834 Colonel Butovskii of the General Staff presented

[9] Chokan Valikhanov, 'Dnevnik poezdki na Issyk-Kul' [1856] & 'Opisanie puti v Kashgar i obratno v Alatavskii Okrug' [1859], in *Izbrannye proizvedeniya* ed. A. Kh. Margulan (Alma-Ata: Kazakhskoe Gosudarstvennoe Izd. Khudozhestvennoi Literatury, 1958), 236–86, 444–86.

[10] M. I. Veniukov, 'Ocherki Zailiiskogo kraya i Prichuiskoi strany', *ZIRGO* (1861), Kn. 4, 79–116.

a proposal for the annexation of 'Semi-rek, in the Great Horde' to the Asiatic Committee of the Ministry of Foreign Affairs. Butovskii, who had recently returned from a trip into the 'Kirgiz Steppe' (whether he had actually penetrated beyond the river Ili himself is not clear), urged that the Qazaqs of the Great Horde and what he called the 'Dikokamennye Kirgizy' (literally 'wild stone' Kirgiz, i.e. the mountain Kyrgyz) had already expressed their desire to become Russian subjects, and that by annexing their territory the empire would acquire 'the very best portion of Kirgiz land, suitable for all forms of agricultural activity', while it would also bring a halt to *baramta* and attacks on caravans in the region. He claimed it would allow the development of trade routes towards Yarkand and Tibet, striking a blow at the pre-eminence of British goods in these markets, and even allow the exploitation of the fabled mineral riches of Badakhshan.[11] This is the only evidence I have found anywhere for the claim made in the standard Soviet account that Russian interest in Semirechie was prompted by the desire for new markets for industrial goods and cheap sources of raw materials.[12] However, the Asiatic Committee was unenthusiastic about Butovskii's proffered cornucopia, saying that conquest would be premature and involve unnecessary expense; they sent the proposal to the archive.

Butovskii's project had referred to 'Sultan Suyuk Ablaikhanov' of the Great Horde as 'wholly given to our government'. The history of the Qazaq Great Horde between the seventeenth and the early nineteenth centuries is extremely shadowy. Its political elites seem to have been crushed by Junghar rule, and unlike those of the Middle and Junior hordes they do not appear to have had regular correspondence with either the Qing or the Russians in the eighteenth century. From the early 1800s a number of Qazaq Chinggissids from Semirechie did begin writing regularly to the Russian authorities in Omsk, making periodic offers of submission – forty-four in 1811 alone.[13] While the documentary record is considerably sparser than for the much longer history of Russian relations with the Junior and Middle Hordes, it displays a similar pattern of approaches by members of Chinggissid elites attracted both by the material rewards of a relationship with Russia and by the prospect of using Russian military resources to strengthen their own authority.[14] This was apparently also true of the

---

[11] 'Proekt o zanyatii Semi-rek, nakhod. v Bol'shoi Kirgizskoi Orde', 03/10/1834 AVPRI F161/4 Op.729/2 D.247 ll. 1–3ob.

[12] B. Dzhamgerchinov, *Prisoedinenie Kirgizii k Rossii* (Moscow: Izd. Sotsial'no-ekonomicheskoi Literatury, 1959), 125.

[13] 'Dokumenty o postuplennii kirgizov na vernopoddanstvo', 28/12/1811 IAOO F.6 Op.1 D.3 ll. 15–16.

[14] Irina Erofeeva's magnificent edition of letters from Qazaq Sultans and Khans to Russian rulers and administrators does not include any from the elites of the Great Horde: Erofeeva, *Epistolyarn'noe nasledie*; Frank, 'The Qazaqs and Russia'.

Northern Kyrgyz, with the first delegation, from the large Bughu tribe, coming to Omsk in 1812, followed by another in 1824.[15]

Suyuk was a son of Ablai Khan, described as the head of the Yusuf (actually the Jalayir) tribe of the Qazaq Great Horde.[16] He had originally written to the West Siberian Governor Grigorii Ivanovich Glazenap (1750–1819) in October 1818 offering to become a Russian subject, and asking for craftsmen to be sent to build him a house and mosque; he despatched a deputation to St Petersburg led by his son, Sultan Jan Khwaja, although Ablaikhanov's intermediary and translator was a Tatar from Tobolsk called Safar Qurbanbaqiev; all funding came from the Ministry of Foreign Affairs.[17] The committee of Ministers considered that building a mosque might be going a bit far, but Tsar Alexander I himself intervened to uphold the Sultan's request, and he was also granted a *chin* at the eighth rank, a gold medal on a sky-blue ribbon and a kaftan and hat. His son received a gold medal on an Alexander ribbon, and other rewards for the two *biis*, the elder and the Sultan's two mullahs who accompanied the delegation were similarly precisely specified.[18] In 1820 the stone house and mosque Suyuk Ablaikhanov had requested had still not been built (the Ministry of Foreign Affairs seems in the end to have baulked at the cost, estimated at over 36,000 roubles, as an armed escort would have been required to protect the construction party in the steppe for six months) but in 1821 he was presented with '10 copies of the Alkoran' at a cost of 191 roubles.[19] This was consistent with the policy the Russians had pursued in the steppe since Catherine the Great's declaration of religious toleration in 1773, seeking to civilise and (they hoped) sedentarise the Qazaqs through the propagation of Tatar forms of Islamic practice.[20] Suyuk Ablaikhanov remained an important intermediary for the Russians as they expanded their influence south: the British artist Thomas Atkinson later claimed that 'a greater robber could not be found in the steppe, and though at this time, being eighty years of age, he could not join in the *baranta*s, many were planned by him', but also noted that when he painted his portrait 'he had on a scarlet coat, a gold medal, and a sabre, sent him by Alexander the First,

[15] Dzhamgerchinov, *Prisoedinenie Kirgizii*, 134–5.
[16] Kilian, 'Allies and Adversaries', 183.
[17] Nesselrode to Glazenap 14/02/1819 IAOO F.6 Op.1 D.38 ll. 4–5*ob*.
[18] 'Vypiska iz zhurnalov komiteta Ministrov 11 i 18 yanvarya 1819 g.'; Nesselrode to Karl Fedorovich von Klot 08/10/1819 IAOO F.6 Op.1 D.38 ll. 16–19.
[19] Nesselrode to Kantsevich 19/11/1820; 'Delo o alkoranakh dlya sultana Siuk Ablaikhanova', 1821 IAOO F.6 Op.1 D.49 ll. 95–8*ob*, 156–8.
[20] Allen Frank, *Islamic Historiography and 'Bulghar' Identity among the Tatars and Bashkirs of Russia* (Leiden: Brill, 1998), 35 & *Muslim Religious Institutions in Late Imperial Russia: The Islamic World of Novouzensk District and the Kazakh Inner Horde, 1780–1910* (Leiden: Brill, 2001), 176–8.

of which he was wonderfully proud.'[21] Atkinson's wife Lucy recalled affectionately how when she and her husband stayed at the fortress of Kapal
shortly after its establishment in 1847, 'old Sultan Souk' was a regular visitor
in their quarters, and was fascinated by her looking-glass.[22]

In 1831 the fortress of Ayaguz was founded as the centre of one of the outer
prikazy of the government of the 'Siberian Kirgiz', and would become the point
of contact between Russia and the Qazaqs of the Great Horde.[23] As the opening
quotation from the Qazaq *zar zaman*[24] poet Dulat Babataiuli (1802–1874)
suggests, its establishment was not part of a 'natural' or organic process of
dobrovol'noe prisoedinenie ('voluntary uniting') as this was usually portrayed
in Soviet historiography, and, as we saw earlier, the establishment of this and
other fortresses such as Karkaraly or Akmolinsk in the 1820s and 1830s was
a major cause of the resistance to the Russian presence led by Kenesary.[25] In its
remoteness and lack of amenities, Ayaguz resembled the steppe fortresses of
the Orenburg region, and seems to have suffered from similar problems of
supply, maintenance and garrison morale, as well as occasional earthquakes.[26]
Even in 1856 Tian-Shanskii described it as 'in such a pitiful and paltry state as
I had never had occasion to see any Russian town', while Choqan Valikhanov,
who passed through in the same year, wrote that it was 'unprepossessing', with
just a few wooden houses and dug-outs and a Tatar mosque, although he
admired the natural beauty of the surrounding area.[27] Despite this, Ayaguz
would become the launching point for the first Russian advance into the south
towards Semirechie. In 1843 a small force of 100 Cossacks with one piece of
artillery was ordered to proceed to the river Lepsu to suppress a case of
baramta committed by Qazaqs of the Sadyr and Arghyn tribes against those
of the Yusuf tribe, in which they apparently carried off 900 horses, 20,000
sheep (*sic* – possibly this was just 2,000), 300 camels, 200 cattle and 200 women

[21] Thomas Atkinson, *Oriental and Western Siberia: A Narrative of Seven Years' Explorations and Adventures in Siberia, Mongolia, the Kirghis Steppes, Chinese Tartary, and Part of Central Asia* (London: Hurst & Blackett, 1858), 568.

[22] Mrs [Lucy] Atkinson, *Recollections of Tatar Steppes and Their Inhabitants* (London: John Murray, 1863), 125–6. On the Atkinsons see Nick Fielding, *South to the Great Steppe: The Travels of Thomas and Lucy Atkinson in Eastern Kazakhstan, 1847–1852* (London: FIRST, 2015); John Massey Stewart, *Thomas, Lucy & Alatau: The Atkinsons' Adventures in Siberia and the Kazakh Steppe* (London: Unicorn, 2018).

[23] Kilian, 'Allies and Adversaries', 246–51.

[24] A school of Qazaq oral poetry which emerged in the middle of the nineteenth century and lamented the social and political changes brought about by Russian rule and the demise of Chinggissid authority.

[25] Kenesary to P. D. Gorchakov, Governor of Western Siberia, 1845 RGVIA F.483 Op.1 D.14 ll. 234–5.

[26] 'Vedomost o proisshestviyakh v Kirgizskoi Stepi', 31/10/1846 IAOO F.3 Op.1 D.2343 l. 104.

[27] Semenov, *Travels*, 51; Valikhanov, 'Dnevnik poezdki na Issyk-Kul', 237–8.

and children, including the daughters of three Sultans.[28] After the usual difficulties with organising supplies (even this small force required 490 *poods* of flour, and 35 good camels to carry this and other rations), *sotnik* Umeshev reported a safe arrival on the river Lepsu in May 1843.[29] Although they had strict instructions not to cross the river at this stage, this advanced picket, named Lepsinsk, would be the seed from which the Russian presence in Semirechie grew.

In 1846 Russian forces penetrated further into Semirechie in a fruitless hunt for Kenesary, who was supposedly to be found around the lower reaches of the Ili, and in the same year, partly it seems in response to this increased Russian presence, Sultan Buteke Abu'lfayz of the 'Kyzaevskii' tribe of Qazaqs of the Great Horde sent a delegation to Ayaguz offering their submission to Russia.[30] Three months later Sultan Dustem of the Yusuf tribe did the same, apparently out of fear of Kenesary,[31] and the further submission of nine Great Horde Sultans at Lepsinsk later in 1846 strengthened Russian claims to sovereignty over the Qazaqs of the Great Horde, and thus by implication over its main territory in Semirechie.[32] Confirmation of Kenesary's death at the hands of the Kyrgyz in spring 1847 did nothing to slow the Russian advance.[33] In the summer of 1847 the Russians despatched another force from Ayaguz to the river Kapal, this time with the explicit intention of constructing a new fortress.[34] The 1,000 Cossacks of this force required 3,000 *chetvert*'s of flour, and initially there was considerable difficulty in finding sufficient camels to carry it – by December the Siberian Frontier Commission had managed to find only 150, barely enough to carry one-tenth of what was required.[35] In 1848 the position of *Pristav* of the Qazaqs of the Great Horde was established at Kapal, the first incumbent being a Cossack captain, Stepan Abakumov. This represented the first attempt at direct administration over the Great Horde, although it fell short of the *okruzhnye prikazy/diwan* system under which the

---

[28] Ayaguz *Prikaz* to Ladyzhenskii, 27/02/1843 TsGARKaz F.374 Op.1 D.2907 ll. 2–4ob.

[29] Ayaguz *Prikaz* to Ladyzhenskii 27/05/1843 TsGARKaz F.374 Op.1 D.2907 l. 32.

[30] 'Vsepoddaneishii Doklad Gos. Kantslera [Count Nesselrode] o prinyatii v poddanstve kirgizy Kyzaevskogo roda', 26/10/1846; P. D. Gorchakov to Chernyshev 23/11/1846, in Serebrennikov, *Sbornik*. Vol. 6. *1847 g.* Docs.44 & 49, 272, 288–9.

[31] 'Vsepoddaneishii Doklad Gos. Kantslera [Count Nesselrode] o prinyatii v poddanstve kirgizy Yusupovskogo roda', 17/12/1846, in Serebrennikov, *Sbornik*. Vol. 5. *1846 g.* Doc.54, 298.

[32] Galiev, 'Prodvizhenie rossiiskikh voisk', 115–16.

[33] Sultan Kambar Alanov to Esaul Niukhalov n.d. (April 1847), in Serebrennikov, *Sbornik*. Vol. 6. *1847 g.* Doc.61, 111.

[34] Kilian, 'Allies and Adversaries', 252–5.

[35] P. D. Gorchakov to the administrator of the Siberian Kirgiz 26/09/1847; Ayaguz *Prikaz* to the head of the Siberian Frontier Commission 03/12/1847; Kokbektinskii *Prikaz* to the head of the Siberian Frontier Commission 23/12/1847 TsGARKaz F.374 Op.1 D.2928 ll. 1ob, 10–13ob.

Middle Horde Qazaqs were administered.[36] In 1849 twelve pickets were established along the new *trakt* linking Ayaguz and Kapal, marking the effective limits of Russian sovereignty and settlement: prior to that date travellers remained reliant on the hospitality of Qazaq *auls*.[37] Despite their claim that the Qazaqs of the Great Horde had been their subjects since 1846, the Russian ability to intervene in Qazaq society or regulate its behaviour remained very limited: in 1851, when the Ayaguz *prikaz* was asked to investigate an apparent robbery by none other than Sultan Suyuk Ablaikhanov (who regularly raided the Naiman tribe of the Middle Horde, with whom he had a long-standing territorial dispute),[38] he referred it back to the newly created *Pristav* of the Great Horde, Abakumov. He in turn declared himself powerless: he merely had some influence over the 'moral and domestic' life of the Qazaqs, and restricted himself to giving advice and attempting to resolve conflicts, without threatening criminal proceedings. He had no judicial authority over the Qazaqs, and would not have been able to exercise it even if he did, given that his entire staff consisted of a translator and a clerk of the second grade.[39]

Thus far the story on the Siberian frontier seems superficially very similar to that which was taking place simultaneously on the Syr-Darya, where in 1847 Fort Raim was already under construction, with similar logistical difficulties in transport, and in finding sufficient camels. However, even at this very early stage, there was one notable difference: the materials for the construction of the fort at Kapal were already to hand, as the advance guard of Cossacks sent to the site had already chopped down 15,000 trees by September 1847.[40] In contrast, as we saw in the previous chapter, at Fort Raim all the wood for construction had to be brought from Bashkiria, over 1,000 *versts* distant. This was an early indication of just how much more favourable the environmental conditions in Semirechie were to the Russian advance, and to the establishment of permanent Cossack and peasant settlements. In 1851 Abakumov submitted a report on the prospects for settlement in the north-eastern region of Semirechie which waxed lyrical over the 'forests and pastures – all these heights and especially the valleys are covered with apple trees, raspberries, blackcurrants, bird cherries (*cheremukhi*) and others – especially notable are

---

[36] Gulmira Sultangalieva, 'The Role of the *pristavstvo* Institution in the Context of Russian Imperial Policies in the Kazakh Steppe in the Nineteenth Century', *CAS* 33/1 (2014), 71–3.

[37] Col. Kleist to the Ayaguz *Prikaz* 26/05/1849 TsGARKaz F.374 Op.1 D.2939 ll. 14–18. Both Atkinsons noted the difficulty and lawlessness of this route in 1847, when Kapal had only just been established: Atkinson, *Oriental and Western Siberia*, 571–9; Atkinson, *Recollections of Tartar Steppes*, 99–103.

[38] Kilian, 'Allies and Adversaries', 258.

[39] Col. Kleist to the Siberian Frontier Commission 03/06/1849; Gasfort to Karl Fedorovich Klots 12/06/1851 IAOO F.3 Op.1 D.2652 ll. 1–3*ob*, 7–*ob*.

[40] 'Vedomost' o chisle vyrublennago lesa kem imenno i skol'ko derev', 22/09/1847 TsGARKaz F.374 Op.1 D.3109 ll. 8–9.

the apples and hops (*khmel'*). The black earth soil and frequent, almost daily rainfall, with a warmer climate than at Kapal, supply all the benefits of strong fertility.[41] There was nothing like an abundance of soft fruit to make Russians (and especially Siberians) feel at home. Even before they established a permanent presence beyond the Ili, Russian settlements in Northern Semirechie were acquiring a permanent character, while their knowledge of the region was rapidly expanding in tandem with their control over it. In 1852 a small topographic party began to survey the eastern shores of Lake Balkhash, travelling by boat down the Lepsu and mapping the south-eastern shore as far as Qaratal.[42] Another important factor was the generally good relations the Russians enjoyed with Qing China in the first half of the nineteenth century, which made this new frontier more secure and stable than that in the western part of the steppe. This was sealed with the Treaty of Ghulja in 1851, negotiated by E. P. Kovalevskii, who had taken part in the winter invasion of Khiva a decade previously. The treaty legalised the extensive trade (much of it in tea) that already existed between Semipalatinsk and Chinese territory in the upper Ili valley, and allowed the Russians to establish a consulate and warehouses in the town of Ghulja.[43]

Also in contrast to the Syr-Darya line, the Russians met no significant military resistance in establishing Lepsinsk and Kapal. This would change once they crossed the River Ili, where they would come up against the same opponent they had faced at Aq Masjid – the khanate of Khoqand. The first significant trans-Ili expedition came in 1850–1, when Gorchakov, with War Minister Chernyshev's assent,[44] began preparing a force to destroy the Khoqandi fortress of Tauchubek (which the Khoqandis themselves called Qurghan-Almaly), located at the junction of the Almaty and Kaskelen rivers. This was in response to complaints from the Qazaqs of the Great Horde that the fortress's Qipchaq garrison had stolen their horses and taken hostages,[45] and, as Gorchakov's successor Gustav Gasfort put it, in order 'to uphold our

---

[41] 'Zapiska o mestakh udobnykh dlya zaselenii v severo-vostochnoi chasti Semirechenskogo kraya', n.d. (before 09/07/1851) RGVIA F.1449 Op.1 D.10, 'Opisanie putei vedushchikh iz Semirechenskogo kraya v Kashkarii, Tashkent i Khokand', l. 17.

[42] Nifantev to Gasfort 26/08/1852; Nifantev to Gasfort 24/09/1852 RGVIA F.1449 Op.1 D.14, 'O komandirovanii iz korpusa topografov Praporshchika Nifanteva s dvumya topografami dlya obozreniya ozeri Balkhash', ll. 31–*ob*, 44–5.

[43] Joseph Fletcher, 'Sino-Russian Relations 1800–62' in *The Cambridge History of China*. Vol. 10, 318–32; Wang, 'The Unofficial Russo-Qing Trade'. For an exhaustive account of the treaty negotiations see Akifumi Shioya, 'The Treaty of Ghulja Reconsidered: Imperial Russian Diplomacy toward Qing China in 1851', *Journal of Eurasian Studies* 10/2 (2019), 147–58.

[44] Chernyshev to Gorchakov 09/08/1850 RGVIA F.1449 Op.1 D.8, 'O vozobnovlenii ekspeditsii po rekoi Ili dlya istrebleniya Tauchubekskogo ukrepleniya', ll. 6–*ob*.

[45] Son of *Bii* Karim Chika to Peremyshil'skii 06/01/1851 RGVIA F.1449 Op.1 D.8 ll. 32–*ob*, 35.

moral influence in the Trans-Ili region'.[46] This force consisted of 1,500 men, comprising one battalion of infantry, four *sotnyas* of Cossacks, two pieces of horse artillery, four 'unicorn' guns, four siege mortars, two rocket batteries and six light fortress guns. This required 550 camels and 100 horses for the transport of ammunition and provisions, which included 100 shells for each mortar, nails, wood and 1,000 sandbags for building embrasures and fortifications, 100 spades for digging trenches, 4,000 *poods* of rusks (*sukhari*) , 500 of pulses and 800 of meat.[47] All the baggage animals, together with 100 bullocks for meat, were to be supplied by the Qazaqs of the Great Horde at Kapal ten days before the expedition set off, while Qazaqs of the Naiman tribe from the Middle Horde would act as scouts. Major M. D. Peremyshil'skii, the new *Pristav*, was also confident of assistance from several Sultans of the Jalayir, Dughlat and Alban tribes of the Great Horde.[48] The garrison at Tauchubek was estimated at just eighty men, and, despite the fact that their leader, Mullah Dewan Haq Quli, sent a defiant letter to Sary *Bii* of the Dughlat tribe condemning him for collaborating with the Russians, writing that 'Muslim subjects will be great, and those who bow down to the *kafirs* – are the enemy!',[49] it seemed unlikely that they would be able to offer serious resistance. News of the Russian expedition clearly spread in advance, as in May the Khoqandi governor of Tashkent, Nar Muhammad Kushpek, wrote to ask on what grounds the Russians, who were supposedly in peaceful relations with Khoqand, were proposing to attack Tauchubek, while referring to the long-standing friendship between the two states and the need to respect each other's borders.[50] By the time this was received the Russian force, led by Lt-Col. Karbyshev, had already left Kapal, and on the 5 June they crossed the Ili. Apart from a brief brush with a '*shaika*' (raiding band) of fifty men from the fortress under the leadership of a Qazaq called Namaz, they encountered no resistance. On the 9 June Karbyshev arrived at Tauchubek to find that it had been abandoned by its garrison. He spent three days blowing up its earthwork walls and bastions, and meanwhile sent a reconnaissance force towards the river Chu to try to catch the fleeing garrison.[51] While they failed to catch up with them, they took prisoner

---

[46] Gasfort to Peremyshil'skii 12/03/1851 TsGARKaz F.3 Op.1 D.2, 'Ob ekspeditsii za reku Iliu i o prochem', l. 20*ob*; Annenkov to Gasfort 09/03/1851; Gasfort to Dolgorukov 24/03/ 1851, in Serebrennikov, *Sbornik*. Vol. 8. *1851 g.*, 44–5, 48–9.

[47] 'Soobrazheniya General ot Infanterii Knyazya Gorchakova', RGVIA F.1449 Op.1 D.8 ll. 27–30.

[48] Peremyshil'skii to Yakovlev 27/02/1851 RGVIA F.1449 Op.1 D.8 ll. 115–*ob*; Peremyshil'skii to the 'Senior Sultans of the Great Horde', 27/03/1851 TsGARKaz F.3 Op.1 D.2 ll. 29–30*ob*.

[49] Peremyshil'skii to Yakovlev 13/02/1851, enclosing Mullah Dewan Haq Quli to Sary *Bii* RGVIA F.1449 Op.1 D.8 ll. 83–6.

[50] Peremyshil'skii to Yakovlev 24/05/1851 RGVIA F.1449 Op.1 D.8 ll. 154–5, 164–5.

[51] Karbyshev to Yakovlev 05/06/1851; 09/06/1851 RGVIA F.1449 Op.1 D.8 ll. 160–2, 169–72.

five men who had been instructed to locate and report on the whereabouts of the Russian column by the commander of the Khoqandi fortress of Pishpek, beyond the Chu, Aq-Qul *Dadkhwah*. Two of these, Aitak Qarakuchukov and Baitak Kalchanov, were members of Khoqand's Qipchaq ruling elite, while the remaining three were Kyrgyz from the Sarybaghysh tribe. These informed the Russians that the appearance of the Russian column had caused panic throughout the Khoqandi strongpoints in Semirechie, causing the evacuation of Toqmaq as well as Tauchubek, and leading to a request from Pishpek to Nar Muhammad in Tashkent for reinforcements. In response a force of 8,000 armed men had recently arrived at Pishpek, but they were there not to fight the Russians, but to drive the Qazaqs of the Great Horde beyond the river Chu so that they could be taxed by Khoqand without Russian interference.[52] Gasfort reported this to the new War Minister, Dolgorukov, noting that more trouble might be expected in that quarter and proposing to write to the Khan of Khoqand asking him to ensure that the Qipchaqs remained on their side of the river Chu and left the Great Horde Qazaqs alone. Dolgorukov replied that he and Nesselrode felt it would be best to wait and see what effect the current expedition had had on the Khoqandis before launching any more military operations, in the hope that it might prompt them to enter into peaceful negotiations. Meanwhile, those they had captured would be retained as prisoners of war. Gasfort's response was to note that the Qazaqs were crossing the Chu in droves to Russian territory, seeking to escape the 'violent yoke' and heavy taxation of the Qipchaqs.[53]

In the summer of 1853, on the eve of the fall of Aq Masjid, Khoqand attempted to re-open dialogue with an embassy to Omsk led by a *caravanbashi* called Yuldash Bai Mirzajan. Gasfort received the embassy coldly, writing to Perovskii in Orenburg that it was clearly prompted by fear at the Russian advance on the Syr-Darya line. Neither he nor the head of the Siberian Frontier Administration, Colonel Ladyzhenskii, believed the embassy's claim that the conflicts of the previous years had all been the result of the ascendancy of the Qipchaqs under Musulmanqul, and that all would be peaceful now Khudoyar Khan had been restored.[54] Instead, after a further punitive expedition beyond the Ili later in 1853, the Russians finally established their own permanent fortress there in 1854: 'His Majesty the Emperor [Nicholas I], having given his agreement on the 4 February last to the establishment of a new fortification among the Great Kirgiz Horde in the valley of Almaty, has graciously decreed

---

[52] Karbyshev to Yakovlev 12/06/1851 RGVIA F.1449 Op.1 D.8 ll. 180–1, 183–5.
[53] Gasfort to Dolgorukov 09/6/1851; Dolgorukov to Gasfort 06/08/1851; Gasfort to Dolgorukov 21/09/1851 RGVIA F.1449 Op.1 D.8 ll. 198–200, 243–4, 250–2.
[54] Gasfort to Perovskii 30/06/1853; Ladyzhenskii to Perovskii 12/07/1853 TsGARUz F.I-715 Op.1 D.14 Docs.76 & 83 ll. 262–3, 288–9.

that this fortification should be named "Vernoe".[55] As Joseph Fletcher suggests, a desire to protect the trade route to Ili, which had grown in importance since the Treaty of Ghulja in 1851, may have played a part in the decision to create a permanent outpost in the region,[56] though the main motivation visible in Russian documents was a desire to exclude Khoqandi influence over the Qazaqs of the Great Horde and the Kyrgyz.[57] Gasfort instructed Peremyshil'skii to pay particular attention when siting the fortress to the availability of building materials and fertile land, which Peremyshil'skii did, reporting that the valley between the 'first and second Almaty' (i.e. what are now called the Greater and Lesser Almatinka rivers) had an abundance of excellent timber, and was already criss-crossed with *ariqs* (no doubt from Qazaq *qishlaqs*, or winter settlements) with land suitable for agriculture and hay-making.[58] The buildings of the new fortress, as at Kapal, would indeed be constructed from what Tian-Shanskii described as the 'magnificent timber, straight as an arrow, of Tian'-Shan' spruce, which had been brought here from the Almaty valley.'[59]

Miraculously one of the barracks constructed around the time of his visit in 1856 still survives amid the ruins of the fort in the centre of modern Almaty, allowing us to appreciate both the skilled craftsmanship and the excellent quality of the timber used – although already by 1858 this new construction had denuded an area two *versts* in radius from the fort of suitable trees.[60] It was from these modest beginnings that the town of Vernyi and the modern city of Almaty would grow.[61]

Almost immediately Gasfort also ordered the construction of a series of new Cossack settlements, to be created along the rivers Almaty, Lepsu and Qarabulak, and along the *trakt* that now ran from Ayaguz to the new fortress of Vernoe. By September 1854 suitable sites had been identified on the upper reaches of the Lepsu, at Urjar on the Qarabulak, at Chubar-Agach and at the pickets of Verkhne-Naryn and Qaraqol. Three and a half *sotnyas* of Cossacks

---

[55] Siberian Frontier Commission to Peremyshil'skii 22/04/1854 RGVIA F.1449 Op.1 D.3, 'O vnov' vozvedennom ukreplenii v kirgizskoi stepi urochishche Almaty', l. 1.

[56] Fletcher, 'Sino-Russian Relations', 331.

[57] Gasfort to Peremyshil'skii 12/07/1853 TsGARKaz F.3 Op.1 D.7, 'O dvizhenii ekspeditsionnogo otryada za r. Ili, o vybore mesta dlya stroitel'stva ukrepleniya "Vernoe"', l. 68.

[58] Gasfort to Peremyshil'skii 12/07/1853; Peremyshil'skii to Gasfort 08/08/1853 TsGARKaz F.3 Op.1 D.7 ll. 69ob, 71.

[59] Semenov, *Travels*, 72.

[60] Kolpakovskii, *Doklad* 30/07/1858 TsGARKaz F.3 Op.1 D.8, 'O stroitel'nykh rabotakh v ukreplenii Vernom na reke Ili', l. 39. By May 1857, shortly after Semenov Tian-Shanskii's visit, three wooden barracks had already been constructed in the Vernoe fortress. Gasfort to Peremyshil'skii 17/05/1857 TsGARKaz F.3 Op.1 D.352 ll. 2–ob.

[61] E. A. Buketova, *Vernenskie istorii* (Almaty: Elnur, 2011) explores the town's later development in the colonial period through five illuminating vignettes, notably the fascinating story of Paul Gourdet, the Frenchman who became Vernyi's municipal architect in the 1870s and 1880s.

Figure 4.1 Early wooden barracks, Fort Vernoe, Almaty. © Berny Sèbe.

from the 6th, 8th and 9th West Siberian Regiments were divided between these outposts to provide the nucleus, and peasant families were encouraged to migrate to them from Western Siberia. Travelling through Semirechie fifty years later, Senator Count Pahlen reported a conversation with 'an old Cossack':

> I was twenty years old at the time [. . .] and had to leave my young wife behind in the *stanitsa* in Siberia. The authorities ordered every *stanitsa*, according to its size, to produce so many young men for emigrating to Semirechie. We were promised good land, and I and twenty other young-sters came to this *stanitsa*, on the river Ili. The younger generation have no idea of what we had to put up with. We were told that we were expected within three years to build a sufficient number of houses, and to lay in supplies of corn and oats sufficient for the next harvest, for three times our number together with their and our own families. Those were hard times. We toiled in the fields by day, spent the night chasing off the Kirgiz who grazed our lands and raided us, built houses and dug wells. It took ten long years to make life more bearable.[62]

Alongside the Cossacks, 440 families of Siberian *starozhiltsy* (old settlers) volunteered: 57 from Tiumen province, 4 from Kurgan, 118 from Omsk, 12 from Tara, 178 from Yalutorsk, 12 from Ishim, 8 from Turgensk, 12 from

---

[62] K. K. Pahlen, *Mission to Turkestan: Being the Memoirs of Count K. K. Pahlen* ed. Richard Pierce & trans. N. J. Couriss (New York: Oxford University Press, 1964), 177.

Tomsk and 43 from Biisk. Those from Biisk were sent to Urjar, and the remainder settled around the new Trans-Ili fortress on the river Almaty – Vernoe.[63]

The striking point in Tian-Shanskii's description of Vernoe is that already, just two years after its foundation, with no houses other than barrack buildings and the residence of the *Pristav*, it was attracting Russian settlers. This was also true of Kapal, which he had visited *en route*. As he wrote, 'what already lent charm to the whole area were the arable lands of the Kapal inhabitants, which were unusually rich in their crops of wheat and oats and in their soil fertility. These lands stretched from the town of Kapal itself across the entire Dzhunke plateau up to the river Biën, which supplied irrigation to them. If one takes into consideration the fact that at that time many of Kapal's inhabitants cultivated up to twenty *desyatinas* per taxed household, it is possible to imagine what a flourishing Russian colony Kapal already was in Semirechie.' He added that the site had first been identified by Karelin in the 1840s, and made similar observations about the fertility of the soil and capacity for colonisation of the region around Arasan.[64] Alongside the Russian settlers, Semenov identified a group of so-called *Cholokazakh* (Shala-Qazaq or 'half-Qazaqs'), who according to his account were Russian fugitives from the penal colonies of Siberia who had initially fled to Tashkent, and then moved to Semirechie and taken Qazaq wives when they learnt of the advent of Russian colonisation there.[65] Valikhanov described them as migrants from the Central Asian khanates who had become Russian subjects after settling in the steppe and marrying Qazaqs.[66] In August 1855 Peremyshil'skii wrote that he believed the Qaratal region (near Balkhash, about 300 km north of Vernoe) would produce a harvest of around 20,000 *chetvert*'s of grain, mostly wheat, that year. The cultivators were

> Tatars, Chalakazaks and Kirgiz; with most of them the standing crops have already been purchased by those who manage transport beyond the Ili [the merchants] Sutiushev, Kuznetsov, Isaev and others. The price for which these individuals have purchased the grain on the spot is 2 r 50 k for wheat, up to a maximum of 3 silver roubles per *chetvert'* . . . I spoke to many of the Chalakazaks and Kirgiz and asked that they themselves bring

[63] Gasfort to head of the Siberian Staff 11/02/1854; Spasskii to Gasfort 30/09/1854 RGVIA F.1449 Op.1 D.17, 'Izbraniya mest pod poseleniya na r. Lepse i Karabulak, bliz uroch. Urdzhara', ll. 1–2*ob*, 38–9; for a complete account of the establishment of these and other settlements along the *trakt* between Ayaguz and Almaty see N. Ledenev, *Istoriya Semirechenskogo Kazach'yago Voiska* (Vernyi: Tip. Semirechenskogo Oblastnogo Upravleniya, 1909), 97–119.
[64] Semenov, *Travels*, 54, 59.
[65] *Ibid.*, 61–4.
[66] Valikhanov, 'Dnevnik poezdki na Issyk-Kul', 237–8.

supplies to Vernoe, and they agreed that they would be willing to do this for 7 silver roubles per *chetvert'* . . .[67]

However, they were afraid of the formalities involved in receiving payment from the treasury, and also the garrison at Vernoe wanted rye, while they had mostly sown wheat. Only one promised to supply 500 *chetvert'*s, half rye, half wheat, if he were paid in advance at a rate of 7 roubles per *chetvert'*. A later report suggested that the real size of the harvest was barely 10,000 *chetvert'*s.[68] Despite these difficulties, and the high cost of transport over even this relatively short distance (which more than doubled the price), this was still an early indication that local supplies of grain were likely to be more reliable and cheaper than on the Syr-Darya. Once the Russians had established a permanent presence beyond the Ili the demands for long-distance transport of supplies would decrease, in a way that they never did on the Syr-Darya, where massive caravans were needed to supply fortifications throughout their existence as military outposts. Lepsinsk, Kapal and Vernoe would all become Cossack *stanitsa*s, initially of the West Siberian host, and then after 1867 of the newly formed Semirechie Cossack host, the only one in Central Asia.[69] These provided not just a military reserve, but food security of a kind that was unimaginable on the Syr-Darya line, whose demoralised garrisons could be supplied only from Orenburg, at vast expense, or else by Bukharan grain merchants. In 1861 there were measures to encourage the Qazaqs of the Great Horde to cultivate more grain, though settlers and Cossacks remained the mainstay.[70] Harvests fluctuated considerably, such that in 1864–5 the central grain stores in Kapal and Vernoe could show a healthy reserve at the end of the year, but were in deficit in 1866, requiring outside supplies,[71] by 1868 the six *stanitsa*s of the new host – Almatinskaya, Sofiiskaya, Kopalskaya, Lepsinskaya, Sergiopolskaya (the new name for Ayaguz) and Urjarskaya – between them had reserves of 3,567 *poods* of grain.[72] The creation of a solid agrarian base for Russian settlement was accompanied by the expansion of the Orthodox Church into the region, foreshadowing its later role as the centre of the Turkestan Eparchate. By the mid 1860s each of the Cossack *stanitsa*s at

[67] Peremyshil'skii to Gasfort 16/08/1855 IAOO F.6 Op.1 D.292 ll. 1–2.
[68] Abakumov to Gasfort 14/10/1855 IAOO F.6 Op.1 D.292 ll. 4–5.
[69] Ledenev, *Istoriya Semirechenskogo Kazach'yago Voiska*, 199.
[70] Kolpakovskii to Sultan Ali Abliev 07/09/1861 TsGARKaz F.3 Op.1 D.572, 'O razreshenii Kazakham zanimat'sya khlebopashchestvom v Zailiiskom krae', ll. 4–5.
[71] 'O zapasnom magazine, sostoiavshchego zernogo khleba stanitsy malo Almatinskoi', 1864; 'Vedomost' o khlebe voiskovoe i obshchestvennoe, sostoyashchem v Kopal'skom zapasnom magazine', 1865; 'O khlebe sostoiavshchem v obshchestvennom zapasnom magazine v stanitse malo-Almatinskoi', TsGARKaz F.39 Op.1 D.1388 ll. 6*ob*–7, 23–5, 76.
[72] 'Vedomost' o chisle zapasnykh khlebnykh magazinakh i sostoyashchikh v nikh zapasakh v stanitsakh Semirechenskogo Kazach'yago Voiska', Aug. 1868 TsGARKaz F.39 Op.1 D.1391 l. 4.

Vernoe (Malo- and Bol'she-Almatinskaya) had its own permanent garrison church, and these also began to appear in smaller settlements. Although Governor Diugamel rejected the proposal from Porfirii, the Bishop of Tomsk, to build a brick church in the fortification next to the bridge across the Ili (Porfirii proposed that it be given a punning dedication to the prophet Eli) on the grounds that the population there was too small, in 1862 churches were built at the Cossack settlements of Sofiiskaya and Nadezhdenskaya. The inhabitants who had requested them defrayed part of the cost through donating surplus grain.[73] Semirechie was well on the way to becoming Russia's only colony of settlement in what would become the new Governor-Generalship of Turkestan even before Russia's main rival in the region – the Khoqand Khanate – had been defeated militarily.

4.2 The Fall of Toqmaq and Pishpek

The establishment of Vernoe saw an uneasy *modus vivendi* established between Russia and Khoqand in the Trans-Ili region, where the Russians claimed the boundary of their new territory to be the river Chu. Khoqandi forces were too weak to besiege Vernoe or expel the Russian forces, but continued to cross the Chu for what the Russians considered to be raiding parties, although it seems probable that the Khoqandis saw this as the legitimate collection of *zakat* from those they claimed as their subjects. Peremyshil'skii sought to persuade the Great Horde Qazaqs and the Northern Kyrgyz tribes, with whom the Russians now came into constant contact for the first time, to submit to his authority as Russia's *Pristav*. They in turn faced a difficult choice, as it cannot have been clear whether the Russian presence would be permanent, or how forcefully they intended to press their claims to sovereignty. The two largest northern Kyrgyz tribes, the Bughu and Sarybaghysh, were in conflict over pastureland, and each sought external support – the Bughu from the Russians and the Sarybaghysh from Khoqand. The bloody conflict which erupted between them *c.* 1853 saw the death of the greatest Sarybaghysh leader, Ormon, but the Bughu were then driven back towards Qing territory by his son, Umbet-'Ali, eventually prompting them to offer their submission to the Russians at Vernyi.[74] Valikhanov, who visited the northern Kyrgyz in 1857, describes an interesting case of the sort of ambivalent and shifting loyalties this produced:

---

[73] Porfirii to Diugamel 26/05/1861; Kolpakovskii to Diugamel 04/02/1862; Prigovor 10/02/1862 & 02/04/1862; Kolpakovskii to Diugamel 11/03/1863 IAOO F.6 Op.1 D.341 ll. 3–*ob*, 11–18*ob*, 33–*ob*.

[74] Jipar Duishembieva, 'Visions of Community: Literary Culture and Social Change among the Northern Kyrgyz, 1856–1924' (Ph.D. Thesis, University of Washington, Seattle, 2015), 49–55; Kilian, 'Allies and Adversaries', 268–72.

A rumour was brought to us that the Pishpek farmanchi [sic – *Parvanachi* – in fact the governor of Pishpek held the rank of *Dadkhwah*] with almost 1,500 men had come to Kutemaldy. The leader of the Sarybaghysh, *Manap*[75] Umbet 'Ali, was said to have been taken prisoner, his cattle stolen. Some talkative members of the Bughu tribe said that their *biis* had spread this rumour around falsely, so that we would not go as far as the lake [Issyq-Kul], the occupation of which would destroy their freedom for ever. Others said that four Tashkentis were now at the *aul* of Borombai, the most influential *manap* of the whole Bughu tribe, and that they had invited them there for the settlement of a dispute with the Sarybaghysh. For the Bughu such a settlement would of course be beneficial: they had already given 30 horses as *zakat*, apart from which Ormon had destroyed Tashkenti [i.e. Khoqandi] *qurghans* [forts], and his successor Umbet 'Ali had not come to them when ordered. It is under-standable that now the Bughu wanted to separate themselves from the Russians and their supplies, and might be victorious over the Sarybaghysh thanks to the Sarts taking part. Anyhow, these are all rumours. We decided regardless to go to the lake.[76]

Valikhanov's sensitive account is a valuable corrective to the assumption found in most Russian documents, and indeed in the standard Soviet account of the conquest of Semirechie, that all the Kyrgyz and Qazaqs of the region viewed the Russian presence as an unqualified good that promised to liberate them from the oppressive yoke of Khoqand.[77] Umbet 'Ali would a few years later call on the *biis* and *batyrs* of the Bughu tribe to embark on a holy war (*ghazat*) against the infidel Russians on behalf of Khoqand.[78] As Daniel Prior notes, the elites of this region were not 'colonial novices' but already 'practiced actors in the give and take of imperial titles and ranks' thanks both to the earlier Qing presence in the region and the claimed suzerainty of Khoqand. Clearly they sought to gain maximum advantage by maintaining relationships

[75] A Kyrgyz leader – Valikhanov himself gives a description of their authority and role – 'Razdeleniya na sosloviya: Manapy i ikh znachenie', *Izbrannye proizvedenii*, 289–92 – in which he says that they had only recently appeared among the Kyrgyz. Daniel Prior has suggested that the emergence of the *Manap* class may in fact have been in response to the Russian presence, as the Russians were used to dealing with the Qazaqs through Chinggissid elites, and sought an analogous group among the Kyrgyz: Daniel G. Prior, 'High Rank and Power among the Northern Kirghiz: Terms and Their Problems, 1845–1864', in *Explorations in the Social History of Modern Central Asia* ed. Paolo Sartori (Leiden: Brill, 2013), 137–79, with a discussion of Valikhanov's text on pp. 156–7. See also Svetlana Jacquesson, *Pastoréalismes: Anthropologie historique des processus d'intégration chez les Kirghiz du Tian Shan intérieur* (Wiesbaden: Ludwig Reichert Verlag, 2010), 45–7; Duishembieva, 'Visions of Justice', 74–9; Dzhamgerchinov, *Prisoedinenie Kirgizii k Rossii*, 53–5.
[76] Valikhanov, 'Dnevnik poezdki na Issyk-Kul', 254.
[77] This is the dominant theme in Dzhamgerchinov, *Prisoedinenie Kirgizii k Rossii*.
[78] Prior, 'High Rank and Power', 166.

with all sides, but this would prove a difficult position to sustain as Russian power grew greater and more assertive, with one Kyrgyz correspondent describing their situation thus (in Prior's translation): 'we are between two forts; we have no recourse [but to you]: though the frog may be on the steppe, his eyes are [always] on the lake'. The first formal submission of the Northern Kyrgyz to Russia would be made by the Bughu tribe in Omsk in January 1855, and Umbet 'Ali of the Sarybaghysh would eventually submit in 1867.[79]

In April 1858 tensions with Khoqand flared up once again when Peremyshil'skii received a report that Atabek *Dadkhwah*, the new governor of Pishpek, had crossed the river Chu with a force variously estimated at 3,000 to 5,000 men and was sending threatening letters to Qazaq leaders exhorting them to abandon the Russian unbelievers and pay *zakat*.[80] They duly passed these on to the Russians at Vernoe, which allows us to reconstruct a fascinating exchange that tells us a good deal about how Russian and Khoqandi ideas of sovereignty came into conflict. Most letters described the Russians as *kafirs*, condemned Qazaq leaders for consorting with them,[81] and urged them to renew their loyalty to Khoqand, in one case referring to the heroic defence of Aq Masjid as an example to be emulated.[82] One of the longest came from Atabek *Dadkhwah* to the Qazaq leaders Andas-Batyr, Suranchi-Batyr, Supotai-Batyr, Syat-Batyr and Narbuta-Batyr. This contained mingled threats and promises, appealing to their common faith: 'if you do not come to us, then neither children nor wives will remain to you; we repeat this a thousand times. Do not fear, but believe us, that if we take from you so much as one kid [i.e. a baby goat] then you will receive it back on the same day'. Crucially, the Russian translation, made by a Cossack officer called *Khorunzhii* Borodin 'from the Tashkenti' (i.e. Chaghatai), contained the phrase 'considering you our subjects' (*poddannye*).[83] This term, which had been the source of so many misunderstandings between the Russians and Qazaqs in the eighteenth century, here became a bone of contention between the Russian and Khoqandi authorities in their tussle for sovereignty over the Qazaqs of the Great Horde and the Northern Kyrgyz. The Khoqandi leaders Muhammad Reza *Dadkhwah*, Rustambek *Dadkhwah*, Atabek *Dadkhwah*, Pir Muhammad

---

[79] Prior, 'High Rank and Power', 148–9, 155, 160, 169; Dzhamgerchinov, *Prisoedinenie Kirgizii*, 179.

[80] Peremyshil'skii to Gasfort 04/04/1858 RGVIA F.1449 Op.1 D.26 l. 1.

[81] Muhammad Reza *Dadkhwah*, Rustambek *Dadkhwah*, Atabek *Dadkhwah*, Pir Muhammad *Dadkhwah*, Karim Qul *Bii*, Bardabek *Bii* and Qalandar *Bii* to Supotai Batyr, Andas Batyr and Daulat-Bek Batyr RGVIA F.1449 Op.1 D.26 ll. 20–*ob* (trans.), 21 (orig.).

[82] Mirza Ahmad Parvanachi to Sultan Tezek RGVIA F.1449 Op.1 D.26 ll. 14–*ob* (trans.), 19 (orig.).

[83] Translation enclosed in Peremyshil'skii to Gasfort 04/04/1858 RGVIA F.1449 Op.1 D.26 l. 2.

Dadkhwah, Karim Qul *Bii*, Bardabek *Bii* and Qalandar *Bii* wrote to '*Fristab*' Peremyshil'skii that they knew well that 'the children of four Dughlat fathers from ancient to current times were slaves of our state; their fathers and ancestors used water and grass in the realm of our Khan'. Now they were refusing to pay *zakat* and fleeing to the Russian side of the river Chu. They warned him that, while they had no quarrel with his master, the Tsar, 'if you listen to the lying words of those Kirgiz and act on their behalf we can fight you'. This, at least, was the message Peremyshil'skii read in Russian translation. However, the word which was translated as 'slave' seems to have been *fuqara*, a term meaning simply the poor or common people.[84]

Peremyshil'skii responded by saying that the Qazaqs of the Great Horde could not be the 'slaves' of Khoqand as they were their co-religionists. If by 'slave' they actually meant 'subject' (and here Peremyshil'skii was perhaps conscious that he might be the victim of his translator) then this had never been voluntary, and dated back only thirty years to the time of Khan Muhammad 'Ali Qushbegi Lashkar, while the Qazaqs had voluntarily become Russian subjects ten years before.[85] The response from the commanders of Pishpek was highly revealing of Khoqandi assumptions about their own sovereignty and the illegitimacy of Russian claims:

> We called them so that they would cross over to the side of the Muslims, and when they did not listen and went over to you, we chastised them [*ikh chebarili*].[86] God and the law allow us to chastise those who do not give *zakat* and we chastised them according to the law. You are a *kafir* and do not know the true law, and equally do not understand the lawfulness of the collection of *zakat* and taxes, and your law does not have it, and ours does. Why should it not be in accordance with the law – when we chastise at will according to our law. This people from ancient times have paid us *zakat* and taxes. Further we say, we wrote to you, that you should return to us our former slaves – Kirgiz, payers of *zakat* who have fled, and besides this we chastise and carry off into bondage your unhappy Kirgiz. We, thanks to the blessings of the Most High, are not without strength and came to seek our people. Your Khan was friendly with our Padshah, which is why we have not come to you. But if you meddle with the affairs of our people, we will come to you – Thanks be to Allah![87]

The letter continued at some length in a similar vein, accusing Peremyshil'skii of lying when he said that the Qazaqs of the Great Horde were Russian

---

[84] Prior, 'High Rank and Power', 170.
[85] Peremyshil'skii to Rustam Bek and Atabek *Dadkhwah* n.d. RGVIA F.1449 Op.1 D.26 l. 39.
[86] This seems to be an archaic version of a verb meaning to rustle, rake over or stir up, and my translation here is tentative – I was unable to establish the term used in the original Turki.
[87] Atabek *Dadkhwah*, Pir Muhammad and Rustam Bek to Peremyshil'skii n.d. RGVIA F.1449 Op.1 D.26 ll. 36–7.

subjects, that they had been subjects of the Khoqand Khan 'since ancient times', and that their betrayal had come only last year, and was motivated purely by the desire to avoid paying *zakat*. Peremyshil'skii responded by writing over their heads to Mirza Ahmad Bahadur Parvanachi, the governor of Tashkent, complaining about the raids carried out by Atabek and Rustam Bek on the Qazaqs and Kyrgyz, in which he also used the expression 'from ancient times' to describe the submission of the Great Horde to Russia. He added that, ever since the Russians had established their fortress in the Almaty valley, 'the river Chu has since been the boundary between two states'.[88] This letter never reached its intended recipient: Rustam Bek and Pir Muhammad replied that Peremyshil'skii had exceeded his authority by writing directly to the Parvanachi. It was for Governor Gasfort in Omsk to write to him, as one equivalent in rank. They continued to insist that the Qazaqs were their subjects (*fuqara*), a word that was translated into Russian as 'slaves'. What is striking in this correspondence is that, although the Khoqandis made use of religious language, suggesting that the Qazaqs and Kyrgyz had betrayed their faith by seeking Russian protection, the root of their objection was that these peoples were Khoqandi subjects who had submitted to their state and owed its ruler duty and obedience. This conception of sovereignty was remarkably similar to that which the Russians felt they should enjoy over the Qazaqs, and had done since the 'submission' of Abu'l-Khayr Khan of the Junior Horde in 1731. Khivan, Bukharan and Khoqandi interference with that sovereignty had provided a recurrent justification for the Russian advance. For the Qazaqs themselves, as Tom Welsford has shown, sovereignty seems to have been a much less bounded, exclusive and absolute concept than it was in neighbouring sedentary societies, and this was a permanent source of tension on the steppe frontier.[89] Here, though, the Russians were coming up against – and brushing aside – claims to sovereignty very similar to their own, although control over people seems to have been more important than control over territory for the Khoqandis, and it is unlikely that they thought of the Chu as a territorial frontier in quite the same way as the Russians did.

At the end of 1858 Gerasim Alexeevich Kolpakovskii (1819–1896), who had served under Gasfort during the suppression of the Hungarian revolution in 1848, succeeded Peremyshil'skii as *Pristav* of the Qazaqs of the Great Horde and commander of the Ala-Tau district.[90] He would remain in post until 1889, from 1867 as Governor of the new Semirechie province, and from 1882 as Governor-General of the steppe region. More than any other individual,

---

[88] Peremyshil'skii to Parvanachi Mirza Ahmad Bahadur n.d. RGVIA F.1449 Op.1 D.26 ll. 41–2.

[89] Welsford, 'The Disappearing Khanate'.

[90] V. E. Nedvetskii, *Uzun-Agachskoe delo i ego znachenie v istorii Semirechenskago kraya* (Vernyi: Tip. Semirechenskogo Oblastnogo Pravleniya, 1910), 35.

Figure 4.2 Gerasim Alexeevich Kolpakovskii (*Turkestan Album*, 1871).

Kolpakovskii (Figure 4.2),[91] who, unusually, had begun his career in the ranks, would set his stamp on the new Russian colony, bringing in peasant settlers from his native region of Voronezh – together with their *Aport* apples, which would grow to enormous size in the benign climate of Semirechie – and overseeing the early urban development of Vernyi, which became a town in 1867. At this stage he was a relatively junior officer, and still forging his military reputation. Opportunities for this would not be lacking, not least as his superiors needed little convincing of the uselessness of negotiating with Khoqand.

In September 1858 Gasfort wrote to Kolpakovskii that the relentless aggressiveness of Khoqand meant that armed force would soon be needed again to 'bring everything into necessary order'.[92] 1859 saw further Khoqandi raids, including an attack on the newly constructed Russian fortress at Kastek led by Rustam Bek, which convinced St Petersburg of the need for a further punitive expedition.[93] When Khoqand attempted to negotiate by sending an embassy to Vernoe early in 1860, Kolpakovskii received strict instructions that it was not to be received: instead Gasfort instructed him to draw the Qazaq and Kyrgyz in the

---

[91] 'Voennyi gubernator Semirechenskoi oblasti General-leitenant G. A. Kolpakovskii', in Kun (ed.), *Turkestanskii al'bom*. Part 4, plate 5, No. 3 (Library of Congress, Prints & Photographs Division LC-DIG-ppmsca-09957–00003).

[92] Gasfort to Kolpakovskii 25/09/1858 TsGARKaz F.3 Op.1 D.11, 'Sobraniiu geograficheskikh i drugikh svedenii o khanstve Kokandskoi i nakhodyashchikhsya v nei kreposti', l. 1.

[93] Terent'ev, *Istoriya zavoevaniya*. I, 244–6.

region away from their allegiance to Khoqand, using a frankly cynical appeal to their self-interest:

> Try as far as possible to convince the Kyrgyz (*Dikokamennye Kirgizy*) at Issyq-Kul and the Dughlats [Qazaqs] beyond the Chu that they themselves should not give and should try to persuade others not to give *zakat* to the Khoqandis. As our Qazaqs (*Kirgizy*) do not pay anything to the government, so you can present this to them as a reason why they should not pay the Khan, all the more so as these levies on them do not go to mosques or matters of faith, but solely for the use of the Khan's officials (*chinovniki*).[94]

In other words, the Russians were continuing a policy of actively undermining the sovereignty and destabilising the rule of Khoqand in the southern *Dasht-i Qipchaq*. A few days later Gasfort instructed Kolpakovskii to break off all direct communication with the commander of Pishpek, 'as it is clear that in this matter the last argument remains the force of arms'. He claimed that the Khoqand Khan himself had recognised Russian sovereignty over the region between the Ili and the Chu, over both shores of Lake Issyq-Kul, and over the Qazaqs and Kyrgyz who lived there. While Russia had no aggressive intentions against Khoqand, they had the right to defend their subjects.[95] What this did not acknowledge, of course, was that so long as the Russians levied no taxes on their side of the River Chu, those Qazaqs and Kyrgyz which Khoqand claimed as its subjects would have a powerful incentive to migrate there, with a consequent catastrophic loss of revenue. Gasfort himself had already admitted that this was a deliberate Russian ploy, and it was one the Khoqandis could hardly be expected not to resist.

Despite these fiscal incentives it is not clear that all Qazaqs and Kyrgyz were necessarily willing to abandon Khoqand and submit to Russia in response. In March Gasfort ordered Kolpakovskii to send two forces towards Lake Issyq-Kul to persuade the Kyrgyz of the region to accept Russian sovereignty and disperse Khoqandi forces: 'you must announce to the *Dikokamennye* [i.e. the Kyrgyz] that our goal is not conquest, but on the contrary the bringing of peace and calm to our Kirgiz subjects'.[96] Whether this distinction would have been clear to the inhabitants of the region seems doubtful: the effect of this expedition, under *sotnik* Zherebyat'ev, was to reinforce Russian claims to control of Issyq-Kul.[97] Two months later, when the Bughu Kyrgyz showed signs of restiveness, Gasfort assumed this was the work of Khoqandi agitators, and ordered Kolpakovskii to identify and root them out, using much more

---

[94] Gasfort to Kolpakovskii 18/02/1860 TsGARKaz F.3 Op.1 D.33, 'Sekretnye predpisaniya i pis'ma komandira otdel'nogo Sibirskogo Korpusa', l. 10.
[95] Gasfort to Kolpakovskii 16/02/1860 TsGARKaz F.3 Op.1 D.33 l. 17.
[96] Gasfort to Kolpakovskii 31/03/1860 TsGARKaz F.3 Op.1 D.33 l. 20*ob*.
[97] Dzhamgerchinov, *Prisoedinenie Kirgizii*, 179–82.

threatening language: 'not one Kara-Kirgiz Yurt will be disturbed by the Russians, if their inhabitants will conduct themselves calmly. But they all know that for each hostile step against us they will pay with their heads.'[98] In July he was complaining that there was a party among the Great Horde Qazaqs who were hostile to Russia, and that it was they who were responsible for burning down a group of Cossack homesteads (khutor) near the Ili, not the Khoqandis. In an echo of Russian tactics among the Junior Horde 100 years before, he suggested taking hostages (amanat) from among them to be held at Vernoe, as a guarantee of good behaviour.[99] One thing which is clear from this correspondence is that it was not Kolpakovskii, the 'man on the spot', who was pushing for a more aggressive and expansionist policy beyond the Chu: had he wished to, he could perhaps have embarked on adventures of his own, not least as it took over a month for messages to travel from Vernoe along the trakt to Omsk, but in this instance the initiative came from above – and would receive willing endorsement from St Petersburg.

In the summer of 1860 the famous military geographer Mikhail Veniukov was despatched to conduct a reconnaissance of what the Russians called the 'Khoqand military line on the river Chu'. Veniukov described a chain of fortresses – Toqmaq, Pishpek, Aq-su, Merke, It-Kichu, Aulie-Ata, Chulaq-Qurghan and Suzaq, which were cut off from the main territories of the khanate by a low mountain range – the Qara-Tau – that ran parallel with the Syr-Darya. As we will see in the following chapter, the idea that the Chu and the Qara-Tau constituted 'natural frontiers' that could be used to delineate a new imperial boundary in the steppe would exercise a determinant influence over later Russian campaigns in the region, and Veniukov's report played an important part in this. More important at this stage was that Veniukov dismissed the Khoqandi fortifications as 'insignificant . . . a very weak defence for such a weak state as Khoqand'. Toqmaq had a garrison of just seventy men, poorly armed and without artillery, who spent most of their time growing vegetables around the fort.[100] Pishpek was more formidable, with perhaps 150–170 men, plus some merchants and other civilians. They had a few light cannon, which were served by 'Sarts' and fugitive Russians, but otherwise the locality was mainly notable for its apricot trees.[101] Veniukov was contemptuous of the fighting qualities of the Khoqandis, and had scathing things to say

---

[98] Gasfort to Kolpakovskii 09/05.1860 TsGARKaz F.3 Op.1 D.33 ll. 22ob–3.

[99] Gasfort to Kolpakovskii 27/07/1860 TsGARKaz F.3 Op.1 D.33 ll. 33ob–4.

[100] An image of the fortress can be found under 'Syr-dar'inskaya oblast': Tsitadel' Tokmaka' in Kun (ed.) Turkestanskii al'bom. Chast' 4, plate 20, No. 22 (Library of Congress, Prints & Photographs Division LC-DIG-ppmsca-09957–00022).

[101] 'Kokanskaya voennaya liniya na r. Chu', 15/07/1860 RGVIA F.1449 Op.1 D.7, 'Opisanie kokandskoi voennoi linii na r. Chu, sostavlennago General'nogo Shtaba Kapitanom Veniukovym', l. 2; a version of this report was published the following year as Veniukov, 'Ocherki Zailiiskogo kraya'.

about their wardrobe – *khalats*, turbans 'of the Persian type, high, like a sugar loaf', and poor-quality boots.[102] He thought only half their infantry had firearms, mostly matchlocks. 'The bronze cannons of the *Kokandtsy* hardly deserve the name of artillery, as they do not have carriages or any means for judging range.' Their lack of discipline and of tactical nous, as well as what he described as the 'inborn cowardice of Asiatics' at the first sign of a reverse, meant that there could be no doubt of the result of a clash between the Khoqandis and Russian troops, or those of any European army. Were it not for the existence of fortifications 'in which, as is known, Asiatics defend themselves very bravely', 450 men would probably suffice to capture and destroy all the fortresses of the Chu line.[103] Veniukov's combination of pride in European technical accomplishments and essentialist descriptions of Asiatic inferiority were highly characteristic of colonial military specialists of this period; sometimes this arrogance led to a fall (it had done so at Aq Masjid in 1852, and would do so again at Tashkent in 1864 and Gök-Tepe in 1879), but in this case Veniukov's assessment proved to be largely correct. The assurance that the campaign would be a pushover only whetted the Russian appetite for action.

Shortly after the submission of Veniukov's report, Gasfort wrote to War Minister Dolgorukov explaining that there could never be peace and security in the Ala-Tau district so long as the Khoqandis continued intriguing among the Qazaqs of the Great Horde. They still believed that they could destroy Fort Vernoe and drive the Russians back beyond the Ili. He urged that they be taught a lesson through the destruction of Toqmaq and Pishpek.[104] The Russian force set out from Vernoe in August 1860 – 2,000 men including six companies of infantry, six *sotnyas* of Cossacks, two *sotnyas* of Qazaq auxiliaries, two heavy guns, four light horse guns, two mountain guns, four rocket batteries, and four light and three heavy mortars with 1,172 rounds, under the command of Colonel Apollon Ernestovich Zimmerman (1825–1884) of the Main Staff.[105] Circumstances seemed favourable to Russian success; relations between Khoqand and Bukhara were frosty, and Malla Khan had been unable to persuade Amir Sayyid Muzaffar ad-Din (1834–1885) to join him in fighting the Russians.[106] There were reports of a force of 2,000 Khoqandis under

---

[102] Confirming the description of the Khoqandi ambassador to the East India Company in 1854, who described the Khoqand troops as wearing the 'kura koolee' or long Persian cap (see the Introduction).

[103] Kokanskaya voennaya liniya na r. Chu', 15/07/1860 RGVIA F.1449 Op.1 D.7 ll. 3–5ob.

[104] Gasfort to Dolgorukov 27/07/1860 RGVIA F.1449 Op.1 D.35, 'O komandirovanii iz ukrepleniya Vernago ekspeditsionnago otryada za reku Chu dlya vzyatiya i razrusheniya kokandskikh krepostei Tokmaka i Pishpeka', ll. 15–18.

[105] Terent'ev, *Istoriya zavoevaniya*. I, 247; see also Dzhamgerchinov, *Prisoedinenie Kirgizii*, 195–9.

[106] Kolpakovskii to Gasfort 08/07/1860 RGVIA F.1449 Op.1 D.35 ll. 23–6.

Qana'at Shah, the governor of Tashkent, beyond the Chu, and that Malla Khan was gathering reinforcements around Aulie-Ata in preparation for a campaign against the Russians once the harvest was in. However, intelligence from Qazaq scouts suggested that there was a garrison of just 500 men at Pishpek, and 100 at Toqmaq.[107] Zimmerman reported that Jantai and Bulekbai, leaders of the Kyrgyz tribes in the Chu region, were offering submission to Russia – another *manap* called Jangarach was angry at a fine of 100 horses levied on his sons by Khoqandi officials, reportedly saying 'soon God will bring the Russians here to destroy Pishpek', and that they would live better under the Russians, where their Muslim kinfolk lived in complete peace.[108] Zimmerman added that he was pretty sure of success, noting that Karbyshev's expedition across the Ili in 1851 had been of similar size, and had induced the Khoqandis to give up Tauchubek without a fight.[109]

At Toqmaq this was more or less what happened. On arrival Zimmerman was greeted by two 'Sarts', who on being told to give up the fortress asked for permission to wait for an answer from the commander of Pishpek, Atabek *Dadkhwah*. When Zimmerman refused, they returned to the fortress, and he sent a Qazaq called Kuat to parley with the commander, Khan Quli. The latter replied that he 'could not surrender the fortress, nor could he defend it'. After an hour of mortar fire, in which the Russians used about fifty shells, a figure appeared crying surrender:

> We later learnt that our fire, although weak [. . .] made a strong impression on the Sarts. The greater part of them concealed themselves; but the commander Khan Quli, as his men said afterwards, remained sitting on the wall and decided to die; only the cries of the women, of whom there were fifteen in the fortress, persuaded him to agree to surrender.[110]

Some of these women had infants at the breast, and one was slightly wounded by shrapnel from a mortar round (Zimmerman made sure to note that she was given medical attention). Toqmaq was surrendered unconditionally, and its fortifications razed to the ground as those of Tauchubek had been nine years before, while the gardens and irrigation works around it were destroyed.[111]

---

[107] Zimmerman to Gasfort 23/07/1860; Kolpakovskii to Gasfort 02/08/1860; Zimmerman to Gasfort 04/08/1860 RGVIA F.1449 Op.1 D.35 ll. 45–6, 56–8, 60–1.

[108] On Jantai Qarabek-oghli see Prior, 'High Rank and Power', 150.

[109] Zimmerman to Gasfort 19/08/1860 RGVIA F.1449 Op.1 D.35 ll. 94–5.

[110] Zimmerman to Gasfort 28/08/1860 RGVIA F.1449 Op.1 D.35 ll. 117–18. This report was later published in D. I. Romanovskii, *Zametki po sredne-aziyatskomu voprosu* (St Pb.: Tip. 2-go Otdela Sobstvennogo Ego Imperatorskogo Velichestva Kantselyarii, 1868), 123–7.

[111] When Chernyaev's force passed the site of the fortress in 1864, Valikhanov reminisced that it had once been surrounded by gardens, now destroyed: M. S. Znamenskii, 'Dnevnik Aulie-atinskogo pokhoda', *Sobranie sochinenii Ch. Ch. Valikhanova* ed. A. Kh. Margulan (Alma-Ata: Kazakhskaya Sovetskaya Entsiklopediya, 1985), V, 249.

Zimmerman's force then moved on to Pishpek, which proved a somewhat tougher nut to crack. Terent'ev would later write that Zimmerman's siege of the fortress 'served as a model for all subsequent sieges' in Central Asia, comparing it favourably with that of Aq Masjid: 'Pishpek was four times larger than Aq Masjid, had double walls, was better armed, and with a more numerous garrison, and with all this the siege lasted only five days, while that of Aq Masjid took 22. Apart from this, our losses at Pishpek were just seven men, while 165 fell at Aq Masjid.'[112] Certainly Zimmerman seems to have set about his operations with considerable efficiency, although it is clear that his small arms and artillery easily outranged those of the Khoqandis. He noted that the fortress was much larger than they had thought – Veniukov had indicated in his reconnaissance report the previous year that each side was 60–65 *sazhens* (approximately 140 yards) long, while the actual length was 105 *sazhens*. It was much larger than Toqmaq, and he ruled out a frontal assault. Many of the defenders wore the red uniforms of the Khoqandi *sarbaz* infantry, and their artillery had a range of about 400 *sazhens*. In response to their lively fire, the Russian guns fired about 400 shells on the first day of the siege, doing noticeable damage to the walls. Meanwhile their siege works were steadily advancing towards the main gates, which they intended to blow in. In the end this proved unnecessary:

> The enemy began to throw stones. From our side we opened up strengthened mortar and cannon fire. Bombs and shells one after the other flew into the fortress, and at 10 in the evening two men ran out crying 'aman! aman!' [we surrender!] They were seized by our scouts, who were concealed in secret outside the gateway and brought to me at the mortar battery. These men averred that the commanders of Pishpek Atabek *Dadkhwah* and Alisher *Dadkhwah* asked for mercy and were prepared to surrender the fortress.[113]

He sent in two translators to negotiate, in response to which Atabek sent out his sword and a letter saying that while they had been loyal to their Khan's salt for five days, now they could not resist any further. Both the *Dadkhwah*s then emerged to offer their unconditional surrender. Zimmerman demanded that they evacuate the fortress completely and give up all their weapons, but allowed them to take their property with them. In all 627 people surrendered, including 84 merchants and their servants, 63 women and 38 small children – 20 of the garrison had been killed and 25 wounded by the Russian bombardment, which had used 954 shells, 12,869 rounds of ammunition and some rockets. The Russians had lost just one man killed, six wounded and one

---

[112] Terent'ev, *Istoriya zavoevaniya*, I, 251; a complete account of the siege was published the following year as *Opisanie voennykh deistvii v Zailiiskom krae v 1860 godu i zhurnal osady khokandskoi kreposti Pishpek* (St Pb.: Tip. V. Spiridionova, 1861).

[113] Zimmerman to Gasfort 05/09/1860 RGVIA F.1449 Op.1 D.35 ll. 131*ob* –4. This report was published in Romanovskii, *Zametki po sredne-aziyatskomu voprosu*, 27–32.

'contused', thanks to the inaccuracy of the Khoqandi fire.[114] The list of trophies captured sheds some light on why this was, and also on the way in which Khoqand had become a destination for second-hand, mostly South Asian military technology and techniques over the previous half-century, since 'Alim Khan's military reforms and the creation of the *Sipah-i Jadid*.[115] The Russians captured the standards of both *Dadkhwahs*, five bronze cannon firing 5-*funt* balls, 11 small iron cannon firing 1- or 2-*funt* balls, 49 'fortress cannons' of large calibre which he compared to a *pishchal'*, a type of antique gun used in the fifteenth and sixteenth centuries, 367 flintlock and matchlock muskets 'of the most varied calibre: amongst them were many old English and Dutch firearms, six pistols, 366 sabres and swords, 206 pikes, sixteen shields with silver decoration, and one inlaid with gold, seven pieces of armour, a helmet with chain mail, five drums, five small *mitavr* (?) which the Khoqandi commanders carry on their saddles, four trumpets, 114 *poods* of gunpowder, many bullets, cast-iron shot for the fortress guns, lead and other things'.[116] The Russians also captured five suspected deserters who were interrogated and put before a military tribunal. Of these two were Muslims: 'Abdurahman Akhmetiev, a Siberian Tatar, and Halilullah Tokhvatullin, a Bashkir Cossack. One of the other three, Alexander Ivanov, was a baptised Tatar from Buchul'minsk district of Orenburg Province, and the fourth and fifth, Alexei Starshin and Nikita Sukhikh, were both Russian Orthodox. All claimed to have been kidnapped and carried off against their will, although these stories by their nature could not be verified. As on the Syr-Darya line, the idea that soldiers in Russian service, particularly those who were Christians, might have voluntarily gone over to the Muslim enemy raised troubling questions of identity and loyalty. Starshin and Tokhvatullin died in custody, but the remaining three appear to have been given the benefit of the doubt as they were freed and sent to serve in the 3rd Siberian Line Battalion. Sukhikh and Ivanov admitted to having been forced to participate in Muslim rites, and were first sentenced to spiritual chastisement, whilst Ivanov and Akhmet'ev were additionally given 100 lashes each.[117]

The day after the surrender Zimmerman set about demolishing the fortress (Figure 4.3[118]) – his description made it clear that it was more than a purely military outpost, as it contained a mosque and what he called a *Gostiny Dvor*

---

[114] Zimmerman to Gasfort 05/09/1860 RGVIA F.1449 Op.1 D.35 ll. 134*ob* –6.

[115] Levi, *Rise and Fall of Khoqand*, 82–5.

[116] Zimmerman to Gasfort 05/09/1860 RGVIA F.1449 Op.1 D.35 l. 135.

[117] 'Pokazanie vzyatago v Pishpeke …', 20/09/1860; Kolpakovskii to Gasfort 17/11/1860; Gasfort to the Military Governor of Semipalatinsk 26/08/1861 TsGARKaz F.3 Op.1 D.64, 'O russkikh pereezzhikakh, vzyatykh vo vremya osady Pishpeka', ll. 1–6, 57–8, 89–91.

[118] 'Syr-dar'inskaya oblast': Tsitadel' Pishpeka', in Kun (ed.), *Turkestanskii al'bom*. Chast' 4, plate 20, No. 23 (Library of Congress, Prints & Photographs Division LC-DIG-ppmsca -09957–00023).

Figure 4.3 The Pishpek Citadel (*Turkestan Album*, 1871).

(i.e. a bazaar) with seventy stalls, along with dwelling-houses for those who traded in them. The clay walls were battlemented, 2½ *sazhens* high and 4 *sazhens* thick, with towers 5½ *sazhens* high. There was a workshop for making bullets, and a 'laboratory' for manufacturing gunpowder: all indicative of Khoqand's ambition to control the steppe, but also of how inadequate even its reformed military structures were in the face of superior Russian arms. Gasfort proposed building a new Russian fortress on the site, and naming it Alexandrovskii after the Tsar, but this was rejected. Although it would be another four years before the region was permanently annexed, Khoqand had suffered a severe humiliation. In response the Qazaqs of the Dughlat tribe who lived beyond the Chu, as well as several Kyrgyz leaders, came forward to offer their submission. The most notable of the latter was Shabdan, the son of the Sarybaghysh *manap* Jantai: although he is said subsequently to have fought against the Russians at Uzun-Agach, he would go on to be a key ally of the colonial regime.[119] Kolpakovskii sent a letter to the *manaps* Jangarach, Jantai,

[119] On Shabdan Batyr see Tetsu Akiyama, 'Why Was Russian Direct Rule over Kyrgyz Nomads Dependent on Tribal Chieftains "*manaps*"?', *CMR* 56/4 (2015), 625–49; & 'From Collaborator to a Symbol of Revolt against Russia: Socio-political Conditions after the Death of a Kirghiz Chieftain at the Beginning of the Twentieth Century', *Journal of Islamic Area Studies* 11 (2019), 47–59; Prior, *Shabdan Batyr Codex*.

Umbet 'Ali, 'Adil and Bulekbai Kurchi telling them that since the fall of Toqmaq and Pishpek the 'Dikokamennye' Kyrgyz should no longer consider themselves subjects of Khoqand and obliged to pay zakat, and asked them to send representatives to Vernoe to make submission.[120]

However, Gasfort still did not believe that the region had been finally secured for Russia; he wrote to Kolpakovskii on the 1 October urging him to use terror rather than kindness when dealing with what he described as 'Kirgiz traitors', as they would interpret the latter as weakness. 'I am sure that in their souls is still hidden the thought that, if the Khan himself were to come with his forces, this would destroy not only our influence over the Kyrgyz (Dikokamennye), who live in the upper reaches of the river Chu, but even our sovereignty (vlady-chestvo) over the Trans-Ili region, which the Khoqandis consider as before to be their possession, despite all the lessons and disappointments inflicted on them, beginning with the destruction of the fortress of Tauchubek.'[121]

4.3   Uzun-Agach

The battle of Uzun-Agach, also known as Qara-Kastek, was the only armed clash in Semirechie which made it into the Russian military canon of victories during the conquest; Terent'ev devoted seven pages of his history to it and provided a plan of the battle in the Turkestan Album, while it also figured in Russian histories of Semirechie as the moment when the military security of the new colony was assured and the disorderly instincts of the Qazaqs and Kyrgyz finally curbed; in 1910, apparently, one might still hear songs about the victory being sung on the streets of Vernyi.[122]

This sense of its significance seems to have been shared on the Khoqandi side, as it also received fairly extensive treatment in the Ta'rikh-i Shahrukhi, which sheds some important light on divisions in the Khoqandi leadership, although its chronology is a little confused and it presents the battle as a victory.[123] Terent'ev described the clash in dramatic terms: in his account, as soon as Pishpek had been destroyed, the Khoqandis began massing for a counter-attack under the banner of ghazavat – holy war. He estimated the number of Khoqandi troops that gathered at Pishpek in early October under the command of Qana'at Shah, the new governor of Tashkent, at 20,000 men with ten guns.[124] Opposed to this there were just 2,440 Russian troops, divided between garrisons at Kastek, at Vernoe and on the Ili. The Russians initially

---

[120] Kolpakovskii to Gasfort 15/09/1860; Copy of a proclamation from Kolpakovskii 06/10/ 1860 RGVIA F.1449 Op.1 D.35 ll. 195–201, 236.

[121] Gasfort to Kolpakovskii 01/10/1860 TsGARKaz F.3 Op.1 D.33 ll. 48–ob.

[122] Terent'ev, Istoriya zavoevaniya, I, 252–9; Nedvetskii Uzun-Agachskoe delo, 2, 6. See also Dzhamgerchinov, Prisoedinenie Kirgizii, 199–210.

[123] TSh, 216–17; Bartol'd, 'Tuzemets o russkom zavoevanii', 337–8.

[124] Terent'ev, Istoriya zavoevaniya, I, 252.

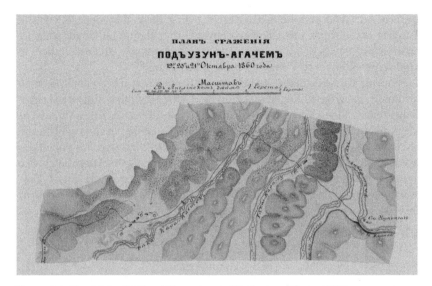

Figure 4.4 Plan of the Battle of Uzun-Agach (*Turkestan Album*, 1871).

ignored reports of the massing of Khoqandi forces.[125] When, on the 15 October, Kolpakovskii sent messages to Qazaq sultans of the Great Horde asking for support, none was forthcoming.[126] On the 18 October Kolpakovskii made his way to the forward post at Kastek, narrowly avoiding an ambush by a group of Qazaqs on the way. The Russians had concentrated the bulk of their forces here, and at the nearby river crossing of Uzun-Agach. On the 19 October a Cossack patrol of ninety men was attacked by a large group of Qazaqs, and according to Terent'ev was saved only by the presence of mind of its commander, *Khorunzhii* Rostovstev, who pretended that the cart he and his men were escorting was a gun-carriage and used it to scare them off.[127] On the 20 October there came an unsuccessful assault on the picket at Uzun-Agach, which prompted Kolpakovskii to move the rest of his forces forward to that point (Figure 4.4).[128] On the night of the 21 October he launched a surprise attack on the Khoqandi forces with three companies of infantry, four *sotnya*s of Cossacks, six guns and two rocket batteries – in all 800 men.[129]

Terent'ev estimates the number of Khoqandis at 13,000, though the force facing Kolpakovskii's men initially was about 5,000, of whom no more than 1,000 were

---

[125] Nedvetskii, *Uzun-Agachskoe delo*, 52.
[126] Terent'ev, *Istoriya zavoevaniya*, I, 252–3.
[127] *Ibid.*, 253–4.
[128] Plan srazheniya pod Uzun-Agachem: 19-go, 20-go i 21-go oktyabrya 1860 goda', in Kun (ed.), *Turkestanskii al'bom*. Chast' 4, plate10, No. 7 (Library of Congress, Prints & Photographs Division LC-DIG-ppmsca-09957–00007).
[129] Nedvetskii, *Uzun-Agachskoe delo*, 60–1, 64–5.

sarbaz infantry.[130] In the *Ta'rikh-i Shahrukhi* Khoqandi gives a figure of 7,000 for the advance guard that crossed the Chu under the leadership of Shadman Khwaja, while the main force, under the joint command of Qana'at Shah and the Kyrgyz governor of Andijan, 'Alim Bek, numbered at least 13,000.[131] Crucially, however, they were without artillery, having been unable to drag it over the pass between Pishpek and Kastek.[132] Predictably enough, it was the Russian artillery, directed by Staff-Captain Obukh, which wrought most of the damage, using both explosive shells and canister shot, and with a commanding position on the heights over-looking the river Qara-Kastek.[133] Although he spared some praise for the bravery of the Khoqandi regular troops or *sarbaz*, one column of which 'attacked bravely and triumphantly with drums, trumpets and flapping standards', and noted that 'the enemy, more than expected, put up a most obstinate resistance: their attacks were very steady, and they threw themselves into hand-to-hand fighting more than once', Terent'ev indicated that the result was never in doubt. The Russians were so exhausted after nine hours of fighting that they were unable to pursue the fleeing enemy, but otherwise victory was complete.

One indication that for all their efforts the Khoqandis were never able to get to close quarters was that the Russians lost just one man killed and 26 wounded, while Terent'ev estimated that the Khoqandis lost at least 350 infantry (including six officers or *pansads*) and up to 1,500 cavalry. A simultaneous Khoqandi assault on the fort at Kastek also failed. Terent'ev compared this to the unsuccessful assault the Khoqandis had made on Fort Perovskii shortly after its capture in 1853, where 13,000 Khoqandis with 17 guns had been beaten off by a garrison of 550. Russian casualties were even lower at Uzun-Agach because of the enemy's lack of artillery. 'Having been burnt by the Orenburgers, now they were also burnt by the Siberians.'[134] Qana'at Shah apparently tried to restore some pride by claiming that the Russians had lost 200 killed, including Kolpakovskii himself, and the narrative in the *Ta'rikh-i Shahrukhi* offers some indications of how Khoqand's elites sought to re-narrate this bruising defeat as a victory – though it also gives clear indications of the divisions that had helped to bring about defeat:

> At that time they received news from Shadman-Khwaja, that he had met with the Russians and entered into battle with them. Immediately the Muslim forces gathered themselves and at the time of breakfast came to *Biket*,[135] between the fortresses of Ashtak [Kastek] and Uch-Almaty [Vernoe], where

[130] P. Pichugin, 'Vtorzhenie Kokandtsev v Alatavskii Okrug v 1860 godu', *VS* (1872), No. 5,15
[131] *TSh*, 216; Bartol'd, 'Tuzemets o russkom zavoevanii', 336.
[132] Nedvetskii notes that the Khoqandi artillery was commanded by a runaway Russian convict called Evgraf: *Uzun-agachskoe delo*, 61.
[133] Terent'ev, *Istoriya zavoevaniya*, I, 255–6.
[134] Terent'ev, *Istoriya zavoevaniya*, I, 256–7.
[135] *Sic* – Bartol'd writes that this is the Russian word *piket*, or military outpost.

they [the Russians] were. The army of Islam, surrounding the unbelievers
(*Kuffar*), arranged themselves in military order. At that time there began an
argument over the command of the troops between the Kyrgyz 'Alim Bek and
the Tajik Qana'at Shah. 'Alim Bek in anger with his enemy distanced himself
[from the battlefield] taking with him his Andijan troops and the Kyrgyz,
leaving all the honour of the battle to Qana'at Shah, and brought upon himself
dishonour, letting fall from his hands the field of honour and courage. A part
of the forces from the capital [Khoqand], Tashkent and Qurama, after saying
the *takbir*,[136] threw themselves like salamanders into the fire of gunpowder[137]
and naphtha[138] (*manand-i samandar khudha ra ba atesh-i daru va naft
zadand*). This unworthy person, the author of these lines, was under the
victorious and high standard of those who had pronounced the *takbir*:
reading the verses 'kill the polytheists' [Qur'an, IX, 5] he inspired the
Muslims; praying for the victory of the true believers, with his own tongue
he repeated the verses 'Oh God! Defend the defenders of the faith.' At that
time, when the army of Islam threw themselves into a sea of the cannonballs
and bullets of the unbelievers (*be darya-yi atesh-i tir o tufang-i kuffar zadand*),
the cannon and rifles (*tup va tufang*) of the unbelievers together with naphtha
threw out such a fire, that it fell on the people of Islam from the heavens
like lightning and hail (*barq-i asman va zhala-i baran dar an biyaban bar sal-i
ahl-i Islam ribakht*). It was possible to imagine that the day of judgement had
come; the sound of firing from the cannon and rifles resembled the sound of
the last trumpet. Many heroes (*dalawaran*) full of courage and strong youths
threw themselves into this valley of fire, like salamanders, and from the bullets
of the unbelievers, from the hands of the cup-bearer of fate, they drank the
sherbet of martyrdom (*sharbat-i shahidat az saqi-i duran nush karda*). Some
heroes with their swords cut off the heads of the unbelievers. [...] Thus the
battle lasted for an hour. Finally, after a lengthy rain of bullets and cannonballs, and after the explosion of burning matter[139] a mass of Qazaqs and
brigand-nomads (*qazaqiyya*), unable to bear the fire of the cannons and rifles,
took to flight and hid themselves in the valleys and depressions of the hills.
But the Sart and Tajik troops (*sartiyya va tajikiyya*), not turning away their
faces from the unbelievers, continued to fight from the time of breakfast until
midday. Finally, the unbelievers, weakened by the firing of the Muslims, drew
away to the top of the hillocks, grieving, and not finding any peace there, took
to flight.[140]

---

[136] The prayer for the dead.

[137] The word here is *daru*, which Bartol'd translates as *porokh*, gunpowder. The common
meaning of this both in Persian and in modern Uzbek is 'drug' or medicinal substance,
an indication that it is a calque from Chinese – Thomas Allsen, 'The Circulation of
Military Technology in the Mongolian Empire', in *Warfare in Inner Asian History* ed.
Nicola Di Cosmo (Leiden: Brill, 2002), 281. My thanks to Scott Levi for confirming this.

[138] Most probably Khoqandi is referring to rocket fire.

[139] Perhaps another reference to rockets.

[140] *TSh*, 217; Bartol'd, 'Tuzemets o russkom zavoevanii', 336–7.

As with Khoqandi's description of the fall of Aq Masjid, we get a sense of how disruptive the coming of the Russians was to the religious assumptions of Khoqand's '*ulama*, and also of the impression made by Russian weapons. Uzun-Agach was of course not a victory for Khoqand, despite the numerical superiority of the khanate's forces, and the account in the *Ta'rikh-i Shahrukhi* indicates clearly enough why this was so: not just the superiority of Russian weaponry, but the deep divisions in Khoqandi society under the fragile leadership of Malla Khan. These expressed themselves both in the dispute between the Kyrgyz 'Alim Bek and the Tajik Qana'at Shah (Khoqandi is careful to attach ethnonyms to both of them) and also in the historian's contemptuous reference to the Qazaq 'brigands' breaking and running, while the Sart and Tajik troops remained steadfast. Since the Bukharan invasion and Qipchaq coup of 1842–4 political power in Khoqand had passed back and forth between nomadic and sedentary groups, usually accompanied by violence.[141] Now the additional pressure brought by the Russian presence was splitting Khoqandi society, or at least its elites, along these lines, and hampering the khanate's ability to resist.

Gasfort wrote to congratulate Kolpakovskii on his victory, assuring him there was no doubt that the Tsar would be gladdened by it.[142] Kolpakovskii lost no time in capitalising on the Russian victory, sending a series of messages to Qazaq Sultans, Kyrgyz *manaps*, *batyrs* and *biis* to inform them that the power of Khoqand was broken and that they should resume their usual pastures and submit to Russia.[143] 'They tell you that they are fighting for the faith. Have they done anything up to now for your faith? On the contrary the Russian government has never prevented anyone from fulfilling the rites of their religion, by laying out the rights of every confession, and [. . .] itself has constructed Muslim mosques in various places on the Kirgiz steppe.'[144] This generous confessional policy would cease after 1867 when the steppe was excluded from the jurisdiction of the Orenburg Mufti, and it is interesting to see its rhetorical use at so late a date.

Gasfort still considered unruly Qazaqs to be a threat to Russian authority and prestige, urging extra care and vigilance, and reiterating once again that they did not understand kindness: 'complete faith in our strength, in the superiority of our arms and in our predestined mission in this region must inspire all and everyone'.[145] Not long after this Gasfort would go into retirement, no doubt still ruminating on the deceitfulness and unruliness of the Qazaqs and Kyrgyz. His successor, A. O. Diugamel, the former Russian envoy to Tehran, was considerably

---

[141] Levi, *The Rise and Fall of Khoqand*, 163–8.
[142] Gasfort to Kolpakovskii 10/11/1860 TsGARKaz F.3 Op.1 D.33 ll. 53–4*ob*.
[143] Kolpakovskii to the Nubuta and Batu *bii* and Surapgi *batyr* 28/10/1860 TsGARKaz F.3 Op.1 D.402, 'O snosheniyakh s kirgizami Bol'shoi i Dikokamennoi Ordy, vozbudiv-shikhsya vsledstvii voennykh deistvii v Zailiiskom krae s kokandtsami v 1860 godu', l. 3.
[144] Kolpakovskii to the Sultans of the Great Horde 20/12/1860 TsGARKaz F.3 Op.1 D.402 l. 10.
[145] Gasfort to Kolpakovskii 24/11/1860 TsGARKaz F.3 Op.1 D.33 ll. 65–74*ob*.

less aggressive and expansionist in his instincts, but this would do little to slow the pace of Russian conquest. Diugamel began by issuing a mild reprimand to Kolpakovskii for a punitive raid carried out beyond the Chu, in which an officer had been killed and forty-seven women and children who were captured had been handed over to Kolpakovskii's Qazaq allies – he asked for them to be freed.[146] In July 1861 he was urging Kolpakovskii to avoid clashes with Khoqand, except in direct response to raids, and then only when he was sure it could be done 'without significant losses on our side', and in August he informed him that the construction of a fortress beyond the Chu had been postponed because relations with Khoqand around the fortress of Julek on the Syr-Darya had apparently improved.[147] In the summer of 1861 the Khoqandis did indeed attempt to re-open dialogue through despatching an embassy to Omsk, at the same time as they also made overtures to the Ottoman Sultan, asking him to intervene and dissuade the Russians from attacking.[148] This followed a common pattern in that it was preceded by a testing of the waters through the agency of a Khoqandi *caravanbashi* called Narynbai, carrying a letter from *Ishan* Mian Khalil, a highly respected religious figure who was their proposed envoy.[149] The response from the Ministry of Foreign Affairs was distinctly unenthusiastic about this approach; while noting the desirability of improving relations with Khoqand given the unstable situation in Kashgar, 'on the other hand [...] the reception in St Petersburg of embassies from Central Asia does not in general bring about the anticipated results, and is extremely expensive'. Given this, and the poor relations with Khoqand in recent years, they recommended receiving the ambassador at Vernoe and carefully vetting him before allowing him to proceed even to Omsk.[150] Here as elsewhere we get the clear sense that the Russian authorities did not view the Central Asian khanates as legitimate interlocutors, and considered attempts at diplomatic dialogue wasted on them. In the event this possible thaw in Russo-Khoqandi relations was put paid to by the attack on and destruction of the fortress of Yangi-Qurghan in the autumn of 1861 by the forces of the Syr-Darya line, who as usual had not kept their Siberian counterparts informed of their plans.

1863 saw a renewal of hostilities in Semirechie as well, as the Russians sent another expeditionary force under Captain Lerkhe to destroy the fortifications which the Khoqandis had reconstructed at Pishpek. The fortress was abandoned

---

[146] Diugamel to Kolpakovskii 30/01/1861 TsGARKaz F.3 Op.1 D.34 l. 3ob.

[147] Diugamel to Kolpakovskii 25/07/1861; 05/08/1861 TsGARKaz F.3 Op.1 D.34 ll. 6–9.

[148] Petition of the Khoqand envoy Khwaja Sudur 30/04/1861, in *The History of Central Asia in Ottoman Documents* ed. Shahin Mustafayev & Mustafa Serin (Samarkand: IICAS, 2001), I, 204

[149] Turki letter from Ishan Mian Khalil to the *Qazaq Hakemi Firishtuf* (i.e. the *Pristav* of the Great Horde, Kolpakovskii) recd. 24/09/1861; Kolpakovskii to Diugamel 25/09/1861 TsGARKaz F.3 Op.1 D.448, 'Perepiska s General-Gubernatorom Zapadnoi Sibiri o posylke posol'stva Kokanskogo khana v Sankt-Peterburg', ll. 2, 4.

[150] MID to Gasfort 04/11/1861 TsGARKaz F.3 Op.1 D.448 ll. 9–10ob.

without a fight, and Lerkhe then proceeded to Aulie-Ata and camped outside its walls. He tried to persuade Kolpakovskii to allow him to attack and seize the town, urging that 'to retreat now would be impolitic and might decisively damage our dignity (*dostoinstvo*)', but on this occasion the prestige argument was overruled.[151] Diugamel reprimanded Kolpakovskii for allowing Lerkhe's scouting party to become a quasi-invading force, and it soon returned to Vernoe. However, Kolpakovskii continued to insist that without the capture of Aulie-Ata it would be impossible to establish full influence over the Kyrgyz, and that Khoqand still had what he called aggressive designs on the Chu Valley, which would be realised as soon as the political situation in the Khanate stabilised – here he referred to the ousting and murder of Malla Khan, and the subsequent struggle between his brother Khudoyar and the Qipchaq ascendancy for control of Khoqand, in which the latter were victorious.[152] It was their leader, 'Alimqul, who would confront the Russians during the final phase of their advance through the steppe towards Tashkent in 1863–5, the subject of the next chapter. Semirechie and its Qazaq and Kyrgyz inhabitants had already largely been subdued, something consolidated with the construction of fortresses in the territory of the northern Kyrgyz at Naryn, on the trade route south to Ferghana and Kashgar in 1868, and at Qaraqol (later renamed Przheval'sk after the famous explorer, who died there in 1888), at the eastern end of Issyq-Kul, in 1869. There remained one more territorial annexation the Russians would make in this region – of the upper valley of the River Ili and the town of Ghulja, which were occupied in 1871 and returned to China in 1881. This forms an intriguing coda to the Russian conquest of Semirechie, one that had profound consequences for its subsequent development under colonial rule, and which is also a unique instance of a conquered territory in Central Asia which was subsequently handed back.

4.4   The Ili Crisis

In 1864 Muslims under Chinese rule – both Turkic and Chinese-speaking – rose up in rebellion and expelled the Qing dynasty's representatives from the whole of the vast Central Asian territory that had been conquered by the Qianlong Emperor just over 100 years before – Jungharia, Kashgaria and Ili.[153] The revolt began among the Dungans (Chinese-speaking Muslims, also known as Hue) in Kucha to the north of the Taklamakan desert in June,

---

[151] Lerkhe to Kolpakovskii 23/03/1863 TsGARKaz F.3 Op.1 D.222 ll. 205–7ob.

[152] Levi, *The Rise and Fall of Khoqand*, 189–91.

[153] The standard work, drawing on an extraordinary range of Chinese, Turkic and Russian sources, is Hodong Kim, *Holy War in China: The Muslim Rebellion and State in Chinese Central Asia, 1864–1877* (Stanford: Stanford University Press, 2004). See also Paine, *Imperial Rivals*, 118–20; Kwang-Ching Liu, 'The Military Challenge: The North-West and the Coast', in *The Cambridge History of China*. Vol. 11 (Cambridge: Cambridge University Press, 1980), 214–44.

and spread rapidly to Urumchi, Yarkand, Kashgar, Khotan and, in October 1864, to Ili, which bordered Russia's new possessions in Semirechie. The most famous figure it produced was Yaqub Beg, a Khoqandi general who had been governor of Aq Masjid at the time of the first, failed Russian assault in 1852 (though he was not actually present when it occurred). By the end of 1865, with a small force from Khoqand, he had placed himself at the head of the rebellion in Kashgar, and successfully stormed the Qing fort outside the city, which had been under siege for over a year. Having established himself as the ruler of almost all the former Qing territories in Central Asia, he was assiduously courted by both Britain and Russia, and attained a certain celebrity. He was the subject of a well-known biography by the Irish journalist Demetrius Boulger, and a more accurate text by the Russian orientalist N. I. Veselovskii.[154]

From the outset the Russians viewed the revolt with dismay, as it replaced a Chinese neighbour that, despite being in their view backward and arrogant, was a known and predictable quantity, with the same 'Islamic fanaticism' that they feared in their own Central Asian territories. Yaqub Beg was also seen as a possible vector of undesirable British influence in the region.[155] The first British visitor to Kashgar in 1868–9 was the tea-planter and orientalist Robert Shaw, and he was followed by an official embassy led by Thomas Forsyth in 1870, by George Hayward in 1871, and by another embassy, led by H. W. Bellew in 1873–4.[156] The Russians responded with their own embassies, the first of which seems to have been that led by Captain Reinthal in 1870,[157] then A. V. Kaul'bars in 1872,[158] and A. N. Kuropatkin in 1876–7, shortly

---

[154] Demetrius Charles Boulger, *The Life of Yakoob Beg, Athalik Ghazi and Badaulet, Ameer of Kashgar* (London: W. H. Allen & Co, 1878); N. I. Veselovskii, *Badaulet Yakub-Bek: Atalyk Kashgarskii* (St Pb.: Tip. Imperatorskoi Akademii Nauk, 1898), originally published in *ZVOIRAO*. Vol. XI (1898), 87–103.

[155] Hsü, *The Ili Crisis*, 13–14.

[156] Robert Shaw, 'Memorandum on the Present Condition of Affairs in Eastern Turkistan', 11/04/1876 IOR/ L/P&S/7/9-Pol.No.131, 159a–k; Robert Shaw, *Visits to High Tartary, Yarkand, and Kashghar* (London: John Murray, 1871); George Henderson & Allan O. Hume, *Lahore to Yarkand: Incidents of the Route and Natural History of the Countries Traversed by the Expedition of 1870 under T. D. Forsyth Esq., C.B.* (London: L. Reeve & Co, 1873); Thomas Forsyth, *Report of a Mission to Yarkund in 1873 under Command of Sir T. D. Forsyth, with Historical and Geographical Information Regarding the Possessions of the Ameer of Yarkund* (Calcutta: Foreign Department Press, 1875); G. Hayward, 'Journey from Leh to Yarkand and Kashgar, and Exploration of the Sources of the Yarkand River', *JRGS* 40 (1871), 33–166; H. W. Bellew, *Kashmir and Kashghar: A Narrative of the Embassy to Kashghar in 1873–4* (London: Trübner & Co, 1875).

[157] 'Otchet Kapitana Reintalya o russkom posol'stve k praviteliu Kashgara', 1870 TsGARKaz F.825 Op.1 D.18.

[158] The records of this mission are in RGVIA F.203 Op.1 D.5 'Dnevnik za 1872 g.' & D.10 'Dokumenty po Kashgarskoi ekspeditsii 1872 goda'.

before Yaqub Beg's death.[159] As we will see subsequently, another mission, which would have been led by M. D. Skobelev in 1875, was overtaken by the outbreak of rebellion in Ferghana. As Ian Campbell has argued, while the British and Russians were ostensibly rivals for Yaqub Beg's favours, they shared many assumptions about the 'savage' nature of his regime and the contrasting benefits which European civilisation was bringing to Central Asia.[160] Accordingly it was not so much fear of British influence that motivated Russian interference in Kashgar as the belief that Yaqub Beg had designs on Russia's protectorate in Khoqand, and presented a potential threat to Russia's ill-defined but mountainous frontier in southern Semirechie, which he had refused to recognise.[161]

This was still truer of the lesser-known Muslim regime which emerged in the upper Ili valley in 1864, where there was no such reassuringly 'natural' barrier to separate it from Russian territory, and which the Russians viewed from the outset as illegitimate and threatening.[162] Ili was a fertile, well-irrigated region with a mixed population, most of whom had either migrated or been forcibly moved there relatively recently, and which had been the main centre of Qing power in Inner Asia. When the Qing destroyed the Junghar confederation in the 1750s they settled Manchu and Mongol Banner troops there to secure their power, and brought in 'Taranchis' (literally 'farmers'), Turkic-speaking Muslims from the Tarim basin, to cultivate the soil. These were also joined by Dungan merchants and peasants.[163] While the revolt here began among the Dungans, who destroyed the local Qing forces, conflict soon broke out between them and the Taranchis, who by the end of 1866 had massacred many of the remaining Han Chinese in the Ili valley and gained control of most of its territory, under the rule of a Taranchi called Abu'l-'Ala Khan, who in Russian sources usually appears as Abil Ogli.[164] Kolpakovskii considered him an erratic and 'fanatical' ruler, and between 1866 and 1870 the Russians recorded a long list of what they considered to be border violations, *baramta* and other outrages.[165] Kolpakovskii also insisted on the necessity of annexing Ghulja

[159] A. N. Kuropatkin, *Kashgariya: Istoriko-geograficheskii ocherk strany, eya voennyya sily, promyshlennost' i torgovlya* (St Pb.: Balashev, 1878), translated as *Kashgaria [Eastern or Chinese Turkestan]: Historical and Geographical Sketch of the Country; Its Military Strength, Industries and Trade* trans. Walter E. Gowan (Calcutta: Thacker, Spink & Co., 1882). On this mission see S. V. Moiseev, 'Diplomaticheskaya i nauchnaya missiya A. N. Kuropatkina v Kashgariiu v 1876–1877 gg.', in *Vostokovednye issledovanie na Altae* ed. S. Moiseev (Barnaul: n.p., 2000), II, 95–104.
[160] Campbell, '"Our Friendly Rivals"'.
[161] Paine, *Imperial Rivals*, 122.
[162] Gorshenina, *Asie Centrale*, 100–3.
[163] Fletcher, 'Ch'ing Inner Asia', 58–9, 64–8.
[164] Kim, *Holy War in China*, 52–7; David Brophy, *Uyghur Nation: Reform and Revolution on the Russia–China Frontier* (Cambridge, MA: Harvard University Press, 2016), 54–7.
[165] Terent'ev, *Istoriya zavoevaniya*, II, 15–20.

to pre-empt any possibility that it might be seized by the more powerful Yaqub Beg, and to gain control of the strategic Muzart Pass which was the main route of communication between Jungharia and the Tarim Basin.[166] He was supported in his aggressive views by Major-General V. Poltoratskii, the governor of Semipalatinsk Province, and by 1870 he had also convinced a receptive Governor-General von Kaufman that Abil Ogli was yet another of those 'Asiatic' rulers who were amenable only to force.[167] That summer von Kaufman ordered Kolpakovskii to occupy the Muzart Pass, and then set about convincing St Petersburg of the need for further military action.[168] War Minister Miliutin quotes a letter from von Kaufman of the 20 February 1871 approvingly in his memoirs:

> On the Chinese frontier our affairs are all in a bad state. There we are dealing with absolute scum (*sovershenno dran'iu*), and there is no other way of finishing with it other than by crushing it, as they do not understand anything else. I would not wish to conquer Ghulja, both because of the categorical order from the Highest Authority and because of my own view of the question; but it could happen that I will be obliged (as General Kolpakovskii, the commander of the forces of Semirechie province, has indicated) to punish the Ghulja Sultan for his conduct towards us. I would dare to assure you, and I think it is clear to all, that I am not quick-tempered and never have been; and because of this, if I decide on some military enterprise or other, then it means that it was not possible to act otherwise.[169]

As Miliutin recalled, 'this was quickly what happened'. In April 1871 Abil Ogli gave Kolpakovskii the pretext he sought. The leader of the Buzum lineage of the Abdan tribe of the Qazaq Great Horde, Tazabek Busurmanov, who held the Russian rank of lieutenant, was found to have been corresponding with the Taranchi Sultan. He had resisted the arrest of two of his relatives for murder, and had been disqualified by the Russian authorities after winning election as a *volost'* administrator. When a force of Cossacks was sent to arrest him he gathered a force of armed followers and attacked them, fleeing to the Ili territory when they were driven off. The Russians then found that a large number of Qazaqs of his lineage had followed him across the frontier – in all over a thousand *kibitkas*.[170] This exercise of nomadic mobility to flee from Russian sovereignty was effectively what the Russians themselves had encouraged the Great Horde Qazaqs to do towards Khoqand ten years earlier, but unsurprisingly they did not like being on the receiving end. Although one

[166] Hsü, *The Ili Crisis*, 18.
[167] Gorshenina, *Asie Centrale*, 104–9.
[168] Terent'ev, *Istoriya zavoevaniya*, II, 19–20.
[169] D. A. Miliutin, *Vospominaniya 1868–nachalo 1873* ed. L. G. Zakharova (Moscow: ROSSPEN, 2006), 433–4.
[170] Terent'ev, *Istoriya zavoevaniya*, II, 26–7.

Taranchi prisoner taken by the Russians, Isen Mullah, claimed that Abil Ogli's
chief adviser Mahpur Shanbegi was largely to blame for the war by advising
against giving Tazabek up,[171] it seems fairly clear that this was an immediate
pretext for a Russian invasion that had long been anticipated. In his proclamation 'To the inhabitants of the Land of Ghulja' in June 1871 Kolpakovskii gave
what would become the standard Russian explanation for the annexation of
the Ili valley:

> From the very beginning of the disorders in your land after the rebellion
> against the Chinese, bandits and cattle-thieves [*barantachi*] frequently
> encroached on Russian domains and disrupted the peace of our subjects.
> Criminals and wicked persons, having carried out some sort of villainous
> enterprise, stole away beyond our boundaries to your side and were then
> taken under protection by the usurper who had seized power over the
> Taranchis by force and the shedding of blood.[172]

The final straw had come when Sultan Abil Ogli gave refuge to the Qazaq
criminal Tazabek, and now Kolpakovskii announced that his forces were
coming to destroy the 'Taranchi' government. He announced that Ghulja
would be occupied, and guaranteed freedom of religion, security of trade
and property: 'those who are oppressed by the Taranchi government –
Solon, Sibo, Chinese, Manchus, Qalmyqs and Dungans! The destruction of
the Taranchi power for you is a liberation from the heavy oppression and
injustice of the Taranchis'. Qazaqs and Kyrgyz were encouraged to dwell on
the benefits their compatriots enjoyed under Russian rule. These and later
proclamations urging the population to abandon resistance were circulated in
Turki translation, though not apparently in Chinese or Manchu.[173]

Despite these exhortations Kolpakovskii's invading force did have to fight
three significant engagements, at the town of Mazar on the 7–8 June, at 'Chin-
cha-go-zi' (Qing-quan-he-zi) on the 18 June and at Suydun on the 19 June.
Kolpakovskii described taking the former town (which was apparently largely
populated by Dungans) with just one and a half *sotnya*s of Semirechie and
Siberian Cossacks, one company of the 11th Turkestan Line Battalion and two
guns. 'The enemy rapidly retreated across the undulating *ariq*s and gullies of
the place' as far as their camp near the village of Ashista, where a Russian
cavalry charge put them to complete flight. Kolpakovskii estimated their

---

[171] 'Pokazanie plennago Isen Mully (vzyat' 28 maya okolo Ketmenya)', n.d. TsGARKaz F.21
   Op.1 D.20, 'Ob okkupatsii gor. Kul'dzhi russkimi voiskami', l. 4*ob*.
[172] 'K naseleniiu Kul'dzhinskoi strany', 06/06/1871 TsGARKaz F.21 Op.1 D.9,
   'Obrashchenie Voennogo Gubernatora Semirechenskoi oblasti k naseleniiu Iliiskogo
   kraya', l. 1.
[173] 'K Iliiskomu naseleniiu', 22/06/1871; 'Narodu i nachal'nikam plemen v Iliiskom krae',
   24/06/1871; 'Naseleniiu Iliiskogo kraya', 27/06/1871; 'Iliiskomu naseleniiu', 11/07/1871
   TsGARKaz F.21 Op.1 D.9 ll. 2–14, 22–*ob*, 26*ob*, 27*ob*.

numbers at 3,000–4,000 under the leadership of 'Abdurrahman Kaznachi,' some armed with falconets but most only with cold steel.[174] While Sultan Abil-Ogli tried to parley, warning the Russians that he would fight if they continued to approach Ghulja, on the 22 June he sent them an embassy led by his son, which gave up the fugitive Tazabek and invited them into Ghulja, where the Sultan surrendered.[175] The Chinese did not learn of the annexation until a month later, at the end of August, when informed by Russia.[176]

Kolpakovskii lost no time in designing an administration for the newly conquered territory, noting in his report to Turkestan Governor-General von Kaufman that 'the will of the government on whether this land will remain in our power or be handed over to the Manchus has still not been finally defined'.[177] He proposed a form of *voenno-narodnoe upravlenie* (military-popular government) similar to that which existed elsewhere in Turkestan, although adapted to what he described as the particular customs of the population which 'in many ways is quite different from that of the settled and nomadic peoples of the Turkestan region'. This would require a complete topographical survey of the region, and the collection of comprehensive statistics on population, livestock, oil, grain and other assets, as well as the amount of tax paid by each town and the volume of trade.[178] The orientalist Nikolai Pantusov (who in 1885 would publish what is still the only edition of the *Ta'rikh-i Shahrukhi*) would be Kolpakovskii's chosen agent for this task, which he began only in 1874.[179] His 120-page report provided both a justification of the annexation and a comprehensive enumeration of the assets Russia had thus acquired (3,361 donkeys, among other things) and made estimates of tax revenues.[180] Kolpakovskii made immediate efforts to

---

[174] Kolpakovskii to Evgenii Andreevich Rossitskii 17/06/1871 TsGARKaz F.21 Op.1 D.20 ll. 11–12; he subsequently wrote again to Rossitskii to tell him that there were 5,000 of the enemy at Chin cha go zi, and a further 6,000 at Suydun, no doubt to ensure he took full note of the scale of the odds: Kolpakovskii to Rossitskii 04/07/1871 TsGARKaz F.21 Op.1 D.20 ll. 65–*ob*.

[175] Sultan Abil Ogli to Kolpakovskii 20/06/1871; Kolpakovskii to Rossitskii 22/06/1871 TsGARKaz F.21 Op.1 D.20 ll. 19, 20–*ob*, 25–6. See also Brophy, *Uyghur Nation*, 58.

[176] Hsü, *The Ili Crisis*, 32–3; Paine, *Imperial Rivals*, 121.

[177] Kolpakovskii to von Kaufman 30/06/1871 TsGARKaz F.21 Op.1 D.20 l. 54.

[178] 'Instruktsiya po voenno-narodnomu upravleniiu'; Kolpakovskii to von Kaufman 30/06/ 1871 TsGARKaz F.21 Op.1 D.20 ll. 42–3, 54*ob*.

[179] He was also the editor of what Hodong Kim describes (*Holy War in China*, xvi) as 'the most important local historical source' on the Muslim rebellion against Chinese rule: Mullah Musa Sayrami's *Ta'rikh-i Amniyya: Taarikh-i Emenie: Istoriya vladetelei Kashgarii: Sochinenie Mully Musy, ben Mulla Aisa, Sairamtsa* ed. N. N. Pantusov (Kazan': Tip. Imperatorskogo Universiteta, 1905).

[180] 'Svedeniya o Kul'tzhinskom [*sic*] raione za 1871–1877 god, sobrannye N. N. Pantusovym', TsGARKaz F.822 Op.1 D.28, published as *Svedeniya o Kuldzhinskom raione za 1871–1877 gody sobrannye N. N. Pantusovym* (Kazan': Universitetskaya Tip., 1881).

revive the trade routes into Kashgar which had been cut off during the rebellion, and to persuade Yaqub Beg to let those Dungan merchants who had fled to Manas and Urumchi to return.[181] From the outset Kolpakovskii was determined to make the case that the occupation of Ghulja should become permanent, not just for reasons of prestige, but for what he presented as its economic advantages. In February 1872 he wrote to von Kaufman that, owing to the Muslim rebellion, the tea trade that formerly flowed from China through Kashgar into Khoqand had been cut off: attempts to import Indian tea instead had foundered as it did not suit Central Asian tastes, and instead Chinese tea now reached Central Asia exclusively through the Siberian customs post at Kiakhta, leaving it in Russian hands. 'If the Manchu power is restored in Urumchi, for which the first step will be the return of Ghulja, all this tea trade will move across to the hands of the Chinese ... losing us millions in turnover on the tea trade across all of Central Asia, the restoration of Manchu power can only give us in return the disposal of our manufactured products in Urumchi, on the Ili and in Kashgar.'[182]

However, there were already signs that St Petersburg was disinclined towards further adventurism in the region. When Kolpakovskii wrote to von Kaufman in August 1872 reporting an appeal from a Dungan leader called Tu-Akhund Lotiya for Russian troops to defend the Dungans of Manas from an attack from Kashgar, Kolpakovskii was ordered to reply that 'The Russian government has so much land and so many people, that our Great Ruler has given a supreme command not to unite to Russian lands any new lands or peoples', and rebuking them for rising against the 'Boghdy Khan' (i.e. the Qing Emperor).[183] This was an early indication that Russian recognition of China's state and monarchical legitimacy would play an important part in the decision to return Ghulja nine years later. As Paine has noted, as early as 1872, the Tsar had indicated that the region should be returned to China as soon as the situation would allow, although the Foreign Ministry was already making plans to extract territorial and trading concessions in return.[184] When in 1873 the Qing began demanding the return of Ghulja, Foreign Minister A. M. Gorchakov sent a lengthy memorandum to General Vlangali, the Russian envoy to Peking, instructing him how to respond. Gorchakov wrote that Russia had shown great forbearance during the first seven years after the outbreak of the Muslim revolt, until the disorders emanating from the Ili valley became intolerable and necessitated annexation. 'The Manchu government should not forget that we took Ghulja at a time when from their side there was

---

[181] Kolpakovskii to Yaqub Beg n.d. (08/1871) TsGARKaz F.21 Op.1 D.22 ll. 21–*ob.*
[182] Kolpakovskii to von Kaufman 23/02/1872 TsGARKaz F.21 Op.1 D.22 ll. 138–*ob.*
[183] Kolpakovskii to von Kaufman 14/08/1872; Kolpakovskii to Tu-Akhund 14/08/1872 F.21 Op.1 D.22 ll. 210–15.
[184] Paine, *Imperial Rivals*, 121–2.

already a positive admission that they themselves did not have the strength to occupy themselves with the pacification of so distant a region.' This and other Russian actions to consolidate the frontier should be presented as a service to the Chinese government, and there could be no question of handing any of it back until Chinese power was once more restored and stable. Vlangali should impress on the Manchus a sense of the obligations they owed to Russia as a neighbouring power 'with which we have treaties'.[185] Though couched in patronising terms, and with a presumption that the Manchus would not be able to reconquer their Muslim Central Asian provinces, it was clear that Gorchakov viewed China as a legitimate diplomatic partner with whom dialogue was possible, a privilege that was not accorded to Khoqand, Bukhara or any of the other Central Asian states and peoples. The implication was that, if the Chinese could vanquish the rebellion and restore order on their frontier, the Russians would be satisfied and withdraw. This might have seemed a distant prospect in 1873, but when it in fact came to pass after 1877, St Petersburg somewhat grudgingly, and in the teeth of strong opposition from von Kaufman and Kolpakovskii, would honour its commitment.[186]

On the 4 March 1879 Miliutin recorded in his diary the results of a three-hour meeting on Chinese affairs, attended by (amongst others) N. K. Giers and Baron A. G. Jomini from the Ministry of Foreign Affairs, and Count Heiden, General N. N. Obruchev (1830–1904) and Colonels A. N. Kuropatkin and A. K. Kaul'bars from the Main Staff:

> We came to the conclusion that the dignity of the state (*dostoinstvo gosudarstva*) demands from us the honourable fulfilment of the promise we have repeated more than once, to return Ghulja to the Chinese, but not before we have received from the Chinese the appropriate concessions, both on some questions of trade and for the satisfaction of many of our previous demands, and also for the correction of our boundary with China to the north of the Tian-Shan, and in particular a guarantee of the fate of the population of the Ili province that we are ceding to China.[187]

The existing, very detailed scholarship on the negotiations surrounding the treaties of Livadia and St Petersburg that followed has largely focused on the Russian attempts to extract these concessions – they appeared to have succeeded with the Livadia treaty, concluded in September 1879, in which the new

---

[185] Gorchakov to Vlangali 07/01/1873 TsGARUz F.I-715 Op.1 D.54 Doc.4 ll. 85–91.

[186] Hsü, *The Ili Crisis*, 15. In October 1878 von Kaufman was protesting about attempts by Qing officials to issue proclamations to the inhabitants of the Ili valley: Russian Mission in Peking to the Chinese Ministry of Foreign Affairs 14/26 Dec. 1878 TsGARUz F.I-1 Op.29 D.380 ll. 2–3ob.

[187] D. A. Miliutin, *Dnevnik 1879–1881* ed. L. G. Zakharova (Moscow: ROSSPEN, 2010), 38; Paine, *Imperial Rivals*, 125 also quotes this passage, though translating *dostoinstvo gosudarstva* as 'national dignity'.

boundary was drawn in such a way as to leave the Muzart Pass in Russian hands.[188] This treaty, which would also have forced China to pay an indemnity of 5 million roubles, was signed by the Chinese envoy Ch'ung-Hou without consulting his government, which refused to ratify it.[189] Russia and China were apparently close to war in the summer of 1880, though neither power really had much appetite for it. In the latter part of that year they negotiated a new treaty, which more or less restored the border as it had been in 1871, leaving the Muzart Pass in Chinese hands, though the Chinese still had to pay 9 million roubles towards what the Russians estimated had been the costs of occupation.[190] However, when contrasted with Russian attempts at diplomatic negotiation with Central Asian states and rulers that took place during this period, what is most striking about the Ili negotiations is that they seem to have been conducted in relatively good faith, and with an underlying assumption that the Chinese constituted a viable, more or less equal, partner, with sovereign territorial rights that should be respected. Miliutin's reference to the 'dignity of the state' and the 'honourable fulfilment' of the promise the Russians had made to China is not the kind of language he or other Russian officials ever used when dealing with Khoqand or Bukhara. This is also suggested by the lengthy correspondence between A. G. Jomini and N. K. Giers (the *de facto* Foreign Minister during Gorchakov's dotage) over the Livadia and St Petersburg Treaties ('*Cette malheureuse affaire chinoise*'), which expresses a degree of respect for their Chinese opposite numbers, and for the Chinese negotiating position: 'You will find in the dossier the note of response from the Marquis of Zeng. It is extremely adroit. He reasons very tightly.'[191] Two weeks later Jomini made this still clearer, albeit in a language of grand condescension:

> I took away the impression that there is a real desire for conciliation on the part of the Marquis [Zeng] and his government . . . it seems to me that in any case we have no reason for declining negotiations here. 1. Morally we have witnessed to the Chinese Government our reprobation of their international conduct [in rejecting the Livadia Treaty] and the lack of confidence which results regarding these negotiations. They recognise our right, they apologise for their conduct, they promise that it will not be repeated. Beyond this they have shown by their acts a better disposition.

---

[188] Hsü, *The Ili Crisis*, 47–77; Paine, *Imperial Rivals*, 132–150; the correspondence between Giers and Jomini regarding these negotiations is published in Jelavich, *Russia in the East*, 91–8.

[189] Hsü, *The Ili Crisis*, 57–8, 69. Brophy, *Uyghur Nation*, 65.

[190] Hsü, *The Ili Crisis*, 171–88; Paine, *Imperial Rivals*, 151–73; Jelavich, *Russia in the East*, 99–139; Voskressenski, *The Sino-Russian St Petersburg Treaty*, 61–129.

[191] Jomini to Giers 20/08/1880 in Jelavich, *Russia in the East*, 102; a similar note of respect for Chinese astuteness is struck in a letter of the 12 October on p. 121.

In this situation it seems to me that we can, without a lack of dignity, condescend to their desire.[192]

Jomini also expressed frustration with what he at one point called this 'less than Celestial Empire', and the fear that if the Russians conceded too much it would result in further Chinese demands rather than the stable relationship they desired – but it was clear that the latter was the goal, not Chinese humiliation or submission.[193] The same correspondence made it clear that, for the Ministry of Foreign Affairs, if not for von Kaufman and Kolpakovskii, securing a substantial indemnity and commercial concessions was much more important than retaining territory.[194] Poor communication between Livadia, St Petersburg and Peking, coupled with Russia's weakness and relative diplomatic isolation at the end of the 'Eastern Crisis' of 1879–81, no doubt also played a role in what came to be seen as a major (and surprising) Chinese diplomatic triumph. The fact that the Chinese could be expected to maintain a stable and orderly frontier, as they had by and large done before the Muslim rebellions, and the unexpected military effectiveness they had shown in reconquering what would come to be known as Xinjiang also played a role, allowing the Russian Ministry of Foreign Affairs to score a rare victory over the 'men on the spot' and the Ministry of War in handing back almost all of the upper Ili valley to China: the only instance during fifty years of relentless Russian territorial expansion in Central Asia when such a retreat occurred.

Article 7 of the Treaty of St Petersburg transferred a portion of the western section of the Ili valley to Russia for the purpose of settling those inhabitants who chose to migrate to Russian territory.[195] At the local level, the end of the Russian occupation of Ghulja meant one thing in particular – the resettlement of 50,000 Taranchis who were unwilling to return to Chinese rule, and chose to become Russian subjects instead. As David Brophy has shown, in the twentieth century it was their descendants, rather than the much more numerous sedentary Turkic Muslims of the Tarim Basin, who would first claim the ancient ethnonym 'Uyghur' as the label for a modern nationalist movement.[196] Their arrival marked a fundamental shift in the demographics of Semirechie. From being a predominantly nomadic region with a scattering of Russian settlers, the arrival of the Taranchis, who were followed not long afterwards by groups of Dungans, began to transform some areas into a settled agricultural landscape. This was particularly true of the region to the east of Vernoe along the Ghulja *trakt*, and the newly annexed territories which became the Zharkent district. Kolpakovskii directed this operation from

[192] Jomini to Giers 07/09/1880 in Jelavich, *Russia in the East*, 105.
[193] Jomini to Giers 03/10/1880 in Jelavich, *Russia in the East*, 117–18.
[194] Jelavich, *Russia in the East*, 138.
[195] Voskressenski, *The Sino-Russian St Petersburg Treaty*, 163.
[196] Brophy, *Uyghur Nation*, 2–7.

Tashkent, where he was the acting Turkestan Governor-General during von Kaufman's illness, his place in Semirechie being taken by Major-General Fride. Pantusov was pressed into service to manage a team of translators from Turki, Manchu and Mandarin, and a theoretically orderly procedure was set up, according to which lists of those desiring to migrate to Russian territory were to be drawn up in advance. They would then be considered Russian subjects under Russian protection even while they were still on Chinese soil.[197] Brophy notes that, while Chinese historians have often claimed that the Russians forced the Taranchis to leave the Ili valley against their will, deliberately depopulating it, the decision seems to have been made collectively, under the leadership of a wealthy grain merchant and power-broker called Vali Bai.[198] Fear of Chinese reprisals also probably played a role, and efforts to reassure the inhabitants that the Chinese authorities had declared an amnesty and that they should remain in Ili seem to have been unsuccessful. In 1879, during the negotiations over the unsuccessful treaty of Livadia, Jomini wrote to Giers that the Russian authorities in Ghulja had objected to the circulation of a Chinese proclamation of amnesty, which had in any case 'produced a disastrous effect on the population who prefer to die at the hands of the Russians rather than the Chinese'.[199] As the final handover approached in 1881, Fride described how a large crowd gathered in the main mosque of Ghulja on the 14 February to listen to the proclamation from the Qing Emperor:

> The Shentai explained the third and fourth points of the agreement, saying that they prescribed the taking of the Ili region with its lands, waters and peoples, and that it was wrong for the population of Ili to prefer Russian rule to Chinese, as the Boghdy Khan loved all his subjects like children, and thus it would be better for them to remain in the wonderful places where they were born. The great courtyard of the mosque was full of Muslims of the Tuguz-Torrau district, and hundreds more had come to the bazaar. All listened calmly to the reading of the proclamation. At the end, in response to the question of the Erkebunya – 'Did you understand?' – the older honoured inhabitants came forward and then all answered directly 'We understood everything, but we now inform you what we earlier told the Russian authorities: everyone is leaving, do not try to stop us.' In the crowd there were isolated cries that they did not believe the proclamation, of deceit.[200]

---

[197] 'Instruktsiya dlya deistvii kommisarov Rossiiskogo i Kitaiskogo Pravitel'stv pri peredache Iliiskogo kraya Daitsinskim vlastyam', TsGARKaz F.21 Op.1 D.691, 'O vodvorenii v Semirechenskoi Oblasti Kul'dzhinskikh vykhodtsev', ll. 37–40.
[198] Brophy, *Uyghur Nation*, 67–70.
[199] Jomini to Giers 28/08/1879, in Jelavich, *Russia in the East*, 94.
[200] Fride to Kolpakovskii (telegram) 15/02/1882 TsGARKaz F.21 Op.1 D.691 l. 169.

214 FROM AYAGUZ TO ALMATY

Over the next few days the same pattern repeated itself elsewhere in Ili – the inhabitants pronounced themselves grateful for the opportunity to migrate, and took it.[201] Fride claimed that, if there had been any doubt on that point, the arrival of the Chinese army in May 1882 decided it. He feared they would clash with the remaining Russian forces, and while there were only a couple of minor incidents of this kind, he recorded fifty-five separate instances of attacks on the local population. Thanks to Pantusov, Fride wrote, he was acquainted with the history of the Muslim rebellion against Chinese rule, and the violence and bitterness it had produced, but he still hoped that perhaps the Muslims of Ili could be reconciled to Chinese rule. Now those hopes had been dashed – the indiscipline of the Chinese army and the weakness of the Chinese authorities showed only too clearly what they could expect at its hands. He fully expected to see the other half of the population migrate to Russian territory as well.[202] This would prove the most significant and long-lasting consequence of Russia's annexation of the Ili valley – but it lies beyond the scope of this book.

Perhaps more than any other phase of the conquest, Russian expansion into Semirechie shows how ambiguous and shifting the boundaries of sovereignty in Central Asia could be. The Russians complained constantly about the lack of clear borders in the region and what they considered illegitimate Khoqandi claims to sovereignty over the Qazaqs of the great horde. They openly encouraged the latter to migrate across the Chu and accept their authority instead, but were furious when some Qazaq groups crossed the frontier to Ghulja in order to escape Russian rule ten years later. Russia, Khoqand and Qing China all claimed sovereignty over this region, most of whose inhabitants were Kyrgyz and Qazaqs with their own tribal divisions and disputes. This cannot be reduced to a simple binary narrative of conquerors and conquered. At the same time, military action proved decisive in establishing Russian claims beyond dispute. Their technological superiority was clear – explosive shells and canister shot made short shrift of Khoqandi resistance at Pishpek and Uzun-Agach, and later that of Ghulja. The logistical challenges were still substantial, but less extreme than along the Syr-Darya. This was partly because the Russians began settling the region well before competing claims to authority over its territory and people by Khoqand and China had been resolved, thus creating what we would now call 'facts on the ground'. Its relatively mild climate and fertile soil facilitated this process, although many Cossacks still had to be compelled to move to Lepsinsk, Kapal and the Trans-Ili region. Until the Muslim rebellion the Russians were also able to obtain supplies through trade with Ghulja. The occupation of the upper Ili valley and its subsequent return to China was significant partly as a rare victory of the Ministry of

---

[201] Fride to Kolpakovskii 18/02/1882 TsGARKaz F.21 Op.1 D.691 ll. 182–3ob.
[202] Fride to Kolpakovskii 06/05/1882; 22/05/1822 TsGarkaz F.21 Op.1 D.691 ll. 254–9, 268–80, 282–ob.

Foreign Affairs over the Ministry of War in Central Asia, but also because of the waves of migration from Chinese territory which followed. Semirechie's special status within Russian Central Asia – a liminal zone between the purely nomadic steppe regions of the north and the settled districts of Turkestan to the south, and a site of settlement both for Russians and for sedentary Muslims from elsewhere in Central Asia – was thus already firmly established within two decades of the Russian conquest.

5

The Search for a 'Natural' Frontier and the Fall of Tashkent, 1863–5

... la plus grande difficulté consiste à savoir s'arrêter ...

Prince A. M. Gorchakov, Minister of Foreign Affairs, 1864

No episode of the Russian conquest of Central Asia has attracted more attention or been more thoroughly mythologised than the fall of Tashkent, Central Asia's largest city, to a force of 1,900 men under General M. G. Chernyaev on the 15 June 1865. In 1915, on the fiftieth anniversary of the city's fall, the then Mayor, Nikolai Mallitskii, sent a congratulatory telegram and letter to the General's widow, outlining the many celebrations that would mark the anniversary of Tashkent's capture by 'Russian *bogatyrs*', which included the renaming of various public buildings and the entire city of Chimkent after Chernyaev.[1] As Jeff Sahadeo has shown, the fall of the city would be marked by ever more elaborate commemorations by its Russian settler community from the 1870s, and its capture was celebrated as a pre-eminent example of Russian heroism, boldness and ingenuity.[2] As the opening quotation suggests, there is also another narrative associated with the fall of Tashkent – one of accident and disobedience. The capture of the city is the pre-eminent example of the 'man on the spot' explanation for the Russian conquest of Central Asia, with Chernyaev supposedly seizing it on his own initiative, without sanction from above. As Petr Valuev, Minister of Internal Affairs, wrote in his diary: 'Tashkent has been taken by General Chernyaev. No one knows why and for what [...] there is something erotic (*nechto eroticheskoe*) about everything we do on the far-flung periphery of the empire.'[3] That this idea was already

The bulk of this chapter was first published as Alexander Morrison, 'Russia, Khoqand, and the Search for a Natural Frontier, 1863–1865', *AI* (2014), No. 2, 165–92, and is republished here by kind permission of that journal. My thanks to Bakhtiyar Babajanov for his detailed comments.

[1] N. N. Mallitskii to A. A. Chernyaeva 29/05/1915 RGVIA F.726 Op.1 D.238 ll. 1–2.

[2] Sahadeo, *Russian Colonial Society in Tashkent*, 47–9.

[3] Diary entry 20/07/1865, in Zaionchkovskii (ed.) *Dnevnik P. A. Valueva*, II, 60–1. Sergei Abashin tells me that the late Anatolyi Remnev always insisted that what Valuev had actually written was 'nechto erraticheskoe' – 'something erratic', and that Zaionchkovskii had made an error when editing the diary. Either interpretation would support the idea of disobedience.

current even before the city's fall can be seen in the classic statement of this 'reluctant imperialist' idea from the Russian Foreign Minister Prince A. M. Gorchakov, in a minute circulated to the Foreign Ministries of all the European powers, in which, after comparing Russian expansion with that of other colonial powers he remarked rather peevishly that 'the greatest difficulty consists in knowing how to stop'.[4] This disavowal of all expansionist ambitions and abdication of responsibility looks wholly hypocritical with hindsight, and was viewed so at the time by the British, who were its principal intended audience. However, there is reason to believe that Gorchakov's sentiments were sincerely felt – even if they were not shared by the man who exercised the greatest influence over the Russian advance, War Minister Dmitrii Miliutin.[5] As we have seen, the Central Asian frontier had been a persistent headache for the Foreign Ministry since at least the 1830s, and most of the territory acquired there since that date was of very dubious strategic and economic value. Later historians have echoed the judgement that Russia's 'men on the spot' got out of control, and that many key episodes were indeed a product of 'not knowing how to stop'.[6] However, a re-examination of contemporary debates and correspondence reveals that this is an over-simplification. St Petersburg did have a plan for expansion in Central Asia in the early 1860s, and Ministers and front line officers shared numerous assumptions about Russia's role in Central Asia, the form her frontier there should take and, above all, how a suitable, *natural* limit to Russian expansion could be identified. In principle, at least, new techniques of surveying, statistics and military topography would make this possible, and in this Russia shared in a wider European imperial military episteme and the formation of what James Hevia has called a 'military techno-elite', which emerged from the 1860s onwards.[7] As David Rich has noted in his study of the Russian Main Staff, the group of officers who created and identi-fied with this spirit of scientific military professionalism (which was still in its infancy in the 1860s): 'Statistical knowledge empowered Russian state servants to act wilfully, yet from motives at once more self-serving and bureaucratically defensible than traditional arbitrariness (*proizvol*).' However, Rich goes on to argue that 'Rogue Generals carved out new territories in Central Asia, either in the absence of unified national policy or oblivious to St Petersburg's demands to the contrary',[8] thus reproducing the conventional 'disobedience' thesis. In fact it was the incommensurability between the Russian military–bureaucratic

---

[4] 'Circular dispatch addressed by Prince Gortchakow to Russian Representatives abroad.' 21/11/1864 *PP* Central Asia No.2 (1873) 'Correspondence Respecting Central Asia' C.704, 70 (French original) – the contemporary English translation (73) has 'knowing when to stop', but I think my rendering is more accurate.

[5] Zaionchkovskii 'K voprosu zavoevaniya Srednei Azii', 52.

[6] Mackenzie, 'Expansion in Central Asia'.

[7] Hevia, *The Imperial Security State*, 34–52.

[8] Rich, *The Tsar's Colonels*, 6, 91.

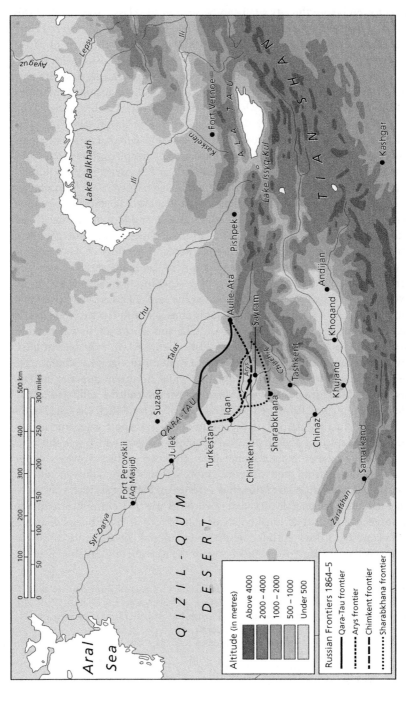

Map 5 Tashkent and its environs

episteme he identifies and the facts of human and physical geography in Central Asia itself that allowed seemingly uncontrolled expansion, and helps to explain Gorchakov's disclaimer. This chapter argues that the 'man on the spot' – in this case Chernyaev – played an important role in determining the timing of the Russian advance, but not its overall goals and direction.[9]

5.1   The Summit of the Qara-Tau

On the 1 August 1863, Gorchakov and War Minister Miliutin jointly presented Tsar Alexander II with a proposal for the uniting of the Orenburg and Western Siberian lines of fortresses through the southern part of the Asian steppe between Fort Vernoe in the Trans-Ili region and Fort Perovskii on the Syr-Darya. As we have seen, this was the product of over four years of argument and wrangling between different ministries in St Petersburg, and between the separate military commands of Orenburg and Omsk. Much of the debate had concerned the fate of the city of Tashkent, whose annexation had been urged by A. P. Bezak, the Governor of Orenburg, and opposed by his counterpart in Western Siberia, A. O. Diugamel.[10] For now though, at least, Tashkent had been left out of the official plans for the year ahead. Miliutin himself probably harboured long-term ambitions of anchoring the planned new Russian frontier on that city, a major trading entrepôt and the centre of a rich agricultural district, and was tacitly encouraging a more aggressive policy of annexation.[11] Officially, however, the line of the Russian advance was to be determined by a process of objective verification based on the natural and human geography of the region. As Miliutin explained to Bezak a week later, after the Tsar had approved the plan:

> In uniting the line, and with the establishment of our frontier on the summit of the Qara-Tau, we are not broadening our frontiers, but on the contrary restricting their extent, and coming closer to the fertile regions of Central Asia.[12]

Miliutin's confident assertion that the new Russian frontier could sit comfortably on the summit of the Qara-Tau (a mountain range that he had never seen, and about whose location and characteristics the Russians, as we shall see, had little accurate knowledge) was entirely characteristic of Russian thinking regarding frontiers in Central Asia in this period, and reflected wider European attitudes. As Alexei Postnikov and Svetlana Gorshenina have shown, rather than acknowledging that frontiers were something imposed on the landscape according to the dictates of political expediency and raw military power,

---

[9] Baumann comes to a similar conclusion: 'The Conquest of Central Asia', 58.
[10] See Chapter 3 and Morrison, 'Nechto eroticheskoe'.
[11] Zaionchkovskii, 'K voprosu zavoevaniya Srednei Azii', 43–6.
[12] Miliutin to Bezak 12/08/1863 TsGARKaz F.382 Op.1 D.47 ll. 33ob–4ob.

officials and statesmen preferred to believe that they were something that could and should be determined according to objective criteria that could be identified in the landscape.[13] These included prominent geographical features such as rivers and watersheds, and also notional human 'civilisational' boundaries, such as those between the steppe and the sown in Central Asia. Existing political arrangements, such as the Khoqand Khanate's control of a large swathe of the southern steppe from its agricultural base in the Ferghana valley, or the ambitions of the ruler of Bukhara, Amir Sayyid Muzaffar, to control Tashkent himself, were either ignored or seen as inherently illegitimate. Instead the science of military geography would allow the Russians to establish a 'frontier' that emerged from the landscape and would allow them to 'obtain a firm state boundary' (*poluchit' tverduiu gosudarstvennuiu granitsu*, in the words of G. K. Gasfort, Governor of Western Siberia in 1859)[14] in the apparently boundless (and boundaryless) Central Asian steppe. Unlike the later creation of the Russian boundary with Afghanistan (which was equally driven by the idea of identifying a 'natural' frontier that could be scientifically fixed),[15] there would be no European partner to this early Russian attempt at boundary-making in Central Asia – and the Russians did not admit the legitimacy of any Central Asian participation in this enterprise.

As we saw in the previous chapter, by the late 1850s Russian surveyors – notably A. G. Vlangali, M. M. Khomentov and, most famously, P. P. Semenov Tian-Shanskii and Choqan Valikhanov, had surveyed and mapped much of the Ili valley and parts of the Tian Shan range in Southern Semirechie.[16] However, the region between Fort Vernoe and the Qara-Tau range remained *terra incognita* as the leadership in St Petersburg began to consider renewing the Russian advance in Central Asia in the early 1860s. In 1859 the military geographer Mikhail Veniukov carried out a crucial survey of what the Russians called the 'Kokan [*sic*] Military Line', a string of fortresses built by the khanate in the valley of the River Chu (Toqmaq, Pishpek, Aq-Su, Merke, It-kichu, Aulie-Ata, Chulaq-Qurghan and Suzaq). These he interpreted as designed to defend a frontier 'which the Khoqandis evidently consider to be the river Chu'.[17] Veniukov was the leading Russian military geographer of his day, and a strong proponent of the idea of the 'natural frontier'. His description here of a frontier defined by a river and by the summits of the Qyzykurt,

[13] Gorshenina, *Asie Centrale*, 37–93; A. V. Postnikov, *Stanovlenie rubezhei Rossii v Tsentral'noi i Srednei Azii (XVIII–XIX vv.)* (Moscow: Pamyatniki Istoricheskoi Mysli, 2007).

[14] 'Zapiska Komandira Otdel'nogo Sibirskogo Korpusa i General Gubernatora Zapadnoi Sibiri o neobkhodimosti zanyatiya verkhov'ev r. Chu i predvaritel'nykh k tomu rasporyazheniyakh', 21/01/1859 RGVIA F.483 Op.1 D.51 ll. 4–5ob.

[15] Hevia, *Imperial Security State*, 92–105.

[16] Postnikov, *Stanovlenie rubezhei*, 228–34; Semenov, *Travels in the Tian'-Shan'*.

[17] 'Kokanskaya voennaya liniya na r. Chu', 15/07/1860 RGVIA F.1449 Op.1 D.7 l. 2.

Buraldai, Qara-Tau and Ala-Tau mountains would prove highly influential in determining the pattern of the Russian advance and the natural features on which statesmen in St Petersburg would try to anchor the Russians' own 'New Khoqand Line' in the mid 1860s.[18] In his later published works Veniukov noted that, with the exception of agreements with China, over the previous 300 years the Russians had never concluded any treaties in Asia that established firm boundaries; this was despite the fact, so he claimed, that the 'state boundary' (*gosudarstvennaya granitsa*) had been extended far to the south by the submission of the Qazaqs of the Junior and Middle Hordes to Russia in 1732 (an interpretation that would become canonical in the Soviet period), even though in many respects (such as the customs boundary) it remained a 'foreign' (*zagranichnyi*) territory until the 1860s.[19] This situation he considered to be anomalous, unacceptable and ripe for revision.

As we have seen, the main culprit in the creation of this zone of uncertainty in the steppe was the Khoqand Khanate, an aggressive, ambitious, expansionist rival to Russia in the steppe. Most frustrating of all was the fact that Khoqand did not appear to the Russians to have a clearly defined northern frontier, although there is some evidence to suggest that the Khanate's own leaders thought otherwise. In 1854, in the aftermath of the fall of Aq Masjid to the Russians, a Khoqandi ambassador to the East India Company stated that 'The boundary between Kokan and Russia was previously Kizzilpir – now it is Akmusjid', although he added that 'I do not know whether Kizzilpir is on the East or West bank of the Sir [Darya].'[20] While this suggests a territorial understanding of sovereignty, this particular account has been mediated through British eyes: as we shall see, evidence from other Khoqandi sources suggests that the khanate's elites thought primarily in terms of control over people rather than territory: at the very least, though, as we saw in the previous chapter, Khoqand claimed sovereignty over the Qazaqs of the Great Horde, whose grazing grounds stretched far to the north and east of the line defined by Veniukov.[21]

---

[18] He published a version of his report the following year as Veniukov, 'Ocherki Zailiiskogo kraya'.

[19] Mikhail Veniukov, *Opyt voennogo obozreniya russkikh granits v Azii* (St Pb.: V. Bezobrazov, 1873), 6, 10.

[20] 'Deposition of Moollah Yar Mahomed, servant of the Padshah or Khan of Kokan, made to Major Edwardes at Peshawur 18 August 1854', NAI/Foreign/S.C./24 November 1854/ Nos. 1–22 *Account of the Khanate of Kokand*, 11.

[21] In this chapter I use four Khoqandi accounts of the Russian conquest as a counterpoint to Russian sources: the most important of these is Beisembiev's magnificent edition of Mullah Muhammad Yunus Jan Shighavul Dadkhwah Tashkandi's *Ta'rikh-i 'Aliquli Amir-i Lashkar* (c. 1901–6, *TA*); all quotations are from Beisembiev's English translation. The other texts are Nikolai Pantusov, *Taarikh Shakhrokhi: Istoriya vladetelei Fergany* (Kazan': Tip Imperatorskogo Universiteta, 1885), an obsolete edition of Mullah Niyaz Khoqandi, *Ta'rikh-i Shahrukhi* (1871, *TSh*) which needs to be read in conjunction with Beisembiev, *Tarikhi Shakhrukhi kak istoricheskii istochnik*, and Muhammad Salih Khwaja

5.2   Searching for a Frontier

Well before Russian troops began to advance west from Vernoe and south from Perovsk in 1863, a notional, 'natural' frontier that would finally set limits to the empire's expansion in Central Asia would be incorporated in the orders issued to their commanders. Shortly before he set out on a reconnaissance mission towards the small Khoqandi fortress of Suzaq early in 1863, General M. G. Chernyaev wrote that, to properly secure the left flank of the Russian frontier, the following would be necessary: 'The taking of Turkestan and the continuation of the line along the Ala-Tau mountains to be united with the Siberian frontier, and the introduction of military settlements along the Syr.'[22] Chernyaev made the first step towards this shortly afterwards by capturing Suzaq almost without a fight, a success which, retrospectively authorised by the War Ministry, finally persuaded the cautious Foreign Minister, A. M. Gorchakov, to accept Miliutin's argument that the uniting of the lines and the creation of a new frontier should take place without further delay.[23] A note from Miliutin to the Foreign Ministry in January 1864 laid out the objectives in Central Asia for the coming year. Chief among these was 'the uniting of the forward Siberian and Orenburg lines, on the basis proposed by General-Adjutant Bezak, that is from Julek along the Syr-Darya, through Suzaq, to Aulie-Ata and further along the summit of the Qara-Tau mountains, having taken Suzaq with the forces of the Orenburg corps and Aulie-Ata with those of the Siberian corps, in order to then transfer the border to the [river] Arys, taking it from Aulie-Ata through Chimkent'.[24] This combination of urban and natural landmarks that would define the new frontier was reproduced verbatim

Tashkandi, *Ta'rikh-i Jadidah-yi Tashkand* (*c.* 1886, *TJT*), Al-Biruni Institute of Oriental Studies, Uzbekistan Academy of Sciences Manuscript No.11073/II, portions transcribed by Bakhtiyar Babajanov at http://zerrspiegel.orientphil.uni-halle.de/t386.html. See further on this text U. A. Sultonov, *Muhammad Solih Khuja va Uning Tarikhi Jadidaii Toshkand* (Tashkent: O'zbekiston, 2009). Finally, N. A Veselovskii, *Kirgizskii rasskaz o russkikh zavoevaniyakh v Turkestanskom krae* (St Pb.: Tip. P. O. Yablonskogo, 1894) falls into a somewhat different category as it was written to order for a Russian orientalist, and the original title of the text is not known. Of these, the *TA* and the *Kirgizskii rasskaz* both reflect the 'Qipchaq' tradition in Khoqandi historiography, while the *TSh* is highly partisan towards Khudoyar Khan and the Ming dynasty: see Beisembiev, *Annotated Indices*, 21–2.

[22] M. G. Chernyaev, 'O vodvorenii spokoistviya v nashikh granitsakh: Napisano do 63 g.' RGIMOPI F.208 Op.1 D.4 l. 70.

[23] Ivanov's suggestion that this approval was owing to a desire to punish the British for their interference in the Polish revolt that year seems to be entirely without foundation – the correspondence reveals that Miliutin's overwhelming concern was for a sustainable and defensible frontier in Central Asia: V. A. Ivanov, 'Rossiya i Turkestan v kontekste Bol'shoi Igry', *Rossiya–Srednyaya Aziya* (Moscow: URSS, 2011), I, 105.

[24] Miliutin to Reutern 09/01/1864, in Serebrennikov, *Sbornik. 1864 g. Pt. I* Doc.45, 81–2; Terent'ev, *Istoriya zavoevaniya*, I, 276.

in the orders issued in March by General Diugamel to Chernyaev, who had been re-assigned from the Orenburg to the Siberian command personally by Miliutin.[25] From the beginning, however, these orders contained a significant ambiguity – there was to be an initial 'natural' frontier between Suzaq and Aulie-Ata along the summit of the Qara-Tau, but, as Bezak wrote to Diugamel in Omsk, 'the War Minister, agreeing entirely with my opinion on the uselessness of despatching any expedition against the Khoqandis without a defined goal, especially in winter, and on the necessity of the rapid uniting of our forward lines, considers the line through Suzaq and Aulie-Ata only temporary'.[26] It would be 'transferred' (an interesting euphemism for an action that would require the conquest of significant further territory) at some unspecified later date to a supposedly equally 'natural' frontier along the River Arys.[27] As we shall see, this ambiguity, combined with the fact that these orders related to a landscape none of the men concerned had actually seen, would allow Chernyaev (Figure 5.1) considerable latitude to interpret his orders as he saw fit, with the assurance that (as in the past), so long as they were victorious, his actions would be retrospectively endorsed.

In the discussions as to where the Siberian section of the new line should run, natural landmarks did not play a prominent role, but human and natural environmental conditions did. G. A. Kolpakovskii, the *Pristav* of the Ala-Tau district (and soon to be Governor of the new province of Semirechie), emphasised the need for fortified points at Merke, Toqmaq and Pishpek in order to defend caravan traffic and prevent *baramta*, noting also that these regions were suitable for settlement and asking for 200 families of Cossacks to be sent there. The main concern, here as in the earlier debates over the desirability of seizing Tashkent, was the importance of having a frontier line that ran through a region with a sedentary population, and thus good supplies of grain and timber. He argued that the supply road for the frontier should run along the Kastek valley because it had good grazing for baggage animals even at the end of summer.[28] On the Orenburg side of the debate, the considerations were more abstract, but Bezak was consistently hawkish, and advocated seizing the town of Turkestan, site of the mausoleum of Khwaja Ahmad Yasavi, at the earliest possible opportunity. He claimed that

> Not that long ago the expanse dividing the Orenburg line from the Siberian was entirely unknown to us, and our information beyond Fort Perovskii was limited to a radius of no more than 100 *versts*. Now we, with

---

[25] Miliutin to Diugamel 12/01/1864; Diugamel to Chernyaev 12/03/1864, in Serebrennikov, *Sbornik. 1864 g. Pt. I* Docs.2 & 6, 4, 7–8.

[26] Bezak to Diugamel 12/01/1864, in Serebrennikov, *Sbornik. 1864 g. Pt. I* Doc.5 & 7.

[27] Zaionchkovskii, 'K voprosu zavoevaniya Srednei Azii', 45.

[28] Kolpakovskii to Diugamel 22/02/1864, in Serebrennikov, *Sbornik. 1864 g. Pt. I* Doc.14, 25–7.

Figure 5.1 Mikhail Grigor'evich Chernyaev. Photograph by A. Den'er, St Petersburg – before 1882.

> a sufficient knowledge of the area, are progressing quickly towards the
> goal laid out by His Imperial Majesty Nikolai Pavlovich, that is to the
> uniting there of our frontier. [. . .] controlling Turkestan is beneficial to us
> in the highest degree, as the central spot for the administration once the
> Orenburg and Siberian Lines are united [. . .] we will be throwing the
> Khoqandis back across the river Arys . . .[29]

As we shall see, Bezak's claims for the improvement of Russian geographical
knowledge of the region turned out to be misplaced, but his representations
had their effect, resulting in a further set of ambiguous instructions, this time
to be passed on to the commander of the Orenburg forces in the region,
Colonel N. A. Verevkin. After consulting with the Tsar, N. P. Ignat'ev, the
new head of the Asiatic department of the Ministry of Foreign Affairs, wrote
that 'Colonel Verevkin is permitted to make use of favourable circumstances
for the taking of Turkestan, without losing sight of the main aim of this
military action – the factual uniting of the Orenburg and Siberian forward

[29] Bezak to Miliutin 04/04/1864, in Serebrennikov, *Sbornik. 1864 g. Pt. I* Doc.53, 95, 97.

lines.'[30] Miliutin passed this message on in slightly different, but no less ambiguous, terms: 'I am permitted on the highest authority to reply, that the plan of action which was resolved upon this summer should not be altered; [. . .] the advance towards Turkestan can be undertaken only when a real and easy opportunity presents itself for seizing this point with a permanent garrison. A simple demonstration towards or bombardment of this city would be more dangerous than useful.'[31] Once again, the decision over when to take a crucial further step into Central Asia was effectively left to the discretion of the 'man on the spot', but with tacit authorisation from the very highest levels of government.

In April 1864 Miliutin once again reminded Bezak that 'the new frontier line, which will initially run along the Qara-Tau summit, will then when the time is favourable be moved, as your Excellency knows, to the Arys, from Aulie-Ata to Chimkent and Turkestan, and then to Suzaq'.[32] There was no indication of how it would be decided when the time was 'favourable', but the 2,500 troops, 800 horses and 4,000 camels of Chernyaev's 'Trans-Chu force' set out from Fort Vernoe on their campaign ten days later on the 1 May.[33] At first they were passing through country which had already been repeatedly ravaged by Russian troops. As we saw in the previous chapter, the Khoqandi fortress of Pishpek had first been seized and destroyed in 1860, and this was followed by the crushing defeat of the Khoqandis by Kolpakovskii at the battle of Uzun-Agach. In the spring of 1863 Pishpek was razed to the ground again in the course of a punitive expedition led by Lt-Col. Lerkhe, who was now Chernyaev's second in command.[34] In March 1864 the Russians intercepted a letter from 'Alimqul to the Kyrgyz *bii/manap* Jantai Batyr *Dadkhwah*, calling upon him to resist the 'accursed Russians' in the name of Islam, but, as we have seen, he had already offered his submission to the Russians after the destruction of Pishpek in 1860; he passed 'Alimqul's letter (Figure 5.2) on to Kolpakovskii at Fort Vernoe, and appealed for Russian protection.[35]

Chernyaev also noted that he had opened negotiations with the 'Kara-Kirgiz', writing to a *Bii* called Choqai of the Besh-Tamghaliq tribe with whom he had

[30] Ignat'ev to Miliutin 14/04/1864, in Serebrennikov, *Sbornik. 1864 g.* Pt. *I* Doc.59, 105.
[31] Resolution by D. A. Miliutin n.d., in Serebrennikov, *Sbornik. 1864 g.* Pt. *I* Doc.53, 98.
[32] Miliutin to Bezak 19/04/1864, in Serebrennikov, *Sbornik. 1864 g.* Pt. *I* Doc.62, 107.
[33] Terent'ev, *Istoriya zavoevaniya*, I, 268–9.
[34] Lerkhe to Kolpakovskii 18/05/1863 TsGARKaz F.3 Op.1 D.222, 'O formirovanii v ukreplenie Vernago otriada i vdvizhenii ego za Chu', l. 168–9ob. On this occasion Lerkhe reached Aulie-Ata but did not attack it; Terent'ev notes that at this point Russian forces were still following the 'Caucasian' practice of mounting punitive expeditions, destroying fortresses and then retreating and allowing the enemy to reoccupy them, which he thought pointless: *Istoriya zavoevaniya*, I, 273.
[35] 'Alimqul to Jantai Batyr Dadkhwah TsGARKaz F.3 Op.1 D.167 l. 140.

Figure 5.2 'Alimqul's appeal to Jantai Batyr Dadkhwah. TsGARKaz F.3 Op.1 D.167 l. 140. © Central State Archive of the Republic of Kazakhstan.

made contact at Suzaq and Chulaq-Qurghan the previous year, whom he described as 'having considerable significance both among the *ordyntsy* and among the Khoqandis'. When his forces reached the Chu, 'near the former Khoqandi fortress of Toqmaq', they were welcomed by a *manap* of the Tanysh clan of the Sarybaghysh tribe called Joriti Khudoyar.[36] The artist M. S. Znamenskii recalled how Valikhanov, travelling with the column as a translator, received a number of letters from local Kyrgyz leaders offering their submission. Perhaps in consequence of these negotiations, Chernyaev's forces encountered no opposition at Merke, Toqmaq or Pishpek, which had all been abandoned by their inhabitants before their advance.[37] They reached Aulie-Ata on the 2 June, and after a brief siege on the 4 June the Russians

[36] Chernyaev to Diugamel 27/05/1864 RGVIA F.483 Op.1 D.77 ll. 76*ob*–7, 90–1*ob*.
[37] Znamenskii, 'Dnevnik Aulie-atinskogo pokhoda', 250–3

stormed the small fortified town. Chernyaev's report described it as having 583 houses, 8 mosques and 237 shops, emphasising its role as a trading mart for the surrounding nomads.[38] Chernyaev wrote to his father on the 6 June that 'before you receive this letter you will no doubt have heard from the newspapers of my capture of Aulie-Ata, *which is the final goal proposed for the force's activities this year* [...] the capture of the fortress hardly cost us any losses, thanks to the constant rain, which prevented the Khoqandis from using their matchlocks' (emphasis added).[39] Apart from offering further evidence of the advantages in military technology enjoyed by the Russians during the conquest of Central Asia, this letter provides evidence that at this stage, at least, Chernyaev understood his orders to have been fulfilled – the further 'transfer' of the frontier to the Arys was not to happen that year. On the 12 June Verevkin's forces captured Turkestan, which put up stiffer resistance than Aulie-Ata had done: Verevkin's report described how 'before us we saw an expanse of gardens surrounding the town, from which was visible only the high dome of the mosque [*sic*] of Hazrat Sultan [i.e. the mausoleum of Khwaja Ahmad Yasavi]'.[40] As Mullah Niyaz Khoqandi put it, 'thus in one year Turkestan and Aulie-Ata, the two most noble fortresses of the *Dasht-i Qipchaq*, were taken by the unbelievers'.[41]

The new Russian frontier had ostensibly been created as planned; however, barely a month later Chernyaev would be advancing on Chimkent. This would appear to offer confirmation of David Mackenzie's 'disobedience' thesis in explaining this phase of the Russian advance into Central Asia, but there were also other factors at work.[42] Terent'ev explained it in the following terms: 'a closer acquaintance with the projected frontier revealed that the Qara-Tau range, which served as the actual frontier, in no way facilitated things, as communications between the forces and their furnishing with supplies were extremely difficult, and the northern slopes of the range, on top of this, were very short of water'.[43] Communications across the Qara-Tau range would certainly not have been easy: in all probability the sum total of Chernyaev's knowledge of the landscape comprised a rough sketch-map (Figure 5.3) drawn up by a Qazaq *lazutchik* (scout) for Kolpakovskii at the beginning of 1864, which gave brief descriptions of routes and distances, and a bare outline of landscape and rivers:

What this map did indicate, however, was that the only road linking Aulie-Ata and Turkestan ran through Chimkent, which was still controlled by

[38] Chernyaev to Diugamel 06/06/1864 RGVIA F.483 Op.1 D.77 ll. 222–5.
[39] M. G. Chernyaev to Grigorii Nikitich Chernyaev 27/06/1864, Aulie-Ata IISH: Archief M. G. Cernjaev Folder 17.
[40] Verevkin to Bezak 12/06/1864 RGVIA F.483 Op.1 D.77 l. 144.
[41] '*Turkestan va Auliya Ata ke ashraf-i qaleha-yi dasht-i qipchaq bud dar yak sal fath-i ahl-i kuffar kardid*', TSh, 268.
[42] Mackenzie, *Lion of Tashkent*, 38.
[43] Terent'ev, *Istoriya zavoevaniya*, I, 278.

Figure 5.3 Sketch map of the Syr-Darya Valley and the Qara-Tau range by 'Abd al-Vali Qarabai-oghli 19/01/1864 TsGARKaz F.3 Op.1 D.167 ll. 114*ob*–15. © Central State Archive of the Republic of Kazakhstan.

Khoqand. In his later memoirs, Miliutin gave this as the key reason for Chernyaev's decision to advance on Chimkent, and approved his reasoning.[44] When Chernyaev was informed that a large Khoqandi force was massing at Chimkent that would sever communications between him and Verevkin, he made the decision to capture the city, and wrote to Verevkin for assistance. This resulted in a famously ill-tempered response from the latter, which Chernyaev would later reproduce (in somewhat altered form) in one of the many self-justifying publications during his retirement.[45] Verevkin claimed that he had more accurate intelligence that there were no more than 600 Khoqandi troops at Chimkent, and added that,

> If the purpose of your proposed advance to Chimkent is simply
> a reconnaissance of the Khoqandi forces, then it seems that this aim is

[44] D. A. Miliutin, *Vospominaniya 1863–4* ed. L. G. Zakharova (Moscow: ROSSPEN, 2003), 515.

[45] IISH Archief M. G. Cernjaev Folder 2 *Tetrad'* 3 p. 137; M. G. Chernyaev, 'Sultany Kenesary i Sadyk', *RV* (1889), No. 8, 27–39; Terent'ev, *Istoriya zavoevaniya*, I, 283.

already fulfilling itself. If you propose to capture Chimkent, with the purpose of its permanent occupation, then, without denying the ease and usefulness of such an enterprise, I must insist that not only the actual siege, but also the creation and supply of a garrison there must fall solely on the Siberian and in no way on the Orenburg forces. As Chimkent lies forty *versts* to the east of the left bank of the Arys, it does not enter at all into our proposed frontier and lies entirely outside the Syr-Darya region.[46]

Curiously enough, on the 27 June Verevkin had apparently sent a message to Bezak reporting a rumour that 'Alimqul was approaching Turkestan with a substantial force.[47] Despite this, he repeated his refusal to Chernyaev verbatim at the beginning of July, and also wrote to Bezak a few days later to insist on the same point.[48] Verevkin's assertion that Chimkent did *not* fall into Russian plans for the frontier might be taken as confirmation that Chernyaev was acting entirely on his own initiative in attacking it, but this was not entirely true: after all, Chimkent had been mentioned by Miliutin as the anchoring-point of the new frontier in the original orders he issued in January 1864. A few days after Chernyaev set out towards Chimkent, this would be reconfirmed by Colonel V. A. Poltoratskii of the Asiatic Section of the General Staff (a personal friend of Chernyaev), who wrote that the purpose of the campaigns was 'To create from the fortresses of Perovskii, Julek, Turkestan, Chimkent, Aulie-Ata, Merke and Toqmaq a new forward Khoqand Line, the centre of administration of which, depending on local circumstances, should be Aulie-Ata or Chimkent.'[49] On the 17 July Miliutin appointed Chernyaev commander of this 'New Khoqand Line', subordinating Verevkin to his authority on the grounds of seniority, although neither officer was yet aware of this. Instead the Chimkent campaign brought into stark relief the dangers of a divided command on the new frontier. Despite his abrupt dismissal of Chernyaev's proposal to attack Chimkent, Verevkin shortly afterwards despatched a small force of two companies of infantry, a *sotnya* of Cossacks, twenty Qazaq auxiliaries, three guns and a rocket battery under Staff-Captain Meyer from Turkestan across the Arys. Whether, as Chernyaev (and later Terent'ev) would allege, this was with the explicit aim of gaining the glory of capturing Chimkent for Orenburg before the Siberian troops could reach it, or was simply intended to secure communications between the forces and Meyer exceeded his orders,

---

[46] Verevkin to Chernyaev 02/06/1864, in Serebrennikov, *Sbornik. 1864 g. Pt. I* Doc.88, 144.

[47] Bezak to Miliutin 17/07/1864 RGVIA F.483 Op.1 D.77 ll. 118–19.

[48] Verevkin to Chernyaev 02/07/1864, in Serebrennikov, *Sbornik. 1864 g. Pt. I* Doc.121, 203; Verevkin to Bezak 08/07/1864, in Serebrennikov, *Sbornik. 1864 g. Pt. I* Doc.131, 217.

[49] 'Zapiska polkovnika Poltoratskogo ob obrazovanii peredovoi Kokanskoi linii', 09/07/1864, in Serebrennikov, *Sbornik. 1864 g. Pt. I* Doc.132, 220.

he advanced directly towards Chimkent without alerting Chernyaev to his presence, and managed to get himself cut off and surrounded in the valley of Aq Bulaq by a much larger Khoqandi force led by 'Alimqul himself.[50] In Terent'ev's account, Meyer managed to extricate himself only at the price of a deceitful and humiliating promise to return Turkestan to the Khoqandis, which was then of course reneged upon when Chernyaev appeared with reinforcements and scattered the Khoqandi troops.[51] Curiously, neither the *Ta'rikh-i Shahrukhi* nor either of the two published Qipchaq narratives of this clash mentions this offer, although 'Alimqul appears to refer to it in an undated letter preserved by Serebrennikov in Russian translation.[52] The *Kirgizskii rasskaz* emphasises the heroism of the Muslims and the fear of the unbelievers:

> Look at the many *Kafirs*! They have placed camels around themselves in defence, laid out cannon, but the *Arvakh* slaughtered the unbelievers: the shots of their own weapons fell among their camels. The Muslims surged over the unbelievers like a torrent, and began to trample and hack at them. The unbelievers heard the voice of Ming-bai [Ming Bai Parvanachi, a Khoqandi commander] and were much afraid.[53]

This account then describes the Russian retreat to the Arys and Aulie-Ata and Turkestan after making a demonstration before the walls of Chimkent, while 'Alimqul appointed a 'Sart' called Nar Muhammad (possibly the same man who had been governor of Tashkent in the early 1850s) as commander of the Chimkent garrison. The *Ta'rikh-i 'Aliquli* offers a much more reflective account, possibly reflecting its later date of composition, and the fact that the author was much closer to the centres of power in Khoqand:

> The Amir-i Lashkar ['Alimqul] sat down alone on the hillock [...] he handed me his own field-glasses and deigned to say: 'Those standing there are Russian forces. Have a look!' I looked through the field-glasses and said: 'There are apparently more than three hundred.' He deigned to answer: 'You also take for people the white packs tied together, there are only a little over two hundred. But the surprising thing is that such an army as ours cannot overpower two hundred Russians!'[54]

Despite Mullah Muhammad Yunus's suggestion that the Khoqandi artillery be brought up closer to bombard the Russians more effectively, their forces were unable to make a breakthrough that day. 'Alimqul sent for his Pashtun artillery commander Jemadar Na'ib and the *sarbaz* infantry to be brought up

---

[50] Terent'ev, *Istoriya zavoevaniya*, I, 284; *TA* trans., 65, text, 71b–2a.

[51] Terent'ev, *Istoriya zavoevaniya*, I, 288–9.

[52] Beisembiev, *Tarikhi Shakhrukhi*, 127; *TSh*, 269; Bartol'd, 'Tuzemets o russkom zavoevanii', 344; 'Alimqul to Chernyaev 1864, in Serebrennikov, *Sbornik. 1864 g. Pt. II* Docs.406 & 407, 295–6.

[53] Veselovskii, *Kirgizskii rasskaz* trans., 19.

[54] *TA* trans. 64, text ff. 72a–b.

from Chimkent, but before they arrived he allowed his commanders to persuade him to make another frontal assault, which failed with heavy losses. Mullah Muhammad Yunus describes negotiations between the Khoqandis and the Russians beginning only *after* Meyer and his men had been relieved by the arrival of Chernyaev and his men from Aulie-Ata. His account of the conversation with the Russian envoy (the naturalist N. A. Severtsov (1827–1885), who had spent a month as a prisoner of the Khoqandi *Bek* of Turkestan in 1858)[55] offers some insight into Khoqandi thinking on the question of frontiers:

> If His Majesty the Emperor orders: 'Leave Aq Masjid', I shall even restore the destroyed walls of Aq Masjid and deliver it to you. But if he says: 'Let that side of Arys belong to the Muslims and this [side] to the Russians', we will act in accordance with this [order]. This proposal was very good and favourable [for us]. But the late Amir-i Lashkar thought: In the event that the town of Turkistan's side of the Arys passes to the Russians, the tribe Besh-Tamghalik will slip out of our hands. Therefore such a favourable opportunity was missed.[56]

In other words, 'Alimqul was reasoning in terms not of territory, but of people: with the benefit of hindsight Mullah Muhammad Yunus saw this as a missed opportunity to keep the Russians on the other side of the Arys, and thus perhaps preserve Tashkent and Khoqand's core territories in Ferghana, which by the time he was writing had been under Russian rule for almost thirty years. Terent'ev's account instead has Chernyaev stating that he did not have authority to negotiate terms, and that all he could do was halt military operations while the Khoqandis despatched an embassy to Russia, while Severtsov was given the delicate task of explaining that Meyer's offer of Turkestan had been a 'misunderstanding'.[57] Even assuming Mullah Muhammad Yunus's memory of the conversation is accurate, it is unlikely that any such agreement would have been kept by the Russians, who were about to discover that the Arys was most unsatisfactory as a 'natural' frontier.

5.3 Before Chimkent

After relieving Meyer and his men, Chernyaev had made a 'reconnaissance' (actually an attempted demonstration of force) before the citadel of Chimkent on the 19–22 July, during which his troops easily beat off another frontal assault, killing the Khoqandi commander Ming Bai Parvanachi, but did not

---

[55] Account of Jukulbai Andeev 27/04/1858 TsGARKaz F.383 Op.1 D.87, 'Perepiska o zakhvate v plen magistra zoologii Severtseva', ll. 1–2; N. A. Severtsov, *Mesyats plena u Kokantsev* (St Pb.: Tip Riumin i Kompanii, 1860).
[56] *TA* trans. 66, text ff. 73a–b.
[57] Terent'ev, *Istoriya zavoevaniya*, I, 289.

attempt to take the citadel. Terent'ev believed that their subsequent retreat owing to lack of supplies was interpreted by some on the Khoqandi side as a victory, and this is borne out by the description in the *Ta'rikh-i Shahrukhi*, which attributes the retreat to Jemadar Na'ib's skill in handling the Khoqandi artillery – so great that the Russians assumed that they were manned by *'farangi'* (English) gunners.[58] Our two Qipchaq sources have a somewhat different perspective – the *Kirgizskii rasskaz* at this point engages in a eulogy to the heroism and discipline of Chernyaev and his men, and mourns the death of Ming-Bai.[59] According to the *Ta'rikh-i 'Aliquli*, 'Alimqul himself was too wise to believe the Russians defeated – he despatched Nar Muhammad Parvanachi, the commander of the Chimkent garrison, to cut off Chernyaev and his men before they could reach Aulie-Ata, knowing they 'wanted food and water desperately', and was furious when he and his men failed to intercept them and lied that the Russians had already escaped. 'Alimqul had one of them, a Qazaq called Baizaq Dadkhwah, blown to pieces from the mouth of a cannon, and the rest executed by firing-squad.[60] The *Kirgizskii rasskaz* described Baizaq as a spy who had helped the Russians, and the latter would interpret this as the brutal punishment of a 'pro-Russian party' in Chimkent, which had had the effect of bringing many over to their side.[61] This understanding was probably based on the *Ta'rikh-i Shahrukhi*, which describes how 'Alimqul had alienated the Qazaqs of the Chimkent region by executing Baizaq, here described as an influential *Bii*.[62] It is unclear how much credence should be lent to this: the *Kirgizskii rasskaz* lays great emphasis on the religious division between Russians and Central Asians,[63] something also clear in the language of the *Ta'rikh-i Shahrukhi*, which consistently refers to the Russians as *'bi din'* and *'kuffar'*. However, the latter text also notes that the Qazaqs of the Turkestan region were so oppressed by the raiding and looting of Mirza Daulat Qarateghini Tajik, 'Alimqul's father-in-law, whom he had appointed as governor of the town, that they preferred to 'recognise the power of the unbelievers'.[64] The most probable explanation is that the approach of the Russians, who represented both a military threat and an alternative source of

---

[58] *TSh*, 270; Bartol'd, 'Tuzemets o russkom zavoevanii', 345.

[59] Veselovskii, *Kirgizskii rasskaz*, trans. 22–9.

[60] *TA* trans. 67–8 text ff. 74a–b.

[61] Veselovskii, *Kirgizskii rasskaz*, 16–17; Mackenzie, *The Lion of Tashkent*, 41.

[62] *TSh*, 272; Bartol'd, 'Tuzemets o russkom zavoevanii', 345–6.

[63] In the *Kirgizskii rasskaz* this is most visible on pp. 20–1, where 'Alimqul is portrayed exhorting his troops, saying 'We are Muslims, they unbelievers' and drawing attention to the desecration of the shrine of Kochkar-Ata by the Russians.

[64] *'Qazaqan-i hauli-yi Turkestan az mahkumat-i an zulm sha'ir gir athar sar eta'at-i khudhara tafta mahkumat-i kufara-ra bar khudha ikhtiyar namudand'*. This is followed by verses reflecting that justice can be more important than Islam for preserving the authority of a ruler: *TSh*, 266–7; Bartol'd, 'Tuzemets o russkom zavoevanii', 342; Beisembiev, *Annotated Indices*, 479.

power and patronage, accentuated what were often already acute political differences within Khoqand.

Although Chernyaev was probably not to blame for the debacle at Aq Bulaq and before Chimkent, it seems that it was at this point that he began to lose the confidence of his superiors in St Petersburg, Orenburg and Omsk. In his memoirs Miliutin blamed Chernyaev for not advancing more quickly to assist Meyer, and gave no credence to the idea that the latter had advanced without informing the Siberian forces in order to have the glory of taking Chimkent for himself.[65] In his private papers Chernyaev kept a copy of a resolution from Miliutin, which complained of Chernyaev's insolence in claiming in a letter to his friend Poltoratskii that his achievement in capturing Aulie-Ata had been insufficiently recognised. Miliutin was clearly very put out at Chernyaev's (entirely characteristic) self-importance and self-pity. In the same letter he went on to express apprehension at Chernyaev's apparent intention of seizing Chimkent, stating that 'such an expansion of our frontiers never entered into our plans; it entirely stretches our line and demands a significant increase in forces', but regretting that communications were so slow that it was unlikely any countermanding order would reach Chernyaev in time.[66] Whilst Chernyaev had not received explicit orders to take Chimkent, Miliutin was being a little selective here: in fact, as we have seen, Chimkent *was* envisaged as a key point on the 'New Khoqand Line', something stated in the orders Miliutin had issued in January 1864, which had been passed on to Chernyaev in March.[67] Chernyaev was guilty not of 'expanding the frontier' *per se*, but of doing so to an accelerated timetable: he took advantage of the vagueness and ambiguity of St Petersburg's vision of where the frontier should run, no doubt encouraged by the fact that the last time he had done this, when capturing Suzaq in 1863, he had been heartily congratulated on his initiative, which had helped Miliutin stir the Foreign Ministry into action.

If Miliutin was now turning against him, Chernyaev still had support from his immediate superior, Diugamel, who accepted his argument that Chimkent's garrison posed an unacceptable threat to Russian communications. The next document in the sequence of Chernyaev's private papers (which were clearly collected both as a record of his numerous vendettas and as an exercise in personal exoneration) was a series of notes excerpted from a letter from Diugamel to Miliutin on the necessity of taking Chimkent to prevent the Khoqandis rupturing communications between Aulie-Ata and Turkestan, clearly intended as proof that his conduct was both justified and

---

[65] Miliutin, *Vospominaniya 1863–4*, 516.
[66] 'Kopiya s rezoliutsii Voennogo Ministra, na pis'mo General-Maiora Chernyaeva, prislannoe Polkovniku Poltoratskomu 18 avgusta 1864 g.', RGIM OPI F.208 Op.1 D.6 ll. 10–*ob*.
[67] This point has also been noted by Jamison, 'Weakness, Expansion and "Disobedience"', 139.

authorised.[68] In any case, as Miliutin had predicted, by the time Diugamel wrote, Russian forces would have captured Chimkent in any case. The city fell on the 21 September after a two-day siege, with Chernyaev himself leading a storming party through a watercourse beneath the walls according to Russian accounts, although the *Ta'rikh-i 'Aliquli* attributed the victory to a clever bluff which had persuaded the Khoqandi garrison to pursue what they thought was a retreating enemy and abandon the protection of their walls.[69] Chernyaev's confidence that his actions would be retrospectively endorsed was not misplaced: Diugamel supported him, writing that 'Insofar as the rewards to General Chernyaev are concerned, his achievements stand out from the range of our recent steppe expeditions', whilst Alexander II himself annotated the letter 'A Glorious Affair' (*Slavnoe Delo*).[70] Chernyaev was congratulated and received the orders of St George 3rd Class and St Stanislaus 1st class: even Miliutin grudgingly accepted that Chernyaev had acted correctly in not leaving Chimkent in Khoqandi hands, because of the threat it posed to communications on the new Russian frontier line.[71] Only the Foreign Ministry was unhappy, but Gorchakov's response inadvertently revealed the degree to which Russian geographical ignorance and the attempt to use 'natural' landmarks to fix the frontier had allowed Chernyaev to exploit the contradictions and ambiguities in his orders: 'Chimkent was made a point on the Arys line only because at that time we thought that this town lay on the right (our) side of the river.'[72] During Chernyaev's later debriefing in St Petersburg, Gorchakov was supposed to have enquired of Ignat'ev 'Quel est ce trou d'Aouliata, dont Tcherniaeff m'a parlé?'[73] Unfortunately for him, it was already much too late to find out.

In response to Chernyaev's conquests, and their consequently improved knowledge of the geography and resources of the region, the War Ministry drew up a new project to define the Central Asian frontier, with four possible variations:

---

[68] Diugamel to Miliutin 23/09/1864 RGIM OPI F.208 Op.1 D.6 ll. 11–12.

[69] Terent'ev, *Istoriya zavoevaniya*, I, 293–4; K. K. Abaza, *Zavoevanie Turkestana* (St Pb.: M. M. Stasiulevich, 1902), 83–4; Mackenzie, *Lion of Tashkent*, 42–3; *TA* trans. 68 text ff. 75b–6a.

[70] Diugamel to Miliutin 31/10/1864, in Serebrennikov, *Sbornik. 1864 g. Pt. II* Doc.270, 139.

[71] Miliutin, *Vospominaniya 1863–4*, 517–18.

[72] Memorandum by Gorchakov 31/10/1864, in Serebrennikov, *Sbornik. 1864 g. Pt. II* Doc.296, 170.

[73] 'What is this hole of an Aulie-Ata, of which Chernyaev spoke to me?', IISH Archief M. G. Cernjaev Folder 3 *Tetrad'* 4 p. 187. Ignat'ev kept a copy of Chernyaev's report of his actions that summer in his private papers, suggesting he too found it perturbing: 'Raport Nachal'nika Zachuiskogo otryada General-Maiora Chernyaeva', 12/06–08/08/1864 GARF F.730 Op.1 D.499 ll. 1–13.

(1) A line from the Syr-Darya through Suzaq and Chulaq-Qurghan and along the Qara-Tau summit to Aulie-ata and Vernoe. This was dismissed because it would run largely though the steppe, and have the same supply problems as the current Syr-Darya Line.

(2) A line along the Syr-Darya to the junction with the river Arys, up the course of this river to Aulie-Ata and along the northern face of the Ala-Tau to Kastek and Vernoe. This was considered better, not least as the Russians still believed the Arys was navigable. The renunciation of Chimkent and the failure to include Lake Issyq-Kul were considered serious drawbacks.

(3) To permanently annex Chimkent, and make Tashkent a client state under Russian protection. This was thought to carry too many risks of sucking Russia deep into Central Asia, and leaving her position in the region unclear.

(4) To permanently annex Tashkent. This would solve supply problems and bring trade benefits, but would be a complex undertaking in a region where 'the russification (*obrusenie*) of the region and its civil administration would be, if not completely impossible, extremely difficult.'[74]

Miliutin's response to this was illuminating in more ways than one, revealing both the continued belief that a 'natural' limit could be placed on Russian expansion in the region and an acknowledgement that this process could not be controlled from St Petersburg:

> I approve the attached note. I would propose to make just one alteration: the river Arys cannot itself serve as a *border*, as beyond it lies Chimkent, already taken by our forces and constituting a forward point which is very beneficial for the enclosing of the whole expanse behind it.
>
> Because of this it seems to me that the river Arys can serve only as an indication (*ukazanie*) of the direction of our forward *line*, and in particular of the communications of the Syr-Darya with Aulie-Ata [...] The *border* line (*pogranichnaya liniya*) will have to be drawn beyond Chimkent. It is possible that we will find between Chimkent and Tashkent some sort of mountain spur (*otrog gor*) or watershed (*vodorazdel'*) that will always be better as a border than the course of a river, particularly such an insignificant river as the Arys. Such a river cannot serve as a *border*, because we are obliged to control both its banks; without this we would not be able to preserve communications along the valley of the Arys with Aulie-Ata.
>
> Where, specifically, we can place the border between Chimkent and Tashkent cannot be decided from here; it would be better to leave this decision to Major-General Chernyaev himself on the spot' (emphasis in original).[75]

[74] 'Proekt soedineniya Orenburgskoi i Sibirskoi Linii', 31/10/1864, in Serebrennikov, *Sbornik. 1864 g. Pt. II* Doc.296, 170–1; Zaionchkovskii, 'K voprosu zavoevaniya Srednei Azii', 49–50.

[75] 'Zapiska Voennago Ministra', 09/11/1864 Serebrennikov, in *Sbornik. 1864 g. Pt. II* Doc.307, 182–3.

Miliutin had (perhaps unwittingly) put his finger on the absurdity of using rivers as supposedly 'natural' frontiers, though one might have added to his purely military observations the fact that river valleys tend to be economic and cultural units, whose division along the watercourse that gives them life is bound to create anomalies – something that would later be clearly illustrated by the Pamir boundary along the river Panj. However, Miliutin had not, of course, abandoned the hope that a 'natural' frontier in the form of a hill or watershed would somehow present itself naturally from the landscape – his acknowledgement that Chernyaev himself would have to identify the necessary natural features once again left substantial latitude to the man on the spot. In any case, events on the frontier had once again moved more rapidly than Miliutin had envisaged: two weeks before he wrote this note, and only a week after Chimkent had fallen on the 27 September, Chernyaev had set out with 1,500 men on a 'reconnaissance' towards Tashkent. This could be tenuously justified with reference to the long-standing Russian intention of separating the city from Khoqand and turning it into a vassal khanate, and rumours that the Amir of Bukhara was also planning to march on the city. In the longer term Miliutin also seems to have thought that Tashkent presented the best long-term solution to the perennial supply problems suffered by Russian garrisons in the steppe, but he had clearly had some difficulty in persuading the Foreign Ministry to accept Chernyaev's *fait accompli* at Chimkent, and did not want any further annexations that year.[76] Once again it was not the fact, but the timing which was objectionable, and this time Chernyaev did not have the defence of a successful action and new military laurels to fall back on – his attack was beaten off with heavy losses (by the standards of Russia's Central Asia's campaigns) of sixteen dead and sixty-two wounded, including four officers.[77] Terent'ev attributed this to the failure to carry out a proper reconnaissance of the walls beforehand, which meant that the Russians were misled by a protruding hillock into thinking that their bombardment had breached the walls, when in fact it had only damaged the upper levels.[78]

Chernyaev finally lost the confidence of his superiors with this first, failed assault on Tashkent. He preserved a letter of rebuke from Diugamel which had clearly wounded him, in which the latter wrote that Chernyaev appeared to have suppressed news of the attack, in which one of his best officers, Obukh, had been killed, and another, Lerkhe, seriously wounded. Chernyaev's reports of the 11, 13 and 17 October had not mentioned the assault, and Diugamel had found out about it from private letters which had reached Semipalatinsk at the beginning of November:

[76] Mackenzie, *Lion of Tashkent*, 45–6.
[77] Chernyaev to Miliutin 14/10/1864, in Serebrennikov, *Sbornik. 1864 g. Pt. II* Doc.268, 134.
[78] Terent'ev, *Istoriya zavoevaniya*, I, 296–7.

Your lengthy silence on the subject of these sad events could have had very undesirable consequences and caused me some considerable difficulties. It would have been easy for news of these events to have reached St Petersburg through Orenburg earlier than it reached me, and then the War Minister could have thought that I was hiding from him the true state of affairs.[79]

He wrote that Chernyaev had no authority to attack the city: 'How a simple reconnaissance changed into the storm of a city with a population of 100,000 is entirely incomprehensible to me.' As usual, Chernyaev preserved his response together with this letter, in which he claimed that he had not sought new laurels, but that he was trying to drive out the Khoqandi garrison from Tashkent to prevent them from re-grouping and gathering a force which he estimated at 15,000 horsemen against his one and a half *sotnyas* of Cossacks. He also claimed to have informed Diugamel of his unsuccessful assault in a despatch of the 11 October.[80]

This controversy would never be entirely settled, although Mackenzie concludes, probably rightly, that Chernyaev deliberately dragged his feet somewhat when filing his reports of the debacle, and feared that he would be dismissed as a result.[81] Miliutin's memoirs, written forty years later, reveal that his irritation at Chernyaev's unauthorised attack on Tashkent had not diminished with the passing of time, although he also made a robust defence of the need to allow local initiative to officers on a frontier so far removed from Russian centres of power, and added the following, highly revealing passage: 'This reverse was especially deplorable because in Asia we are supported not so much through material strength, owing to the small numbers of our troops, as through moral authority.'[82] In other words, Chernyaev's principal crime was not so much the assault itself, as the fact that it had been unsuccessful, and here Miliutin tacitly admitted that a further victory would be needed to wipe out this impression of weakness from the minds of 'Asiatics'. This was the same logic which had led to the launch of V. A. Perovskii's expedition to Khiva thirty years earlier, and had also prevented the Russians from retreating from their unsustainable position on the Syr-Darya in the late 1850s.[83] The need to maintain prestige, and the fear of appearing weak before both their Asian opponents and their European rivals would always be the deciding argument when the Russians were debating whether or not to advance in Central Asia.

---

[79] Diugamel to Chernyaev 12/11/1864 RGIM OPI F.208 Op.1 D.5 l. 27*ob*.

[80] Chernyaev to Diugamel 17/12/1864 RGIM OPI F.208 Op.1 D.5 ll. 29–30.

[81] Mackenzie, *Lion of Tashkent*, 45–7; Jamison disagrees, seeing the week's delay in drawing up the report as entirely understandable: 'Weakness, Expansion and "Disobedience"', 142–4.

[82] Miliutin, *Vospominaniya 1863–4*, 518.

[83] Morrison, 'Twin Imperial Disasters', 282–6 & 'Nechto eroticheskoe'.

5.4   Iqan and After

The famous 'Iqan Affair' (*'Delo pod Ikanom'*) of the 3–5 December 1864, during which a single *sotnya* of Ural Cossacks under Esaul Serov held off a much larger Khoqandi force (the Russians estimated it at 10,000) under 'Alimqul's command, went some way towards soothing their ruffled military pride. Mullah Muhammad Yunus recorded it as another melancholy setback caused by disciplined Russian volley fire,[84] while the *Ta'rikh-i Shahrukhi*, rather surprisingly, given the author's general hostility to 'Alimqul, described it as a victory in which sixty Russians were taken prisoner and the rest killed.[85] However, for the Russians it became one of the most celebrated incidents of all the Turkestan campaigns, commemorated for many years afterwards as an instance of heroism that wiped out the unfavourable impression left both by Chernyaev's reverse at Tashkent and by the earlier duplicity of Captain Meyer – although it did produce another episode of apparent cowardice, by Sub-Lt Sukorko, who failed to relieve Serov and his men, infuriating Chernyaev.[86]

The Iqan affair was the subject of a painting in Vasilii Vereshchagin's Turkestan series (Figure 5.4), and would even find a place in C. E. Callwell's *Small Wars*, where the *doyen* of British strategists of colonial warfare noted the moral effect which the victory had had on the Khoqandis.[87] 'Alimqul had apparently been intending to recapture Turkestan, but after this further disappointment he retreated to Tashkent, which he proceeded to fortify to the best of his ability. During the winter of 1864–5 Russian campaigning came to a halt, awaiting better weather. Whilst Chernyaev complained of boredom, the Khoqandis seem to have interpreted this lull somewhat differently, and they once again opened negotiations with the Russians to try to fix a new frontier. This episode is not mentioned by Terent'ev, nor in Serebrennikov's collection of documents, but, as Mullah Muhammad Yunus Tashkandi described it, the suggestion came from him, and at a guess the negotiations must have taken place in late December, perhaps two weeks or so after the Iqan affair. He first opened correspondence with Chernyaev, and then sent two merchants called Mullah 'Abd as-Sa'id Hajji and Muhammad Karim Bek to Chernyaev, who was

---

[84] *TA* trans. 70–1, text ff. 79a–81a.

[85] *TSh*, 271; Bartol'd, 'Tuzemets o russkom zavoevanii', 245.

[86] Chernyaev to Miliutin 27/12/1864, in Serebrennikov, *Sbornik. 1864 g.* Pt. II Doc.396, 279–83; 'K', 'Delo Ural'tsev pod Turkestanom', *VS* (1865), No. 4, 115–24; Mikhail Khoroshkhin, *Geroiskii podvig Ural'tsev: Delo pod Ikanom 4, 5 i 6 dekabria 1864 goda* (Ural'sk: n.p., 1895); Terent'ev, *Istoriya zavoevaniya*, I, 298–305; Abaza, *Zavoevanie Turkestana*, 85–9; Mackenzie, *Lion of Tashkent*, 49–50. Aleksei Plentsov, *Delo pod Ikanom: Sotnya protiv desyati tysyach* (St Pb.: Istoriko-Kul'turnyi Tsentr Karel'skogo Peresheika, 2014) provides an excellent technical description of the battle framed in very jingoistic terms.

[87] Callwell, *Small Wars*, 79.

Figure 5.4 *'Surrender!' 'Go to the Devil!'* (*Sdavaisya! Ubiraisya k chertu!*) – Vasilii Vereshchagin's imagined portrayal of the Iqan Affair (1874). Tretyakov Gallery, Moscow (Wikimedia Commons).

initially annoyed because he believed that the Khoqandis had been blocking trade between Chimkent and Tashkent. Tashkandi replied that this was because Chernyaev had prevented the Qazaqs of the Jappas clan, who acted as carriers for the Tashkent merchants, from coming to Tashkent. This misunderstanding underscored the need to normalise relations along the impromptu frontier:

> Finally, after neighbourly and friendly relations had sprung up between us by means of our correspondence, I wrote: 'If thanks to us peace is concluded between two padishahs, it will be of benefit and profit for all the creatures of Allah. It would be good if at first the frontier was established and demarcated.' Chernyaev replied: 'If you wish by establishing the frontier to get Chimkent back, it will never happen, because I took Chimkent with great difficulty and reported its conquest to his Majesty the Emperor. It is impossible to draw the border through this place. Let the frontier be at Sharabkhana.'[88]

---

[88] *TA* trans. 72, text ff. 72b–3a. My thanks to Beatrice Penati for drawing my attention to this passage.

Sharabkhana (literally 'alcohol house' or pub) was a caravanserai half-way between Tashkent and Chimkent, which was marked on the sketch map drawn up for Kolpakovskii in 1864 at a junction between two roads, but with no river, 'mountain spur' or other 'natural feature' that might make it a suitable frontier. Like those which had followed the affair at Aq Bulaq, these negotiations also fell through: in a passage which (like many of those in his history) is redolent with a melancholy awareness of the further defeats and losses that awaited Khoqand at Russian hands, Mullah Muhammad Yunus recorded 'Alimqul's supposed response: 'This peace agreement is of course a benefit for Allah's creatures, [and would mean] tranquillity for the yurt, and the flowering of religion and faith. But the people of Turkistan and Ferghana are extremely ignorant, stupid and warlike, of rude temperament, and are unable to tell harm from benefit.'[89] If they agreed to it, he added, then he and Mullah Muhammad Yunus would be accused of thinking only of their own benefit, and leaving many Muslims in the hands of the Russians. Mullah Muhammad Yunus's bitter regret at this outcome (assuming his account is reliable) was probably misplaced, as there is every reason to doubt Chernyaev's sincerity in these negotiations. He had not accepted his reverse before Tashkent in October 1864, and already in December was urging Miliutin and Bezak to take advantage of 'Alimqul's departure from Tashkent to Khoqand with his troops, giving heart to what he claimed was a growing party in Tashkent who wished to break with Khoqand and ally with Russia. He asked what he should do in the event that they appealed to him for protection, as he claimed that he did not have sufficient forces to take the city on his own. His claims were met with scepticism by Bezak, who considered that most rumours passed on by the Qazaqs were likely to be lies, but provided some encouragement by suggesting that these divisions would make it easy to seize Tashkent once the Tsar had given the order. The Quartermaster General of the Orenburg Line, General Verigin, a man with almost forty years' experience of Central Asian affairs, also considered larger forces would be necessary, but began with a phrase that Chernyaev later transcribed into his private archive:

> For the consolidation of the forward Khoqand line the taking of the town of Tashkent is made almost essential, especially after the unsuccessful attempt by Major-General Chernyaev to take this town in the current year.[90]

---

[89] *TA* trans. 73–4, text ff. 85b–6a; this calls into question Jamison's suggestion that 'Alimqul was 'fanatical' and simply unwilling to make peace and give up so many subjects and so much territory, although Mullah Muhammad Yunus's account was written much later with a good deal of hindsight. Jamison, 'Weakness, Expansion and "Disobedience"', 164.

[90] Chernyaev to Bezak 28/12/1864, in Serebrennikov, *Sbornik. 1865 g. Pt. I* Doc.37, 47–8; 'Kopiya s zapiski General-Kvartirmeistera Gen-Adt. Verigina', 01/02/1865 RGIM OPI F.208 Op.1 D.6 ll. 23–*ob.*

This passage had presumably stung Chernyaev's pride, but also reinforced his belief that in taking Tashkent he had only been recognising strategic and 'moral' realities.

Towards the end of January Chernyaev wrote to his old friend Poltoratskii, urging the latter to come to Tashkent: 'when you arrive here, then you will be able to confirm on the spot that the attack on Tashkent was not so senseless as all my friends sought to present it in St Petersburg. If there had not been instructions [to the contrary], then I would now drive out the Khoqandis from this small town with its 200,000 population [*sic*], in response to 'Alimqul's attack on the outskirts of Turkestan.'[91] He added that there were rumours the Bukharan Amir had allied himself with the Khoqandis and that they were advancing together to attack the Russians in Chimkent (this was quite false – Amir Sayyid Muzaffar instead looked on Khoqand's defeats against the Russians as an opportunity to seize territory from the rival khanate, though it is true that he coveted Tashkent for himself). Miliutin meanwhile gave Chernyaev orders not to undertake anything against Tashkent until he received reinforcements, but to maintain relations with its inhabitants.[92] This maintained a certain ambiguity in the messages making their way slowly from Orenburg to Chernyaev in Chimkent, hinting that the capture of Tashkent did fall into future plans for the new frontier, and also that Chernyaev should continue to try to draw the city out of Khoqand's orbit.

Meanwhile, on the 25 January, yet another special committee had met in St Petersburg to decide the question of the administration and frontiers of 'the Orenburg region and Asiatic Russia', and resolved to unite the territory 'from the western limit of Issyq-Kul to the Aral Sea' into a new Turkestan province (*oblast'*).[93] On the 12 February 1865 an order from the War Ministry confirmed the Tsar's agreement to this. The new province comprised almost all the territory conquered by the Russians in Central Asia since 1847; Chernyaev was to administer it, but was still subordinate to Orenburg, where from the 9 February N. A. Kryzhanovskii (1818–1888) replaced A. P. Bezak as the new governor.[94] Among the first instructions Kryzhanovskii received was a lengthy memorandum from Gorchakov, setting out the Foreign Ministry's views on Russia's position in Central Asia. This once again reiterated the need for a 'firm, fixed state boundary' (*prochnoi, nepodvizhnoi gosudarstvennoi granitsy*) in Central Asia, but also noted the following:

---

[91] Chernyaev to Poltoratskii 22/01/1865, in Serebrennikov, *Sbornik. 1865 g. Pt. I* Doc.25, 33.

[92] Miliutin to Bezak 02/02/1865, in Serebrennikov, *Sbornik. 1865 g. Pt. I* Doc.38, 49.

[93] 'Zhurnal komiteta, rassmatrivavshago vopros ob ustroistve Orenb. kraya i Aziatskoi Rossii', 25/01/1865, in Serebrennikov, *Sbornik. 1865 g. Pt. I* Doc.30, 37.

[94] 'Prikaz Voennogo Ministra', 12/02/1865, in Serebrennikov, *Sbornik. 1865 g. Pt. I* Doc.47, 59.

It is essential to add a few specific considerations regarding Tashkent, as our closest neighbour, which will doubtless play a significant role for us in political and trade relations. We have decided not to include this town within the empire, because we consider it incomparably more beneficial to limit ourselves to indirect influence over it, which is very real thanks to the proximity of our military forces. However, it would be much more advantageous for us if Tashkent succeeded in separating itself from Khoqand and constituted itself once more as an independent realm [...] with the restoration of its previous independence, this town would serve as an excellent tool in the event of a necessity to act against Khoqand, and in part against Bukhara.[95]

On the 25 February Kryzhanovskii sent Chernyaev a summary of this document in the form of a list of requests and instructions whose faintly patronising tone can hardly have failed to rile the latter, and noted that he intended to visit Turkestan himself before the end of August (he asked Chernyaev to arrange a meeting for him with the Khan of Khoqand and the Amir of Bukhara, unintentionally revealing his lack of understanding of the situation on the frontier). His letter concluded, however, with a significant injunction regarding Tashkent, passing on the instructions of the Foreign Ministry:

As for Tashkent, I beg your Excellency vigilantly and closely to observe everything that occurs in this town, and to assist the moral party which wishes to separate from hostile Khoqand and through your actions to direct the formation from Tashkent of a polity independent from Khoqand and Bukhara but a vassal of Russia.[96]

Both Zaionchkovskii and Mackenzie noted the ambiguity of these instructions, which did not explicitly forbid an attack on Tashkent, and Matthew Jamison has argued that this order constituted an open invitation, or at the very least an excuse, for Chernyaev to attack Tashkent once he felt his forces were strong enough.[97] It is certainly hard to see how he could have been expected to bring Tashkent within the Russian sphere of influence, or create an independent khanate out of it, without first attacking the city and expelling its Khoqandi garrison. In a later autobiographical account Chernyaev would claim that Kryzhanovskii was very keen to seize Tashkent himself, and in a private letter had urged it happen after his arrival so that he could share in the glory, but that Chernyaev had been compelled to attack sooner because of the threat from Bukhara.[98] Given Kryzhanovskii's behaviour once he had arrived in Turkestan

---

[95] Gorchakov to Kryzhanovskii 23/02/1865, in Serebrennikov, *Sbornik. 1865 g. Pt. I* Doc.60, 83.

[96] Kryzhanovskii to Chernyaev 25/02/1865, in Serebrennikov, *Sbornik. 1865 g. Pt. I* Doc.63, 88.

[97] Zaionchkovskii, 'K voprosu zavoevaniya Srednei Azii', 53–4; Mackenzie, *Lion of Tashkent*, 54; Jamison, 'Weakness, Expansion and "Disobedience"', 171–4, 176–8.

[98] 'Avtobiografija M. G. Cernjaeva', IISH Archief M. G. Cernjaev Folder 5 p. 11.

(see Chapter 6), this is not entirely implausible, but it could equally be one of Chernyaev's many retrospective justifications for his behaviour. He continued to send reports saying that the 'Russian party' in Tashkent were prepared to give up the city if the Russians approached with a military force, although 'Alimqul had strictly forbidden communications, and there was another group that favoured Bukhara.[99] On the 23 April he replied to Kryzhanovskii's message from two months previously in rather bitter language:

> Regarding the permanent state border (*postoyannoi gosudarstvennoi granitsy*) with Khoqand, I have the honour to submit that, in our current relations with this khanate, the implementation of a provisional frontier is clearly impossible, and the existence of such a frontier in the future would not give us any guarantee that the Khoqandis would not breach it during their raids. In order to repel the latter it is essential that peace and order be introduced into the khanate, and this in turn will be possible only with the establishment of our solid influence in the khanate itself. Insofar as the actual border is concerned, I cannot give any indications on this subject, as the map of Khoqand is entirely unknown to us, and any suggestions in this case would be founded solely on speculations, which very often differ from reality.[100]

This last phrase might be taken as emblematic of all Russian attempts to fix their frontier in Central Asia during these turbulent few years. Chernyaev's irritation was palpable, but what he did not acknowledge was how much freedom of action the ignorance and ambiguity in his orders had given him. Within less than a week of despatching this letter Chernyaev had set off with nine and a half companies of infantry and twelve guns towards Tashkent, ostensibly on another reconnaissance, but in fact with a clear intention of capturing the city once and for all. Various sources attest that Kryzhanovskii's request not to make any move before his proposed arrival in Turkestan in the summer helped to prompt this, as Chernyaev did not wish to share his glory with anyone else.[101] The next time he wrote to his nominal superior, on the 2 May, Chernyaev was at the fortress of Niyaz Bek, which he had captured three days earlier, cutting off Tashkent's water supply from the river Chirchik – when the news reached St Petersburg, the Tsar immediately awarded him the order of St Anna First Class, showing that military success would still win favour even if it was notionally unauthorised.[102] The Russian frontier was

[99] Military Commander of the Orenburg Region to the Military Commander of Western Siberia 17/03/1865, in Serebrennikov, *Sbornik. 1865 g. Pt. I* Doc.79, 107.
[100] Chernyaev to Kryzhanovskii 23/04/1865, in Serebrennikov, *Sbornik. 1865 g. Pt. I* Doc.98, 138–9.
[101] Terent'ev, *Istoriya zavoevaniya*, I, 307–8; Mackenzie, *Lion of Tashkent*, 54–5.
[102] Chernyaev to Kryzhanovskii 02/05/1865; Miliutin to Kryzhanovskii 04/06/1865, in Serebrennikov, *Sbornik. 1865 g. Pt. I* Docs.102, 127, 146, 191; Iu. Sokolov, *Tashkent, Tashkenttsy i Rossii* (Tashkent: Uzbekistan, 1965), 138–9.

about to move forward once again, and once again on Chernyaev's initiative: it would be wrong, however, to suppose that, had it not been for his ambition, Tashkent might have escaped Russian rule altogether. Frustration with supposed Khoqandi insolence, the official aim of creating a vassal khanate from the city and Kryzhanovskii's own ambitions for military glory would all, sooner or later, have ensured a Russian assault. Chernyaev determined the timetable, but not the general direction of Russian policy.

5.5   The Fall of Tashkent

From this perspective, then, the final successful assault on Tashkent seems of reduced significance: had the city not fallen to Chernyaev in the summer of 1865, it would almost certainly have been taken a year or two later by some other commander. It still remains to be explained just how a city with an estimated population of 150,000, and a garrison reputed to be 30,000, could fall to a Russian force of just 1,900 men, however ably commanded (and few contemporary observers agreed with Chernyaev's own assessment of his military genius). Part of this is just sleight of hand with numbers, which in this case come from a report submitted by Chernyaev to Kryzhanovskii after the event, designed to justify and magnify his actions.[103] All estimates of Tashkent's population at the time are suspect: although it was certainly a large city by Central Asian standards, and probably the largest in the region, it is unlikely to have had more than 100,000 people. The figure of 30,000 for the garrison would thus represent the entire adult male population, most of whom remained passive in the face of the assault. While Callwell, amongst others, had clearly swallowed the legend that Tashkent fell to a daring *coup de main*, leading to an immediate surrender, in fact the fighting lasted for almost two days, and had resistance been more uniform Chernyaev's feat would indeed have been impossible.[104] It seems most likely that the city's fall was largely a product of internal divisions, and that Chernyaev, who, as we have seen from his reports, was well aware of these, was relying on the existence of a pro-Russian party within the city. Those opposed to Russian rule were further divided between supporters of Khoqand, those of Bukhara and (probably) those who wished to revive the autonomy which the city had enjoyed until its conquest by 'Umar Khan in 1807. Finally, Khoqandi morale and will to resist were severely undermined by the death of 'Alimqul in a preliminary skirmish beneath the walls of the city at Shur-Tepa on the 9 May.

Muhammad Yunus Tashkandi writes that when 'Alimqul heard that Chernyaev had seized Niyaz Bek, he immediately hurried there with all the

---

[103]   Chernyaev to Kryzhanovskii 07/07/1865, in Serebrennikov, *Sbornik. 1865 g. Pt. I* Doc.158, 244–5; also in Grebner, *Osady*, 33.
[104]   Callwell, *Small Wars*, 59.

troops he could find in Khoqand, but the first message he received from the city was that 'General Chernyaev came, stopped at Shur Tepa, and has begun to besiege Tashkent. But the mood of the citizens of Tashkent has changed; they seem to have lost faith.' In a passage clearly meant to underscore the consequences of 'Alimqul's impending death, Tashkandi reassured him, saying that 'As long as your Worship is alive, the attachment to, and confidence in you of the Tashkent citizens will never change or disappear.'[105] When he was struck down by a Russian bullet 'the Muslim army stopped fighting'. While there may be some exaggeration, given that the whole purpose of Tashkandi's biography was to exalt 'Alimqul and his leadership qualities, the death of the commander is always demoralising for an army. 'Alimqul's charisma seems to have made a great impression on his contemporaries, and other chronicles also attach great significance to his death.[106] One modern Uzbek historian has gone so far as to say that Chernyaev's assault would probably not have succeeded had 'Alimqul still been alive.[107] Instead the 6,000 men and 40 guns which he had reportedly brought from Ferghana to stiffen the defence of Tashkent were left leaderless, and seem to have played no part in the defence of the city.[108]

'Alimqul's death left a power vacuum that remained unfilled until the Russian assault one month later; there was an attempt to revive the city's independence by proclaiming one Sultan Sayyid Khan its ruler, but this was not universally accepted – and did not necessarily imply submission to Russia. Instead the city's elders despatched envoys both to Khoqand and to the Amir of Bukhara requesting military support against the Russian forces, and received an enthusiastic response from the latter, who hoped to take over Tashkent himself.[109] Chernyaev reported that he had hoped that 'Alimqul's death might lead to a pro-Russian change of power across the whole khanate, but that disappointingly in Tashkent it had emboldened the Bukharan party, who were now openly treating with the Amir. Conveniently enough, this gave him a further reason to press on, and he had sent a small force to seize the fortress of Chinaz, southwest of Tashkent where the Chirchik joined the Syr-Darya and there was an important river crossing. His forces were far too few to place Tashkent under full siege, but, as he described it, light patrols would harass the inhabitants seeking to gather crops or pasture their animals in the gardens surrounding the city, in an attempt to interfere with its food supply,

---

[105] *TA* trans. 75, text f. 87b.
[106] *TA* trans. 76, text f. 90b, n. 284; Sokolov, *Tashkent, Tashkenttsy i Rossii*, 151–2.
[107] Bakhtiyar Babajanov, personal communication. See also Mackenzie, *Lion of Tashkent*, 56–7.
[108] Levengof to Kryzhanovskii 03/06/1865, in Serebrennikov, *Sbornik. 1865 g. Pt. I* Docs.124–5, 189.
[109] Sokolov, *Tashkent, Tashkenttsy i Rossii*, 154–5.

Figure 5.5 The seal of 'Alimqul, military leader of Khoqand 1863–5. TsGARKaz F.3 Op.1 D.167 l. 140. © Central State Archive of the Republic of Kazakhstan.

while a light battery under Colonel Kraevskii bombarded and partly destroyed the Khoqand Gate.[110]

While Chernyaev was preparing his assault, Gorchakov at the Foreign Ministry continued to pen memoranda which betrayed his complete ignorance of the state of relations with Bukhara and Khoqand. He insisted that they be brought into a relationship of 'subjection' or 'vassalage' in which they would be completely obedient to Russia, but which fell short of outright annexation, but he apparently expected this to be achieved through the delivery of wordy threatening letters from himself and the Orenburg Governor-General, translated into Turki – one to the Bukharan Toqsaba, and another to 'the military and civil leaders of the Khoqand Khanate'.[111] Gorchakov, Kryzhanovskii and Chernyaev all complained of the instability of Khoqand, and later Bukhara, and the consequent difficulty of maintaining diplomatic relations with them, but did not appreciate that much of this instability was owing to the Russian presence and repeated military defeats, which placed enormous strain on their political fabric. When Chernyaev's men approached the Kamelan Gate of Tashkent on the night of the 14–15 June, the bulk of the population were surely aware that a Russian assault was imminent, but few were prepared to resist either for Khudoyar of Khoqand or for Sayyid Muzaffar of Bukhara, and some may have at least passively welcomed the Russians. The standard Soviet

[110] Chernyaev to Kryzhanovskii 11/06/1865, in Serebrennikov, *Sbornik. 1865 g. Pt. I* Doc.135, 201–3.
[111] Gorchakov to Kryzhanovskii 05/06/1865 & 08/06/1865; Kryzhanovskii to Levengof 05/06/1865, in Serebrennikov, *Sbornik. 1865 g. Pt. I* Docs.129, 130 & 133, 192–5, 198–203.

account of these events by F. Azadaev suggests that this was true above all of the merchant class of the city, who depended heavily on trade with Russia – at the beginning of 1865 they apparently despatched an envoy to St Petersburg called Tura Khan Zeibukhanov, who in the name of '50 of the wealthiest and most influential merchants' of the city requested Russian protection. Zeibukhanov lost his letters and accreditation documents *en route*, and was not received in St Petersburg, although Severtsov vouched for the genuineness of his mission. Frustration at the halt to trade and cultivation provoked by the Russian blockade very probably was growing.[112]

As Mackenzie has noted, it is unclear precisely when Chernyaev decided on an assault – according to one uncorroborated account, it was a product of desperation, as he and his officers had decided that any retreat from their advanced and exposed position was impossible, and would bring the 'Asian hordes' down on them like locusts.[113] Chernyaev's retrospective justification was that the capture of the city was to prevent it from being seized by Bukhara, and, as we shall see in the following chapter, that would become the rationale for garrisoning the city and making it a permanent Russian possession rather than a protectorate, as had originally been envisaged. The idea of seizing Tashkent and the cultivated region around it as the keystone of Russia's new frontier in the steppe had been mooted for at least six years, and Chernyaev would have known that, if successful, his *fait accompli* would almost certainly be endorsed by the War Ministry and the Tsar, as had all his previous conquests. He had also received, from some Tashkentis who went over to him in the winter of 1864 – notably Sharafi Bai, Yuzbashi 'Abd Rahim Bai Muhammad, 'Abdurrahman Bek (former *aqsaqal* (elder) of the eastern part of the city) and the merchant Said 'Azim Bai, who had been fined heavily by 'Alimqul for communicating with Chernyaev – assurances that Russian forces would be welcomed and resistance lukewarm if they attacked the city again.[114] However, the most pressing factor for Chernyaev was surely the memory of his failed assault the previous year, which, if left unavenged, would have permanently marred his career, to say nothing of the lasting damage to Russian prestige.

On the 17 June, after two days of fighting, Chernyaev reported, in a characteristically portentous tone, to Kryzhanovskii that the city was in his hands: 'with the capture of Tashkent, we have acquired in Central Asia a status consonant with the interests of the Empire and the might of the Russian people'.[115] It had been a close-run thing. The initial capture of the Kamelan

[112] F. Azadaev, *Tashkent vo vtoroi polovine XIX veka: Ocherki sotsial'no-ekonomicheskoi i politicheskoi istorii* (Tashkent: Izd AN UzSSR, 1959), 72–3, 77.
[113] Mackenzie, *Lion of Tashkent*, 57.
[114] Azadaev, *Tashkent vo vtoroi polovine XIX veka*, 74–6; Sokolov, *Tashkent, Tashkenttsy i Rossii*, 136–7.
[115] Chernyaev to Kryzhanovskii 17/06/1865, Serebrennikov, *Sbornik. 1865 g. Pt. I* Doc.140, 212–13.

Gate using scaling-ladders, led by Rotmistr Gustav Alexandrovich Wulfert (1840–1894), Chernyaev's future brother-in-law, was relatively straightforward – it was the resistance within the walls of Tashkent which caused the assault to last almost two days. According to a vivid account by Lt Soltanovskii, the defenders on the walls did not notice their stealthy approach with ladders in the darkness, and they even heard the Khoqandis discussing the failure of the Russians to take the city so far. At about 4 am the paces of the *qaraul* (watchman) could no longer be heard, and they assumed he had gone to sleep: 'in one moment we ran with our ladders from the garden to the wall, placed our ladders against it, and from the first rungs I together with Wulfert and the riflemen were on the walls of the city, with a cry of "Ura!", which produced alarm amongst them, and although some threw themselves on their weapons, by then they were already in our hands'.[116] Instead they came under fire from within the city, where there were musket men concealed among the gardens and '*saklyas*' (a Caucasian term for a fortified village, widely used by Russian officers who had served there) and from artillery in the neighbouring turrets. After an hour exchanging fire they had several wounded, including Rotmistr Wulfert, so Soltanovskii assumed command. Once the storming column had opened the gate and admitted the artillery, it took only a couple of salvoes for the Khoqandis to retreat from their positions – Soltanovskii estimated that by then it was about 5.30 am. Meanwhile a second column under Colonel Kraevskii mounted an assault close to the Salar Gate, first bombarding the turrets with explosive shells to destroy their artillery cover, and firing canister shot at the defenders on the walls. The officer commanding the battery of Orenburg horse artillery noted that their position was exposed, and they were hampered by soft soil, which meant the guns had to be dug out after each recoil, while the enemy's fire was heavy – but it was also inaccurate, and after an hour's bombardment, which used up most of their remaining stock of shells, they had silenced the Khoqandi guns, with the loss of just seven horses.[117] Just as they were bombarding the Salar Gate, they were ordered to attack a group of the enemy that was escaping to the north, and after two *versts* they came across a large body of cavalry near the crossing of the Chirchik, which broke under canister shot, abandoning several of their standards. Four *versts* further on they encountered another body of cavalry and infantry, who also scattered under canister shot, pursued by the Cossacks. Returning to the city, Kraevskii's force entered through the Kashgar Gate without resistance, and were able to replenish their stores of gunpowder

---

[116] Praporshchik Soltanovskii, 'Zapiska o deistviyakh vzvoda strelkovoi roty 7 Zapadno-Sibirskago Bataliona pri shturme gor. Tashkenta 15, 16 i 17 iiunya 1865 g.' 22/06/1865, in Serebrennikov, *Sbornik. 1865 g. Pt. I* Doc.143, 215–16.

[117] Khorunzhii Bukharin (1st Orenburg Cossack Horse Artillery) to Kryzhanovskii 26/06/1865, in Serebrennikov, *Sbornik. 1865 g. Pt. I* Doc.145, 220–1.

from an artillery park, which included 'two cases of explosive shells and more than 500 fuses of very good workmanship'[118] – evidence perhaps of Jemadar Naib's management of 'Alimqul's artillery. The Russians were now inside the walls of the city at two different points, but it was here that the most effective resistance began.

As Soltanovskii's column made their way towards the Samarkand Gate, they came under heavy small arms and artillery fire from a barricade which the defenders had constructed across the road – once again Russian artillery fire cleared the obstacle, with one salvo of canister shot scattering the defenders. As they forged deeper into the city they came under fire once again: 'Many Khoqandis in large parties had gathered in the saklyas and on the roofs, and some were in the trees, firing on our column.' He ordered the artillery to destroy the saklyas, and his riflemen to pick off the musketeers in the trees, and in this fashion they proceeded for three versts, destroying more barricades along the way, until they reached the Samarkand Gate, where they halted to await fresh ammunition supplies. They encountered further resistance as they continued onward for another two versts, in the form of musketry and artillery fire from behind garden walls, which one by one were first destroyed with artillery and then taken with a bayonet charge. As evening fell, the column retraced its steps, only to find that the Khoqandis had brought up a new battery of five guns covering the road which had to be captured by skirmishers.[119] On the other side of the city Kraevskii's column had a very similar experience as it attempted to force its way deeper into the city, coming under continuous fire from the surrounding houses and gardens, and periodically having to destroy barricades across the road – they were unable to join the main force at the Kamelan Gate on the night of the 15 June, and spent the night in the citadel, repelling attacks on the breach they had made in its walls with canister fire.[120] Soltanovskii's column reached the Kamelan Gate once again at 10 pm, and the besiegers effectively found themselves besieged behind a temporary barricade, which they reinforced by setting the surrounding buildings on fire – Muhammad Salih Tashkandi describes this as scaring the inhabitants.[121] The Russian force drove off the Khoqandis with rifle and canister volleys when they tried to extinguish it. After repelling an attack at 5 am and pursuing the Khoqandis with a bayonet charge, Soltanovskii's column set about clearing another road which led from the right of the Kamelan Gate through the city, repeating the pattern of the previous day, as they cleared the barricades

---

[118] Bukharin to Kryzhanovskii 26/06/1865, in Serebrennikov, *Sbornik. 1865 g. Pt. I* Doc.145, 222–3.

[119] Soltanovskii, 'Zapiska o deistviyakh vzvoda', 216–18; Mackenzie, *Lion of Tashkent*, 58.

[120] Bukharin to Kryzhanovskii 26/06/1865, in Serebrennikov *Sbornik. 1865 g. Pt. I* Doc.145, 223–4.

[121] 'Ahl-i nasura atesh bedarun shahr midad [...] va marduman parishan hal budeand', *TJT*, f. 1a–b.

constructed by the defenders with canister shot from their field guns before going in with the bayonet, the only casualties being two riflemen who were mortally wounded by explosives which the Khoqandis set off in one of the houses they were exploring.[122] Kraevskii's column encountered similar resistance, finding that many of the barricades they had destroyed the previous day had been resurrected and provided with artillery, though a few volleys of rifle fire usually sufficed to clear them – for some reason he wrote that 'the use of artillery in these slums was impossible'. His column reached the main force at the Kamelan Gate that evening, as did Soltanovskii's. The following day, the 17 June, resistance seems to have ended – Soltanovskii and his men were gathering up all the abandoned weapons they could find.[123]

While Russian casualties were relatively light, given the size of the city – twenty-five dead and eighty-eight wounded, including three officers – the resistance had been more than symbolic. Whether it came mainly from the Bukharan party, as Mackenzie suggests, from Khoqandi loyalists, or from those who wished to reassert the city's independence is unclear – most Russian accounts simply refer to the enemy generically as '*Kokandtsy*', while Azadaev, basing his judgement on Muhammad Salih Tashkandi, suggests they were small, uncoordinated groups of 'Alimqul loyalists, supporters of the Khoqandi governor of Tashkent and those who followed Sultan Sadiq (Syzdyq), Kenesary's son.[124] Of the eight St George's Crosses awarded for the assault, one went to Wulfert, one to A. K. Abramov (1836–1886), future governor of the Zarafshan region (*Okrug*) and a major figure in Turkestan's administration until his death in 1886, and another to N. A. Ivanov, who would succeed Abramov in Samarkand and later become Turkestan Governor-General.[125] Chernyaev had his prize – the question was whether he could continue to hold it with his tiny force. It would take a good deal of bluff and conciliation.

In his first full report to Kryzhanovskii after Tashkent's capture, on the 29 June, Chernyaev gave full voice to his fears: he described his forces as wholly inadequate, and reported rumours of a three-way alliance between Khiva, Bukhara and Khoqand to defeat the Russians – in fact, as we know from reading the Khoqand chronicles, this prospect, which had haunted the Russians since the 1850s, was as far away from reality as ever. While

---

[122] Soltanovskii, 'Zapiska o deistviyakh vzvoda', 22/06/1865, in Serebrennikov, *Sbornik. 1865 g. Pt. I* Doc.143, 218–19.

[123] Bukharin to Kryzhanovskii 26/06/1865, in Serebrennikov, *Sbornik. 1865 g. Pt. I* Doc.145, 224–5; Soltanovskii, 'Zapiska o deistviyakh', 22/06/1865, in Serebrennikov, *Sbornik. 1865 g. Pt. I* Doc.143, 219.

[124] Mackenzie, *Lion of Tashkent*, 58–9; Azadaev, *Tashkent vo vtoroi polovine XIX veka*, 83.

[125] 'Spisok Georgievskikh Kavalerov, nagrazhdennykh za otlichiya vo vremya shturma g. Tashkenta 15 iiunya 1865 g.', in Serebrennikov, *Sbornik. 1865 g. Pt. I* Doc.138, 209–10.

'Alimqul, who was notionally to have led this alliance, was safely dead, Chernyaev insisted that the Amir of Bukhara still had designs on the city, and that he had massed 80,000 men and 100 guns at Khujand.[126] While this was fantastical, Chernyaev's position in Tashkent was extremely precarious – with his usual talent for self-dramatisation, he later reminisced that 'The situation of a small force (1,100 men with 85 wounded on its hands) between a just-conquered population of a hundred thousand and a Bukharan army almost as strong [sic] was truly tragic.'[127] For all his rhetoric about the triumph of Russian arms and civilisation Chernyaev badly needed local allies. Accordingly, despite the fact that an Orthodox priest, Father Efim Malov, had led the storming party into battle bearing a cross, and in stark contrast to his later anti-Muslim fulminations in the run-up to the Russo-Turkish War, Chernyaev's policy towards Islam and representatives of Islamic authority in Tashkent was extremely conciliatory.[128] He sought to reassure the population by visiting the main mosque, the bazaar, the hammam and several maktabs, and paid a house-call on the Qazi-Kalan, Ishan Hakim Khwaja – whose son, Muhyi al-Din Khwaja, would become a key intermediary between the Russian colonial regime and local society after he succeeded his father in 1870.[129] Muhammad Salih Tashkandi also refers to Chernyaev 'seeing the bazaars, and sarais, and every alleyway, before coming to the haveli of Ishan Hakim Khwaja the Qazi-Kalan'.[130] This came after he had attended a gathering of the most important 'ulama of Tashkent, including 'Abu'l Qasim Khan Ishan, Domla Saleh Bek, six other Qazis, and four of the city's aqsaqals, presided over by Ishan Hakim Khwaja, which produced a shartnama (agreement) that guaranteed to Muslims the practice of their religion and the Shari'a.[131] This is almost certainly a reference to the well-known proclamation of the 18 June, in which Chernyaev promised not only to respect and uphold Islam and the Shari'a, but to stamp out various immoral practices: 'it is forbidden to drink buza [a type of millet beer], to drink vodka, to play games of hazard or engage in prostitution or sodomy … and you should not engage in sodomy with juveniles (bacha-bozliq), or organise playing on the doira [tambourine] or dances'. This proclamation became widely known in its contemporary Russian translation, with the American Consul Eugene Schuyler devoting

---

[126] Chernyaev to Kryzhanovskii 29/06/1865, in Serebrennikov, Sbornik. 1865 g. Pt. I Doc.154, 238–40.
[127] IISH Archief M. G. Cernjaev Folder 3 Tetrad' No. 4 p. 167.
[128] Bakhtiyar Babadzhanov, 'Rossiiskii General-Konkvistador v Russkom Turkestane: Vzlety i padeniya M. G. Chernyaeva', CIAS Discussion Paper No. 35 (2013), 28–9; Mackenzie, Lion of Tashkent, 61.
[129] Mackenzie, Lion of Tashkent, 61; Sartori, Visions of Justice, 111–13, 142.
[130] 'bazarha va saraiha va kucheha dida ta be houli-yi Hakim Khwaja Qazi Kalan raftani shod', TJT, f. 1a–b.
[131] TJT, f. 1b–2a.

considerable attention to it in his account of his journey through Turkestan in 1871-2.[132] However, it was drafted not by Chernyaev, but by members of the Tashkent *'ulama* acting on his instructions. Bakhtiyar Bababajanov, working with the Chaghatai original, remarks that it is 'something one would expect from a Muslim war leader or ruler who had conquered Tashkent, but never from a Russian general, who within a few years would be "defending the Orthodox faith against Islam" ... nevertheless it was a thoughtful diplomatic move, entirely able to calm popular opinion in a city which had only just been captured and, most importantly, to overcome the confessional fears of Muslims regarding "faith and custom"'.[133] This, rather than a conscious con-tinuation of earlier Russian policies towards Islam, is surely the key to under-standing the alliance Chernyaev forged with the Tashkent *'ulama* in the immediate aftermath of the city's fall.[134] With fewer than 2,000 soldiers and in almost complete ignorance of existing administrative arrangements, he could not control the city by force, and he had just fought and crushed its Khoqandi and Bukharan political leadership. The *'ulama* were the only influ-ential collaborators left, and they saw an opportunity to use Russian power to advance their own agenda, which, as is evident from the proclamation, was not just about maintaining freedom of worship and the existing status of Islam, but advancing social and moral reform.

Although I have not been able to make a full survey of evidence from the Khoqandi side on the campaigns that led up to the fall of Tashkent, certain points seem reasonably clear. Firstly, the belief that a 'natural' boundary would present itself between Aulie-Ata and Turkestan, combined with Russian ignor-ance of the geography of the region, played directly into Chernyaev's hands. He could quite legitimately argue that the orders he had received, which simul-taneously told him to capture Chimkent and not to advance beyond the line of the River Arys, were wholly contradictory, and thus exploit them as he saw fit. It is also clear that Miliutin accepted the geographical logic of Chernyaev's decision to advance beyond the Arys – namely that it was too shallow to constitute a 'natural' frontier, and that in any case military security demanded that the Russians control both banks. Secondly, Russian negotiations with the Khoqandis were not conducted in good faith; there were opportunities in 1864 to draw up a peace treaty that might have been recognised by both sides. While the *Ta'rikh-i 'Aliquli*, the *Ta'rikh-i Shahrukhi*, the *Ta'rikh-i Jadidah-yi*

---

[132] The contemporary shortened Russian translation is in Azadaev, *Tashkent vo vtoroi polovine XIX veka*, 85–6, and it was on this that Eugene Schuyler based his comments in *Turkistan: Notes of a Journey in Russian Turkistan, Khokand, Bukhara, and Kuldja* (London: Sampson, Lowe, Marston, Searle & Rivington, 1876) I, 115–16. See also Sokolov, *Tashkent, Tashkenttsy i Rossii*, 167–8.

[133] Babadzhanov, 'Rossiiskii General-Konkvistador v Russkom Turkestane', 32–3, where the Chaghatai text is translated in full.

[134] Crews, *For Prophet and Tsar*, 242.

Tashkand and the *Kirgizskii rasskaz* all indicate that the Russian advance had severely destabilised the already-turbulent politics of the Khoqand khanate, its leaders had recognised the need to negotiate, but were rebuffed because Russian decisions in Orenburg and St Petersburg were made without reference to them. When Chernyaev was on the spot he entered into direct negotiations, partly perhaps to buy time for his forces to rest and resupply, but he was simultaneously urging on his superiors the danger posed first by Chimkent and then by Tashkent so long as they remained under Khoqandi control. Finally, the move from Muslim to Christian rule was profoundly disruptive to the world-view of Central Asia's literate elites. For all Khoqandi authors the Russians were identified primarily in terms of their faith, either with pejorative epithets (*bi din, kuffar* – unbelievers) or more neutral, archaic terms such as *Nasuranie* ('Nazarenes'), while the Khoqandis themselves were the 'people of Allah' or the 'people of Islam' (*ahl-i Islam*). Mullah Niyaz Khoqandi bemoaned the lack of Muslim unity which had allowed the Russians to conquer the 'people of Islam of *Mawara' al-nahr* ', and this even overcame his distaste for the Qipchaq usurpers who had overthrown the Ming dynasty, as he presented 'Alimqul as a heroic defender of Islam to the last, while 'the darkness of unbelief made the *Dasht-i Qipchaq* into "Tarikistan"' ('the land of shadows' – a pun on 'Turkestan').[135] The Russian conquest meant the end of Central Asia as *Dar al-Islam*, a theme which preoccupied Muhammad Salih Tashkandi in particular, even if in time most of the Central Asian *'ulama* became reconciled to Russian rule, which rarely interfered actively with their faith.[136] Looking back in the early twentieth century, Mullah Muhammad Yunus noted that 'the will of the most High God was that the *vilayat* of Turkistan and Ferghana would be passed into the possession of the emperor', but also recalled how 'Alimqul 'to his last breath inspired the emirs and warriors to *ghazat* and the defence of the fortress' of Tashkent.[137]

As we will see in the following chapter, the fall of Tashkent did not provide the Russians with the 'natural frontier' they desired either. While it solved their immediate supply problems on the Syr-Darya, it also helped to provoke the Amir of Bukhara into declaring war, once again impelled at least in part by the religious agitation that the Russian advance had provoked among the *'ulama*

---

[135] *'Zulmat-i kafir Dasht-i Qipchaq ra Tarikistan kardanid'*, TSh, 199, 268, 274; Bartol'd, 'Tuzemets o russkom zavoevanii', 343, 347. *'Zulmat'* can also be translated as 'oppression'.

[136] See Babadhzanov, *Kokandskoe khanstvo*, 267–8; Bakhtiyar Babajanov, 'Russian Colonial Power in Central Asia as Seen by Local Muslim Intellectuals', in *Looking at the Coloniser* ed. Beate Eschment & Hans Harder (Würzburg: Ergon Verlag, 2004), 75–90; Hisao Komatsu, 'Dar al-Islam under Russian Rule as Understood by Turkestani Muslim Intellectuals', in *Empire, Islam, and Politics* ed. Tomohiko Uyama (Sapporo: Slavic Research Centre, 2007), 3–21.

[137] *TA* trans. 76, text f. 91a.

and the wider population of the emirate. By August 1865 Chernyaev had obtained grudging permission from A. M. Gorchakov to establish a Russian outpost south of Tashkent on the Syr-Darya at Chinaz, and after initial scepticism his superior, Kryzhanovskii, would agree that Tashkent itself could not live from its own resources.[138] The new Turkestan governor, General D. I. Romanovskii (1825–1881), then used similar arguments to justify the capture of Khujand in 1866, and the Russian frontier advanced yet again. Ultimately, of course, the notion that the landscape itself would signal to the Russians the location of a 'natural' frontier where they should halt their advance was a fallacy. Instead it would be determined by diplomatic factors, notably the Empire's relations with Britain, Persia and Afghanistan, which in the 1880s and 1890s led to a final demarcation following the line of the Amu-Darya in the east, and a largely arbitrary, trigonometrically determined boundary in the west. Even then, many Russian officers continued to hanker after the watershed of the Hindu Kush as the truly 'natural' frontier to the Empire's expansion in Central Asia.

[138] Gorchakov to Miliutin 31/08/1865, in Serebrennikov, *Sbornik. 1865 g. Pt. I* Doc.215, 42–4.

6

War with Bukhara, 1866–8

'All'armi, Sarti!'

Emilio Salgari, *Le aquile della steppa* (1905)

In the summer of 1865 it appeared that the Russians had succeeded in their main strategic aim in Central Asia, which was to create a secure new frontier running through a settled grain-producing region, anchored on the trading entrepôt of Tashkent. There were no plans for a further advance beyond Tashkent, and St Petersburg hoped to turn the city into the centre of a puppet khanate, withdrawing most Russian garrisons to the fortresses of the steppe lines. Had they succeeded then the political geography of Central Asia would have remained very different, with Russian rule limited to the steppe region, and Khoqand, Khiva and Bukhara surviving, like Afghanistan, as buffer states between Russian and British territory. Instead this strategy unravelled almost immediately, as war broke out with the Emirate of Bukhara in 1866, leading to the further annexations of Jizzakh and Khujand that year. This was followed by a year and a half's uneasy truce, during which Konstantin Petrovich von Kaufman (1818–1882) was appointed the first Governor-General of what the Russians were now calling 'Turkestan'.[1] In 1868 war with Bukhara broke out again, leading to the capture of the ancient city of Samarkand, and the annexation of the upper portion of the Zarafshan valley.[2] Bukhara became a Russian protectorate in all but name, a status that was formalised after 1885. As James Pickett has argued, the imposition of external boundaries by the Russian empire, and the support it would come to offer to the ruling Manghit dynasty, profoundly transformed the nature of Bukharan statehood, making it more centralised and able to impose its will on outlying regions such as Shahrisabz and Hissar in a way that had never been possible

---

My thanks to James Pickett and Paolo Sartori for their detailed comments on this chapter.

[1] Historically this was the name given to the region of the middle and lower Syr-Darya valley between the Aral Sea and Tashkent – the liminal zone between the steppe (*Dasht-i Qipchaq*) and Transoxiana (*Ma wara' al-nahr*), but it was often applied to the whole of settled Central Asia even before the Russian conquest.

[2] The only up to date account of these campaigns is A.M. Malikov, 'The Russian Conquest of the Bukharan Emirate: Military and Diplomatic Aspects', *CAS* 33/2 (2014), 180–98.

before.[3] In 1866 all this lay in the future – instead the Russians were swallowing Bukharan territory with the same enthusiasm with which in the 1850s and early 1860s they had that of Khoqand.

What drove these further territorial annexations? As with the fall of Tashkent, the idea that the Russian military was fulfilling a 'cotton' agenda set by the Moscow textile industry remains deeply implausible: in fact, throughout the first part of 1865 the military authorities in Orenburg and the other northern steppe fortresses detained all Bukharan merchants and impounded their goods, thus cutting off the supply of low-grade Central Asian cotton to the Nizhny Novgorod fair, something which prompted a petition for their release from the Orenburg merchants.[4] As General Kryzhanovskii's Bashkir translator, Mirsalih Bekchurin, who toured the region with the Orenburg Governor in 1865-6, observed, the temporary spike in cotton prices caused by the American Civil War had already eased by the time the Russians moved south of Tashkent, and an influx of cheap, higher-quality cotton from India and the southern United States meant that the Moscow manufacturers were no longer buying Bukharan cotton, a short-staple variety known as *ghuza* which was in any case unsuited to industrial manufacture.[5] Had the Russians been primarily concerned with cotton they would have invaded the Ferghana valley, the core of the later cotton economy, but at this stage they continued to maintain it as a protectorate, annexing it only after a revolt in 1875, as we shall see in Chapter 8. Nor did the Russians continue to advance because they wished to threaten the British in India either: although, as we have seen, this argument was used tactically by Miliutin in 1863 to convince the more cautious Gorchakov that the uniting of the Siberian and Syr-Darya lines of fortresses was absolutely necessary, it never figured in decision-making during 1866-8.[6] Nor was it purely down to the ambition of 'men on the spot' in Tashkent, although this played a greater role at this stage of the Russian conquest than at any other. In this relatively densely populated region of riverine oases, troops could live off the land in a way that was impossible in steppe or desert.[7] The existence of roads meant that carts (*arba*s) could be used as well as the ubiquitous camel, so that baggage trains were smaller and draught animals fewer, thus facilitating spontaneous

---

[3] James Pickett, 'Written into Submission: Reassessing Sovereignty through a Forgotten Eurasian Dynasty', *AHR* 123/3 (2018), 817–45.

[4] Kryzhanovskii to Miliutin 12/08/1865, in Serebrennikov, *Sbornik. 1865 g. Pt. II*, Doc.196, 14–16.

[5] M. M. Bekchurin, *Turkestanskaya Oblast': Zametki Statskogo Sovetnika Bekchurina* (Kazan: Universitetskaya Tip., 1872), 46.

[6] Miliutin to A. M. Gorchakov 01/?/1863 RGVIA F.483 Op.1 D.62 ll. 198ob–9ob.

[7] D. Ivanov, 'Pod Samarkandom (rasskaz Novichka)', *VS* (1876), No. 1, 181–212 & No. 2, 362–92 makes frequent reference to gifts or purchases of food from the population of Samarkand in 1868.

campaigns.[8] At the same time the telegraph had not yet reached Tashkent, giving local military leaders greater autonomy than they would have after it did so in 1873. In the substantial chapters which he devoted to these campaigns Terent'ev, characteristically, considered the wars of 1866–8 to be caused by Bukharan dishonesty and bad faith, and their refusal to accept Russian control of Tashkent.[9] However, the most fundamental reason was, on the one hand, the Russian inability to understand the degree to which their conquests and campaigns had upset the balance of power between Bukhara and Khoqand and created chronic political instability within both states, and on the other the inability of political and religious elites within Bukhara to appreciate the gravity of the Russian threat and the military hopelessness of resisting it – mutual incomprehension led to severe miscalculations on both sides.

Reading Bukharan sources alongside Russian ones is crucial to explaining what often seem some rather baffling military and political decisions. Although Bukhara was the most powerful of the three Central Asian states in the 1850s and 1860s, for reasons that are unclear its historiography is somewhat sparser than that of Khoqand.[10] Until the 1860s Russia's relations with Bukhara, its principal trading partner in Central Asia, had been better than those with Khiva and Khoqand. Bukhara was cut off from direct rivalry with Russia by territory held by Khiva and Khoqand, and its influence on the steppe and amongst the nomadic peoples who inhabited it was less than that of its rivals. As in Khiva and Khoqand, early mentions of Russian movements in the region in the Bukharan chronicles are mainly second-hand, and only after the Emirate came into direct conflict with Russia in 1866 are there accounts written by eyewitnesses. Two of the most important late-nineteenth-century chronicles were published and translated into Russian in the Soviet period: Mirza 'Abd al-'Azim Sami's (1839–1908) *Ta'rikh-i Salatin-i Manghitiyya*, originally written in Persian *c.* 1907,[11] and Ahmad-i Donish's *Risala ya Mukhtasari az Ta'rikh-i Saltanat-i Khanadan-i Manghitiyya*,

---

[8] M. Lyko, *Ocherk voennykh deistvii 1868 goda v doline Zaryavshana* (St Pb.: Tip. Deputata Udelov, 1871), 46 refers to the ease with which carts could be hired for the 1868 campaign, many of them from inhabitants of Samarkand, the object of the Russian advance.

[9] Terent'ev, *Istoriya zavoevaniya*, I, 322–510.

[10] James Pickett and Kimura Satoru have suggested to me that this may have been because of Bukhara's survival as a protectorate, which meant both that there was less of an urge to memorialise than in defunct Khoqand and that the Amir's court continued to exercise greater control over historical writing. Paolo Sartori has reminded me that Bukhara's importance as a centre of education and lithographic publishing remained undiminished until 1917.

[11] Mirza 'Abd al-'Azim Sami, *Ta'rikh-i Salatin-i Mangitiya: Istoriya Mangitskikh gosudarei pravivshikh v stolitse, Blagorodnoi Bukhare* ed. L. M. Epifanova (Moscow: Vostochnaya Literatura, 1962) (henceforth *TSM*). For a discussion of Sami and his text, see Jo-Ann Gross, 'Historical Memory, Cultural Identity and Change: Mirza 'Abd al-'Aziz Sami's Representation of the Russian Conquest of Bukhara', in *Russia's Orient: Imperial Borderlands and Peoples 1700–1917* ed. Daniel Brower & Edward J. Lazzerini (Bloomington, IN: Indiana University Press, 1997), 203–26.

originally written in Persian *c.* 1878.[12] Both these authors were mentors to the first generation of Bukharan *Jadids*, or Muslim reformers, and critics of the Manghit dynasty:[13] Sami's work is in the form of a 'secret' history to accompany an official chronicle (the *Tuhfa-yi Shahi*)[14] which he had written for the Amir. This helps to explain the favour their texts found in Soviet times, as both authors could be considered staunch enemies of the 'feudal' old order. Donish (also known as Ahmad-i Kalla) was a major figure, much revered in modern-day Tajikistan as the originator, along with Sadriddin 'Aini, of modern Tajik literature.[15] Donish's reminiscences and Sami's two chronicles all contain vivid accounts of the Russian campaign against Bukhara in 1866-8, including the battles at Jizzakh, Irjar, Yangi-Qurghan, Samarkand and the Zirabulak heights. There is also a group of short Persian texts describing more or less the same period preserved in the personal *Fond* of the orientalist Alexander Kuhn (1840-1888) at the St Petersburg branch of the Oriental Institute of the Russian Academy of Sciences, describing events in the Ura-Tepe region, the Upper Zarafshan Valley and Shahrisabz, all of which have been transcribed on Halle's *Zerrspiegel* website.[16] Finally, there are the oral testimonies of two Samarqandis – Kamalbai and Muhammad Sufi – who were caught up in the Russian assault on their city in 1868, recorded by L. Khokhriakova in Kiakhta (where they had been exiled) in the early 1900s. These provide an unusual perspective from below, and give a greater insight into how ordinary Central Asians experienced and viewed the Russian invasion than any other source.[17]

---

[12] Ahmad Makhdum-i Danish, *Risala ya Mukhtasari az Ta'rikh-i Saltanat-i Khanadan-i Manghitiyya* ed. Abulghani Mirzoev (Stalinabad: Nashriyat-i Daulati-i Tajikistan, 1960); *Istoriya Mangitskoi Dinastii*. ed. & trans. I. A. Nadzhafova (Dushanbe: Donish, 1967).

[13] Franz Wennberg, *On The Edge: The Concept of Progress in Bukhara during the Rule of the Later Manghits* (Uppsala: Acta Universitatis Uppsaliensis, 2013), 146–75; Evelin Grassi, 'The Manuscripts of the Works by Ahmad Danish and His Popularity as a Precursor of the Bukharan Jadids', in *Iranian Languages and Literatures of Central Asia: From the 18th Century to the Present* ed. Matteo De Chiara and Evelin Grassi, *Cahiers de Studia Iranica* 57 (2015), 233–58.

[14] 'Abd al-'Azim Bustani Bukharayi, *Tuhfa-yi Shahi* ed. Nadira Jalali (Tehran: Anjuman-i athar va mafakhir-i farhangi, 2010).

[15] This is in particular for his memoirs – Ahmadi Donish, *Novodir ul-vaqoe'* (Dushanbe: Donish 1988) 2 volumes. See further Siamak Adhami, 'Toward a Biography of Ahmad Danesh' (Ph.D. Dissertation, University of California, Los Angeles, 2006).

[16] *Bayan-i ahvalat-i 'Abdullah Bik Avdaichi*, 'Zhizneopisanie Abdully bek, odnogo iz pridvornykh emira Muzafara', AV F.33 Op.1 D.149 (http://zerrspiegel.orientphil.uni-halle.de /t1190.html); *Hikayat-i Damulla 'Abad Akhund*, 'Rasskaz ochevidtsa o sobytiyakh vremen prisoedineniya Srednei Azii k Rossii (o russkikh v Samarkande i Bukhare)', AV F.33 Op.1 D.147 & 184 ff. 8b–14b (http://zerrspiegel.orientphil.uni-halle.de/t21.html); *Ta'rif-i hakemran-i Shahrisabz dar zaman-i piruzi-yi urusiya*, 'Rasskaz o pravitelyakh Shakhrisabza pered russkim zavoevaniem', AV F.33 Op.1 D.142 (http://zerrspiegel .orientphil.uni-halle.de/t1189.html).

[17] L. Kh. Simonova [Khokhriakova], 'Rasskazy ochevidtsev o zavoevanii russkimi Samarkanda i o semidnevnom sidenii', *IV* 97 (1904), No. 9, 844–66.

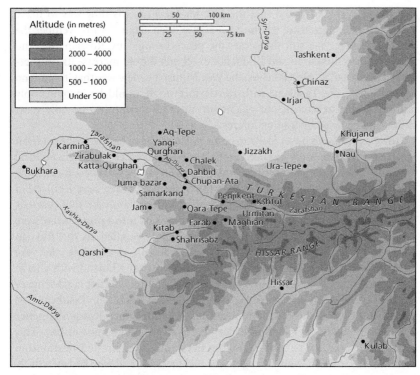

Map 6 The Zarafshan valley

6.1 The Renewal of War with Bukhara

Although, as we have seen, Russian military leaders were already advocating the annexation of Tashkent and the Chirchik valley in the late 1850s, at the time of General Chernyaev's assault on the city in June 1865 the future administration and political geography of the region were still undecided. Tashkent's fall did not necessarily entail outright annexation: once the city had been removed from Khoqandi control, the initial intention was that the Russians would withdraw, having set up a puppet regime that would give preference to Russian trade and, above all, provide the fortresses of the Syr-Darya line with a secure supply of grain.[18] The Russians were aware that prior to the city's capture by 'Umar Khan of Khoqand in 1807, Tashkent had effectively been an independent city-state.[19] *Voennyi Sbornik*'s report on the

---

[18] Azadaev, *Tashkent vo vtoroi polovine XIX veka*, 86–7.
[19] 'Zapiski neizvestnogo litsa: 'Etnograficheskie zametki o Zachuyskom krae (o mestnikh usloviyakh russkoi politiki v Srednei Azii)', Russian State Archive of Ancient Acts (RGADA) F.1385 Op.1 D.661 l. 4 – my thanks to James Pickett for providing me with his notes on this file.

capture of Tashkent noted that the task for the Russians now was to make Tashkent 'self-supporting' (*samostoyatel'nyi*) once again.[20] In November the official message was still the same: the peace brought by Russian rule and freedom from Bukharan and Khoqandi exactions should increase its prosperity and importance. Nevertheless, the War Ministry's view was that 'there is no necessity to unite Tashkent with Russia forever. It would be incomparably more desirable to have as our neighbour an independent, but friendly state, closely linked to us by trading interests.'[21]

However, this was never likely to be an easy task. Even before Tashkent fell it was clear that successive Russian campaigns had caused considerable political turmoil, as Bukhara had taken advantage of Khoqand's weakness to sack the khanate's capital for the second time in thirty years, and then seize Khujand in March 1865.[22] In August Chernyaev reported to Kryzhanovskii that evacuating Russian troops from Tashkent and turning the city into a protectorate were simply not feasible: the Amir of Bukhara had responded to the Russian advance by making his own claims to Tashkent, demanding that the Russians withdraw to Chimkent.[23] He was currently at Khujand with a large force, and could be expected to seize the city if the Russians left it. Chernyaev claimed that, whilst a permanent occupation was essential, Tashkent had proved so easy and cheap to administer that only a minimal Russian presence would be required to maintain order and keep the Bukharans at bay. This could be achieved in part by exploiting the Amir's complicated relationship with Khudoyar Khan, whose daughter he had married, and who had effectively been re-installed in Khoqand as a Russian puppet.[24] In a letter to his close friend Colonel V. A. Poltoratskii in mid August, Chernyaev noted that the Amir of Bukhara, having set off proudly from Samarkand, was now being a little more conciliatory, and that both Khiva and Khoqand had sent missions to Tashkent.[25] Towards the end of August there were clear signs that the Amir was trying to conciliate the Russians, as Chernyaev reported to Poltoratskii his surprise that a demand for the release of two prisoners of war led to the men being sent back to the Russian lines almost immediately, wearing rich *khalats*, and accompanying a Tatar soldier who had deserted from the garrison at Chinaz a few days before.[26]

[20] 'Vzyatie Tashkenta', *VS* (1865), No. 9, 76–7.

[21] 'Izvestiya iz Turkestanskoi Oblasti', *VS* (1865), No. 11, 206–8.

[22] 'Izvestiya iz Turkestanskoi Oblasti', *VS* (1865), No. 7, 70–2.

[23] Ahmad-i Donish claims that the Amir saw the Russian attack on Tashkent primarily as an opportunity to seize territory from Khoqand, and forbade those who wished to help their fellow Muslims resist the Russians from doing so. Donish, *Risala*, 39–40 & *Istoriya*, 42–3.

[24] Chernyaev to Kryzhanovskii 06/08/1865, in Serebrennikov, *Sbornik. 1865 g. Pt. II*, Doc.193, 8.

[25] Chernyaev to V. A. Poltoratskii 15/08/1865, *Ibid.*, Doc.202, 23.

[26] Chernyaev to V. A. Poltoratskii 31/08/1865, *Ibid.*, Doc.213, 39.

While Kryzhanovskii was sceptical about Chernyaev's claims, and clearly at this stage would have preferred to withdraw troops from Tashkent and create a vassal state there, he wrote to Miliutin that he would have to travel to the region himself to assess whether or not it was feasible.[27] Gorchakov gave his reluctant blessing to Chernyaev's creation of fortified garrisons on the Syr-Darya south of Tashkent at Chinaz and Niyaz-Bek, whilst adding piously that, once the situation had stabilised, the Bukharans had withdrawn and (he still fondly hoped) Tashkent had been turned into an independent khanate, they would become surplus to requirements. He still did not see the Russian military presence as permanent, and considered that in future they would merely need to offer 'moral support' to whatever regime they succeeded in establishing in the city.[28] Kryzhanovskii, writing from Fort No. 1 (Kazalinsk) on the road to Tashkent, still appeared to think that it would be possible to create weak vassal states in Khoqand and Tashkent, although he noted the possibility that the Bukharans would have to be severely chastised by the 'heroic Turkestan forces' in order to ensure that they left them alone. He added some observations on Russia's 'civilising mission' in the region which were more than usually patronising, and which give a clear indication of the cultural arrogance with which he proposed to approach negotiations with Central Asia's barbaric rulers:

> I mentioned to the Amir's emissary *inter alia* that I would conduct all relations with the rulers of Central Asia not otherwise than in Russian, and that if the Amir did not have someone who knew Russian well, then I would give him one. It seems to me that the time has come to cease to indulge the morals, language and customs of our weak neighbours, and to start to accustom them a little to our manners and impose our language on them. In Central Asia we must be the only lords, so that with time through our hands may be propagated civilisation and improvement in the lives of those unhappy pariahs of the human race.[29]

The emissary in question was Najmuddin Khwaja, whose embassy to St Petersburg had been detained at Kazalinsk at the end of July.[30] One clear manifestation of Russian arrogance towards Bukhara was that they would not allow Amir Sayyid Muzaffar to negotiate directly with the Tsar as an equal, but only through the military commanders in Orenburg and Tashkent, which was an additional source of tension.[31] The Amir's envoy responded to these overtures by saying that Sayyid Muzaffar (Figure 6.1) would have liked to seal his friendship with Russia in person, but that until he had introduced 'calm

---

[27] Kryzhanovskii to Miliutin 14/08/1865, *Ibid.*, Doc.200, 19–20.
[28] Gorchakov to Miliutin 31/08/1865, *Ibid.*, Doc.215, 42–4.
[29] Kryzhanovskii to Stremoukhov 03/09/1865, *Ibid.*, Doc.218, 48.
[30] Malikov, 'Russian Conquest', 184.
[31] Terent'ev, *Istoriya zavoevaniya*, I, 324.

MOZAFFAR-EDDIN, AMIR OF BUKHARA.

Figure 6.1 Amir Sayyid Muzaffar of Bukhara (Schuyler, *Turkistan* II, 83)

and quiet' to Shahrisabz, Hissar, Kulab and Khoqand, 'where there have been considerable disturbances', this was impossible, and that he was compelled to send a representative.[32]

Local accounts suggest that, as had happened with Khoqand, the Russian advance had caused considerable turmoil in the internal politics of Bukhara, prompting local governors and power-brokers to assert their independence from the capital. Apart from Shahrisabz and Hissar, areas which had long defied

---

[32] Sudur Najmuddin Khwaja Muhammad Amin Khojin to Kryzhanovskii trans. from the Persian by Bekchurin 03/09/1865, in Serebrennikov, *Sbornik. 1865 g. Pt. II*, Doc.219 2nd Enclosure, 52.

Bukharan control, this instability was particularly marked in the region around Khujand and Ura-Tepe, which had been annexed from Khoqand only a few months before, and where the local ruler, 'Abd al-Ghafar Bek, had begun raiding what the Russians considered to be their territory. Terent'ev claimed that this was a cunning campaign by the Amir to harass the Russians and starve Tashkent while disclaiming responsibility.[33] It seems much more likely that the Amir was genuinely unable to exert control, Sami noting of 'Abd al-Ghafar Bek that 'he submitted neither to the Khan of Khoqand nor to the state of Bukhara.'[34] On the 13 September Chernyaev sent a small force under Lt-Col. Pistolkors beyond the Chirchik to quell these depredations and secure territory which, as *Voennyi Sbornik* put it, was vital to the productivity of Tashkent, and where many of the city's inhabitants owned land, but the Russians were still unable to stabilise their frontier.[35]

By the autumn of 1865 Russian official opinion began to shift in favour of the outright annexation of Tashkent.[36] Kryzhanovskii loathed Chernyaev, and was always inclined to believe the opposite of whatever the general told him. Nevertheless, after touring the region, he reported to Gorchakov that, whilst any further conquests should be prevented, Tashkent itself would need a permanent garrison, and should become part of the empire:

> Tashkent really cannot live from its own resources. It obtains all its meat from the north from the nomadic Kirgiz, our subjects, and all its bread from the south, and a little from the north-west, from the arable farming Kirgiz of the Qurama tribe, who live in the valley of the Chirchik and along the whole expanse as far as the river Syr-Darya. In exchange for these Tashkent carried out trade both in own products and in others, and this is so firm and lively that even the Asiatic administration and plundering of the khans, amirs and Alimqul from Ferghana was unable to kill it off completely.
>
> Having considered all the above, we come to the choice of how we can best direct progress towards aims that will be worthy of Russia? Is it essential for this to conquer Tashkent, Khujand, Namangan, Khoqand and others and thus endlessly expand the frontiers of the Empire? In my opinion, there is nothing essential about this. In my opinion the best outcome would be achieved if we were to enclose our frontier with independent, but weak states, closely linked to us through trading interests; but in order that this state should be truly independent of Asiatic rulers and trade, it is absolutely necessary to guarantee it against the Khan

---

[33] Terent'ev, *Istoriya zavoevaniya*, I, 325.

[34] 'na be Khan-i Khuqand ita'at dasht va na be daulat-i Bukhara enqiyad mikard', in Sami, *Tuhfa-yi Shahi*, 143; in this official history Sami then goes on to assert that Amir Sayyid Muzaffar later brought him to heel, which, as we shall see, was not the case.

[35] 'Izvestiya iz Turkestanskoi Oblasti', *VS* (1865), No. 11, 206; Terent'ev, *Istoriya zavoevaniya*, I, 325–6.

[36] Terent'ev, *Istoriya zavoevaniya*, I, 327.

of Khoqand and the Amir of Bukhara, and such a guarantee can only be achieved by leaving Russian garrisons in certain points of the new country.

In Asia the strength and sacredness of agreements do not exist, here almost every day the outward relations of one to another can change, and it is sometimes difficult to distinguish who is allied to whom and who is an enemy, here only force, only weapons can be reliable and constant, in Asia the *ultima ratio* – the cannon – is not the last, but the only instrument of a healthy policy. If Tashkent is announced to be an independent city and our forces are withdrawn to the [Syr-Darya] line, then the Uzbeks who live in the city will soon begin to stir, a party will form in favour of the Amir, and even before the latter appears with his forces the town will become Bukharan.[37]

Kryzhanovskii's conviction that the Central Asian states were not amenable to the ordinary niceties of diplomacy and negotiation is clear. He wrote that an evacuation of Tashkent would lead to a renewed outbreak of war, and necessitate a further assault on the city, leaving the Russians back where they had started, 'but without our current moral influence, which would be badly shaken by our retreat if, having given our word to the Tashkandis when they submitted to our power, we gave them back into the hands of the local rulers'. Kryzhanovskii concluded by saying that he had instead announced to the Tashkandis that the city would be permitted to retain a degree of independence, but with Russian garrisons located at strategic points.[38] He was also deeply suspicious of the city's religious elites, and their claims to political authority:

> Taking advantage of our mistaken belief in the importance of the clergy, which had taken root in the immediate aftermath of the conquest, The *Qazi-Kalan* naturally found it very convenient not to sow seeds of doubt in the minds of the conquerors, and passing himself off as the head of the clergy, took for himself from those very conquerors powers to which he was in no way entitled. In order to strengthen his position still further in 1865, when the chief officer of the region [Chernyaev] was in Tashkent, the *Qazi-Kalan* composed an address requesting Russian citizenship, but accompanied by conditions which would have placed the entire region in dependence on him personally, and on the entire clergy; this address could not in any way be accepted by our government.[39]

As we have seen in the previous chapter, in the aftermath of Tashkent's capture the *'ulama* had taken full advantage of Chernyaev's desperate need for local

[37] Kryzhanovskii to Dolgorukov 23/10/1865 AVPRI F.133 Op.469 D.121 1865, 'Orenbourg, G^e Kryjanovsky', ll. 4ob–5ob.
[38] Kryzhanovskii to Dolgorukov 23/10/1865 AVPRI F.133 Op.469 D.121 1865 ll. 5ob–6ob.
[39] Annual Report of the Orenburg Governor-General to Alexander II, March 1866–February 1867 GARF F.678 Op.1 D.622 l. 59.

figures he could negotiate with to strengthen their authority in the city. Quite apart from Kryzhanovskii's misgivings, granting political control to a *Qazi-Kalan* to rule the city would have been a radical break with local precedent, and there did not appear to be any other credible candidates. Although it was only in June 1866 that Gorchakov would finally accept that the plan to turn Tashkent into an independent khanate had to be abandoned, and only at the end of August of that year that its inhabitants would be informed by proclamation that they were now Russian subjects, in effect the decision had been clear six months previously.[40] A new Turkestan *oblast'* (province) was created with Chernyaev at its head, but it was still subordinated to Kryzhanovskii in Orenburg.

Thus Chernyaev would achieve his initial object of a permanent annexation of Tashkent, but he did not consider this to be sufficient. In his eyes Bukhara was still dangerously independent, and whilst Khoqand had been greatly weakened by the Russian conquest, it was likely either to fall under Bukharan influence, or else to fragment and become a source of Muslim resistance to the Russians, analogous to that which he had encountered in the Caucasus earlier in his career:

> Khoqand as an independent dominion already does not exist [...] – it would suffice for us to build a fortification at Khujand and at Namangan in order for it all to fall into our hands.[41]

In the same letter to his friend Poltoratskii he added that it was essential for the Russians to keep the British on the other side of the Hindu Kush, 'as otherwise we will exchange roles: instead of us threatening the position of the British in India, we ourselves will find out position in Central Asia threatened', whilst he claimed there were rumours that the Amir of Bukhara had already been in communication with the British.[42] Meanwhile Chernyaev's mother chose this moment of high tension to suggest a change of scene:

> And you, *très cher ami*, could you not change your service from Tashkent to that of Governor of Taganrog? which will be the best province of this country and which should be declared after the New Year? You could rest after all your fatigues and efforts. If war is declared somewhere and you want to take part you would be free to do so. But it seems to me that you have already worked and suffered enough for your Fatherland. You must now think of your precious health, and conserve it for the one you have chosen as your companion and see that her days flow with good fortune

---

[40] Gorchakov to Kryzhanovskii 22/06/1866, in Serebrennikov, *Sbornik. 1866 g. Pt. I*, Doc.173, 304–5; Kryzhanovskii to Miliutin 31/08/1866, in Serebrennikov, *Sbornik. 1866 g. Pt. II*, Doc.215, 47–8.

[41] Chernyaev to V. A. Poltoratskii 20/12/1865 RGIM OPI F.208 Op.1 D.5 l. 35*ob*.

[42] Chernyaev to V. A. Poltoratskii 20/12/1865 RGIM OPI F.208 Op.1 D.5 l. 35*ob*.

and joy. What good fortune would it be for us, *cher ami*, if you were the Governor of Taganrog. We could see you often . . .[43]

Sadly Chernyaev's reply to this tender maternal missive does not survive, though it seems likely that he set an even higher value on the services he had rendered to Russia than his mother did. Certainly a man of his ambition was not yet ready to yield the prospect of further military laurels in Turkestan for a soft billet in Taganrog. In January 1866 Chernyaev's fears of Bukharan aggression appeared to be confirmed: the embassy which he had despatched there in November, led by Court Counsellor Struve and A. Tatarinov, had been detained, and the Bukharans were preparing for war. He wrote a characteristically melodramatic note to his fiancée, announcing the resumption of hostilities:

> The Amir of Bukhara has detained my embassy charged with negotiations with him, and I have no means left other than the bayonet to bring him to reason. I cannot predict the outcome of this new struggle, any more than the time of my departure from here.
>
> > My love will be my guide,
> > I am yours to my last sigh.
>
> > > > M. Tcherniaeff[44]

6.2   Bukharan Bravado

Why had the Bukharans indulged in such a provocation? On one level it is easy enough to comprehend – Najmuddin Khwaja's embassy had been detained at Kazalinsk from July to November until Kryzhanovskii's arrival there, and the Bukharans were responding in kind. Chernyaev's detention of 138 Bukharan merchants was intended to bring the Bukharans to the negotiating table, and

---

[43] 'Et toi, très cher ami, ne pourrais-tu pas changer ton service de Tachkente à celui de Gouverneur à Tanganrok [*sic*] qui sera le meilleur Gouvernement de ces pays et qui doit après le nouvel an être déclaré? Tu pourrais te reposer de toutes tes fatigues et peines. Si la guerre se déclarait, quelque part et que tu veuilles y prendre part tu serais libre. Mais il me semble que tu as assez travaillé et souffert pour ta Patrie. Tu dois à présent penser à ta précieuse sante, et la conserver pour celle que tu choisis pour amie et tacher de lui faire couler les jours dans le bonheur et la joie. Quel bonheur, cher ami, serait pour nous si tu étais le Gouverneur de Tanganrok. Nous pourrions te voir souvent . . .', Aimée Esther Charlotte Chernyaeva (née Lecuyer) to M. G. Chernyaev, 10/12/1865 IISH Archief M. G. Cernjaev Folder 17.

[44] 'L'Emir de Bokhara retient mon ambassade chargée de pourparlers avec lui et il ne me reste d'autres moyens que la bayonnette pour le ramener à la raison. Je ne peux prévoir la fin de cette nouvelle lutte, ainsi que fixer le temps de mon départ d'ici. Mon amour sera mon guide. Je suis à Vous jusqu'à mon dernier soupir.' M. G. Chernyaev to A. A. Vul'fert 14/01/1866 RGVIA F.726 Op.1 D.74 l. 7.

had perhaps been modelled on Perovskii's tactic against Khiva thirty years earlier. Terent'ev considered it to be a clear own goal which needlessly antagonised the Bukharans and, as we have seen, actually damaged Russian commercial interests by cutting off the flow of raw cotton to Russian markets.[45] However, there are also indications that the Amir was unable to control events. Sami's account of the imprisonment of the Russian embassy emphasises the role played by the *'ulama* of Bukhara in instigating it, but he reserves his strongest criticism for what he calls the *ghulaman* (slaves) – i.e. the low-born Shi'i officials – also known as *mahram* – with whom Amir Muzaffar had surrounded himself:

> When [the amir] arrived in Samarkand, Governor Kaufman [*sic* – Chernyaev was still the head of Turkestan Province at this point] wrote him a letter with expressions of friendship, advising him of the taking of Tashkent, and sent the letter with one Chahar Laila Tura, whom he made his envoy. When the ambassador of the Governor came to the Amir, and gave him the letter with verbal communications, they replied to him with accommodations and according to the laws of civilized governments tried to [show] him respect. But after some time, at the instigation and incitement of the dull-witted, fanatical [*ta'asib*] malevolent and evil-intentioned slaves [*ghulaman*] they arrested the Russian ambassador, giving voice to their hostility and enmity towards Russia and began to prepare for resistance. At this time occurred the revolt [*balwa*][46] of the mullahs and students [of the Bukharan madrasas]. The story of this is as follows. The *Ra'is* of Bukhara, Ishan Baqa Khwaja Sadr, for the protection of Islam [*az ru-yi himayat-i Islam*] and from his natural energy was not happy with friendly relations with the Christians, and strove for holy war [*ghazat*]. Some zealous students also considered it necessary to join with this high personage and incited other students. The mullahs of all the madrasas rose up at the same time and called for Jihad [*sala jihad*]. Mulla Akram Khwaja, a Khoqand *'alim*, the best known in the city and the town for the beauty of his writing and other dignities, with some other people wrote a *fatwa* and obliged all Muslims to engage in holy war. He compelled the *'ulama*, willingly and unwillingly to affix their seals to this *fatwa*. A numerous crowd of mullahs and other partisans of holy war, having received in the presence of witnesses the legal *rivayat* [i.e. the *fatwa*], came to the Registan, threw themselves against the gate of the *Arg* [citadel], and exclaimed: 'Al-Jihad, al-Jihad'.[47]

The account given by Sami in his official *Tuhfa-yi Shahi* also asserts that the *'ulama* played a prominent role in inflaming the sentiments of the crowd, and

---

[45] Terent'ev, *Istoriya zavoevaniya*, I, 323, 330.
[46] This term is rare in Central Asian Persian, but is used in Urdu and Indian Persian for the Indian 'Mutiny' of 1857 – it is just possible this was the association Sami intended. My thanks to James Pickett for this insight.
[47] *TSM* text ff. 68a–b, trans. 60–1.

in many places uses very similar language.[48] On the basis of this account, it seems very possible that the Amir was not able to control either the response of the Bukharan 'ulama to the approach of an infidel army to what was a major centre of Islamic learning, or popular hostility to the Russians among his subjects.

The evidence from Russian sources is ambivalent: Tatarinov's captivity memoir describes an initial meeting with the Amir at which, after several days cooling their heels, the Russian delegation had not been allowed to exchange a single word with the Bukharan ruler. Tatarinov blamed Sayyid Muzaffar himself for deliberately stirring up the 'fanaticism' of the population, but the evidence of his own account suggests that the large Russian delegation, which included several armed Cossacks, attracted considerable popular hostility from the crowds that accompanied them as they travelled. Although they were unable either to see the Amir or communicate with Tashkent, at no stage during the first two months of their captivity, under house arrest in Bukhara, do they seem to have been ill-treated or in any real danger: indeed, they were presented with cigars and a bottle of wine to celebrate Christmas, and at one point the Amir seems to have tried to release them to return to Tashkent.[49] This changed when Chernyaev's forces moved on Jizzakh, which seems to have emboldened and infuriated the anti-Russian party in Bukhara, and in early February the embassy and its escort were disarmed in a violent scuffle – even at this stage there were signs that Bukharan officials were actually trying to protect them from the mob, and had brought them to Samarkand as a preliminary to releasing them.[50] When Chernyaev's forces retreated from Jizzakh on the 10 February their captivity was instead prolonged, this time in the much less agreeable conditions of the prison inside the Samarkand citadel.[51] In his official report after the embassy's release Struve described Bukharan counsels as divided, stating that the merchants and a portion of the Uzbek nobility urged the Amir to make peace with the Russians, but that 'the party of war carried all before it', urging instead an immediate attack on Tashkent. He claimed that one of the foremost voices in the agitation was a 'renegade Tatar', a former watchmaker from Orenburg, whom he described as literate, intelligent and possessing a powerful influence over the Amir.[52] Quite probably this reflects no more than common Russian prejudices about 'sly' and 'fanatical' Tatars – Tatarinov, clearly referring to the same individual (whose name was 'Ali Muhammad Qarataev, originally from Saratov), writes

[48] Sami, *Tuhfa-yi Shahi*, 172–3.
[49] A. Tatarinov, *Semimesyachnyi plen v Bukharii* (St Pb.: Izd. M. O. Vol'fa, 1867), 20–45.
[50] *Ibid.*, 49–52, 56–8.
[51] *Ibid.*, 59, 63–4.
[52] Struve to Stremoukhov 07/07/1866, in Serebrennikov, *Sbornik. 1866 g. Pt. I*, Doc.161, 282.

that he had strongly advised the Amir *not* to quarrel with Russia, and was instrumental in arranging their release after the battle of Irjar.[53]

Donish's *Risala* also has a somewhat different emphasis on the reasons for Bukharan intransigence. While he poured scorn on the agitation of the *'ulama* for a holy war (noting particularly the iniquity of their claim that it was the responsibility of all able-bodied males to fight, and not just professional soldiers), Donish's account of Sayyid Muzaffar's negotiations with the Russians placed greater stress on the Amir's delusions of strength. He wrote that Sayyid Muzaffar, emboldened by an easy victory over Khoqand, boasted that he could ignore Tashkent and march directly on Moscow:

> because he was convinced that the Russian government – was like the rulers of *Ma wara' al-nahr*, and as he had enjoyed victory over them, so he reasoned that he would have victory over the Russians as well [...] As for the Amir, being by nature stupid and narrow-minded, he was unable to comprehend the difference between governments.[54]

Donish's loathing for the Manghits clearly led him to exaggerate, and he was also exhibiting a certain amount of wisdom after the event, as his own knowledge of Russia's power stemmed from a later journey to St Petersburg. Tatarinov wrote that the Bukharans recognised clearly that the struggle with Russia was an unequal one.[55] Nevertheless, there may have been a grain of truth in Donish's description of Sayyid Muzaffar's very circumscribed world-view. In 1813 the Indo-Bukharan traveller Mir 'Izzatullah had written that 'The people of this region [Central Asia] have not seen a war of the great powers for nearly a hundred years, and by warfare (*kar-i sipahgari*) they understand nothing but assault and pillage (*takht u taz*).'[56] The three Central Asian khanates had not faced attack by a stronger neighbouring power since Nadir Shah's invasion in the 1740s, when Bukhara had been utterly defeated.[57] For more than 100 years since then they had become accustomed to measuring

---

[53] Tatarinov, *Semimesyachnyi plen*, 80–1, 103–6; Malikov, 'Russian Conquest', 185.

[54] '*In sukhun az an jihat gufta, ki daulat-i Rus-ra hamchu hukum-i daulat-i Ma wara' al-nahr e'tiqad karda bud, va bar anha chun ghalaba namud, guman kard ki ba urus niz ghalib bashad* [...] *chun balahat o safahat dar tinat-i amir jibbili bud, tashkhis-i mian-i daulatain natavanest kard*', Donish, *Risala*, 40–1 & *Istoriya*, 43–4.

[55] Tatarinov, *Semimesyachnyi plen*, 87.

[56] Holzwarth, 'Bukharan Armies and Uzbek Military Power', 316, quoting the Persian MS in the British Library. It can also be found in Mir 'Izzatullah, *Travels in Central Asia by Meer Izzat-Oollah in the years 1812–13* trans. Capt. P. D. Henderson (Calcutta: Foreign Department Press, 1872), 61. On Mir 'Izzatullah's journey see Maria Szuppe, 'En quête de chevaux turkmènes: Le journal de voyage de Mir 'Izzatullah de Delhi à Boukhara en 1812–1813', in *CAC*. Vols. 1–2. *Asie Centrale–l'Inde: Routes du commerce et des idées* (Tashkent & Aix-en-Provence: IFEAC, Éditions De Boccard, 1996), 91–113.

[57] Holzwarth, 'The Uzbek State'; Sela, *Legendary Biographies*, 117–33; Levi, *Rise of Khoqand*, 48.

their strength against each other, and Bukhara had usually emerged as the strongest, both it and Khoqand having done much to modernise their armed forces with disciplined infantry formations and artillery trained by Anglo-Indian and Persian adventurers. For a century and a half, since the Bekovich-Cherkassky expedition of 1717, geography had been an effective barrier against military incursions from the north. In principle, Russia's series of shattering victories over Khoqand since 1853 should have alerted the Bukharans (and indeed the Khivans) to the Russian threat, but instead they seem to have seen it primarily as an opportunity to seize territory at their neighbour's expense. This turned out to be a grave miscalculation.

What does seem clear is that Bukharan counsels were divided – and this is probably what accounts for the initial detention of the Russian embassy in Bukhara in November–December 1866: nobody could decide what to say to them. Meanwhile, the fact that no word was received from them in Tashkent for two months suggested to Chernyaev that they had been imprisoned with hostile intent, and gave him the pretext for advancing on Jizzakh, which in turn strengthened the hand of those in Bukhara advocating war with Russia. Even Donish was prepared to admit that with the fall of Tashkent the Amir had realised the importance of defending Jizzakh, which was the key to the pass which led to Samarkand, and he writes that 100,000 *tanga*s had been spent strengthening and improving the defences.[58] It was perhaps owing to this that Chernyaev decided the double walls of the city were too formidable to tackle with the small force at his disposal and retreated to Tashkent on the 11 February. Terent'ev defended Chernyaev's decision, writing that had an assault failed the consequences would have been disastrous, while had it succeeded it would have cost the lives of the envoys.[59] Unknown to Chernyaev, three days earlier, on the 8 February, Miliutin had issued orders for his recall to St Petersburg, writing that his explanations regarding the Bukharan embassy and the administration of the Tashkent territory were 'incomplete and unsatisfactory', which was a prelude to his dismissal.[60] Chernyaev himself, characteristically, would later claim that this was entirely because of Kryzhanovskii's jealousy at being denied a share in the glory of capturing Tashkent, and Chernyaev's failure to organise a suitable set of laurels for him in an expedition against Khoqand.[61] Chernyaev's replacement, Major-General D. I. Romanovskii (1825–1881), did his best to imply that Chernyaev's military failure at Jizzakh was to blame, in part to confer additional lustre on his own subsequent victory. As Terent'ev pointed out, Chernyaev's dismissal

[58] Donish, *Risala*, 30 & *Istoriya*, 52.
[59] Terent'ev, *Istoriya zavoevaniya*, I, 332.
[60] Miliutin to Kryzhanovskii 08/02/1866, in Serebrennikov, *Sbornik. 1866 g. Pt. I*, Doc.33, 52–3.
[61] 'Avtobiografija M. G. Cernjaeva', IISH Archief M. G. Cernjaev Folder 5 pp. 13–15.

came about largely because of Kryzhanovskii's hostile reports on the state of Turkestan's administration, not because of the retreat from Jizzakh, which happened after the decision to recall him had been taken.[62] Perhaps, quite simply, Miliutin's patience with this wayward subordinate had finally run out.

It is significant that neither Donish nor Sami chose to mention that the Russians retreated from Jizzakh in early February 1866, and instead in both cases their narratives jump straight to the Bukharan defeat at Irjar in May 1866 (Sami is doubly inaccurate in describing the Russian forces as despatched by von Kaufman and led by Chernyaev). Donish also describes the Russian forces proceeding immediately from Jizzakh to attack Samarkand, whereas in fact after taking Jizzakh the Russian advance halted again for almost eighteen months. This underlines the fact that both authors were intent on writing a chronicle of unremitting disaster caused by Manghit ineptitude: hostility to the dynasty, rather than to the Russians, is by far the dominant sentiment of their work.[63]

The detention of the ambassadors was not the only grievance which the Russians felt they had against the Bukharans. Minor raids by 'shaiki' continued throughout late February and March, prompting punitive expeditions in return, the most important of which, on the 6 April, was directed against a force commanded by Kenesary's son, Sadiq.[64] In his report on military activities in Central Asia for April 1866, Romanovskii's chief of staff, Colonel Count Vorontsov-Dashkov, noted that small bands of what he referred to as *barantovshchiki* were conducting constant small raids in the environs of Tashkent, and along the notional frontier near Chinaz, and had overwhelmed an outlying picket of *jigits* at Niyaz-bek. This prompted Romanovskii to organise a punitive expedition of 150 men under Staff-Captain Grebenkin on the 26 April.[65] Writing to Miliutin from Chinaz a month later, after the battle of Irjar and the fall of Khujand, Vorontsov-Dashkov would claim that the failure of the Russians to avenge immediately their reverse at Jizzakh had emboldened the Amir, to the extent that he had sent a force under Rustam Bek well across the Syr-Darya to raid Russian territory.[66] Romanovskii, meanwhile, considered that Bukharan interference on Russian territory went beyond mere raiding, and extended to the fomenting of anti-Russian feeling in Tashkent:

> The disturbances and agitation in our Trans-Chirchik region were not only a consequence of the appearance of the party of the Amir and

[62] Terent'ev, *Istoriya zavoevaniya*, I, 335; Romanovskii, *Zametki po sredneaziatskomu vopros*, 36–7.

[63] *TSM* text ff. 68b–9a, trans. 62–3; Donish, *Risala*, 30–2; *Istoriya*, 52–3.

[64] Terent'ev, *Istoriya zavoevaniya*, I, 339–43.

[65] 'Zhurnal voennykh deistvii i proisshestvii na sredne-aziatskikh granitsakh s 10 aprelya po 1 maya 1866 g.', in Serebrennikov, *Sbornik. 1866 g. Pt. I*, Doc.116, 199–200.

[66] Vorontsov-Dashkov to Miliutin 06/06/1866, *Ibid.*, Doc.159, 267–8.

represented the result of a broader conspiracy, the threads of which had found themselves a place in Tashkent itself. Thank God that it was granted to us to prevent this conspiracy in time.[67]

Whether there was truly a 'conspiracy' is highly doubtful. The accompanying note from Major Serov (the hero of the battle of Iqan) alleged that the Amir and Rustam Bek had somehow contrived to spread rumours across Tashkent that they would soon attack the city, and Rustam Bek himself did appear with a significant force near Parkent, about 17 *versts* from Tashkent. Serov believed that he had sent a spy into the city with a letter from the Amir, who had been captured and handed over to Serov thanks to the good services of a Tatar, called Sharafi, and two Tashkandis who favoured the Russians, Sayyid 'Azim and his brother Sayyid Qasim.[68] The Sayyid 'Azim mentioned here, described as someone who, with his brother, had rendered signal service to the Russians 'not for the first time', is surely the well-known Sayyid 'Azim Bai, one of Tashkent's richest merchants, who by throwing in his lot with the conquerors from the very beginning secured for himself a position of great privilege and influence under the colonial regime.[69] Under these circumstances, there is every chance that this 'conspiracy' was a fiction concocted by these men in order that their apparent unmasking of it could raise their credit with the Russians still further – in January 1868, indeed, Sayyid Qasim would accuse his brother of plotting with Khudoyar Khan of Khoqand against the Russians.[70] Either way, it can only have added to the atmosphere of mutual suspicion in which Russo-Bukharan relations were conducted.

6.3   The Battle of Irjar and Its Aftermath

The upshot of these disagreements and misunderstandings was the crushing defeat of the Bukharans at the battle of Irjar on 8 May 1866. With characteristic ambiguity, the instructions Romanovskii received on his appointment urged him to establish friendly trading relations with Bukhara and avoid further territorial annexations, but also reminded him that 'the Asiatic only respects force' and that the slightest sign of indecision or retreat would be taken as weakness. Romanovskii considered that Chernyaev's retreat from Jizzakh was already in danger of damaging Russian prestige, and that Chernyaev himself had told him that, despite the unbroken series of Russian victories in Central Asia since 1853, the 'half-savage' people still needed to be educated in the

---

[67]   Romanovskii to Kryzhanovskii 30/05/1866, *Ibid.*, Doc.149, 241.

[68]   Serov to Romanovskii 10/05/1866, *Ibid.*, Doc.149 Pril.I, 248.

[69]   Terent'ev, *Istoriya zavoevaniya*, I, 327; on Sayyid 'Azim Bai see Sahadeo, *Russian Colonial Society*, 20–1.

[70]   The investigating officer, Alexander Khoroshkhin, thought that this was probably an attempt to gain control of Sayyid 'Azim's property. Khoroshkhin to Serov 25/01/1868 TsGARUz F.I-1 Op.29 D.11a ll. 5–8.

superiority of Russian arms.[71] Unsurprisingly, Romanovskii interpreted this as requiring an advance to dislodge the force which the Amir had stationed in the Irjar depression near one of the crossings of the Syr-Darya.[72] In the long report which he sent to Kryzhanovskii three days after the battle, which was subsequently viewed and approved by the Tsar, Romanovskii wrote that, ever since the Amir had constructed a crossing over the Syr-Darya at Irjar in late March, and based his army on either side of the river there, it had been clear that decisive action on the battlefield would be needed to dislodge him and make him see sense. It was only a shortage of men and money which had delayed the assault by a month. On the 7 May Romanovskii advanced from Chinaz, with 14 companies of infantry, 5 *sotnyas* of Cossacks and 20 guns and rockets (around 3,000 men in all), against a force of Bukharans which his spies claimed numbered up to 100,000, but which Romanovskii himself estimated at about 5,000 *sarbaz* infantry and up to 35,000 cavalry levies.[73] The usual commissariat problems were partly obviated, as Romanovskii noted, because he was able to rely on the steamer *Perovskii*, which carried many of the supplies his men needed up the Syr-Darya from Chinaz. The battle itself was perhaps the most one-sided of the entire conquest. Romanovskii described successive waves of Bukharan cavalry dashing themselves pointlessly against the volley fire of his infantry whilst suffering terribly under artillery bombardment. The Russians then attacked in two infantry columns, one led by Abramov and the other by Pistolkors, until the Bukharans broke in panic, pursued by the Ural Cossacks.[74] The accounts that reached Tatarinov in captivity suggested that the battle had been 'comic' in its one-sidedness, with a sudden wind blowing dust in the Bukharans' eyes as the Russians attacked, while 10,000 troops from Shahrisabz (surely an exaggeration) had abandoned the field almost immediately.[75] Romanovskii's official despatch to the military forces of the Turkestan *oblast'* in the aftermath of the battle claimed that over 1,000 Bukharan corpses had been left behind on the field of battle, together with their entire artillery park and two camps full of booty, whilst the Russians had suffered only one dead and ten wounded.[76] Donish's account was scathing:

> Willy-nilly [*char o nachar*] there occurred a clash, like that at Siffin [a reference to the battle between 'Ali and Mu'awiya]. The sounds of trumpets and drums rang out. The Russian forces consisted of one and a half or two thousand men. They came forward like a wall of steel [*hamchu divar-i*

[71] Romanovskii, *Zametki po sredneaziatskomu voprosu*, 38–41.
[72] Ibid., 58; Malikov, 'Russian Conquest', 185.
[73] Romanovskii, *Zametki po sredneaziatskomu voprosu*, 61.
[74] Romanovskii to Kryzhanovskii 11/05/1866, in Serebrennikov, *Sbornik. 1866 g. Pt. I*, Doc.130, 215–23; Terent'ev, *Istoriya zavoevaniya*, I, 345–9.
[75] Tatarinov, *Semimesyachnyi plen*, 97–8.
[76] 'Prikaz po voiskam Turkest. Oblasti', 9/05/1866, in Serebrennikov, *Sbornik. 1866 g. Pt. I*, Doc.128, 213.

ahanin miamadand]. With each step the *ghazis* of our forces gave ground
to them more and more, in order to bring the Russians onto soft ground
and, encircling them, take them prisoner. There where the Amir had
halted rose a ceremonial pavilion [*sarparda-yi ikhlal*]. From it to the
field of battle it was half a *farsang*, so the sound of the kettledrums reached
it. The Amir sat in the shade of the tent engaged in a game of chess.
A crowd of readers sang songs and *ghazals* [*qawwalan qawwal va ghazal
miguftand*]. From his throne the Amir tapped his leg in time to the sound
of the drums. Occasionally he ordered a messenger to be sent to Salim *Bii*,
the chief of artillery and to the commander of the forces Shir ʻAli [Inaq]
with an order to secure the Russian treasury, that it might not fall into the
hands of *naukars* and that they might not plunder it and might not kill
many Russians, but take them alive, so they could be included in the ranks
of *sarbaz*es, and fulfil military service. And at the rear of the troops Yahya
Khwaja-i Turkman, who bore the title of *Akhund*, and who was exceptional for his stupidity [*safih*], threw the end of his turban over his back
and, holding in his hands a large sheet [of paper], read about the superiority of holy war and called for steadfastness. But at that time the
Russians, beginning their attack, seized the cannon and blasted the fight-
ers for the faith of Islam two or three times with grape-shot. It was as if
everyone had just been waiting for the possibility of flight, and preferred
flight to steadfastness. The first to run was Yahya Akhund, discarding his
turban. Then he reported to his Highness that the forces had wavered and
gave himself up to flight. The Amir in complete disarray jumped onto an
unsaddled horse, without succeeding in putting on his *khalat* or putting
his turban on his head. Thus, abandoning chess, he mounted a horse and
scuttled off. [*hamchonin az sar-i shatranj bar khaste bala-yi zin {bar}
neshast va asb merond*].[77]

He further noted that many of the Uzbek tribes had refused to fight with the
Amir's forces, as they were led by Shiʻi slave commanders who had been the
Amir's schoolmates, and they considered it shameful to serve under them.[78]
He was referring both to Shir ʻAli Inaq,[79] later to be an unpopular governor of
Samarkand, and to Yaqub Bek, the governor of Jizzakh, whom Tatarinov notes
was a Persian slave raised to the dignity of Bek after Amir Nasrullah had noted
his gifts as a boy at court.[80] Hostility to Shi'ism is a consistent theme in
Donish's work, prompted not just by sectarian prejudice but by the fact that
since the early nineteenth century the Manghit dynasty had sought to reduce
its dependence on the Uzbek tribal nobility by placing administration in the
hands of *Iran*is, Persian Shiʻi slaves and their descendants – the *mahram* or

---

[77] Donish, *Risala*, 47–8 & *Istoriya*, 47–8.
[78] Holzwarth, 'Bukharan Armies and Uzbek Military Power', 336–8.
[79] Tashkandi refers to this figure, whom we will encounter again later, as 'Shir Ali Shiʻi
Irani', *TJT*, ff. 42b–3a; he was the brother of one of Amir Sayyid Muzaffar's wives.
[80] Tatarinov, *Semimesyachnyi plen*, 16–17.

ghulaman whom we have already encountered in Sami's work.[81] This was another fault line in Bukharan politics which the Russian conquest would brutally expose.

Two members of the Russian embassy held captive in Samarkand, Court Counsellor Struve and Lt-Col. Glukhovskoi, reported that six days after the battle a Tatar who spoke fluent Russian (i.e. Qarataev) had come to them and said that they would be released and sent to the Russian lines the following day in an attempt to restore peaceful relations, saying that 'the affair of the 8 May did not come about because of a wish to enter into open struggle with Russia, but was undertaken in fulfilment of Muslim law'.[82] Sayyid Muzaffar's subsequent letter to Romanovskii mingled conciliatory phrases with complaints about Russian inconsistency. He complained about Chernyaev having failed to address him with sufficient friendliness (probably referring to the lack of polite forms of address, or more broadly to the general's arrogance), and accused him (with some justification) of launching an unprovoked attack on Jizzakh. He also bemoaned the fact that his ambassadors to St Petersburg had been detained at Tashkent and prevented from going any further. However, he added that he hoped that friendship could now be established, and that Romanovskii would release his merchants and allow him to send an embassy directly to the Tsar.[83] This was not to be the case, however, as Romanovskii promptly advanced south-east to Khujand, subsequently rationalising his decision as follows:

> In order to make best use of our success at Irjar and to attain the goals with which the expedition onto the right bank [of the Syr-Darya] was undertaken in January, i.e. to return our embassy and punish the Amir for his perfidy, we were presented with two courses of action: either the immediate pursuit of the defeated enemy, directed towards Ura-Tepe, Samarkand and onwards, or to direct ourselves to Nau and Khujand.
>
> The experience of the past few years has shown clearly that all decisive offensives of our forces in these regions, when successful, bring with them an inescapable necessity to, if not remain in the region for ever, then at least retain our forces there for a considerable time. The victorious advent of our forces always forms a party of those favourable towards the Russians amongst the natives, whom to then abandon to the oppression of half-savage rulers, without a loss of faith in us, is impossible. In view of these very points, I considered it in all respects more advantageous and

---

[81] Holzwarth, 'The Uzbek State'; Kimura Satoru, 'Sunni–Shi'i Relations in the Russian Protectorate of Bukhara, as Perceived by the Local *'ulama'*, in *Asiatic Russia: Imperial Power in Regional and International Contexts*, ed. Tomohiko Uyama (London: Routledge, 2012), 192–4; Wennberg, *On the Edge*, 150–2. Thanks also to Paolo Sartori for his comments on this.

[82] Struve & Glukhovskoi to Romanovskii 14/05/1866, in Serebrennikov, *Sbornik. 1866 g. Pt. I*, Doc.132, 224.

[83] Amir Sayyid Muzaffar to Romanovskii 20/05/1866, *Ibid.*, Doc.137, 228–9.

less extreme to avoid a movement into the bounds of Bukhara and to move towards Nau and Khujand, the first of which consists of a fortress, albeit not a large one, but nevertheless very strong, and has an important strategic significance, as a point lying on the main route between Bukhara and Khoqand, and secondly, apart from its trading significance, it will always constitute the main obstacle to all disorderly persons threatening our trans-Chirchik region.[84]

Terent'ev poured scorn on this explanation, writing that to seize a city which, whilst in Bukharan hands, was historically part of Khoqand, was an odd way of punishing the Amir.[85] Khujand was a liminal city, long contested between Bukhara and Khoqand and owing unqualified allegiance to neither: instead it had long enjoyed a large degree of autonomy, developing its own notarial practices and even hosting its own *Qazi-Kalan*, something very unusual for a subordinate city.[86] There was a strong sense of local identity and patriotism, which persists to this day. While in Khujand, as in Tashkent, there was a party in favour of the Russians (in this case led by the *Qazi-Kalan*), the leader of the 'warlike party', Khwaja Amin, the *aqsaqal* of the city, had had him and his principal followers imprisoned. The fortress was stronger than most of those the Russians had encountered, and the garrison resisted fiercely, but a heavy bombardment followed by an attack in twin columns soon settled the matter in familiar fashion.[87] Romanovskii claimed that 2,500 Khujandis had died, whilst 71 Russian soldiers were killed or wounded, 65 suffered 'contusions' and 6 were missing.[88] Almost immediately after the fall of Khujand, a deputation arrived from the Bek of Jizzakh, saying that the Amir was now willing to agree terms and return the imprisoned ambassadors. However, Romanovskii wrote, 'as at the head of this embassy was a Bukharan who was already known to me as an extremely shady individual (*lichnost' ves'ma podozritel'naya*)', he decided that it was probably a delaying tactic, and had them welcomed courteously but informed that he would speak to them only once the ambassadors had actually been returned to the Russian camp.[89] Romanovskii added that he considered Nau, Khujand and the surrounding area to be much the most attractive, prosperous and fertile region the

[84] Romanovskii to Kryzhanovskii 30/05/1866, *Ibid.*, Doc.149, 241–2.

[85] Terent'ev, *Istoriya zavoevaniya*, I, 349.

[86] My thanks to James Pickett for explaining this to me. On Khujand's unusual notarial and administrative practices see T. Welsford & N. Tashev (ed.), *A Catalogue of Arabic-Script Documents from the Samarqand Museum* (Samarkand: International Institute for Central Asian Studies, 2012), 14, 475–9.

[87] Terent'ev, *Istoriya zavoevaniya*, I, 350–4. For a detailed description of the siege and capture of Khujand see Inomjon Mamadaliev, 'The Defence of Khujand in 1866 through the Eyes of Russian Officers', *CAS*, 33/2 (2014), 170–9.

[88] Romanovskii to Kryzhanovskii 30/05/1866, in Serebrennikov, *Sbornik. 1866 g. Pt. I*, Doc.149, 244.

[89] *Ibid.*, 245.

Russians had yet conquered, and he also claimed the local inhabitants had informed them that their control of the city would be sure to lead to the full submission of Khoqand as well.[90] His proclamation to the inhabitants claimed that Russia 'had not come for conquest', simultaneously saying that without Russian troops in Khujand, there would be no peace in the surroundings of Tashkent.[91] Romanovskii's missive to the Amir left the latter in no doubt that any further renewal of hostilities would lead to an advance towards Samarkand and the Bukharan capital.[92]

The ambassadors had returned safely to Tashkent on the 1 June, but this did not end Russian discontents and suspicions. Shortly afterwards Romanovskii wrote to Amir Sayyid Muzaffar, complaining that Rustam Bek of Ura-Tepe was still sending out parties of horsemen to harass the population of the territory around Khujand and Nau.[93] He expressed his suspicions more fully a few days later in a long despatch to Orenburg:

> Apart from the fact that the very government of Asiatic states is extremely unstable, the conduct of the Amir, even now, when he is conducting negotiations and making concessions, is already beginning to give rise to misgivings. There are rumours that already at the start of peace negotiations with us, which he was driven to only in extremity, the ruler of Bukhara had already sent off two embassies: one to the Afghans, and the other to the English. Up until now it has not fallen to me to gather accurate information on this point, and because of this I cannot vouch for the accuracy of rumours, but I find them not implausible. [...] There are many reasons to think that secretly the Amir will never make peace with us. Up until now he has been considered all-victorious, and, really, one cannot but acknowledge that he has some military gifts. In recent years he has very skilfully used our war with the Khoqandis and, conquering Nau and Khujand, succeeded in making Khoqand and the Qipchaqs submit to him. This year, emboldened by his previous successes, having in his hand at all events our embassy, he undertook a still more serious enterprise, and, in his own fashion, managed affairs very intelligently. The choice by him of the main position at Irjar, if nothing else, showed his forethought.[94]

He urged that the Russians exercise extreme caution and make preparations for a renewal of hostilities, perhaps even involving a pre-emptive attack in the autumn, before the Bukharans could rebuild their shattered forces. Romanovskii's jumpiness and borderline paranoia were further illustrated by his decision to expel P. I. Pashino, an employee of the Ministry of Foreign

---

[90] *Ibid.*, 246.

[91] 'The Military Governor of the Turkestan *Oblast*' to the wise and honourable people of Khujand', *Ibid.*, Doc.149 Pril.4, 250.

[92] Romanovskii to Amir Sayyid Muzaffar (n.d.), *Ibid.*, Doc.149 Pril.6, 251–2.

[93] Romanovskii to Amir Sayyid Muzaffar 15/06/1866, *Ibid.*, Doc.167 Pril.5, 298.

[94] Romanovskii to Kryzhanovskii 23/06/1866, *Ibid.*, Doc.174, 306.

Affairs who had come to Turkestan on an unofficial trip,[95] whom he accused of being much too thick with the 'natives' (including his own translator, Bekchurin) and of spreading rumours, apparently still current in the Tashkent bazaar, that Romanovskii would soon be recalled and the city turned into an independent khanate under the rule of the *Qazi-Kalan*, Ishan Hakim Khwaja.[96] In August 1866 Romanovskii complained to Miliutin about

> our still unsettled relations with Bukhara and the repeated attacks by small *shaikas* of the Bek of Ura-Tepe on the inhabitants of the Nau region and on our border forces, the reason for which can be explained either as some sort of secret project of the Amir, or, plausibly, as a striving for independence by the Ura-Tepe Bek himself.[97]

On the 20 August Romanovskii again wrote to the Amir, asking why he was still waiting for an answer to a letter sent to him two months previously, and warning the Amir that unless he released those Russian merchants who were still detained in Bukhara, and restrained Rustam Bek of Ura-Tepe, the Russians would be forced to renew hostilities.[98] His suspicions of the Amir's good faith extended to a belief, perhaps derived from the testimony of Tatarinov and other members of the detained embassy, that he was deliberately whipping up religious feeling amongst his subjects:

> I am more and more convinced that fanaticism here is something grafted on (*delo privitoe*), supported by the influence of the Amir: the people long to rid themselves of the tight, self-interested oppression of their clergy.[99]

This delusion that the population of Turkestan would freely abandon Islam once it was deprived of state support would inform Russian religious policy throughout the period of colonial rule.[100] Kryzhanovskii, who by this time had arrived in the region himself, shared these suspicions, or at any rate was equally willing to use Bukharan untrustworthiness and bad faith as an excuse for further annexations – he was evidently anxious for victories of his own:[101]

> The Amir has not replied to General Romanovskii's letters of the 20 July; it has become known that, from fear of an advance from our side, he is gathering a quantity of forces at Samarkand; from all of this it was evident

---

[95] Pashino wrote some of the earliest articles describing the new province to appear in the 'Thick' journals, culminating in the publication of P. I. Pashino, *Turkestanskii krai v 1866 g.: Putevye zametki* (St Pb.: Tiblen & Nekliudov, 1866), which contained a remarkable series of lithographs of Central Asian scenes, the first to be seen by the Russian public.

[96] Romanovskii to Stremoukhov 26/06/1866, in Serebrennikov, *Sbornik. 1866 g. Pt. I*, Doc.181, 316–18.

[97] Kryzhanovskii to Miliutin 10/08/1866, *Ibid.*, Doc.210, 39.

[98] Romanovskii to Amir Sayyid Muzaffar 20/08/1866, *Ibid.*, Doc.212, 43.

[99] Romanovskii to Miliutin 05/09/1866, *Ibid.*, Doc.220, 58–9.

[100] Morrison, *Russian Rule in Samarkand*, 51–87.

[101] Terent'ev, *Istoriya zavoevaniya*, I, 328, 365–6.

that the Amir wanted to renege on all agreements, and to renew with us the trade which is essential to him and to his subjects, leaving matters in the same state as they were before the war, i.e. to free himself from all reparations which he ought to bear owing to the failure of his attack. [. . .] The Amir quickly replied that he was sending a plenipotentiary. However, I cannot refrain from saying that I have small hopes of the compliance of the Amir, and would suggest that, even if he accepts our conditions, he is unlikely to do so in good faith, and because of this I cannot, unfortunately, hope that it will be possible to conclude peace without taking up arms once again. It would be more certain, I may suggest, that it will be necessary to turn to force and take Jizzakh, behind which lies a very valuable defile.[102]

In early October Miliutin wrote to Kryzhanovskii urging caution owing to the delicate situation in Europe (he meant the Austro-Prussian war), at the same time saying that he wanted more information about Bukharan activities, as he had still not heard whether the Russian merchants there had been freed, or whether there was any build-up of forces near Samarkand.[103] He was already much too late, however. On the 20 September a force under Romanovskii set out from Khujand, and on the 2 October Ura-Tepe was taken by storm, after heavy fighting in which, for once, the Russians suffered quite heavy casualties, 151 of the 500 men who carried out the initial assault on the gates of the fortress being killed or wounded, the total casualties standing at 17 dead, 103 seriously wounded and 106 lightly wounded.[104] The resistance had been determined, and the small-arms fire of the city's defenders had been unusually accurate: like Khujand, Ura-Tepe was a fiercely independent city which had long resented the authority of both Khoqand and Bukhara, something vividly evoked by the local poet and historian Dilshod, when she wrote about how its inhabitants had defied 'Umar Khan of Khoqand in 1810.[105] Terent'ev wrote that the heavy Russian casualties were owing to the use of scaling ladders by the first two storming columns under the inexperienced

---

[102] Kryzhanovskii to Miliutin 05/09/1866, in Serebrennikov, *Sbornik. 1866 g.*, Pt. I, Doc.223, 61–2.

[103] Miliutin to Kryzhanovskii 06/10/1866, *Ibid.*, Doc.246, 93–4.

[104] 'Vsepoddanneishii doklad komanduiushchago voiskami Orenb. okr. 06/10/1866 g. Ura-Tyube', *Ibid.*, Doc.246, 93–4; Romanovskii to Kryzhanovskii 07/10/1866, *Ibid.*, Doc.248, 107, 111.

[105] 'Brother Turks and Persians [*baradaran Turk va Fars*]! Men of the town and villages of Ura-Tepa [*mardom-i shahr va dehat-i Ura-tepa*]! May my soul fall victim for my brothers [*baradaram*] and fellow townsmen [*hamshahram*], and afterwards if I say something false or unworthy you may throw stones at my head. Why are this realm and this city seeing such distress and destruction? ... The rulers of Ferghana and Bukhara have rent and thrown this city and reduced it to the earth [*Be in nauh bar hakemranan-i Farghana va Bukhara rakhte andakhte shahr-ra chak tarab kardand*]. Dilshod, *Ta'rikh-i Muhajiran*, in A. Mukhtarov, *Dil'shod i ee mesto v istorii obshchest-vennoi mysli tadzhikskogo naroda* (Dushanbe: Donish, 1969), 193–4.

leadership of what he rather contemptuously referred to as '*gvardeitsy*' (Guards Officers) – Shafus and Glukhovskii – who drew attention to themselves prematurely by shouting 'Ura' and running forward when still too far from the walls. In contrast, the canny veteran Colonel Nazarov (whom we will meet again at the siege of Samarkand) had kept his head down and brought his men quietly up to the walls with minimal losses. Terent'ev concluded his account with an almost certainly inflated estimate of 2,000 dead among the defenders.[106]

Miliutin and the War Ministry were far from pleased with this turn of events, but their annoyance paled when compared with the reaction of the Ministry of Foreign Affairs, where the Director of the Asiatic Department, P. N. Stremoukhov, was incandescent with rage:

> The letter from Romanovskii is reasonably reassuring, although even in this one sees the desire for annexations flickering; but the letter from Kryzhanovskii clearly shows that he really wishes to turn himself into Alexander the Great [*on reshitel'no zhelaet sdelat'sya Aleksandrom Makedonskim*]. If the telegram sent to him has not succeeded in catching him before undertaking the expedition, then, it seems to me, we can still set matters right with the most categorical order in the name of the Emperor telling him point-blank to refrain from all annexations [*prisoedinenii*]. [. . .] all rumours about the hostile activities of Khoqand are absolute fraudulent nonsense. The Khoqandis are ready to do everything that we tell them to do, and if there have been some violations of the frontier [. . .] a force of Cossacks is sufficient to teach them a good lesson. Kryzhanovskii so wishes for achievements and conquests that for him the Khoqandi will always be guilty, like the lamb before the wolf. I beg you, thrice-respected Dmitri Alexeevich [Miliutin], for the sake of the true interests of Russia, to send a decisive order bringing to a halt the military enterprises of these gentlemen.[107]

Once again, this reaction came too late: on the 12 October Kryzhanovskii sent a threatening letter to the Bek of Jizzakh, reminding him of all the fortresses that had already fallen to the Russians and of the Bukharan defeat at Irjar, and telling him any attempt to defend the town would be a useless blood-letting.[108] In the event the Bukharans resisted fiercely once more – since Chernyaev's abortive attack on the city eight months before, they had strengthened its walls and created a clear field of fire around them, and the garrison consisted of around 10,000 men, although only 2,000 of these were regular *sarbaz* infantry.[109] Sami (in his official history) writes that an important part

[106] Terent'ev, *Istoriya zavoevaniya*, I, 369–71.
[107] P. N. Stremoukhov to D. A. Miliutin 08/10/1866, in Serebrennikov, *Sbornik. 1866 g. Pt. I*, Doc.249, 112.
[108] Kryzhanovskii to the Bek of Jizzakh 12/10/1866, *Ibid.*, Doc.252, 114.
[109] Terent'ev, *Istoriya zavoevaniya*, I, 373.

was played by a group of Afghan soldiers under a leader called Iskander Khan 'Janril' (i.e. 'general'): he and many of his men would subsequently enter Russian service.[110] The siege lasted five days; at 100 men and officers killed or wounded Russian casualties were lower than at Ura-Tepe, as they had eschewed scaling-ladders in favour of bombardment.[111] The slaughter on the Bukharan side seems to have been horrific: Terent'ev described a 'hecatomb' of 3,000 corpses, men and horses mingled, in front of the Tashkent Gate, where they had been cold-bloodedly shot down even as they threw aside their weapons, though as is so often the case he may have exaggerated the numbers.[112] Miliutin's reply to the news of Jizzakh's fall was mild, merely asking him to see what he could do to restrain expenses and make the new annexations pay for themselves, but Stremoukhov's response was still more furious:

> This telegram demonstrates clearly that the brave general, without regard to any other considerations, simply wanted cheap laurels and rewards: in his last report, he was preparing to threaten the Khoqandis, and now he is practising conquering exploits at the expense of the Bukharans. Having acquired at the cost of Russian blood, God knows what for, some fortress or other, he now, naturally, extols its strategic and political significance; then, to satisfy his growing appetite, he takes Jizzakh, and who knows, maybe then Samarkand. *Pourquoi s'arrèter en si beau chemin?* [...] I do not understand why, when we have entire Ministries of War and of Foreign Affairs, we then leave all political matters, the declaration of peace and war, the extension of our frontiers and trans-border relations to each local commander. At the very least, this power was given to them by the very highest levels of Government, and now they take it wilfully into their own hands and compel the government to submit blindly *aux faits accomplis.*
>
> If they give Kryzhanovskii the [Order of St] George now, then you can be certain that not only will this encourage him to further exploits, but also that both his and Romanovskii's successor will undertake new exploits and conquests, disobeying the most definite instructions.[113]

Kryzhanovskii, predictably enough, defended his actions by saying that the further annexations had been a strategic necessity to prevent the Russian forces at Khujand being caught between a twin advance from Khoqand and Bukhara,

---

[110] Sami, *Tuhfa-yi Shahi*, 187, 192–3; F. F. Pospelov, 'Seid-Khan Karimkhanov', *Spravochnaya kniga Samarkandskoi Oblasti.* Vyp. 10 (Samarkand: Tip-Lit. Tovarishchestva B. Gazarov i K. Sliyanov, 1912), 126–31.

[111] Kryzhanovskii to Miliutin 19/10/1866, in Serebrennikov, *Sbornik. 1866 g. Pt. II,* Doc.255, 119.

[112] Terent'ev, *Istoriya zavoevaniya,* I, 381.

[113] Stremoukhov to Miliutin 25/10/1866, in Serebrennikov, *Sbornik. 1866 g. Pt. II,* Doc.263, 124–5.

and that now he was quite certain that the frontier would remain secure. This was accepted wearily by the Ministers of War and Foreign Affairs, and Alexander II wrote 'God willing, that the results he anticipates can be achieved without new military actions.'[114] In this he was to be disappointed. Neither Kryzhanovskii nor Romanovskii was reprimanded – and Kryzhanovskii did indeed receive a St George's Cross, 3rd Class, which, as Zaionchkovskii observed, was hardly likely to dampen military adventurism in the future.[115] More importantly still, it was not until the Russians came to understand that they had to bolster the authority of the Bukharan Amir rather than undermining it that they would succeed in maintaining a stable relationship with what would become their protectorate.

6.4   The Samarkand Campaign of 1868

The end of 1866 saw a pause in the Russian advance. Romanovskii was dismissed and left Tashkent in December of that year, replaced by an acting Governor, Major-General N. M. Manteufel, while Turkestan's administrative future was decided. This was seen very much as an exercise in creating a colonial administration on the European model, informed by the notion of a 'civilising mission'.[116] As Miliutin put it: 'It seemed that this savage, unattractive region was awakening from a many-centuries sleep and was being summoned to new life under the aegis of Russia.'[117] Throughout 1865–6, a military–judicial commission had been touring the newly conquered regions of Semirechie and the Syr-Darya Valley and drawing up recommendations for their future administration.[118] Despite Kryzhanovskii's advocacy of continued control from Orenburg, it was clear that the region was too remote, and communications across the steppe too difficult. Instead, in July 1867 a new Governor-Generalship of Turkestan was created by statute, consisting of two provinces – Syr-Darya and Semirechie – with extensive plenipotentiary powers granted to its Governor-General.[119] The post was given to Konstantin Petrovich von Kaufman, an engineer officer who had served at the siege of Kars during the Crimean War, and most recently had been governor of Vilna.

---

[114] Kryzhanovskii to Miliutin 31/10/1866, *Ibid.*, Doc.268, 130–3.

[115] Zaionchkovskii, 'K voprosu zavoevaniya Srednei Azii', 62.

[116] Ulrich Hofmeister, 'Civilization and Russification in Tsarist Central Asia, 1860–1917', *JWH* 27/3 (2016), 411–42.

[117] Miliutin, *Vospominaniya 1868–nachalo 1873*, 58.

[118] Terent'ev, *Istoriya zavoevaniya*, I, 400–1. The work of the steppe commission, which drafted both the Turkestan Statute and the Steppe Statute of 1867–8, lies beyond the scope of this book, but see Martin, *Law and Custom*, 49–54; Campbell, *Knowledge and the Ends of Empire*, 31–62; D. V. Vasil'ev, *Bremya Imperii: Administrativnaya politika Rossii v Tsentral'noi Azii: Vtoraya polovina XIX v.* (Moscow: ROSSPEN, 2018), 120–53.

[119] 'Ob uchrezhdenii Turkestanskogo General-Gubernatorstva', 11/07/1867, *PSZ* 2nd Series Vol. 42 Pt. I (1867), No. 44831, 1150–1.

Von Kaufman was not a Baltic German aristocrat, but descended from an Austrian mercenary who had entered Russian service in the late eighteenth century.[120] A Russian-speaking Orthodox Christian, the only German thing about him was his name. Terent'ev noted that he had a 'purely Russian view on the aims of the Russian state', though this did not prevent Terent'ev from directing numerous anti-German jibes against von Kaufman elsewhere in his history. He was a solid professional officer in the mould preferred by Miliutin, and for several years had been his Head of Chancery at the War Ministry.[121] The expectation was clearly that von Kaufman would bring a halt to the uncontrolled campaigning and annexations of 1865–6 and 'avoid further conquests'.[122] In the event, less than a year after his arrival in Tashkent in November 1867, von Kaufman (Figure 6.2[123]) would have embarked on new conquests of his own.

Alongside the injunction to avoid further conquests, Miliutin noted that 'the goal of our policy in the region was meant to ensure that the neighbouring khanates submit to our moral influence (*nravstvennoe vliyanie*), institute peaceful trading relations with us and end raiding on our territory'.[124] In his account this proved impossible in the case of Bukhara owing to the 'contrivances (*ukhishchreniyam*) of essentially Asiatic diplomacy' employed by the Bukharans, the 'fanaticism' of their religious elites and the continued raids along the Russian frontier.[125] He had clearly accepted von Kaufman's explanation for the conquests that were to follow.

One of the many tasks von Kaufman faced on taking up his post in November 1867 was to finalise a permanent peace treaty with Bukhara. This had first been drafted by Kryzhanovskii, and demanded an indemnity, the recognition of Russian conquests to date and permission for Russian merchants to trade freely in Bukhara. After some minor changes it had been presented to the Bukharan ambassador in Orenburg in September 1867, but in December it had still not been signed by the Amir.[126] According to one source this was because he feared that raising taxes to pay the indemnity was likely to provoke a rebellion, but the Russians saw it as 'Asiatic diplomacy', to

[120] See David Mackenzie, 'Kaufman of Turkestan: An Assessment of His Administration 1867–1881', *SR* 26/2 (1967), 265–85; D. V. Vasil'ev, 'Ustroitel' Turkestanskogo kraya (k biografii K. P. von Kaufmana), in *SRIO*. Vol. 5 (Moscow: Russkaya Panorama, 2002), 45–57.
[121] Terent'ev, *Istoriya zavoevaniya*, I, 383.
[122] Miliutin, *Vospominaniya 1868–nachalo 1873*, 58.
[123] 'Turkestanskii general-gubernator, i komanduiushchii voiskami Turkest. Voennago Okruga General Leitenant, Gener-ad'iutant [*sic*] K. P. fon-Kaufman I-i', in *Kun Turkestanskii al'bom* Pt. 4, plate 4, No. 2 (Library of Congress, Prints & Photographs Division LC-DIG-ppmsca-09957-00002).
[124] Miliutin, *Vospominaniya 1868–nachalo 1873*, 58.
[125] *Ibid.*, 59–60.
[126] Becker, *Russia's Protectorates*, 36–9.

Figure 6.2 Konstantin Petrovich von Kaufman, first Governor-General of Turkestan (*Turkestan Album*, 1871).

use Miliutin's phrase.[127] Meanwhile the situation along the frontier deteriorated further. During the interregnum before von Kaufman's appointment Manteufel had allowed another unauthorised annexation, of the fortified town of Yangi-Qurghan, near Jizzakh on the road to Samarkand, which was taken by a force under A. K. Abramov on the 26 May 1867; the ostensible justification (ridiculed by Terent'ev) was that Jizzakh depended on the region for food and its water supply.[128] The Bukharans made repeated attempts to recapture it over the next two months, in vain, and this further damaged relations. The Russians complained of repeated raids along the Syr-Darya by 'the bandit Sadiq', Kenesary's son, some of them as far north as Fort No. 1, and the capture of an artillery officer called Sluzhenko and three soldiers in a raid near Chinaz.[129] At the same time it is clear that the aggression was mutual – the Russians simply termed their own raids on Bukharan territory 'punitive expeditions', one example being Abramov's destruction of the village of

---

[127] M. G. Bogdanov, 'Materialy dlya opisaniya bukharskoi ekspeditsii 1868 goda', in *Materialy dlia statistiki Turkestanskogo kraya: Ezhegodnik*. Vyp. II ed. N. A. Maev (St Pb.: n.p., 1873), 428.
[128] Terent'ev, *Istoriya zaveovaniya*, I, 391–3; Malikov, 'Russian Conquest', 186.
[129] Lyko, *Ocherk voennykh deistvii*, 4–6.

Ukhum in December 1867.[130] In February 1868 von Kaufman reported occasional raids and exchanges of fire with '*shaiki*' near Bogdan-ata, and noted that one Jura-Bek was recruiting men for the Amir's forces in the region. In fact this was an indication of von Kaufman's lack of understanding of the political situation in Bukhara, since Jura-Bek was the ruler of Kitab, to the south of the Zarafshan range, and at least since the accession of Sayyid Muzaffar had not acknowledged the Amir of Bukhara's authority: the men he was recruiting were almost certainly for his own forces.[131] Von Kaufman also noted that the frontier with Bukhara remained largely undefined, and that around the advanced fortified Russian positions many of the inhabitants had still not seen any Russians or paid any taxes to the Russian administration.[132] In March there was a more serious attack by what von Kaufman again described as Bukharan '*shaiki*' from Chalek in the northern Zarafshan valley on a small force led by sub-lieutenant Mashina at a point midway between Jizzakh and Yangi-Qurghan. Von Kaufman noted that 'although this affair is of no particular importance, and shouldn't have any harmful consequences, nevertheless the reason for this unexpected attack of *shaiki* on our force, it is clear, was the insufficient caution and order in the despatch of the force, and doubtless the wilfulness (*samovol'stvo*) of officers who relied on their own boldness in breaching the established rules'.[133] Von Kaufman wrote again the following day to explain that the region in question around Bogdan-Ata was a sort of no man's land, nominally ceded to Russia under the 1866 peace agreement, but whose *bek*s did not consider themselves to be under Russian rule, whilst the inhabitants were 'bandits', and that all the raids along the frontier line emanated from here. He hoped that the dispute could be resolved through negotiations, but a week later reported that these were getting nowhere, the raids were increasing, and that a force would need to be despatched to conquer the area definitively – a force of twenty companies of infantry, sixteen guns and seven *sotnyas* of Cossacks had been sent to the frontier fortress of Kliuchevoe in preparation.[134] This was about 4,000 men, or over a third of all the forces available to von Kaufman at the time – thanks to an

[130] Terent'ev, *Istoriya zaveovaniya*, I, 399.

[131] Jura-Bek had originally been appointed as governor of Kitab by Amir Nasrullah in 1852, but his tribe, the Keneges, had effectively ruled the region independently for the previous eighty years. When Nasrullah's successor Sayyid Muzaffar attempted to dismiss Jura-Bek and replace him with his own candidate, Zakir Bek, the Keneges rose up in rebellion and restored Jura Bek to his position: von Kaufman to Miliutin 11/01/1873 RGVIA F.400 Op.1 D.352, 'Po khodataistvu Turkestanskogo General-Gubernatora o vydache soderzhanii byvshim sredneaziatskim bekam', l. 1.

[132] Von Kaufman to the War Ministry 07/02/1868 & 15/02/1868 RGVIA F.1396 Op.2 D.44, 'Perepiska s Kokandskim Khanom i Bukharskim Emirom ob ustanovlenii granits', ll. 24–35ob.

[133] Von Kaufman to Miliutin 22/03/1868 RGVIA F.1396 Op.2 D.44 l. 64.

[134] Von Kaufman to Miliutin 23/03/1868 & 30/03/1868 RGVIA F.1396 Op.2 D.44 ll. 67–77.

unusually wet winter, hastily constructed barracks and an often contaminated water supply, of his total command of some 16,000 officers and men, some 4,200 were incapacitated with sickness (probably cholera) in the spring of 1868, while 820 had died over the previous eight months.[135]

In the middle of April the Russians managed to obtain fairly accurate intelligence of what was going on in Bukhara from a merchant who had recently returned from there. He reported that the Amir had summoned *beks*, substantial merchants and *'ulama* to a council in the Arg (palace-citadel) at Bukhara to discuss whether to make war or peace with the Russians. The Amir himself had not taken part, but had watched the debate secretly from behind a wall. The debate had lasted all day, and, whilst there had been voices for peace, many were in favour of war 'to uphold the *shari'a*'. While the question of war or peace had remained unresolved, almost all those present had been unanimous that the Amir himself was not fit to rule, and should be replaced by his eldest son, 'Abd al-Malik Tura, currently serving with Bukharan forces at Samarkand. The Amir had then fled to Karmina, returning a few days later to be confronted with a crowd demanding war. The merchant was of the opinion that the Amir himself did not want war and would prefer to conclude peace as quickly as possible in order to concentrate on pacifying his own dominions and re-establishing his control over the population. 'The people, who previously did not want war, now look on war as a means for ridding themselves of the hated Amir'.[136] Clearly the Russian presence was once again putting considerable strain on Bukhara's fragile political fabric.

The Ural Cossack officer Alexander Khoroshkhin (1841–1875) wrote in his memoir of the campaign that on the 14 April his men, encamped near the 'Kliuchevoe' fortress on the frontier, had managed to capture a 'Sart' spy, sent by Shir 'Ali Inaq, the newly appointed *bek* of Samarkand, to assess the strength of the Russian forces.[137] The following day the commandant of the Jizzakh District, Colonel Troitskii, reported to General Nikolai Nikitich Golovachev (1823–1887), the commander of Russian forces in Syr-Darya Province, that at 4 am that morning a large Bukharan force had attacked the assembled Russian forces in the fortified camp at Kliuchevoe. They had been beaten off with heavy losses on their side, whilst amongst the Russians the only casualty was a cornet who had received a heavy blow with a stick. The Cossacks had pursued and scattered the Bukharans, only returning in the evening. Troitskii claimed that the attack had been led by 'Umar-Bek, the Bukharan administrator of Chalek, and added: 'I submit that this assault by the Bukharans was not carried out by vagabonds and bandits and undesired by the Amir; it is an open military

---

[135] Lyko, *Ocherk voennykh deistvii*, 23–5; Terent'ev, *Istoriya zavoevaniya*, I, 408–9.

[136] 'Chastnyya svedeniya iz Bukhary', 14/04/1868 RGVIA F.1396 Op.2 D.44 ll. 82–4ob.

[137] A. P. Kh[oroshkhi]n, 'Vesna 1868 g. v Srednei Azii', *VS* (1875), No. 9, 167–9.

action, initiated against us by the Bukharan authorities.'[138] Not long after this skirmish came the desertion of Iskander Khan and his Afghans, who arrived in Jizzakh on the 19 April and offered their services to the 'White Tsar', which von Kaufman, conscious of the limited numbers at his disposal, gratefully accepted.[139]

The Russian invasion of Bukharan territory followed two weeks later, led by von Kaufman in person. Von Kaufman claimed that the negotiations over a permanent peace treaty with Bukhara which had been going on for the previous six months finally looked as if they were coming to fruition, and that he had brought his forces to the Bukharan frontier to persuade the Amir to sign.[140] At Tash-Kupruk ('Stone Bridge'), halfway between Yangi-Qurghan and Samarkand, the Amir attempted to parley, once again sending Najmuddin Khwaja, who had been Bukhara's ambassador to St Petersburg in 1859 and 1866, to carry out negotiations. He attempted unsuccessfully to persuade the Russians to halt, and accompanied them as they advanced another ten *versts* to the village of Aq-Qurghan in the Miankal Valley, part of the middle portion of the Zarafshan.[141] As they approached the river they came under the gaze of a large, hostile force occupying the Chupan-Ata heights – so called because they were crowned by the domed mausoleum of the eponymous 'shepherd saint', who was supposed to be Samarkand's protector – on the other side of the Zarafshan. Here Najmuddin Khwaja presented peace terms signed by the Amir, but von Kaufman claimed that these were significantly different from those he had originally sent to Sayyid Muzaffar for signature, while the Persian text apparently contained many words which his translators did not understand.[142] Von Kaufman's response to Najmuddin Khwaja was that, unless the Bukharan forces began to withdraw within three-quarters of an hour, he would attack.[143] The troops on the Chupan-Ata heights were made up of a poorly armed popular levy from Samarkand itself, some irregular Uzbek cavalry, and 4,000 *sarbaz* infantry under an Ottoman military specialist known as Hajji Rumi. Overall command was nominally in the hands of Osman, a deserter from the Ural Cossacks who had converted to Islam, although the different portions of the force do not seem to have been well coordinated.[144] Najmuddin Khwaja's attempt to persuade them to withdraw simply led to them opening fire with their artillery (commanded by another Russian deserter called Bogdanov), suggesting that they were no longer fully

---

[138] Troitskii to Golovachev 15/04/1868 RGVIA F.1396 Op.2 D.46 ll. 30–1.
[139] Lyko, *Ocherk voennykh deistvii*, 39–41.
[140] Von Kaufman to Miliutin 08/05/1868 RGVIA F.846 Op.1 D.6 ll. 69–81.
[141] Terent'ev, *Istoriya zavoevaniya*, I, 418.
[142] Lyko, *Ocherk voennykh deistvii*, 55–6; Terent'ev, *Istoriya zaveovaniya*, I, 419.
[143] Von Kaufman to Alexander II 01/05/1868 RGVIA F.1396 Op.2 D.46 ll. 45–50; RGVIA F.1392 Op.1 D.2 ll. 4–8.
[144] Malikov, 'Russian Conquest', 189.

obedient to the Amir and his agents. The same dynamic visible in 1866 – of a hostile *'ulama* stirring up the population to a 'holy war' that the Bukharan authorities did not necessarily want – seems to have been playing out once more. Kamalbai recalled that, while the *bek* of the city (Shir 'Ali Inaq) had equivocated over whether to resist the Russians or not, the 'mullahs' had encouraged the population of Samarkand to defend their native city and its mosques against the Russians. This had led to violence when Shir 'Ali sent *sarbaz* infantry to break up a public meeting in the Tilla-Qari madrasa, one of the three magnificent buildings on Samarkand's Registan (marketplace), calling for resistance to the Russians, resulting in several deaths. Shir 'Ali then fled Samarkand, and the Amir's forces joined the townsfolk on the Chupan-Ata heights, quite possibly on their own initiative – Kamalbai at first did not even know whether the Amir had given orders to defend the city or not. When the Amir's envoys were negotiating with the Russians on the morning of the battle, it seemed that he had in fact ordered Samarkand to be surrendered, though Muhammad Sufi believed that this was a slander.[145]

The highly inaccurate Bukharan bombardment did little damage, but prompted a renewed Russian advance through the houses and gardens across the river, towards the heights, from which the enemy fled precipitately, abandoning all their artillery – so rapidly that according to von Kaufman his troops could not pursue them.[146] The real reason was that the Russian forces were exhausted after fording two branches of the Zarafshan breast-deep – they had to lie on their backs on the bank and shake their legs in the air to empty the water out of their boots – and then advancing through flooded rice fields. One young officer, Ivanov, described the marshy conditions underfoot as a far greater challenge than the erratic Bukharan artillery and small-arms fire, and wrote that by the time they reached the summit of the heights they were physically unable to pursue the fleeing Bukharan forces.[147] Kamalbai remembered a feeling of awe at the ease with which the Russians crossed the two branches of the river, and growing fear at the relentlessness of their advance, which seemed entirely unaffected by Bukharan fire:

> We thought they were sorcerers. Those at the front were in dense ranks, and behind them were row after row of others. Our cannonballs flew over their heads, bullets did not reach them. It seemed that these were not people, but spirits of war. And so they formed up and moved on us. A solid wall advancing. We fired, again some began to fall. I myself saw how a soldier would fall here and there, and they would close up ranks and

[145] Simonova, 'Rasskazy ochevidtsev', 845–8, 859.
[146] Von Kaufman to Alexander II 01/05/1868 RGVIA F.1396 Op.2 D.46 ll. 45–50; RGVIA F.1392 Op.1 D.2 ll. 4–8.
[147] D. Ivanov, 'Pod Samarkandom (rasskaz Novichka)', *VS* (1876), No. 1: 193–202; see also Lyko, *Ocherk voennykh deistvii*, 61–2; Terent'ev *Istoriya zavoevaniya*, I, 421–2.

Figure 6.3 The site of the battle of Chupan-Ata (*Turkestan Album*, 1871).

continue the advance, as if our shots did not bother them. They came on and on. Their caps with large protruding visors (*kepis*), their legs, which like a palisade went up and down, instilled fear in us. I stopped firing, I stood there, as if petrified. They were getting closer and closer. A dull thudding of footsteps could be heard: *tup-tup, tup-tup*. It seemed that an uncanny force was coming, which could not be stopped or dispersed, and which would crush and destroy everything that would get in its way. Our people began to retreat in horror. I remember how I threw down my pistol and began to run as fast as I could, everyone was running, trying to save themselves. Behind us we heard the cry 'Ur-ra'![148]

The superiority of Russian discipline and the poor accuracy of Bukharan artillery and small-arms fire could hardly have been more clearly demonstrated, and it is noteworthy that Kamalbai used the same imagery of the Russian infantry as an advancing 'wall' as Donish had employed in his description of the battle of Irjar. The Russians lost just two dead and thirty-eight wounded at Chupan-Ata (Figure 6.3[149]), and the way to Samarkand now lay open.

[148] Simonova, 'Rasskazy ochevidtsev', 848–9.
[149] 'Chopan-Atinskiia vysoty oznamenovannyia pobiedoiu nad reguliarnymi voiskami Bukharskago Emira 1 maia 1868 g.', in Kun (ed.), *Turkestanskii al'bom* Pt. 4, plate

The capture of Samarkand was of particular significance to the Russians: 'the pride and glory of the Muslim world, the goal of our campaign – *Samarkand*' according to Ivanov, or, as a later traveller put it: 'Samarkand is the Moscow of Central Asia.'[150] Initially the city fell without a struggle, and Ivanov recorded how, after their victory at Chupan-Ata, he and his comrades wandered into the suburbs of the city and were able to refresh themselves with dried apricots (*uriuk*) and loaves (*lepeshki*). While they were nervous as they approached the gates, wondering whether they would encounter gunfire from the houses and gardens within the city walls (perhaps recalling the house-to-house fighting during Chernyaev's capture of Tashkent), there was no further resistance.[151] Kamalbai recalled good relations with the Russians in the first few days after the occupation of the town, noting that they paid well and promptly for their supplies, something his father profited from.[152]

According to Khoroshkhin, once von Kaufman had entered the city at the invitation of its inhabitants, he and his entourage went straight to the palace of the Bek, where he made a rather melodramatic speech before the 'blue–green stone' (*Kök Tash*) which was believed to be the throne of Tamerlane, or Timur, saying that their victory would be a form of revenge for the earlier subjugation of Russia by the 'Tatars'.[153] Certainly von Kaufman reported the initial capture of the city to Alexander II in the following terms: 'I have the honour to congratulate your Imperial Majesty on a new triumph: the most ancient and famous city of Central Asia, a centre of Islam – Samarkand, proud in its historical glory, has fallen to the troops of your Majesty without a shot being fired'. He went on to describe his ceremonial entry into the city in exhaustive detail: 'everything was fulfilled as had been arranged. The inhabitants before the gate and in the streets met us in welcoming fashion and with gladness. In the name of your Majesty I let them know that they should carry on occupying themselves with their affairs, open stalls and return their families to the city, as they had been hidden in the surrounding areas.' He added that he had appropriated the local symbols of sovereignty, as he was writing from what he described as the 'Khan's palace, known in Asia under the name of the "Kok-Tash" (blue–green stone)', which had once been part of the throne of Tamerlane.[154] Ron Sela has suggested that both the idea of the *Kök Tash* as a symbol of sovereignty and its association with Timur were of relatively recent origin, as he has not found any explicit reference to it before the eighteenth

54, No. 130 (Library of Congress, Prints & Photographs Division LC-DIG-ppmsca-09957–00130).
[150] Ivanov, 'Pod Samarkandom', *VS* (1876), No. 1, 184; V. V. Krestovskii, *V gostyakh u Emira Bukharskogo* (St Pb.: A. S. Suvorin, 1887), 46.
[151] Ivanov, 'Pod Samarkandom', *VS* (1876), No. 1, 207–8; No. 2, 362–74.
[152] Simonova, 'Rasskazy ochevidtsev', 850.
[153] Khoroshkhin, 'Vesna 1868 goda', 180.
[154] Von Kaufman to Alexander II 02/05/1868 RGVIA F.1396 Op.2 D.46 ll. 53–4ob.

century.[155] Von Kaufman's understanding of it was probably based upon the account by Nikolai Khanykov, who visited Samarkand in 1841 and wrote that every Khan needed to sit on it in order to be legitimised.[156]

According to Sami, who claims to have been present, the inhabitants of Samarkand had despatched a letter to von Kaufman asking for the Russians to take Samarkand, as they were suffering so much from the oppression and tyranny (*zulm va jor*) of Shir 'Ali Inaq, the Shi'i governor and commander whom the Amir had placed in charge of the city's defence:

> As there was no other road other than that to the town [Samarkand] – everywhere there were disorders, and the strong robbed the weak – in order to save our lives, we went into the town. [...] The writer of these words became acquainted with Mufti Mullah Kamaladdin, son of Damullah 'Alim Kuz-Falak, and went to him and gave himself under his protection [... on the following day] the aforementioned Mulla Kamaladdin-mufti with six *aqsaqals* of Samarkand, bringing with them hen's eggs and a cow [*gerefta murgh tokhm va gau*] went out to make expressions of submission to a meeting with the Governor-General at Chupan-Ata and, when they saw him, acknowledged their guilt. The Governor-General was welcoming and affectionate to them and freed the Samarkand *vilayat* from taxes. After this together with the *aqsaqals* through the gate of the Holy Shah-i Zindah the Governor came into Samarkand and stayed at the Kok Tash.[157]

Mufti Kamaladdin would be rewarded for his role by being made the first Russian-appointed *qazi* of the city.[158] Despite this peaceful beginning, Samarkand would subsequently provide the Russians with one of the more important heroic epics of the conquest. Samarkand's surrender was followed by a series of small expeditions to subdue resistance in the outlying towns of Urgut, Chalek and Qara-Tepe.[159] Significantly the last of these was fought against a force assembled by Jura Bek, the ruler of Kitab, who had brought a large body of men over the Zarafshan range. While the Russians succeeded in scattering them with volley fire, they were ambushed while returning through the village of Muhala near the Dargom canal, in which a translator and some soldiers were killed, and two officers wounded: according to Kamalbai over 300 men, women and children were killed in the subsequent reprisals.[160]

---

[155] Ron Sela, 'The "Heavenly Stone" (Kök Tash) of Samarqand: A Rebels' Narrative Transformed', *Journal of the Royal Asiatic Society* 17/1 (2007), 21–32.

[156] Khanikoff, *Bokhara, Its Amir and People*, 131; Tatarinov also mentions it as Tamerlane's 'throne': *Semimesyachnyi plen*, 20, 91.

[157] *TSM* text ff. 79a–b, trans. 77–8.

[158] See Morrison, *Russian Rule in Samarkand*, 254–5; Wilde, *What Is beyond the River*, II, 785–7.

[159] Lyko, *Ocherk voennykh deistvii*, 75–9, 89–96.

[160] Simonova, 'Rasskazy ochevidtsev', 851.

At the end of May, evidently believing that resistance in the Samarkand region was now at an end, von Kaufman then moved on to confront the Bukharan army which had retreated further up the Zarafshan Valley to Katta-Qurghan. He left behind a garrison of just 658 infantry, 94 artillerymen, two guns and two mortars under Baron Friedrich Karlovich von Stempel (1829–1891) to occupy the Samarkand citadel.[161] On the 3 June, as we will see, the Bukharan army was once again soundly defeated at the Zirabulak heights,[162] but by this time von Stempel and his small force had been attacked from another quarter. Jura Bek's force re-formed after the clash at Qara-Tepe, and he was joined by the ruler of nearby Shahrisabz, Baba Bek, and by 'Abd al-Malik Tura, the rebellious elder son of Amir Muzaffar, who was accompanied by 'Abd al-Ghafar Bek, the former troublesome ruler of Ura-Tepe, who had now abandoned Amir Sayyid Muzaffar in favour of his son.[163] Kitab and Shahrisabz, whilst nominally subject to Bukhara, had in fact been independent for at least eighty years.[164] 'Abd al-Malik's quarrel with his father derived in part from the poisonous politics of succession in Bukhara, but, as we have seen, he had apparently also advocated more vigorous resistance to the Russians, thus making himself the chosen leader of the 'clerical party' who advocated holy war. Shir 'Ali Inaq had accused him of riot and rebellion, and with the Amir's consent had sent him away from Samarkand to Ghuzar, south of the Zarafshan range.[165] His decision to ally himself with Amir Muzaffar's mortal enemies, Baba Bek of Shahrisabz and Jura Bek of Kitab, was further evidence of the shredding of Bukhara's fragile political fabric under the pressure of the Russian advance. Jura Bek also began to negotiate with the leader of a powerful religious lineage, 'Umar Khwaja Makhdum-i A'zami of the village of Dahbid near Samarkand.[166] He in turn was in touch with leaders from the city of Samarkand, including 'Abd as-Samad, the Persian adventurer who had helped to reform the Bukharan army over the previous decade.[167] The bazaar was rife with rumours of an impending uprising, but: 'the Russians knew nothing, they did not understand our language and could not listen to the gossip in the bazaar. Sometimes a soldier or an officer passed by a *divana* [dervish] at the time when he called for the complete extermination of the Russians, but, not

---

[161] Von Kaufman to Miliutin 26/05/1868 RGVIA F.1392 Op.1 D.2 ll. 33–4.

[162] Petrushevich to von Stempel 03/06/1868 RGVIA F.1392 Op.1 D.2 l. 45.

[163] Kaufman to Miliutin 11/01/1873 RGVIA F.400 Op.1 D.352, 'Po khodataistvu Turkestanskogo General-Gubernatora o vydache soderzhanii byvshim sredneaziatskim bekam', ll. 3–*ob*.

[164] Pickett, 'Written into Submission'.

[165] Malikov, 'Russian Conquest', 187.

[166] This was the site of the tomb of his ancestor, the Naqshbandi sheikh Ahmad Kasani Makhdum-i A'zam. See N. I. Veselovskii, 'Dagbid', *ZVOIRAO* (1888), No. 2, 85–7.

[167] Simonova, 'Rasskazy ochevidtsev', 852.

knowing the Sart language, willy-nilly he was deaf.'[168] On the 1 and 2 June shops in the city were closed, and many families began to move their women and children out to the surrounding villages. Kamalbai's father, who had been due to deliver some sheep for slaughter to the Russian garrison in the fortress on the 1 June, hid himself.[169]

Von Stempel's report on the subsequent attack gives a vivid sense of the confusion and increasing suspicion in relations between the Russian garrison and the inhabitants of the town. He wrote that on the evening of the 1 June some of the *aqsaqals* of the city requested that he send a force to the Khwaja Ahrar gate in order to beat off a *shaika* from Shahrisabz which was threatening it. When Major Al'bedil arrived with a platoon of the 6th Turkestan Line Battalion there was no sign of any enemy, and the inhabitants around the gate said that none had been there. That evening the Russians saw a large party of cavalry and infantry on the Chupan-Ata heights above the city, whom they identified as members of the Khitai-Qipchaq and Qaraqalpaq tribes, together with other groups from the regions neighbouring the city. On the 2 June at 3 am Stempel and his men were again disturbed by a group of *aqsaqals*, who asked them to come to the Khwaja Ahrar Gate. This time a small group from Shahrisabz were there, but they fired a few shots and then disappeared. The local inhabitants asked the Russians not to fire back, as they claimed that the attackers had groups of Samarqandis held captive in the gardens surrounding the city walls. They told him that the enemy were moving off towards the Bukhara Gate (Figure 6.4),[170] but again von Stempel found nothing there:

> From this it is very clear that the inhabitants wanted to distract my attention from the real movements of the enemy. About an hour later across the whole city arose the sound of drumming, the noise of horns and cries of *ur! ur!* which became stronger and stronger, spreading across the time. A mob of the enemy, having entered the city, together with the inhabitants drew near to the citadel from all sides, with the evident intention of storming it.[171]

That first night saw four frontal assaults on the gate of the citadel, each of which was beaten off with heavy losses to the attackers. Fighting continued fiercely on the 3 June until 3 pm, when most of the Shahrisabzi forces were seen leaving the city along the Urgut road – the Russians later discovered from a Persian spy whom they sent out into the city that this was because news had reached them of the disastrous

---

[168] *Ibid.*, 853.

[169] *Ibid.*, 854.

[170] 'Bukharskiya vorota g: Samarkanda', in Kun (ed.), *Turkestanskii Al'bom* Pt. 4, plate 54, No. 131 (Library of Congress, Prints & Photographs Division LC-DIG-ppmsca -09957–00131).

[171] 'Kopiya s raporta i. d. komendanta g. Samarkanda k komanduiushchemu voiskami Syr-Dar'inskoi Oblasti', 15/06/1868 RGVIA F.1396 Op.2 D.46 l. 108.

Figure 6.4 The Bukhara Gate of the city of Samarkand (*Turkestan Album*, 1871).

defeat of the Amir's forces at Zirabulak.[172] Kamalbai meanwhile recalled that both Jura-Bek and Baba-Bek felt that neither 'Abd al-Malik nor the inhabitants of the city had given them enough support, and did not want to risk the lives of their soldiers further.[173] 'Abd al-Ghafar Bek retreated with some of his men into the region of Urmitan and Penjikent in the upper Zarafshan valley, where at least one local source suggests he oppressed the local population.[174] Whilst the Samarqandis and Uzbeks from the surrounding areas of the Zarafshan valley attempted to maintain the siege, the heart seems to have gone out of them. Sami's account is quite vivid:

> The Governor with the main Russian force was facing the Bukharan Army at Katta-Qurghan. A small portion of the Russian force was left in Samarkand,

---

[172] 'Kopiya s raporta i. d. komendanta g. Samarkanda k komanduiushchemu voiskami Syr-Dar'inskoi Oblasti' 15/06/1868 RGVIA F.1396 Op.2 D.46 ll. 116*ob*–19.

[173] Simonova, 'Rasskazy ochevidtsev', 857.

[174] *Hikayat-i Damulla 'Abad Akhund*, 'Rasskaz ochevidtsa o sobytiyakh vremen prisoedineniya Srednei Azii k Rossii (o russkikh v Samarkande i Bukhare)', AV F.33 Op.1 D.147 & 184 ff. 8b–14b (http://zerrspiegel.orientphil.uni-halle.de/t21.html). Domla 'Abad Akhund's 'description of the Russian conquest' is in fact mainly a chronicle of the oppression (*zulm*) meted out by 'Abd al-Ghafar Bek.

which was surrounded in the citadel together with a group of Samarkand Jews and *Iranis* [*Samarqandi-yi irani va yahudi*]. The army of the *Tura*, having seized the approaches to the fortress, placed it under siege. At that time *Ishan* 'Umar Khan Makhdum-i Azami arrived with a large force, and joined with the *Tura's* forces. Many people from the tribes of the Khitai-Qipchaqs and Qaraqalpaqs, together with the Samarkand Tajiks [*Samarqandi-yi tajiki*] also concluded an agreement [with the *Tura*] to unite and tried to restrain the besieged and destroy the fortress wall. Over three days and nights they breached [the walls] in a few places, and some heroes [*bahaduran*] fought through the breaches [in the fortress], until fickle fate changed once more and played a trick, which was the reason for the flight of the Muslims and the salvation of the besieged. The *Tura* and the army were forced to leave the fortress and set off for Shahrisabz. Such a throng [of people], the number of whom could not be calculated, and such bravery and daring which is beyond the bounds of description, – [all] at once grew confused, dispersed and disappeared.[175]

Von Stempel concluded that at its height the force besieging the city was led by Jura-Bek and Baba-Bek – he did not mention 'Abd al-Malik and does not seem to have realised that he was there. He estimated that there were about 25,000 men from Shahrisabz, 15,000 Khitai-Qipchaqs under 'Adil Dadkhwah and 15,000 Urgutis, Panjikandis, Naimans, Tuya-Tatars, Qaraqalpaqs, Samarqandis and people from the surrounding villages under the leadership of Hussain Bek, 'Abd al-Ghafar Bek and 'Umar Bek.[176] Khoroshkin believed that this and the almost simultaneous attack on the Russian forces near Katta-Qurghan were a result of careful planning by the Bukharans,[177] and the notion that the siege was the result of a deep-laid Bukharan plot became ingrained in Russian accounts.[178] However, given that the force that was defeated at Zirabulak was more or less obedient to the Amir, whilst 'Abd al-Malik, Jura Bek and Baba Bek were in open rebellion against him, this seems most unlikely. Any coordination of forces seems to have been entirely accidental.[179]

Von Kaufman had caught up with the main Bukharan army at the Zirabulak heights near Katta-Qurghan on the 1 June, and the battle was fought the following day. At the time General Golovachev estimated the Bukharan numbers at 20,000 cavalry and 10,000 *sarbaz* infantry, though a later account gives the more modest figure of 15,000 men, of whom 6,000–8,000 were regular *sarbazes*.[180] The most vivid account of the battle comes from the pen of Nikolai Nikolaevich Karazin

[175] *TSM* text. ff. 84b–5a, trans. 85.
[176] 'Kopiya s raporta i. d. komendanta g. Samarkanda k komanduiushchemu voiskami Syr-Dar'inskoi Oblasti', 15/06/1868 RGVIA F.1396 Op.2 D.46 l. 121.
[177] Khoroshkhin, 'Vesna 1868 goda', 182.
[178] Lyko, *Ocherk voennykh deistvii*, 98–9; Terent'ev, *Istoriya zavoevaniya*, I, 439.
[179] Malikov, 'Russian Conquest', 190.
[180] Golovachev to von Kaufman 28/05/1868 RGVIA F.846 Op.1 D.6 ll. 57–8; Lyko, *Ocherk voennykh deistvii*, 102.

Figure 6.5 N. N. Karazin *The Entry of Russian Forces into Samarkand on the 8 June 1868 (Vstuplenie Russkikh voisk v Samarkand 8 iiunya 1868)* (1877). Russian State Museum, St Petersburg (Wikimedia Commons).

(1842–1908), later to become a well-known author and artist, most of whose work had Turkestani themes (Figure 6.5).[181] He fought at Zirabulak as a lieutenant in the 5th Turkestan Line Battalion, and first published his account of the affray in 1874.[182] According to Karazin, what turned into an easy victory for von Kaufman's force of 3,000 Russians, reinforced by Iskander Khan's Afghans from Jizzakh (a large and 'solid' force by local campaigning standards, as he noted), began in chaos, as they advanced towards the village of Zirabulak near Katta-Qurghan without realising that the red-coated Bukharan *sarbazes* had occupied the heights on their flank: only poor Bukharan gunnery saved them from heavy casualties when their artillery opened fire – after a brief period of confusion as their officers formed the marching columns into firing order (one of them crying out '*kasha, kasha!*' [porridge] in an attempt to shame his men into responding more quickly),[183] the Russians fired several volleys at the massed Bukharan ranks, and then charged:

> The regular cries of '*Ura*' that one hears on parade and manoeuvres do not give any understanding of the Hades-like chaos of sound, which one hears at the moment of a desperate scrimmage (*v minutu otchayannoi svalki*). Those who at that moment have ceased to be people, are not able to make human sounds – roars, whistles, piercing screams, something like mad

---

[181] On Karazin's *œuvre* see E. Shafranskaya, *Turkestanskii tekst v russkoi kul'ture: Kolonial'naya proza Nikolaya Karazina* (St Pb.: Self-published, 2016).

[182] Karazin, 'Zarabulakskie vysoty' [1874], in *Pogonya za nazhivoi*, 471–501.

[183] Karazin, 'Zarabulakskie vysoty', 478–9.

laughter and plaintive, almost dog-like howls mingle with the characteristic sound of copper-clad rifle butts striking human skulls.[184]

The Bukharans resisted at first – Karazin, in a fine orientalist touch, attributed this bravery to their being drugged with opium – before turning to flee: 'it
was not flight, it was not a retreat, it was something incomprehensible,
perplexing even our Turkestantsy, who were never perplexed. They went
quietly, drooping their heads, crowded together in thick masses, not one
looking back.'[185] Khoroshkhin estimated that, of the 6,000 Bukharan sarbazes
who fought there, at least 3,000 were killed or wounded, whilst only 1,000
retreated and reformed at Karmina.[186] The remainder scattered, and Sami
writes contemptuously that the Bukharans 'as usual, preferred flight'.[187] He
also believed that it was only the siege of Samarkand and von Kaufman's
consequent hasty retreat which prevented the fall of the Emirate altogether.

One officer who fought at Zirabulak described how, almost as soon as the
battle was won, a message in German from von Stempel was brought to von
Kaufman by a Persian slave from Samarkand, in which he informed him that
they had already beaten off five attempted stormings, and lost 210 men killed
or wounded, almost half the garrison. Von Kaufman's force had to march back
as quickly as possible to relieve them. They arrived just in time, and, according
to Muhammad Salih Tashkandi, were once again welcomed at the Shah-i
Zinda Gate of the city by the group of Iranis who had taken refuge with the
garrison in the citadel – if the inhabitants had hoped that the Russian arrival
would end what seems to have been a temporary Shi'i ascendancy in the city,
they were mistaken. Part of the bazaar was then burned to the ground as
a reprisal for the attack.[188] Muhammad Sufi recalled that for a few days it was
dangerous to go out into the streets because of the possibility of being shot by
Russian troops, but that things rapidly returned to normal.[189]

The siege of the Samarkand citadel produced many heroes of Russian arms,
many of whom would have their portraits recorded in the Turkestan Album
three years later. The most famous of these is the artist Vasilii Vereshchagin,
then an ensign in one of the Turkestan line battalions and a protégé of von
Kaufman: several of his best-known paintings, notably At the Fortress Walls
(1871) (Figure 6.6), made direct reference to the siege, though it was not until
much later that he published his own memoir of it.[190]

---

[184] Karazin, 'Zarabulakskie vysoty', 480.
[185] Karazin, 'Zarabulakskie vysoty', 482.
[186] Khoroshkhin, 'Vesna 1868 goda', 184.
[187] TSM text ff. 85a–b, trans. 86–7.
[188] TJT ff. 45a–b.
[189] Simonova, 'Rasskazy ochevidtsev', 864–5.
[190] V. Vereshchagin, 'Samarkand 1868', Na voine v Azii i Evrope: Vospominaniya (Moscow:
I. N. Kushnerev, 1894), 1–55. On Vereshchagin's Central Asian career see
Schimmelpenninck van der Oye, Russian Orientalism, 76–91.

Figure 6.6 *At the Fortress Walls – Let Them Enter!* (*U krepostnoi steny – pust voidut!*), Vasilii Vereschagin's memory of the 1868 siege of Samarkand (1871). Tretyakov Gallery Moscow (Wikimedia Commons).

Most accounts also celebrate the role of Lt-Colonel Nazarov, commander of the 9th Orenburg Line Battalion, who had remained behind in the citadel only because he was ill.[191] Stempel described him in his report as 'experienced', writing that, just as it looked as if the assault might carry the Bukhara Gate, 'Lt-Col. Nazarov with a cry of Ura! charged with the bayonet; the *mêlée* lasted for 15 minutes, the enemy was thrown back from the gate, and our men [*nashi*] threw themselves after them into the city.'[192] A fellow-officer described Nazarov as 'a remarkable individual – he spent all his life getting drunk and losing at cards. Wherever Nazarov is, there you will find drunkenness and cards,'[193] while Vereshchagin wrote that he was a '*bol'shoi kutila*' (a great hell-raiser).[194] According to Khokhriakova, the Russian renegade Bogdanov also played a key role – he had been captured at Chupan-Ata and was still under arrest. His initial offer of assistance was refused as von Stempel and the other officers did not trust him, but as the situation grew more desperate they relented. Bogdanov, who was intimately familiar with the fortifications, did a circuit of the walls, dropping grenades on the groups of Samarqandis who were seeking to undermine them,

---

[191] Shtabs-Kapitan Cherkasov, 'Zashchita Samarkand v 1868 godu', *VS* (1870), No. 9, 36.
[192] 'Kopiya s raporta i. d. komendanta g. Samarkanda k komanduiushchemu voiskami Syr-Dar'inskoi Oblasti', 15/06/1868 RGVIA F.1396 Op.2 D.46 ll. 109, 114.
[193] RGIA F.954 Op.1 D.336, 'Pis'mo ofitsera (familiya neustanovlena) s opisaniem voennykh deistvii otryada Konst. Petr. Fon Kaufmana', l. 10*ob*.
[194] Vereshchagin, 'Samarkand 1868', 5.

and so demoralising them that most withdrew.[195] Nazarov singled Vereshchagin out for particular praise in his report, noting that: 'Ensign Vereshchagin, regardless of the hail of stones and murderous gun fire, at the critical moment, with a gun in his hands rushed forward on the enemy; the soldiers, heartened by this heroic feat, followed him.'[196] He was praised in similar terms by a brother officer, Cherkasov, for having set an inspiring example to the men, leading from the front under heavy fire in order to expel an enemy foray into the citadel.[197] According to one anonymous account, Vereshchagin also felt bold enough to criticise von Kaufman's decision to leave the fortress so weakly garrisoned:

> The conduct of Vereshchagin, the artist who was in Samarkand, occasioned considerable surprise. This individual is remarkable both for his bravery and for his eccentricity. When upon his return Kaufman addressed himself with kindness to Vereshchagin, the latter replied 'Everyone here has been cursing you from first to last.' What? Why? 'Because you abandoned the citadel without reinforcing it.'[198]

Like Vereshchagin, the author of this letter was highly critical of von Kaufman's military judgement in leaving Samarkand so lightly garrisoned, and considered that, had the citadel fallen, it might have been the signal for a general uprising. He accused the general of being heavily under the influence of the Cossack officer Pistolkors (whom he described as a disgraced adventurer), who had urged von Kaufman to press on to Katta-Qurghan, leaving Samarkand exposed.[199] The account of the siege by a participant officer published in *Voennyi Sbornik* was careful, unsurprisingly, to voice no explicit criticisms of von Kaufman, nor indeed did Vereshchagin in his memoir.[200] If not quite as important to the Russians as the siege of Lucknow was to the British,[201] the attack on the Samarkand citadel gave the military in Central Asia a heroic narrative of their own: as von Kaufman put it: 'the defence of Samarkand by Russian forces can be provisionally placed in the series of the most glorious feats of Russian arms'.[202] It also instilled a deep suspicion of the 'fanatical' townsfolk of the city who had lent their support to the Shahrisabz forces. The Russians survived, albeit by the skin of their teeth, and the loss of

---

[195] Simonova, 'Rasskazy ochevidtsev', 856 – she claimed to have heard this story from a veteran NCO of the 6th Turkestan Line Battalion.

[196] Nazarov to von Shtempel 15/06/1868 RGVIA F.1392 Op.1 D.2 ll. 112–13.

[197] Cherkasov, 'Zashchita Samarkanda', 52.

[198] 'Pis'mo ofitsera', RGIA F.954 Op.1 D.336 l. 11*ob*.

[199] RGIA F.954 Op.1 D.336 ll. 1–4; Lt. Col Pistolkors had been Chernyaev's subordinate in Tashkent.

[200] Cherkasov, 'Zashchita Samarkanda'. See further Barooshian, *V. V. Vereshchagin*, 23–5, 39–40.

[201] Skrine makes this comparison – see *The Heart of Asia*, 395.

[202] Von Kaufman to Miliutin 08/06/1868 RGVIA F.1392 Op.1 D.2 l. 50.

Samarkand was a heavy blow to the Amir of Bukhara, which forced him to sue for terms.

The subsequent treaty between the Russian empire and Bukhara obliged the latter to pay an indemnity of 500,000 roubles, to allow Russian merchants to trade freely, and to cede Ura-Tepe, Jizzakh and Samarkand, though the latter remained a separate military division, raising the tantalising prospect that it might one day be returned.[203] The treaty did not refer to Russian protection or any cession of sovereignty – Bukhara did not formally become a protectorate of Russia in the sense of giving up control over its external affairs until a later treaty in 1885 – but it was clear that, like Khoqand, it was now a vassal state of the Russian empire.[204]

Possession of Samarkand meant that both branches of the Zarafshan (the Aq-Darya and Qara-Darya), upon which Bukhara depended for all its water, were now in the Zeravshan *Okrug* (later the Samarkand *Oblast'*) in Russian territory. In principle this gave the Russians considerable leverage, and, together with the familiar invoking of prestige, it became one of the main arguments for retaining Samarkand and the territory around it.[205] The technical difficulties involved in actually blocking the water supply altogether were enormous, however, as the commission charged with defining the new boundary with Bukhara quickly realised:

> Really, if 5,000 Sarts who are accustomed to this type of work need three weeks to construct a dam across the Qara-Darya, then how many hands and how much time it would take in order to divert the enormous and rapidly flowing mass of water of the Aq-Darya into a new direction! To say nothing of the fact that such a diversion of the water would flood the regions of Katta-Qurghan and Samarkand.[206]

A more realistic tactic was to alter the ratio of water use between canals in the Samarkand region and Bukhara in favour of the former, but even this proved extremely difficult to enforce owing to lack of technical knowledge on the Russian side – only in 1902 would a permanent formula for sharing water between Russian and Bukharan territory be agreed.[207] Even without this potential weapon, the Russian ascendancy over Bukhara seemed firm – but whether it would lead to a stable frontier and a stable diplomatic relationship or to the complete collapse of the emirate's political structures was still unclear.

[203] Morrison, *Russian Rule in Samarkand*, 103.
[204] Becker, *Russia's Protectorates*, 41–3.
[205] Von Kaufman to Miliutin 08/05/1868 RGVIA F.846 Op.2 D.6 l. 79*ob*.
[206] 'Zhurnal otryada sledovavshego pri kommissii dlya razgranicheniya Bukharskikh zemel' ot Zaryavshanskogo Okruga', 21/11/1868 RGVIA F.1396 Op.2 D.46 l. 145.
[207] Morrison, *Russian Rule in Samarkand*, 205–9.

6.5 Consolidating the Bukharan Protectorate

In the summer of 1868 Bukhara had been soundly defeated, humiliated and stripped of territory – but this had also been true in the summer of 1866, and war had broken out again less than two years later, with almost constant frontier conflict in between. This time, the arrangement proved more long-lasting – indeed, one could argue that it outlived the Tsarist regime itself, as the Manghit dynasty would rule in Bukhara until 1920, and the territory of the Emirate would be incorporated into the new Uzbek SSR only in 1924. Why was this? It was not simply that the Amir, the 'ulama and the ordinary population of Bukhara had been taught the futility of resisting Russian military superiority: that lesson was already clear after the Battle of Irjar. As we have seen, a key cause of conflict between Russia and Bukhara was the failure of the Bukharan state to conform to Russian expectations of what a state should be, and the inability of the Amir to control actors within it – whether these were the beks of frontier regions, the 'ulama and madrasa students, the townsfolk of Samarkand or indeed his own son. While Bukhara had never been a Westphalian state with clear external frontiers, this chronic instability was in part a function of the Russian presence, and the repeated humiliations heaped on Central Asian rulers through military defeat since 1853. There are clear signs that by 1868 the Russians had finally realised that they would need to strengthen Sayyid Muzaffar's authority, legitimacy and territorial grasp if they wanted him to be a reliable partner. In September Abramov reported that an attempt by the Amir to capture Shahrisabz had failed, and that this would further damage his authority as Jura-Bek and Baba-Bek continued to defy him. This was compounded by the continued presence there of 'Abd al-Malik Tura, who, even without forces of his own, was a continued threat to his father's authority owing to his personal popularity. Abramov considered that active measures needed to be taken to neutralise him and bolster Sayyid Muzaffar's authority.[208] In late October Abramov reported his return from Qarshi, where, after two small skirmishes, he had successfully put 'Katta-Tura' to flight. He had settled his men into winter quarters in the village of Jam, near the Bukharan frontier, so that they would be immediately available if needed.[209]

A year later, in December 1869, von Kaufman reported that the Amir was still fighting to subdue what he described as a rebellion by the Beks of Kulab and Hissar – in fact these regions well to the south-east of the Zarafshan range, though claimed by Bukhara, had effectively been independent for over 100 years.[210] Von Kaufman added that there were bands of armed raiders causing trouble along the new frontiers of the Zarafshan Region. The Bek of Ziauddin

---

[208] Abramov to von Kaufman ?/09/1868 RGVIA F.846 Op.2 D.6 ll. 177–185ob.
[209] Abramov to von Kaufman 30/10/1868 RGVIA F.846 Op.2 D.6 ll. 210–12.
[210] Wilde, *What Is beyond the River*, II, 754, 776.

was powerless to stop them, but detachments of Ural Cossacks sent out from
Katta-Qurghan had succeeded in killing and capturing a number of them.[211]

> The Amir himself, through his accredited envoy, intends to strongly stand
> by the union with Russia as the main support of his power within the
> khanate. In confirmation of these words, Seid-Muzafar [*sic*] in his letter to
> me and through Nasyr Toqsaba explains with complete openness his
> relations with Constantinople, Egypt, the East-India Company and
> Afghanistan, and asks for my advice on how to reply to the letters he
> has received from them.[212]

Von Kaufman naturally advised him that it would be 'inconvenient' for him
to maintain these contacts with such distant neighbours, which might end up
endangering his close ties with Russia. Later that year he wrote to the director
of the Asiatic Department, P. N. Stremoukhov, that 'The Bukharan Amir is
now beginning, it seems, to conduct himself as he ought to', whilst also noting
that the Amir's appeals to outside help at the time of the conquest had proved
of little use in any case, as the Ottoman Sultan's reply to the letter the Amir had
despatched after the defeat at Irjar in 1866 had not arrived until May 1870,
whilst the East India Company (as he still referred to the Government of India)
had been distinctly discouraging, and the Amir had still not replied to them.[213]
The Viceroy (who at that date was Sir John Lawrence, implacably opposed to
the 'forward school' of British frontier thinking) had asked the Amir what was
the reason for his dispute with the Russians, saying that he could not imagine
that war would have erupted unless Bukhara were somehow at fault. 'As we are
not your neighbours and live far from your realm, your affairs are not known
to us and we cannot give you any advice at the moment.'[214]

In his letter to the Tsar asking for his royal assent to the agreement on trade
drawn up between von Kaufman and Khudoyar Khan of Khoqand, Prince
Gorchakov also noted that Russian influence over Bukhara should be preserved, but that under no circumstances could outright annexation be considered. The Amir should be assured of this, and the Russians would offer to
recognise one of his sons as his successor, 'all the more so, because his eldest
son, Katta-Tura, having rebelled against his father, excels in his fanaticism and
hostility to us'.[215] In August 1870, partly in belated retaliation for the attack on
the Samarkand garrison, but also because the Amir's own efforts in this

---

[211] Von Kaufman to Gorchakov 24/12/1869 AVPRI F.147 Op.485 D.1260, 'Svedeniya
o polozhenii del v sosednykh s Turkestanskim kraem nezavisimykh sredneaziyatskikh
vladeniyakh', ll. 4–5*ob*.

[212] Von Kaufman to Gorchakov 23/09/1870 AVPRI F.147 Op.485 D.1260 ll. 12–*ob*.

[213] Von Kaufman to P. N. Stremoukhov 23/09/1870 AVPRI F.147 Op.485 D.1260 ll. 13–14.

[214] 'Ofitsial'nyya svedeniya o snosheniyakh Seid Muzafara s inostrannymi gosudaryami,
soobshchenyya poslannika Emira Nasyrom Toksaboyu', AVPRI F.147 Op.485 D.1260 ll.
18–19*ob*.

[215] Gorchakov to Alexander II 09/12/1872 AVPRI F.161/4 Op.729/2 D.326 ll. 1–2.

direction had clearly failed, General A. K. Abramov led a column over the pass through the Zarafshan mountains to the south of the city in order to attack Kitab and Shahrisabz, whose rulers, Jura-Bek and Baba-Bek, had defied both Bukhara and the Russians for so long. The small citadel at Kitab was stormed after a brief bombardment on the 13 August, for the relatively heavy loss of 19 killed and 108 wounded on the Russian side, and an estimated 600 dead among the defenders – with this the whole valley, including Shahrisabz, which was not defended, fell into Russian hands.[216] The two *beks* fled, first to the upper Zarafshan valley and then to Khoqand, where Khudoyar Khan promptly handed them over to the Russians. They would eventually be reconciled to Russian rule and given pensions and honorary military rank.[217] Abramov, on von Kaufman's instructions, handed over the Shahrisabz region to Amir Muzaffar of Bukhara rather than making a further annexation. A contemporary Persian account states that in thus destroying Shahrisabz's independence the *Nim-Padshah* ('Half-Emperor', i.e. the Governor-General, von Kaufman) had succeeded in doing what no Bukharan Amir (not even the notorious Amir Nasrullah, Bahadur Khan) had managed over the previous eighty-seven years.[218] This account, significantly, was commissioned and collected by the orientalist Alexander Kuhn, who had been assigned to von Kaufman's command in 1868.[219] He was sent on the Shahrisabz expedition with the express purpose of collecting topographical and other information – his role in many ways a textbook example of the orientalist as the servant of imperial power. Kuhn discovered a small collection of twenty-three manuscripts in Jura-Bek's palace in Kitab, which he sent, together with seventy-five others he had purchased, to the Imperial Public Library in St Petersburg.[220] This included a copy of the *Sharafnama-yi Shahi* by Hafiz-i Tanish, an important history of the reign of the sixteenth-century Abu'l-Khayrid Uzbek ruler 'Abdullah II, very probably that which is now in the manuscript

---

[216] 'Izvlechenie iz donesenie General-Maiora Abramova ob ekspeditsii v Shakhrisyabz, 1870 g.', in *Russkii Turkestan: Sbornik izdannyi po povodu Politekhnicheskoi vystavki.* Vyp. 3 ed. V. N. Trotskii (St Pb.: n.p., 1872), 207–17. In garbled form the Shahrisabz expedition made its way into the Italian adventure novelist Emilio Salgari's *Le aquile della steppa* (Genoa: Donath, 1907), a ripping yarn which I highly recommend.

[217] Kaufman to Miliutin 11/01/1873 RGVIA F.400 Op.1 D.352 ll. 1–5*ob*; Beisembiev (ed.), *The Life of Alimqul*, 26. See further V. V. Bartol'd, *Istoriya kul'turnoi zhizni Turkestana* (Leningrad: Izd. Akademii Nauk SSSR, 1927), 190.

[218] *Ta'rif-i Hakemran-i Shahrisabz dar zaman-i piruzi-yi urusiya,* 'Rasskaz o pravitelyakh Shakhrisabza pered russkim zavoevaniem', AV F.33 Op.1 D.142 (http://zerrspiegel .orientphil.uni-halle.de/t1189.html).

[219] On Kuhn's Central Asian career see Olga Yastrebova & Arezou Azad, 'Reflections on an Orientalist: Alexander Kuhn (1840–88), the Man and His Legacy', *IS* 48/5 (2015), 675–94.

[220] Chancery of the Turkestan Governor-General to Abramov n.d. TsGARUz F.I-1, Op.15 D.69 ll. 66–9.

Figure 6.7 'Abd al-Ghafar Bek, the former ruler of Ura-Tepe (*Turkestan Album*, 1871).

collection of the Oriental Institute of the Russian Academy of Sciences in St Petersburg.[221] As we shall see in subsequent chapters, this prefigured Kuhn's role as an 'embedded orientalist' in the 1873 Khiva and 1875-6 Khoqand campaigns.[222]

Following Shahrisabz's fall 'Abd al-Malik Tura fled to Afghanistan and eventually ended his days in Peshawar, where in 1877 he would be joined by 'Abd al-Ghafar Bek (Figure 6.7),[223] who had rejected the pension offered him by the Russians. Both received pensions from the Government of India, and dropped out of Bukharan politics.

In 1882 a wealthy Tashkent pilgrim called Ishan Sayyid Vali Khan, who had travelled from Mecca to Turkestan via British India, reported to the Russian authorities on his return that 'Abd al-Malik, or 'Katta-Tura', was now addicted to opium and quite incapable of playing any future role in Bukhara, and that an

---

[221] This was published in facsimile by M. A. Salakhetdinova as *Sharaf-nama-i shakhi: Kniga shakhskoi slavy, faksimile rukopisi D 88* (Moscow: Nauka, 1983 & 1989). See Thomas Welsford, *Four Types of Loyalty in Early Modern Central Asia: The Tuqay-Timurid Takeover of Greater Mawara al-nahr* (Leiden: Brill, 2013), 308.

[222] Yastrebova & Azad, 'Reflections on an Orientalist', 678-9; Morrison, 'Applied Orientalism', 637-9.

[223] 'Abdul-Gafar bek byvshii ura-tiubinskii-bek', in Kun (ed.), *Turkestanskii al'bom* .Pt. 2, Vol. 1, plate 8, No. 24 (Library of Congress, Prints & Photographs Division LC-DIG-ppmsca-09951-00024).

attempt the year before to arrange a reconciliation between him and Sayyid Muzaffar had failed.[224] The subjugation of Shahrisabz, and the neutralization of the threat from the Amir's eldest son by the Russians, demonstrated their new determination to transform Bukhara into a subordinate but viable partner – a protectorate similar to an Indian princely state, a model Miliutin had cited when the idea of transforming Tashkent into an independent khanate was still being mooted.

As Terent'ev put it, referring to Abramov's attack on Yangi-Qurghan in 1867: 'This was the whole secret: any consequences or reprimands came with rewards attached … in this way we created a peculiar system of action in Central Asia: the commanders of small forces were presented with freedom of initiative, often against the views of the government: the results of their enterprises were recognised by the government as *faits-accomplis*, 'a property of history', and the enterprising hustler (*peredovik*), instead of a reprimand, received a reward.'[225] The campaigns of 1866–8, which added Khujand, Jizzakh, Samarkand and the Zarafshan valley to the Russian possessions in Central Asia, were perhaps the only phase of the conquest of Central Asia where the 'man on the spot' genuinely slipped from the centre's control. The reasons are not difficult to find – the centre of command had shifted from Orenburg and Omsk to Tashkent, but communications had not yet caught up with this rapid advance (the telegraph would reach Tashkent only in 1873). The huge difficulties of transport and supply which ensured that steppe campaigns required months of preparation and large budgets for food, fodder and baggage animals did not apply once the Russians were operating in the cultivated, densely populated oases of the Chirchik, Ferghana and Zarafshan valleys. They could use carts rather than camels, purchase or requisition food from the local population, and were never far from water, though its poor quality did cause problems with sickness. Even so, the importance of local initiative should not be exaggerated. The War Ministry was much less concerned by this disobedience than the Foreign Ministry, while von Kaufman could always rely on steadfast support and approval from Miliutin in St Petersburg.

The other factor driving the Russian advance was the hostile relations with Bukhara: these were in many ways unexpected. Bukhara was not a steppe power, and was Russia's main trading partner in Central Asia. Prior to the early 1860s relations had been fairly good, even under the notorious Amir Nasrullah (who in local sources is remembered not as a crazed maniac, but as 'Bahadur Khan' – the brave ruler). Amir Sayyid Muzaffar took advantage of Khoqand's

[224] Memorandum from the acting Turkestan Governor-General (G. A. Kolpakovskii) 26/10/1877; Kolpakovskii to N. K. Giers 03/03/1882 AVPRI F.147 Op.485 D.1260 ll. 72, 82*ob*–4.
[225] Terent'ev, *Istoriya zavoevaniya*, I, 394.

weakness to seize territory from his neighbour, and then set his sights on Tashkent, something the Russians were never likely to tolerate. He probably underestimated Russian strength to begin with, and was clearly angered and humiliated by the Russian refusal to allow his ambassadors to proceed to St Petersburg and treat with the Tsar on equal terms. At the same time the Russian presence in Tashkent was clearly deeply destabilising for Bukhara's internal politics. It emboldened the rulers of regions that had never really acknowledged Bukharan authority – Ura-Tepe, Shahrisabz – to mount attacks on Russian outposts and patrols on their own account. It enraged the *'ulama* and *madrasa* students in Bukhara and Samarkand, an anger which seems to have extended to much of the urban and possibly the rural population. After Irjar it is clear that the Amir did not want further war, but was forced to prosecute it if he wanted to retain his throne, the biggest political threat being posed by his own eldest son, 'Abd al-Malik Tura, who presented himself as the champion of the anti-Russian party.

The cycle of warfare and rebellion ended after 1868 because the Russians realised that they would either have to reinforce the Amir's authority, or conquer and garrison all of the emirate's territory, something for which there was no appetite in either Tashkent or St Petersburg. They suppressed his internal enemies, made it clear to the population that the threat of Russian arms lay behind his authority, and brought outlying territories that had only ever been nominally subject to Bukhara under the Amir's rule.[226] In many ways Bukharan statehood, as it came to be understood by a later generation of the region's intellectuals, was a creation of Russian power.[227]

---

[226] Wilde, *What Is beyond the River*, II, 787–9.
[227] Khalid, *Politics of Muslim Cultural Reform*, 184–215; Khalid, *Making Uzbekistan*, 117–55.

7

The Fall of Khiva, 1872–3

Поля неведомой земли,
И гибель роты несчастливой,
И Уч-Кудук, и Киндерли,
И русский флаг над белой Хивой.

A battlefield in unknown lands
The doom of all our sad platoons
And Uch-Kuduk, and Kinderli
And Russian flags above white Khiva

Nikolai Gumilev, *Turkestanskie generaly* (1912)

No other campaign of Central Asian conquest was so carefully coordinated, choreographed and chronicled as Konstantin Petrovich von Kaufman's assault on Khiva in 1873. This was to be the first Turkestan Governor-General's personal triumph, one that he would not have to share in any way with his hated predecessor Chernyaev. The fall of Khiva had a powerful symbolism that would not be lost on any of its planners and participants, or on the educated public in Russia – where Bekovich-Cherkasskii had failed in 1717, and Perovskii in 1839–40, von Kaufman would succeed.[1] Although during the campaign itself press reports were censored,[2] in its immediate aftermath the Khiva expedition received extensive coverage in newspapers and periodicals, both in Russia

---

My thanks to Ulfatbek Abdurasulov and Paolo Sartori for their detailed comments on this chapter.

[1] Both these earlier unsuccessful campaigns had recently been the subject of publications in the Main Staff journal *Voennyi Sbornik*: D. Golosov, 'Pokhod v Khivu v 1717 godu', *VS* Vol. XXI (1861), 303–64; M. Ivanin/D. Golosov, 'Pokhod v Khivu v 1839 godu otryada russkikh voisk, pod nachal'stvom General-Ad'yutanta Perovskago', *VS* Vol. XXIX (1863), No. 1, 3–72 & No. 2, 309–58; Vol. XXX (1863), No. 3, 3–71. Von Kaufman referred to these precedents explicitly in a memorandum which successfully urged a Russian attack on Khiva: von Kaufman to Miliutin 31/10/1872 TsGARUz F.I-715 Op.1 D.53 l. 109*ob*.

[2] Ministry of Interior circular, 'Glavnoe upravlenie po delam pechati', 10/01/1873 TsGARUz F.I-1 Op.29 D.82, 'O nepropuske tsenzur'noi statei, kasaiushchikhsya Khivy i Srednei Azii', l. 4.

and abroad.[3] The only professional journalist who accompanied the column was in fact an American, the magnificently named Januarius Macgahan, whose best-selling account ensured the campaign would become almost as well known in the English-speaking world, though not all his judgements were welcome to the Russians.[4] Still less welcome were those of the American Consul in St Petersburg, Eugene Schuyler, who visited Turkestan in 1871-2 when an expedition to Khiva was already being mooted, and made use of his contacts among the Russian officer corps to make a series of embarrassing revelations about mismanagement owing to personal rivalries and ambition, and atrocities committed by Russian troops during the notorious massacre of the Yomud Turkmen which followed the fall of Khiva.[5] More surprisingly, perhaps, similar criticisms were made by Mikhail Terent'ev in his standard history, which contains a number of scathing judgements on von Kaufman and other officers.[6] In the khanate's own historiography the Russian conquest

[3] *Turkestanskii sbornik*. Vol. 46, 1-260 is dedicated entirely to press cuttings on the expedition, from *Moskovskie Vedomosti, Peterburgskie Vedomosti, Birzhevye Vedomosti, Peterburgskii Listok* and many other daily newspapers. Among the many longer pieces see in particular F. Lobysevich, 'Vzyatie Khivy i Khivinskaya ekspeditsiya 1873 g.', *VE* (1873), Nos. 8 & 10. Lt Hugo Stumm of the 8th Westphalian Hussars accompanied the Mangishlaq column and published his impressions in a series of columns for the *Norddeutsche Allgemeine Zeitung*, collected as Hugo Stumm, *Der russische Feldzug nach Chiwa* (Berlin: Mittler, 1875) and translated as Hugo Stumm, *The Russian Campaign against Khiva in 1873* trans. F. Henvey & P. Mosa (Calcutta: Foreign Department Press, 1876); see Terent'ev, *Istoriya zavoevaniya*, II, 222-3; M. Alikhanov-Avarskii, *Pokhod v Khivu (kavkazskikh otryadov): Step' i oazis* (St Pb.: Ya. I. Liberman, 1899), 2-3, 122; Mark, *Im Schatten des „Great Game"*, 161-2.

[4] J. A. Macgahan, *Campaigning on the Oxus and the Fall of Khiva* (London: Sampson, Low, Marston, Low and Searle, 1874), translated into Russian the following year as *Voennye deistviya na Oksus i padenie Khivoi* (Moscow: Universitetskaya Tip., 1875). MacGahan's arrival was neither authorised nor welcomed by the Russians, who at first mistook him for Eugene Schuyler, whose tour of Turkestan had ended the year before – the Commandant of the Kazalinsk district wrote to von Kaufman admitting that he had escaped their surveillance, and saying he did not know what had possessed Captain Rodionov, the assistant to the Commandant of Perovsk district, or Captain Geitsev, the commander of the Blagoveshchensk fortress at Irkibai, to allow him to proceed to Khiva: Kazalinsk district commandant to von Kaufman 08/04/1873 RGVIA F.1393 Op.1 D.23, 'O pribytii v otryad deistvuiushchikh voisk amerikanskogo poddannogo Mak Kokhan [sic]', ll. 1-ob.

[5] Eugene Schuyler, *Turkistan: Notes of a Journey in Russian Turkistan, Khokand, Bukhara, and Kuldja* (London: Sampson, Lowe, Marston, Searle & Rivington, 1876), II, 328-86; the appearance of Schuyler's book caused considerable disquiet in Russian military circles, and led them to look more favourably on Macgahan's account, which was considered more objective: 'Dokladnaya zapiska Generala Gorlova kak otvet na knigu amerikantsa Skailera', 1878 TsGARUz F. I-1 Op.27 D1524a 'Dokladnaya zapiska Generala Gorlova kak otvet na knigu amerikantsa Skailera, v kotoroi poslednii obvinil russkie voiska v zlodeniyakh, sovershennykh pri zavoevanii Srednei Azii', ll. 1-8.

[6] Terent'ev, *Istoriya zavoevaniya*, II, 59-321.

THE FALL OF KHIVA, 1872–3

was seen as a calamity, but one which had to be borne, although the most detailed account, the court historian Muhammad Yusuf Bek Bayani's *Shajara-yi Khwarazmshahi* (1914), would not become well known until the Soviet period.[7] Despite this tarnish on the shiny image of the campaign, it was widely celebrated in memoirs, official histories and even painting, with Nikolai Karazin producing a series of vast elaborate canvases portraying its most important moments, such as the crossing of the Amu Darya and the surrender of the city of Khiva.[8] At the time, at least, it was seen as a personal triumph for von Kaufman.

Despite this there was no question in this case of St Petersburg's 'man on the spot' getting out of control; while certainly serving von Kaufman's personal ambition, the 1873 Khiva expedition was an extremely elaborate, expensive operation which required months of planning, all stages of which were discussed and approved in St Petersburg: as Dmitri Miliutin, the War Minister, later recalled: 'despite all General Kaufman's peaceableness, and the complete desire of the higher government to avoid new conquests in Central Asia, there was no possibility of leaving the insolence of the Khivan Khan unpunished'.[9] As we shall see, von Kaufman's behaviour in his relations with Khiva was anything but peaceable, but Miliutin's reference to Khivan 'insolence' (*der-zost'*) is extremely significant: it is a theme that can be traced in Russian writings about Khiva since at least the 1820s, and, as we have seen in Chapter 2, was also cited by Perovskii when advocating his ultimately unsuccessful expedition in 1835. As Khrebtov, the author of a popular account of the campaign in a series of readings 'for soldiers and the people', wrote, 'the Khivans belong among those barbarous people who from the outset, from the very beginnings of the Russian state, were implacable and deadly foes of the Russians', something he traced back all the way to the 'Mongol yoke'.[10] As much as any real or imagined material damage to Russian interests through the plundering of caravans or slave raiding, it was this memory of earlier humiliations, and Khiva's perceived propensity to cock a snook at Russian authority, which was unforgiveable. Just as in 1837–9, in 1872–3 the Khivan Khan, Muhammad Rahim II, made repeated attempts to secure a peaceful settlement

---

[7] Yuri Bregel, 'Sochinenie Bayani "Shadzhara-ii khorezmshakhi" kak istochnik po istorii Turkmen', *Kratkie soobshcheniya instituta narodov Azii* Vyp. 44 (1961), 125–57 & 'Bayani: The Russian Conquest of Khiva and the Massacre of the Yomut Turkmens' trans. Ron Sela, in *Islamic Central Asia: An Anthology of Historical Sources* ed. Ron Sela & Scot Levi (Bloomington, IN: Indiana University Press, 2010), 300–5.

[8] 'Khudozhestvennoe izvestie: Khivinskii pokhod: Al'bom khromolitografii, ispolnennykh zavedeniem "Vinkel'man" po original'nym risunkam N. N. Karazina', *Niva* (1875), No.10 in *TS* Vol. 196, 34–6.

[9] Miliutin, *Vospominaniya 1869–nachalo 1873*, 543.

[10] A. N. Khrebtov, *Khivinskii pokhod: Chetyre chteniya dlya voisk i naroda* (St Pb.: Tip. A. M. Kotomina, 1875), 1.

with Russia, but was consistently rebuffed by Kaufman, who was single-mindedly bent on military glory.

Schuyler suggests that von Kaufman was anxious for a successful campaign to distract attention from the criticisms of Turkestan's administration which were appearing in the press, most of them inspired by Chernyaev's hostility, and that 'there was perhaps too, in the Governor-General's mind a feeling that a successful Khivan expedition, while being in itself an achievement of considerable merit, would in a satisfactory way round off his whole Asiatic career'.[11] Von Kaufman was an engineering officer, and overcoming the logistical difficulties of the campaign was for him a question of professional pride. Khiva's isolation by deserts had perhaps been somewhat exaggerated in the Russian mind by the failures of previous expeditions, but it was nevertheless real. As Paolo Sartori has put it: 'Khvārazm presented distinctive ecological features that made it less easy for anyone to connect with it than with other parts of Central Asia.'[12] It was widely recognised that the main difficulties of the campaign would consist in getting to Khiva in the first place; as V. A. Poltoratskii of the Caucasian Staff recalled:

> This expedition, debated and permitted from above, was so complicated by conditions and methods that, of course, it had to be considered more important than Shahrisabsz, Ghulja, Qarshi and even the capture of Samarkand. As a result of previous repeated failures of ours when trying to take possession of Khiva, the present campaign was of interest not only for Russia, but for the whole of Europe. Legends of past unsuccessful campaigns to Khiva, beginning with the invasion of Prince Bekovich-Cherkasskii, at the time of Peter the Great, to fresher stories about the attempts of Count Perovskii during the reign of Nicholas I to ravage this nest of predators, established some fantastic idea of the inaccessibility of the Khivan Khanate, which, on more sober consideration was found to be no more than a disorganised, savage, but not very terrible tribe of Central Asia, to which only access was very difficult and complicated.[13]

The 1873 Khiva campaign was the first of the Turkestan campaigns to have a special medal minted for its participants, a further sign of official approval and 'legend creation'.[14] It attracted large numbers of what the officers in regular Central Asian service called 'pheasants' – well-connected aristocratic officers who gained a temporary transfer to Turkestan, Orenburg or the Caucasus for the duration of the campaign in the hope of gaining medals or promotion.[15]

[11] Schuyler, *Turkistan*, II, 333; on Chernyaev's press campaign through *Russkii Mir*, the paper that he owned, see Mackenzie, 'Kaufman of Turkestan', 276 & *The Lion of Tashkent*, 108–14.
[12] Paolo Sartori, 'On Khvārazmian Connectivity: Two or Three Things That I Know about It', *JPS* 9/2 (2016), 141.
[13] V. A. Poltoratskii, 'Vospominaniya', *IV* (1895), No. 5, 415.
[14] See http://medalirus.ru/sobitiya1865-1914/medal-za-khivanskiy-pokhod.php.
[15] Alikhanov-Avarskii, *Pokhod v Khivu*, 11–12.

Subsequently the most famous of these would be Mikhail Dmitr'evich Skobelev (1843–1881), who in 1870 had been sent away from Turkestan by von Kaufman after fighting a duel with a superior officer.[16] While serving in Tiflis he had submitted a short memorandum urging the necessity of taking Khiva in order to consolidate Russian power in Central Asia, and he now successfully contrived to get himself assigned to the Caucasian column that would set out from Mangishlaq.[17] Less distinguished militarily, though even better connected socially, were Prince Evgenii Maximilianovich Romanovskii of Leuchtenberg (1847–1901), a grandson of Nicholas I who would later marry Skobelev's sister; Prince Alexander Konstantinovich Bagration-Imeretinskii (1837–1900), known for some reason as 'Pineapple';[18] Count Pavel Petrovich Shuvalov (1847–1902), whose correspondence from the march with his father Petr Pavlovich, Grand Duke Alexei Alexandrovich and Count Boris Alexeevich Perovskii is one of the best sources for the advance from Orenburg;[19] and Grand Duke Nikolai Konstantinovich Romanov (1850–1918), the Tsar's nephew, who, after a series of lurid sexual misdemeanours, would eventually be exiled permanently to Turkestan.[20] Shuvalov described his journey as one of a group of well-connected officers who travelled from St Petersburg to Orenburg in February 1873 specifically to take part in the forthcoming campaign, for the duration of which they were assigned temporary commands in Orenburg Line and Cossack regiments.[21] To his father he added that he had chosen the Orenburg force rather than the one setting out from Tashkent after von Kaufman had made it clear that the practice of introducing officers 'whose rank gives them the right to command separate units [i.e. Guards Officers and Staff Officers] outrages his sense of justice and military privilege'[22] – though this

[16] A. N. Maslov, *Zapiski o M. D. Skobeleve (materialy dlya biografii)* (St Pb.: A. S. Suvorin, 1887), 219–20. Skobelev was the son of Lt-General Dmitrii Ivanovich Skobelev, and spent his early life in the Peter & Paul Fortress in St Petersburg (where his grandfather was Commandant) and then in Paris. He had very good St Petersburg connections.
[17] 'Zapiska o zanyatii Khivy', 05/08/1871 GARF F.728 Op.1 D.2943, published in 'Posmertnye bumagi M. G. Skobeleva', *IV* (1883), No. 10, 130–8.
[18] Alikhanov-Avarskii, *Pokhod v Khivu*, 14.
[19] BL Add. MS. 47841 ff. 75–101, 'Zapiska Grafa P. Shuvalova o khivinskom pokhode', 1873; RGIA F.1092 Op.1 D.287, 'Pis'ma Pavla Petr. Shuvalova (Gr. Bor. Aleks) Perovskomu ob uchastii ego v khivinskom pokhode (s risunkami i kartami)'; D.288 'Pis'ma Pavla Petr. Shuvalova otsu Gr. Petru Pavl. Shuvalovu iz khivinskoi ekspeditsii'. My thanks to Yuan Gao for consulting the letters held in RGIA for me.
[20] Morrison, *Russian Rule in Samarkand*, 204–5; and for a much fuller account A. M. Lavrenova & M. O. Chernichenko, '"Avgusteishii bol'noi", zhandarmy i psikhiatry: "Krymskie kanikuly" velikogo knyazya Nikolaya Konstantinovicha (1901–1904 gody)', *Novyi Istoricheskii Vestnik* Vol. 51 (2017), 116–51 (www.nivestnik.ru /2017_1/51.pdf).
[21] Shuvalov to Grand Duke Alexei Alexandrovich Letter 1 19/02/1873 BL Add. MS. 47841 ff. 75–6v.
[22] Shuvalov Jr to Shuvalov Sr 21/01/1873 RGIA F.1092 op.1 D.288 l. 1.

did not apparently extend to those with royal connections, as Prince Romanovskii and Grand Duke Nikolai Konstantinovich would both be given commands by von Kaufman. This jostling for position also ensured that the campaign generated numerous memoirs by participants anxious to demonstrate the part they had played,[23] and an elaborate official history, ostensibly authored by Major V. N. Trotskii, who had been von Kaufman's Chief of Staff for the campaign, but actually part of a collective enterprise overseen by the indefatigable and indispensable N. I. Grodekov (1843–1913), who would also go on to be the chronicler of Skobelev's victories and eventually Turkestan Governor-General himself.[24] Von Kaufman's editorial hand is frequently visible in this narrative, which was published in 1881–2 with funds from the War Ministry.[25] Von Kaufman also conceived a series of volumes (not all of which were published) on the history, economy, flora and fauna of the Khwarazm oasis. For this purpose the columns that marched to Khiva included a team of six 'embedded experts' under the leadership of Baron Alexander Kaul'bars.[26] The best-known of these, the orientalist Alexander Ludwigovich Kuhn, had gained his first experience of this kind of work during the Shahrisabz campaign of 1870, and would play a similar role in Khoqand in 1875–6.[27] He was tasked with taking possession of the khanate's archives and libraries, so that they could be used to understand its history, administration and tax system. The manuscripts he collected were whisked off to the Oriental Insitutute in St Petersburg, but languished unused until the 1930s, when they became the main source for P. P. Ivanov and Yuri Bregel's pioneering work on nineteenth-century

[23] See most notably Polkovnik Kolokol'tsov, *Ekspeditsiya v Khivu v 1873 godu: Ot Dzhizaka do Khivy: Pokhodnyi dnevnik* (St Pb.: Tip. Departamenta Udelov, 1873); E. Saranchov, 'Khivinskiya ekspeditsiya 1873 goda (zapiski ochevidtsa sapera)', *Inzhenernyi Zhurnal* (1874), Nos. 1–5; Poltoratskii, 'Vospominaniya', *IV* (1895), Nos. 5–6, 414–44, 760–82; Maslov, *Zapiski o M. D. Skobelev*; Alikhanov-Avarskii, *Pokhod v Khivu*.

[24] V. N. Trotskii (ed.) [N. I. Grodekov], *Materialy dlya opisaniya khivinskago pokhoda 1873 goda: Opisanie deistvii kavkazskikh otryadov* (Tashkent: Izdano, na pravakh rukopisi, po rasporyazheniiu Turkestanskogo General-Gubernatora, Gen-Ad. K. P. Fon-Kaufmana, 1881) – Grodekov's name does appear on the title page of the second edition: N. I. Grodekov, *Khivinskii pokhod 1873 g.: Deistviya kavkazskikh otryadov* (St Pb.: V. S. Balashov, 1883); V. N. Trotskii (ed.) [Grodekov/Verevkin], *Opisanie deistvii orenburgskago otryada v khivinskuiu ekspeditsiiu 1873 g., sostavlennoe pod redaktsieiu svity Ego Velichestva General-Maiora Trotskago* (Tashkent: n. p., 1881); V. N. Trotskii (ed.) [Grodekov], *Opisanie deistvii Turkestanskago otryada v khivinskuiu ekspeditsiiu 1873 goda* (Tashkent: Tip. F. V. Basilevskim, 1882).

[25] 'Zamechaniya Gen-ad' f. Kaufman 1 na sostavlennoe polkov: Grodekovym opisanie khivinskago pokhoda 1873 goda', RGIM OPI F.307 Op.1 D.7 ll. 98–102. See further Morrison, 'The Turkestan Generals'.

[26] AV F.33 Op.1 D.6, 'Zametka o razlichnykh oblastei russkikh issledovaniya v Turkestanskom krae', ll. 15–19.

[27] Morrison, '"Applied Orientalism"', 637–9; Yastrebova & Azad, 'Reflections on an Orientalist'.

Khiva.[28] While Kuhn's volumes never appeared, M. N. Bogdanov, the naturalist who accompanied the expedition, did publish a description of its animal, bird and fish life, including the Amu-Darya sturgeon, which he named after von Kaufman.[29]

While there was certainly a reality to the Khivan campaign – a reality which, as with most other steppe and desert campaigns in Central Asia, consisted largely of dead and dying camels, to which in this case we can add thousands of men desperate with thirst – we are never far away from a sense that the whole event was conceived to fit a pre-determined historical narrative; the initial quarrel, the meticulous planning, the logistical difficulties overcome, the carefully stage-managed triumphal entry into the city, the many medals awarded, the pious utterances about slavery, and the subsequent presentation of all these in memoirs, historiography, paintings and even poetry: none of this was spontaneous or accidental. If, after his death, von Kaufman came to be known as the *pokoritel'* (conqueror) as well as the *ustroitel'* (builder) of the Turkestan region, it was largely thanks to this campaign.[30]

7.1   Russia–Khiva Relations 1869–72

The fall of Tashkent in 1865 had bridged the gap between the Syr-Darya and Siberian lines of fortresses, encircling most of the Qazaq steppe; from 1867 the new steppe statute began to close this formerly open frontier, internalising its administration and transforming it into a series of military provinces of the empire – with districts, *volosts* and numbered *auls* as units of administration,

---

[28] P. P. Ivanov, *Arkhiv khivinskikh khanov XIX v.: Issledovanie i opisanie dokumentov s istoricheskim vvedeniem* (Leningrad: Izd. Gosudarstvennoi Publichnoi Biblioteki, 1940); Iu. E. Bregel, *Khorezmskie turkmeny v XIX veke* (Moscow: Nauka, 1961) & *Dokumenty Arkhiva Khivinskikh Khanov po istorii i etnografii Karakalpakov* (Moscow: Nauka 1967); Sartori, 'On Khvārazmian Connectivity', 135–8 & 'Seeing Like a Khanate: On Archives, Cultures of Documentation, and Nineteenth-Century Khvārazm', *JPS* 9/2 (2016), 228–57.

[29] M. N. Bogdanov, *Ocherki prirody Khivinskogo Oazisa i pustyni Qizil-Qum: Opisanie khivinskago pokhoda 1873 goda, sostavlennoe pod redaktsieiu General'nogo Shtaba General-Leitenanta V. N. Trotskago.* Vyp. XII (Tashkent: Tip. F. V. Basilevskim, 1882). *Pseudoscaphirhynchus kaufmanii* is now severely endangered – see Vadim J. Birstein, 'Threatened Fishes of the World: *Pseudoscaphirhynchus spp. (Acipenseridae)' Environmental Biology of Fishes* 48 (1997), 381–3.

[30] A. A. Semenov, 'Pokoritel' i ustroitel' Turkestanskogo kraya: General-Ad'iutant K. P. fon-Kaufman 1-i', in *Kaufmanskii sbornik: Izdannyi v pamyat' pokoritelya i ustroitelya Turkestanskogo kraya, General-Ad'iutanta K. P. fon-Kaufmana 1-ogo* (Moscow: Tip. I. N. Kushnerev, 1910), i–lxxxiv; see also G. P. Fedorov, 'Moya sluzhba v Turkestanskom krae (1870–1910 goda)', *IV* (1913), No. 12, 810–11. The association continues to this day, in part thanks to Gumilev's specific referencing of the campaign in Turkestanskie generaly: Yadgor Norbutaev 'Sekrety "Turkestanskikh Generalov": i Uch-Kuduk, i Kinderli', fergana.ru 09/08/2016 (www.fergananews.com/articles/9053).

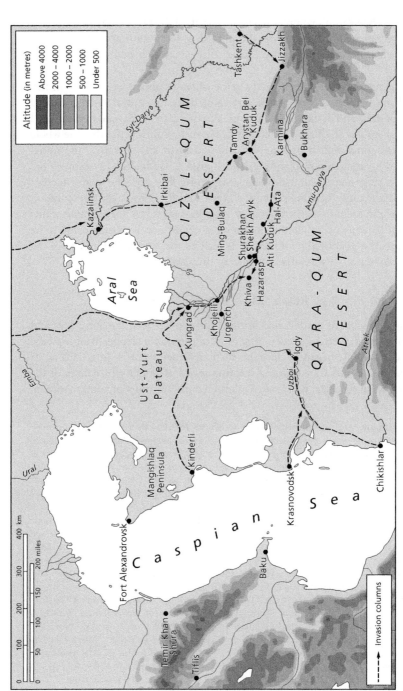

Map 7 Khiva and the routes to it

providing at least an appearance of regularity and order.³¹ This left the Qizil-
Qum desert in the East and the Mangishlaq peninsula in the West as open
frontiers between newly conquered Russian territory and Khwarazm, separ-
ated from it by inhospitable territory, but still in Russian eyes allowing the
khanate's undesirable influence to leach out and cause disruption. In
January 1870 Miliutin still considered that the construction of a ring of
fortifications around the khanate by the Orenburg, Caucasus and Turkestan
commands might be sufficient to contain it without the need for a costly
expedition or the annexation of Khivan territory.³² Later the same year, in
an incident that became notorious, the Qazaqs of the Adai tribe on the
Mangishlaq peninsula rebelled and attacked a patrol commanded by the
head of the Mangishlaq Division, Colonel Rukin, who committed suicide
rather than let himself be captured; those of his men who survived were carried
off as prisoners of war and enslaved.³³ The Russians assumed that the Adai
must have been acting under Khivan instigation, and this episode would be
brought up two years later by Governor Kryzhanovskii of Orenburg as a reason
to refuse negotiations with the Khivan Khan.³⁴ Other grievances frequently
cited by the Russians were Khiva's earlier support of the Qazaq freebooter and
rebel Iset Kutebar (though he had made his peace with the Russians in 1858
when the Ignat'ev mission came to Khiva, and in 1873 he would actually serve
as a guide for the Orenburg column), and more recently of 'the bandit Sadiq',
son of Kenesary, who had rebelled against the Russians after receiving his early
education in Orenburg and had helped to organise resistance to the Russians at
Tashkent in 1864.³⁵

As Jeff Eden has recently shown, the most long-standing grievance claimed
by Russia – that Khiva had large numbers of enslaved Russian subjects – was
almost certainly untrue by the 1870s.³⁶ The 400 captives released by Richmond

³¹ Martin, *Law and Custom*, 39–40; Campbell, *Knowledge and the Ends of Empire*, 31–62.
³² Miliutin to Grand Duke Mikhail Romanov 19/01/1870 TsGARUz F.I-715 Op.1 D.45 ll.
107–9.
³³ V. A. Potto, 'Gibel otryada Rukina v 1870 godu', *IV* (1900), No. 7, 110–35; Terent'ev,
Istoriya zavoevaniya, II, 62; Alikhanov Avarskii, *Pokhod v Khivu*, 15.
³⁴ Kryzhanovskii to Miliutin 13/03/1872 RGVIA F.400 D.301, 'O vysylke khivinskim khanom poslantsev v Tiflis dlya ustanovleniya mirnykh otnoshenii s Rossiei', ll. 13–16; the
Khivan historian Agahi does suggest that the attack on Rukin by the Adai was at the
instigation of the Khan, but it seems more likely that he sought to claim it as a victory after
the event: V. V. Bartol'd, 'Sobytiya pered khivinskim pokhodom 1873 goda po rasskazu
khivinskogo istorika' [1910], in *Sochineniya* II (2) (Moscow: Izd. Vostochnoi Literatury,
1964), 412.
³⁵ Ignat'ev, *Missiya v Khivu i Bukharu*, 59–79; Akhmet Kenesarin, *Sultany Kenisara i Sadyk*
ed. E. T. Smirnov (Tashkent: Tip. S. I. Lakhtina, 1889); Kilian, 'Allies and Adversaries',
224–5, 238–9.
³⁶ Jeff Eden, 'Beyond the Bazaars: Geographies of the Slave Trade in Central Asia', *MAS* 51/4
(2017), 919–55.

Shakespear in 1841 probably represented almost the sum total of Russians held in Khwarazm at that time, and they would not be replenished.[37] The twenty-one Russian prisoners whom Muhammad Rahim Khan released in early 1873 in a last attempt to avert a Russian attack were very probably all those left in the khanate by that date, and all of them seem to have been captured in the previous two or three years.[38] The Russians also emphasised the humane objective of liberating the much more numerous Persian slaves in the khanate, which did much to reconcile British public opinion to the expedition.[39] Even before Khiva's surrender, von Kaufman wrote to Foreign Minister Gorchakov from the line of march that, thanks to Russian pressure, the Khan had proclaimed the liberation of all slaves in the khanate (which he estimated at 16,000) and that most of the Persians were now on their way home, something he believed would secure Russia's moral influence in Central Asia.[40] This was a means of burnishing Russia's claim to a *mission civilisatrice* in Central Asia after the event, not a major factor in the original decision to invade.

It was questions of prestige and security, not the economic motivations invented by Soviet historians, which dominated the debate over whether to send an expedition to Khiva over the next two years.[41] Von Kaufman urged that it was necessary to 'finish with' the khanate (*nado pokonchit' s neiu*), noting that this did not necessarily imply annexation – the attack on Shahrisabz the previous year had shown that a punitive expedition could have a sufficiently salutary effect.[42] He added that, while he respected the Tsar's injunction that there be no more territorial annexations in Central Asia (he described Kolpakovskii's actions in the Ili valley as an exception, provoked by the aggression of the Taranchis), he did not think they could confine themselves to a purely defensive position towards Khiva, whose ruler would simply interpret this as weakness: 'not one embassy to Khiva has had the desired result, not one letter or exhortation has had the desired effect, and the more modest our demands, the more obstinate the Asiatic ruler is in his cunning (*kovarstvo*), in his insolence (*derzost'*) against us.'[43] He also made

---

[37] Perovskii to Chernyshev, 26/11/1840, in Serebrennikov, *Sbornik*. Vol. 2. *1841 g.*, Doc.133, 217; Shakespear, 'A Personal Narrative'.

[38] Kazalinsk District Commandant to von Kaufman 25/03/1873 RGVIA F.1393 Op.1 D.16, 'O pribytii khivinskogo poslantsa s russkimi plennymi', ll. 3–*ob*; Bayani, *Shajara-yi Khwarazmshahi* trans. Sela, in *Islamic Central Asia*, 301; Grodekov estimated the total number of Russian captives at thirty: *Khivinskii pokhod*, 276; see Eden, *Slavery and Empire*, 186.

[39] Richard Huzzey, *Freedom Burning: Anti-slavery and Empire in Victorian Britain* (Ithaca, NY: Cornell University Press, 2012), 204–10; Eden, *Slavery and Empire*, 183.

[40] Von Kaufman to Gorchakov 16/05/1873 TsGARUz F.I-715 Op.1 D.56 ll. 105–8.

[41] T. G. Tukhtametov, *Rossiya i Khiva v kontse XIX–nachale XX veka* (Moscow: Nauka, 1969), 11–30.

[42] Von Kaufman to Miliutin 17/03/1871 TsGARUz F.I-715 Op.1 D.45 l. 323.

[43] Von Kaufman to Miliutin 18/03/1871 TsGARUz F.I-715 Op.1 D.45 ll. 339*ob*–40.

an argument from the standpoint of economy, pointing out that a fortress at
Irkibai in the Qizil-Qum, which Miliutin had agreed to, made little sense
except as an advance post for an attack on Khiva, and that it would be even
more expensive and difficult to supply than the Syr-Darya forts had been.
Instead, he suggested, Khiva could be tamed by constructing a fortress on the
right bank of the Amu-Darya (he either did not know, or did not recognise,
that this was Khivan territory) and annexing the delta of the river. There would
be no need to annex Khiva itself. The enterprise, he recognised, was fraught
with logistical difficulties, which had caused the failure of previous expeditions
since 1717 (a reference to Bekovich-Cherkasskii), but he was confident that the
5,000 camels which he estimated would be needed could be found among the
Qazaqs and Turkmen, and he was already engaged in active preparations for
the expedition. In characteristically paranoid style he concluded by invoking
the spectre of a rumoured holy war brewing between Bukhara and
Afghanistan, making the need to reinforce Russian prestige all the more
urgent.[44] While von Kaufman rattled his sabre in Turkestan, Colonel
N. G. Stoletov was doing the same from the Caucasian command, sending
a memorandum to Miliutin which suggested using the new Russian outpost of
Krasnovodsk on the Caspian shore, which he had established in 1869, as the
base for an expedition that would seize Kungrad in the delta of the Amu-Darya
and all the khanate's territory to the north of the dry bed of the Lauzan canal.[45]

According to Agahi's *Jami' ul-waq'iat-i Sultani*, Khoqand had sent an
embassy to Khiva requesting assistance against the Russians after the fall of
Aq Masjid in 1853 and urging the Qunghrats to join them in a Jihad against the
Russians.[46] In 1854 the Khivan Khan sent a letter to the Ottoman Sultan
requesting assistance against the Russians, described as occupying
a considerable amount of Khivan territory – no doubt a reference to their
newly established presence on the Syr-Darya.[47] In 1858 the Ignat'ev mission
had alarmed the Khivans owing to its size and the presence of the steamers
Obruchev and *Perovskii*, and had left without managing to negotiate
a treaty; it had also confirmed Russian opinion of Khiva's relative military

[44] Von Kaufman to Miliutin 18/03/1871 TsGARUz F.I-715 Op.1 D.45 ll. 340–2.
[45] Stoletov to Miliutin n.d. (1871) TsGARUz F.I-715 Op.1 D.46 ll. 328–35; on the significance of the Lauzan to Russian thinking about Khiva see Akifumi Shioya, 'Povorot and
the Khanate of Khiva: A New Canal and the Birth of Ethnic Conflict in the Khorazm
Oasis, 1870s–1890s', *CAS* 33/2 (2014), 232–45.
[46] *MPITT* Vol. II, 539; Muhammad Riza Mirab Agahi, *Jami' al-vaqi'at-i Sultani* ed.
Nouryaghdi Tashev (Samarkand & Tashkent: International Institute for Central Asian
Studies, 2012); Paolo Sartori informs me that the original of this missive is today
preserved in the Archive of the Khans of Khiva – he describes it as 'a crude attempt by
Khoqandis to persuade the Qunghrats to join their armed resistance' against the Russian
'infidels' (personal communication).
[47] Petition for assistance from the Khivan Khan to the Ottoman Sultan 25/06/1854, in *The
History of Central Asia in Ottoman Documents* ed. Mustafayev & Serin, I, 191.

weakness.[48] Agahi's *Shahid-i Iqbal* describes another embassy from Khoqand to Khiva requesting assistance after the fall of Turkestan in 1864, and repeated emissaries from Bukhara during the period of its ongoing subjection to Russia in 1866-8, while Muhammad Rahim Khan also hosted Amir Sayyid Muzaffar's rebellious son, 'Abd al-Malik Tura, after the latter's failure to recapture Samarkand in the summer of 1868.[49] Although distracted by a rebellion amongst the Yomud Turkmen in 1864-6, Khiva's ruling elite were thus well aware of the growing threat posed by Russian expansion, although it played a limited role in the khanate's historiography. If the defeats suffered by Khoqand and Bukhara between 1864 and 1868 had not alerted them to this, the establishment of a Russian fortress on the Caspian shore at Krasnovodsk (Qizil-su) in 1869, in a region claimed by Khiva, and an armed reconnaissance expedition by Transcaspian troops under Colonel V. I. Markozov (1838-1908) towards the Sary-Kamish depression in the autumn of 1871 certainly did (see Chapter 9).[50] Thanks to Qazaq informants who spent winters close to the Russian lines, they were also aware of Russian military superiority, and the ineffectiveness of their irregular cavalry against Russian infantry.[51] Unsurprisingly, then, as in 1837-9, the Khivans made numerous efforts to negotiate with the Russians and stave off an attack.[52] Becker refers to Muhammad Rahim Khan's 'obstinate rejection of Russian demands',[53] but this simply echoes the Russian understanding of their relationship with Khiva, whose attempts to find a diplomatic solution are invisible in Russian accounts. Grodekov refers to the 'refusal of the Khivan Khan to fulfil the just and proportionate demands of our government'.[54] Terent'ev presents a series of negotiations between Tashkent and Khiva in which he assumes the bad faith of the latter, and consistently presents the Khan as disrespectful, intransigent and badly advised by his anti-Russian *Diwan-begi*, Muhammad Murad. The latter emerges as the chief villain in most Russian accounts, and also in Mullah Shayda'i's poem on the fall of Khiva he becomes the scapegoat for Khivan misfortunes ('his concern was not the homeland, but money').[55] Muhammad Murad's influence over the Khan probably derived from the prominent role he

---

[48] Ignat'ev, *Missiya v Khivu i Bukharu*, 143-55; Strong, 'The Ignat'ev Mission'.

[49] Bartol'd, 'Sobytiya pered khivinskim pokhodom 1873 goda', 403-6.

[50] Terent'ev, *Istoriya zavoevaniya*, II, 73.

[51] Bartol'd, 'Sobytiya pered khivinskim pokhodom 1873 goda', 403-6.

[52] D. Kh. Ziyaeva, 'Khivinskoe khanstvo v period ustanovleniya protektorata Rossiiskoi Imperii', in *Khorezm v istorii gosudarstvennosti Uzbekistana* ed. D. A. Alimova & E. V. Rteveladze (Tashkent: Uzbekistan Failasuflari Milliy Jamiyati, 2013), 233-9.

[53] Becker, *Russia's Protectorates*, 65.

[54] Trotskii [Grodekov], *Opisanie deistvii kavkazskikh otryadov*, 1.

[55] Aftandil Erkinov, 'The Conquest of Khiva from a Poet's Point of View', in *Looking at the Coloniser: Cross-Cultural Perceptions in Central Asia and the Caucasus, Bengal, and Related Areas* ed. Beate Eschment & Hans Harder (Würzburg: Ergon Verlag, 2004), 95, 100.

had played in the suppression of the Yomud rebellion in 1864–6, but it seems doubtful that he can be held solely responsible for the breakdown in negotiations with Russia.[56] The Khivans believed, with some reason, that the Russians had repeatedly threatened their subjects and territory by constructing fortresses at Alexandrovsk in Mangishlaq, at Kazalinsk on the Syr-Darya and finally at Krasnovodsk.[57] Even Terent'ev's account makes it clear that the Khivans considered that the Russians had encroached on their territory and violated their sovereignty by claiming all the territory along both banks of the Syr-Darya, and by constructing the fortresses on the Caspian, though he presents their demands for redress as further evidence of their insolence.[58]

Reading between the lines, what we actually see here is an intense attempt by the Khivans to negotiate and settle differences by diplomatic means. As in Bukhara in the 1860s, the Khan and his advisers probably underestimated the threat from Russia until it was too late, but the failure of these negotiations was not solely or even primarily down to Khiva. It is true that the Khivan leadership refused to abandon what the Russians considered to be undesirable, uncivilised and disorderly behaviour – harbouring caravan raiders, receiving enslaved Russians and Persians from the Qazaqs and Turkmen, and refusing to admit Russian merchants. While the Russians assumed that these practices arose purely from Khivan insolence, savagery and barbarity – that they were a form of engrained Oriental vice – in fact many of these activities were simply an ordinary and essential part of the Khanate's economy. Beyond this, the raids carried out on neighbouring regions by their Turkmen and Qazaq clients were also expressions of loyalty to the dynasty by these groups, and as such 'constitutive of the Qunghrats' sovereignty'.[59] Eliminating them when the Russians offered no economic incentives to do so was not straightforward. In any case, the persistent sticking-point in the negotiations was not the direct Khivan rejection of Russian demands, but the Khan's insistence that as a fellow sovereign ruler he be allowed to negotiate directly with the Tsar in St Petersburg on equal terms, rather than with von Kaufman in Tashkent, something the latter consistently refused. In 1870 Miliutin had stated that von Kaufman had chief responsibility for negotiations with Khiva, and that the Orenburg and Caucasian commands were to communicate with the khanate only when it was absolutely necessary, on matters of purely local political importance.[60] This was a prerogative which von Kaufman guarded jealously. In April 1872 a Khivan envoy called Ataliq Bala Irnazar Kabylov, a Qaraqalpaq, requested permission to proceed to St Petersburg to discuss the question of Russia's

---

[56] MPITT, II, 611–38.
[57] Bartol'd, 'Sobytiya pered khivinskim pokhodom 1873 goda', 407.
[58] Terent'ev, Istoriya zavoevaniya, II, 60–71.
[59] Paolo Sartori (personal communication).
[60] Miliutin to Grand Duke Mikhail Romanov 19/01/1870 TsGARUz F.I-715 Op.1 D.45 l. 111.

borders with the khanate, but he was refused, detained for three days and then sent back to Khiva, having only been allowed to leave a letter.[61] The last and most serious attempt by the Khivans to avert war reflected their frustration with von Kaufman, as they attempted to bypass him altogether by negotiating with the Russian forces on the Caspian shore, which were under the authority of the Caucasian Military District. As this case is unusually well documented, it is worth examining in detail to understand why Russo-Khivan negotiations failed.[62]

In January 1872 the Commandant of Mangishlaq reported that the previous week an envoy had arrived at Fort Alexandrovsk. He described him as 'one of the Turkmen elders of the Abbol tribe' called Abrek Khuji Nazar, who enjoyed considerable respect and confidence among the Turkmen and among local merchants. He conveyed the following account of the discussions in Khiva that followed Markozov's expedition to Sary-Kamish:

> being fully convinced that the Russians would quickly come once again, to Khiva itself, [Khan Muhammad Rahim] in depression called together the elders from all the tribes living and nomadising in Khiva and asked for their advice as to what he should do if the Russians were to come to Khiva. The majority of the elders responded that it would be ill-advised to attempt any resistance to the Russians: at their first appearance all the Turkmen: Chaudar, Irdir, Khoja and Yomud would go over to the Russian side; as for the Sarts, Uzbeks and Qaraqalpaqs, although they were not against offering resistance to the Russians, the Khan does not have the means to be sure of supplying for long any force he gathered, which would need to be significant in order to handle even the weakest Russian force.[63]

At this point one of the Turkmen elders present, one Hajji Mambet, proposed inviting an *ishan* from Mangishlaq who had frequently travelled to the Russian-ruled Caucasus to join the gathering, and ask him to act as an intermediary. This man, Nur Muhammad Bek Turdy *Ishan*, was welcomed with honour, and when asked by the Khan what attitude he should take to the Russians, cried out that he had been advising the Khan's *Diwan-begi* to make peace with Russia ever since he first travelled to the Caucasus in 1867 and became acquainted with the extent of Russian power:

> He knows that each time he reported to the Khan or advised him, the Khan would laugh at him; not once up until now has he invited him to his presence; he has continued to shelter and give refuge to all thieves, bandits

---

[61] Ballozek to Miliutin 17/04/1872 RGVIA F.400 Op.1 D.301 ll. 75-6.

[62] Terent'ev dismisses both these missions in the space of a paragraph: *Istoriya zavoevaniya*, II, 73-4; the account in Zhukovskii, *Snosheniya Rossii s Bukharoi i Khivoi*, 164-6 is equally perfunctory.

[63] Report of the Mangishlaq Commandant to the Head of Daghestan Province 20/01/1872 RGVIA F.400 Op.1 D.301 l. 18.

and robbers, to purchase prisoners and even to pay money and reward those who bring him Russian heads.[64]

The elderly Nur Muhammad *Ishan* made a suitably dramatic speech of denunciation, accusing the Khan of arrogance, of refusing to listen to him for years, casting his words to the wind. Only now, with the enemy at the gates, would he listen, but it was already too late. The *ishan* offered to take and release all the remaining Russian prisoners in Khiva, but this the Khan forbade, as with a large Russian force approaching he wanted to be able to retain a bargaining card. Nur Muhammad eventually persuaded him to let him take four of them, either to the Emba or to Krasnovodsk, and hand them over to the Russians as part of an embassy designed to forestall a Russian attack.[65]

In the middle of February 1872 the Khivan embassy arrived at Fort Alexandrovsk in Mangishlaq. It was led by the eighty-five-year-old Nur Muhammad *Ishan* himself, accompanied by his son-in-law Muhammad Amin, forty-five years old and also a senior Khivan *ishan*, and by his eldest son Nur Muhammad Qul Muhammad, who was forty. This use of members of religious lineages for diplomatic exchanges had a long pedigree in Central Asia, where both their prestige and their relative neutrality in dynastic or tribal disputes made them ideal intermediaries. In his study of the Yomud Turkmen, Irons notes that sacred lineages acted as channels of communication between hostile tribes, who were all expected to remain perpetually at peace with these groups, known as *awlad*.[66] As Sherzodhon Mahmudov has shown, in the eighteenth and nineteenth centuries Khoqandi and Bukharan embassies to neighbouring powers were routinely led by Khwajas or Ishans, in the belief that they would be held in greater respect.[67] Nur Muhammad *Ishan* had once dwelt permanently in Mangishlaq and been on good terms with the Russian authorities, receiving a gold medal from the Governor of Orenburg in 1859. In 1868 he had moved to Khiva after a disagreement with the then commander of the Alexandrovsk fortress, Zelenin, as he had many relatives there among the Turkmen of the Chaudar tribe. He now had a mosque and madrasah there, was very close to the Khan, and had acquired the sobriquet of the '*Sary ishan*' (yellow or blonde ishan). The other members of the party included a younger son of Nur Muhammad, Yusuf Makhsum, aged twenty-five, Mullah Quman,

---

[64] Report of the Mangishlaq Commandant to the Head of Daghestan Province 20/01/1872 RGVIA F.400 Op.1 D.301 l. 19*ob*.

[65] Report of the Mangishlaq Commandant to the Head of Daghestan province 20/01/1872 RGVIA F.400 Op.1 D.301 ll. 20–1*ob*.

[66] William Irons, *The Yomut Turkmen: A Study of Social Organization among a Central Asian Turkic-Speaking Population* (Ann Arbor, MI: University of Michigan Anthropological Papers, 1975), 65–6.

[67] Sherzodhon Mahmudov, 'The Role of Sufis in Diplomatic Relations between the Khanate of Khoqand and India', in *Sufism in India and Central Asia* (Delhi: Manakin Press, 2017), 39–52.

the imam of Nur Muhammad's mosque at Khiva, and Sufi Anaqliq, the
ishan's favourite pupil, together with three Turkmen who apparently were
just the escort, as they had no particular standing in Khiva – all but one of the
Russian prisoners had been left behind because of the season and would
follow later.[68] The embassy bore a letter from Muhammad Rahim Khan
which contained the Khan's acquiescence to all Russia's conditions, namely
(1) to establish peaceful relations; (2) to release all prisoners; (3) to open up
the most extensive caravan trade possible; and (4) to obey the Viceroy of the
Caucasus. They asked to be allowed to send the younger members of the
party on to Tiflis to treat with the Viceroy, as Nur Muhammad himself was
too frail to make the longer journey. In his deposition to the commander of
the Mangishlaq force, Nur Muhammad confirmed the account given by
Abrek Khuji Nazar, but further embellished it:

> As we came to the house of the Khan, the Khan saw us, and said to me
> *khosh geldi, yakshi geldi* [welcome, may you be well]. Then he asked me
> 'was it true that I had been in Daghestan not long ago and saw his Majesty
> the Emperor and his brother the Grand Duke?' I said 'it's true' and added
> that his Majesty the Emperor said to all of us that he was happy to see me,
> and before that, when I was in the group being presented to the Grand
> Duke, he asked me how I earned my medal, which I was wearing, and said
> he hoped that I would continue to serve that well in the future.
>   After this the Khan asked me 'is it true that the Russian forces have
> come in our direction?' and I said 'It's true!' The Khan then said to me
> 'you are an old man, experienced – tell me: what do you think about this?
> I replied 'the Russian forces are surprisingly strong and powerful, like an
> angry lion, and no one can stand against them. I would propose that for
> you it would be best if you made peace in this matter. The Khan replied 'I
> also think so; but I don't know if the Russians will take my envoy, even if
> I send to them the most peaceful and friendly proposals.' I said 'It seems to
> me that His Majesty the Emperor will not refuse your kind proposals.'
> After this the Khan ordered his *Yasawul-bashi* to take me with my son and
> offer us hospitality. The morning of the following day the uncle of the
> Khan Amir 'Umar summoned me; he asked me the same questions as the
> Khan, and I gave the same answers I had given to the Khan.[69]

He had also brought letters from the Russian prisoners in Khiva, which
revealed that in the city itself they numbered just twenty, with another forty
in the surrounding area. The only prisoner who had accompanied the embassy,
a thirty-year-old fisherman called Sergei Deburin, also made a short deposition

---

[68] Commandant of Daghestan province to Prince Svyatopolk-Mirskii 11/03/1872 RGVIA
F.400 Op.1 D.301 ll. 24–5.
[69] Translation of the testimony of Nur Muhammad the Mangishlaq Ishan to the head of the
Mangishlaq division RGVIA F.400 Op.1 D.301 l. 31*ob.*

which focused mainly on the fertility of the soil in Khiva and the honey-like sweetness of its melons.[70]

Grand Duke Mikhail Romanov, the Viceroy of the Caucasus, reported the Khivan request to be allowed to send an embassy to Tiflis 'no doubt under the strong impression made by the current reconnaissance of the Krasnovodsk force', and asked whether it could be received despite the fact that relations with Khiva were formally the responsibility of the Turkestan Governor-General.[71] The response from Gorchakov at the Ministry of Foreign Affairs was not encouraging – he wrote that allowing any Khivan envoy to proceed as far as Baku or Tiflis would simply waste time, as the Khan would only meet Russian demands if he were still under a sense of threat. Instead he suggested that the envoy should only be permitted to go as far as Temir-Khan-Shura, where his stay should be as brief as possible.[72] Once von Kaufman got wind of it he was furious, asking that Nur Muhammad *Ishan* and the rest of the embassy be sent immediately to Tashkent, as relations with the Central Asian Khanates were the exclusive responsibility of the Turkestan Governor-General.[73] In his letter to Stremoukhov, the head of the Asiatic Department at the Ministry of Foreign Affairs, he wrote of the failure of his own attempts to negotiate with Khiva, using Amir Sayyid Muzaffar of Bukhara as an intermediary. He attributed this partly to Khivan intransigence, and while acknowledging the suspicions that Sayyid Muzaffar might not be acting as an honest broker, insisted that he had no reason to doubt him. He took the appearance of another Khivan envoy at Mangishlaq as further evidence of Khivan duplicity.[74] Possibly von Kaufman saw here the prospect of a peaceful resolution to a dispute which he was anxious should be settled by military means, and certainly unwarranted interference from the Caucasian military district, which was in constant rivalry with Turkestan.

Despite von Kaufman's objections, the embassy was allowed to proceed as far as Temir-Khan-Shura, though not to Tiflis. There they presented a letter from Muhammad Rahim Khan, which was forwarded by the head of Daghestan province to Grand Duke Mikhail. The Khan's letter promised friendship in fulsome terms, and asserted that Khiva had never done anything to breach the peace with Russia; he asked the Russians to recognise his frontiers in return for the release of all remaining prisoners.[75] In return they

---

[70] Sergei Deburin, *Doznanie* 17/02/1872 RGVIA F.400 Op.1 D.301 l. 39.
[71] Grand Duke Mikhail Romanov to Gorchakov 17/02/1872 RGVIA F.400 Op.1 D.301 ll. 2–3.
[72] Gorchakov to Grand Duke Mikhail Romanov 11/02/1872 RGVIA F.400 Op.1 D.301 ll. 4–5.
[73] Von Kaufman to Miliutin 10/04/1872 RGVIA F.400 Op.1 D.301 l. 67.
[74] Von Kaufman to Stremoukhov 09/04/1872 RGVIA F.400 Op.1 D.301 l. 68.
[75] Muhammad Rahim Khan to Alexander II ?/01/1872 RGVIA F.400 Op.1 D.301 ll. 87–8*ob* (trans.) & 90–*ob* (original).

were presented with a list of eighty-one Russian demands, which included the release of all Russian prisoners and a letter of explanation to be written to von Kaufman. Nur Muhammad promised to send his two sons back to Khiva with the letter for the Khan, and asked permission to be allowed to return to Mangishlaq to await the outcome of the embassy, as the climate at Temir-Khan-Shura did not agree with him.[76] However, Grand Duke Mikhail had already decided that because the offer made by Muhammad Rahim Khan in the letter they had brought did not correspond to what they had said at Fort Alexandrovsk, this embassy, like previous Khivan embassies, could be safely ignored. Repeating a phrase used by Gorchakov, he wrote that, although, given Khiva's proximity to the Caspian, the Caucasus authorities did have a legitimate role to play in negotiations, these were likely to be a waste of time: 'from long and wearisome experience we know that discussions with such Central Asian envoys do not lead to any positive results'. He referred to Khiva's unfriendly behaviour in sheltering 'the bandit Sadiq' (Kenesary's son) who had raided the Syr-Darya post road in 1867, and above all to the 'insolent' (*derzko*) replies the Khan had given to the friendly envoys of the Turkestan Governor General. Now he was simply acting out of fear and trying to play for time.[77]

In July the head of the Mangishlaq Division reported the Khivan response, relayed to him by Muhammad Amin and Qul Muhammad, the *ishan*'s son-in-law and son. The ambassador had returned to Khiva and met with the Khan and with his influential uncles, conveying the message that all the prisoners must be released at once without conditions, and a letter of apology and submission sent to von Kaufman. The *Diwan-begi*, Muhammed Murad, 'a well-known fanatic, who has much influence with the Khan, received them very coldly'. A council of thirty-two elders was held, and the *Diwan-begi* held forth against any concessions. The two sons reported that they had told Muhammad Murad that the curses of thousands would be on his head if he brought down punishment on Khiva through his failure to appease the Russians, and that they would continue to repeat this 'so long as they have tongues' and 'so long as they have hairs on their heads', but to no avail. Muhammad Murad refused to listen, saying that they were too young, and the Khan himself said that he could not reply to the Russian demands until he had received a formal answer from the Tsar to his own letter. Muhammad Murad said that the Khan would lose all respect and honour if he simply let the prisoners go, and that the threat to the khanate was small, since the Russian forces at Krasnovodsk were insignificant, and he could rely on the Teke,

[76] Grand Duke Mikhail to Miliutin 27/04/1872 RGVIA F.400 Op.1 D.301 l. 80*ob*.

[77] Grand Duke Mikhail to the commander of Daghestan Province 30/03/1872 RGVIA F.400 Op.1 D.301 l. 83. Gorchakov to Grand Duke Mikhail 29/02/1872 TsGARUz F.I-715 Op.1 D.49 ll. 264–6.

Yomud and other Turkmen to defend them. If the Russians did attack, he could forestall them by sending the prisoners out to meet the force. The *ishan* and his sons meanwhile were accused of being Russian stooges, and hoping for a reward from that quarter. The final argument was that the Russians had shown discourtesy and bad faith in their treatment of Khivan envoys; the last one they had sent to Tashkent had been detained by the Amir of Bukhara – after all, the Russian Emperor was the same everywhere, was he not? So why should they not be permitted to negotiate with him through any of his deputies, rather than just Tashkent?[78]

In the letters which accompanied their verbal depositions the ambassadors apologised for the delay in responding, saying that they had waited twenty-three days for a reply after presenting their papers to the Khan, who had detained them while he conferred with elders (*amaldar*) and the *Diwan-begi* and awaited a response to a message he had sent to the 'Inglis' in 'Kabulistan'. They suggested that, while the Khan himself might have been willing to release the prisoners and write to von Kaufman, the *Diwan-begi* was implacably against it, while the *amaldar*s were divided among themselves, but generally opposed the Khan. While the *ishan* and his sons were away, the Qaraqalpaq ambassador Irnazar had also returned from Orenburg, saying that the Russians were enemies who did not wish to negotiate, which further stiffened resolve. They concluded with final professions of loyalty and regret, announcing their return to Mangishlaq.[79]

Despite the fact that all these communications were composed for a Russian audience, they do give us some insight into the debates that took place at Muhammad Rahim Khan's court as the threat of Russian invasion began to loom, and the reasons why there was no negotiated settlement of Russian grievances. The Russians did not allow the fact that this Muslim religious figure was one of the leaders of the peace party at Khiva to disturb their fixed ideas about Muslim 'fanaticism' as a major factor in Khivan intransigence – however, they believed the *Diwan-begi* Muhammad Murad to be the main villain of the piece, and would insist on his immediate exile after Khiva fell, first to Kazalinsk and then to Kaluga.[80] Certainly Muhammad Murad seems to have underestimated the seriousness of the Russian threat, but Khivan counsels were always likely to be divided between doves and hawks: we need to understand why the hawks prevailed. Here the refusal of the Russians to

---

[78] Report of the Commander of the Mangishlaq force 18/07/1872 RGVIA F.400 Op.1 D.301 ll. 109*ob*–13.

[79] Muhammad Amin and Qul Muhammad to Lomakin n.d. (June 1872); Qul Muhammad Nur Muhammad-oghli and Yusuf Muhammad Amin Ishan-oghli to Prince Melikov 07/06/1872 RGVIA F.400 Op.1 D.301 l. 114, 119–20*ob*.

[80] 'Po povodu vysylke byvshago divanbegi Mat Murada iz Kazalinska vnutr Rossii', 26/02/1874 RGVIA F.400 Op.2 D.376, 'O vysylke byvshego khivinskogo divan begi Mat Murada i esaula Rakhmet ullu iz Kazalinska vnutr Rossii', l. 1.

allow any Khivan envoys to travel beyond Orenburg, Tashkent or Temir-Khan-Shura to the seat of power in St Petersburg reveals their contempt for Khiva as a savage, 'pirate' state which was not amenable to the usual niceties of diplomatic negotiation: this was precisely the attitude taken by Perovskii forty years earlier. As the head of the Mangishlaq Division put it:

> The character of Asiatic rulers is everywhere the same: when the danger is near they are willing to engage in any kind of trade-off, but let the danger diminish and they will seek to deflect all unpleasant events to the last degree, employing for this purpose the usual, in these circumstances, deceit, resourcefulness and distrust. It is for this reason that in place of the speedy freeing of our unhappy prisoners (prisoners from the most mighty Power in the world) we see them tormented already for some years in captivity, in insignificant (*nichtozhneishii*) Khiva.[81]

We see the same recurring themes: Russia's status as a great (here 'the greatest') power, which rendered the defiance of 'insignificant' Central Asian rulers and peoples simply intolerable, proof of their deceitfulness and amenability only to force. This meant that, rather than negotiating in good faith, the Russians simply presented the Khivans with long lists of demands – so long in some cases (eighty-one items!) that it hardly seems likely that they either wished or expected the Khivans to comply with them. Certainly they proposed no concessions in return – none of the usual give and take of diplomatic negotiation – other than a vague promise to hold off from invading the khanate. The Amir of Bukhara reportedly informed Muhammad Rahim Khan that the Russians were planning to invade anyway, whether he released the prisoners or not, which was not far from the truth and may have stiffened his resolve.[82] In his later correspondence with the Russians, Muhammad Rahim Khan would refer bitterly to their refusal to accept the envoys he had sent to the Caucasus and Orenburg in 1872.[83]

At the end of October von Kaufman cited the failure of the embassy and the Khan's refusal to fulfil 'our just and reasonable demands' in a lengthy memorandum to Miliutin urging the necessity of an attack on Khiva. He expatiated at length on the continued intransigence of the Khivans, and the general inability of 'Asiatics' to understand any language but force, citing Bukhara's continued opposition even after Khoqand had been crushed by Russian forces: 'the state of things forces us to change the peace-loving policy we have strictly maintained up until now, punish this khanate and take away from it the possibility of threatening us'. Khiva's 'fanatical pride' had prevented the khanate from

---

[81] Report of the commander of the Mangishlaq Division 18/06/1872 RGVIA F.400 Op.1 D.301 l. 107.

[82] Kryzhanovskii to Miliutin 20/07/1872 RGVIA F.400 Op.1 D.301 l. 98.

[83] Muhammad Rahim Khan to Verevkin 14/06/1873 TsGARUz F.I-715 Op.1 D.57 Doc.321 l. 158.

learning this lesson up until now.[84] When the inevitable *soveshchanie* was held at the War Ministry in November 1872 to decide the fate of the khanate, Kaufman got what he wanted: Khiva would be invaded and brought decisively to heel in the most elaborate and expensive campaign of conquest undertaken in Central Asia to date.[85] The decision was confirmed by the Tsar on the 12 December 1872.[86] Sergeev's suggestion that the invasion of Khiva was a response to the Granville–Gorchakov agreement of January 1873 (which the 'war party' in St Petersburg saw as making too many concessions to Britain) thus reveals a lack of attention to chronology, as the final decision to invade the khanate had already been taken well before the agreement was signed; the attitude of the British barely figures in any of the Russian discussions on Khiva.[87]

While Lomakin and Markozov's forays in Transcaspia (see the following chapter) had revealed that a single well-supplied and organised column from that quarter would probably have been sufficient to secure Khiva's surrender, this would have left the glory to the Caucasians, which was certainly not part of von Kaufman's plan. From the outset he intended that Khiva should be attacked from two sides, the Caucasus and Turkestan: the detailed plan he presented to Miliutin at the end of October 1872, which he claimed could be fulfilled for a relatively modest 287,000 silver roubles, showed that he had been planning the expedition for some time.[88] Eventually there would be four columns: two of these, from Krasnovodsk and Mangishlaq, would indeed depart from the Caspian shore and be made up largely of Caucasian troops, but one would cover the vast distance from Orenburg in the north, following almost exactly the route which had proved fatal for Perovskii's expedition in the winter of 1839–40, and the largest column would set out from Turkestan with von Kaufman himself in command, to cross the sands of the Qizil-Qum. The four columns had different experiences – the Krasnovodsk column failed altogether, much of the Turkestan column barely saw action, except for the notorious massacre of the Yomud Turkmen which followed the capture of Khiva, while the Orenburg and Mangishlaq columns did most of what fighting there was. Accordingly, rather than describing the campaign strictly chronologically, I will describe the experience of each column separately, before bringing them together in Khiva's fall – mimicking, in fact, the Russian invasion plan itself (Figure 7.1).

---

[84] Von Kaufman to Miliutin 31/10/1872 TsGARUz F.I-715 Op.1 D.53 ll. 109–10.
[85] Terent'ev, *Istoriya zavoevaniya* II, 106–7; Schuyler suggests that von Kaufman's 'winning manners and social popularity' when he came to St Petersburg to argue the case for the campaign in the autumn of 1872 also played a role: *Turkistan*, II, 334.
[86] Editor's note by Serebrennikov, TsGARUz F.I-715 Op.1 D.53 l. 120.
[87] Sergeev, *The Great Game*, 142–8 & *Bol'shaya Igra*, 130–4.
[88] Von Kaufman to Miliutin 31/10/1872 TsGARUz F.I-715 Op.1 D.53 ll. 112–20.

Figure 7.1 Map of the Khivan invasion routes (Khrebtov, *Khivinskii Pokhod*, 1875).

7.2 The Turkestan Column

The route to be taken by the Turkestan column was the most challenging of all, and indeed it made little logistical sense to despatch any troops to Khiva from the east – but to launch the invasion only from the Caucasus or Orenburg would have left military command in their hands, rather than von Kaufman's, so a Turkestan column was a necessity. It was made up of twenty-one companies of infantry (all from the Turkestan rifle and line battalions), seven *sotnyas* of Cossacks (Ural, Orenburg and one *sotnya* of Semirechie Cossacks, the first time they had seen action since the creation of the host six years before), twenty guns and eight rocket batteries.[89] Because of the supply and

---

[89] Terent'ev, *Istoriya zavoevaniya*, II, 147; he alleges that the inclusion of the 5th *sotnya* of Semirechie Cossacks was because its commander, von Grünewald, was German, and that

water problems that would be caused by gathering too many men and animals in one place, from the outset the force had to be divided. One portion set off from the river Kly, near Jizzakh, the other from the Irkibai depression near Kazalinsk, following the main caravan route from Kazalinsk to Bukhara. The two were then to unite at Tamdy near the Bukan Hills, then proceed via Ming-bulak and Shurakhan to the Amu-Darya, a relatively well-known route.[90]

The initial plan was for the Jizzakh column of the Turkestan force to march in three separate echelons with substantial gaps between them to avoid placing too much strain on the wells along the route. The last echelon would set off thirty-eight days after the first, while there would need to be a complex relay system of camels being sent back as they completed each stage to reinforce the columns coming up behind them.[91] Lt-Col. Tikhmenev, the head of the commissariat, reflected that dividing and thus weakening one's forces in this way would be considered madness in any European field of war, but that the terrain made it essential – he also noted that the Khivans would suffer from the same difficulties.[92] In the event the Jizzakh column was divided into four echelons; the first two were a little lighter and included the horse artillery and the rocket division. The third contained the siege artillery park and the engineers, and the fourth was the rearguard.[93] While in principle this division of the force and the need to protect the enormous baggage train did make it more vulnerable to attack *en route*, in practice the Khivans were unable to take advantage of this.[94]

In total, according to the official history, the Turkestan column required 111,688 *poods* of supplies, of which 78,791 *poods* was carried with the column, the remainder having been sent on ahead to supply dumps.[95] As always, the main form of transport was camels, and as always the Russians had to rely on the Qazaqs who bred them, in this case with Tashkent *caravanbashis* acting as intermediaries. Of the camels needed by the Jizzakh column, 1,547 came from

---

'Kaufman, although he was Orthodox, always protected Germans'. This remark is a product of the politics of the early twentieth century, when Terent'ev completed his history.

[90] Trotskii to Golovachev 25/02/1873 RGVIA F.1393 Op.1 D.5, 'O vystuplenii otryada iz g. Tashkenta k Khive', ll. 13–15, 111; von Kaufman to Miliutin 31/10/1872 TsGARUz F. I-715 Op.1 D.53 ll. 114–15; Trotskii [Grodekov], *Opisanie deistvii Turkestanskago otryada*, 5, 60; Terent'ev, *Istoriya zavoevaniya*, II, 164.

[91] Lt-Col. Tikhmenev, 'Ob"yasnitelnaya zapiska k marshrutu', 26/01/1873 TsGARUz F. I-715 Op.1 D.54 Doc.24 ll. 137–41.

[92] Lt-Col. Tikhmenev, 'Proekt boevogo marsha chrez Kizyl Kummy na Khivu', 01/02/1873 TsGARUz F.I-715 Op.1 D.54 Doc.34 l. 158.

[93] 'Raspredelenie voisk Dzhizakskogo otryada po eshelonam, dlya sledovaniya ot sbornogo punkta na r. Kly do Bukanskikh gor', RGVIA F.1393 Op.1 D.5 ll. 11–12; Kolokol'tsov, *Ekspeditsiya v Khivu*, 1.

[94] Baumann, 'The Conquest of Central Asia', 60.

[95] Trotskii [Grodekov], *Opisanie deistvii Turkestanskogo otryada*, 15.

the Tashkent (Qurama) district, 1,497 from the Chimkent district and 1,800 from the Aulie-Ata district.[96] These were all hired rather than purchased, with the name of every owner recorded individually – most had rented just one, none more than three.[97] The drivers also came from all over these three districts, almost 800 of them in all. The original intention was to transport the infantry on camels, with two per beast; Trotskii was apparently so sanguine about sufficient numbers being available that he even suggested that once the first echelon had reached the first set of wells half the camels could be sent back and returned to their owners to save the cost of hire and fodder (this was 24 roubles a month for hire, with one driver for every seven camels paid 15 silver kopeks a day, while fodder cost 6 r 50 k per camel per month).[98] This proved much too optimistic, and in this, as in all previous and subsequent steppe and desert campaigns, the Russians would be desperately short of camels, the availability of which made the difference between success or failure. The expedition was carrying three and a half months' worth of supplies, and there were no camels to spare to transport the infantry – Trotskii no doubt had in mind an ingenious system for carrying infantry on wooden chairs slung on either side of the camel, as first proposed to the Main Staff by the then Governor of Orenburg, General Katenin, in 1858, but apparently never put into practice.[99] Trotskii also suggested that the owners of some camels would deliberately supply sickly beasts in the hope that they would die, for the sake of the compensation the Russians were offering.[100] Whether this was really the case or not, the hardships of the journey and the poor management of the camels meant that the mortality rate was extremely high. The initial estimate of 2,491 camels needed for the Kazalinsk column had to be substantially revised upwards, while the column from Jizzakh eventually set off with over 6,000 camels, carrying a load of 12 *poods* each – the official total was 9,374, though Schuyler, referring to 'private information', suggests that eventually over 14,000 camels were needed for the Turkestan force.[101] While the expedition was launched in early spring to avoid the heat of summer, this meant that the camels had only had sparse winter grazing over the previous months and were

[96] 'Vedomost o chisle caravan bashei, lauchi i verbliudov sdannykh v chasti voisk', RGVIA F.1383 Op.1 D.6 'Khivinskii pokhod: Podgotovka i osushchestvlenie plana', ll. 27–*ob*.
[97] 'Spisok khozyaev verbliudov, karavan bashei, lauchei i chisla verbliudov naznachennykh ot Aulie-Atinskogo uezda', RGVIA F.1393 Op.1 D.6 ll. 7–26.
[98] Trotskii to Golov 11/02/1873; 'Rasschet', 22/02/1873 RGVIA F.1393 Op.1 D.5 ll. 23–4; D.6 l. 65.
[99] A. A. Katenin, 'O pokhodnykh dvizhenii pekhota po stepi', 06/12/1858 RGVIA F.483 Op.1 D.49 ll. 114–18; 'Pokhody v stepi: Upotreblenie verbliudov dlya voennykh nadobnostei', *VS* (1862), No. 2, 357–88.
[100] Trotskii to Golov 11/02/1873 RGVIA F.1393 Op.1 D.5 l. 25*ob*.
[101] Ivanov to Golovachev 01/03/1873 RGVIA F.1393 Op.1 D.7 ll. 11–14; Trotskii [Grodekov], *Opisanie deistvii Turkestanskogo otryada*, 25; Schuyler, *Turkistan*, II, 337.

often in poor condition even before they set out.[102] Eventually 8,000 of the camels used by the Turkestan column would perish on the journey, and, as compensation to their owners was fixed at 50 r per camel, this alone cost 400,000 roubles, or 25 per cent more than von Kaufman's original estimate for the entire expedition.[103]

Ironically enough, given the extreme shortages of water the expedition would later encounter, the initial departure of the Jizzakh column was hampered by heavy rain, which made it difficult to load the camels, which struggle when it is wet underfoot, and over 400 of them perished on the 6-verst stretch between Jizzakh and the camp on the river Kly.[104] Already by the end of April, of the 1,500 camels supplied from the Chimkent district, 729 had died.[105] Golovachev reported to von Kaufman that, while the first echelon of the Kazalinsk column had reached Irkibai on the 18 March, and the second on the 19 March, the remaining two had been held up by the weakness of their camels after the winter. All the beasts required an additional four or five days of rest. As most of the Qazaqs of the Perovsk district had already migrated north to Turgai for the summer, it was almost impossible to find fresh camels, so he decided to leave the camels which had brought supplies to the depot there for the use of the column from Kazalinsk, noting that he did not think they would have been capable of making the return journey across the Qizil-Qum.[106] The shortage of camels would produce serious shortages of supplies until the expedition reached the Khwarazm oasis: Poltoratskii remarked with characteristic *hauteur* that around the camp on the river Kly 'the whole native bazaar from the town [Jizzakh] had relocated itself [. . .] and from dawn you could hear around our tents the cries of the Sarts trading *lepeshki* (loaves), eggs, oil, milk and all types of rubbish (*dryan'*)'.[107] The troops of the Turkestan force would be only too grateful for the opportunity to buy this sort of 'rubbish' when they encountered their first bazaar in Khwarazm.

Lack of water also became a problem early on – the commander of the first echelon, von Kaufman's adjutant, Colonel Kolokol'tsov, recalled that, within the first three days, when they reached the wells at Balta-Sadyr on the 15 March, the echelon was forced to divide because there was too little water, with the portion under his command taking a more difficult northern

---

[102] Terent'ev, *Istoriya zavoevaniya*, II, 165.
[103] Saranchov, 'Khivinskiya ekspeditsiya 1873 goda', *Inzhenernyi Zhurnal* (1874) No. 1, 38.
[104] Kolokol'tsov, *Ekspeditsiya v Khivu*, 4–6; Trotskii [Grodekov], *Opisanie deistvii Turkestanskogo otryada*, 29, 34; Poltoratskii, 'Vospominaniya', *IV* (1895), No. 5, 417, 419.
[105] 'Vedomost o chisle vozvrashchennykh, pavshikh ostavshikhsya verbliudov Chimkentskogo uezda na puti sledovaniya Turkestanskogo otryada iz Tashkent do Khalata', 25/04/1873 RGVIA F.1393 Op.1 D.6 ll. 224–5.
[106] Golovachev to von Kaufman 20/03/1873 RGVIA F.1393 Op.1 D.5 ll. 138–9.
[107] Poltoratskii, 'Vospominaniya', *IV* (1895), No. 5, 418.

route through the Tamdy depression.[108] On the 21 March von Kaufman
reported the safe arrival of the main portion of the column at the first stage,
the wells of Temir-Kobuk, in the foothills of the Qara-Tau. While only 28 men
out of 3,500 were sick, the same was not true of the camels. He complained that
many of these had been weak and sick when they were first supplied, and large
numbers had either died or were no longer fit to carry loads. However, he
expected the imminent arrival of 200–300 camels from Bukhara at the next
well, Balta-Saldyr, to make up part of his losses.[109]

The most difficult stretch of the march as originally planned lay from Balta-
Sadyr through Ming-Bulak to the Amu-Darya, estimated at anything from 80
to 160 versts, which initial reports suggested was entirely without water.[110]
Schuyler alleges that at this point the plan of march was changed, because 'it
appears that, by the rules of the order, the Cross of St George can be given to
the chief of staff of an expedition only when the route successfully followed has
been prepared by him. Now Colonel Trotzky [sic], who was the chief of staff of
the expedition, had not personally engaged in the preparation of the route
which was to be followed [. . .] Therefore, in order to render him eligible for the
military decoration [. . .] it was resolved [. . .] to follow a new road through
Khalata to Utch-Utchak, which seemed to be shorter, but of which absolutely
nothing was known.'[111] Unsurprisingly, the official history gives a somewhat
different explanation – namely that the route beyond Ming-Bulak was also
unknown, that they believed the Khivans would have poisoned or blocked the
wells, and that it was twice as long as the possible alternatives. Accordingly, on
the 23 March, while the Jizzakh column was at Balta-Sadyr, von Kaufman
decided to follow a route through the Hal-Ata depression, where there were
abundant wells, and which would become the new forward point for the
collection of supplies and the site of a temporary fortification, christened
Fort St George.[112] Terent'ev was scathing about this decision, which he said
was based on intelligence gathered from some 'unknown Sarts' in Samarkand
and Jizzakh by Baron Johann Friedrich Gustav Aminov (1844–1899, Figure
7.2),[113] a Swede who, he alleged, did not speak Russian properly.

He argued that it was extraordinarily irresponsible to launch the expedition
on a route which had never been surveyed and was not used by caravans, and

[108] Kolokol'tsov, *Ekspeditsiya v Khivu*, 7; on Kolokol'tsov, an elderly former Guards Officer
who had moved to Turkestan after the 'upset of his affairs', see Poltoratskii,
'Vospominaniya', *IV* (1895), No. 5, 420.
[109] Von Kaufman to Miliutin 21/03/1873 TsGARUz F.I-715 Op.1 D.55 Doc.132 ll. 144–7.
[110] Kolokol'tsov, *Ekspeditsiya v Khivu*, 13.
[111] Schuyler, *Turkistan*, II, 339.
[112] Trotskii [Grodekov], *Opisanie deistvii Turkestanskogo otryada*, 41–4.
[113] 'Nagrazhdennye zolotym oruzhiem: Za vziatie uk. Kitab 13-go avgusta 1870 g. Baron.
G. A. Aminov', in Kun (ed.), *Turkestanskii al'bom*. Pt. 4, plate 75, No. 205 (Library of
Congress, Prints & Photographs Division LC-DIG-ppmsca-09957-00205).

Figure 7.2 Baron Johann Friedrich Gustav Aminov (*Turkestan Album*, 1871).

which forced the Kazalinsk column to march an additional 385 *versts*.[114] Whatever the real reason for the change, the reality seems to have been that Russian intelligence on the routes to the Amu-Darya was faulty and incomplete – the subsequent course of events seems to bear this out.

On the 26 March von Kaufman gave the dispositions for the passage of the force across the Qizil-Qum to Hal-Ata, which show the complexity and precision required – the arrival at the wells had to be staggered to allow them to re-fill between waterings. The first echelon was to reach the wells of Arystan-Bel-Kuduk by the 28 March and spend two days there before proceeding. The second echelon should reach the wells of Maschi by the 28 March, and then proceed to Arystan-Bel-Kuduk on the 30 March. The third was to reach the wells of Bajan Tapta by the 27 March, spend one day there and proceed to Maschi on the 29 March. The fourth was to reach the wells of Qosh-Baji on the 27 March, and move on from there to Bajan Tapta on the 29 March.[115] The bulk of the Jizzakh column eventually reached Arystan-Bel-Kuduk on the

---

[114] Terent'ev, *Istoriya zavoevaniya*, II, 171–2.
[115] Von Kaufman to Trotskii 26/03/1873 RGVIA F.1393 Op.1 D.5 l. 103.

30 March.[116] These arrangements for marching in echelons were easily disrupted, both because it might take longer than predicted for an echelon to complete each stage and also because the amount of water available was unpredictable – Terent'ev suggested that von Kaufman had not divided the force sufficiently, and that the echelons were too large to be watered at a single set of wells.[117] Poltoratskii noted an 'unexpected shortage of water' at Arystan-Bel-Kuduk, and his first echelon was forced to water at the wells of Momandzan, but here too there was too little water for camels, horses and men.[118] On the 14 April von Kaufman reported that a forward reconnaissance by Baron Aminov had revealed that the wells at Churk-Kuduk did not have enough water, and that the first echelon would therefore have to be split into three and travel by three different routes, to unite at the wells of Suli-Kujumdi. The third echelon would also have to be divided.[119] A week later Golov wrote that the second column of the third echelon had failed to complete the stage from Churk-Kuduk to Sultan Bibi in a single day because of the weakness of the camels – this had also forced them to abandon all the kibitkas they were carrying for sick men and officers, as well as a good deal of fuel.[120]

The first echelon of the Jizzakh force finally reached Hal-Ata on the 21 April, followed by the Kazalinsk column on the 24 April; here, while there was plenty of water, the column faced a serious shortages of supplies. Many of the sukhari (rusks) they had brought with them turned out to be rotten and alive with maggots – Poltoratskii, asked to inspect them, reported to von Kaufman that 'your Excellency, if you point them in the right direction, they themselves without any assistance or means of transport will make their way to Khiva'.[121] They were saved by the timely despatch of 3,200 poods of flour by the Amir of Bukhara, which allowed them to bake fresh bread. Amir Sayyid Muzaffar's gesture was almost certainly not entirely altruistic – apart from his desire to curry favour with von Kaufman, without the supplies the force would probably have had to turn south onto Bukharan territory, where they would have caused mayhem.[122] Though paid for by the Amir, the merchant who provided the supplies was in fact a Russian called Gromov, the agent of Khludov, one of the greatest Moscow trading firms.

The Russians feared that the wells in the desert beyond Hal-Ata had all been destroyed or poisoned by the Khivans, and von Kaufman was faced with a difficult choice, as there were too few healthy camels left to allow the

[116] Trotskii [Grodekov], *Opisanie deistvii Turkestanskogo otryada*, 48.
[117] Terent'ev, *Istoriya zavoevaniya*, II, 175.
[118] Poltoratskii, 'Vospominaniya', IV (1895), No. 5, 422.
[119] Von Kaufman to Trotskii 14/04/1873 RGVIA F.1393 Op.1 D.5 ll. 212–14.
[120] Golov to Trotskii 21/04/1873 RGVIA F.1393 Op.1 D.5 ll. 242–ob.
[121] Poltoratskii, 'Vospominaniya', IV (1895), No. 5, 422, 424.
[122] Terent'ev, *Istoriya zavoevaniya*, II, 173, 178; Callwell cites a similar instance of spoiled biscuit disrupting the British expedition to Khartoum in 1884: *Small Wars*, 43.

expedition to carry enough water with it. Poltoratskii recalled that 'Kaufman became very anxious and silent, and no wonder, the responsibility was no joke.'[123] On the 29 April the *jigits* sent out ahead for reconnaissance returned with reports that for the first 100 *versts* there were wells along the route to the Amu-Darya, although those for the last 60 *versts* were without water. Von Kaufman waited until this report was confirmed by the leader of the advance guard, Colonel Bardovskii, before ordering a first echelon of five companies of infantry, one battery of horse artillery and 3,000 baggage camels to advance to the first set of wells, at Adam-Krylgan (Figure 7.3).[124]

The following stage was by far the most difficult – the crisis of the whole expedition. Within a day of leaving the wells, the column found itself almost without water or transport, and began to abandon or destroy much of its baggage, including elements of the siege train and ammunition for the artillery – one unexpected problem was that the barrels which they had brought to transport water, unused up until this point, had dried out and were no longer watertight.[125] Von Kaufman's account of this stage of the march in his later report to Miliutin is highly circumspect,[126] but Macgahan vividly imagines what was at stake for him:

Figure 7.3 N. N. Karazin, *The Khiva Expedition of 1873. The Crossing of the Dead Sands to the Wells of Adam-Krylgan by the Turkestan Force (Khivinskii pokhod 1873 goda. Perekhod Turkestanskogo otryada cherez mertvye peski k kolodtsam Adam-Krylgan)* (1888). Russian State Museum, St Petersburg (Wikimedia Commons).

[123] Poltoratskii, 'Vospominaniya', *IV* (1895), No. 5, 423.
[124] Kolokol'tsov, *Ekspeditsiya v Khivu*, 19–20.
[125] *Ibid.*, 26; Poltoratskii, 'Vospominaniya', *IV* (1895), No. 5, 426–7.
[126] Von Kaufman to Miliutin 10/06/1873 TsGARUz F.I-715 Op.1 D.57 Doc.314 ll. 135–7.

General Kaufmann passed through one of those moments of despair which every general who has ever commanded an army has probably experienced at least once in his life. The situation was hopeless. The men were without water, the camels almost exhausted, the artillery horses already suffering. The thermometer marked 100 of Fahrenheit. He was on the very verge of a similar disaster to that which, unknown to him, had overtaken Colonel Markosoff only a few days before, in the Turcoman desert, on the other side of the Amu-Darya; but failure to him entailed consequences a hundred times more tremendous. The Russians only maintain their authority in Central Asia by convincing the people that they are invincible and infallible. One mistake, one defeat, and this illusion would be destroyed; for the people finding the Russians could be beaten would rise.[127]

At this point, according to Kolokol'tsov, Macgahan and Schuyler, the column was saved by a Qazaq *jigit* (two of them according to Poltoratskii), who had been despatched to search for wells, and on returning informed von Kaufman of the existence of a well 7 *versts* away from the line of march: 'the *jigit* who had been despatched returned, having found wells with water no more than seven *versts* from here!!! You had to see that moment, when all the people aroused themselves and leapt up from their places, having heard the news that returned them their boldness of spirit, and the strength to endure more privations – in one word, life!'[128] This did not prove sufficient – the wells at Alty-Kuduk were very deep, two of the six were blocked (in one, 20 *arshins* deep, two sappers suffocated from the stale air while trying to dig it out), and the men and horses could only be watered slowly. By the evening of the 3 May they were all dry, and Poltoratskii remarked again how the strain was telling on von Kaufman: 'His face was sunk and wrinkled, the lines on his forehead stood out sharply, and his eyes were not burning with ordinary fire, but had somehow faded.'[129] That evening, in his account, discipline amongst the troops collapsed completely as they struggled with each other around the wells for water, and refused to obey their officers:

> Having reached the well, we could not immediately push through to it. A thick crowd of people surrounded it like a wall, desperately defending it against all comers. Neither demands, nor threats, nor caresses – nothing could move us a step closer to this source, not of earthly blessings, but a muddy liquid that during those minutes decided the question of life and death [. . .] not paying attention to what lay under their feet, like wild beasts they rushed to the water, mercilessly trampling on their almost

[127] Macgahan, *Campaigning on the Oxus*, 167.
[128] Kolokol'tsov, *Ekspeditsiya v Khivu*, 26, 28–9; Schuyler, *Turkistan*, II, 341; Poltoratskii, 'Vospominaniya', IV (1895), No. 5, 428.
[129] Poltoratskii, 'Vospominaniya', IV (1895), No. 5, 429.

insensible companions. With their inflamed eyes popping outward, these ill-fated sufferers seemed to see and understand nothing.[130]

Von Kaufman was forced to abandon his plans to continue the advance, and instead sent all the cavalry, artillery and baggage animals back to Adam-Krylgan under Bardovskii's command to collect as much water as possible, while the bulk of the infantry remained at Alty-Kuduk, where the wells produced just enough water to sustain them until Bardovskii's return a week later. On the 9 May the reunited column finally set off for the Amu-Darya.[131]

The correspondence generated by the Turkestan column before it reached the Amu-Darya is almost entirely concerned with the questions of water and transport – there is hardly any mention of the enemy because they had little contact with them until they had reached the oasis of Khiva itself: instead the letters and reports speak of sick and dying camels, of shortages of forage or meat, of the failure of new beasts to arrive, thus delaying departures, and above all of inadequate supplies of water at the wells *en route*. Colonel Weimarn, the head of the second echelon, wrote in early May that he had been delayed at Fort St George, because he had only enough camels to carry two and a half days' worth of supplies.[132] Kolokol'tsov noted that the two camels carrying his personal baggage collapsed during the worst part of the journey, from Adam-Krylgan to the Amu-Darya, despite the fact that he had carefully picked out two of the strongest.[133] On the 15 May the commander of the 3rd Turkestan Infantry Battalion, which was under Weimarn's command in the second echelon, wrote that his men 'were in a very difficult condition; the work on the wells for watering the horses and camels goes on day and night', while they also had to maintain a constant guard, and had run out of meat, existing solely on pulses cooked in water.[134] The exceptions to this gloomy picture were reports of a skirmish between the advance guard and some Turkmen cavalry on the 27 April, in which according to Bardovskii's official report there were no Russian casualties, although Poltoratskii wrote that two officers, Ivanov and Tikhmenev, were lightly wounded;[135] another on the 7 May, when about 200

---

[130] *Ibid.*, 431–2.

[131] Kolokol'tsov, *Ekspeditsiya v Khivu*, 36; Poltoratskii, 'Vospominaniya', *IV* (1895), No. 5, 433–5.

[132] Weimarn to von Kaufman 06/05/1873 RGVIA F.1393 Op.1 D.5 l. 278; for a description of the fortress see Kolokol'tsov, *Ekspeditsiya v Khivu*, 8–9 & Macgahan *Campaigning on the Oxus*, 106–13.

[133] Kolokol'tsov, *Ekspeditsiya v Khivu*, 24–5.

[134] Commander of the 3rd Turkestan Infantry Battalion to Weimarn 15/05/1873 RGVIA F.1393 Op.1 D.5 l. 322.

[135] Bardovskii to von Kaufman 27/04/1873 RGVIA F.1393 Op.1 D.21, 'Dela s nepriyatelem, raznyya svedeniya pro etim', l. 1; Kolokol'tsov, *Ekspeditsiya v Khivu*, 17–18; Poltoratskii, 'Vospominaniya', *IV* (1895), No. 5, 425; this is probably the engagement referred to by Bayani, *Shajara-yi Khwarazmshahi* trans. Sela in *Islamic Central Asia*, 302.

Turkmen horsemen attacked Bardovskii's column for two and a half hours; and another on the 11 May (both again without inflicting casualties).[136]

Von Kaufman's own reports were invariably more fulsome than this, especially when referring to the exploits of his commanders – Golovachev, Trotskii and of course Grand Duke Nikolai Konstantinovich. The advance guard of the Turkestan column fought a small action on the 10–11 May at Lake Sardoba Kul, where the troops were commanded by one of the *fazany*, his Highness Prince Evgenii Maximilianovich Romanovskii, Herzog of Leuchtenberg – there were no Russian casualties, but ten to fifteen dead on the Khivan side.[137] On the 16 May von Kaufman wrote to both Miliutin and Gorchakov that his column had reached the Amu-Darya, with no encounters with the enemy other than some slight skirmishes with some Turkmen.[138] In contrast to the dry language of the reports, Kolokol'tsov described this as a moment of emotion and epiphany, but all his emphasis was on the natural obstacles overcome, not the enemy:

> I cannot convey that feeling, with which we gazed on this great mass of water, which had until so recently been the subject of all our prayers and hopes. Here, on the banks of the Amu-Darya, some thousands of *versts* distant from the fatherland, in the deepest depths of barbarous Asia, to which, since the time of Alexander the Great, not one European army had penetrated, now stood a small Russian force of a few thousand men, which had over two months struggled with the most awful, lifeless nature, with terrible squalls, with scorching and stifling heat, and had emerged victorious.[139]

Poltoratskii was similarly lyrical, and provided the additional detail that Kolokol'tsov had serenaded the column with Schubert's *Ständchen*, played on the cornet-a-piston.[140] The following day they stormed the small Khivan fortress of Tulaqul on the Amu-Darya, once again with no Russian casualties, but supposedly killing 150 Khivans and wounding 400.[141]

As the Turkestan column moved into the cultivated oasis of Khiva, its supply problems began to ease. On the 18–19 May, after capturing the fortress of Shura Khan, they crossed the Amu-Darya (Figure 7.4) in a flotilla of small boats (*kayuks*) commandeered from the local population, who began to bring foodstuffs to sell while they were bivouacked on the riverbank, despite a rumoured prohibition

---

[136] Kolokol'tsov, *Ekspeditsiya v Khivu*, 35; von Kaufman to Miliutin 13/05/1873 TsGARUz F.I-715 Op.1 D.56 l. 78.

[137] Bardovskii to von Kaufman 12/05/1873 RGVIA F.1393 Op.1 D.21 ll. 18, 24–35; Kolokol'tsov, *Ekspeditsiya v Khivu*, 42–3.

[138] Von Kaufman to Gorchakov 16/05/1873 TsGARUz F.I-715 Op.1 D.56 Doc.252 ll. 105–8.

[139] Kolokol'tsov, *Ekspeditsiya v Khivu*, 45.

[140] Poltoratskii, 'Vospominaniya', *IV* (1895), No. 5, 436–8.

[141] *Svedenie* 17/05/1873 RGVIA F.1393 Op.1 D.21 ll. 45–6.

Figure 7.4 N. N. Karazin, *The Crossing of the Amu-Darya by the Turkestan Force, 1873* (*Pereprava Turkestanskogo otryada cherez Amu-Dar'iu v 1873 godu*) (1889). Military-Historical Museum of Artillery & Engineers, St Petersburg (Wikimedia Commons).

from the *Diwan-begi*.[142] Lt-Col. Chaikovskii, who had been sent ahead on a *furazhirovka* (a forage-gathering expedition), reported contact with the inhabitants of the villages around Hazarasp, the town which was traditionally the seat of the heir to the throne of the khanate. Near the village of Sheikh-Ariq he had seen some villagers hiding in the reeds. When he asked them to furnish the necessary forage, they had said they were too scared to do so, as a large Khivan force had arrived at Hazarasp and warned them not to supply the Russians. On investigating Chaikovskii saw large numbers of laden *arba*s heading towards Hazarasp, and then he and his men were fired on. Between the villages of 'Umar and Karavan they encountered a large force of infantry under the command of the Khivan *Yasawulbashi* Mahmud Niyaz, but they scattered when Chaikovskii opened fire with his one piece of artillery, and his cavalry were able to hold them off.[143] While some villagers had fled their homes on the approach of Russian troops, they were already returning, and their *aqsaqals* had come forward to ask for peaceful relations. Chaikovskii had replied in the affirmative, but had asked them to bring supplies: 'this morning at dawn the bazaar opened in the place indicated by me, and all sections purchased enough meat, grain and forage'. It was no longer necessary to send out forage parties, and he had given strict instructions to forbid all troops from entering the villages.[144]

---

[142] Kolokol'tsov, *Ekspeditsiya v Khivu*, 56–60.
[143] Chaikovskii to von Kaufman 22/05/1873 RGVIA F.1393 Op.1 D.5 ll. 337–8; Kolokol'tsov, *Ekspeditsiya v Khivu*, 60–1.
[144] Chaikovskii to Golovachev 21/05/1873 RGVIA F.1393 Op.1 D.5 ll. 337–8.

The capture of Hazarasp itself followed a few days later – Kolokol'tsov remarked how 'after the desert we had crossed, this place seemed to us like a paradise, and our unaccustomed eyes feasted on the variety and richness of flora'.[145] In his report Golovachev was more prosaic, dwelling on the difficulties of the surrounding terrain, and using the Caucasian term 'saklya' to describe the houses and walled gardens surrounding the town through which they had had to fight.[146] Von Kaufman's description of the same engagement to Miliutin was enormously long and detailed – one suspects because it was the first action of the campaign which he was directing. He noted that the Khivan artillery was hopelessly inaccurate, the shot either falling short or sailing harmlessly overhead. Of the twenty rounds that were more or less on target, none hit anybody. The Russian troops marched into Hazarasp itself without firing a shot. Von Kaufman issued a proclamation offering amnesty to the inhabitants if they would agree to provide supplies, and an impromptu bazaar quickly sprang up, selling loaves, vegetables and dried fruit to the Russian forces, while they also appropriated 1,000 poods of wheat, 800 of jugara (sorghum) and 680 of rice which they found in the town's citadel.[147] Macgahan provides a vivid description of abundance, a stark contrast to the privations of the march:

> Upon setting foot on shore, my comrade and I made a rush for the bazaar, which had been opened that day for the first time by the Khivans, in response to a friendly proclamation of General Kaufmann . . . the Khivans had responded to Kaufman's proclamation with cartloads of flour, fruit, chickens, sheep, fresh wheaten cakes, 'hot and hot', apricots, rice, sugar, tea, great quantities of white mulberries, together with clover and djugera [sorghum] for the horses. They had drawn up their great lumbering wooden carts just outside the camp, and were now surrounded by the Russian soldiers, with whom they seemed on excellent terms. A few of the soldiers spoke Tartar, or Kirghiz, but those who could not managed to get on somehow by signs, and the most lively exchange was going on between them and the natives when we arrived upon the scene.[148]

Kolokol'tsov, meanwhile, waxed lyrical about the beauty of the place, and the pleasures of listening to birdsong once more.[149] From this point onwards the Turkestan column's supply problems were at an end, and they met no more serious resistance – Kolokol'tsov described the disappointment (among the officers, at least) when they heard that the Khan wished to surrender and there

---

[145] Kolokol'tsov, Ekspeditsiya v Khivu, 61.
[146] Golovachev to von Kaufman 26/05/1873 TsGARUz F.I-715 Op.1 D.56 Doc.276 ll. 204–6.
[147] Von Kaufman to Miliutin 26/05/1873 TsGARUz F.I-715 Op.1 D.56 Doc.279 ll. 213, 223, 225, 227–8, 230.
[148] Macgahan, Campaigning on the Oxus, 177–8.
[149] Kolokol'tsov, Ekspeditsiya v Khivu, 63.

would be no climactic storming of the city.[150] The question became whether von Kaufman and his column would arrive at Khiva in time to accept the Khan's surrender, since they had been outpaced by the forces arriving from Orenburg and Mangishlaq.

7.3   The Caucasian Columns

The two columns which set out from the Caspian shores were both under the jurisdiction of the Caucasian military district, and, while they included some Turkestani military officers (notably Grodekov with the Mangishlaq column), their composition reflected this, being made up of Daghestan, Apsheron, Shirvan, Samur and Kabardian regiments, with many Georgian and Armenian officers and at least one – the well-known Mahsud Alikhanov-Avarskii (1846–1907) – who was a Muslim Lezghin, and fluent in Turki. His memoir of the Mangishlaq column's march is punctuated with vivid vignettes derived from his ability to speak directly to the Qazaq drivers on whom the column relied.[151] The Caucasian forces had a shorter distance to cover than the Turkestan and Orenburg columns (520 *versts* from Mangishlaq, 570 *versts* from Chikishlar), but if anything through a more hostile landscape – the Ust-Yurt plateau for the Mangishlaq column, and the Qara-Qum desert for that from Krasnovodsk.[152] While some of them had served in Transcaspia since the Russian occupation of Krasnovodsk in 1869, many were much less experienced than the Turkestan forces in steppe and desert campaigning.

The omens for the force commanded by Colonel Markozov, which, although the bulk of it set out from Chikishlar, was known as the Krasnovodsk column, were not good. In June 1872, already certain that a full-scale expedition to Khiva was imminent, he had sent out what was ostensibly an armed reconnaissance force whose real object was to be within striking distance of Khiva as soon as negotiations broke down, so that he could seize the glory of capturing the city for himself and the Caucasian command. His attempts to requisition camels from the Turkmen by force met with failure, and the two platoons he sent out for this purpose were provided with only 6 days' worth of supplies and too little water. As the heat rose to 50 degrees, they were reduced to drinking their own urine, and only just managed to return to Chikishlar with 200 camels, which was far too few.[153] In autumn 1872 he attempted a repeat, this time breaking his agreement with the Göklan and Atabai Yomud Turkmen around the Atrek and Gurgan that he would not

[150] *Ibid.*, 65–6.
[151] Alikhanov-Avarskii, *Pokhod v Khivu*, 24; the British journalist George Dobson left a fine portrait of Alikhanov-Avarskii after travelling with him in 1888: *Russia's Railway Advance into Central Asia* (London: W. H. Allen & Co., 1890), 224.
[152] Terent'ev, *Istoriya zavoevaniya*, II, 83.
[153] *Ibid.*, II, 74–5.

violate Persian territory by raiding them and carrying off 200 camels. This provoked a cross-border retaliatory raid in which Turkmen under Russian jurisdiction lost over 1,000 head of livestock, further deepening their resentment at Russian actions.[154] The lack of camels meant that Markozov was forced instead to launch his reconnaissance from Krasnovodsk; they made it as far as the wells of Topi-Ata, where Markozov received definitive orders not to proceed any further towards Khiva. At this point his force was attacked by a large band of Akhal-Teke Turkmen, and retreated with difficulty to Krasnovodsk.[155] Always contemptuous of Caucasian troops, Terent'ev suggests that it was this failure which led the Main Staff to decide that an assault on Khiva solely from the Caspian side would fail, and led to the decision to have a three-pronged assault.[156] Markozov himself, in a later, rather self-serving memoir, while he laid great stress on the enormous challenges he faced in securing enough transport, did not acknowledge either that his forcible approach to the Turkmen might have been counter-productive or that he had repeatedly violated Persian sovereignty in pursuing it.[157]

After receiving his orders in Tiflis, at the end of January 1873 Markozov despatched a small force to the Atrek to attempt to obtain camels from the Atabai branch of the Yomud Turkmen by means of a peaceful agreement – in the official history Grodekov describes the hopes of such an agreement as being faint because of the unprovoked hostility of the Atabai, but, as we have seen, they had real grievances against Markozov and his men. Sure enough, after much procrastination, the negotiations with a leading Yomud Qazi broke down, and Markozov resorted to force once more.[158] In February 1873 Markozov's men once again violated the Persian frontier in search of camels, fighting a sharp action on the Atrek and returning with 430 beasts, which they handed over to 'loyal' Russian Turkmen to pasture until they were needed. Markozov's superior, the head of the Caucasian Staff, urged him instead to simply pay for them, but this he seems to have been unwilling to do.[159] At the beginning of March the Consul at Astrabad forwarded a report from Markozov to Tiflis in which he reported that the Turkmen were spreading rumours about the presence of a large Russian force at Chikishlar, which they

[154] *Ibid.*, II, 77.
[155] Consul at Astrabad to the Minister at Tehran 25/09/1872, 26/10/1872, 12/11/1872 21/11/1872 NAG F.5 Op.1 D.2241, 'Doneseniya Rossiiskogo Imperatorskogo Poslannika v Tegerane po raznym predmentam', ll. 275–9*ob*, 319–21, 322–4 & *PT*, 87–9; Terent'ev, *Istoriya zavoevaniya*, II, 78–80; see Chapter 9.
[156] Terent'ev, *Istoriya zavoevaniya*, II, 82.
[157] V. Markozov, *Krasnovodskii otryad: Ego zhizn' i sluzhba so dnya vysadki na vostochnyi bereg Kaspiiskogo Morya po 1873 g. vkliuchitel'no* (St Pb.: V. A. Berezovskii, 1898), 155–68.
[158] Trotskii [Grodekov], *Opisanie deistvii kavkazskikh otryadov*, 22–5.
[159] Terent'ev, *Istoriya zavoevaniya*, II, 86–7.

were giving as a reason not to hire camels for the use of his column. He attributed this both to Persian interference and to the baleful influence of a religious leader whom he called 'Chaputov Yarachi Kazy';[160] the real reason was almost certainly Markozov's repeated forcible seizure of camels from the Göklan and Atabai Yomuds over the previous year. As Terent'ev put it, imagining how Markozov had reasoned: 'What was to be done? The Turkmen do not come to us with camels, and camels are needed, as God knows – without them we cannot go on the expedition. We were supposed to leave in February, the Orenburgers and Turkestanis have already set out.'[161] This prompted Markozov to send three columns totalling 350 men across the Atrek into Persian territory on the 27 February, prompting a protest from the Persian government, to which Markozov replied that it was a punitive exped-ition against hostile Turkmen.[162] In fact – as Markozov himself admitted in his later published account – it was another camel raid, which returned with 2,200 beasts – but this was still too few, and the camels were weak and in poor condition, unable to carry more than 5–7 poods.[163] While Grodekov's official history justified Markozov's actions and dignified his camel-raiding as a well-organised preparatory campaign,[164] Terent'ev's verdict was blunt: 'In the eyes of the Turkmen the Krasnovodtsy, and through them, as a result, all Russians, were simply barantachi (livestock-raiders), and if the Turkmen accompanied the force throughout and harassed it, then it is entirely obvious that such swallows will bring vultures in their wake . . .' Markozov's reputation for dishonesty with the Turkmen had crippled his ability to obtain camels from them.[165]

News of Markozov's transport difficulties had reached St Petersburg by late February, and Count Heiden suggested sending his supplies and part of his force to reinforce the column which the Caucasian command now proposed to despatch from Mangishlaq, but Markozov was determined to preserve his independent command.[166] He compounded his errors by choosing a route, via the wells of Bugdaily and Aidin, which, while shorter than the alternative via the Sary-Kamish depression which he had successfully navigated before, was very short of water and subject to extremes of heat. Markozov's response to

160 Astrabad Consul to the Russian Minister in Tehran 02/03/1873 TsGARUz F.I-715 Op.1 D.55 Doc.80 ll. 6–7.
161 Terent'ev, Istoriya zavoevaniya, II, 88.
162 'Copie d'une dépêche du Conseiller Poiré Beges en date de Téhéran le 19 mars 1873', TsGARUz F.I-715 Op.1 D.54 ll. 309–13.
163 Markozov, Krasnovodsksii otryad, 171; Terent'ev, Istoriya zavoevaniya, II, 88–90.
164 Trotskii [Grodekov], Opisanie deistvii kavkazskikh otryadov, 25–35.
165 Terent'ev, Istoriya zavoevaniya, II, 137, 142.
166 Telegram Heiden to Kryzhanovskii 17/03/1873 RGVIA F.1393 Op.1 D.11 l. 5; Telegram Heiden to von Kaufman 17/03/1873 RGVIA F.1393 Op.1 D.13, 'O sledovanii Mangishlakskogo otryada v Khivu', ll. 1–2.

the shortage of transport was to reduce the size of his force, which, when it set out on the 19 March, consisted of just 2,250 men – 12 companies of infantry from the Kabardian, Daghestan, Samur and Shirvan regiments, 4 *sotnyas* of Terek Cossacks, 4 field and 12 mountain guns, 7 rocket frames and a small group of sappers.[167] Markozov took various measures to save weight and thus economise on camels – no dried peas, as they took so long to cook, dried cabbage instead of salted, garlic instead of onions, crystallised citric acid instead of vinegar and, perhaps most controversially, tea and sugar instead of vodka.[168] None of these measures would make any difference, since the crucial factor was the amount of water that could be carried along the near-waterless route Markozov had chosen. Already on the first stage of the march, between Chikishlar and the wells of Aidin, the Terek Cossacks lost 350 of their camels.[169] From the 13 April the temperature began to rise sharply, and they were forced to switch to marching at night, which greatly slowed their progress. On the 16 April the advance guard of Cossacks under Prince Chavchavadze fought a short action in which they captured 450 Turkmen, 1,000 camels and 5,000 sheep.[170] It was to do them little good. The crisis point came at the stage between the wells of Igdy and those of Ortakoy, which they reached on the 17 April – Markozov believed that the distance of three *manzils* (a measurement of distance equal to a day's journey) given by his Turkmen guides was about 70 *versts*, which could be crossed in three days. In reality it was almost twice as far. Terent'ev gives a very full account of the disaster that ensued, explaining how it was mathematically impossible for Markozov's force to carry enough water for its needs on that march. The troops used one-third of their water after the first day, and the advance guard of Terek Cossacks, who were attempting to make the traverse more quickly but with a lighter load, soon found themselves tortured by thirst and heat, their horses struggling through the sand. As dawn broke on the 20 April and the heat returned, discipline broke down altogether: 'people fell in desperation with each step, and many of them already in an almost senseless condition. There was no help for them, the cognac had all been drunk. Those who were still in a condition to continue, threw down all their clothing and even their weapons by the way … some, entirely naked, dug holes and lay in them, seeking shade and moisture …' Never slow to apportion blame or to draw a moral when it could be used to attack the Caucasian command (though he coyly disavowed this intention), Terent'ev added:

> Let this awful picture serve as a warning to all future leaders of steppe expeditions: not to undertake an expedition on the fly (*na avos'*), without

---

[167] Markozov, *Krasnovodskii otryad*, 172–6; Terent'ev, *Istoriya zavoevaniya*, II, 113–14.
[168] Terent'ev, *Istoriya zavoevaniya*, II, 115.
[169] Markozov, *Krasnovodskii otryad*, 178.
[170] *Ibid.*, 181–2.

consideration for bread and water, not to rush to seize laurels from the hands of other forces, not to sacrifice to this a more feasible, if less direct route, and not in this way to stake on a hand of cards the honour of the fatherland, the glory of arms and the lives of those you command.[171]

He compared it to an incident described by Marshal Saint-Arnaud in Algeria, between Mostanegem and Mascara, to demonstrate that the men could not be blamed for abandoning their weapons and equipment 'whether it is the steppe of the Kabyles, or the Turkmens – it is all the same; French, or Russian, before dying they will discard all their burdens'.[172] Markozov's command saved their lives only by heading for the wells of Bala-Ishem, 15 versts away from their route – that evening, among the infantry barely 60 men were still capable of carrying their weapons, while the Cossacks had lost 126 horses. With far longer desert marches awaiting them if they tried to resume, and a desperate shortage of water barrels and camels to carry them, it was clear that the column could not carry on any further, and on the 21 April a military council of his unit commanders decided to return to Krasnovodsk, overruling Markozov's desire to continue.[173] According to Terent'ev the losses were less heavy than might have been expected – over 200 men were temporarily incapacitated by heat, thirst and sunstroke, but only three died, although over 300 horses were lost.[174] Schuyler, however, citing an article in *Birzhevye Vedomosti*, alleges that sixty men died of sunstroke.[175] Markozov did not even attempt to justify the debacle in his later account, simply reproducing Grodekov's description from the official history, which refrained from criticising the decisions he had made, and instead emphasised the intense heat.[176]

The second Caucasian column which set out from Mangishlaq was an afterthought, conceived once it became clear that Markozov's difficulties in finding camels would mean that his force would be very small, if it were able to march at all.[177] The order to form it came on the 4 March, and, although the forces began concentrating on Caucasian side from the 12 March, they did not begin crossing the Caspian to the Kinderli inlet on the Mangishlaq peninsula until two weeks later – in all one steamer and eight schooners were needed to transport supplies.[178] This delay was partly because they were still awaiting news from Markozov, and also because it was clear that the camels needed for

---

[171] Terent'ev, *Istoriya zavoevaniya*, II, 125.
[172] *Ibid.*, II, 128.
[173] *Ibid.*, II, 131, 134–6, 141–2, 146.
[174] *Ibid.*, 140.
[175] Schuyler, *Turkistan*, II, 345.
[176] Markozov, *Krasnovodskii otryad*, 183–97; Trotskii [Grodekov], *Opisanie deistvii kavkazskikh otryadov*, 55–64.
[177] Trotskii [Grodekov], *Opisanie deistvii kavkazskikh otryadov*, 35.
[178] Grodekov, *Khivinskii pokhod*, 67.

346 THE FALL OF KHIVA, 1872-3

the force could not be rounded up any sooner.[179] The Mangishlaq column had fewer problems collecting transport than Markozov, largely because the Qazaqs of Mangishlaq were less alienated from the Russians than the Turkmen of the Atrek. By the 22 March 2,600 had been assembled.[180] However, here too the beasts were weak after the long winter, and often in poor condition, and in fact, just like Markozov, the Mangishlaq force would eventually have to resort to raiding to make up its complement of camels, using a force specially designated for the purpose under Colonel Navrotskii.[181] The force consisted of 12 companies of infantry from the Daghestan, Shirvan, Samur and Kabardian regiments, 4 *sotnyas* of Terek Cossacks, 16 guns and 7 rocket batteries – in all 2,200 men and 500 horses, under the command of General N. P. Lomakin.[182]

While Grodekov's narrative is the most reliable source for the numerical details of the Mangishlaq column's march, it is dry, and circumspect about many of the more embarrassing details. The liveliest and frankest accounts come from Alikhanov-Avarskii, and from the pen of Captain Alexei Nikolaevich Maslov (1852–1922), the pseudonym of a sapper officer whose real name was Bezhetskii, who also served as a correspondent for the Slavophile newspaper *Novoe Vremya*, and who, according to Alikhanov, earned the nickname of the 'expeditionary nightingale' because of his fine voice and cheerful disposition, which comes across to the full in his memoir, written when he was only twenty-two.[183] Focusing on Skobelev, and written after his death for biographical purposes, it nevertheless catches details which eluded other observers – indeed, much of what he writes about Skobelev is so frank you catch yourself wondering whether it was really intended to enhance his reputation, or whether Maslov in fact had a hidden agenda:

> Skobelev, notwithstanding that he was already suffering from haemor-
> rhoids, was always joking and unfailingly welcoming to those serving
> under him [. . .] At the same time Skobelev demolished all the rum and
> cognac that we had extraordinarily quickly. The rest of us used it only in
> small quantities to improve the disgusting well-water – but Mikhail
> Dmitrievich, notwithstanding the terrible heat, drank both one and the
> other in unadulterated form, calling it 'grog'.[184]

Reading Alikhanov and Maslov, it seems that, as with Markozov's column, the early omens were not good. Alikhanov described how on his arrival the Kinderli inlet presented a picture of complete disorder, with piles of provisions

---

[179] Trotskii [Grodekov], *Opisanie deistvii kavkazskikh otryadov*, 36–7, 73–4.
[180] Grodekov, *Khivinskii pokhod*, 68.
[181] Alikhanov-Avarskii, *Pokhod v Khivu*, 27; Terent'ev, *Istoriya zavoevaniya*, II, 212–14.
[182] Grodekov, *Khivinskii pokhod*, 69.
[183] Alikhanov-Avarskii, *Pokhod v Khivu*, 14.
[184] Maslov, *Zapiski o M . D. Skobeleve*, 230.

stacked almost at random on the beach.[185] He also claims that part of the Mangishlaq column very nearly met the same fate as Markozov's, owing to a lack of water vessels and an inexperienced colonel who chose a route that missed the wells, but his description seems remarkably similar to those of the Krasnovodsk column, and it is not clear that he actually witnessed it himself.[186] Maslov wrote that

> In general one must admit that the force was entirely improvised; the men did not know their commanders, the commanders did not know their men; most had never seen the desert before; the soldiers did not know how to handle camels, and the route proposed was known only from hearsay.[187]

On the 18 April, at the wells of Senek, a large portion of the Mangishlaq force – two *sotnyas*, three field guns and a portion of the infantry – had to return to Kinderli, as the mortality among the camels meant there were insufficient baggage animals to carry supplies for them.[188] The remainder did reach Khiva without enduring the same trauma as the Turkestan column or Markozov's, despite crossing almost equally difficult country. What saved the Mangishlaq column from suffering the same fate as Markozov or the same near-disaster as von Kaufman was the skill and loyalty of its Qazaq drivers and guides – this is abundantly clear from Alikhanov's account, as, unlike most officers, he could communicate with them in their own language: 'the Kirgiz move as if by inborn instinct, more accurate than a compass'. When he asked one of the 'old *stepniaks*', a 'Kirgiz mullah', how they managed this, he explained that in this region, where water was so scarce, they could not pasture their flocks but moved across them as quickly as possible, and always by the same routes, which left traces that to them were clear and easy to follow.[189] The specialised skills of the Qazaqs were also vital whenever the force arrived at the wells which determined its route. Alikhanov focuses overwhelmingly on wells, and it is clear how their number and accessibility, and above all the quality of their water, was the single most important factor in the welfare of the force and the success of the expedition. This ranged from the twenty-five wells at Kinderli which he eschewed in favour of Caucasus and seltzer water on the waiting steamers, to that at the end of their first march at Kaundy ('even worse than Kinderli'), to the well of Kuruk that saved them on the Ust-Yurt, whose water was 'cold and pure as a mountain spring in the Caucasus', and which he christened 'unforgettable'.[190] At Ilteje, where all but one of the wells were

---

[185] Alikhanov-Avarskii, *Pokhod v Khivu*, 9.
[186] *Ibid.*, 47–53.
[187] Maslov, *Zapiski o M . D. Skobeleve*, 224.
[188] Alikhanov-Avarskii, *Pokhod v Khivu*, 64–5.
[189] *Ibid.*, 42–3.
[190] *Ibid.*, 17.

blocked, the Qazaq guides saved them again, quickly digging out six of them.[191] Alikhanov remarked with admiration on the skill and energy shown by the Qazaqs in watering the camels, hauling the heavy camel-skin bag swiftly hand over hand when the water was twenty fathoms down, and their ability to water their horses quickly from a well forty fathoms deep which had defeated the Cossacks.[192]

It was not until the 5 May, when the advance guard under Skobelev's command reached the wells of Itebai on the fringes of the Khivan oasis, that the Mangishlaq column had their first 'engagement'. Watering at the wells the Russians found not Khivan forces, but a trade caravan of 50 Qazaqs with 200 camels loaded with sorghum and barley, who were preparing to leave. In Maslov's account, Skobelev went forward with two other officers and seven Cossacks and ordered them to turn back towards Khiva, so that the Russian forces could make use of their camels and the supplies they were carrying:

> The Kirgiz informed them that they had already paid their taxes [zakat], and for this reason refused to carry out Skobelev's demand. Skobelev then threw himself at them with his sword, at which some of the Kirgiz quickly started to drive the camels away, and those who had weapons began to defend themselves. Skobelev's Karabakh [a horse from the Karabakh region of Transcaucasia], which up until then had taken everything in its stride, began to rear and threw its rider to the ground. Skobelev beat them off with his hands and feet, and received some minor wounds. They struck Kedrin [a Cossack officer] in the mouth with a pike and he was also prostrate on the ground. Getting to his feet, he began to defend himself with Skobelev's sabre, which was near him, and this allowed Mikhail Dmitrievich to rise as well.[193]

At this point the Qazaq traders, seeing the approach of the advance guard's infantry, galloped off, abandoning their camels with their load. Skobelev himself was apparently very pleased with this farcical episode, was officially listed as 'wounded', and attempted to use it to claim a St George's Cross. The incident was dignified as the Delo pod Itebaem, thus putting it on a par with the Delo pod Ikanom and other heroic episodes in the conquest of Central Asia, though it was effectively nothing more than an armed robbery, which netted the Mangishlaq column 200 camels and 800 poods of grain that they sorely needed.[194] However, as accounts of it circulated Maslov claimed it provoked jealousy of Skobelev, who fell out with Lomakin over his behaviour, and was deprived of his independent command, while he did not get his coveted

---

[191] Ibid., 98-9; Grodekov, Khivinskii pokhod, 189.
[192] Alikhanov-Avarskii, Pokhod v Khivu, 61, 93.
[193] Maslov, Zapiski o M. D. Skobeleve, 231.
[194] Grodekov, Khivinskii pokhod, 198-9.

citation for a 'George'.[195] Alikhanov and Terent'ev both describe it as a real engagement, in which Skobelev and Kedrin had showed a foolhardy level of bravery in attacking a much larger force of Qazaqs.[196]

On the 6 May the bulk of the Mangishlaq column reached the abandoned fortress of Alan which marked the beginning of the Khivan oasis.[197] The fort, which Alikhanov described as clearly of European construction, was a reminder of the earlier humiliations which their force was supposed to revenge: their Qazaq guides informed them that it had been built by Daulat-Girei, Bekovich-Cherkasskii's Muslim name: from them and from the Turkmen whom they encountered, Alikhanov recorded several stories connected with the earlier expedition.[198] They completed the last stage to the Amu-Darya in a series of three forced marches, partly because their food was running low, but principally because it was clear that the Orenburg column was ahead of them, and Lomakin did not want to be constantly lagging behind their advance, and hence miss out on the chance of military glory. Eventually, on the 16 May, the two forces met on the road between Kungrad and Khojeili; Terent'ev noted that the Caucasians advanced with music and singing, alarming the Orenburgers, who took the sound of kettledrums for gunfire and almost opened fire on their comrades.[199]

7.4 The Orenburg Column

Von Kaufman had originally proposed that Orenburg would provide reinforcements for the Turkestan column at Kazalinsk, rather than constituting an independent command, but General Kryzhanovskii, the Governor, objected that this would require them to make a much longer journey than was really necessary across the steppe and along the eastern shore of the Aral, and leave an escape route for the Khivans onto the Ust-Yurt plateau.[200] The Orenburg column, commanded by Gen. N. A. Verevkin (last encountered capturing Turkestan in 1864), would thus follow the same route as that attempted by Perovskii in 1839–40: south to the river Emba, then across the Ust-Yurt plateau and along the western shores of the Aral to the northern part of the Amu-Darya delta (Figure 7.5). It set out with 3,233 men (including 75 musicians) and 1,449 horses, and over 10,000 camels for transport (5,000 to stock the forward post on the Emba and another 5,000 to accompany the

[195] Maslov, *Zapiski o M. D. Skobeleve*, 231–2.
[196] Alikhanov-Avarskii, *Pokhod v Khivu*, 116–17; Terent'ev, *Istoriya zavoevaniya*, II, 218.
[197] Grodekov, *Khivinskii pokhod*, 197.
[198] Alikhanov-Avarskii, *Pokhod v Khivu*, 25, 39, 95, 108–9; Terent'ev, *Istoriya zavoevaniya*, II, 219–20.
[199] *Ibid.*, 208, 223–4.
[200] Kryzhanovskii to Miliutin 13/11/1872 TsGARUz F.I-715 Op.1 D.53 ll. 167–8; Schuyler, *Turkistan*, II, 335–6.

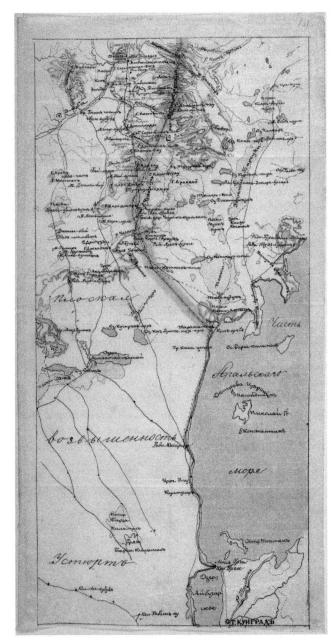

Figure 7.5 The route of the Orenburg column from the Emba to Kungrad (BL Add. MS 47841 f. 101).

column), for the hiring of which they ended up paying the enormous sum of 766,275 roubles.[201] Terent'ev was full of admiration for the Orenburg column's supply and commissariat arrangements, devoting almost ten pages to listing them and noting Kryzhanovskii and Verevkin's forethought and consideration for the men – the supplies included the latest in preserved food: dried cabbage, 'Kitara' potato groats, 'Danilevskii' dried *shchi*, a special type of biscuit developed by war minister Prince Dolgorukov and Liebig's condensed bouillon, as well more homely comforts such as bay leaves.[202] Water was less of a problem than it would be for the Turkestan or Mangishlaq columns because in March there was still snow on the ground in the northern part of the route, though like Perovskii forty years earlier they ran the risk of seeing their camels die of cold. As they neared Khwarazm and marched along the shores of the Aral, they found that in some places the seawater was fresh enough for men and beasts to drink.[203] Forage for horses and camels alike was very scarce, however, and the order of march still had to be meticulously planned, and was distributed to commanders in the form of printed tables.[204]

The column set out in nine echelons, four each from Orenburg and Orsk, and one from Ural'sk, between the 13 and the 24 February.[205] There was clearly no expectation of attack during the first part of the journey to the Emba, as Shuvalov noted that they were accompanied by two officers' wives, one of whom, the 'beautiful and clever' Mrs Engelke, wife of the battery commander at Emba, he gallantly rescued after she fell through the ice into the river Temir.[206] On the 8 March Verevkin reported to von Kaufman that the column had arrived safely at the Emba post, in good health, though after a trying journey.[207] While he initially planned to halt for ten days, in the end his force would rest and recruit their strength for almost three weeks before setting off for the most difficult part of their route, across the Ust-Yurt, having been

---

[201] 'Vedomost' o chislennosti sostave ekspeditsionago otryada Orenburgskogo voennogo okruga', RGVIA F.1393 Op.1 D.11, 'O sledovaniya Orenburgskogo otryada v Khive', ll. 16–17; Terent'ev, *Istoriya zavoevaniya*, II, 185; Saranchov, 'Khivinskiya ekspeditsiya', *Inzhenernyi Zhurnal* (1874), No. 1, 38.

[202] Terent'ev, *Istoriya zavoevaniya*, II, 184, 193. These 'Dolgorouki biscuits' were apparently made of 'flour, beef and sour krout [*sic*] in equal parts' and could be eaten as they were or dissolved in water to make soup. Captain F. Chenevix Trench, 'The Russian Campaign against Khiva, in 1873', *RUSI Journal* 18/77 (1874), 212–26.

[203] Shuvalov to Grand Duke Alexei Alexandrovich 25/04/1873 BL Add. MS.47841 f. 99; Terent'ev, *Istoriya zavoevaniya*, II, 201.

[204] RGVIA F.1393 Op.1 D.11 ll. 1–2. Apart from Shuvalov's letters a vivid account of the march of this column can be found in Saranchov, 'Khivinskiya ekspeditsiya', *IZ* (1874), No. 2, 159–221.

[205] Terent'ev, *Istoriya zavoevaniya*, II, 195.

[206] Shuvalov to Grand Duke Alexei Alexandrovich 16/03/1873 BL Add. MS.47841 f. 78; Shuvalov Jr to Shuvalov Sr 16/03/1873 RGIA F.1092 Op.1 D.288 ll. 12–13.

[207] Verevkin to von Kaufman 08/03/1873 RGVIA F.1393 Op.1 D.11 ll. 3–4.

further delayed by heavy snow and, according to Shuvalov, by a lack of transport as their camels had suffered severely from the cold.[208] Verevkin added that 'as Khiva, without doubt, will be taken by the troops of the Turkestan District' it might be more useful for his column to head for the northern part of the Amu-Darya delta and seize the towns and fortresses there.[209] Verevkin was no doubt aware of von Kaufman's anxiety to be the first to accept Khiva's surrender, but in fact he was being over-pessimistic: his small force would see far more fighting than von Kaufman's.

The advance guard set out from the Emba on the 26 March, and it took almost forty-five days for Verevkin's column to reach the Khwarazm oasis from there.[210] On the 4 April he reported to Kryzhanovskii in Orenburg that, while they were making quite good progress, their camels were dying at an alarming rate:

> We are meeting much more serious difficulties on the side of the camels: some dozens are normally turning out to be unable to carry loads until the halting-point, which makes it necessary to send others in exchange for them. Many have simply collapsed or have had to be abandoned as they are not fit for the road ahead. Along with this the unfit camels cannot be exchanged for fresh ones because of the complete absence of nomadising Kirgiz not only on the route we are following, but around it.[211]

This was because of continued deep snow, which the camels hated, and which slowed their progress – Shuvalov noted that on the 1 April 200 of the 425 camels with the advance guard simply refused to move and spent the night 10 *versts* away from the camping-place, requiring a separate guard.[212] Help was at hand, however, in the form of a Qazaq agent called Minbai Utagulov, who agreed to supply an additional 800 camels to the Emba fortification by a certain date, at a hiring rate of 3 roubles per month per camel.[213] On the 3 April Shuvalov noted that they had been joined by the administrator of the Kabakov canton, Iset Kutebar, whose romantic history as a brigand and rebel against Tsarist rule he was fully acquainted with, but who was now to serve as a guide on the last stage into Khiva, where he had been protected by the Khan in the 1840s and 1850s.[214] Terent'ev notes that much of the relatively smooth and easy passage of the Orenburg column was due to the assistance that it received from the Qazaqs, who provided hospitality and accommodated as many soldiers

---

[208] Shuvalov to Grand Duke Alexei Alexandrovich 16/03/1873 BL Add. MS 47841 ff. 78–9.
[209] Verevkin to von Kaufman 30/03/1873 RGVIA F.1393 Op.1 D.11 ll. 13–15.
[210] Terent'ev, *Istoriya zavoevaniya*, II, 200.
[211] Verevkin to Kryzhanovskii 04/04/1873 RGVIA F.1393 Op.1 D.11 ll. 125–6.
[212] Shuvalov to Grand Duke Alexei Alexandrovich 01/04/1873 BL Add. MS 47841 f. 91.
[213] Verevkin to Kryzhanovskii 18/04/1873 RGVIA F.1393 Op.1 D.11 ll. 130–3.
[214] Shuvalov to Grand Duke Alexei Alexandrovich 03/04/1873 BL Add. MS 47841 ff. 93–v. He wrote that Iset 'appeared somewhat distrustful but good-natured, although alongside this somewhat arrogant'.

as they could in *auls* along the route.[215] Shuvalov wrote in the middle of April that he and other officers were staying in a Qazaq *kibitka*,[216] and, despite the problems with the camels, his description made the march sound like a picnic – a stark contrast to the reports from the other two columns: 'life is healthy and merry: fresh air, fresh food, constant movement: only the enemy is lacking'.[217]

On the 21 April Verevkin received his first communication from Lomakin and the Mangishlaq column, and on the 1–2 May most of the force arrived at Urga, on the Aral not far from Kungrad. Kungrad was taken on the 6 May, with very little Khivan resistance, and Verevkin found it deserted by its inhabitants – Bayani writes that the elders of the city did not have enough ammunition to fight, and asked Verevkin to wait until it arrived. Unsurprisingly, 'Verevkin ignored their request and decided to enter the city anyway.'[218] By a curious twist of fate, he appointed the former bandit Iset Kutebar as assistant to the commander of the small garrison he left behind there.[219] On the 19 May he reported that they were already advancing from Kungrad to Khojeili.[220] They had lost only two men in battle so far, one when the advance guard of Cossacks was attacked in the middle of the night by a small force of about 300 men, and the other when the surveying party travelling with the rearguard was surrounded by a *shaika* of about 50 men – according to Verevkin both attacks were easily beaten off, although Bayani claims that the attack on the advance guard resulted in the death of 13 Russians (which seems unlikely) and the capture of 13 horses.[221] Shortly before reaching Khojeili they found a large abandoned fortified camp, which Verevkin estimated must have held 3,000–5,000 Khivan troops. He judged that they had left only the evening before, as they had left freshly cut bundles of reeds behind them. His scouts reported that this was the main fighting force of the Khanate, led by an Uzbek called Yaqub Bai, and accompanied by the Khivan *Mehtar* and *Inaq*: they included 1,000 infantry and three guns. As we have seen, that evening (16 May) they were joined by the Mangishlaq column, whose members looked jealously on the Orenburgers' comparatively lavish supplies and comfortable marching order; Verevkin assumed command of both columns.[222]

---

[215] Terent'ev, *Istoriya zavoevaniya*, II, 196–7.

[216] Shuvalov to B. A. Perovskii 14/04/1873 RGIA F.1092 Op.1 D.288 l. 3*ob.*

[217] Shuvalov to Grand Duke Alexei Alexandrovich 25/04/1873 BL Add. MS 47841 f. 87*v.*

[218] Bayani, *Shajara-yi Khwarazmshahi* trans. Sela, in *Islamic Central Asia*, 302.

[219] Verevkin to von Kaufman 12/04/1873 RGVIA F.1393 Op.1 D.11 ll. 56–62; Terent'ev, *Istoriya zavoevaniya*, II, 204.

[220] Verevkin to von Kaufman 19/05/1873 RGVIA F.1393 Op.1 ll. 21–31 – also copied by Serebrennikov and available in TsGARUz F.I-715 Op.1 D.56 ll. 126–35.

[221] Verevkin to von Kaufman 19/05/1873 RGVIA F.1393 Op.1 D.11 ll. 21–3. Verevkin wrote that he did not know if the attackers were Khivans or Adai Qazaqs, but Bayani's account confirms that they were Khivans. Bayani, *Shajara-yi Khwarazmshahi* trans. Sela, in *Islamic Central Asia*, 302.

[222] Verevkin to von Kaufman 19/05/1873 RGVIA F.1393 Op.1 D.11 l. 25; Terent'ev, *Istoriya zavoevaniya*, II, 224–5.

The now combined forces of the Mangishlaq and Orenburg columns captured Khojeili the following day without firing a shot, as the Khivan cavalry retreated before them. According to Verevkin,

> The local inhabitants consist almost exclusively of Khwajas (Uzbeks who consider themselves descendants of Muhammad) and are remarkable for their entirely peaceful character, they did not participate in any military operations, and on the contrary, regardless of the general respect in which they are held by Muslims, had endured oppression from the Khivan army which halted here, against which they asked for protection.[223]

Bayani also writes that after the fall of Khojeili the Uzbek troops dispersed, and only the Turkmen continued to offer resistance, though, as we shall see, this was not entirely true.[224]

No doubt much to his satisfaction, Skobelev was given charge of the advance guard as the column proceeded south.[225] The advance from Khojeili towards Khiva was marked by repeated skirmishes in which he played a prominent role – leading a flying column tasked with burning down Turkmen *zimovki* (winter settlements), and beating off an attempted Khivan attack on the baggage transport.[226] Maslov noted that 'Skobelev's role consisted in the main in capturing crossing-points, although at the main Kilich-Niyaz bridge he was late and arrived only when it had already been burnt by the enemy.'[227] The combined column was responsible for capturing the towns of Manghit and Qipchaq, where they engaged in house-to-house fighting, finding large numbers of dead and wounded in the courtyards of the houses: 'All this demonstrated that the inhabitants (Uzbeks) had taken part in actions against the column, which is why, on the capture of the town, some of them paid for this with their lives, and their houses were looted.'[228] The Russians lost one officer and two men killed, and another three wounded – Verevkin could not estimate the number of casualties on the other side, though believed them to be significant. The column continued on to the town of Khitai, and their baggage train was attacked *en route* with the loss of a horse and a few camels. On the 22 May, between Yangi-yapa and Gurlen, came the most significant military action of the whole campaign, where the Russians beat off a Khivan force which Verevkin estimated at 10,000 men, sustaining just six casualties to what he claimed was 200 on the enemy side, largely owing to their crushing superiority in artillery. Verevkin believed that it had broken Khivan morale:

---

[223] Verevkin to von Kaufman 19/05/1873 RGVIA F.1393 Op.1 D.11 l. 29.
[224] Bayani, *Shajara-yi Khwarazmshahi* trans. Sela, in *Islamic Central Asia*, 303.
[225] Maslov, *Zapiski o M. D. Skobeleve*, 233.
[226] Verevkin to von Kaufman 31/05/1873 02/06/1873 RGVIA F.1393 Op.1 D.11 l. 68*ob*, 71.
[227] Maslov, *Zapiski o M. D. Skobeleve*, 233–4.
[228] Verevkin to von Kaufman 31/05/1873 TsGARUz F.I-715 Op.1 D.56 Doc.292 l. 265.

This affair must have produced a tremendous effect on the enemy: here they had gathered all their available forces, they had made use of all their energy and, judging by the accounts of our scouts, had counted on a victory, in that the Yomuds had promised the Khan not to return without complete success. Further developments confirm this conclusion: after the affair of the 22 May the Yomuds in large part returned to their houses and surrounding *qishlaq*s for looting, and the Uzbeks and Sarts who remained in the service of the Khan turned to a different kind of tactic.[229]

On the 25 May Skobelev's advance guard captured the strategic bridge of Katta Köpru, which was followed by an action in the dense walled gardens surrounding the village of 'Shanamikh avli' in which he reported that both Shuvalov and Alikhanov-Avarskii had distinguished themselves – the only casualties were two Cossacks lightly wounded, and some horses killed.[230] The advanced guard of Verevkin's force reached Khiva on the 26 May, and fought another minor action almost under the walls of the city on the following day, when two *sotnya*s of Cossacks under Skobelev's command drove off an attack by what Verevkin estimated to be 3,000 Khivans, who attempted to carry off the baggage camels from the Russian camp. The Russians lost one killed and nine wounded, together with 30 camels lost in an *ariq*. Verevkin claimed that the Khivans had lost over 300 men killed.[231] While the numbers of casualties on the Khivan side were probably consistently exaggerated in Russian reports, the Russian casualties were noticeably low. Maslov's account gives a clear idea of the unequal nature of the fighting:

> Between Khojeili and Khiva we had a few clashes with the enemy; they were partly Uzbeks, partly Yomud Turkmen, who had come at the request of the Khan, poorly armed and a thoroughly undisciplined rabble, running away at the first shots from our not very numerous artillery. It is enough to say that in all before Khiva in six affairs we lost one officer and 28 other ranks killed and wounded.[232]

Though the column had reached Khiva on the 26 May, Verevkin claimed, at least, that it was only two days later that he received any direct communication from von Kaufman and the Turkestan column; in von Kaufman's absence, he decided to assault the city himself.[233]

---

[229] Verevkin to von Kaufman 31/05/1873 RGVIA F.1393 Op.1 D.11 ll. 70–71; also copied by Serebrennikov in TsGARUz F.I-715 Op.1 D.56 Doc.292 l. 270.

[230] Skobelev to Lomakin 02/06/1873 RGVIA F.1393 Op.1 D.11 ll. 169–78 – also copied by Serebrennikov in TsGARUz F.I-715 Op.1 D.57 Doc.297 ll. 23–34.

[231] Skobelev to Lomakin 02/06/1873; Verevkin to von Kaufman 06/06/1873 RGVIA F.1393 Op.1 D.11 ll. 76, 172–4.

[232] Maslov, *Zapiski o M. D. Skobeleve*, 233–4.

[233] Verevkin to von Kaufman 31/05/1873 RGVIA F.1393 Op.1 D.11 l. 78; Terent'ev, *Istoriya zavoevaniya*, II, 247–51.

7.5   The Fall of Khiva

With the arrival of all three columns of Russian troops in the Khivan oasis, the only question that remained was whether the crowning triumph of the campaign – the fall of the city and the surrender of the Khan – could be stage-managed to von Kaufman's satisfaction. The competing ambitions of the officers involved would instead ensure that it smacked strongly of farce. Von Kaufman had received a letter from Muhammad Rahim Khan on the 26 May in which he noted the previous rejection of the envoys he had sent to Russia, repeated that he had already fulfilled all Russian demands and did not understand why the Russians had invaded his realm, and asked von Kaufman to halt his forces at Hazarasp while they negotiated peace terms.[234] Kaufman did not reply – nothing less than the unconditional surrender of Khiva would satisfy him, and that this could be achieved was no longer in doubt. An envoy from Verevkin arrived at his camp at the same time as the Khivan envoy, reporting that he was closing in on the city, and on the 28 May the Khan's cousin, Iltuzar Inaq, came to von Kaufman promising surrender. He immediately sent orders to Verevkin telling him not to fire on the town, and to remain 25 *versts* distant.[235] Verevkin, however, had no intention of conceding any of the glory to the Turkestan Governor-General. Terent'ev is once again scathing about what followed on the 28 May: 'Was it meant to be an assault? But who attempts to storm a three-*sazhen* wall without breaches or scaling ladders? Was it a "reconnaissance in strength"? But nobody attempted to inspect anything.'[236] Maslov describes the bungled attack with characteristic frankness:

> The two detachments were drawn into the gardens surrounding Khiva, without any dispositions, and first came under artillery fire from the walls, then finally stumbled upon the Palwan-ata canal. The Caucasian detachment, which was on the right flank, met a barricade on the way, seizing it and two guns behind it; pursuing the defenders of the barricades and excited by gunfire from the walls, which they had almost not heard throughout the expedition, they rushed across the bridge, located 80 *sazhens* from the city gates, and with shouts of *Ura* continued the offensive. It was about noon. There was dust and smoke in the hot air and, strangely enough, no one saw the gate between two half-bastions, despite it being so close; apart from this, on the eastern side of the wall, a breach was subsequently seen, through which it would also be possible to easily seize the city. Crossing the bridge, the Caucasian infantry occupied a spot under the wall of the cemetery to the right of the gate and exchanged fire

---

[234] Kaufman to Miliutin 10/06/1873; Muhammad Rahim Khan to von Kaufman n.d. TsGARUz F.I-715 Op.1 D.57 Doc.314 ll. 116, 237–8.

[235] Kaufman to Miliutin 10/06/1873 TsGARUz F.I-715 Op.1 D.57 Doc.314 ll. 116–18; Poltoratskii, 'Vospominaniya', IV (1895), No. 5, 441.

[236] Terent'ev, *Istoriya zavoevaniya*, II, 254.

with the enemy. At the same time our artillery placed itself at the bridge and to the left along the canal, and fired without any specific aim at the wall and around the city. There were no arrangements for an assault, and within an hour and a half or two hours Verevkin gave the order to end the 'reconnaissance' and retreat.[237]

The bombardment resumed, and at it was at this point that the Khan fled to Tashauz with an escort of Yomud Turkmen – as Maslov drily remarked, despite divisions within Khiva the bombardment 'was not to their taste', and a deputation then came forward to surrender the town. As von Kaufman had not yet arrived, the Khivans agreed to send a deputation to meet him, escorted by Lomakin – Verevkin having been severely wounded in the face during the earlier fighting.[238]

Alikhanov mentioned how from the outset the officers of the Mangishlaq column had hoped for a climactic storming of Khiva, remembering the reputation that Central Asians had for fighting stoutly behind fortifications, as they had at Ura-Tepe and Jizzakh.[239] While they were waiting for the deputation to return with von Kaufman, Skobelev, who had been disappointed at not having been involved in the '*goryachee delo*' the previous day, decided to put this to the test. According to his official report, on reaching the city he had immediately set up a battery of two field guns and four mortars opposite the Shahabad Gate. Early on the morning of the 29 May, on the pretext that two shots had been fired on them, and that he had learned (from what source he left vague) that the party that wished to prolong the conflict with the Russians had gained in strength in that part of the city, he ordered his battery to open fire. After twenty-four shots a breach was visible in the gate, and he ordered an assault – three men were killed while crossing the 250 yards of open ground before the gates, when they were taken in the flank by an attack from the cemetery. At that point, Skobelev reported, 'there was an order to cease fighting, as the town had surrendered itself to his Excellency, the commander of the forces of the Turkestan District'.[240]

Skobelev was being more than a little economical with the truth – as we have seen, Khiva had in fact already agreed to surrender the day before. Von Kaufman reported to Miliutin that he considered the fighting 'untimely and entirely unwarranted', given that even the Yomuds and Muhammad Murad had surrendered, and that he had ordered an immediate ceasefire.[241] Grodekov wrote that the attack on the Shahabad Gate was 'entirely unnecessary, and can

---

[237] Maslov, *Zapiski o M. D. Skobeleve*, 234–5.
[238] Von Kaufman to Miliutin 10/06/1873 TsGARUz F.I-715 Op.1 D.57 Doc.314 l. 121; Trotskii [Grodekov], *Opisanie deistvii Turkestanskogo otryada*, 211.
[239] Alikhanov-Avarskii, *Pokhod v Khivu*, 30.
[240] Skobelev to Lomakin 02/06/1873 TsGARUz F.I-715 Op.1 D.57 Doc.297 ll. 32–4.
[241] Von Kaufman to Miliutin 10/06/1873 TsGARUz F.I-715 Op.1 D.57 Doc.314 l. 120; Trotskii [Grodekov], *Opisanie deistvii Turkestanskogo otryada*, 212.

be explained only through the desire of Verevkin to show that in fact he had captured Khiva, and not the Turkestan force'. He noted that everything on the 29 May had been peaceful, with the Khivan surrender having been agreed.[242] Quoting Grodekov, Maslov wrote 'one should add that the commander of the advance guard, Skobelev, in his turn burned with the wish to excel', and as usual he gives the clearest account of what actually happened.[243] As Verevkin was wounded and Lomakin had been sent to Kaufman, the senior officer present was an artillery colonel called Konstantinovich, who seems to have been no match for Skobelev's ability to manipulate. There were three bodies still lying in the cemetery below the walls from the fight the previous day. When the Cossacks recovered these, they claimed that the Khivans had muti-lated them. This of course filled Skobelev with righteous indignation:

> Then Skobelev, turning to Rotmistr Count Shuvalov, said: 'Count! Go to the commander of the detachment and ask him whether in view of such a disgrace he will give permission to punish the city and resume the bombardment!' The permission was obtained. Then, with several shells, the gate and part of the tower were destroyed and Skobelev burst into the city. The defenders rushed headlong from the walls and sought refuge in flight. All this was a matter of a few minutes. Whether the forces with Skobelev suffered losses or not, I do not remember.[244] Entering the city, Skobelev captured the gate leading to the citadel, which turned out not be closed, and also the khan's palace.
>
> General Kaufman was displeased overall by the fact that Verevkin, without waiting for him, took possession of the city, and in particular was angry with Skobelev. To this we must add that among the many staff officers commanding the troops there were not a few individuals who were hostile to Skobelev. Lomakin, in his turn, was angry with him, saying that he had ruined the affair of the 28 May, since he considered the fall of Khiva to have happened thanks to this. He told Skobelev this rather harshly, but nevertheless, at the request of the latter, he proposed him for a 'George' [i.e. the order of St George for bravery]. This proposal, however, was rejected by the council of chivalry. For our part, we laughed at Mikhail Dmitr'evich and even composed a satirical song called 'Storming Incognito', which Mikhail Dmitr'evich liked to remember later. At the time he was not in the mood for songs; He was terribly upset and considered himself slighted. And indeed: if he did not deserve the St George Cross for the business on the 29 May, then his service throughout the entire expedition was at any rate outstanding; during this

---

[242] Grodekov, *Khivinskii pokhod*, 263; Terent'ev also quotes this line: *Istoriya zavoevaniya*, II, 259.

[243] Maslov, *Zapiski o M. D. Skobeleve*, 235.

[244] Macgahan, whose account is otherwise very similar to Maslov's, says that fourteen soldiers were wounded, one of them Shuvalov, who was struck by a falling beam: *Campaigning on the Oxus*, 230.

time he managed to attract the attention not only of the authorities, but of all the officers of the detachment.[245]

Skobelev would remain skilled at attracting attention for the rest of his career. What this episode reveals clearly is not just his overweening ambition, but the degree to which the fall of Khiva had ceased to be a military question at all, but instead had become a petty, rather sordid dispute between the commanders involved as to who should get the credit. Schuyler, whose sources evidently mainly came from the Orenburg detachment, was decidedly of the opinion that most of it belonged to them, and this was also what Shuvalov wrote to his father, stressing that it was their detachment that took the city.[246] Von Kaufman's annoyance perhaps expressed itself in the refusal of the 'council of chivalry' which he chaired on the 3 June to award more than one of the St George's Crosses out of the eighteen proposed by Verevkin, and none at all to the Caucasian troops.[247] Among the disappointed was Skobelev, who would eventually win his George's Cross for a reconnaissance expedition from Ili Ali towards Imdy-Kuduk and Ortakuy, a somewhat contrived exploit which was apparently suggested to him by another of the 'pheasants', the War Minister's son, Alexei Dmitr'evich Miliutin.[248]

Despite Verevkin and Skobelev's best attempts to rain on his parade, von Kaufman entered the city in triumph later that afternoon through the Hazarasp gate, to the stirring sounds of the Dargo march, played by the band of the Shirvan regiment, an aural link with earlier Russian expeditions in the Caucasian War.[249] He was met not by the Khan, who had fled, but by Sayyid Amir ul-'Umar, an elderly uncle of the previous Khan (Schuyler refers to him as 'an imbecilic old man') who had supposedly headed the peace party in the city in opposition to the Diwan-begi Muhammad Murad.[250] As von Kaufman later reported, at first the Russians did not know where Muhammad Rahim Khan had hidden himself, and there were rumours that he planned to

---

[245] Maslov, Zapiski o M. D. Skobeleve, 235–7.

[246] Shuvalov Jr to Shuvalov Sr 28/06/1873 RGIA F.1092 Op.1 D.288 ll. 16–17; Schuyler, Turkistan, II, 351–2.

[247] Poltoratskii, 'Vospominaniya', IV (1895), No. 6, 761.

[248] Ibid., 775–7; Maslov, Zapiski o M. D. Skobeleve, 238–9; Macgahan Campaigning on the Oxus, 427–8.

[249] The song commemorates the disastrous expedition to Dargo (one of Shamil's auls) in 1845 – the only text I have been able to find is at http://militarysong.ru/polkovoj-darginskij-marsh. On the Dargo expedition see N. Gorchakov, 'Ekspeditsiya v Dargo (1845 g.)', Kavkazskii sbornik II (Tiflis, 1877), 117–42; Gammer, Muslim Resistance to the Tsar, 149–61; Alexander Statiev, At War's Summit: The Red Army and the Struggle for the Caucasus Mountains in World War II (Cambridge: Cambridge University Press, 2018), 14–16.

[250] Von Kaufman to Miliutin 10/06/1873 TsGARUz F.I-715 Op.1 D.57 Doc.314 ll. 119–22; Trotskii [Grodekov], Opisanie deistvii Turkestanskogo otryada, 213–14; Schuyler, Turkistan, II, 349.

prolong resistance to the Russians from Tashauz, but he appeared in the camp
of the Turkestan column on the 2 June to offer his unconditional surrender.[251]
According to Bayani, the leader of the Yomuds hosting him, Sary Sardar, had
urged him to accept von Kaufman's safe conduct and offer his surrender to the
Russians, which if true sheds a still grimmer light on what was to happen to the
Yomuds afterwards.[252] So long as the Russian forces remained in Khiva von
Kaufman imposed a set of requirements for supplying them, and specified that
the Khan would rule with the assistance of a council, with four Russian and
three Khivan members.[253] When von Kaufman submitted his report to
Miliutin on the 10 June, he noted that the atmosphere in the city had calmed,
and that the shops and stalls were beginning to re-open.[254] This calm was
perhaps a form of numbness: both Bayani and the poet Shayda'i give a clear
impression of how much of a shock the fall of Khiva to an invading non-
Muslim army had been, but also express the hopeless acquiescence of its
inhabitants and the ruling elite:

You have abandoned your good guns and your troops, strange days have come upon
   you, Khorezm.
The ill-fated sky has undergone a turn of fortune, none of the Muslims' affairs succeeds.
This destiny was written down from the very beginning, and you were resigned to this
   to the very end, Khorezm.
It was God's will that the Russians came, whoever complains about this is heedless.[255]

   Von Kaufman would later write of Muhammad Rahim Khan that 'a greater
acquaintance with him assures me that he is an able man, but who up until the
current catastrophe had never occupied himself with anything, giving over
himself and all his khanate into the hands of his bad adviser, the former
Diwan-begi Muhammad-Murad', who had now been exiled.[256] Nevertheless
the treaty terms imposed on Khiva were somewhat harsher than those von
Kaufman had applied to Bukhara. This supposedly reflected the khanate's
greater intransigence prior to the campaign, but, given that Bukhara, unlike
Khiva, had actually attacked Russian outposts and sent a large army towards
Russian territory, it seems more likely that it reflected both the difficulties of
the campaign and the symbolic importance of the victory to von Kaufman.
Certainly the size of the indemnity demanded by von Kaufman, 2 million

[251] Von Kaufman to Miliutin 10/06/1873; von Kaufman to Alexander II 16/06/1873
   TsGARUz F.I-715 Op.1 D.57 Docs.314 & 331 ll. 123–5, 190.
[252] Bayani, Shajara-yi Khwarazmshahi trans. Sela, in Islamic Central Asia, 303.
[253] 'Polozhenie ob upravlenii Khivinskim khanstvom vo vremya prebyvaniya v nem russkikh voisk', 06/06/1873 von Kaufman to Miliutin 29/06/1873 TsGARUz F.I-715 Op.1
   D.57 Doc.305 ll. 81–2; Becker, Russia's Protectorates, 73.
[254] Von Kaufman to Miliutin 10/06/1873 TsGARUz F.I-715 Op.1 D.57 Doc.314 l. 124.
[255] Erkinov, 'The Conquest of Khiva', 102.
[256] Von Kaufman to Miliutin 29/06/1873 TsGARUz F.I-715 Op.1 D.57 Doc.351 l. 288.

roubles, was based on his estimated cost of the campaign (almost ten times the figure he had projected in the autumn of 1872).[257] Bukhara also had not been subjected to the indignity of having its archives removed – during the weeks that followed Khiva's fall Alexander Kuhn and his Tajik assistant Mirza 'Abd al-Rahman were hard at work packing up all the manuscripts he could find in the Khan's palace and elsewhere:[258] 'Many of the books, as I was informed by Mr Kuhn, the Orientalist of the expedition, were very curious and valuable. They were all written by hand, many of them beautifully; for the most part, they were bound in leather or parchment. Among them were a history of the world and a history of Khiva from the beginning of time. They have all been sent to the Imperial Library of St Petersburg' (some also went to the Asiatic Museum).[259] On the 12 June, with considerable fanfare, von Kaufman proclaimed the abolition of slavery in the khanate, and required that all remaining slaves be released, something that would long be celebrated as a key event in Russia's 'civilising mission' in Central Asia.[260] While this might have been the intention, Jeff Eden believes that slavery continued in Khiva, although the cases he cites are all from Bukhara.[261]

Von Kaufman insisted to Miliutin that, if the Russians simply left behind a garrison on the territory of the khanate, it would be isolated and constantly preoccupied with its own defence, and thus unable to exercise the requisite moral influence over the population. He insisted that the right bank of the Amu-Darya should become Russian territory, with a new fortress and Russian settlement: 'They need to understand well that, if it was difficult for us to get here the first time, and we got here all right, then the next time we will get here with considerably less effort ... and that the next time we will not conduct ourselves so generously.'[262] St Petersburg acquiesced to this, although it contradicted von Kaufman's original instructions, and the assurances that the Russians had given to the British that there would be no further territorial annexations as a result of the expedition.[263] Khiva, like Bukhara, would become a protectorate, and remain in an ambiguous state, maintaining a good deal of internal autonomy, which produced a remarkable flowering of literature and architecture in the last fifty years of its existence, but at the same

[257] Von Kaufman to Miliutin 10/06/1873 TsGARUz F.I-715 Op.1 D.57 Doc.314 l. 131.
[258] Bregel, *Dokumenty Arkhiva Khivinskikh Khanov*, 9–62.
[259] Macgahan, *Campaigning on the Oxus*, 250.
[260] Grodekov, *Khivinskii pokhod*, 275–9; see e.g. 'Dvadtsatipyatiletie pokoreniya Khivy', *Niva* (1898), No. 24, 477–8.
[261] Eden, 'Beyond the Bazaars', 946–53.
[262] Von Kaufman to Miliutin 25/07/1873 TsGARUz F.I-715 Op.1 D.57 Doc.408 ll. 452–3.
[263] 'Usloviya mira Rossii s Khivoi', 12/08/1873 TsGARUz F.I-1 Op.27 D.7 ll. 1–5; Becker, *Russia's Protectorates*, 75; the full text of the treaty in English can be found in Macgahan, *Campaigning on the Oxus*, 416–20.

time fully under Russian control in its external affairs.[264] Unlike in Bukhara, the Khan would not even have direct relations with the Turkestan Governor-General, but would be answerable to the commander of the Amu-Darya Division at Petroalexandrovsk (modern Tortkol), and would face the constant threat of intervention from the garrison under his command.[265] Having attacked Khiva and humiliated Muhammad Rahim Khan, von Kaufman now wished to re-establish him firmly on his throne on Russian terms; the need to bolster his authority against his most unruly subjects, the Yomud Turkmen, would become the pretext for the most notorious incident of the entire campaign.

7.6   The Yomud Massacre and After

In his first full report to Miliutin von Kaufman noted that two of the most important questions confronting him were the freeing of the Persian slaves, which he believed would produce a social revolution in the khanate, and the question of how to settle with the Turkmen, who in his eyes were 'desperate robbers', who had not only led the resistance to the Russian advance, but had taken the opportunity to plunder the settled inhabitants of the khanate: 'When we began discussions on the ending of hostilities, the Yomuds were the only ones who were in favour of continuing the war to the bitter end, and when the Khan left Khiva for General Verevkin's force, they took advantage of his absence to produce a revolution in the city and chose as Khan his younger brother Ata-Jan, and when he returned to the city, closed the gates and refused to admit him.' He believed they had intended to carry the Khan off to the region of their 'nomadising' and force him to prolong the fight, until the arrival of all three forces beneath the walls of Khiva forced them to come to terms. In other words, they were a threat to Khiva's internal stability, just as Shahrisabz had been to Bukhara, and if the khanate was to become a Russian protectorate they would need to be curbed.[266] The best means of doing this, von Kaufman urged, would be a heavy financial indemnity, which they could not be expected to pay willingly – this would necessitate an expedition into their lands: 'A satisfactory resolution of the Turkmen question is essential at this time. The seizing from them of the due part of the contribution should be carried out in the most determined fashion and, in the case of their resistance or refusal . . .

---

[264] On the ambiguities of Khiva's status as a protectorate see Ulfat Abdurasulov & Paolo Sartori, 'Neopredelonnost' kak politika: razmyshlenyaya prirode rossikogo protektorata v Srednei Azii', *AI* (2016), No. 3, 118–64; on the culture of Muhammad Rahim Khan's court after 1873 see Aftandil Erkinov, 'How Muhammad Rahim Khan II of Khiva (1864–1910) Cultivated His Court Library as a Means of Resistance against the Russian Empire', *Journal of Islamic Manuscripts* 2 (2011), 36–49.

[265] Becker, *Russia's Protectorates*, 81–5.

[266] Von Kaufman to Miliutin 10/06/1873 TsGARUz F.I-715 Op.1 D.57 Doc.314 ll. 127–9.

we will bring our forces to cruelly (*zhestoko*) conquer and crush (*razgromit'*) the regions where they nomadise and produce with this a strong moral impression.'[267] He believed that this would have a calming effect on the population of the khanate as a whole.

Von Kaufman mentioned his intention to impose an indemnity on the Turkmen once again on the the 29 June, saying it would apply to the Chaudar, Göklan and Imrali tribes as well as the Yomuds.[268] None of these groups were prolonging their resistance to the Russians, and as Becker observed, the reasons for the campaign were by no means clear to von Kaufman's contemporaries and fellow officers.[269] MacGahan notes that von Kaufman was criticised by many of his officers for insisting on the indemnity:

> He knew very well, they said, it was not possible for the Turcomans to pay in the specified time: he had allowed himself to be hoodwinked by the Khan; and was becoming a mere tool in his hands for the furtherance of his schemes of conquest over the Turcomans [. . .] I do not think that Kaufmann was so easily hoodwinked, nor that he allowed himself to be unduly influenced by the Khan's assertions. What he did, he did with a full knowledge of the case, and upon his own judgement. Rightly or wrongly, he professed to place no reliance on the Turcomans' promises to pay; and not to believe their professions of future good conduct. They could not, he said, be relied upon to keep the peace until they should be completely crushed. Besides, he wishes to conciliate the Uzbegs, who would be only too rejoiced to see their turbulent neighbours conquered, and reduced to submission. In addition to this, they were an independent people, who flouted all authority – the unpardonable sin in the eyes of the Russian government. It was necessary to make an example of them, and enforce obedience to royal authority, even though that authority were only per-sonified in the person of the Khan of Khiva.[270]

This is borne out by the reasoning visible in von Kaufman's reports to Miliutin, and certainly the reference to authority rings true – however, there were other interpretations. Schuyler alleged that it was the ambition of the officers of the Turkestan detachment which was to blame:

> The officers of the Tashkent detachment were not satisfied. They had started on the campaign for the purpose of obtaining decorations and increased rank. There had been great intrigues before the campaign began as to the persons who should accompany it, and further intrigues during the course of it for prominent and advantageous commands. Decorations, it is true, had been distributed with a lavish hand for the skirmish near Khalata, as well as for all those on the banks of the Amu Darya. Nearly

---

[267] Von Kaufman to Miliutin 10/06/1873 TsGARUz F.I-715 Op.1 D.57 Doc.314 l. 130.
[268] Von Kaufman to Miliutin 29/06/1873 TsGARUz F.I-715 Op.1 D.57 Doc.351 l. 290.
[269] Becker, *Russia's Protectorates*, 74.
[270] MacGahan, *Campaigning on the Oxus*, 353–4.

every officer had, three times at least, been presented for reward – for having safely made the march over the desert, for having crossed the Amu Darya, and for having reached and entered Khiva. Still there had been no actual fight, and the Cross of St George – the highest esteemed reward – could not be given without that. Something had to be done, and it was suggested to make a campaign against the Turkomans.[271]

Schuyler's account of the Khiva expedition would be vigorously contested when it was published;[272] however, Terent'ev suggested the same, noting that the officers of the force sent against the Turkmen – Blok, Novomlinskii, Dreshern, Esipov and Grünewald – were all those who had arrived after Khiva had already fallen, and that this was a means of allowing them 'to smell gunpowder'. 'One thing was strange – the Turkmen had still not refused to pay the indemnity, and yet an execution was already being sent against them . . .'[273] These are retrospective judgements, but there is also contemporary evidence, though it comes from the commander of the Caucasian detachment, who had no love for the *Turkestantsy*. On the 6 July Lomakin wrote what seems to have been a private note to Grand Duke Mikhail Romanov in Tiflis explaining what he believed had prompted the punitive expedition against the Yomuds:

> The expedition against the Yomuds, about which I have already written to your Radiance in my last letter, it seems will happen in the next few days. It is very miserable. All the elders have come forward, all our demands have been fulfilled with accuracy; and all the same we are going to ravage them. [. . .] On the eve of our return we will exhaust our cavalry to no purpose whatsoever. They say that it is essential that the 8th Turkestan Battalion, which has not yet fired a single shot in the course of the expedition, should be given an opportunity to distinguish itself. No doubt there can be only one result of all this: when we leave *en route* the Yomuds will rob both our caravans and the Khivans with renewed energy. Thank God that at least our infantry isn't going.[274]

Von Kaufman's instructions to Golovachev (Figure 7.6),[275] issued the same day, referred once again to the 'final resolution of the Turkmen question'. He informed Golovachev that, of the twenty-three Turkmen leaders he had summoned, only seventeen had appeared, and he had informed them that the total amount demanded was 300,000 roubles, of which 100,000 roubles should

[271] Schuyler, *Turkistan*, II, 354–5.
[272] Gorlov, *Dokladnaya zapiska* (1878), TsGARUz F.I-1 Op.27 D.1524a ll. 1–8.
[273] Terent'ev, *Istoriya zavoevaniya*, II, 267.
[274] Lomakin to Grand Duke Mikhail 06/07/1873 TsGARUz F.I-715 Op.1 D.57 Doc.364 ll. 332–3.
[275] 'Voennyi Gubernator Syr-Dar'inskoi Oblasti General-Maior N. N. Golovachev', in Kun (ed.), *Turkestanskii al'bom* Pt. 4, plate 9, No. 6 (Library of Congress, Prints & Photographs Division LC-DIG-ppmsca-09957-00006).

Figure 7.6 Nikolai Nikitich Golovachev (*Turkestan Album*, 1871).

be brought within ten days, and the remaining 200,000 roubles five days later, to which they had agreed.

Golovachev's task was to proceed along the length of the Ghazavat canal, surround the Turkmen and prevent them from dispersing into the steppe – if he saw any signs of them massing for an attack, or of trying to escape, he was to 'give over these nomadic Yomud and their families to complete ruin and extermination, and their property and herds to confiscation'.[276] Saranchov, who had taken over command of the Orenburg force from the wounded Verevkin, was simultaneously ordered to keep the Turkmen around Qizil-Tahir under surveillance and prevent them from coming to the aid of the Yomuds, and to assist Golovachev if necessary, with a similar injunction to destroy if the Turkmen showed any signs of resistance.[277] Macgahan wrote that, once Golovachev's force had reached the Ghazavat canal, 'Here the army encamped all next day; ostensibly for the purpose of seeing if the Turcomans would come forward and pay; really, I believe, because General Golovatchoff, who did not much relish the expedition, wished to give them an opportunity of escaping'.[278] Schuyler, quoting an anonymous source who served with the expedition, gives a contrasting account:

---

[276] '*Predat'* eti kochev'ya Yomudov i sem'i ikh polnomu i sovershennomu razoreniiu i istrebleniiu, a imushchestvo ikh, stada i prochee konfiskovaniiu', Kaufman to Golovachev 06/07/1873 TsGARUz F.I-715 Op.1 D.57 Doc.361 ll. 325–6; also quoted in Grodekov *Khivinskii pokhod*, 292; Terent'ev, *Istoriya zavoevaniya*, II, 269.

[277] Kaufman to Saranchov 06/07/1873 TsGARUz F.I-715 Op.1 D.57 Doc.363 l. 329.

[278] MacGahan, *Campaigning on the Oxus*, 357.

When we had gone about twenty-five miles from Khiva, General Golovatchef said before a large number of officers in my presence: 'I have received an order from the Commander-in-Chief – I hope you will remember it and give it to your soldiers. This expedition does not spare either sex or age. Kill all of them.' After this the officers delivered this command to their several detachments. The detachment of the Caucasus army had not then arrived, but came that evening. Golovatchef called together the officers of the Caucasus and said: 'I hope you will fulfil all these commands strictly in the Circassian style, without a question. You are not to spare either sex or age. Kill all of them.' The old Colonel of the Caucasus said, 'Certainly, we will do exactly as you say.'[279]

The killing of the Turkmen and the burning of their villages began on the 7 July. The most vivid description of the massacre was Macgahan's, though he went much further than Schuyler to exculpate the Russians from the most damaging charge, that of killing women and children, which helps explain why his account would be characterised as more 'objective' by Russian sources:[280]

Everywhere, lying among the thickly standing arbas, were the bodies, with sabre-cuts on head and face, bloody and ghastly. But worse still to see were the women cowering under the carts, like poor dumb animals, watching us with fear-stricken faces and beseeching eyes, but never uttering a word, with the dead bodies of their husbands, lovers, and brothers lying around them. They expected to be treated as they knew their own husbands, brothers, and lovers would have treated the vanquished under like circumstances [...] But worst of all to see was a number of little mites of children, whose parents had probably been killed. Some were crawling among the wheels, crying; others, still sitting in the carts among the baggage, watched us with curious, childish eyes; one little girl crowed and laughed at the sight of General Golovatchoff's banner ... I must say, however, that cases of violence towards women were very rare; and although the Russians here were fighting barbarians who commit all sorts of atrocities upon their prisoners, which fact might have excused a good deal of cruelty on the part of the soldiers, their conduct was infinitely better than that of European troops in European campaigns.[281]

He did see one old woman killed by a sabre-cut to the neck, but thought she had probably been mistaken for a man. Ron Sela has shown that the account of the Yomud massacre in Bayani's Shajara-yi Khwarazmshahi is partly based on an Ottoman translation of Macgahan's description of the massacre of the

[279] Schuyler, Turkistan, II, 359.
[280] Gorlov, 'Dokladnaya zapiska' (1878), TsGARUz F.I-1 Op.27 D.1524a ll. 1–8.
[281] Macgahan, Campaigning on the Oxus, 399–400.

Yomud Turkmen.[282] Meanwhile Grodekov's account of the massacre occupies just two paragraphs: he referred coldly to large numbers of Turkmen dead, but did not specify their sex or age.[283]

On the 13 July the Turkmen attacked Golovachev's camp and succeeded in killing Lt Kamenetskii of the first *sotnya* of Ural Cossacks and one of his men who had been stationed on picket duty before reinforcements could reach them; Schuyler's source blamed Golovachev's slowness, and noted that the bodies were mutilated, angering the men of the force.[284] On the night of the 15 July, when the Russians were encamped at Ili Ali, there was a much more serious attack, which inspired Golovachev to new heights of descriptive prose in his report, although it could not entirely disguise either the confusion which had reigned, or the ultimately one-sided nature of a battle in which only the Russians had artillery. The Russians had formed a *wagenburg* for protection, but it was still incomplete when the neighing of horses in the darkness warned them of the approach of the Turkmen. 'The Turkmen threw themselves on us with desperate determination: pushing their hats over their eyes, they came running with swords and knives in their hands, throwing themselves onto the bayonets [. . .] the canister did dreadful execution: the cries all of a sudden died down, and the enemy retreated from the battery [. . .] everyone unanimously avers that never so far in Central Asia have the natives shown such desperate courage and energy – they fought for life or death.' He took care to note the bravery and good service of Prince Evgenii Maximilianovich Romanovskii of Leuchtenberg, who had shot down a Turkmen with his revolver, while his aide-de-camp, Colonel von Meyer, was wounded in the head and hand. Golovachev described the losses as heavy, but they amounted to one officer (Lt-Col. Esipov of the Orenburg Cossacks) and three men killed, with another five officers (including Golovachev himself) and thirty-two men wounded, two of the latter fatally. Golovachev estimated that there had been 10,000 Turkmen attackers, of whom at least 800 had been killed, both numbers probably grossly exaggerated.[285] Schuyler's source gave a somewhat less flattering account of the affair:

> The *wagenburg* was only half done when the order was given to advance, and contrary to all rules the cavalry was sent out first. They went along a narrow road intersected with canals, not noticing that many Turkomans were lying hidden in the grass on each side. After going some distance they

---

[282] Bayani, *Shajara-yi Khwarazmshahi* trans. Sela, in *Islamic Central Asia*, 304–5; Ron Sela, 'Invoking the Russian Conquest of Khiva and the Massacre of the Yomut Turkmens: The Choices of a Central Asian Historian', *AS* 60/2 (2006), 459–77.

[283] Grodekov, *Khivinskii pokhod*, 301–2.

[284] Golovachev to von Kaufman 14/07/1873 TsGARUz F.I-715 Op.1 D.57 Doc.384 ll. 373–4; Terent'ev, *Istoriya zavoevaniya*, II, 274; Schuyler, *Turkistan*, II, 360.

[285] Golovachev to von Kaufman 23/07/1873 TsGARUz F.I-715 Op.1 D.57 Doc.396 ll. 403–12.

suddenly found themselves face to face with a large body of Turkoman cavalry across the road, whose intention was to take the camp. The Cossacks turned face and fled, followed by the Turkomans, and all hurried in one mass into the camp. The utmost confusion ensued, and for twenty minutes I did not hear a single command or see any order, and we thought that the whole affair was lost, until the commander of the rocket battery brought his rockets into play.[286]

It was during the initial panicked retreat of the Cossacks that their commander, Esipov, had been killed, and ultimately it was the infantry who had saved the day, with disciplined volley fire after the Turkmen had been panicked by the rockets – here again Terent'ev's account accords with Schuyler's, though he is less critical of Golovachev's leadership.[287] Irrespective of whether Golovachev was at fault or not, the failure of this attack seems to have broken the Turkmen resistance. On the 25 July von Kaufman wrote a lengthy official report to Miliutin explaining how the Turkmen question had been settled, in which he set forth still more explicitly why he considered them a threat to Khiva's peace and stability:

> I have come to the certainty that in order to give the Khan's government the ability to carry out our requests in future and uphold the terms of the peace agreement which I intend to propose to him soon, it is essential to change those relations which have been established and exist between the Turkmen and the government of the Khivan Khan. Now it is already obvious, that the power of the Khan over the Turkmen living in the Khivan oasis was only nominal, and that on the contrary these last used the authority of the Khan exclusively for their benefit and their purposes. It was not the Khan who ruled and had at his disposition the mass of semi-nomadic Turkmen, but they who held him always in their hands. With strength in numbers, up to 30,000 *kibitkas*, the population of Turkmen presented a threatening element to the Khivan government, all the more so as they are a particularly warlike tribe and extremely wilful and thieving; they can raise up, estimating one man per *kibitka*, up to 30,000 armed warriors, extremely brave, insolent and cunning, on superb, fast, sturdy horses [. . .] this unbridled tribe cannot by any means enter into the programme of our actions for Khiva. Even the annexation of the right bank of the Amu-Darya [. . .] does not present in this case a sufficient guarantee of the cowing (*izumlenie*) of the abnormal relations of the Khan to the population under his rule.[288]

---

[286] Schuyler, *Turkistan*, II, 361.
[287] Terent'ev, *Istoriya zavoevaniya*, II, 275–6; Macgahan, *Campaigning on the Oxus*, 384–5 describes the battle as a close-run thing, in which they were saved by the steadiness of the infantry. See also Grodekov, *Khivinskii pokhod*, 298–300.
[288] Von Kaufman to Miliutin 25/07/1873 TsGARUz F.I-715 Op.1 D.57 Doc.404 ll. 427–8.

All of this was clearly leading up to a justification of the violence which Golovachev's force had inflicted on them, about which von Kaufman was oblique. He noted that Golovachev had been attacked on the 13 and 15 July, and that on the 17 July his force had 'overtaken the Turkmen who were moving away from it into the sands, after which the Yomuds scattered themselves in different directions'.[289] He then went on to say that the force had shown ability, courage and cool-headedness. Rather than describing the violence (which he had not witnessed himself), von Kaufman instead described its results, which he saw after leading another force to join Golovachev's along the Ghazavat canal on the 19 July:

> The condition of the Turkmen in these areas is excellent; they present the same kinds of carefully maintained pastures, gardens and fields that one sees among the Uzbeks and other settled peoples of the khanate. All this we found abandoned, the fields unharvested; in the houses and saklya, everywhere were the traces of the sudden abandonment of their homes by the Yomuds [. . .] the pogrom carried out by our forces among the Yomuds was very considerable. They lost many killed and wounded. Up to 9,000 of their cattle were driven off; their houses, grain, various stores along the route of Major-General Golovachev's force from Ghazavat to Zmukhshir, all was given over to the flames. At various times the force destroyed and burned up to 3,000 arbas containing Yomud property. Materially weakened and morally shattered, the Yomuds scattered in different directions.[290]

A few days later deputations from some Yomud clans – the Ushak, Salah and Uruskushi, presented themselves to von Kaufman begging to be allowed to resettle in their previous spot, to which von Kaufman agreed. 'If they really do return, then I propose in any case to obtain from them at least a part of the indemnity that they still owe.' He wrote that the chastising of the Yomuds had produced a strong impression across the whole khanate, and that the settled population was relieved to be free of Yomud depredations, while the Khan was delighted. On the 21 July he called together the representatives of the remaining Turkmen tribes – the Chaudar, Imrali, Karadashi Aliele, Göklan and Qara-Jalandy – at Ili Ali, and informed them that they too would have to pay an indemnity of 310,000 roubles.[291] In what appears to have been a private letter on the same day, von Kaufman did allow some doubt, or possibly even pangs of conscience, to creep in:

> From my representations on the Turkmen question I hope your Excellency will deign to see the reasons which caused me to raise it now, and also the direction which it took [. . .] to close one's eyes and leave the

[289] Von Kaufman to Miliutin 25/07/1873 TsGARUz F.I-715 Op.1 D.57 Doc.404 l. 430.
[290] Von Kaufman to Miliutin 25/07/1873 TsGARUz F.I-715 Op.1 D.57 Doc.404 l. 432.
[291] Von Kaufman to Miliutin 25/07/1873 TsGARUz F.I-715 Op.1 D.57 Doc.404 ll. 433–4.

question open, meant it would have to be resolved in the future, and this according to my custom I could not do, and so it arose. The first scene of this drama was pretty bloody; what will happen further – I do not know, but hope it will end more peacefully than it began, and more than anything else I hope for the authority I have earned in Asia – but I may be mistaken.[292]

A further indication that von Kaufman was not proud of the Yomud massacre was that reference to his orders and descriptions of the massacre were excluded from the original three volumes of the official history. Grodekov did include a description in the second edition of his volume on the Caucasian columns, published after von Kaufman's death, in which he justified it in terms of the disruptive and hostile relationship the Turkmen had with the Khivan government and with their settled neighbours, and by claiming that it was provoked by the refusal of the Turkmen to release their Persian slaves, something von Kaufman never mentioned in any of his reports.[293] Terent'ev followed Grodekov in claiming that the failure to release slaves was what provoked the demand for an indemnity, but he was scathing about the elisions in the official history, and dismissed contemporary attempts to pretend that von Kaufman's orders did not exist or had been misinterpreted – for him their meaning was clear: 'in other words, if you see a suitable occasion, then use it, . . . so that the troops will have the right to decorations not for the privations of a difficult expedition, but for fighting excellence'.[294] He also mocked the suggestion that the massacre was a result of the uncontrollable savagery of the Caucasian troops, whom Schuyler suggested had been urged to handle the affair 'in the Circassian manner': 'Evgenii Maximilianovich of Leuchtenberg, Baron Kridner, von Grünewald. Were they really Circassians?' (they were, of course, all German). Terent'ev concluded that overall 'Schuyler did not lie' – the order had been given and carried out, and Terent'ev did not even consider that it had been necessary to secure Muhammad Rahim Khan's authority – it was 'causeless and needless cruelty'.[295]

On the 11 August von Kaufman wrote to Miliutin to say that the deadline for the remaining Turkmen to pay the indemnity had expired on the 2 August, by which time they had brought in only one-third of the amount – without any apparent sense of incongruousness, he noted that 'I did not find it just to inflict punishment on them, as their desire and attempts to settle with us and bring in the tax demanded of them were so clear. On the other hand, I did not find it possible or convenient to forgive them the remaining two-thirds of the indemnity demanded from them; this half-savage people would take any

[292] Von Kaufman to Miliutin 25/07/1873 TsGARUz F.I-715 Op.1 D.57 Doc.408 l. 451.
[293] Grodekov, *Khivinskii pokhod* (1883), 290.
[294] Terent'ev, *Istoriya zavoevaniya*, II, 270.
[295] *Ibid.*, II, 272, 278–9; Schuyler, *Turkistan*, II, 359.

announcement that they had been forgiven part of the indemnity as a sign of weakness and indecisiveness on our side.'[296] His appetite for violence seems to have been sated, and there was no further expedition against the Turkmen. Autumn 1873 marked the end of the active phase of the Khivan campaign, and telegrams of congratulation came to Kaufman from Kryzhanovskii at Orenburg, from Kolpakovskii in Vernyi and, most importantly, from the Tsar at Livadia.[297] Von Kaufman had his triumph.

From a purely pragmatic perspective the 1873 Khiva expedition appears wholly unnecessary, at least in the form that it took. A diplomatic solution to the long-standing disagreements between the Russian empire and Khiva could probably have been found without the need for violence had the Russians been willing to treat the Khan as a sovereign ruler, and to make some economic concessions that would have compensated for the loss of income from plundering of caravans and slave-raiding. It is less clear whether Khiva could have become the kind of subordinate and stable partner the Russians desired without some show of military force: as in Bukhara, the Russian conquest was the prelude to the reconstitution of what had been a loosely governed polity with blurred sovereign boundaries to a more centralised state with defined frontiers along European lines. The Russians smashed the Khan's authority in order to reconstitute it afresh in a manner that served their interests better, and which probably gave him greater internal control over his subjects than he had had before. Even so, a single well-equipped column of troops from Orenburg or Mangishlaq would have been enough to achieve this, and this was clear even without the benefit of hindsight. The acute suffering which befell the Turkestan column under von Kaufman's command, and the disaster and failure which befell Markozov, were largely a product of individual ambition trumping more sober military considerations. This is why the *Khivinskii pokhod* was so large, elaborate and expensively organised, and why (on von Kaufman's insistence) it received the tribute of an official history funded by the Ministry of War, something neither the preceding campaign against Bukhara nor the one that followed against Khoqand would have. The smallest and weakest of Central Asia's states would be inflated into Russia's most ancient, hostile, intractable and above all insolent foe, and its downfall milked for every last drop of symbolism. Macgahan wrote that, 'apart from the prestige thus gained, the conquest of Khiva has little importance',[298] by which he meant little importance for the Russian advance towards India which his English-speaking audience was primarily interested in. However, Macgahan missed the point – the conquest of Khiva was precisely about prestige, not

---

[296] Von Kaufman to Miliutin 11/08/1873 TsGARUz F.I-715 Op.1 D.58 Doc.437 l. 42.

[297] Telegrams 28/08/1873, 13/09/1873, 01/10/1873 RGIA F.954 Op.1 D.66 ll. 3, 6, 8; my thanks to Yuan Gao for looking at these for me.

[298] Macgahan, *Campaigning on the Oxus*, 424.

about any rational calculation of economic or strategic advantage vis-à-vis the British or anyone else. It was about avenging Bekovich-Cherkasskii and Perovskii, and wiping out the memory of over 150 years of 'insolence'. What is more telling is that von Kaufman's stage management was not perfect: the failure of Markozov, the near-disaster that befell his own column, the farcical circumstances of the city's surrender and the subsequent massacre of the Yomuds all served to tarnish his triumph.

As with all the desert and steppe expeditions in Central Asia, the greatest challenge was logistical: the expense of hiring camels made up over half the projected cost of the expedition, and once compensation had been paid for all the beasts that had died, over a third of the actual expenditure. As always, also, this threw the Russians into an uneasy relationship of dependence on the nomads who bred and managed these indispensable but intractable beasts. Paolo Sartori has called for a reappraisal of Khivan 'connectivity', urging that historians neither exaggerate Khiva's isolation, nor suggest that it enjoyed the same levels of integration into global networks as Bombay or Macau, but instead pay more attention to evidence of regional connections.[299] It was these regional connections which the Russians had to make use of to conquer Khiva: where their columns stuck to established caravan routes – those between Kazalinsk and Bukhara, Orenburg and the Emba, and Mangishlaq and Kungrad – they had few difficulties. What made the difference between success and failure was the support of the nomadic population and the use of its specialist knowledge. Markozov failed because he had so alienated the Atrek Turkmen through his camel-raiding, and because he chose an untried route. Von Kaufman very nearly failed as well through ignoring an established caravan route, and was saved only by the skill of his Qazaq guides, who found water at the very last minute. The relatively smooth passage of the Orenburg and Mangishlaq columns was largely down to the much better relations the Russians enjoyed with the Qazaqs in these regions: without their navigation skills and ability to use steppe and desert wells, none of the Russian columns would have reached its destination. Does this make them somehow complicit in the conquest of their fellow Central Asians and co-religionists? This is really an anachronistic question; the solidarity it suggests was contingent and conditional, where it existed at all – these men were professionals doing their job, and, luckily for the Russians, doing it well. They were not decision-makers. The Khiva campaign, like all the other campaigns in Central Asia, was an enterprise of the Russian imperial state, and above all its military – there were plenty of instances during the campaign where Russian technological superiority was clear and decisive: volleys of Berdan rifle-fire and salvoes of canister

---

[299] Sartori, 'On Khvārazmian Connectivity', 141.

scattered the Khivan forces, and later the Yomuds. It is worth remembering, though, that the Russians would never have been able to exercise this technological superiority in the first place had it not been for their harnessing of local forms of knowledge, on which they ultimately remained dependent.

8

'Those Who Should Be Spared': The Conquest of Ferghana, 1875–6

It was on the first day of the month of Muharram al-haram, 1293 [1875], that the governor of the city of Namangan, by the name of Skobelev, general of the Nazarenes and Russians, brought news from Tashkent that he had cleansed the district of Ferghana of the foulness and dust of the evil provocateurs and thugs of that region.

> Muhammad Salih Khwaja Tashkandi, *Ta'rikh-i Jadidah-yi Tashkand* (*c*. 1886), f. 124a

The final extinction of the Khoqand Khanate and the annexation of its remaining territory in the fertile, densely populated Ferghana valley came after an uneasy decade in which it had existed as a Russian protectorate. Perhaps it was for this reason that, unlike the earlier capture of Tashkent, Samarkand and Khiva, or the later Russian campaigns in Transcaspia, this stage of the Russian conquest of Central Asia attracted little international attention at the time. In consequence, as Sergei Abashin has argued, it has been given very little attention within the grand narrative of the Russian conquest, which focuses on the set-piece sieges of Tashkent and Gök-Tepe.[1] As Khoqand was already assumed to be a Russian puppet, British 'Great Gamers' were not unduly alarmed or interested when its territory passed from indirect to direct Russian rule. Curiously enough, the one exception at the time came from C. E. Callwell, who analysed Russia's campaigns against Khoqand in his *Small Wars* as a model of successful colonial warfare, though he concentrated mainly on the period prior to the fall of Tashkent in 1865.[2] The main contemporary account in English is from Eugene Schuyler, and while it is an accurate summary of events, unlike his gossip-laden description of the Khiva campaign, it is colourless and uncontroversial.[3] The standard accounts of the Ferghana campaign in Russian, whilst indispensable and extremely detailed, were composed in the Tsarist period, and carry some

My thanks to Bakhtiyar Babajanov for his comments on this chapter.
[1] Sergei Abashin, 'The "Fierce fight" at Oshoba: A Microhistory of the Conquest of the Khoqand Khanate', *CAS* 33/2 (2014), 215–16.
[2] Callwell, *Small Wars*, 17, 242.
[3] Schuyler, *Turkistan*, II, 274–302.

heavy ideological baggage.[4] This historiographical neglect is unjustified: as we shall see, whilst Ferghana's incorporation into Russian Turkestan came about almost by accident, as a consequence of political processes about which the Russians had little understanding, its longer-term consequences were profound.

For the inhabitants of southern Central Asia perhaps no other Russian campaign of conquest was of greater significance. Khoqand was the only one of the 'three khanates' of sedentary Central Asia to be completely destroyed, its ruling Uzbek Ming dynasty exiled. In Bukhara and Khiva there was at least the appearance of political continuity, and indeed, as we have seen earlier, argu-ably it was Russian support that transformed what had been loose congeries of sovereignty into Anglo-Indian style princely states. In cultural terms the continuity was real, and the ruling Manghit and Qunghrat dynasties continued to act as patrons of the arts, poetry and pious learning.[5] Khoqand was not granted this extra stay of execution, and it is important to understand both why this happened, given von Kaufman's preference for indirect rule where pos-sible, and the local reaction to the destruction of this, Central Asia's newest and in many ways most successful polity.

The Khoqand Khanate has sometimes been seen as a flash in the pan, lacking the imperial pedigree of Khwarazm or Bukhara. It first emerged as a semi-independent dominion under nominal Bukharan suzerainty in the 1740s, its rulers would not assume the title of 'khan' until 1801, and, although they expanded aggressively into the *Dasht-i Qipchaq* in the 1820s and 1830s to claim a larger territory than either Bukhara or Khiva, Khoqand's rulers controlled this steppe empire for barely thirty years. However, Khoqand was in many ways the most dynamic of all the Central Asian states, as its Ming rulers presided over a boom in trade with India, Russia and China in the early nineteenth century, and substantially expanded the irrigation network in its core territory of Ferghana.[6] It was these canals which would allow Ferghana to become the centre of the future cotton economy of Turkestan which emerged in the 1890s. The last of them, the Ulugh-nahr, was constructed after the khanate had already become a Russian protectorate in 1868–71, and was remembered by the poet Furqat as one of Khudoyar Khan's greatest

[4] The first, dryly factual official narrative was published as 'Voennyya deistviya v byvshem Kokanskom khanstve s 25 dekabrya 1875 goda po 7go fevralya 1876 goda', *VS* (1876), No. 8, 119–77. The later accounts by Serebrennikov and Terent'ev are rather more opinion-ated. A. G. Serebrennikov, 'K istorii Kokanskago pokhoda', *VS* (1897), No. 9; (1899), No. 4; (1901), Nos. 4, 7–11; Terent'ev, *Istoriya zavoevaniya*, II, 322–426.
[5] Erkinov, 'How Muhammad Rahīm Khān II of Khiva (1864–1910) Cultivated His Court Library'.
[6] Levi, *Rise and Fall of Khoqand* & 'India, Russia'; Newby, *The Empire and the Khanate*, 45–50.

achievements.[7] The cotton boom would transform the rural landscape and economy of Ferghana, where the flat, intensively cultivated lowlands end abruptly at the stony slopes of the Qurama hills to the north, and the Zarafshan and Alai ranges to the south. By 1915 70 per cent of arable land in the valley was under cotton, and the city of Khoqand itself became a brash *fin-de-siècle* boom town.[8] The greatest manifestation of Khoqand's lasting legacy in colonial Turkestan lies in the extraordinarily voluminous historiography which it generated. It is difficult to think of any comparably sized state in the Muslim world which produced so many chronicles: the majority, however, were written after the khanate's demise at the hands of Russia, and much of this literary flowering seems to have been an exercise in nostalgia and recrimination, and also a function of the disappearance of any political control over what could be written and circulated about the defunct khanate. Some of this writing, notably the *Tar'rikh-i Shahrukhi*, was known to the Russians and became the basis of the earliest writing on the khanate's history.[9] However, most of the Khoqand chronicles still exist only in manuscript, and their sheer extent and richness have only recently been fully demonstrated thanks to the pioneering work of the late Timur Beisembiev, who devoted a lifetime of research to studying their contents, composition, authorship and language. One of his main conclusions was that Khoqand's internal political rivalry between its sedentary ('Sart') and nomadic ('Qipchaq') elements, which spilled over into open warfare in 1842, is closely reflected in the khanate's historiography, with most authors writing as partisans of one side or the other.[10] The longest of all the Khoqand chronicles, Muhammad Salih Khwaja Tashkandi's Persian-language *Ta'rikh-i Jadidah-yi Tashkand*, which we have already encountered in earlier chapters, contains a description of the final conquest of the Ferghana valley by General Skobelev in 1875–6.[11] As the opening quotation suggests, this reflects a characteristic sedentary 'Sart' disapproval of the mostly nomadic rebels, Qipchaqs and Kyrgyz, who rose against Khudoyar Khan in 1875 – a division which plagued the last thirty years of

[7] S. Khalilov, 'Iz istorii kanala Ulughnakhr', in *Iz istorii Srednei Azii (dorevoliutsionnyi period): Sbornik statei* (Tashkent: Nauka, 1965), 37–44; N. P. Ostroumov, 'Pesnya o Khudoyar Khane', *ZVORIAO* Vol. 2 (1887), 194; Beisembiev notes, however, that 'Aziz ibn Riza Marghinani in his *Tasnif-i Gharib*, composed in Marghelan *c.* 1910, condemns the high mortality amongst those who constructed the Ulugh-nahr. Beisembiev, *Kokandskaya istoriografiya*, 290.

[8] Penati, 'The Cotton Boom and the Land Tax'; Obertreis, *Imperial Desert Dreams*, 96–102.

[9] Notably V. P. Nalivkin, *Kratkaya istoriya Kokandskogo khanstva* (Kazan': Tip. Imperatorskogo Universiteta, 1885); Bartol'd, 'Tuzemets o russkom Zavoevanii'.

[10] In 1842 the Qipchaqs under Musulman Quli had deposed and exiled the young Khudoyar Khan, who was then restored after a rebellion and massacre of the Qipchaqs in 1852. Beisembiev divides the extant chronicles roughly equally between pro-Khudoyar Khan and pro-Qipchaq narratives. Beisembiev, *Annotated Indices*, 21–2.

[11] *TJT*, f. 124a.

Khoqand's existence, and partly explains its fragmentation under Russian pressure.[12] The latest of the chronicles, 'Ishaq Khan 'Ibrat's *Ta'rikh-i Farghana*, composed in 1914–16 by an author who was only fifteen years old when Ferghana was annexed, also contains descriptions of the Russian campaigns of 1875–6, and has been used extensively by Bakhtiyar Babajanov in his *magnum opus* on Khoqand.[13] This recent research on Khoqand by Central Asian and Western scholars has enormously enriched our understanding of the internal structures of the khanate and its external relations, and ensured that it now takes its proper place in the history of nineteenth-century Eurasia.[14] This chapter, on Khoqand's final destruction and annexation to Russian Turkestan as the *Ferganskaya Oblast'* (Ferghana Province), inevitably relies primarily on Russian sources, but I will also attempt to draw upon elements of Khoqand's rich literary tradition, not least in order to demonstrate just how disruptive and painful the destruction of the khanate was, at least for its elites, which helps to explain the ghostly afterlife which its political structures and literary culture had in colonial Central Asia.

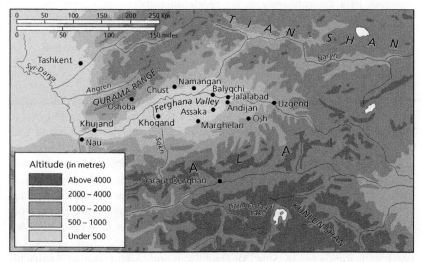

Map 8 The Ferghana valley

[12] Abashin, 'The Fierce Fight', 223.
[13] Babadzhanov, *Kokandskoe khanstvo*, 285–304.
[14] Levi, *The Rise and Fall of Khoqand* & 'The Ferghana Valley at the Crossroads of World History'.

8.1   Rumours of Rebellion

Russian concerns about the internal stability of their protectorate in Ferghana long pre-dated the collapse of 1875. The turbulent modern history of Khoqand was well known in Russia even before the conquest: an 1856 article by a Russian orientalist described the poor relations which existed between that khanate and Bukhara, Amir Nasrullah's invasion of the Ferghana valley in 1842, the Qipchaq ascendancy under Musulmanqul in Khoqand which followed, and the overthrow of Musulmanqul and restoration of Khudoyar Khan in 1852.[15] In 1871 a Russian naturalist and geographer, A. P. Fedchenko, had been allowed to travel in the khanate, penetrating as far as the village of Daraut-Qurghan in the Alai valley. He produced an extensive survey of its territories which appeared just as the crisis in Khoqand reached its height.[16] Russian officials were thus well aware of the fragile nature of Khudoyar Khan's authority. As early as 1865, General Chernyaev observed that Khudoyar was heavily reliant both on Bukharan support (Amir Sayyid Muzaffar was his son-in-law) and on Russian forbearance:

> Khudoyar is not remarkable either for his spirit or his character, and does not have the confidence of the people, in particular as regards the Qipchaqs, who, in these circumstances, will always be our weapon against the Khan. The Bukharan emir, linked to this appointment, will value our friendship all the more, because he is not always in the position to support his father-in-law, who, situated much closer to us than he is to Bukhara, is unwillingly subject exclusively to our influence.[17]

A few months later Chernyaev wrote to his close friend Colonel Poltoratskii that Khoqand had been so greatly weakened by the Russian conquest that it was likely either to fall under Bukharan influence, or else to fragment and become a source of Muslim resistance to the Russians: 'It is essential for us to destroy Khoqand, in order not to make for ourselves a second Caucasus – we are capable of this: Khoqand as an independent dominion already does not exist.'[18] In 1868, in the midst of negotiations over the treaties drawn up between Khoqand and newly defeated Bukhara, Governor-General von Kaufman noted that Khudoyar Khan was anxious to conclude peace in order to secure his own fragile position, and that there was a strong party opposed to peace with Russia led by Shir 'Ali Dadkhwah and 'Abdurrahman Aftabachi, a son of the former Qipchaq ruler Musulmanqul, who would lead the revolt

[15] Velyaminov-Zernov, 'Istoricheskiya izvestiya o Kokanskom khanstve', 333–9, 353.
[16] A. P. Fedchenko, 'Puteshestvie v Turkestan', *Izvestiya Imperatorskogo Obshchestva Lyubitelei Estestvoznaniya*. Vol. I, Pt. 2. *V Kokanskom khanstve* (St Pb. & Moscow: Tip. M. Stasiulevicha, 1875), 1–137.
[17] Chernyaev to Kryzhanovskii 06/08/1865, in Serebrennikov, *Sbornik. 1865 g. Pt. II*, Doc.193, 8.
[18] Chernyaev to V. A. Poltoratskii 20/12/1865 RGIM OPI F.208 Op.1 D.5 l. 35ob.

against Khudoyar in 1875.[19] In 1872 the Russians signed a further agreement with Khudoyar Khan regarding trade and guarantees for Russian merchants, notwithstanding Khudoyar's claims that he would be unable to protect them from his own 'fanatical' people.[20]

In 1873 Khoqand was shaken by a serious uprising led by a Kyrgyz leader called Pulad Khan, who claimed to be (and according to some local sources was) the youngest son of the former Khoqandi ruler 'Alim Khan.[21] In September Kolpakovskii, then Acting Governor-General, wrote that the uprising had begun among the Kyrgyz in the highlands to the south of the Ferghana valley, after an attempt to levy double the usual rate of *zakat* on livestock, and that it threatened 'the final downfall' of the Khan.[22] Khudoyar sent a force under 'Abdurrahman Aftabachi to suppress the revolt; he had come to an agreement with the erstwhile rebel in 1866, and appears to have attempted to co-opt him as a military leader.[23] This succeeded at first, but then Khudoyar reignited opposition by executing the envoys whom Aftabachi had persuaded the Kyrgyz to send to the court at Khoqand, and the rebels then captured Uzgend, Uch-Qurghan and several other towns. Kolpakovskii wrote that the 'Sart' (i.e. sedentary) inhabitants of Andijan and Khoqand were only awaiting the arrival of the Kyrgyz to rise up in rebellion against Khudoyar as well, while there were rumours that Khudoyar's son and heir, Nasruddin, had gone over to them.[24] In November Baron Nol'de, the District Commandant of Khujand, reported the arrival of two Kyrgyz, envoys from the insurgents, with a letter explaining their reasons for rebelling against Khudoyar – namely that he was 'acting against the *shari'a*' and had captured and was holding hostage 270 of their compatriots. The tone of the letter was not hostile – it requested advice and support from Nol'de as a 'great commander', and also informed him that they had despatched two envoys with a similar request to the Sarybaghysh Kyrgyz leader Shabdan Jantai-oghli, better known as Shabdan *Batyr* (see Chapter 4), in the Toqmaq district: they claimed that he had advised them to seize Andijan.[25]

---

[19] Von Kaufman to A. M. Gorchakov 21/03/1868 RGVIA F.1396 Op.2 D.44 ll. 43–4ob.

[20] A. M. Gorchakov to Alexander II 09/12/1872 AVPRI F.161/4 Op.729/2 D.326, 'Zakliuchenie dopolnitel'nogo dogovor s khanom Kokanskim o torgovle', ll. 1–2; Terent'ev, *Istoriya zavoevaniya*, II, 328.

[21] Beisembiev cites the *TJT* on this point: *Kokandskaya istoriografiya*, 290; however, Babajanov suggests this was a myth designed to secure legitimacy, *Kokandskoe khanstvo*, 288.

[22] Kolpakovskii to Miliutin 04/09/1873 TsGARUz F.I-715 Op.1 D.58 part I Doc.476 l. 177.

[23] Babadzhanov, *Kokandskoe khanstvo*, 280.

[24] Kolpakovskii to Miliutin 04/09/1873 TsGARUz F.I-715 Op.1 D.58 part I Doc.476 ll. 178–9.

[25] Nol'de to Major-General Eiler n.d. (Nov. 1873) enclosing 'Perevod pis'mo insurgentov kirgizov Kokandskogo khanstva Nachal'niku Khodzhentskogo uezda' TsGARUz F.I-715 Op.1 D.58 Pt.II ll. 325–6.

In December 1873 Kolpakovskii reported to the War Ministry that the uprising in Khoqand seemed to have collapsed, and that the discontent of the nomadic population with Khudoyar Khan's rule was expressing itself through migration to Russian territory rather than open rebellion.[26] Four months later he was once again reporting widespread rebellion, as the people ran out of patience with Khudoyar's exactions and cruelty, while he had executed his *Mehtar* (finance minister) Mullah Mir Kamil, who had always been friendly to Russia, prompting a letter of rebuke from von Kaufman which also referred to his poor treatment of Russian merchants.[27] That summer the intrigues against Khudoyar became ever more complex – in June a Russian report suggested that the discontented Kyrgyz and Qipchaqs were seeking a figurehead, and had put forward a sixteen-year-old, 'Abd al-Karim Bek,[28] the grandson of Khudoyar's uncle, and indeed Khudoyar's own son, Nasruddin, now governor of Andijan: 'although the nomadic population has not yet decided to act openly against the Khan, nevertheless combustible material continues to mount up, and it will only take a spark to renew the flame of rebellion'.[29] By August the leader of the rebellion was said to be a Kyrgyz called Musulmanqul, a name which he shared with the Qipchaq ruler of Khoqand from 1842–52, and which thus had a powerful resonance – however, he also claimed to be a descendant of one of the earlier Ming dynasty Khans.[30] As their choice of potential leaders shows, this was not a rebellion against the Ming dynasty as a whole, still less against the idea or legitimacy of Khoqand as a state, but against Khudoyar (Figure 8.1)[31] in person – this is important for understanding the subsequent course both of the rebellion in Ferghana and of local resistance to the Russian invasion.

[26] Kolpakovskii to Miliutin 20/12/1873 AVPRI F.147 Op.485 D.1260, 'Svedeniya o polozhenii del v sosednikh s Turkestanskim kraem nezavisimykh sredne-aziatskikh vladeniyakh', ll. 345*ob.*

[27] Kolpakovskii to von Kaufman 23/04/1874; von Kaufman to Khudoyar Khan 31/05/1874 TsGARUz F.I-715 Op.1 D.60 Docs.113 & 154, ll. 49–50, 165–6.

[28] Beisembiev notes that he was a son of Sadiq Bek Ming – *Annotated Indices*, 307. He had lived for many years in Khujand, and was accused by Kolpakovskii of stirring up trouble amongst the Kyrgyz, but he escaped from the surveillance of Baron Nol'de and fled to the mountains. Terent'ev, *Istoriya zavoevaniya*, II, 414. In March 1875 'Abd al-Karim and two sons of 'Abd al-Ghafar Bek, the former Bukharan governor of Ura-Tepe, were about to lead a party of Kyrgyz in an attack on Khudoyar when they were surprised and scattered by his troops: Weinberg to ? 28/05/1875 TsGARUz F.I-715 Op.1 D.62 l. 288.

[29] 'Nekotoryya svedeniya o polozhenii del v Kokanskom khanstve, lichnosti Khudoyar Khana i otnosheniyakh ego k narodu i priblizhennym', 10/06/1874 TsGARUz F.I-715 Op.1 D.60 Doc.164 ll. 197–200.

[30] Golovachev to Kolpakovskii 11/08/1874 TsGARUz F.I-715 Op.1 D.61 Doc.227 ll. 71–2.

[31] 'Seid Mukhamed Khudayar-Khan, Kokanskii khan', in Kun (ed.), *Turkestanskii al'bom*. Pt. 2, Vol. 1, plate 11, No. 32 (Library of Congress, Prints & Photographs Division LC-DIG-ppmsca-09951–00032).

Figure 8.1 Khudoyar Khan of Khoqand (*Turkestan Album*, 1871).

Late in 1874 von Kaufman despatched an envoy, Arkady Avgustovich Weinberg, to give a first-hand account of how events in Khoqand were developing. After visiting Assaka, Andijan and Khoqand itself, he gave a pessimistic assessment, considering that Khudoyar showed no signs of learning from his earlier mistakes, and that the state of affairs was 'unworthy of the dignity of Russia, thrust by fate into the role of civiliser (*tsivilizator*) in Central Asia'. He suggested a personal meeting between von Kaufman and Khudoyar in Khujand or Tashkent, though acknowledging the Governor-General's reluctance to intervene directly in the internal affairs of the protectorate.[32] He did not suggest sending troops to prop up Khudoyar's authority. Terent'ev claims that the Russian military authorities in Turkestan had decided to leave Khudoyar Khan to sink or swim on his own, as retaliation for his failure to fulfil the commercial clauses of the peace treaties he had signed, and von Kaufman does indeed seem to have washed his hands of him at this stage.[33] As we have seen, this was in stark contrast to Bukhara, where, after peace was signed in 1868, Amir Sayyid Muzaffar's authority was bolstered by carefully staged displays of Russian military might, most notably the punitive expedition to Shahrisabz in 1870. Without overt Russian support, weakened by two decades of warfare and defeat, Khudoyar Khan's authority finally crumbled in the summer of 1875.

---

[32] Weinberg to von Kaufman 29/12/1874 TsGARUz F.I-715 Op.1 D.62 Doc.331 ll. 328–34.
[33] Terent'ev, *Istoriya zavoevaniya*, II, 333.

According to Babajanov, the decisive factor which brought about Khudoyar's downfall was taxation, more specifically what were viewed as the extortionate and illegitimate levies he used in an increasingly desperate attempt to fund his bloated army of *sarbaz* infantry, which was mainly officered by Afghan, Indian, Persian and Russian military adventurers. The final straw was an attempt to impose an inheritance tax, which was widely condemned by the *'ulama* as contrary to all principles of *fiqh* (Islamic jurisprudence).[34] It was perhaps because of this criticism that Khudoyar wrote to von Kaufman rather defensively that he had always ruled his people in accordance with the *shari'a*, but that 'immoral, worthless people' had been stirring up trouble among his nomadic subjects.[35] Despite this, the Russian authorities would come to assume that the revolt was directed primarily against them – an Islamic uprising against the Russian *kafirs* similar to what they had seen in Bukhara ten years before. Khudoyar himself seems to have done his best to encourage this idea, no doubt realising that it increased his chances of receiving Russian support.

Terent'ev suggested that it was the arrival of a small Russian delegation in Khoqand on the 13 July 1875 which accelerated the revolt in the capital, as the 'Mullah-ishans' began preaching that it was the Russians who were responsible for all the poverty in the khanate, as they were supporting the hated Khan.[36] Whatever the truth of this, it is certainly significant that one of the party was Fligel'-Ad'iutant Colonel Mikhail Dmitrievich Skobelev (Figure 8.2),[37] who was meant to be on his way to Yaqub Beg in Kashgar, but whose presence in Ferghana when the revolt broke out would be the making of his military reputation.

Some sources suggest that Skobelev was aware that trouble was brewing in Khoqand, and had sought a transfer to Turkestan precisely so that he could be in the thick of it, with the accompanying possibilities of promotion and decorations. Skobelev's most interesting biographer, A. N. Maslov, reports that early in spring 1875 a general (unnamed) visiting St Petersburg from Tashkent reported that there would soon be a campaign in Khoqand, owing to the growing discontent of the population with the Khan, and that already in April Skobelev predicted he would be asked to command the cavalry in the forthcoming campaign.[38] V. P. Nalivkin (1852–1918), in his very hostile memoir, suggests that Skobelev engineered a meeting with von Kaufman

[34] Babadzhanov, *Kokandskoe khanstvo*, 285–9.
[35] Khudoyar Khan to von Kaufman 09/10/1873 TsGARUz F.I-715 Op.1 D.58 part II Doc.511 ll. 263–4.
[36] Terent'ev, *Istoriya zavoevaniya*, II, 335.
[37] Photograph by Levitskii & Sons, St Petersburg, presented to the French Geographical Society by A. N. Kuropatkin and now in the Bibliothèque Nationale de France (http://gallica.bnf.fr/ark:/12148/btv1b8449929j/f1.item).
[38] Maslov, *Zapiski o M. D. Skobeleve*, 245.

Source gallica.bnf.fr / Bibliothèque nationale de France

Figure 8.2 Mikhail Dmitr'evich Skobelev, 1881.

(who had barred him from service in Turkestan after a series of youthful misdemeanours, compounded by his antics at the fall of Khiva) on a railway journey through Poland, in order to win over 'the old boy' (*starikashka*) as Skobelev apparently called him.[39] Some of this may be hindsight, given the importance of this campaign to establishing Skobelev's later reputation. There is little doubt that the Russian force of twenty-two Cossacks which accompanied Skobelev's mission was far too small to constitute a serious show of force in Khudoyar's support, and that it might have been seen instead as a provocation,

---

[39] V. P. Nalivkin, 'Moi vospominaniya o Skobeleve', *Russkii Turkestan* (1906), No. 119, reprinted in *Polveka v Turkestane: V. P. Nalivkin: biografiya, dokumenty, trudy* ed. T. V. Kotiukova (Moscow: Izd. Mardzhani, 2015), 535–6.

or even an indication that no serious military support would be forthcoming. The immediate trigger for a renewed uprising was 'Abdurrahman Aftabachi's decision to turn against Khudoyar. On the 19 July 1875 Weinberg sent a report to Tashkent in a tone of some panic:

> The state of affairs in the Khoqand Khanate is very disquieting. The government force of 4,000 men, sent against the rebels in the Uzgend hills, have gone over to the insurgents together with their leaders Isa-Auliya and 'Abdurrahman Aftabachi, and the *Bek* of Qara-su Khan Nazar Ishiq Agassy. The Khan-zada [Khudoyar's son, Nasruddin] and the Andijan garrison of 5,000 men with artillery have also gone over to the rebels. The towns of Osh, Namangan, Andijan and Assaka are in the hands of the rebels, who are heading towards Marghelan, which up until now has remained loyal to the legitimate ruler. The Khan is very agitated, and does not hope for the Khoqand garrison. He has sent representatives to the camp of the rebels for talks: if these diplomatic attempts do not have a fortunate outcome then he thinks he will turn to the Governor-General for help. I don't know what Konstantin Petrovich [von Kaufman] will make of all this, perhaps it will be necessary to meddle in the affairs of Khoqand [?].[40]

According to Babajanov, the Khoqandi sources are divided as to Aftabachi's motivation in turning on his erstwhile sovereign, with some suggesting he wanted revenge for the murder of his father and the other Qipchaq leaders when Khudoyar was restored to the throne in 1852, and others emphasising his anti-Russian sentiments.[41] His later willingness to treat with the Russians suggests the former was more important, but it is clear that neither the Russians nor Khudoyar had anticipated that he would switch sides. In his report to von Kaufman on the same day, Weinberg wrote of the possibility of anarchy, and noted that it might be necessary to support Khudoyar by force of arms.[42] In an audience on the 20 July Khudoyar insisted that the uprising was a 'jihad against the Russians' and officially requested Russian assistance.[43] Weinberg asked whether it might be possible to send a battalion of Russian troops from Khujand as far as Besh-Ariq, thirty *versts* from Khoqand, even without von Kaufman's authorisation, as the situation was now extremely bad and likely to get much worse if they waited any longer.[44]

In Tashkent, news of the situation had already spread, and according to one account was greeted with a loud 'Hurrah' in military circles, as officers immediately saw the prospect of action and its attendant possibilities of

---

[40] Weinberg to Golovachev 19/07/1875 RGVIA F.1396 Op.2 D.91, 'O voennykh deistviyakh v Kokandskom khanstve', ll. 17–18.

[41] Babadzhanov, *Kokandskoe khanstvo*, 290.

[42] Weinberg to von Kaufman 19/07/1875 TsGARUz F.I-715 Op.1 D.63 Doc.137 ll. 44–6.

[43] Skobelev to Trotskii 20/07/1875 TsGARUz F.I-715 Op.1 D.63 Doc.142 ll. 52–3.

[44] Weinberg to Golovachev 21/07/1875 RGVIA F.1396 Op.2 D.91 ll. 19–*ob*.

promotion and medals.[45] Von Kaufman was in Vernyi when news of the rebellion reached the Russians, and had to be alerted by a telegram from General N. N. Golovachev, commander of the military forces of Syr-Darya province, suggesting that the Governor-General had not anticipated any dangerous developments in Ferghana.[46] Before he could respond, Khudoyar Khan had already fled to Russian territory, accompanied by his family, an entourage of 500 people and a baggage train of 50 *arbas*, together with the Russian envoy, and escorted by a force of 50 mounted infantrymen sent from Khujand by its district commandant, Baron Nol'de.[47] Events in Khoqand unrolled with bewildering speed, and Khudoyar's authority seems to have collapsed within a few days of 'Abdurrahman Aftabachi's revolt. On the night of the 21–22 July, as drums and rockets sounded in Khoqand's streets, half the Khoqand garrison, 4,000 men, deserted to the rebels, led by Khudoyar's second son Muhammad Amin Bek. The following morning Weinberg, Skobelev and their small escort of Cossacks had to struggle through streets thronged with unruly crowds who joked that they would soon cut off all their heads, to reach the Khan's palace and escort Khudoyar away. At this point his remaining troops deserted him, and Weinberg noted that he preferred to trust his family to his Russian escort than to the scattering of *jigits* who remained.[48] Had the Russians decided that they did, after all, wish to keep Khudoyar in place, it would already have been too late. Weinberg wrote on the day of their arrival in Khujand that the now ex-Khan 'is tired and ill from the severe strain on his physical and moral strength; he gives over himself and his khanate to the mercy of His Majesty the Emperor, but strongly hopes that the Governor-General will again restore him.'[49] In this he was to be disappointed. Whilst the Russians had not yet given up on the idea of maintaining at least a truncated part of Khoqand as an independent khanate, Khudoyar's legitimacy, after thirty years in which he had already been overthrown and restored by external forces three times, was finally felt to be exhausted.[50] The following day Nol'de reported that Khudoyar's son, Nasruddin (Figure 8.3),[51] had been 'triumphantly proclaimed Khan' by the rebels (according to at least one Khoqandi source, 'Abdurrahman Aftabachi had also given a speech denouncing the Ming

[45] M. Mikhailov, *Pokhod v Kokand v 1875 g.: Otdel'nyi ottisk iz gazety Turkestanskie Vedomosti* 1884, Nos. 3, 10, 11, 12, 13 (Tashkent: Turkestanskie Vedomosti, 1884), 290.

[46] Telegram Golovachev to von Kaufman 22/07/1875 RGVIA F.1396 Op.2 D.91 l. 1.

[47] Nol'de to Golovachev 24/07/1875 RGVIA F.1396 Op.2 D.91 ll. 30–2.

[48] Weinberg to von Kaufman 28/07/1875 TsGARUz F.I-715 Op.1 D.63 Doc.162 ll. 86–8, 95.

[49] Weinberg to Golovachev 24/07/1875 RGVIA F.1396 Op.2 D.91 l. 33.

[50] The eyewitness 'Ibrat, in his *Ta'rikh-i Farghana*, remarked on the bitterness of Khudoyar's thoughts at this point: Babadzhanov, *Kokandskoe khanstvo*, 293.

[51] 'Seid Mukhamed Nasretdin Bek (starshii syn Kokanskago khana)', in Kun (ed.), *Turkestanskii al'bom*. Pt. 2, Vol. 1, plate 11, No. 31 (Library of Congress, Prints & Photographs Division LC-DIG-ppmsca-09951–00031).

Figure 8.3 Nasruddin *Bek*, eldest son of Khudoyar Khan (*Turkestan Album*, 1871).

dynasty and its many iniquities, giving some sense of the difficulties the new Khan would have to overcome),[52] and asked whether Khudoyar could be removed from Khujand to Tashkent, as his presence could complicate negotiations, and would be awkward if open hostilities were to break out.[53]

Khudoyar himself was reluctant, as he fully recognised that this would be an admission that he would never return to Khoqand, but eventually he went into exile, first in Tashkent, and then in Orenburg, where his handsome figure and reputed wealth apparently caused a sensation among the officers' wives of the garrison there.[54] On the 4 August von Kaufman wrote to Nasruddin offering to recognise him as Khan in succession to his father, provided he abided by the terms of the 1868 treaty, compensated the Russians for the loss of their embassy's property and the two *jigits* who had been killed during their flight to Khujand, and agreed to pay his father a pension.[55] These relatively mild terms suggest that von Kaufman was still not thinking in terms of annexation, and hoped to preserve Khoqand's integrity under the Ming dynasty. Instead over the next few weeks it

---

[52] Babadzhanov, *Kokandskoe khanstvo*, 295.
[53] Nol'de to Golovachev 25/07/1875 RGVIA F.1396 Op.2 D.91 ll. 53–6. A copy is in TsGARUz F.I-715 Op.1 D.63 ll. 68–70.
[54] Nol'de to Golovachev 28/07/1875 RGVIA F.1396 Op.2 D.91 ll. 68–70; Terent'ev, *Istoriya zavoevaniya*, II, 338; Frederick Burnaby, *A Ride to Khiva* (London: Cassell, Petter & Galpin, 1877), 97–8.
[55] Von Kaufman to Nasruddin 04/08/1875 TsGARUz F.I-715 Op.1 D.63 Doc.171 ll. 121–2.

would become clear that Nasruddin's authority and ability to control events were extremely limited. Only three days later a party of 1,000 horsemen with two cannon attacked the customs post at Ablyk in the Angren valley above Tashkent. Von Kaufman despatched a punitive expedition of one infantry company, four Cossack *sotnyas* and four guns under Golovachev, noting that 'in this way the Khoqandis have begun a war'.[56]

Almost from the outset, the Russians attributed a religious motivation to the uprising against Khudoyar, and it was this aspect – the spectre of '*musulmans-kii fanatizm*' – which troubled them most.[57] Golovachev reported to von Kaufman that all the rumours coming from Khoqand to Khujand suggested that a Holy War had been declared against the Russians, and that the chief culprit was 'Abdurrahman Aftabachi, and von Kaufman duly reported to Miliutin that they were facing a 'holy war' and a 'Muslim movement' in Khoqand.[58] This seems to have been more than simply a Russian perception: Muhammad Salih Tashkandi also suggests that 'Abdurrahman Aftabachi declared a '*ghazat*' against the Russians, although possibly only in response to their advance into Ferghana.[59] On the 28 July Nol'de reported the arrival of a letter from Aftabachi to Khudoyar, and appended a translation from the Persian to his report. In it Aftabachi invoked 'the honour of Islam, the strength of the *shari'a* of our Prophet, and carrying out *ghazat*, which for all true believers is considered a particularly needful thing'. Aftabachi wrote that he had sent three letters to Khudoyar in Khoqand, but that the latter had not replied to these, instead fleeing the capital. He concluded by suggesting that Khudoyar take the opportunity to make the pilgrimage to Mecca, a traditional means of getting rid of unwanted former rulers, and something which speaks for the letter's authenticity, despite the lack of a seal.[60] A letter addressed by him to von Kaufman which arrived the same day noted Khudoyar's 'departure from the path of the *shari'a*', which would now be upheld under the rule of his son, Nasruddin.[61] Whether these letters were genuine or not, and despite their lack of any overt threat towards the Russians, their language fanned Russian fears, and on the 13 August Nol'de wrote once again to say that rumours of

---

[56] Von Kaufman to Trotskii 07/08/1875 TsGARUz F.I-715 Op.1 D.63 Doc.181 ll. 137–8.

[57] A. G. Serebrennikov, 'Iz istorii Kokanskago pokhoda', *VS* (1901), No. 10, 70.

[58] Golovachev to von Kaufman 02/08/1875 RGVIA F.1396 Op.2 D.91 l. 40*ob*; von Kaufman to Miliutin 01/09/1875 TsGARUz F.I-715 Op.1 D.63 Doc.304 l. 362.

[59] *TJT*, f. 114b.

[60] 'Abdurrahman Aftabachi to Khudoyar Khan, n.d., enclosed in Nol'de to Golovachev 28/07/1875 RGVIA F.1396 Op.2 D.91 ll. 71–2; Thomas Welsford, 'The Re-opening of Iran to Central Asian Pilgrimage Traffic, 1600–1650', in *Central Asian Pilgrims: Hajj Routes and Pious Visits between Central Asia and the Hijaz* ed. Alexandre Papas, Thomas Welsford & Thierry Zarcone (Berlin: Klaus Schwarz Verlag, 2011), 153–4.

[61] 'Abdurrahman Aftabachi to von Kaufman 28/07/1875 TsGARUz F.I-715 Op.1 D.63 Doc.161 l. 82.

a Holy War launched against the Russians from Khoqand were becoming still more credible.[62]

These fears soon spread well beyond Ferghana: while Terent'ev claims that the inhabitants of Tashkent, remembering their previous oppression at the hands of the Khoqandis, remained loyal in the face of Aftabachi's call to *jihad*, and that only those in regions neighbouring the khanate sided with the Khoqandi *'shaiki'* out of fear, this confidence seems to have been retrospective.[63] Weinberg considered that Aftabachi was a 'fanatic' who loved power, and that he expected him to seize control of Khoqand with the support of Yaqub Beg, 'who is the same sort of "Condottiere"'.[64] In the middle of August Golovachev wrote that there were rumours that the 'Sart' inhabitants of Tashkent might rise up in revolt in the event of an assault by the Khoqandis, and made plans for the defence of the Russian city and its population.[65] A few days later the district commandant in distant Aulie-Ata also reported considerable alarm and agitation in his district.[66] Raiders ravaged the Angren Valley above Tashkent, and attacked the post-roads between Khujand, Ura-Tepe and Tashkent, as well as the post-station of Murza-Rabat, whose *starosta*, Stepan Yakovlev, died defending it after a two-day siege, providing Terent'ev with a suitable *bogatyr* for his narrative. They also attacked the dismantled fortress at Nau, where a band of raiders decapitated one Dr Petrov in front of his young daughter, whom they kidnapped, which in turn provided Terent'ev with an Indian 'Mutiny'-style atrocity.[67] Whilst this disorder and violence was probably the inevitable result of the collapse of central authority in a region which had always resisted Khoqandi rule,[68] the Russians interpreted these attacks as part of a concerted plan and evidence of 'fanaticism'. This culminated on the 8–9 August in an assault on Khujand itself by 15,000 Khoqandis, which was not fully beaten off and dispersed until five days later.[69]

It was unsurprising then that von Kaufman decided to launch a direct attack on the khanate, the first target of which was the fortress of Makhram, on the

[62] Nol'de to von Kaufman 13/08/1875 RGVIA F.1396 Op.2 D.91 l. 153.
[63] Terent'ev, *Istoriya zavoevaniya*, II, 339.
[64] Private letter from Weinberg to an unknown correspondent ?/08/1875 TsGARUz F.I-715 Op.1 D.63 Doc.185 l. 142.
[65] Golovachev to von Kaufman 15/08/1875 RGVIA F.1396 Op.2 D.92, 'Ob ekspeditsii protiv Kokandskogo khanstva', ll. 1–2.
[66] Aulie-Ata D. C. to the Military Governor of Syr-Darya Province 18/08/1875 RGVIA F.1396 Op.1 D.91 ll. 140–1.
[67] Von Kaufman to Miliutin 01/09/1875 TsGARUz F.I-715 Op.1 D.63 Doc.304 ll. 362–80; Terent'ev, *Istoriya zavoevaniya*, II, 339–41, 360.
[68] On the less than enthusiastic reception offered to 'Alim Khan of Khoqand when he captured Ura-Tepe in 1816, see the accounts by the poetess Dilshod: *Ta'rikh-i Mahasura* (*History of the Siege*) and *Ta'rikh-i Muhajiran* (*History of the Refugees*), in Mukhtarov (ed.), *Dil'shod i ee mesto*, 13–14, 29, 134–8.
[69] Terent'ev, *Istoriya zavoevaniya* II, 340–8.

border near Khujand, which Nasruddin Khan had reinforced with a garrison of 5,000 *sarbaz* infantry and ten cannon.[70] Preparations for this had already begun under the authority of General Golovachev, since the first word of the disturbances in the khanate had reached the Russians in July. The force assembled at Khujand consisted of sixteen companies of infantry, twenty guns, eight rocket batteries and eight *sotnyas* of Cossacks, the latter under Skobelev's command. The assault on Makhram, which would come to be commemorated as an iconic moment of the Khoqand campaign,[71] exemplified the main features of the Russian conquest of Ferghana, namely the prominent personal role played by Skobelev (who was promoted to General on the strength of the victory here) and the huge disparity between the casualties on the Russian and Khoqandi side. The fortress fell on the 22 August in just four hours, and a surprise attack by Skobelev's Cossacks from the heights above proved decisive. Russian losses were six killed and eight wounded, while there were an estimated 1,200 dead on the Khoqandi side.[72] In the aftermath, one of Aftabachi's associates, Isa-Auliya, gave himself up to the Russians – characteristically Terent'ev noted that 'this Sart, obviously, was much more intelligent than the Qipchaq Aftabachi' as he had realised that resistance to the Russians was useless. Meanwhile Nasruddin Khan attempted to sue for peace.[73] Von Kaufman refused these overtures, replying to Nasruddin's letter with a promise only to conduct negotiations at Khoqand itself, and issuing a series of proclamations calling on the governors of Marghelan, Osh, Andijan, Assaka and other Ferghana towns to submit to Russian authority, which did not at first produce the desired response. According to Serebrennikov, von Kaufman was already lobbying St Petersburg for the khanate's annexation, on the grounds that without this, if a similar 'Muslim movement' arose in Bukhara, the Russians would be in no position to contain and defeat it, whilst exemplary punishment of the Khoqandis was needed to discourage the Bukharans and also Yaqub Beg in Kashgar.[74] Weinberg wrote in late August that von Kaufman had told him privately that he considered that trying to maintain Khoqand's vassal status would be more trouble than it was worth, and that he would prefer

---

[70] *Ibid.*, II, 338.

[71] A. I. Bryanov, *Na pamyat' o Fergane: 1876–1901 g.* (Novyi Margelan: Tip. Ferganskogo Oblastnogo Pravleniya, 1901).

[72] Skobelev to Golovachev 25/05/1875 TsGARUz F.I-715 Op.1 D.63 Doc.278 ll. 300–7. One of the dead, the only Russian officer to perish, was the Ural Cossack Officer Alexander Khoroshkhin, who had published extensively on legal and agrarian questions connected with Turkestan's administration. His articles were collected and published posthumously by his friend N. A. Maev as *Sbornik statei kasaiushchikhsya do Turkestankogo kraya* (St Pb.: Tip. A. Transhelya, 1876). See Mikhailov, 'Pokhod v Kokand v 1875 g.', 9–10 for a description of Khoroshkhin's death.

[73] Terent'ev, *Istoriya zavoevaniya*, II, 356–9.

[74] Serebrennikov, 'Iz istorii Kokanskago pokhoda', *VS* (1901), No. 4, 30–1.

outright annexation.[75] St Petersburg did not agree, however. On the 29 August von Kaufman wrote to the Tsar that Khoqand had fallen without a fight and now humbly begged for his mercy: as his forces advanced from Makhram, everywhere the inhabitants had come forward with bread and salt, and Nasruddin had emerged from the town to receive and escort them within the walls.[76] In response Miliutin wrote that any extension of the empire's borders was undesirable: 'for his Majesty the Emperor it is desirable that the troops should not remain in Khoqand, but that native rule should be established on the model of Khiva', where he praised von Kaufman's success in re-establishing the Khan under the 'moral influence' of a Russian post across the frontier.[77] The question of the future political settlement became urgent as Marghelan and Osh quickly fell to Skobelev's forces over the next few days. On the 13 September von Kaufman wrote to Miliutin explaining the difficulties he faced, firstly from 'an element which, like the Turkmens in Khiva, presents a savage and unbridled force that has always been a threat to the other peoples of the khanate, and which refused to submit to the power of the Khan – the Qipchaqs, Kara-Kirgiz and other nomadic and semi-nomadic tribes', and the fact that Nasruddin was inexperienced and had no effective forces under his control.[78] Von Kaufman proposed dividing Ferghana along the line of the Syr-Darya and annexing the northern part around Namangan to provide a permanent presence for Russian power, and these were the terms of the peace treaty drawn up on the 28 September.[79] In this he was consciously imitating the precedent set after his defeats of Bukhara in 1868 and Khiva in 1873, when each conceded a swathe of territory (respectively the Zarafshan *Okrug* and the Amu-Darya *Otdel*) which allowed the Russians to control the rump which remained. The reference to the Qipchaqs and Kyrgyz of Ferghana being analogous to the Turkmen of Khiva boded ominously for the future.

Even before this treaty could be ratified in St Petersburg (which happened on the 17 October), it was overtaken by events, as the strained political fabric of the khanate crumpled once more under this renewed humiliation. On the 20 September Nasruddin wrote to von Kaufman saying that he had been no more than Aftabachi's puppet, unable to resist as the rebels swept him along,

[75] Private letter from Weinberg to an unknown correspondent 19/08/1875 TsGARUz F. I-715 Op.1 D.63 Doc.289 ll. 309–10.

[76] Von Kaufman to Alexander II 29/08/1875 TsGARUz F.I-715 Op.1 D.63 Doc.291 l. 346.

[77] Miliutin to von Kaufman 02/09/1875 TsGARUz F.I-715 Op.1 D.63 Doc.302 l. 360.

[78] Von Kaufman to Miliutin 13/09/1875 TsGARUz F.I-715 Op.1 D.63 Doc.340 ll. 514–25; Chillingly, Terent'ev notes that in Ferghana the Qipchaqs 'played the same role as the Turkmen in Khiva', a reference to von Kaufman's massacre of the Yomuds during the campaign of 1873, very likely the analogy the latter was drawing. Terent'ev, *Istoriya zavoevaniya*, II, 384.

[79] Terent'ev, *Istoriya zavoevaniya*, II, 362, 366–8.

and that he felt betrayed by the treaty, which attributed guilt to him and required payment of an indemnity: he asked to be relieved of his duties as Khan.[80] News soon came of a fresh uprising against Nasruddin and the Russians in Andijan, where 'Abdurrahman Aftabachi and Pulad Khan had proclaimed a *ghazat*.[81] The city was duly stormed on the 1 October by a force of Orenburg and Ural Cossacks and infantry of the 2nd and 4th Turkestan Line Battalions under von Kaufman's chief of staff, Major-General Trotskii, who described fierce house-to-house fighting: 'Continuing the advance to the bazaar, the Cossacks seized three more barricades by storm, and following immediately after them Baron Aminov's column engaged in incessant, lively fire with the enemy, who along the whole route, from huts (*saklya*), gardens and mosques, stubbornly and fiercely defended the town.'[82] Trotskii then withdrew his forces, considering that the city and its inhabitants had been sufficiently chastised and pacified,[83] a decision for which, revealingly, Terent'ev criticises him severely, writing that he should at least have burned part of it down. Andijan rebelled once again as soon as the Russian forces had left, and during their retreat they were repeatedly attacked, with Skobelev and his Cossacks once again to the fore in Terent'ev's narrative. Further revolts duly broke out in Marghelan and in Khoqand itself, leading Nasruddin to flee to the Russians at Khujand in his turn.[84] Whilst the new Khan would make a temporary return, Khoqand's fragile sovereignty had finally collapsed under the twin pressures of Russian force and popular revolt. It remained for the Russians to pacify and stamp their authority on the territory of Ferghana, something they proceeded to do over the succeeding months with considerable brutality.

8.2 'Cleansing' Ferghana

On the 11 October Russian forces launched their second assault on Andijan, described by Trotskii as the centre of 'Abdurrahman Aftabachi and Pulad Khan's renewed uprising. Much of Trotskii's information on the situation in Andijan came from the orientalist Alexander Kuhn, fresh from his exploits in Khiva (where he had secured the khanate's archives, which were carried off to Russia).[85] Kuhn had arrived in Andijan in search of materials from the library

---

[80] Nasruddin to von Kaufman 20/09/1875 TsGARUz F.I-715 Op.1 D.63 Doc.360 ll. 577–8.

[81] Serebrennikov, 'Iz istorii Kokanskago pokhoda', *VS* (1901), No. 4, 40.

[82] Trotskii to von Kaufman 10/10/1875 TsGARUz F.I-715 Op.1 D.64 Doc.394 ll. 53–5.

[83] Trotskii, *Raport Nachal'nika otryada, deistvovavshego na levom beregu Syrdar'i* (Tashkent: n.p., 1875), 40–1.

[84] Weinberg to Miliutin 10/10/1875 TsGARUz F.I-715 Op.1 D.64 Doc.414 l. 96; Terent'ev, *Istoriya zavoevaniya*, II, 376–81.

[85] Trotskii to von Kaufman 15/10/1875 RGVIA F.1396 Op.2 D.91 l. 401; Trotskii *Raport*, 1; Bregel, *Dokumenty Arkhiva Khivinskikh Khanov*, 59–62.

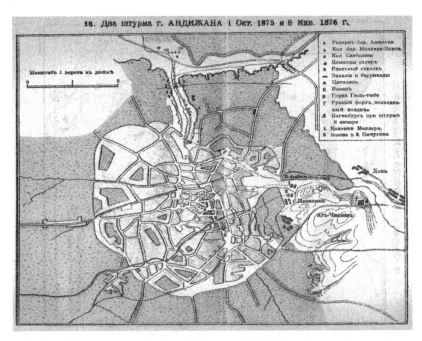

Figure 8.4 The two stormings of Andijan (Terent'ev, *Istoriya zavoevaniya*).

of the khans of Khoqand, and barely escaped with his life when the rebellion broke out again two days later: he would later put the experience to good use in producing one of the first post-conquest Russian descriptions of the khanate.[86] The siege was organised by Skobelev, who, after siting the rocket batteries, found his reconnaissance party temporarily cut off by a sally from the city when they attempted to return to the main Russian force, since 'as always in Asia, when they saw our forces retreating, the enemy became particularly bold and brave'. This caused a few moments' worry, but the sally was soon crushed. The main assault on the city was followed by more 'bitter fighting in the streets, the huts (*saklya*), the mosques and courtyards' of Andijan (Figure 8.4). 'The enemy used every form of cover; fired from behind walls, roofs and trees', and it was only Skobelev's use of artillery in the city which finally crushed resistance. Trotskii remarking admiringly that he exposed himself repeatedly to enemy fire.

Over the following days, as he rather chillingly put it, Skobelev and Baron A. N. Meller-Zakomel'skii (1844–1928) occupied themselves with 'cleaning

---

[86] N. A. Maev, 'A. L. Kun', *TV* 22/11/1888 No. 46; A. L. Kun, *Ocherk Kokandskogo khanstva: Otdel'nyi ottisk iz izvestii Imperatorskogo Russkogo Geograficheskogo Obshchestva.* Vol. 12 (St Pb.: n.p., 1876).

up' (*ochistit'*) the villages around Andijan.[87] 'Abdurrahman Aftabachi fled towards Chartak, Yangi-Qurghan and Kasan, pursued by another punitive expedition under Colonel Fride which burned farms and houses, but had only one brief skirmish with Qipchaq forces.[88] Serebrennikov notes the importance of exemplary violence and collective punishment in order to secure submission to Russian authority, and his account is littered with references to the destruction of settlements, including 'Abdurrahman Aftabachi's native village, which was burnt to the ground by a force under Meller-Zakomel'skii.[89] A subsequent assault on the citadel of Chust, which had also rebelled against the new dispensation, according to Skobelev's own calculations saw 3,800 Muslim lives lost, and just 6 dead and 29 wounded on the Russian side. A few days later a force of 20,000 Qipchaqs was routed at Balyqchi, losing 2,000 of their number for just 1 Russian dead and 8 wounded. But, as Terent'ev put it, the former subjects of Khoqand, and in particular the Qipchaqs, had still not learned their lesson.[90] Skobelev's reports to von Kaufman from Namangan warned that another uprising was imminent, and that further annexations and punitive expeditions would be necessary to secure submission. At the end of October he reported that a large force of some 10,000 Qipchaqs, commanded by two of Pulad Khan's subordinates, Hamam Khan and Batyr-Tura, had appeared on the other bank of the Naryn and were threatening the town. He described how the urban population – 'Yids, Indians, Tatars, a few Sarts' – were working energetically to reinforce the fortifications in expectation of attack, which came on the 24 October and was easily repulsed with volleys of canister, leaving piles of corpses behind.[91] A few days later Skobelev reiterated the need for decisive measures to be taken against the Qipchaqs – and, no doubt playing on von Kaufman's considerable vanity, he invoked the Governor-General's own earlier triumphs in Samarkand:

> Recalling examples from the past, we saw that in 1866, when the occupation of Ura-Tepe and Jizzakh was over, after a terrible *pogrom* and the occupation of the territory by force, notwithstanding the intimidatory effect on the inhabitants, the authority of the administration was represented by a fictitious active force, which, throwing itself first in one, then in another direction, was unable to revive its activities in 1867 and 1868, and only with the occupation of Samarkand did administrative power assume its due rights. With Samarkand this was repeated too, although to

---

[87] Trotskii to von Kaufman 15/10/1875 RGVIA F.1396 Op.2 D.91 ll. 405–*ob*, 408*ob*–10, 428*ob*–9.

[88] Fride to Golovachev 12/10/1875 TsGARUz F.I-715 Op.1 D.64 Doc.418 ll. 111–18.

[89] Serebrennikov, 'Iz istorii Kokanskago pokhoda', *VS* (1901), No. 4, 47–8, 53; No. 9, 44–5; No. 10, 85, 89.

[90] Terent'ev, *Istoriya zavoevaniya*, II, 384–6.

[91] 'Zapiska o polozhenii del v Namangane', 31/10/1875 TsGARUz F.I-715 Op.1 D.63 Doc.512 ll. 365–70.

a lesser extent due to special conditions (peace with the Amir, which destroyed the possibility of military operations and the agitation of minds); there the administration occupied its proper position only by pacifying neighbours or after the expeditions to Qarshi, Shahrisabz and Matcha.[92]

Certainly opposition to the Russian forces was far from crushed at this stage – as Sergei Abashin has shown in meticulous detail, individual villages, in this case Oshoba in the Qurama range at the western end of the Ferghana valley, put up astonishingly fierce resistance to Russian punitive expeditions. According to Colonel Pichugin, the commander of this force, when they attacked the village on the 18 November, 'not one of the *Ashabintsy* would surrender, and they all perished with weapons in their hands. The women threw themselves with knives at the soldiers or threw stones at them from the roofs.' While the Russians prevailed, this defeat was re-imagined and narrated by the inhabitants as a victory, which is still recalled today.[93] The affair at Oshoba is also important as it demonstrates that opposition to the Russian conquest came from sedentary 'Sart' villages as well as nomadic Kyrgyz and Qipchaqs, and they would suffer accordingly as the campaign progressed.

On the 21 November 1875 what would become one of the most memorialised episodes of the Khoqand campaign took place – the murder of Foma Danilov.[94] One of the Commissaries of the 2nd Turkestan Sharpshooter Battalion, Danilov (originally from Bugulinsk district in Samara Province), who had remained with a cart carrying regimental supplies when it broke an axle, was carried off by a band of Qipchaqs near Marghelan. His fate remained unknown until the following March, when Marghelan was finally captured by Skobelev's forces. The narrative which then emerged resembled British tales of rugged European defiance in the face of Oriental cruelty, such as the murder of George Hayward by Shah Dil Iman near the Darkot pass in Gilgit in 1870 (which inspired Sir Henry Newbolt's fanciful 'He Fell among Thieves'), or the execution of Private Moyse for refusing to kow-tow to his Chinese captors near the Taku Forts in 1860 (which inspired an even worse poem – 'The Private of the Buffs' – by Sir Francis Hastings Doyle).[95] The story, based on a report from Skobelev, first appeared in *Russkii Invalid* in 1876. It described how Danilov

---

[92] 'Zapiska Gen. M. Skobelev o polozhenii del v Namanganskom otdele', 04/11/1875 TsGARUz F.I-715 Op.1 D.65 Doc.532 ll. 31–3a.

[93] Abashin, 'The Fierce Fight', 220–6.

[94] Serebrennikov, 'Iz istorii Kokanskago pokhoda', *VS* (1901), No. 9, 54

[95] 'Last night, among his fellow roughs/He jested, quaffed, and swore/A drunken private of the Buffs/Who never looked before/To-day, beneath the foeman's frown/He stands in Elgin's place/Ambassador from Britain's crown/And type of all her race.' See James Hevia, *English Lessons: The Pedagogy of Imperialism in Nineteenth-Century China* (Durham, NC: Duke University Press, 2003), 66–7; G. J. Alder, 'He Fell among Thieves', *Journal of the Royal Central Asian Society* 52/1 (1965), 42–8.

was taken to Marghelan and brought before Pulad Khan, painted as a monstrous figure who enjoyed nothing so much as slitting the throats of his enemies 'as if they were sheep'. Called upon three times to convert to Islam, he defiantly refused, reportedly saying 'I will die in the faith that I was born in, I swore an oath to my Tsar, and will not betray it [...] you dogs are exerting yourselves in vain, you will take nothing from me, but if you wish to kill me, kill me.' He was bound to the wheel of a cart and shot by a firing squad, but the volley was inaccurate, and he lived for another hour before dying.[96] This account was taken up by Dostoevskii in his 'Diary of a Writer' as an example of the simple heroism and faith of the ordinary Russian people.[97] In slightly altered form it would then reappear in the *Brothers Karamazov* in the opening dispute between Grigory and Smerdyakov, though here Danilov's execution by firing squad was transformed into a lurid flaying alive, and there was no explicit mention of who his cruel captors were. The message, however, was the same – the stark contrast between the simple faith and dignity of the Russian people, and the savagery and barbarism of their opponents.[98] Narratives such as this not only served to legitimise the Russian presence in Central Asia, but also, in this particular instance, would overshadow the violence which Skobelev had by then unleashed on Ferghana's population.

Skobelev wrote to von Kaufman from the 'Jardin du Bek' in Namangan in November 1875, saying that he thought there was imminent danger of an attack by 'Abd al-Ghafar Bek, the former ruler of Ura-Tepe, who was now making trouble around Matcha. Skobelev made characteristic claims about the importance of his own presence and charisma, and stressed the persistent danger posed by the Qipchaq forces to order and stability, themes which he reiterated at greater length the following day, noting that they were spreading agitation amongst the 'Sart' population who might otherwise be expected to favour Russia.[99] In support of this he appended a translation of a letter from 'six Khoqandis', which stated that Khudoyar Khan had maintained friendly relations with the Russians in defiance of the 'wishes of the people', which had

---

[96] 'O geroiskoi smerti Unter-ofitsera Danilova', *Russkii Invalid* (1876), No. 90, in *TS*, Vol. 424, 77–8.

[97] F. Dostoevskii, 'Foma Danilov, zamuchennyi russkii geroi', in *Dnevnik pisatel'ya* Jan. 1877, in *Sobranie sochinenii* (St Pb.: Nauka, 1995), Vol. 14, 14–19.

[98] Yuan Gao, 'Captivity and Empire: Russian Captivity Narratives in Fact and Fiction' (M.A. Thesis, Nazarbayev University, 2016), 28–31. (http://nur.nu.edu.kz/handle/123456789/1672).

[99] 'Ma présence ici est indispensable; je suis certain qu'après mon départ l'ennemi se portera de nouveau sur notre rive en masse, ce qu'il faut, à mon avis, éviter de faire départ, au point de vue du maintien du prestige de notre autorité et aussi, vu la difficulté d'appro-visionner les chevaux; cela a toujours été la conséquence direct de l'apparition des bandes Kipchaks sur notre territoire', Skobelev to von Kaufman 23/11/1875, Skobelev to von Kaufman 24/11/1875 RGVIA F.1396 Op.2 D.93, 'O voennykh deistviyakh v Kokandskom khanstve', ll. 12, 20*ob*.

led to the uprising, and that if the Russians now wished to live in harmony with the 'high-ranking Khan' then they should retreat to their own region.[100] Despite initial misgivings, prompted by his fear that St Petersburg would take a dim view of further military action, Skobelev's representations quickly convinced von Kaufman that further violence was necessary.[101] On the 29 November he launched a further punitive expedition towards Uzgend against the Qipchaqs.[102] Despite the capture of all the major cities of Ferghana, in December von Kaufman still did not consider the khanate to be sufficiently pacified, noting that 'at present in the Khoqand khanate the disorderly, savage element, the nomadic population of the khanate – Kyrgyz and Qipchaqs – is still in control, that element which has always dodged our blows in the current Khoqand campaign, and which is clearly determined to continue the struggle against us through hostility to our dominion (*vlady-chestvo*), this uncivilized (*grubyi*) force, by its very nature, will not submit and is not submitting to any lawfulness, any order'.[103] His solution was to give Skobelev more or less *carte blanche* to use whatever means were necessary to establish Russian sovereignty with a view to complete annexation:

> From the experience of the history of this khanate, and also from the recent example from the campaigns of this year, it is possible to say decisively that the final restraint of this wild force will be possible only under one condition – the annexation by us of the whole Khoqand khanate [...] Trading and manufacturing Khoqand, and the other big centres of the khanate, more than any of the other Central Asian domains neighbouring Russian Turkestan, have many common interests and direct economic ties to Tashkent and with other parts of the Turkestan *krai*.[104]

Von Kaufman's reference here to Ferghana's economic integration with the rest of Turkestan (the implicit contrast was probably with Khiva) is interesting, and appears to anticipate the key role Ferghana would later enjoy within the Turkestan economy. It is certainly notable that as soon as Makhram had fallen, and well before the khanate had been conquered and pacified, von Kaufman ordered the collection of the land taxes of *tanap* and *kharaj* from the conquered territory (though this had as much symbolic as economic importance), whilst much of Skobelev's personal correspondence with him from Namangan also concerns calculations of the former khanate's *dokhodnost'* (revenue capacity) and the best means of levying land tax in order to make the newly

---

[100] Translation of a letter from Qoshpetar, Atabai Ishiq-aga, Khan Quli Parwanachi and three others (seals illegible), RGVIA F.1396 Op.2 D.93 ll. 63–4.
[101] Judging by the original correspondence, Terent'ev may have rather exaggerated this reluctance: Terent'ev, *Istoriya zavoevaniya*, II, 383, 388.
[102] Skobelev to von Kaufman 29/11/1875 TsGARUz F.I-715 Op.1 D.65 Doc.619 ll. 271–288.
[103] Von Kaufman memorandum to Miliutin 05/12/1875 RGVIA F.1396 Op.2 D.92 l. 20.
[104] Von Kaufman memorandum to Miliutin 05/12/1875 RGVIA F.1396 Op.2 D.92 ll. 20ob–21ob.

conquered territory fiscally productive as soon as possible.[105] In the later 1870s Ferghana would become the site of a particularly elaborate set of land-settlement works, designed to establish with much greater accuracy than the Russians had hitherto achieved in Central Asia what was being grown, who was growing it and where, in order to levy taxes directly on the producers, so far as possible, but this would founder owing to the great expense involved and a lack of local knowledge.[106] In 1875 all this lay in the future, however. Von Kaufman's arguments were probably being offered to sweeten the pill with the Ministry of Finance, which was already thoroughly weary of expensive Central Asian conquests encouraged by Miliutin and the War Ministry. In the event the annexation of the former khanate would be officially approved in February 1876, by which time Skobelev's exploits had already gone some way to making Russian rule a reality.[107]

8.3 'Pacification' Continues

The pacification campaign continued in characteristically bloody fashion with an assault on the village of Uljibai in early December 1875. Here Skobelev described with relish how a whole column of the enemy 'not less than 600 men, were cut down on the spot' by his force of Orenburg Cossacks, led by an officer familiar to all historians of colonial Turkestan, *Sotnik* Vladimir Petrovich Nalivkin. Skobelev reported that 'our losses in the glorious affair at Uljibai were one officer wounded (*Sotnik* Nalivkin was lightly wounded in the hand), seven other ranks whose wounds meant they had to be sent to hospital [. . .], and fourteen wounded who remained at the front. The enemy, who had 6,000 cavalry and 600 infantry, lost at least 600 men, left lying at the scene.'[108] Nalivkin's own later description of this attack accused Skobelev of cowardice and irresponsibility in ordering the charge of his Cossacks on the enemy infantry, and claimed that Skobelev actually took satisfaction from the fact that two Cossacks were killed, as it would make his report of the fierceness of

---

[105] Terent'ev, *Istoriya zavoevaniya*, II, 359; Skobelev to von Kaufman 09/06/1876 RGVIA F.1396 Op.2 D.97 ll. 82–9.

[106] Beatrice Penati, 'Notes on the Birth of Russian Turkestan's Fiscal System: A View from the Ferghana *Oblast*'', *JESHO* 53/4 (2010), 739–69.

[107] Terent'ev suggests that Skobelev, with his personal connections in high places in St Petersburg, almost certainly found out about the decision to annex before Kolpakovskii, who was then standing in for von Kaufman in Tashkent. Terent'ev, *Istoriya zavoevaniya*, II, 395. This no doubt emboldened him. Miliutin's diary suggests he learnt (and approved) of von Kaufman's annexation plan on the 3 February 1876: L. G. Zakharova (ed.), *Dnevnik General-Fel'dmarshala Grafa Dmitriya Alekseevicha Miliutina 1876–1878* (Moscow: ROSSPEN, 2009), 41–2.

[108] Skobelev to von Kaufman 07/12/1875 RGVIA F.1396 Op.2 D.93 ll. 106–7*ob*. There is also a description in Serebrennikov, 'Iz istorii Kokanskago pokhoda', *VS* (1901), No. 9, 52–3.

the fighting more convincing.[109] This engagement, like many others in the numerous campaign reports on the conquest of Ferghana, underlines both the unequal nature of the warfare the Russians were engaged in (perhaps only comparable to the British conquest of the Sudan twenty years later in the disparity in casualties) and the apparent relish Skobelev took in slaughter, something that would be a hallmark of his later campaigns in Transcaspia as well. Nalivkin's own description of Skobelev's Ferghana *razzia* must be handled with some care: as Sergei Abashin has shown, he had become a fierce anti-militarist and opponent of the Tsarist regime by the time he published it in the post-revolutionary atmosphere of 1906, which no doubt coloured his recollections.[110] While his accusation that Skobelev was a coward may have been made with the benefit of hindsight, the allegations of wanton violence directed against civilians are corroborated in A. N. Kuropatkin's later memoir, where he attributes this partly to the baleful influence of Meller-Zakomel'skii, who had been at school with Skobelev.[111] Nalivkin vividly evokes the sense of disgust and shame he felt at the wanton slaughter of unarmed men, women and children, a sentiment he says was shared by other officers:

> I said in French, so that the lower ranks wouldn't understand: 'What a disgrace! Why are you doing this!' Bogoliubov [a fellow officer] replied to me more or less like this: 'What can I do? The General flies into a passion, goes too far, listens to nothing and nobody.' One of the other officers, I don't remember exactly who, explained further: 'Now for us this has become an entirely normal affair; it hasn't been possible to arrange "battles"; we cannot submit reports without substance, so we vent ourselves on those who should be spared.'[112]

According to this later account, it was because of his experiences during this campaign that Nalivkin asked to be transferred to military administration and embarked on a long and distinguished career as an orientalist-administrator in colonial Turkestan. In 1878 he would resign his commission altogether and go off to live with his wife (Maria, née Sartori) in the Ferghana *qishlaq* of Nanay,

---

[109] Nalivkin, 'Moi vospominaniya o Skobeleve', *Russkii Turkestan* (1906), No. 120, reprinted in Kotiukova (ed.), *Polveka v Turkestane*, 541–2.

[110] S. N. Abashin, 'V. P. Nalivkin: "Budet to, chto neizbezhno dolzhno byt'; i to, chto neizbezhno dolzhno byt', uzhe ne mozhet ne byt'.": Krizis orientalizma v Rossiiskoi Imperii?', in *Aziatskaya Rossiya: Liudi i struktury Imperii* ed. Iu. P. Rodionov & A. V. Yakub (Omsk: Izd. OMGU, 2005), 43–96.

[111] Ian Campbell, 'Violent Acculturation: Alexei Kuropatkin, the Central Asian Revolt, and the Long Shadow of Conquest', in *The Central Asian Revolt of 1916: A Collapsing Empire in the Age of War and Revolution* ed. Aminat Chokobaeva, Cloé Drieu and Alexander Morrison (Manchester: Manchester University Press, 2020), 196.

[112] Nalivkin, 'Moi vospominaniya o Skobeleve', *Russkii Turkestan* (1906), No. 120, in Kotiukova (ed.), *Polveka v Turkestane*, 538.

where the two of them wrote a pioneering ethnography of the 'Sart' women of Ferghana.[113]

A month after the clash in which Nalivkin was wounded, Skobelev sent a telegram to Kolpakovskii in Tashkent, warning that a large force under Aftabachi was heading towards Andijan, which was once again about to go over to the party of war. The third Russian assault on the city produced similar bloodshed, as Skobelev described how the Russian artillery sowed panic in the ranks of the Khoqandis: 'the impression made in the khanate was enormous' and most of the inhabitants fled to Assaka. He asked to be allowed to continue towards Assaka and Marghelan in order to defeat what he described as the 'party of *ghazat*'.[114] Just two weeks later, Aftabachi gave himself up: Skobelev telegraphed the contents of a letter (which it seems likely he had dictated) from the Qipchaq leader to Kolpakovskii, to be sent on to von Kaufman: 'Feeling my powerlessness against the brave and invincible forces of the White Tsar, and also wishing to bring to an end the poverty of war which is ravaging my fatherland, I have given myself up to General Skobelev, hoping in the merciful kindness of the world-powerful White Tsar.' Skobelev added a note asking that he be shown mercy as he had promised, and he was eventually exiled to Russia together with the deposed Nasruddin.[115] Pulad Khan proved more elusive. After heavily defeating him at Uch-Qurghan, a force under Meller-Zakomel'skii managed to seize all of his property and 200 camels, but the man himself escaped with ten followers into the Pamir Alai, where Skobelev finally captured him on the 18 February 1876.[116] With that, it seemed, the rebellion was at an end, and so was the rule of the Ming dynasty. Nasruddin was dismissed as weak and incapable of controlling the 'fanatical' elements of the khanate.[117] Already on the 2 February, von Kaufman had telegraphed from St Petersburg that the annexation of the Khanate of Khoqand to the Russian empire as Ferghana province, with Skobelev at its head, had been agreed. The campaign ended with an unedifying episode recalling the fall of Khiva, in

---

[113] V. P. Nalivkin & M. Nalivkina, *Ocherk byta zhenshchiny osedlago tuzemnago naseleniya Fergany* (Kazan: Tip. Imperatoskogo Universiteta, 1886), translated as Vladimir Nalivkin & Maria Nalivkina, *Muslim Women of the Fergana Valley: A 19th-Century Ethnography from Central Asia* trans. Maria Markova & ed. Marianne Kamp (Bloomington, IN: Indiana University Press, 2016). For a survey of other early Russian works on the newly conquered khanate see S. N. Abashin, 'Naselenie Ferganskoi doliny: K stanovleniiu etnograficheskoi nomenklatury v kontse XIX–nachale XX veka', in *Ferganskaya dolina: Etnichnost', etnicheskie protsessy, etnicheskie konflikty* ed. S. N. Abashin & V. I. Bushkov (Moscow: Vostochnaya Literatura, 2004), 40–6.

[114] Telegram Skobelev to Kolpakovskii 14/01/1876 RGVIA F.1396 Op.2 D.93 ll. 170–1.

[115] Telegram Skobelev to Kolpakovskii 28/01/1876 RGVIA F.1396 Op.2 D.93 ll. 244, 250.

[116] Meller-Zakomelskii to Skobelev 31/01/1876; Kolpakovskii to Golovachev 24/02/1876 RGVIA F.1396 Op.2 D.93 ll. 330–9, 386; Serebrennikov, 'Iz istorii Kokanskago pokhoda', *VS* (1899), No. 4, 217.

[117] *Ibid.*, 220–1.

400 THOSE WHO SHOULD BE SPARED

which Skobelev disobeyed Kolpakovskii's orders to delay entry into the city of Khoqand until the 19 February, the day Alexander II had acceded to the throne, and made a triumphal entry on the 5 February – Kolpakovskii, furious, did not arrive until ten days later.[118] Khoqand was no more, and it would live on only in the numerous works of its historians.[119] However, there was an epilogue in the mountains surrounding the fertile valley floor of Ferghana, which suggests how deeply this loss was felt, at least in some quarters.

8.4   Loss of Sovereignty

In May 1876 Skobelev led another punitive expedition into the Qizil-su valley to the south of Marghelan partly because, as he put it, its Kyrgyz inhabitants were 'still little acquainted with Russian power' and hence had not made their formal submission to the new district commandant in Marghelan,[120] and partly in order to track down various Khoqandi dignitaries and officials who had fled the Russian advance. Notable amongst these were 'Abd al-Karim Bek, one of Khudoyar's relatives, who, as we have seen, was already being touted as an alternative claimant to the khanship in June 1875, Valikhan Tura, Omar Bek, Taniqul Pansad, Suleiman Awdaichi and 'Abdullah Bek *Dadkhwah*.[121] It was the last of these, a Kyrgyz leader and former governor of Osh, whose mother, Qurmanjan *Dadkhwah* (1811–1907), is today a Kyrgyz national icon, who would provide the most startling note of defiance.[122]

By June Skobelev's forces were pursuing the fugitives through the Osh region and into the Pamir Alai, whence Skobelev sent frequent bulletins (once again in French) to von Kaufman reporting on the progress of his punitive columns: 'I am counting on the impressionability of the Asiatic masses who, feeling the two columns suspended like a sword of Damocles,

---

[118] Terent'ev, *Istoriya zavoevaniya*, II, 405–10.

[119] An early, wistful response to Skobelev's proclamation of Russian rule over Ferghana is in the *TJT*, ff. 123b–5b. Muhammad Salih Khwaja Tashkandi was highly ambivalent about the advent of Russian rule, although, like most of the Turkestan *'ulama*, his attitude to the conquerors was pragmatic. Babajanov, *Kokandskoe khanstvo*, 268.

[120] Skobelev to Golovachev 18/05/1876 RGVIA F.1396 Op.2 D.97, 'O polozhenii del v Ferganskoi Oblasti', ll. 29*ob*–33.

[121] Serebrennikov suggests that all of these were Kyrgyz, except for Vali Khan Tura, who was a 'Sart'. If so, it is an interesting reflection both on the political alliances which were forged during the resistance to the Russians and on the enduring utility of the khanate's political traditions in Kyrgyz areas. Serebrennikov, 'K istorii Kokanskago pokhoda', *VS* (1897), No. 9, 15.

[122] 'Abdullah Bek does not figure in Beisembiev's index to the Khoqand chronicles; Terent'ev writes that he was 'the son of the famous Marmandan-*Dadkhwah*' (*sic*) and the head of two Kyrgyz lineages of the Alai, the Adygei and the Mongushi. Terent'ev, *Istoriya zavoevaniya*, II, 412. See I. Yuvachev, 'Kurban-Dzhan-Datkha [*sic*], kara-kirgizskaya Tsaritsa Alaya', *IV* (1907), No. 12, 954–80.

will not fail to be demoralised at the moment when we appear, if they are expecting it.'[123] After fighting an indecisive action near Sary-Qurghan in July, he returned to Marghelan to take up the post of Military Governor of the new province, leaving Captain Bogoliubov in charge of the Alai region, and warning him of the danger that either Yaqub Beg in Kashgar or the British might intervene if the last pockets of Khoqandi resistance were not eliminated. Shortly thereafter, Bogoliubov was presented with a proclamation from 'Abd al-Karim Bek which had been intercepted by one of his agents, Bii Yerdaulat, whom he had sent out with a few men to collect *zakat* from the Kyrgyz. In the translation which he forwarded to Skobelev, 'Abd al-Karim appealed to the local Kyrgyz Biis of the Naiman, Tait, Khizr-Shah, Bustan and Qipchaq lineages, to Timur Bii Hal Muhammad Bii, Aqshi Bai Bii, Yerdaulat Bii, Cholpanqul Bii, Haji Murad Bii, Muhammad Yusuf Bii, Omar Bii Qipchaq, Nur Muhammad Bii, Artiq Bii, Mullah Hal Qazi, Yusuf Batyr and Juma'a Bii. The Russian translation read as follows:

> Let it be known that thanks to *'ghazat'* against the anathematised unbe-lievers, we, placing our reliance firstly in God, have come to this place and have joined with Omar Bek Dadkhwah and 'Abdullah Bek Mingbashi. All great and small – Sarts, Tajiks, Qirghiz and Qipchaqs, all with general agreement have proclaimed us Khan. Because of this we have gathered together some thousands of troops from the Musulmans, who have arrived at the gully of Talika.[124]

The original was clearly considerably longer, but has been cut into four within the file – amongst those parts which are decipherable, the term *'ghazat'* is visible, whilst the list of those who had proclaimed 'Abd al-Karim a khan mingles the ethnic and tribal terms of the Russian version with geographical locations such as Andijan and Osh, indicating that identification with the political geography of the khanate was at least as important as tribal loyalties in motivating resistance. Skobelev responded with a letter to 'Abdullah Bek, in which he stated that he was no longer willing to parley with him, something which prompted a remarkable response (Figure 8.5) addressed directly to the Russian military leader. The Russian translation, which Skobelev himself would have read, is given below, with some phrases reproduced from the original where they diverge:

> To the high-ranking commander Governor General [*sic*] Skobelev [*Eskubuluf*]

---

[123] 'Je compte sur l'impressionabilité des masses asiatiques, qui, sentant les deux autres colonnes suspendues comme une épée de Damoclès, ne manqueront pas de se démoraliser au moment ou nous apparaîtrons, si toutefois elles attendent ce moment.' Skobelev to von Kaufman 02/07/1876 RGVIA F.1396 Op.2 D.97 l. 165*ob.*

[124] Bogoliubov to Skobelev 29/07/1876 RGVIA F.1396 Op.2 D.97 ll. 282–4a.

Figure 8.5 'Abdullah Bek's letter to Skobelev. RGVIA F.1396 Op.2 D.97 l. 290.
© Russian State Military-Historical Archive.

After the usual native greetings, the words are as follows:

> You wrote a letter relating to peace, and we on receiving it were very satisfied. Your letter concluded with the following sentiments: 'You can already appreciate the impossibility of resisting the heroic Russian forces [*urusiyah-ning bahadur-liq-ka hich kim-ni aqwati yitmay-dur-ghan 'askar-lari-ghah qarshi turub bulmasiqin*], they are not halted by mountains, or rivers, or by the enemy. Because of this you can imagine that you will become harried refugees, and that sooner or later you will be taken by us. Therefore you should throw yourselves on the inexhaustible mercy of the Yarim Padshah [Half-Emperor, i.e. the Governor-General of Turkestan], relying on his kindness.'
>
> Placing our reliance in God and his Prophet, we up until now have gathered men and used every means to resist. We did this because you yourself have broken the agreed conditions: for instance, the Yarim Padshah, having given the Khoqand Khanate to Nasruddin in complete authority, afterwards repudiated all this, and sent him to Siberia [*janab Nasr al-Din Bik-ga Yarim Padishah-ni uzi 'ahd-i payman qilib Khwaqand (sic) mamlakati-ga hakim qilib sahib-i ikhtiyar-sin dib*

quyub irdi // yanah yarim Padishah uzi qilghan 'ahd wa'da-si-ni buzub Nasr al-Din Bik-ni Sibir qilib]. And you, General Skobelev, who also in the same way concluded an agreement with Aftabachi and promised to establish him in Khoqand, you also sent him to Siberia, together with some of our *biis*. All of this serves as a reason for us to fear and through this fear to distance ourselves to different parts of the mountains. Having no faith in any of your conditions, we have decided, as a few men of Islam, to resist strongly [*siz-lar qurqunchi salib tagh tash-lar-ga chiqarding-lar shul sabab-din sizlar-ni 'ahd-i payman-lar-ing-ga i'tiqad wa imtidad-imiz qalmay shul ishlar-ni bir nichi ahl-i Islam bilan bu jan-imiz-ni awwal khuda-ni yuli-ghah* (towards the path of God) *Ikkinchi uz din-i pak-imiz-ni yuli-gha* (towards the path of the purity of our faith) *hadiyah ilab* (dedicating our lives [*jan*]) *sizlar bilan ru bih ru bulush-ga* (to meet with you face to face)]. You take pride in your great and victorious exploits; we are humble people, without strength, who only trust in God, and ask help of him. Because of this, for the reasons given above, we will struggle in every way so long as there is a soul in our bodies. We are nomads, we need neither a treasury, nor property [*wa biz ilatiyah khalqi-ghah khazinah dafinah dargar imas*]. Beginning with Toqmaq [taken by the Russians in 1860], you have brought under your sway the Qirghiz, Qipchaqs and Sarts, always fulfilling your stated promises. But when you seized Khoqand, all this changed and from this stems all the disturbances, which would not have been had you kept your word.[125]

Apart from the omission of the conventional compliments at the outset, the Russian translation of this letter was unusually accurate, possibly reflecting an appreciation of the letter's powerful language and message by Skobelev's translator, the Tatar Captain Bekchurin.[126] 'Abdullah Bek himself was still at large in September, when Skobelev wrote to von Kaufman to say that he was still negotiating 'Abdullah Bek's surrender, and suspected that he and the other rebellious Kyrgyz *biis* seemed to be in league with the (still independent) Shah of Qarateghin. Thereafter he disappears from the Russian documentary record, though Terent'ev asserts that he and the other 'rebels' did indeed make their

[125] Translation of a letter from 'Abdullah Bek *Dadkhwah* (n.d.) RGVIA F.1396 Op.2 D.97 ll. 286 (Russian), 290 (original). The Russian text of this letter (with some elisions and sarcastic commentary) is published in Terent'ev, *Istoriya zavoevaniya*, II, 418. My thanks to a friend who prefers to remain anonymous for reading through the Chaghatai text and providing me with a transcription and translation.

[126] We can gain some idea of the procedure for the receipt and translation of this letter from a romanticised account of the pacification campaign in the southern mountains of the khanate which draws heavily on the conventions of Caucasian military memoirs and short stories: D. Ivanov, 'V Gorakh (iz turkestanskoi pokhodnoi zhizni)', *VS* (1876), No. 4, 457, in which a *jigit* appears bearing a letter from one 'Hussein-Bek', which the translator immediately begins reading and translating for his commanding officer.

Figure 8.6 A modern statue of Qurmanjan *Dadkhwah*, the 'Queen of the Alai', in central Bishkek. © A. Morrison.

way to Qarateghin.[127] It was apparently at this point that Skobelev began negotiations with 'Abdullah Bek's mother, Qurmanjan *Dadkhwah* (Figure 8.6).

Having inherited the title of *Dadkhwah* from her second husband, 'Alim Bek, she had effectively ruled the Alai Kyrgyz under Khoqandi auspices since 1861. Russian accounts describe Skobelev receiving her with honour at a ceremonial *dastarkhan* (spread of food), praising the bravery of her sons, and then asking her to use her influence in the Alai to bring further Kyrgyz

---

[127] Telegram Skobelev to von Kaufman 05/09/1876 RGVIA F.1386 Op.2 D.97 ll. 307–9; Terent'ev, *Istoriya zavoevaniya*, II, 418.

resistance to an end, promising to respect her authority in return.[128] Whether this romantic encounter actually occurred is not clear – it does not figure in the archival record – but Kyrgyz resistance did peter out, and – like Shabdan Batyr among the Sarybaghysh Kyrgyz in the north – Qurmanjan maintained her status and authority among the Alai Kyrgyz as a key intermediary with the Russian authorities. By the time of her death in 1907 at the age of ninety-six, she had become a legendary figure, the so-called 'Queen of the Alai', sought out by passing travellers such as Paul Pelliot and Carl Gustav Mannerheim, who left an account of their meeting.[129] Her son 'Abdullah Bek remains a more shadowy figure, but the terms in which he framed his defiance of the Russians are almost startling clear. Islam was clearly one basis for resistance, but so was pride in nomadism and, perhaps most strikingly of all, loyalty to the idea of Khoqandi statehood, and a sense that that statehood had been betrayed and destroyed by Russian power. This is all the more striking in that it came from a group of Kyrgyz nomads, often assumed to have been oppressed under Khoqandi rule and to have had limited engagement with its political structures.[130]

If we compare this brief outline of the Khoqand campaign with earlier and later examples of Russian expansion in Central Asia, together with conventional explanations for the Russian advance, certain elements are striking. One is that, for all the efforts made by Terent'ev and Serebrennikov to construct a consistent and heroic narrative of the campaign, both their accounts and the documents on which they were based indicate that all the military encounters were so one-sided as to be massacres: Serebrennikov himself admitted that, whilst the Russians were always heavily outnumbered, many of those on the opposing side were unarmed. Nalivkin's memoirs, while they should be read with caution as a condemnation penned thirty years after the event, nevertheless inject a still more sinister element – the deliberate and unprovoked targeting of unarmed men, women and children as part of the unnecessary prolongation of a 'pacification' campaign whose main purpose was to inflate the reputation of Skobelev and his fellow officers. This violent collective punishment had first been seen two years earlier with the Yomud massacre, and would be repeated by Skobelev during the Akhal-Teke campaign five years later. It is also striking that the principal constraint on Russian military activities – the difficulties of logistics and supply, which hugely complicated both their earlier campaigns in the Qazaq steppe and their later ones in Transcaspia – did not apply in the rich lands of Ferghana,

[128] Yuvachev, 'Kurban-Dzhan-Datkha', 965–8; Terent'ev, Istoriya zavoevaniya, II, 416–17.
[129] C. G. Mannerheim, Across Asia from West to East in 1906–1908 (Oosterhout: Anthropological Publications, 1969), I, 26.
[130] This is the basic argument of V. M. Ploskikh, Kirgizy i Kokandskoe khanstvo (Frunze: Ilim, 1977).

with their relatively smooth roads and highly developed agriculture. The Russians were able to move their equipment and supplies on *arba*s, which were much less costly than camels.[131] They invaded in the summer, when food was plentiful, and they could live off the land: when von Kaufman's troops first encamped at Khoqand in August 1875, a local contractor supplied the troops with *lepeshki* – Central Asian bread (*non*).[132] Mikhailov also noted how cheaply the Cossacks were able to obtain forage for their horses.[133]

Secondly, it is clear that Russian policy was made on the hoof, haphazardly, and in response to events that moved to a political dynamic rooted in the Khoqand Khanate's own troubled history, which the Russians only partially understood. None of the usual explanations given for Russian expansion here or elsewhere was of great importance compared with this. The British, supposed rivals in Russia's 'Great Game' for the control of Central Asia, are almost invisible in the documents and were invoked only well after the event by Terent'ev (in the form of an imaginary threat to Turkestan's undefined southern frontier) thirty years after Ferghana was annexed. The Russians were rather more concerned that Yaqub Beg might take advantage of the disorders in his native Ferghana to invade and set himself up as Khan, and Weinberg and Skobelev had been on an embassy to him with the aim of defining the khanate's eastern frontier when they found themselves caught up in the revolt, but even this was seen as a rather remote possibility.[134] The independent initiative of the 'man on the spot', commonly invoked as an important factor in the Russian conquest of Central Asia,[135] was also of little importance in determining whether Ferghana would be annexed or not.[136] A hallmark of Russian correspondence at the time was the desire for authorisation from above, and whilst Skobelev certainly acted more or less independently in December 1875–February 1876, this was because rumours had already reached him through his personal connections in St Petersburg that the annexation was more or less

---

[131] Serebrennikov, 'Iz istorii Kokanskago pokhoda', *VS* (1901), No. 9, 37; No. 10, 73–9.

[132] Terent'ev, *Istoriya zavoevaniya*, II, 362.

[133] Mikhailov, 'Pokhod v Kokand', 10.

[134] Kolpakovskii to Skobelev 30/04/1876 RGVIA F.1396 Op.2 D.97 ll. 19–21*ob*; Terent'ev, *Istoriya zavoevaniya* II, 330–3, 420–6.

[135] MacKenzie, 'Expansion in Central Asia'.

[136] Here I would disagree with Babajanov's use of A. E. Snesarev's later work (*Indiya kak glavnyi faktor v sredne-aziatskom voprose*, St Pb.: A. Suvorin, 1906) to prove that St Petersburg was simply duped by the 'local atamans'. The documentary record does not bear this out. In the Ferghana campaign Miliutin was nobody's dupe; he shared the aims of his 'man on the spot', von Kaufman, received regular reports from him and from Weinberg, and ensured ministerial support for Russian conquests. Babadzhanov, *Kokandskoe khanstvo*, 280–1; Zakharova (ed.), *Dnevnik D. A. Miliutina 1876–1878*, 41–2.

a *fait accompli*.[137] Still less relevant was rational economic calculation. Ferghana would become the wealthiest and most agriculturally productive province of Russian Turkestan, and the core of the late Imperial cotton economy, but this was entirely fortuitous. It was neither known nor foreseen by those who ordered and authorised the invasion and annexation. Though von Kaufman did note the province's economic potential in his memorandum on the need for annexation, by then the deed was effectively done, and the khanate's political structures had already been shattered by Russian military action.

The annexation of Khoqand did not proceed from any particular Russian initiative. The khanate was undone by internal political instability, partly owing to tension between 'Sarts' and nomads which stretched back at least to the 1840s, but also to its repeated defeats and loss of territory to Russia in the 1850s and 1860s, and the additional ideological and religious tensions generated by its proximity and subordination to an overtly Christian power. This in itself is not a sufficient explanation, however. The Bukharan state was similarly unstable and riven by internal rivalries, in this instance primarily between the Uzbek tribal nobility and the Shi'i *Irani* slaves who served the Amir, whilst it too had areas which refused to acknowledge central authority (notably Hissar and Shahrisabz), had lost substantial territory to the Russian advance, and had seen a *jihad* declared against Russia in 1866–8. The difference was that, after the capture of Samarkand and the defeat of the Bukharan Amir at Zirabulak, the Russians set out very consciously to strengthen Sayyid Muzaffar's authority and provide some external stiffening to the weak and porous structures of the Bukharan state, most notably in the punitive expedition to Shahrisabz in 1870. In Khoqand, by contrast, Khudoyar was left to sink or swim as best he could. The reasons for this are not entirely clear – it may have been because, as Terent'ev said, Khudoyar had failed to abide by the terms of the peace treaty (though this was itself a sign of his political weakness, as the Russians well understood), but it also seems to have been rooted in a deep distrust and contempt for the khanate as a polity. Russia had maintained reasonably friendly relations with Bukhara throughout the nineteenth century, apart from the three years which followed the fall of Tashkent. From the Russian perspective, Khoqand was a trouble-maker, contesting Russian claims to sovereignty over the Qazaqs, expanding its territory in the steppe, and launching continued raids on Russian fortresses and territory: between 1853 and 1866 warfare had been fairly constant. The Russians also felt that Khoqand also lacked the imperial aura of Bukhara or Samarkand, and there seems to have been a widespread assumption that its recent origin meant that its political identity was weak, although, as we have seen, there is strong evidence to the

---

[137] Terent'ev accused Kolpakovskii of indecision and pusillanimousness when events in Ferghana reached their crisis at the end of 1875 – *Istoriya zavoevaniya*, II, 396.

contrary in the khanate's historiography, in the correspondence of its leaders with the Russians and in the sheer extent, persistence and desperation of local resistance to the Russian advance, which was far greater than in either Bukhara or Khiva. The case of Khoqand thus emphasises the importance of writing microhistories when seeking to explain and describe the Russian conquest of Central Asia. Each stage of the advance involved a different set of external political factors, different personalities, environmental and logistical conditions, and, perhaps above all, different situations on the ground. The Central Asian khanates maintained an independent political identity and existence even when they were being over-run by Russian forces, and should not be relegated to the status of pawns in a European 'Great Game'.

9

'The Harder You Hit Them, the Longer They Will Be Quiet Afterwards': The Conquest of Transcaspia, 1869–85

> I hold it as a principle that in Asia the duration of peace is in direct proportion to the slaughter you inflict on the enemy. The harder you hit them, the longer they will be quiet afterwards. We killed nearly 20,000 Turcomans at Geok Tepé. The survivors will not soon forget the lesson.
>
> Mikhail Dmitrievich Skobelev in conversation
with Charles Marvin, 1882

The advance through the deserts of Transcaspia is perhaps the best known of all the Russian military campaigns in Central Asia. In its final phase, from 1879 until 1885, Russia's war against the Turkmen was eagerly commented on in the international press,[1] and became the subject of more campaign memoirs and narrative accounts by participants than any other phase of the conquest.[2] British paranoia was one

---

My thanks to Victoria Clement and Anton Ikhsanov for their comments on this chapter.

[1] The best-known European accounts were both by journalists: Edgar Boulanger, 'Voyage à Merv', in *Le Tour du Monde* (1886), 145–208 & *Voyage à Merv* (Paris: Hachette, 1888); Edmund O'Donovan, *The Merv Oasis: Travels and Adventures East of the Caspian, 1879-80-81, Including Five Months' Residence among the Tekkés of Merv* (London: Smith, Elder & Co., 1882) 2 volumes.

[2] A. Kuropatkin, *Turkmeniya i Turkmenii* (St. Pb.: Tip. A. Poletiki, 1879); M. Arnol'di, *V Zakaspiiskom krae v 1877 godu (vospominaniya ofitsera)* (St Pb.: Tip. Departamenta Udelov, 1885); P. Bobrovskii, 'Akhal-Tekinskaya ekspeditsiya 1879 goda', *VS* (1898), No. 10, 259–95; Shtabs-Kapitan Chernyak, 'Ekspeditsiya v Akhal-Teke 1879 goda (iz dnevnika sapernago ofitsera)', *VS* (1887), No. 6, 283–93; No. 7, 129–44; No. 9, 125–38; No. 10, 261–78; N. I. Grodekov, *Voina v Turkmenii: Pokhod Skobeleva v 1880–1881 gg.* (St Pb.: Tip. V. A. Balasheva, 1883–4) 4 volumes, translated as Major-General N. Grodekoff, *The War in Turkumania [sic]: Skobeleffs Campaign of 1880–81* trans. J. M. Grierson (Simla: Government Central Branch Press, 1884–5) 4 volumes and in abbreviated form as A. Prioux, *Les Russes dans l'Asie Centrale: La dernière campagne de Skobelev* (Paris: Librairie Militaire de L. Baudoin et Cie., 1886); V. A. Tugan-Mirza-Baranovskii, *Russkie v Akhal-Teke 1879 g.* (St Pb.: Tip. V. V. Komarova, 1881); A. Maslov, 'Rossiya v Srednei Azii: Ocherk nashikh noveishikh priobretenii', *IV* (1885), No. 5, 372–423; V. Shakhovskoi, 'Ekspeditsiya protiv Akhal-Tekintsev v 1879–1880–1881 gg.: Posvyashchaetsya pamyati M. D. Skobeleva', *RS* XLVI (1885), No. 4, 161–286; No. 5, 377–410; No. 6, 531–58; V.N.G., 'Ocherk ekspeditsii v Akhal-Teke 1879–1880', *VS* (1888), No. 5, 204–30; No. 6, 396–426; A. N. Kuropatkin, *Zavoevaniya Turkmenii (pokhod v Akhal-Teke v 1880–1881 gg.) s ocherkom voennykh deistvii v Srednei Azii s 1839 po 1876 g.* (St Pb.: V. Berezovskii, 1899).

important factor generating interest in the Transcaspian advance. The defeat of the Akhal-Teke Turkmen in 1881 was followed by the supposedly 'voluntary' annex-ation of Merv in 1884.[3] In 1885 the Transcaspian region assumed its final form with the annexation of the Panjdeh oasis from Afghanistan, a Russian advance almost to the outskirts of the Afghan city of Herat, and a skirmish with Afghan troops. Having been firmly convinced since the 1830s that Herat was the 'key to India', Russian moves in that city's general vicinity were always likely to provoke British fears.[4] Like Semirechie thirty years earlier, or the Pamirs in the 1890s, Transcaspia was a region where the Russians rubbed up not just against Central Asian peoples and rulers, but also against neighbouring states with which they already had diplomatic relationships. Afghanistan was viewed (not entirely accurately) as a British puppet, but Qajar Persia had in many ways been a Russian client state since the treaty of Turkmanchai in 1828. While the Russians would annex some territory claimed by Persia, they were also to some degree solicitous of Persian sovereignty and in particular of the stability of its monarchy.[5] Unlike the Turkmen, but like Qing China, Qajar Persia was seen by the Russians as an inferior but nevertheless legitimate state that was a viable partner for mutual boundary-drawing, with the new Transcaspian frontier settled by treaty in 1881 – in many ways to the relief of the Qajars, who had always struggled to maintain their sovereignty in the region and had been powerless to prevent Turkmen raids on their subjects.[6] Despite one skirmish with Afghan forces in 1885 which provoked a war scare with Britain, a joint Anglo-Russian boundary commission would also complete its work delineating the Russo-Afghan frontier amicably and with few serious disagreements – the first, but not the last, occasion when Russian and British officers worked closely together to create a territorial delimitation in Central Asia, united by a shared commitment to European science and the 'civilising mission', and largely excluding the inhabitants of the region from the process. The British came to view Russian rule over the Turkmen as a decided improvement on the chaos and savagery that had gone before.[7]

[3] M. N. Tikhomirov, *Prisoedinenie Merva k Rossii* (Moscow: Izd. Vostochnoi Literatury, 1960), 1–10, 209–10.

[4] G. J. Alder, 'The Key to India?: Britain and the Herat Problem 1830–1863', *MES* 10/2 (1974), 188–9.

[5] Moritz Deutschmann, '"All Rulers Are Brothers": Russian Relations with the Iranian Monarchy in the Nineteenth Century', *IS* 46/3 (2013), 383–413; Elena Andreeva, *Russia and Iran in the Great Game: Travelogues and Orientalism* (Abingdon: Routledge, 2007), 13–21; Denis Volkov *Russia's Turn to Persia: Orientalism in Diplomacy and Intelligence* (Cambridge: Cambridge University Press, 2018), 60.

[6] Firuz Kazemzadeh, *Russia and Britain in Persia, 1864–1914: A Study in Imperialism* (Newhaven, CN: Yale University Press, 1968), 78–99; Abbas Amanat, 'Central Asia viii: Relations with Persia in the 19th Century', in *Encyclopædia Iranica*, V/2, 205–7; Moritz Deutschmann, *Iran and Russian Imperialism: The Ideal Anarchists 1800–1914* (London: Routledge, 2016), 58–70.

[7] Skrine & Ross, *The Heart of Asia*, 338–9.

As the opening quotation suggests, another major reason why the conquest of Transcaspia took place in the full glare of international publicity was the presence on the battlefield for the latter part of the campaign of Mikhail Dmitrievich Skobelev, basking in recent celebrity from his victories in the Russo-Turkish War. His victory in 1880–1 would long be remembered as the most violent and brutal of all Russian campaigns of conquest, which accounted for much of the horrified (and hypocritical) fascination with which it was viewed by other Imperial powers.[8] When the great Akhal-Teke Turkmen fortress at Gök-Tepe[9] finally fell in January 1881 after a three-week siege in which 6,000 Turkmen and 1,000 Russian soldiers perished, it was followed by a massacre in which another 8,000 fleeing men, women and children were killed by Skobelev's troops, something even the General's many apologists found hard to defend.[10] Famously this did not prevent Fyodor Dostoevskii from responding to it with a triumphalist reflection on Russia's destiny in Asia, one of the very last things he wrote.[11]

The extreme violence unleashed at Gök-Tepe is well known, but until recently there has been little attempt to analyse its significance: it suggests clear parallels with the violence the French inflicted on the population of the Algerian Sahara from the 1840s to the early 1900s – was there something about the harshness of the desert landscape, or the reputation shared by the Turkmen and the Touareg for savagery, insolence and slave-raiding which prompted similar, almost atavistic European responses?[12] As Ian Campbell has argued, there is a sense in much Russian writing that both land and people in Transcaspia needed to be forcibly subdued and bent to the Imperial will; this drew upon older discourses about the Qazaq steppe, another region where population and environment combined to make conquest difficult.[13] There were clear precedents for the massacre of the Akhal-Teke at Gök-Tepe, notably General Golovachev's massacre of the Yomud Turkmen in Khwarazm eight years before, prompted by a similar sense that violence was the only language Asiatics in general, and nomads in particular, were able to understand (see Chapter 7). A still more immediate precedent was the brutal campaign of pacification in Ferghana in 1875–6; this was directed against sedentary peoples

---

[8] Marvin, *The Russian Advance towards India*, 98–9.
[9] There is some confusion over the naming of the fortress, referred to indiscriminately in Russian sources as both Gök (Geok)-Tepe and Denghil-Tepe. The locality was known as Gök-Tepe, but the fortress contained a small hill called Denghil-Tepe.
[10] O. A. Novikova, *Skobeleff and the Slavonic Cause* (London: Longmans, Green & Co., 1883), 213.
[11] Fedor Dostoevskii, 'Dnevnik pisatelya. III. Geok-Tepe – Chto takoe dlya nas Aziya?', in *Polnoe sobranie sochinenie*. Vol. 21 (St Pb.: A. F. Marks, 1896), 513–23.
[12] Brower, *A Desert Named Peace*, 21–6.
[13] Ian Campbell, 'Bloody Belonging: Writing Transcaspia into the Russian Empire', in *Empire and Belonging in the Eurasian Borderlands* ed. Lewis Siegelbaum & Krista Goff (Ithaca, NY: Cornell University Press, 2019), 35–47.

and nomads alike, but the common factor here, of course, was the presence of Skobelev in command (see Chapter 8). As we shall see, Russian military failures against the Akhal-Teke in the previous decade before the victory and massacre at Gök-Tepe also played a role.

In Transcaspia the Russians had to overcome greater human and environmental obstacles than in any of their previous Central Asian campaigns. To the extreme logistical challenges they had already faced when attempting to cross the Qara-Qum desert during the Khiva expedition was added fierce and effective local resistance, something that had been largely lacking in 1873. While remembered subsequently as the crowning triumph of the Russian conquest, and of Skobelev's career (he would die unexpectedly in 1882), this was a campaign that began in humiliation and defeat for the Russian empire. The initial repulse of General N. P. Lomakin's (1830–1902) assault on Gök-Tepe in 1879 received unwelcome international attention, and the need to wipe out the memory of this earlier reverse played a decisive role in shaping the subsequent campaign.[14] This chapter will focus primarily on this earlier, lesser-known period – the decade from the foundation of Krasnovodsk in 1869 to Lomakin's defeat and removal from command in 1879, when Russian forces on the Caspian shore were in a state of constant tension and friction with the Akhal-Teke Turkmen. Skobelev's campaign in 1880–1 and the circumstances surrounding the annexation of Merv and Panjdeh in 1884–5 are better-known, and need not detain us as long.[15]

Although the Russian sources on the conquest of Transcaspia, both archival and published, are extremely abundant, the same cannot be said for contemporary Turkmen accounts. Apart from songs and poetry, which give some sense of the trauma, suffering and humiliation the Russian forces inflicted, the only narrative account I have found is *Goni-Bek*, an oral narrative collected by the Turkmen ethnographer (and former Tsarist officer) Seid Murad Ovezbaev in the 1920s, and published in Russian translation in the journal *Turkmenovedenie* in 1927.[16] This concentrates on the first, unsuccessful

---

[14] Charles Marvin, *The Eye Witnesses' Account of the Disastrous Russian Campaign against the Akhal Tekke Turcomans* (London: W. H. Allen & Co., 1880); Callwell seems to have relied on this in *Small Wars*, 45–6.

[15] Notably Terent'ev devotes just 25 pages to the Russians in Transcaspia from 1869–1880, and 225 to the period 1880–5: *Istoriya zavoevaniya*, III, 1–26, 27–252.

[16] Seid Murad Ovezbaev, 'Goni Bek (rasskaz Turkmena o bitve s russkimi pod Geok-Tepe)', *Turkmenovedenie* (1927), No. 1, 23–9. There is a modern Turkmen edition, Seýitmyrat Öwezbaýew, *Gönübek (Gökdepe söwesine gatnaşan türkmeniň gürrüňi)* (Ashgabat: Altyn gushak, 1991), but this is a re-translation of the 1927 Russian text – thanks to Uli Schamiloglu for this reference. *Turkmenovedenie* was the Russian-language journal of Turkmenkul't, the early Soviet Turkmen Cultural Institute – see Victoria Clement, *Learning to Become Turkmen: Literacy, Language, and Power 1914–2014* (Pittsburgh, PA: Pittsburgh University Press, 2018), 62–3. Ovezbaev himself is a fascinating figure, decorated for bravery for his service in the First World War, he later

Russian assault on Gök-Tepe in 1879, and, although it is difficult to know how the narrative had evolved in the forty years between the battle and the first written record, it provides a vivid sense of how the Akhal-Teke elites, at least, saw their conflict with the Russians, and how they later memorialised it.

Though Russian relations with Persia have been extensively studied, there is relatively little modern historiography on the Russian conquest of Transcaspia. The only complete account in English is Mehmet Saray's 1989 monograph, which makes good use of British archival sources and available published materials in Russian, though it is sometimes a little simplistic in its assessments of Russian motives.[17] Evgeny Sergeev's chapter in *The Great Game* is the only work on the subject in English that uses Russian archival sources, though it was originally written in Russian; here as always he has a tendency to exaggerate the importance of Anglo-Russian rivalry.[18] The standard Soviet-era works by Masson, Tikhomirov, Davletov and Il'yasov adhered closely to the usual *prisoedinenie* narrative, seeking evidence of the 'voluntary' submission of the Turkmen even in this most violent of campaigns, and asserting that rule by Tsarist Russia was a 'lesser evil', compared with domination of the Turkmen by their 'feudal' neighbours, Khiva, Bukhara and Persia, or by the imperialist and expansionist British.[19] The violence of the Russian conquest was largely glossed over, and blamed on the actions of 'feudal' Turkmen elites and the machinations of the British.[20] In the early 1990s the sacrifices and heroism of the Turkmen defenders of the fortress began to be remembered and celebrated in Turkmenistan,[21] and post-independence Gök-Tepe has become a major site of commemoration, with the anniversary of its fall celebrated as a national holiday, but this phenomenon is intimately bound up with the cult of former President Saparmurat Niyazov and modern Turkmen national ideology, and seems to have little in common with earlier Turkmen memories and practices of commemoration.[22]

joined the Red Army and worked for Gosplan in the early Soviet period. He was arrested in 1932 and shot in 1937. Thanks to Anton Ikhsanov for these biographical details.

[17] Mehmet Saray, *The Turkmens in the Age of Imperialism: A Study of the Turkmen People and Their Incorporation into the Russian Empire* (Ankara: Turkish Historical Society Printing House, 1989), 138–239.

[18] Sergeev, *The Great Game*, 189–210 & *Bol'shaya Igra*, 167–85.

[19] Tikhomirov, *Prisoedinenie Merva k Rossii*; Dzh. Davletov & A.Il'yasov, *Prisoedinenie Turkmenii k Rossii* (Ashkhabad: Ilim, 1972); A. Il'yasov (ed.), *Prisoedinenie Turkmenii k Rossii: Sbornik arkhivnykh dokumentov* (Ashkhabad: Izd. AN Turkmenskoi SSR, 1960), 5–16 (hereafter *PT*). While the interpretation Ily'asov places on them is questionable, as source material this large published collection of archival documents is invaluable.

[20] M. E Masson et al. (eds.), *Istoriya Turkmenskoi SSR* (Ashkhabad: Izd. AN Turkmenskoi SSR, 1957), I, Pt. 2, 114–28.

[21] For example Nargylyç Hojageldiýew, *Gökdepe galasy: Gysgaça taryhy oçerk* (Ashgabat: 'Çäç' döredijilik-önümçilik birleşigi, 1991). My thanks to Uli Schamiloglu for this reference.

[22] Slavomír Horák, 'The Battle of Gökdepe in the Turkmen Post-Soviet Historical Discourse', *CAS* 34/2 (2015), 149–61.

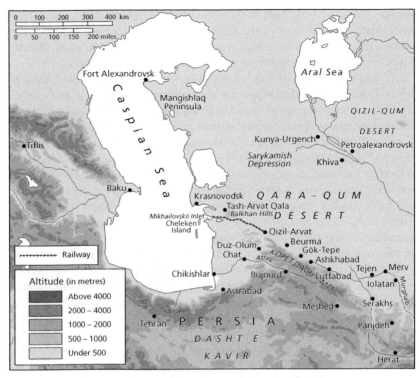

Map 9 Transcaspia

9.1   The Russians in Transcaspia, 1869–76

The Russian empire's troubled relations with the Turkmen stretched back well into the seventeenth century, when they generally appeared in Russian documents and accounts as '*trukhmeny*', usually in connection with slave raids.[23] In 1833 V. A. Perovskii had ordered the erection of Fort Novoalexandrovskii at Qizil-tash on the Qaidaq inlet in the northern Caspian as a means of guarding against such raids.[24] In 1846, ostensibly at the request of a local religious leader, Nur Muhammad *Ishan*, in an attempt to control both the Turkmen of the region and the Adai Qazaqs the fortress was relocated to the Mangishlaq peninsula as Fort Novopetrovskii (from 1857 Fort Alexandrovsk, now Fort Shevchenko near modern Aqtau).[25] Throughout the 1850s there were numerous proposals to establish a permanent Russian presence further south on the Caspian shore: as early as 1836 Perovskii had suggested occupying Cheleken

---

[23] See e.g. Filipp Efremov, 'Stranstvovaniya Filipp Efremova', in *Puteshestviya po vostoku v epokhu Ekateriny II* ed. A. A. Vigasin (Moscow: Vostochnaya Literatura, 1995), 185.

[24] Perovskii to G. S. Karelin 1833, in *RTO*, 271.

[25] Nurmuhammad Ishan to V. A. Obruchev 04/07/1846, in *RTO*, 394–5.

island, both for strategic reasons and to exploit its reserves of oil and salt, a proposal revived in 1857 by M. N. Galkin (1832–1916), who was then working as an ethnographer for General A. A. Katenin, the governor of Orenburg.[26] However, when the council of ministers met in 1859 to discuss Katenin's proposal to make the Turkmen Russian subjects, it concluded that 'not only subjecthood, but even an official announcement of protection (*pokrovitel'stvo*) over the Turkmen would be undesirable'.[27]

Instead a permanent Russian presence in Transcaspia came only in 1869, when, at the urging of Turkestan Governor-General von Kaufman, War Minister Miliutin authorised the construction of a fortress on the south-eastern shore of the Caspian at the Krasnovodsk (Qizil-su) inlet.[28] This was initially justified as a means of reminding the Persian Shah of his obligations under the treaty of Turkmanchai, suppressing Turkmen raids and providing an additional anchorage for the cruisers of the Caspian squadron.[29] Later it would be presented as a defensive measure, to allow the transport of Caucasian troops across the Caspian 'in the event of a coalition against us' and to foster caravan traffic.[30] However, it is clear that one of the reasons why von Kaufman wanted Krasnovodsk to be occupied was so that it could be used as a base for the already anticipated attack on the Khanate of Khiva, which would take place in 1873.[31] The Russian force occupying Krasnovodsk was led by Colonel N. G. Stoletov, who almost immediately began urging the occupation of territory further inland, in particular the Balkhan hills, which he argued offered a more favourable climate than the Krasnovodsk inlet and a secure source of fresh water; in August 1870 he sent a small force there to occupy Tash-Arvat Qala.[32] Stoletov also occupied the inlets at Mikhailovskoe and Chikishlar, the latter near the Atrek river which formed the *de facto* frontier with Persia, where the Russians erected a small fortification of sand.[33] He led

---

[26] M. N. Galkin, 'Istoricheskoe obozrenie snoshenii Rossii s narodom Turkmenskim', 24/12/1857 NAG F.I-1087 Op.1 D.610 ll. 9–11. My thanks to Tom Welsford for this reference.

[27] 'Iz zhurnal osobogo soveshchaniya Komiteta ministrov po voprosu zanyatiya iugo-vostochnogo poberezh'ya Kaspiiskogo morya i prinyatii Turkmen v poddanstvo Rossii', 02–09/01/1859 in *RTO*, 463–5.

[28] Von Kaufman to Miliutin 10/07/1869 in *RTO*, 532; for a description of the strange, artificial Russian settlement that sprang up there see O'Donovan, *Merv Oasis*, I, 64–5.

[29] Gorchakov to Krabbe 15/10/1869, in *PT*, 19–24.

[30] 'Otchet Nachal'nika Zakaspiiskogo Voennago Otdela 1874–1877 g.', 22/12/1877 NAG F.545 D.1891 l. 18.

[31] 'Iz zapiski Ministerstva inostrannykh del "O znachenii Kaspiiskogo morya v politicheskom i ekonomicheskom otnosheniyakh', 20/12/1869 & von Kaufman to Miliutin 18/01/1870, in *PT*, 32–4, 43–5; Zaionchkovskii, 'K voprosu zavoevaniya Srednei Azii', 70–1.

[32] Stoletov to Grand Duke Mikhail 08/12/1869, in *PT*, 27–9.

[33] Saray, *The Turkmens*, 98; Valentine Baker, *Clouds in the East* (London: Chatto & Windus, 1876), 64–5; O'Donovan, *Merv Oasis*, I, 42.

a series of reconnaissances further inland, one of which came within a day's march of the fortress of Qizil-Arvat at the edge of the Akhal-Teke oasis.[34] These tactics were continued by his successor, Markozov, who in the autumn of 1871 led an expedition to reconnoitre the route from Krasnovodsk to the Sarykamish depression on the road to Khiva, seizing the 500 camels he needed by force from the Yomud Turkmen.[35] In the autumn of 1872 he embarked on a similar show of strength towards Khiva, this time with a much larger force of 1,800 men, in what was explicitly described as a *karatel'naya* (punitive) expedition against the Turkmen. This time he ran into more serious difficulties with transport: the Yomuds refused to furnish him with the 3,500 camels he demanded, partly because the Göklan, the main camel-rearing tribe, were in their summer pastures in the Balkhan hills, and also rumoured to be ill-disposed towards the Russians.[36] While the main force which set out from Krasnovodsk managed to secure 1,800 camels, a smaller party from Chikishlar, led by Markozov himself, was able to secure only 150, and was forced to turn back well before the intended rendezvous with the main column at the wells of Topi-Ata. The other column did not fare much better – after stealing 1,000 Turkmen sheep at Shukur-köy, they lost 150 camels to Turkmen attacks, and were unable to continue on the road to Khiva because of a shortage of water. Turning south instead towards Jamal-Togalak, they were attacked by another party of Akhal-Teke Turkmen led by Sufi Khan. As they advanced towards Qizil-Arvat, they found that the Turkmen retreated before them, burning their *auls* and their crops. It was only with considerable difficulty that they managed to return to the Caspian shore, and there were persistent rumours among the Turkmen that they had died of thirst, which spread into northern Persia and reached the ears of the Russian consul at Astrabad, who feared the damaging effects this might have on prestige.[37] This was a foretaste of the logistical difficulties the Russians would face as they sought to establish larger territorial claims on the eastern shore of the Caspian.

As we have seen, the following year Markozov's column from Krasnovodsk also failed to reach Khiva owing to the refusal of the Turkmen to supply his force with camels. Despite this setback, newly established Russian control over Khiva encouraged them to seek secure routes from the Caspian across the desert to the Amu-Darya. In the aftermath of the Khiva campaign Colonel Glukhovskii of the General Staff was assigned the task of exploring commercial

---

[34] Consul, Astrabad to Minister Tehran 31/01/1871, in PT, 53–4.
[35] Saray, *The Turkmens*, 100.
[36] On the Göklan, who were among the most prosperous Turkmen groups, see Irons, *The Yomut Turkmen*, 9.
[37] Astrabad Consul to the Minister at Tehran 25/09/1872, 26/10/1872, 12/11/1872 & 21/11/1872 NAG F.5 Op.1 D.2241, 'Doneseniya Rossiiskogo Imperatorskogo Poslannika v Tegerane', ll. 275–9ob, 319–21, 322–4 & PT, 87–89; Saray, *The Turkmens*, 102; Terent'ev, *Istoriya zavoevaniya*, II, 81–99.

routes to the khanate from Russia and the Caspian. Among his many recommendations was that the Russians extend their defensive line on the Atrek until it met the newly expanded Bukharan dominions at Charjui, which would effectively turn the whole of the Transcaspian region into Russian territory.[38] While before the fall of Khiva both the Turkestan command and the Caucasus command had repeatedly invoked the need to maintain pressure on its supposedly hostile Khan as a reason for the occupation of Transcaspia, the successful outcome of the campaign only meant that they found new reasons to argue for the same thing. In February 1874 Grand Duke Mikhail wrote to Miliutin suggesting that, now that Khiva was a vassal state, it was all the more imperative to have a fixed military presence in Transcaspia to allow the rapid transfer of forces from the Caucasus to Bukhara and Khiva in the event of a revolt, or a threat from the Turkmen. What he bizarrely characterised as the earlier policy of 'gradual cultural assimilation' of the Turkmen by the force of Russia's superior civilisational example would no longer be sufficient.[39] Miliutin duly called a meeting with the Minister of Finance, Baron Reutern, and the Director of the Asiatic Department of the Ministry of Foreign Affairs, P. N. Stremoukhov, to discuss future Russian policy in Transcaspia; they agreed that there seemed no grounds for attempting to introduce anything other than the most basic form of military rule, and that attempts to provide education or medical care to the Turkmen would be premature; at the same time, despite Reutern's pleas, they decided that it would also be premature to introduce a standard taxation system, meaning that the administration of the region would continue to be funded out of the budget of the Caucasus Military District.[40] A temporary statute for the Transcaspian region, a simplified form of the temporary Turkestan Statute of 1867, was approved in March 1874. It created two divisions, Mangishlaq and Krasnovodsk, to be governed from the latter.[41] In June 1874, on the recommendation of Grand Duke Mikhail and Miliutin, the Tsar approved the creation of a new Transcaspian Military Division, administered from Tiflis as part of the 'Caucasus Mountain Administration' (*Kavkazskoe Gorskoe Upravlenie*) whose head was Major-General Franchini – this odd combination came about because the North Caucasus was also under military administration.[42] Miliutin was aware of the possible negative response from the British, and sought to anticipate it, writing to Grand Duke Mikhail that local commanders in Transcaspia, while they

---

[38] Glukhovskii to Geiden 14/01/1874 NAG F.545 Op.1 D.965, 'Zapiski sostavlennyya General'nogo Shtaba Polkovnikom Glukhovskim, vo vremya ego poezdki v 1873 godu v Sredniuiu Aziiu dlya izsledovaniya torgovykh putei', l. 10*ob*.

[39] Grand Duke Mikhail to Miliutin 22/02/1874, in *PT*, 137–9.

[40] Mishcherinov to Miliutin 27/02/1874, in *PT*, 140–2.

[41] 'Vremennoe polozhenie o voennom upravlenii v Zakaspiiskom krae', 06/03/1874, in *PT*, 142–51.

[42] *Protokol soveshchaniya* 27/08/1874 NAG F.545 Op.1 D.965, ll. 93–104*ob*.

Figure 9.1 Nikolai Pavlovich Lomakin. *Vsemirnaya Illiustratsiya* Vol. 17 (1877), No. 428, p. 224 (Wikimedia Commons).

could send out reconnaissance missions, would be expected to exercise particular caution and avoid clashes with the Turkmen tribes. He noted that beyond the Atrek there was no defined frontier.[43] General Nikolai Pavlovich Lomakin (Figure 9.1) was placed in charge of the new *otdel*, apparently on the strength of his successful command of the Mangishlaq column during the Khiva campaign.

Lomakin lost no time in embarking on a series of expeditions from his base at Chikishlar deep into the territory of the Atrek Yomud and Akhal-Teke Turkmen. The first of these came in August 1874, when he advanced along the Atrek to the little Balkhan, reporting that the local Yomud Turkmen were friendly, and recommending that a careful survey be made of the oil wells in the region.[44] In April 1875 General Franchini ordered Lomakin on another reconnaissance along the Atrek, in order to survey what the Russians now claimed as their frontier with Persia.[45] In June 1875 he reported that a reconnaissance towards the Uzboi (the depression believed to be the original course of the Amu-Darya) had resulted in the presentation of gifts and an offer

---

[43] Miliutin to Grand Duke Mikhail 03/04/1875 NAG F.545 Op.1 D.1154, 'Doklad Nachal'nika Kavkazskogo Gorskogo Upravleniya o rezul'tatakh rekognostsirovki voisk Zakaspiiskogo otdela po Uzboiu i Atrek', ll. 4–8; also in *PT*, 183–5.
[44] Lomakin to Franchini 16/08/1874, in *PT*, 174–6.
[45] Franchini to Lomakin 22/04/1875, in *PT*, 185–6.

of submission from all the leaders of the Akhal-Teke, including Sufi Khan and Tykma Sardar.[46] Franchini considered this a promising development, and suggested that, rather than attempting direct annexation either to Khiva or to the Transcaspian Division, the Russians should seek to exercise their 'moral influence' over the Akhal-Teke through a single, authoritative plenipotentiary, who would form the point of contact between the Teke tribes and the Russian administration: in effect indirect rule through a single Khan.[47] While Grand Duke Mikhail was sceptical that this would mean a permanent end to the 'disorderliness and predatory behaviour (*buistvo i khishchnichestvo*)' of the Turkmen, he argued that Russia should try to take advantage of their apparent willingness to enter a vassal relationship to establish a 'firm state frontier' in a region where 'we cannot allow any other power access' and impose direct rule over the Akhal-Teke oasis. He claimed this would not meet with any significant resistance, and would save money in the long term. Miliutin responded that the Tsar considered the proposal '*neudobno*' (inconvenient) at this time, and added that an advance over the desert terrain presented significant challenges, would upset the British and the Afghans, and might provoke the Turkmen of Merv to aggression.[48]

The fragility of Lomakin's communication and supply chain with the Caucasus was highlighted when on 30 June 1876 the steamer *Krasnovodsk*, specially built for Caspian service just four years before, blew up at her moorings at Cheleken island. The cause of the blast was unclear, but thought to be a faulty boiler; five men were killed and seven wounded, and all the supplies she was carrying were lost.[49] In any case, getting men and matériel across the Caspian was the easy part, and the enormous difficulties in securing baggage animals and keeping them alive which had prevented Markozov from reaching Khiva persisted. As early as 1876 Lomakin advocated the construction of a railway, noting that the country presented particular challenges for camels and bemoaning the terrible mortality among them, caused largely by the military requirement to have them move during the heat of the day.[50] This explained both why they died in such numbers and why the Qazaqs and Turkmen were so reluctant to hire them out for military purposes, preferring to hire them to a trade caravan for 7½ roubles rather than for 15 roubles to a military expedition, even if the distance was the same. Lomakin added that supplies for just 800 men weighed 8,000 *poods*, requiring 800 camels and 120 drivers, at a cost of 15,000 roubles one way. At the same time the country was flat, with an abundance of oil for fuel, and a single steam locomotive could

[46] Lomakin to Franchini 22/06/1875, in *PT*, 186–8.
[47] Franchini to Grand Duke Mikhail 14/01/1876, in *PT*, 199–203.
[48] Grand Duke Mikhail to Miliutin 24/01/1876; Miliutin to Grand Duke Mikhail 19/02/1876 NAG F.545 Op.1 D.1154 ll. 34–5*ob*, 74–8, also in *PT*, 204–8, 209–11.
[49] Lomakin to Franchini 30/06/1876 NAG F.545 Op.1 D.1252 ll. 58–61*ob*.
[50] Lomakin to Franchini 20/11/1876 NAG F.545 Op.1 D.1255 l. 34*ob*.

move 1200 *poods* at a time. The railway would indeed come to Transcaspia
before any other region of Central Asia, but not in time to help Lomakin.

9.2   Lomakin's Command, 1877–8

Lomakin's contacts with the Akhal-Teke continued, but he was frustrated by
the fragmentation of political authority among the Turkmen, and the absence
of a single figure with whom he could negotiate, insisting that there could only
be peace in the region 'when the Akhal-Teke have one Khan, whom all the
people will respect, fear and listen to'. This in turn he believed would be
possible only if the Russians occupied the oasis and threw their weight behind
a single candidate to be their Khan in chief, 'making of him a person answerable to us'.[51] This was always likely to be a challenge, given the fragmented and
horizontal nature of Turkmen social structure. In their dealings with Turkmen
elites the Russians were reasoning by analogy with the Qazaqs, among whom
those of Chinggissid descent formed a clearly identifiable elite with whom, as
we have seen, the Russian empire had been able to establish a relationship of
indirect rule in the 1820s and 1830s. The Turkmen had no Chinggissid
lineages, and the title of 'Khan' among them did not imply even the limited
authority which these figures had within the wider Qazaq aristocratic elite. The
two main anthropological studies of Turkmen groups, by Irons and König,
both note the absence of centralised authority among them, with a segmentary
system of descent groups cutting across potential vertical hierarchies. While
David Sneath's model of the 'headless state' has some purchase in understanding power structures among the Qazaqs, it is much less applicable to the
Turkmen, whose nobility, while it certainly existed, was much less
powerful.[52] While Irons notes the existence of the office of *thaqlau* or chief
among the Yomud Turkmen in northern Persia, efforts by the Qajars to
transform the *thaqlau* into instruments of indirect rule failed – the Qajars
supplied them with armed retainers, but the Yomuds mobilised along descent
lines to thwart this, resorting where necessary to violence and flight.[53] While
Irons notes that the Russians had more success than the Qajars in bringing the
Turkmen under control, as we shall see this came about through violence
rather than indirect rule through Turkmen aristocratic intermediaries.

---

[51] Lomakin to Franchini 21/02/1876 NAG F.545 Op.1 D.1251, 'O polozhenii del
v Zakaspiiskom voennom otdele', ll. 69–71*ob.*

[52] Sneath, *The Headless State*, 142–56; see the reviews by David Durand-Guédy in the
International Journal of Asian Studies, 8 (2011), 119–22 & Devin DeWeese in the
International Journal of Turkish Studies 16/1–2 (2010), 142–51.

[53] Irons, *The Yomut Turkmen*, 67–8, 73; Wolfgang König, *Die Achal-Teke: Zur Wirtschaft
und Gesellschaft einer Turkmenen-Gruppe im XIX Jahrhundert* (Berlin: Akademie-Verlag,
1962), 151–2.

Lomakin's preferred candidate to be the agent of Russian influence was Nurberdy Khan (1826–1880), to whom he wrote pledging Russian support in strengthening his authority if he would persuade his people to stop raiding, though almost simultaneously he also wrote to Franchini to insist that there would be no peace among the Akhal-Teke until Russian forces had made a show of strength throughout the oasis.[54] The difficulty of negotiation with Turkmen elites was underlined a few days later when a Teke caravan of forty camels arrived at Krasnovodsk, bringing with it several senior *sardars*. These reported that Nurberdy Khan had been deposed at a recent gathering at Gök-Tepe, as the leaders of the four divisions of the Akhal-Teke had asserted that he had no authority beyond his own division. The 'Khivan party' then asked Musa Mutavali, a Khivan envoy, to be their Khan instead, although he demurred, saying he would need permission from the Khan of Khiva. Lomakin described the outcome as follows:

> The comedy was played out in this way: Nurberdy Khan was offended and left the assembly, saying: 'If I won't be your Khan, then no one will.' The principal *Ishan* of the Teke, Qurban Murad Ishan, who was considered to be at the head of the earlier system of rule by four khans, did not arrive at the assembly at all, and nor did the Teke military leader Tykma-Sardar. The four khans, former rulers, who had continued to nurture a secret hostility towards Nurberdy-Khan, were left visibly satisfied with this result, saying that it was better to hand over power to a negligible person, whom nobody would listen to, than anyone else.[55]

Whether this description was accurate or not, it reinforced Lomakin's conviction that the divisions and lack of clear authority among the Akhal-Teke made them impossible to deal with by diplomatic means, but ripe for subjection by military ones: 'So long as the Russians do not come to us', Lomakin claimed his Turkmen informants said, 'and do not appoint a Khan for us, then there cannot and will not be one; but disorder, robbery, brigandage and violence will continue as before.' One alternative, proposed by the head of the Amu-Darya Division, Ivanov, was to ask Muhammad Rahim Khan of Khiva to use his influence. He had asked the Khan to despatch as his envoy Musa Mutavali, whom some of those who gathered at Gök-Tepe had attempted to make their Khan.[56] Now he suggested that Muhammad Rahim Khan issue Nurberdy Khan with a *yarliq* that would bolster his authority. Lomakin objected that it would be highly undesirable to recognise Khivan suzerainty over the Akhal-Teke, although so long as his forces were not allowed to advance beyond Qizil-Arvat

---

[54] Lomakin to Nurberdy Khan 20/02/1876; Lomakin to Franchini 21/02/1876, in *PT*, 211–15.

[55] Lomakin to Ivanov 25/02/1876 NAG F.545 Op.1 D.1251 l. 97*ob*, also in *PT*, 216.

[56] Translation of a letter from the Turkmen elders Khan Muhammad Ataliq, Avaz Durdy-Khan and Khwaja Khan to Lomakin 03/02/1876, in *PT*, 208–9.

there might be no alternative to reinforcing Nurberdy Khan's authority in this way.[57] In his following report he would complain that the Teke were communicating independently with the Khivan Khan, and thus, by implication, with Ivanov. Ivanov meanwhile pointedly noted in his letters to Muhammad Rahim Khan that he was not informed of the movements of Lomakin's Caucasian troops.[58] This was only the first of a series of turf wars between Lomakin in Krasnovodsk and Ivanov in Petro-Alexandrovsk, another expression of the rivalry between the Caucasian and Turkestan military districts.[59] Miliutin continued to resist the calls for military action against the Akhal-Teke from Lomakin, Franchini and Grand Duke Mikhail, and explicitly forbade Lomakin from exploring the upper Atrek towards Ashkhabad, instructing him instead to focus on the potential trade route through Sarykamish to Khiva.[60] Lomakin continued to insist vehemently that nothing less than a full-blown military expedition to the heart of Akhal-Teke territory would bring a halt to their raiding and banditry.[61] At the same time he continued to exhort the Akhal-Teke to recognise Nurberdy Khan's authority, and communicate with the Russians only through him.[62]

In September 1876 Lomakin led a small force from Krasnovodsk to Khiva in order to reconnoitre the road, and also, apparently, to remind the Khan of the strength of Russian forces. Muhammad Rahim Khan took advantage of the Russian presence to collect taxes from the Yomud Turkmen around Kunya-Urgench. Lomakin's reports stressed the enormous potential of this trade route if only the Teke could be pacified, and once again urged the importance of leading a full-blown expedition against them, citing numerous outrages they had committed which he claimed had gone unpunished.[63] He proposed a fortress and trading-post at Ushaq-Bent to protect and promote trade with Khiva across the Qara-Qum. This ran into strong objections from von Kaufman, who squashed this idea as impractical and too expensive, noting that a single large fort on a caravan route 600 *versts* long would be quite useless, and that its construction on Khivan territory would undermine the authority of the Khan. Behind the latter objection lay von Kaufman's fear that the

---

[57] Lomakin to Franchini 06/05/1876 NAG F.545 Op.1 D.1251 ll. 160–2*ob*, also in *PT*, 228–30.

[58] Ivanov to von Kaufman 12/05/1876; Ivanov to Muhammad Rahim Khan 07/05/1876 NAG F.545 Op.1 D.1252 ll. 14–19.

[59] This is a major theme in Terent'ev's history, in which he is unashamedly partisan on the Turkestan side: *Istoriya zavoevaniya* II, 134–46; III, 1–4, 31–8.

[60] Miliutin Grand Duke Mikhail to 27/03/1876, in *PT*, 221–2.

[61] Lomakin, 'Zapiski ob ustroistve Krasnovodsko-Amu-Dar'inskogo puti', 29/04/1876, in *PT*, 227–8.

[62] Lomakin to the Akhal-Teke elders 22/06/1876, in *PT*, 245–6.

[63] Ivanov to von Kaufman 21/09/1876; Lomakin to Franchini 23/09/1876; Lomakin to Franchini 20/11/1876 NAG F.545 Op.1 D.1255, 'O dvizhenii russkogo otryada v Khive, i ustroistve Krasnovodsko-Khivinskogo puti', ll. 1–4, 33, also in *PT*, 258–62.

9.2 LOMAKIN'S COMMAND, 1877-8

Caucasus Military District would seek to interfere in the internal affairs of Turkestan's new protectorate. The Caucasians responded that it was high time the two disparate halves of Russia's Central Asian possessions were united, something they expected would be achieved by Lomakin's expedition against the Akhal-Teke Turkmen at Qizil-Arvat, which was planned for 1877.[64]

At the end of February 1877 Lomakin wrote to the leaders of the Jafarbai Yomuds, explaining that the purpose of his forthcoming expedition was to chastise the Akhal-Teke for their attacks on Turkmen who were Russian subjects (i.e. the Jafarbai Yomuds themselves), and ordering them to provide camels, for which he would pay 50 kopeks per day, with 50 kopeks per day for their drivers and 10 roubles a month for those who joined the force as auxiliary horsemen – Colonel Navrotskii, Lomakin's chief of staff, succeeded in raising a company of these, from among the Qazaqs of Mangishlaq rather than the Turkmen.[65] While the camels did materialise, this expedition proved an early lesson in the sheer difficulties of terrain in Transcaspia. Lomakin reported that, from an initial stage of 50 *versts* through sand dunes without water in unbearable heat, they passed to marsh and bog, and then had three days of almost uninterrupted rain. All the horses (apart from the 'Kirgiz' ones) refused the grazing and became bogged down,[66] together with all the artillery, while each halt had no more than two or three wells, meaning the camels could only be watered slowly. He also anticipated a 'warm welcome' from the Teke, whose scouts shadowed the column; while he claimed that the Russians had done everything possible to bring about a peaceful outcome (he did not, apparently, consider that leading a large armed force into Teke territory might not be understood in these terms), he attributed Turkmen hostility to manipulation by Persian border officials and a British agent, Captain G. C. Napier, who was then thought to be at Merv.[67] When they reached Qizil-Arvat on the 8 May, it proved a disappointment: 'Once it was a fortress perhaps – there were walls, and even a citadel; but now it is more of a cattle-pen.'[68] Not only was the campaigning hard, but the rewards appeared small. Lomakin's observation of the weak and ruinous state of the walls may also have encouraged him to think

---

[64] Von Kaufman to Miliutin 05/07/1876 & 18/02/1877; Doklad No. 181 NAG F.545 Op.1 D.1154 ll. 100–8*ob*; 121–4*ob*; 128*ob*–40.

[65] Lomakin to the Jafarbai Yomuds 25/02/1877, in *PT*, 290–2; M. Arnol'di, 'V Zakaspiiskom krae v 1877godu', *VS* (1885), No. 9, 135. Arnol'di was dismissive of the military capabilities of the Qazaq auxiliaries, though he acknowledged (p. 146) that it was only thanks to their expertise that the Russians were able to find water at all.

[66] Arnol'di noted the superiority of the horses supplied by the Qazaqs under these conditions, and the fact that the Kabardian horses brought across the Caspian disdained the wormwood which formed much of the available grazing, and 'wasted away, until they looked like Borzoi dogs': 'V Zakaspiiskom krae v 1877 godu', 137, 143.

[67] Lomakin to Franchini 29/04/1877 NAG F.545 Op.1 D.1438 ll. 26–8*ob*, also in *PT*, 305–6.

[68] Lomakin to Franchini 08/05/1877 NAG F.545 Op.1 D.1438 ll. 30–2, also in *PT*, 308–10.

that all Turkmen fortresses were equally feeble, which would lead him to miscalculate fatally two years later at Gök-Tepe.

While one group of Teke Turkmen leaders, including Tykma Sardar, sent Lomakin a letter acknowledging their submission, the 'warm welcome' he had anticipated was not long in coming.[69] On the 14 May Lomakin reported a serious clash at Qizil-Arvat with a large force under Nurberdy Khan, who had clearly decided he did not want the role of Russian stooge. Hearing rumours that the Akhal-Teke were on the march, and noting that the apparently friendly nearby Turkmen had all disappeared, at 4.30 am on the 12 May Lomakin sent a small cavalry reconnaissance party to investigate a cloud of dust which had appeared in the Yangi-Ata valley to the south-west of the Russian camp the evening before. The first shots rang out an hour later, as the Russian scouts spotted a group of 5,000–6,000 Akhal Teke, 'with all their khans, *ishans* and *aqsaqals*', and 3,000 camels. Characteristically, he attributed their hostility to Islam:

> Aroused by their clergy, some of whom had recently returned from Mecca and Constantinople, all the remote Turkmen had gathered to die or destroy our small force; as the Koran demands, they would not give up to us a scrap of their land without a struggle. They have tried by force to join together the Teke of the nearby fortresses, with all their khans and elders.[70]

He believed their original plan had been for the Turkmen cavalry to descend on the Russian baggage camels and drive them off – when the Russian cavalry set off in pursuit, they would attack the camp with their remaining forces, surround it and cut off the water supply. This might well have worked, so Lomakin believed, but 'The Lord saved us' (*Gospod spas nas*), since the plan depended on complete surprise, and the Turkmen panicked when the Russian scouts appeared in the valley; however, the Russians were outnumbered twenty to one, and initially their situation was 'critical' – 'but each time, the murderous fire of the Berdan rifles, and the cool-headedness, energy, courage and good management' of their commander, Colonel Navrotskii, allowed them to hold on until reinforcements arrived. The battle lasted over four hours, and Lomakin was forced to commit almost all his men and artillery, leaving the camp practically undefended, before the Turkmen finally broke and ran, leaving behind sixty dead. Their prisoners informed them that they had lost over 200 casualties, and (so Lomakin claimed) that they had learned that they could not stand up against Russian small arms and artillery fire: "'Half of our bullets", the prisoners said, "did not even reach you, while yours even overshot

---

[69] Letter from Sufi Khan, Shih-Quli Khan, Avaz Murad Sardar (Tykma Sardar) & Qaraja Khan to Lomakin 05/05/1877, trans. & original NAG F.545 Op.1 D.1438 ll. 33–4*ob*, also in *PT*, 306–8.

[70] Lomakin to Franchini 14/05/1877 NAG F.545 Op.1 D.1438 l. 44*ob*, also in *PT*, 312.

us: how could we stand it?"[71] Arnol'di counted 100 Turkmen corpses left behind in the defile.[72] The Russians lost eleven wounded and one killed.

Lomakin wrote that this engagement (Figure 9.2) would have taught the Turkmen a good lesson, and expressed his satisfaction that 'the most warlike people in these steppes' were now convinced that they could not withstand Russian weapons.[73] However, he was able neither to pursue his defeated enemy, nor to maintain his position at Qizil-Arvat. By the end of the month he reported that Nurberdy Khan was gathering his forces once again, and seeking to prevent any communication between Gök-Tepe and Qizil-Arvat. Supplies were running low, and he could not weaken his force by sending a portion of it back to Krasnovodsk to replenish them. On the 9 June he decided to retreat, citing the severe supply problems and a decline in the health both of camels and of men, as the latter succumbed to fever and eye problems brought on by the dust.[74] While he was assured by the Caucasus command there was no shame in this, it does not seem to have been perceived this way at the time,[75] and Lomakin urged the need for a more ambitious expedition deep into the territory of the Akhal-Teke.

While Lomakin might have won a short-term tactical victory over the Akhal-Teke, he had not succeeded in destroying or dispersing them, and had been forced to retreat and leave them in possession. Referring to unspecified 'Persian sources', probably from the British consulate at Meshed, Marvin claimed that 'Lomakin was besieged in his camp, that he was reduced to great straits, and that he had to bury his cannon in the sand and retire in disorder to Krasnovodsk; the Turkmen pursuing him hotly the whole way and blockading the fort for several weeks after he had entered it.'[76] The Akhal-Teke, meanwhile, had learnt that they were at a disadvantage when fighting the Russians in open ground, and that they would need to challenge their superiority in firearms and artillery from behind fortifications, something they would later do to great effect. In the Ministry of Foreign Affairs there was some disquiet at the possibility that Lomakin's clash with the Akhal-Teke would lead to more military adventurism in Transcaspia, disquiet which Count Heiden, the chief of the Main Staff, did his best to dispel by assuring them that it had been no more than an ordinary reconnaissance expedition, undertaken to protect the caravan route to Khiva in accordance with the Tsar's

---

[71] Lomakin to Franchini 14/05/1877 NAG F.545 Op.1 D.1438 l. 47, also in *PT*, 313.

[72] Arnol'di, 'V Zakaspiiskom krae v 1877 godu', *VS* (1886), No. 10, 326.

[73] Lomakin to Franchini 14/05/1877 NAG F.545 Op.1 D.1438 l. 47*ob*, also in *PT*, 314.

[74] Lomakin to Franchini 28/05/1877; 09/06/1877 NAG F.545 Op.1 D.1438 ll. 56–7*ob*, 70, also in *PT*, 319–20, 323–5.

[75] Terent'ev roundly condemns Lomakin for giving an impression of a Russian retreat: *Istoriya zavoevaniya*, III, 4; Callwell in *Small Wars*, 77 also disparages Lomakin's tactics in 1876–7.

[76] Marvin, *Disastrous Russian Campaign*, 13.

Figure 9.2 Plan of the engagement with the Turkmen at Qizil-Arvat, 1877. NAG F.545 Op.1 D.1438 l. 49. © National Archives of Georgia.

wishes, and that there was no question of any force being allowed to proceed further towards Merv and upset the British.[77]

At the end of 1877, in a report on his first three years as commandant, Lomakin described the Akhal-Teke in the following, revealing terms:

> [The] Akhal-Teke oasis occupies a narrow, 20 or 30 *verst* strip of land, stretching for 250 *versts* from Qizil-Arvat to Anu and Ghiaurs, between the north-eastern slopes of the Köpet-Dagh and the Qara-Qum desert. This oasis is inhabited by Turkmen of the Teke tribe, who are semi-sedentary and live in 40–50 clay fortresses, or around them, occupying themselves primarily with robbery and brigandage, the passion for which is, we might say, rooted in them, innate, inherited by them as their only means of living. This nest of brigands (*razboinichn'e gnezdo*) is now the sole obstacle to the introduction of order and calm to the local steppes, and to the establishment in this region of uninterrupted and correct caravan trade with Khiva. These Turkmen are considered the most war-like and fanatical tribe among all the Turkmen tribes and keep all the Yomuds, both local and Khivan, in permanent terror. The name Teke alone (which means a monastery of dervish-mullah-fanatics) – demonstrates the extreme fanatical temper of these savages.[78]

Predictably enough, Lomakin characterised all the bad blood between the Russians and the Akhal-Teke as the fault of the latter, and prior to 1873 of the Khivan Khan, who had stirred them up. He also noted that the future of the region, and all its economic potential, was inextricably bound up in the development of the oil industry, noting that the Nobel company already had a presence on Cheleken island, renting five wells from the local population, and that other Baku-based oil firms – Kokorev & Co, Baranovskii & Co, Devur & Co – were also investing there.[79] Leaving aside the curious etymological fetishism of Lomakin's explanation for Turkmen 'fanaticism', he expressed the usual Russian convictions regarding Russia's Central Asian foes here, a set of essentialised attributes which placed them beyond any possibility of normal diplomacy, and rendered them amenable only to violence.

Lomakin's next expedition the following year was no more successful. This time the destination was originally meant to be the Merv oasis, but, as we have seen, this was countermanded in July, and the operation was rebranded as a reconnaissance along the line of the River Atrek. The expedition set off from Chikishlar in an attempt to reduce the distance involved. While they created

---

[77] Geiden to Girs 18/06/1877, in *PT*, 326–7.

[78] 'Otchet Nachal'nika Zakaspiiskogo Voennago Otdela 1874–1877 g.', 22/12/1877 NAG F.545 Op.1 D.1891 l. 14.

[79] 'Otchet Nachal'nika Zakaspiiskogo Voennago Otdela 1874–1877 g.', 22/12/1877 NAG F.545 Op.1 D.1891 ll. 89–96; these were themes he dwelt on in his private correspondence as well: Lomakin to F. A. Bakulin 03/03/1876, in *Pis'ma Konsulu F. A. Bakulinu (o sredne-aziatskikh delakh) 1874–1878* ed. V. Alekseev (St Pb.: P. Usov, 1914), 22–3.

a new fortified post at Chat, they soon ran into difficulties.[80] Logistical problems manifested themselves early on when the steam schooner *Persiyanin*,
which had been ferrying supplies from Krasnovodsk to Chikishlar, broke
down. Supplies had to be brought to Chat directly from Krasnovodsk,
a distance of 500–600 *versts*. Owing to the delay in collecting sufficient
supplies, the 3,000 camels which had been assembled on the Atrek consumed
all the available grazing and began to die. When the expedition did finally
advance towards Qizil-Arvat, the order was almost immediately countermanded as 'premature', and they were forced to return to Chat, where
Lomakin was ordered to carry out a thorough reconnaissance of the surrounding country.[81] Terent'ev's account of this expedition drips with sarcasm:

> Chat was taken on the 3 August without a shot being fired. Lomakin was
> not satisfied with this and, in order to have some gunplay (*dobitsya
> vystrelov*), he went forward decisively without any need for it. Evidently
> he still did not know then, that after any needless movement forwards one
> also has to come back, and in Asia this is always considered as a defeat.[82]

On their way back to Chat the Russian column was repeatedly harassed by
Turkmen cavalry: six artillerymen who had strayed from the main column
were captured. Once the column had reached Chat, the Turkmen, knowing
that the Russians were weak in cavalry with just 180 Cossacks, effectively
blockaded them for several weeks, before the main force retreated to
Chikishlar, leaving a small garrison behind.[83] In December 1878 the Akhal-
Teke were sufficiently emboldened to attack the main depot and fortification at
Chikishlar itself, and Lomakin enumerated, in outraged tones, all the various
attacks to which his force had been subjected in the previous six months,
making the familiar argument from prestige: 'There is only one course left to
us – to finally finish with this nest of brigandage, with this disgrace and stain of
our times [. . .] All Central Asia, Khorasan, Afghanistan, Bukhara, Khiva is
looking at us, and waiting for us to finish with these savage barbarians, with
these insolent brigands.' He urged an immediate attack on the Akhal-Teke,
though leaving Merv to one side.[84] A week later, Lt-Gen. Pavlov, Chief of Staff
of the Caucasian Military District, informed him that the Tsar had agreed.[85]

[80] Lomakin to Staff of the Caucasus Army 08/08/1878 & 16/10/1878, in *PT*, 339–42, 350–1.

[81] Staff of the Caucasus Army to Lomakin 14 or 15/08/1878, in *PT*, 342–4.

[82] Terent'ev, *Istoriya zavoevaniya*, III, 4.

[83] Lomakin to Staff of the Caucasus Army 16/09/1878, in *PT*, 347–8; 'Zapiska Nachal'nika
Zakaspiiskogo Voennogo Otdela o polozhenii del v etom krae posle Akhal-Tekinskoi
ekspeditsii', 15/06/1879 NAG F.545 Op.1 D.1893 ll. 13–16*ob*; Terent'ev, *Istoriya zavoevaniya*, III, 5.

[84] Lomakin to Staff of the Caucasus Army 02/01/1879, in *PT*, 356–8, 360–1; the Russian
officers O'Donovan spoke to in 1879 gave him very similar justifications for the campaign
against the 'untameable, predatory' Akhal-Teke: *Merv Oasis*, I, 70.

[85] Pavlov to Lomakin 11/01/1879, in *PT*, 362.

9.3 Britain and Afghanistan

How far, then, can the 1879 expedition against the Akhal-Teke be seen as a move in the 'Great Game', whose aim was to discomfit or alarm the British? As we have seen, in general the British threat, such as it was, received far less emphasis in Ivanov and Lomakin's correspondence than their problematic relations with the Turkmen themselves, and it usually appeared in tandem with fears of Persian interference, as despite the preponderant Russian influence in Tehran, they generally assumed that any attempt by the Qajars to assert their sovereignty over the Atrek, Akhal-Teke or Merv Turkmen must be down to British machinations.[86] Throughout 1877 and the first half of 1878 the Russians believed that what the Turkmen called an 'Inglis-Tura' – Captain Napier, a British agent from Meshed – was stirring up the Merv Turkmen against them.[87] This was the latest in a line of similar reports on the activities of British emissaries, who were supposedly supplying the Turkmen with arms and (ironically, given Lomakin's desire for the same thing) encouraging them to unite under a single leader. Sergeev suggests that resistance from Kurds and Armenians prevented British plans from succeeding, but, given that both groups were present only in very small numbers, the many sources of disunity among the Turkmen themselves would seem a more likely cause.[88] In his final report Lomakin described Napier as bribing the Turkmen leader Avaz-Durdy Khan to acknowledge Persian suzerainty: 'For the Teke this was a good calculation: on the one hand, becoming subjects of Persia would deliver them from Russia, and on the other, it would present them with perfect freedom to give themselves up to their most savage instincts and ingrained passion for robbery and violence without punishment, which the Persian government would be wholly unable to interfere with.'[89] Lomakin's language here and elsewhere, and the attitudes towards the Turkmen found in all Russian official correspondence on Transcaspia, suggest that sooner or later the Russians would have felt the need to punish their 'insolence' and bring

---

[86] For example Ivanov to von Kaufman 21/09/1876; Lomakin to Franchini 23/09/1876; Astrabad Consul to Lomakin 15/02/1877; Astrabad Consul to the Minister in Tehran 24/06/1877, in *PT*, 255–63, 289–90, 328–9.

[87] Miliutin to Grand Duke Mikhail 10/02/1877 (telegram) & Lomakin to Franchini 02/03/1877, in *PT*, 288, 294–6; Astrabad Consul to the Russian Minister in Tehran 04/04/1877; Miliutin to Svyatopolk-Mirskii, 10/?/1877, cypher telegram in numerical code; Astrabad Consul to Lomakin 20/03/1878; Lomakin to Franchini 16/04/1878 NAG F.545 Op.1 D.1154 ll. 152, 180–2, 187–8; D.1440, 'Raporta o polozhenii del v Asterbadskoi i Khorasanskoi provintsiyakh', ll. 24–5; Napier's reports of an earlier mission are in IOR/L/P&S/20/228, *Collections of Journals and Reports Received from the Hon. Capt. G. C. Napier, on Special Duty in Persia 1874* (London: Eyre & Spottiswoode, 1876).

[88] Sergeev, *The Great Game*, 191.

[89] 'Otchet Nachal'nika Zakaspiiskogo Voennago Otdela 1874–1877 g.', 22/12/1877 NAG F.545 Op.1 D.1891 l. 53.

them to heel, regardless of whether or not they thought the British were behind their intransigence, and they do not seem to have taken the idea that the British might have designs on the territory themselves very seriously.

However, the timing of the campaign against the Akhal-Teke, if not the fact, did have something to do with worsening relations with Britain over Afghanistan. Once again, it was not a direct competition for territory or influence that proved significant, but a more nebulous question of prestige. In the spring of 1878, at the end of the Russo-Turkish War, anticipating the pressure which would be applied to have Russia's territorial gains from the Ottoman Empire under the treaty of San Stefano reversed, Miliutin and von Kaufman had resolved to launch a military operation in Central Asia with the aim of panicking the British in India and possibly provoking a revolt there. One prong of the advance was an expedition to the Afghan frontier from Tashkent, Samarkand and Ferghana, which proved abortive because many of the men died of cholera when they halted at the village of Jam in the Zarafshan valley. As we have seen, the other prong was supposed to be launched across the Caspian Sea from the Caucasus Military District through Transcaspia to Merv, but this had still not set out by the time the Congress of Berlin was held, bringing the 'Eastern Crisis' to an end. On the 18 July Miliutin passed on the Tsar's order that the operation had been cancelled, and the force based at Krasnovodsk should confine itself to local operations.[90] However, the embassy the Russians sent to Kabul under Colonel Stoletov to reassure Amir Shir 'Ali Khan that these manoeuvres were not directed at him inadvertently helped to trigger the Second Anglo-Afghan War; although this ended disastrously for the British, the Russians initially believed that their prestige in Central Asian had suffered a severe blow.[91]

In December 1878 A. N. Kuropatkin, then Director of the Asiatic Section of the Main Staff, submitted a lengthy memorandum on the 'Afghan question', in which he urged the need for an aggressive response to the British invasion of the country. While Kuropatkin ruled out direct involvement in the ongoing war in Afghanistan, he also argued against complete neutrality, suggesting that Russia offer covert support (including despatching officer volunteers to train and lead Afghan troops). Without this, he claimed, Russia would lose all influence in Afghanistan, abandoning any ambition of using Central Asia as a lever to exert pressure on the 'Eastern Question' and opening the way for the British to supply arms to the Turkmen and other troublesome tribes. He also urged the need for a further military demonstration from the Caucasus side through Transcaspia along the line of the Atrek. His memorandum was

[90] Miliutin to Grand Duke Mikhail 18/07/1878, in *PT*, 338.
[91] On this episode see Morrison, 'Beyond the Great Game'. The standard contemporary account of the embassy is by I. L. Yavorskii, *Puteshestvie Russkoi Missii po Avganistanu i Bukharskomu khanstvu v 1878–79 gg.* (St Pb.: Tip. M. A. Khana, 1882).

enthusiastically endorsed both by General N. N. Obruchev of the Main Staff Academy and by Miliutin himself.[92] Partly in response to the collapse of organised government in Afghanistan, in November 1878 von Kaufman had given Colonel N. I. Grodekov four months' leave for the purpose of reconnoitring routes through Bukhara, Afghanistan and Persia.[93] This would become a celebrated episode of the 'Great Game', largely because of the publication by Charles Marvin of an English translation of Grodekov's account of the journey.[94] While this is well known, the original of Grodekov's travel account was preceded by a secret memorandum which he had prepared six months earlier on Russia's strategic position in Afghanistan, which was not published.[95] His assessment was bitter and pessimistic: even if the new agreement between the British and the Afghans still supposedly guaranteed the independence of Afghanistan, the British could now place whomever they wanted on the throne of the country, which would become no more than a puppet state, and from there they would interfere in Russia's Central Asian territories. Grodekov concluded that the Russian advance towards the Afghan frontier had had a salutary effect on Afghan opinion, and urged both the strategic necessity of sending a punitive expedition to Merv, occupying both the Akhal-Teke oasis and the town of Charjui on the Amu-Darya, and the moral need to suppress Turkmen raiding of the surrounding Persian and Afghan settled population.[96]

Another lengthy memorandum urging an expedition against the Akhal-Teke came early in 1879 from Colonel Petrusevich of the Main Staff, who had been sent to conduct a survey of Khorasan the previous year. While he referred briefly to British machinations in the region, and the abortive expeditions of 1878, his focus was above all the Turkmen themselves, and the threat they posed to Russian prestige and Russian trade. Above all, he concluded, recent tactics had only emboldened them: 'If the indecisiveness of the Krasnovodsk force persists, then there is no doubt that the Teke will become accustomed to our means of war, and with each despatch of a force they will become bolder and bolder, and victory over them will cost us more and more.' He also referred

[92] 'Zapiska zaveduiushchego Aziatskoi Chast'iu Glavnogo Shtaba Polkovnika A. N. Kuropatkina po afganskomu voprosu', 25/11/1878 RGVIA F.846 Op.1 D.28 ll. 18–42, in Zagorodnikova, 'Bol'shaya Igra', 209, 213–14.
[93] Von Kaufman to Miliutin 13/11/1878 RGVIA F.400 Op.1 D.577, 'O poezdke Polkovnika Grodekova po avganskomu Turkestanu', l. 1.
[94] Charles Marvin (trans.), Colonel Grodekoff's Ride from Samarcand to Herat through Balkh and the Uzbek States of Afghan Turkestan: With His Own Map of the March-Route from the Oxus to Herat (London: W. H. Allen & Co., 1880).
[95] 'Doklad General'nogo Shtaba Polkovnika Grodekova', 18/03/1879 RGVIA F.400 Op.1 D.577 ll. 11–100ob.
[96] 'Doklad General'nogo Shtaba Polkovnika Grodekova', 18/03/1879 RGVIA F.400 Op.1 D.577 ll. 53–74; Sergeev, Bol'shaya Igra, 192.

to the probable friendly attitude of Persia, which would welcome the definition of her northern frontier and an end to Turkmen raids.[97]

For Lt-Gen. Pavlov of the Caucasus Military District the priority was to create a definite border in the undefined region between Persia, Afghanistan and Bukhara, and he noted that this would of necessity require the annexation of Merv as well as the Akhal-Teke oasis.[98] When the Caucasian Viceroy Grand Duke Mikhail Romanov presented the results of a meeting of the General Military Council on the Turkmen question which he had convened in Tiflis, he noted that the expeditions of the previous year had damaged Russian prestige, something that British agents in Persia were ready to take advantage of: 'In the interests of Russian influence we cannot accept such attempts to strengthen themselves in Persia, and because of this, for the restoration of our prestige, it is essential to severely punish the Teke and prevent the renewal of their insolent encroachments.' He added that the lesson of the campaigns in the Qazaq steppe thirty years earlier had been that only when the nomads' winter pastures were occupied would there be a secure frontier and an end to raiding.[99] His deputy, Prince Svyatopolk-Mirskii, wrote that he entirely shared the opinion of Count Shuvalov, the Russian ambassador in London, that 'We cannot respond to the actions of the British in Afghanistan with negotiation, but with action, and that this action must be along the Atrek.' He clearly expected the ongoing British military actions in Afghanistan to be fully successful, and feared that they would establish a permanent foothold in Herat or beyond.[100] He concluded that

> The actions towards us of the Teke, and the impossibility of any negotiation or agreement whatsoever with a people that has no fixed government, fully justify our use of the force of arms against them.[101]

Transcaspia thus emerged as the one place where the Russians could dispel the unfortunate impression of weakness which they believed had been created by their failure to protect Shir 'Ali Khan from British aggression.[102] The destruction of British resident Major Louis Cavagnari's mission at Kabul in September 1879, Sergeev argues, provided them with the opportunity, as the British were once more distracted by Afghan affairs, and he claims this

---

[97] 'Voenno-statisticheskogo opisaniya Polkovnikom Petrusevichem Khorasana', 1879, in *PT*, 368, 370.

[98] 'Soobrazheniya Nachal'nika Shtaba Kavkazskogo Voennogo Okruga', 01/1879, in *PT*, 374.

[99] Grand Duke Mikhail to Miliutin 22/01/1879, in *PT*, 377, 379.

[100] Svyatopolk-Mirskii to Grand Duke Mikhail 07/02/1879, in *PT*, 391–3.

[101] Svyatopolk-Mirskii to Grand Duke Mikhail 07/02/1879, in *PT*, 392.

[102] See further 'O predstoyashchikh voennykh deistviyakh v Zakaspiiskom krae', 22/01/1880, in *PT*, 465–70, which also states that the expedition was prompted by the need to respond to British aggression.

'precipitated' Lomakin's unsuccessful campaign.[103] Once again this betrays a lack of attention to chronology. In fact Count Heiden had submitted a lengthy proposal for an expedition to the Akhal-Teke oasis to Alexander II in February 1879, placing the emphasis not just on the pacification of the Akhal-Teke, but on the need to 'finally settle' Russia's frontiers with Persia and Afghanistan.[104] The expedition was launched in April, when the British position in Kabul still looked impregnable. Cavagnari himself lived long enough for news of the expedition's disastrous outcome to reach him, and gave the following shrewd assessment:

> The object of this expedition is said to be the punishment of the Akhal-Tekes in order to put a stop to their predatory habits. The slave-trade carried on by these habitual robbers has also been prominently put forward by the Russian press as a kind of appeal to the sympathies of Europe in this work of civilization! A season fraught with domestic difficulties and financial embarrassment is not the time that any nation would select for the prosecution of such philanthropical designs. The true object Russia has in view in fitting out, regardless of expense, an expedition superior in every way to any she has yet organized for her Central Asian campaigns, is not difficult to discover. Lomakin's repulse by the Turkomans, and the diplomatic defeat Russia has recently sustained in Afghanistan, make it imperative for her to take steps for the recovery of her lost prestige.[105]

Far from being a response to British weakness, the 1879 Akhal-Teke expedition was once again an attempt to restore Russian prestige in the face of what still looked like a British triumph.

9.4 The Campaign of 1879

The clearest indication that his superiors did not look favourably on Lomakin's actions in 1877 and 1878 was the decision to give the command of the 1879 expedition not to him, but to General Ivan Davidovich Lazarev (1820–1879), despite Lomakin's many years of experience serving in Transcaspia. While Lazarev's leadership and charisma were lavishly praised by Marvin, who based his account on contemporary newspapers, and O'Donovan also found him physically impressive, Terent'ev was much more dismissive, considering that Lazarev knew too little about the specifics of Central Asian campaigning, and

---

[103] Sergeev, *The Great Game*, 195.

[104] Heiden to Alexander II 02/1879, in *PT*, 385–90. Baranovskii remarks that among the officers it was thought the purpose of the expedition was both to respond to the British occupation of Kabul and to chastise the Turkmen: *Russkie v Akhal-Teke*, 2–3.

[105] Cavagnari to A. C. Lyall, Secretary to the Foreign Dept, Government of India, 30/08/1879 IOR/L/P&S/20/MEMO/35 *Memoranda on Miscellaneous Subjects*. Vol. 5. *1874–1880*, 35.

that his initial proclamation to the Turkmen, in which he made reference to the
Qur'an and offered payment to any man who presented himself with a sound
horse, was extremely ill-judged: 'Is this the language of force? To promise pay
to all those who have a horse and a desire to receive money – this is a purely
Armenian way of going about things.'[106] This was both a sneer at Lazarev's
Armenian background and a dig at the competence of the Caucasian command. The prospect of what it appeared would be easy military laurels, as in
previous Central Asian campaigns, also attracted a number of well-born and
well-connected officers to what was normally considered an obscure hardship
posting. As one British diplomat reported:

> General Tergukasoff, on taking over the command after Lazareff's death,
> found on arrival at headquarters some 40 or 50 officers of various grades
> belonging to high families and show regiments stationed at St Petersburg
> and Moscow, who had, with a view to receiving orders and decorations
> got themselves appointed to the staff. As these gentlemen did nothing but
> drink and impair the efficiency of the force by idleness, extravagance, and
> luxury, they were forthwith ordered to return to their regiments. Most of
> them belonged to influential families, and as, in consequence of the
> disastrous result of the expedition to which they had contributed they
> received no decorations, their friends are supposed to have had something
> to do with General Tergukasoff's subsequent resignation. NOTE – these
> officers abound in Caucasian campaigns, and are commonly nicknamed
> 'Fasans' or 'Pheasants'. They carry an enormous quantity of baggage,
> regard with contempt the regimental officer, and when a battle takes
> place take up a good position in the rear, so as to enjoy a view of the
> fighting without risk of a bullet.[107]

Unlike in the 1873 Khiva expedition, they were to be disappointed even in this.

Meanwhile Lomakin was instead placed in command of the advanced post
at Chat, and was soon able to report a skirmish with a party of 1,500 Turkmen
at the wells of Aqcha-Koy, after they had tried to drive off 10,000 sheep and
3,000 camels that were being delivered to the Russian advance post under
escort. Captain Ter-Gazarov and his men successfully beat them off, and
Lazarev reported with satisfaction what he described as the first significant
victory for Russian arms over the Turkmen, which he believed would have
a salutary effect.[108]

[106] Marvin, *Disastrous Russian Campaign*, 52–7; O'Donovan, *Merv Oasis*, I, 18; Terent'ev,
Istoriya zavoevaniya, III, 9–10. Terent'ev's phrase definitely smacks of Turkestani contempt for the Caucasian military.
[107] Sir Oliver J. Byrne, 'Russia in Central Asia No. 3', 31/12/1880 IOR/L/P&S/20/MEMO/35
Memoranda on Miscellaneous Subjects. Vol. 5. *1874–1880*, No. 11, 8.
[108] Lomakin to Lazarev 10/04/1879, 17/04/1879; Lazarev to Svyatopolk-Mirskii 04/05/1879
RGVIA F.1300 Op.1 D.77, 'Doneseniya ot komandovaniya Zakaspiiskago otryada
i Zakaspiiskogo Voennogo Otdela ob operatsiyakh protiv Tekintsev', ll. 3–11, 12–*ob*.

While a new telegraph line from Chikishlar to the Russian consulate at Astrabad allowed relatively swift communication with Baku and Tiflis, the commissariat arrangements underlined the particular difficulties of the campaign. The total force was 15,123 men and 6,181 horses, much larger than the individual columns that had been used for the assault on Khiva in 1873, or the forces used in earlier campaigns in the Qazaq steppe. They would need a total of 97,285 *poods* of supplies, 59,000 of which were fodder for the horses. The initial estimate was that this would require 7,350 camels to transport it on from the port at Chikishlar. These cost 15 roubles a month to hire, meaning an estimated cost of 460,800 roubles for four months, which was the expected duration of the campaign, and a total transport cost of 1,352,556 roubles.[109] Preparations began in early March, and demonstrated an attempt to learn from the experience of previous expeditions and adapt to local conditions. Because Russian horses were unsuited to a steppe expedition, many of these were left on the western shore of the Caspian and replaced with 'Kirgiz' (i.e. Qazaq) horses. The troops were given lightweight summer uniforms and service caps with scarves to protect them from the sun, baggy trousers and, perhaps more unexpectedly, 'pans with tripods for the baking of *lavash*, local bread, which is prepared very quickly in the Persian manner'.[110] They were equipped with four months of supplies, including 88,790 portions of tinned soup (27,302 of *shchi-kasha* and 61,488 of pea soup), 165,000 rations of tinned horsemeat and, in place of the usual dried pickled cabbage, a new type of preserved vegetable manufactured in St Petersburg. Their daily ration is specified in Table 9.1.

To this were added black pepper, bay leaves, onion, garlic, salt in proportion, citric acid for adding to their food and water, the aforementioned preserved vegetables, 1 *funt* of tea and 3 *funts* of sugar for every 100 men (they supplied

Table 9.1 *Daily summer ration for a soldier in Transcaspia, 1879*

Item	Quantity
Sukhari (rusks)	2½ *funts* (approx. 1 kg)
Pulses	½ *funt* (approx. 200 g)
Meat	1 *funt* (approx. 400 g)
Wheat flour	4 *zolotniks* (approx. 20 g)
Buckwheat	32 *zolotniks* (approx. 135 g)
Fat (butter or sheep's tail)	5 *zolotniks* (approx. 20 g)

[109] 'Vedomost', 20/08/1879 RGVIA F.1300 Op.1 D.77 ll. 52ob–53, 60, 68ob.
[110] I. D. Lazarev, 'Zhurnal zanyatii i voennykh deistvii Akhal-Tekinskogo ekspeditsionnogo otryada', 01/06/1879 RGVIA F.1300 Op.1 D.80, 'Zhurnal voennykh deistviyakh Akhal-Tekinskogo ekspeditsionnogo otryada', ll. 4ob–7ob.

their own teapots), and two measures of spirits per man. Alongside all this they had to bring fuel from Persia, as the region around Chikishlar had already been stripped bare of saxaul, and also carry forage for the horses – in all 8,000 *chetvert*'s of 'horse galettes' made of barley and 50,000 *poods* of hay, divided between the supply depots at Chikishlar and Chat. Lazarev noted that they had already encountered severe transport difficulties. The contractor Korganov was proving very slow at getting supplies from Baku to Chikishlar because of a shortage of transport on the Caspian, while storms also hampered communications. The horses they had brought over from the Caucasus were suffering from catarrh because of the sudden change of temperature. Of the 3,500 camels they had secured from the Qazaqs of Mangishlaq to transport supplies from Krasnovodsk to Chikishlar, only 2,500 remained, the rest having perished or been carried off by the Turkmen. Of these only 1,000 were strong enough to face the onward journey to Chat. They had managed to hire another 2,100 and purchase 3,000, and would hire 3,000 more – Lazarev estimated that they should have 8,300 camels for the expedition, with around 1,000 drivers.[111] Eventually the expedition would set off with almost 13,000 camels, and even this turned out to be insufficient. Marvin, O'Donovan and Terent'ev all noted the error of bringing across the men before all the supplies for the expedition had been delivered, meaning that they spent months in idleness at Chikishlar, developing disease and consuming rations uselessly.[112] According to British sources, these inherent problems were compounded by rampant corruption:

> The peculation and embezzlement which occurred during General Lazareff's command are said to have been unprecedented, and the great mortality and sickness which prevailed to be in great part a consequence of it. The chief of the medical staff was compelled by threats to pass meat and provisions not fit for consumption supplied by the head contractor, one of the most influential Armenians of Tiflis, and a connection of the late General.[113]

Reports from the expedition's commanders returned constantly to the same theme – lack of transport, which was crippling their ability to move even as far as Chat, which was less than a quarter of the way to the Akhal-Teke oasis. In particular, the decision to rely partly on *arba*s (high-wheeled carts) turned out to be mistaken. A healthy camel could carry around 9 *poods* for the four-day journey to Chat. They could manage three of these journeys a month, meaning one camel could carry 27 *poods* in that time. While the carts could carry 15

[111] V. I. Lazarev, 'Zhurnal zanyatii i voennykh deistvii Akhal-Tekinskogo ekspeditsionnogo otryada', 01/06/1879 RGVIA F.1300 Op.1 D.80 ll. 8–10*ob*.
[112] Marvin, *Disastrous Campaign*, 315–16; O'Donovan, *Merv Oasis*, I, 141; Terent'ev, *Istoriya zavoevaniya*, III, 11.
[113] Byrne, 'Russia in Central Asia No. 3', 31/12/1880 IOR/L/P&S/20/MEMO/35, *Memoranda on Miscellaneous Subjects*. Vol. 5. *1874–1880*, No. 11, 8.

*pood*s at a time, they took seven days to make the journey, so they could travel only twice a month, and they cost more than twice as much to hire for that time (53 roubles for a cart, as opposed to 19–20 roubles for a camel with its driver). It was true that camels would need to rest after a month's journeying, but unlike the horses pulling carts they could go three or four days without water, and even longer without food. Purchased camels were even better value, provided they survived for at least four months – if they lasted six months they cost just 15 roubles a month.[114] It was clear that more camels were needed – the problem was persuading the Turkmen to supply them. While there was often no love lost between the Yomuds of the Atrek and the Akhal-Teke, the fact that their fellow Turkmen were the object of the Russian expedition made the Yomuds understandably reluctant to provide it with transport. At the beginning of August Prince Dolgorukov and his Kabardian regiment were despatched on an expedition against the Atabai Yomuds – ostensibly this was a punitive measure, but in fact it was quite simply a raiding party, of precisely the kind the Russians themselves so deplored among the Turkmen. Dolgorukov and his men succeeded in carrying off 1,250 camels, and the easy victory they won here was treated as further proof of the pusillanimity of the enemy.[115]

The transport question meant that, whilst most of the force had already crossed the Caspian to Chikishlar by the 14 June, the advance guard did not set out for Chat until the beginning of August, by which time a considerable portion of the stock of supplies had already been consumed. During this long period of waiting in severe heat, Lazarev's health began to deteriorate, as he himself described:

> The illness began in the middle of July with what looked like a simple boil on the left shoulder, and I, not paying it attention, proposed to move together with the troops, but by the end of July the illness had taken on such a serious character that the doctor forbade me to leave. The boil turned into a carbuncle, and the inflammation brought on a feverish state and since the last days of July I was confined to bed. On the 1 August I agreed to have it lanced in the hope to gain some relief and leave on the 6 August, but the operation did not bring any real improvement, and has brought me to a pass where I have completely lost my strength and am not in a state to get up from my bed.[116]

He asked to be relieved of his command, and urged that it be passed instead to Lt-Gen. Petrov, the commander of the infantry division. Despite the

---

[114] Malama, 'Zhurnal zanyatii i voennykh deistvii Akhal-Tekinskogo ekspeditsionnogo otryada', 01/08/1879 RGVIA F.1300 Op.1 D.80 ll. 69–70ob.

[115] Malama, 'Zhurnal zanyatii i voennykh deistvii Akhal-Tekinskogo ekspeditsionnogo otryada', 01/08/1879; 01/09/1879 RGVIA F.1300 Op.1 D.80 ll. 102–4, 108ob–9.

[116] Lazarev to Vitold Vikent'evich Gurchin 10/08/1879 RGVIA F.1300 Op.1 D.77 ll. 49–50.

excruciating pain, and the insistence of his doctor that he return to the Caucasus, Lazarev insisted on being transported by *tarantass* (post-wagon) to Chat, but expired almost immediately upon his arrival.[117] On the 20 August Zinoviev, the Russian Minister in Tehran, reported to Tiflis that, owing to Lazarev's death, Lomakin as the senior general remaining in the field had taken over temporary command.[118] Grand Duke Mikhail informed Lomakin that he had appointed Lt-Gen. Tergukasov to replace Lazarev, and that Lomakin would retain temporary command until his arrival in the middle of September.[119] It is not clear when this telegram reached him, but the day before it was sent Lomakin had already ordered the advance-guard to make a reconnaissance in strength towards Gök-Tepe. Lomakin was probably aware that there was only a brief window in which he could wipe out the memory of the retreats of 1877 and 1878 with a decisive victory over the Turkmen: Terent'ev asserts that Lomakin and the other staff officers 'were glad' of Lazarev's death, and 'champing at the bit', and that the former deliberately made haste to advance before a new commander could be appointed.[120] Because of the shortage of camels, only one-quarter of the 12,000-strong force – just over 3,000 men – would actually advance towards Gök-Tepe – far too few, as it turned out.[121]

To understand the reasons why the 1879 expedition was so poorly planned, and ended in such humiliating failure, we need some insight into the state of mind of its unintended commander. Lomakin clearly resented his replacement by Lazarev, and worried about how his record was viewed in Tiflis and St Petersburg. Already in June 1879, two months before Lazarev's death, when Lomakin was commanding the advance-guard, his communications were full of anxiety and paranoia about his military reputation:

> At the beginning of this year, when the current expedition to the Akhal-Teke oasis was under consideration, several opinions were expressed which were pretty unpleasant for the current administration of the Transcaspian region. They said and wrote that our position in the region over the last ten years, rather than growing more solid and defined with the passage of time, has deteriorated; that the means we have used to introduce order and calm in this region were in general impractical; that the undertaking for this purpose of a whole series of expeditions was in

---

[117] O'Donovan, who was himself prostrate with dysentery at the time, says the rumour was that Lazarev had caught the infection from a rug he purchased in plague-ridden Astrakhan: *Merv Oasis*, I, 136–7.

[118] Telegram Zinov'ev to Svyatopolk-Mirskii 20/08/1879 RGVIA F.1300 Op.1 D.77 ll. 32–ob.

[119] Grand Duke Mikhail to Lomakin, cipher telegram 23/08/1879 RGVIA F.1300 D.77 l. 73, also in *PT*, 432–3.

[120] Terent'ev, *Istoriya zavoevaniya*, III, 14.

[121] *Ibid.*, 22.

general not beneficial for our influence in the region: the Turkmen have taken the reverse movement of our forces as a retreat, and seen in this a sign of our weakness, have pursued our forces and by degrees become more and more bold. It has been portrayed as if the fortress of Chat was blockaded; that some of our soldiers were carried off as prisoners; that the Teke attacked Chikishlar; and that all this has produced an impression on Persia that is not favourable to us.[122]

Lomakin wrote that there had been only two genuine expeditions in the region – that to Khiva in 1873, and the current one against the Akhal-Teke. He had been restricted by his orders to carrying out temporary reconnaissances, in accordance with the Tsar's will, although he had repeatedly assured his superiors that there would be no peace in the region until the Akhal-Teke were suppressed. He had asked to be allowed to send a punitive expedition against the Akhal-Teke after abandoning Qizil-Arvat the previous year, and had been refused. He made a series of excuses for his failures in 1878, and claimed credit for pacifying the Turkmen around Krasnovodsk and Cheleken, as well as the Adai Qazaqs of the Mangishlaq peninsula. He concluded with an emotional appeal: 'Everyone who has served in this region, everyone who has been in Krasnovodsk, or on the local expeditions, knows how conscientiously and honourably I have laboured in this matter, not knowing fatigue, not sparing my health, or any efforts or means; and it will thus be understood with what sorrow I learnt of these personal opinions, these reports, from these clearly mistaken people.'[123]

A few days later, in a private letter to Alexander Vissarionovich Komarov (1830–1904) – a fellow Caucasian officer who would later become governor of Transcaspia himself – Lomakin laid bare his anxieties still more clearly. He was commenting on a memorandum by Kuropatkin which had severely criticised the state of affairs in Transcaspia and implied not only that Russian prestige had been damaged by so many apparent retreats, but also that the Caucasian troops were having their morale sapped and becoming cowardly.[124] Kuropatkin had made a number of unfavourable comparisons with the Turkestani way of dealing with unruly 'natives', prompting Lomakin to write the following:

The fact is that Mr Colonel Kuropatkin is a *Turkestanets* to the marrow of his bones. It is with this that all the squabbles between Turkestan and the Caucasus began, of which the Mountain Administration has entire

[122] 'Zapiska Nachal'nika Zakaspiiskogo Voennogo Otdela o polozhenii del v etom krae posle Akhal-Tekinskoi ekspeditsii', 15/06/1879 NAG F.545 Op.1 D.1893 l. 2, also in *PT*, 413.
[123] 'Zapiska Nachal'nika Zakaspiiskogo Voennogo Otdela o polozhenii del v etom krae posle Akhal-Tekinskoi ekspeditsii', 15/06/1879 NAG F.545 Op.1 D.1893 l. 19, also in *PT*, 425–6.
[124] Kuropatkin, *Doklad* 16/02/1879, in *PT*, 394–400.

volumes of copies of hostile judgements: against the construction of the Krasnovodsk–Khiva road, against the direction of Central Asian trade through Krasnovodsk, or the flooding of the Uzboi, the construction of the fortress at Ushaq-Bent and so on. Because of this it is only natural that he cannot relate sympathetically to the administration of this region; he has been joined by other partisans of malice and slander, such as Glukhovskii – who thanks to his dirty, petty mercenary ways left a not entirely pleasant memory behind him in this region – or Yomudskii, Dzerzhinskii and others, who were forced to leave a region where they were not only entirely useless, but harmful . . . I am presenting you with these notes, Alexander Vissarionovich, in an entirely private way, in a private letter . . . it will perhaps spare me from these so unjust and undeserved reproaches, which torture me, and from which I now know no rest by night or day.[125]

He asked Komarov to make representations to Prince Dmitrii Ivanovich, and through him to Grand Duke Mikhail, reflecting that, if this proved impossible, 'I will not be the last to be a victim of intrigue.' It seems clear, then, that Lomakin's military judgement was severely compromised by his anxiety to restore his reputation with a quick and easy victory. The weak ego, over-strong need for approval and closed mind which Norman Dixon identified as common factors in catastrophically bad military decision-making are all on prominent display.[126]

As the advance-guard pressed forward, the supply problems became more and more acute – with just 2,350 camels, Lomakin's small force could only carry supplies for 15 days and 120 bullets per man.[127] They crossed the Köpet Dagh on the 23 August with considerable difficulty, but there was no sign of the enemy until they reached Durun, where they dispersed some advanced pickets: the *auls* they came across were mostly deserted. There they learned from some of the Beurma and Qizil-Arvat Turkmen that 'With a few exceptions, all the population of the oasis, with their wives, children and property, had gathered in part at Gök-Tepe, in part at Ashkhabad, with the aim of defending themselves against our advance.'[128] Lomakin's small force pressed on for another 25 *versts* until the fortifications of Gök-Tepe came into view. Figure 9.3[129] shows the route taken.

[125] Lomakin to Alexander Vissarionovich Komarov 20/06/1879 NAG F.545 Op.1 D.1893 ll. 24–5ob.

[126] Norman Dixon, *On the Psychology of Military Incompetence* (London: Jonathan Cape, 1976), 166–7.

[127] Terent'ev, *Istoriya zavoevaniya*, III, 15.

[128] Lomakin to Grand Duke Mikhail Romanov Telegram 24/08/1879, in *PT*, 435; 'Zhurnal zanyatii i voennykh deistvii Akhal-Tekinskogo ekspeditsionnogo otryada', 01/09/1879 RGVIA F.1300 Op.1 D.80 ll. 120–1.

[129] G. Demurov, 'Boi s tekintsami pri Denghil-Tepe, 28 avgusta 1879 goda', *IV* (1881), No. 3, 623.

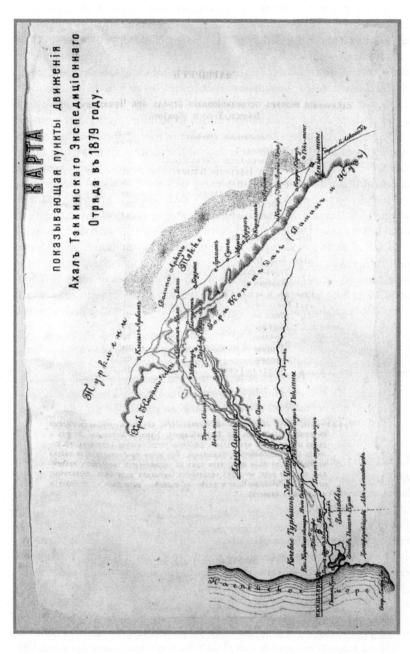

Figure 9.3 Route of the Akhal-Teke expeditionary force from Chikishlar to Denghil-Tepe, 1879.

The first report of the repulse of Lomakin's forces came in the form of a telegram, composed on the 4 September and received in Tiflis from Chikishlar on the 15 September. Lomakin described the strong fortifications the Turkmen had constructed around the small hill of Denghil-Tepe, which he estimated was occupied by up to 15,000 armed men, with another 30,000 elderly, women and children. His twelve guns bombarded the fortress, causing what he claimed were several thousand casualties. 'In view of their tendency to run away at night', he wrote, 'it was essential to quickly inflict a decisive blow on them which could immediately end the expedition. At 5 pm the general assault began. The troops bravely threw themselves against the enemy with bayonets fixed and seized the outer face of the fortress, but, meeting insurmountable resistance with every step, they began to lose many men, and because of this with the coming of evening they were recalled.' The losses he gave initially were 7 officers and 178 men killed, and 16 officers and 234 men wounded.[130] Grand Duke Mikhail immediately passed on the contents of Lomakin's telegram to Alexander II, but added a gloss that described the attack as a 'reconnaissance in strength' and emphasised the 'thousands' of Turkmen losses rather than the repulse of Russian troops.[131] A fuller description of the battle came in Lomakin's general report on the activities of the expedition, compiled on the 1 September, which made the scale of the Russian defeat much clearer. He began by describing the strong position the Turkmen had occupied:

> The enemy had occupied the position in the following fashion. Their main strength, consisting of infantry, armed on the whole with cold steel, such as pikes, *yatagans* [knives] and axes, with only a few armed with smooth-bore, percussion-cap and flint-lock firearms, had gathered in the village of Denghil-Tepe, surrounded by a clay wall about a *sazhen* in height. A part of their infantry occupied a small *qala*, a mill, an *ariq* and some dry gullies that lay before it. On the mill, hidden behind trees, was stationed a falconet, which fired balls about an inch in diameter.[132]

The left and right wings of the position were protected by cavalry, with about 1,000 men on each wing. As the Russian advance guard approached, the Turkmen cavalry also advanced, raising a great cloud of dust, and sought to outflank the Russian column and attack the baggage train. The Cossack sent to warn its commander, Count Borch, was captured by the Turkmen, hacked to pieces and stripped: 'They cut open his chest and left his epaulettes inside, which is how he was identified.' However, the Yerevan infantry managed to beat off the 700 Turkmen who attacked the baggage, and a bombardment with

---

[130] Telegram Lomakin to Grand Duke Mikhail Romanov 04/09/1879 RGVIA F.1300 Op.1 D.77 ll. 118–20, also in *PT*, 438–9.
[131] Grand Duke Mikhail Romanov to Alexander II 15/09/1879, in *PT*, 441–2.
[132] 'Zhurnal zanyatii i voennykh deistvii Akhal-Tekinskogo ekspeditsionnogo otryada', 01/09/1879 RGVIA F.1300 Op.1 D.80 l. 128, also in *PT*, 442–55, misdated to 15/09/1879.

shrapnel and case shot forced them to retreat to the fortress. The Russians surrounded and bombarded the fortress, with the Turkmen unable to return fire except from their falconets, and one larger gun whose shot did not reach the Russian besiegers.[133] As the infantry advanced, a crowd of 500 Turkmen, armed with pikes, *yatagans* and axes, emerged from the advanced positions before the fortress and 'crying "Allah", without firing a shot advanced in a single line to the attack'. The Russians halted this with artillery and volley fire, and then returned to the attack themselves. They managed to storm the little *qala*, the mill, and the *ariqs* and dried gullies before the main fortress, but they were too few to risk an assault on the latter, and settled down to defend those positions until the rest of the column arrived at about 3.30 pm. There followed a bombardment from all twelve Russian guns for about an hour, the *kibitkas* inside the walls making an 'excellent target'. The dry prose of Lomakin's report is in stark contrast to the description in the *Goni-Bek* narrative, which makes it clear that many, if not most, of those crammed within the fortress walls were women and children, and gives some sense of the appalling conditions they suffered under fire:

> ... individual moments and snippets revive in my memory. I remember a clear, sunny day. I was recovering from wounds, but they had still not healed fully. Rifle bullets were hitting the fortress, and occasionally shells. Children were running around and collecting the bullets – their fathers in a spare hour would melt them down into round balls for *hirla* [rifled weapons]. For some children this occupation ended in death – all the same it was necessary to collect them, and the collection – which was within a child's powers – continued. The Russians came close to the fortress wall. From the bustle and conversations around it was clear that there was a danger of the enemy breaking in. I came out of the *tiuma* [dugout] with my weapon. Some with *klych* [curved sabres], others with knives, others with sticks, to the end of which were tied *kirkilyk* [sheepshears] – walked and ran in the direction of the assault. All those who had firearms and pistols had already been there for some time and were firing. Following all of them with my good wishes, I gazed on the sombre faces of all of them. Ahead of me, eighty paces off, came an old woman, carrying at her side a piece of freshly baked *churek* [flatbread]. She came on, paying no attention to the whine of the bullets around her. I was suddenly absorbed by a whole crowd of those running to say farewell. When I looked once again in the direction of the old woman – she lay dead, partly covering the piece of *churek* with her body, drenched with her warm blood. Those passing and running by stopped by her corpse. Squatting down by her, they broke off a piece of the bloodied bread and,

---

[133] According to the *Goni-Bek* narrative this had been captured by the Turkmen from the Persians near Qara-Qala: Ovezbaev, 'Goni-Bek', 25.

putting it into their mouths, continued on their way, saying 'Send to us too, oh Lord, such an easy death.'[134]

When the Russian forces moved to storm the walls, some soldiers did manage to gain a foothold at the top, but, as Lomakin's report explained, the Turkmen resistance was too strong:

> Beyond the walls were numerous defenders, with firearms, bayonets, yatagans and who with blows from their pikes and bullets threw down our soldiers who had raised themselves on the walls. The Georgians also, under strong enemy fire, headed towards the kibitkas and captured them, but they then encountered ditches and ramparts made out of sandbags, felt, kibitkas and the corpses of men and camels, and beyond those ramparts still more defenders, who routed our troops with well-directed fire.[135]

The Turkmen, seeing how small the number of attackers was, then made a sortie to attack the Russian infantry in the flank:

> Seeing the danger, both the grenadiers and the riflemen, beginning from the threatened flank, began to move back, and then after them from all along the ramparts poured a mass of Turkmen, up to 2,000 men, who from the front supported their flank attack. The grenadiers, weakened by their losses during the storming, could not stand it and began to retreat. The Teke followed them right up to the guns, and our artillery was endangered. Our officers were obliged to use their revolvers and the gunners their swords. At that point all four guns fired a salvo of case shot; and when the smoke cleared, before the battery lay the corpses of the foremost Teke, and those behind them halted in hesitation. There followed a second salvo, after which the whole mass of Turkmen retreated back to the aul.[136]

With their line broken, the other infantry battalions were also forced to retreat: one last attempt by the Shirvan battalion to advance towards the walls, band playing, in order to cut off the Turkmen retreat failed, and they lost sixty men before they could return to their previous position.[137] Terent'ev wrote that someone on the Russian side had cried 'back' – and the troops had broken in panic, and rushed back to their artillery, leaving 175 bodies unretrieved and

[134] Ovezbaev, 'Goni-Bek', 25.
[135] 'Zhurnal zanyatii i voennykh deistvii Akhal-Tekinskogo ekspeditsionnogo otryada', 01/09/1879 RGVIA F.1300 Op.1 D.80 l. 137ob.
[136] 'Zhurnal zanyatii i voennykh deistvii Akhal-Tekinskogo ekspeditsionnogo otryada', 01/09/1879 RGVIA F.1300 Op.1 D.80 l. 137ob; this accords almost exactly with the account given by G. Demurov, 'Boi s tekintsami pri Denghil-Tepe, 28 avgusta 1879 goda', IV (1881), No. 3, 620.
[137] 'Zhurnal zanyatii i voennykh deistvii Akhal-Tekinskogo ekspeditsionnogo otryada', 01/09/1879 RGVIA F.1300 Op.1 D.80 l. 139ob–40.

over 600 Berdan rifles in Turkmen hands.[138] As the *Goni-Bek* narrative put it: *'Allah* rang out powerfully, *Ura* feebly, and after a short time *Ura* could not be heard at all.'[139] Turkmen casualties were heavy, and included Berdy Murad Khan, their young commander, killed in the blast of case shot that had turned back the Turkmen sally, and also Tykma Sardar's son, Khan Berdy Sardar.

In his subsequent full report Lomakin gave more details of the casualties, which were almost unprecedentedly severe for Russia's Central Asian campaigns. The heaviest losses were borne by the 3rd Battalion of the 13th Yerevan Grenadier Regiment, which lost 2 officers and 29 men killed, 3 officers and 26 men wounded and 6 missing out of its total strength of 314, a 40% casualty rate among officers and nearly 20% among the men. The 3rd battalion of the 14th Georgian Grenadier Regiment lost 1 officer and 31 men killed and 1 officer and 37 men wounded out of a total strength of 305, a 22% casualty rate. Overall the infantry suffered a 21% casualty rate, almost half of them killed.[140] The artillery and cavalry got off relatively lightly, though another eighteen men were killed there. In the course of the eight hours of the assault, Lomakin's troops fired 218,333 Berdan rifle rounds, 2,100 musket rounds, 1,782 revolver rounds, 269 explosive shells, 291 of canister shot and 569 cartridges.[141] In view of the fact that one-fifth of their small force were now *hors de combat*, and they had enough ammunition left for only one day's further fighting, Lomakin and his officers decided that another assault was not feasible – eyewitness accounts describe a situation of complete chaos, with confusion as to whether the fortress had been taken or not, exhausted men, no facilities for the wounded, no forage for horses and camels, and a lack of leadership from the demoralised officers.[142] The subsequent retreat to Bendessen was difficult because of the heat, but Lomakin's forces were not actively harassed by the Turkmen, although a small group of 200 dogged their steps all the way and prevented them from grazing their remaining camels, for fear they be carried off.[143] One of these parties captured a Turkmen called Mullah Dungdor, who had supposedly acted as a guide for the Russians; he was burnt alive by being pushed head down into a giant *tandur* oven.[144]

[138] Terent'ev, *Istoriya zavoevaniya*, III, 21, 24.
[139] Ovezbaev, 'Goni-Bek', 28.
[140] Lomakin, *Otchet* 15/09/1879 RGVIA F.1300 Op.1 D.77 ll. 162–7.
[141] 'Vedomost' o kolichestve boevykh metallicheskikh patronov i artilleriiskikh snaryadov vypushchennykh pekhotoiu, artilleriiu i kavalerieiu Akhal-Tekinskogo ekspeditsionnogo otryada', 28/08/1829 RGVIA F.1300 Op.1 D.77 ll. 168–9ob.
[142] Demurov, 'Boi s tekintsami', 620; Baranovskii, 'Russkie v Akhal-Tekke', 123–8; Chernyak, 'Ekspeditsiya v Akhal-Teke 1879 goda', VS (1887), No. 10, 266–9.
[143] 'Zhurnal zanyatii i voennykh deistvii Akhal-Tekinskogo ekspeditsionnogo otryada', 01/09/1879 RGVIA F.1300 Op.1 D.80 ll. 141, 152ob.
[144] Ovezbaev, 'Goni-Bek', 28.

On the 6 September, eight days after the assault and the retreat to Bendessen, Lomakin called a council of war to discuss the fate of the expedition, attended by all the senior officers of the force, including Colonel Malama (Main Staff), Major-General Count Borch (Infantry), Prince Sayn-Wittgenstein-Berleburg (Cavalry), Colonel Prozorkevich (Artillery), Prince Dolgorukov, and Colonels Grodekov and Navrotskii of the Main Staff. Grodekov made the familiar argument that a retreat from the oasis would be damaging for Russian prestige, and bolster resistance to Russia in Persia and Afghanistan: 'The best decision would be to remain in the oasis forever, but unfortunately we have no means to do this.'[145] Supplies were so low and so limited that there was a real danger of scurvy breaking out among the men. He believed that their retreat to Beurma had been measured enough that the Turkmen would be unlikely to dare attack them. All the commanders agreed, with Prozorkevich and Wittgenstein noting that the artillery horses were in a pitiful state for lack of fodder. The latter added 'If we leave the force in the oasis, it will just be so that they can write in the newspapers that the Russians remained at Akhal-Teke. We should look on this expedition as a reconnaissance. It will be possible to conquer the Akhal-Teke only by using the same system that was practised to conquer the western Caucasus [i.e. through gradual encirclement and a scorched earth policy]. The system of raids should have no place.'[146] While Malama suggested lingering as long as possible to avoid any impression of retreat, the majority were in favour of moving off immediately. So many of the force's camels had died that not only had it been impossible for the main body to reinforce the advance guard, but also the advance guard itself had been forced to retreat to the nearest supply depot.[147]

Lomakin's first report to Tergukasov, his new commander, was largely an exercise in self-exoneration. He blamed everything on supply problems; already by the middle of August they had used up over half of the supplies stored at Chikishlar, and had only one and a half months' worth left. Of the nearly 13,000 camels they had started out with, those from Mangishlaq were already under-nourished and unusable after three months' waiting in the hinterland of Chikishlar; the Atabai Yomuds took back the 1,500 camels they had rented to the Russians, 900 others escaped, and 2,000 that had been taken from the Jafarbai Yomuds had to be returned. Of the remainder, another 1,000 camels had died by the middle of August, leaving them just 4,000 camels. Of these, 1,500 were used to carry supplies for the advance force, leaving just 2,500 for the main force, enough to carry food for just 15 days. Dolgorukov's

[145] 'Protokol zasedanie voennogo soveta, obsuzhdavshago vopros o polozhenii Akhal-Tekinskogo otryada', 06/09/1879 RGVIA F.1300 Op.1 D.77 ll. 404–7.

[146] 'Protokol zasedanie voennogo soveta, obsuzhdavshago vopros o polozhenii Akhal-Tekinskogo otryada', 06/09/1879 RGVIA F.1300 Op.1 D.77 ll. 409–10.

[147] Grand Duke Mikhail to Miliutin 01/10/1879 RGVIA F.1300 Op.1 D.77 ll. 171–ob.

unprovoked attack on the Atabai Yomuds had brought them another 2,000 camels, but there was still a snag – they had only 400 saddles, all of them in bad condition.[148] With the commissariat in such disarray, Lomakin claimed, there was only one possibility left if the expedition was not to be abandoned altogether, which was to send a light, flying column forward. This, Lomakin claimed, had been the late General Lazarev's intention, which he had continued in obedience to his orders. Some form of armed reconnaissance was absolutely necessary because 'we up until then had only the most vague and shadowy understanding of the Teke and their oasis; you cannot find reliable scouts here for any amount of money; we could only cast light of some sort on this region and its savage inhabitants through our own means.'[149] As the supply problems increased, it became clear that, rather than eight battalions as originally planned, this advance force could be made up of only three or four. The remaining camels were so weak that sending them back to Chat to resupply the force, a distance of 300–400 *versts* there and back, was impossible, and would only have deprived them of transport altogether.

> They say we shouldn't have gone on further; but how would that have been possible, how could any of us have dared even to think of it, after we found ourselves already almost in the oasis and had already had two or three encounters with the enemy? We would then have been forced to return all the same after three to four weeks in the same deplorable state that we find ourselves in now; that is, to return not only from Bam and Beurma, but from Bendessen, Khwaja Qala, Ters Akana, and to return without any result; in such circumstances they could indeed reproach us with indecisiveness, weakness, say that we had lost the vital moment, become scared, cowardly. No alternative was left to us but to go on, in order to attain some kind of result . . .[150]

When Tergukasov finally reached his new command in the middle of October, he submitted a damning report on the poor state of the troops – undernourished and sick – which also mercilessly dissected the failings which had led to defeat. The report was heavily annotated by Grand Duke Mikhail, with numerous comments, underlinings and exclamation marks. Tergukasov began by noting that there was no permanent communication between Chikishlar and the other fortified posts the Russians had established. None of the correspondence received from Baku and Tiflis after the 1 August was forwarded onwards until the 17 September (Comment: 'unforgivable'). Even the priest who accompanied the expedition was not properly supplied with the robes, utensils, bread

[148] Lomakin to Tergukasov 30/09/1879 RGVIA F.1300 Op.1 D.77 ll. 226–8, also in *PT*, 458–61, though Il'yasov describes the document as without an addressee, having apparently seen a different copy.
[149] Lomakin to Tergukasov 30/09/1879 RGVIA F.1300 Op.1 D.77 l. 228.
[150] Lomakin to Tergukasov 30/09/1879 RGVIA F.1300 Op.1 D.77 l. 231.

and wine he needed to celebrate the eucharist (this note was underlined three times with the comment 'And this! Why was it not communicated in time?'). 'In the administration of the transport *complete chaos* ruled' – the ostensible head of transport was too distant from his charges to see that they were properly looked after and found grazing, and the officers who were supposed to be in charge of the transport divisions in reality did not assume their responsibilities: 'The drivers [Turkmen and Qazaqs], seeing that the camels were being passed from one hand to another by ones and twos, refused to look after them, and it was necessary to make ordinary soldiers the drivers.' The entire carrying strength of the force now consisted of just 300 camels, effectively meaning that it was immobile.[151] Meanwhile the troops had not received either their regular or their campaign pay for several months (marginal comment: *Turetskie poryadki!* – 'Turkish customs!') as the commissariat had no money – the only exceptions were those attached to the Staff (marginal comment: 'Shameful!').

> Finally, and most importantly, there was no unity of command in the force – each did what he wanted to, and obeyed only when he chose, and if he didn't like one order or the other, then he did not fulfil it, or even cancelled it, and nobody at any point was reprimanded for this. This last circumstance was the reason for all the remaining irregularities enumerated above, and all the disorders which crept into all branches of the force's arrangements . . . [marginal comment: 'and this will serve as a good lesson for the future!'][152]

Tergukasov also noted that the conditions in Transcaspia were very different from those the troops were used to in the Caucasus, or during the recent war with Turkey, and that those serving on the eastern shore of the Caspian should receive additional allowances because of the 'appalling climate'.

An even more revealing verdict came from Colonel Malama of the Main Staff, commanding at Chikishlar, who had been with the force throughout and witnessed its problems at first hand. He explicitly set out to correct what he saw as inaccuracies in Lomakin's report, which had tried to foist the blame on the late General Lazarev. Lazarev, he wrote, had intended to establish an advanced magazine at Beurma or Bent-Hassan, and had ordered the commanders of the three columns of the expedition to send their camels back to Chat or Duz-Olum to resupply once they arrived there. Malama had been at Duz Olum awaiting the arrival of the camels of the advanced column when he received the news of Lazarev's death. He immediately suggested to Lomakin that he take command, assuming that he would continue to follow Lazarev's plan. Lomakin, however, proposed to move out immediately, without awaiting the arrival of the baggage camels:

[151] Tergukasov to Grand Duke Mikhail 18/10/1879 RGVIA F.1300 Op.1 D.77 ll. 280–2.
[152] Tergukasov to Grand Duke Mikhail 18/10/1879 RGVIA F.1300 Op.1 D.77 ll. 283, 285, 291.

On the morning of the 16 August I informed Major-General Lomakin that we could not and should not move out before the arrival of the camels, and that because of this it was mistaken to take the companie of the Daghestan battalion, without having any baggage transport for them; but in reply I heard 'Never mind, it will be worse still ahead, and we must move on.' All these arrangements were in the first place not in agreement with the views of the late Adjutant-General Lazarev, and in the second place profoundly mistaken. That they were not in agreement is visible from the report, and that they were mistaken is evident from the following: (1) in setting off without waiting for the camels we were rejecting even the idea of creating a supply depot at Bent Hasan and Khwaja Qala, which we should not have neglected. Finally, with the non-arrival of the camels the echelon could not carry all the supplies earmarked for it, and the dragoons even left some of the fodder behind at Duz-Olum.[153]

Malama accused Lomakin of neglecting supply arrangements and exhausting the camels unnecessarily, adding that there was no reason to hurry, but 'the slogan became onward and onward!' When they did arrive before the fortifications at Gök-Tepe, Lomakin called a council of war with the heads of the infantry, cavalry and artillery, but they couldn't agree on the best tactics to follow. Dolgorukov wanted to outflank the fortified position with cavalry, while others thought they should attack from the side facing the *aul* of Yangi-Qala, but neither of these proposals found favour. In the end they decided on the most obvious course – a frontal assault on the side facing them – which proved the worst possible option: 'Suffice to say that we attacked, as you can judge from the plan, the strongest part of the *aul* – namely the corner C3 [referring to a numbered plan in the report], on the faces of which there was a breastwork', ignoring other sections of the walls that were weaker. The decision to storm, he added, was of course the responsibility of the commander, who would not have undertaken it had he not had some hope of success. However, Malama attributed the Russians' failure overall to their underestimation of the enemy:

> Above all it was our lack of knowledge of the enemy that was to blame, and in part the raid by Colonel Prince Dolgorukov [to capture camels from the Atabai Yomuds, at the beginning of the expedition] after which many concluded that the Teke were *khalatniki*[154] who were not worthy of any attention, and we feared only that they might run away.[155]

---

[153] Report by Colonel Malama 05/11/1879 RGVIA F.1300 Op.1 D.77 ll. 379–90.
[154] Literally 'wearers of dressing-gowns' – a term that is almost impossible to translate accurately, but which carries overtones of carelessness, idleness and oriental sloth (the Russian word for dressing-gown – *khalat* – is derived from the Arabic/Persian term for a robe of honour). Terent'ev, clearly drawing on Malama's report, uses the same phrase and comes to the same conclusion – *Istoriya zavoevaniya*, III, 18.
[155] Report by Colonel Malama 05/11/1879 RGVIA F.1300 Op.1 D.77 ll. 391–2.

In other words, what Patrick Porter has called 'Military Orientalism' caused the Russians to severely underestimate their opponents.[156] This judgement was echoed by V. Shakhovskoi, one of the officers with the expedition, who also wrote that Lomakin had made a serious error in surrounding the fortress entirely to prevent the enemy from running away: 'Every Caucasus military man, old or young, knows that you can subdue an Asiatic *aul* only when you leave a loophole for the fleeing enemy – otherwise the Asiatic will be driven to terrible desperation.'[157] Lomakin himself continued to insist that the failure was owing to difficulties of supply that could not have been foreseen. As late as the 4 September, six days after the repulse of the assault, he claimed that he had not been informed of the parlous state of the commissariat, which is why he had not mentioned it in his first report; it was only subsequently he learned that, rather than having 2,500 camels able to carry 20,000 *poods* of supplies, they had only 500 still fit for work, which would not be able to carry more than 2,000 between them.[158] The recriminations and finger-pointing would continue, but there was no doubt that the expedition had ended in humiliating failure.

9.5 Skobelev's Campaign

There was never any question of allowing Lomakin's reverse to remain unavenged; nor does there seem to have been any doubt as to who should carry out that vengeance. Tergukasov ruled himself out because of ill-health, and confirmed this by dying shortly afterwards. The Caucasus military command proposed one of their own, General Arnold Wilhelmovich von Schach, but the Tsar, probably following Miliutin's advice, thought differently. Fresh from his recent triumphs at Lovcha and Plevna in the Russo-Turkish War (later also assiduously chronicled by his constant lieutenant, A. N. Kuropatkin),[159] which had been immortalised in paint (in somewhat ambiguous terms) by Vasilii Vereshchagin,[160] it had to be Mikhail Dmitrievich Skobelev. On the 6 January 1880 Miliutin sent a telegram to Grand Duke Mikhail announcing the following:

> ... on the proposed appointment of General Schach, His Imperial Majesty, while doing full justice to the worthiness of that general, finds it more prudent and necessary to entrust the direction of affairs in the

[156] Patrick Porter, *Military Orientalism: Eastern War through Western Eyes* (Oxford, Oxford University Press, 2013), 27–48.

[157] Shakhovskoi, 'Ekspeditsiya protiv Akhal-Tekintsev', *RS* (1885), No. 4, 171.

[158] Lomakin to Tergukasov 15/11/1879 RGVIA F.1300 Op.1 D.77 ll. 402–3.

[159] A. N. Kuropatkin, *Deistvie otryadov General Skobeleva v Russko-Turetskoi Voine 1877–78 g.: Lovcha i Plevna* (St Pb.: Tip. Glavnogo Shtaba, 1885).

[160] Vereshchagin's famous painting *Skobelev at Shipka* (1878) shows the 'White General' receiving the cheers of his men as he rides along their front – but the foreground of the painting is dominated by the corpses of the dead.

Transcaspian region, under the current circumstances, to a general who is more acquainted with the *modus operandi* [*obraz deistvii*], and proposes to commission for this purpose, under the guidance of your Highness, General Skobelev.[161]

This was also a victory for the Turkestanis over the Caucasians; while Skobelev had served with the Mangishlaq force during the Khiva expedition owing to his differences with von Kaufman, he had cut his teeth in Turkestan, and his bloody exploits in Ferghana were surely what the Tsar and Miliutin had in mind when they referred to his familiarity with the *modus operandi* needed in Transcaspia. In this they would not be disappointed. In September Skobelev sent a message to Kuropatkin asking him whether he wished to form a force in the Amu-Darya Division to take part in the forthcoming expedition against the Akhal-Teke.[162] In October von Kaufman agreed to the despatch of a small Turkestani force of 500 men and 200 horses, though he noted that it could not arrive before the middle of December at the earliest, even though part of the route was by water along the Amu-Darya.[163] Given that a force of this size could hardly make any difference to the outcome, and Skobelev's specific request that it be commanded by his old comrade in arms Kuropatkin (who would end up directing the siege works at Gök-Tepe and leading the main storming column), it seems probable that this was simply a means of giving the *Turkestantsy* their share of the forthcoming laurels, and perhaps even for Skobelev to have a suitable chronicler of his exploits on hand. Certainly *Turkestantsy* – Grodekov, Kuropatkin, Terent'ev – would have the decisive say in how the Transcaspian campaign was recorded and remembered, as their works became by far the most influential.[164] While initially Transcaspia would be administered largely by Caucasian officers under General A. V. Komarov,

[161] Miliutin to Grand Duke Mikhail Romanov 06/01/1880, in *PT*, 464.
[162] Fride to Kuropatkin 19/09/1880 RGVIA F.1392 Op.1 D.34, 'O komandirovanii Polkovnika Kuropatkina s otryadom v Akhal-Tekinskuiu ekspeditsiu', l. 1.
[163] Von Kaufman to Miliutin 31/10/1880, in *PT*, 481–2; in the end the expedition took the more direct route across the desert, meeting the main column from Krasnovodsk at Bami. Captain Muravtsev published an account of the march, which was also later partly translated into English: Kapitan Muravtsev, 'Turkestanskii otryad v Akhal-Tekinskoi ekspeditsii 1880 god', *VS* (1882), No. 3, 159–83; No. 4, 358–76; No. 5, 167–92; No. 12, 292–9; (1883), No. 1, 149–58; No. 2, 288–332; 'March of the Turkestan Detachment across the Desert from the Amu', trans. J. J. Leverson, *Journal of the Royal United Service Institution* 26 (1883), 568–85.
[164] Grodekov, *Voina v Turkmenii*; A. N. Kuropatkin, *Zavoevaniya Turkmenii (pokhod v Akhal-Teke v 1880–1881 gg.) s ocherkom voennykh deistvii v Srednei Azii s 1839 po 1876 g.* (St Pb.: V. Berezovskii, 1899); Terent'ev, *Istoriya zavoevaniya*, III, 1–228. Visiting Grodekov in 1882, Charles Marvin noted that he 'is writing an official history of Skobelev's great campaign, under the supervision of Skobeleff himself': *The Russian Advance towards India*, 40. See further Campbell, 'Bloody Belonging'.

Figure 9.4 Alexei Nikolaevich Kuropatkin (Wikimedia Commons).

from 1890 its Governor was Kuropatkin (Figure 9.4), who forged the provincial administration very much in his own image.[165]

Along with the appointment of Skobelev, the other crucial early decision that set this campaign apart from all those which had preceded it in Central Asia was the order to construct a light railway from the Mikhailovskoe (Uzun-Ada) inlet to Qizil-Arvat, the forerunner of the Transcaspian Railway.[166] Preceding Kitchener's celebrated advance through the Sudan by fifteen years, this would be the first steam-powered European imperial conquest on land. At the same time a submarine telegraph cable was laid between Baku and Krasnovodsk, replacing the indirect line via Astrabad and Tehran.[167] This did not entirely free Skobelev from the transport and communication difficulties that had afflicted Lomakin, as his force still required over 20,000 camels to transport supplies from the railhead deeper into Akhal-Teke territory, but it did cut out the most difficult part of the route nearest the coast. For all his violent impulsiveness, Skobelev was also well aware that the careful preparation of commissariat and supplies would be key to the success of his campaign.[168] With characteristic and chilling bombast he wrote that

[165] Alexander Morrison, 'The Pahlen Commission and the Restoration of Rectitude in Transcaspia, 1908–1909', *Monde(s). Histoire, Espaces, Relations* No. 4 (2013), 45–64.
[166] Gurchin to Pavlov 07/02/1880, 06/03/1880, in *PT*, 471.
[167] *Opisanie ustroistva podvodnoi telegrafnoi linii chrez Kaspiiskoe more mezhdu gg. Baku i Krasnovodsk* (St Pb.: n.p., 1880), in *TS*, Vol. 349, 137–55.
[168] 'Osobennosti voiny v Srednei Azii i podgotovka k ekspeditsii 1880–1881 gg.', NAG F. I-1087 Op.1 D.605 ll. 4–ob; Callwell makes particular note of this paradox in *Small Wars*, 46.

I feel that the forces entrusted to me must act both swiftly and decisively, but I am constrained by the insufficiency of means in both supplies and transport. Here in Asia risk in warfare is much less justifiable than in Europe. Asia has always understood victory and defeat in its own way; victory must without fail bring material loss to the enemy; here it is necessary to act without risks and deal the final blow after victory, and these two necessities exclude haste in the period of preparation.[169]

The obvious parallel is with the siege of Aq Masjid almost thirty years before, where Blaramberg's repulse in 1852, and Perovskii's own memories of failure in the 1839–40 Khiva expedition, made the restoration of Russian prestige paramount. Perovskii took no risks during the summer of 1853, as his troops carefully dug and sapped their way towards the mud walls of the little fortress, despite complaints that the siege was taking too long (see Chapter 3). A similarly methodical approach was visible at Gök-Tepe in 1880–1: in the sheer numbers involved (11,000 men and 3,000 horses),[170] in the massive accumulation of supplies, in the construction of the railway, in careful advance reconnaissance, including the despatch of a small force to explore and sketch the fortifications in August, and in the time and effort spent on siege works, digging trenches and saps, and mining the walls before the final assault in January 1881.[171] All this cost money: in February 1881 the Main Staff estimated that the conquest of Transcaspia, from 1869 to the victory at Gök-Tepe, had cost over 29 million roubles. While this included almost 8 million roubles for the construction of the railway, it was notable that Skobelev's expedition of 1880–1 had cost twice as much as Lomakin's the year before – 11 as opposed to 5.5 million roubles.[172] Skobelev's campaign was a juggernaut, crushing all before it until its final, bloody climax. Designed to wipe out the memory of Lomakin's humiliation, it certainly succeeded, at least in the Russian mind[173] – and yet it was crucially informed by the campaigning experiences of 1869–79. This was most obviously true when it came to the commissariat arrangements, but also of the exemplary violence which Skobelev unleashed on the Turkmen after defeat. There were to be no more aspersions cast on Russian prestige, of

[169] Skobelev to the Minister in Tehran 13/05/1880, in *PT*, 475.
[170] Kuropatkin, *Zavoevanie Turkmenii*, 107–8.
[171] Makarov to the Minister of Marine 05/08/1880, in *PT*, 479.
[172] Heiden to Miliutin 06/02/1881, in *PT*, 484.
[173] This was also a function of the posthumous cult of Skobelev, who died in mysterious circumstances the following year. Apart from the official histories and campaign memoirs, the Akhal-Teke campaign of 1880–1 quickly became the subject of short popular works aimed at a school audience: see for instance L. K. Artamonov (ed.), *Pokorenie Turkmen-Tekintsev russkimi voiskami pod nachal'stvom General Skobeleva v 1880–1881 g.* Trudy Pedagogicheskogo Muzeya po sostavleniiu chteniya dlya voisk i naroda (St Pb.: Tip. M. M. Stasiulevicha, 1884); K. M. Fedorov *Akhal-Tekinskaya ekspeditsiya 1880–1 gg.: Geok-Tepinskii boi M. D. Skobeleva* (Askhabad: Elektropechatnya K. M. Fedorova, 1904).

the 'Asiatics' claiming victory after a strategic Russian retreat, or regrouping to fight once again.[174] Skobelev would no doubt have indulged the sadistic tendencies he displayed in Ferghana in any case, but the need to wipe out the impression of weakness that Lomakin's repeated forays and retreats had supposedly created provided him with the perfect justification.

The proverb that victory has 100 fathers is amply confirmed by the Transcaspian campaign of 1880–1, where, apart from the official histories written by Kuropatkin and Grodekov (which barely mentioned the prior campaigns), those participating produced a plethora of book-length campaign memoirs or shorter journal and newspaper articles.[175] Most of these are formulaic descriptions of blazing heat, savage orientals and Russian bravery (with a particular emphasis on the dazzling figure of Skobelev himself), but some do rise above the genre and enable us to acquire a clearer sense of the lived experience of the long march, siege and final storming. Here we return again to Alexei Maslov's often unintentionally revealing memoirs. Maslov noted that from Mikhailovskoe he travelled as light as he could, carrying no more than a sack of barley, a pair of boots, an overcoat, a few changes of linen, a pound of sugar, a teapot and two bottles of cognac – a contrast, he added, to the baggage of the Irish journalist O'Donovan, which according to contemporaries consisted *exclusively* of cognac.[176] He was dismissive of the Qazaq auxiliaries from Mangishlaq who accompanied the column, writing that they 'were not distinguished for their heroism' and complaining that they did not speak a word of Russian, though he did grudgingly concede that they were more dependable than the Turkmen auxiliaries and made good drivers and messengers. He also noted that the armed Qazaq militia formed by Lomakin and Lazarev had been disbanded by Skobelev, on the grounds that 'it does not do to revive in them the spirit of military comradeship'.[177] Maslov's party of six seems to have travelled without an escort of any kind until they reached Fort Qazanjik, where the Akhal-Teke oasis could be said to begin. On the 25 November Tykma Sardar did attack the Russian supply lines back to Mikhailovskoe, killing 35 men, carrying off 2,000 camels (which were later recovered) and disrupting the laying of telegraph lines by a small force which included Baranovskii.[178] Partly thanks

---

[174] Kuropatkin lays particular emphasis on this aspect: *Zavoevanie Turkmenii*, 101.

[175] See e.g. K. Geins, 'Ocherk boevoi zhizni Akhaltekinskogo otryada 1880–1881 gg.', *VS* (1882), No. 6, 340–59; No. 7, 151–9; No. 8, 336–48; No. 9, 155–67; No. 10, 317–28; No. 11, 128–42; A. A. Maier, *God v peskakh: Nabroski i ocherki Akhal-Tekinskoi ekspeditsii 1880–1881 (iz vospominanii ranenago)* (Kronstadt: Pechatano v Tip. Kronshtadtnogo Vestnika, 1886); A. V. Shcherbak, *Akhal-Tekinskaya ekspeditsiya Generala Skobeleva v 1880–81 godakh* (St Pb.: A. S. Suvorin, 1887). On the broader genre of writing that emerged from the campaign see Campbell, 'Bloody Belonging'.

[176] A. N. Maslov, *Zavoevanie Akhal-Tekke* (St Pb.: A. S. Suvorin, 1887), 2.

[177] *Ibid.*, 3–4.

[178] *Ibid.*, 19–24.

to the railway, partly thanks to cautious and careful planning, the logistical disasters which had repeatedly beset Lomakin were avoided, and the bulk of Skobelev's force reached Gök-Tepe and laid siege to it on the 18 December 1880.

Grodekov's official report or diary of the siege, compiled five months later, and Skobelev's official published report both make it clear that the three weeks which passed from the investing of Gök-Tepe to the final storming on the 12 January 1881 were marked by a regular, grinding routine – constant bombardment of the enclosure behind the thick mud walls of the fortress, frequent sallies by Turkmen horsemen, which were beaten off at the cost of a small trickle of casualties, occasional ragged small-arms fire on the Russian camp from the fortress walls, and all the while the gradual advance of the siege works, a zig-zag of saps that allowed the Russians to approach closer and closer, with the aim of exploding a mine beneath them. After the 4 January the Turkmen sallies ceased, as they had sent most of their horses away, and they awaited the storming of the fortress.[179] Maslov noted that the walls of the fortress had been greatly strengthened since 1879, while the Turkmen had managed to acquire some Berdan rifles from the unsuccessful assault.[180]

Maslov described the atmosphere in the camp as utter chaos, as officers and men hunted for their baggage and horses, but 'charlatans and conjurors always carve out a road for themselves'. He and his companions spent their time wandering from *kibitka* to *kibitka*, playing cards and hunting pheasants and hares while they waited for the siege to begin.[181] As bullets flew from the Turkmen positions through the Russian camp, Maslov sketched the following vignette:

> And here comes a batman in an old officers' tunic without epaulettes and a crumpled overcoat with a canary-coloured kepi: under his armpit he carries a portable samovar; at his side, in a dirty napkin, tied in a knot, and on a knapsack on his shoulder unwashed glasses and plates are shaking and clinking; near him is a platoon clerk. They are clearly in good relations with each other, but occasionally use '*Vy*' [the polite form of address] ...
>
> – 'Why didn't you put the samovar in the wagon?'
> – 'Out of the question. The spigot would break, or something else. I need to keep it under my eye ... there are only two or three samovars for the entire force, the rest are kettles. Thank God I'm carrying the last batch – I've been carrying things from the old spot since this morning.'

---

[179] Grodekov, 'Zhurnal voennykh deistvii za yanvar' mesyats' 1881 goda', 05/05/1881 RGVIA F.1300 Op.1 D.90 ll. 2–50, also in *PT*, 497–529, misdated to 2 May; M. D. Skobelev, 'Osada i shturm kreposti Dengil-Tepe (Geok-Tepe)', *VS* (1881), No. 4, 3–64.

[180] Maslov, *Zavoevanie Akhal-Tekke*, 30–2.

[181] *Ibid.*, 41.

- ‘Perhaps you could give me some tea . . . I’ve had a hard time myself, carrying all the stationery . . .’
- ‘Come in the evening; the *barins* [nobles – i.e. officers] will be on duty at night – and as those Teke have started firing, one may get a bullet in the leg, God forgive!’
- ‘Now the artilleryman said that the battery commander’s cow was killed with a huge bullet – see how they’re firing!’
- ‘It’s nothing, this is just what they do at the beginning, firing at the camp. They’ll get into the habit, then ease off and stop.’[182]

He went on to describe other homely details of the siege, such as the cooks boiling up cabbage and chopping meat for *shchi* (cabbage soup) – only to be interrupted by the arrival of a body, the first death Maslov had seen, shot through the eye: ‘It was pitiful to look on that old, dusty uniform.’ These juxtapositions of the domestic and the sanguinary recur throughout his text – a few pages on he described a young doctor trying to staunch the blood of a wounded NCO, while beside them his orderly brewed tea.[183] The siege also produced a martyr on the Russian side when a gunner called Agafon Nikitin, from the appropriately named district of Calvary, was captured by the Turkmen during a sortie from the fortress on the 30 December 1880, and suffered death by torture rather than serve his captors by directing their one cannon against his comrades (Figure 9.5).[184]

However, the casualties in the Russian camp were minor compared with the destruction wrought on the Turkmen crammed into the fortified enclosure by Russian artillery and mortar fire. A Persian slave called Medjifir [*sic*], who escaped from the Turkmen camp during the siege, told the Russians during his debriefing that he thought there were 10,000 *kibitkas* in total in the fortress, and that already by the 5 January the number of those killed was like ‘a large town’.[185] In his official report, Grodekov noted that the advanced observation post had counted 9,280 *kibitkas* inside the fortress, with a total population they estimated at 45,000. There was little movement during the day, as the Turkmen avoided exposing themselves to Russian fire, only manning the ramparts *en masse* at night, in fear of a surprise attack. He expressed satisfaction at the effect of Russian shelling, which forced the Turkmen to constantly shift their *kibitkas*.[186] All the while Skobelev’s sappers dug steadily, approaching the south-eastern corner of the fortress by a series of

---

[182] *Ibid.*, 49.

[183] *Ibid.*, 53, 57.

[184] Anon., *Russkim voinam na pamyat’ ob Agafon Nikitine, pogibshem mucheniskoiu smer-t’iu v 1880 godu za Veru, Tsarya i Otechestvo, pri vzyatii nashimi voiskami kreposti Geok-Tepé* (St Pb.: n.p., 1902), 1, 19–21.

[185] ‘Pokazaniya Persiyanina Medzhifir, zhitelya Bishkalminskoi kreposti, bezhavshego 5 yanvarya 1881 goda iz ukrepleniya Dengli-Tepe’, RGVIA F.165 Op.1 D.248 ll. 97*ob*, 99.

[186] Grodekov, ‘Zhurnal voennykh deistvii za yanvar’ mesyats’ 1881 goda’, 05/05/1881 RGVIA F.1300 Op.1 D.90 ll. 2–50, in *PT*, 507.

Figure 9.5 An anonymous depiction of the martyrdom of Agafon Nikitin (1902).

zig-zags. Skobelev himself seems to have had some concerns over morale, judging from an impatient note in French which he despatched to Kuropatkin on the 29 December:

> I beg you my dear Colonel to take well into consideration that, notwith-
> standing that our losses have been quite considerable, what matters is
> victory. Restore morale whatever it may cost: you know me well enough,
> dear Colonel, not to doubt that, having burnt up our reserves, I will know
> how to make the last of our soldiers pass the Rubicon. I hear a lot of jokes
> [...] make them all shut up. I will have the chatterboxes shot, whatever
> their rank might be. The greatest battles have been lost through having
> allowed chattering in the ranks.[187]

[187] 'Vous prie cher Colonel de bien prendre en considération que désormais cela c'est de
pertes plus du moins considérables, qu'il s'agit mais bien de victoire. Remontez le moral
coute que coute; vous me connaissez assez cher Colonel, pour ne pas douter qu'ayant
brulé nos raisseaux, je saurais faire passe le Rubican du dernier de nos soldats. J'entends
dire un tas de blagues [...] Fuire taisez tout le monde. Je ferais fusiller sur les bavards s'il
le faut quoi que soit son grade. Les plus grands batailles ont été perdues pour avais permis
le bavardage dans le rangs.' Skobelev to Kuropatkin 29/12/1880 RGVIA F.165 Op.1
D.248 'Perepiska nachal'nika Turkestanskogo otryada Polkovnika Kuropatina
s komanduishchim voiskami Generalom Skobelevym M.' ll.40ob – 41.

Initially the assault was planned for the morning of the 10 January, but the chief engineer then advised that the mine chambers underneath the walls of the fortress could not be made ready in time, and it was postponed to the 12 January, when 72 *poods* of gunpowder were to be exploded beneath the walls.[188] Even then, Maslov remarked that several officers thought that the trenches needed to be put in better order and the soldiers given a few days' rest before the assault, to which Skobelev's response was 'We didn't come here to dig holes, but to press forward! We must hurry! We must finish!'[189] The final assault began at 7 am on the 12 January. The artillery had already succeeded in opening up one breach on the left flank of the siege works, and the mines were detonated at 11.20 am, opening up a vast breach on the eastern side of the fortress. 'All right lads? The enemy are scum (*dryan'*)', Maslov reported Skobelev as saying at this point, drawing a loud *Ura* from his men as he exposed himself to enemy fire.[190] A column under Major Sivinis, in Kuropatkin's division, made the first attempt to storm this breach, where 'Notwithstanding the strength and unexpectedness of the blast, which annihilated all the defenders of the walls who were in that section, the enemy flung themselves into the crater, forming themselves up along where the walls had been, and meeting Major Sivinis's column with accurate fire, pikes and cold steel.'[191] Another column under Colonel Kozelkov simultaneously attacked the breach formed by artillery on the opposite side. While the latter column had to be reinforced before they could overcome the fierce small-arms fire and bombardment with stones, by half-past twelve the Russians had firmly established themselves within the fortress and occupied the small hill of Denghil-Tepe at its centre which commanded the whole of the interior (Figure 9.6). Despite continued fierce resistance and hand-to-hand fighting among the *kibitkas* within it, the Turkmen began to break and flee, and were pursued into the surrounding desert.[192]

Here we come to the single most notorious aspect of the storming of Gök-Tepe – the massacre of fleeing and unarmed Turkmen which followed it. Colonel Gaidarov's column reported counting 6,500 corpses within the walls of the fortress, and another 8,000 scattered about it – though they did not specify their age or sex.[193] Grodekov's report noted that 'It was only after

[188] Grodekov 'Zhurnal voennykh deistvii za yanvar' mesyats' 1881 goda' 05/05/1881 RGVIA F.1300 Op.1 D.90 ll.2–50, in *PT*, 508–9.

[189] Maslov, *Zavoevanie Akhal-Tekke*, 64.

[190] *Ibid.*, 89.

[191] Grodekov, 'Zhurnal voennykh deistvii za yanvar' mesyats' 1881 goda', 05/05/1881 RGVIA F.1300 Op.1 D.90 ll. 2–50, in *PT*, 513–14; see also Kuropatkin, *Zavoevanie Turkmenii*, 206–7; Grodekov, *Voina v Turkmenii*, III, 284.

[192] Grodekov, 'Zhurnal voennykh deistvii za yanvar' mesyats' 1881 goda', 05/05/1881 RGVIA F.1300 Op.1 D.90 ll. 2–50, in *PT*, 514–16.

[193] Grodekov, 'Zhurnal voennykh deistvii za yanvar' mesyats' 1881 goda', 05/05/1881 RGVIA F.1300 Op.1 D.90 ll. 2–50, in *PT*, 520.

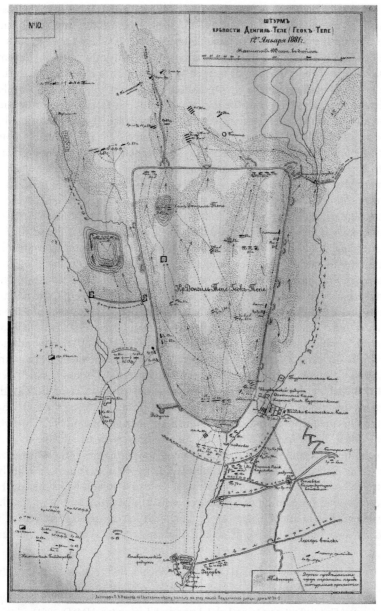

Figure 9.6 Plan of the storming of Denghil-Tepe (Gök-Tepe) (Skobelev, 'Osada i shturm kreposti Dengil-Tepe').

the capture of the fortress that it was possible to appreciate the terrible losses which the enemy had suffered during the siege from artillery and small-arms fire. Within the fortress it was possible to see *kibitka*s where entire groups of the dead lay in the same condition in which death had come to them. In some *kibitka*s up to twenty corpses lay heaped up. From this it was visible that during the last days of the siege the enemy did not bury their dead, but simply piled them up in different parts of the fortress.'[194] Skobelev's official report (which was almost immediately translated into English) stated that the pursuing troops killed 8,000 Turkmen 'of both sexes' (*oboego pola*).[195] On this point both he and Grodekov were specifically questioned by Charles Marvin, and both apparently confirmed it, this being the occasion for Skobelev's notorious remark that 'I hold it as a principle, that in Asia the duration of peace is in direct proportion to the slaughter you inflict on the enemy. The harder you hit them, the longer they will be quiet afterwards. We killed nearly 20,000 Turcomans at Geok Tepé. The survivors will not soon forget the lesson.'[196] In subsequent accounts this aspect – the killing of women and (presumably) children – faded into the background. In his private notes on the Gök-Tepe campaign Kuropatkin wrote that most of the Turkmen found dead around the fortress had been wounded during the siege and died while fleeing, and that the claim that 8,000 Turkmen were deliberately 'chopped up' (*porublennye*) was exaggerated.[197] In their official histories Kuropatkin and Grodekov both wrote that the 'pursuit and hewing' (*rubka*) of the Turkmen by the cavalry continued for up to 15 *verst*s, without specifying whether these included women and children – though Kuropatkin wrote that, while all the Turkmen males were either killed or driven away, 5,000 women and children remained in the fortress that night.[198] Maslov did not shy away from describing the sufferings of the Turkmen women and children under bombardment, and the many who were killed; he expressed admiration for the bravery of the defenders both during the siege and during the storming of the fortress, writing of one tall, muscular Turkmen warrior that as he lay dying 'he was somehow with his outstretched hands defending that scrap of his native soil on which he lay'. He also described the looting of the fortress which followed, and the mania this created in Russia and Europe for Turkmen carpets in subsequent years ('in 1883 I saw them in a shop selling Eastern artefacts on the Boulevard

---

[194] 'Polozhenie Tekintsev v kreposti Geok-Tepe vo vremya osady eya', 05/05/1881 RGVIA F.1300 Op.1 D.90 ll. 30*ob*–5*ob*, also in *PT*, 520–1.

[195] Skobelev, 'Osada i shturm kreposti Dengil-Tepe', 52; *Siege and Assault of Denghil-Tépé: General Skobeleff's Report* trans. Lt J. J. Leverson R.E. (London: HMSO, 1881), 54.

[196] Marvin, *The Russian Advance towards India*, 98–9.

[197] A. N. Kuropatkin, 'Neskol'ko zametok po ekspeditsii v Akhal-Tekke', *Dnevnik Kuropatkina A. N.: Za vremya pokhoda v Turtsii 1877–1881*, RGVIA F.165 Op.1 D.1833 l. 116.

[198] Kuropatkin, *Zavoevanie Turkmenii*, 210–11; Grodekov, *Voina v Turkmenii*, III, 292–3.

Haussmann in Paris'); however, he did not mention any deliberate massacre of fleeing Turkmen women and children after the fall of the fortress.[199] Terent'ev remains wholly silent on Turkmen casualties, mentioning only briefly the pursuit of those who fled the fortress.[200] A final echo of the massacre comes from an unexpected source – a brief note by Leo Tolstoy, written in 1889 but first published in England in 1902, in which he recalled a young officer telling him that the soldiers had baulked at being told to 'cut up' (*pererezat'*) the Turkmen at Gök-Tepe, whereupon Skobelev had got them drunk to steel them to the task.[201]

The Persian slave Medjifir thought that there were about 10,000 Turkmen of fighting age who were actively defending the fortress, only half of whom had firearms, while they had just three cannon.[202] In his official history Grodekov estimated the number of males of fighting age within the fortress at 11,000–12,000, of whom only one-sixth were equipped with firearms, with a severe shortage of ammunition.[203] This meant that the Turkmen barely had a numerical advantage over Skobelev's forces, and that their technological disadvantage was severe. It also meant that a substantial proportion of the dead must have been non-combatants, mostly women and children. Under the circumstances, then, it was a remarkable testament to the fierceness of Turkmen resistance that the Russians lost as many as 1,000 men in the siege and assault, heavier than usual for one of their Central Asian campaigns, but dwarfed by the dead on the Turkmen side.[204] The aftermath, in which the ground was strewn with corpses and severed limbs, must have been as horrific as the massacre itself, and the Russians do not seem to have buried the dead – in March the monthly report noted that 'In view of the development of typhus from the mass of corpses and filth in the camp beneath Gök-Tepe, on the 14 March the hospital division was moved 6 *versts* away to the mountains.'[205]

---

[199] Maslov, *Zavoevanie Akhal-Tekke*, 108, 148–9, 163–9. Grodekov also referred to looting in his conversation with Marvin, *The Russian Advance towards India*, 49–50, and it is the main theme of the first part of a Turkmen song about Gök-Tepe recorded and published in 1902: A. Semenov, 'Turkmenskaya pesnya pro vzyatie Geok-Tepe (zapisana v Akhal-Tekinskom oazise, v seleniya "Kipchak")', *Etnograficheskoe Obozrenie* (1903), No. 4, 125–7.

[200] Terent'ev, *Istoriya zavoevaniya*, III, 198–9.

[201] 'Po povodu knigi A. I. Ershova "Sevastopol'skie Vospominaniya"', in *L. N. Tolstoi protiv voiny* ed. V. G. Chertkov (Christchurch: Izd. Svobodnogo Slova, 1902); Leo Tolstoy, 'Preface', in *Sevastopol and Other Stories* trans. Louise Maude & Aylmer Maude (London: Grant Richards, 1903), vii.

[202] 'Pokazaniya Persiyanina Medzhifir, zhitelya Bishkalminskoi kreposti, bezhavshego 5 yanvarya 1881 goda iz ukrepleniya Dengli-Tepe', RGVIA F.165 Op.1 D.248 ll. 97*ob*–8.

[203] Grodekov, *Voina v Turkmenii*, III, 267–8.

[204] Kuropatkin, *Zavoevanie Turkmenii*, 211.

[205] Grodekov, 'Zhurnal voennykh deistvii za marta' mesyats' 1881 goda', 18/05/1881 RGVIA F.1300 Op.1 D.90 l. 88*ob*.

We can get some idea of the lasting memory the defeat and massacre created among the Turkmen from a song recorded twenty years later in the village of Qipchaq, near Ashkhabad, by Ahmed-Bek Efendiev, chief translator to the governor of Transcaspia, and published by the orientalist Alexander Semenov in 1903:

> Under every bush of steppe herbs
> Lie the abandoned bodies of the fallen
> Who were – hundreds of thousands
> And only a few prisoners escaped death at the hands
> Of the victors – called the unbeliever Urus
> After them Sunnis and Shi'i hurried to rob us
> They abducted beautiful women and girls
> Grenades and bombs buried us in the ground,
> And arms and legs lay everywhere on the steppe
> One mourned a son, another a daughter,
> And each parted company from the other
> 'Do not reproach me with lying!' said the singer
> On the hill of Gök-Tepe blood is spilled
> Of which I am a witness, of which I sang
> In the world the Teke have become pitiful prisoners
> And their good name has become without glory.[206]

9.6   Settling the Frontier: Merv, Kushk, Persia and the Afghan Boundary Commission

After this crushing victory, and the exemplary violence that followed it, there was no further armed resistance from the Akhal-Teke; as Grodekov put it, 'after the 12 January there was not a single further shot fired'.[207] Objections from Persia, over whose territorial claims Skobelev's forces literally rode rough-shod as they advanced further east to Ashkhabad, were muted and swiftly dissipated. O'Donovan noted that the Persian authorities seemed in awe of Skobelev's success in destroying the resistance of the Akhal-Teke, and that they quickly resumed trade, despatching 2,000 camel loads of grain from Meshed to feed the Russian forces, thus further easing their supply problems.[208] The treaty establishing the new frontier from the Caspian to the region just north of Meshed was agreed within a year of the victory at Gök-Tepe, though the delineation of the new boundary between Khorasan and the Akhal-Teke oasis by a joint Russo-Persian commission was not completed until 1886.[209] The interpreter to the

[206] Semenov, 'Turkmenskaya pesnya pro vzyatie Geok-Tepe', 127.
[207] Grodekov, 'Zhurnal voennykh deistvii za fevral' mesyats' 1881 goda', 05/05/1881 RGVIA F.1300 Op.1 D.90 ll. 73–5, partly reproduced in *PT*, 529–30.
[208] O'Donovan, *The Merv Oasis*, II, 76.
[209] Kazemzadeh, *Russia and Britain in Persia*, 80–84; Deutschmann, *Iran and Russian Imperialism*, 58–70, 134–47; the Russian text of the border treaty with Persia, dated 09/12/1881, is in *PT*, 602–5.

Persian commission, Mirza Reza Khan Danesh, recalled how he had persuaded the Russians to make some minor territorial concessions around the village of Lutfabad, to preserve access to pasture and agricultural land for its inhabitants. This was despite a lack of support from Tehran, from where the Shah wrote that he had at one point feared that Skobelev might try to seize the whole of Khorasan, and that the loss of territory around Lutfabad was insignificant compared with the danger which Persia had avoided.[210] The Qajars were reluctant to provoke conflict with Russia even on their own behalf, let alone at the behest of the British.

The Russians swiftly set about regularising the administration of their newly conquered territories. At the beginning of February Major Spolatbog was appointed administrator of the Akhal-Teke oasis, including the whole region from Qizil-Arvat to Ashkhabad. On the 23 April Count Heiden proposed to Alexander II the creation of a new Transcaspian Province (*Oblast'*) out of the current territories in Mangishlaq and Krasnovodsk, together with the newly conquered Akhal-Teke lands.[211] The administrative centre of the new province was fixed at Ashkhabad, a small and entirely deserted settlement when O'Donovan passed through it shortly after Gök-Tepe fell, but with good supplies of timber and water.[212] There was disagreement as to where Transcaspia should be administered from – for the time being it remained under the authority of the Viceroy of the Caucasus in Tiflis and within the Caucasian sphere, but Grodekov, Kuropatkin and other Turkestani officers advocated its transfer to Tashkent, while Skobelev considered it should be an autonomous province whose governor was placed directly under the War Ministry.[213]

Terent'ev referred scornfully to the enthusiasm with which former enemies among the 'half-savage nomad' Turkmen came forward to offer their submission, and were rewarded with gold medals and *khalats*.[214] Following the formal submission by Tykma Sardar, another Teke Turkmen leader called Muhammad Ovez Sayyid Geldi and a representative of the Merv Turkmen called Halli Khan Berdy at the court in St Petersburg in May, this process got rapidly under way.[215] While the Russians sought to use those Akhal-Teke leaders they identified as 'influential', which included both Tykma Sardar (granted the rank of Major and a salary, he died in June 1882) and Sufi

[210] Prince 'Arfa, *Memories of a Bygone Age: Qajar Persia and Imperial Russia, 1853–1902* (London: Gingko Library, 2016), 78–89.
[211] Heiden to Alexander II 23/04/1881, in *PT*, 496.
[212] O'Donovan, *The Merv Oasis*, II, 71–3.
[213] Notes by Skobelev and Grodekov on a report regarding Russia's relations with Merv 09/11/1881, in *PT*, 591–6.
[214] Terent'ev, *Istoriya zavoevaniya*, III, 240.
[215] 'Ob obrazovanii iz territorii turkmen tekinskogo roda i zemel' Zakaspiiskogo Voennogo Otdela Zakaspiiskoi Oblasti', 15/05/1881; Heiden to ? 16/05/1881, in *PT*, 532–3.

Khan,[216] there was no question of making Transcaspia a protectorate under indirect rule: Turkmen political structures were seen as far too weak and chaotic for this to be possible, and, even if this had not been the case, Russian military action had smashed them. In May 1881 almost 8,500 Akhal-Teke households returned from Merv, to which they had fled after the massacre, and settled once more across the oasis, in a state of destitution.[217] In October the governor of Transcaspia appealed to the Russian Red Cross to do something to relieve the poverty of these 'newest members of the Russian family', as his administration did not have the funds.[218] The Akhal-Teke leader Makhtum Quli Khan, Nur Berdy Khan's son, remained at Merv, to which Russian attention was now directed.[219]

It was only Russian qualms about upsetting the British – paranoid as always about the approaches to Herat – which prevented the immediate annexation of Merv and the valley of the Murghab, and the creation of a new Russian frontier stretching to the Bukharan protectorate. In August 1881 the then commander of the Transcaspian region, General P. F. Rerberg (1835–1912), wrote that the Turkmen of Merv and Tejen did not understand why the Russian advance had halted where it did. He urged the elimination of all remaining Qajar influence and a speedy annexation of Merv and the region around it.[220] The Foreign Ministry as usual attempted to sit on the fence, arguing that, while strenuous efforts should be made to keep British influence (and above all British weapons) out of Merv, the Russians had no pretensions towards that region, and desired nothing but friendly relations with its inhabitants.[221] Almost immediately reports had begun to come in of the continued undesirable presence of a British 'envoy' in the Merv oasis.[222] This was Edmund O'Donovan, correspondent of the *Daily News*, who had no official capacity and in fact was effectively being held prisoner by the Merv Turkmen, with the British appealing to the Russians to help secure his release.[223] Despite this his role would be systematically exaggerated in both contemporary Russian writings and subsequent Soviet historiography as a cunning agent of British imperialism. While O'Donovan, the rest of the British press and the public opinion which they helped to stimulate considered

[216] 'Spisok vliyatel'nykh lits mezhdu naseleniem Tekinskogo oazisa', n.d. (May 1881) & Rerberg to Caucasian Command 30/10/1881, in *PT*, 534–6, 589; Terent'ev *Istoriya zavoevaniya*, III, 242.

[217] Spolatbog, *Raport*, c. July 1881, in *PT*, 543–5.

[218] Commandant of the Transcaspian District to the Chairman of the Russian Red Cross 18/10/1881, in *PT*, 571–2.

[219] O'Donovan, *Merv Oasis*, II, 206.

[220] Lt-Gen. Rerberg, 'Dokladnaya zapiska Nachal'nika Zakaspiiskoi Oblasti', n.d. (Aug. 1881), in *PT*, 556–63.

[221] 'Instruktsiya Ministerstva inostrannykh del o politike Rossii v otnoshenii Ateka i Merva', in *PT*, 546–8.

[222] Kidyaev to Spolatbog 26/05/1881, in *PT*, 537.

[223] O'Donovan, *Merv Oasis*, II, 116–37; Obruchev to Spolatbog 07/07/1881, in *PT*, 541.

Merv to be an independent principality, the Russians held very different views. Already in January 1879 the Commandant of the Amu-Darya Division had reported a request from Baba Khan, the nominal head of the Tokhtamysh lineage of Merv Turkmen, for them to become Russian subjects,[224] and, as we have seen, a representative of the Turkmen of Merv accompanied Tykma Sardar when he went to make his submission to the Tsar in St Petersburg in May 1881. Baba Khan also informed the Russians that there was no organised government in Merv, and that in peace time the Turkmen there did not even have elders, whilst the title of 'khan' had no real significance – from which the Russians concluded that any agreements O'Donovan might have signed with Turkmen leaders there had no political value.[225] Despite this, when Spolatbog reported that thirty-two English armaments craftsmen had appeared in Merv to assist the inhabitants in overhauling their artillery, it caused alarm and annoyance, even though by early 1882 the Russians had realised that this was an 'untrue rumour', which they blamed on promises made by O'Donovan.[226] According to the latter, the Turkmen had about thirty-five guns at Merv, including four 18-pounders, a 7-inch howitzer and two 6-inch mortars, but they were old pieces captured from the Persians in 1860, mostly dismounted, their ventholes enlarged through repeated use, and their bores 'so scraped, apparently by the passage of heterogeneous projectiles, such as gravel and horse nails, that at first sight the guns might pass as having been formerly rifled'. The Mervis informed O'Donovan that they would be able to build new carriages (he did not think there was enough timber), that they had some people who knew how to make gunpowder (they had none in reserve) and that, while they had no ammunition, they could dig up shot which had remained buried in the ground from the last Persian attack. 'All this was extremely melancholy from the point of view of military precision; and I inwardly congratulated myself on the fact that I was not one of the officers charged with "haunting the oasis and stirring up the Turcomans".'[227] No serious military opposition to the Russians was likely at Merv.

In the summer of 1881 Makhtum Quli Khan reported that Baba Khan of Merv was now placing his hopes in the English, although he still believed in the might of Russia, but after O'Donovan's departure in July fears of British interference receded.[228] In February 1882 a Russian caravan set out for

---

[224] Baba Khan to Muhammad Rahim Khan of Khiva; Ivanov to von Kaufman 24/01/1879, in *PT*, 380–1.

[225] Report to the Main Staff from the Caucasian Military District 19/01/1882, in Tikhomirov, *Prisoedinenie Merva*, 213–14.

[226] Telegram Spolatbog to Komarov 13/05/1881, in *PT*, 531–2; report to the Main Staff from the Caucasian Military District 19/01/1882, in Tikhomirov, *Prisoedinenie Merva*, 210.

[227] O'Donovan, *Merv Oasis*, II, 147–9, 153–4.

[228] Makhtum Quli Khan to Spolatbog n.d., in *PT*, 545–6; Report to the Main Staff from the Caucasian Military District 19/01/1882, in Tikhomirov, *Prisoedinenie Merva*, 211 & *PT*, 614–19.

Merv, led by Shtabs-rotmistr Mahsud Alikhanov-Avarskii, whom we last met with the Mangishlaq column during the invasion of Khiva in 1873 (he had subsequently been reduced to the ranks after fighting a duel, and gradually worked his way up again to a commission).[229] Being a Muslim and fluent in Turki, he was able to communicate directly with the Turkmen. While the purpose of the caravan was ostensibly commercial, Alikhanov made little secret of its political objectives either at the time or in the account he published of the journey in *Moskovskie Vedomosti*, whose abbreviated translation by the British journalist Charles Marvin helped make Alikhanov an object of fascination for Anglo-Indian officers.[230] Terent'ev claimed that, while most of the Turkmen leaders in Merv favoured becoming Russian subjects (notably Sary-Khan and the widow of Nur-Berdy Khan, Guljamal), throughout 1881–3, a British agent who went under the name of '*Siah-push*' (black shirt), accompanied by an Afghan and two Indians, was stirring up the Merv Turkmen to resist the Russians.[231] Alikhanov, who met him, thought he was probably an agent of Ayub Khan, a pretender to the Afghan throne who hoped to use the Turkmen to overthrow the rule of 'Abdurrahman Khan in northern Afghanistan, but nevertheless attributed most of the resistance to Russian annexation at Merv to his machinations.[232]

That the annexation of Merv was an authorised goal of Russian policy is not in doubt: at an official gathering to discuss the question in June 1882, which included Foreign Minister Girs and General N. N. Obruchev, the Chief of the Main Staff, it was agreed at the highest level that Russia's territories in Turkestan and Transcaspia should be united, and that Merv was the only remaining obstacle to this.[233] This goal was brought appreciably closer early in 1883 when the Merv Turkmen were alarmed by a visit by the Qajar Shah Nasruddin to Khorasan, a ceremonial procession designed to assert the shaky Persian sovereignty over that province.[234] They believed this might be a preliminary to a Persian annexation of Merv, and sent an envoy to A. V. Komarov, who had been appointed governor of Transcaspia in

[229] Alikhanov to the Chief of staff, Transcaspian District 08/02/1882, in *PT*, 623–5.
[230] 'Russkie v Merve', *Moskovskie Vedomosti* (1882); Charles Marvin, 'Lieutenant Alikhanoff's Journey with a Russian Caravan to Merv', in *Reconnoitring Central Asia: Pioneering Adventures in the Region Lying between Russia and India* (London: Swan Sonnenschein, 1884), 363–83; the following year Alikhanov published an ethnographic account of the Merv Turkmen and a detailed topographical description of the roads leading to the oasis: M. Alikhanov-Avarskii, *Mervskii Oazis i dorogi vedushchie k nemu* (St Pb.: A. Transhelya, 1883).
[231] Terent'ev, *Istoriya zavoevaniya*, III, 244–5.
[232] M. Alikhanov-Avarskii, 'Zakaspiiskiya vospominaniya 1881–5', *VE* (1904), No. 10, 445–56.
[233] 'Iz protokola "osobogo soveshchaniya" o merakh po dal'neishemu ukrepleniiu russkogo vliyaniya na tekintsev Merva', 24/06/1882, in *PT*, 638–41.
[234] Deutschmann, '"All Rulers are Brothers"', 293.

March 1883, asking what they should do in the face of a Persian attack. Komarov sent a force to the river Tejen, from where he despatched Alikhanov as his envoy to the Turkmen leaders of the oasis, whom he visited in turn to persuade them to become Russian subjects.[235] In response twenty-four Turkmen leaders who favoured Russia appeared at Ashkhabad and swore allegiance to the Tsar on the 31 January 1884, receiving a guarantee of freedom of religion, plus the assurance that the authority of their 'khans' would be upheld (under the supervision of a Russian officer) and that they would retain their own 'popular' judges.[236] Alikhanov was duly made the first commandant of the Merv district, in which position he would later be guilty of extensive corruption and abuses of the local population.[237] His role in the submission of the Turkmen of Merv became internationally celebrated, and was later adduced by Soviet historians as evidence of the 'voluntary' uniting of the region to the Russian empire.[238] Quite apart from the impression that had been made by the Gök-Tepe massacre, which surely played a role in their decision, some of the Merv Turkmen had not participated in and did not accept the agreement. When Komarov sent an expedition (four companies, two *sotnya*s and four guns) to Iolatan and Merv to make the Russian annexation a reality, it resulted in a skirmish in which one Russian soldier and forty Turkmen were killed.[239] This was followed swiftly in May 1884 by the despatch of a force of Caucasian cavalry to seize Sarakhs, opposite the Persian fortress of Ruknabad, creating a *de facto* frontier with Persia along the line of the river of the same name. On this occasion the Qajars did protest and sought British support to reverse this, but to no avail.[240]

The annexation of Merv still left the frontier with Afghanistan undefined, and prompted a storm of hysterical comment in the British press (an outbreak of 'Mervousness', as the 8th Duke of Argyll apparently called it).[241] Having annexed Iolatan, which was inhabited by Sariq Turkmen, the Russians now

---

[235] Komarov to Dondukov-Korsakov 07/02/1884, in Tikhomirov, *Prisoedinenie Merva*, 216–19 & *PT*, 706–12.

[236] The text of this agreement is published in Tikhomirov, *Prisoedinenie Merva*, 209–10, and in K. K. Palen, *Otchet, revizuiushchago, po vysochaishemu poveleniiu, Turkestanskogo kraya: Kraevoe Upravlenie* (St Pb.: Senatskaya Tip., 1910), 31–2.

[237] Morrison, 'The Pahlen Report and the Restoration of Rectitude in Transcaspia', 56.

[238] Marvin, *Reconnoitring Central Asia*, 363–83; Tikhomirov, *Prisoedinenie Merva*, 1–10.

[239] Komarov to Dondukov-Korsakov 29/05/1884, in *PT*, 737–43; N. V. Charykov, 'Mirnoe zavoevanie Merva (iz vospominanii o pokhode generala A. V. Komarova v 1885 g.', *IV* (1914), No. 11, 486–518; Terent'ev, *Istoriya zavoevaniya*, III, 243–5.

[240] Komarov to Dondukov-Korsakov 29/10/1884, in *PT*, 773–4; Anon., 'Boi na Kushke 18 marta 1885 g. i territorial'nye priobreteniya v tsarstvovanie imperatora Aleksandra III', *RS* (1910), No. 3, 651; Kazemzadeh, *Russia and Britain in Persia*, 87–93.

[241] The Duke was a former Lord Privy Seal and author of *The Eastern Question from the Treaty of Paris 1836 to the Treaty of Berlin 1878 and to the Second Afghan War* (London: Strahan & Co., 1879).

turned their attention south, where another group of Sariq inhabited the Panjdeh oasis north of Herat.[242] A sudden solicitude for the tribal cohesion of the Sariq (something which had been signally absent when the Russians were defining their boundary with Persia and divided the territory of the Atrek Yomuds in two) would become the basis of Russia's claim to Panjdeh. Here they entered into direct rivalry with the Afghan Amir 'Abdurrahman Khan, whose claims were dismissed by the Caucasian commander, Prince A. M. Dondukov-Korsakov (1820–1893).[243] Effectively it was only since 'Abdurrahman Khan's accession in 1881 that the writ of the Afghan government in Kabul had run anywhere north of the Hindu Kush, and he had only asserted control of Herat and Maimuna earlier that year.[244] In reality, as at least some Russian commentators realised, Panjdeh, like Merv, and indeed the Akhal-Teke oasis itself, had been part of a zone of blurred and undefined sovereignty along the frontiers of the Persian, Afghan and Russian states.[245] The Russians and Persians had now agreed a frontier as far as Sarakhs, while British surveyors had been hard at work over the previous twenty years defining the Persian frontiers with British India and Afghanistan in Seistan to the south.[246] The last surviving patch of uncertainty was about to be squeezed between the Russian advance and a newly assertive Afghan state, funded and armed by the British. It was one of the few occasions when Russian and British forces came into direct contact with each other in Central Asia, and is a celebrated episode of the so-called 'Great Game', another moment when that nineteenth-century cold war supposedly almost became hot.[247] Ultimately the British and Russians resolved their differences relatively easily by means of a boundary commission which began work in the autumn of 1884 to draw up a mutually agreed line – but not before a clash of arms between Russian and Afghan forces.[248]

---

[242] On the earlier history of the Sariq Turkmen see William A. Wood, 'The Sariq Turkmen of Merv and the Khanate of Khiva in the early nineteenth century' (Ph.D. Dissertation, Indiana University, Bloomington, 1998).

[243] Dondukov-Korsakov to Vannovskii 14/06/1884, in PT, 745–56.

[244] Jonathan L. Lee, The Ancient Supremacy: Bukhara, Afghanistan and the Battle for Balkh, 1731–1901 (Leiden: Brill, 1996), 445–60.

[245] A. D. Shemanskii, Boi na Kushke i ego 25-letnii iubilei (St Pb.: V. Berezovskii, 1910), 10.

[246] Pirouz Mojtahed-Zadeh, Small Players of the Great Game: The Settlement of Iran's Eastern Borderlands and the Creation of Afghanistan (Abingdon: Routledge, 2004) offers an extremely one-eyed account of this process which makes anachronistic assumptions about Iranian claims to sovereignty in the region. Much better is Benjamin Hopkins, 'The Bounds of Identity: The Goldsmid Mission and the Delineation of the Perso-Afghan Border in the Nineteenth Century', JGH 2 (2007), 233–54, which emphasises how each side sought to exploit British imperial power in pursuit of their often rather newly minted sovereign claims.

[247] Hopkirk, The Great Game, 425–9.

[248] Apparently they were encouraged in this by Bismarck, who was anxious to avoid an open Anglo-Russian conflict: Mark, Im Schatten des „Great Game", 329–39.

According to Fayz Muhammad Katib's *Siraj al-Tawarikh*, the most famous Afghan court history, the contested claim to Panjdeh first became apparent to the Afghans in November 1884 when an unidentified Russian Colonel together with eight men approached a group of Afghan border guards on the road to the village and were turned back. In this account the role of the British in defending the frontier and maintaining Afghan claims to sovereignty is minimised – instead they are portrayed as trying to moderate Afghan behaviour to prevent a clash – but the Russians assumed that Afghan resistance was entirely down to British machinations behind the scenes.[249] Terent'ev, as usual, considered that the British had acted in bad faith throughout, firstly by claiming the Sariq Turkmens of Panjdeh as Afghan subjects, and then by encouraging the Afghans to resist the Russians and supplying them with arms (5,000 breech-loading Snider rifles) and military advisers – however, according to the *Siraj al-Tawarikh* this was agreed with the Viceroy, Lord Dufferin, only in April, after the clash at Panjdeh, where the Afghans were still armed solely with muzzle-loaders.[250] The British military presence around Herat at the time consisted of an escort of 200 Bengal lancers, under the overall command of the Chief Boundary Commissioner, Sir Peter Lumsden, based in Herat. The chief of the Indian section of the Commission, Colonel Joseph Ridgway (who later succeeded Lumsden as chief commissioner), was encamped with the Afghan forces at Panjdeh, together with his deputy Captain Charles Yate. Along with his brother, Arthur, also serving with the commission, he provided the best-known account of events from the British side.[251] The British had received strict instructions not to intervene directly in any dispute with the Russians, who at this stage, rather than sending commissioners of their own, had instead advanced in force to occupy disputed territory and create 'facts on the ground'.

Early in March 1885 Komarov advanced to a small village called Aq-Tepe, near the confluence of the Kushk and Murghab rivers, where the Afghans had a small fort. His force of eight companies, four *sotnyas* and four guns was made up partly of Turkestan and partly of Caucasian troops, with the addition of a Turkmen militia recruited in Merv and under Alikhanov's command.[252] The direct confrontation came on the 18/30 March 1885 with an Afghan force of 4,000 men under *Jarnail* (General) Ghiyasuddin Khan and *Naib Salar* Timur

[249] Fayz Muhammad Katib Hazarah, *The History of Afghanistan: Fayz Muhammad Katib Hazarah's Siraj al-Tawarikh* trans. & ed. R. D. McChesney & M. M. Khorrami (Leiden: Brill, 2013), III, 132–3.
[250] Terent'ev, *Istoriya zavoevaniya*, III, 248–9; Fayz Muhammad Katib Hazarah, *The History of Afghanistan*, III, 167, 172.
[251] Major C. E. Yate, *Northern Afghanistan, or, Letters from the Afghan Boundary Commission* (Edinburgh: Blackwood, 1888); Lt. A. C. Yate, *England and Russia Face to Face in Asia: Travels with the Afghan Boundary Commission* (Edinburgh: Blackwood, 1887).
[252] Anon., 'Boi na Kushke 18 marta 1885 g.', *RS* (1910), No. 4, 34.

Shah Khan, at a crossing of the river Kushk at Pul-i Khishti/Tash-Köpru (Stone Bridge).[253] In a published report, Komarov wrote that the 'insolence' (*derzost*) of the Afghans had become insupportable, as their cavalry harassed his forward posts, and they were heard to shout 'Get out of here – here there are no Mervis, none of your Turkmen, only Afghans. We have beaten off the British, and we will beat you too.' Seeing Russian prestige thus insulted, fearing (so he claimed) that it would undermine the loyalty of his Turkmen levies, and believing an attack to be imminent, he resolved to pre-empt it.[254] According to his and subsequent Russian accounts, unable to withstand Russian volley fire, and attacked on their flank by Alikhanov's Turkmen cavalry, the Afghan forces broke and fled back across the river.[255] In what was probably a *post facto* attempt to preserve face, Fayz Muhammad Katib wrote that Timur Shah Khan had received orders from Amir 'Abd al-Rahman not to resist any Russian attack, since it was more important to preserve his force intact to defend Maimuna and Herat, and Panjdeh was worthless anyway. He added (perhaps more plausibly) that 'their weapons were muzzle-loaders, and because of the heavy rain, when they poured in the powder, water got mixed in and made a (non-combustible) paste' and that in consequence 300 soldiers 'attained martyrdom', while an additional 73 were wounded, including General Ghiyasuddin Khan.[256] Terent'ev claimed that the Afghans suffered 500 casualties – another source suggested the number was 1,000, indicating just how vague and probably exaggerated all such Russian estimates were – but it seems clear enough that the Afghans lost all their artillery, supplies and camels.[257] The Russian forces lost just nine killed and eighteen wounded.[258] The British contested many aspects of the Russian account, alleging that it was a reconnaissance in force by the latter on Afghan territory which had provoked the conflict.[259] Alikhanov considered that 'in reality it was the English who

---

[253] M. Gornyi, *Pokhod na Afgantsev i boi na Kushke (1885)* (Moscow: E. I. Konovalova, 1901), 77–101; Anon., 'Boi na Kushke', *RS* (1910), No. 3, 588–9; No. 4, 26–44.

[254] Komarov to Dondukov-Korsakov, published in *Kavkaz* No. 113 (30/03/1885) and reprinted in *PT*, 776–88.

[255] Anon., 'Boi na Kushke 18 marta 1885 g.', *RS* (1910), No. 4, 35–7; Shemanskii, *Boi na Kushke*, 63–8; Rob Johnson, *The Afghan Way of War* (London: Hurst, 2011), 144–5.

[256] Fayz Muhammad Katib Hazarah, *The History of Afghanistan*, III, 151–2; Yate, *England and Russia Face to Face*, 328.

[257] These guns, according to Charles Yate, who saw some of them mounted on a memorial to the dead in Ashkhabad in 1887, were 'old Cossipore smooth-bores cast some fifty years ago', i.e. they came from the East India Company's ordnance factory near Calcutta: Yate, *Northern Afghanistan*, 415.

[258] Terent'ev, *Istoriya zavoevaniya*, III, 249–50; Anon., 'Boi na Kushke 18 marta 1885 g.', *RS* (1910), No. 4, 37.

[259] 'Telegram from Lieutenant-General Sir Peter Lumsden Relative to the Fight between Russians and the Afghans at Ak Tépé', *PP Central Asia* No. 1 (1885) C.4363 Vol. LXXXVII (April 1885), 21–3.

were beaten off at Kushk',[260] and in general the Russians refused to believe that the Afghans would have been so defiant without British encouragement and connivance. However, Charles Yate, deputising for the absent Colonel Ridgway, was probably sincere when he assured the Russians that he could not control the actions of the Afghan commanders.[261] His brother noted that the Afghans were furious at the British failure to support them fully against the Russians, and it is clear that at no point were the British willing to risk war over Panjdeh.[262] 'Abdurrahman Khan's regime was almost as aggressively expansionist as that of Russia, and still in the process of consolidating its control over Afghan Turkestan when the Russian challenge arose – indeed, in the *Siraj al-Tawarikh* the Afghans are presented as laying claim to Merv, Sarakhs and the Akhal-Teke oasis, and speak consistently in the language of hard borders and defined territorial sovereignty.[263] It is a staple of the 'Great Game' mentality that no agency or initiative is ever attributed to Central Asian rulers and peoples, but there is no reason to reproduce this assumption in modern historiography.[264]

In the end perhaps the most notorious result of the skirmish on the Kushk was the almost complete demolition of the wonderful fifteenth-century Musalla complex, built by the Timurid queen Gawhar Shad, to make way for fortifications outside Herat in case the Russians advanced further. Most sources blame this on British military advice, although Yate claimed that it was done on the Amir's own initiative, something partially borne out in the *Siraj al-Tawarikh* in which 'Abd al-Rahman refers to 'mining' the Musalla in order to blow it up if the Russians attacked. However, according to the same source, the decision to destroy it pre-emptively does indeed seem to have been because of the advice of Colonel Stewart, the military engineer sent to prepare Herat's defence. As the arcades and walls of the Musalla were covered with inscriptions from the Qur'an, which would be cast down and defiled when the buildings were demolished, the people of Herat were angry and protested, cursing the British – only when a group of *'ulama* provided a *fatwa* authorising the destruction, and the Amir instructed that the inscriptions should be removed first, wrapped in shrouds and cast into the river, did they acquiesce.[265] When Robert Byron visited in 1933 only the minarets remained to give some idea of the glory of what had been destroyed so needlessly.[266]

---

[260] Alikhanov-Avarskii, 'Zakaspiiskiya vospominaniya', 486–8.

[261] Anon., 'Boi na Kushke 18 marta 1885 g.', *RS* (1910), No. 4, 31.

[262] Yate, *England and Russia Face to Face*, 330; Yapp, 'British Perceptions', 657.

[263] Fayz Muhammad Katib Hazarah, *The History of Afghanistan*, III, 137–40.

[264] See further Morrison, 'Beyond the Great Game'.

[265] Yate, *Northern Afghanistan*, 16, 30–2; Fayz Muhammad Katib Hazarah, *The History of Afghanistan*, III, 160, 174.

[266] Robert Byron, *The Road to Oxiana* (London: Jonathan Cape, 1937), 97–9, 251–8.

After the clash on the Kushk, negotiations over the Russo-Afghan boundary continued. P. M. Lessar (1851–1905), the Russian agent at Bukhara, who had recently been travelling in the region, was present when Colonel T. H. Holdich, the commission's principal surveyor, read his initial report of the boundary commission's activities to a meeting of the Royal Geographical Society on the 23 March (N.S.), a few days before the clash at Aq-Tepe. Responding to the paper in French, Lessar noted that 'Before the fall of Geuk-Tepeh, and even the occupation of Merv, we could have very little knowledge of the claims of Turkomans in these regions; only quite lately began the surveying of the country, and from that time our maps largely differ from General Walker's. The permanent frontier between Turkomania and Afghanistan ought certainly to be defined according to the mutual rights of both parties, and not on the basis of a fancy line drawn on a map previous to the study of the country.' What Lessar was referring to here was the claim that blood ties between the Sariq Turkmen of the region and the Akhal-Teke meant that they too should come under Russian rule, a logic rejected by his British audience, who pointed out (reasonably enough) that the same logic had not been followed in demarcating the Russo-Persian frontier in 1881, which had left the Yomud Turkmen on both sides of the border.[267] Fayz Muhammad Katib also refers to Lessar's arguments, which seem to have prompted a proposal from the head of the boundary commission, General Lumsden, to expel the Sariq Turkmen from Panjdeh in order to pre-empt the Russian claim, something the Afghans rejected.[268]

While this indicated continued disagreement over where exactly the boundary should run, what is perhaps more significant is Lessar's presence at this gathering in the first place. It indicates the relatively free exchange of information between Russian and British scholar-administrators, and the shared intellectual assumptions and culture which lay behind it. It was the two European powers who would determine the course of the new frontier, using standard shared European land surveying techniques – although the commission did have an Afghan representative, Qazi Sa'd al-Din, when he and the governor of Herat protested about the siting of a boundary marker at Aq-Tepe Colonel Ridgway instead accepted the Russian position, which was based on the claim that all territory cultivated by Turkmen should be assigned to them: 'Those two informed his Majesty by letter saying, "Colonel Ridgway, having decided that he is the final judge and we are only the people who bring provisions and are mere servants of his government, never asks us about anything (neither matters weighty nor trivial) and continues to advance the

---

[267] T. H. Holdich, 'Afghan Boundary Commission; Geographical Notes. III', *PRGS* (1885), No. 5, 287; Terent'ev also refers to Lessar's objections, suggesting the British were being entirely cynical: *Istoriya zavoevaniya*, III, 248.

[268] Fayz Muhammad Katib Hazarah, *The History of Afghanistan*, III, 149–50.

business of delineating the border".' While noting that Ridgway was supposed to be an impartial arbitrator between Russian and Afghan claims, and displaying palpable irritation at his failure to stand up for Afghan rights, in effect the Amir would advise his representatives to submit to Ridgway's verdict, and forbade them from communicating directly with the Russian officials. The British, as Ridgway apparently made clear, had a strong interest in establishing a fixed border even at the expense of some Afghan territorial claims, rather than seeing it remain undefined and thus leaving open the possibility of further Russian aggression.[269]

From the Afghan perspective, then, the British and the Russians were effectively collaborating to exclude them, and indeed the two boundary commissions seem to have enjoyed excellent social relations. According to Yate, communications with the small party of Kuban Cossacks who arrived first were difficult as their officers did not speak French or German, but the arrival of their commander, Colonel Kuhlberg, who spoke fluent English, together with some other French- and German-speaking officers, smoothed over this initial awkwardness. The rounds of entertainment were lavish, and Yate remarked on how agreeable he and his fellow officers found the custom of taking vodka and *zakuski* before dinner, and the good quality of the Caucasian wines they drank with it when entertained by the Russians.[270] Captain Varenik, one of the officers of the Cossack escort, seems to have found Anglo-Indian hospitality a little more bemusing – the food too spicy, and the custom of having a savoury after pudding very strange.[271] The new frontier line gave the Russians the right bank of the river Kushk and the western part of the Maruchak valley along the left bank of the Murghab, territory which Yate suggested they valued rather more than the Afghans would have done. The erection of the final boundary pillar on Christmas Day 1887 was a festive occasion, marked by yet another 'capital dinner'.[272] The establishment of the boundary ushered in a period of what Sergeev rightly calls 'fragile equilibrium' in Anglo-Russian relations and, as we shall see in the following chapter, established an important precedent for the amicable resolution of a similar dispute in the Pamirs a decade later.[273]

The campaigns and events I have explored in this chapter are better-known to English-speaking audiences than any of those earlier in this book. This is

[269] Fayz Muhammad Katib Hazarah, *The History of Afghanistan*, III, 199, 205–10, 217–20, 254.

[270] Yate, *Northern Afghanistan*, 72–82.

[271] Varenik, 'S russko-avganskoi granitsy', *Severnyi Kavkaz* (1886), Nos. 28–9, in *TS*, Vol. 411, 186a–96a – in an earlier publication I mistakenly assumed that 'Varenik' was a pseudonym (although it does indeed mean 'dumpling'): Morrison, 'Russian Rule in Turkestan', 690.

[272] Yate, *Northern Afghanistan*, 384–7.

[273] Sergeev, *The Great Game*, 209; Sergeev, *Bol'shaya Igra*, 184.

because the Transcaspian conquests were the first where the Russians came into direct contact with British agents and officials – where the 'Great Game' might finally be said to have been played between them in anything more than a metaphorical sense – and indeed the British did figure more prominently in Russian decision-making than in earlier campaigns of conquest. Nevertheless, it is clear that it was the Turkmen themselves, and to a lesser extent Persia, which were the objects of conquest and the main focus of Russian concern. The Akhal-Teke Turkmen were considered particularly savage, intractable and insolent, thumbing their noses at Russian power from their desert fastness. Relations with the Yomud and Göklan Turkmen along the Atrek were initially somewhat better, but they were alienated by the Russian requisitioning of camels for military expeditions, which often descended into precisely the kind of unprovoked raiding and theft which the Russians had so long condemned in their nomadic neighbours. From the moment the Russians established an outpost on the Caspian shore – prompted in large part by the desire for a base from which to launch the conquest of Khiva – conflict with the Turkmen and ultimately annexation were likely. Relations with the British seem merely to have determined the timing of the decisive push in 1879 – when the Russians felt they had been outmanoeuvred in Afghanistan. The humiliating failure of Lomakin's expedition then required an immediate and emphatic response, and that – combined with the presence of Skobelev – helps to explain the extreme violence that was unleashed after the fall of Gök-Tepe. The precedent of the Yomud massacre – prompted by a similar assumption of the savagery and intransigence of the Turkmen – also played a role. As Lessar put it, in response to a challenge from Sir Henry Rawlinson regarding the character of the Sariq Turkmen:

> The Russians certainly do not boast of having in one year civilised the Turkomans. They claim to have pacified the desert, abolished the slave trade, and made it possible for the surrounding countries to live in peace. To this end it was necessary to subdue and chastise the Turkomans, and it is fear, and not the civilisation of their character, which produces this change in their conduct.[274]

The fate of the Akhal-Teke was terrible, but we should not idealise the situation in the region before the Russian conquest. Their economy did indeed depend to some degree on slave-raiding among the settled Persian communities to the south, which were no doubt as relieved as their Qajar rulers to see this brought to an end by Russian conquest.

It was also with the conquest of Transcaspia that the process of border-drawing became more definitive, as the Russian empire found partners – Britain,

---

[274] T. H. Holdich, 'Afghan Boundary Commission; Geographical Notes. III', *PRGS* (1885), No. 5, 292.

Afghanistan and Persia – with whom it could mutually delineate a hard border, in a way that had not been possible either with Khiva or Bukhara, or with the Turkmen and Qazaqs. This was partly because these were states which the Russians were prepared to recognise as enjoying sovereign rights akin to their own, and also because – as Ben Hopkins has argued – the Durrani and Qajar dynasties and their servants had begun to assimilate European ideas of borders and sovereignty, forming what Thongchai Winichakul famously called 'the Geo-body of the nation' and supplanting older ideas of sovereignty based on control over people, resources or routes, and areas of blurred, shared or non-existent state sovereignty.[275] With the conquest of Transcaspia almost the last area of vagueness on the Central Asian map had been eliminated – the only one that remained was in the Pamirs, the subject of the next chapter. The Russian empire now had what it had sought for so long in Central Asia – a firm frontier, mutually agreed with neighbouring states, whose sovereignty it was prepared to respect – for the time being at least. While Afghanistan would continue to sit under an umbrella of British protection, the situation in Persia became steadily more complicated throughout the 1890s and early 1900s, as its economic and fiscal independence was progressively undermined by British and Russian encroachments. The division of the country into spheres of influence under the Anglo-Russian agreement of 1907 did not halt this process. By 1914, as Jennifer Siegel has shown, the Russian consuls in Tabriz and Meshed were effectively acting as local governors, encouraging the local inhabitants to become Russian subjects and making plans to bring Russian peasant settlers into the region.[276] Thus even these frontiers did not prove absolutely definitive – but in the end they outlasted Tsarist Russia: Panjdeh would ultimately become the southernmost point of the USSR.

---

[275] Hopkins, 'The Bounds of Identity'; Thongchai Winichakul, *Siam Mapped: A History of the Geo-body of the Nation* (Honolulu, HI: University of Hawai'i Press, 1993).
[276] Siegel, *Endgame*, 154–66, 187.

10

Aryanism on the Final Frontier of the Russian Empire: The Exploration and Annexation of the Pamirs, 1881–1905

I know that you won't cheat me because you're white people – sons of Alexander – and not like common, black Mohammedans.

Rudyard Kipling, The Man Who Would Be King (1888)

The final phase of Russian expansion in Central Asia took place in some of the remotest and least-known terrain on the planet – Badakhshan, the High Pamirs, and the neighbouring mountainous regions of Qarateghin, Darvaz, Roshan, Shughnan and Wakhan – but it is also one of the best-known portions of the conquest.[1] This is largely because it was here, finally, that the British and Russian empires came into direct contact, and the resulting individual encounters between officers and explorers immediately became part of the mythology of the 'Great Game'; as with the Transcaspian campaigns, the extension of Russia's frontier here took place in the full glare of international, Anglophone publicity.[2] It was also,

My thanks to Daniel Beben, Markus Hauser, Oybek Mahmudov, Robert Middleton and Paul Richardson for their comments on this chapter, which have enormously improved it.

[1] Badakhshan is the historic term that was applied to the whole of this mountainous region in Persian sources. Strictly speaking, 'the Pamirs' should refer only to the elevated but shallow valleys of the eastern plateau, not the steeper valleys of Roshan, Shughnan and Wakhan in the west along the river Panj, but most contemporary Russian and British sources use it to refer to the entire region, and I too will do so in this chapter.

[2] The most famous of these accounts is Francis Younghusband, *The Heart of a Continent: A Narrative of Travels in Manchuria, across the Gobi Desert, through the Himalayas, the Pamirs, and Hunza 1884–1894* (London: John Murray, 1896). See also Gabriel Bonvalot, *Du Caucase aux Indes, à travers le Pamir* (Paris: Librairie Plon, 1889); G. Littledale, 'A Journey across the Pamir from North to South', *PRGS* 14/1 (1892), 1–35; Earl of Dunmore, *The Pamirs; Being a Narrative of a Year's Expedition on Horseback and Foot through Kashmir, Western Tibet, Chinese Tartary and Russian Central Asia* (London: John Murray, 1893) 2 volumes; G. N. Curzon, *The Pamirs and the Source of the Oxus* (London: The Royal Geographical Society, 1896) & *On the Indian Frontier* ed. Dhara Anjaria (Karachi: Oxford University Press, 2012); Sven Hedin, *Through Asia* (London: Methuen & Co., 1898) 2 volumes; Algernon Durand, *The Making of a Frontier: Five Years' Experiences and Adventures in Gilgit, Hunza, Nagar, Chitral, and the Eastern Hindu-Kush* (London: John Murray, 1899); Ralph Cobbold, *Innermost Asia: Travel and Sport in the Pamirs* (London: William Heinemann, 1900); Wilhelm Filchner, *Ein Ritt über den Pamir* (Berlin: Ernst Siegfried Mittler und Sohn, 1903); O. Olufsen, *Through the Unknown Pamirs: The Second Danish Pamir Expedition, 1898–99* (London: William Heinemann, 1904).

perhaps, because there was a certain romance and heroism attached to this wild and majestic terrain, 'where men and mountains meet', to use John Keay's evocative phrase, which was lacking from the domesticated landscapes of fields, poplars and irrigation canals in the lowland oasis regions of Central Asia.[3] The equally picturesque inhabitants of the mountains attracted interest from philologists and ethnographers out of all proportion to their numbers, and rapidly became mythologised in equal measure, as the innocent 'guardians of edenic sanctuaries' (like the hill-peoples of India), as practitioners of a less 'fanatical' form of Islam than that of the lowlands, and as providing linguistic and racial evidence of the original 'Aryan' population of Central Asia.[4] This was the one phase of the Russian conquest which almost justifies the use of the old Soviet term *prisoedinenie* – if not in its literal translation as 'uniting', then as the looser 'annexation' or 'occupation'. Apart from a few skirmishes with Afghan troops, the Russians occupied the Pamir region more or less without violence – and indeed would soon cast themselves as the protectors of its population against the rapacity both of the Afghans and of the lowland officials of their own protectorate, the Emirate of Bukhara. The mountainous region north and east of the river Panj saw the emergence of a self-consciously elite 'frontier cadre' of Russian officers, many of them from the Main Staff, who had much in common with their counterparts on the North-West frontier of British India; men who claimed to 'know the native mind', and did much to create the image of the Pamir region as a world apart, uncontaminated by the sordid, moneygrubbing world of the lowlands, with a distinct culture that required paternalist protection – a view that persists to this day.

Perhaps the best-known of this cadre, Andrei Evgen'evich Snesarev (1865–1937),[5] was also one of the initiators of an unusually rich and detailed historiography, which grew out of a nexus between Persianate chronicles, military

[3] John Keay, *Where Men & Mountains Meet: The Explorers of the Western Himalayas 1820–1875* (Karachi: Oxford University Press, 1977) &*The Gilgit Game: Explorers of the Western Himalayas 1865–1895* (London: John Murray, 1979).

[4] Dane Kennedy, 'Guardians of Edenic Sanctuaries: Paharis, Lepchas, and Todas in the British Mind', *South Asia* 14/2 (1991), 57–77; Laruelle, *Mythe aryen et rêve impérial*, 133–67.

[5] Snesarev had a doctorate in mathematics from Moscow University and had sung professionally at the Bolshoi Theatre, but made his mark primarily as a Military Orientalist both before and after the revolution. He was the author of many standard works on the Pamirs, British India and Afghanistan. See in particular A. E. Snesarev, 'Religiya i obychai gortsev zapadnogo Pamira', *TV* Nos. 89–93, 29/06–07/07/1904; *Indiya kak glavnyi faktor v sredneaziatskom voprose* (St Pb.: A. Suvorin, 1906) & A. E. Snesarev (ed.), *Svedeniya kasaiushchiyasya stran, sopredel'nykh s Turkestanskim Voennym Okrugom* (Tashkent: Tip. Shtaba Turkestanskogo Voennogo Okruga, 1898–1900) 19 volumes. See further Volkov, *Russia's Turn to Persia*, 180–2, 220–2; M. K. Baskhanov, *'U vorot angliiskogo mogushchestva': A. E. Snesarev v Turkestane 1899–1904* (St Pb.: Nestor-Istoriya, 2015); Oybek Mahmudov, '"Po Pamiram … na angel'skikh vysotakh …": Andrei Evgen'evich Snesarev o Pamire i pamirtsakh' (forthcoming); for a full list of Snesarev's publications see his entry in M. K. Baskhanov's indispensable *Russkie voennye vostokovedy do 1917 goda: Biobibliograficheskii slovar'* (Moscow: Vostochnaya Literatura, 2005), 217–20.

ethnography and geography, oriental studies (*vostokovedenie*) and, later, Soviet academic scholarship, which continued to accord a special status to this region, most of which was included in the Gorno-Badakhshan autonomous *oblast'* of the Tajik SSR. Three important Persian-language chronicles describing the Russian annexation were produced in the early twentieth century, and subsequently published, all of which give a generally positive account of the advent of Russian rule.[6] Apart from Snesarev, other Tsarist officers and orientalists who wrote detailed accounts of their journeys and service in the region include B. L. Grombchevskii, A. A. Semenov, A. G. Serebrennikov and B. L. Tageev; their works often rise well above the genre of military orientalism, although they still have to be handled with caution.[7] The Pamir region continued to generate some excellent scholarship in the Soviet period. N. A. Khalfin, whose tendentious studies of the Russian conquest I have often had occasion to criticise elsewhere in this book, produced by far his best work on relations between Russia and the Bukharan emirate in the western Pamirs.[8] Despite its not always very subtle anti-Uzbek and anti-lowland-Tajik agenda, the exhaustive work of Bahodur Iskandarov on the history of the Pamirs is also indispensable.[9] Partly as a result of this, and also because of the generous funding that has been available from the Aga Khan foundation for research on the Isma'ilis of Badakhshan since the Soviet collapse, the quality and quantity of modern scholarship on the region is also

---

[6] Mirza Sang Muhammad Badakhshi & Fazl 'Ali-bek Surkh Afsar, *Ta'rikh-i Badakhshan – Istoriya Badakhshana* ed. & trans A. N. Boldyrev (Leningrad: Izd. Leningradskogo Gosudarstvennogo Universiteta, 1959; reprinted Moscow: Nauka, 1997). The main part of this text by Badakhshi was composed in the early nineteenth century, the continuation (*tattimah*) was provided by Surkh-Afsar in 1907. See Farid Ullah Bezhan, 'The Enigmatic Authorship of "*Tārikh-i Badakhshān*"', *East and West* 58/1–4 (2008), 107–21 for a description of this text, which questions the authorship attributed to it by Boldyrev; Seiid Khaidar-Sho, *Istoriya Shugnana (Ta'rikh-i Shugnan)* trans. A. A. Semenov (Tashkent: Tip. pri Kantselyarii Turkestanskogo General-Gubernatora, 1916) & *TKLA* 21 (1917), i–iii, 1–23; Qurban Muhammadzadah & Muhabbat Shahzadah, *Tā'rīkh-i Badakhshan* [*c.* 1930] ed. A. A. Egani (Moscow: Nauka, 1973). My thanks to Daniel Beben for his guidance on all these sources.

[7] B. L. Grombchevskii, *Na sluchai voiny s Indieiu: Ozero Shiva kak strategicheskii punkt: Voenno-politicheskii ocherk* (Novyi Margelan: Tip. Ferganskogo Oblastnogo Pravleniya, 1891) & *Doklad Podpolkovnika B. L. Grombchevskago, chitannyi v Nikolaevskoi Akademii General'nogo Shtaba 14 marta 1891 g.* (Moscow: n.p., 1891); A. A. Semenov, 'Po granitsam Bukhary i Afganistana (putevye ocherki 1898 g.)', *IV* (1898), No. 3, 961–92; No. 4, 98–122; A. G. Serebrennikov, *Ocherki Pamira* (St Pb.: Tip. Glavnoe Upravlenie Udelov, 1900); B. L. Tageev, 'Pamirskii pokhod (vospominaniya ochevidtsa)', *IV* (1898), No. 7, 111–63; *Pamirskie pokhody 1892–1895 g.* (Warsaw: Gubernskaya Tip., 1900) & 'Russkie nad Indiei: Ocherki i rasskazy iz boevoi zhizni na Pamire', in *Poludennye ekspeditsii: Ocherki* (Moscow: Voennoe Izd., 1998), 163–350.

[8] N. A. Khalfin, *Rossiya i Bukharskii emirat na Zapadnom Pamire* (Moscow: Nauka, 1975).

[9] See in particular Bakhodur Iskandarov, *Vostochnaya Bukhara i Pamir vo vtoroi polovine XIX v.* (Dushanbe: AN Tadzhikskoi SSR, 1962–3; reprint Dushanbe: Donish, 2012).

unusually high. The standard work on Badakhshan before the Russian conquest remains that of Grevemeyer, but alongside this Thomas Welsford has explored its place in the appanage system of the Uzbek Khans, Alexandre Papas the history of Badakhshani Sufi lineages and Gabrielle van den Berg the rich legacies of oral and written poetry, while Daniel Beben's Ph.D. thesis contains a wealth of new research on narratives of Islamisation and the origins of the Isma'ili *da'wa* in the region.[10] A. V. Postnikov's *Struggle on the 'Roof of the World'* is the definitive account of the exploration and annexation of the Pamirs in Russian, and the debt which I owe to his work will be obvious in this chapter.[11] The best general account of Russian explorations and annexations in English is Robert Middleton's excellent series of chapters on the subject in the *Odyssey Guide to Tajikistan and the High Pamirs*.[12] In Tajik we have Khaidarsho Pirumshoev's history of Darvaz, a fruitful union of older traditions of local history with modern academic scholarship.[13] Current research by Matthias Battis, Daniel Beben, Hakim Elnazarov and Oybek Mahmudov also promises to transform our understanding of nineteenth- and early-twentieth-century Badakhshan and the scholars who studied it.[14] Accordingly, in this

[10] Jan-Heeren Grevemeyer, *Herrschaft, Raub und Gegenseitigkeit: Die politische Geschichte Badakhshans 1500–1883* (Wiesbaden: O. Harrassowitz, 1982); Welsford, *Four Types of Loyalty*, 185–195; Alexandre Papas, 'Soufis du Badakhshân: Un renouveau confrérique entre l'Inde et l'Asie centrale', in *CAC*. Vols. 11–12. *Les Montagnards d'Asie centrale* ed. Svetlana Jacquesson (Tashkent & Aix-en-Provence: IFEAC, Éditions De Boccard, 2004), 87–102; G. R. van den Berg, *Minstrel Poetry from the Pamir Mountains: A Study on the Songs and Poems of the Isma'ilis of Tajik Badakhshan* (Wiesbaden: Reichert Verlag, 2004); Daniel Beben, 'The Legendary Biographies of Nasir-i Khusraw: Memory and Textualisation in Early Modern Persian Isma'ilism' (Ph.D. Dissertation, Indiana University, Bloomington, 2015).

[11] A. V. Postnikov, *Skhvatka na 'Kryshe mira': Politiki, razvedchiki i geografy v bor'be za Pamir v XIX veke: Monografiya v dokumentakh* (Moscow: Pamyatniki Istoricheskoi Mysli, 2001).

[12] Robert Middleton, 'The Pamirs: Exploration and Adventure on the Roof of the World', in *Tajikistan and the High Pamirs: A Companion and Guide* ed. Robert Middleton & Huw Thomas (Hong Kong: Odyssey Books and Guides, 2012), 260–513.

[13] Khaidarsho Pirumshoev, *Ta'rikhi Darvoz (az qadim to zamoni muosir)* (Dushanbe: Irfon, 2008).

[14] See Matthias Battis, 'Soviet Orientalism and Nationalism in Central Asia: Aleksandr Semenov's Vision of Tajik National Identity', *IS* 48/2 (2015), 729–45; Daniel Beben, 'Local Narratives of the Great Game in Badakhshan' (unpublished paper, cited with the kind permission of the author); Hakim Elnazarov, 'Anglo-Russian Rivalry in the Pamirs and Hindukush, 1860–1914' (Ph.D. Thesis, King's College London, 2018); Oybek Mahmudov, 'I. D. Yagello na Pamire: Maloizvestnye stranitsy deyatel'nosti Nachal'nika Pamirskogo otryada (po arkhivnym materialam)', *O'zbekiston Tarixi* (2015), No. 3, 64–71; 'Pamir i pamirtsy v trudakh russkikh puteshestvennikov i issledovatelei poslednei treti XIX–nachala XX veka (po materialam turkestanskogo sbornika)', in *Rossiisko-uzbekistanskie svyazi v kontekste mnogovekovoi istoricheskoi retrospektivy* (Tashkent: n.p., 2013), 324–39; '"Odichalye frantsuzy" Pamira: Naselenie Pamira pripamirskikh vladenii glazami russkikh voennykh i issledovatelei', *CIAS Discussion Paper* (Kyoto, 2013), No. 35, 47–71 & 'Skvoz dzhungli instruktsii po "Kryshe Mira": Politika Rossi i Pamirskaya okraina

chapter I will concentrate on establishing the motivations and chronology of the Russian advance into and eventual annexation of the region, and the emergence of a fierce debate as to whether it should be administered directly by Russian officials, or by those of the Emirate of Bukhara, to which Shughnan, Roshan and Wakhan were initially annexed when the Pamir boundary was drawn in 1895. I argue that, while the older 'Great Game' narrative emphasising rivalry with Britain is of some relevance, Russian and British interests in the region were in the end quite easily and amicably reconciled – something largely ignored in the dominant historiography.[15] Their common European identity, and common sense of imperial mission, helped to ensure the success of what was effectively a gentleman's agreement which pointedly excluded both the local population and the other two states whose territory met in the region – Afghanistan and China.[16] Indeed, reading Russian sources it is clear that their contempt and hostility were directed primarily towards these 'native' powers, especially the Afghans, with whom they had their only violent clashes. What is also striking is the unusually sympathetic Russian attitude towards the local population– above all the Pamiri 'highlanders' (*gortsy*) of Shughnan, Roshan and Wakhan – which stood in stark contrast to the brutality with which they had treated their lowland neighbours in Ferghana fifteen years before. Like Daniel Dravot and Peachey Carnahan in Kipling's *The Man Who Would Be King*, they saw the mountain-dwellers as special – Aryans, white men, not ordinary 'black Mohammedans' like the Sunni lowlanders of Ferghana, Bukhara and Afghanistan. While the Russians also evoked the supposed link with the legions of Alexander the Great (an important source of legitimacy for some local lineages),[17] for them the Pamiris of Roshan, Shughnan and Wakhan were the last remnants of the autochthonous population of Central Asia, driven into the mountains by successive waves of Turkic migration, but still preserving racial and linguistic purity.[18]

imperii glazami russkogo kolonial'nogo chinovnika' (unpublished paper, cited with the kind permission of the author).

[15] See notably Terent'ev, *Istoriya zavoevaniya*, III, 394–426; Hopkirk, *The Great Game*, 447–501; Sergeev, *The Great Game*, 212–28 & *Bol'shaya Igra*, 186–99.

[16] Morrison, 'Russian Rule in Turkestan and the Example of British India', 689–91; Campbell, "'Our Friendly Rivals'".

[17] Sergei Abashin, 'Le culte d'Iskandar Zu-l-Qarnayn chez les montagnards d'Asie centrale', *CAC* 11/12 (2004), 61–86.

[18] This is seen particularly clearly in the materials produced by the expedition to the western Pamirs led by Count A. A. Bobrinskii in 1898: A. A. Bobrinskii, *Gortsy verkhov'ev Piandzha (Vakhantsy i Ishkashimtsy: Ocherki byta)* (Moscow: n.p., 1908), 13–14; V. V. Eggert, 'Ocherk Pamirov (svedeniya sobrannye v Pamirskom otryade s avgusta 1896 goda po iiul' 1897 goda)', in *Sbornik geograficheskikh, topograficheskikh i statisticheskikh materialov po Azii* (St Pb.: n.p., 1902), Vyp. 16–17. See Matthias Battis, 'Aleksandr A. Semenov (1873–1958) and His Vision of Tajik Identity: On the Origins of Soviet Nationalities Policy in Late Imperial Russian Oriental Studies' (D.Phil. Thesis,

This discourse played a key legitimising role in the Russian conquest: as early as 1877 the well-known military geographer Mikhail Veniukov wrote that Russia was fulfilling her historical destiny by liberating the Aryan population of the mountain massifs of Central Asia from Turkic oppression, and reuniting them with their brethren in Europe.[19] As Marlène Laruelle has shown, the 'Aryan Myth' was widely disseminated among intellectuals in the Russian empire, although I would disagree with her conclusion that in Russia it remained a largely cultural and philological idea, without overtones of race.[20] Given that the main outgrowth of racial 'Aryanism' in Western Europe was a virulent form of anti-Semitism, and that the Russian state and society in the nineteenth century were the most anti-Semitic in Europe, this distinction is hard to sustain.[21] It is clear that Aryanism in Russia was often an explicitly racial idea, especially among officers and orientalists in Central Asia. Snesarev, writing to his sister in 1901, may have emphasised language when he observed that 'In the valley of the Panj I became acquainted with the Tajiks, who turn out to be the most purely preserved Aryans: many of their words so remind you of our, or German, or French words, that you are simply astonished.'[22] However, he also argued that the reason Indians had been feeble, passive and ripe for conquest over the previous 1,000 years was because of the admixture of Dravidian blood in the Aryan stock of the upper classes, an observation which mirrors much British writing on the subject.[23] Serebrennikov wrote that 'the Tajiks of Shughnan, Roshan and Wakhan have been less subject to mixing with peoples of Turko-Mongol blood than other representatives of the

University of Oxford, 2016), Chapter 5; D. Khudonazarov, *Pamirskie ekspeditsii Grafa A. A. Bobrinskogo 1895–1901 godov: Etnograficheskii al'bom* (Moscow: Nauka, 2013).

[19] Veniukov, 'Postupatel'noe dvizhenie Rossii v Srednei Azii', 60; Laruelle, *Mythe aryen*, 138–9.

[20] *Ibid.*, 180–1.

[21] There is a vast literature on anti-Semitism in late Tsarist Russia. See, notably, Hans Rogger, 'The Beilis Case: Anti-Semitism and Politics in the Reign of Nicholas II', *SR* 25/4 (1966), 615–29; Eugene M. Avrutin, 'Racial Categories and the Politics of (Jewish) Difference in Late Imperial Russia', *Kritika* 8/1 (2007), 13–40; Laura Engelstein, 'The Old Slavophile Steed: Failed Nationalism and the Philosophers' Jewish Problem', in *Slavophile Empire: Imperial Russia's Illiberal Path* (Ithaca, NY: Cornell University Press, 2009), 192–203. On ideas of race in physical anthropology in late Imperial Russia see Marina Mogilner, 'Russian Physical Anthropology of the Nineteenth–Early Twentieth Centuries: Imperial Race, Colonial Other, Degenerate Types, and the Russian Racial Body', in *Empire Speaks Out* ed. Gerasimov, Kusber & Semyonov, 155–89; Marina Mogil'ner, *Homo Imperii: Istoriya fizicheskoi antropologii v Rossii* (Moscow: Novoe Literaturnoe Obozrenie, 2008).

[22] A. E. Snesarev to K. E. Komarova, Khorog, 05/06/1901, *Pis'ma A. E. Snesareva iz Indii i Srednei Azii 1899–1904* (Moscow: Tsentrizdat, 2006), 474.

[23] Snesarev, *Indiya kak glavnyi faktor*, 71; see further Joan Leopold, 'British Applications of the Aryan theory of Race to India, 1850–1870', *EHR* 89/352 (1974), 578–603 & T. R. Trautmann, *Aryans and British India* (Berkeley, CA: University of California Press, 1997).

Aryan tribes, and therefore present themselves as members of the Aryan family who have most preserved the purity of type' – he then gave a detailed description of their phrenological characteristics.[24] However, while she downplays racial thinking in Russian Aryanism, Laruelle does demonstrate how useful the 'Aryan myth' could be in providing Russia with a superior identity that was not necessarily overtly European, and in establishing a justification – through kinship – for reconquering Central Asia and Siberia from the Turkic nomads who had supposedly usurped them.[25] It also produced a strong imperative to demonstrate the benevolence and paternalism of rule by the Russians over their racial brethren on the Pamirs.

Like the steppe campaigns of the 1850s and 1860s, but unlike the campaigns in the neighbouring Zarafshan and Ferghana valleys, local environmental conditions were the main challenges the Russians had to overcome on the Pamirs, and determined the nature and progress of their advance. The steepness of the terrain, the lack of grazing, the very limited local grain supply and the extremely harsh winters of this highland region ensured that the Russian military presence remained minimal. The Pamir expeditions were one of the very few instances in the nineteenth century when the Russian army was called upon to engage in mountain warfare.[26] The main constraint was animal transport: here ponies took the place of the camels of the steppe campaigns, but the limitation on numbers remained the same – given the lack of grazing available for them on the Pamir plateau, the ponies had to carry their own fodder.[27] Thus, while the first proper expeditionary force in 1892 consisted of 900 men, the permanent garrison the Russians established that year numbered just 150, scattered between several small outposts, while it was reconnaissance parties of just 25 men which engaged the Afghans in 1892–3. This demonstrates what James C. Scott describes as the increased friction of extending state power into upland areas: the costs of effective occupation and administration were extremely high, and the rewards for the state in the Pamirs were even lower than in the Southeast Asian Massif which forms the focus of his work, given the greater elevation and more northerly latitude.[28] Quite simply, the Pamirs were incapable of providing enough agricultural produce to pay for their military occupation, and the greater exploitation of their fabled mineral resources (Badakhshan rubies, lapis lazuli) hardly figured in Russian calculations, as creating a modern mining industry would have required a massive investment in transport infrastructure. The Russians had no economic interest in occupying the Pamirs, and it was the mountains' strategic geographical

---

[24] A. G. Serebrennikov, 'Ocherk Pamira', VS (1899), No. 10, 447–9.
[25] Laruelle, Mythe aryen, 133–9.
[26] Statiev, At War's Summit, 11–32 summarises the other cases.
[27] Morrison, 'Camels and Colonial Armies'.
[28] James C. Scott, The Art of Not Being Governed: An Anarchist History of Upland Southeast Asia (Newhaven, CN: Yale University Press, 2009), 1–63.

location which gave them their importance.[29] Indeed, historically Badakhshan had rarely produced enough even for the subsistence of the local sedentary population, who had a long history of migrating to find work in the lowlands, in particular as soldiers. A substantial proportion of the armies of the Mughal emperors in India, as well as part of Khoqand's *sarbaz* infantry in the early nineteenth century, were *ghalchas*, the slightly derogatory lowland term for the mountain-dwellers.[30]

As might be expected then, following Scott's thesis, the inhabitants of the Pamirs historically had a largely antagonistic relationship with neighbouring lowland states, but they were more dependent on neighbouring lowland regions than their equivalents in Southeast Asia owing to lower agricultural productivity.[31] This in turn seems to have made it considerably more difficult for them to withdraw altogether from state control. In the course of this chapter we will encounter the Kyrgyz and Tajiks of the Pamirs entering under and seeking to escape from the Chinese, British Indian, Afghan, Bukharan and Russian states; and, at the risk of reproducing the rose-tinted Soviet narrative, for both religious and fiscal reasons the Russians were probably the most appealing of these options.

10.1 Russian Expeditions to the Pamirs

Britain and Russia began negotiations over their relative spheres of influence in Badakhshan in the late 1860s, when it became clear that their colonial possessions were growing more adjacent. The 1873 Gorchakov–Granville Agreement took the line of the Panj as the limit of Afghan sovereignty; Postnikov notes that, although the Russians had at first contested Afghan claims to Badakhshan and Wakhan, their negotiating position was weakened by their almost complete reliance on British maps and travelogues, principally the account by Captain John Wood of his journey in 1838 from Qunduz along the Oxus (Panj) to Zor Kul, which he considered naming Lake Victoria, and mistakenly believed to be the river's source.[32] Although Alexei Fedchenko had explored the foothills of the Alai range neighbouring Ferghana in the early 1870s, it was

[29] A. G. Serebrennikov, 'Ocherk Pamira', *VS* (1899), No. 7, 223–4.

[30] Zahiruddin Muhammad Babur, *The Baburnama: Memoirs of Babur, Prince and Emperor* trans. & ed. Wheeler M. Thackston (New York, NY: Random House, 2002), 396; Nur ud-Din Muhammad Jahangir, *The Jahangirnama: Memoirs of Jahangir, Emperor of India* trans. & ed. Wheeler M. Thackston (Oxford: Oxford University Press, 1999), 83; Levi, 'The Ferghana Valley', 228.

[31] See further on this point Daniel Beben, 'Religious and Ethnic Identity in the Pamirs: The Ismāʿīlī Daʿwa in Shughnan in the 17th to 19th Centuries', in *Revisiting Pamiri Identity in Central Asia and Beyond* ed. Carole Faucher and Dagikhudo Dagiev (London: Routledge, 2019), 123–42.

[32] A. V. Postnikov, "'Istoricheskie prava" sosednikh gosudarstv i geografiya Pamira kak argumenty v "Bol'shoi Igre" Britanii i Rossii (1869–1896 gg.)', *Acta Slavica Iaponica* 17 (2000), 40–8; John Wood, *A Journey to the Source of the River Oxus* (London: John

484   ARYANISM ON THE FINAL FRONTIER

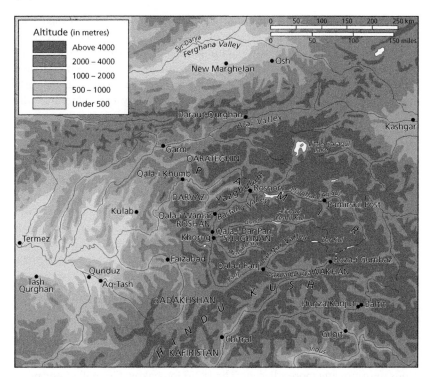

Map 10 The Pamirs. Redrawn by Cox Cartographic Ltd from S. Umanets 'Pamirskii Vopros i ego znachenie' IV (1892) No.1 pp. 196–208 and 'Map of the Pamir Mountains' by Markus Hauser, with the kind permission of the Pamir Archive.

only after the annexation of Khoqand and the creation of the new Ferghana province in 1876 that the Russian authorities really began to turn their attention to this remote and unexplored region.[33] Osh and New Marghelan were the starting points for their earliest scientific and military expeditions, and Khoqand's vague claims to sovereignty over the plateau would later form the basis of those put forward by Russia, though they were always contested by the British.[34] In May 1876, when Russian punitive expeditions against so-called

Murray, 1872); see also Chikhachev, 'O issledovanii vershin Syr i Amu-dar'i', 28–9; Anon., 'On Badakhshán and Wakhán' *PRGS* 17/2 (1872), 108–16.

[33] A. Fedchenko, *Iz Kokana: Svedeniya o puteshestvii po Kokandskomu khanstvu A. P. Fedchenko v 1871 g. iz turkestanskikh vedomostei* (Tashkent: Tip. Okruzhnogo Shtaba, 1871) & 'Puteshestvie v Turkestan', 131–60.

[34] For example Grombchevskii, *Doklad*, 18; S. Umanets, 'Pamirskii vopros i ego znachenie', IV (1892), No. 1, 202; A. G. Serebrennikov, 'Ocherk Pamira' *VS* (1899) No.9, 226; see IOR/L/P & S/18/A89 *Note on the Connection between the Khanate of Khokand and the Pamirs* 21/10/1892, 1: 'Such evidence as I have gathered is of necessity almost entirely negative. If the sovereignty of Khokand over the Pamirs had existed as a fact, or even as a

'*shaiki*' (bands) led by former Khoqandi officials in the Alai were still in full flow, Rahim Shah, the ruler of the neighbouring region of Qarateghin, wrote to M. D. Skobelev offering him presents as the new ruler of Ferghana, and asking him to suppress a band of Kyrgyz who were making trouble for him with raids and banditry in the Alai region. In his reply, Skobelev took this as a request from Rahim Shah to preserve the same relationship with Russia that he had previously had with Khoqand, which he interpreted as one of suzerainty: 'I have presented to the attention of the *Yarim Padshah* (the Turkestan Governor-General, von Kaufman) the desire of your Highness to be obedient and fulfil all the orders of the Russian government'.[35] A few months later Skobelev reported disturbances in Qarateghin, where the Amir of Bukhara had taken advantage of Khoqand's demise to expel Rahim Shah (who had fled to Garm) and impose his own administration – this was probably what had prompted Rahim Shah to make his nominal submission to the Russians in the first place. This had led to a rebellion against the Amir's authority, and an appeal from the population for the Russians to intervene; this was not the last time they would be asked to protect the peoples of this region from the activities of their own vassal, although on this occasion it did not meet with a positive response. Just a week later, the Russians signed a *shartnama* (agreement) with Bukhara, agreeing the boundaries between Ferghana and Qarateghin, leaving the Amir in firm control.[36] As this indicates, so long as the mountainous regions to the south of their new possessions remained either under the nominal sovereignty of the Chinese, or persisted as small, semi-independent khanates under their own rulers, the Russians had little interest in extending direct sovereignty over them; it was only the annexation of Roshan and Shughnan by the Afghan Amir, 'Abdurrahman Khan, in 1883–4, coupled with the appearance of British agents at Gilgit and Hunza in the late 1880s, which led to a growing uneasiness about the security of their southern frontier.[37] Even before this, however, they sought more accurate knowledge of the geography of the region.

The first major Russian expeditions to the Pamir region both took place in 1878.[38] The first, led by the zoologist N. A. Severtsov (he who had been

---

well-understood claim, one would have inevitably found references to it in a careful study of contemporaneous accounts of the Khanate . . . '.

[35] Rahim Shah to Skobelev (trans.) n.d. [April–May 1876]; Skobelev to Rahim Shah 24/05/1876 RGVIA F.1396 Op.2 D. 97 ll. 39–43.

[36] Telegram Skobelev to von Kaufman 22/08/1876; 'Dogovor o provedenii granitsy mezhdu Ferganskuiu oblast'iu i vladeniem Emira Bukharskogo Karateginom', RGVIA F.1396 Op.2 D.97 ll. 291–2, 419–20a. See further Pirumshoev, *Ta'rikhi Darvoz*, 69.

[37] Robert A. Huttenback, 'The 'Great Game' in the Pamirs and the Hindu-Kush: The British Conquest of Hunza and Nagar', *MAS* 9/1 (1975), 1–29.

[38] A. G. Serebrennikov, 'Ocherk Pamira', *VS* (1899), No. 6, 438–44 contains a summary description of Russian expeditions, with more detailed accounts in Postnikov, *Svkhatka*, 133–77 and Middleton, 'The Pamirs', 386–435.

captured and imprisoned by the Khoqandis in Turkestan twenty years earlier), crossed the Alai range through the Qizil-Art pass as far as lake Yeshil-Qul. Severtsov's party concentrated mainly on carrying out a topographical survey of the Pamir peaks and watersheds, but he died before most of his results could be published.[39] In October of that year Colonel Matveev, Chief of Staff of the forces in Syr-Darya Province, was despatched on a mission with a more military focus, to Badakhshan through Eastern Bukhara, with a brief to explore the routes south of Ferghana through Kafiristan to India. He was accompanied by Franz von Schwarz, a German astronomer at the Tashkent Observatory, and a German zoologist, Friedrich Johann Wilhelm Russow, with a small escort of two riflemen and six Cossacks. The expedition travelled via Qara-Tepe and Kitab to Kulab, where Russow turned back, pleading the cold. They crossed the Amu-Darya with some difficulty at Sary-Chashma, when they were delayed by Muhammad Nabi Khan, the governor of Rustak, who had to send to the Khan of Tokhtapul for permission to allow them to proceed. Matveev described how, once on the left bank, they were received 'coldly' by the Afghans, and told that all communications with Chitral and Kafiristan were cut off by snow, and that in any case the Badakhshanis had no intercourse with Kafiristan, while the fierce 'Siahpushi'[40] who inhabited the region did not allow travellers through. Matveev was shown a group of these 'Siahpushi', whom he described as having 'a wholly savage aspect, with long loose hair, and their appearance strongly recalled that of American Indians, as portrayed by [James Fenimore] Cooper'.[41] Matveev noted that that the local Tajik population 'hate the Afghans, who conduct themselves as if they were in an enemy country', a refrain that would be often repeated in future years.[42] The Russians were regarded with great suspicion by the Afghan authorities, who kept them under close guard throughout their time there, and 'looked on us as agitators stirring up the population against Amir Shir 'Ali, on behalf of 'Abdurrahman Khan, who has great popularity among the people'. The rest of Matveev's report consisted mainly of reflections on the timidity of the local population

---

[39] N. A. Severtsov, 'Kratkii otchet o Pamirskikh issledovaniyakh i obshchikh nauchnykh rezul'tatakh Ferganskoi uchenoi ekspeditsii', *IIRGO* (1879), No. 2, 66–86, also in *TS* Vol. 349, 65–75A, & trans. Alexis Lomonossof as 'M. Severtsof's Journey in Ferghana and the Pamir in 1877-8', *PRGS* 2/8 (1880), 499–506 & *Orograficheskii ocherk Pamirskoi gornoi sistemy* (St Pb.: Tip. Imperatorskoi Akademii Nauk, 1886).

[40] Matveev meant the *Siah-push*, or 'black shirts', one of the divisions of the Kafir people. See G. S. Robertson, *The Kafirs of the Hindu-Kush* (London: Lawrence & Bullen, 1896), 74–8. Olufsen surveyed a number of large fortresses in Wakhan which the local inhabitants said had been constructed during a period of Kafir rule two or three hundred years before: *Through the Unknown Pamirs*, 165–96.

[41] Matveev to commander of the Syr-Darya *Oblast'* 24/10/1878 RGVIA F.400 Op.1 D.578, 'O poezdke Polkovnika Matveeva v Badagshan', ll. 3–8.

[42] Matveev to commander of the Syr-Darya *Oblast'* 24/10/1878 RGVIA F.400 Op.1 D.578 l. 8.

and their sufferings since the conquest of Badakhshan by the Afghans in 1873, though he also noted the discovery of Greek silver coinage at the ruined fortress of Kafir-Qala, near Rustak.[43] Despite his failure to penetrate any further into Badakhshan, von Kaufman pronounced himself well satisfied with the surveying work done by this party, which had established the precise locations of a number of towns in the eastern part of the Bukharan protectorate. In 1881 Dr E. A. Regel followed the same route to the Western Pamir, visiting Shughnan for botanical research.[44] A more elaborate military expedition to the region was despatched by M. G. Chernyaev when he became Governor-General in 1883, led by Staff-Captain D. V. Putyata, and including a mining engineer called D. L. Ivanov and the military topographer N. A. Benderskii, who would later play an important role in delineating the Pamir boundary. This expedition followed what would become the standard route for Russian explorers, travelling via the Alai valley as far as the valley of the Aq-Su/Murghab river, where the Russians would establish their first permanent post ten years later.[45]

Between 1884 and 1887 the famous Polish explorer and lepidopterist G. E. Grumm-Grzhimailo (1860–1936) undertook a series of expeditions in pursuit of butterflies through the Alai valley to Qarateghin, Darvaz, Rang-Qul and the Aq-Su/Murghab valley.[46] N. F. Petrovskii (1837–1908), the Russian consul in Kashgar, took against Grumm-Grzhimailo (possibly because he was Polish, though Petrovskii's misanthropy was fairly universal).[47] He described him as

[43] 'Otchet o poezdke Nachal'nika Shtaba voisk Syr-Dar'inskoi Oblasti po Bukharskim i Avganskim vladeniyam', 06/02/1879 RGVIA F.400 Op.1 D.578 ll. 23, 53.

[44] E. A. Regel, 'Poezdka v Karategin i Darvaz', IIRGO 18/2 (1882), 127–41; 'Puteshestvie v Shugnan', TV (1884), No. 17 & 'Puteshestvie v Shugnan', IIRGO 20/4 (1884), 268–74.

[45] D. V. Putyata, 'Pamirskie Ekspeditsii 1883 g.', IIRGO 19 (1883), 332–40 – this includes an excellent map, showing their route, and was published in English a year later as 'The Russian Pamir Expedition of 1883', PRGS 6/3 (1884), 135–42 & 'Ocherk ekspeditsii v Pamir, Sarykol, Vakhan i Shugnan v 1883 g.', Sbornik geograficheskikh, topograficheskikh i statisticheskikh materialov po Azii (1884), Vyp. 10, 1–88; D. L. Ivanov, 'Puteshestvie na Pamir', IIRGO 20 (1884), 209–52; 'Chto nazyvat' Pamirom', IIRGO 21/2 (1885), 131–45 & 'Shugnan: Afganskie ocherki', VE 4/7 (1885), 49–52. On Putyata, see Baskhanov, Voennye vostokovedy, 197–8.

[46] G. E. Grumm-Grzhimailo, 'Ocherk pripamirskikh stran', IIRGO 22/2 (1886), 81–109 in TS Vol. 405, 36–50; Gr. Groum-Grshimaïlo, Le Pamir et sa faune lépidoptérologique: Mémoires sur les lépidoptéres ed. N. M. Romanoff Vol. IV (St Pb.: M. M. Stassuléwitsch, 1890); this detail made its way into an anxious British intelligence report that year: Huttenback, 'The Great Game', 11. See further Tatiana Yusupova, 'Grigorii Efimovich Grumm-Grzhimailo (1860–1936)', in The Quest for Forbidden Lands: Nikolai Przheval'skii and His Followers on Inner Asian Tracks ed. Alexandre Andreyev, Mikhail Baskhanov & Tatiana Yusupova (Leiden: Brill, 2018), 311–47.

[47] My thanks to Oybek Mahmudov for this insight into Petrovskii's character. For an account of the Russian presence in Kashgar, where Petrovskii wielded considerable influence, see D. Arapov, 'Vy posylaetes v stranu, kotoruiu my malo znaem: Razvedyvatel'naya "programma" russkogo konsula v Kashgare N. F. Petrovskogo',

enormously conceited, writing that 'his reserves of knowledge are small, his ability to conduct research and use instruments nil, and his self-importance is colossal. In conversation all one hears is "Humboldt was mistaken, Richthofen is mistaken, Przheval'skii could have done a lot more, I found, I determined etc." You know better than I do, how highly, in the world of geographical exploration, the work of our travellers in Central Asia stands. I fear that these new travellers, of the type of Mr Grumm, will end up discrediting all these previous researches through their unfounded work and frivolousness.'[48] Petrovskii's fears for the authority enjoyed by Russian exploration would prove unfounded.

It was another Pole, Bronislav Ludvigovich Grombchevskii (1855–1926 – Figure 10.1),[49] a nobleman from Kovno, educated in Warsaw, who became the most prominent advocate of a permanent Russian presence on the Pamirs, and certainly their best-known military explorer. He transferred to the 14th Turkestan Line Battalion in 1876 and participated in the conquest of Ferghana, where he was a member of Skobelev's punitive expedition into the Alai range. He would remain in the region until 1900, when he became boundary commissioner in Kwantung (Port Arthur), and ended his active career as Governor-General of Astrakhan.[50] Many accounts by western travellers refer to Grombchevskii, whom they often approached for advice before undertaking their own Pamir journeys, and he published a series of memoirs and travel accounts of his own after the revolution, in his native Polish.[51]

Grombchevskii's first intelligence mission came in 1885, when he was sent to conduct a military survey of routes between Ferghana and Kashgar.[52]

Istochnik. Dokumenty russkoi istorii No. 6 (2002), 52–5 and A. Kolesnikov, *Russkie v Kashgarii: Missii, ekspeditsii, puteshestviya* (Bishkek: Raritet, 2006).

[48] N. F. Petrovskii to F. R. Osten-Saken 22/08/1887, in N. F. Petrovskii, *Turkestanskie pis'ma* ed. V. S. Myasnikov (Moscow: Pamyatniki Istoricheskoi Mysli, 2010), 202.

[49] Archive of the Russian Geographical Society (RGO) F.45 Op.1 No. 4 (with thanks to Sergei Andreyev).

[50] Baskhanov, *Voennye vostokovedy*, 69–70; for comprehensive accounts of Grombchevskii's travels and publications see Postnikov, *Skhvatka*, 167–187; A. Iu. Rudnitskii, *Etot groznyi Grombchevskii ... Bol'shaya Igra na granitsakh imperii* (St Pb.: Aleteia, 2013); 'K poslednemu perevalu: Zhizn' i stranstviya Bronislava Grombchevskogo', in *Dervish Gindukusha: Putevye dnevniki tsentral'no-aziatskikh ekspeditsii Generala B. L. Grombchevskogo* ed. M. K. Baskhanov, A. A. Kolesnikov & M. A. Matveeva (St Pb.: Nestor-Istoriya, 2015), 7–50 & M. K. Baskhanov, 'Bronislav Liudvigovich Grombchevskii (1855–1926)', in *The Quest for Forbidden Lands: Nikolai Przheval'skii and His Followers on Inner Asian Tracks* ed. Alexandre Andreyev, Mikhail Baskhanov & Tatiana Yusupova (Leiden: Brill, 2018), 255–310.

[51] For example Bonvalot, *Du Caucase*, 261.

[52] B. L. Gronbchevskii [*sic*], *Otchet o poezdke v Kashgar i iuzhnuiu Kashgariiu v 1885g (Sekretno)* (New Margelan: Pechataetsya na Pravakh Rukopisi, 1886); in retirement he also published an account of this journey in Polish: Bronisław Grąbczewski, *Kaszgarja: Kraj i ludzie: Podróż do Azji Środkowej* (Warsaw: Gebethner i Wolff, 1924).

Figure 10.1 Bronislav Ludwigovich Grombchevskii (RGO F.45 Op.1 No. 4).

Despite his Polish origins, which aroused Petrovskii's distrust,[53] he seems to have gained the full confidence of the Russian high command early in his career, something he clearly remained proud of. In his later memoirs Grombchevskii recalled that in 1888, on A. N. Kuropatkin's recommendation, he had been summoned at short notice from New Marghelan to St Petersburg to advise the War Minister, P. S. Vannovskii (1822–1904) – he claimed that this was at the express desire of Alexander III, who was looking for a way to annoy the British in Central Asia and distract them from European affairs.[54] Grombchevskii's suggestion was to support Ishaq Khan, the pretender to the Afghan throne, then living as a Russian pensioner in Samarkand, in an invasion of Afghan Turkestan, which met with Kuropatkin and Vannovskii's approval. Whilst the then Turkestan governor-general, N. O. Rosenbach,

[53] Petrovskii compared him to Jan Witkewicz, the Polish exile whose embassy to Dost Muhammad Khan had helped provoke the first Afghan war (see Chapter 1): 'Just as then a Russian officer (a Pole) Vitkevich alarmed the English, so now the same type of Russian officer (a Pole) Grombchevskii has alarmed the British with his journey to Kanjut.' Petrovskii to Osten-Sacken 14/05/1892, *Turkestanskie pis'ma*, 226.
[54] This was a *reprise* of Russian tactics during the 'Eastern Crisis' of 1876–8. See Morrison, 'Beyond the Great Game'.

wanted nothing to do with this scheme,[55] Grombchevskii claimed he organised 10,000 rifles and 100,000 silver roubles for Ishaq Khan, and escorted him across the Amu-Darya towards Mazar-i Sharif. After initial successes the rebellion failed, and 'Abdurrahman Khan reconquered his northern provinces.[56] In a lecture to the General Staff Academy three years later Grombchevskii lamented this as a missed opportunity for Russia to 'plant her feet firmly on the Hindu Kush', but added that by November 1888, when Ishaq Khan's rebellion was in full swing, he was already in Kanjut (the northern part of Hunza), on a mission which, while he claimed it had a purely 'scientific' character, was fairly clearly aimed at bringing the petty khanates of the Pamirs into the Russian camp.[57]

Grombchevskii's journey to Kanjut and Hunza did not get off to a smooth start, as there were differing views in the Russian hierarchy as to how far it was safe or desirable to provoke the British. Initially he was instructed by War Minister Vannovskii to take a route directly across the Pamir plateau, returning via Wakhan and Shughnan, but Governor-General Rosenbach suggested that this might upset the British, and recommended a route via Kashgar.[58] The head of the Asiatic Department of the Ministry of Foreign Affairs was equally concerned about the possible effect of Grombchevskii's presence on Anglo-Russian relations, no doubt remembering the morbid sensitivity the British had exhibited on frontier matters after the annexation of the Panjdeh oasis in 1885. He suggested that Grombchevskii present himself to Safdar 'Ali Khan, the ruler of Hunza, as a private traveller rather than an envoy from the emperor, and Foreign Minister N. K. Giers underlined the importance of Grombchevskii comporting himself 'as cautiously and carefully as possible', to avoid awakening British disquiet.[59] From Kashgar that June N. F. Petrovskii reported a visit from Muhammad Nazim, Safdar 'Ali Khan's brother, who had requested Russian support against British plans to bring all the petty kingdoms of the region under the power of the Maharajah of Kashmir. He added that he

---

[55] A letter from Petrovskii to the explorer N. M. Przheval'skii 09/09/1888 offers some independent confirmation of this: Turkestanskie pis'ma, 208.

[56] Bronisław Grąbczewski, Na służbie rosyjskiej: Fragmenty wspomnień (Warsaw: Gebethner i Wolff, 1926), 30–44. See further N. A. Khalfin, 'Vosstanie Iskhak-khana v iuzhnom Turkestane i pozitsiya russkogo tsarizma (1888 g.)', in Trudy Sredneaziyatskogo Gosudarstvennogo Universiteta im. V. I. Lenina: Istoriya stran vostoka. Vyp. LXVIII, Kn. 9 (Tashkent: Izd. SAGU, 1955), 107–26.

[57] Grombchevskii, Doklad, 2–3; Baskhanov, 'Bronislav Liudvigovich Grombchevskii', 268–77.

[58] Vannovskii to Girs 08/04/1888 AVPRI F.147 Op.485 D.1296, 'Po povodu poezdki sostoyashchago dlya poruchenii pri Voennym Gubernatorom Ferganskoi Oblasti Sht. Kapitana Grombchevskogo v Kanzhud, dlya poputnogo obsledovaniya prokhodov cherez mustag', l. 3.

[59] Zinov'ev to Petrovskii; Giers to Vannovskii 16/04/1888 AVPRI F.147 Op.485 D.1296 ll. 5–6.

had been very surprised by Rosenbach's refusal to allow Grombchevskii to travel to Kanjut via the Pamirs, particularly as it was ostensibly based on a report in which Petrovskii had described the poor relations between that state and Kashgar, and recommended that Grombchevskii be allowed to proceed forthwith.[60] He followed this up with his own letter to Grombchevskii, in which he explained the history of Kanjut as a 'nest of banditry', and the inevitable fate which awaited it of being annexed to a larger neighbouring power, as the Russians had annexed the mountainous *bekstvo*s of Magian, Farab and Kshtut in the upper Zarafshan valley, Bukhara had taken Hissar, Kulab and Darvaz, and Afghanistan Maimuna, Balkh, Shirabad and most recently Shughnan and Wakhan.[61] However, July found Grombchevskii still languishing in New Marghelan, sending plaintive telegrams requesting permission to depart. Petrovskii wrote again in August, saying that Grombchevskii was already too well-known in the region for there to be any point in maintaining the pretence that he was a private traveller; he recommended that he be allowed to drop his incognito status and travel in uniform, and reiterated the threat from British expansionism in a region where borders and spheres of influence remained insufficiently defined: 'Above all it is essential to say that this region, whilst it is sufficiently defined and denoted to the west, loses this definition in the eastern direction: if even Badakhshan, thanks to the incorrect inquiries made by the late General Kaufman, should now be considered as falling into the zone of [British] influence, this cannot in any way be said of Roshan, Shughnan and Wakhan, the independent existence of which was agreed by us with the British government.'[62] The legitimate limits of British control were the borders of Kashmir, and the fate of the places to its north (i.e. Gilgit and Hunza) would be determined by the 'scale, reality and character of influence over them – ours or that of the English'. He concluded that Grombchevskii's mission should be of an observational character.[63]

By August Grombchevskii had finally left Marghelan, and travelled via Osh into the Alai range. The first report from his expedition did not reach Petrovskii until early October. Grombchevskii had followed a route that would become the standard one for future military expeditions to the

---

[60] Petrovskii to Zinov'ev 07/06/1888 AVPRI F.147 Op.485 D.1296 ll. 15–16ob.

[61] Petrovskii to Grombchevskii 07/06/1888 AVPRI F.147 Op.485 D.1296 ll. 25–8ob.

[62] This was a reference both to the 1873 agreement with the British on spheres of influence in the western Pamirs and to the provisions in the 1881 Treaty of St Petersburg with China on the boundary in the Eastern Pamirs, which was widely viewed as inadequate and based on a lack of geographical knowledge of the region: see L. Kornilov, *Kashgariya ili Vostochnyi Turkestan: Opyt voenno-statisticheskogo opisaniya* (Tashkent: Tip Shtaba Turkestanskogo Voennogo Okruga, 1903), 31–5; Paine, *Imperial Rivals*, 151–67, 272–4.

[63] Grombchevskii to Vannovskii telegram 08/07/1888; Petrovskii to Zinov'ev 14/08/1888 AVPRI F.147 Op.485 D.1296 ll. 19, 20–3ob.

Pamirs.[64] It took him twenty-three days to travel from Marghelan to the Boza-i Gumbaz[65] pass, and the horses had suffered a great deal from the cold. The Wakhjir pass was also partly blocked by heavy snow, but despite these obstacles, and being delayed by the Bek of Kurumcha on the Murghab river, and by Tughra Muhammad Bek at Aq-Tash, his party reached Kanjut on the 15 August, and Baltit on the 1 September: 'You already know how many difficulties and losses we have endured on this route; there is no need to describe it to you; I will only say that, if Dante had come to Kanjut, then the description of the route would be more characteristic and have greater verisimilitude.'[66] His party lost half their horses and many of their yaks along the way. In the end Grombchevskii remained in Baltit for just a week, citing as the reasons for his speedy return the sudden illness of the Mir, an outbreak of cholera and the seizing of Wakhan by 'Ali Mardan Shah. On his return route he set out to explore the valley of the Raskam-Darya, which gave another foretaste of the sheer physical difficulties the Russians would encounter in this surprisingly arid terrain: 'This trip almost cost us our lives. We passed through four great passes, without encountering a drop of water, and that night came to the banks of the river Raskam, which flowed at our feet through a deep ravine, with entirely sheer banks, so that we were unable to descend to the river.' The following morning they stumbled across a route down by sheer chance, but not without losing another of their horses to thirst.[67] Grombchevskii concluded his reports by stating that Safdar 'Ali Khan had treated him as an official envoy, and was anxious to become a Russian subject, entrusting Grombchevskii with letters to the Foreign Ministry and the Turkestan Governor-General to that effect – in his later address to the Academy of the General Staff he elaborated on this, saying that the Khan, despite his illness, had granted him a ceremonial audience in which he showed him a letter from the Viceroy of India, promising him weapons and financial support, but had told him 'I hate the English, and drove away their envoys. I know the English will revenge themselves on me for this, but I do not fear them as I rest on the same unshakeable rock as the Great White Tsar.' Grombchevskii claimed that this placed him in an embarrassing position owing to his lack of official authority to negotiate, and he recommended that Safdar 'Ali Khan send his request to Petrovskii at Kashgar, the Turkestan Governor-General and the Ministry of Foreign Affairs. Petrovskii complained in a private letter to Fyodor Romanovich Osten-Saken that the

[64] A preliminary report describing the route and the difficulties he encountered was published as 'Vesti iz ekspeditsii B. L. Grombchevskogo', IIRGO 26 (1890), 85–107.
[65] This was the domed tomb of a Kyrgyz chieftain, who had apparently held the title of Dadkhwah from the court of Khoqand, for which he collected zakat. The Russians used this as a basis for their claim to sovereignty over the Pamirs, although in the end they did not annex this territory, which became part of Afghanistan's Wakhan corridor.
[66] Grombchevskii to Petrovskii 26/09/1888 AVPRI F.147 Op.485 D.1296 ll. 35–41ob.
[67] Grombchevskii to Petrovskii 24/10/1888 AVPRI F.147 Op.485 D.1296 l. 48ob.

Asiatic Department had not sufficiently considered the effect of the arrival in Kanjut of Grombchevskii, 'whom every dog on the frontier knows is an officer and government adviser', as it would encourage Safdar 'Ali Khan to believe the Tsar was offering military protection against the British, which they were not in a position to do, and would later complain that the Polish officer had needlessly provoked the British on this journey in order to advance his own career.[68] In Grombchevskii's account, Petrovskii detained Safdar 'Ali Khan's ambassador at Kashgar, and forwarded his letters to Tashkent and St Petersburg, but 'the ruler of Kanjut was not considered worthy of an answer' from the Asiatic Department (a dig at overly cautious diplomats that no doubt went down well with his military audience).[69] In his original report Grombchevskii also noted that he had received several requests from 'Ali Mardan Shah of Wakhan to visit, but had not wished to do so without Petrovskii's permission.[70] In his later report he added that by this stage his expedition's total treasury amounted to 37 silver roubles, he had no suitable presents to offer, and many of his horses had perished, making a return to Kashgar essential.[71] There Petrovskii forbade him to travel to Wakhan and sent him back to Ferghana, and on the 22 November he telegraphed his safe return to Osh, having completed a series of geographical and ethnographic surveys, and brought back a small collection of specimens.[72] Grombchevskii returned to the Pamirs in 1889, when he attempted to travel to Kafiristan via Chitral; it was on this expedition that he had his celebrated encounter with Francis Younghusband at Khayan-Aqsai in the valley of the Yarkand river. Younghusband's impressions of Grombchevskii – 'tall and well built, with a pleasant, genial manner' – were positive, and led him to the oft-quoted conclusion that 'We and the Russians *are* rivals, but I am sure that individual Russian and English officers like each other a great deal better than they do the individuals of nations with which they are not in rivalry. We are both playing at a big game, and we should not be one jot better off for trying to conceal the fact.'[73]

Grombchevskii did not refer to his friendly encounter with Younghusband in his March 1891 address to the General Staff Academy: instead his tone was

[68] Petrovskii to Osten-Sacken 17/11/1888 & 14/05/1892, *Turkestanskie pis'ma*, 211, 226.
[69] Grombchevskii, *Doklad*, 3; this is corroborated in a letter from Petrovskii to Osten-Sacken 05/10/1891, *Turkestanskie pis'ma*, 220.
[70] Grombchevskii to Petrovskii 24/10/1888 AVPRI F.147 Op.485 D.1296 ll. 50–1*ob*.
[71] Grombchevskii, *Doklad*, 5.
[72] Telegram Grombchevskii to Vannovskii 22/11/1888 AVPRI F.147 Op.485 D.1296 l. 56; see also his later account of this journey: Bronisław Grąbczewski, *Przez Pamiry i Hindukusz do źródeł rzeki Indus* (Warsaw: Gebethner i Wolff, 1924).
[73] Younghusband, *The Heart of a Continent*, 235–8; see Postnikov, *Skhvatka*, 218–22 & Baskhanov, 'Bronislav Liudvigovich Grombchevskii', 281–300 for a more detailed account.

much more alarmist. He drew attention to Afghan, British and Chinese encroachments on the Pamirs, territory which, he claimed, was rightfully Russian since the annexation of Khoqand, and referred to his successful spying on Younghusband's negotiations with the Chinese authorities in the summer of 1890, which had revealed a plan to divide the Pamir plateau between the British and Chinese empires, cutting out Russia.[74] During the same journey he had also discovered to his dismay that Safdar 'Ali Khan of Kanjut had now accepted a British subsidy and become a vassal of 'East India', and was seeking to extend his control (and hence, by proxy, that of the British) into Chinese territory in the Taghdumbash Pamir and the Aq-Su/Murghab valley.[75] In his speech he gave numerous examples of the friendliness of the Pamir peoples and their rulers for the Russians, and their hatred of the English, and noted that the difficulties of the paths through the mountains for military forces had been exaggerated (somewhat disingenuously, given his earlier description of the road to Kanjut as like something out of Dante's *Inferno*) and that it could be a useful subsidiary theatre of war in the event of a Russian campaign against India.[76] Grombchevskii was, more than any other Russian officer, the public face of Pamir exploration, and one of the most eloquent advocates of further Russian expansion in the region. While Petrovskii believed he was stirring up public opinion on his own account,[77] Grombchevskii would not have been invited to give a public lecture with such potentially inflammatory content at the Main Staff Academy without official encouragement.[78] His often exaggerated warnings about British, Chinese and Afghan encroachments on the Pamir plateau, and a possible agreement between them to divide the region, had already met with a ready audience in the War Ministry. In November 1890 Baron A. V. Vrevskii (1834–1910), the new Turkestan Governor-General, had written to N. N. Obruchev, the Chief of the Main Staff, noting Younghusband's presence at Yarkand and asserting that this was part of a plan to divide the Pamir region between Afghanistan and China, thus cutting off Russia's one route to Chitral and Kashmir and violating the rights she had inherited from

---

[74] Grombchevskii, *Doklad*, 17–18. Petrovskii boasted to Cobbold that the Chinese *Taotai* had kept him fully informed of all Younghusband's attempts to persuade the Chinese to send their forces to annex the Eastern Pamirs, and ridiculed the decision to entrust this delicate mission to an officer who did not speak Chinese: *Innermost Asia*, 67; he wrote to Baron Osten-Sacken that he had paid just 3 roubles to intercept Younghusband's letters to Davison: Petrovskii to Osten-Sacken 05/10/1891, *Turkestanskie pis'ma*, 221.

[75] Grombchevskii to Petrovskii 08/07/1890, in A. V. Stanishevskii, *Sbornik arkhivnykh dokumentov po istorii Pamira i Ismailizmu* (Moscow & Leningrad: n.p., 1933), 51–2. My thanks to Daniel Beben for providing me with an electronic copy of this very rare edition.

[76] Grombchevskii, *Doklad*, 18–28.

[77] Petrovskii to Osten-Sacken 14/05/1892, *Turkestanskie pis'ma*, 226.

[78] Baskhanov, 'Bronislav Liudvigovich Grombchevskii', 304–5.

Khoqand in the region.[79] Obruchev and the War Minister, Vannovskii, had agreed that something should be done, and in February 1891 Foreign Minister Giers had already given his consent to the despatch of a small force to assert Russian rights on the Pamir plateau.[80]

10.2 The Beginnings of the Russian Military Occupation

Thus July 1891 saw the first serious Russian military expedition into the Pamirs under Colonel Mikhail Efremovich Ionov (1846–1924), who was also from Poland, but of Russian origin.[81] He led a force of eight officers (including two other Polish officers, Lts Brzhezitskii and Skerskii), eighty infantry, thirty-three Cossacks, a doctor and military topographer Benderskii, at a total cost of approximately 6,000 roubles.[82] While Grombchevskii had urged once again the provision of military support to Safdar 'Ali Khan at Kanjut, this did not enter into the expedition's plans.[83] Ionov's brief was to complete a topographical survey of the Pamir plateau (this resulted in the first detailed Russian military map, published the following year), and Governor-General Vrevskii also instructed him to remove obvious signs of British or Chinese sovereignty. These included Chinese boundary-markers at Yeshil-Kul[84] and the persons of two British officers, Captain Davison (who was forced to return to India via Ferghana and Russia) and, most famously, Francis Younghusband, in the second, and marginally less friendly, of his celebrated encounters with Russian officers, this time at Boza-i Gumbaz:[85]

> Colonel Yonoff [sic] said he had something very disagreeable to say to me. He then courteously and civilly, and with many apologies, informed me that he had that morning, while at Lake Victoria, on the Great Pamir, received a despatch from his Government, in which he was instructed to escort me from Russian territory back to Chinese territory [. . .] I told him

[79] Vrevskii to Obruchev 23/11/1890 RGVIA F.846 Op.1 D.106, 'O predpolozheniyakh angliiskogo pravitel'stva razgranichit' Pamir mezhdu Kitaem i Afganistanom', ll. 1–2.
[80] Giers to Vannovskii 02/02/1891 RGVIA F.846 Op.1 D.106 ll. 15–16ob.
[81] On Ionov see Baskhanov, *Voennye vostokovedy*, 96–7; N. L. Luzhetskaya, 'Materialy Arkhiva vostokovedov IVR RAN o dvizhenii letuchego otryada Polkovnika Ionova na r. Bartang v Rushane: 1893 g.', *PPV* 1/12 (2010), 223–5; N. D. Kareeva, 'Moi prapraded dal Rossii "Kryshu mira"', *Rodina* (2015), No. 8, 84–5. Thanks to Oybek Mahmudov for the latter reference.
[82] 'Vedomost' raskhodov, vyzyvaemykh otpravleniem na Pamir svodnago rekognostsirovochnogo otryada', RGVIA F.846 Op.1 D.106 ll. 57–8.
[83] Grombchevskii to Obruchev 06/04/1891 RGVIA F.846 Op.1 D.106 ll. 28–32.
[84] This infuriated Petrovskii in Kashgar, who had not been informed, and believed that Vrevskii had misinterpreted the Foreign Office's instructions and needlessly offended the Chinese. Petrovskii to Osten-Sacken 05/10/1891; Petrovskii to Osten-Sacken 25/10/1891, *Turkestanskie pis'ma*, 220, 222.
[85] Postnikov, *Skhvatka*, 245–6.

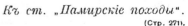

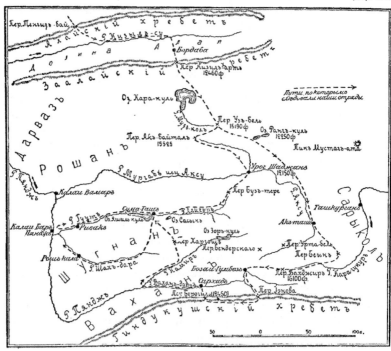

Figure 10.2 Map of the Pamir military expeditions (Novitskii, *Voennaya Entsiklopedia*
17, 271).

that I did not consider I was on Russian territory at all, and that, in any
case, I was returning to India; but Colonel Yonoff replied that by his maps
Bozai-Gumbaz was included in the Russian territory [. . .] Colonel Yonoff
and his companions came out to wish me good-bye, and express their
sincerest regrets at having to treat a friend as they had been obliged to treat
me. They presented me with a haunch of *Ovis poli*, from an animal they
had shot on the previous day, and we parted on as friendly terms as were
possible in the circumstances.[86]

---

[86] Younghusband, *The Heart of a Continent*, 293–4; the account of his expulsion which he
gave in a letter to his father at the time (20/08/1891) is almost identical to that he
published five years later: IOR MSS Eur F197/142, quoted in Postnikov, *Skhvatka*, 229–
230. However, he did not mention it in his address to the Royal Geographical Society in
1892: F. E. Younghusband, 'Journeys in the Pamirs and Adjacent Countries', *PRGS* 14/4
(1892), 205–34.

Younghusband signed a declaration in French promising to return voluntarily to Chinese territory via the Wakhajai pass, and not to return without express permission.[87] As he noted, this caused a considerable diplomatic stir at the time, but what is striking reading his account now is how many common assumptions regarding the European imperial mission (and notions of 'gentlemanliness') he shared with his Russian counterpart. While Ionov told Younghusband that he was now on Russian territory, and that they intended to claim not just the Pamir plateau, but Shughnan and Roshan, his reconnaissance force did not did not enter those regions, under Afghan occupation, and they also withdrew from the Pamir plateau with the onset of winter, whereupon (according to Petrovskii) the Chinese promptly reoccupied the territory claimed by Russia, and reinstated their own officials.[88] However, Vrevskii reported that Ionov's mission had been a complete success – a '*blistatel'naya rekognostsirovka*' (brilliant reconnaissance) – which had managed to avoid upsetting the Chinese or Afghans. He noted the encounter with Younghusband at Boza-i Gumbaz, and his forced return to China, as well as Davison's arrest and despatch to St Petersburg via Marghelan.[89] In fact the Chinese Legation in St Petersburg did issue a formal protest at what they described as the Russian violation of their frontiers, but the only response was a re-assertion of Russian claims to the region.[90] When the Governor of Xinjiang made similar objections in a letter to Vrevskii, he received a remarkably rude response from Petrovskii informing him that he had no right to address the Turkestan Governor-General as an equal.[91]

In December 1891 Vrevskii was already advocating sending a larger force of two *sotnya*s of Cossacks and two mountain guns to consolidate the claims made the previous year.[92] This was lent greater urgency a few days later when Petrovskii reported the arrival of 1,500 British Indian troops at Kanjut (Hunza), under the command of Younghusband and Mortimer Durand, alleging that their aim was to annex not just Kanjut but Boza-i Gumbaz, and urging the despatch of a flying column of four *sotnya*s of Cossacks under Grombchevskii's command to aid Safdar 'Ali Khan's resistance. Vrevskii supported the proposal despite the

---

[87] The original of this celebrated document, dated 17/08/1891, is in RGVIA F.846 Op.1 D.110, 'O Pamirskom voprose i o merakh k eiu razresheniiu', l. 32. It carries the note 'Cette déclaration est faite sous proteste'.

[88] Petrovskii to Osten-Sacken 14/05/1892, *Turkestanskie pis'ma*, 227.

[89] Cipher Telegram Vrevskii to Vannovskii 19/08/1891 RGVIA F.846 Op.1 D.110 ll. 87–*ob*.

[90] 'Les militaires russes entreprennent, sans aucun motif, d'occuper une possession étrangère et complètement au mépris de nos Traités', RGVIA F.846 Op.1 D.106 ll. 109–*ob*.

[91] Copy of a translation of a letter from the Governor of Sinkiang to the Turkestan Governor-General, 6th day of the 8th Moon; Petrovskii to the Governor of Sinkiang 30/10/1891 RGVIA F.846 Op.1 D.110 ll. 89–93.

[92] 'O neobkhodimosti komandirovanii otryada na Pamiry v 1892 godu', 18/12/1891 RGVIA F.846 Op.1 D.110 ll. 72–9.

difficulties of despatching a force in winter, but, after some dithering by Vannovskii, Foreign Minister Giers insisted that there could be no question of helping Kanjut – the Khan was already beaten and in flight, and the news that the British planned to annex parts of the Pamirs had come exclusively from letters from him and his envoys, which were not to be trusted.[93] Shortly afterwards the Tsar authorised a special commission on the Pamir question, which, after much discussion of Russia's rights and the beneficial results of Ionov's expedition, resolved to send another flying column to the region in the spring, though not, at this stage, a permanent garrison.[94]

April 1892 saw two further meetings of the Pamir commission, whose members included War Minister Vannovskii, Prince Lobanov-Rostovskii from the Ministry of Foreign Affairs, General N. N. Obruchev (Chief of the Main Staff) and A. N. Kuropatkin. These were prompted by a proposal from Vrevskii to follow Ionov's reconnaissance mission with a larger force which, this time, would remain on the Pamirs throughout the winter and establish a permanent Russian presence there. This was in response to the threat of incursions by other powers, notably the Chinese, who were said to be establishing garrisons at Rang-Qul and Boza-i Gumbaz, and the British in Hunza and Chitral. As usual, the Ministry of Foreign Affairs urged caution, suggesting that a force be sent only as far as the Alai valley, and avoid penetrating the southern Pamir region because of the risk of European repercussions. However, Vannovskii, Obruchev and Kuropatkin all urged the necessity of a more aggressive strategy:

> Insofar as the Pamir region is concerned, in the opinion of these individuals, we must take a clearly defined, firm position, recognising that this region has a significance and is essential for Russia, as a useful portion of our territory and as a protective position for the maintenance of calm and safety of the Turkestan region, and that it is not possible to yield it to other governments. Persuaded of this, we cannot confine ourselves solely to an announcement of the inclusion of the Pamirs in our sphere of influence and distant supervision over it. It is essential to take active measures to confirm our influence and power within the boundaries of this region, and for this we must occupy the most important points in the region, amongst which the most significant are the Bozai-i Gumbaz depression and Aq-Tash, as the main junctions of the roads and most important positions, where if we establish ourselves we will have the possibility of firmly fixing our frontier in the foothills of the Hindu Kush.[95]

These arguments won the day, as usually happened when the War Ministry and Foreign Ministry clashed. The invocation of the Hindu Kush may have

---

[93] Vrevskii to Vannovskii 22/12/1891; Girs to Vannovskii 06/01/1892 RGVIA F.846 Op.1 D.110 ll. 107–*ob*, 170–1*ob*. On the British annexation of Hunza and Nagar see Huttenback, 'The "Great Game" in the Pamirs'.

[94] *Protokol* 12/01/1892 RGVIA F.846 Op.1 D.110 ll. 178–80.

[95] 'Otnositel'no posylki otryada na Pamir', 05/05/1892, in Stanishevskii, *Sbornik*, 53.

played a part in this, as Russian officers and military topographers had long argued that this range represented the 'natural' limits of Russian expansion in the region.[96] While urging caution, and the avoidance of all open clashes with neighbouring powers, the commission recommended the despatch of a permanent military force as far as the Aq-Su/Murghab valley 'to protect our interests in that region', and to begin the process of drawing the boundaries with Afghan, British and Chinese territory, something they already envisaged might be undertaken by a joint Anglo-Russian commission.[97]

Thus, when the time came to organise this second Pamir expedition in 1892, the Russians were determined to leave a force permanently stationed in the Aq-Su/Murghab valley throughout the harsh Pamir winter. As is so often the case, it is the logistical side of the Russian advance which has been neglected in earlier scholarship (in his otherwise excellent account Postnikov, for instance, has little to say about how the soldiers of the Pamir force kept themselves warm),[98] and this proved a particular challenge. The first stage was selecting the right men; the senior doctor of the 2nd Turkestan Line Battalion, stationed at Marghelan, reported that he had carried out a careful inspection and selection of the 'other ranks' of the battalion, in order to select at least 300 of the strongest and healthiest, and had accepted 359 of them as fit for this arduous posting, rejecting another 92 as under-nourished or with insufficient musculature.[99] The next stage was ordering sufficient warm clothing – for this battalion that meant 94 *arshins* of camel-wool cloth for shirts, horsehair face masks, warm puttees and *sapogi* (felt boots). The Cossacks were additionally given 'Sart furs', at a total cost of 1,133 r 50 k. Overall the cost of equipping the 906 men of the force to cope with the cold was 7,118 roubles, or 7 r 85 k per man.[100] As with the steppe expeditions of thirty years previously, but unlike the more recent campaigns against Khoqand and Bukhara, they had to prepare and carry all their supplies with them – the *sukhari* would have to be baked in several batches at the barracks bakery at New Marghelan, which would take two weeks. Of the total cost of 95,365 roubles, by far the single greatest item was transport (Table 10.1).

---

[96] See further Morrison, 'Russia, Khoqand, and the Search for a Natural Frontier'.
[97] 'Otnositel'no posylky otryada na Pamir', 05/05/1892, in Stanishevskii, *Sbornik*, 53–9.
[98] Postnikov, *Skhvatka*, 270–95.
[99] Lebedev to the commander of the 2nd Turkestan Line Battalion, 31/05/1892 RGVIA F.1438 Op.1 D.18, 'O formirovanii otryada na Pamir/Alai i o snabzhenii ego teploi odezhdy', ll. 15–16.
[100] 'Vedomost' 2go Turkestanskogo Lineinogo Bataliona den'gam izraskhodovannym iz sum batal'ona na veshchi i materialy dlya nizhnikh chinov okhotnich'ei komandy pri vystuplenii v pokhode v sostave Pamirskogo otryada'; Khoroshkhin to the commander of forces in Ferghana 11/12/1893; Vr. Intendanta Turk. V.O. to Vrevskii 13/05/1892 RGVIA F.1438 Op.1 D.18 ll. 32, 57–8, 123.

Table 10.1 *Major items of equipment and supplies for the second Pamir expedition*[a]

Item	Quantity	Cost (roubles and kopeks)
Warm clothing	94 *arshins* of camel-wool cloth, furs, horsehair masks, *sapogi*	7,118 r
Sukhari and pulses	3,752 *poods* (61 tonnes)	4,315 r 75 k
Baggage ponies	1,175	38,700 r (75 k per day)
Fodder	10,000 *poods* (164 tonnes)	14,883 r

[a] Vr. Intendanta Turk. V.O. to Vrevskii 13/05/1892; 'Vedomost' summam otpushchennym ot intendantstva avansom Nachal'niku Alaiskogo otryada dlya chastei voisk, vkhodyashchikh v sostav otryada', 26/05/1892 RGVIA F.1438 Op.1 D.18 ll. 114–18, 128–*ob*, 142, 213–14.

From Marghelan the bulk of the Pamir force made its way via the villages of Avval and Uch-Qurghan through the Langar valley up to the Tengiz Bai pass, then rested for a day in Daraut Qurghan (the village which had marked the furthest point of Fedchenko's explorations twenty years previously). They then passed by Qizil Ungur and the river Jyptik and along the Archa-Bulaq valley, arriving eventually at Bor-Baba, eleven days and 260 *versts* later. A smaller group of 125 men took the longer route (363 *versts*) via Osh and Ghulcha, arriving at Bor-Baba in sixteen days.[101] From there the reunited force would march together to the Aq-Su/Murghab valley, where they would establish the first permanent Russian post on the Pamirs.

Ionov described how even on the very first part of the route into the Kishi-Alai through the Isfara valley the force found its way barred by deeply packed snow and had to scramble up almost to the summit to find a way across, while he had to send the artillery round by a pass further to the south, delaying their arrival at Daraut-Qurghan.[102] Well before their arrival at the site of the Pamir post, at Archa-Bulaq, Ionov was already reporting Afghan and Chinese intrigues. He claimed that 100 Kyrgyz 'natives' had come to him to complain about their ill-treatment by their Chinese-appointed headman, Sahibjan, asking him to defend them, as Russian subjects, against this oppression.[103] They also, perhaps not unconnectedly, asked for permission to move their flocks into the Alai range. More sinisterly, the head of Ionov's forward reconnaissance party, Lt Brzhezitskii, reported that he had encountered a Chinese

[101] 'Marshrut dlya sledovaniya Pamirskogo otryada priblizitel'no v 800 nizhnikh chinov', RGVIA F.1438 Op.1 D.18 l. 246.
[102] Ionov to Korol'kov 09/06/1892 RGVIA F.1438 Op.1 D.18 l. 254.
[103] Ionov to Korol'kov 15/06/1892 RGVIA F.1438 Op.1 D.18 ll. 257–8*ob*.

astronomer called 'Uyan-His-Dalla' at the little Qara-kul lake, and that there were about sixty Afghans in the same valley under a captain 'Kamardin' (presumably Qamar al-din). They had two forward posts, one at the village of Sarez, the other on the river Murghab, opposite the shrine of Shah-Jan. They were supplied from Wakhan through the Khorgosh pass and, so he claimed, had been oppressing the surrounding inhabitants, most of whom had moved to Aq-Baizal and were thinking of migrating to the Alai. As he put it, the boundaries in the region were dangerously unclear:

> Who considers the Pamir their own? At the moment it is difficult to say, but according to our information we can posit that the left bank of the Murghab and the right bank of the Wakhan-Darya have gone to the Afghans, and everything on this side – to the Chinese.[104]

Meanwhile Brzhezitskii warned that Younghusband was in Kanjut, where he was gathering troops and supplies, and despatching his agents all across the Pamirs. The inhabitants suggested to him that the Chinese and the British had agreed on a division of the plateau, which only awaited the despatch of British forces from Kanjut for it to become a reality; Younghusband's movements around Qara Chukur and the river Ming-tepe continued to attract Russian attention for the next two weeks, but they eventually concluded that he did not have any troops at Kanjut after all.[105] Brzhezitskii also reported on the activities of the Afghans: there had been a substantial flight of population from Roshan, seeking to escape the oppression of the Afghan governor 'Ibadullah Khan. In early July a group of Pamir-Alai Kyrgyz reported that they had been attacked by the Afghans, and requested Russian protection, while Grombchevskii also reported a dispute with the commander of the Afghan garrison at Summa-Tash, Ghulam Haidar Khan, over a Kyrgyz whom he claimed had stolen 200 Kabuli rupees and then fled to Russian protection.[106]

It was in response to Afghan, rather than British movements, that Ionov embarked on a reconnaissance which on the 12 July 1892 (O.S.) led to the most serious military clash between rival powers on the Pamirs. Ionov despatched a lengthy message to Korol'kov describing how he had approached the Afghan post at Yeshil-Kul (Alichur) with three small groups of Cossacks, and asked the commander to come out and parley with him, unarmed:

> In contradiction to my numerous requests to come unarmed, the captain came up to me with fourteen Afghans with their weapons loaded and even cocked. The Afghan bore himself disrespectfully (*derzko*), provokingly,

[104] Brzhezitskii to Ionov 06/06/1892 RGVIA F.1438 Op.1 D.18 l. 260.
[105] Brzhezitskii to Ionov 13/06/1892; 24/06/1892; 27/06/1892; 29/06/1892 RGVIA F.1438 Op.1 D.18 ll. 291–2, 308–9, 327–*ob*, 329.
[106] Brzhezitskii to Ionov 20/06/1892; telegram Ionov to Korol'kov 02/07/1892; Grombchevskii to Kholmskii 08/07/1892 RGVIA F.1438 Op.1 D.18 ll. 305–6, 345–6, 460–1.

and to my proposal to lay down their weapons and withdraw he gave the response that they would give up their weapons with their lives. My sincere desire to terminate the discussion peacefully only encouraged the Afghan. I was forced to give the order to fall on and disarm the Afghans. Grabbing their weapons, the Afghans fired a volley; a soft-nosed bullet seriously wounded *Prikaznyi* Borisov. In the struggle the following were killed: Captain Ghulam Haidar Khan and nine Afghans; two were seriously wounded and six surrendered. On our side apart from Borisov two were lightly wounded, two contused. I request permission to seize Shughnan with my reconnaissance force.[107]

The brief account of this clash from the Afghan side, in Fayz Muhammad Katib's *Siraj al-Tawarikh*, asserts that twelve of Ionov's men were killed, along with nine Afghans, and does not mention that Ghulam Haidar Khan himself perished.[108] In his initial brief despatch alerting Korol'kov to the fate of Ghulam Haidar Khan's force, Ionov had written that, apart from the small garrison at Qala-i Bar Panj, he did not think there was any significant body of Afghan troops in Shughnan, and that a rapid advance with two columns along the Gund and Shakhdara rivers would cut off the remaining 100 Afghan soldiers in Roshan, thus achieving what he interpreted as his instructions – the peaceful acquisition of Shughnan and Roshan – within a week.[109] He followed this up with a report that two Shughnis had arrived at the Russian camp, informing him that their compatriots were so fed up with Afghan rule that they would rise up if they advanced, and kill every Afghan in Qala-i Bar Panj.[110] Korol'kov immediately responded in the negative to Ionov's request, urging that he avoid all breaches of the frontier with Roshan and Shughnan, not least as it would violate the agreement with the British, and noting that 'Lord Dokmor' (i.e. the Earl of Dunmore) and Major Roche would soon be visiting the region, and that Ionov should offer them every assistance.[111] Ionov responded reluctantly that he would stay put, but also claimed that the Afghans had established a new picket on the Shakhdara, and that the Shughnis were

[107] Telegram Ionov to Korol'kov 19/07/1892 RGVIA F.1438 Op.1 D.18 ll. 474–7.
[108] Muhammad Fayz Katib Hazarah, 'The Completion of the Brick Bridge at Fayzabad, Badakhshan and Other Events of the Time', in *The History of Afghanistan: Fayz Muhammad Katib Hazarah's Siraj al-Tawarikh* trans. and ed. R. D. McChesney & M. M. Khorrami (Brill Online, 2016), unpaginated & *Siraj al-Tawarikh* (Kabul: Matba'ah-i Hurufi Dar al-Saltanah, 1912–14), III, 883. Petrovskii confirmed Ghulam Haidar Khan's death, with the detail that he had narrowly failed to kill Ionov before being shot. Petrovskii believed the violence to have been unnecessary: Petrovskii to V. R. Rosen 03/09/1892; Petrovskii to F. R. Osten-Sacken 07/09/1892, *Turkestanskie pis'ma*, 230–1. Terent'ev's account is clearly based on Ionov's telegram: *Istoriya zavoevaniya*, III, 409–10.
[109] Ionov to Korol'kov 17/07/1892 RGVIA F.1438 Op.1 D.18 l. 550ob.
[110] Ionov to Korol'kov 21/07/1892 RGVIA F.1438 Op.1 D.18 ll. 547–8.
[111] Korol'kov to Ionov 22/07/1892 RGVIA F.1438 Op.1 D.18 l. 488. Middleton, 'The Pamirs', 460–79.

requesting Russian protection against them.[112] He informed Korol'kov that 'as our retreat towards the Murghab might be taken by the natives and the Afghans as a sign of our weakness', he had resolved to remain where he was for the time being, although on the 26 July he returned to Murghab, having released his nine Afghan prisoners.[113]

When Ionov handed over his command to his replacement, Captain P. A. Kuznetsov, who would command the detachment throughout the long Pamir winter, he instructed him that his task was to strengthen Russian power in those areas not claimed by the Afghans and Chinese, to preserve peace and order among the local population, to avoid armed clashes (as Ionov himself had failed to do) and to avoid interference in the internal affairs of Shughnan and Roshan. He was to communicate with Ferghana by letter no less frequently than twice a week, and by telegram from the nearest telegraph station no less frequently than three times a week.[114] The detachment was to be housed in Kyrgyz yurts, partly buried in the ground. The population of the region surrounding the new outpost was sparse; a Russian name list of members of the two Kyrgyz lineages living in the valley of the Aq-Su/Murghab – the Allahyar Shahin and Rosa Keshak – came to just ninety-six male individuals.[115]

In the spring of 1893, when Major V. N. Zaitsev took over command of the post, the annual changing over of the Pamir forces had settled down to something like a routine, with regular amounts allocated for warm clothing and baggage transport. The year 1893 also saw the construction of the first permanent Russian fortifications on the Pamirs in the valley of the Aq-Su/ Murghab, which would come to be known as the *Pamirskii Post* (Figure 10.3),[116] close to the site of the modern town of Murghab on the Pamir highway. This followed a series of complaints about the freezing and insanitary conditions in the yurts which had hitherto been the only accommodation for officers and men, with earthen stoves that disintegrated into dust. Replacing these with permanent constructions, even basic *zemlyanki* (dug-outs), would be expensive as there was no construction wood available locally, but at least twelve would be necessary, including a bath-house.[117] The new buildings were designed and constructed by Adrian Georgevich Serebrennikov (1863–?), a

[112] Ionov to Korol'kov 26/07/1892 RGVIA F.1438 Op.1 D.18 ll. 501–2.
[113] Ionov to Korol'kov 17/07/1892; Ionov to Korol'kov 26/07/1892 RGVIA F.1438 Op.1 D.18 ll. 521, 550.
[114] Ionov to Sofonov 25/08/1892 RGVIA F.1438 Op.1 D.18 ll. 630–2.
[115] 'Imennoi spisok Kirgizam kochuiushchim na verkhov'yakh r. Ak Su', RGVIA F.1438 Op.1 D.18 ll. 592–3.
[116] B. L. Tageev, 'Cherez Alai i Pamir', *Vsemirnoi Illiustratsii* 53 (1895), 459 (courtesy of The Pamir Archive, with thanks to Markus Hauser).
[117] Report from Major-General von Zigern-Korn 01/02/1893 RGVIA F.1438 Op.1 D.19, 'O smene Shadzhanskogo otryada novym', ll. 323–9.

Figure 10.3 *Pamirskii Post* from the south-west (Tageev, 'Cherez Alai i Pamir', 459).
© The Pamir Archive.

young officer in the engineer corps, who was later to play a significant role in establishing the historical record of the Russian conquest. The total cost was 6,000 roubles, and the buildings included earthwork fortifications, with crenellations 8½ feet high, and a series of *zemlyanki*, mud huts slightly sunk in the ground and lined with wood, with stoves made of bricks and iron sheets that would have to be carried up to Murghab on the backs of ponies.[118] The new post also received two Nordenfelt guns, which barely survived the long journey up, but were considered necessary to meet a possible renewed Afghan threat.[119] The foundations of the new *zemlyanki* and fortifications were begun on the 22 July, and the ceremony included a rocket and artillery salute and the singing of the imperial anthem, while 'a ceremonial march and frugal breakfast completed the day of arrangements for great Russia on the road to the Hindu Kush'. In an attempt to reduce the post's dependence on imported supplies, Zaitsev accompanied the new construction with an experimental plantation of

---

[118] A. G. Serebrennikov, 'Zapiska po ustroistvu zimnikh pomeshchenii dlya otryada, ostavlyaemogo na Pamire na zimu 1893–1894 g.', RGVIA F.1438 Op.1 D.19 ll. 154–161.

[119] Turkestan General Staff to the Chief of the Turkestan Artillery Brigade, 07/05/1893; *Akt* 13/08/1893; RGVIA F.1438 Op.1 D.19 ll. 432, 473. Hedin, Cobbold and Filchner all refer to these Nordenfelt guns on their visits in 1894, 1897 and 1900, respectively: *Through Asia*, I, 188–201; *Innermost Asia*, 199; *Ein Ritt über den Pamir*, 72.

wheat, rye, barley, turnips, maize, beans, cabbage, radishes, onions and potatoes, although of these only the barley, turnips and potatoes survived early
frosts.[120] The new buildings (Figure 10.3) were completed by the middle of
October, just in time for winter, although already by then the average night-
time temperature was −8, with lows of −15 Celsius.[121] Other outposts, notably
that at Kudar, were also preparing for total winter isolation even from the main
post at Murghab.

10.3   Expansion into Roshan and Shughnan

The Kudar post was to become a site of particular importance that winter
owing to repeated appeals from the inhabitants of Roshan and Shughnan to be
protected from Afghan exactions, which led to a creeping of the Russian
presence from the Pamir plateau into the upper valleys of these regions. In a
report on the actions of a flying column which he led on patrol through the
upper Bartang Valley in Roshan in the summer of 1893, Ionov described the
area around Kudar as an 'improvised canton (*volost'*), recognising itself as
Russian', and centred on the large village of Roshorv (Oroshar in Russian
sources).[122] This growing Russian presence on what was nominally Afghan
territory came about largely owing to a series of importunate letters from the
aqsaqal of Roshorv, known to the Russians as 'Yazghulam'.[123] In June 1893
Captain Kuznetsov, now in command of the Kudar post, received a series of
letters sent by one Shahidullah Khan, on behalf of the Afghan commander of
Roshan, 'Ibadullah Khan, to the Aqsaqals of Roshorv, Kukany and Maska. In
these he threatened them with dire consequences if they did not appear before
him and make submission, and warned them not to expect any help from the
Russians. Yazghulam accompanied copies of these threatening missives with a

---

[120] 'Otchet o deistviyakh Pamirskogo otryada Kapitana Zaitseva v period s 26 IV 1893 g. po
18 X 1894 g.', in N. L. Luzhetskaya, 'Otchet Nachal'nika Pamirskogo otryada Kapitana V.
N. Zaitseva 1893–1894', *PPV* 1/8–11 (2008), 157, 159.

[121] Zaitsev to Korol'kov 16/10/1893; 'Svedeniya srednikh nabliudenii na meteorologicheskoi
stantsii v novom ukreplenii na Pamirakh', 8–15/10/1893 RGVIA F.1438 Op.1 D.19 ll. 609–10.

[122] Ionov to Vannovskii, Report 14/02/1894 in Luzhetskaya, 'Materialy Arkhiva vostokovedov', 230.

[123] Yazghulam is the name of a river and mountain-range in Roshan, north of the Bartang
valley where Roshorv is located, but all Russian correspondence assumes that
'Yazghulam' was the aqsaqal of Roshorv's *name*. Very probably he had acquired the
epithet Yazghulami, so called because he was not local to the Bartang Valley, and the
Russians mistook this for a personal name (my thanks to Daniel Beben for suggesting
this explanation). Ionov writes that 'in all our preparatory work we received great
assistance from the Oroshar *volostnoi upravitel'*, the Tajik Yazghulam. This Tajik has
been in Russian Turkestan, speaks Turki excellently and stands out noticeably from his
compatriots, by whom he has been chosen to carry out the duties of a *volost'* administrator.' Ionov to Vannovskii, Report 14/02/1894, in Luzhetskaya, 'Materialy Arkhiva
vostokovedov', 230.

plaintive appeal to 'Kuznetsov-Tura' for protection, saying that 'Ibadullah Khan had threatened to burn down their houses.[124] In response Staff-Captain S. P. Vannovskii of the Preobrazhenskii Guards (son of the Minister of War, he received a transfer to the Pamirs in the summer of 1893, no doubt in the hope of seeing promotion and medal-worthy action) was sent by Zaitsev on a 'reconnaissance mission' with twenty-five men down the Bartang valley.[125] Vannovskii left his infantry to establish a forward post at Roshorv under Sub-Lt Rukin, who immediately reported that Afghan 'marauders' had been crossing the Panj and raiding the Bartang valley, sowing continued uneasiness among the local population.[126] Vannovskii himself continued with eight Cossacks towards the Afghan fortress of Qala-i Wamar on the Panj. Its commander, Shah Sayyid 'Jarnail', refused to allow him to proceed without authorisation from 'Ibadullah Khan. After three days of fruitlessly exchanging notes, Vannovskii found himself besieged at the village of Yamch by a larger Afghan force of forty men, who kept him and his patrol under fire for 7½ hours until he took the decision to retreat under cover of darkness to the village of Baghu.[127] When Vannovskii protested, 'Ibadullah Khan wrote defiantly that the Russians were at fault for failing to specify their peaceful intentions, and that 'all my men are brave, trained and enjoy fighting'.[128]

This reverse, with all its implications for Russian prestige, seems to have made the officers of the Pamir force still more determined to assert the Russian right to protect the population of Roshan and Shughnan from Afghan incursions. Zaitsev wrote to 'Ibadullah Khan, urging him to desist and reminding him that according to the 1873 agreement the border ran along the Panj and he should prevent his men from crossing it.[129] Later in October Zaitsev received a letter from one Mullah Mumin Shah Nazar Avsat Khan stating that he was a spiritual leader (pir) with a following of 3,000 households, and that he and all

---

[124] Letter from Shahidullah Khan 03/06/1893; Yazghulam to 'Kuznetsov-Tura' n.d. RGVIA Fond 5369 Op.1 D.2, 'O Kudarinskom nabliudatel'nom poste so svedenii iz Roshana', ll. 2–7ob.

[125] Baskhanov, Voennye vostokovedy, 44–5; N. L. Luzhetskaya, 'Materialy k istorii razgranicheniya na Pamire v Arkhive vostokovedov SPbF IV RAN (fond A. E. Snesareva): "Otchet General'nogo Shtaba Kapitana Vannovskogo po rekognostsirovke v Rushane" (1893 g.)', PPV 2/3 (2005), 134–6.

[126] Rukin to Zaitsev 27/08/1893 RGVIA F.5369 Op.1 D.2 ll. 19–20.

[127] Vannovskii to Rukin 30/08/1893 RGVIA F.5369 Op.1 D.2 l. 26; S. P. Vannovskii, 'Otchet po rekognostsirovke v Rushane', in Luzhetskaya, 'Materialy k istorii razgranicheniya na Pamire', 142–6; Tageev, 'Russkie nad Indiei', 306–19. The account in the Siraj al-Tawarikh alleges that this action was led by Captain Ghulam Haidar Khan, whom the Russians believed had been killed in the clash at 'Alichur in 1892: Fayz Muhammad Katib Hazarah, 'The Russians Plan a Move toward Pamhir and Murghabi and the Border Guards Prevent It', in The History of Afghanistan trans. & ed. McChesney & Khorrami (Brill Online), unpaginated & Siraj al-Tawarikh, III, 936–7.

[128] 'Ibadullah Khan to Vannovskii n.d. RGVIA F.5369 Op.1 D.2 ll. 75–ob.

[129] Zaitsev to 'Ibadullah Khan 07/09/1893 RGVIA F.5369 Op.1 D.2 ll. 35–ob.

his followers wished to become Russian subjects without further delay: he was awaiting Zaitsev at Roshorv.[130] Yazghulam also continued to bombard Zaitsev with letters in which he repeated that Kuznetsov and Brzhezitskii had promised that they would become Russian subjects, and that he was currently hosting 'fifty friends' who had been robbed mercilessly by the Afghans 'The eyes of all of them are turned to the White Tsar and they await an answer, as they have lost blood and all their property to the *kaprali* [corporals] (*subadars*), and 100 Tajiks have been carried off forcibly by the Afghans.' In his reply, Zaitsev promised that the White Tsar would not withhold his protection: three Cossacks and two armed *jigits* would be permanently stationed at Roshorv without further ado.[131] However, unknown to him St Petersburg had belatedly decided that the Turkestan authorities were exceeding their instructions by attempting to establish a post at Roshorv, and the War Ministry gave instructions for its withdrawal, and the recall of Rukin and Vannovskii's forces, which Rukin complied with on the 10 October.[132] This met with some resistance from Zaitsev and Ionov, who claimed that the error lay in the original instructions, which had indeed specified the need for a Russian post at Roshorv – the confusion lay over whether or not the village lay within the boundaries of Roshan. They added that the purpose of the post was to uphold the authority of the Russian-appointed canton administrator of the region, Yazghulam, and to prevent repeated Afghan raiding.[133] As they wrangled with St Petersburg, the petitions continued to flood in. In early–mid November the villagers of Bardan-Kucha, Shukur *mingbashi* and Mullah Usan Qazi from the village of Qurban Bek, and Mirza Vafa and Muzaffar of the village of Shahdar also wrote asking to become Russian subjects – Shukur *mingbashi* adding that he had been summoned to Fayzabad to receive a *farman* from Amir 'Abdurrahman Khan and acknowledge Afghan suzerainty, and had heard complaints from villagers and their *aqsaqals* all along his route about the oppression meted out by their Afghan governors (*zulm o jur besyar guftand*), and a desire to be ruled by the White Tsar (*daulat-i Aq Padshah*).[134] In October 1893 the War Minister reported to the Foreign Ministry that over 100 families of Shughnis had fled to Russian territory as a result of the annexation of

---

[130] Mullah Mumin Shah Nazar Avsat Khan to Zaitsev n.d. (10/1893) RGVIA F.5369 Op.1 D.2 ll. 117–19.

[131] Yazghulam to Zaitsev 15/10/1893; Zaitsev to Yazghulam RGVIA F.5369 Op.1 D.2 19/10/ 1893 ll. 120–1.

[132] War Ministry to Zaitsev 02/10/1893; Chief of Staff of the Ferghana *Oblast'* to Ionov 20/ 09/1893; Instructions to Sub-Lt Rukin 16/10/1893 RGVIA F.5369 Op.2 D.2 ll. 61ob–6, 72; Luzhetskaya, 'Otchet Nachal'nika Pamirskogo otryada', 162

[133] Rukin to Zaitsev 30/10/1893. Instructions to Rukin from General Povalo-Shvyikovskii, commander of the Ferghana Military District RGVIA F.5369 Op.1 D.2 ll. 107–8, 110.

[134] Petition from Bardan-Kucha 07/11/1893; Petition to the '*Rusiya Tura*' 12/11/1893 RGVIA F.5369 Op.1 D.2 ll. 122–6ob.

Shughnan by the Afghans, and were now squatting on the outskirts of Osh, where it was proving extremely difficult to find sufficient land to settle them. The Turkestan Governor-General, Baron Vrevskii, suggested granting each family three *desyatinas* of land, and freeing them from taxation for ten years. The unusually paternalistic Russian attitude towards the mountain peoples was clearly in evidence, albeit possibly with an eye to the effect such generosity would have among those under Afghan rule.[135]

In the middle of November Zaitsev wrote once again to convince his superiors that the post at Roshorv should be restored.[136] At first Korol'kov, the governor of Ferghana province, stuck to the view that the Russians should not interfere in Shughnan and Roshan, and instructed Zaitsev accordingly. However, Major-General M. P. Khoroshkhin, chief of staff of the Turkestan military district, argued that a correct reading of the 1872–3 agreement with England on the Pamir boundary had it running along the line of the river Panj, meaning that Shughnan and Roshan did indeed fall within the Russian sphere of influence and that consequently they had every right to establish a post at Roshorv.[137] In December 1893 Russia's encroachment into Roshan appeared to have borne fruit, in the form of the defection of the Afghan governor of the region, 'Ibadullah Khan, who had opened contact with Vannovskii. The explanation was that

> Although 'Ibadullah Khan considers himself to be a Badakhshan Kirgiz, his ancestors were Turks, of Moghul descent, who left Ferghana and transferred their service from Khudoyar Khan to the ruler of Badakhshan. In 1878, with the seizing of Badakhshan by the Afghans, the last Khan Jandar Shah fled from Uch-Qurghan, and all those close to him were slaughtered, including two relatives of 'Ibadullah Khan: Palwan Usaev and Mahmet Esaul.[138]

He had supposedly been nursing a deadly grievance ever since, and, seeing the desire of the local Tajiks to become Russian subjects, had sought contact with Vannovskii's reconnaissance party. This turned out to be less of a breakthrough than it appeared, as Yazghulam reported that the Afghans soon got wind of 'Ibadullah Khan's treachery, removed him from his post and imprisoned him in Shughnan. To make matters worse, the following month Rukin reported that the tables had been turned – he had arrested none other than Yazghulam himself on suspicion of spying for the Afghans and stirring up trouble among the people of Roshan, but the latter had managed to escape; despite a thorough search they had been unable to catch

[135] War Minister to the Foreign Minister 08/10/1893 AVPRI F.147 Op.485 D.1220 ll. 1–2.
[136] Zaitsev to Korol'kov 14/11/1893 RGVIA F.5369 Op.1 D.2 ll. 128–9*ob*.
[137] Khoroshkhin to Korol'kov 08/12/1893 RGVIA F.1438 Op.1 D.19 ll. 652–3.
[138] Zaitsev to Korol'kov 01/12/1893 RGVIA F.5369 Op.1 D.2 l. 137.

him. This followed a denunciation by one Amin Nazar *Bek*, who claimed that Yazghulam had openly disavowed his connection with the Russians, no longer wishing to serve them, that he had treacherously informed the Afghans as soon as the advanced Russian post at Roshorv had been withdrawn, that he had been in secret communication with the *Bek* of Qala-i Wamar, and had passed on false information to the Russians. Zaitsev responded forlornly that 'unfortunately the news recently received from your honour is so contradictory that it is almost impossible to believe it' and he suggested that possibly lack of knowledge of the local dialect had led to a misunderstanding, but Rukin asserted that Yazghulam's flight proved it.[139] From these sources it is impossible to know whether Yazghulam had really 'betrayed' the Russians or not – he had probably been denounced by a jealous rival – but it does help to put the numerous petitions requesting Russian protection into perspective.[140] He was probably trying to play the Russians and Afghans off against each other, in the hope of securing the best possible terms from each, and is unlikely to have been the only local leader doing so.

What matters for our purposes, however, is how the Russians themselves responded to such appeals for assistance. For the men on the spot, they provided powerful ammunition for an expansionist agenda that could be presented in almost purely humanitarian terms. As Zaitsev had observed the year before:

> In response to all requests from Afghan subjects I reply that the great White Tsar does not want new lands without the agreement of the Amir, does not want bloodshed – and that therefore my advice is to live peacefully with their neighbours, to fulfil all demands of the Kabul government and to suppress among the inhabitants what are for now idle dreams about Russia, but such advice is incomprehensible to the children of the savage mountains, they cannot explain to themselves the peaceful desires of a strong state, and its refusal only more strongly ignites

[139] Rukin to Zaitsev 18/05/1894; Zaitsev to Rukin 22/05/1894; Rukin to Zaitsev 04/06/1894 RGVIA F.5369 Op.1 D.2 ll. 180–3, 191–4.
[140] In 1898 Ralph Cobbold met an individual whom he described (with a characteristically tin ear for local terms) as 'Shur Chor' [Shir Char, Shukur?], the 'mimbashi' [mingbashi] of 'Roshar' [Roshorv], who, together with his father, had recently been suspected of forwarding reports to the British and spent time in Murghab gaol, but was now back in office, and did not appear to bear resentment. Possibly this was the same man, or his son: 'He seemed well-informed and intelligent, had been to Petersburg for the Tsar's coronation, which he seemed to have greatly enjoyed, and wore a number of decorations on the breast of his dark blue frock coat, which he wore with loose white trousers, a Kabul puggaree, and Russian boots. He was a good-looking, athletic young man, with well-cut features, sunburnt complexion, and piercing black eyes. He wore his head shaved, and round his waist was a black leather belt with silver fittings, while on his coat and waistcoat were brass buttons bearing the mark of a German firm.' *Innermost Asia*, 159–60.

their desire to be freed from the hated Afghans, be placed on the same footing as the inhabitants of the Pamirs, and finally find relief beneath a great hand from historical affliction.[141]

The immediate result of the Yazghulam debacle was that Korol'kov in Ferghana authorised Zaitsev to re-establish the forward post at Roshorv in order to prevent the Afghans from oppressing and forcibly deporting the local population – a *de facto* Russian annexation of part of Roshan.[142] In April 1894 Zaitsev was succeeded as commander of the Pamir force by A. G. Skerskii, another Polish officer, who had been one of Ionov's subordinates in 1892.[143] The Russian posts on the Pamirs reported that all Afghan outposts had now been withdrawn to the left bank of the Panj, to Qala-i Panj and Qala-i Bar Panj. They interpreted this as the British having finally persuaded the Afghans to honour the 1872–3 agreement between Britain and Russia. There were still fears that the Afghans might try to deport the entire population from the areas they had been forced to cede into Afghan Badakhshan. This did not material-ise, and, while there continued to be rumours of Afghan interference and minor frontier skirmishes throughout 1895, even after the Russians had established posts at Khorog and Qala-i Wamar, the Afghans were in fact gone for good.[144]

The narrative of Afghan oppression or '*zulm*' was thus one of the key justifications for the Russian annexation of Roshan, Shughnan and Wakhan. It could be seen already in Matveev's report of 1878, and in Grombchevskii's speech at the General Staff Academy in 1891: 'The population grew faint beneath Afghan oppression, and in the future saw only famine and the poverty that comes with it. In general Amir 'Abdurrahman breached all boundaries of cruelty.'[145] The context here was the reconquest of Roshan, Shughnan and Wakhan after 'Abdurrahman's suppression of the 1889 uprising under Ishaq Khan (which Grombchevskii himself later claimed to have had a hand in instigating), but this was how the Russians generally portrayed Afghan rule even in normal times. As we have seen, this was a reflection of the language used by the local population when they appealed to the Russians for protection, so it was not a purely Russian discourse by any means. In many ways this is unsurprising – whatever the inhabitants of the western Pamirs really thought about the Afghans, they clearly had a strong interest in playing off one side

---

[141] Zaitsev to Korol'kov 01/12/1893 RGVIA F.1438 Op.1 D.19 l. 721.

[142] Korol'kov to Zaitsev 04/06/1894 RGVIA F.5369 Op.1 D.2 ll. 195, 198–9.

[143] Baskhanov, *Voennye vostokovedy*, 212–13.

[144] 'Svedeniya o sobytiyakh v Avganistane', 01/04/1894; 01/05/1894; 01/06/1894; 01/09/1894; 01/11/1894; 01/01/1895 RGVIA F.1438 Op.1 D.22, 'Rekognostsirovki i svedeniya iz zagranitsy', ll. 16–17; 33–9*ob*; 47–62; 77–80; 'Otchet byv. Nachal'nika Pamirskogo otryada Kapitana Sulotskogo za vremya s 14-ogo maya 1895 g. po 17 avgusta 1896 g.', n. d., after 11/1896 RGVIA F.400 Op.1 D.2028 ll. 25–45.

[145] Grombchevskii, *Doklad*, 12.

against the other, as the episode of Yazghulam suggests. However, there were a number of reasons why the Pamiris might genuinely have preferred Russian to Afghan rule: the Russians were not particularly interested in extracting revenue from the Pamirs, and accepted the fact that they would hold these territories at a loss, which was not something 'Abdurrahman Khan's regime was prepared to tolerate to the same degree. Equally, as they were Isma'ilis, 'Muslim' (i.e. Sunni) rule was considerably less attractive to the Pamiris, whom the Afghans considered it legitimate to enslave. The Russians proclaimed religious neutrality throughout their Central Asian territories. Orthodoxy had certain privileges (though given the over-representation of Polish officers, many of the Pamir cadre were not Orthodox themselves), but proselytisation was banned. Russian colonial rule could mean safety from religious persecution. As Bobrinskii put it, in a pamphlet advocating protection and patronage for the Isma'ilis of the Pamirs, on the model of that offered to their counterparts in British India: 'we should not be surprised that the highlanders are well-disposed towards the Russians; they calculate that they will find in the Russians patrons of their sects and support in their senseless, but hard and constant struggle with Sunnism'.[146] The British were coming to very similar conclusions about Isma'ilism in India at the time, leading to a close relationship of patronage with the Aga Khan – something which prompted Russian misgivings.[147] However, the Russians had their own reasons for patronising Isma'ilism – quoting the orientalist V. P. Nalivkin, Snesarev believed that the Pamirs could play a key role in the 'struggle with Islam', and that they should be considered a 'wedge, hammered into the Muslim body'.[148]

A number of these themes appear in contemporary histories by Badakhshani authors, and whilst some of these were written under Russian auspices and have to be handled with caution, they do suggest a strong dislike of Afghan rule, and a welcoming of the arrival of the Russians to protect them from something worse. As Daniel Beben has argued, these 'local narratives of the Great Game' either imply that Russian rule was a very light imposition (at least before 1917), or else actively welcome it.[149] Fazl 'Ali Bek Surkh Afsar, author of the late continuation of the best-known history of Badakhshan, described the conquest by the Afghans in relatively neutral terms, focusing on the shame defeat brought to Badakhshani forces rather than on Afghan

---

[146] A.A. Bobrinskii, *Sekta Ismail'ya v russkikh i bukharskikh predelakh Srednei Azii* (Moscow: Obshchestva Liubitelei Estestvoznaniya, Antropologii i Etnografii, 1902), 22.

[147] See Daniel Beben, 'Introduction', in *The Memoirs of Aga Khan I: Text Edition and English Translation of the Tārīkh-i 'ibrat-afzā of Ḥasan 'Alī Shāh Āqā Khān Mahallātī* ed. Daniel Beben (London: I.B. Tauris, 2018), 47–60.

[148] A. E. Snesarev, 'O Pamirakh', n.d. (07/1901) RGVIA D.1396 Op.2 D.2134 ll. 1–57, published in Baskhanov, 'U vorot angliiskogo mogushchestva', 233–304, here 302.

[149] Beben, 'Local Narratives of the Great Game in Badakhshan', 15–16.

cruelty – but he was not an Isma'ili, and his account was appended to a text originally produced under Afghan patronage.[150] However, in his *Ta'rikh-i Shughnan*, written at the request of the orientalist Alexander Semenov, the Isma'ili author Sayyid Haidar Shah described the Afghans as establishing their power in Shughnan by deceit and maintaining it by terror. He portrays not just the Afghans, but also the local rulers of Shughnan who preceded them, in a negative light: Yusuf 'Ali Khan, whom the Afghans tricked and then executed in 1883, is described as a tyrant, while Muhammad Akbar Khan, a descendant of the Yarid ruling lineage who came from Hissar and briefly assumed power during Ishaq Khan's rebellion, 'through deceit brought the people onto his side, saying that he was an Isma'ili. The people began to defend him and resisted the Afghans. Many were killed.'[151] These sufferings at the hands of the Afghans continued 'until that time when the Sun of Righteousness, spreading justice, the Lord of Time, his Majesty the Great Emperor, the White Tsar, threw his Shadow over half of Shughnan, and the people, living both on this side of the Amu-Darya and on that side, through the mercy of the Tsar became calm'.[152] Whilst the rhetoric reflects the circumstances under which the text was composed, it is noteworthy that Mirza Haidar Shah refers here to the division of historic Shughnan into two halves along the Panj – the protection of the White Tsar came at a price. As Fazl 'Ali Bek Surkh Afsar described it:

> The representatives of both sides met on the Pamirs, and clearly laid out the boundary between unclearly defined lands, which belonged to Bukhara, Afghanistan, Russia and England.[153]

Although he used neutral language, this represented a dramatic change in the organisation of territory in the Pamir region. As Beben has pointed out, the earlier histories of Badakhshan never regard the Panj as a barrier, political or otherwise. River valleys formed natural agricultural and social units in the region, whose historic divisions – Wakhan, Shughnan, Roshan and Darvaz – were strung out on both sides of the Panj.[154] This was about to change, without any involvement of the Pamiris themselves, and with only minimal input from the Afghan government whose frontier it would also become. In the long term this would have a profound impact on both settled and nomadic populations.

---

[150] Fazl 'Ali Bek Surkh Afsar, *Ta'rikh-i Badakhshan* trans. 95. My thanks to Daniel Beben for this observation.

[151] Fazl 'Ali Bek Surkh Afsar also had little good to say about Muhammad Akbar Khan, writing that he had numerous illegitimate sons; *Ta'rikh-i Badakhshan* trans. 99.

[152] Seiid Khaidar-Sho, *Istoriya Shugnana*, 14–17.

[153] *Ta'rikh-i Badakhshan* trans. 99.

[154] Beben, 'Local Narratives of the Great Game in Badakhshan', 6–8.

10.4   Drawing the Boundary

There was an obvious precedent for the use of a joint Anglo-Russian boundary commission to survey and define the Afghan frontier in the Pamirs, namely the commission which had defined the frontier between Transcaspia, Afghanistan and Persia in 1884–7. As we have seen, the Russian commission on the Pamir question had already proposed such a body for the Pamirs in 1892, indicating that they did not consider their disagreements with Britain to be particularly fundamental.[155] The minor clashes and skirmishes of the following three years did not really jeopardise this understanding, confirming once again that the interests of the supposed rivals of the 'Great Game' were much more closely aligned with each other than is usually assumed. Younghusband himself took the Russian annexation quite philosophically, acknowledging that it reflected shared assumptions, motives, and norms of imperial 'manliness':

> A little further on we also came across a Shughni with a letter for me. He had come straight from Shughnan & reported that the whole of trans-Oxus Shughnan & Roshan had just been annexed by the Russians. There had been a small fight between the Russians and the Afghans but the latter had very soon retired. This move of the Russians is what we had been expecting for some time. A year or two ago before we had become established in this country this might have been rather a serious matter for us but now that we are comfortably established in the Hindu Kush I don't think it need trouble us very much. The Russians are drawn on in much the same way as we are – mainly I think by frontier officers. Frontier officers & officials at headquarters who have much to do with the frontier become too sensitive, I think, of the intentions of the opposite party. A forward policy seems the most manly & even the most prudent & to anticipate the designs of the other a forward move is suggested & carried out. The other seeing this makes a counter-move & so the game goes on. Our move to Gilgit was a case in point & addenda to it were the moves to Hunza & Chitral. The present move by the Russians is but the reply which would be expected.[156]

The 1895 Russo-British agreement on the Pamir boundary essentially confirmed the division agreed in 1873, but this time each party agreed to despatch a survey team, who would agree the boundary line together with rather greater geographical accuracy.[157] For most of its length the line between Russian and Afghan territory would run along the Panj, or upper Oxus, despite the fact that

[155] 'Zapis' materialov osobogo soveshchaniya po Pamirskomu voprosu', 15 & 29/04/1892, in Stanishevskii, *Sbornik*, 60–7.

[156] IOR MSS Eur F197/257 F. E. *Younghusband. Private Journal. 1894*, Entry for 26/09/1894, Khoghazi.

[157] 'Agreement between the Governments of Great Britain and Russia with Regard to the Spheres of Influence of the Two Countries in the Region of the Pamirs. London, March 11, 1895', *PP* C.7643 Treaty series No. 8 (1895), 1–4.

closer acquaintance with the region had taught even European observers that
this would cut through existing political, cultural and economic units. As
Curzon wrote, with characteristic *hauteur*:

> The blunders resulting from geographical ignorance were more notable
> still. The Oxus was accepted, almost without demur, as a boundary,
> simply because it was a river, and because in European countries rivers
> are frequently the lines of division between states; whereas in very moun-
> tainous regions, like these under discussion, watersheds and not rivers are
> the almost invariable boundaries, while in the particular region affected,
> neither ethnographically, historically, nor administratively, had the Upper
> Oxus ever been a dividing line.[158]

The Russian side of the commission set off from New Marghelan on the 17
May 1895, arriving at the Pamir post on the 2 July. Here they were later joined by
George Macartney, the British Consul at Kashgar, who was taking a long way
round to return to his posting, and awaited the English section of
the Commission under Major-General Gerard, which arrived on the 9 July
(O.S.).[159] Sven Hedin's account focuses mainly on the festivities that followed
the setting up at the last boundary pillar, as the Russians and British feasted each
other on Champagne, caviar, *pâté de foie gras*, crayfish soup, lobster mayonnaise,
asparagus, and ices: 'What! Champagne on the Pamirs? Yes, even so.'[160] The
spirit of bonhomie and good fellowship he describes is confirmed by the report
of the British members of the commission, which is replete with praise of
Russian hospitality, and spends almost as much time discussing the shooting
of game as the technicalities of boundary drawing.[161] This was tempered with
only the mildest degree of mutual suspicion, emphasising once again that the
European protagonists of the 'Great Game' always felt closer to each other than
to their native subjects. The Commission had completed its work and returned
by the 5 September.[162] Although Olufsen observed that when he first passed
through in 1896 the Pamirs were still in a state of interregnum, as the Afghans
had been driven out without the Russians establishing full control, when he
returned in 1898 their presence seemed stable and permanent.[163]

---

[158] Curzon, *On the Indian Frontier*, 147.

[159] The 22 July according to the Gregorian Calendar: M. G. Gerard, *Report on the Proceedings of the Pamir Boundary Commission* (Calcutta: Office of the Superintendent of Government Printing, 1897), 17.

[160] Hedin, *Through Asia*, II, 686–700.

[161] Gerard, *Report on the Proceedings of the Pamir Boundary Commission*, 4–11, 20, 25–6.

[162] 'Otchet byv. Nachal'nika Pamirskogo Otryada Kapitana Sulotskogo za vremya s 14-ogo maya 1895 g. po 17 avgusta 1896 g.', n.d., after 11/1896 RGVIA F.400 Op.1 D.2028 ll. 5–17.

[163] Olufsen, *Through the Unknown Pamirs*, 168. This remained true almost to the present day, given the continued role played by the Russian armed forces in securing Tajikistan's border with Afghanistan. The Russian garrison in Khorog was withdrawn only in 2004 – see Ian

Thus by the late 1890s relations with the British on the Pamir frontier had stabilised. While Petrovskii in Kashgar was still agitated at the prospect of Kanjut being finally drawn into the British sphere of influence, his superiors were content with the territorial settlement that had been reached in the region. As Staff-Captain Stasov wrote from the Pamir frontier to the new War Minister, A. N. Kuropatkin, in 1898, an aggressive war launched by Britain against Russia's Asian territories was now 'beyond the boundaries of the believable' – and Russia's interests in the region now lay in maintaining the status quo and keeping things quiet, so long as the British were prepared to behave themselves, although he considered that, given the sympathy the populations of neighbouring regions of Afghanistan had with Russia, if it suited their interests they could stir up a rebellion there (something Kuropatkin had underlined with a question mark). The Russians were more concerned about the possibility of political instability in Afghanistan after the apparently imminent death of 'Abdurrahman Khan. Having small, unstable states on the frontier was undesirable, as the earlier examples of Ghulja, Khoqand and Kashgar had shown.[164] It was understood that both sides spied on each other, but there was also an understanding that this should not lead to an open breach where detected. In February 1899 W. Klemm from the Ministry of Foreign Affairs reported to S. M. Dukhovskoi, the Turkestan Governor-General, that they had recently captured a Nepali who had strayed onto Russian territory in the Pamirs, and whom he suspected of being a spy, but that even if this were the case it would be better simply to expel him to British territory, as anything more drastic might provoke British reprisals against three Main Staff Officers (one of whom was Snesarev) who were due to cross the Pamirs into India soon.[165] This and similar reports indicate that, while the rivalry with Britain never entirely disappeared, after the Pamir boundary commission had done its work the territorial question was effectively settled. In 1915, when Aurel Stein travelled through the region, he was full of praise for its Russian administration, and the assistance he was given by the then commander of the Pamir detachment, Colonel Ivan Dionisevich Jagello (1865–1942).[166]

MacWilliam, 'Pamirs Adapt to Life without Russia', *BBC News* 22/02/2005 (http://news.bbc .co.uk/2/hi/asia-pacific/4284083.stm).

[164] Stasov to Kuropatkin 12/03/1898 RGVIA F.1396 Op.2 D.1544, 'Perepiska po politicheskoi chasti', ll. 1–3ob.

[165] Polozov to Sakharov 25/01/1899; Klemm to Dukhovskoi 13/02/1899 RGVIA F.1396 Op.2 D.1539, 'Perepiska po politicheskoi chasti 1899 g.', ll. 20–1, 42–3. Snesarev would indeed encounter difficulties on this journey, where he was severely delayed at Gilgit, and then only permitted to make a very formal public tour of Indian cities, under constant surveillance and without the possibility of remaining anywhere for an extended period of time, as he complained in a letter to his sister written from Murree: A. E. Snesarev to K. E. Komarova 16/28 Sept. 1899, *Pis'ma A. E. Snesareva*, 462.

[166] Sir Aurel Stein, 'A Third Journey of Exploration in Central Asia, 1913–1916', *GJ* 48/3 (1916), 212–19.

Whilst in the long term the new frontier would cause severe difficulties for the local population, after it was effectively closed in the 1930s,[167] initially, and perhaps unexpectedly, it also created new opportunities for them. Till Mostowlansky has argued that, so long as they found themselves on the frontier of an empire, rather than a nationalising state, the religious minority communities of the highland regions in what are now Pakistan and Tajikistan could exploit their strategic position for their own benefit, receiving subsidy and substantial investments in infrastructure, while the British and Russian (or Soviet) imperial regimes did not see them as a threat to the national community, and hence did not seek to forcibly assimilate them.[168] Their position on the frontier also could allow them to escape state-imposed obligations. In November 1896 the Amir of Bukhara's new Governor in Roshan, Mirza 'Isa Khwaja Qaraulbegi, reported that thirty-five families from the Afghan village of Chastu had rebelled against the conscription of their menfolk for military service and crossed the Panj to the Russian side, destroying the bridges behind them, and firing on the Afghan soldiers, who were forced to abandon pursuit once they were on Russian territory.[169] Whilst the Russians viewed cross-border movement towards them with satisfaction, as a demonstration of their superior benevolence, this was of course something that cut both ways. The threat to migrate to Afghan or British territory and thus damage Russian prestige would be made frequently by the inhabitants of Roshan, Shughnan and Wakhan over the next ten years. This was because, as Khalfin and Iskandarov noted, even as the Anglo-Russian 'Pamir Question' was settled, a new one reared its head. While the Pamir plateau, with its sparse Kyrgyz population, came under direct Russian rule in 1895 as part of Ferghana province, Roshan, Shughnan and Wakhan were handed over to the Amir of Bukhara, as part of the Russian protectorate in the region.[170] It was in the clash between Bukharan and Russian assumptions about governance that some of the peculiarities of the Russian attitude to the Pamir region and its peoples would come to the fore most strongly.

---

[167] The classic study remains M. Nazif Shahrani, *The Kirghiz and Wakhi of Afghanistan: Adaptation to Closed Frontiers and War* (Seattle, WA: University of Washington Press, 2002 [1979]), esp. Chapter 7.

[168] Till Mostowlansky, 'Where Empires Meet: Orientalism and Marginality on the Former Russo-British Frontier', in *Études de Lettres*. Nos. 2–3. *L'Orientalisme des marges: Éclairages à partir de l'Inde et de la Russie* ed. Philippe Bornet & Svetlana Gorshenina (Lausanne: Université de Lausanne, 2014), 179–96.

[169] Mirza 'Isa Khwaja Qaraulbegi to Amir 'Abd al-Ahad 23/11/1896, in Stanishevskii, *Sbornik*, 81–2.

[170] Khalfin, *Bukharskii Emirat*, 3; Iskandarov, *Vostochnaya Bukhara i Pamir*, 472–82; Becker, *Russia's Protectorates*, 155–8.

10.5   Russian–Bukharan conflict

Bukharan influence in and claims to the western Pamir region pre-dated the 1895 decision to include it within the Emirate. In 1877 Amir Sayyid Muzaffar had taken advantage of the demise of Khoqand, Bukhara's historic rival in the region, by occupying first Qarateghin and then Darvaz, and installing a *bek* in the central town of Qala-i Khumb.[171] Whilst Bukharan expansionism was a product of the general consolidation and centralisation of the Amir's rule which the Russian protectorate made possible, there was no direct Russian presence in the region, or Russian oversight of its administration. In 1892, when Captain Kuznetsov visited Darvaz, he reported that he had only been able to buy sheep from the local inhabitants thanks to the intervention of the Bukharan officials he was travelling with, as the local population did not recognise Russian money.[172] In Shughnan, Roshan and Wakhan the situation would be different from the start, as the Russian garrison at Khorog represented an alternative, and – in the eyes of the local inhabitants – more credible and sympathetic centre of power and authority. Khalfin suggests that, while the official explanation for giving Shughnan, Roshan and Wakhan to the Amir was to compensate him for the loss of the portion of Darvaz that lay to the south of the Panj, the real reason lay in the unwillingness of the Turkestani authorities to shoulder the considerable costs of administering a remote, desperately poor region that was unlikely ever to pay its own way.[173] Whilst Khalfin offers no direct evidence for this, subsequent events suggest that such reasoning may have played a part, but there were always powerful voices within the Turkestan administration for whom considerations of prestige, combined with a paternalistic attitude to the Pamiri Tajiks, trumped fiscal prudence.

This internal 'Pamir Question' divided Turkestani officialdom, throwing the officers on the spot into conflict with Tashkent, and Tashkent into conflict with St Petersburg and the agency of the Ministry of Foreign Affairs in Bukhara.[174] Amir 'Abd al-Ahad himself was not particularly keen on accepting the new territories, and seems to have done so partly because the alternative financial payment would have been too low and partly because for reasons of prestige he needed some public compensation for the loss of his territories beyond the Panj. It also appears that he had not been informed of the Tsar's decision to grant a three-year moratorium on taxation to the local population, a demonstration of Russian benevolence that would reinforce the Tsar's prestige at his vassal's expense. 'Abd al-Ahad complained bitterly when he discovered this, and also protested that the territories he had lost in Darvaz were much more fertile. The question of exemption from taxes remained unresolved – the

---

[171]   Pirumshoev, *Ta'rikhi Darvoz*, 70–92; Iskandarov, *Vostochnaya Bukhara i Pamir*, 135–42.
[172]   Kuznetsov to Nikolai Ivanovich 26/07/1892 RGVIA F.1438 Op.1 D.18 l. 565*ob.*
[173]   Khalfin, *Bukharskii Emirat*, 5–7.
[174]   Becker, *Russia's Protectorates*, 215–18.

Russian authorities insisted on the moratorium, whilst the Amir was reluctant to accept its legitimacy.[175] In July 1896 the first Bukharan officials arrived after a long and difficult journey from Qala-i Khumb in Bukharan Darvaz – Ishanqul Toqsaba in Roshan, Sayyid Akbar Shah (a former ruler) in Shughnan and his brother Mansur Shah in Wakhan.[176] By November the first conflict had already erupted between the former and Captain V. V. Eggert, the commander of the new Pamir post at Khorog. None of the Bukharan officials had received any salary, and in any case, as they complained, there were no bazaars where they could make ordinary purchases, so they resorted to requisitioning meat, oil and grain from the local population without payment in order to feed themselves and their suites. This was usual elsewhere in Bukhara, where officials received a portion of their pay and subsistence in kind in this way.[177] This prompted Eggert to intervene: he informed Ishanqul publicly that he would have to reimburse the inhabitants for the cost of what he and his suite had requisitioned, and that he would be sending a detailed list to the Turkestan Governor-General. As the beleaguered *Divan-begi* put it, 'When these words came to the naked and hungry inhabitants, they produced confusion amongst them, and my authority as a ruler suffered a heavy loss.' To add injury to this insult, Eggert also expelled Ishanqul Toqsaba from the house where he had taken up residence, and used it to establish the Russian post.[178] In a stormy audience with V. I. Ignat'ev, the Russian agent in Bukhara, the Amir asked whether he could really be considered sovereign in the region or not, given this treatment of his officials, decried once again the granting of exemption from taxes over his head, and threatened to renounce the region altogether.[179]

In January 1897 the chief of the Turkestan Staff, General Fedorov, wrote to War Minister Kuropatkin suggesting that, as it seemed impossible to prevent officers of the Pamir force from making undesirable interference in and criticism of Bukharan affairs, it would be best to withdraw the permanent garrisons from Shughnan and Roshan, and only mount occasional patrols in these territories.[180] Kuropatkin did not take this suggestion up, writing that, according to a report he had received from a group of Danish officers (Olufsen's Pamir expedition), the local inhabitants were considerably stirred

[175] Khalfin, *Bukharskii Emirat*, 10–13.
[176] *Ibid.*, 13–17.
[177] A. A. Semenov, *Ocherk ustroistva tsentral'nogo administrativnogo upravleniya Bukharskogo khanstva pozdneishego vremeni* (Stalinabad: AN Tadzhikskoi SSR, 1954), 10–13; Alexander Morrison, 'Amlākdārs, Khwājas and Mulk Land in the Zarafshan Valley after the Russian Conquest', in *Explorations in the Social History of Modern Central Asia (19th–Early 20th Century)* ed. Paolo Sartori (Leiden: Brill, 2013), 36–8.
[178] Khalfin, *Bukharskii Emirat*, 19–22.
[179] *Ibid.*, 24–7.
[180] Fedorov to Kuropatkin 05/01/1897 RGVIA F.400 Op.1 D.2129 ll. 3–6ob.

up against the newly appointed Bukharan administration, whose officials had been sent without any funds and had resorted to extortion from the local population. Only the presence of the Russian posts had prevented a full-scale uprising, and any abandonment of them would unnecessarily alarm the inhabitants; in view of this and the continued Afghan threat they would need to remain.[181] In May 1897 the Turkestan Governor-General, Baron Vrevskii, included in his instructions to the new commander of the Pamir force, Staff-Captain Karl-Edvard Kivekäs (1866–1942), an exhortation to be watchful for oppressive behaviour by Bukharan officials. He authorised him to investigate the claims of injustice on their part presented in petitions by the local population, although he did warn that care needed to be taken when assessing their veracity, and noted that good Russo-Bukharan relations were the best guarantee of the good treatment of the locals.[182] In the event Kivekäs, a Finnish officer who would go on to command the Pamir post three times for a total of six years between 1897 and 1907, would become a persistent champion of Russian annexation, and of the protection of the inhabitants of the Pamir region from Bukharan cruelty.[183]

In December 1898 the new Turkestan Governor-General, S. M. Dukhovskoi, decided on his own initiative to despatch Kuznetsov to Bukhara to initiate discussions with the Amir about annexing Wakhan, Shughnan and Roshan to Russia, on the grounds that the Amir found trying to rule these regions a burden, one which the commander of the Pamir force would be well placed to relieve him of. When the Ministry of Foreign Affairs learnt of this through Ignat'ev, they were highly displeased, and insisted that Kuznetsov be recalled immediately. War Minister Kuropatkin reprimanded Dukhovskoi, telling him that all such discussions had to be cleared first with the Ministry of Foreign Affairs, and conducted through the agency in Bukhara.[184] Despite the abortive end to Kuznetsov's mission, Dukhovskoi's initiative did prompt a renewal of the debate over Bukharan rule in the western Pamirs, and the acceptance by the War

---

[181] 'Dokladnaya Zapiska po Glavnomu Shtabu', 08/03/1897 RGVIA F.400 Op.1 D.2129 ll. 19–20.

[182] 'Instruktsiya Nachal'niku Pamirskogo Otryada', 26/05/1897 RGVIA F.1396 Op.2 D.1544 l. 8; Khalfin, *Rossiya i Bukharskii Emirat*, 38–9.

[183] Hedin, who met him in Marghelan in 1893, described him as a 'light-hearted son of Finland' and noted that he was a Swedish-speaker: *Through Asia*, I, 104. See Baskhanov, *Voennye vostokovedy*, 111–12; D. Khudonazarov, 'Pervyi russkii pravitel' Pamira (pamyati Eduarda Karlovicha Kivekesa)', in *Pamirskaya ekspeditsiya* (Moscow: IV RAN, 2006), 219–32; T. V. Kotiukova, 'Ya dal bukhartsam znat', chto podrobnogo nasiliya ne dopushchu …', *Voenno-istoricheskii Zhurnal* (2008), No. 9, 61–5. Thanks to Oybek Mahmudov for the latter two references.

[184] Dukhovskoi to Kuznetsov 09/12/1898; Asiatic Department to Kuropatkin 18/12/1898; Kuropatkin to Ivanov 19/12/1898; Kuropatkin to Dukhovskoi 17/01/1899 RGVIA F.400 Op.1 D.2329, 'Po voprosu o vkliuchenii v predely Rossii bukharskikh vladenii v Shugnane, Roshane i Vakhane i o sbore podatei s naselenii sikh vladenii', ll. 1–18.

Ministry that the transfer of the region to Russia was desirable in principle.[185] Hard on its heels came a damning report from Kivekäs detailing Bukharan abuses of the local population. Aqsaqal Dauruk-Bek of Shakhdara had come to him, claiming that two Bukharan officials called Sultan Murad and Mullah-Pir had been extorting flour, barley and fat, and paying less than half the usual price for them. When he ventured to protest:

> For this impudence he was sentenced to fifty strokes with a rod. They beat him across the spine, and each blow with the rod affected the region of the heart and the main nervous centre of the spine, such that already after the fifteenth blow he lost consciousness. When he came to they told him that he was the same kind of *Kafir* (unbeliever) as the Russians, as he had done them service, and confronted him with the fact that in return for the service he had done the force he had received a *khalat* from me.[186]

Kivekäs alleged that the Bukharans hated the Russians owing to their religious 'fanaticism', flaunting their superior piety, and that they despised the local population both for their loyalty to the Russian unbelievers, and because they were 'indifferent' to normal Muslim practices. They constantly sought to levy unreasonable fines – attempting to collect 120 roubles from a Tajik whose unhappy lover had drowned herself in the Panj, and attempting to collect *zakat* in defiance of the moratorium on taxes. When he questioned lower officials they invariably responded that it was the Bukharan *bek*, Ishanqul, who had given the order, something which the latter systematically denied. He concluded that 'everything the Bukharans do is exclusively for profit, and only for profit', that the absence of any defined laws or rules gave free rein to Bukharan officials, who were clearly only sent there to enrich themselves, and that centuries of bad administration in the Emirate ensured that they were all 'the most refined type of scoundrel'. He called for them to be expelled, or at the very least placed in complete subordination to the Russian commander, adding that were war to break out it was essential that the local *aqsaqals* be reliable Russian appointees.[187] Kivekäs reinforced his argument by enclosing the original of a petition 'to the honoured *Sahib*-General from the poor of Shughnan': this lamented that they had long been under the oppression (*zulmat*) of the Afghans, who had passed all limits; the Russians had freed them from this – so why had they now been handed over to the Bukharans, under whose rule day by day things got worse (*ruz ba ruz kharab shod*), who extorted money and grain, and who despised them and would not sit or eat with them? The petition ended with a list

[185] Khalfin, *Rossiya i Bukharskii Emirat*, 44.
[186] Kivekäs to Chaikovskii 06/01/1899 RGVIA F.400 Op.1 D.2329 l. 36.
[187] Kivekäs to Chaikovskii 06/01/1899 RGVIA F.400 Op.1 D.2329 ll. 37–*ob*.

of twenty-four inhabitants who had had money or grain extorted from them, presumably the petitioners.[188] We see here the same impulses which had prompted and legitimised the original extension of Russian rule over the Pamirs coming into play once again: a powerful narrative of the oppression of innocent mountain peoples by their rapacious Sunni neighbours. There is no reason to doubt the sincerity of Kivekäs's outrage, but his views of Bukharan administration were clearly influenced by standard stereotypes of Oriental despotism, similar to those which later appeared in D. N. Logofet's lurid critique of the Emirate as a 'lawless land'.[189] Equally, it is clear that the local population, or at any rate the local officials, knew exactly how to appeal to Russian sensibilities and prejudices on this point. None of this is to say that Bukharan rule in the western Pamirs was not corrupt and oppressive – probably it was more so than elsewhere in the emirate, given the newness of Bukharan administration and the religious difference between rulers and ruled. Perhaps even more importantly, in the western Pamirs Bukharan rule was subjected to constant Russian scrutiny, and there were particular cultural factors – notably the idealisation of the local population as the original 'Aryan' inhabitants of Central Asia and adherents of a less 'fanatical' form of Islam – which caused Russian officers to respond to this in a particular way. In the case of Kivekäs, his identification with them was so complete that he and his wife adopted a Shughni girl called Gulbegim Barakat as their daughter.[190]

Unsurprisingly, the Bukharan perspective on these problems was different. The following month Ignat'ev had an audience with Amir 'Abd al-Ahad in which he brought up the question of the three Pamiri principalities, to which the Amir responded as follows:

> Since the time that Shughnan and Roshan were joined to my realm, these provinces have brought me nothing but affliction and unpleasantness. The exchange of Darvaz for these provinces was carried out against my will. I myself never wanted it. Mr Lessar [Ignat'ev's predecessor as Russian agent in Bukhara] obliged me to agree to this exchange. If I now renounce these provinces and do not receive in exchange some territorial compensation, or some form of satisfaction for my self-respect, then it could significantly damage my prestige among my subjects. At the same time, I repeat that the possession of Shughnan and Roshan is a burden for me. All the officials whom I send there quickly return, having spoiled their reputations, regardless of the fact that I ordered worthy people there. I incessantly hear petitions and offensive accusations towards myself for the

---

[188] *'ariza bara-yi hurmatli sahib-janarul, az taraf-i faqirha-i Shughnan* (Persian original) plus Russian translation by Lt Vygornitskii RGVIA F.400 Op.1 D.2329 ll. 41–3ob.

[189] D. N. Logofet, *Strana bespraviya: Bukharskoe khanstvo i ego sovremennoe sostoyanie* (St Pb.: B. Berezovskii, 1909); see Becker, *Russia's Protectorates*, 212–14.

[190] Middleton, 'The Pamirs', 434.

governance of these provinces, and yet I rule them in accordance with the dictates of the *shari'a*. Why, after the transfer of the governance of these provinces to me, do Russian officers continue to interfere in my internal affairs? Under these circumstances ruling is difficult.[191]

He went on to complain that even at the most favourable time of year it took three months to travel there from Bukhara, and that for much of the year it was impossible to get there at all. At most the provinces might bring in 23,000 *tangas* a year, while they cost at least a *lakh* (100,000 *tangas*) to administer. Darvaz, in contrast, had brought in a clear profit of 13,000–15,000 *tangas* a year. Ignat'ev commented that the Amir might be prepared to give up the region in return for adequate financial compensation; a few days later he qualified this judgement, saying that the *Qush-begi* (Prime Minister), Astanaqul, had indicated that what the Amir really wanted was some public sign of imperial favour, such as the title of *Vysochestva* (Highness) which he bore becoming hereditary, the rank of full General, or the order of St Andrew 1st Class.[192]

The following month Major-General Putyata, who had led an early expedition to the Pamirs in 1883, contributed a pair of memoranda on the question in which humanitarian and intelligence concerns were combined – he claimed that the Amir's officials had ignored a three-year moratorium on the collection of taxes introduced in 1898, and that their exactions were at risk of causing famine, while the Russian posts in the region were besieged with petitions. Direct Russian supervision over the local population might allow them to collect intelligence from their relations across the Afghan frontier and their co-religionists in British Chitral. He advocated handing over control to the commander of the Pamir force at Khorog, estimating the annual cost at a relatively trifling 5,160 roubles per year.[193] Dukhovskoi drew up a proposal which essentially followed Kivekäs's recommendation, suggesting that, while the Amir could remain nominally sovereign, real authority should be handed over to the commander of the Pamir post – this, he argued, would make an excellent impression on the population of neighbouring regions of India and Afghanistan once they saw how the lot of the Pamiris had improved, although he accepted that some form of compensation would be needed to salve the Amir's *amour-propre*, not least as the Russians were also negotiating with him to have a garrison placed at Termez. He suggested an arrangement similar to that governing the Amu-Darya Division, which had been annexed from Khiva

---

[191] Ignat'ev to Dukhovskoi 06/02/1899 RGVIA F.400 Op.1 D.2329 ll. 22–3*ob*.

[192] Secret telegram from Ignat'ev to Dukhovskoi 11/03/1899 RGVIA F.400 Op.1 D.2329 ll. 26–*ob*.

[193] D. V. Putyata, 'O znachenii dlya nas Shugnana i Roshana peredavaemykh Emirom Bukharskim', 18/03/1899; 'Dokladnaya zapiska', 23/03/1899 RGVIA F.1396 Op.2 D.1544 ll. 9–10*ob*; RGVIA F.400 Op.1 D.2329 ll. 27–9*ob*.

in 1873.[194] In the face of this onslaught from the Turkestani authorities, the Ministry of Foreign Affairs mounted a robust defence of the Amir, but one which ultimately tended to the same conclusion. Ignat'ev wrote that the Bukharan system of governance in the western Pamirs was no different from that which obtained in other Bukharan provinces, and blamed the continued petitioning and complaints of the Amir's subjects there on the meddling presence of Russian officers, who assured the inhabitants that they could always appeal to them against the Amir's officials. He dismissed Dukhovskoi's proposal for *de facto* annexation with nominal Bukharan sovereignty, saying that this was precisely the opposite of what the Amir had requested, and would simply perpetuate the current problems. Instead now the only possibility was a complete annexation by Russia – but some form of compensation was essential.[195] In July 1899 A. P. Chaikovskii, the military governor of Ferghana province, also advocated annexation: 'The inclusion of Roshan, Shughnan and Wakhan in our possessions is possible in my view. So far as I know, these provinces, which lie in our direct sphere of influence and border surveillance, were handed over to the Bukharan Amir only because it was essential to compensate the latter for the loss of part of Darvaz, which was taken away from him and given to Afghanistan. However, this did not accord either with the desires of the local population, which had anticipated the uniting of the provinces with the Empire, or with the establishment of desirable frontiers, which require the creation of military posts at Khorog and Langar Gisht.' The British might object, but this should not be a serious consideration. He suggested that a new Pamir district could be established with a minimum of expense, and no increase in the Russian military presence.[196]

Despite this apparent consensus, Dukhovskoi found reasons to delay – namely the extension of British authority (via the Mir of Hunza) over the Taghdumbash Pamir, over which the Chinese claimed sovereignty.[197] He worried that the removal of Shughnan and Roshan from Bukharan authority might be seen as retaliation, and that it would be better to delay the annexation until Russian discussions with China about resisting British incursions had been settled (something which in the event proved impossible because of the eruption of the Boxer Rebellion). The Ministry of Foreign Affairs agreed, and asked Dukhovskoi to remind his officers not to interfere with Bukharan affairs while the matter was being resolved; at the same time they decided to extend

[194] Dukhovkskoi to Sakharov 06/04/1899; 'Soobrazheniya ob organizatsii upravleniya Shugnanom i Roshanom', RGVIA F.400 Op.1 D.2329 ll. 34–5ob, 44–5ob.
[195] Ignat'ev to Dukhovskoi 03/06/1899 RGVIA F.400 Op.1 D.2329 ll. 50–5ob.
[196] A. P. Chaikovskii to Mikhail Dmitrievich (?) 24/07/1899 RGVIA F.1396 Op.2 D.1544 ll. 24–7.
[197] On this see further Alder, *British India's Northern Frontier*, 283–4.

the moratorium on tax collection until the following year.[198] Early in 1900
Dukhovskoi noted that the Amir had actually written to him asking to be
relieved of the burden of administering the troublesome provinces,[199] but a
combination of administrative inertia and worries about the British response
meant that the debate continued for another four years. Instead, in the summer
of 1900 the tax moratorium came to an end, and Dukhovskoi asked the new
commander of the Pamir post, Captain N. S. Anosov, to establish a revenue
regime in consultation with Bukharan officials.[200] This appears to have been a
simplified version of the system which existed elsewhere in Bukhara, consisting of *kharaj* at a rate of 10 per cent of the harvest, plus *zakat* on livestock at a
rate of 1/40, and a certain amount in kind for the *amlakdar* and another official
called the 'mushrup [*mushrif*]', plus a large number of miscellaneous taxes on
oil and other cash crops, and on marriages.[201] Despite claims that this system
was wholly in accordance with the best principles of *shari'a*, it immediately led
to a renewal of complaints, from local inhabitants and Russian officers alike. In
September 1900 Dukhovskoi responded to a report from the Governor of
Ferghana province on Bukharan tax collection practices in Shughnan,
Roshan and Darvaz (he had enclosed a petition of complaint from the inhabitants) by stating that Bukharan methods of collecting *zakat* were entirely in
accordance with local customs. He reminded him that 'Our forces on the
Pamirs are prohibited from all interference with the internal affairs of the
Pamir khanates which lie within the domains of the Amir of Bukhara.'[202] Two
months later Dukhovskoi had to defend the Bukharan administration from the
Main Staff, who in the midst of the international crisis provoked by the Russian
occupation of Manchuria after the Boxer Rebellion somehow found the time to
produce a memorandum specifically on the taxation system in the western
Pamirs, objecting that it was both too complicated and too heavy, that the
people were notoriously poor, many of them living 'off wild herbs', and that as
it would soon be annexed by Russia the moratorium on taxation should be
extended.[203] Dukhovskoi countered that the system might be complicated, but
that it was founded on 'Shariat', that the Bukharans would not accept any other

---

[198] Dukhovskoi to Sakharov 18/08/1899; Sakharov to Dukhovskoi 24/09/1899; Ignat'ev to
Dukhovskoi 16/12/1899 RGVIA F.400 Op.1 D.2329 ll. 57–9.
[199] Dukhovskoi to Sakharov 17/03/1900 RGVIA F.400 Op.1 D.2329 ll. 68–9.
[200] Dukhovskoi to Sakharov 28/09/1900 RGVIA F.400 Op.1 D.2329 ll. 74–5.
[201] 'Razmer i poryadok vzimaniya podatei Bukharskim pravitel'stvom s podvlastnogo emu
naseleniya Rushana, Shugnana i Vakhana', 04/07/1900 RGVIA F.400 Op.1 D.2329 ll. 76–
8*ob*; on the Bukharan taxation system see Morrison, 'Amlākdārs, Khwājas and Mulk
Land', 21–38.
[202] Dukhovskoi to Korol'kov 20/09/1900 RGVIA F.1396 Op.2 D.16, 'O narodnom sude', ll.
24–*ob*.
[203] 'Dokladnaya zapiska po Glavnomu Shtabu', 10/11/1900 RGVIA F.400 Op.1 D.2329; they
seem to have borrowed this phrase from a report from Captain Anosov to the Governor
of Ferghana, A. P. Chaikovskii: Khalfin, *Rossiya i Bukharskii Emirat*, 51.

basis for it, and that the Turkestan authorities simply did not have enough understanding of the economic life of the regions to devise a system that would accord with Russian ideas or norms.[204] Owing to a harvest failure in 1900 the taxation moratorium was once again extended, much to the disgust of the Bukharans, while the question of Russian annexation was allowed to drift, partly because of Dukhovskoi's unexpected death in March 1901. When, in the spring of 1902, an attempt by Bukharan officials to collect taxes in Shughnan led to an uprising, prompting Amir 'Abd al-Ahad to raise the matter again, he was told once again that the transfer would not be timely – although the real reason seems to have been a realisation of just how expensive the direct administration of the region would be.[205] General F. N. Vasil'ev, the new director of the Asiatic Section of the General Staff, estimated the cost at 20,000 roubles a year, or four times what Putyata had suggested in 1899 when the problem was first debated.[206] The Turkestani authorities, however, now argued that, for urgent reasons of prestige, the territories should be taken from Bukhara and handed over to direct Russian control.[207]

As a sop to the Amir, in July 1902 the Acting Turkestan Governor-General, N. A. Ivanov, removed Kivekäs from the command of the Pamir post at Khorog, replacing him with Andrei Evgen'evich Snesarev.[208] Snesarev's views on the need for reform in the administration of the Pamir region would have been well known to his superiors, as in 1901 he had authored a lengthy memorandum which accused the Bukharans of being as cruel and oppressive as the Afghans, and urged a direct Russian annexation.[209] Khalfin claimed that Snesarev received strict instructions not to interfere with the doings of Bukharan officials.[210] In fact, these instructions retained the same ambiguous formula as before, simultaneously telling Snesarev that he had the right to 'attentively follow the actions of the Bukharan administration [. . .], with the aim of attracting the sympathy of the population to the Russian side, and with the aim of preventing violence and corruption on the part of the Bukharan authorities', but that he should not intervene directly in Bukharan

---

[204] Dukhovskoi to Viktor Viktorovich 28/12/1900 RGVIA F.400 Op.1 D.2329 l. 88.

[205] Khalfin, *Rossiya i Bukharskii Emirat*, 54–5.

[206] F. N. Vasil'ev, 'Po voprosu o peredache name Pamirskikh khanstv – Shugnana i Roshana', 16/08/1902 RGVIA F.400 Op.1 D.2329 ll. 103–6.

[207] This was the tenor of a memorandum prepared by Prince Shakhovskii, the Acting Diplomatic Official in the Turkestan Governor-General's chancery, which outlined at considerable length the negotiations over the Pamir boundary, the historical reasons for handing over the western Pamirs to Bukhara, and the undesirable consequences of this: 'Doklad diplomaticheskogo chinovnika pri Turkestanskom General-Gubernatore ot 21 iiulya 1902 godu', in Stanishevskii, *Sbornik*, 85–155.

[208] Baskhanov, 'U vorot angliiskogo mogushchestva', 172–3.

[209] A. E. Snesarev, 'O Pamirakh', n.d. (07/1901) RGVIA D.1396 Op.2 D.2134 ll. 1–57, published in Baskhanov, 'U vorot angliiskogo mogushchestva', 233–304, here 264–80.

[210] Khalfin, *Rossiya i Bukharskii Emirat*, 56–7.

Figure 10.4 Andrei Evgen'evich Snesarev with other Turkestani officers, *c.* 1904 (Wikimedia Commons).

affairs but rather seek to influence them by advice and example, while he should not accept any petitions from the local population, instead simply passing them on to the Russian agent in Bukhara.[211] Snesarev was clearly disgusted by this muddled compromise, and no more inclined to accept the legitimacy of Bukharan authority than his predecessor, writing to his sister as follows:

> Here I have confusion, uproar and chaos. I am plunged into a maze of life: before me I see worshippers of Mammon, whose first aim is to steal; formalists, warming themselves around the dead letter of the law, idle loafers, who are so lazy that you cannot arouse them either with sticks or reproaches [...] and I walked straight into all this chaos through my own hot-headedness, idealism (sometimes sentimentalism) and a big dose of over-confidence [...] For now all is calm between me and the Bukharans, though I have already received a scolding from them [...] You cannot imagine how keenly, nervously, tensely things are unfolding [...] The general direction of things in Tashkent is flaccid, unprincipled and muddled.[212]

---

[211] 'Instruktsiya Nachal'nika Pamirskogo Otryada', 27/09/1902, in Stanishevskii, *Sbornik*, 156–65.

[212] A. E. Snesarev to K. E. Komarova, Khorog, 05/10/1902 in *Pis'ma A. E. Snesareva*, 485–7; see also Baskhanov, *'U vorot angliiskogo mogushchestva'*, 187–8.

His one comfort, he added, was his relations with the people – their smiles, and those of their children. They brought him apples, flowers, pumpkins, pieces of bread: 'The children pester me even more, those former little wild animals: they run to meet me, laugh, bring something – often flowers, and still more often – a merry bow [. . .] I sense that, if I manage to salvage something in this place, it will be because of this cowed, unhappy people, for whom I have already nagged at the bek and insulted his officials, and for whom I will stand, whatever it may cost me.'[213] Once again, we see a very particular paternalism and solicitude in Russian attitudes towards the Pamiris.

By January 1903 the Amir's impatience was palpable, and he complained that the inhabitants of Shughnan and Roshan had now been completely exempted from taxes for eight years. In response Acting Governor-General Ivanov wrote to Kuropatkin suggesting that the time had finally come to do as the Amir wanted and take over Shughnan and Roshan, but this was met with objections from Baron A. A. Cherkasov, the Secretary to the new Agent of the Ministry of Foreign Affairs in Bukhara, Ya. Ya. Liutsh, who said the international situation was not favourable, and that the British might protest – however, Cherkasov did concede that the time had come to introduce regular taxation.[214] This had predictable results: the tension and frustration Snesarev described found an outlet in June 1903, when a serious revolt against Bukharan rule broke out at Langar Gisht, the easternmost point of Shughnan and Roshan, on the borders of Wakhan. Snesarev reported that a large portion of the population was preparing to flee either to the Russian half of the Pamirs, or into Afghan Wakhan. The reason, he insisted, was the enduring hatred of the 'Mountain Tajiks' (i.e. the Pamiris) for the Bukharans, and their inability to make peace with the idea that 'The White Tsar, having taken them, for some reason gave them over to the Bukharans, a people worse than the Afghans.' This was familiar language, clearly derived both from local petitions and from the reports submitted by his predecessors. Snesarev considered the immediate cause to be an attempt by the Bukharans to introduce zakat on livestock, after a winter in which he estimated that 30 per cent of the sheep and 50 per cent of the cattle in Wakhan had died. He added that, if this caused the inhabitants of Russian Wakhan to flee to their compatriots in Afghanistan, 'it would place a shame and stamp on the Russian interest and name in Central Asia, and the breadth and depth of the results of such a misfortune are difficult to foresee'. Here too the language, though hyperbolic, was familiar – appeals to prestige had been part of the stock in trade of officers on the Central Asian frontier seeking territorial expansion since the beginning of the previous century. To

---

[213] A. E. Snesarev to K. E. Komarova, Khorog, 05/10/1902 in Pis'ma A. E. Snesareva, 485–7.
[214] Ivanov to Kuropatkin 18/01/1903; Bukharan Agency to Ivanaov 08/01/1903; Bukharan Agency to Ivanov 20/01/1903 RGVIA F.400 Op.1 D.2329 ll. 112–17ob. Khalfin, Rossiya i Bukharskii Emirat, 59.

reinforce the sense of *déjà vu*, Snesarev also included a petition from various *aqsaqal*s of Shughnan pleading their poverty and inability to pay *zakat*, and claiming that thanks to Bukharan oppression (*zulm*) they found themselves in the same state of poverty as they had been under the Afghans.[215] Ivanov passed Snesarev's report to Cherkasov in Bukhara, asking him try to calm things down, and also wrote to the Governor of Ferghana province noting that it was unclear whether Snesarev (Figure 10.4) proposed to use force against the Bukharans or against the local population, but that either would be undesirable.[216]

The Amir was away, and Cherkasov reported that the Bukharan *Qush-begi*, Astanaqul, expressed complete disbelief in Snesarev's report, but that he was sure it would cause the Amir to raise the question of transferring the region to Russia again. Cherkasov himself wondered whether the agitation might not be the work of the '*murids*' (disciples) of Ishan Shahzada Laiza, whom he claimed received instructions from a *pir* who was ('as everyone knows') a tool of the British agent in Chitral.[217] A few days later another report, from a Bukharan official called Mirza Yuldash-Bii, suggested a different culprit – none other than the Russian commander of the outpost at Langar-Gisht, Khorunzhii Goliavinskii. Mirza Yuldash claimed that he had begun collecting *zakat* in Wakhan without difficulties, but that he then received a letter from Goliavinskii saying he had promised the people of Wakhan that no *zakat* would be collected this year, and that Mirza Yuldash should not attempt to do so, or the population would all emigrate to Afghanistan. When Mirza Yuldash asked Snesarev for an explanation, the latter replied that his officer had acted rashly, and that he would write to tell him so. However, when Mirza Yuldash and the *zakatchi*s he had appointed arrived in Wakhan, Goliavinskii told them that they were collecting too much, and that they should spend the night in the village of Qurghan. There they were attacked by a mob, led by the local *aqsaqal*s, robbed and imprisoned. There had been four Russian soldiers stationed outside the house, who failed to protect them. Seeing that their horses had been stolen, and fearing for their lives, they escaped to the hills. There they sent a message to the Russian officer in charge of the post at Langar, who appeared in person with ten men and said 'If you carry on talking about *zakat* I'll have you shot.' He did disperse the crowd in Qurghan – but they returned the next day, shouting that they did not want to be Bukharan

---

[215] Snesarev to Chaikovskii 16/06/1903 RGVIA F.400 Op.1 D.2329 ll. 130–2; also in Stanishevskii, *Sbornik*, 170–3.

[216] Ivanov to Cherkasov 30/06/1903; Ivanov to Chaikovskii 30/06/1903 RGVIA F.400 Op.1 D.2329 ll. 132–4.

[217] Cherkasov to Ivanov 15/07/1903 RGVIA F.400 Op.1 D.2329 ll. 135–7.

subjects and pay *zakat*. Mirza Yuldash described the people as 'wild and undisciplined', and claimed that he was lucky to escape with his life.[218] The precise extent of Snesarev and Goliavinskii's connivance in the Wakhan rebellion remains in doubt: Cherkasov grumbled that Snesarev had done nothing to protect Bukharan officials from the local population. The report from the Main Staff noted that the question of the uniting of the region to Russia had been decided in unfortunate fashion by the current political situation, and that the rebellion in Wakhan seemed to have been the work of the officer in command of the post at Langar Gisht.[219] However, Ivanov wrote that he 'refused to believe that any Russian officer would take such an action upon himself', and despatched the head of his chancery's diplomatic section, A. A. Polovtsov, to conduct an official investigation.[220] His report exonerated Snesarev and Goliavinskii, and claimed that his interrogation of Mirza Yuldash exposed this Bukharan official's testimony as a tissue of lies. Instead he said that the revolt was spontaneous, having been provoked by the oppression of Bukharan rule – and that if this continued most of the population would probably migrate to British or Afghan territory, damaging Russian prestige.[221] A series of reports from Cherkasov (in which his growing idealisation of and advocacy for the Pamiris is clearly visible) finally convinced the Ministry of Foreign Affairs to concede the point.[222] In January 1905 a committee including General Sakharov, the Chief of the General Staff, Polovtsov, Cherkasov and Kivekäs met in Tashkent to agree on the transfer of Shughnan to Russia; they also (rather hypocritically) outlined a proposed taxation system for the new province, though their estimate was that it would not produce enough revenue to cover the cost of administration. A few days later the Turkestan Governor-General issued new instructions for the commander of the Pamir force, making him a district commandant under the authority of the Governor of Ferghana province. Whilst he still had a Bukharan official subordinate to him, the position of Bek was abolished, and the western Pamirs came under *de facto* direct Russian rule.[223]

The story of the Russian annexation of the Pamirs, their last territorial acquisition in Central Asia, is much more than a chapter in the 'Great

---

[218] Cherkasov to Ivanov 28/07/1903 enclosing Mirza Yuldash-Bii's report RGVIA F.400 Op.1 D.2329 ll. 138*ob*–41.

[219] 'Dokladnaya zapiska po Glavnomu Shtabu', 17/09/1903 RGVIA F.400 Op.1 D.2329 ll. 142–3*ob*.

[220] Khalfin, *Rossiya i Bukharskii Emirat*, 61–2.

[221] A. A. Polovtsov, 'Doklad diplomaticheskogo chinovnika pri Turkestanskom General-Gubernatore', 25/09/1903, in Khalfin, *Rossiya i Bukharskii Emirat*, 77–81.

[222] All of these are printed in Khalfin, *Rossiya i Bukharskii Emirat*, 90–123. On Cherkasov and his journeys see Mahmudov, 'Skvoz dzhungli instruktsii po "Kryshe Mira"'.

[223] 'Zhurnal soveshchaniya po voprosu o prisoedinenii k Rossii zemel', vkhodyashchikh v sostav Shugnanskogo bekstva', ?/01/1905 & 'Vremennaya instruktsiya Nachal'nika Pamirskogo Otryada', 12/01/1905, in Stanishevskii, *Sbornik*, 245–57, 258–65.

Game'. Fear that the British or their Afghan satellite would occupy the region
and pose a strategic threat to Russian possessions did provide the initial
impulse for annexation, but the nature, timing and extent of the Russian
advance were all determined by environmental factors, and by the Russians'
relations with the local population. These in turn were strongly coloured by
their identification of the Pamiris as 'Aryans', something which emerges
consistently in all Russian writing on the region. Grombchevskii, Zaitsev,
Skerskii, Kivekäs, Snesarev and other Russian commanders of the Pamir post
all remarked on this in their private and official correspondence.[224] The notion
that 'Aryans' constituted the original population of Central Asia, and that the
mountain-dwellers represented the last remnants of their culture and racial
type, also became a dominant theme in Russian ethnographic and orientalist
scholarship, notably in the works of Bobrinskii, Semenov, and V. V.
Bartol'd.[225] Alongside this arose a powerful discourse which asserted that the
Pamiris were less 'fanatical' Muslims than lowland Sunnis, and that Isma'ilism,
uniquely among the forms of Islam in Central Asia, was worthy of Russian
protection and support. Finally, the genuine poverty of the inhabitants of the
Pamirs, scratching a marginal existence in one of the most inhospitable regions
of Central Asia, and hugely vulnerable to crop failure, seems to have touched a
genuine vein of compassion and sympathy amongst Russian officers, and
aroused all their paternalistic instincts. Russian officers on the frontier also
repeatedly borrowed from the language of the petitions they received from the
local population when referring to Afghan and Bukharan oppression as a
reason for Russian annexation. Set alongside this, the rivalry with Britain
usually fades into the background. Finally, it is striking how many of the
debates over the racial and cultural peculiarity of the Pamiris that arose during
the annexation of their territory, and the subsequent wranglings over
Bukharan rule, would find echoes in the decision to create a Tajik SSR in the
1920s, and can still be encountered in modern Tajik national ideology.[226]

---

[224] Luzhetskaya, 'Otchet Nachal'nika Pamirskogo otryada', 158; L. G. Skerskii, 'Kratkii
Ocherk Pamira', *Sbornik geograficheskikh, topograficheskikh i statisticheskikh materialov
po Azii* Vyp. L (1892), 35; Serebrennikov, 'Ocherk Pamira', *VS* (1899), No. 10, 447; A. E.
Snesarev to K. E. Komarova, Khorog, 05/06/1901, *Pis'ma A. E. Snesareva*, 474; N. L.
Korzhenevskii, *Poezdka na Pamiry, Vakhan i Shugnan v 1903 g.* (St Pb.: Obshchestva
Zemlevedeniya pri Sankt-Peterburgskogo Universiteta, 1906), 12; Tageev, 'Pamirskii
pokhod', 152.

[225] For example V. V. Bartol'd, 'Neskol'ko slov ob ariiskoi kul'ture v Srednei Azii', *TKLA* 1/6
(1896), reprinted in *Sochineniya*, II (2), 322–32.

[226] Bergne, *The Birth of Tajikistan*, 3–14, 20–7, 39–54; Battis, 'Aleksandr A. Semenov',
Chapter 5.

Epilogue: After the Conquest

When the Soviet Union invaded Afghanistan in 1979, it took Russian troops beyond the limits established by the Russian Empire's Central Asian conquests, seemingly reviving a nineteenth-century drive for imperial expansion. Svetlana Alexievich opened *Boys in Zinc*, her harrowing collection of oral testimonies from the Soviet–Afghan War, with an epigraph referring to Paul I's crazed despatch of Cossacks to invade India in 1801.[1] If 1980s Afghanistan did indeed see the last phase of the Russian conquest of Central Asia, it was incomparably bloodier, more destructive and less successful than what had preceded it – 13,000 Soviet dead, over 40,000 wounded and perhaps a million Afghan casualties, with nothing to show for it other than a wrecked and broken country.[2] In contrast the amount of actual fighting in the nineteenth-century Russian conquest of Central Asia seems disproportionately small set against both its span of almost a century and its momentous and lasting consequences. With the exception of the Akhal-Teke Turkmen, in each individual case the armed resistance offered to Russian expansion by Central Asia's peoples and states was not particularly prolonged, and certainly not comparable either to Afghanistan or to the fifty-year war fought against the Russians in Daghestan and Chechnya in the first half of the nineteenth century.

Although it is possible to set chronological limits to the overall process of Russian territorial expansion in Central Asia, it is often difficult to know when to break off the tale of any of the individual campaigns which made it up. Sometimes they merged into each other almost without a break, as was the case between the capture of Tashkent and the outbreak of war with Bukhara. Sometimes – as with the Khiva expeditions – there was a clearer starting and end-point to the conflict and violence, but in all cases the process of conquest and annexation led seamlessly to the establishment of the structures of colonial rule – the creation of a bureaucracy or a protectorate, the administration of justice, the collection of taxes, the introduction of settlers. Even as the Russians annexed more territory, these processes were occurring simultaneously in regions that had already been subdued. As Chernyaev advanced on Tashkent

---

[1] Svetlana Aleksievich, *Tsinkovkye mal'chiki* (Moscow: Vremya, 2015).
[2] Kalinovsky, *A Long Goodbye*, 1.

531

in 1865, in Semirechie a new Cossack host was being established, and the first taxes were being levied on the Qazaq population. As von Kaufman made elaborate plans for the expedition to Khiva in 1872–3, new Russian quarters were being laid out next to the old cities of Tashkent and Samarkand. Over the following decade entirely new Russian towns were constructed at Vernyi, Ashkhabad, New Marghelan in Ferghana and Kagan in Bukhara. While in Bukhara and Khiva the existence of protectorates ensured some continuity, the nature of their statehood was transformed by the relationship with Russia. Perhaps the most dramatic change had come in Ferghana, where Khoqandi statehood was destroyed but not forgotten. Once the railway reached Andijan in 1898 cotton cultivation took off, completely transforming the social and economic landscape of the region. By 1914 Khoqand would have its own stock exchange, and a visiting geographer could write that 'I've heard it said that nowhere in Russia, apart from Moscow and St Petersburg, does one drink as much Champagne of the best French *marques* as in Khoqand.'[3]

In other ways, though, this social, economic and administrative transform-ation remained incomplete when the Tsarist regime collapsed. Like so many colonial states, that of the Russians in Central Asia was weak, and had limited penetration of local society. The administration of taxation and of justice, irrigation and agriculture remained largely in the hands of local elites in 1914.[4] Even the cotton boom, the main factor in Central Asia's economic transformation, was the largely accidental product of a set of fiscal policies introduced for different reasons, but which led thousands of individual small-holders to adopt the crop as it suddenly became profitable.[5] It was only in 1906 that the railway between Orenburg and Tashkent opened, finally providing a direct link between Central Asia and European Russia. It was only immediately before the First World War that Turkestan began to recoup some of the costs of its occupation, as the cotton economy began to flourish and revenues rose. In 1912 Agriculture Minister Alexander Krivoshein presented a ruthless vision for a 'new Turkestan', flooded with Russian settlers and with large private and state-owned cotton plantations.[6] The implementation of this much more exploitative vision of *nasha koloniya* – 'our colony' – was interrupted by the outbreak of the First World War, and then by a widespread revolt against Tsarist rule in 1916 which revealed the very shallow roots which the Russian colonial state had put down in Central Asian society over the previous fifty years.[7] The Soviet regime

---

[3] A. Woeikoff, *Le Turkestan russe* (Paris: Armand Colin, 1914), 138, 148.

[4] This is a major argument of my first book, Morrison, *Russian Rule in Samarkand*.

[5] See Penati, 'The Cotton Boom and the Land Tax'.

[6] A. P. Krivoshein, *Zapiska Glavnoupravlyaiushchago Zemleustroistvom i Zemledeliem o poezdke v Turkestanskii krai v 1912 godu* (St Pb.: Gosudarstvennaya Tip., 1912).

[7] On the 1916 revolt see Jörn Happel, *Nomadische Lebenswelten und zarische Politik: Der Aufstand in Zentralasien 1916* (Stuttgart: Franz Steiner, 2010) and the essays in Chokobaeva, Drieu and Morrison (eds.), *The Central Asian Revolt of 1916*.

which followed differed from its Tsarist predecessor in many important respects, but it was still dominated by Russia, and led to much greater levels of cultural and linguistic russification in Central Asia than had ever been the case under the Romanovs. At the time of writing the Central Asian Republics have been independent for almost thirty years, and yet the importance of the link with Russia remains – it is far stronger than that between the United Kingdom and the British Commonwealth, or even the ties of *Françafrique*. The complicated, messy, process of conquest outlined in this book, with its sometimes accidental or trivial causes, had very long-lasting consequences.

If we return to the themes mentioned in the introduction – sovereignty, prestige, local agency, violence, personality, environment, camels – we see that all of these figured at virtually every stage of the conquest. Conflicts over sovereignty were at the heart of the Russian decision to advance into Central Asia – not just contested sovereignty over particular lands and peoples, but the nature of sovereignty itself. The Russian desire for hard borders, exclusive loyalty and stable populations could never be satisfied on a frontier populated by nomads, nor even in relations with states whose external boundaries were as amorphous as those of Khoqand, Bukhara and Khiva. Often the very presence of Russian power helped to generate the instability that its leaders complained of, whether this was the construction of new outposts in the steppe in the 1820s and 1830s, which provoked Kenesary's resistance, the repeated hammer blows which they landed on the fragile political fabric of Khoqand and Bukhara in the 1850s and 1860s, or their meddling with the internal politics of the Turkmen. As we have seen, there were indigenous ideas of sovereignty in Central Asia – even when the reigning Khan, Khudoyar, was despised, the idea of Khoqandi statehood persisted, with highland Kyrgyz becoming the last defenders of the khanate as a sovereign polity. Khiva's receipt of tribute – in the form of slaves – from Qazaq and Turkmen raiders, and Kenesary's demand for recognition of his status as Qazaq Khan suggest something similar. The Russian refusal to recognise these forms of sovereignty as legitimate, or to countenance the usual nomadic practice of maintaining relations of nominal submission with multiple neighbouring sedentary powers, was always likely to draw the empire into conflict once it ceased to tolerate this earlier messiness on the steppe frontier, as it had (by and large) until the end of the Napoleonic Wars. This was closely connected to a sense of Russia's prestige as a great, imperial power, the maintenance of which was an absolutely overriding aim, more important than any rational calculation of economic or strategic advantage. Time and again we see the appeal to prestige – from Simonich urging support for the Sardars of Qandahar in the 1830s, to the decision to maintain the Syr-Darya line in the late 1850s in the face of all the evidence that it was a useless burden, to the almost theatrical orchestration of the 1873 Khiva campaign and the enormous expense of Skobelev's advance to Gök-Tepe, which was required in order to wipe out the shame of Lomakin's defeat the year before. In nearly all cases the Russians were responding first and foremost to what they saw as challenges or threats from Central Asian rulers and Central Asian peoples – not the British. Even the winter invasion of Khiva was planned well before the Russians learnt of the British invasion of Afghanistan, though that gave them another reason to press ahead with it. The same was true during the second Anglo-Afghan War in 1878–80, which helped determine the timetable but not the fact of the Russian advance into Transcaspia. Time and again we see that local actors had agency, even if the Russians saw their exercise of it as inherently illegitimate: Kenesary's defiance of the new administration in the steppe; the Russian reliance on Bukharan grain traders in their steppe fortresses; 'Alimqul's military leadership; the agitation of the Bukharan *'ulama* in their call for *jihad*; the complete Russian reliance on Qazaq scouts and guides during both invasions of Khiva; the Kyrgyz–Qipchaq rebellion against Khudoyar Khan; or indeed the way in which Pamiri villagers deliberately involved the Russians in their affairs in order to drive out the Afghans: these factors were crucial at different stages of the conquest, regardless of Russian desires. The inseparable twin of Russian prestige was Central Asian insolence – *derzost'* – a term used at different times to describe the behaviour of Kenesary, Khivan and Khoqandi Khans, Bukharan Amirs, Akhal-Teke tribal leaders, even the unfortunate Captain Ghulam Haidar Khan of the Afghan army, one of the handful of victims of the last stage of the Russian advance into the Pamirs.

Although the numbers of dead and wounded were tiny by the grim standards of the twentieth century, the conquest was far from being the bloodless 'uniting' of Soviet myth. As with other European colonial conquests in Asia and Africa, violence was an essential part of the process, and the Russian case bears a clear 'family resemblance' to those of the British and French, although it has not attracted the same degree of attention.[8] Local resistance, while usually not prolonged, was often fierce, whether that of Kenesary, the Khoqandi defenders of Aq Masjid, the Kyrgyz and Qipchaqs of Ferghana or the Turkmen of Gök-Tepe. Casualties on the Central Asian side were exaggerated in Russian accounts but still relatively heavy, especially from artillery. Nevertheless, the conquest of Central Asia was less brutal and provoked less resistance than either the conquest of the Caucasus or the French conquest of Algeria, with which the Russians themselves often compared it.[9] It is also noticeable that the nature of Russian violence changed over time. In the eighteenth century and until at least the 1840s the Russians participated in a common economy of steppe raiding, whose aim was not intimidation through violence but the seizing of livestock and people for barter. Once the

[8] Walter, *Colonial Violence*, 4–5.
[9] Brower, *A Desert Named Peace*; Porch, *The Conquest of the Sahara*; Marcel Emerit, *L'Algérie à l'époque d'Abd-el-Kader* (Paris: Bouchene, 2002).

Russians began to encroach on the sedentary zone to the south, until the late 1860s conflict was between garrisons and armies in set-piece battles or sieges. While civilians, women and children might be killed or wounded, as at Aq Masjid or Toqmaq, once the initial conflict was over, it was not generally followed by reprisals against non-combatants or the wider civilian population. An early sign that this was changing was perhaps the massacre in the village of Muhala near the Dargom canal in 1868, where apparently 300 people were killed after a Russian patrol was ambushed. There can be no doubt at all about the Yomud massacre of 1873, denounced by Terent'ev as 'wanton and unnecessary cruelty', followed by the appalling violence inflicted on unarmed men, women and children during Skobelev's 'pacification' campaign in Ferghana, which seems to have disgusted at least some of his fellow officers, and the massacre of the Turkmen at Gök-Tepe ordered by the same commander. There is no doubt that Skobelev was a revolting sadist, but this growing pattern of violence in the later Russian campaigns in Central Asia (the Pamirs excepted) cannot just be explained by the presence of a single individual. Nor can it be fully explained by the nature of the opposition the Russians encountered. Von Kaufman ordered the Yomud massacre despite there having been very limited resistance once the Russians had reached Khiva: the same man at Samarkand five years before had contented himself with only burning down the city's bazaar after a much more serious attempt to destroy the Russian garrison.

The growth in violence towards non-combatants may have been partly a function of growing Russian self-confidence and power: in 1868, when Samarkand fell, the Russians' position in Central Asia was still very precarious, and they had greater need to conciliate and work with local elites than they did at Khiva five years later. It may also have been a product of a growing racialisation of violence of the kind seen in British, French and German colonial warfare in the later nineteenth and early twentieth centuries.[10] Isabel Hull has suggested that, in the notorious case of the genocide of the Herero by the German army in South-West Africa, it was German military doctrine which was to blame, as counsels of restraint from colonial officials and soldiers were overridden by the Prussian General Staff.[11] As this suggests, colonialism and racial difference per se are not an adequate explanation for a growth in the use of violence and collective punishment towards civilians: the suppression of the Polish revolt of 1863–4 saw much greater indiscriminate violence and collective punishment than anything which happened during the

---

[10] Kim A. Wagner, 'Savage Warfare: Violence and the Rule of Colonial Difference in Early British Counterinsurgency', History Workshop Journal 85 (2018), 217–37.

[11] Isabel Hull, Absolute Destruction: Military Culture and the Practices of War in Imperial Germany (Ithaca, NY: Cornell University Press, 2006), 44–69.

conquest of Central Asia.[12] In the course of the twentieth century the violence that Europeans were willing to inflict on each other dwarfed what they did in their colonies. Although the Turkmen in particular were dehumanised in Russian accounts, and there was a tendency to extend that belief in their essential 'savagery' to other nomadic groups such as the Qipchaqs, even Skobelev did not go as far as von Trotha did with the Herero. The language of race – as opposed to religion, civilisation or culture – was rarely used in Russian accounts, and these forms of violence do not seem to have been fully normalised or accepted among the Russian military, possibly because most of them were long-serving *Turkestantsy* who spent most of their careers in the region. Terent'ev's condemnation of von Kaufman for the Yomud massacre may have been a product of his prejudice against Germans, but it was still strikingly frank. Nalivkin's denunciation of Skobelev was still more so. The elision of the massacres of Turkmen from the official accounts of the Khiva and Akhal-Teke campaigns tells its own tale – their author, Grodekov, was ashamed.

What about the importance of personality? Skobelev's role in accentuating the violence of some of the later campaigns has already been mentioned, and amongst the Russians the petty rivalries, jealousies and ambitions of individuals – both those on the spot and in St Petersburg – were sometimes important. Chernyaev's touchiness and neurotic desire for glory led him to take much greater risks than a more stolid commander like Verevkin. Lomakin's fear that he was being undermined by *Turkestantsy* on the Main Staff led him to make a series of disastrous misjudgements that culminated in the humiliating repulse from Gök-Tepe. The absence of personal correspondence and my limited linguistic skills make this much more difficult to assess on the Central Asian side, but certainly they do not seem to have been fortunate in their leaders – Khudoyar Khan misjudged the mood of his people repeatedly; Amir Sayyid Muzaffar vacillated in the face of the Russian threat. Kenesary and 'Alimqul clearly had much greater charisma and ability, but the former never managed to create a state structure to support his bid for power, while the latter was killed just when his leadership was most needed to repel the Russian assault on Tashkent.

Environmental factors were crucial: they explain the far greater ease and success the Russians enjoyed in their advance across the Ili into Semirechie, as opposed to along the Syr-Darya. They explain the ability of Kryzhanovskii and Romanovskii to make merry with a series of unauthorised attacks and annexations in 1866, and the lack of any major logistical obstacles to either the Bukharan campaign of 1868 or that in Ferghana in 1875–6. Moving and fighting in steppe or desert and over cultivated, populated land were two

[12] Norman Davies, *God's Playground: A History of Poland*. Vol. II (Oxford: Oxford University Press, 1982), 268–9.

completely different experiences. It was the former which captured the Russian military imagination, and found its place in the limited body of military doctrine tailored to Central Asian campaigning. Without the use of tens of thousands of camels the conquest of Central Asia would never have happened at all – and the Russians could not rear, supply or manage them themselves. The steppe campaigns of the 1840s, 1850s and early 1860s would have been impossible without the assistance of Qazaq scouts and auxiliaries, and above all Qazaq *vozhaks* – camel breeders and drivers. The columns of the 1873 Khiva expedition would never have reached their destination without Qazaq expertise. Time and again, the real challenge of fighting in Central Asia was logistical – it was rounding up the requisite number of camels and keeping them alive which mattered. Unless the military leadership was unusually incompetent the rest would look after itself.

How far did the nature of the conquest determine the nature of the future colonial regime? The men who made the conquest, at least in its latter stages – Chernyaev, von Kaufman, Grodekov, Kuropatkin, Alikhanov – were also those who ended up governing Central Asia. Alikhanov became the commandant of Merv, the oasis he had helped to annex, before being dismissed for corruption and abuse of office in 1890 – this does not seem to have affected his military career, and in 1906–7 he would acquire a new notoriety as the General commanding the punitive expedition which suppressed the Gurian peasant republic in Kutaisi Province.[13] Grodekov, who was first Governor of Syr-Darya Province and then Governor-General of Turkestan, died only in 1913. Kuropatkin (Governor of Transcaspia, Minister of War) became the last Governor-General in 1916 and died in 1924. They carried with them into administration many of the assumptions that they had acquired during the conquest – that the 'Sarts' were unwarlike, that the Turkmen were savage, that Islam was a source of 'fanaticism' – although they had already learnt this last lesson during the earlier conquest of the Caucasus, where both von Kaufman and Chernyaev had served.[14] The colonial regime would be governed by a constant fear of rebellion, of a renewal of resistance to what was until the early twentieth century a very skeletal Russian presence.[15] The irony was that this was unnecessary: once the original campaigns of conquest were over, there was remarkably little violent resistance to Russian rule. The Andijan Uprising of 1898, in which a religious leader called the Dukchi Ishan led an uncoordinated attack by 2,000 of his followers on a Russian garrison, was the only significant rebellion in Central Asia before the First World War. While it

[13] Morrison, 'The Pahlen Report and the Restoration of Rectitude in Transcaspia', 56; S. F. Jones, 'Marxism and Peasant Revolt in the Russian Empire: The Case of the Gurian Republic', *SEER* 67/3 (1989), 429–30.
[14] Alexander Knysh, 'Sufism as an Explanatory Paradigm: The Issue of the Motivations of Sufi Movements in Russian and Western Historiography', *Die Welt des Islams* 42 (2002), 139–73.
[15] Babajanov, 'How Will We Appear in the Eyes of *inovertsy* and *inorodtsy*?'

generated significant alarm and paranoia among colonial officials, this was out of all proportion to its scale – only twenty soldiers were killed.[16] After the initial shock and humiliation of defeat, Muslim elites in the sedentary regions of Turkestan, at least, reconciled themselves to Russian rule – and, indeed, we have seen some of the most important local collaborators, such as Shabdan *Batyr* among the Kyrgyz, and Ishan Hakim Khwaja and Sayyid 'Azim Bai in Tashkent, already reaching an accommodation with the Russians in the 1860s.[17] With the partial exception of Transcaspia, where the extreme bloodiness of the conquest was prolonged into a particularly corrupt and oppressive colonial administration,[18] the violence of the Russian colonial regime remained latent, expressed in small garrisons of Russian troops (approximately 30,000 for the region as a whole) who were only rarely called upon to suppress unrest. Russian colonial rule acquired the minimum level of legitimacy needed to function without constant and expensive resort to force. It did so in large part by not attempting to govern too intensely. As Norman Stone wrote of the empire as a whole, 'like most autocracies, its great strength was not that it governed harshly, but that it governed less', and what was true in the peasant heartlands of European Russia was still truer in the remote colonial periphery of Turkestan.[19] One lesson the Russians believed they had learnt from the conquest was that the costs and difficulties of mounting military expeditions in Central Asia were so great that it was better to tread softly to avoid resistance in the first place. This was the logic which lay behind the decisions to reduce the tax burden in the 'core' provinces of Turkestan (Syr-Darya, Samarkand and Ferghana), to devolve most of the fiscal and judicial administration to local structures of self-government, and to exempt Central Asian Muslims from conscription.[20] Turkestan became a drain on the imperial budget, but it remained largely peaceful.[21]

This relative equilibrium was disturbed in the last decade before the out-break of war, as ever larger numbers of settlers from European Russia flooded into Central Asia along the newly constructed Orenburg–Tashkent railway, and were granted land that was already under cultivation by sedentarised Kyrgyz and Qazaqs, something which local officials opposed, but in vain.[22] After the outbreak of the First World War the combination of this with

---

[16] Alexander Morrison, 'Sufism, Pan-Islamism and Information Panic: Nil Sergeevich Lykoshin and the Aftermath of the Andijan Uprising', *Past & Present* 214/1 (2012), 255–304.

[17] Komatsu, 'Dār al-Islām under Russian Rule as Understood by Turkestani Muslim Intellectuals'; Babadzhanov, 'Russian Colonial Power in Central Asia as Seen by Local Muslim Intellectuals'.

[18] Morrison, 'The Pahlen Report and the Restoration of Rectitude in Transcaspia'.

[19] Norman Stone, *The Eastern Front 1914–1917* (London: Hodder & Stoughton, 1975), 214.

[20] Morrison, *Russian Rule in Samarkand*, 172–200.

[21] Pravilova, *Finansy Imperii*, 271–301.

[22] Alexander Morrison, 'Sowing the Seed of National Strife in This Alien Region: The Pahlen Report and *Pereselenie* in Turkestan 1908–1910', *Acta Slavica Iaponica* 31 (2012), 1–29.

livestock requisition, higher taxation and an attempt to conscript Central
Asian men into labour battalions would prove explosive. The rebellion
which Tsarist colonial officials had dreaded for so long finally came to
Central Asia in the summer of 1916, as 3,000 Russian settlers were killed in
a series of uncoordinated attacks in Semirechie. The man entrusted with
suppressing the revolt was one of Central Asia's conquerors, Alexei
Nikolaevich Kuropatkin, the last Turkestan Governor-General. His diary
reveals that he was haunted by memories of his earlier campaigns, and the
lessons these held for defeating the 1916 rebels.[23] But while the initial indigenous resistance to conquest could sometimes be viewed as having a certain
legitimacy or even heroism – think, for instance, of Maslov's commentary on
the fallen Turkmen warriors at Gök-Tepe[24] – this rebellion against the established authority of the Russian colonial state, combined with the presence of
settlers, unleashed forms of eliminationist violence far more horrific than
anything that happened during the original campaigns of conquest. At least
150,000 Central Asians, mostly Kyrgyz, perished at the hands of Russian
punitive expeditions and settler vigilantes. A concerted programme of ethnic
cleansing ensued as Russian settlers sought revenge for their losses and the
expropriation of fertile land, justified by what Walter calls 'discourses of
retribution'.[25] The violence of 1916–17 offers clear parallels with the genocide
of the Herero, or indeed the savage and indiscriminate retribution inflicted by
the British during their suppression of the Indian 'Mutiny' of 1857.[26] Far more
Central Asians died from violence, famine and disease in the five years between
the outbreak of the 1916 Revolt and the establishment of Soviet power in 1921
than during all the campaigns of conquest which had made Central Asia
Russian over the previous 100 years.[27] Having been forcibly incorporated
into the Russian empire, Central Asia's peoples suffered all the tragic consequences of its collapse as the twentieth century dawned.

[23] Ian Campbell, 'Violent Acculturation: Alexei Kuropatkin, the Central Asian Revolt, and
the Long Shadow of Conquest', in *The Central Asian Revolt of 1916* ed. Chokobaeva,
Morrison & Drieu, 191–208.
[24] Compare Belich, *The New Zealand Wars*, 166, 173, 186, 319–20.
[25] See Aminat Chokobaeva, 'When the Nomads Went to War: The Uprising of 1916 in
Semirech'e', in *The Central Asian Revolt of 1916* ed. Chokobaeva, Drieu and Morrison,
145–168; Walter, *Colonial Violence*, 180–2.
[26] On the latter see Kim Wagner, *The Skull of Alum Bheg: The Life and Death of a Rebel of
1857* (London: Hurst, 2017).
[27] M. Buttino, 'Study of the Economic Crisis and Depopulation in Turkestan, 1917–1920',
CAS 9/4 (1990), 59–74

SOURCES AND BIBLIOGRAPHY

Russian State Military-Historical Archive, Moscow (RGVIA)
  Fond 69 Danzas, Aleksandr Loginovich
  Fond 165 Kuropatkin, Aleksei Nikolaevich
  Fond 203 Kaul'bars, Aleksandr Vasil'evich
  Fond 289 Blaramberg, Ivan Fedorovich
  Fond 400 Glavnyi Shtab. Opis' 1. Aziatskaya Chast'
  Fond 483 Voenno-Uchenogo Arkhiva. Voennye Deistvii v Srednei Azii
  Fond 726 Chernyaev, Mikhail Grigor'evich, Gen-Lt.
  Fond 1300 Shtab Kavkazskogo Voennogo Okruga
  Fond 1392 Pokhodnoi Kantselyarii Komanduiushchego voiskami
    Turkestanskogo Voennogo Okruga
  Fond 1393 Polevogo pokhodnogo shtaba Turkestanskogo Voennogo Okruga
  Fond 1396 Shtab Turkestanskogo Voennogo Okruga
  Fond 1433 Upravleniya Komanduiushchego Syr-Dar'inskoi Linii
  Fond 1435 Shtaba Voisk Syr-Dar'inskoi Linii
  Fond 1438 Shtaba Voisk Ferganskoi Oblasti
  Fond 1441 Shtaba Otdel'nogo Orenburgskogo Korpusa
  Fond 1449 Shtaba Voisk Zapadnoi Sibiri
  Fond 5369 Smennogo Pamirskogo Otryada
Archive of the Foreign Policy of the Russian Empire, Moscow (AVPRI)
  Fond 133 Kantselyariya Ministerstva Inostrannykh Del
  Fond 147 Sredne-Aziatskii Stol
  Fond 154 Aziatskii Departament
  Fond 161 Sankt-Peterburgskii Glavnyi Arkhiv
  Fond 161/4 Dela Aziatskogo Departamenta, ne vshedshie v opisi glavnogo
    arkhiva
  Fond 194 Missiya v Persii
Central State Archive of the Russian Federation, Moscow (GARF)
  Fond 678 Alexander II
  Fond 728 Skobelev, Mikhail Dmitr'evich
  Fond 730 Ignat'ev, Nikolai Pavlovich
Documentary Division of the Russian Historical Museum, Moscow (RGIM OPI)
  Fond 208 M. G. Chernyaev

Fond 307 N. I. Grodekov
Central State Historical Archive, St Petersburg (RGIA)
Fond 19 Departament Vneshnei Torgovli
Fond 954 von Kaufman, Konstantin Petrovich
Fond 1092 Shuvalovy, Grafy
Archive of Orientalists, St Petersburg Oriental Insitute (AV)
1-i Razryad Aziatskiya Politika
Fond 33 Kun, Aleksandr Ludwigovich
Central State Archive of the Republic of Kazakhstan, Almaty (TsGARKaz)
Fond 3 Nachal'nik Alatavskogo Okruga Kirgizov Bol'shoi Ordy
Fond 4 Oblastnoe Pravlenie Orenburgskimi Kirgizami
Fond 21 Kantselyariya Voennogo Gubernatora Semirechenskoi Oblasti po Kul'dzhinskim delam
Fond 118 Upravlenie Komendanta g. Turkestan 1865–69
Fond 345 Oblastnoe Pravlenie Sibirskimi Kirgizami
Fond 374 Pogranichnoe Upravlenie Sibirskimi Kirgizami
Fond 382 Upravlenie Komanduiushchego Syr-Dar'inskoi Linii
Fond 383 Upravlenie Kirgizami Syr-Dar'inskoi Linii
Fond 384 Upravlenie Komendanta Forta No. 1
Fond 385 Kantselyariya Upravlyaiushchego Mestnym Naseleniem Pravogo Flanga Turkestanskoi Oblasti
Fond 822 Pantusov, Nikolai Nikolaevich
Fond 825 Kolpakovskii, Gerasim Alekseevich
State Archive of Orenburg Province (GAOrO)
Fond 6 Kantselyariya Orenburgskogo Voennogo Gubernatora
Fond 153 Orenburgskaya Pogranichnaya Tamozhnya g. Orenburg
Fond 166 Gens, Grigorii Fedorovich
Fond 167 Chernov, Ivan Vasil'evich
Fond 169 Sevast'yanov, Sergei Nikonorovich
Fond 339 Kantselyariya Nachal'nika Orenburgskogo Tamozhennogo Okruga
Historical Archive of Omsk Province (IAOO)
Fond 3 Glavnoe Upravlenie Zapadnoi Sibiri
Fond 6 Shtab Otdel'nogo Sibirskogo Korpusa
Central State Archive of the Republic of Uzbekistan, Tashkent (TsGARUz)
Fond I-1 Kantselyariya Turkestanskogo General-Gubernatora
Fond I-715 Serebrennikov, A. G.
National Archives of Georgia (NAG)
Fond 11 Diplomaticheskaya Kantselariya Namestnika Kavkazskogo
Fond 545 Kavkazskoe Gorskoe Upravlenie
British Library
BL Add. MS.47841 Zapiski Grafa P. Shuvalova o Khivinskom Pokhode
India Office Records (IOR)
Political and Secret Proceedings
MSS Eur F197 Younghusband Papers

National Archives of India, Delhi (NAI)
  Foreign Department Proceedings
International Institute for Social History, Amsterdam (IISH)
  Archief M. G. Cernjaev

Published Collections of Documents

AGADZHANOV, S. G. (ed.): *Russko-turkmenskie otnosheniya v XVIII–XIX vv.: Do prisoedineniya Turkmenii k Rossii: Sbornik arkhivnykh dokumentov* (Ashkhabad: Izd. Akademii Nauk Turkmenskoi SSR, 1963)

BEKMAKHANOVA, N. E.: *Prisoedinenie Kazakhstana i Srednei Azii k Rossii (XVIII–XIX veka): Dokumenty* (Moscow: Institut Rossiiskoi Istorii RAN, 2008)

BERZHE, A. (ed.): *Akty, sobrannye Kavkazskoi Arkheograficheskoi Kommissii.* Vol. 8. *1831–7* (Tiflis: Tip. Glavnogo Upravleniya Namestnik Kavkazskogo, 1881)

BREGEL, Iu. E.: *Khorezmskie Turkmeny v XIX veke* (Moscow: Izd. Vostochnoi Literatury, 1961)

BREGEL, Iu. E.: *Dokumenty iz arkhiva Khivinskikh Khanov po istorii i etnografii Karakalpakov* (Moscow: Nauka, 1967)

EROFEEVA, I. V. (ed.): *Istoriya Kazakhstana v russkikh istochnikakh XVI–XX vekov.* Vol. III. *Zhurnaly i sluzhebnye zapiski diplomata A. I. Tevkeleva po istorii i etnografii Kazakhstana (1731–1759 gg.)* (Almaty: Daik-Press, 2005)

EROFEEVA, I. V (ed.) *Epistolyarnoe nasledie kazakhskoi pravyashchei elity 1675–1821 godov* (Almaty: abdi, 2014) 2 volumes

EROFEEVA, I. V. & ZHANAEV, B. T.: *Istoriya Kazakhstana v russkikh istochnikakh XVI–XX vekov.* Vol. VI. *Putevye dnevniki i sluzhebnye zapiski o poezdakh po iuzhnym stepyam XVIII–XIX veka* (Almaty: Daik-Press, 2007)

JELAVICH, Charles & JELAVICH, Barbara: *Russia in the East 1876–1880: The Russo-Turkish War and the Kuldja Crisis as Seen through the Letters of A. G. Jomini to N. K. Giers* (Leiden: E. J. Brill, 1959)

KIREEV, F. N. *et al.* (ed.): *Kazakhsko-russkie otnosheniya v XVI–XVIII vekakh (1594–1770)* (Alma-Ata: Nauka, 1961)

KIREEV, F. N. *et al.* (ed.): *Kazakhsko-russkie otnosheniya v XVIII–XIX vekakh (1771–1867 gody): Sbornik dokumentov i materialov* (Alma-Ata: Nauka, 1964)

MUSTAFAYEV, Shahin & SERIN, Mustafa (eds.): *The History of Central Asia in Ottoman Documents.* Vol. I. *Political and Diplomatic Relations* (Samarkand: IICAS, 2001)

NODA, Jin & ONUMA, Takahiro (eds.): *A Collection of Documents from the Kazakh Sultans to the Qing Dynasty* (Tokyo: TIAS, 2010)

Parliamentary papers:

  Central Asia No. 2 (1873) C.704
  Central Asia No. 1 (1885) C.4363
  Treaty series No. 8 (1895) C.7643

SEREBRENNIKOV, A. G. (ed.): *Sbornik materialov dlya istorii zavoevaniya Turkestanskogo kraya.* Vol. 1. *1839 g.* (Tashkent: Tip. Shtaba Turkestanskogo Voennogo Okruga, 1908), Vol. 2. *1840 g.* & Vol. 3. *1841 g.* (Tashkent: Tip. Shtaba Turkestanskogo Voennogo Okruga, 1912), Vol. 4. *1842–3 gg.* (Tashkent: Tip. Shtaba Turkestanskogo Voennogo Okruga, 1913)

SEREBRENNIKOV, A. G. (ed.): *Turkestanskii krai: Sbornik materialov dlya istorii ego zavoevaniya.* Vol. 5. *1844–46 g.*, Vol. 6. *1847 g.*, Vol. 7. *1848–1850 g.* & Vol. 8. *1851–52 g.*; *1864 g. Pt. I; 1864 g. Pt. II; 1865 g. Pt. I; 1865 g. Pt. II* (Tashkent: Tip. Shtaba Turkestanskogo Voennogo Okruga, 1914), *1866 g. Pt. I; 1866 g. Pt. II* (Tashkent: Tip. Shtaba Turkestanskogo Voennogo Okruga, 1915)

SHASTITKO, P. M. *et al.* (eds.): *Russko-indiiskie otnosheniya v XIX v.* (Moscow: Izd. Firma Vostochnaya Literatura RAN, 1998)

SHASTITKO, P. M. *et al.* (eds.): *Russko-indiiskie otnosheniya v 1900–1917 gg.* (Moscow: Izd. Firma Vostochnaya Literatura RAN, 1999)

STANISHEVSKII, A. V.: *Sbornik arkhivnykh dokumentov po istorii Pamira i Ismailizmu* (Moscow & Leningrad: n.p., 1933)

STRUVE, V. V., VOROVKOV, A. K. & ROMASKEVICH, A. A. (eds.): *Materialy po istorii Turkmen i Turkmenii* (Moscow & Leningrad: Izd. AN SSSR, 1938) 2 volumes

Turkestanskii sbornik, Navoi Library, Tashkent

Vneshnyaya politika Rossii XIX i nachala XX veka: Dokumenty Rossiiskogo Ministerstva inostrannykh del. Series I & II (Moscow: Gosudarstvennoe Izd. Politicheskoi Literatury, 1960–1995)

WELSFORD, Thomas & TASHEV, Nuryoghdi (eds.): *A Catalogue of Arabic-Script Documents from the Samarqand Museum* (Samarkand: International Institute for Central Asian Studies, 2012)

ZAGORODNIKOVA, T. N. (ed.): *'Bol'shaya igra' v Tsentral'noi Azii: 'Indiiskii pokhod' russkoi armii: Sbornik arkhivnykh dokumentov* (Moscow: Institut Vostokovedeniya, 2005)

ZHANAEV, B. T. (ed.): *Istoriya Kazakhstana v russkikh istochnikakh XVI–XX vekov.* Vol. VIII. *O pochetneishikh i vliyatel'neishikh ordyntsakh* (Almaty: Daik-Press, 2006)

Persian Sources

Bayan-i ahvalat-i 'Abdullah Bik Avdaichi [*c.* 1870] 'Zhizneopisanie Abdully bek, odnogo iz pridvornykh emira Muzafara', Sankt-Peterburgskii filial Instituta Vostokovedeniya RAN Arkhiv Vostokovedov [AV] F.33 Op.1 D.149. Available at http://zerrspiegel.orientphil.uni-halle.de/t1190.html.

Hikayat-i Damulla 'Abad Akhund [*c.* 1870] 'Rasskaz ochevidtsa o sobytiyakh vremen prisoedineniya Srednei Azii k Rossii (o russkikh v Samarkande i Bukhare)', AV F.33 Op.1 D.147 & 184 ff8b–14b. Available at http://zerrspiegel.orientphil.uni-halle.de/t21.html.

544 SOURCES AND BIBLIOGRAPHY

Mirza Sang Muhammad Badakhshi: *Ta'rikh-i Badakhshan – Istoriya Badakhshana* [*c*. 1900] ed. A. N. Boldyrev (Leningrad: Izd. Leningradskogo Gosudarstvennogo Universiteta, 1959)

Ahmad Makhdum-i Danish: *Risala ya Mukhtasari az Ta'rikh-i Saltanat-i Khanadan-i Mangitiyya* [1898] ed. Abulghani Mirzoev (Stalinabad: Nashriyat-i Daulati-yi Tajikistan, 1960)

Muhammad Fayz Katib Hazarah: *Siraj al-Tawarikh* (Kabul: Matba'ah-i Hurufi Dar al-Saltanah, 1912–14) 3 volumes

Muhammad Hakim Khan: *Muntakhab al-Tawarikh. Ta'lif-i Muhammad Hakim Khan* [1845] ed. Yayoi Kawahara & Koichi Haneda. Vol. II (Tokyo: Toyo Bunko, 2006)

Mullah Niyazi Muhammad b. 'Ashur Muhammad Khoqandi: *Ta'rikh-i Shahrukhi* [1871] ed. N. N. Pantusov as *Taarikh Shakhrokhi. Istoriya Vladetelei Fergany Sochinenie Molly Niyazi Mukhammed Ben Ashur Mukhammed Khokandtsa* (Kazan': Tip. Imperatorskogo Universiteta, 1885)

Qurban Muhammadzadah & Muhabbat Shahzadah: *Tā'rīkh-i Badakhshan* [*c*. 1930] ed. A. A. Egani (Moscow: Nauka, 1973)

Mirza 'Abd al-'Azim Sami: *Ta'rikh-i Salatin-i Manghitiyya*. [*c*. 1907] *Istoriya Mangitskikh Gosudarei Pravivshikh v stolitse, Blagorodnoi Bukhare* ed. L. M. Epifanova (Moscow: Izd. Vostochnoi Literatury, 1962)

'Abd al-'Azim Bustani [Sami] Bukharayi: *Tuhfa-yi Shahi* [*c*. 1907] ed. Nadira Jalali (Tehran: Anjuman-i athar va mafakhir-i farhangi, 2010)

Ta'rif-i Hakemran-i Shahrisabz dar Zaman-i Piruzi-yi Urusiya [*c*. 1870] 'Rasskaz o pravitelyakh Shakhrisabza pered Russkim zavoevaniem', AV F.33 Op.1 D.142. Available at http://zerrspiegel.orientphil.uni-halle.de/t1189.html.

Muhammad Salih Khwaja Tashkandi: *Ta'rikh-i Jadidah-yi Tashkand* [*c*. 1886]. Al-Biruni Institute of Oriental Studies, Tashkent MS IVAN RUz-1, 11073/II. Available at http://zerrspiegel.orientphil.uni-halle.de/t386.html. (This transcription includes only extracts from ff. b1a1–294 of the 1,000-folio manuscript.)

Persian and Chaghatai Sources in Russian Translation

BARTOL'D, V. V.: 'Sobytiya pered khivinskim pokhodom 1873 goda po rasskazu khivinskogo istorika' [1910], in *Sochineniya* Vol. II, Part 2 (Moscow: Izd. Vostochnoi Literatury, 1964) pp. 400–13

BARTOL'D, V. V.: 'Tuzemets o russkom zavoevanii', in *Sochineniya* Vol. II, Part 2 (Moscow: Nauka, 1964) pp. 333–49

CHEKHOVICH, O. D.: 'Skazanie o Tashkente' (1808), in *PPV* (Moscow: Nauka, 1970) pp. 172–6

Akhmad Donish: *Istoriya Mangitskoi dinastii* (1898) ed. & trans. I. A. Nadzhafova (Dushanbe: Donish, 1967)

MUKHTAROV, A.: *Dil'shod i ee mesto v istorii obshchestvennoi mysli tadzhikskogo naroda* (Dushanbe: Donish, 1969)

OSTROUMOV, N. P. (ed.): 'Razskaz v stikakh o srazhenii russkikh s musulmanami v gor. Chimkente Syr-Dar'inskoi Oblasti Turkestanskogo Kraya, v 1864 godu', in *Sbornik materialov dlya statistiki Syr-Dar'inskoi Oblasti*. Vol. III (Tashkent: Tip. Syr-Dar'inskoi Oblastnogo Statisticheskogo Komiteta 1894) pp. 1–64

OVEZBAEV, Seid Murad (ed. & trans.): 'Goni Bek (rasskaz Turkmena o bitve s russkimi pod Geok-Tepe)', *Turkmenovedenie* (1927) No. 1, pp. 23–29

SEMENOV, A. A. (ed.): 'Turkmenskaya pesnya pro vzyatie Geok-Tepe (zapisana v Akhal-Tekinskom oazise, v seleniya "Kipchak"', *Etnograficheskoe Obozrenie* (1903) No. 4, pp. 125–7

Mirza 'Abdal-'azim Sami: *Ta'rikh-i Salatin-i Mangitiia*. (1907) *Istoriya Mangitskikh Gosudarei Pravivshikh v stolitse, Blagorodnoi Bukhare* ed. & trans. L. M. Epifanova (Moscow: Izd. Vostochnoi Literatury, 1962)

Seiid Khaidar-Sho: *Istoriya Shugnana (Ta'rikh-i Shugnan)* trans. A. A. Semenov (Tashkent: Tip. pri Kantselyarii Turkestanskogo General-Gubernatora, 1916) & *TKLA* Vol. 21 (1917) pp. i–iii, 1–23

Fazl 'Ali-Bek Surkhafsar & Sang-Mukhammad Badakhshi: *Ta'rikh-i Badakhshan (Istoriya Badakhshana)* trans. A. N. Boldyrev & S. E. Grigor'ev (Moscow: Nauka, 1997)

VESELOVSKII, N. I. (ed.): *Kirgizskii razskaz o russkikh zavoevaniyakh v Turkestanskom Krae* (St Pb.: P. O. Yablonskii, 1894)

Persian and Chaghatai Sources in English Translation

Prince 'Arfa: *Memories of a Bygone Age: Qajar Persia and Imperial Russia, 1853–1902* (London: Gingko Library, 2016)

Zahiruddin Muhammad Babur: *The Baburnama: Memoirs of Babur, Prince and Emperor* trans. & ed. Wheeler M. Thackston (New York, NY: Random House, 2002)

Muhammad Yunus Bek Bayani: *Shajara-yi Khwarazmshahi* [1914] trans. Ron Sela, in *Islamic Central Asia: An Anthology of Historical Sources* ed. Ron Sela & Scott Levi (Bloomington, IN: Indiana University Press, 2010) pp. 300–6

ERKINOV, Aftandil (ed. & trans.): 'The Conquest of Khiva from a Poet's Point of View', in *Looking at the Coloniser: Cross-Cultural Perceptions in Central Asia and the Caucasus, Bengal, and Related Areas* ed. Beate Eschment & Hans Harder (Würzburg: Ergon Verlag, 2004) pp. 91–115

Fayz Muhammad Katib Hazarah: *The History of Afghanistan: Fayz Muhammad Katib Hazarah's Siraj al-Tawarikh* trans. & ed. R. D. McChesney & M. M. Khorrami (Leiden: Brill, 2013 & Brill Online 2016) 4 volumes

Mir 'Izzatullah: *Travels in Central Asia by Meer Izzat-Oollah in the Years 1812–13* trans. Capt. P. D. Henderson (Calcutta: Foreign Department Press, 1872)

Nur ud-Din Muhammad Jahangir: *The Jahangirnama: Memoirs of Jahangir, Emperor of India* trans. & ed. Wheeler M. Thackston (Oxford: Oxford University Press, 1999)

Qurban 'Ali Khalidi: *An Islamic Biographical Dictionary of the Eastern Kazakh Steppe, 1770–1912* ed. Allen J. Frank & Mirkasym Usmanov (Leiden: Brill, 2005)

Shir Muhammad Mirab Munis & Muhammad Riza Mirab Agahi: *Firdaws al-iqbal: History of Khorezm* [*c.* 1840] trans. & ed. Yuri Bregel (Leiden: Brill, 1999)

PRIOR, Daniel (ed. & trans.): *The Shabdan Baatyr Codex: Epic and the Writing of Northern Kirghiz History* (Leiden: Brill, 2013)

Mullah Muhammad Yunus Jan Shighavul Dadkhwah Tashkandi: *Ta'rikh-i 'Aliquli, Amir-i Lashkar* [*c.* 1903] trans. & ed. Timur Beisembiev as *The Life of 'Alimqul: A Native Chronicle of Nineteenth Century Central Asia* (London: Curzon Press, 2003)

Published Sources in Russian

ABAZA, K. K.: *Zavoevanie Turkestana: Razskazy iz voennoi istorii, ocherki prirody, byta i nravov tuzemtsev – v obshchedostupnom izlozhenii* (St Pb.: Tip. M. M. Stasiulevicha, 1902)

ABRAMOV, A. K.: 'Izvlechenie iz donesenie General-Maiora Abramova ob ekspeditsii v Shakhrisyabz, 1870 g.', in *Russkii Turkestan: Sbornik izdannyi po povodu Politekhnicheskoi vystavki* ed. V. N. Trotskii. Vyp. 3 (St Pb.: n.p., 1872) pp. 207–17

ABRAMOV, N.: 'Chernyaev: K Turkestanskim boevym iubileem 1865–1915', *VS* (1915) No. 6, pp. 171–8; No. 7, pp. 167–71; No. 8 pp. 137–42; No. 9, pp. 109–15; No. 10, pp. 141–51; No. 11, pp. 65–81; No. 12, pp. 87–96; *VS* (1916) No. 1, pp. 85–95

ABRAMOV, N.: 'K biografii Chernyaeva (pereskaz posluzhnogo spiska), *VS* (1915) No. 3, pp. 175–84

ALEKSEEV, V. (ed.): *Pis'ma Konsulu F. A. Bakulinu (o sredne-aziatskikh delakh) 1874–1878* (St Pb.: P. Usov, 1914)

ALEKSIEVICH, Svetlana: *Tsinkovye Mal'chiki* (Moscow: Vremya, 2015)

ALIKHANOV-AVARSKII, M.: 'Russkie v Merve', *Moskovskie Vedomosti* (1882)

ALIKHANOV-AVARSKII, M.: *Mervskii Oazis i dorogi vedushchie k nemu* (St Pb.: A. Transhelya, 1883)

ALIKHANOV-AVARSKII, M.: *Pokhod v Khivu (kavkazskikh otryadov) 1873: Step' i oazis* (St Pb.: Ya. I. Liberman, 1899)

ALIKHANOV-AVARSKII, M.: 'Zakaspiiskiya vospominaniya 1881–5', *VE* (1904) No. 9, pp. 74–125; No. 10, pp. 445–95

ANDREEV, I. G.: *Opisanie srednei ordy Kirgiz-kaisakov* [1790] (Almaty: Gylym, 1998)

ANNENKOV, Gen. M.: *Akhal-Tekhinskii Oazis i puti k Indii* (St Pb.: Tip. Shtaba Voisk Gvardii, 1881)

ARNOL'DI, M.: *V Zakaspiiskom krae v 1877 godu (vospominaniya ofitsera)* (St Pb.: Tip. Departamenta Udelov, 1885)

ARANDARENKO, G. A.: *Dosugi v Turkestane 1874–1889* (St Pb.: Tip. M. M. Stasiulevicha, 1889)

ARTAMONOV, L. K. (ed.): *Pokorenie Turkmen-Tekintsev russkimi voiskami pod nachal'stvom General Skobeleva v 1880–1881 g*. Trudy Pedagogicheskogo Muzeya po sostavleniiu chteniya dlya voisk i naroda (St Pb.: Tip. M. M. Stasiulevicha, 1884)

BARTOL'D, V. V.: 'Neskol'ko slov ob ariiskoi kul'ture v Srednei Azii', *TKLA* Vol. 1/6 (1896); also in *Sochineniya* Vol. II, Part 2 (Moscow: Izd. Vostochnoi Literatury, 1964) pp. 322–32

BEKCHURIN, A.: *Turkestanskaya oblast': Zametki statskogo Sovetnika Bekchurina* (Kazan: Tip. Imperatorskogo Universiteta, 1872)

BEZAK, A. P.: 'Yany-Kurgan', *VS* (1861) No. 12, pp. 511–25

BLARAMBERG, I. F.: *Voenno-statisticheskoe obozrenie Rossiiskoi Imperii*. Vol. 14, Pt. 3. *Zemli Kirgiz-kaisakov vnutrennei (Bukeevskoi) i zaural'skoi (Maloi) Ordy, Orenburgskogo vedomstva* (St Pb.: n.p., 1848)

BLARAMBERG, I. F.: *Vospominaniya* (Moscow: Nauka, 1978)

BOBRINSKII, A. A.: *Sekta Ismail'ya v russkikh i bukharskikh predelakh Srednei Azii* (Moscow: Obshchestva Liubitelei Estestvoznaniya, Antropologii i Etnografii, 1902)

BOBRINSKII, A. A.: *Gortsy verkhov'ev Pyandzha: Vakhantsy i ishkashimtsy: Ocherki byta* (Moscow, n.p., 1908)

BOBROVSKII, P.: 'Akhal-Tekinskaya ekspeditsiya 1879 goda', *VS* (1898) No. 10, pp. 259–95

BOBROVSKII, P.: 'Zametki k stat'e "Akhal-Tekinskaya ekspeditsiya 1879 goda"', *VS* (1899) No. 1, pp. 56–8

BOGDANOV, M. G.: 'Materialy dlya opisaniya bukharskoi ekspeditsii 1868 goda', in *Materialy dlya statistiki Turkestanskogo kraya: Ezhegodnik*. ed. N.A. Maev Vyp. II. (St Pb.: n.p., 1873)

BOGDANOV, M. N.: *Ocherki prirody Khivinskogo Oazisa i pustyni Qizil-Qum: Opisanie khivinskago pokhoda 1873 goda, sostavlennoe pod redaktsieiu general'-nogo shtaba General-Leitenanta V. N. Trotskago*. Vyp. XII (Tashkent: Tip. F. V. Basilevskim, 1882)

'Boi na Kushke 18 marta 1885 g.', *RS* (1910) No. 3, pp. 644–64; No. 4 pp. 26–44

BOLOTOV, S.: 'S Syr-Dar'i', *RV* (1866) No. 3, pp. 174–94

BUTAKOV, A. I. *Dnevnye zapiski A. I. Butakova po Aral'skomu Moryu v 1848–1849 gg*. (Tashkent: Izd. AN UzSSR, 1953)

BUTTINO, Marko: *Revoliutsiya naoborot* (Moscow: Zven'ya, 2007)

BRYANOV, A. I.: *Na pamyat' o Fergane: 1876–1901 g*. (Novyi Margelan: Tip. Ferganskogo Oblastnogo Pravleniya, 1901)

CHERKASOV, Shtabs-Kapitan: 'Zashchita Samarkanda v 1868 godu', *VS* (1870) No. 5, pp. 33–58

CH[ERNYAEVA], A: 'M. G. Chernyaev v Srednei Azii (na Syr-Dar'inskoi linii)', *IV* (1915) No. 6, pp. 840–72

CHERNYAEV, M. G.: 'Sultany Kenesary i Sadyk', *RV* (1889) No. 8, pp. 27–39

CHERNYAK, Shtabs-Kapitan: 'Ekspeditsiya v Akhal-Teke 1879 goda (iz dnevnika sapernogo ofitsera)', *VS* (1887) No. 6, pp. 283–93; No. 7, pp. 129–44; No. 9, pp. 125–38; No. 10, pp. 261–78

548 SOURCES AND BIBLIOGRAPHY

CHERNYSHEV, A. I.: 'Zhizneopisanie Grafa Aleksandra Ivanovicha Chernysheva', *SIRIO* Vol. 122 (St Pb., 1905)

CHERNYSHEV, A. I.: 'Bumagi A. I. Chernysheva za Tsarstvovanie Imperatora Aleksandra I', *SIRIO* Vol. 121 (St Pb., 1906)

[CHERNYSHEV, A. I.:] *Voennye deistviya otryada General Ad"iutanta Chernysheva v 1812, 1813 i 1814 godakh* (St Pb.: Voennaya Tip., 1839)

CHERTKOV, V. G. (ed.): *L. N. Tolstoi protiv voiny* (Christchurch: Izd. Svobodnogo Slova, 1902)

CHIKHACHEV, P.: 'O issledovanii vershin Syr i Amu-dar'i i nagornoi ploshchadi Pamir', *ZIRGO* Kn. III (1849) pp. 1–41.

DAL', V. I.: 'Pis'ma k druzyam iz khivinskoi ekspeditsii', *RA* (1867) No. 3, pp. 402–31; No. 4, pp. 606–39

DESINO, K. N.: 'Izvlechenie iz otcheta o puteshestvii Kapitana Yungkhezbanda po Pamiram i sopredel'nym stranam', in *Sbornik geograficheskikh, topograficheskikh i statistecheskikh materialov po Azii.* Vyp. L (St Pb., 1892) pp. 246–252

DIUGAMEL', A. O.: 'Avtobiografiya A. O. Diugamelya', *RA* (1885) No. 5, pp. 82–126; No. 10, pp. 161–224

'Dmitrii Vasil'evich Volkov: Materialy k ego biografii 1718–1785', *Russkaya Starina* (September 1874) No. 9, pp. 478–96

DOBROMYSLOV, A.: 'Zaboty Imperatritsy Ekateriny II o prosveshchenii Kirgizov', *TOUAK* Vyp. IX (1902) pp. 51–63

DOBROMYSLOV, A. I.: *Tashkent v proshlom i nastoiashchem: Istoricheskii ocherk* (Tashkent: A. I. Portsev, 1912)

DOSTOEVSKII, F.: 'Foma Danilov, zamuchennyi russkii geroi', in *Dnevnik pisatelya* Jan. 1877, *Sobranie sochinenii.* Vol. 14 (St Pb.: Nauka, 1995) pp. 14–19

DOSTOEVSKII, F.: 'Geok-Tepe – chto takoe dlya nas Aziya?', in *Dnevnik pisatelya* Jan. 1881, *Polnoe sobranie sochinenie.* Vol. 21 (St Pb.: A. F. Marks, 1896) pp. 513–23

EFREMOV, Filipp: 'Stranstvovanie Filippa Efremova, rossiiskogo unterofitsera, kotoryi nyne praporshchikom, devyatiletnee stranstvovanie i priklyucheniya v Bukharii, Khive, Persii i Indii i vozvrashchenie ottuda chrez Angliyu v Rossiyu, pisannoe im samim v Sankt-Peterburge 1784 goda', in *Puteshestviya po Vostoku v epokhu Ekaterina II* (Moscow: Vostochnaya Literatura, 1985)

EGGERT, V. V.: 'Ocherk Pamirov (svedeniya sobrannye v Pamirskom otryade s avgusta 1896 goda po iiul' 1897 goda)', *Sbornik geograficheskikh, topograficheskikh i statisticheskikh materialov po Azii.* Vyp. 16 (St Pb.: n.p., 1902) pp. 1–29

ERMOLOV, A. P.: *Materialy dlya istorii voiny 1812 goda: Zapiski Alekseya Petrovicha Ermolova* (Moscow: Tip. V. Got'e, 1863)

ERMOLOV, N. P.: (ed.): *Zapiski Alekseya Petrovicha Ermolova. Chast' I. 1801–1812 g.* & *Chast' II. 1816–1827 g.* (Moscow: Universitetskaya Tipografiya, 1865–8)

EVDOKIMOV, L. V.: '"Slavnyi liubimyi General" – M. G. Cherniaev', *VS* (1915) No. 11, pp. 111–28; No. 12, pp. 151–60; *VS* (1916) No. 1, pp. 129–44

FEDCHENKO, A. P.: *Iz Kokana: Svedeniya o puteshestvii po Kokandskomu Khanstvu A. P. Fedchenko v 1871 g. iz turkestanskikh vedomostei* (Tashkent: Tip. Okruzhnogo Shtaba, 1871)

FEDCHENKO, A. P.: 'Puteshestvie v Turkestan', in *Izvestiya Imperatorskogo Obshchestva Liubitelei Estestvoznaniya*. Vol. I, Part II. *V Kokanskom khanstve* (St Pb. & Moscow: Tip. M. Stasiulevicha, 1875)

FEDOROV, G. P.: 'Moya sluzhba v Turkestanskom krae', *IV* (1913) No. 9, pp. 786–812; No. 10, pp. 30–55; No. 11, pp. 437–65; No. 12, pp. 860–90

FEDOROV, K. M.: *Akhal-Tekinskaya ekspeditsiya 1880–1 gg.: Geok-Tepinskii boi M. D. Skobeleva* (Askhabad: Elektropechatnya K. M. Fedorova, 1904).

G[AGEMEISTER, Iu. A.]: 'O torgovom znachenii Srednei Azii v otnoshenii k Rossii', *RV* Vol. 41 (1862) No. 10, 706–36

GEINS, A. K.: 'Kirgizskie ocherki', *VS* (1866) No. 1, pp. 145–78

GEINS, K.: 'Ocherk boevoi zhizni Akhaltekinskogo otryada 1880–1881 gg.', *VS* (1882) No. 6, pp. 340–59; No. 7, pp. 151–9; No. 8, pp. 336–48; No. 9, pp. 155–67; No. 10, pp. 317–28; No. 11, 128–42

GOLOSOV, D.: 'Pokhod v Khivu v 1717 godu', *VS* (1861) No. 10, pp. 303–64

GOLOVNINA, Iu. D.: *Na Pamirakh: Zapiski russkoi puteshestvennitsy* (Moscow: Tip. M. N. Kushnerev, 1902)

GORNYI, Mikhail: *Pokhod na Afgantsev i boi v Kushke (1885 g.): Vospominaniya byvshego ryadovogo Andreya Bolandina* (Moscow: E. I. Konovalova, 1901)

'Graf Vasilii Alekseevich Perovskii', *RA* (1878) No. 3, pp. 373–4

GREBNER, A.: *Osady i shturmy sredne-aziyatskikh krepostei i naselennykh punktov* (St Pb.: V. A. Tikhanov, 1897)

GREN, A.: 'Pis'ma iz Forta Perovskii (Ak-Mechet') 31/08/1859', *VS* (1859) No. 12, pp. 445–62

GREN, A.: 'Zametki ob ukrepleniyakh v Orenburgskom krae voobshche i na Syr-Dar'inskoi linii v osobennosti', *Inzhenernyi Zhurnal* (1861) No. 5, pp. 433–65

GRIGOR'EV, V. V.: 'Russkaya politika v otnoshenii k Srednei Azii', in *Sbornik Gosudarstvennykh Znanii*. Vyp. I ed. V. P. Bezobrazov (St Pb.: Tip. V. P. Bezobrazov, 1874), pp. 233–61

GRODEKOV, N. I.: *Khivinskii pokhod 1873 g.: Deistviya kavkazskikh otryadov* (St Pb.: V. S. Balashov, 1883)

GRODEKOV, N. I.: *Voina v Turkmenii: Pokhod Skobeleva v 1880–1881 gg.* (St Pb.: Tip. V. A. Balasheva, 1883–4) 4 volumes

GROMBCHEVSKII, B. L.: 'Vesti iz ekspeditsii B. L. Grombchevskogo', *IIRGO* Vol. 26 (1890) No. 1, pp. 85–107

GROMBCHEVSKII, B. L.: *Nashi interesy na Pamire: Voenno-politicheskii ocherk: Doklad Podpolkovnika B. L. Grombchevskago, chitannyi v Nikolaevskoi Akademii General'nogo Shtaba 14 marta 1891 g.* (Moscow: n.p., 1891)

550 SOURCES AND BIBLIOGRAPHY

GROMBCHEVSKII, B. L.: *Na sluchai voiny s Indieyu: Ozero Shiva kak strategicheskii punkt: Voenno-politicheskii ocherk* (Novyi Margelan: Tip. Ferganskogo Oblastnogo Pravleniya, 1891)

GRONBCHEVSKII [*sic*], B. L.: *Otchet o poezdke v Kashgar i iuzhnuiu Kashgariiu v 1885 g. (sekretno)* (Novyi Margelan: Pechataetsya na pravakh rukopisi, 1886)

GRUMM-GRZHIMAILO, G. E.: 'Ocherk pripamirskikh stran', *IIRGO* Vol. 22 (1886) No. 2, pp. 81–109, also in *TS* Vol. 405, pp. 36–50

IGNAT'EV, N. I.: *Missiya v Khivu i Bukharu v 1858 g. Fligel'-ad"yutanta Polkovnika N. Ignat'eva* (St Pb.: Gosudarstvennaya Tip., 1897)

IUDIN, M. L.: *Vzyatie Ak-Mecheti v 1853 godu kak nachalo zavoevaniya Kokandskogo Khanstva* (Moscow: Izd. Vladimira Bolasheva, 1917)

IUZHAKOV, Iu. D.: *Shestnadtsatiletnyaya godovshchina vzyatiya Tashkenta (vospominamie starago Turkestantsa)* (St Pb.: Tip. V. V. Komarova, 1881)

IVANIN, M. I.: 'Zametki po povodu napechatannoi vo 2 i 3 numerakh "Voennogo Sbornika" nyneshnogo goda stat'i "pokhod v Khivu 1839 g."', *VS* (1863) No. 4, pp. 484–502

IVANIN, M. I.: *Opisanie zimnego pokhoda v Khivu v 1839–40 g.* (St Pb.: Tip. Obshchestvennaya Pol'za, 1874)

IVANIN, M. I.: *O voennom iskusstve i zavoevaniyakh mongol-tatar i sredneaziyatskikh narodov pri Chingis-Khane i Tamerlane* ed. N. S. Golitsyn (St Pb.: Tip. Obshchestvennaya Pol'za, 1875)

IVANIN, M. I./GOLOSOV, D.: 'Pokhod v Khivu v 1839 godu otryada russkikh voisk, pod nachal'stvom General-Ad'iutanta Perovskago', *VS* (1863) No. 1, pp. 3–72; No. 2, pp. 309–58; No. 3, pp. 3–71

IVANOV, D. L.: 'Pod Samarkandom (rasskaz Novichka)', *VS* (1876) No. 1, pp. 181–212; No. 2, pp. 362–92

IVANOV, D. L.: 'V gorakh (iz turkestanskoi pokhodnoi zhizni)', *VS* (1876) No. 4, pp. 449–80; No. 5, pp. 189–213; No. 6, pp. 407–30

IVANOV, D. L.: 'Puteshestvie na Pamir', *IIRGO* Vol. 20 (1884) No. 3, pp. 209–52

IVANOV, D. L.: 'Chto nazyvat' Pamirom', *IIRGO* Vol. 21 (1885) No. 2, pp. 131–45

IVANOV, D. L.: 'Shugnan: Afganskie ocherki', *VE* Vol. 4 (1885) Kn. 7, pp. 49–52

IVANOV, D. L.: 'Iz vospominanii Turkestantsa', *IV* (1896) No. 5, pp. 830–59

'Izvestiya s Syr-Dar'inskoi linii', *VS* (1864) No. 4, pp. 191–2

'Izvestiya iz Orenburgskogo kraya: Deistviya pod Chemkentom', *VS* (1864) No. 11, pp. 40–3

'Izvestiya iz Vostoka', *VS* (1864) No. 12, pp. 150–2

'Izvestiya iz Turkestanskoi Oblasti', *VS* (1865) No. 7, pp. 70–2; No. 11, pp. 204–9

'Iz zapisok Gr. Vasiliya Alekseevicha Perovskago o prebyvanii ego v plenu u frantsuzov 1812–1814', *RA* (1865) No. 3, pp. 258–86

K: 'Delo Ural'tsev pod Turkestanom', *VS* (1865) No. 5, pp. 115–24

K. M. V.: 'Kaspiiskoe More', *VS* (1900) No. 4, pp. 405–22

KAMENSKII, Gavriil: 'Angliya strashnyi sopernik Rossii v torgovle i promyshlennosti', *Vestnik Promyshlennosti* (1859) No. 2, 141–61

KARAZIN, N. N.: 'Zarabulakskie vysoty', in *Pogonya za Nazhivoi* [1876] (St Pb.: Lenizdat, 1993) pp. 471–501

KENESARIN, Akhmet: *Sultany Kenisara i Sadyk* ed. E. T. Smirnov (Tashkent: Tip. S. I. Lakhtina, 1889)

KAZANSKII, K. K.: *Vblizi Pamirov* (Tashkent: Tip Brat'ev Izmenskie, 1895)

KHANYKOV, N.A.: *Opisanie Bukharskogo Khanstva* (St Pb.: Tip. Imperatorskoi Akademii Nauk, 1843)

'Khivinskaya ekspeditsiya 1839 goda', *RS* Vol. 7 (1873) No. 2, pp. 236–53

KH[OROSHKHI]N, A. P.: 'Vesna 1868 g. v Srednei Azii', *VS* (1875) No. 9, pp. 154–87

KHOROSHKHIN, A. P.: *Sbornik statei kasaiushchikhsya do Turkestanskogo kraya* (St Pb.: Tip. A. Transhelya, 1876)

KHOROSHKHIN, M.: *Geroiskii podvig ural'tsev: Delo pod Ikanom 4, 5 i 6 dekabrya 1864 goda* (Ural'sk: n.p., 1895)

KHREBTOV, A. N.: *Khivinskii pokhod: Chetyre chteniya dlya voisk i naroda* (St Pb.: Tip. A. M. Kotomina, 1875)

KILEVEIN, E. B.: 'Otryvok iz puteshestviya v Khivu, i nekotorye podrobnosti o khanstve vo vremya pravleniya Seid-Mohammed Khana, 1856–1860 g.', *ZIRGO* (1861) Kn. 1, pp. 1–14

KIYASKO, Podpolkovnik: 'Ocherki Zakaspiiskoi Oblasti', *VS* (1897) No. 8, pp. 342–74; No. 9, pp. 150–82; No. 10, pp. 358–88; No. 11, pp. 188–212; No. 12, pp. 372–9

KOLOKOL'TSOV, Polkovnik: *Ekspeditsiya v Khivu v 1873 godu: Ot Dzhizaka do Khivy: Pokhodnyi dnevnik* (St Pb.: n.p., 1873)

KORITSKII, Ivan: *Khiva, ili geograficheskoe i statisticheskoe opisanie Khivinskago Khanstva, sostoyashchago teper' v voine s Rossiei* (Moscow: Universitetskaya Tip., 1840)

KORNILOV, L.: *Kashgariya ili Vostochnyi Turkestan: Opyt voenno-statisticheskogo opisaniya* (Tashkent: Tip Shtaba Turkestanskogo Voennogo Okruga, 1903)

KORSAKOV, A.: 'Vospominaniya o Karse', *RV* Vol. 34 (1861) pp. 337–430

KORZHENEVSKII, N. L.: *Poezdka na Pamiry, Vakhan i Shugnan* (St Pb., Obshchestva Zemlevedeniya pri Sankt-Peterburgskogo Universiteta, 1906)

KORZHENEVSKII, N. L.: 'Cherez Pamir k Gindukushu (ot Osha do Pamirskogo posta)', *IV* (1912) No. 2, pp. 691–732

KORZHENEVSKII, N. L. (ed.): *Dnevnye zapiski plavaniya A. I. Butakova po Aral'skomu Moriu v 1848–1849 gg.* (Tashkent: Izd. AN UzSSR, 1957)

KORZHINSKII, S.: *Ocherk Roshana i Shugnana s sel'skokhozyaistvennoi tochki zreniya* (St Pb.: Tip. Sankt-Peterburgskogo Gradonachal'stva, 1898)

KOSTENKO, L. F.: *Puteshestvie v Bukharu russkoi missii v 1870 godu* (St Pb.: A. Morigerovskii, 1871)

KOSTENKO, L. F.: *Srednyaya Aziya i vodvorenie v nei russkoi grazhdanstvennosti* (St Pb.: Tip. B. Bezobrazov, 1871)

KOSTENKO, L. F.: 'Turkestanskiya voiska i usloviya ikh bytovoi, pokhodnoi i boevoi zhizni', *VS* (1875) No. 4, pp. 203–22; No. 5, pp. 61–82; No. 6, pp. 294–312

KOSTENKO, L. F.: 'Istoricheskii ocherk rasprostranenie russkogo vladychestva v Srednei Azii', *VS* (1887) No. 8, pp. 145–78; No. 9, pp. 5–37; No. 10, pp. 139–160; No. 11, pp. 5–35

KOSYREV, E. M.: 'Pokhod v Khivu v 1839 godu (iz zapisok uchastnika)', *IV* (1898) No. 8, pp. 538–45

KRESTOVSKII, V. V.: *V gostyakh u Emira Bukharskogo* (St Pb.: A. S. Suvorin, 1887)

KRIVOSHEIN, A. P.: *Zapiska Glavnoupravlyaiushchago Zemleustroistvom i Zemledeliem o poezdke v Turkestanskii krai v 1912 godu* (St Pb.: Gosudarstvennaya Tip., 1912).

KUN, A. L. (ed.): *Turkestanskii al'bom: Po rasporiazheniiu turkestanskago General-Gubernatora General-ad'iutanta K. P. fon Kaufmana 1-go* (Tashkent: Literatura Voenno-Topograficheskogo Otdela Turkestanskogo Voennogo Okruga, 1871–2) 4 volumes

KUN, A. L.: 'Nekotorye svedeniya o Ferganskoi doline', *VS* (1876) No. 4, pp. 417–48

KUN, A. L.: *Ocherk Kokandskogo Khanstva: Otdel'nyi ottisk iz 'Izvestii Imperatorskogo Russkogo Geograficheskogo Obshchestva'* Vol. 12 (St Pb.: n. p., 1876)

KUROPATKIN, A. N.: *Alzhiriya* (St Pb.: Tip. V. A. Poletiki, 1877)

KUROPATKIN, A. N.: *Kashgariya: Istoriko-geograficheskii ocherk strany, eya voennyya sily, promyshlennost' i torgovlya* (St Pb.: V. Balashev, 1878)

KUROPATKIN, A. N.: *Turkmeniya i Turkmenii* (St. Pb.: Tip. A. Poletiki, 1879)

KUROPATKIN, A. N.: *Deistvie otryadov General Skobeleva v Russko-Turetskoi Voine 1877–78 g.: Lovcha i Plevna* (St Pb.: Tip. Glavnogo Shtaba, 1885)

KUROPATKIN, A. N.: *Zavoevanie Turkmenii: Pokhod v Akhal-Teke v 1880–1881 gg.: Ocherk voennykh deistvii v Srednei Azii s 1839 po 1876-i god* (St Pb.: V. Berezovskii, 1899)

Kratkaya Istoriya 6-ogo Turkestanskogo Strelkovago Batal'ona (Samarkand: Tip. Trud, 1904)

LEDENEV, N.: *Istoriya Semirechenskogo Kazach'yago voiska* (Vernyi: Tip. Semirechenskogo Oblastnogo Upravleniya, 1909)

LEVSHIN, A. I.: *Opisanie kirgiz-kazach'ikh ili kirgiz-kaisatskikh gor i stepei* [1832] (Almaty: Sanat, 1996)

LIPSKII, V. I.: *Gornaya Bukhara: Rezul'taty trekhletnikh puteshestvii v Sredniuiu Aziiu v 1896, 1897 i 1899 godu* (St Pb.: Tipo-Lit. 'Gerol'da', 1892–1905) 3 volumes

LITVINOV, B.: 'Cherez Bukharu na Pamiry', *IV* (1904) No. 10, pp. 297–331; No. 11, pp. 698–729; No. 12, pp. 1045–87

LOBYSEVICH, F.: 'Syr-Dar'inskaya liniya', *VS* (1864) No. 6, pp. 397–410

LOBYSEVICH, F. 'Vzyatie Khivy i Khivinskaya ekspeditsiya 1873 g.', *VE* (1873) No. 8, pp. 583–619; No. 12, pp. 583–600

LOBYSEVICH, I.: 'Orenburg, ego zhiteli, torgovlya, promyshlennost'', *VS* (1861) No. 1, pp. 211–22

LOGOFET, D. N.: *Strana bezpraviya: Bukharskoe khanstvo i ego sovremennoe sostoyanie* (St Pb.: V. Berezovskii, 1909)

LYKO, M.: *Ocherk voennykh deistvii 1868 goda v doline Zaryavshana* (St Pb.: Tip. Deputata Udelov, 1871)

MACGAHAN, J. A.: *Voennye deistviya na Oksus i padenie Khivoi* (Moscow: Universitetskaya Tip., 1875)

MAEV, N. A. (ed.): *Materialy dlya statistiki Turkestanskago Kraya: Ezhegodnik.* Vyp. I (St Pb.: Izd. Turkestanskogo Statisticheskogo Komiteta, 1873)

MAEV, P.: 'Aziyatskii Tashkent', in *Materialy dlya statistiki Turkestanskago kraya: Ezhegodnik* ed. N. A. Maev. Vyp. IV (St Pb.: Tip. A. Transhelya, 1876) pp. 260–313

MAEV, N. A.: 'A. L. Kun', *TV* Vol. 22/11 (1888) No. 46

MAIER, A. A.: *God v peskakh: Nabroski i ocherki Akhal-Tekinskoi ekspeditsii 1880–1881 (iz vospominanii ranenogo)* (Kronstadt: Pechatano v Tip. Kronshtadtnogo Vestnika, 1886)

MAKSHEEV, A. (ed.): *Voenno-statisticheskoe obozrenie Rossiiskoi Imperii* (St Pb.: Tip. F. S. Sushchinskogo, 1867)

MARKOZOV, V.: *Krasnovodskii otryad: Ego zhizn' i sluzhba so dnya vysadki na vostochnyi bereg Kaspiiskogo Morya po 1873 g. vkliuchitel'no* (St Pb.: V. A. Berezovskii, 1898)

MASLOV, A. N.: 'Rossiya v Srednei Azii: Ocherk nashikh noveishikh priobretenii', *IV* (1885) No. 5, pp. 372–423

MASLOV, A. N.: *Zapiski o M. D. Skobelev (materialy dlya biografii)* (St Pb.: A. S. Suvorin, 1887)

MASLOV, A. N.: *Zavoevanie Akhal-Tekke* (St Pb.: A. S. Suvorin, 1887)

MEIER, A. A. & TAGEEV, B. L.: *Poludennye ekspeditsii* (Moscow: Voennoe Izd., 1998)

MEIER, L.: 'Obzor Zapadnoi okonechnosti Karatauskikh gor i neskol'ko slov o vzyatii kokanskoi kreposti Yany-Kurgan', *VS* (1862) No. 10, pp. 263–78

MEIER, L. (ed.): *Kirgizskaya step' Orenburgskago vedomstva: Materialy dlya geografii i statistiki Rossii sobrannye ofitserami general'nogo shtaba* (St Pb.: Tip. E. Veimar & F. Person, 1865)

MEIENDORF, E. K.: *Puteshestviya iz Orenburga v Bukharu* (Moscow: Nauka, 1975)

MIKHAILOV, M.: *Pokhod v Kokand v 1875 g.: Otdel'nyi ottisk iz gazety 'Turkestanskie Vedomosti' 1884 Nos. 3, 10, 11, 12, 13* (Tashkent: Turkestanskie Vedomosti, 1884)

MILIUTIN, D. A.: *Dnevnik D. A. Milyutina 1873–82* ed. P. A. Zaionchkovskii (Moscow: Biblioteka SSSR imeni V. I. Lenina, 1947–50) 4 volumes

MILIUTIN, D. A.: *Vospominaniya General-Fel'dmarshala Grafa Dmitriya Alekseevicha Milyutina 1860–1862* ed. L. G. Zakharova (Moscow: Rossiiskii Arkhiv, 1999)

MILIUTIN, D. A.: *Vospominaniya General-Fel'dmarshala Grafa Dmitriya Alekseevicha Milyutina 1843–1856* ed. L. G. Zakharova (Moscow: Rossiiskii Arkhiv, 2000)

MILIUTIN, D. A.: *Vospominaniya General-Fel'dmarshala Grafa Dmitriya Alekseevicha Milyutina 1863–1864* ed. L. G. Zakharova (Moscow: ROSSPEN, 2003)

MILIUTIN, D. A.: *Vospominaniya General-Fel'dmarshala Grafa Dmitriya Alekseevicha Milyutina 1856–1860* ed. L. G. Zakharova (Moscow: ROSSPEN, 2004)

MILIUTIN, D. A.: *Vospominaniya General-Fel'dmarshala Grafa Dmitriya Alekseevicha Milyutina 1868–nachalo 1873* ed. L. G. Zakharova (Moscow: ROSSPEN, 2006)

MILIUTIN, D. A.: *Dnevnik General-Fel'dmarshala Grafa Dmitriya Alekseevicha Miliutina 1876–1878* ed. L. G. Zakharova (Moscow: ROSSPEN, 2009)

MILIUTIN, D. A.: *Dnevnik General-Fel'dmarshala Grafa Dmitriya Alekseevicha Miliutina 1879–1881* ed. L. G. Zakharova (Moscow: ROSSPEN, 2010)

MURAV'EV, N. N.: *Puteshestvie v Turkmeniyu i Khivu v 1819 i 1820 godakh* (Moscow: Tip. Avgusta Semena, 1822)

MURAVTSEV, Kapitan: 'Turkestanskii otryad v Akhal-Tekinskoi ekspeditsii 1880 god', *VS* (1882) No. 3, pp. 159–83; No. 4, 358–76; No. 5, 167–92; No. 12, 292–9; (1883) No. 1, pp. 149–58; No. 2, pp. 288–332.

NALIVKIN, V. P.: 'Moi vospominaniya o Skobeleve', *Russkii Turkestan* (1906) No. 119, reprinted in *Polveka v Turkestane: V. P. Nalivkin: biografiya, dokumenty, trudy* ed. T. V. Kotiukova (Moscow: Izd. Mardzhani, 2015) pp. 525–53

NALIVKIN, V. P.: *Kratkaya istoriya Kokandskago Khanstva* (Kazan': Tip. Imperatorskogo Universiteta, 1885)

NALIVKIN, V. P. & NALIVKINA, M.: *Ocherk byta zhenshchiny osedlago tuzemnogo naseleniya Fergany* (Kazan: Tip. Imperatorskogo Universiteta, 1886).

NEDVETSKII, V. E.: *Uzun-Agachskoe delo i ego znachenie v istorii Semirechenskago kraya* (Vernyi: Tip. Semirechenskogo Oblastnogo Pravleniya, 1910)

NESSELRODE, K. V. 'Zapiski Grafa Karla Vasil'evicha Nessel'rode', *Russkii Vestnik* Vol. 59 (1865) pp. 519–68

NOVITSKII, V. F. (ed.): *Voennaya entsiklopediya* (St Pb.: Tip. Tovarishchestva I. D. Sytina, 1911–15) 18 volumes

'O geroiskoi smerti Unter-ofitsera Danilova', *Russkii Invalid* (1876) No. 90

OBERUCHEV, K.: 'Artileriya v Kokanskom pokhode 1875–1876 godov', *VS* (1896) No. 9, pp. 36–62; No. 11, pp. 173–93; No. 12, pp. 388–408

'Obozreniya Kokanskogo Khanstva v nyneshnem ego sostoyanii', *ZIRGO* Kn. III (1849) pp. 96–116

OBRUCHEV, N. N. (ed.): *Voenno-statisticheskii sbornik.* Vyp. III (St Pb.: Voennaya Tip., 1868) & Vyp. IV (St Pb.: Voennaya Tip., 1871)

Opisanie voennykh deistvii v Zailiiskom krae v 1860 godu i zhurnal osady Khokandskoi kreposti Pishpek (St Pb.: Tip. V. Spiridionova, 1861)

OSTROUMOV, N. P.: *Kitaiskie emigranty v Semirechenskoi oblasti Turkestanskogo kraya i rasprostranenie sredi nikh Pravoslavnogo Khristianstva* (Kazan': Tip. Imperatorskogo Universiteta, 1879)

OSTROUMOV, N. P.: 'Pesnya o Khudoyar Khane', *ZVORIAO* Vol. 2 (1887) pp. 189–94

OSTROUMOV, N. P.: 'Neskol'ko dokumentov, otnosyashchikhsya k zavoevaniiu Tashkenta', *TKLA* Vol. 19 (1915) pp. 5–10

PALEN, K. K.: *Otchet, revizuiushchago, po vysochaishemu poveleniiu, Turkestanskogo kraya: Kraevoe upravlenie* (St Pb.: Senatskaya Tip., 1910)

PANTUSOV, N. N.: *Svedeniya o Kuldzhinskom raione za 1871–1877 gody sobrannye N. N. Pantusovym* (Kazan': Universitetskaya Tip., 1881)

PASHINO, P. I. *Turkestanskii Krai* (St Pb.: Tiblen & Nekliudov, 1866)

PEROVSKII, V. A.: 'Pis'ma Grafa V. A. Perovskago k A. Ya. Bulgakovu', *RA* (1878) No. 7, pp. 34–46

PESLYAK, Aloizii: 'Zapiski Peslyaka', *IV* (1883) No. 9, pp. 576–94

PETROVSKII, N. F.: *Turkestanskie pis'ma* ed. V. S. Myasnikov (Moscow: Pamyatniki Istoricheskoi Mysli, 2010)

PICHUGIN, P.: 'Vtorzhenie Kokandtsev v Alatavskii Okrug v 1860 godu', *VS* (1872) No. 5, pp. 5–40

'Pokhody v stepi: Upotreblenie verbliudov dlya voennykh nadobnostei', *VS* (1862) No. 2, pp. 357–88

POLTORATSKII, V. A.: 'Vospominaniya', *IV* (1895) No. 5, pp. 414–44; No. 6, pp. 760–82

POSPELOV, F. F.: 'Seid-Khan Karimkhanov', in *Spravochnaya kniga Samarkandskoi Oblasti.* Vyp. 10 (Samarkand: Tip-Lit. Tovarishchestva B. Gazarov i K. Sliyanov, 1912) pp. 126–31

POTTO, V. A.: 'O stepnykh pokhodakh', *VS* (1873) No. 4, pp. 5–36; No. 5, pp. 33–62; No. 6, pp. 209–36; No. 7, 229–66

POTTO, V. A.: 'Iz putevykh zametok po stepi', *VS* (1876) No. 8, pp. 383–409

POTTO, V. A.: 'Gibel otryada Rukina v 1870 godu', *IV* (1900) No. 7, pp. 110–35

PUTINTSEV, Mikhail: 'Obshchii ocherk Kirgizskoi Stepi: ot Semipalatinsk do Kopala', *VS* (1865) No. 11, pp. 359–86

PUTYATA, D. V.: 'Pamirskie ekspeditsii 1883 g.', *IIRGO* Vol. 19 (1883) No. 4, pp. 332–40

PUTYATA, D. V.: 'Ocherk ekspeditsii v Pamir, Sarykol, Vakhan i Shugnan v 1883 g.', *Sbornik geograficheskikh, topograficheskikh i statisticheskikh materialov po Azii.* Vyp. 10 (1884) pp. 1–88

RAZGONOV, A. K.: *Po vostochnoi Bukhare i Pamiru* (Tashkent: Izd. Turkestanskogo Voennogo Okruga, 1910)

REGEL, A. E.: 'Puteshestvie v Shugnan', *IIRGO* Vol. 20 (1884) No. 4, pp. 268–73

REGEL, A. E.: 'Puteshestvie v Shugnan', *TV* (1884) No. 17

REGEL, A. E.: 'Poezdka v Karategin i Darvaz', *IIRGO* Vol. 18 (1882) No. 2, pp. 127–41

ROMANOVSKII, D. I.: *Zametki po sredne-aziyatskomu voprosu* (St Pb.: Tip. 2-go Otdela Sobstvennogo Ego Imperatorskogo Velichestva Kantselyarii, 1868) *Russkim voinam na pamyat' ob Agafon Nikitine, pogibshem mucheniskoiu smert'iu v 1880 godu za veru, Tsarya i otechestvo, pri vzyatii nashimi voiskami kreposti Geok-Tepé* (St Pb.: n.p., 1902)

SARANCHOV, E.: 'Khivinskiya ekspeditsiya 1873 goda', *Inzhenernyi Zhurnal* (1874) No. 1, pp. 1–38; No. 2, pp. 159–221; No. 3, pp. 297–334; No. 4, pp. 447–79

SHCHERBAK, A. V.: *Akhal-Tekinskaya ekspeditsiya Generala Skobeleva v 1880–81 godakh* (St Pb.: A. S. Suvorin, 1887)

SEMENOV, A. A.: 'Po granitsam Bukhary i Afganistana (putevye ocherki 1898 g.)', *IV* (1898) No. 3, pp. 961–92; No. 4, 98–122

SEMENOV, A. A.: *Etnograficheskie ocherki Zaravshanskikh gor, Karategina i Darvaza* (Moscow: n.p., 1903)

SEMENOV, A. A.: 'Pokoritel' i ustroitel' Turkestanskogo kraya: General-Ad'iutant K. P. fon-Kaufman 1-i', in *Kaufmanskii Sbornik: Izdannyi v pamyat' pokoritelya i ustroitelya Turkestanskogo kraya, General-Ad'iutanta K. P. fon-Kaufmana 1-ogo* (Moscow: Tip. I. N. Kushnerev, 1910) pp. i–lxxxiv

SEMENOV, P. P.: 'Znachenie Rossii v kolonizatsionnom dvizhenii evropeiskikh narodov', *IIRGO* Vol. 38 (1892) pp. 349–69

SEMENOV, P. P.: 'Pervaya poezdka na Tian'-shan ili nebesnyi khrebet do verkhov'ev r. Yaksarta ili Syr-Dar'i v 1857 g.', *VIRGO* Chast' 23, Otd. 5 (1858) pp. 1–25

SEMENOV, V. P. (ed.): *Rossiya: Pol'noe geograficheskoe opisanie nashego otechestva.* Vol. XVIII. *Kirgizskii krai* (St Pb.: Izd. A. F. Devriena, 1903)

SEMENOV-TIAN-SHANSKII, P. P.: *Puteshestvie v Tian'-Shan' v 1856–7 godakh* ed. L. S. Berg (Moscow: OGIZ, 1946)

SEREBRENNIKOV, A. G.: 'Ocherki Shugnana', *VS* (1895) Nos. 11–12, pp. 406–35

SEREBRENNIKOV, A. G.: 'K istorii Kokanskogo pokhoda', *VS* (1897) No. 9, pp. 5–28; (1899) No. 4, pp. 211–26; (1901) No. 4, pp. 29–55; No. 9, pp. 28–55; No. 10, pp. 69–96; No. 11, pp. 37–74

SEREBRENNIKOV, A. G.: 'Ocherk Pamira', *VS* (1899) No. 6, pp. 432–44; No. 7, pp. 219–36; No. 8, pp. 442–64; No. 9, pp. 216–26; No. 10, pp. 447–66; No. 11, pp. 227–36 & reprinted as *Ocherki Pamira* (St Pb.: Tip. Glavnoe Upravlenie Udelov, 1900)

SEREDONIN, S. M.: 'Istoricheskii ocherk zavoevaniya Aziatskoi Rossii', in *Aziatskaya Rossiya*. Vyp. I (St Pb.: Izd. Pereselencheskago Upravleniya, 1914) pp. 1–44

SEVAST'YANOV, S. N.: 'Sobytiya v Orenburgskom krae pogotovivshiya ekspeditsiyu v Khivu 1839–1840 gg.', *TOUAK* Vyp. XVI (1906) pp. 108–42

SOURCES AND BIBLIOGRAPHY 557

SEVAST'YANOV, S. N.: 'Grigorii Fedorovich Gens', *TOUAK* Vyp. XIX (1907) pp. 148–67

SEVERTSOV, N. A.: *Mesyats plena u Kokandtsev* (St Pb.: Tip. Riumin i Kompanii, 1860)

SEVERTSOV, N. A.: 'Kratkii otchet o Pamirskikh issledovaniyakh i obshchikh nauchnykh rezul'tatakh Ferganskoi uchenoi ekspeditsii', *IIRGO* (1879) No. 2, pp. 66–86; also in *TS* Vol. 349, pp. 65–75A

SEVERTSOV, N. A.: *Orograficheskii ocherk Pamirskoi gornoi sistemy* (St Pb.: Tip. Imperatorskoi Akademii Nauk, 1886)

SHEVCHENKO, Taras: *Polnoe Sobranie Sochinenii v 10-i tomakh* (Kiev: Izd. AN USSR, 1962) 10 volumes

SHAKHOVSKOI, V. 'Ekspeditsiya protiv Akhal-Tekintsev v 1879–1880–1881 gg.: Posvyashchaetsya pamyati M. D. Skobeleva, *RS* Vol. XLVI (1885) No. 4, pp. 161–286; No. 5, 377–410; No. 6, 531–58

SHEMANSKII, A. D.: *Boi na Kushke i ego 25-letnii iubilei* (St Pb.: V. Berezovskii, 1910)

SHUMIGORSKII, E.: 'Odin iz revnosteishikh nasaditelei nemetskago zasil'ya v Rossii: Graf Karl Vasil'evich Nessel'rode', *RS* Vol. 161 (1915) No. 1, pp. 160–5

SIMONOVA [Khokhriakova], L. Kh.: 'Rasskazy ochevidtsev o zavoevanii russkimi Samarkanda i o semidnevnom sidenii', *IV* 97 (1904) No. 9, pp. 844–66

SKER'SKII, A. G.: 'Kratkii ocherk Pamira', *Sbornik geograficheskikh, topograficheskikh i statisticheskikh materialov po Azii* Vyp. L (1892) pp. 13–39

SKOBELEV, M. D. 'Osada i shturm kreposti Dengil-Tepe (Geok-Tepe)', *VS* (1881) No. 4, pp. 3–64

SKOBELEV, M. D. 'Posmertnye bumagi M. D. Skobeleva', *IV* (1883) No. 11, pp. 109–294

SNESAREV, A. E. (ed.): *Svedeniya kasaiushchiyasya stran, sopredel'nykh s Turkestanskim Voennym Okrugom* (Tashkent: Tip. Shtaba Turkestanskogo Voennogo Okruga 1898–1900) 19 volumes

SNESAREV, A. E.: 'Religiya i obychai gortsev zapadnogo Pamira', *TV* (1904) Nos. 89–93

SNESAREV, A. E.: *Indiya kak glavnyi faktor v sredne-aziatskom voprose* (St Pb.: A. Suvorin, 1906)

SNESAREV, A. E.: *Pis'ma A. E. Snesareva iz Indii i Srednei Azii 1899–1904* (Moscow: Tsentrizdat, 2006)

SOBOLEV, L. N.: *Vozmozhen-li pokhod Russkikh v Indiyu?* (Moscow: n.p., 1901)

SYARKOVSKII, Gilyarii: 'Vospominaniya ofitsera o Turkestanskikh pokhodakh 1864–5 gg.', *VS* (1891) No. 2, pp. 357–81; No. 3, pp. 157–64

TAGEEV, B. L.: 'Cherez Alai i Pamir', *Vsemirnoi Illiustratsii* (1895) Vol. 53, p. 459

TAGEEV, B. L.: 'Pamirskii pokhod (vospominaniya ochevidtsa)', *IV* (1898) No. 7, pp. 111–63

TAGEEV, B. L.: *Pamirskie pokhody 1892–1895 g.* (Warsaw: Gubernskaya Tip., 1900)

TAGEEV, B. L.: *Russkie nad Indiei: Ocherki i rasskazy iz boevoi zhizni na Pamire* (St Pb.: Tip. V. S. Ettingera, 1900) reprinted in *Poludennye ekspeditsii: Ocherki* (Moscow: Voennoe Izd., 1998) pp. 163–350

TATARINOV, A.: *Semimesyachnyi plen v Bukharii* (St Pb.: Izd. M. O. Vol'fa, 1867)

TERENT'EV, M. A.: *Rossiya i Angliya v Srednei Azii* (St Pb.: P. P. Merkulev, 1875)

TERENT'EV, Gen-Lt. M. A.: *Istoriya zavoevaniya Srednei Azii* (St Pb.: A. V. Komarov, 1906) 3 volumes

TOLBUKHOV, E.: 'Skobelev v Turkestane (1869–1877 g.)', *IV* (1916) No. 10, pp. 107–32; No. 11, pp. 369–403; No. 12, pp. 638–67

TROTSKII, V. N.: *Raport Nachal'nika otryada deistvovavshego na levom beregu Syr-Dar'i, Svity ego Velichestva General-Maiora Trotskogo, Komanduiushchemu voiskami deistvovavshimi v Kokandskom khanstve* (Tashkent: n.p., 1875)

TROTSKII, V. N.: *Materialy dlya opisaniya Khivinskago pokhoda 1873 goda: Opisanie deistvii Kavkazskikh otryadov* (Tashkent: Izdano, na pravakh rukopisi, po rasporyazheniiu Turkestanskogo General-Gubernatora, Gen-Ad. K. P. Fon-Kaufmana, 1881)

TROTSKII, V. N.: *Opisanie deistvii Orenburgskago otryada v khivinskuiu ekspeditsiiu 1873 g.* (Tashkent: n.p., 1881)

TROTSKII, V. N.: *Opisanie deistvii Turkestanskago otryada v khivinskuiu ekspeditsiiu 1873 goda* (Tashkent: Tip. F. V. Vasilevskim, 1882)

TUGAN-MIRZA-BARANOVSKII, V. A.: *Russkie v Akhal-Teke 1879 g.* (St Pb.: Tip. V. V. Komarova, 1881)

'Turkestanskaya Oblast'', *VS* (1865) No. 3, pp. 57–61

UMANETS, S.: 'Pamirskii vopros i ego znachenie', *IV* (1892) No. 1, pp. 196–208

URALEV, N.: *Na verbliudakh: Vospominaniya iz zhizni v Srednei Azii* (St Pb.: Tip. P. P. Soikina, 1897)

V.N.G.: 'Ocherk ekspeditsii v Akhal-Teke 1879–1880', *VS* (1888) No. 5, pp. 204–30; No. 6, pp. 396–426

VALUEV, D. A.: *Dnevnik P. A. Valueva 1815–1890* ed. P. Zaionchkovskii (Moscow: Izd. AN SSSR, 1961) 2 volumes

VALIKHANOV, Chokan Chingisovich: *Sochineniya Chokana Chingisovicha Valikhanova* ed. N. I. Veselovskii, *ZIRGO po otdeleniu etnografii*. Vol. XXIX (St Pb.: Tip. Glavnogo Upravleniya Udelov, 1904)

VALIKHANOV, Chokan Chingisovich: 'Dnevnik poezdki na Issyk-Kul' [1856], in *Izbrannye proizvedeniya* ed. A. Kh. Margulan (Alma-Ata: Kazakhskoe Gosudarstvennoe Izd. Khudozhestvennoi Literatury, 1958) pp. 236–86, 444–86

VALIKHANOV, Chokan Chingisovich: 'Opisanie puti v Kashgar i obratno v Alatavskii Okrug' [1859], in *Izbrannye proizvedeniya* ed. A. Kh. Margulan (Alma-Ata: Kazakhskoe Gosudarstvennoe Izd. Khudozhestvennoi Literatury, 1958) pp. 444–86

VALIKHANOV, Chokan Chingisovich: *Sobranie sochinenii Ch. Ch. Valikhanova* ed. A. Kh. Margulan (Alma-Ata: Kazakhskaya Sovetskaya Entsiklopediya, 1985) 5 volumes

VARENIK: 'S Russko-Avganskoi granitsy', *Severnyi Kavkaz* (1886) Nos. 28–29
VASIL'EV, Shtabs-Kapitan: 'Statisticheskii ocherk Karategina', *VS* (1888) No. 10, pp. 422–36
VELYAMINOV-ZERNOV: V. V.: 'Istoricheskiya izvestiya o Kokanskom Khanstve ot Mukhammed-Ali do Khudoyar Khana', *TVOIRAO* Chast' II (St Pb.: n.p., 1856) pp. 329–70
VENIUKOV, M. I.: 'Zametki o stepnykh pokhodakh v Srednei Azii', *VS* (1860) No. 12, pp. 269–98
VENIUKOV, M. I.: 'Ocherki Zailiiskogo kraya I: Prichuiskoi strany', *ZIRGO* (1861) No. 4, pp. 79–116
VENIUKOV, M. I.: *Puteshestviya po okrainam Russkoi Azii i zapiski o nikh* (St Pb.: Tip. Imperatorskoi Akademii Nauk, 1868)
VENIUKOV, M. I.: *Opyt' voennogo obozreniya russkikh granits v Azii* (St Pb.: Tip. B. Bezobrazov, 1873–6) 2 volumes
VERESHCHAGIN, V. V.: *Na voine v Azii i Evrope: Vospominaniya khudozhnika V. V. Vereshchagina* (Moscow: I. N. Kushnerev, 1894)
VESELOVSKII, N. I.: 'Dagbid', *ZVOIRAO* (1888) No. 2, pp. 85–95
VESELOVSKII, N. I.: *Badaulet Yakub-Bek: Atalyk Kashgarskii* (St Pb.: Tip. Imperatorskoi Akademii Nauk, 1898)
VITKEVICH, I. V.: 'Zapiska, sostavlennaya po rasskazam Orenburgskogo Lineinoga Batal'ona No. 10 Praporshchika Vitkevicha otnositel'no puti ego v Bukharu i obratno', in *Zapiski o Bukharskom Khanstve* ed. N. A. Khalfin (Moscow: Nauka, 1983)
'Voennoe predpriyatie protiv Khivu', in *Chteniya v Imperatorskom obshchestve istorii i drevnostei rossiiskikh pri Moskovskom Universitete. Kn. 1-aya* (1860) pp. 147–66
'Voennye deistvii v byvshem Kokandskom khanstve s 25-go dekabrya 1875 goda po 7-go fevral'ya 1876 goda', *VS* (1876) No. 8, pp. 119–77
'Vzyatie Tashkenta', *VS* (1865) No. 9, pp. 67–77
YAVORSKII, I. L.: *Puteshestvie russkoi missii po Avganistanu i Bukharskomu khanstvu v 1878–79 gg.* (St. Pb.: Tip M. A. Khana, 1882) 2 volumes
YUVACHEV, I.: 'Kurban-Dzhan-Datkha [sic], kara-kirgizskaya tsaritsa Alaya', *IV* (1907) No. 12, pp. 954–80
ZAITSEV, V. N.: *Istoriya 4-ogo Turkestanskogo Lineinogo Batal'ona za period s 1771 do 1882 god kak material k dvizheniiu russkikh v Sredniuiu Aziiu* (Tashkent: n.p., 1882)
ZAKHAR'IN, I. N.: *Khiva: Zimnii pokhod v Khivu Perovskago v 1839 godu, – i 'Pervoe posol'stvo v Khivu' v 1842 godu* (St Pb.: Tip. P. P. Soikina, 1898)
ZAKHAR'IN, I. N.: *Graf V. A. Perovskii i ego zimnii pokhod v Khivu* (St Pb.: Tip. P. P. Soikina, 1901)
ZAKHAR'IN, I. V.: 'Nachalo zavoevaniya Kokanda (k 25-letiiu prisoedineniya Ferganskoi oblasti)', *IV* (1901) No. 6, pp. 1065–74
ZALESOV, I.: 'Pis'mo iz stepi', *VS* (1858) No. 8, pp. 487–91

ZALESOV, I.: 'Pis'mo iz Khivy', *VS* (1858) No. 8, pp. 492–7; (1859) No. 1 pp. 273–95

ZALESOV, I.: 'Pis'mo iz Bukhary', *VS* (1860) No. 4, pp. 335–48

ZALESOV, I.: 'Posol'stvo v Khivu Kapitana Nikiforova v 1841 g.', *VS* (1861) No. 11, pp. 41–92

ZALESOV, I.: 'Posol'stvo v Khivu Podpolkovnika Danilevskogo v 1842 g.', *VS* (1866) No. 5, 41–75

ZHUKOVSKII, S. V.: *Snosheniya Rossii s Bukharoi i Khivoi za poslednee trekhsotletie* (Petrograd: Obshchestvo Russkikh Orientalistov, 1915)

ZINOV'EV, M.: *Osada Ura-Tyube i Dzhizaka: Vospominaniya ob osennoi ekspeditsii 1866 goda v Turkestanskoi Oblasti* (Moscow: Russkii Vestnik, 1868)

ZNAMENSKII, M. S.: 'Dnevnik Aulie-atinskogo pokhoda', in *Sobranie sochinenii Ch. Ch. Valikhanova* ed. A. Kh. Margulan. Vol. 5 (Alma-Ata: Kazakhskaya Sovetskaya Entsiklopediya, 1985) pp. 247–54

ZYKOV, S. 'Khivinskiya dela s 1839–1842', *Russkoe Slovo* (March 1862) pp. 1–58

Published Sources in Other Languages

A Narrative of the Russian Military Expedition to Khiva under General Perofski, in 1839. Translated from the Russian for the Foreign Department of the Government of India (Calcutta: Office of the Superintendent of Government Printing, 1867)

ABBOT, Capt. James: *Narrative of a Journey from Heraut to Khiva, Moscow and St Petersburgh during the Late Russian Invasion of Khiva, with Some Account of the Court of Khiva and the Kingdom of Khaurism* (London: W. H. Allen & Co., 1843) 2 volumes

ALISON, Sir Archibald: *History of Europe from the Commencement of the French Revolution [. . .] to the Restoration of the Bourbons* (Edinburgh: Wm Blackwood, 1835–1842) 12 volumes

ATKINSON, Mrs [Lucy]: *Recollections of Tatar Steppes and Their Inhabitants* (London: John Murray, 1863)

ATKINSON, Thomas: *Oriental and Western Siberia: A Narrative of Seven Years' Explorations and Adventures in Siberia, Mongolia, the Kirghis Steppes, Chinese Tartary, and Part of Central Asia* (London: Hurst & Blackett, 1858)

BADDELEY, J. F. *The Russian Conquest of the Caucasus* (London: Longmans, Green & Co., 1908)

BAKER, Valentine: *Clouds in the East* (London: Chatto & Windus, 1876)

BELLEW, H. W.: *Kashmir and Kashghar: A Narrative of the Embassy to Kashghar in 1873–4* (London: Trübner & Co, 1875)

BONVALOT, Gabriel: *Du Caucase aux Indes, à travers le Pamir* (Paris: Librairie Plon, 1889)

BOULANGER, Edgar: 'Voyage à Merv', *Le Tour du monde. Nouveau journal des voyages* Vol. 53 (1887) pp. 145–208

BOULANGER, Edgar: *Voyage à Merv* (Paris: Hachette, 1888)

BOULGER, Demetrius Charles: *The Life of Yakoob Beg, Athalik Ghazi and Badaulet, Ameer of Kashgar* (London: W. H. Allen, 1878)

BURNABY, Capt. Fred: *A Ride to Khiva* (London: Cassel, Petter & Galpin, 1877)

BURNES, Capt. Sir Alexander: *Travels into Bokhara* (London: John Murray, 1834) 3 volumes

BUTAKOFF, Alexey: 'Survey of the Sea of Aral', *JRGS* Vol. 23 (1853) pp. 93–101

BYRON, Robert: *The Road to Oxiana* (London: Jonathan Cape, 1937)

CALLWELL, Charles E.: *Small Wars: Their Principles and Practice* 2nd ed. (London: HMSO, 1899)

CASTLE, John: 'Journal von der AO 1736 aus Orenburg zu dem Abul Geier Chan der Kirgis-Kaysak tartarischen Horda', in *Materialen zu der russischen Geschichte* (Riga: n.p., 1784) trans. Sarah Tolley & ed. Beatrice Teissier as *Into the Kazakh Steppe: John Castle's Mission to Khan Abu'lkhayir (1736)* (Oxford: Signal Books, 2014)

CHENEVIX TRENCH, Captain F.: 'The Russian Campaign against Khiva, in 1873', *RUSI Journal*, 18/77 (1874) pp. 212–26

COBBOLD, Ralph: *Innermost Asia: Travel and Sport in the Pamirs* (London: William Heinemann, 1900)

CONOLLY, Arthur: *Journey to the North of India Overland from England through Russia, Persia and Affghaunistan* (London: Richard Bentley, 1834)

CURZON, G. N.: *Russia in Central Asia in 1889 and the Anglo-Russian Question* (London: Longmans, 1889)

CURZON, G. N.: 'The Transcaspian Railway', *PRGS* Vol. 11 (1889) No. 5, pp. 273–95

CURZON, G. N.: *The Pamirs and the Source of the Oxus* (London: Royal Geographical Society, 1896)

CURZON, G. N.: *On the Indian Frontier* ed. Dhara Anjaria (Karachi: Oxford University Press, 2012)

DAVIS, Jefferson: *Report of the Secretary of War, Communicating, in Compliance with a Resolution of the Senate of February 2, 1857, Information Respecting the Purchase of Camels for the Purposes of Military Transportation* (Washington, DC: A. O. P. Nicholson, 1857)

DE NESSELRODE, A. (ed.): *Lettres et papiers du Chancelier Comte de Nesselrode 1760–1850: Extraits de ses archives* (Paris: A. Lahure, 1907) 12 volumes

DUNMORE, Earl of: *The Pamirs: Being a Narrative of a Year's Expedition on Horseback & on Foot through Kashmir, Western Tibet, Chinese Tartary and Russian Central Asia* (London: John Murray, 1893) 2 volumes

DURAND, Algernon: *The Making of a Frontier: Five Years' Experiences and Adventures in Gilgit, Hunza, Nagar, Chitral and the Eastern Hindu Kush* (London: John Murray, 1899)

FEDCHENKO, A.: 'Topographical Sketch of the Zarafshan Valley', *JRGS* Vol. 40 (1870) pp. 448–62

FILCHNER, Wilhelm: *Ein Ritt über den Pamir* (Berlin: Ernst Siegfried Mittler und Sohn, 1903)

FORSYTH, Thomas: *Report of a Mission to Yarkund in 1873 under Command of Sir T. D. Forsyth, with Historical and Geographical Information Regarding the Possessions of the Ameer of Yarkund* (Calcutta: Foreign Department Press, 1875)

GARBER, Johann Garber: *Journal von der Reise aus Astrachan nach Chiwa und Bucharen, 1732* (St Pb.: Buchdruckerei der kaiserlichen Akademie der Wissenschaften, 1902)

GERARD, M. G.: *Report on the Proceedings of the Pamir Boundary Commission* (Calcutta: Office of the Superintendent of Government Printing, 1897)

GRĄBCZEWSKI, Bronisław: *Kaszgarja: Kraj i ludzie: Podróż do Azji Środkowej* (Warsaw: Gebethner i Wolff, 1924)

GRĄBCZEWSKI, Bronisław: *Przez Pamiry i Hindukusz do źródeł rzeki Indus* (Warsaw: Gebethner i Wolff, 1924)

GRĄBCZEWSKI, Bronisław: *Na służbie rosyjskiej: Fragmenty wspomnień* (Warsaw: Gebethner i Wolff, 1926)

GRODEKOFF, Major-General N. I.: *The War in Turkumania: [sic] Skobeleff's Campaign of 1880–81* trans. J. M. Grierson (Simla: Government Central Branch Press, 1884–5) 4 volumes

GROUM-GRSHIMAÏLO, Gr.: *Le Pamir et sa faune lépidoptérologique: Mémoires sur les lépidoptéres* ed. N. M. Romanoff. Vol. IV (St Pb.: M. M. Stassuléwitsch, 1890)

HAYWARD, George: 'Journey from Leh to Yarkand and Kashgar, and Exploration of the Sources of the Yarkand River', *JRGS* Vol. 40 (1871) pp. 33–166

HEDIN, Sven: *Through Asia* (London: Methuen & Co, 1898) 2 volumes

HENDERSON, George & HUME, Allan Octavian: *Lahore to Yarkand: Incidents of the Route and Natural History of the Countries Traversed by the Expedition of 1870 under T. D. Forsyth Esq., C.B.* (London: L. Reeve & Co, 1873)

HOLDICH, T. H.: 'Afghan Boundary Commission; Geographical Notes. III', *PRGS* (1885) No. 5, pp. 273–92

IGNATIEV, N. P.: *Mission to Khiva and Bukhara, 1858* (Newtonville, MA: Oriental Research Partners, 1984)

KHANIKOFF, Nikolai: *Bokhara, Its Amir and Its People* trans. Baron Clement A. de Bode (London: James Madden, 1845)

KUROPATKIN, A. N.: *Kashgaria [Eastern or Chinese Turkestan]: Historical and Geographical Sketch of the Country; Its Military Strength, Industries and Trade* trans. Walter E. Gowan (Calcutta: Thacker, Spink & Co., 1882)

LEONARD, Arthur Glyn: *The Camel: Its Uses and Management* (London: Longmans, Green & Co., 1894)

LERCH, Peter: *Khiva oder Kharezm: Seine historischen und geographischen Verhältnisse* (St Pb.: Verlag der Kaiserlichen Hofbuchhandlung, 1873)

LITTLEDALE, St George R.: 'A Journey across the Pamir from North to South', *PRGS* Vol. 14 (1892) No. 1, pp. 1–35

LOMONOSOFF, Alexis: 'M. Severtsof's Journey in Ferghana and the Pamir in 1877–8', *PRGS* Vol. 2 (1880) No. 8, pp. 499–506

MACGAHAN, J. A. *Campaigning on the Oxus and the Fall of Khiva* (London: Sampson, Low, Marston, Low and Searle, 1874)

MANNERHEIM, C. G.: *Across Asia from West to East in 1906–1908* (Oosterhout: Anthropological Publications, 1969) 2 volumes

MARVIN, Charles: *Colonel Grodekoff's Ride from Samarcand to Herat, through Balkh and the Uzbek States of Afghan Turkestan* (London: W. H. Allen & Co., 1880)

MARVIN, Charles: *The Eye Witnesses' Account of the Disastrous Russian Campaign against the Akhal Tekke Turcomans* (London: W. H. Allen & Co., 1880)

MARVIN, Charles: *Merv, the Queen of the World, and the Scourge of the Man-Stealing Turcomans* (London: W. H. Allen & Co., 1881)

MARVIN, Charles: *The Russian Advance towards India: Conversations with Skobeleff, Ignatieff, and Other Distinguished Russian Generals and Statesmen, on the Central Asian Question* (London: W. H. Allen & Co., 1882)

MARVIN, Charles: 'Lieutenant Alikhanoff's Journey with a Russian Caravan to Merv', in *Reconnoitring Central Asia: Pioneering Adventures in the Region Lying Between Russia and India* (London: Swan Sonnenschein, 1884) pp. 363–83

MEYENDORFF, Georges de: *Voyage d'Orenbourg à Boukhara fait en 1820* (Paris: Librairie Orientale de Dondey-Dupré Père et Fils, 1826)

MICHELL, John & **MICHELL**, Robert (eds.): *The Russians in Central Asia: Their Occupation of the Kirghiz Steppe and the Line of the Syr-Daria: Their Political Relations with Khiva, Bokhar and Kokan: Also Descriptions of Chinese Turkestan and Dzungaria by Capt. Valikhanof, M. Veniukof and Other Russian Travellers* (London: Edward Stanford, 1865)

MICHELL, Robert: 'The Russian Expedition to the Alai and Pamir in 1876', *PRGS* Vol. 21 (1876–7) No. 2, pp. 122–40

MICHELL, Robert: 'The Russian Expedition to the Alai and Pamir', *JRGS* Vol. 47 (1877) pp. 17–47

MICHELL, Robert: 'The Regions of the Upper Oxus', *PRGS* Vol. 6 (1884) No. 9, pp. 489–512

MONTGOMERIE, T. G. (ed.): 'A Havildar's Journey through Chitral to Faizabad in 1870', *JRGS* Vol. 16 (1871–2) No. 3, pp. 253–61

[**MURAVTSEV**, Captain]: 'March of the Turkestan Detachment across the Desert from the Amu', trans. J. J. Leverson, *Journal of the Royal United Service Institution* Vol. 26 (1883) pp. 568–85

MURAV'YOV, Nikolay: *Journey to Khiva through the Turcoman Country* [Calcutta: 1871] (London: Oghuz Press, 1977)

NALIVKIN, Vladimir & **NALIVKINA**, Maria: *Muslim Women of the Fergana Valley: A 19th-Century Ethnography from Central Asia* trans. Maria

Markova & ed. Marianne Kamp (Bloomington, IN: Indiana University Press, 2016)

NAPIER, Capt.G. C.: *Collections of Journals and Reports Received from the Hon. Capt. G. C. Napier, on Special Duty in Persia 1874* (London: Eyre & Spottiswoode, 1876)

NOVIKOVA, O. A.: *Skobeleff and the Slavonic Cause* (London: Longmans, Green & Co., 1883),

O'DONOVAN, Edmund: *The Merv Oasis: Travels and Adventures East of the Caspian, 1879-80-81, Including Five Months' Residence among the Tekkés of Merv* (London: Smith, Elder & Co., 1882) 2 volumes

OLUFSEN, Ole: *Through the Unknown Pamirs: The Second Danish Pamir Expedition 1898-99* (London: W. Heinemann, 1904)

OLUFSEN, Ole: *The Emir of Bokhara and His Country: Journeys and Studies in Bokhara (with a Chapter on My Voyage on the Amu Darya to Khiva)* (Copenhagen: Gyldendal, Nordisk forlag; London: Heinemann, 1911)

OOKHTOMSKY, Prince E. E.: *Travels in the East of Nicholas II, Emperor of Russia When Cesarewitch 1890-1* trans. Robert Goodlet (Westminster: Constable, 1896) 2 volumes

PAHLEN, K. K.: *Mission to Turkestan: Being the Memoirs of Count K. K. Pahlen* ed. Richard Pierce & trans. N. J. Couriss (London: Oxford University Press, 1964)

PRIOUX, A.: *Les Russes dans l'Asie Centrale: La dernière campagne de Skobelev* (Paris: Librairie Militaire de L. Baudoin et Cie., 1886)

[PUTYATA, D. V.]: 'The Russian Pamir Expedition of 1883', *PRGS* Vol. 6 (1884) No. 3, pp. 135-42

RANKE, Leopold: 'Die grossen Mächte', *Historisch-Politische Zeitschrift* Vol. II (1833) pp. 1-51

RENNELL, James: 'On the Rate of Travelling, as Performed by Camels: And Its Application, as a Scale, to the Purposes of Geography', *Philosophical Transactions of the Royal Society of London* Vol. 81 (1791) pp. 129-45

ROBERTSON, G. S.: *The Kafirs of the Hindu-Kush* (London: Lawrence & Bullen, 1896)

SALGARI, Emilio: *Le aquile della steppa* (Genoa: Donath, 1907)

SEVERTSOF, N. A.: 'M. Severtsof's Journey in Ferghana and the Pamir in 1877-8', trans. Alexis Lomonossof, *PRGS* Vol. 2 (1880) No. 8, pp. 499-506

SCHUYLER, Eugene: 'A Month's Journey in Kokand in 1873', *PRGS* Vol. 18 (1873-4) No. 4, pp. 408-14

SCHUYLER, Eugene: *Turkistan: Notes on a Journey in Russian Turkestan, Khokand, Bukhara and Kuldja* (London: Sampson, Lowe, Marston, Searle & Rivington, 1876) 2 volumes

SEMENOV TIAN-SHANSKII, P. P.: *Travels in the Tian-Shan 1856-1857* ed. Colin Thomas (London: The Hakluyt Society, 1998)

SEREBRENNIKOV, A.: 'On the Afghan Frontier: A Reconnaissance in Shugnan', *GJ* Vol. XVI (1900) No. 6, pp. 669–71

SHAKESPEAR, Richmond: 'A Personal Narrative of a Journey from Heraut to Ourenbourg, on the Caspian [*sic*] in 1840', *Blackwood's Edinburgh Magazine* Vol. 51 (June 1842) pp. 691–720

SHAW, Robert: *Visits to High Tartary, Yarkand, and Kashghar* (London: John Murray, 1871)

SKOBELEFF, M. D.: *Siege and Assault of Denghil-Tépé: General Skobeleff's Report* trans. Lt J. J. Leverson R.E. (London: HMSO, 1881),

SKRINE, Francis Henry & ROSS, Edward Denison: *The Heart of Asia: A History of Russian Turkestan and the Central Asian Khanates from the Earliest Times* (London: Methuen & Co., 1899)

STEIN, Aurel: 'A Third Journey of Exploration in Central Asia, 1913–1916', *GJ* Vol. 48 (1916) No. 3, pp. 212–19

STUMM, Hugo: *Der russische Feldzug nach Chiwa* (Berlin: Mittler, 1875)

STUMM, Hugo: *The Russian Campaign against Khiva in 1873* trans. F. Henvey & P. Mosa (Calcutta: Foreign Department Press, 1876)

TOLSTOY, L. N.: *Sevastopol and other Stories* trans. Louise Maude & Aylmer Maude (London: Grant Richards, 1903)

TOLSTOY, Leo: *War and Peace* trans. Louise Maude & Aylmer Maude (Oxford: Humphrey Milford for Oxford University Press, 1942)

TROTTER, Henry: 'The Proceedings of the Pamir Boundary Commission', *GJ* Vol. 13 (1899) No. 1, pp. 50–6

VAMBERY, Arminius: 'Sketch of a Journey through Central Asia to Khiva, Bokhara and Samarcand', *PRGS* Vol. 8 (1863–4) No. 6, pp. 267–74

VAMBERY, Arminius: *Travels in Central Asia* (London: John Murray, 1864)

WOEIKOFF, A.: *Le Turkestan russe* (Paris: Armand Colin, 1914)

WOLFF, Rev. Joseph: *Narrative of a Mission to Bokhara in the Years 1843–5* 6th ed. (Edinburgh: Wm Blackwood & Sons, 1852)

WOOD, Capt.John: *A Journey to the Source of the River Oxus* (London: John Murray, 1872)

YATE, A. C.: *England and Russia Face to Face in Asia: Travels with the Afghan Boundary Commission* (Edinburgh: Wm Blackwood & Sons, 1887)

YATE, C. E.: *Northern Afghanistan or Letters from the Afghan Boundary Commission, with Route Maps* (Edinburgh: Wm Blackwood & Sons, 1888)

YOUNGHUSBAND, Francis: 'Journeys in the Pamirs and Adjacent Countries', *PRGS* Vol. 14 (1892) No. 4, pp. 205–34

YOUNGHUSBAND, Francis: *The Heart of a Continent: A Narrative of Travels in Manchuria, across the Gobi Desert, through the Himalayas, the Pamirs and Hunza 1884–1894* (London: John Murray, 1896)

Secondary Works in Russian

ABAEVA, T. G.: *Ocherki istorii Badakhshana* (Tashkent: Nauka, 1964)

ABDIROV, Murat: *Zavoevanie Kazakhstana Tsarskoi Rossiei i bor'ba Kazakhskogo naroda za nezavisimost'* (iz istorii voenno-kazach'ei kolonizatsii kraya v kontse XVI–nachale XX vekov) (Astana: Elorda, 2000)

ABDURASULOV, Ulfat & SARTORI, Paolo: 'Neopredelonnost' kak politika: Razmyshlenyaya prirode rossiiskogo protektorata v Srednei Azii', *AI* (2016) No. 3, pp. 118–64

ABASHIN, S. N.: 'V. P. Nalivkin. "Budet to, chto neizbezhno dolzhno byt'; i to, chto neizbezhno dolzhno byt', uzhe ne mozhet ne byt'.": Krizis orientalizma v Rossiiskoi Imperii?', in *Aziatskaya Rossiya: Liudi i struktury Imperii* ed. Iu. P. Rodionov & A. V. Yakub (Omsk: Izd. OMGU, 2005) pp. 43–96

ABASHIN, S. N.: *Natsionalizmy v Srednei Azii: V poiskakh identichnosti* (St Pb.: Aleteia, 2007)

ABASHIN, S. N.: & BUSHKOV, V. I. (ed.): *Ferganskaya dolina: Etnichnost', etnicheskie protsessy, etnicheskie konflikty* (Moscow: Nauka, 2004)

ABASHIN, S. N., ARAPOV, D.A. & BEKMAKHANOVA, N. A. (ed.): *Tsentral'naya Aziya v sostave Rossiiskoi Imperii* (Moscow: Novoe Literaturnoe Obozrenie, 2008)

AKHMEDZHANOV, G. A.: *Rossiiskaya Imperiya v Tsentral'noi Azii (istoriya i istoriografiya kolonial'noi politiki Tsarizma v Turkestane)* (Tashkent: FAN, 1995)

AKRAMOV, N: *Voprosy istorii, arkheologii i etnografii narodov Pamira i Pripamir'ia v trudakh B. L. Grombchevskogo* (Dushanbe: Irfon, 1974)

AMINOV, A. M. & BABAKHODZHAEV, A. Kh.: *Ekonomicheskie i politicheskie posledstviya prisoedineniya Srednei Azii k Rossii* (Tashkent: Izd. Uzbekistan, 1966)

ARAPOV, D.: 'Vy posylaetes v stranu, kotoruiu my malo znaem: Razvedyvatel'naya "programma" russkogo konsula v Kashgare N. F. Petrovskogo', *Istochnik. Dokumenty russkoi istorii* (2002) No. 6, pp. 52–5

ASIMOV, M. S. & MUKHTAROV,A. M. (ed.): *Pamirovedenie* (Dushanbe: Donish, 1984–5)

AZADAEV, F.: *Tashkent vo vtoroi polovine XIX-go veka* (Tashkent: Izd. Akademii Nauka Uzbekskoi SSR, 1959)

BABADZHANOV, Bakhtiyar: *Kokandskoe Khanstvo: Vlast', politika, religiya* (Tokyo & Tashkent: NIHU Programme Islamic Area Studies Centre, 2010)

BABADZHANOV, Bakhtiyar: 'Rossiiskii General-Konkvistador v Russkom Turkestane: Vzlety i padeniya M. G. Chernyaeva', *CIAS Discussion Paper* No. 35 (Kyoto, 2013) pp. 17–45

BARTOL'D, V. V.: *Istoriya kul'turnoi zhizni Turkestana* (Moscow: Izd. Akademii Nauk SSSR, 1927)

BARTOL'D, V. V.: 'Ocherk istorii Semirech'ya', in *Sochineniya* Vol. II, Part 1 (Moscow: Izd. Vostochnoi Literatury, 1963) pp. 23–106

BASKHANOV, M. K.: *Russkie voennye vostokovedy do 1917 goda: Biobibliograficheskii slovar'* (Moscow: Izd. Firma Vostochnaya Literatura RAN, 2005)

BASKHANOV, M. K.: *'U vorot angliiskogo mogushchestva': A. E. Snesarev v Turkestane 1899–1904* (St Pb.: Nestor-Istoriya, 2015)

BASKHANOV, M. K., KOLESNIKOV, A. A. & MATVEEVA, M. A. (ed.): *Dervish Gindukusha: Putevye dnevniki tsentral'no-aziatskikh ekspeditsii Generala B. L. Grombchevskogo* (St Pb.: Nestor-Istoriya, 2015)

BEISEMBIEV, Timur: *Tarikh-i Shakhrukhi kak istoricheskii istochnik* (Alma-Ata: Nauka, 1987)

BEISEMBIEV, Timur: 'Vysshaya Administratsiya Tashkenta i yuga Kazakhstana v period Kokandskogo Khanstva: 1809–1865 gg.' in *Istoriko-kul'turnye vzaimos-vyazi Irana i Dasht-i Kipchaka v XIII–XVIII vv.* (Almaty: Daik-Press, 2004) pp. 291–313

BEISEMBIEV, Timur: *Kokandskaya istoriografiya: Issledovanie po istochnikove-deniiu Srednei Azii XVIII–XIX vekov* (Almaty, TOO Print-S, 2009)

BEKMAKHANOV, Erumzhan Bekmakhanovich: *Kazakhstan v 20–40 gody XIX veka* (Alma-Ata: Kazakhskoe Ob"edinennoe Gosudarstvennoe Izd., 1947)

BOBROVNIKOV, V. O.: *Musul'mane Severnogo Kavkaza: nasilie* (Moscow: Vostochnaya Literatura, 2002)

BOBROVNIKOV, V. O.: 'Pochemu my marginaly? Zametki na poliakh russkogo perevoda "Orientalizma" Edwarda Saida', *AI* (2008) No. 2, pp. 325–44

BREGEL, Iurii: 'Sochinenie Bayani "Shadzhara-ii khorezmshakhi" kak istochnik po istorii Turkmen', *Kratkie soobshcheniya instituta narodov Azii* Vyp. 44 (1961) pp. 125–57

BREZHNEVA, S. N.: *Prisoedinenie Turkestana k Rossii: diskussionye problemy dorevoliutsionnoi i sovetskoi istoriografii* (Tol'yatti: Tol'yattinskaya Gosudarstvennaya Akademiya Servisa, 2004)

BUKETOVA, E. A.: *Vernenskie istorii* (Almaty: Elnur, 2011)

CHEKHOVICH, O. D.: 'O nekotorykh voprosakh istorii Srednei Azii XVIII–XIX vekov', *Voprosy Istorii* (1956) No. 3, pp. 84–95

DEMIDOVA, E. Iu., MORRISON A. S. & SABITOV A. R.: 'Rossiiskie ukreplen-nye poseleniya Raim i Vernyi: Graficheskaya rekonstruktsiya', *Vestnik TiumGASU* (2015) No. 3, pp. 73–9

DZHAMGERCHINOV, B.: *Prisoedinenie Kirgizii k Rossii* (Moscow: Izd. Sotsial'no-ekonomicheskoi Literatury, 1959)

EPIFANOVA, L. M.: *Rukopisnye istochniki po istorii Srednei Azii perioda prisoe-dineniya ee k Rossii* (Tashkent: Nauka, 1965)

EROFEEVA, I. V.: *Khan Abulkhair: Polkovodets, pravitel', politik* (Almaty: Daik-Press, 2007)

FON KIUGELGEN, Anke: *Legitimatsiya sredneaziatskoi dinastii Mangitov v proizvedeniyakh ikh istorikov (XVII–XIX vv.)* (Almaty: Daik-Press, 2004)

GALIEV, B. Z.: 'Prodvizhenie rossiiskikh voisk po territorii iuzhnogo Kazakhstana', in *Istoriya kolonizatsii Kazakhstana v 20–60x godakh XIX veka* ed. B. Z. Galiev & S. F. Mazhitov (Almaty: Mektep, 2009) pp. 111–130

GLUSHCHENKO, E. A.: *Rossiya v Srednei Azii: Zavoevaniya i preobrazovaniya* (Moscow: Tsentropoligraf, 2010)

HODIZODA, Rasul: *Akhmad Danish: Ego biografiya i literaturnoe nasledstvie* (Dushanbe: Irfon, 1976)

IL'YASOV, A.: *Prisoedinenie Turkmenii k Rossii* (Ashkhabad: Ilim, 1972)

ISKANDAROV, B. I.: *Iz istorii Bukharskogo emirata: Vostochnaya Bukhara i zapadnyi Pamir v kontse XIX veka* (Moscow: Izd. Vostochnoi Literatury, 1958)

ISKANDAROV, B. I.: *Vostochnaya Bukhara i Pamir v period prisoedineniya Srednei Azii k Rossii* (Stalinabad: Tadzhikskoe Gosudarstvennoe Izd., 1960)

ISKANDAROV, B. I.: *Vostochnaya Bukhara i Pamir vo vtoroi polovine XIX v.* (Dushanbe: AN Tadzhikskoi SSR, 1962–3)

IVANOV, P. P.: *Vosstanie Kitai-Kipchakov v Bukharskom Khanstve 1821–1825 gg.: Istochniki i opyt ikh issledovaniya.* Trudy Instituta Vostokovedeniya XXVII (Moscow & Leningrad: Izd. AN SSSR, 1937)

IVANOV, P. P.: *Arkhiv khivinskikh khanov XIX v.: Issledovanie i opisanie dokumentov s istoricheskim vvedeniem* (Leningrad: Izd. Gosudarstvennoi Publichnoi Biblioteki, 1940)

IVANOV, S. M., D'YAKOV, N. N. & SULTANOV, T. I. (eds.): *Rossiya, Zapad i Musul'manskii Vostok v kolonial'nuiu epokhu* (St Pb.: Izd. Dmitrii Bulanin, 1996)

IVANOV, V. A.: 'Rossiya i Turkestan v kontekste Bol'shoi Igry', in *Rossiya– Srednyaya Aziya.* Vol. I (Moscow: URSS, 2011) pp. 96–123

KAREEVA, N. D.: 'Moi prapraded dal Rossii "Kryshu mira"', *Rodina* (2015) No. 8, pp. 84–5

KASTEL'SKAYA, Z. D.: *Iz istorii Turkestanskogo kraya* (Moscow: Nauka, 1980)

KHALFIN, N. A.: 'Vosstanie Iskhak-khana v iuzhnom Turkestane i pozitsiya russkogo tsarizma (1888 g.)', in *Trudy Sredneaziyatskogo Gosudarstvennogo Universiteta im. V. I. Lenina: Istoriya stran vostoka.* Novaya Seriya, Vyp. LXVIII, Vostokovedcheskie Nauki, Kn. 9 (Tashkent: Izd. SAGU, 1955) pp. 107–26

KHALFIN, N. A.: *Politika Rossii v Srednei Azii (1857–1868)* (Moscow: Izd. Vostochnoi Literatury, 1960)

KHALFIN, N. A.: *Prisoedinenie Srednei Azii k Rossii* (Moscow: Nauka, 1965)

KHALFIN, N. A.: 'Drama v nomerakh "Parizh"', *Voprosy Istorii* (1966) No. 10, pp. 216–20

KHALFIN, N. A.: *Rossiya i khanstva Srednei Azii* (Moscow: Nauka, 1974)

KHALFIN, N. A.: *Rossiya i Bukharskii Emirat na Zapadnom Pamire* (Moscow: Nauka, 1975)

KHALILOV, S.: 'Iz istorii kanala Ulughnakhr', in *Iz istorii Srednei Azii (dorevoliutsionnyi period): Sbornik statei* (Tashkent: Nauka, 1965) pp. 37–44

KHARIUKOV, L. N.: *Anglo-russkoe sopernichestvo v Tsentral'noi Azii i Ismailizm* (Moscow: Izd. Moskovskogo Universiteta, 1995)

KHIDOYATOV, G. A.: *Iz istorii anglo-russkikh otnoshenii v Srednei Azii v kontse XIX veka* (Tashkent: FAN, 1969)

KHIDOYATOV, G. A.: *Britanskoe ekspansiya v Srednei Azii* (Tashkent: FAN, 1981)

KHUDONAZAROV, D.: 'Pervyi russkii pravitel' Pamira (pamyati Eduarda Karlovicha Kivekesa)', in *Pamirskaya ekspeditsiya* (Moscow: IV RAN, 2006) pp. 219–32

KHUDONAZAROV, D.: *Pamirskie ekspeditsii Grafa A. A. Bobrinskogo 1895–1901 godov: Etnograficheskii al'bom* (Moscow: Nauka, 2013)

KINYAPINA, N. S., BLIEV, M. M. & DEGOEV, V. V.: *Kavkaz i Srednyaya Aziya vo vneshnei politike Rossii* (Moscow: Izd. MGU, 1984)

KOLESNIKOV, A.: *Russkie v Kashgarii: Missii, ekspeditsii, puteshestviya* (Bishkek: Raritet, 2006)

KOTIUKOVA, T. V.: 'Ya dal bukhartsam znat', chto podrobnogo nasiliya ne dopushchu . . .', *Voenno-istoricheskii Zhurnal* (2008) No. 9, pp. 61–5

KOTIUKOVA, T. V. (ed.): *Polveka v Turkestane. V. P. Nalivkin: Biografiya, dokumenty, trudy* (Moscow: Izd. Mardzhani, 2015)

KOZYBAEV, M. K. (ed.): *Istoriya Kazakhstana s drevneishikh vremen do nashikh dnei.* Vol. III. *Kazakhstan v Novoe Vremya* (Almaty: Atamura, 2010)

KUZNETSOVA, A.: 'M. I. Veniukov i Imperskie proekty Rossii v Srednei Azii', *Vestnik Evrazii* Vol. 4 (2002) No. 19, pp. 72–84

LARIN, Andrei: 'Yan Vitkevich: Raporty iz Afganistana', in *Istoriya i istoriografiya zarubezhnogo mira v litsakh* ed. V. V. Kutyavin. Vyp. IX (Samara: Izd. 'Samarskii Universitet', 2009) pp. 171–95

LAVRENOVA, A. M. & CHERNICHENKO M. O.: '"Avgusteishii bol'noi", zhandarmy i psikhiatry: "Krymskie kanikuly" velikogo knyazya Nikolaya Konstantinovicha (1901–1904 gody)', *Novyi Istoricheskii Vestnik* Vol. 51 (2017) pp. 116–51

LEVTEEVA, L. G.: *Prisoedinenie Srednei Azii k Rossii v memuarnykh istochnikakh* (Tashkent: FAN, 1986)

LITVINOV, P. P.: *Gosudarstvo i Islam v Russkom Turkestane (1865–1917) (po arkhivnym materialam)* (Elets: Eletskii Gosudarstvennyi Pedagogicheskii Institut, 1998)

LUNIN, B. V.: *Istoriya Uzbekistana v istochnikakh* (Tashkent: FAN, 1990)

LUZHETSKAYA, N. L.: 'Materialy k istorii razgranicheniya na Pamire v Arkhive vostokovedov SPbF IV RAN (fond A. E. Snesareva): "Otchet General'nogo Shtaba Kapitana Vannovskogo po rekognostsirovke v Rushane" (1893 g.)', *PPV* Vol. 2 (2005) No. 3, pp. 134–52

LUZHETSKAYA, N. L.: 'Otchet Nachal'nika Pamirskogo otryada Kapitana V. N. Zaitseva 1893–1894', *PPV* Vol. 1/8 (2008) No. 11, pp. 154–64

LUZHETSKAYA, N. L.: 'Materialy Arkhiva vostokovedov IVR RAN o dvizhenii letuchego otryada Polkovnika Ionova na r. Bartang v Rushane: 1893 g.', *PPV* Vol. 1 (2010) No. 12, pp. 223–36

MAHMUDOV, Oybek: '"Po Pamiram . . . na angel'skikh vysotakh . . .": Andrei Evgen'evich Snesarev o Pamire i pamirtsakh' (unpublished paper, cited with the kind permission of the author)

MAHMUDOV, Oybek: 'Skvoz dzhungli instruktsii po "Kryshe Mira": Politika Rossi i Pamirskaya okraina imperii glazami russkogo kolonial'nogo chinovnika' (unpublished paper, cited with the kind permission of the author)

MAHMUDOV, Oybek: '"Odichalye frantsuzy" Pamira: Naselenie Pamira pripamirskikh vladenii glazami russkikh voennykh i issledovatelei', *CIAS Discussion Paper* No. 35 (Kyoto, 2013) pp. 47–71

MAHMUDOV, Oybek: 'Pamir i pamirtsy v trudakh russkikh puteshestvennikov i issledovatelei poslednei treti XIX–nachala XX veka (po materialam turkestanskogo sbornika)', in *Rossiisko-uzbekistanskie svyazi v kontekste mnogovekovoi istoricheskoi retrospektivy* (Tashkent: n.p., 2013) pp. 324–39

MAHMUDOV, Oybek: 'I. D. Yagello na Pamire: Maloizvestnye stranitsy deyatel'-nosti Nachal'nika Pamirskogo otryada (po arkhivnym materialam)', *O'zbekiston Tarixi* (2015) No. 3, 64–71

MASSON, M. E *et al.* (ed.): *Istoriya Turkmenskoi SSR* (Ashkhabad: Izd. AN Turkmenskoi SSR, 1957)

MATSUZATO, Kimitaka: 'General-Gubernatorstva v Rossiiskoi Imperii', in *Novaya imperskaya istoriya postsovetskogo prostranstva* (Kazan': Tsentr Issledovanii Natsionalizma i Imperii, 2004) pp. 427–58

MAVRODIN, V. V.: *Iz istorii otechestvennogo oruzhiya: Russkaya Vintovka* (Leningrad: Izd. Leningradskogo Universiteta, 1981)

MIKHALEVA, G. A.: *Torgovye i posol'skie svyazi Rossii so sredneaziatskimi khanstvami cherez Orenburg* (Tashkent: FAN, 1982)

MIRZAEVA, L.: *Sbornik 'Turkestanskii Krai A. G. Serebrennikova i ego znachenie dlya sredneaziatskoi istoriografii'*. Avtoreferat dissertatsii v soiskanii uchenoi stepeni kandidata istoricheskikh nauk (Tashkent: Izd. AN Uzbekskoi SSR, 1963)

MOGIL'NER, Marina *Homo Imperii: Istoriya fizicheskoi antropologii v Rossii* (Moscow: Novoe Literaturnoe Obozrenie, 2008)

MOISEEV, S. V.: 'Diplomaticheskaya i nauchnaya missiya A. N. Kuropatkina v Kashgariiu v 1876–1877 gg.', in *Vostokovednye issledovanie na Altae* ed. S. Moiseev. Vol. II (Barnaul: n.p., 2000) pp. 95–104

MOISEEV, S. V.: *Rossiya i Kitai v Tsentral'noi Azii (vtoraya polovina XIX v.–1917 g.)* (Barnaul: AzBuka, 2003)

MOISEEV, S. V.: *Vzaimootnosheniya Rossii i uigurskogo gosudarstva Iettishar, 1864–1877 gg.* (Barnaul: AzBuka, 2006)

NABIEV, R. N.: *Iz istoriya Kokandskogo Khanstva (feodal'noe Khozyaistvo Khudoyar-Khana)* (Tashkent: Izd. FAN Uzbekskoi SSR, 1973)

NORBUTAEV, Yadgor: 'Sekrety "Turkestanskikh Generalov": i Uch-Kuduk, i Kinderli', *fergana.ru* 09/08/2016 (www.fergananews.com/articles/9053)

PIRUMSHOEV, Khaidarsho: *Rossiisko-sredneaziatskie otnosheniya XVI–serediny XIX vekov v russkoi istoriografii* (Dushanbe: MAORIF, 2000)

PLENTSOV, Aleksei: *Delo pod Ikanom: Sotnya protiv desyati tysyach* (St Pb.: Istoriko-kul'turnyi Tsentr Karel'skogo Peresheika, 2014)

PLOSKIKH, V. M.: *Kirgizy i Kokandskoe Khanstvo* (Frunze: Izd. ILIM, 1977)

POKROVSKII, M. N.: *Diplomatiya i voiny tsarskoi Rossii v XIX stoletii: Sbornik statei* (Moscow: Izd. Krasnaya Nov', 1923)

POPOV, A. L.: 'Bor'ba za sredneaziatskii platsdarm', *IZ* (1940) No. 7, 182–235

POSTNIKOV, A. V.: '"Istoricheskie prava" sosednikh gosudarstv i geografiya Pamira kak argumenty v "Bol'shoi Igre" Britanii i Rossii (1869–1896 gg.)', *Acta Slavica Iaponica* Vol. 17 (2000) pp. 33–99

POSTNIKOV, A. V.: *Skhvatka na "Kryshe Mire": Politiki, razvedchiki i geografy v bor'be za Pamir v XIX veke* (Moscow: Pamyatniki Istoricheskoi Mysli, 2001)

POSTNIKOV, A. V.: *Stanovlenie rubezhei Rossii v Tsentral'noi i Srednei Azii (XVIII–XIX vv.)* (Moscow: Pamyatniki Istoricheskoi Mysli, 2007)

PRAVILOVA, Ekaterina: *Finansy Imperii: Den'gi i vlast' v politike Rossii na natsional'nykh okrainakh* (Moscow: Novoe Izd., 2006)

REMNEV, A. V.: "'Omskii pasha" – general-gubernator knyaz' P. D. Gorchakov', *Izvestiya Omskogo Gosudarstvennogo Istoriko-kraevedcheskogo Muzeya* (2008) No. 14, 179–96

REMNEV, A. V.: 'U istokov Rossiiskoi Imperskoi geopolitiki: Aziyatskie pogranichnye prostranstva v issledovaniyakh M. I. Venyukova', *IZ* Vol. 4 (2001) No. 122, pp. 344–69

ROZHKOVA, M. K.: *Ekonomicheskiya politika tsarskogo pravitelstva na srednem vostoke vo vtoroi chetverti XIX veka i russkaya burzhuaziya* (Moscow & Leningrad: Izd. AN SSSR, 1949)

ROZHKOVA, M. K.: *Ekonomicheskie svyazi Rossii so Srednei Azii 40–60e gody XIX veka* (Moscow: Izd. AN SSSR, 1963)

RUDNITSKII, A. Iu.: *Etot groznyi Grombchevskii . . . Bol'shaya Igra na granitsakh imperii* (St Pb.: Aleteia, 2013)

SEMENOV, A. A.: *Ocherk ustroistva tsentral'nogo administrativnogo upravleniya Bukharskogo Khanstva pozdneishego vremeni* (Stalinabad: AN Tadzhikskoi SSR, 1954)

SERGEEV, E.: *Bol'shaya Igra: Mify i realii rossiisko-britanskikh otnoshenii v Tsentral'noi i Vostochnoi Azii* (Moscow: KMK, 2012)

SHAFRANSKAYA, E.: *Turkestanskii tekst v russkoi kul'ture: Kolonial'naya proza Nikolaya Karazina* (St Pb.: self-published, 2016)

SOKOLOV, Iu. A.: *Tashkent, tashkenttsy i Rossiya* (Tashkent: Izd. Uzbekistan, 1965)

TIKHOMIROV, M. N.: *Prisoedinenie Merva k Rossii* (Moscow: Izd. Vostochnoi Literatury, 1960),

TUKHTAMETOV, T. G.: *Rossiya i Khiva v kontse XIX–nachale XX veka* (Moscow: Nauka, 1969)

VASIL'EV, D. V.: 'Ustroitel' Turkestanskogo kraya (k biografii K. P. von Kaufmana)' in *SRIO* Vol. 5 (Moscow: Russkaya Panorama, 2002) pp. 45–57

VASIL'EV, D. V.: *Rossiya i Kazakhskaya step': Administrativnaya politika i status okrainy XVIII–pervaya polovina XIX veka* (Moscow: ROSSPEN, 2014)

VASIL'EV, D. V.: *Bremya Imperii: Administrativnaya politika Rossii v Tsentral'noi Azii: Vtoraya polovina XIX v.* (Moscow: ROSSPEN, 2018)

YAROSHEVSKAYA, A. M., KIRILLOVA, O. D. & LEUS, L. A. (ed.): *Istoriya Uzbekistana. Vol. III. XVI–pervaya polovina XIX veka* (Tashkent: FAN, 1993)

ZAIONCHKOVSKII, P.A.: 'K voprosu zavoevaniya Srednei Azii', in *Petr Andreevich Zaionchkovskii: Sbornik statei i vospominanii k stoletiiu istorika* ed. L. G. Zakharova *et al.* (Moscow: ROSSPEN, 2008) pp. 36–95

ZIYAEV, Kh. Z.: *Istoriya Uzbekskoi SSR*. Vol. II. *Ot prisoedineniya Uzbekskikh Khanstv k Rossii do Velikoi Oktyabrskoi Sotsialisticheskoi Revolyutsii* (Tashkent: FAN, 1967)

ZIYAEVA, D. Kh.: 'Khivinskoe khanstvo v period ustanovleniya protektorata Rossiiskoi Imperii', in *Khorezm v istorii gosudarstvennosti Uzbekistana* ed. D. A. Alimova & E. V. Rteveladze (Tashkent: Uzbekistan Failasuflari Milliy Jamiyati, 2013) pp. 233–45

Secondary Works in Other Languages

ABASHIN, Sergei: 'Le culte d'Iskandar Zu-l-Qarnayn chez les montagnards d'Asie centrale', *CAC* Vol. 11 (2004) No. 12, pp. 61–86

ABASHIN, Sergei: 'The 'Fierce Fight' at Oshoba: A Microhistory of the Conquest of the Khoqand Khanate', *CAS* Vol. 33 (2014) No. 2, pp. 215–31

ADHAMI, Siamak: 'Toward a Biography of Ahmad Danesh' (Ph.D. Dissertation, University of California, Los Angeles, 2006)

AFINOGENOV, Gregory: 'Languages of Hegemony on the Eighteenth-Century Kazakh Steppe', *The International History Review* Vol. 41 (2018) No. 5, pp. 1020–38

AKIYAMA, Tetsu: 'Why Was Russian Direct Rule over Kyrgyz Nomads Dependent on Tribal Chieftains "manaps"?', *CMR* Vol. 56 (2015) No. 4, 625–49

AKIYAMA, Tetsu: 'From Collaborator to a Symbol of Revolt against Russia: Socio-political Conditions after the Death of a Kirghiz Chieftain at the Beginning of the Twentieth Century', *Journal of Islamic Area Studies* Vol. 11 (2019) pp. 47–59

ALDER, G. J.: *British India's Northern Frontier 1865–95; a Study in Imperial Policy* (London: Longmans, 1963)

ALDER, G. J.: 'He Fell among Thieves', *Journal of the Royal Central Asian Society* Vol. 52 (1965) No. 1, 42–8

ALDER, G. J.: 'The Key to India?: Britain and the Herat problem 1830–1863 – part 1', *Middle Eastern Studies* Vol. 10 (1974) No. 2, pp. 287–311

ALEXANDER, John T.: *Autocratic Politics in a National Crisis: The Imperial Russian Government and Pugachev's Revolt, 1773–1775* (Bloomington, IN: Indiana University Press, 1969)

ALLSEN, Thomas 'The Circulation of Military Technology in the Mongolian Empire', in *Warfare in Inner Asian History* ed. Nicola Di Cosmo (Leiden: Brill, 2002) pp. 265–93

AMANAT, Abbas: 'Central Asia viii: Relations with Persia in the 19th Century', in *Encyclopædia Iranica*, Vol. V, No. 2, pp. 205–7

ANDERSON, M. S.: *The Eastern Question 1774–1923: A Study in International Relations* (London: Macmillan, 1966)

ANDREEVA, Elena: *Russia and Iran in the Great Game: Travelogues and Orientalism* (Abingdon: Routledge, 2007)

ATKIN, Muriel: *Russia and Iran, 1780-1828* (Minneapolis, MN: University of Minnesota Press, 1980)

AVRUTIN, Eugene M.: 'Racial Categories and the Politics of (Jewish) Difference in Late Imperial Russia', *Kritika* Vol. 8 (2007) No. 1, pp. 13–40

BABADJANOV, Bakhtiyar: 'Russian Colonial Power in Central Asia as Seen by Local Muslim Intellectuals', in *Looking at the Coloniser: Cross-Cultural Perceptions in Central Asia and the Caucasus, Bengal, and Related Areas* ed Beate Eschment & Hans Harder (Würzburg: Ergon Verlag, 2004) pp. 75–90

BABAJANOV, Bakhtiyar: 'How Will We Appear in the Eyes of *inovertsy* and *inorodtsy*? Nikolai Ostroumov on the Image and Function of Russian Power' *CAS* Vol. 33 (2014) No. 2, pp. 270–88

BAROOSHIAN, Vahan D.: *V. V. Vereshchagin, Artist at War* (Gainesville, FL: University Press of Florida, 1993)

BARRETT, Thomas M.: 'Lines of Uncertainty: The Frontiers of the Northern Caucasus', in *Imperial Russia: New Histories for the Empire* ed. Jane Burbank and David L. Ransel (Bloomington, IN: Indiana University Press, 1998) pp. 148–73

BASKHANOV, M. K.: 'Bronislav Liudvigovich Grombchevskii (1855–1926)', in *The Quest for Forbidden Lands: Nikolai Przheval'skii and His Followers on Inner Asian Tracks* ed. Alexandre Andreyev, Mikhail Baskhanov & Tatiana Yusupova (Leiden: Brill, 2018) pp. 255–310

BASSIN, Mark: *Imperial Visions: Nationalist Imagination and Geographical Expansion in the Russian Far East, 1840-1865* (Cambridge: Cambridge University Press, 1999)

BATTIS, Matthias: 'Soviet Orientalism and Nationalism in Central Asia: Aleksandr Semenov's Vision of Tajik National Identity', *IS* Vol. 48 (2015) No. 2, pp. 729–45

BATTIS, Matthias: 'Aleksandr A. Semenov (1873–1958) and His Vision of Tajik Identity – on the Origins of Soviet Nationalities Policy in Late Imperial Russian Oriental Studies' (D.Phil. Thesis, University of Oxford, 2016)

BAUMANN, Robert F.: *Russian–Soviet Unconventional Wars in the Caucasus, Central Asia, and Afghanistan* (Fort Leavenworth, KS: Combat Studies Institute, 1993)

BAYLY, C. A.: *Imperial Meridian: The British Empire and the World, 1780-1830* (London: Longmans, 1989)

BAYLY, C. A.: *Empire and Information: Intelligence-Gathering and Social Communication in India, 1780-1870* (Cambridge: Cambridge University Press, 1996)

BAYLY, C. A.: *The Birth of the Modern World 1780-1914* (Oxford: Blackwell, 2004)

BEBEN, Daniel: 'Local Narratives of the Great Game in Badakhshan' (unpublished paper, cited with the kind permission of the author)

BEBEN, Daniel: 'The Legendary Biographies of Nasir-i Khusraw: Memory and Textualisation in Early Modern Persian Ismailism' (Ph.D. Dissertation, Indiana University, Bloomington, 2015)

BEBEN, Daniel (ed.): *The Memoirs of Aga Khan I: Text Edition and English Translation of the Tārīkh-i 'ibrat-afzā of Ḥasan 'Alī Shāh Āqā Khān Mahallātī* (London: I.B. Tauris, 2018)

BEBEN, Daniel: 'Religious and Ethnic Identity in the Pamirs: The Ismā'īlī Da'wa in Shughnan in the 17th to 19th Centuries', in *Revisiting Pamiri Identity in Central Asia and Beyond* ed. Carole Faucher and Dagikhudo Dagiev (London: Routledge, 2019) pp. 123–42

BECKER, Seymour: *Russia's Protectorates in Central Asia, Bukhara and Khiva* (Cambridge, MA: Harvard University Press, 1968)

BECKER, Seymour: 'Russia's Central Asian Empire, 1885–1917', in *Russian Colonial Expansion to 1917* ed. Michael Rywkin (London: Mansell Publishing, 1988) pp. 235–56

BECKERT, Sven: *Empire of Cotton: A New History of Global Capitalism* (London: Allen Lane, 2014)

BECKERT, Sven: 'Emancipation and Empire: Reconstructing the Worldwide Web of Cotton Production in the Age of the American Civil War', *AHR* Vol. 109 (2004) No. 5, pp. 1405–38

BEISEMBIEV, Timur: 'Farghana's Contacts with India in the 18th & 19th Centuries (According to the Kokand Chronicles)', *JAH* Vol. 28 (1994) pp. 124–35

BEISEMBIEV, Timur: *Annotated Indices to the Kokand Chronicles* (Tokyo: ILCAA, 2008)

BELICH, James: *The New Zealand Wars and the Victorian Interpretation of Racial Conflict* (Auckland: Auckland University Press, 1986)

BENNETT, Huw, FINCH, Michael, MAMOLEA, Andrei & OWEN-MORGAN, David: 'Studying Mars and Clio: Or How Not to Write about the Ethics of Military Conduct and Military History', *History Workshop Journal* Vol. 88 (2019) pp. 274–80

BERGNE, Paul: *The Birth of Tajikistan: National Identity and the Origins of the Republic* (London: I.B. Tauris, 2007)

BERLIN, Isaiah: 'The Hedgehog and the Fox: An Essay on Tolstoy's View of History', in *Russian Thinkers* ed. Henry Hardy & Aileen Kelly (London: Penguin, 2013) pp. 24–92

BEZHAN, Farid Ullah: 'The Enigmatic Authorship of "*Tārikh-i Badakhshān*"', *East and West* Vol. 58 (2008) Nos. 1–4, pp. 107–21

BIRSTEIN, Vadim J.: 'Threatened Fishes of the World: *Pseudoscaphirhynchus spp. (Acipenseridae)*', *Environmental Biology of Fishes* Vol. 48 (1997) 381–3

BITIS, Alexander: *Russia and the Eastern Question: Army, Government and Society 1815–1833* (Oxford: Oxford University Press, 2006)

BODGER, Alan: 'Abulkhair, Khan of the Kazakh Little Horde, and His Oath of Allegiance to Russia of October 1731', *SEER* Vol. 58 (1980) No. 1, 40–57

BODGER, Alan: *The Kazakhs and the Pugachev Uprising in Russia, 1773–1775* (Bloomington, IN: Research Unit for Inner Asian Studies, Indiana University, 1988)

BRADLEY, Joseph: *Guns for the Tsar: American Technology and the Small Arms Industry in Nineteenth-Century Russia* (DeKalb, IL: Northern Illinois University Press, 1990)

BREGEL, Yuri: *Bibliography of Islamic Central Asia* (Bloomington, IN: Indiana University Press, 1995) 3 volumes

BREGEL, Yuri: *Notes on the Study of Central Asia.* Papers on Inner Asia No. 28 (Bloomington, IN: Indiana University Research Institute for Inner Asian Studies, 1996)

BREGEL, Yuri: *The Administration of Bukhara under the Manghits and Some Tashkent Manuscripts.* Papers on Inner Asia No. 34 (Bloomington, IN: Indiana University Research Institute for Inner Asian Studies, 2000)

BREGEL, Yuri: 'The New Uzbek States: Bukhara, Khiva and Khoqand *c.* 1750–1886', in *The Cambridge History of Inner Asia: The Chinggisid Age* ed. Nicola di Cosmo, Allen J. Frank & Peter B. Golden (Cambridge: Cambridge University Press, 2009) pp. 392–411

BROPHY, David: *Uyghur Nation: Reform and Revolution on the Russia–China Frontier* (Cambridge, MA: Harvard University Press, 2016)

BROWER, Benjamin Claude: *A Desert Named Peace: The Violence of France's Empire in the Algerian Sahara 1844–1902* (New York, NY: Columbia University Press, 2009)

BROWER, Daniel & LAZZERINI, Edward (eds.): *Russia's Orient. Imperial Borderlands and Peoples 1700–1917* (Bloomington, IN: Indiana University Press, 1997)

BROWER, Daniel: *Turkestan and the Fate of the Russian Empire* (London & New York, NY: RoutledgeCurzon, 2003)

BULLIET, Richard W.: *The Camel and the Wheel* (Cambridge, MA: Harvard University Press, 1975)

BURTON, Audrey: 'Itinéraires commerciaux et militaires entre Boukhara et l'Inde', in *CAC.* Vols. 1–2. *Asie Centrale–l'Inde: Routes du commerce et des idées* (Tashkent & Aix-en-Provence: IFEAC, Éditions De Boccard, 1996) pp. 13–35

BURTON, Audrey: *The Bukharans, a Dynastic, Diplomatic and Commercial History 1550–1702* (London: Curzon, 1997)

BUTTINO, Marco: 'Study of the Economic Crisis and Depopulation in Turkestan, 1917–1920', *CAS* Vol. 9 (1990) No. 4, pp. 59–74

CAIN, P. J. & HOPKINS, A. G.: *British Imperialism: Innovation and Expansion 1688–1914* (London: Longmans, 1990)

CAMPBELL, Ian W.: '"Our Friendly Rivals": Rethinking the Great Game in Ya'qub Beg's Kashgaria, 1867–77', *CAS* Vol. 33 (2014) No. 2, 199–214

CAMPBELL, Ian W.: *Knowledge and the Ends of Empire: Kazak Intermediaries and Russian Rule on the Steppe, 1731–1917* (Ithaca, NY: Cornell University Press, 2017)

CAMPBELL, Ian W.: 'Bloody Belonging: Writing Transcaspia into the Russian Empire', in *Empire and Belonging in the Eurasian Borderlands* ed.

Lewis Siegelbaum & Krista Goff (Ithaca, NY: Cornell University Press, 2019) pp. 35–47

CAMPBELL, Ian W.: 'Violent Acculturation: Alexei Kuropatkin, the Central Asian Revolt, and the Long Shadow of conquest', in *The Central Asian Revolt of 1916: A Collapsing Empire in the Age of War and Revolution* ed. Aminat Chokobaeva, Cloé Drieu & Alexander Morrison (Manchester: Manchester University Press, 2020) pp. 191–208

CARRÈRE D'ENCAUSSE, Hélène: 'Systematic Conquest, 1865 to 1884', in *Central Asia: A Century of Russian Rule* ed. Edward Allworth (New York, NY: Columbia University Press, 1967) pp. 131–50

CHOKOBAEVA, Aminat: 'When the Nomads Went to War: The Uprising of 1916 in Semirech'e', in *The Central Asian Revolt of 1916: A Collapsing Empire in the Age of War and Revolution* ed. Aminat Chokobaeva, Cloé Drieu & Alexander Morrison (Manchester: Manchester University Press, 2020) pp. 145–68

CLEMENT, Victoria: *Learning to Become Turkmen: Literacy, Language, and Power 1914–2014* (Pittsburgh, PA: Pittsburgh University Press, 2018)

COOPER, Randolf G. S.: *The Anglo-Maratha Campaigns and the Contest for India: The Struggle for Control of the South Asian Military Economy* (Cambridge: Cambridge University Press, 2003)

CREWS, Robert D.: *For Prophet & Tsar: Islam and Empire in Russia and Central Asia* (Cambridge, MA: Harvard University Press, 2006)

CURTISS, John Shelton: *The Russian Army under Nicholas I 1825–1855* (Durham, NC: Duke University Press, 1965)

DARWIN, John: *The Empire Project: The Rise and Fall of the British World-System 1830–1970* (Cambridge: Cambridge University Press, 2009)

DARWIN, John: 'Imperialism and the Victorians: The Dynamics of Territorial Expansion', *English Historical Review* Vol. CXII (1997) No. 447, pp. 614–42

DAVIES, Brian L.: *Warfare, State and Society on the Black Sea Steppe 1500–1700* (London: Routledge, 2007)

DAVIES, Brian L.: *The Russo-Turkish War, 1769–1774* (London: Bloomsbury, 2016)

DAVIES, Norman: *God's Playground: A History of Poland* Vol. II (Oxford: Oxford University Press, 1982)

DEUTSCHMANN, Moritz: '"All Rulers Are Brothers": Russian Relations with the Iranian Monarchy in the Nineteenth Century', *IS* Vol. 46 (2013) No. 3, pp. 383–413

DEUTSCHMANN, Moritz: *Iran and Russian Imperialism: The Ideal Anarchists 1800–1914* (London: Routledge, 2016)

DEWEESE, Devin: 'Review of Sneath *The Headless State*', *International Journal of Turkish Studies* Vol. 16 (2010) Nos. 1–2, pp. 142–51

DI COSMO, Nicola (ed.): *Warfare in Inner Asian History* (Leiden: Brill, 2002)

DIXON, Norman: *On the Psychology of Military Incompetence* (London: Jonathan Cape, 1976)

DUISHEMBIEVA, Jipar: 'Visions of Community: Literary Culture and Social Change among the Northern Kyrgyz, 1856–1924' (Ph.D. Thesis, University of Washington, Seattle, 2015)

DUMETT, Raymond (ed.): *Gentlemanly Capitalism and British Imperialism: The New Debate on Empire* (London: Longmans, 1999)

DURAND-GUÉDY, David: 'Review of Sneath *The Headless State*', *International Journal of Asian Studies*, Vol. 8 (2011) pp. 119–22

ECKSTEIN, A. M.: 'Is There a "Hobson–Lenin Thesis" on Late Nineteenth-Century Colonial Expansion?', *EcHR* Vol. 44 (1991) No. 2, pp. 297–318

EDEN, Jeff: *Slavery and Empire in Central Asia* (Cambridge: Cambridge University Press, 2018)

EDEN, Jeff: 'Beyond the Bazaars: Geographies of the Slave Trade in Central Asia', *Modern Asian Studies* Vol. 51 (2017) No. 4, pp. 919–55

EDGAR, Adrienne: *Tribal Nation: The Making of Soviet Turkmenistan* (Princeton, NJ: Princeton University Press, 2004)

ELNAZAROV, Hakim: 'Anglo-Russian Rivalry in the Pamirs and Hindukush, 1860–1914' (Ph.D. Thesis, King's College London, 2018)

EMERIT, Marcel: *L'Algérie à l'époque d'Abd-el-Kader* (Paris: Bouchene, 2002)

ENGELSTEIN, Laura: 'The Old Slavophile Steed: Failed Nationalism and the Philosophers' Jewish Problem', in *Slavophile Empire: Imperial Russia's Illiberal Path* (Ithaca, NY: Cornell University Press, 2009) pp. 192–203

ERKINOV, Aftandil: 'How Muhammad Rahim Khan II of Khiva (1864–1910) Cultivated His Court Library as a Means of Resistance against the Russian Empire', *Journal of Islamic Manuscripts* Vol. 2 (2011) pp. 36–49

ESDAILE, Charles: *Napoleon's Wars: An International History 1803–1815* (London: Allen Lane, 2007)

ETKIND, Alexander: *Internal Colonization: Russia's Imperial Experience* (Cambridge: Polity Press, 2001)

FERRET, Carole: 'Des chevaux pour l'empire', in *CAC*. Vols. 17–18. *Le Turkestan russe: Une colonie comme les autres?* ed. Svetlana Gorshenina and Sergej Abašin (Tashkent and Aix-en-Provence: IFEAC, Éditions De Boccard, 2009) pp. 211–53

FIELDING, Nick: *South to the Great Steppe: The Travels of Thomas and Lucy Atkinson in Eastern Kazakhstan, 1847–1852* (London: FIRST, 2015)

FIGES, Orlando: *Natasha's Dance: A Cultural History of Russia* (London: Allen Lane, 2002)

FISHER, Alan W.: *The Annexation of Crimea by the Russian Empire* (Cambridge: Cambridge University Press, 1970)

FISHER, Michael H.: *The Politics of the British Annexation of India 1757–1857* (Delhi: Oxford University Press, 1997)

FLETCHER, Joseph: 'Ch'ing Inner Asia c. 1800', in *The Cambridge History of China*. Vol. 10 (Cambridge: Cambridge University Press, 1978) pp. 58–90

FLETCHER, Joseph: 'Sino-Russian Relations 1800–62', in *The Cambridge History of China*. Vol. 10 (Cambridge: Cambridge University Press, 1978) pp. 318–32

FRANK, Allen J.: *Islamic Historiography and 'Bulghar' Identity among the Tatars and Bashkirs of Russia* (Leiden: Brill, 1998)

FRANK, Allen J.: *Muslim Religious Institutions in Imperial Russia: The Islamic World of Novouzensk District and the Kazakh Inner Horde 1780–1910* (Leiden: Brill, 2001)

FRANK, Allen J.: 'The Qazaqs and Russia', in *The Cambridge History of Inner Asia: The Chinggisid Age* ed. Nicola di Cosmo, Allen J. Frank & Peter B. Golden (Cambridge: Cambridge University Press, 2009) pp. 363–79

FRANK, Allen J.: 'Islam and Ethnic Relations in the Kazakh Inner Horde: Muslim Cossacks, Tatar Merchants and Kazakh Nomads in a Turkic Manuscript 1870–1910', in *Muslim Culture in Russia and Central Asia from the 18th to the Early 20th Centuries*. Vol. II. *Inter-regional & Inter-ethnic Relations* ed. Anke von Kügelgen, Michael Kemper & Allen J. Frank (Berlin: Klaus Schwarz Verlag, 1998) pp. 211–42

FRANKEL, Joseph: 'Towards a Decision-Making Model in Foreign Policy', *Political Studies* 7 (1959) No. 1, pp. 1–11

FULLER, William C.: *Strategy and Power in Russia 1600–1914* (Toronto: The Free Press, 1992)

GALBRAITH, John S. and **MARSOT**, Afaf Lutfi al-Sayyid: 'The British Occupation of Egypt: Another View', *IJMES* Vol. 9 (1978) No. 4, 471–88

GAMMER, Moshe: 'Russian Strategies in the Conquest of Chechnia and Daghestan 1825–1859', in *The North Caucasus Barrier: The Russian Advance towards the Muslim World* ed. Marie Bennigsen Broxup (London: Hurst & Co., 1992) pp. 45–61

GAMMER, Moshe: *Muslim Resistance to the Tsar: Shamil and the Conquest of Chechnya and Daghestan* (London: Frank Cass, 1994)

GAO, Yuan: 'Captivity and Empire: Russian Captivity Narratives in Fact and Fiction' (M.A. Thesis, Nazarbayev University, 2016) (http://nur.nu.edu.kz/han dle/123456789/1672)

GAUTHIER-PILTERS, Hilde & **DAGG**, Anne Innis: *The Camel: Its Evolution, Ecology, Behaviour and Relationship to Man* (Chicago, IL: University of Chicago Press, 1981)

GERASIMOV, Ilya, **KUSBER**, Jan & **SEMYONOV**, Alexander (eds.): *Empire Speaks Out: Languages of Rationalization and Self-Description in the Russian Empire* (Leiden & Boston: Brill, 2009)

GEYER, Dietrich: *Russian Imperialism: The Interaction of Domestic and Foreign Policy 1860–1914* trans. Bruce Little (Leamington Spa: Berg, 1987)

GOMMANS, Jos: 'The Horse Trade in 18th-Century South Asia', *JESHO* Vol. 37 (1994) No. 3, pp. 228–50

GORSHENINA, Svetlana: *Asie Centrale: L'invention des frontiers et l'heritage russo-soviétique* (Paris: CNRS Éditions, 2012)

GRASSI, Evelin: 'The Manuscripts of the Works by Ahmad Danish and His Popularity as a Precursor of the Bukharan Jadids', in *Iranian Languages and Literatures of Central Asia: From the 18th Century to the Present* ed. Matteo

De Chiara and Evelin Grassi. *Cahiers de Studia Iranica* Vol. 57 (2015) pp. 233–58

GREVEMEYER, Jan-Heeren: *Herrschaft, Raub und Gegenseitigkeit: Die politische Geschichte Badakhshans 1500–1883* (Wiesbaden: O. Harrassowitz, 1982)

GROSS, Jo-Ann: 'Historical Memory, Cultural Identity and Change: Mirza 'Abd al-'Aziz Sami's Representation of the Russian Conquest of Bukhara', in *Russia's Orient:Imperial Borderlands and Peoples 1700–1917* ed. Daniel Brower & Edward J. Lazzerini (Bloomington, IN: Indiana University Press, 1997) pp. 203–26

HAIJIT, Baymirza: 'Some Reflections on the Subject of the Annexation of Turkestani Kazakhstan by Russia', *CAS* Vol. 3 (1984) No. 4, pp. 61–76

HAPPEL, Jörn: *Nomadische Lebenswelten und zarische Politik: Der Aufstand in Zentralasien 1916* (Stuttgart: Franz Steiner, 2010)

HAUGEN, Arne: *The Establishment of National Republics in Soviet Central Asia* (Basingstoke: Palgrave Macmillan, 2003)

HARTLEY, Janet M.: *Russia 1762–1825: Military Power, the State and the People* (Westport, CN & London: Praeger, 2008)

HAULE, Sébastien: "'... us et coutumes adoptées dans nos guerres d'orient": L'expérience coloniale russe et l'expédition d'Alger', *CMR* Vol. 45 (2004) Nos. 1–2, pp. 293–320

HAUNER, Milan: *What Is Asia to Us? Russia's Asian Heartland Yesterday and Today* (London: Routledge, 1997)

HEADRICK, Daniel R.: *The Tools of Empire: Technology and European Imperialism in the Nineteenth Century* (Oxford: Oxford University Press, 1981)

HEVIA, James: *English Lessons: The Pedagogy of Imperialism in Nineteenth-Century China* (Durham, NC: Duke University Press, 2003)

HEVIA, James: *The Imperial Security State: British Colonial Knowledge and Empire-Building in Asia* (Cambridge: Cambridge University Press, 2012)

HEVIA, James: *Animal Labor and Colonial Warfare* (Chicago, IL: University of Chicago Press, 2018)

HIRSCH, Francine: *Empire of Nations: Ethnographic Knowledge and the Making of the Soviet Union* (Ithaca, NY: Cornell University Press, 2005).

HOFMEISTER, Ulrich: *Die Bürde des Weißen Zaren: Russische Vorstellungen einer imperialen Zivilisierungsmission in Zentralasien* (Stuttgart: Franz Steiner, 2019)

HOFMEISTER, Ulrich: 'Civilization and Russification in Tsarist Central Asia, 1860–1917', *JWH* Vol. 27 (2016) No. 3, pp. 411–42

HOJAGELDIÝEW, Nargylyç: *Gökdepe galasy: Gysgaça taryhy oçerk* (Ashgabat: 'Çäç' döredijilik-önümçilik birleşigi, 1991)

HOPKIRK, Peter: *The Great Game: On Secret Service in High Asia* (London: John Murray, 1990)

HOPKINS, Benjamin: *The Making of Modern Afghanistan* (Basingstoke: Palgrave Macmillan, 2008)

HOLZWARTH, Wolfgang: 'Relations between Uzbek Central Asia, the Great Steppe and Iran, 1700–1750', in *Shifts and Drifts in Nomad–Sedentary*

Relations ed.Stefan Leder & Bernard Streck (Wiesbaden: Dr Ludwig Reichert Verlag, 2005) pp. 179–216

HOLZWARTH, Wolfgang: 'The Uzbek State as Reflected in Eighteenth Century Bukharan Sources', *AS* Vol. LX (2006) No. 2, pp. 321–53

HOLZWARTH, Wolfgang: 'Bukharan Armies and Uzbek Military Power, 1670–1870: Coping with the Legacy of a Nomadic Conquest', in *Nomad Military Power in Iran and Adjacent Areas in the Islamic Period* ed. Kurt Franz & Wolfgang Holzwarth (Wiesbaden: Ludwig Reichert Verlag, 2015) pp. 273–354

HOPKINS, A. G.: 'The Victorians and Africa: A Reconsideration of the Occupation of Egypt, 1882', *Journal of African History* Vol. 27 (1986) No. 2, 363–91

HOPKINS, Benjamin: 'The Bounds of Identity: The Goldsmid Mission and the Delineation of the Perso-Afghan Border in the Nineteenth Century', *JGH* Vol. 2 (2007) pp. 233–54

HOPKINS, Benjamin: *The Making of Modern Afghanistan* (Basingstoke: Palgrave Macmillan, 2008)

HORÁK, Slavomír: 'The Battle of Gökdepe in the Turkmen Post-Soviet Historical Discourse', *CAS* Vol. 34 (2015) No. 2, pp. 149–61

HOSKING, Geoffrey: *Russia, People and Empire 1552–1917* (London: HarperCollins, 1997)

HULL, Isabel *Absolute Destruction: Military Culture and the Practices of War in Imperial Germany* (Ithaca, NY: Cornell University Press, 2006)

HUZZEY, Richard Huzzey: *Freedom Burning: Anti-slavery and Empire in Victorian Britain* (Ithaca, NY: Cornell University Press, 2012)

HSÜ, Immanuel C. Y.: *The Ili Crisis: A Study of Sino-Russian Diplomacy 1871–1881* (Oxford: Clarendon Press, 1965)

INGLE, Harold N.: *Nesselrode and the Russian Rapprochement with Britain, 1836–1844* (Berkeley, CA: University of California Press, 1976)

INGRAM, Edward: *In Defence of British India: Great Britain in the Middle East, 1775–1842* (London: Frank Cass, 1984)

INGRAM, Edward: *The Beginning of the Great Game in Asia, 1828–1834* (Oxford: Clarendon Press, 1979)

IRONS, William: *The Yomut Turkmen: A Study of Social Organization among a Central Asian Turkic-Speaking Population* (Ann Arbor, MI: University of Michigan Anthropological Papers, 1975)

JACQUESSON, Svetlana: *Pastoréalismes: Anthropologie historique des processus d'intégration chez les Kirghiz du Tian Shan intérieur* (Wiesbaden: Ludwig Reichert Verlag, 2010)

JAMISON, Matthew: 'Weakness, Expansion and "Disobedience": The Beginnings of Russian Expansion into the Heart of Central Asia, 1864–1865' (D.Phil. Thesis, University of Oxford, 2007)

JOHNSON, Rob: '"Russians at the Gates of India": Planning the Strategic Defence of India, 1884–1899', *JMH* Vol. 67 (2003) pp. 697–743

JOHNSON, Rob: *Spying for Empire: The Great Game in Central and South Asia 1757–1947* (London: Greenhill, 2006)

JOHNSON, Rob: *The Afghan Way of War* (London: Hurst, 2011)

JOLL, James: *1914: The Unspoken Assumptions: An Inaugural Lecture Delivered 25 April 1968* (London: Weidenfeld & Nicholson, 1968)

JONES, David R. (ed.): *Military–Naval Encyclopaedia of Russia and the Soviet Union* (Gulf Breeze, FL: Academic International press, 1978) 8 volumes

JONES, S. F.: 'Marxism and Peasant Revolt in the Russian Empire: The Case of the Gurian Republic', *SEER* Vol. 67 (1989) No. 3, pp. 403–34

KALBANOVA, E. E.: 'Les Cosaques de l'Oural au Karakalpakistan', in *CAC*. Vol. 10. *Karakalpaks et autres gens de l'Aral: Entre rivages et déserts* (Tashkent & Aix-en-Provence: IFEAC, Éditions De Boccard, 2002)

KALINOVSKY, Artemy: *A Long Goodbye: The Soviet Withdrawal from Afghanistan* (Cambridge, MA: Harvard University Press, 2011)

KAMP, Marianne: *The New Woman in Uzbekistan: Islam, Modernity and Unveiling under Communism* (Seattle, WA: University of Washington Press, 2006)

KANYA-FORSTNER, A. S.: *The Conquest of the Western Sudan: A Study in French Military Imperialism* (Cambridge: Cambridge University Press, 1969)

KAPPELER, Andreas: *The Russian Empire: A Multiethnic History* (London: Longmans, 2001)

KAZEMZADEH, Firuz: 'Anglo-Russian Convention of 1907', in *Encyclopædia Iranica*, Vol. II, Part 1, pp. 68–70

KAZEMZADEH, Firuz: *Russia and Britain in Persia, 1864–1914: A Study in Imperialism* (Newhaven, CN: Yale University Press, 1968)

KEAY, John: *The Gilgit Game: Explorers of the Western Himalayas 1865–1895* (London: John Murray, 1979)

KEAY, John: *Where Men & Mountains Meet: The Explorers of the Western Himalayas 1820–1875* (Karachi: Oxford University Press, 1977)

KEENAN, Edward, 'Muscovy and Kazan: Some Introductory Remarks on the Patterns of Steppe Diplomacy', *SR* Vol. 26 (1967) No. 4, 548–58

KEEP, John L. H. (ed.): *Soldiers of the Tsar: Army and Society in Russia 1462–1874* (Oxford: Clarendon Press, 1985)

KELLER, Shoshana: *To Moscow, not Mecca: The Soviet Campaign against Islam in Central Asia, 1917–1941* (New York, NY: Praeger, 2001)

KELLY, Laurence: *Diplomacy and Murder in Tehran: Alexander Griboyedov and Imperial Russia's Mission to the Shah of Persia* (London: I.B. Tauris, 2002)

KENNEDY, Dane: 'Guardians of Edenic Sanctuaries: Paharis, Lepchas, and Todas in the British Mind', *South Asia* Vol. 14 (1991) No. 2, pp. 57–77

KENNEDY, Paul: *The Rise and Fall of the Great Powers: Economic Change and Military Conflict from 1500–1980* (London: Unwin Hyman, 1988)

KHALID, Adeeb: *The Politics of Muslim Cultural Reform: Jadidism in Central Asia* (Berkeley, CA: University of California Press, 1998)

KHALID, Adeeb: 'Society and Politics in Bukhara, 1868–1920', *CAS* Vol. 19 (2000) Nos. 3–4, pp. 364–93

KHALID, Adeeb: 'Culture and Power in Colonial Turkestan', in *CAC*. Vols. 17–18. *Le Turkestan russe, une colonie comme les autres?* ed. Svetlana Gorshenina & Sergej Abašin (Tashkent & Aix-en-Provence: IFEAC, Éditions De Boccard, 2009) pp. 413–47

KHALID, Adeeb: *Making Uzbekistan: Nation, Empire and Revolution in the Early USSR* (Ithaca, NY: Cornell University Press, 2015)

KHALID, Adeeb, KNIGHT, Nathaniel & TODOROVA, Maria: 'Ex Tempore – Orientalism', *Kritika* Vol. 1 (2000) No. 4, pp. 691–727

KHAZANOV, Anatoly: *Nomads and the Outside World* (Madison, WI: University of Wisconsin Press, 1994)

KHAZANOV, Anatoly: 'Review of David Sneath *The Headless State*', *Social Evolution & History* Vol. 9 (2010) No. 2, pp. 135–8

KHAZENI, Arash: 'Across the Black Sands and the Red: Travel Writing, Nature and the Reclamation of the Eurasian Steppe *circa* 1850', *IJMES* Vol. 42 (2010) No. 4, pp. 591–614

KHODARKOVSKY, Michael: *Where Two Worlds Met: The Russian State and the Kalmyk Nomads 1600–1771* (Ithaca, NY: Cornell University Press, 1992)

KHODARKOVSKY, Michael: *Russia's Steppe Frontier: The Making of a Colonial Empire, 1500–1800* (Bloomington, IN: Indiana University Press, 2002)

KHODARKOVSKY, Michael: *Bitter Choices: Loyalty and Betrayal in the Russian Conquest of the North Caucasus* (Ithaca, NY: Cornell University Press, 2011)

KILIAN, Janet: 'Allies and Adversaries: The Russian Conquest of the Kazakh Steppe' (Ph.D. Dissertation, George Washington University, 2013)

KIM, Hodong: *Holy War in China: The Muslim Rebellion and State in Chinese Central Asia* (Palo Alto, CA: Stanford University Press, 2004)

KIMURA, Satoru: 'Sunni–Shi'i Relations in the Russian Protectorate of Bukhara, as Perceived by the local *'ulama'*, in *Asiatic Russia: Imperial Power in Regional and International Contexts* ed. Tomohiko Uyama (London: Routledge, 2012) pp. 189–215

KNIGHT, Nathaniel: 'Grigoriev in Orenburg, 1851–1862: Russian Orientalism in the Service of Empire?', *SR* Vol. 59 (2000) No. 1, pp. 74–100

KNYSH, Alexander: 'Sufism as an Explanatory Paradigm: The Issue of the Motivations of Sufi Movements in Russian and Western Historiography', *Die Welt des Islams* Vol. 42 (2002) pp. 139–73

KOMATSU, Hisao: 'Dar al-Islam under Russian Rule as Understood by Turkestani Muslim Intellectuals', in *Empire, Islam, and Politics in Central Eurasia* ed. Tomohiko Uyama (Sapporo: Slavic Eurasian Research Centre, 2007) pp. 3–21

KOMATSU, Hisao & DUDOIGNON, Stéphane (eds.): *Islam and Politics in Russia and Central Asia (Early Eighteenth to Late Twentieth Centuries)*. Islamic Area Studies (London: Kegan Paul, 2001)

KÖNIG, Wolfgang: *Die Achal-Teke: Zur Wirtschaft und Gesellschaft einer Turkmenen-Gruppe im XIX. Jahrhundert* (Berlin: Akademie-Verlag, 1962)

LARUELLE, Marlène *Mythe aryen et rêve impérial dans la Russie du XIXe siècle* (Paris: CNRS Éditions, 2005)

LATTIMORE, Owen: *Inner Asian Frontiers of China* (New York, NY: American Geographical Society, 1940)

LAYTON, Susan: *Russian Literature and Empire: Conquest of the Caucasus from Pushkin to Tolstoy* (Cambridge: Cambridge University Press, 1994)

LEDONNE, John P.: *The Russian Empire and the World, 1700–1917: The Geopolitics of Expansion and Containment* (Oxford: Oxford University Press, 1997)

LEDONNE, John P.: 'The Russian Governors General 1775–1825: Territorial or Functional Administration?', *CMR* Vol. 42 (2001) No. 1, pp. 5–30

LEDONNE, John P.: *The Grand Strategy of the Russian Empire, 1650–1831* (Oxford: Oxford University Press, 2004)

LEE, J. L.: *The 'Ancient Supremacy': Bukhara, Afghanistan and the Battle for Balkh, 1731–1901* (Leiden: Brill, 1996)

LEOPOLD, Joan: 'British Applications of the Aryan Theory of Race to India, 1850–1870', *EHR* Vol. 89 (1974) No. 352, pp. 578–603

LÉTOLLE, René: 'Les expéditions de Bekovitch-Tcherkassky en Turkestan (1714–1717) et le début de l'infiltration russe en Asie centrale', in *CAC.* Vols. 5–6. *Boukhara la noble* (Tashkent &Aix-en-Provence: IFEAC, Éditions De Boccard, 1998) pp. 259–85

LEVI, Scott: 'India, Russia and the Transformation of the Central Asian Caravan Trade', *JESHO* Vol. 42 (1999) No. 4, pp. 519–48

LEVI, Scott: 'The Ferghana Valley at the Crossroads of World History: The Rise of Khoqand 1709–1822', *JGH* Vol. 2 (2007) No. 2, pp. 213–32

LEVI, Scott: *The Rise and Fall of Khoqand 1709–1876: Central Asia in the Global Age* (Pittsburgh, PA: Pittsburgh University Press, 2017)

LIEVEN, Dominic: *Empire: The Russian Empire and Its Rivals* (London: John Murray, 2000)

LIEVEN, Dominic: 'Russia and the Defeat of Napoleon (1812–14)', *Kritika* Vol. 7 (2006) No. 2, pp. 283–308

LIEVEN, Dominic: 'Introduction', in *The Cambridge History of Russia* . Vol. II ed. Dominic Lieven (Cambridge: Cambridge University Press, 2006) p. 3

LIEVEN, Dominic (ed.): *The Cambridge History of Russia*. Vol. II. *Imperial Russia 1689–1917* (Cambridge: Cambridge University Press, 2006)

LIEVEN, Dominic: *Russia against Napoleon: The Battle for Europe, 1807–1814* (London: Allen Lane, 2009)

LIEVEN, Dominic: 'Tolstoy on War, Russia, and Empire', in *Tolstoy on War: Narrative Art and Historical Fiction in 'War and Peace'* ed. Rick McPeak & Donna Tussing Orwin (Ithaca, NY: Cornell University Press, 2012)

LINCOLN, W. Bruce: *Nicholas I: Emperor and Autocrat of All the Russias* (DeKalb, IL: Northern Illinois University Press, 1989)

584   SOURCES AND BIBLIOGRAPHY

LIU, Kwang-Ching: 'The Military Challenge: The North-West and the Coast', in *The Cambridge History of China*. Vol. 11 (Cambridge: Cambridge University Press, 1980) pp. 214–44

MACKAY, Joseph: 'International Politics in Eighteenth- and Nineteenth-Century Central Asia: Beyond Anarchy in International Relations Theory', *CAS* Vol. 32 (2013) No. 2, pp. 210–24

MACKENZIE, David: 'Kaufman of Turkestan: An Assessment of His Administration 1867–1881', *SR* Vol. 26 (1967) No. 2, pp. 265–85

MACKENZIE, David: 'Expansion in Central Asia: St. Petersburg vs. the Turkestan Generals (1863–1866)', *Canadian Slavic Studies* Vol. 3 (1969) No. 2, pp. 286–311

MACKENZIE, David: *The Lion of Tashkent: The Career of General M. G. Cherniaev* (Athens, GA: University of Georgia Press, 1974)

MACWILLIAM, Ian: 'Pamirs Adapt to Life without Russia', *BBC News* 22/02/2005 (http://news.bbc.co.uk/2/hi/asia-pacific/4284083.stm).

MAHMUDOV, Sherzodhon: 'The Role of Sufis in Diplomatic Relations between the Khanate of Khoqand and India', in *Sufism in India and Central Asia* (Delhi: Manakin Press, 2017) pp. 39–52

MALIKOV, A. M.: 'The Russian Conquest of the Bukharan Emirate: Military and Diplomatic Aspects', *CAS* Vol. 33 (2014) No. 2, pp. 180–98

MAMADALIEV, Inomjon: 'The Defence of Khujand in 1866 through the Eyes of Russian Officers', *CAS* Vol. 33 (2014) No. 2, pp. 170–9

MARK, Rudolf A.: *Im Schatten des „Great Game": Deutsche „Weltpolitik" und russischer Imperialismus in Zentralasien 1871–1914* (Paderborn: Ferdinand Schoeningh, 2012).

MARSHALL, Alexander: 'Turkfront: Frunze and the Development of Soviet Counter-insurgency in Central Asia', in *Central Asia: Aspects of Transition* ed. Tom Everett-Heath (London: Routledge, 2003) pp. 5–29

MARSHALL, Alexander: *The Russian General Staff and Asia, 1800–1917* (London: Routledge, 2006)

MARSOT, Afaf Lutfi al-Sayyid: *Egypt and Cromer: A Study in Anglo-Egyptian Relations* (London: John Murray, 1968)

MARTIN, Alexander M.: *Romantics, Reformers, Reactionaries: Russian Conservative Thought and Politics in the Reign of Alexander I* (DeKalb, IL: Northern Illinois University Press, 1997)

MARTIN, Terry Martin: *The Affirmative Action Empire: Nations and Nationalism in the Soviet Union, 1923–1939* (Ithaca, NY: Cornell University Press, 2001)

MARTIN, Virginia: 'Barimta: Nomadic Custom, Imperial Crime', in *Russia's Orient: Imperial Borderlands and Peoples 1700–1917* ed. Daniel Brower & Edward J. Lazzerini (Bloomington, IN: Indiana University Press, 1997) pp. 249–70

MARTIN, Virginia: *Law and Custom in the Steppe: The Kazakhs of the Middle Horde and Russian Colonialism in the Nineteenth Century* (Richmond: Curzon Press, 2001)

MARTIN, Virginia: 'Kazakh Chinggisids, Land and Political Power in the Nineteenth Century: A Case Study of Syrymbet', *CAS* Vol. 29 (2010) No. 1, pp. 79–102

MARTIN, Virginia: 'Using Turki-Language Qazaq Letters to Reconstruct Local Political History of the 1820s–30s', in *Explorations in the Social History of Modern Central Asia (19th Early 20th Century)* ed. Paolo Sartori (Leiden: Brill, 2013) pp. 207–45

MARTIN, Virginia: 'Engagement with Empire as Norm and in Practice in Kazakh Nomadic Political Culture (1820s–1830s)', *CAS* Vol. 36 (2017) No. 2, pp. 175–94

MCNEILL, William H.: 'The Eccentricity of Wheels, or Eurasian Transportation in Historical Perspective', *AHR* Vol. 92 (1987) No. 5, pp. 1111–26

MCPEAK, Rick & ORWIN, Donna Tussing: *Tolstoy on War: Narrative Art and Historical Fiction in 'War and Peace'* (Ithaca, NY: Cornell University Press, 2012)

MENNING, Bruce: 'A. I. Chernyshev: A Russian Lycurgus', *Canadian Slavonic Papers* Vol. 30 (1988) No. 2, pp. 190–219

MENNING, Bruce: *Bayonets before Bullets: The Imperial Russian Army, 1861–1914* (Bloomington, IN: Indiana University Press, 1992)

MEYER, Karl and BRYSAC, Shareen: *Tournament of Shadows: The Great Game and the Race for Empire in Asia* (Washington, D.C.: Counterpoint, 1999)

MIDDLETON, Robert & THOMAS, Huw: *Tajikistan and the High Pamirs: A Companion and Guide* (Hong Kong & London: Odyssey Books & Guides, 2008)

MILLER, Alexei & RIEBER, Alfred: *Imperial Rule* (Budapest: Central European University Press, 2004)

MIKABERIDZE, Alexander: *The Russian Officer Corps in the Revolutionary and Napoleonic Wars, 1795–1815* (Staplehurst: Spellmount, 2005)

MOGILNER, Marina: 'Russian Physical Anthropology of the Nineteenth–Early Twentieth Centuries: Imperial Race, Colonial Other, Degenerate Types, and the Russian Racial Body', in *Empire Speaks Out: Languages of Rationalization and Self-Description in the Russian Empire* ed. Ilya Gerasimov, Jan Kusber & Alexander Semyonov (Leiden: Brill, 2009) pp. 155–89

MOJTAHED-ZADEH, Pirouz: *Small Players of the Great Game: The Settlement of Iran's Eastern Borderlands and the Creation of Afghanistan* (Abingdon: Routledge, 2004)

MORRISON, Alexander: 'Russian Rule in Turkestan and the Example of British India', *SEER* Vol. 84 (2006) No. 4, pp. 666–707

MORRISON, Alexander: *Russian Rule in Samarkand 1868–1910: A Comparison with British India* (Oxford: Oxford University Press, 2008)

MORRISON, Alexander: '"Applied Orientalism" in British India and Tsarist Turkestan', *CSSH* Vol. 51 (2009) No. 3, 619–47

MORRISON, Alexander: 'Metropole, Colony and Imperial Citizenship in the Russian Empire', *Kritika* Vol. 13 (2012) No. 2, pp. 327–64

MORRISON, Alexander: 'Sowing the Seed of National Strife in This Alien Region: The Pahlen Report and *Pereselenie* in Turkestan 1908–1910', *Acta Slavica Iaponica* Vol. 31 (2012) pp. 1–29

MORRISON, Alexander: 'Sufism, Pan-Islamism and Information Panic: Nil Sergeevich Lykoshin and the Aftermath of the Andijan Uprising', *Past & Present* Vol. 214 (2012) No. 1, pp. 255–304

MORRISON, Alexander: 'Amlākdārs, Khwājas and Mulk Land in the Zarafshan Valley after the Russian Conquest', in *Explorations in the Social History of Modern Central Asia (19th–Early 20th Century)* ed. Paolo Sartori (Leiden: Brill, 2013) pp. 23–64

MORRISON, Alexander: 'The Pahlen Commission and the Restoration of Rectitude in Transcaspia, 1908–1909', *Monde(s). Histoire, Espaces, Relations* (2013) No. 4, pp. 45–64

MORRISON, Alexander: 'Camels and Colonial Armies: The Logistics of Warfare in Inner Asia in the Early 19th century', *JESHO* Vol. 57 (2014) pp. 443–85

MORRISON, Alexander: 'Introduction: Killing the Cotton Canard and Getting Rid of the Great Game: Rewriting the Russian Conquest of Central Asia, 1814–1895', *CAS* Vol. 33 (2014) No. 2, pp. 131–42

MORRISON, Alexander: '"Nechto eroticheskoe?" "Courir après l'ombre?" Logistical Imperatives and the Fall of Tashkent, 1859–1865', *CAS* Vol. 33 (2014) No. 2, pp. 153–69

MORRISON, Alexander: 'Russia, Khoqand, and the Search for a Natural Frontier, 1863–1865', *AI* (2014) No. 2, pp. 165–92

MORRISON, Alexander: 'Twin Imperial Disasters: The Invasions of Khiva and Afghanistan in the Russian and British Official Mind, 1838–1842', *MAS* Vol. 48 (2014) No. 1, pp. 253–300

MORRISON, Alexander: 'Russia's Colonial Allergy', *eurasianet.org* 19/12/2016 (https://eurasianet.org/russias-colonial-allergy)

MORRISON, Alexander: 'Beyond the "Great Game": The Russian Origins of the Second Anglo-Afghan War', *MAS* Vol. 51 (2017) No. 3, pp. 686–735

MORRISON, Alexander: '"The Extraordinary Successes Which the Russians Have Achieved" – the Conquest of Central Asia in Callwell's *Small Wars*', *Small Wars and Insurgencies* Vol. 30 (2019) Nos. 4–5, pp. 913–36

MORRISON, Alexander: 'The "Turkestan Generals" and Russian Military History', *War in History* Vol. 26 (2019) No. 2, pp. 153–84

MOSELY, Philip E.: 'Russian Policy in Asia (1838–9)', *SEER* Vol. 14 (1936) No. 42, pp. 670–81

MOSTOWLANSKY, Till : 'Where Empires Meet: Orientalism and Marginality on the Former Russo-British Frontier', in *Études de Lettres*. Nos. 2–3. *L'Orientalisme des marges: Éclairages à partir de l'Inde et de la Russie* ed. Philippe Bornet & Svetlana Gorshenina (Lausanne: Université de Lausanne, 2014) pp. 179–96

NEWBY, L. J.: *The Empire and the Khanate: A Political History of Qing Relations with Khoqand ca. 1760–1860* (Leiden: Brill, 2005)

NOELLE, Christine: *State and Tribe in Afghanistan: The Reign of Amir Dost Muhammad Khan (1826–1863)* (London: Curzon Press, 1997)

OBERTREIS, Julia: *Imperial Desert Dreams: Cotton Growing and Irrigation in Central Asia* (Göttingen: V & R Unipress, 2017).

O'NEILL, Kelly *Claiming Crimea: A History of Catherine the Great's Southern Empire* (Newhaven, CN: Yale University Press, 2017)

OTTE, T. G.: *The Foreign Office Mind: The Making of British Foreign Policy, 1865–1914* (Cambridge: Cambridge University Press, 2011)

OTTE, T. G. and PAGEDAS, Constantine A. (eds.): *Personalities, War and Diplomacy: Essays in International History* (London: Frank Cass, 1997)

PAINE, S. C. M.: *Imperial Rivals: China, Russia, and Their Disputed Frontier* (Armonk, NY: M. E. Sharpe, 1996)

PALAT, Madhavan K.: 'Tsarist Russian Imperialism', *Studies in History* Vol. 4 (1988) Nos. 1–2, pp. 157–297

PAPAS, Alexandre: 'Soufis du Badakhshân: Un renouveau confrérique entre l'Inde et l'Asie centrale', in *CAC*. Vols. 11–12. *Les Montagnards d'Asie centrale* ed. Svetlana Jacquesson (Tashkent & Aix-en-Provence: IFEAC, Éditions De Boccard, 2004) pp. 87–102

PENATI, Beatrice: 'Notes on the Birth of Russian Turkestan's Fiscal System: A View from the Ferghana *Oblast*' ', *JESHO* Vol. 53 (2010) No. 4, pp. 739–69

PENATI, Beatrice: 'The Cotton Boom and the Land Tax in Russian Turkestan (1880s–1915)', *Kritika* Vol. 14 (2013) No. 3, pp. 741–74

PERDUE, Peter C.: *China Marches West: The Qing Conquest of Central Eurasia* (Cambridge, MA: Belknap Press, 2005)

PICKETT, James: 'Written into Submission: Reassessing Sovereignty through a Forgotten Eurasian Dynasty', *AHR* Vol. 123 (2018) No. 3, pp. 817–45

PIRUMSHOEV, Khaidarsho: *Ta'rikhi Darvaz az qadim ta zamani muosir* (Dushanbe: Irfon, 2010)

POMFRET, Richard: *The Central Asian Economies in the Twenty-First Century: Paving a New Silk Road* (Princeton, NJ: Princeton University Press, 2019)

PORCH, Douglas: *The Conquest of the Sahara* (London: Jonathan Cape, 1984)

PORTER, Patrick: *Military Orientalism: Eastern War through Western Eyes* (Oxford: Oxford University Press, 2013)

POUJOL, Catherine: 'Les voyageurs Russes et l'Asie Centrale: Naissance et declin de deux mythes, les réserves d'or et la voie vers l'Inde', *CAS* Vol. 4 (1985) No. 3, pp. 59–73

PRIOR, Daniel G.: 'High Rank and Power among the Northern Kirghiz: Terms and Their Problems, 1845–1864', in *Explorations in the Social History of Modern Central Asia* ed. Paolo Sartori (Leiden: Brill, 2013) pp. 137–79

RAEFF, Marc: *Siberia and the Reforms of 1822* (Seattle, WA: University of Washington Press, 1956)

RAM, Harsha: *The Imperial Sublime: A Russian Poetics of Empire* (Madison, WN: University of Wisconsin Press, 2003)

REYNOLDS, David: *Britannia Overruled: British Policy and World Power in the Twentieth Century* (London: Longmans, 1991)

RIASANOVSKY, Nicholas V.: 'Asia through Russian Eyes', in *Russia and Asia* ed. W. S. Vucinich (Stanford, CA: Hoover Institution Press, 1972)

RIEBER, Alfred J.: *The Struggle for the Eurasian Borderlands: From the Rise of Early Modern Empires to the End of the First World War* (Cambridge: Cambridge University Press, 2014)

RICH, David Alan: *The Tsar's Colonels: Professionalism, Strategy, and Subversion in Late Imperial Russia* (Cambridge, MA: Harvard University Press, 1998)

ROBINSON, Ronald & GALLAGHER, John 'The Imperialism of Free Trade', *EcHR* Vol. 4 (1953) No. 1, pp. 1–15

ROBINSON, Ronald & GALLAGHER, John with DENNY, Alice: *Africa and the Victorians: The Official Mind of Imperialism* (London: Collins, 1965)

ROGGER, Hans: 'The Beilis Case: Anti-Semitism and Politics in the Reign of Nicholas II', *SR* Vol. 25 (1966) No. 4, pp. 615–29

ROGGER, Hans: 'The Skobelev Phenomenon: The Hero and his Worship', *Oxford Slavonic Papers* Vol. 9 (1976) pp. 46–78

ROY, Kaushik: 'Military Synthesis in South Asia: Armies, Warfare and Indian Society, *c*. 1740–1849', *JMH* Vol. 69 (2005) No. 3, pp. 651–90

SABOL, Stephen: 'Kazak Resistance to Russian Colonization: Interpreting the Kenesary Kasymov Revolt 1837–1847', *CAS* Vol. 22 (2003) Nos. 2–3, pp. 231–52

SAHADEO, Jeffery: 'Conquest, Colonialism and Nomadism on the Eurasian Steppe', *Kritika* Vol. 4 (2003) No. 4, pp. 942–54

SAHADEO, Jeffery: *Russian Colonial Society in Tashkent 1865–1923* (Bloomington, IN: University of Indiana Press, 2007)

SAID, Edward: *Orientalism: Western Conceptions of the Orient* (London: Routledge & Kegan Paul, 1978)

SARAY, Mehmet: 'The Russian Conquest of Central Asia', *CAS* Vol. 1 (1982) Nos. 2–3, pp. 1–31

SARAY, Mehmet: *The Turkmens in the Age of Imperialism: A Study of the Turkmen People and Their Incorporation into the Russian Empire* (Ankara: Turkish Historical Society Printing House, 1989)

SARTORI, Paolo: 'Judicial Elections as a Colonial Reform: The Qadis and Biys in Tashkent, 1868–1883', *CMR* Vol. 49 (2008) No. 1, pp. 79–100

SARTORI, Paolo: 'Behind a Petition: Why Muslims' Appeals Increased in Turkestan under Russian Rule', *AS* Vol. LXIII (2009) No. 2, pp. 401–34

SARTORI, Paolo: 'Colonial Legislation Meets Shari'a: Muslims' Land Rights in Russian Turkestan', *CAS* Vol. 29 (2010) No. 1, pp. 43–60

SARTORI, Paolo (ed.): *Explorations in the Social History of Modern Central Asia (19th–20th Centuries)* (Leiden: Brill, 2013)

SARTORI, Paolo: 'On Khvārazmian Connectivity: Two or Three Things That I Know about It', *JPS* Vol. 9 (2016) No. 2, pp. 133–57

SARTORI, Paolo: 'Seeing Like a Khanate: On Archives, Cultures of Documentation, and Nineteenth-Century Khvārazm' *JPS* Vol. 9 (2016) No. 2, 228–57

SARTORI, Paolo: *Visions of Justice: Sharī'a and Cultural Change in Russian Central Asia* (Leiden: Brill, 2016)

SARTORI, Paolo: 'Archival Silences: On 18th-Century Russian Diplomacy and the Historical Episteme of Central Asian Hostility', *Itinerario* (forthcoming)

SCHIMMELPENNINCK VAN DER OYE, David: *Towards the Rising Sun: Russian Ideologies of Empire and the Path to War with Japan* (Dekalb, IL: Northern Illinois University Press, 2001)

SCHIMMELPENNINCK VAN DER OYE, David & MENNING, Bruce (ed.): *Reforming the Tsar's Army: Military Innovation in Imperial Russia from Peter the Great to the Revolution* (Cambridge: Cambridge University Press, 2004)

SCHIMMELPENNINCK VAN DER OYE, David: 'Vasilij V. Vereshchagin's Canvases of Central Asian Conquest', in *CAC*. Vols. 17–18. *Le Turkestan russe: Une colonie comme les autres?* ed. Svetlana Gorshenina & Sergej Abašin (Tashkent & Aix-en-Provence: IFEAC, Éditions De Boccard, 2009) pp. 179–209

SCHIMMELPENNINCK VAN DER OYE, David: *Russian Orientalism: Asia in the Russian Mind from Peter the Great to the Emigration* (Newhaven, CN: Yale University Press, 2010)

SCHIMMELPENNINCK VAN DER OYE, David: 'Paul's Great Game: Russia's Plan to Invade British India', *CAS* Vol. 33 (2014) No. 2, pp. 143–52

SCHÖLCH, Alexander: 'The "Men on the Spot" and the English Occupation of Egypt in 1882', *HJ* Vol. 19 (1976) No. 3, 773–85

SCHUMPETER, Joseph: 'The Sociology of Imperialisms', trans. Heinz Norden, in *Imperialism and Social Classes* ed. Paul Sweezy (Oxford: Oxford University Press, 1951) pp. 65–98

SCOTT, James C.: *The Art of Not Being Governed: An Anarchist History of Upland Southeast Asia* (Newhaven, CN: Yale University Press, 2009)

SELA, Ron: 'Invoking the Russian Conquest of Khiva and the Massacre of the Yomut Turkmens: The Choices of a Central Asian Historian', *AS* Vol. LX (2006) No. 2, pp. 459–77

SELA, Ron: 'The "Heavenly Stone" (Kök Tash) of Samarqand: A Rebels' Narrative Transformed', *Journal of the Royal Asiatic Society* Vol. 17 (2007) No. 1, pp. 21–32

SELA, Ron: *The Legendary Biographies of Tamerlane: Islam and Heroic Apocrypha in Central Asia* (Cambridge: Cambridge University Press, 2011)

SELA, Ron: 'Prescribing the Boundaries of Knowledge: Seventeenth-Century Russian Diplomatic Missions to Central Asia', in *Writing Travel in Central Asian History* ed. Nile Green (Bloomington, IN: Indiana University Press, 2014) pp. 69–88

SERGEEV, Evgeny: *The Great Game 1856–1907* (Washington, D.C.: Woodrow Wilson Centre & Johns Hopkins University Press, 2013)

SHAHRANI, M.Nazif: *The Kirghiz and Wakhi of Afghanistan: Adaptation to Closed Frontiers and War* (Seattle, WA: University of Washington Press, 2002 [1979])

SHIOYA, Akifumi: '*Povorot* and the Khanate of Khiva: A New Canal and the Birth of Ethnic Conflict in the Khorazm Oasis, 1870s–1890s', *CAS* Vol. 33 (2014) No. 2, 232–45

SHIOYA, Akifumi 'The Treaty of Ghulja Reconsidered: Imperial Russian Diplomacy toward Qing China in 1851', *Journal of Eurasian Studies* Vol. 10 (2019) No. 2, pp. 147–58

SIEGEL, Jennifer: *Endgame: Britain, Russia and the Final Struggle for Central Asia* (London: I.B. Tauris, 2002)

SINOR, Dennis: 'The Inner Asian Warriors', *Journal of the American Oriental Society* Vol. 101 (1981) No. 2, pp. 133–44

SMITH, Jeremy: *Red Nations: The Nationalities Experience in and after the USSR* (Cambridge: Cambridge University Press, 2013)

SMOLARZ, Elena: 'Speaking about Freedom and Dependency: Representations and Experiences of Russian Enslaved Captives in Central Asia in the First Half of the 19th Century', *Journal of Global Slavery* Vol. 2 (2017) pp. 44–71

SNEATH, David: *The Headless State: Aristocratic Orders, Kinship Society, and Misrepresentations of Nomadic Inner Asia* (New York, NY: Columbia University Press, 2007)

STATIEV, Alexander: *At War's Summit: The Red Army and the Struggle for the Caucasus Mountains in World War II* (Cambridge: Cambridge University Press, 2018)

STEENSGAARD, Niels: *The Asian Trade Revolution of the Seventeenth Century: The East India Companies and the Decline of the Caravan Trade* (Chicago, IL: Chicago University Press, 1973)

STEINER, Zara S.: *The Foreign Office and Foreign Policy, 1898–1914* (Cambridge: Cambridge University Press, 1969)

STEWART, John Massey: *Thomas, Lucy & Alatau: The Atkinsons' Adventures in Siberia and the Kazakh Steppe* (London: Unicorn, 2018)

STOKES, Eric: 'Late Nineteenth-Century Colonial Expansion and the Attack on the Theory of Economic Imperialism: A Case of Mistaken Identity?', *HJ* Vol. 12 (1969) No. 2, pp. 285–301

STOKES, Eric: 'Bureaucracy and Ideology: Britain and India in the Nineteenth Century', *TRHS* Vol. 30 (1980) pp. 131–56

STONE, Norman: *The Eastern Front 1914–1917* (London: Hodder & Stoughton, 1975)

STRONG, John W. 'The Ignat'ev Mission to Khiva and Bukhara in 1858', *Canadian Slavonic Papers* Vol. 17 (1975) Nos. 2–3, pp. 236–60

SULTANGALIEVA, Gulmira; 'The Role of the *pristavstvo* Institution in the Context of Russian Imperial Policies in the Kazakh Steppe in the Nineteenth Century', *CAS* Vol. 33 (2014) No. 1, pp. 62–79

SULTONOV, U. A.: *Muhammad Solih Khuja va Uning Tarikhi Jadidaii Toshkand* (Tashkent: O'zbekiston, 2009)

SUNDERLAND, Willard: *Taming the Wild Field: Colonization and Empire on the Russian Steppe* (Ithaca, NY: Cornell University Press, 2004)

SUNDERLAND, Willard: 'The Ministry of Asiatic Russia: The Colonial Office That Never Was but Might Have Been', *SR* Vol. 69 (2010) No. 1, pp. 120–50

SZUPPE, Maria: 'En quête de chevaux turkmènes: Le journal de voyage de Mîr 'Izzatullâh de Delhi à Boukhara en 1812–1813', in *CAC*. Vols. 1–2. *Asie Centrale–l'Inde: Routes du commerce et des idées* (Tashkent & Aix-en-Provence: IFEAC, Éditions De Boccard, 1996) pp. 91–113

TILLETT, Lowell: *The Great Friendship: Soviet Historians on the Non-Russian Nationalities* (Chapel Hill, NC: University of North Carolina Press, 1969)

TUCHSCHERER, Michel: 'Some Reflections on the Place of the Camel in Ottoman Egypt', in *Animals and People in the Ottoman Empire* ed. Suraiya Faroqhi (Istanbul: Eren, 2010) pp. 171–86

TRAUTMANN, T. R.: *Aryans and British India* (Berkeley, CA: University of California Press, 1997)

URE, John: *Shooting Leave: Spying out Central Asia in the Great Game* (London: Constable, 2010)

VAN DEN BERG, G. R.: *Minstrel Poetry from the Pamir Mountains: A Study on the Songs and Poems of the Ismailis of Tajik Badakhshan* (Wiesbaden: Reichert Verlag, 2004)

VAN DYKE, Carl: *Russian Imperial Military Doctrine and Education 1832–1914* (New York, NY: Greenwood Press, 1990)

VOLKOV, Denis: *Russia's Turn to Persia: Orientalism in Diplomacy and Intelligence* (Cambridge: Cambridge University Press, 2018)

VOLODARSKY, Mikhail: 'The Russians in Afghanistan in the 1830s', *CAS* Vol. 3 (1984) No. 1, pp. 63–86

VON KÜGELGEN, Anke; KEMPER, Michael & FRANK, Allen J.: *Muslim Culture in Russia and Central Asia from the 18th to the Early 20th Centuries*. Vol. II. *Inter-regional & Inter-ethnic Relations* (Berlin: Klaus Schwarz Verlag, 1998)

VOSKRESSENSKI, Alexei D.: *The Sino-Russian St Petersburg Treaty of 1881: Diplomatic History* (Commack, NY: Nova Science Publication, 1996)

WALTER, Dierk. *Colonial Violence: European Empires and the Use of Force* (London: Hurst, 2017)

WANG, Di: 'The Unofficial Russo-Qing Trade on the Eastern Kazakh Steppe and in Northern Xinjiang in the First Half of the 19th Century' (M.A. Thesis, Nazarbayev University, 2018) (https://nur.nu.edu.kz/handle/123456789/3316)

WAGNER, Kim A.: 'Seeing Like A Soldier: The Amritsar Massacre and the Politics of Military History', in *Decolonization and Conflict: Colonial Comparisons and Conflicts* ed. Martin Thomas and Gareth Curless (London: Bloomsbury Academic, 2017) pp. 24–37

WAGNER, Kim A.: *The Skull of Alum Bheg: The Life and Death of a Rebel of 1857* (London: Hurst, 2017)

WAGNER, Kim A.: *Thuggee: Banditry and the British in Early Nineteenth-Century India* (Basingstoke: Palgrave Macmillan, 2007)

WAGNER, Kim A.: 'Savage Warfare: Violence and the Rule of Colonial Difference in Early British Counterinsurgency', *History Workshop Journal* Vol. 85 (2018) No. 1, 217–37

WELSFORD, Thomas: 'The Re-opening of Iran to Central Asian Pilgrimage Traffic, 1600–1650', in *Central Asian Pilgrims: Hajj Routes and Pious Visits between Central Asia and the Hijaz* ed Alexandre Papas, Thomas Welsford & Thierry Zarcone (Berlin: Klaus Schwarz Verlag, 2011) pp. 149–67

WELSFORD, Thomas: *Four Types of Loyalty in Early Modern Central* Asia. *The Tuqay-Timurid takeover of Greater Mawara al-nahr* (Leiden: Brill, 2013)

WELSFORD, Thomas: 'The Disappearing Khanate', in *Turko-Persian Cultural Contacts in the Eurasian Steppe: Festschrift in Honour of Professor István Vásáry* ed. B. Péri and F. Csirkes (Leiden: Brill, forthcoming)

WENNBERG, Franz: *On The Edge: The Concept of Progress in Bukhara during the Rule of the Later Manghits* (Uppsala: Acta Universitatis Uppsaliensis, 2013), pp. 146–75

WHITMAN, John: 'Turkestan Cotton in Imperial Russia', *American Slavic and East European Review* Vol. 15 (1956) No. 2, 190–205

WILDE, Andreas: *What Is Beyond the River? Power, Authority and Social Order in Transoxiana in the 18th–19th Centuries* (Vienna: Verlag der Österreichischen Akademie der Wissenschaften, 2016) 3 volumes

WINICHAKUL, Thongchai: *Siam Mapped: A History of the Geo-body of the Nation* (Honolulu, HI: University of Hawai'i Press, 1993)

WOOD, William A.: 'The Sariq Turkmen of Merv and the Khanate of Khiva in the Early Nineteenth Century' (Ph.D. Dissertation, Indiana University, Bloomington, 1998)

WORTMAN, Richard: *Scenarios of Power: Myth and Ceremony in the Russian Monarchy*. Vol. I. *From Peter the Great to the Death of Nicholas I* (Princeton, NJ: Princeton University Press, 1995); Vol. II. *From Alexander II to the Abdication of Nicholas II* (Princeton, NJ: Princeton University Press, 2000)

YAPP, M. E.: *Strategies of British India: Britain, Iran, and Afghanistan, 1798–1850* (Oxford: Clarendon Press, 1981)

YAPP, M. E.: 'British Perceptions of the Russian Threat to India', *MAS* Vol. 21 (1987) No. 4, pp. 647–65

YAPP, M. E.: 'The Legend of the Great Game', *Proceedings of the British Academy* Vol. 111 (2001) pp. 179–98

YAROSHEVSKI, Dov: 'Imperial Strategy in the Kirghiz Steppe in the Eighteenth Century', *JBFGO* Vol. 39 (1991) No. 2, pp. 221–4

YASTREBOVA, Olga & **AZAD**, Arezou: 'Reflections on an Orientalist: Alexander Kuhn (1840–88), the Man and his Legacy', *IS* Vol. 48 (2015) No. 5, 675–94

YOUSEF, M. K., **WEBSTER**, M. E. D. & **YOUSEF**, O. M.: 'Energy Costs of Walking in Camels, *Camelus dromedarius*', *Physiological Zoology* Vol. 62 (1989) No. 5, pp. 1080–8

YUSUPOVA, Tatiana: 'Grigorii Efimovich Grumm-Grzhimailo (1860–1936)', in *The Quest for Forbidden Lands: Nikolai Przheval'skii and His Followers on Inner Asian Tracks* ed. Alexandre Andreyev, Mikhail Baskhanov & Tatiana Yusupova (Leiden: Brill, 2018) pp. 311–47

INDEX

Page numbers in bold refer to illustrations.

capture of Suzaq by, 1863, 165, 222
capture of Tashkent by, 1865, 216,
    243, 244, 245, 246, 247, 250, 251,
    254, 259, 290, 532
conflict with Bukhara, 1865–6, 260,
    263, 266, 268, 275
correspondence with mother, 1865,
    265
dismissal as Turkestan governor,
    1866, 270
disobedience of, 166, 216, 219, 223,
    227, 233, 237, 252
family background, 152
first assault on Tashkent, 1864, 236,
    238, 240
in the Caucasus, 537
negotiations with Khoqand, 1864–5,
    238, 253
reasons for assaulting Tashkent,
    1865, 242, 247
renaming of Chimkent after, 114
retreat from Jizzakh, 1866, 268, 270,
    272, 280
rivalry with K. P. von Kaufman, 310
Chernyshev, Prince A. I. (1785–1857),
    Minister of War, 56, 63, 65, 88, 90,
    123, 128
Chikishlar, 341, 342, 344, 415, 416, 418,
    427, 428, 435, 436, 437, 439, 442,
    446, 447, 448
occupation of, 1870, 415
Chimkent, 33, 167, 222, 225, 229, 241,
    260
as the site of Russia's border, 234,
    235, 239
capture of, 1864, 30, 31, 169, 227,
    229, 231, 233, 236, 252
defence of by 'Alimqul, 1864, 231, 232
district, 330, 331
renaming of after M. G. Chernyaev,
    216
China, 35, 64, 75, 111, 221, 410, 497,
    523
frontier, 48, 169, 177, 480, 494
Ili Crisis, 1871–1881, 203, 209, 210,
    211, 212, 214
Khoqand trade with, 3, 375
relations with the Kyrgyz, 214
relations with the Qazaqs, 76, 214

Russian trade with, 16, 17, 19, 157,
    161, 167, 177, 209
Chinggissid, 72, 73, 74, 75, 76, 77, 79,
    95, 170, 172, 420
Chirchik (river), 157, 243, 245, 248,
    259, 263, 305
Chitral, 81, 114, 486, 493, 494, 498, 513,
    522, 528
Christianity
    Anglican, 63
    Catholic, 51, 63
    Lutheran, 51
    Monophysite, 51
    Old Believers, 40
    Orthodoxy, 2, 26, 51, 80, 101, 153,
        183, 195, 251, 252, 253, 267, 283,
        407, 511
Chu (river), 129, 155, 178, 179, 184,
    186, 187, 188, 190, 191, 192, 193,
    199, 202, 203, 214, 220
Chulaq-Qurghan, 81, 191, 220, 226, 235
Chupan-Ata, Battle of, 1868, 31, 36,
    287, 288, **289**, 289, 290
Cobbold, Ralph (1869–1965), 509
cognac, 344, 346, 454
Cossacks, 39, 42, 62, 140
    Orenburg, 39, 40, **100**, **106**, 124, 138,
        154, 328, 367, 391, 397
    Semirechie, 39, 183, 207, 328
    Siberian, 39, 122, 153, 181, 207
    Terek, 344, 346
    Ural, 39, 40, 103, 124, 138, 238, 273,
        286, 287, 302, 328, 367, 391
cotton
    boom of the early 1900s, 15, 376, 532
    'Canard' as an explanation for the
        Conquest, 13, 14, 15
    'Famine' of the 1860s, 7, 14, 15, 107,
        159, 256
    ghuza, 256
    raw imports from Central Asia, 18,
        267
    textiles, 14, 16, 17, 18, 84,
        159, 256
Crimean khanate, 55
Crimean Tatars, 72
Crimean War (1853–6), 7, 11, 14, 16,
    20, 30, 38, 57, 154, 282
Curzon, G. N. (1859–1925), 514

604 INDEX